PSYCHOLOGY

Almost everyone who sees this image by Lois Greenfield stops, stares, and then whispers the word "Wow." We did too. Why is this image so captivating?

Throughout history, human beings have seen themselves as creatures that exist somewhere between the mundane and the divine. The figure in this image appears to be both descending from the heavens and rising from the earth, briefly suspended between two worlds, engaged in some uniquely human ritual that neither the gods above him nor the beasts below him can fully comprehend. For us, this moment of balance captures the essential tension between the mind and the body, between our higher and lower natures, between the aspirations and the origins of our species.

Lois Greenfield has been photographing dancers and dance movement since 1973. In the last three decades, her work has appeared in such diverse publications as *American Photographer, Dance Magazine, Elle, Esquire, Life, The New York Times, Newsweek, Rolling Stone, Vanity Fair, The Village Voice,* and *Vogue.* She has been featured in one-woman exhibitions in the United States, Europe, China, and most recently Japan. She has published two books, *Breaking Bounds: The Dance Photography of Lois Greenfield* (Chronicle Books, 1992) and *Airborne: The New Dance Photography of Lois Greenfield* (Chronicle Books, 1998). She currently lives in New York City.

PSYCHOLOGY

DANIEL L. SCHACTER
Harvard University

DANIEL T. GILBERT
Harvard University

DANIEL M. WEGNER
Harvard University

WORTH PUBLISHERS

Publisher: Catherine Woods
Senior Acquisitions Editor: Charles Linsmeier
Executive Marketing Manager: Katherine Nurre
Senior Development Editor: Mimi Melek
Development Editors: Phyllis Fisher, Barbara Brooks
Senior Media Editor: Andrea Musick
Associate Managing Editor: Tracey Kuehn
Project Editor: Jane O'Neill
Photo Editor: Ted Szczepanski
Photo Researchers: Elyse Rieder and Lyndall Culbertson
Art Director and Cover Designer: Babs Reingold
Text Designer: Lissi Sigillo
Layout Designer: Lee Mahler
Illustration Coordinator: Susan Timmins
Illustrations: Matt Holt, Christy Krames, Don Stewart
Cover Photograph: Lois Greenfield
Production Manager: Sarah Segal
Composition: TSI Graphics
Printing and Binding: RR Donnelley

Chapter opening art credits: p. xxxiv, Brand X Pictures; p. 38, Michael Gibbs; pp. 72 and 208, Dung Hoang; pp. 120 and 404, Jonathan Barkat; p. 166, Stephanie Dalton Cowan; p. 252, Noma Bliss; p. 292, Brian Stauffer; p. 336, Gerard Dubois; p. 366, Colin Anderson/Brand X/Corbis; p. 448, Karen Klassen; p. 488, Lynn Foster; p. 536, John Lund/Corbis; p. 580, Eric Field; p. 620, Andrew Steward.

Library of Congress Project Control Number: 2007939064

ISBN-13: 978-0-7167-5215-8
ISBN-10: 0-7167-5215-8

Printed in the United States of America

First printing

Worth Publishers
41 Madison Avenue
New York, NY 10010
www.worthpublishers.com

To our children and their children

Hannah Schacter

Emily Schacter

Arlo Gilbert

Shona Gilbert

Daylyn Gilbert

Sari Gilbert

Kelsey Wegner

Haley Wegner

About the Authors

DANIEL L. SCHACTER is a professor of psychology at Harvard University. Schacter received his BA degree from the University of North Carolina at Chapel Hill in 1974. He subsequently developed a keen interest in memory disorders. He continued his research and education at the University of Toronto, where he received his PhD in 1981. He taught on the faculty at Toronto for the next 6 years before joining the psychology department at the University of Arizona in 1987. In 1991, he joined the faculty at Harvard University. His research explores the relation between conscious and unconscious forms of memory and the nature of memory distortions. He has received the Phi Beta Kappa teaching prize and several research awards, including the Troland Award from the National Academy of Sciences. Many of Schacter's studies are summarized in his 1996 book, *Searching for Memory: The Brain, the Mind, and the Past*, and his 2001 book, *The Seven Sins of Memory: How the Mind Forgets and Remembers*, both winners of the APA's William James Book Award.

DANIEL T. GILBERT is a professor of psychology at Harvard University. After attending the Community College of Denver and completing his BA at the University of Colorado at Denver in 1981, he earned his PhD from Princeton University in 1985. He taught on the faculty of the University of Texas at Austin for the next 11 years. In 1996, he joined the faculty of Harvard University. Gilbert received the American Psychological Association's Distinguished Scientific Award for an Early Career Contribution to Psychology. He has also won numerous teaching awards, including the Phi Beta Kappa Teaching Prize. His research on "affective forecasting" is an attempt to understand how and how well people predict their emotional reactions to future events. He is the author of the 2006 national best seller *Stumbling on Happiness*, winner of the Royal Society General Book Prize given for the year's best popular science book.

DANIEL M. WEGNER is a professor of psychology at Harvard University. He received his BS in 1970 and PhD in 1974, both from Michigan State University. He began his teaching career at Trinity University in San Antonio, Texas, before his appointments at the University of Virginia in 1990 and then Harvard University in 2000. He is Fellow of the American Association for the Advancement of Science and former associate editor of *Psychological Review*. His research focuses on thought suppression and mental control, social memory in relationships and groups, and the experience of conscious will. His seminal work in thought suppression and consciousness served as the basis of two trade titles, *White Bears and Other Unwanted Thoughts* and the *Illusion of Conscious Will*, both of which were named *Choice* Outstanding Academic Books.

Brief Contents

Preface xvii

CHAPTER 1   Psychology: The Evolution of a Science 1

CHAPTER 2   The Methods of Psychology 39

CHAPTER 3   Neuroscience and Behavior 73

CHAPTER 4   Sensation and Perception 121

CHAPTER 5   Memory 167

CHAPTER 6   Learning 209

CHAPTER 7   Language and Thought 253

CHAPTER 8   Consciousness 293

CHAPTER 9   Intelligence 337

CHAPTER 10   Emotion and Motivation 367

CHAPTER 11   Development 405

CHAPTER 12   Personality 449

CHAPTER 13   Psychological Disorders 489

CHAPTER 14   Treatment of Psychological Disorders 537

CHAPTER 15   Stress and Health 581

CHAPTER 16   Social Psychology 621

Glossary G-1

References R-1

Name Index NI-1

Subject Index SI-1

Contents

Preface xvii

Chapter 1 Psychology: The Evolution of a Science 1

Psychology's Roots: The Path to a Science of Mind 5
Psychology's Ancestors: The Great Philosophers 5
From the Brain to the Mind: The French Connection 6
From Physiology to Psychology: A New Science Is Born in Germany 7
Titchener Brings Structuralism to the United States 9
James and the Functional Approach 9
→ THE REAL WORLD Improving Study Skills 11

Errors and Illusions Reveal Psychology 12
Illusions of Movement and the Birth of Gestalt Psychology 12
Mental Disorders and Multiple Selves 13
Freud and Psychoanalytic Theory 14
Influence of Psychoanalysis and the Humanistic Response 16

Psychology in the 20th Century: Behaviorism Takes Center Stage . . 17
Watson and the Emergence of Behaviorism 18
B. F. Skinner and the Development of Behaviorism 19

Beyond Behaviorism: Psychology Expands 21
The Emergence of Cognitive Psychology 21
The Brain Meets the Mind: The Rise of Cognitive Neuroscience 24
The Adaptive Mind: The Emergence of Evolutionary Psychology 26
→ HOT SCIENCE New Connections 27

Beyond the Individual: Social and Cultural Perspectives 28
The Development of Social Psychology 28
The Emergence of Cultural Psychology 29

The Profession of Psychology: Past and Present 31
Psychologists Band Together: The American Psychological Association 31
What Psychologists Do: Research Careers 33
→ WHERE DO YOU STAND? The Perils of Procrastination 35

Chapter 2 The Methods of Psychology 39

Empiricism: How to Know Things 40

The Science of Observation: Saying What 41
Measurement 41
Samples 44
→ THE REAL WORLD Taking a Chance 46
Bias 49

The Science of Explanation: Saying Why 52
Correlation 52
Causation 56
→ HOT SCIENCE Establishing Causality in the Brain 63
Drawing Conclusions 64

The Ethics of Science: Saying Please and Thank You 68
→ **WHERE DO YOU STAND?** The Morality of Immoral Experiments   70

Chapter 3 Neuroscience and Behavior 73

Neurons: The Origin of Behavior 74
Components of the Neuron   75
Major Types of Neurons   77
→ **HOT SCIENCE** Mirror, Mirror, in My Brain   78

Electric Signaling: Communicating Information within a Neuron . . . 79
The Resting Potential: The Origin of the Neuron's Electrical Properties   79
The Action Potential: Sending Signals over Long Distances   80

Chemical Signaling: Synaptic Transmission between Neurons 81
Types of Neurotransmitters   83
How Drugs Mimic Neurotransmitters   85

The Organization of the Nervous System 87
Divisions of the Nervous System   87
Components of the Central Nervous System   90
Exploring the Brain   91
→ **HOT SCIENCE** Thought Control   92
→ **THE REAL WORLD** Brain Plasticity and Sensations in Phantom Limbs   100

The Development and Evolution of Nervous Systems 101
Prenatal Development of the Central Nervous System   102
Evolutionary Development of the Central Nervous System   102
Genes and the Environment   104

Investigating the Brain 107
Learning about Brain Organization by Studying the Damaged Brain   108
Listening to the Brain: Single Neurons and the EEG   111
Brain Imaging: Watching the Brain in Action   113
→ **WHERE DO YOU STAND?** Brain Death   116

Chapter 4 Sensation and Perception 121

The Doorway to Psychology 123
Psychophysics   124
Measuring Thresholds   124
Signal Detection   126
Sensory Adaptation   128
→ **THE REAL WORLD** Multitasking   129

Vision: More Than Meets the Eye 130
Sensing Light 130
Perceiving Color   135
The Visual Brain   138
Recognizing Objects by Sight   141
Perceiving Depth and Size   144
Perceiving Motion   148

Audition: More Than Meets the Ear 150
Sensing Sound   150
The Human Ear   151
Perceiving Pitch   152
→ **HOT SCIENCE** Cochlear Implants   154
Localizing Sound Sources   154

The Body Senses: More Than Skin Deep 155
Touch 155
Pain 156
Body Position, Movement, and Balance 157

The Chemical Senses: Adding Flavor 158
Smell 158
Taste 161
→ THE REAL WORLD **Supertasters** 162
→ WHERE DO YOU STAND? **Perception and Persuasion** 163

Chapter 5 Memory 167

Encoding: Transforming Perceptions into Memories 169
Elaborative Encoding 170
Visual Imagery Encoding 171
Organizational Encoding 172

Storage: Maintaining Memories over Time 173
Sensory Storage 173
Short-Term Storage and Working Memory 174
Long-Term Storage 176
Memories in the Brain 178
→ HOT SCIENCE **A Memory Drug?** 179

Retrieval: Bringing Memories to Mind 180
Retrieval Cues: Reinstating the Past 180
Separating the Components of Retrieval 182

Multiple Forms of Memory: How the Past Returns 182
Implicit and Explicit Memory 182
Semantic and Episodic Memory 185

Memory Failures: The Seven Sins of Memory 187
Transience 187
Absentmindedness 189
Blocking 191
Memory Misattribution 193
→ THE REAL WORLD **Deadly Misattributions** 196
Suggestibility 197
Bias 199
Persistence 201
Are the Seven Sins Vices or Virtues? 203
→ WHERE DO YOU STAND? **The Mystery of Childhood Amnesia** 204

Chapter 6 Learning 209

**Defining Learning: Experience That Causes
a Permanent Change** 210
The Case of Habituation 210
Learning and Behaviorism 211

Classical Conditioning: One Thing Leads to Another 212
Pavlov's Experiments on Classical Conditioning 212
The Basic Principles of Classical Conditioning 214
→ THE REAL WORLD **Understanding Drug Overdoses** 215
Conditioned Emotional Responses: The Case of Little Albert 218

A Deeper Understanding of Classical Conditioning   219

→ **HOT SCIENCE Can Animals Learn Language?**   221

Operant Conditioning: Reinforcements from the Environment   . . . 224

The Early Days: The Law of Effect   224

Reinforcement, Punishment, and the Development of Operant Conditioning   225

The Basic Principles of Operant Conditioning   229

A Deeper Understanding of Operant Conditioning   236

Observational Learning: Look at Me   242

Learning without Direct Experience   242

Observational Learning in Humans   243

Observational Learning in Animals   245

Implicit Learning: Under the Wires   246

Ways to Study Implicit Learning   246

→ **THE REAL WORLD Can You Sleep on It?**   248

Implicit and Explicit Learning Use Distinct Neural Pathways   248

→ **WHERE DO YOU STAND? Learning for Rewards or for Its Own Sake?**   250

Chapter 7   Language and Thought   253

Language and Communication: Nothing's More Personal   254

The Complex Structure of Human Language   254

Language Development   257

Theories of Language Development   259

The Neurological Specialization That Allows Language to Develop   262

Can Other Species Learn Human Language?   263

→ **THE REAL WORLD Does Bilingualism Interfere with Cognitive Development?**   264

Language and Thought: How Are They Related?   266

Concepts and Categories: How We Think   267

The Organization of Concepts and Category-Specific Deficits   268

Psychological Theories of Concepts and Categories   269

Judging, Valuing, and Deciding: Sometimes We're Logical, Sometimes Not   273

Decision Making: Rational, Optimal, and Otherwise   274

→ **HOT SCIENCE The Neuroscience of Risky Decision Making**   278

Other Approaches to Human Decision Making   279

Problem Solving: Working It Out   280

Means-Ends Analysis   281

Analogical Problem Solving   281

Creativity and Insight   282

Transforming Information: How We Reach Conclusions   285

→ **WHERE DO YOU STAND? Choosing a Mate**   289

Chapter 8   Consciousness   293

Conscious and Unconscious: The Mind's Eye, Open and Closed   . . . 294

The Mysteries of Consciousness   295

The Nature of Consciousness   298

The Unconscious Mind   305

→ **HOT SCIENCE How Smart Is the Unconscious Mind?**   307

Sleep and Dreaming: Good Night, Mind 309
Sleep 309
Dreams 314
➜ HOT SCIENCE Dreaming and the Brain 316

Drugs and Consciousness: Artificial Inspiration 318
Drug Use and Abuse 318
Types of Psychoactive Drugs 320
➜ THE REAL WORLD Drugs and the Regulation of Consciousness 324

Hypnosis: Open to Suggestion 327
Induction and Susceptibility 327
Hypnotic Effects 328

Meditation and Religious Experiences: Higher Consciousness . . .331
Meditation 332
Ecstatic Religious Experiences 332
➜ WHERE DO YOU STAND? Between NORML and MADD: What Is Acceptable Drug
Use? 333

Chapter 9 Intelligence 337

The Measurement of Intelligence: Highly Classified 338
The Intelligence Quotient 339
The Logic of Intelligence Testing 341
Consequential Behaviors 343
➜ THE REAL WORLD Look Smart 345

The Nature of Intelligence: Pluribus or Unum? 345
General and Specific Abilities 345
Middle-Level Abilities 347

The Origins of Intelligence: From SES to DNA 351
Intelligence and Genes 352
Intelligence and Groups 356

The Future of Intelligence: Wising Up 359
Changing Intelligence 359
Improving Intelligence 360
➜ HOT SCIENCE The Plot Thickens 361
➜ WHERE DO YOU STAND? Making Kids Smart or Making Smart Kids? 363

Chapter 10 Emotion and Motivation 367

Emotional Experience: The Feeling Machine 368
What Is Emotion? 369
The Emotional Body 370
The Emotional Brain 373
The Regulation of Emotion 376

Emotional Communication: Msgs w/o Wrds 377
➜ THE REAL WORLD The Pleasures of Uncertainty 378
Communicative Expression 379
➜ HOT SCIENCE That's Gross! 382
Deceptive Expression 383

Motivation: Getting Moved 386
The Function of Emotion 386
The Conceptualization of Motivation 389

Eating and Mating   390
Kinds of Motivation   397
→ WHERE DO YOU STAND? Here Comes the Bribe   401

Chapter 11   Development 405

Prenatality: A Womb with a View 406
Prenatal Devlopment   407
Prenatal Environment   408

Infancy and Childhood: Becoming a Person 410
Perceptual and Motor Development   410
Cognitive Development   412
Social Development   420
→ HOT SCIENCE An Accountant in the Crib?   421
Moral Development   425
→ THE REAL WORLD The Truth about Day Care   426

Adolescence: Minding the Gap 430
The Protraction of Adolescence   432
Sexuality   433
Parents and Peers   436

Adulthood: The Short Happy Future 438
Changing Abilities   439
Changing Orientations   441
Changing Roles   443
→ WHERE DO YOU STAND? Licensing Parents   445

Chapter 12   Personality 449

Personality: What It Is and How It Is Measured 450
Describing and Explaining Personality   450
Measuring Personality   451

The Trait Approach: Identifying Patterns of Behavior 454
Traits as Behavioral Dispositions and Motives   454
The Search for Core Traits   456
Traits as Biological Building Blocks   458
→ THE REAL WORLD Do Different Genders Lead to Different Personalities?   459

The Psychodynamic Approach: Forces That Lie beneath Awareness 462
Unconscious Motives   463
The Structure of the Mind: Id, Ego, and Superego   464
Dealing with Inner Conflict   465
Psychosexual Stages and the Development of Personality   468

The Humanistic-Existential Approach: Personality as Choice 470
Human Needs and Self-actualization   471
Conditions for Growth   471
Personality as Existence   472

The Social Cognitive Approach: Personalities in Situations 473
Consistency of Personality across Situations   474
Personal Constructs   475
Personal Goals and Expectancies   476

The Self: Personality in the Mirror 477

Self-concept   478

Self-esteem   480

→ **HOT SCIENCE** Implicit Egotism: Liking Ourselves without Knowing It   483

→ **WHERE DO YOU STAND?** Personality Testing for Fun and Profit   485

Chapter 13 Psychological Disorders 489

Identifying Psychological Disorders: What Is Abnormal? 490

Defining the Boundaries of Normality   492

Classification of Psychological Disorders   494

Classification and Causation   497

→ **THE REAL WORLD** Cultural Variants of Abnormal Behavior   499

Consequences of Labeling   500

Anxiety Disorders: When Fears Take Over 501

Generalized Anxiety Disorder   501

Phobic Disorders   503

Panic Disorder   505

Obsessive-Compulsive Disorder   506

Dissociative Disorders: Going to Pieces 508

Dissociative Identity Disorder   508

Dissociative Amnesia and Dissociative Fugue   510

Mood Disorders: At the Mercy of Emotions 511

Depressive Disorders   511

Bipolar Disorder   515

→ **THE REAL WORLD** Suicide Risk and Prevention   516

Schizophrenia: Losing the Grasp on Reality 519

Symptoms and Types of Schizophrenia   519

Biological Factors   522

Psychological Factors   525

Personality Disorders: Going to Extremes 526

Types of Personality Disorders   527

Antisocial Personality Disorder   529

→ **HOT SCIENCE** Positive Psychology: Exterminating the Mindbugs   530

→ **WHERE DO YOU STAND?** Normal or Abnormal   532

Chapter 14 Treatment of Psychological Disorders 537

Treatment: Getting Help to Those Who Need It 539

Why People Need Treatment   539

Why People Cannot or Will Not Seek Treatment   540

Approaches to Treatment   541

Psychological Therapies: Healing the Mind through Interaction . . . 541

→ **THE REAL WORLD** Types of Psychotherapists   542

Psychodynamic Therapy   543

Behavioral and Cognitive Therapies   547

Humanistic and Existential Therapies   553

Groups in Therapy   555

Medical and Biological Treatments: Healing the Mind through the Brain 559

Antipsychotic Medications   560

→ THE REAL WORLD **Tales from the Madhouse** 561

Antianxiety Medications 562

Antidepressants and Mood Stabilizers 563

Herbal and Natural Products 564

Medications in Perspective 565

Biological Treatments beyond Medication 567

Treatment Effectiveness: For Better or for Worse 569

Evaluating Treatments 570

Which Treatments Work? 573

→ THE REAL WORLD **Controversial Treatment: Eye Movement Desensitization and Reprocessing** 575

→ WHERE DO YOU STAND? **Should Drugs Be Used to Prevent Traumatic Memories?** 577

Chapter 15 Stress and Health 581

Sources of Stress: What Gets to You 582

Stressful Events 582

Chronic Stressors 584

Perceived Control over Stressful Events 585

Stress Reactions: All Shook Up 585

Physical Reactions 586

→ HOT SCIENCE **Why Sickness Feels Bad: Psychological Effects of Immune Response** 589

Psychological Reactions 591

Stress Management: Dealing with It 595

Mind Management 595

Body Management 598

→ THE REAL WORLD **Rubbing the Right and Wrong Way: Massage and Therapeutic Touch** 599

Situation Management 601

The Psychology of Illness: When It's in Your Head 604

Sensitivity to Illness 604

→ HOT SCIENCE **This Is Your Brain on Placebos** 606

On Being a Patient 608

The Psychology of Health: Feeling Good 610

Personality and Health 611

Health-Promoting Behaviors and Self-regulation 612

→ WHERE DO YOU STAND? **Consider Yourself Warned** 618

Chapter 16 Social Psychology 621

Social Behavior: Interacting with People 622

Survival: The Struggle for Resources 622

Reproduction: The Quest for Immortality 631

→ THE REAL WORLD **An Affair to Remember** 634

→ HOT SCIENCE **Beautifully Average** 637

Social Influence: Controlling People 640

The Hedonic Motive: The Power of Pleasure 640

The Approval Motive: The Power of Social Acceptance 641

The Accuracy Motive: The Power of Being Right 645

→ THE REAL WORLD **This Just In** 649

Social Cognition: Understanding People 652

Stereotyping: Drawing Inferences from Categories   652

Attribution: Drawing Inferences from Actions   657

→ **WHERE DO YOU STAND?** **Are You Prejudiced?**   660

Glossary G-1

References R-1

Name Index NI-1

Subject Index SI-1

Preface

For most of our adult lives, the three of us have been studying the human mind and teaching our students what we and other psychologists have learned about it. We've each written articles in professional journals to convey our findings and ideas to our colleagues, and we've each published popular nonfiction titles to communicate with the general public. For each of us, though, something important has been missing: a text written specifically for students. Reading a textbook should be just as engaging as reading a popular book, and we've worked hard to make sure that happens in *Psychology*.

Telling the Story of Psychology from a Fresh Perspective

As we wrote this textbook, we found ourselves confronting a question: Why were we attracted to psychology in the first place? Although we each have different interests in psychology that cover a broad range of the field—from cognitive psychology to social psychology to clinical psychology and neuroscience—we all share a common fascination with the errors, illusions, biases, and other mental mistakes that reveal how the mind works.

We believe psychology is interesting in large part because it offers insights into the errors of human thought and action. Some of these errors are familiar and amusing (why do we forget jokes the moment we've heard them?), and others are exceptional and tragic (what causes a pilot to fail to deploy his landing gear on approach?). But all of them cry out for explanation. Indeed, if our thoughts, feelings, and actions were error free, our lives would be orderly, predictable, and dull—and there would be few mysteries for psychology to illuminate.

But human behavior is endlessly surprising, and its surprises are what motivates us to understand the psychological complexities that produce them. Why is memory so prone to error, and what can be done to improve it? How can people discriminate against others even when they're trying hard not to? How can mobs make normal people behave like monsters? What allows a child with an IQ of 50 to compose a symphony? How can newborn babies know about kinetics and occlusion when they can't even find their own fingers? Psychology offers the possibility of answering such questions from a scientific perspective, and it is this possibility that drew us to the field.

Troubleshooting the Mindbugs

Every rambunctious child knows that you can learn how a toy works by breaking it. If you want to understand things so that you can eventually fix them and even build new ones, knowing how they break is invaluable. When things break, we learn about the pieces and processes that normally work together. Breakdown and error are not just about destruction and failure—they are paths to knowledge. Psychology has long followed these paths. The "bugs" of the human mind reveal a great deal about its function, structure, and design. For example: Freud and other pioneers studied psychological disorders not only to alleviate human misery, but because the disordered mind provides a window through which to view normal psychological functioning; the social blunders of autistic people teach us how human beings usually manage to have such seamless interactions; depression teaches us how most people deal so effectively with the losses and heartbreaks of everyday life; violence and antisocial behavior teach us how most people manage to live relatively peaceful lives characterized by morality and self-control; visual illusions teach us how the eye and brain normally generate visual experiences that correspond so faithfully to the realities they represent; errors of inference and memory teach us how people ordinarily make successful decisions and how they remember so much, so well, for so long. These and other examples of mindbugs are integrated throughout the chapters:

- Automatic behaviors, such as when an individual says "Thank you" to a machine that has just delivered a stamp, provide important insights into the role of habit in mental life (Chapter 1, page 4)

- The tendency to underestimate the likelihood of coincidences helps us understand why people believe in magical abilities such as ESP (Chapter 2, page 46)

- Phantom limb syndrome, in which amputees can feel their missing limbs moving and even feel pain in their absent limbs, sheds light on plasticity in the brain (Chapter 3, page 100)

- The experience of synesthesia, where certain musical notes can evoke visual sensations of certain colors or certain sounds can produce an experience of specific tastes, provides clues about how perception works (Chapter 4, pages 121–123)

- The "seven sins" of memory are aspects of forgetting and distortion that show how people reconstruct their pasts and also reveal the adaptive functions of memory (Chapter 5, pages 187–203)

- Rewarding an individual can result in a decrease in the rewarded behavior when an external award undermines the intrinsic satisfaction of performing a task, thereby illuminating some of the limits of reinforcement (Chapter 6, page 229)

- Savants, such as an English boy named Christopher who was fluent in 16 languages yet lacked the cognitive capacities to live on his own, provide striking evidence that cognition is composed of distinct abilities (Chapter 7, page 253)

- Trying not to think about something can make you obsessed with it and quickly reveals one of the key problems we have in controlling our minds and actions (Chapter 8, pages 303–304)

- The pattern of people's errors on intelligence tests teaches us about how different abilities—such as language and reasoning—are related (Chapter 9, page 348)

- The mistakes people make when identifying their own emotions helps us understand the role that cognition plays in emotional experience (Chapter 10, page 378)

- The mistakes young children make when trying to answer questions about other people's beliefs and desires tell us how human beings come to understand their own minds and the minds of others (Chapter 11, pages 416–417)

- People often report that their favorite letter of the alphabet is the one that begins their own name, revealing an irrational bias to think of "me" first (Chapter 12, page 483)

- Some personality problems—such as being extremely dramatic, shy, or dishonest—are not recognized by the people who have them, showing how little insight we have into our own disorders (Chapter 13, pages 528–529)

- Placebo treatments such as sugar pills or therapies with no "active ingredients" can still sometimes be effective and so show how susceptible we are to psychological influences on our health (Chapter 14, pages 571–572)

- Students taking a boring class cough more often than those in an exciting class, revealing how disease symptoms can be modified by processes of attention (Chapter 15, pages 604–605)

- Stereotyping teaches us how people use categories to make predictions about objects and events they have never seen before (Chapter 16, pages 652–656)

Our experience as teachers suggests that students are every bit as fascinated by these mental oddities as we are. So we've incorporated these inherently interesting examples of human behavior throughout the text. Derived from the idea of "computer bugs," we refer to these examples as "mindbugs." Mindbugs are useful in illuminating the mechanisms of human psychology: They relate seemingly different topics to one another and highlight the strengths of the human mind as well as its vulnerabilities. We have used these errors, mistakes, and behavioral oddities as a thematic focus in each of the domains traditionally covered by introductory textbooks.

This approach has at least two benefits. First, it provides a conceptual linkage between chapters on normal psychological functions (such as memory, perception, and emotion) and chapters on pathology (such as psychological disorders, therapy, and stress and health). Second, psychologists know that most errors occur when normally adaptive mechanisms temporarily misbehave. For example, the tendency to stereotype others is not merely a bad habit acquired from ignorant parents but rather a misuse of the normally adaptive tendency to categorize objects and then use what one knows about the category to prejudge the object itself. A focus on mindbugs invites students to think of the mind as an adaptive solution to the problems that human beings face in the real world.

The Brain and the Classic Questions of Psychology

Just as psychologists come to understand the mind by observing the instances in which it fails and by considering the problems that it has adapted to solve, they also understand the mind by examining the brain. Traditionally, psychologists have relied on nature's occasional and inexact experiments to teach them about the function of the brain, and the study of brain-damaged patients continues to be an important source of new information. In the last two decades, emerging neuroimaging technologies (such as functional magnetic resonance imaging and positron emission tomography) have allowed psychologists to peer deep into the healthy, living brain as well. These two methods have led to the birth of a new field called cognitive neuroscience, and the findings from this field are already shedding light on some interesting and familiar problems. Consider these examples:

- When people have hallucinations, do they actually see pink elephants and hear the voice of God? Neuroimaging studies have shown that both visual and auditory hallucinations are accompanied by increased activity in the regions of the brain that are normally activated by real visual and auditory experience. This suggests that people really are seeing and hearing during hallucinatory episodes.

- When people claim to remember satanic rituals and childhood sexual abuse, are they really remembering? Neuroimaging studies have revealed that false memories are accompanied by activity in the regions of the brain that are normally associated with true memories, suggesting that people who claim to remember such events are, in fact, having a memorial experience.

- When people fail to get what they wanted and then claim to like what they got, is this just a case of "sour grapes" or do they really prefer the outcome they received to the one they originally desired? Studies of amnesiac patients have revealed that people like the outcomes they receive even when they cannot remember what those outcomes are, suggesting that unreachable grapes really do taste sour.

Cases such as these provide a natural entry to discussions of fundamental issues in perception, memory, and motivation. The brain is the basis of all psychological phenomena, and imaging technologies reveal how the brain creates the miracle of the mind. Our decision to integrate neuroscience in this way reflects the current direction in which the field of psychology is moving. The brain is no longer just the province of specialists—the widespread use of imaging techniques has allowed a whole generation of researchers who study cognition, development, personality, emotion, and social psychology to become excited about the possibility of learning how the brain and the mind are interrelated. We have attempted to bring this excitement and new knowledge to introductory students through vivid case illustrations, brain images, and nontechnical explanations.

Choices That Inspire, Teach, and Respect Students' Intelligence

An introduction to psychology should focus on what is most important and what is most compelling. It should not be a rehashing of all things psychological. In fact, no single author—nor any three authors—can be expert in all the various domains of psychology. To ensure that *Psychology* offers the very best of psychological science, we formed our Contributing Consultants board of accomplished researchers and master teachers in areas outside our areas of expertise. They advised us on early drafts and throughout the writing process, explaining what is important, what is true, and how to think about the issues and data in their respective fields. Taking this information, we have addressed topics in each subfield of psychology in the greater context of that field as a whole. Each chapter has a narrative arc that tells the story of that field of psychology and provides a thematic context that will hook students from the start. In writing *Psychology*, we have made informed choices about our topic coverage weighing classic studies and current research to produce a contemporary perspective on the field. We believe that our approach engages students, teaches students, entertains students, and above all inspires them as the three of us are inspired by psychology.

Effective Pedagogy

Captivating and entertaining our readers are not our only goals in *Psychology*. Helping students learn and remember what they have learned remains paramount. We have devised a pedagogical program that reinforces the book's themes and supports student learning.

Chapter-Opening Vignette Each chapter begins with a story of an incident from everyday life or a case study to capture students' attention and preview the topics covered in the chapter. The stories typically describe a mindbug that helps explain the chapter topic.

Special-Topic Boxes

- *Hot Science:* Each chapter has one or more boxes that feature exciting, cutting-edge research on one of the chapter's core topics. Often this research points toward some big question that psychologists hope to answer in the next few decades. For example, in the chapter on consciousness (Chapter 8), one of the Hot Science boxes looks at recent research suggesting that decisions made without conscious thought can sometimes be better than those made with intensive conscious deliberation. These boxes are meant to help students see that psychology is a living enterprise with many uncharted territories, an enterprise that has room for "hot" new insights and future contributions—perhaps from the students themselves.

- *The Real World:* Psychology is about things we experience every day. These boxes focus on these experiences and apply the chapter content to some pressing real-world phenomenon. Some of The Real World boxes focus on issues straight from the news (Chapter 3, "Neuroscience and Behavior," includes a box on the legal status of brain death and discusses the Terry Schiavo case), whereas others focus on issues that may be relevant to their personal lives (Chapter 16, "Social Psychology," has a box on secret romantic relationships).

Where Do You Stand? (End of Chapter) Each chapter ends with a "critical thinking" feature that discusses a topic related to the chapter content. Students are presented with questions that encourage them to consider more deeply the implications of these topics and require them to report their own experiences or to generate defensible arguments and cogent opinions—rather than to remember factual answers. For example, Chapter 11, "Development," presents students with arguments for and against parental licensing, and Chapter 10, "Emotion and Motivation," asks students whether governments should pay citizens to vote.

Interim Summaries To promote study and learning of the material, each major section concludes with *In Summary* features that recap the major points in the section and provide a transition to the next section.

Only Human Features These funny-but-true accounts of oddities and errors in human behavior provide a bit of comic relief that relates to the issues under discussion.

Definitions and Glossary Each key term—a central concept, experimental procedure, or theory—is set apart from the text in boldface type, with its definition immediately following in italic type. The terms and their definitions are provided in a marginal glossary as well as an alphabetical, end-of-text glossary. The terms themselves appear at the end of the chapter with page numbers for easy reference.

Chapter Review In addition to the interim summaries, a bulleted summary at the end of the chapter summarizes the main concepts in each major section.

Recommended Readings Each chapter concludes with recommended readings, including trade books accessible to students, classic articles from the professional literature, online articles, and occasionally films related to a key concept or phenomenon discussed in the chapter.

Media and Supplements to Accompany *Psychology*
Web/CD-ROM

NEW! Worth Publishers Student Video Tool Kit for *Psychology*
With its superb collection of brief (1 to 13 minutes) clips and emphasis on the biological basis of behavior, the **Student Video Tool Kit** gives students a fresh way to experience both the classic experiments at the heart of psychological science and cutting-edge research conducted by the field's most influential investigators.

The **Student Video Tool Kit** provides 51 video clips with a balance of contemporary news footage and classic experiments (both original and re-created) to help illustrate key concepts of the introductory psychology course. The **Student Video Tool Kit** is correlated to each Worth introductory psychology textbook, providing students with book-specific activities and multiple-choice questions. Students can print their answers to these questions, making the **Student Video Tool Kit** a seamless part of your course.

NEW! Video Tool Kit for *Psychology*: Online Version
The online version of the **Video Tool Kit for *Psychology*** includes the 51 video clips found on the student CD and is easily accessible through an access code packaged with *Psychology*. Fully customizable, the **Online Video Tool Kit** offers instructors the option of incorporating videos into assignments as well as annotating each video with notes or instructions, making the tool kit an integral part of the introductory course. Instructors also have the option of assigning the tool kit to students without instructor involvement. Videos are correlated to the textbook, and each video is accompanied by multiple-choice questions so that students can assess their understanding of what

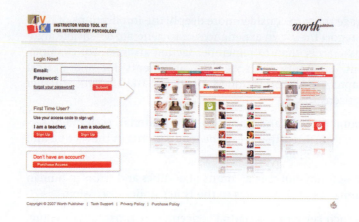

they have seen. Student responses/grades are sent to an online grade book, allowing instructors to easily assign and assess as much of the **Online Video Tool Kit** as desired.

NEW! PsychInvestigator: Laboratory Learning in Introductory Psychology by Arthur Kohn, PhD, Dark Blue Morning Productions

This exciting new Web-based product is a virtual laboratory environment that enables students to participate in real experiments. Students are introduced—step by step—to the various research techniques that are used in psychology. In **PsychInvestigator**, students participate in classic psychology experiments, generate real data, and are trained to create lab reports that summarize their findings. In each experiment, students participate in compelling video tutorials that are displayed before *and* after the actual experiment. **PsychInvestigator** requires no additional faculty time. Students' quiz scores can be automatically uploaded into an online grade book if instructors wish to monitor students' progress.

eLibrary to Accompany *Psychology* (worthpublishers.com/elibrary)

The **eLibrary** brings together text and supplementary resources in a single, easy-to-use Web site and includes a sophisticated, straightforward search engine (similar to Google) that allows a quick search for resources related to specific topics (not just by chapter). Through simple browse and search tools, users can quickly access content from the text and ancillary package and either download it or create a Web page to share with students.

PsychSim 5.0 CD-ROM and Booklet by Thomas Ludwig, Hope College

These 42 interactive simulations involve students in the practice of psychological research by having them play the role of experimenter (conditioning a rat, probing the hypothalamus electrically, working in a sleep lab) or subject (responding to tests of memory or visual illusions, interpreting facial expressions). Other simulations provide dynamic tutorials or demonstrations. In addition, five-question multiple-choice quizzes are available for each activity on the **Book Companion site.**

Psychology **Book Companion Website at www.worthpublishers.com/schacter**
The *Psychology* **Book Companion Website** offers students a virtual study guide 24 hours a day, 7 days a week. Best of all, these resources are free and do not require any special access codes or passwords. The site includes

- Annotated Web links
- Online quizzing
- Interactive flash cards
- Online version of 20 PsychSim 5.0 modules (by Thomas Ludwig, Hope College), accompanied by five-question, multiple-choice quizzes for each PsychSim activity
- Audio downloads
- A **password-protected Instructor site** offers a full array of teaching resources, including a new suite of PowerPoint slides, electronic lecture guides, an online quiz grade book, and links to additional tools.

PsychInquiry for *Psychology:* Student Activities in Research and Critical Thinking CD-ROM by Thomas Ludwig, Hope College
Customized to work specifically with *Psychology,* this CD-ROM contains dozens of interactive activities designed to help students learn about psychological research and to improve their critical-thinking skills.

Course Management

NEW! PsychPortal—One click. One place. For all the psychology tools you need!

- Easy integration of all resources
- Easy-to-assign content
- Easy customization
- Easy to afford

PsychPortal is Worth's nationally hosted learning management solution. It combines standard course management features (such as course announcements, a syllabus manager, a calendar, and discussion forums) with state-of-the-art content and interactive-learning features. **PsychPortal** is organized into three main teaching and learning components: the **Interactive eBook and Study Center, Course Materials,** and **Quizzes and Assignments,** all fully customizable by the instructor. In addition, **PsychPortal** includes **PsychInvestigator,** a virtual laboratory environment that enables students to participate in real experiments and introduces them to the various research techniques that are used in psychology.

PsychPortal Features

- The **Interactive eBook and Study Center** offers a complete online version of the text, equipped with interactive note taking and highlighting capability and fully integrated with all the media resources available with *Psychology.*

- **Course Materials** organizes all the resources for *Psychology* in one location for both students' and instructors' ease of use. In addition, it allows instructors to post their own materials for use or assignment.

- **Quizzes and Assignments** enable instructors to automatically assign and grade homework and quizzes for their classes. Student assignments are collected in one location and allow students immediate feedback on their progress.

Enhanced Course Management Solutions: Superior Content All in One Place www.bfwpub.com/lms
The most powerful course management tools are worthless without solid teaching and learning resources that have been meaningfully integrated. Our enhanced *Psychology*

turnkey course in Blackboard, WebCT (Campus Edition and Vista), and Angel course management systems offers a completely integrated solution that you can easily customize and adapt to meet your teaching goals and course objectives. Student content is organized by book chapters and instructor content by content type (e.g., PowerPoint slides). On demand, we can also provide our enhanced *Psychology* solution to those using Desire2Learn, Sakai, and Moodle.

Sample Instructor Content

- Video clip library of more than 40 digitized video clips organized by the text chapters
- Complete test bank
- Complete instructor's resources (in Word and PDF formats)
- Complete suite of PowerPoint slides
- Chapter art PowerPoint slides
- Enhanced lecture PowerPoint slides
- Step-up psychology review game
- Personal response system/clicker questions
- PsychSim 5.0 work sheet answer key
- Link to the instructor's eLibrary

Sample Student Content

- PsychSim 5.0 (20 activities, work sheets, and quizzes)
- Interactive flash cards (in both Spanish and English)
- Critical thinking and applications exercises
- Anatomical art self-quizzes (for select chapters)
- Crossword puzzles
- Additional simulations and demonstrations (for select chapters)
- Annotated web links
- Link to American Psychological Association style guide

To learn more about the course management solution to accompany *Psychology,* go to www.bfwpub.com.

NEW! We Now Offer Customized ePacks and Course Cartridges
Through the custom program, we can also help you tailor *Psychology* content to meet your course needs as well as provide you with technical support and services such as customizing your tests and quizzes, adding new student premium resources, adding Web links, reorganizing content, and adding a customized course banner. For more details, contact your Worth representative.

Assessment

Printed Test Bank by Russell Frohardt and Helen Just, St. Edward's University
The **Test Bank** provides more than 2,000 multiple-choice, true/false, and essay questions. Each question is keyed to a chapter objective and APA Outcome, referenced to the textbook pages, and rated for level of difficulty. Web quizzes from the Book Companion site and Quick Quizzes from the Study Guide (for instructors who incorporate or require the Study Guide in their courses) are also included.

Diploma Computerized Test Bank (available in Windows and Macintosh on one CD-ROM)
The CD-ROM allows you to add an unlimited number of questions, edit questions, format a test, scramble questions, and include pictures, equations, or multimedia links. With the accompanying grade book, you can record students' grades throughout a

course, sort student records and view detailed analyses of test items, curve tests, generate reports, and add weights to grades. This CD-ROM is the access point for **Diploma Online Testing**. Blackboard- and WebCT-formatted versions of the **Test Bank** are also available in the Course Cartridge and ePack.

Diploma Online Testing at www.brownstone.net

With **Diploma**, you can easily create and administer exams over the Internet with questions that incorporate multimedia and interactivity. Students receive instant feedback and can take the quizzes multiple times. Instructors can sort and view results and can take advantage of various grade-book and result-analysis features as well as restrict tests to specific computers or time blocks.

Online Quizzing at worthpublishers.com/schacter

Now you can easily and securely quiz students online using prewritten multiple-choice questions for each chapter. Students receive instant feedback and can take the quizzes multiple times. As the instructor, you can view results by quiz, student, or question or you can get weekly results via e-mail.

iClicker Radio Frequency Classroom Response System
Offered by Worth Publishers in partnership with iClicker

iClicker is Worth's hassle-free new polling system, created by educators for educators. This radio frequency system makes your class time more efficient and interactive. **iClicker** allows you to pause to ask questions and instantly record responses as well as take attendance, direct students through lectures, and gauge students' understanding of the material.

Presentation

ActivePsych: Classroom Activities Project and Video Teaching Modules

Recognizing that professors want out-of-the-box tools to make introductory psychology more applied and class presentations more interactive, Worth Publishers is proud to launch **ActivePsych**, a suite of instructor presentation CD-ROMs that include the following:

- Interactive activities designed for in-class presentation and group participation. **ActivePsych** activities require very little instructor preparation (allowing adopters to simply load the CD-ROM and launch the activity) and are designed to foster class discussion. Activities include animations, video clips, illustrations and photographs, and critical thinking questions. A number of activities have been adapted from Martin Bolt's Instructor's Resources and Thomas Ludwig's PsychSim 5.0 (and are now classroom-presentation friendly). **ActivePsych** also includes a significant number of completely original, creative activities all written (and class-tested) by veteran introductory psychology teachers.

- **ActivePsych: Classroom Activities Project** This segment of ActivePsych includes

  32 flash-based interactive demonstrations designed to promote classroom discussion and critical thinking.

  22 PowerPoint-based demonstrations, inventories, and surveys designed to assess student understanding of various psychological topics. These demonstrations can easily work with the iClicker classroom response systems.

- **NEW!** **Digital Media Archive, Second Edition** Housed in **ActivePsych** and edited by Joe Morrissey, State University of New York at Binghamton (with the assistance of Ann Merriwether, State University of New York at Binghamton and Meredith Woitach, University of Rochester), the second edition offers 33 sections of completely new short video clips and animations drawn from a variety of sources.

- **NEW!** *Scientific American* Frontiers Teaching Modules, **Third Edition** Housed in **ActivePsych** and edited by Martin Bolt, Calvin College, the third edition offers 15 edited clips from *Scientific American* Frontiers segments produced between 2003 and 2005.

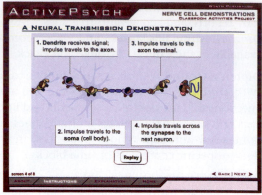

Instructor's Resource CD-ROM

Customized for *Psychology,* this CD-ROM contains prebuilt PowerPoint presentation slide sets for each chapter, a digital photograph library, an electronic version of the Instructor's Resources, and a complete illustration library. A new intuitive browser interface makes it easy to preview and use all elements in this CD-ROM.

- **Chapter Art PowerPoint Slides** feature all of the text art and illustrations (including tables, charts, and graphs) in a PowerPoint format. We also offer a number of layered PowerPoint slides for key biological processes.

- **Step Up to Psychology: A PowerPoint Review Game** In this PowerPoint-based "game show," teams of students climb the pyramid by answering questions related to chapter material. Questions are ranked for difficulty (four levels) and include both factual/definitional and conceptual/application formats.

- **Lecture PowerPoint Presentation Slides** focus on key concepts and themes from the text and feature tables, graphs, and figures from both the text and outside sources.

- **Digital Photo Library** provides all the photographs from *Psychology* organized by chapter.

Worth Image and Lecture Gallery at www.worthpublishers.com/ilg

Using the Image and Lecture Gallery, you can browse, search, and download text art, illustrations, outlines, and prebuilt PowerPoint slides for *all* Worth titles. Users can also create personal folders for easy organization of the materials.

Video/DVD Resources

NEW! Worth Publishers Video Tool Kit for Introductory Psychology • Available in Dual Platform CD-ROMs, VHS, and DVD

With its superb collection of brief (1 to 13 minutes) video clips and emphasis on the biological bases of behavior, the **Instructor Video Tool Kit** allows you to introduce central topics, illustrate and reinforce specific core concepts, or stimulate small-group and full-classroom discussions. The **Video Tool Kit** includes a set of 72 digitized video clips combining both research and news footage from the BBC Motion Gallery, CBS News, and other sources. These clips can be easily used with PowerPoint or other presentation resources for classroom lectures and are accompanied by a faculty guide by Martin Bolt (Calvin College).

Moving Images: Exploring Psychology through Film • Available in VHS and DVD
Edited by Martin Bolt (Calvin College), this completely new series (drawn from the Films for the Humanities and Sciences) contains 25 1- to 8-minute clips of real people, real experiments, and real patients, combining historical footage with cutting-edge research and news programming. Some highlights include "Brain and Behavior: A Contemporary Phineas Gage," "Firewalking: Mind over Matter," and "Social Rejection: The Need to Belong."

Worth Digital Media Archive • Available in Dual Platform CD-ROMs, VHS, and DVD
This rich presentation tool contains 42 digitized video clips of classic experiments and research. Footage includes Bandura's Bobo doll experiment, Takooshian's bystander studies, Piaget's conservation experiment, Harlow's monkey experiments, and Milgram's obedience studies. The **Digital Media Archive** CD-ROM clips are available in MPEG for optimal visual presentation and are compatible with PowerPoint.

***Psychology: The Human Experience* Teaching Modules • Available in VHS and DVD**
This series includes more than 3 hours of footage from the introductory psychology telecourse *Psychology: The Human Experience,* produced by Coast Learning Systems in collaboration with Worth Publishers. Footage contains noted scholars, the latest research, and striking animations.

***The Many Faces of Psychology* Video**
Created and written by Frank J. Vattano, Colorado State University, and Martin Bolt, Calvin College (Produced by the Office of Instructional Services, Colorado State University) • Available in VHS and DVD
A terrific way to begin your psychology course, *The Many Faces of Psychology* introduces psychology as a science and a profession, illustrating basic and applied methods. This 22-minute video presents some of the major areas in which psychologists work and teach.

***The Brain* Video Teaching Modules, Second Edition**
Edited by Frank J. Vattano and Thomas L. Bennet, Colorado State University, and Michelle Butler, United States Air Force Academy • Available in VHS and DVD
This collection of 32 short clips provides vivid examples for myriad topics in introductory psychology.

***Scientific American* Frontiers Video Collection, Second Edition • Available in VHS and DVD**
Hosted by Alan Alda, these 8- to-12-minute teaching modules from the highly praised *Scientific American* series feature the work of such notable researchers as Steve Sumi, Renee Baillargeon, Carl Rosengren, Laura Pettito, Steven Pinker, Barbara Rothbaum, Bob Stickgold, Irene Pepperberg, Marc Hauser, Linda Bartoshuk, and Michael Gazzaniga.

***The Mind* Video Teaching Modules, Second Edition**
Edited by Frank J. Vattano, Colorado State University, in consultation with Charles Brewer, Furman University, and David Myers, Hope College, in association with WNET • Available in VHS and DVD
These 35 brief, engaging video clips will dramatically enhance and illustrate your lectures. Examples include segments on language processing, infant cognitive development, genetic factors in alcoholism, and living without memory (featuring a dramatic interview with Clive Wearing).

Print Supplements

For Instructors

Instructor's Resources by Russell Frohardt and Helen Just, St. Edwards University
Written and compiled by experienced instructors of introductory psychology, the **Instructor's Resources** includes the following:

- An **Outline of Resources** for each chapter, organized by text topic, includes the relevant Instructor's Resources items by type (classroom exercise, lecture/discussion topic, etc.) with a cross-reference to its appropriate Instructor Resource page number.

- **Chapter Outlines** follow the major text section headings (with page references), providing relevant instructional materials for each topic—including dozens of ready-to-use, detailed lecture/discussion ideas, student projects, classroom exercises (many with ready-to-use handouts for in-class or out-of-class use), suggestions of multimedia resources provided by Worth Publishers (see pages xxi–xxvii), and feature films (as they apply to psychological concepts discussed in the text). Other film resources are outlined at the end of each chapter of the Instructor's Resources.

- **Chapter Objectives** from the text highlight main concepts and terms and detail the key points of each text chapter. They can be used as essay questions in classroom examinations. Test Bank and Study Guide questions are keyed to the Chapter Objectives as well.

Instructor's Media Guide
This handy guide quickly and visually organizes the extensive instructor and student media resources available for *Psychology*, including every video, Web activity (including PsychInvestigator and PsychSim), PowerPoint, and more—all organized by chapter.

For Students

Study Guide by Russell Frohardt and Helen Just, St. Edwards University
Following the text's content, the **Study Guide** offers the following for each main chapter:

- **"The Big Picture,"** a brief wrap-up of the chapter's main ideas and concepts
- **Chapter Objectives**, which also appear in the Instructor's Resources and Test Bank
- **Chapter Overview**, a fill-in-the-blank summary that is divided by major section
- Three 10-question **"Quick Quizzes"** and a conceptual/analytical essay question
- **Answers section** with page references, corresponding chapter objectives, and explanations of why a choice is correct or incorrect
- **"Things to Ponder,"** a section that helps students extend and apply knowledge and think about where the material might be going.

Pursuing Human Strengths: A Positive Psychology Guide by Martin Bolt, Calvin College
By using the scientific method in its efforts to assess, understand, and then build human strengths, positive psychology balances the investigation of weakness and damage with a study of strength and virtue. This brief positive psychology guide gives instructors and students alike the means to learn more about this relevant approach to psychology.

Critical Thinking Companion, Second Edition
Jane Halonen, University of West Florida, and Cynthia Gray, Alverno College
Tied to the main topics in psychology, this engaging handbook includes six categories of critical thinking exercises: pattern recognition, practical problem solving, creative problem solving, scientific critical thinking, psychological reasoning, and perspective taking, which connect to the six categories used in the Critical Thinking Exercises available in the student Study Guide.

Scientific American Reader to Accompany *Psychology* by Daniel L. Schacter, Daniel T. Gilbert, and Daniel M. Wegner
Exclusive to Worth Publishers and in partnership with *Scientific American*, this collection of articles features pioneering and cutting-edge research across the fields of psychology. Selected by the authors themselves, this collection provides further insight into the fields of psychology through articles written for a popular audience.

Scientific American Mind
Scientific American Mind is a new magazine from the editors of *Scientific American*. The magazine explores riveting breakthroughs in psychology, neuroscience, and related fields. *Scientific American Mind* investigates, analyzes, and reveals new thinking on a variety of contemporary psychological theories and ideas.

Improving the Mind and Brain: A *Scientific American* Special Issue
This single-topic issue from *Scientific American* magazine features findings from the most distinguished researchers in the field.

Scientific American Explores the Hidden Mind: A Collector's Edition
This collector's edition includes feature articles that explore and reveal the mysterious inner workings of our minds and brains.

Acknowledgments

Despite what you might guess by looking at our photographs, we all found women who were willing to marry us. We thank Susan McGlynn, Marilynn Oliphant, and Toni Wegner for that particular miracle and also for their love and support during the years when we were busy writing this book.

Although ours are the names on the cover, writing a textbook is a team sport, and we were lucky to have an amazing group of professionals in our dugout. Our contributing consultants not only shaped our understanding of key areas of psychology but provided us with original material, expert ideas, and overviews that allowed us to write knowledgeably about topics not our own. We owe them a significant debt of thanks. They are Martin M. Antony, Mark Baldwin, Patricia Csank, Denise D. Cummins, Ian J. Deary, Howard Eichenbaum, Paul Harris, Arthur S. Reber, Alan Swinkels, Richard M. Wenzlaff, and Steven Yantis.

We are grateful for the editorial, clerical, and research assistance we received from Celeste Beck, Amy Cameron, Beth Mela, Betsy Sparrow, Adrian Gilmore, and Alana Wong.

In addition, we would like to thank our core supplements authors from St. Edward's University in Austin, Texas. They provided insight into the role our book can play in the classroom and adeptly developed the materials to support it. Helen Just, Russ Frohardt, and supplements coordinator Alan Swinkels, we appreciate your tireless work in the classroom and the experience you brought to the book's supplements.

Over 1,000 students have class-tested chapters of *Psychology* in various stages of development. Not only are we encouraged by the overwhelmingly positive responses to *Psychology,* but we are also pleased to incorporate these students' insightful and constructive comments. In particular, we would like to thank the introductory psychology students at the following institutions who learned from these chapters in their classrooms and contributed to the development of *Psychology* with a level of engagement we have come to expect from our best students: Baker University; Baldwin Wallace College; Boston University; Bowling Green State University; College of Lake County; College of St. Elizabeth; Curry College; Dominican University; Gainesville College; Hiwassee College; Illinois Wesleyan University; Kennesaw State University; Loyola University, Lakeshore; McKendree College; Morrisville State College, SUNY; Nazareth College of Rochester; Oregon State University; Regis University; Rochester Institute of Technology; Rowan University; Shepherd University; State University of West Georgia; Texas A&M University; University of Arizona; University of Arkansas-Fayetteville; University of Idaho; University of Kansas; University of Minnesota-Duluth; University of Nebraska at Kearney; University of San Diego; University of Texas at Austin; Villanova University; Wake Forest University; Washburn University; Washtenaw Community College.

We also learned a lot from focus group attendees, survey respondents, chapter reviewers, and class testers who read parts of our book, and we thank them for their time and insights, both of which were considerable. They include

George Alder
Simon Fraser University

Brad Alford
University of Scranton

John Allen
University of Arizona

Amber Alliger
Hunter College

Erica Altomare
University of Pittsburgh at Titusville

Eileen Astor-Stetson
Bloomsburg University

Raymond Baird
University of Texas, San Antonio

Scott Bates
Utah State University

Phillip Batten
Wake Forest University

Kyle Baumbauer
Texas A&M University

Kimberly Bays-Brown
Ball State University

Denise Berg
UCLA

Frank Bernieri
Oregon State University

Joan Bihun
University of Colorado, Denver

Wendi Born
Baker University

Deborah Briihl
Valdosta State University

Sara Broaders
Northwestern University

Cliff Brown
Wittenberg University

Krisanne Bursik
Suffolk University

Adam Butler
University of Northern Iowa

Peter Carole
Regis University

Isabelle Cherney
Creighton University

Sharon Claffey
University of Georgia

Samuel Clay
BYU-Idaho

Carl Clements
University of Alabama

Lawrence Cohen
University of Delaware

David Copeland
University of Nevada, Las Vegas

Gregory Corso
Georgia Institute of Technology

Renee Countryman
Illinois Wesleyan University

Cynthia Craig
Thomas Jefferson University

Susan Cross
Iowa State University

Mary Ellen Dello Stritto
Western Oregon University

Cathy DeSoto
University of Northern Iowa

Mary Devitt
Jamestown College

Tracy Dunne
Boston University

Steven Dworkin
Jacksonville State University

Jennifer Dyck
SUNY Fredonia

Vanessa Edkins
University of Kansas

Tami Eggleston
McKendree University

Lisa End-Berg
Kennesaw State University

Oney Fitzpatrick
Lamar University

Bill Flack
Bucknell University

Sandra Frankmann
Colorado State University–Pueblo

Phyllis R. Freeman
SUNY at New Paltz

Perry Fuchs
University of Texas, Arlington

Shira Gabriel
University at Buffalo, SUNY

Danielle Gagne
Alfred University

Anne Garcia
Washtenaw Community College

Luis Garcia
Rutgers University–Camden

Wendi Gardner
Northwestern University

Afshin Gharib
Dominican University

Diane Gillmore
Loyola University, Lakeshore

Wendell Goesling
De Anza College

Jamie Goldenberg
University of South Florida

Nicholas Greco
College of Lake County

Erinn Green
Wilmington College

Anthony Greene
University of Wisconsin–Milwaukee

Sarah Grison
University of Illinois, Urbana Champaign

Robert Guttentag
The University of North Carolina at Greensboro

Darlene Hannah
Wheaton College

Deletha Hardin
University of Tampa

David Harrison
Virginia Tech University

Mike Havens
Montana State University, Billings

Stephen Heinrichs
Regis College

Gloria Henderson
University of San Diego

Patricia Hinton
Hiwassee College

Debra Hollister
Valencia Community College

Jeffrey Holmes
Ithaca College

Herman Huber
College of St. Elizabeth

Allen Huffcutt
Bradley University

Linda Jackson
Michigan State University

James Jakubow
Florida Atlantic University

Norine Jalbert
Western Connecticut State University

Alisha Janowsky
University of Central Florida

Lance Jones
Bowling Green State University

Steve Joordens
University of Toronto at Scarborough

Deana Julka
University of Portland

Cynthia Kaschub
University of Florida

Mary-Louise Kean
University of California, Irvine

Craig Kinsley
University of Richmond

Michael Knepp
Virginia Tech University

Steve Kohn
Valdosta State University

Kim Krinsky
Georgia Perimeter College

Jose Lafosse
Regis University

Pamela Landau
Eastern Michigan University

Ann Leonard-Zabel
Curry College

Cheyanne Lewis
Shephard University

Pam MacDonald
Washburn University

Brian Malley
University of Michigan

Abe Marrero
Rogers State University

Karen Marsh
University of Minnesota, Duluth

Rona McCall
Regis University

David McDonald
University of Missouri, Columbia

Russell McGuff
Tallahassee Community College

Dani McKinney
SUNY Fredonia

Anca Miron
University of Wisconsin, Oshkosh

John Moritsugu
Pacific Lutheran University

Jane Noll
University of South Florida

Peggy Norwood
Red Rocks Community College

Rory O'Brien McElwee
Rowan University

Kristy Olin
Robert E. Lee High School

John Pierce
Villanova University

Joan Porcaro
Pace University

Gabriel Radvansky
University of Notre Dame

Celia Reaves
Monroe Community College

Cynthia Riedi
Morrisville State College

Bonnie Rosenblatt
Kutztown University

Gail Rothman-Marshall
Rochester Institute of Technology

Michael Russell
Washburn University

Catherine Sanderson
Amherst College

Nelly SantaMaria
University of Pittsburgh

Katie Saulsgiver
University of Florida

David Schroeder
University of Arkansas

Doyce Scott
Southern University, Shreveport

Marc Sebrechts
Catholic University of America

Janet Seide
Bridgewater State College

Ines Segert
University of Missouri, Columbia

Don Sharpe
University of Regina

David Simpson
Carroll College

Alice Skeens
University of Toledo

Jeffrey Skowronek
University of Tampa

John Skowronski
Northern Illinois University

Louisa Slowiaczek
Bowdoin College

Christine Smith
Antioch College

Claire St. Peter Pipkin
West Virginia University

David Steitz
Nazareth College of Rochester

Barry Stennett
Gainesville College

Deborah Stote
University of Texas, Austin

Jim Stringham
University of Georgia

George Taylor
University of Missouri, St. Louis

Brian Thomas
Baldwin-Wallace College

Lisa Thomassen
Indiana University

Inger Thompson
Glendale Community College

David Topor
The University of North Carolina at Greensboro

Michael Trent
Triton College

Julie Turchin
College of San Mateo

Julie Van Dyke
Pace University

Frank Vattano
Colorado State University

David Washburn
Georgia State University

Shannon Welch
University of Idaho

Robin Lea West
University of Florida

Julia Whisenhunt
State University of West Georgia

Len Williams
Rowan University

William Wozniak
University of Nebraska at Kearney

John William Wright
Washington State University

Jay Wright
Washington State University

Karen Yanowitz
Arkansas State University

Barbara Young
Middle Tennessee State University

Tricia Yurak
Rowan University

We are especially grateful to the extraordinary people of Worth Publishers. They include our publisher, Catherine Woods, who provided guidance and encouragement at all stages of the project; our acquisitions editor, Charles Linsmeier, who managed the project with intelligence, grace, and good humor; our senior development editor, Mimi Melek, who beat us mercilessly with her green pen and greatly improved our book in the process, as well as Barbara Brooks, Phyllis Fisher, and Michael Kimball, who also improved the text with their incisive edits; our narrative editor Alan Swinkels, who whipped a lumpy Dan soup into a smooth Dan puree; our associate managing editor Tracey Kuehn, project editor Jane O'Neill, copy editor Karen Taschek, production manager Sarah Segal, and assistant editor Justin Kruger, who through some remarkable alchemy turned a manuscript into a book; our art director Babs Reingold, layout designer Lee Mahler, photo editor Ted Szczepanski, and photo researcher Elyse Rieder, who made that book an aesthetic delight; our senior media editor Andrea Musick, and production manager Stacey Alexander, who guided the development and creation of a superb supplements package; and our executive marketing manager Kate Nurre, and associate director of market development Carlise Stembridge, who served as tireless public advocates for our vision. Thank you one and all. We look forward to working with you again.

Daniel L. Schacter   Daniel T. Gilbert   Daniel M. Wegner

Cambridge, 2007

PSYCHOLOGY

1

Psychology: The Evolution of a Science

Psychology's Roots: The Path to a Science of Mind
Psychology's Ancestors: The Great Philosophers
From the Brain to the Mind: The French Connection
From Physiology to Psychology: A New Science Is Born in Germany
Titchener Brings Structuralism to the United States
James and the Functional Approach
THE REAL WORLD Improving Study Skills

Errors and Illusions Reveal Psychology
Illusions of Movement and the Birth of Gestalt Psychology
Mental Disorders and Multiple Selves
Freud and Psychoanalytic Theory
Influence of Psychoanalysis and the Humanistic Response

Psychology in the 20th Century: Behaviorism Takes Center Stage
Watson and the Emergence of Behaviorism
B. F. Skinner and the Development of Behaviorism

Beyond Behaviorism: Psychology Expands
The Emergence of Cognitive Psychology
The Brain Meets the Mind: The Rise of Cognitive Neuroscience
The Adaptive Mind: The Emergence of Evolutionary Psychology
HOT SCIENCE New Connections

Beyond the Individual: Social and Cultural Perspectives
The Development of Social Psychology
The Emergence of Cultural Psychology

The Profession of Psychology: Past and Present
Psychologists Band Together: The American Psychological Association
What Psychologists Do: Research Careers
WHERE DO YOU STAND? The Perils of Procrastination

A LOT WAS HAPPENING IN 1860. ABRAHAM Lincoln had just been elected president, the Pony Express had just begun to deliver mail between Missouri and California, and a woman named Anne Kellogg had just given birth to a child who would one day grow up to invent the cornflake. But none of this mattered very much to William James, a bright, taciturn, 18-year-old boy who had no idea what to do with his life. He loved to paint and draw but worried that he wasn't talented enough to become a serious artist. He had enjoyed studying biology in school but doubted that a naturalist's salary would ever allow him to get married and have a family of his own. And so like many young people who are faced with difficult decisions about their futures, William abandoned his dreams and chose to do something in which he had little interest but of which his family heartily approved. Alas, within a few months of arriving at Harvard Medical School, his initial disinterest in medicine blossomed into a troubling lack of enthusiasm, and so with a bit of encouragement from the faculty, he put his medical studies on hold to join a biological expedition to the Amazon. The adventure failed to focus his wandering mind (though he learned a great deal about leeches), and when he returned to medical school, both his physical and mental health began to deteriorate. It was clear to everyone that William James was not the sort of person who should be put in charge of a scalpel and a bag of drugs.

Had William become an artist, a biologist, or physician, we would probably remember nothing about him today. Fortunately for us, he was a deeply confused young man who could speak five languages, and when he became so depressed that he was once again forced to leave medical school, he decided to travel around Europe, where at least he knew how to talk to people. And as he talked and listened, he learned about a new science called *psychology* (from a combination of the Greek *psyche*, which means "soul," and *logos*, which means "to study"), which was just beginning to develop. As William read about psychology and talked with those who were developing it, he began to see that this new field was taking a modern, scientific approach to age-old questions about human nature—questions that had become painfully familiar to him during his personal search for meaning, but questions to which only poets and philosophers had ever before offered answers (Bjork, 1983; Simon, 1998). Excited about the new discipline, William returned to America and quickly finished his medical degree. But he never practiced medicine and never intended to do so. Rather, he became a professor at Harvard University and devoted the rest of his life to psychology. His landmark book—*The Principles of Psychology*—is still widely read and remains one of the most influential books ever written on the subject (James, 1890).

William James (1842–1910) was excited by the new field of psychology, which allowed him to apply a scientific approach to age-old questions about the nature of human beings.

A lot has happened since then. Abraham Lincoln has become the face on a penny, the Pony Express has been replaced by a somewhat slower mail system, and the Kellogg Company sells about $9 billion worth of cornflakes every year. If William James (1842–1910) were alive today, he would be amazed by all of these things. But he would probably be even more amazed by the intellectual advances that have taken place in the science that he helped create. Indeed, the sophistication and diversity of modern psychology are nothing short of staggering: Psychologists today are exploring perception, memory, creativity, consciousness, love, anxiety, addictions, and more. They use state-of-the-art technologies to examine what happens in the brain when people feel anger, recall a past experience, undergo hypnosis, or take an intelligence test. They examine the impact of culture on individuals, the origins and uses of language, the ways in which groups form and dissolve, and the similarities and differences between people from different backgrounds. Their research advances the frontiers of basic knowledge and has practical applications as well—from new treatments for depression and anxiety to new systems that allow organizations to function more effectively.

Psychology is *the scientific study of **mind** and **behavior**.* The **mind** refers to our *private inner experience,* the ever-flowing stream of consciousness that is made of perceptions, thoughts, memories, and feelings. **Behavior** refers to *observable actions of human beings and nonhuman animals,* the things that we do in the world, by ourselves or with others. As you will see in the chapters to come, psychology is an attempt to use scientific methods to address fundamental questions about mind and behavior that have puzzled people for millennia. For example, psychologists are curious about the bases of perceptions, thoughts, memories, and feelings, or our subjective sense of self. We'd like to understand how the mind usually functions so effectively in the world, allowing us to accomplish tasks as mundane as tying our shoes, as extraordinary as sending astronauts to the moon, or as sublime as painting the *Mona Lisa.* Importantly, psychologists also want to understand why the mind occasionally functions so *in*effectively in the world, causing us to make errors in reasoning and mistakes in judgment or to experience illusions in perception and gaps in memory. The answers to these questions would have astonished William James. Let's take a look at some examples:

■ *What are the bases of perceptions, thoughts, memories, and feelings, or our subjective sense of self?* For thousands of years, philosophers tried to understand how the objective, physical world of the body was related to the subjective, psychological world of the mind, and some philosophers even suggested that the pineal gland in the brain might function as the magic tunnel between these two worlds. Today, psychologists know that there is no magic tunnel, and no need for one, because all of our subjective experiences arise from the electrical and chemical activities of our brains. Our mental lives are nothing more or less than "how it feels to be a brain." (Of course, this is a bit like saying that becoming wealthy involves nothing more or less than making money: It makes something sound simple that isn't.)

As you will see throughout this book, some of the most exciting developments in psychological research focus on how our perceptions, thoughts, memories, and feelings are related to activity in the brain. Psychologists and neuroscientists are using new technologies to explore this relationship in ways that would have seemed like science fiction only 20 years ago. The technique known as *functional magnetic resonance imaging,* or fMRI, allows scientists to "scan" a brain and see which parts are active when a person reads a word, sees a face, learns a new skill, or remembers a personal experience. William James was interested in how people acquire complex skills such as the ability to play the violin, and he wondered how the brain enabled great musicians to produce virtuoso performances. What William James could only ponder, modern psychologists can discover.

As one example, in a recent study, the brains of professional and novice pianists were scanned as they made complex finger movements like those involved in piano playing, and the results showed that professional pianists have *less* activity than novices in those parts of the brain that guide these finger movements (Krings et al.,

PSYCHOLOGY The scientific study of mind and behavior.

MIND Our private inner experience of perceptions, thoughts, memories, and feelings.

BEHAVIOR Observable actions of human beings and nonhuman animals.

2000). This result suggests that extensive practice at the piano changes the brains of professional pianists and that the regions controlling finger movements operate more efficiently than they do in novices. You'll learn more about this in Chapter 6 and see in the coming chapters how studies using fMRI and related techniques are beginning to transform many different areas of psychology.

■ *How does the mind usually allow us to function effectively in the world?* Scientists sometimes say that form follows function; that is, if we want to understand *how* something works (e.g., an engine or a thermometer), we need to know what it is working *for* (e.g., powering vehicles or measuring temperature). As William James often noted, "Thinking is for doing," and the function of the mind is to help us do those things that sophisticated animals have to do in order to prosper, such as acquiring food, shelter, and mates. Psychological processes are said to be *adaptive,* which means that they promote the welfare and reproduction of organisms that engage in those processes.

For instance, perception allows us to recognize our families, see predators before they see us, and avoid stumbling into oncoming traffic. Language allows us to organize our thoughts and communicate them to others, which enables us to form social groups and cooperate. Memory allows us to avoid solving the same problems over again every time we encounter them and to keep in mind what we are doing and why. Emotions allow us to react quickly to events that have "life or death" significance, and they enable us to form strong social bonds. The list goes on and on, and as far as anyone can tell, there is no psychological equivalent of the body's appendix; that is, there's no thoroughly useless mental process that we'd all be better off without.

Given the adaptiveness of psychological processes, it is not surprising that those people with deficiencies in those processes often have a pretty tough time. The neurologist Antonio Damasio described the case of Elliot, a middle-aged husband and father with a good job, whose life was forever changed when surgeons discovered a tumor in the middle of his brain (Damasio, 1994). The surgeons were able to remove the tumor and save his life, and for a while Elliot seemed just fine. But then odd things began to happen. At first, Elliot seemed more likely than usual to make bad decisions (when he could make decisions at all), and as time went on, his bad decisions became truly dreadful ones. He couldn't prioritize tasks at work because he couldn't decide what to do first, and when he did, he got it wrong. Eventually he was fired, and so he pursued a series of risky business ventures, all of which failed, and he lost his life's savings. His wife divorced him, he married again, and his second wife divorced him too.

So what ruined Elliot's life? The neurologists who tested Elliot were unable to detect any decrease in his cognitive functioning. His intelligence was intact, and his ability to speak, to think, and to solve logical problems was every bit as sharp as it ever was. But as they probed further, they made a startling discovery: Elliot was no longer able to experience emotions. For example, Elliot didn't experience anxiety when he poured his entire bank account into a foolish business venture, he didn't experience any sorrow when his wives packed up and left him, and he didn't experience any regret or anger when his boss gave him the pink slip and showed him the door. Most of us have wished from time to time that we could be as stoic and unflappable as that; after all, who needs anxiety, sorrow, regret, and anger? The answer is that we all do. Emotions are adaptive because they function as signals that tell us when we are putting ourselves in harm's way. If you felt no anxiety when you thought about an upcoming exam, about borrowing your friend's car without permission, or about cheating on your taxes, you would probably make a string of poor decisions that would leave you without a degree and without a friend, except perhaps for your cellmate. Elliot didn't have those feelings, and he paid a big price for it. The ability of a basic psychological process (i.e., the experience of emotion) to perform its normally adaptive function was missing in poor Elliot's life.

■ *Why does the mind occasionally function so ineffectively in the world?* The mind is an amazing machine that can do a great many things quickly. We can drive a car while talking to a passenger while recognizing the street address while remembering the name of the song that just came on the radio. But like all machines, the mind often

ONLY HUMAN
DÉJÀ VU ALL OVER AGAIN In Troy, NY, Todd W. Bariteau Sr., 32, pleaded guilty to robbing, for the second time, a store called Déjà vu. In the second robbery, he broke through the same window and stole some of the same kinds of merchandise that he had stolen in the earlier theft.

trades accuracy for speed and versatility. This can produce "bugs" in the system, such as when a doughnut-making machine occasionally spews out gobs of gooey mush rather than dozens of delicious doughnuts. Our mental life is just as susceptible to *mindbugs,* or occasional malfunctions in our otherwise-efficient mental processing. One of the most fascinating aspects of psychology is that we are *all* prone to a variety of errors and illusions. Indeed, if thoughts, feelings, and actions were error free, then human behavior would be orderly, predictable, and dull, which it clearly is not. Rather, it is endlessly surprising, and its surprises often derive from our ability to do precisely the wrong thing at the wrong time.

For example, in two British airline crashes during the 1950s, pilots mistakenly shut down an engine that was operating perfectly normally after they became aware that another engine was failing (Reason & Mycielska, 1982, p. 5). Though the reasons for such catastrophic mental lapses are not well understood, they resemble far more mundane slips that we all make in our day-to-day lives. Consider a few examples from diaries of people who took part in a study concerning mindbugs in everyday life (Reason & Mycielska, 1982, pp. 70–73):

- *I meant to get my car out, but as I passed the back porch on my way to the garage, I stopped to put on my boots and gardening jacket as if to work in the yard.*
- *I put some money into a machine to get a stamp. When the stamp appeared, I took it and said, "Thank you."*
- *On leaving the room to go to the kitchen, I turned the light off, although several people were there.*

If these lapses seem amusing, it is because, in fact, they are. But they are also potentially important as clues to human nature. For example, notice that the person who bought a stamp said, "Thank you," to the machine and not, "How do I find the subway?" In other words, the person did not just do *any* wrong thing; rather, he did something that would have been perfectly right in a real social interaction. As each of these examples suggest, people often operate on "autopilot," or behave automatically, relying on well-learned habits that they execute without really thinking. When we are not actively focused on what we are saying or doing, these habits may be triggered inappropriately. William James thought that the influence of habit could help explain the seemingly bizarre actions of "absentminded" people: "Very absent-minded persons," he wrote in *The Principles of Psychology,* "on going into their bedroom to dress for dinner have been known to take off one garment after another and finally get into bed."

William James understood that the mind's mistakes are as instructive as they are intriguing, and modern psychology has found it quite useful to study such mindbugs. Things that are whole and unbroken hum along nicely and do their jobs while leaving no clue about how they do them. Cars gliding down the expressway might as well be magic carpets as long as they are working properly because we have no idea what kind of magic is moving them along. It is only when automobiles break down that we learn about their engines, water pumps, and other fine pieces and processes that normally work together to produce the ride. Breakdowns and errors are not just about destruction and failure—they are pathways to knowledge. In the same way, understanding lapses, errors, mistakes, and the occasionally buggy nature of human behavior provides a vantage point for understanding the normal operation of mental life and behavior. The story of Elliot, whose behavior broke down after he had brain surgery, is an example that highlights the role that emotions play in guiding normal judgment and behavior.

Psychology is exciting because it addresses fundamental questions about human experience and behavior, and the three questions we've just considered are merely the tip of the iceberg. Think of this book as a guide to exploring the rest of the iceberg. But before we don our parkas and grab our pick axes, we need to understand how the iceberg got here in the first place. To understand psychology in the 21st century, we need to become familiar with the psychology of the past.

Psychology's Roots: The Path to a Science of Mind

When the young William James interrupted his medical studies to travel in Europe during the late 1860s, he wanted to learn about human nature. But he confronted a very different situation than a similarly curious student would confront today, largely because psychology did not yet exist as an independent field of study. As James cheekily wrote, "The first lecture in psychology that I ever heard was the first I ever gave." Of course, that doesn't mean no one had ever thought about human nature before. For 2,000 years, thinkers with scraggly beards and poor dental hygiene had pondered such questions, and in fact, modern psychology acknowledges its deep roots in philosophy. We will begin by examining those roots and then describe some of the early attempts to develop a scientific approach to psychology by relating the mind to the brain. Next we'll see how psychologists divided into different camps or "schools of thought": *structuralists,* who tried to analyze the mind by breaking it down into its basic components, and *functionalists,* who focused on how mental abilities allow people to adapt to their environments.

Psychology's Ancestors: The Great Philosophers

The desire to understand ourselves is not new. Greek thinkers such as Plato (428 BC–347 BC) and Aristotle (384 BC–322 BC) were among the first to struggle with fundamental questions about how the mind works (Robinson, 1995). Greek philosophers debated many of the questions that psychologists continue to debate today. For example, are cognitive abilities and knowledge inborn, or are they acquired only through experience? Plato argued in favor of **nativism**, which maintains that *certain kinds of knowledge are innate or inborn.* Children in every culture figure out early on that sounds can have meanings that can be arranged into words, which then can be arranged into sentences. Before a child is old enough to poop in the proper place, she has already mastered the fundamentals of language without any formal instruction. Is the propensity to learn language "hardwired"—that is, is it something that children are born with? Or does the ability to learn language depend on the child's experience? Aristotle believed that the child's mind was a *"tabula rasa"* (a blank slate) on which experiences were written, and he argued for **philosophical empiricism**, which holds that *all knowledge is acquired through experience.*

Although few modern psychologists believe that nativism or empiricism is entirely correct, the issue of just how much "nature" and "nurture" explain any given behavior is still a matter of controversy. In some ways, it is quite amazing that ancient philosophers were able to articulate so many of the important questions in psychology and offer many excellent insights into their answers without any access to scientific evidence.

NATIVISM The philosophical view that certain kinds of knowledge are innate or inborn.

PHILOSOPHICAL EMPIRICISM The philosophical view that all knowledge is acquired through experience.

Many current ideas in psychology can be traced to the theories of two Greek philosophers from the fourth century BC: Plato (left), who believed in nativism, and Aristotle (right), who was Plato's student and believed in empiricism.

**Figure 1.1 René Descartes
(1595–1650)** Descartes made contributions
to many fields of inquiry, from physiology to
philosophy. He is probably best known for
his suggestion that the body and soul are
fundamentally different.

Figure 1.2 Phrenology Francis Gall
(1758–1828) developed a theory
called phrenology, which suggested that
psychological capacities (such as the
capacity for friendship) and traits (such as
cautiousness and mirth) were located in
particular parts of the brain. The more of
these capacities and traits a person had, the
larger the corresponding bumps on the skull.

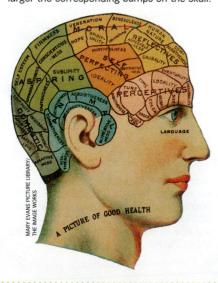

Their ideas came from personal observations, intuition, and speculation. Although they were quite good at arguing with one another, they usually found it impossible to settle their disputes because their approach provided no means of testing their theories. As you will see in Chapter 2, the ability to test a theory is the cornerstone of the scientific approach and the basis for reaching conclusions in modern psychology.

From the Brain to the Mind: The French Connection

We all know that the brain and the body are physical objects that we can see and touch and that the subjective contents of our minds—our perceptions, thoughts, and feelings—are not. Inner experience is perfectly real, but where in the world is it? The French philosopher René Descartes (1596–1650) argued that body and mind are fundamentally different things—that the body is made of a material substance, whereas the mind (or soul) is made of an immaterial or spiritual substance (**FIGURE 1.1**). But if the mind and the body are different things made of different substances, then how do they interact? How does the mind tell the body to put its foot forward, and when the body steps on a rusty nail, why does the mind say, "Ouch"? This is the problem of *dualism,* or how mental activity can be reconciled and coordinated with physical behavior.

Descartes suggested that the mind influences the body through a tiny structure near the bottom of the brain known as the pineal gland. Unfortunately, he was largely alone in this view, as other philosophers at the time either rejected his explanation or offered alternative ideas. For example, the British philosopher Thomas Hobbes (1588–1679) argued that the mind and body aren't different things at all; rather, the mind *is* what the brain *does*. From Hobbes's perspective, looking for a place in the brain where the mind meets the body is like looking for the place in a television where the picture meets the flat panel display.

The French physician Franz Joseph Gall (1758–1828) also thought that brains and minds were linked, but by size rather than by glands. He examined the brains of animals and of people who had died of disease, or as healthy adults, or as children, and observed that mental ability often increases with larger brain size and decreases with damage to the brain. These aspects of Gall's findings were generally accepted (and the part about brain damage still is today). But Gall went far beyond his evidence to develop a psychological theory known as **phrenology**, which held that *specific mental abilities and characteristics, ranging from memory to the capacity for happiness, are localized in specific regions of the brain* (**FIGURE 1.2**). The idea that different parts of the brain are specialized for specific psychological functions turned out to be right; as you'll learn later in the book, a part of the brain called the hippocampus is intimately involved in memory, just as a structure called the amygdala is intimately involved in fear. But phrenology took this idea to an absurd extreme. Gall asserted that the size of bumps or indentations on the skull reflected the size of the brain regions beneath them and that by feeling those bumps, one could tell whether a person was friendly, cautious, assertive, idealistic, and so on.

Gall's phrenological approach was based entirely on anecdotes and casual observations (Fancher, 1979). For example, Gall recalled that someone he knew had a good memory and large protruding eyes, and thus he suggested that the part of the brain behind the eyes must play a special role in memory. Phrenology made for a nice parlor game and gave young people a good excuse for touching each other, but in the end it amounted to a series of strong claims based on weak evidence. Not surprisingly, his critics were galled (so to speak), and they ridiculed many of his proposals. Despite an initially large following, phrenology was quickly discredited (Fancher, 1979).

While Gall was busy playing bumpologist, other French scientists were beginning to link the brain and the mind in a more convincing manner. The biologist Pierre Flourens (1794–1867) was appalled by Gall's far-reaching claims and sloppy methods, and so he conducted experiments in which he surgically removed specific parts of the brain from dogs, birds, and other animals and found (not surprisingly!) that their actions and movements differed from those of animals with intact brains.

The surgeon Paul Broca (1825–80) worked with a patient who had suffered damage to a small part of the left side of the brain (now known as Broca's area). The patient, Monsieur Leborgne, was virtually unable to speak and could utter only the single syllable "tan." Yet the patient understood everything that was said to him and was able to communicate using gestures. Broca had the crucial insight that damage to a specific part of the brain impaired a specific mental function, clearly demonstrating that the brain and mind are closely linked. This was important in the 19th century because at that time many people accepted Descartes' idea that the mind is separate from, but interacts with, the brain and the body. Broca and Flourens, then, were the first to demonstrate that the mind is grounded in a material substance; namely, the brain. Their work jump-started the scientific investigation of mental processes.

THE GRANGER COLLECTION

Surgeon Paul Broca (1824–80) worked with a brain-damaged person who could comprehend but not produce spoken language. Broca suggested that the mind is grounded in the material processes of the brain.

From Physiology to Psychology: A New Science Is Born in Germany

In the middle of the 19th century, psychology benefited from the work of German scientists who were trained in the field of **physiology**, which is *the study of biological processes, especially in the human body.* Physiologists had developed methods that allowed them to measure such things as the speed of nerve impulses, and some of them had begun to use these methods to measure mental abilities. William James was drawn to the work of two such physiologists: Hermann von Helmholtz (1821–94) and Wilhelm Wundt (1832–1920). "It seems to me that perhaps the time has come for psychology to begin to be a science," wrote James in a letter written in 1867 during his visit to Berlin. "Helmholtz and a man called Wundt at Heidelberg are working at it." What attracted James to the work of these two scientists?

Helmholtz Measures the Speed of Responses

A brilliant experimenter with a background in both physiology and physics, Helmholtz had developed a method for measuring the speed of nerve impulses in a frog's leg, which he then adapted to the study of human beings. Helmholtz trained participants to respond when he applied a **stimulus**—*sensory input from the environment*—to different parts of the leg. He recorded his participants' **reaction time**, or *the amount of time taken to respond to a specific stimulus,* after applying the stimulus. Helmholtz found that people generally took longer to respond when their toe was stimulated than when their thigh was stimulated, and the difference between these reaction times allowed him to estimate how long it took a nerve impulse to travel to the brain. These results were astonishing to 19th-century scientists because at that time just about everyone thought that mental processes occurred instantaneously. When you move your hands in front of your eyes, you don't feel your hands move a fraction of a second before you see them. The real world doesn't appear like one of those late-night movies in which the video and the audio are off by just a fraction of a second. Scientists assumed that the neurological processes underlying mental events *must* be instantaneous for everything to be so nicely synchronized, but Helmholtz showed that this wasn't true. In so doing, he also demonstrated that reaction time could be a useful way to study the mind and the brain.

Wundt and the Development of Structuralism

Although Helmholtz's contributions were important, historians generally credit the official emergence of psychology to Helmholtz's research assistant, Wilhelm Wundt (Rieber, 1980). Wundt published two books outlining his vision of a scientific

HULTON ARCHIVE/GETTY IMAGES

By measuring a person's reaction times to different stimuli, Hermann von Helmholtz (1821–94) estimated the length of time it takes a nerve impulse to travel to the brain.

PHRENOLOGY A now defunct theory that specific mental abilities and characteristics, ranging from memory to the capacity for happiness, are localized in specific regions of the brain.

PHYSIOLOGY The study of biological processes, especially in the human body.

STIMULUS Sensory input from the environment.

REACTION TIME The amount of time taken to respond to a specific stimulus.

Wilhelm Wundt (1832–1920), far right, founded the first laboratory devoted exclusively to psychology at the University of Leipzig in Germany.

ARCHIVES OF THE HISTORY OF AMERICAN PSYCHOLOGY

approach to psychology and describing experiments on sensory perception that he had conducted in a makeshift laboratory in his home (Schultz & Schultz, 1987). In 1867, Wundt taught at the University of Heidelberg what was probably the first course in physiological psychology, and this course led to the publication of his book *Principles of Physiological Psychology* in 1874. Wundt called the book "an attempt to mark out [psychology] as a new domain of science" (Fancher, 1979, p. 126). In 1879, at the University of Leipzig, Wundt opened the first laboratory ever to be exclusively devoted to psychological studies, and this event marked the official birth of psychology as an independent field of study. The new lab was full of graduate students carrying out research on topics assigned by Wundt, and it soon attracted young scholars from all over the world who were eager to learn about the new science that Wundt had developed.

Wundt believed that scientific psychology should focus on analyzing **consciousness,** *a person's subjective experience of the world and the mind.* Consciousness encompasses a broad range of subjective experiences. We may be conscious of sights, sounds, tastes, smells, bodily sensations, thoughts, or feelings. As Wundt tried to figure out a way to study consciousness scientifically, he noted that chemists try to understand the structure of matter by breaking down natural substances into basic elements. So he and his students adopted an approach called **structuralism,** or *the analysis of the basic elements that constitute the mind.* This approach involved breaking consciousness down into elemental sensations and feelings, and you can do a bit of structuralism right now without leaving your chair.

Consider the contents of your own consciousness. At this very moment you may be aware of the meaning of these words, the visual appearance of the letters on the page, the key ring pressing uncomfortably against your thigh, your feelings of excitement or boredom (probably excitement), the smell of curried chicken salad, or the nagging question of whether the War of 1812 really deserves its own overture. At any given moment, all sorts of things are swimming in the stream of consciousness, and Wundt tried to analyze them in a systematic way using the method of **introspection,** which involves *the subjective observation of one's own experience.* In a typical experiment, observers (usually students) would be presented with a stimulus (usually a color or a sound) and then be asked to report their introspections. The observers would describe the brightness of a color or the loudness of a tone. They were asked to report on their "raw" sensory experience rather than on their interpretations of that experience. For example, an observer presented with this page would not report seeing words on the page (which counts as an interpretation of the experience), but instead might describe a series of black marks, some straight and others curved, against a bright white background. Wundt also attempted to carefully describe the feelings associated with ele-

CONSCIOUSNESS A person's subjective experience of the world and the mind.

STRUCTURALISM The analysis of the basic elements that constitute the mind.

INTROSPECTION The subjective observation of one's own experience.

mentary perceptions. For example, when Wundt listened to the clicks produced by a metronome, some of the patterns of sounds were more pleasant than others. By analyzing the relation between feelings and perceptual sensations, Wundt and his students hoped to uncover the basic structure of conscious experience.

Wundt tried to provide objective measurements of conscious processes by using reaction time techniques similar to those first developed by Helmholtz. Wundt used reaction times to examine a distinction between the perception and interpretation of a stimulus. His research participants were instructed to press a button as soon as a tone sounded. Some participants were told to concentrate on perceiving the tone before pressing the button, whereas others were told to concentrate only on pressing the button. Those people who concentrated on the tone responded about one tenth of a second more slowly than those told to concentrate only on pressing the button. Wundt reasoned that both fast and slow participants had to register the tone in consciousness (perception), but only the slower participants had to also interpret the significance of the tone and press the button. The faster research participants, focusing only on the response they were to make, could respond automatically to the tone because they didn't have to engage in the additional step of interpretation (Fancher, 1979). This type of experimentation broke new ground by showing that psychologists could use scientific techniques to disentangle even subtle conscious processes. In fact, as you'll see in later chapters, reaction time procedures have proven extremely useful in modern research.

Titchener Brings Structuralism to the United States

The pioneering efforts of Wundt's laboratory launched psychology as an independent science and profoundly influenced the field for the remainder of the 19th century. Many European and American psychologists journeyed to Leipzig to study with Wundt. Among the most eminent was the British-born Edward Titchener (1867–1927), who studied with Wundt for 2 years in the early 1890s. Titchener then came to the United States and set up a psychology laboratory at Cornell University (where, if you'd like to see it, his brain is still on display in the psychology department). Titchener brought some parts of Wundt's approach to America, but he also made some changes (Brock, 1993; Rieber, 1980). For instance, whereas Wundt emphasized the relationship between elements of consciousness, Titchener focused on identifying the basic elements themselves. He trained his students to provide detailed descriptions of their conscious images and sensations—a demanding process that Titchener called "hard introspective labor." In his textbook *An Outline of Psychology* (1896), Titchener put forward a list of more than 44,000 elemental qualities of conscious experience, most of them visual (32,820) or auditory (11,600) (Schultz & Schultz, 1987).

The influence of the structuralist approach gradually faded, due mostly to the introspective method. Science requires replicable observations—we could never determine the structure of DNA or the life span of a dust mite if every scientist who looked through a microscope saw something different. Alas, even trained observers provided conflicting introspections about their conscious experiences ("I see a cloud that looks like a duck"—"No, *I* think that cloud looks like a horse"), thus making it difficult for different psychologists to agree on the basic elements of conscious experience. Indeed, some psychologists had doubts about whether it was even possible to identify such elements through introspection alone. One of the most prominent skeptics was someone you've already met—a young man with a bad attitude and a useless medical degree named William James.

James and the Functional Approach

After William James pulled out of his downward spiral in the early 1870s, he was still inspired by the idea of approaching psychological issues from a scientific perspective. He received a teaching appointment at Harvard (primarily because the president of the

Edward Titchener (1867–1927) brought structuralism to America, setting up a psychology laboratory at Cornell University. Titchener studied under Wundt in Germany.

CARL A. KROCH LIBRARY

FUNCTIONALISM The study of the purpose mental processes serve in enabling people to adapt to their environment.

NATURAL SELECTION Charles Darwin's theory that the features of an organism that help it survive and reproduce are more likely than other features to be passed on to subsequent generations.

university was a neighbor and family friend) and in 1875 offered a course called "The Relations between Physiology and Psychology." More importantly, his position at Harvard enabled him to purchase laboratory equipment for classroom experiments, making his the first course at an American university to draw on the new experimental psychology developed by Wundt and his German followers (Schultz & Schultz, 1987). These courses and experiments led James to write his masterpiece, *The Principles of Psychology* (James, 1890).

James agreed with Wundt on some points, including the importance of focusing on immediate experience and the usefulness of introspection as a technique (Bjork, 1983), but he disagreed with Wundt's claim that consciousness could be broken down into separate elements. James believed that trying to isolate and analyze a particular moment of consciousness (as the structuralists did) distorted the essential nature of consciousness. Consciousness, he argued, was more like a flowing stream than a bundle of separate elements. So James decided to approach psychology from a different perspective entirely, and he developed an approach known as **functionalism:** *the study of the purpose mental processes serve in enabling people to adapt to their environment.* In contrast to structuralism, which examined the structure of mental processes, functionalism set out to understand the functions those mental processes served. (See The Real World box for some strategies to enhance one of those functions—learning.)

James's thinking was inspired by the ideas in Charles Darwin's recently published book on biological evolution, *The Origin of Species* (1859). Darwin proposed the principle of **natural selection**, which states that *the features of an organism that help it survive and reproduce are more likely than other features to be passed on to subsequent generations.* From this perspective, James reasoned, mental abilities must have evolved because they were adaptive—that is, because they helped people solve problems and increased their chances of survival. Like other animals, people have always needed to avoid predators, locate food, build shelters, and attract mates. Applying Darwin's principle of natural selection, James (1890) reasoned that consciousness must serve an important biological function and the task for psychologists was to understand what those functions are. Wundt and the other structuralists worked in laboratories, and James felt that such work was limited in its ability to tell us how consciousness functioned in the natural environment. Wundt, in turn, felt that James did not focus enough on new findings from the laboratory that he and the structuralists had begun to produce. Commenting on *The Principles of Psychology,* Wundt conceded that James was a topflight writer but disapproved of his approach: "It is literature, it is beautiful, but it is not psychology" (Bjork, 1983, p. 12).

The rest of the world did not agree, and James's functionalist psychology quickly gained followers, especially in North America, where Darwin's ideas were influencing many thinkers. G. Stanley Hall (1844–1924), who studied with both Wundt and James, set up the first psychology research laboratory in North America at Johns Hopkins University in 1881. Hall's work focused on development and education and was strongly influenced by evolutionary thinking (Schultz & Schultz, 1987).

Hall believed that as children develop, they pass through stages that repeat the evolutionary history of the human race. Thus, the mental capacities of a young child resemble those of our ancient ancestors, and children grow over a lifetime in the same way that a species evolves over aeons. Hall founded the *American Journal of Psychology* in 1887 (the first psychology journal in the United States), and he went on to play a key role in founding the American Psychological Association (the first national organization of psychologists in the United States), serving as its first president.

The efforts of James and Hall set the stage for functionalism to develop as a major school of psychological thought in North America. Psychology departments that embraced a functionalist approach started to spring up at many major American universities, and in a struggle for survival that would have made Darwin proud, functionalism became more influential than structuralism had ever been. By the time Wundt and Titchener died in the 1920s, functionalism was the dominant approach to psychology in North America.

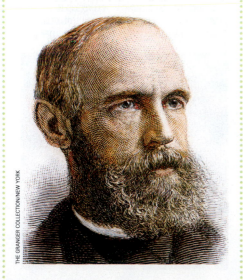

G. Stanley Hall (1844–1924) contributed greatly to the growth of psychology in North America. He founded the continent's first psychology laboratory at Johns Hopkins University, the first academic journal devoted to psychology, and the first professional organization (the American Psychological Association).

THE GRANGER COLLECTION/NEW YORK

{ THE REAL WORLD } Improving Study Skills

By reading this book and taking this introductory course, you will learn a great deal about psychology, just as you learn about subjects ranging from religion to literature to history in other courses. Unlike other disciplines, psychology can provide a kind of insight that is applicable to everyday life: Psychology can help you to learn about psychology.

Psychologists have progressed a great deal in understanding how we remember and learn. We'll explore the science of memory and learning in Chapters 5 and 6, but here we focus on the practical implications of psychological research for everyday life: how you can use psychology to improve your study skills. Such knowledge should help you to perform your best in this course and others, but perhaps more importantly, it can help to prepare you for challenges you will face after graduation. With the rapid pace of technological change in our society, learning and memory skills are more important than ever. Experts estimate that the knowledge and skills required for success in a job will change completely every 3 to 7 years during an individual's career (Herrmann, Raybeck, & Gruneberg, 2002). Enhancing your learning and memory skills now should pay off for you later in life in ways we can't even yet predict.

Psychologists have focused on mental strategies that can enhance your ability to *acquire* information, to *retain* it over time, and to *retrieve* what you have acquired and retained. Let's begin with the process of acquiring information—that is, transforming what you see and hear into an enduring memory. Our minds don't work like video cameras, passively recording everything that happens around us. To acquire information effectively, you need to actively manipulate it. One easy type of active manipulation is rehearsal: repeating to-be-learned information to yourself. You've probably tried this strategy already, but psychologists have found that some types of rehearsal are better than others. A particularly effective strategy is called *spaced rehearsal*, where you repeat information to yourself at increasingly long intervals. For example, suppose that you want to learn the name of a person you've just met named Eric. Repeat the name to yourself right away, wait a few seconds and think of it again, wait for a bit longer (maybe 30 seconds) and bring the name to mind once more, then rehearse the name again after a minute and once more after 2 or 3 minutes. Studies show that this type of rehearsal improves long-term learning more than rehearsing the name without any spacing between rehearsals (Landauer & Bjork, 1978). You can apply this technique to names, dates, definitions, and many other kinds of information, including concepts presented in this textbook.

Simple rehearsal can be beneficial, but one of the most important lessons from psychological research is that we acquire information most effectively when we think about its meaning and reflect on its significance. In fact, we don't even have to try to remember something if we think deeply enough about what we want to remember; the act of reflection itself will virtually guarantee good memory. For example, suppose that you want to learn the basic ideas behind Skinner's approach to behaviorism. Ask yourself the following kinds of questions: How did behaviorism differ from previous approaches in psychology? How would a behaviorist like Skinner think about psychological issues that interest you, such as whether a mentally disturbed individual should be held responsible for committing a crime, or what factors would contribute to your choice of a major subject or career path? In attempting to answer such questions, you will need to review what you've learned about behaviorism and then relate it to other things you already know about. It is much easier to remember new information when you can relate it to something you already know.

You'll also learn later in this book about techniques for visualizing information, first developed by the ancient Greeks, that modern psychological research has proven to be effective memory aids (Paivio, 1969). One such technique, known as the *method of loci*, involves "mentally depositing" information you wish to remember into familiar locations and then later searching through those locations to recall the information.

For example, suppose you want to remember the major contributions of Wundt, Freud, and Skinner to the development of psychology. You could use your current or former home as the location and imagine Wundt's reaction time apparatus lying on your bed, Freud's psychoanalysis couch sitting in your living room, and Skinner's rats running around your bathroom. Then when you need this information, you can "pull up" an image of your home and take a mental tour through it in order to see what's there. You can use this basic approach with a variety of familiar locations—a school building you know well, a shopping mall, and so forth—in order to remember many different kinds of information.

You can use each of the mental manipulations discussed here to help you remember and learn the material in this textbook and prepare for your tests:

- Think about and review the information you have acquired in class on a regular basis. Begin soon after class, and then try to schedule regular "booster" sessions.
- Don't wait until the last second to cram your review into one sitting; research shows that spacing out review and repetition leads to longer-lasting recall.
- Don't just look at your class notes or this textbook; test yourself on the material as often as you can. Research also shows that actively retrieving information you've acquired helps you to later remember that information more than just looking at it again.
- Take some of the load off your memory by developing effective note-taking and outlining skills. Students often scribble down vague and fragmentary notes during lectures, figuring that the notes will be good enough to jog memory later. But when the time comes to study, they've forgotten so much that their notes are no longer clear. Realize that you can't write down everything an instructor says, and try to focus on making detailed notes about the main ideas, facts, and people mentioned in the lecture.
- Organize your notes into an outline that clearly highlights the major concepts. The act of organizing an outline will force you to reflect on the information in a way that promotes retention and will also provide you with a helpful study guide to promote self-testing and review.

To follow up on these suggestions and find much more detailed information on learning and study techniques, see the Recommended Reading by Hermann, Raybeck, & Gruneberg (2002).

"As I get older, I find I rely more and more on these sticky notes to remind me."

In summary, philosophers have pondered and debated ideas about human nature for millennia, but, given the nature of their approach, they did not provide empirical evidence to support their claims. Some of the earliest successful efforts to develop a *science* linking mind and behavior came from the French scientists Pierre Flourens and Paul Broca, who showed that damage to the brain can result in impairments of behavior and mental functions. Hermann von Helmholtz furthered the science of the mind by developing methods for measuring reaction time. Wilhelm Wundt, credited with the founding of psychology as a scientific discipline, created the first psychological laboratory and taught the first course in physiological psychology. His structuralist approach focused on analyzing the basic elements of consciousness. Wundt's student, Edward Titchener, brought structuralism to the United States. William James emphasized the functions of consciousness and applied Darwin's theory of natural selection to the study of the mind, thus helping to establish functionalism and scientific psychology in the United States. Scientific psychology in America got a further boost from G. Stanley Hall, who established the first research laboratory, journal, and professional organization devoted to psychology. ■ ■

Errors and Illusions Reveal Psychology

At about the same time that some psychologists were developing structuralism and functionalism, other psychologists were beginning to think about how illusions and disorders might illuminate psychological functioning. They began to realize that one can often understand how something works by examining how it breaks. Let's look first at the illusion that launched a new movement known as Gestalt psychology and then consider how observations of mental disorders influenced the development of psychology. In each case, a careful examination of some mindbugs led to a clearer understanding of human mental functioning.

Illusions of Movement and the Birth of Gestalt Psychology

Magicians and artists could not earn a living unless people were susceptible to **illusions**, that is, *errors of perception, memory, or judgment in which subjective experience differs from objective reality.* For example, if you measure the dark horizontal lines shown in **FIGURE 1.3** with a ruler, you'll see that they are of equal length. And yet, for most of us, the top line appears longer than the bottom one. As you'll learn in Chapter 4, this is because the surrounding vertical lines influence your perception of the horizontal lines. A similar visual illusion fired the imagination of a German psychologist named Max Wertheimer (1880–1943), who was enjoying a train ride during his vacation when he had a sudden insight into the nature of visual perception. Wertheimer was so excited by his idea that he went to a store as soon as he

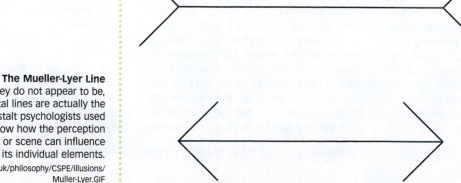

Figure 1.3 **The Mueller-Lyer Line Illusion** Although they do not appear to be, these two horizontal lines are actually the same length. The Gestalt psychologists used illusions like this to show how the perception of a whole object or scene can influence judgments about its individual elements.

http://www.gla.ac.uk/philosophy/CSPE/illusions/Muller-Lyer.GIF

got off the train and purchased equipment for an experiment (Benjamin, 1988). In Wertheimer's experiment, a person was shown two lights that flashed quickly on a screen, one after the other. One light was flashed through a vertical slit, the other through a diagonal slit. When the time between two flashes was relatively long (one fifth of a second or more), an observer would see that it was just two lights flashing in alternation. But when Wertheimer reduced the time between flashes to around one twentieth of a second, observers saw a single flash of light moving back and forth (Fancher, 1979; Sarris, 1989).

Creating the illusion of motion was not new. Turn-of-the-century moviemakers already understood that quickly flashing a series of still images, one after the other, could fool people into perceiving motion where none actually existed. But Wertheimer's *interpretation* of this illusion, conceived during his train ride, was the novel element that contributed to the growth of psychology (Benjamin, 1988; Steinman, Pizlo, & Pizlo, 2000). He reasoned that the perceived motion could not be explained in terms of the separate elements that cause the illusion (the two flashing lights) but instead that the moving flash of light is perceived as a *whole* rather than as the sum of its two parts. This unified whole, which in German is called *Gestalt*, makes up the perceptual experience. Wertheimer's interpretation of the illusion led to the development of **Gestalt psychology**, *a psychological approach that emphasizes that we often perceive the whole rather than the sum of the parts.* In other words, the mind imposes organization on what it perceives, so people don't see what the experimenter actually shows them (two separate lights); instead they see the elements as a unified whole (one moving light). This analysis provides an excellent illustration of how illusions can offer clues about the basic principles of the mind.

The Gestaltists' claim was diametrically opposed to the structuralists' claim that experience can be broken down into separate elements. Wertheimer and later Gestalt psychologists such as Kurt Koffka (1886–1941) and Wolfgang Kohler (1887–1967) developed the theory further and came up with additional demonstrations and illusions that strengthened their contention that the mind perceives the whole rather than the sum of its parts. Although Gestalt psychology no longer exists today as a distinct school of thought, its basic claims have influenced the modern study of object perception (as you'll see in Chapter 4) as well as social perception (as you'll see in Chapter 16). Indeed, the notion that the mind imposes structure and organization was a central claim of the philosopher Immanuel Kant (1724–1824), and it remains one of modern psychology's most widely accepted principles. And imagine: All of this came from a lovely little train ride.

DAVID LEE

Max Wertheimer's (1880–1943) insights about the perception of motion offered a scientific explanation of why we see movement when viewing a series of rapidly flashed still pictures, a method used by moviemakers in the early 1900s.

Mental Disorders and Multiple Selves

Just as Gestalt psychologists were discovering that illusions in visual perception can help us understand how the eye and the brain normally work so well, other psychologists were discovering how the bizarre behaviors of patients with psychological disorders could shed light on the workings of the ordinary mind. For example, in 1876 a startling report in a French medical journal described a woman called Felida X (Azam, 1876). Felida was normally shy and quiet, but sometimes she would suddenly become much bolder and more outgoing. Then, without warning, she would just as suddenly return to her usual shy and reserved state. Stranger still, the shy Felida had no memory of what the outgoing Felida had done. Once while riding in a carriage, Felida suddenly switched from outgoing to shy and seemed to completely forget that she had just been to the funeral of a close friend. The barrier between the two states was so strong that the shy Felida forgot that she had become pregnant while in her outgoing state!

ILLUSIONS Errors of perception, memory, or judgment in which subjective experience differs from objective reality.

GESTALT PSYCHOLOGY A psychological approach that emphasizes that we often perceive the whole rather than the sum of the parts.

Figure 1.4 Dissociative Identity Disorder Shirley Ardell Mason's (left) struggle with dissociative identity disorder was described first in the book *Sybil* (a pseudonym given to protect her privacy), which chronicles her mental illness as revealed through her therapy with Dr. Cornelia Wilbur. Sybil's story was told in the 1973 book (right) and later made into a television movie starring Sally Field, who won an Emmy for her portrayal of Sybil.

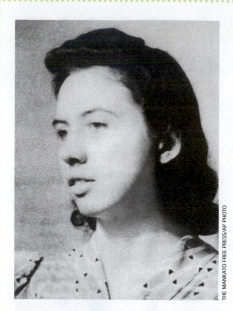
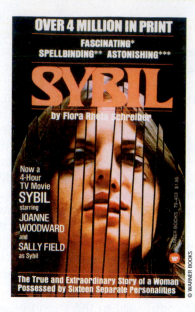

Felida X was an early example of an unusual condition now called **dissociative identity disorder** (see Chapter 13), which *involves the occurrence of two or more distinct identities within the same individual* (**FIGURE 1.4**). The French physicians Jean-Marie Charcot (1825–93) and Pierre Janet (1859–1947) reported similar observations when they interviewed patients who had developed a condition known then as **hysteria**, or a *temporary loss of cognitive or motor functions, usually as a result of emotionally upsetting experiences*. Hysterical patients became blind, paralyzed, or lost their memories, even though there was no known physical cause of their problems. However, when the patients were put into a trancelike state through the use of hypnosis (an altered state of consciousness characterized by suggestibility), their symptoms disappeared: Blind patients could see, paralyzed patients could walk, and forgetful patients could remember. After coming out of the hypnotic trance, however, the patients forgot what had happened under hypnosis and again showed their symptoms. Like Felida X, the patients behaved like two different people in the waking versus hypnotic states.

These peculiar disorders were ignored by Wundt, Titchener, and other laboratory scientists, who did not consider them a proper subject for scientific psychology (Bjork, 1983). But William James believed they had important implications for understanding the nature of the mind (Taylor, 2001). He discerned an important mindbug at work, capitalizing on these mental disruptions as a way of understanding the normal operation of the mind. During our ordinary conscious experience we are only aware of a single "me" or "self," but the aberrations described by Charcot, Janet, and others suggested that the brain can create many conscious selves that are not aware of each other's existence (James, 1890, p. 400). These striking observations also fueled the imagination of a young physician from Vienna, Austria, who studied with Charcot in Paris in 1885. His name was Sigmund Freud (1856–1939).

Freud and Psychoanalytic Theory

After his visit to Charcot's clinic in Paris, Freud returned to Vienna, where he continued his work with hysteric patients. (The word *hysteria*, by the way, comes from the Latin word *hyster*, which means "womb." It was once thought that only women suffered from hysteria, which was thought to be caused by a "wandering womb.") Working with the physician Joseph Breuer (1842–1925), Freud began to make his own observations of hysterics and develop theories to explain their strange behaviors and symptoms. Freud theorized that many of the patients' problems could be traced to the effects of painful childhood experiences that the person could not remember, and he

DISSOCIATIVE IDENTITY DISORDER A condition that involves the occurrence of two or more distinct identities within the same individual.

HYSTERIA A temporary loss of cognitive or motor functions, usually as a result of emotionally upsetting experiences.

FREUD MUSEUM

In this photograph, Sigmund Freud (1856–1939) sits by the couch reserved for his psychoanalytic patients.

suggested that the powerful influence of these seemingly lost memories revealed the presence of an unconscious mind. According to Freud, the **unconscious** is *the part of the mind that operates outside of conscious awareness but influences conscious thoughts, feelings, and actions.* This idea led Freud to develop **psychoanalytic theory,** *an approach that emphasizes the importance of unconscious mental processes in shaping feelings, thoughts, and behaviors.* From a psychoanalytic perspective, it is important to uncover a person's early experiences and to illuminate a person's unconscious anxieties, conflicts, and desires. Psychoanalytic theory formed the basis for a therapy that Freud called **psychoanalysis,** which focuses on *bringing unconscious material into conscious awareness.* During psychoanalysis, patients recalled past experiences ("When I was a toddler, I was frightened by a masked man on a black horse") and related their dreams and fantasies ("Sometimes I close my eyes and imagine not having to pay for this session"). Psychoanalysts used Freud's theoretical approach to interpret what their patients said.

In the early 1900s, Freud and a growing number of followers formed a psychoanalytic movement. Carl Gustav Jung (1875–1961) and Alfred Adler (1870–1937) were prominent in the movement, but both were independent thinkers, and Freud apparently had little tolerance for individuals who challenged his ideas. Soon enough, Freud broke off his relationships with both men so that he could shape the psychoanalytic movement himself (Sulloway, 1992). Psychoanalytic theory became quite controversial (especially in America) because it suggested that understanding a person's thoughts, feelings, and behavior required a thorough exploration of the person's early sexual experiences and unconscious sexual desires. In those days these topics were considered far too racy for scientific discussion.

DANNY SHANAHAN/CARTOONBANK.COM

UNCONSCIOUS The part of the mind that operates outside of conscious awareness but influences conscious thoughts, feelings, and actions.

PSYCHOANALYTIC THEORY Sigmund Freud's approach to understanding human behavior that emphasizes the importance of unconscious mental processes in shaping feelings, thoughts, and behaviors.

PSYCHOANALYSIS A therapeutic approach that focuses on bringing unconscious material into conscious awareness to better understand psychological disorders.

This famous psychology conference, held in 1909 at Clark University, was organized by G. Stanley Hall and brought together many notable figures, such as William James and Sigmund Freud. Both men are circled, with James on the left.

CORBIS

Most of Freud's followers, like Freud himself, were trained as physicians and did not conduct psychological experiments in the laboratory (though early in his career, Freud did do some nice laboratory work on the sexual organs of eels). By and large, psychoanalysts did not hold positions in universities and developed their ideas in isolation from the research-based approaches of Wundt, Titchener, James, Hall, and others. One of the few times that Freud met with the leading academic psychologists was at a conference that G. Stanley Hall organized at Clark University in 1909. It was there that William James and Sigmund Freud met for the first time. Although James worked in an academic setting and Freud worked with clinical patients, both men believed that mental aberrations provide important clues into the nature of mind. Each thinker, in his own way, recognized the value of pursuing mindbugs as a clue to human functioning.

Influence of Psychoanalysis and the Humanistic Response

Most historians consider Freud to be one of the two or three most influential thinkers of the 20th century, and the psychoanalytic movement influenced everything from literature and history to politics and art. Within psychology, psychoanalysis had its greatest impact on clinical practice, but over the past 40 years that influence has been considerably diminished.

This is partly because Freud's vision of human nature was a dark one, emphasizing limitations and problems rather than possibilities and potentials. He saw people as hostages to their forgotten childhood experiences and primitive sexual impulses, and the inherent pessimism of his perspective frustrated those psychologists who had a more optimistic view of human nature. In America, the years after World War II were positive, invigorating, and upbeat: Poverty and disease were being conquered by technology, the standard of living of ordinary Americans was on a sharp rise, and people were landing on the moon. The era was characterized by the accomplishments and not the foibles of the human mind, and Freud's viewpoint was out of step with the spirit of the times.

Freud's ideas were also difficult to test, and a theory that can't be tested is of limited use in psychology or other sciences. Though Freud's emphasis on unconscious processes has had an enduring impact on psychology, psychologists began to have serious misgivings about many aspects of Freud's theory.

It was in these times that psychologists such as Abraham Maslow (1908–70) and Carl Rogers (1902–87) pioneered a new movement called **humanistic psychology**, *an approach to understanding human nature that emphasizes the positive potential of human beings*. Humanistic psychologists focused on the highest aspirations that people had

HUMANISTIC PSYCHOLOGY An approach to understanding human nature that emphasizes the positive potential of human beings.

Carl Rogers (1902–87) (left) and Abraham Maslow (1908–70) (right) introduced a positive, humanistic psychology in response to what they viewed as the overly pessimistic view of psychoanalysis.

for themselves. Rather than viewing people as prisoners of events in their remote pasts, humanistic psychologists viewed people as free agents who have an inherent need to develop, grow, and reach their full potential. This movement reached its peak in the 1960s when a generation of "flower children" found it easy to see psychological life as a kind of blossoming of the spirit. Humanistic therapists sought to help people to realize their full potential; in fact, they called them "clients" rather than "patients." In this relationship, the therapist and the client (unlike the psychoanalyst and the patient) were on equal footing. In fact, the development of the humanistic perspective was one more reason why Freud's ideas became less influential.

In summary, psychologists have often focused on mindbugs as a way of understanding human behavior. The errors, illusions, and foibles of mental functioning offer a glimpse into the normal operations of the mind. Max Wertheimer founded Gestalt psychology by examining the illusion that causes us to see the whole instead of its parts. Clinicians such as Jean-Marie Charcot and Pierre Janet studied unusual cases in which patients acted like different people while under hypnosis, raising the possibility that each of us has more than one self. Through his work with hysteric patients, Sigmund Freud developed psychoanalysis, which emphasized the importance of unconscious influences and childhood experiences in shaping thoughts, feelings, and behavior. But happily, humanistic psychologists offered a more optimistic view of the human condition, suggesting that people are inherently disposed toward growth and can usually reach their full potential with a little help from their friends. ■ ■

Psychology in the 20th Century: Behaviorism Takes Center Stage

The schools of psychological thought that had developed by the early 20th century—structuralism, functionalism, psychoanalysis, Gestalt psychology, and humanism—differed substantially from one another. But they shared an important similarity: Each tried to understand the inner workings of the mind by examining conscious perceptions, thoughts, memories, and feelings or by trying to elicit previously unconscious material, all of which were reported by participants in experiments or patients in a clinical setting. In each case it proved difficult to establish with much certainty just what was going on in people's minds, due to the unreliable nature of the methodology. As the 20th century unfolded, a new approach developed as psychologists challenged the idea that psychology should focus on mental life at all. This new approach was called **behaviorism,** which advocated that psychologists should restrict themselves to *the scientific study of objectively observable behavior.* Behaviorism represented a dramatic departure from previous schools of thought.

BEHAVIORISM An approach that advocates that psychologists restrict themselves to the scientific study of objectively observable behavior.

In 1894, Margaret Floy Washburn (1871–1939), a student of Edward Titchener at Cornell, became the first woman to receive a PhD degree in psychology. Washburn went on to a highly distinguished career, spent mainly in teaching and research at Vassar College in Poughkeepsie, New York. Washburn wrote an influential book, *The Animal Mind*, developed a theory of consciousness, and contributed to the development of psychology as a profession.

After leaving Johns Hopkins University amid a scandal, John B. Watson (1878–1958) embarked on a successful career with the J. Walter Thompson advertising firm in New York City. He was responsible for developing several memorable ad campaigns, such as this one for toothpaste.

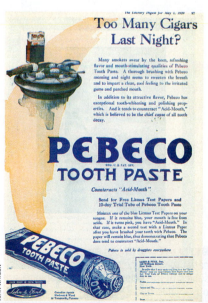

Watson and the Emergence of Behaviorism

John Broadus Watson (1878–1958) received his PhD in 1904 from the University of Chicago (the first psychology PhD ever awarded there), where he was strongly influenced by James Angell (1869–1949), who had worked within the functionalist tradition. But Watson believed that private experience was too idiosyncratic and vague to be an object of scientific inquiry. Science required replicable, objective measurements of phenomena that were accessible to all observers, and the introspective methods used by structuralists and functionalists were far too subjective for that. So instead of describing conscious experiences, Watson proposed that psychologists focus entirely on the study of behavior—what people *do*, rather than what people *experience*—because behavior can be observed by anyone and it can be measured objectively. Watson thought that a focus on behavior would put a stop to the endless philosophical debates in which psychologists were currently entangled, and it would encourage psychologists to develop practical applications in such areas as business, medicine, law, and education. The goal of scientific psychology, according to Watson, should be to predict and control behavior in ways that benefit society.

Why would someone want to throw the mind out of psychology? This may seem excessive, until you notice that Watson studied the behavior of animals such as rats and birds. In such studies, inferring a mind is a matter of some debate. Shall we say that dogs have minds, for instance, but leave out pigeons? And if we include pigeons, what about worms? Animal behavior specialists staked out claims in this area. In 1908 Margaret Floy Washburn (1871–1939) published *The Animal Mind,* in which she reviewed what was then known about perception, learning, and memory in different animal species. She argued that nonhuman animals, much like human animals, have conscious mental experiences (Scarborough & Furumoto, 1987). Watson reacted to this claim with venom. Because we cannot ask pigeons about their private, inner experiences (well, we can *ask*, but they never tell us), Watson decided that the only way to understand how animals learn and adapt was to focus solely on their behavior, and he suggested that the study of human beings should proceed on the same basis.

Watson was influenced by the work of the Russian physiologist Ivan Pavlov (1849–1936), who carried out pioneering research on the physiology of digestion. In the course of this work, Pavlov noticed something interesting about the dogs he was studying (Fancher, 1979). Not only did the dogs salivate at the sight of food, they also salivated at the sight of the person who fed them. The feeders were not dressed in Alpo suits, so why should the mere sight of them trigger a basic digestive response in the dogs? To answer this question, Pavlov developed a procedure in which he sounded a tone every time he fed the dogs, and after a while he observed that the dogs would salivate when they heard the tone alone. In Pavlov's experiments, the sound of the tone was a stimulus—*sensory input from the environment*—that influenced the salivation of the dogs, which was a **response**—*an action or physiological change elicited by a stimulus*. Watson and other behaviorists made these two notions the building blocks of their theories, which is why behaviorism is sometimes called "stimulus-response" or "S-R" psychology.

Watson applied Pavlov's techniques to human infants. In a famous and controversial study, Watson and his student Rosalie Rayner taught an infant known as "Little Albert" to have a strong fear of a harmless white rat (and other white furry animals and toys) that he had previously not feared. Why would they do such a thing? You'll learn more about this study in Chapter 6, but the short answer is this: Watson believed that human behavior is powerfully influenced by the environment, and the experiments with Little Albert provided a chance to demonstrate such influence at the earliest stage of life. Neither Watson nor later behaviorists believed that the environment was the *only* influence on behavior (Todd & Morris, 1992), but they did think it was the most important one. Consistent with that view, Watson became romantically involved with someone prominent in his environment: Rosalie Rayner. He refused to end the affair when confronted by colleagues, and the resulting scandal forced Watson to leave his position at Johns Hopkins University. He found work in a New York advertising agency, where he applied behaviorist principles to marketing and advertising (which certainly involves manipulating the environment to influence behavior!).

Watson also wrote popular books that exposed a broad general audience to the behaviorist approach (Watson, 1924, 1928). The result of all these developments—Pavlov's work in the laboratory, Watson and Rayner's applications to humans, and Watson's practical applications to daily life—was that by the 1920s, behaviorism had become a dominant force in scientific psychology.

B. F. Skinner and the Development of Behaviorism

In 1926, Burrhus Frederick Skinner (1904–90) graduated from Hamilton College in upstate New York. Like William James, Skinner was a young man who couldn't decide what to do with his life. He aspired to become a writer, and his interest in literature led him indirectly to psychology. Skinner wondered whether a novelist could portray a character without understanding why the character behaved as he or she did, and when he came across Watson's books, he knew he had the answer. Skinner completed his PhD studies in psychology at Harvard (Wiener, 1996) and began to develop a new kind of behaviorism. In Pavlov's experiments, the dogs had been passive participants that stood around, listened to tones, and drooled. Skinner recognized that in everyday life, animals don't just stand there—they do something! Animals *act* on their environments in order to find shelter, food, or mates, and Skinner wondered if he could develop behaviorist principles that would explain how they *learned* to act in those situations.

Skinner built what he called a "conditioning chamber" but what the rest of the world would forever call a "Skinner box." The box has a lever and a food tray, and a hungry rat could get food delivered to the tray by pressing the lever. Skinner observed that when a rat was put in the box, it would wander around, sniffing and exploring, and would usually press the bar by accident, at which point a food pellet would drop into the tray. After that happened, the rate of bar pressing would increase dramatically and remain high until the rat was no longer hungry. Skinner saw evidence for what he called the principle of **reinforcement**, which states that *the consequences of a behavior determine whether it will be more or less likely to occur again*. The concept of reinforcement became the foundation for Skinner's new approach to behaviorism (see Chapter 6), which he formulated in a landmark book, *The Behavior of Organisms* (Skinner, 1938).

Skinner set out to use his ideas about reinforcement to help improve the quality of everyday life. Skinner often worked with pigeons, and he wanted to see whether he could use reinforcement to teach pigeons to do something that they did not do naturally. Careful scientific observation revealed that pigeons in the wild almost never take up Ping-Pong, so Skinner decided to use the principle of reinforcement to teach some pigeons to play the game. He first broke the task down into small parts and used the principle of reinforcement to teach the pigeons each of the parts—reinforcing them when they made the right move (e.g., turning their paddles toward the ball) but not when they made the wrong one (e.g., yelling at the referee). Soon, the pigeons were able to bat the ball back and forth in a relatively entertaining display of athletic prowess.

Skinner was visiting his daughter's fourth-grade class when he realized that he might be able to improve classroom instruction by

NINA LEEN/TIME LIFE PICTURES/GETTY IMAGES

Inspired by Watson's behaviorism, B. F. Skinner (1904–90) investigated the way an animal learns by interacting with its environment. Here, he demonstrates the "Skinner box," in which rats learn to press a lever to receive food.

RESPONSE An action or physiological change elicited by a stimulus.

REINFORCEMENT The consequences of a behavior that determine whether it will be more likely that the behavior will occur again.

 ONLY HUMAN

"A" TRAIN FROM THE COOP TO HEATHROW A full page of letters from readers in an issue of *New Scientist* magazine reported sightings by London, England, subway riders of pigeons boarding, and disembarking from, subway cars in "purposeful" ways that suggest they have figured out where they are going.

breaking a complicated task into small bits and then using the principle of reinforcement to teach children each bit (Bjork, 1993). He developed automatic devices known as "teaching machines" that did exactly that (Skinner, 1958). The teaching machine asked a series of increasingly difficult questions that built on the students' answers to the simpler ones. To learn a complicated math problem, for instance, students would first be asked an easy question about the simplest part of the problem. They would then be told whether the answer was right or wrong, and if a correct response was made, the machine would move on to a more difficult question. Skinner thought that the satisfaction of knowing they were correct would be reinforcing and help students learn.

If fourth graders and pigeons could be successfully trained, then why stop there? In the controversial books *Beyond Freedom and Dignity* and *Walden II,* Skinner laid out his vision of a utopian society in which behavior was controlled by the judicious application of the principle of reinforcement (Skinner, 1971). In those books he put forth the simple but stunning claim that our subjective sense of free will is an illusion and that when we think we are exercising free will, we are actually responding to present and past patterns of reinforcement. We do things in the present that have been rewarding in the past, and our sense of "choosing" to do them is nothing more than an illusion. In this, Skinner echoed the sentiments of the philosopher Benedict Spinoza (1632–1677), who several centuries earlier had noted that "men are deceived in thinking themselves free, a belief that consists only in this, that they are conscious of their actions and ignorant of the causes by which they are determined. As to their saying that human actions depend on the will, these are mere words without any corresponding idea" (1677/1982, p. 86).

Skinner argued that his insights could be used to increase human well-being and solve social problems. Not surprisingly, that claim sparked an outcry from critics who believed that Skinner was giving away one of our most cherished attributes—free will—and calling for a repressive society that manipulated people for its own ends. The criticism even extended to *TV Guide,* which featured an interview with Skinner and called his ideas "the taming of mankind through a system of dog obedience schools for all" (Bjork, 1993, p. 201). Given the nature of Skinner's ideas, the critics' attacks were understandable—he had seriously underestimated how much people cherish the idea of free will—but in the sober light of hindsight, they were clearly overblown. Skinner did not want to turn society into a "dog obedience school" or strip people of their personal freedoms. Rather, he argued that an understanding of the principles by which behavior is generated could be used to increase the social welfare, which is precisely what happens when a government launches advertisements to encourage citizens to drink milk or quit smoking. The result of all the controversy, however, was that Skinner's fame reached a level rarely attained by psychologists. A popular magazine that listed the 100 most important people who ever lived ranked Skinner just 39 points below Jesus Christ (Herrnstein, 1977).

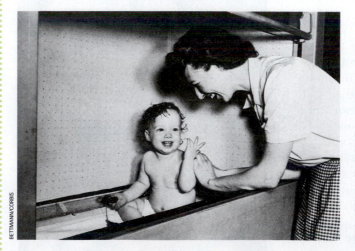

Skinner's well-publicized questioning of such cherished notions as free will led to a rumor that he had raised his own daughter in a Skinner box. This urban legend, while untrue, likely originated from the climate-controlled, glass-encased crib that he invented to protect his daughter from the cold Minnesota winter. Skinner marketed the crib under various names, including the "Air-crib" and the "Heir Conditioner," but it failed to catch on with parents.

BETTMANN/CORBIS

In summary, behaviorism advocated the study of observable actions and responses and held that inner mental processes were private events that could not be studied scientifically. Ivan Pavlov and John B. Watson studied the association between a stimulus and response and emphasized the importance of the environment in shaping behavior. Influenced by Watson's behaviorism, B. F. Skinner developed the concept of reinforcement using a "Skinner box." He demonstrated that animals and humans repeat behaviors that generate pleasant results and avoid performing those that generate unpleasant results. Skinner extended Watson's contentions about the importance of the environment in shaping behavior by suggesting that free will is an illusion and that the principle of reinforcement can be used to benefit society. ■ ■

COGNITIVE PSYCHOLOGY The scientific study of mental processes, including perception, thought, memory, and reasoning.

Beyond Behaviorism: Psychology Expands

Watson, Skinner, and the behaviorists dominated psychology from the 1930s to the 1950s. The psychologist Ulric Neisser recalled the atmosphere when he was a student at Swarthmore in the early 1950s:

> Behaviorism was the basic framework for almost all of psychology at the time. It was what you had to learn. That was the age when it was supposed that no psychological phenomenon was real unless you could demonstrate it in a rat (quoted in Baars, 1986, p. 275).

Behaviorism wouldn't dominate the field for much longer, however, and Neisser himself would play an important role in developing an alternative perspective. Why was behaviorism replaced? Although behaviorism allowed psychologists to measure, predict, and control behavior, it did this by ignoring some important things. First, it ignored the mental processes that had fascinated psychologists such as Wundt and James and, in so doing, found itself unable to explain some very important phenomena, such as how children learn language. Second, it ignored the evolutionary history of the organisms it studied and was thus unable to explain why, for example, a rat could learn to associate nausea with food much more quickly than it could learn to associate nausea with a tone or a light. As we shall see, the approaches that ultimately replaced behaviorism met these kinds of problems head-on.

The Emergence of Cognitive Psychology

For almost two decades, psychologists dismissed the problem of the mind as an intractable fairy tale that could not be studied scientifically. There were some exceptions to this rule (including most clinical and social psychologists, who remained deeply committed to the scientific study of mental processes), but by and large, psychologists happily ignored mental processes until the 1950s, when something important happened: the computer. The advent of computers had enormous practical impact, of course, but it also had an enormous conceptual impact on psychology. Computers are information-processing systems, and the flow of information through their circuits is clearly no fairy tale. If psychologists could think of mental events—such as remembering, attending, thinking, believing, evaluating, feeling, and assessing—as the flow of information through the mind, then they might be able to study the mind scientifically after all. The emergence of the computer led to a reemergence of interest in mental processes all across the discipline of psychology, and it spawned a new approach called **cognitive psychology**, which is *the scientific study of mental processes, including perception, thought, memory, and reasoning.*

Early Cognitive Pioneers

Even at the height of behaviorist domination, there were a few quiet revolutionaries whose research and writings were focused on mental processes. For example, Sir Frederic Bartlett (1886–1969) was a British psychologist interested in memory. He was dissatisfied with existing research and especially with the research of the German psychologist

"What about that! His brain still uses the old vacuum tubes."

Hermann Ebbinghaus (1850–1909), who had performed groundbreaking experiments on memory in 1885 that we'll discuss in Chapter 5. Serving as his own research subject, Ebbinghaus had tried to discover how quickly and how well he could memorize and recall meaningless information, such as the three-letter nonsense syllables *dap, kir,* and *sul.* Bartlett believed that it was more important to examine memory for the kinds of information people actually encounter in everyday life, and so he gave people stories to remember and carefully observed the kinds of errors they made when they tried to recall them some time later (Bartlett, 1932). Bartlett discovered many interesting things that Ebbinghaus could never have learned with his nonsense syllables. For example, he found that research participants often remembered what *should* have happened or what they *expected* to happen rather than what actually *did* happen. These and other errors led Bartlett to suggest that memory is not a photographic reproduction of past experience and that our attempts to recall the past are powerfully influenced by our knowledge, beliefs, hopes, aspirations, and desires.

Jean Piaget (1896–1980) was a Swiss psychologist who studied the perceptual and cognitive errors of children in order to gain insight into the nature and development of the human mind. For example, in one of his tasks, Piaget would give a 3-year-old child a large and a small mound of clay and tell the child to make the two mounds equal. Then Piaget would break one of the clay mounds into smaller pieces and ask the child which mound now had more clay. Although the amount of clay remained the same, of course, 3-year-old children usually said that the mound that was broken into smaller pieces was bigger, but by the age of 6 or 7, they no longer made this error. As you'll see in Chapter 9, Piaget theorized that younger children lack a particular cognitive ability that allows older children to appreciate the fact that the mass of an object remains constant even when it is divided. For Piaget, mindbugs such as these provided key insights into the mental world of the child (Piaget & Inhelder, 1969).

The German psychologist Kurt Lewin (1890–1947) was also a pioneer in the study of thought at a time when thought had been banished from psychology. Lewin (1936) argued that one could best predict a person's behavior in the world by understanding the person's subjective experience of the world. A television soap opera is a meaningless series of unrelated physical movements unless one thinks about the characters' experiences—how Karen feels about Bruce, what Van was planning to say to Kathy about Emily, and whether Linda's sister, Nancy, will always hate their mother for meddling in the marriage. Lewin realized that it was not the stimulus, but rather the person's *construal* of the stimulus, that determined the person's subsequent behavior. A pinch on the cheek can be pleasant or unpleasant depending on who administers it, under what circumstances, and to which set of cheeks. Lewin used a special kind of mathematics called *topology* to model the person's subjective experience, and although his topological theories were not particularly influential, his attempts to model mental life and his insistence that psychologists study how people construe their worlds would have a lasting impact on psychology.

BILL ANDERSON/PHOTO RESEARCHERS, INC.

Jean Piaget (1896–1980) studied and theorized about the developing mental lives of children, a marked departure from the observations of external behavior dictated by the methods of the behaviorists.

Technology and the Development of Cognitive Psychology

Although the contributions of psychologists such as Bartlett, Piaget, and Lewin provided early alternatives to behaviorism, they did not depose it. That job required the army. During World War II, the military had turned to psychologists to help understand how soldiers could best learn to use new technologies, such as radar. Radar operators had to pay close attention to their screens for long periods while trying to decide whether blips were friendly aircraft, enemy aircraft, or flocks of wild geese in need of a good chasing (Aschcraft, 1998; Lachman, Lachman, & Butterfield, 1979). How could radar operators be trained to make quicker and more accurate decisions? The answer to this question clearly required more than the swift delivery of pellets to the radar operator's food tray. It required that those who designed the equipment think about and talk about cognitive processes, such as perception, attention, identification, memory, and decision making. Behaviorism solved the problem by denying it, and thus some psychologists decided to deny behaviorism and forge ahead with a new approach.

The British psychologist Donald Broadbent (1926–93) was among the first to study what happens when people try to pay attention to several things at once. For instance, Broadbent observed that pilots can't attend to many different instruments at once and must actively move the focus of their attention from one to another (Best, 1992). Broadbent (1958) showed that the limited capacity to handle incoming information is a fundamental feature of human cognition and that this limit could explain many of the errors that pilots (and other people) made. At about the same time, the American psychologist George Miller (1956) pointed out a striking consistency in our capacity limitations across a variety of situations—we can pay attention to, and briefly hold in memory, about seven (give or take two) pieces of information. Cognitive psychologists began conducting experiments and devising theories to better understand the mind's limited capacity, a problem that behaviorists had ignored.

As you have already read, the invention of the computer in the 1950s had a profound impact on psychologists' thinking. People and computers differ in many ways, but both seem to register, store, and retrieve information, leading psychologists to wonder whether the computer might be used as a model for the human mind. A computer is made of hardware (e.g., chips and disk drives today, magnetic tapes and vacuum tubes a half century ago) and software (stored on optical disks today and on punch cards a half century ago). If the brain is roughly analogous to the computer's hardware, then perhaps the mind was roughly analogous to a software program. This line of thinking led cognitive psychologists to begin writing computer programs to see what kinds of software could be made to mimic human speech and behavior (Newell, Shaw, & Simon, 1958).

This navy radar operator must focus his attention for long stretches of time, while making quick, important decisions. The mental processes involved in such tasks are studied by cognitive psychologists.

This 1950s computer was among the first generation of digital computers. Although different in many ways, computers and the human brain both process and store information, which led many psychologists at the time to think of the mind as a type of computer. Researchers currently adopt a more sophisticated view of the mind and the brain, but the computer analogy was helpful in the early days of cognitive psychology.

Noam Chomsky's (b. 1928) critique of Skinner's theory of language signaled the end of behaviorism's dominance in psychology and helped spark the development of cognitive psychology.

Ironically, the emergence of cognitive psychology was also energized by the appearance of a book by B. F. Skinner called *Verbal Behavior*, which offered a behaviorist analysis of language (Skinner, 1957). A linguist at the Massachusetts Institute of Technology (MIT), Noam Chomsky (b. 1928), published a devastating critique of the book in which he argued that Skinner's insistence on observable behavior had caused him to miss some of the most important features of language. According to Chomsky, language relies on mental rules that allow people to understand and produce novel words and sentences. The ability of even the youngest child to generate new sentences that he or she had never heard before flew in the face of the behaviorist claim that children learn to use language by reinforcement. Chomsky provided a clever, detailed, and thoroughly cognitive account of language that could explain many of the phenomena that the behaviorist account could not (Chomsky, 1959).

These developments during the 1950s set the stage for an explosion of cognitive studies during the 1960s. Cognitive psychologists did not return to the old introspective procedures used during the 19th century, but instead developed new and ingenious methods that allowed them to study cognitive processes. The excitement of the new approach was summarized in a landmark book, *Cognitive Psychology*, written by someone you met earlier in this chapter: Ulric Neisser (1967). His book provided a foundation for the development of cognitive psychology, which grew and thrived in years that followed.

The Brain Meets the Mind: The Rise of Cognitive Neuroscience

If cognitive psychologists studied the software of the mind, they had little to say about the hardware of the brain. And yet, as any computer scientist knows, the relationship between software and hardware is crucial: Each element needs the other to get the job done. Our mental activities often seem so natural and effortless—noticing the shape of an object, using words in speech or writing, recognizing a face as familiar—that we fail to appreciate the fact that they depend on intricate operations carried out by the brain. This dependence is revealed by dramatic cases in which damage to a particular part of the brain causes a person to lose a specific cognitive ability. Recall that in the 19th century, the French physician Paul Broca described a patient who, after damage to a limited area in the left side of the brain, could not produce words—even though he could understand them perfectly well. As you'll see later in the book, damage to other parts of the brain can also result in syndromes that are characterized by the loss of specific mental abilities (e.g., prosopagnosia, in which the person cannot recognize human faces) or by the emergence of bizarre behavior or beliefs (e.g., Capgras syndrome, in which the person believes that a close family member has been replaced by an imposter). These striking—sometimes startling—cases remind us that even the simplest cognitive processes depend on the brain. The high level of interest psychologists now have in the link between brain and mind is rooted in the achievements of pioneering researchers working in the middle of the 20th century.

Karl Lashley (1890–1958) conducted experiments that he hoped would reveal a brain area that stores learned information. He removed different parts of animals' brains and observed the effects on the animals' behavior. Though he never found a specific area where learning is stored, his general approach had a major influence on behavioral neuroscience.

Karl Lashley (1890–1958), a psychologist who studied with John B. Watson, took an approach similar to the one that Flourens used a century earlier. By training rats to run mazes, surgically removing parts of their brains, and then measuring how well they could run the maze again, Lashley hoped to find the precise spot in the brain where *learning* occurred. Alas, no one spot seemed to uniquely and reliably eliminate learning (Lashley, 1960). Rather, Lashley simply found that the more of the rat's brain he removed, the more poorly the rat ran the maze. Lashley was frustrated by his inability to identify a specific site of learning, but his efforts inspired other scientists to take up the challenge. They developed a research area called *physiological psychology*. Today, this area has grown into **behavioral neuroscience**, which *links psychological processes to activities in the nervous system and other bodily processes*. To learn about the relationship

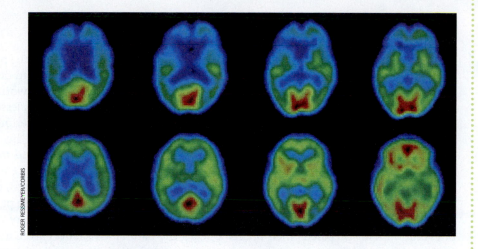

ROGER RESSMEYER/CORBIS

Figure 1.5 PET Scans of Healthy and Alzheimer's Brains PET scans are one of a variety of brain-imaging technologies that psychologists use to observe the living brain. The four brain images on the top each come from a person suffering from Alzheimer's disease; the four on the bottom each come from a healthy person of similar age. The red and green areas reflect higher levels of brain activity compared to the blue areas, which reflect lower levels of activity. In each image, the front of the brain is on the top and the back of the brain is on the bottom. You can see that the patient with Alzheimer's disease, compared with the healthy person, shows more extensive areas of lowered activity toward the front of the brain.

between brain and behavior, behavioral neuroscientists observe animals' responses as they perform specially constructed tasks, such as running through a maze to obtain food rewards. The neuroscientists can record electrical or chemical responses in the brain as the task is being performed or later remove specific parts of the brain to see how performance is affected (**FIGURE 1.5**).

Of course, experimental brain surgery cannot ethically be performed on human beings, and thus psychologists who want to study the human brain often have had to rely on nature's cruel and inexact experiments. Birth defects, accidents, and illnesses often cause damage to particular brain regions, and if this damage disrupts a particular ability, then psychologists deduce that the region is involved in producing the ability. For example, in Chapter 5 you'll learn about a patient whose memory was virtually wiped out by damage to a specific part of the brain, and you'll see how this tragedy provided scientists with remarkable clues about how memories are stored (Scoville & Milner, 1957). (See the Hot Science box on p. 27 for a related example of amnesia.) But in the late 1980s, technological breakthroughs led to the development of noninvasive "brain-scanning" techniques that made it possible for psychologists to watch what happens inside a human brain as a person performs a task such as reading, imagining, listening, and remembering. Brain scanning is an invaluable tool because it allows us to observe the brain in action and to see which parts are involved in which operations (see Chapter 3).

For example, researchers used scanning technology to identify the parts of the brain in the left hemisphere that are involved in specific aspects of language, such as understanding or producing words (Peterson et al., 1989). Later scanning studies showed that people who are deaf from birth but who learn to communicate using American Sign Language (ASL) rely on regions in the right hemisphere (as well as the left) when using ASL. In contrast, people with normal hearing who learned ASL after puberty seemed to rely only on the left hemisphere when using ASL (Newman et al., 2002). These findings suggest that although both spoken and signed language usually rely on the left hemisphere, the right hemisphere also can become involved—but only for a limited period (perhaps until puberty). The findings also provide a nice example of how psychologists can now use scanning techniques to observe people with various kinds of cognitive capacities and use their observations to unravel the mysteries of the mind and the brain (**FIGURE 1.6**). In fact, there's a name for this area of research. **Cognitive neuroscience** is the *field that attempts to understand the links between cognitive processes and brain activity* (Gazzaniga, 2000).

BEHAVIORAL NEUROSCIENCE An approach to psychology that links psychological processes to activities in the nervous system and other bodily processes.

COGNITIVE NEUROSCIENCE A field that attempts to understand the links between cognitive processes and brain activity.

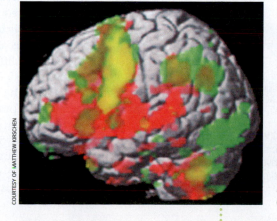

COURTESY OF MATTHEW KIRSCHEN

Figure 1.6 More Ways to Scan a Brain fMRI scanners produce more precise images than PET scans, allowing researchers to more accurately localize brain activity. fMRIs are also quicker at capturing images, allowing researchers to measure brain activity over briefer periods. Here, green areas of the brain were active when research participants remembered information presented visually, and red areas were active when they remembered information presented aurally. Yellow areas were active during both types of presentations.

Today's evolutionary psychologists embrace Charles Darwin's (1809–82) ideas, just as William James did 100 years ago. Darwin's theories of evolution, adaptation, and natural selection have provided insight into why brains and minds work they way they do.

EVOLUTIONARY PSYCHOLOGY A psychological approach that explains mind and behavior in terms of the adaptive value of abilities that are preserved over time by natural selection.

The Adaptive Mind: The Emergence of Evolutionary Psychology

Psychology's renewed interest in mental processes and its growing interest in the brain were two developments that led psychologists away from behaviorism. A third development also pointed them in a different direction. Recall that one of behaviorism's key claims was that organisms are blank slates on which experience writes its lessons, and hence any one lesson should be as easily written as another. But in experiments conducted during the 1960s and 1970s, the psychologist John Garcia and his colleagues showed that rats can learn to associate nausea with the smell of food much more quickly than they can learn to associate nausea with a flashing light (Garcia, 1981). Why should this be? In the real world of forests, sewers, and garbage cans, nausea is usually caused by spoiled food and not by lightning, and although these particular rats had been born in a laboratory and had never left their cages, millions of years of evolution had "prepared" their brains to learn the natural association more quickly than the artificial one. In other words, it was not only the rat's learning history—but the rat's *ancestors'* learning histories—that determined the rat's ability to learn. Although that fact was at odds with the behaviorist doctrine, it was the credo for a new kind of psychology.

Evolutionary psychology *explains mind and behavior in terms of the adaptive value of abilities that are preserved over time by natural selection.* Evolutionary psychology has its roots in Charles Darwin's (1809–82) theory of natural selection, which inspired William James's functionalist approach. But it is only since the publication in 1975 of *Sociobiology,* by the biologist E. O. Wilson, that evolutionary thinking has had an identifiable presence in psychology. That presence is steadily increasing (Buss, 1999; Pinker, 1997a; Tooby & Cosmides, 2000). Evolutionary psychologists think of the mind as a collection of specialized "modules" that are designed to solve the human problems our ancestors faced as they attempted to eat, mate, and reproduce over millions of years. According to evolutionary psychology, the brain is not an all-purpose computer that can do or learn one thing just as easily as it can do or learn another; rather, it is a computer that was built to do a few things well and everything else not at all. It is a computer that comes with a small suite of built-in applications that are designed to do the things that previous versions of that computer needed to have done.

Consider, for example, how evolutionary psychology treats the emotion of jealousy. All of us who have been in romantic relationships have been jealous, if only because we noticed our partner noticing someone else. Jealousy can be a powerful, overwhelming emotion that we might wish to avoid, but according to evolutionary psychology, it exists today because it once served an adaptive function. If some of our hominid ancestors experienced jealousy and others did not, then the ones who experienced it might have been more likely to guard their mates and aggress against their rivals and thus may have been more likely to reproduce their "jealous genes" (Buss, 2000).

Critics of the evolutionary approach point out that many current traits of people and other animals probably evolved to serve different functions than those they currently serve. For example, biologists believe that the feathers of birds probably evolved initially to perform such functions as regulating body temperature or capturing prey and only later served the entirely different function of flight. Likewise, people are reasonably adept at learning to drive a car, but nobody would argue that such an ability is the result of natural selection; the learning abilities that allow us to become skilled car drivers must have evolved for purposes other than driving cars.

Complications like these have lead the critics to wonder how evolutionary hypotheses can ever be tested (Coyne, 2000; Sterelny & Griffiths, 1999). We don't have a record of our ancestors' thoughts, feelings, and actions, and fossils won't provide much information about the evolution of mind and behavior. Testing ideas about the evolutionary origins of psychological phenomena is indeed a challenging

{ HOT SCIENCE } New Connections

In this chapter we've looked at the development of numerous subfields in psychology, including behaviorism, psychoanalysis, cognitive psychology, cognitive neuroscience, evolutionary psychology, and social psychology. Each takes a different approach to understanding human behavior, and each has its own research journals and scientific jargon. As a result, psychologists in the various subfields usually work separately from one another. No matter how different their approaches, most psychologists have a common goal: understanding the mind and behavior. Instead of tackling this difficult task from just a single viewpoint, combining approaches from different subfields can help generate new insights that might not be obtained otherwise. Research during the past decade bears out this idea: Many of the most exciting new findings in psychology have resulted from making new connections across different subfields.

Two of your textbook authors, Daniel Gilbert and Daniel Schacter, were among the authors of a research study that illustrates the benefits of combining different perspectives: social psychology (Gilbert's area) and cognitive neuroscience (Schacter's area). The study explored the process of *cognitive dissonance*, which is the psychological discomfort that occurs when our behavior conflicts with our beliefs about ourselves (Lieberman, Ochsner, Gilbert, & Schacter, 2001). As you'll learn in Chapter 16, this topic has long interested social psychologists. People will do almost anything to reduce dissonance, such as changing what they believe to fit their behavior or discrediting evidence that threatens their beliefs. An unhappily married woman who believes that her marriage should be successful may distort the past to make the present seem more bearable. A man who purchased an expensive car and then read a bad review

claiming that the car is a lemon might belittle the reviewer as an ignoramus who has no business writing about cars.

Social psychologists have assumed that the experience of cognitive dissonance requires the ability to recall the behavior that produced conflict in the first place. If the man who bought the car doesn't remember making the purchase, presumably the bad magazine review won't bother him, so he won't have any dissonance to reduce. Or will he?

Lieberman and his colleagues examined psychological conflict in a special group of individuals: patients suffering from amnesia as a result of damage to parts of the brain that are needed to form new memories. As you'll see in Chapter 5, these patients have little or no ability to remember their recent experiences. If people with amnesia show cognitive dissonance even though they can't remember the experience that created it, social psychologists would have to modify their ideas about the dissonance process.

To get a sense of the procedure these researchers used, consider the following scenario. You visit an art gallery and fall in love with two prints by the same artist but only have enough money to purchase one. After almost deciding on one and then the other, you finally make your choice. Though you feel conflicted about passing over the remaining print, you rationalize your decision by convincing yourself that you like the print you purchased quite a bit more than the one you passed up. Happily, the dissonance and discomfort created by the difficult decision go away.

Studies have shown that just this sort of dissonance reduction occurs when people are forced to decide between two art prints (Brehm, 1956; Gerard & White, 1983). After making the choice, people

claim to like the chosen print *more* and the bypassed print *less* than they had earlier. We showed art prints to amnesic patients and people without memory problems; they ranked the prints according to how much they liked them. The two groups then made a choice between two prints, indicating which one they would prefer to hang in their homes, and later ranked all the prints again for liking. We found that amnesic patients inflated how much they liked the chosen print relative to the print they had passed over. In other words, people with amnesia reduced the dissonance created by choosing between the two prints in much the same way as non-amnesiacs would. But the patients with amnesia didn't have any conscious memory of making the choice that produced dissonance in the first place! These results suggest that we don't need to *remember* a past conflict in order to be influenced by the rationalizations we used to reduce cognitive dissonance.

By combining a patient population that is usually studied by cognitive neuroscientists with a traditional social psychology procedure, this study encourages us to think in a new way about what happens when people reduce psychological discomfort brought about by cognitive dissonance. When we (or others) rationalize our choices in everyday life, it may seem like we are just "making excuses" for our behavior. Saying that we really like the art print we chose a lot more than the one we bypassed—even though initially we didn't—may seem like a flimsy attempt to make ourselves feel better. The fact that amnesic patients do exactly the same thing, without any memory of the conflict, shows that these rationalizations are much more than just flimsy "excuse making"; they reflect deep and enduring changes in our beliefs.

---

task, but not an impossible one (Buss, Haselton, Shackelford, Bleske, & Wakefield, 1998; Pinker, 1997b). Evolutionary psychologists hold that behaviors or traits that occur universally in all cultures are good candidates for evolutionary adaptations. For example, physical attractiveness is widely valued by both men and women in many cultures, and people from different cultures tend to agree in their judgments of facial attractiveness (Cunningham, Roberts, Barbee, Druen, & Wu, 1995). Several aspects of facial attractiveness, such as symmetrical facial features, have been linked with enhanced physical and mental health, also suggesting the possibility that it is an evolutionary adaptation (Shackelford & Larsen, 1999).

Evolutionary adaptations should also increase reproductive success. So, if a specific trait or feature has been favored by natural selection, it should be possible to find some evidence of this in the numbers of offspring that are produced by the trait's bearers. Consider, for instance, the hypothesis that men tend to be tall because women prefer to mate with tall men. To investigate this hypothesis, researchers conducted a study in which they compared the numbers of offspring from short and tall men. They did their best to equate other factors that might affect the results, such as the level of education attained by short and tall men. Consistent with the evolutionary hypothesis, they found that tall men do indeed bear more offspring than short men (Pawlowski, Dunbar, & Lipowicz, 2000). This kind of study provides evidence that allows evolutionary psychologists to test their ideas. Not every evolutionary hypothesis can be tested, of course, but evolutionary psychologists are becoming increasingly inventive in their attempts.

In summary, psychologists such as Frederic Bartlett, Jean Piaget, and Kurt Lewin defied the behaviorist doctrine and studied the inner workings of the mind. Their efforts, as well as those of later pioneers such as Donald Broadbent, paved the way for cognitive psychology to focus on inner mental processes such as perception, attention, memory, and reasoning. Cognitive psychology developed as a field due to the invention of the computer, psychologists' efforts to improve the performance of the military, and Noam Chomsky's theories about language. Cognitive neuroscience attempts to link the brain with the mind through studies of both brain-damaged and healthy people. Evolutionary psychology focuses on the adaptive function that minds and brains serve and seeks to understand the nature and origin of psychological processes in terms of natural selection. ■ ■

Beyond the Individual: Social and Cultural Perspectives

The picture we have painted so far may vaguely suggest a scene from some 1950s science-fiction film in which the protagonist is a living brain that thinks, feels, hopes, and worries while suspended in a vat of pink jelly in a basement laboratory. Although psychologists often do focus on the brain and the mind of the individual, they have not lost sight of the fact that human beings are fundamentally social animals who are part of a vast network of family, friends, teachers, and coworkers. Trying to understand people in the absence of that fact is a bit like trying to understand an ant or a bee without considering the function and influence of the colony or hive. People are the most important and most complex objects that we ever encounter, and thus it is not surprising that our behavior is strongly influenced by their presence—or their absence. The two areas of psychology that most strongly emphasize these facts are social and cultural psychology.

The Development of Social Psychology

Social psychology is the study of *the causes and consequences of interpersonal behavior.* This broad definition allows social psychologists to address a remarkable variety of topics. Historians trace the birth of social psychology to an experiment conducted in 1895 by the psychologist and bicycle enthusiast, Norman Triplett, who noticed that cyclists seemed to ride faster when they rode with others. Intrigued by this observation, he conducted an experiment that showed that children reeled in a fishing line faster when tested in the presence of other children than when tested alone. Triplett was not trying to improve the fishing abilities of American children, of course, but rather was trying to show that the mere presence of other people can influence performance on even the most mundane kinds of tasks.

Social psychology's development began in earnest in the 1930s and was driven by several historical events. The rise of Nazism led many of Germany's most talented

"You're certainly a lot less fun since the operation."

GAHAN WILSON/CARTOONBANK.COM

SOCIAL PSYCHOLOGY A subfield of psychology that studies the causes and consequences of interpersonal behavior.

scientists to immigrate to America, and among them were psychologists such as Solomon Asch (1907–96) and Kurt Lewin. These psychologists had been strongly influenced by Gestalt psychology, which you'll recall held that "the whole is greater than the sum of its parts," and though the Gestaltists had been talking about the visual perception of objects, these psychologists felt that the phrase also captured a basic truth about the relationship between social groups and the individuals who constitute them. Philosophers had speculated about the nature of sociality for thousands of years, and political scientists, economists, anthropologists, and sociologists had been studying social life scientifically for some time. But these German refugees were the first to generate theories of social behavior that resembled the theories generated by natural scientists,

and more importantly, they were the first to conduct experiments to test their social theories. For example, Lewin (1936) adopted the language of midcentury physics to develop a "field theory" that viewed social behavior as the product of "internal forces" (such as personality, goals, and beliefs) and "external forces" (such as social pressure and culture), while Asch (1946) performed laboratory experiments to examine the "mental chemistry" that allows people to combine small bits of information about another person into a full impression of that person's personality.

Other historical events also shaped social psychology in its early years. For example, the Holocaust brought the problems of conformity and obedience into sharp focus, leading psychologists such as Asch (1956) and others to examine the conditions under which people can influence each other to think and act in inhuman or irrational ways. The civil rights movement and the rising tensions between Black and White Americans led psychologists such as Gordon Allport (1897–1967) to study stereotyping, prejudice, and racism and to shock the world of psychology by suggesting that prejudice was the result of a perceptual error that was every bit as natural and unavoidable as an optical illusion (Allport, 1954). Allport identified a mindbug at work: The same perceptual processes that allow us to efficiently categorize elements of our social and physical world allow us to erroneously categorize entire groups of people. Social psychologists today study a wider variety of topics (from social memory to social relationships) and use a wider variety of techniques (from opinion polls to neuroimaging) than did their forebears, but this field of psychology remains dedicated to understanding the brain as a social organ, the mind as a social adaptation, and the individual as a social creature.

Social psychology studies how the thoughts, feelings, and behaviors of individuals can be influenced by the presence of others. Members of Reverend Sun Myung Moon's Unification Church are often married to one another in ceremonies of 10,000 people or more; in some cases couples don't know each other before the wedding begins. Social movements such as this have the power to sway individuals.

The Emergence of Cultural Psychology

Americans and Western Europeans are sometimes surprised to realize that most of the people on the planet are members of neither culture. Although we're all more alike than we are different, there is nonetheless considerable diversity within the human species in social practices, customs, and ways of living. Culture refers to the values, traditions, and beliefs that are shared by a particular group of people. Although we usually think of culture in terms of nationality and ethnic groups, cultures can also be defined by age (youth culture), sexual orientation (gay culture), religion (Jewish culture), or occupation (academic culture). **Cultural psychology** is *the study of how cultures reflect and shape the psychological processes of their members* (Shweder & Sullivan, 1993). Cultural psychologists study a wide range of phenomena, ranging from visual perception to social interaction, as they seek to understand which of these phenomena are universal and which vary from place to place and time to time.

CULTURAL PSYCHOLOGY The study of how cultures reflect and shape the psychological processes of their members.

Perhaps surprisingly, one of the first psychologists to pay attention to the influence of culture was someone recognized today for pioneering the development of experimental psychology: Wilhelm Wundt. He believed that a complete psychology would have to combine a laboratory approach with a broader cultural perspective. Wundt wrote extensively about cultural and social influences on the mind, producing a 10-volume work on culture and psychology, in which he covered a vast range of topics, such as how people gesture in different cultures or the origins of various myths and religions (Wundt, 1908). But Wundt's ideas failed to spark much interest from other psychologists, who had their hands full trying to make sense of results from laboratory experiments and formulating general laws of human behavior. Outside of psychology, anthropologists such as Margaret Mead (1901–78) and Gregory Bateson (1904–80) attempted to understand the workings of culture by traveling to far-flung regions of the world and carefully observing child-rearing patterns, rituals, religious ceremonies, and the like. Such studies revealed practices—some bizarre from a North American perspective—that served important functions in a culture, such as the painful ritual of violent body mutilation and bloodletting in mountain tribes of New Guinea, which initiates young boys into training to become warriors (Mead, 1935/1968; Read, 1965). Yet at the time, most anthropologists paid as little attention to psychology as psychologists did to anthropology.

Cultural psychology only began to emerge as a strong force in psychology during the 1980s and 1990s, when psychologists and anthropologists began to communicate with each other about their ideas and methods (Stigler, Shweder, & Herdt, 1990). It was then that psychologists rediscovered Wundt as an intellectual ancestor of this area of the field (Jahoda, 1993).

Physicists assume that $e = mc^2$ whether the m is located in Cleveland, Moscow, or the Orion Nebula. Chemists assume that water is made of hydrogen and oxygen and that it was made of hydrogen and oxygen in 1609 as well. The laws of physics and chemistry are assumed to be universal, and for much of psychology's history, the same assumption was made about the principles that govern human behavior (Shweder, 1991). *Absolutism* holds that culture makes little or no difference for most psychological phenomena—that "honesty is honesty and depression is depression, no matter where one observes it" (Segall, Lonner, & Berry, 1998, p. 1103). And yet, as any world traveler knows, cultures differ in exciting, delicious, and frightening ways, and things that are true of people in one culture are not necessarily true of people in another. *Relativism* holds that psychological phenomena are likely to vary considerably across cultures and should be viewed only in the context of a specific culture (Berry, Poortinga, Segall, & Dasen, 1992). Although depression is observed in nearly

The Namgay family from Shingkhey, Bhutan (left), and the Skeen family from Texas, USA (right), display their respective family possessions in these two photos, both taken in 1993. Cultural psychology studies the similarities and differences in psychological processes that arise between people living in different cultures.

every culture, the symptoms associated with it vary dramatically from one place to another. For example, in Western cultures, depressed people tend to devalue themselves, whereas depressed people in Eastern cultures do not (Draguns, 1980).

Today, most cultural psychologists fall somewhere between these two extremes. Most psychological phenomena can be influenced by culture, some are completely determined by it, and others seem to be entirely unaffected. For example, the age of a person's earliest memory differs dramatically across cultures (MacDonald, Uesiliana, & Hayne, 2000), whereas judgments of facial attractiveness do not (Cunningham et al., 1995). As noted when we discussed evolutionary psychology, it seems likely that the most universal phenomena are those that are closely associated with the basic biology that all human beings share. Conversely, the least universal phenomena are those rooted in the varied socialization practices that different cultures evolve. Of course, the only way to determine whether a phenomenon is variable or constant across cultures is to design research to investigate these possibilities, and cultural psychologists do just that (Cole, 1996; Segall et al., 1998).

In summary, social psychology recognizes that people exist as part of a network of other people and examines how individuals influence and interact with one another. Social psychology was pioneered by German émigrés, such as Kurt Lewin, who were motivated by a desire to address social issues and problems. Cultural psychology is concerned with the effects of the broader culture on individuals and with similarities and differences among people in different cultures. Within this perspective, absolutists hold that culture has little impact on most psychological phenomena, whereas relativists believe that culture has a powerful effect. Together, social and cultural psychology help expand the discipline's horizons beyond just an examination of individuals. These areas of psychology examine behavior within the broader context of human interaction. ■ ■

The Profession of Psychology: Past and Present

If ever you find yourself on an airplane with an annoying seatmate who refuses to let you read your magazine, there are two things you can do. First, you can turn to the person and say in a calm and friendly voice, "Did you know that I am covered with strange and angry bacteria?" If that seems a bit extreme, you might instead try saying, "Did you know that I am a psychologist, and I'm forming an evaluation of you as you speak?" as this will usually shut them up without getting you arrested. The truth is that most people don't really know what psychology is or what psychologists do, but they do have some vague sense that it isn't wise to talk to one. Now that you've been briefly acquainted with psychology's past, let's consider its present by looking at psychology as a profession. We'll look first at the origins of psychology's professional organizations, next at the contexts in which psychologists tend to work, and finally at the kinds of training required to become a psychologist.

Psychologists Band Together: The American Psychological Association

You'll recall that when we last saw William James, he was wandering around the greater Boston area, expounding the virtues of the new science of psychology. In July 1892, James and five other psychologists traveled to Clark University to attend a meeting called by G. Stanley Hall. Each worked at a large university where they taught psychology courses, performed research, and wrote textbooks. Although they were too few to make up a jury or even a decent hockey team, these seven men decided that it was time to form an organization that represented psychology as a profession, and on that day the American Psychological Association (APA) was born. The seven psychologists could scarcely have imagined that today their little club would have more than 150,000 members—approximately the population of a decent-sized city in the United

States. Although all of the original members were employed by universities or colleges, today academic psychologists make up only 20% of the membership, while nearly 70% of the members work in clinical and health-related settings. Because the APA is no longer as focused on academic psychology as it once was, the American Psychological Society (APS) was formed in 1988 by 450 academic psychologists who wanted an organization that focused specifically on the needs of psychologists carrying out scientific research. The APS, renamed the Association for Psychological Science in 2006, grew quickly, attracting 5,000 members within six months; today it comprises nearly 12,000 psychologists.

Mary Whiton Calkins (1863–1930), the first woman elected APA president, suffered from the sex discrimination that was common during her lifetime. Despite academic setbacks (such as Harvard University refusing to grant women an official PhD), Calkins went on to a distinguished career in research and teaching at Wellesley College.

WELLESLEY COLLEGE ARCHIVES—MARGARET CLAPP LIBRARY

The Growing Role of Women and Minorities

In 1892, APA had 31 members, all of whom were White and all of whom were male. Today, about half of all APA members are women, and the percentage of non-White members continues to grow. Surveys of recent PhD recipients reveal a picture of increasing diversification in the field. The proportion of women receiving PhDs in psychology increased nearly 20% between the mid-1980s and mid-1990s, and the proportion of minorities receiving PhDs in psychology nearly doubled during that same period. Clearly, psychology is increasingly reflecting the diversity of American society.

The current involvement of women and minorities in the APA, and psychology more generally, can be traced to early pioneers who blazed a trail that others followed. In 1905, Mary Calkins (1863–1930) became the first woman to serve as president of the APA. Calkins became interested in psychology while teaching Greek at Wellesley College. She studied with William James at Harvard and later became a professor of psychology at Wellesley College, where she worked until retiring in 1929. In her presidential address to the APA, Calkins described her theory of the role of the "self" in psychological function. Arguing against Wundt's and Titchener's structuralist ideas that the mind can be dissected into components, Calkins claimed that the self is a single unit that cannot be broken down into individual parts. Calkins wrote four books and published over 100 articles during her illustrious career (Calkins, 1930; Scarborough & Furumoto, 1987; Stevens & Gardner, 1982).

Francis Cecil Sumner (1895–1954) was the first African American to hold a PhD in psychology, receiving his from Clark University in 1920. Sumner conducted research on race relations, equality, and the psychology of religion.

ARCHIVES OF THE HISTORY OF AMERICAN PSYCHOLOGY

Today, women play leading roles in all areas of psychology. Some of the men who formed the APA might have been surprised by the prominence of women in the field today, but we suspect that William James, a strong supporter of Mary Calkins, would not be one of them.

Just as there were no women at the first meeting of the APA, there weren't any non-White people either. The first member of a minority group to become president of the APA was Kenneth Clark

A student of Francis Cecil Sumner's, Kenneth B. Clark (1914–2005) studied the developmental effects of prejudice, discrimination, and segregation on children. In one classic study from the 1950s, he found that African American preschoolers preferred white dolls to black ones. Clark's research was cited by the U.S. Supreme Court in its decision for the landmark *Brown v. Board of Education* case that ended school segregation.

WILLIAM E. SAURO/NEW YORK TIMES CO./GETTY IMAGES

(1914–2005), who was elected in 1970. Clark worked extensively on the self-image of African American children and argued that segregation of the races creates great psychological harm. Clark's conclusions had a large influence on public policy, and his research contributed to the Supreme Court's 1954 ruling (*Brown v. Board of Education*) to outlaw segregation in public schools (Guthrie, 2000). Clark's interest in psychology was sparked as an undergraduate at Howard University when he took a course from Francis Cecil Sumner (1895–1954), who was the first African American to receive a PhD in psychology (from Clark University, in 1920). Little known today, Sumner's main interest focused on the education of African American youth (Sawyer, 2000).

What Psychologists Do: Research Careers

So what should you do if you want to become a psychologist—and what should you fail to do if you desperately want to avoid it? You can become "a psychologist" by a variety of routes, and the people who call themselves psychologists may hold a variety of different degrees. Typically, students finish college and enter graduate school in order to obtain a PhD (or doctor of philosophy) degree in some particular area of psychology (e.g., social, cognitive, developmental). During graduate school, students generally gain exposure to the field by taking classes and learn to conduct research by collaborating with their professors. Although William James was able to master every area of psychology because the areas were so small during his lifetime, today a student can spend the better part of a decade mastering just one.

After receiving a PhD, you can go on for more specialized research training by pursuing a postdoctoral fellowship under the supervision of an established researcher in their area or apply for a faculty position at a college or university or a research position in government or industry. Academic careers usually involve a combination of teaching and research, whereas careers in government or industry are typically dedicated to research alone.

The Variety of Career Paths

As you saw earlier, research is not the only career option for a psychologist. Most of the people who call themselves psychologists neither teach nor do research, but rather, they assess or treat people with psychological problems. Most of these *clinical psychologists* work in private practice, often in partnerships with other psychologists or with psychiatrists (who have earned an MD, or medical degree, and are allowed to prescribe medication). Other clinical psychologists work in hospitals or medical schools, some have faculty positions at universities or colleges, and some combine private practice

ONLY HUMAN

A TREASURY OF THERAPEUTIC TECHNIQUES The *Austin American-Statesman* reported that then Texas treasurer Martha Whitehead had hired a psychologist, for $1,000, to counsel several employees of her office who were despondent about Whitehead's recommendation to abolish her agency.

Figure 1.7 **The Major Subfields in Psychology** Psychologists are drawn to many different subfields in psychology. Here are the percentages of people receiving PhDs in various subfields. Clinical psychology makes up almost half of the doctorates awarded in psychology. Source: 2004 Graduate Study in Psychology. Compiled by APA Research Office.

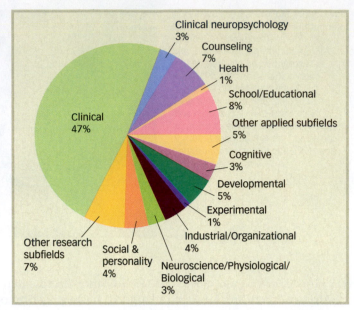

with an academic job. Many clinical psychologists focus on specific problems or disorders, such as depression or anxiety, whereas others focus on specific populations, such as children, ethnic minority groups, or elderly adults (**FIGURE 1.7**).

Just over 10% of APA members are *counseling psychologists,* who assist people in dealing with work or career issues and changes or help people deal with common crises such as divorce, the loss of a job, or the death of a loved one. Counseling psychologists may have a PhD or an MA (master's degree) in counseling psychology or an MSW (master of social work).

Psychologists are also quite active in educational settings. About 5% of APA members are *school psychologists,* who offer guidance to students, parents, and teachers. A similar proportion of APA members, known *as industrial/organizational psychologists,* focus on issues in the workplace. These psychologists typically work in business or industry and may be involved in assessing potential employees, finding ways to improve productivity, or helping staff and management to develop effective planning strategies for coping with change or anticipated future developments.

Even this brief and incomplete survey of the APA membership provides a sense of the wide variety of contexts in which psychologists operate. You can think of psychology as an international community of professionals devoted to advancing scientific knowledge; assisting people with psychological problems and disorders; and trying to enhance the quality of life in work, school, and other everyday settings.

In summary, the American Psychological Association (APA) has grown dramatically since it was formed in 1892 and now includes over 150,000 members, working in clinical, academic, and applied settings. Psychologists are also represented by professional organizations such as the Association for Psychological Science (APS), which focuses on scientific psychology. Through the efforts of pioneers such as Mary Calkins, women have come to play an increasingly important role in the field and are now as well represented as men. Minority involvement in psychology took longer, but the pioneering efforts of Francis Cecil Sumner, Kenneth B. Clark, and others have led to increased participation of minorities in psychology. Psychologists prepare for research careers through graduate and postdoctoral training and work in a variety of applied settings, including schools, clinics, and industry. ■ ■ ■

The Perils of Procrastination

As you've read in this chapter, the human mind and behavior are fascinating in part because they are not error free. Mindbugs interest us primarily as paths to achieving a better understanding of mental activity and behavior, but they also have practical consequences. Let's consider a mindbug that can have significant consequences in your own life: procrastination.

At one time or another, most of us have avoided carrying out a task or put it off to a later time. The task may be unpleasant, difficult, or just less entertaining than other things we could be doing at the moment. For college students, procrastination can affect a range of academic activities, such as writing a term paper or preparing for a test. Academic procrastination is not uncommon: Over 70% of college students report that they engage in some form of procrastination (Schouwenburg, 1995). Procrastination can be thought of as a mindbug because it prevents the completion of tasks in a timely manner. Although it's fun to hang out with your friends tonight, it's not so much fun to worry for three days about your impending history exam or try to study at 4:00 a.m. the morning before the test. Studying now, or at least a little bit each day, robs the procrastination mindbug of its power over you.

Some procrastinators defend the practice by claiming that they tend to work best under pressure or by noting that as long as a task gets done, it doesn't matter all that much if it is completed just before the deadline. Is there any merit to such claims, or are they just feeble excuses for counterproductive behavior?

A study of 60 undergraduate psychology college students provides some intriguing answers (Tice & Baumeister, 1997). At the beginning of the semester, the instructor announced a due date for the term paper and told students that if they could not meet the date, they would receive an extension to a later date. About a month later, students completed a scale that measures tendencies toward procrastination. At that same time, and then again during the last week of class, students recorded health symptoms they had experienced during the past week, the amount of stress they had experienced during that week, and the number of visits they had made to a health care center during the previous month.

Students who scored high on the procrastination scale tended to turn in their papers late. One month into the semester, these procrastinators reported less stress and fewer symptoms of physical illness than did nonprocrastinators. But at the end of the semester, the procrastinators reported *more* stress and *more* health symptoms than did the nonprocrastinators and also reported more visits to the health center. The procrastinators also received lower grades on their papers and on course exams.

This study shows, then, that procrastination did have some benefits: Procrastinators tended to feel better early on, while they were procrastinating and their deadline was far in the future. But they paid a significant cost for this immediate relief: Procrastinators not only suffered more stress and health problems as they scrambled to complete their work near the deadline, but also reported more stress and health symptoms across the entire semester. There was also no evidence to support the idea that procrastinators do their "best work under pressure," since their academic performance was worse than that of nonprocrastinators. Therefore, in addition to making use of the tips provided in the Real World box on increasing study skills (p. 11), it would seem wise to avoid procrastination in this course and others.

Where do you stand on procrastination? Calculate your procrastination score by rating the statements below on a scale of 1–5, where

1 = not at all; 2 = incidentally;
3 = sometimes; 4 = most of the time;
5 = always

How frequently last week did you engage in the following behaviors or thoughts?

1. Drifted off into daydreams while studying
2. Studied the subject matter that you had planned to do
3. Had no energy to study
4. Prepared to study at some point but did not get any further
5. Gave up when studying was not going well
6. Gave up studying early in order to do more pleasant things
7. Put off the completion of a task
8. Allowed yourself to be distracted from your work
9. Experienced concentration problems when studying
10. Interrupted studying for a while in order to do other things
11. Forgot to prepare things for studying
12. Did so many other things that there was insufficient time left for studying
13. Thought that you had enough time left, so that there was really no need to start studying

Chapter Review

Psychology's Roots: The Path to a Science of Mind

- Psychology is the scientific study of mind and behavior. Behavior is usually adaptive because it helps us meet the challenges of daily living; similarly, the brain and mind usually function effectively and efficiently. Disruptions to the mind and behavior, in the form of mindbugs, allow us to better understand the normal functions of the mind and behavior.

- Early efforts to develop a science of mind were pioneered by French scientists Pierre Flourens and Paul Broca, who observed the effects of brain damage on mental abilities of people and animals, and by German scientists such as Hermann von Helmholtz and Wilhelm Wundt, who applied methods from physiology to the study of psychology.

- In Germany, Wilhelm Wundt and Edward Titchener developed a school of thought called structuralism, which focused on analyzing the basic elements of consciousness.

- In America, William James pioneered the school of functionalism, which emphasized the functions of consciousness, and applied Darwin's theory of natural selection to the mind. G. Stanley Hall helped organize psychology with the formation of the first professional laboratory, organization, and journal in the field.

Errors and Illusions Reveal Psychology

- Max Wertheimer founded Gestalt psychology based on the interpretation of an illusion of apparent motion, in which people perceive flashing lights as a moving whole instead of the sum of its parts.

- Clinicians such as Jean-Marie Charcot and Pierre Janet studied unusual cases in which patients acted like different people while under hypnosis, raising the possibility of more than one conscious self.

- Based on his own observations of clinical patients, Sigmund Freud developed the theory of psychoanalysis, which emphasized the importance of unconscious influences and childhood experiences in shaping thoughts, feelings, and behavior. A more optimistic view of the human condition, espoused by humanistic psychologists such as Abraham Maslow and Carl Rogers, held that people need to grow and reach their full potential.

Psychology in the 20th Century: Behaviorism Takes Center Stage

- Behaviorism studies observable actions and responses and holds that inner mental processes are private events that cannot be studied scientifically.

- John Watson launched behaviorism in 1913, studied the association between a stimulus and response, and emphasized the importance of the environment over genetics in shaping behavior.

- B. F. Skinner developed the concept of reinforcement, demonstrating that animals and humans will repeat behaviors that generate positive outcomes and avoid those that are associated with unpleasant results.

Beyond Behaviorism: Psychology Expands

- Cognitive psychology is concerned with inner mental processes such as perception, attention, memory, and reasoning. Cognitive psychology developed as a field due to psychologists' efforts to improve cognitive performance, the invention of the computer, and Noam Chomsky's ideas concerning the development of language.

- Cognitive neuroscience attempts to link the brain with the mind through studies of brain-damaged and healthy patients using neuroimaging techniques that allow glimpses of the brain in action.

- Evolutionary psychology focuses on the adaptive value of the mind and behavior and seeks to understand current psychological processes in terms of abilities and traits preserved by natural selection.

Beyond the Individual: Social and Cultural Perspectives

- Social psychology recognizes that people exist in a network of other people and examines how individuals influence and interact with one another.

- Cultural psychology is concerned with the effects of the broader culture on individuals and with similarities and differences among people in different cultures.

The Profession of Psychology: Past and Present

- The American Psychological Association (APA), the largest organization of professional psychologists, has grown dramatically since it was formed in 1892 and now includes over 150,000 members.

- Through the efforts of pioneers such as Mary Calkins, women have come to play an increasingly important role in psychology. Minority involvement in psychology took longer, but the efforts of Francis Cecil Sumner, Kenneth B. Clark, and others have been followed by increased participation by minorities.

- Psychologists prepare for research careers through graduate and postdoctoral training and also work in a variety of applied settings, including schools, clinics, and industry.

Key Terms

psychology (p. 2)	reaction time (p. 7)	dissociative identity disorder (p. 14)	response (p. 18)
mind (p. 2)	consciousness (p. 8)	hysteria (p. 14)	reinforcement (p. 19)
behavior (p. 2)	structuralism (p. 8)	unconscious (p. 15)	cognitive psychology (p. 21)
nativism (p. 5)	introspection (p. 8)	psychoanalytic theory (p. 15)	behavioral neuroscience (p. 24)
philosophical empiricism (p. 5)	functionalism (p. 10)	psychoanalysis (p. 15)	cognitive neuroscience (p. 25)
phrenology (p. 6)	natural selection (p. 10)	humanistic psychology (p. 16)	evolutionary psychology (p. 26)
physiology (p. 7)	illusions (p. 12)	behaviorism (p. 17)	social psychology (p. 28)
stimulus (p. 7)	Gestalt psychology (p. 13)		cultural psychology (p. 29)

Recommended Readings

Fancher, R. E. (1979). *Pioneers of psychology.* New York: Norton. This engaging book examines the history of psychology by painting portraits of the field's pioneers, including many of the psychologists featured in this chapter. A great way to learn more about the history of psychology is by becoming familiar with the lives of its founders.

Hermann, D., Raybeck, D., & Gruneberg, M. (2002). *Improving memory and study skills.* Seattle: Hogrefe and Huber. This excellent book offers a nice introduction to many aspects of cognitive psychology. More importantly, it offers several practical suggestions for improving memory, improving study habits, and mastering material that you are trying to learn.

James, W. (1890). *The principles of psychology (1890/1955).* New York: Holt. Considered by many psychologists to be the "bible" of psychology, this masterpiece by William James is still exciting to read over a century after it was published. If you do have a chance to read it, you will understand why thousands of psychologists are so thankful that James bypassed a career in medicine for one in psychology.

Skinner, B. F. (1948/1986). *Walden II.* Englewood Cliffs, NJ: Prentice Hall. Skinner's provocative novel describes a modern utopia in which scientific principles from behavioristic psychology are used to shape a model community. This controversial book raises intriguing questions about how knowledge from psychology could or should be used to influence day-to-day living in modern society.

American Psychological Association Web site: www.apa.org

Association for Psychological Science Web site: www.psychologicalscience.org

These Web sites provide a wealth of information about the APA and the APS and about news and research in all areas of psychology. Both sites have sections specially designed for students and contain many links to other useful and informative sites in psychology. An excellent way to learn about what is going on in the field today.

2

The Methods of Psychology

Empiricism: How to Know Things

The Science of Observation: Saying What
Measurement
Samples
THE REAL WORLD Taking a Chance
Bias

The Science of Explanation: Saying Why
Correlation
Causation
HOT SCIENCE Establishing Causality in the Brain
Drawing Conclusions

The Ethics of Science: Saying Please and Thank You
WHERE DO YOU STAND? The Morality of Immoral Experiments

LORI AND REBA SCHAPPELL ARE HAPPY to be twins. One is an award-winning country music singer; one is a wisecracking hospital worker who likes strawberry daiquiris. Despite their different interests and different temperaments, they get along quite well and love each other dearly. That's a good thing because Lori and Reba not only share the same parents and the same birthday, but they also share a blood supply, part of a skull, and some brain tissue. Lori and Reba are conjoined twins who have been attached at the forehead since birth. When asked whether they would ever consider being surgically separated, Reba seems perplexed: "Our point of view is no, straight-out no. Why would you want to do that? For all the money in China, why? You'd be ruining two lives in the process" (Angier, 1997). If you find this hard to believe, then welcome to the club. Conjoined twins are routinely separated at birth even when this means crippling both or killing one of them because surgeons and parents—like most of us—can't imagine that a conjoined life is really worth living. And yet, conjoined twins don't seem to share that view. As one medical historian noted, "The desire to remain together is so widespread among communicating conjoined twins as to be practically universal. . . . I have yet to find an instance in which conjoined twins have sought out separation" (Dreger, 1998).

Are conjoined twins really as happy as they claim, or are they simply fooling themselves? Do parents and doctors have the right to impose dangerous surgery on infants who would otherwise grow up to refuse it? Such questions have moral, religious, and philosophical answers, but they can have scientific answers as well. If we could find some way to measure a psychological property such as happiness, then we could use scientific methods to determine who has it and who doesn't and to discover what kinds of lives promote or preclude it. Is a conjoined life a wonderful life, or is it society's responsibility to separate conjoined twins whenever possible? As you are about to see, psychological methods are designed to provide answers to questions like this one.

AP PHOTO/READING EAGLE, JOHN A. SECOGES

Are conjoined twins less happy than singletons? Reba (left) and Lori (right) Schappell are sisters who say that the answer is no.

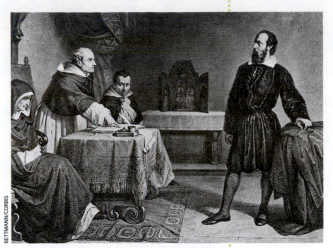

The 17th-century astronomer Galileo Galilei was excommunicated and sentenced to prison for sticking to his own observations of the solar system rather than accepting the teachings of the church. In 1597 he wrote to his friend and fellow astronomer Johannes Kepler, "What would you say of the learned here, who, replete with the pertinacity of the asp, have steadfastly refused to cast a glance through the telescope? What shall we make of this? Shall we laugh, or shall we cry?" As it turned out, the correct answer was *cry*.

Empiricism: How to Know Things

When ancient Greeks sprained their ankles, caught the flu, or accidentally set their togas on fire, they had to choose between two kinds of doctors: dogmatists (from *dogmatikos*, meaning "belief"), who thought that the best way to understand illness was to develop theories about the body's functions, and empiricists (from *empeirikos*, meaning "experience"), who thought that the best way to understand illness was to observe sick people. The rivalry between these two schools of medicine didn't last long, however, because the people who chose to see dogmatists tended to die, which wasn't very good for repeat business. It is little wonder that today we use the word *dogmatism* to describe the tendency for people to cling to their assumptions and the word **empiricism** to describe *the belief that accurate knowledge of the world requires observation of it*. The fact that we can answer questions about the world by observation may seem obvious to you, but this obvious fact is actually a relatively new discovery. Throughout most of human history, people have trusted authority to answer important questions about the world, and it is only in the last millennium (and especially in the past three centuries) that people have begun to trust their eyes and ears more than their elders. The shift from dogmatism to empiricism was a long time coming, but when it came, it laid the foundation of modern science.

Of course, some of the sick people who visited empiricists died too because empiricism is by no means infallible. If you glance out the window right now, you will see that the earth is flat and the sun is making a slow circle around it. Neither of these observations is accurate, of course, but until fairly recently most people believed them to be true—not because people were dogmatists, but because they were empiricists who could see the flatness of the earth and the orbit of the sun for themselves. Alas, the naked eye is blind to many things. No matter how long you stare out the window, you will never see a black hole, an atom, a germ, a gene, evolution, gravity, or the true shape of the planet on which you are standing. Empiricism has proved to be a profitable approach to understanding natural phenomena, but using this approach requires a **method**, which is *a set of rules and techniques for observation that allow observers to avoid the illusions, mistakes, and erroneous conclusions that simple observation can produce.*

In many sciences, the word *method* refers primarily to technologies that enhance the powers of the senses. Biologists use microscopes and astronomers use telescopes because the phenomena they seek to explain are invisible to the naked eye. Human behavior, on the other hand, is relatively easy to observe, so you might expect psychology's methods to be relatively simple. In fact, the empirical challenges facing psychologists are among the most daunting in all of modern science, and thus psychological methods are among the most sophisticated. Three things make people especially difficult to study:

- *Complexity:* Psychologists study the single most complex object in the known universe. No galaxy, particle, molecule, or machine is as complicated as the human brain. Scientists can describe the birth of a star or the death of a cell in exquisite detail, but they can barely begin to say how the 500 million interconnected neurons that constitute the brain give rise to the thoughts, feelings, and actions that are psychology's core concerns.
- *Variability:* In almost all the ways that matter, one *E. coli* bacterium is pretty much like another. But people are as varied as their fingerprints. No two individuals ever do, say, think, or feel exactly the same thing under exactly the same circumstances, which means that when you've seen one, you've most definitely not seen them all.

"Are you just pissing and moaning, or can you verify what you're saying with data?"

- *Reactivity:* An atom of cesium-133 oscillates 9,192,631,770 times per second regardless of who's watching. But people often think, feel, and act one way when they are being observed and a different way when they are not. When people know they are being studied, they don't always behave as they otherwise would.

In short, human beings are tremendously complex, endlessly variable, and uniquely reactive, and these attributes present a major challenge to the scientific study of their behavior. As you'll see, psychologists have developed a variety of methods that are designed to meet these challenges head-on.

People are variable. Three identical men may stick identical footballs in their ears and still levitate quite differently.

SPENCER RESEARCH LIBRARY, UNIVERSITY OF KANSAS

The Science of Observation: Saying What

There is no escaping the fact that you have to observe *what* people do before you can try to explain *why* they do it. To *observe* something means to use your senses to learn about its properties. For example, when you observe a round, red apple, your brain is using the pattern of light that is falling on your eyes to draw an inference about the apple's identity, shape, and color. That kind of informal observation is fine for buying fruit but not for doing science. Why? First, casual observations are notoriously unstable. The same apple may appear red in the daylight and crimson at night or spherical to one person and elliptical to another. Second, casual observations can't tell us about many of the properties in which we might be interested. No matter how long and hard you look, you will never be able to discern an apple's crunchiness or pectin content simply by watching it. If you want to know about those properties, you must do more than observe. You must *measure*.

Measurement

For most of human history, people had no idea how old they were because there was no simple way to keep track of time. Or weight, or volume, or density, or temperature, or anything else for that matter. Today we live in a world of tape measures and rulers, clocks and calendars, odometers, thermometers, and mass spectrometers. Measurement is not just the basis of science, it is the basis of modern life. All of these measurements have two things in common. Whether we want to measure the intensity of an earthquake, the distance between molecules, or the attitude of a registered voter, we must first *define* the property we wish to measure and then find a way to *detect* it.

Definition and Detection

You probably think you know what *length* is. But if you try to define it without using the word *long,* you get tongue-tied pretty quickly. We use words such as *weight, speed,* or *length* all the time in ordinary conversation without realizing that each of these terms has an **operational definition**, which is *a description of a property in measurable terms.* For example, the operational definition of the property we casually refer to as *length* is "the change in the location of light over time." That's right. When we say that a bookshelf is "a meter long," we are actually saying how long it takes a particle of light to travel from one end of the shelf to the other. (In case you're interested, the answer is 1/299,792,458th of a second. In case you're not interested, that's still the answer.) According to this operational definition, the more time it takes for a photon to travel from one end of a bookshelf to the other, the more "length" that bookshelf has. Operational definitions specify the concrete events that count as instances of an abstract property. The first step in making any measurement is to define the property we want to measure in concrete terms.

EMPIRICISM Originally a Greek school of medicine that stressed the importance of observation, and now generally used to describe any attempt to acquire knowledge by observing objects or events.

METHOD A set of rules and techniques for observation that allow researchers to avoid the illusions, mistakes, and erroneous conclusions that simple observation can produce.

OPERATIONAL DEFINITION A description of an abstract property in terms of a concrete condition that can be measured.

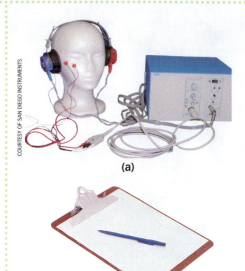

(a)

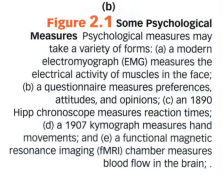

(b)

(c)

(d)

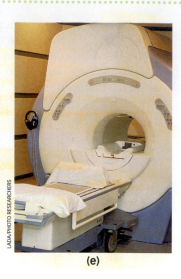

(e)

Figure 2.1 **Some Psychological Measures** Psychological measures may take a variety of forms: (a) a modern electromyograph (EMG) measures the electrical activity of muscles in the face; (b) a questionnaire measures preferences, attitudes, and opinions; (c) an 1890 Hipp chronoscope measures reaction times; (d) a 1907 kymograph measures hand movements; and (e) a functional magnetic resonance imaging (fMRI) chamber measures blood flow in the brain; .

The second step is to find a way to detect the concrete terms that our definition describes. To do this we must use a **measure**, which is *a device that can detect the events to which an operational definition refers*. For example, length is the change in the location of light over time, and we can detect such changes by using a photon detector (which tells us the location of a particle of light) and a clock (which tells us how long it took the particle of light to travel from one location to another). Once we have determined just how far a photon travels in 1/299,792,458th of a second, we can make our next measurement a lot less expensive by marking that distance on a piece of wood and calling it a ruler. Keep in mind that measures (such as clocks and photon detectors) detect the concrete conditions described by our operational definitions (such as "change in the location of light over time"), but *they do not detect the property itself* (such as length). Indeed, properties such as shape, color, length, or duration are best thought of as abstract ideas that can never be measured directly. **FIGURE 2.1** shows a variety of old and new measures used by psychologists.

Defining and *detecting* are the two tasks that allow us to measure physical properties, and these same two tasks allow us to measure psychological properties as well. If we wanted to measure Lori Schappell's happiness, for example, our first task would be to develop an operational definition of that property—that is, to specify some concrete, measurable event that will count as an instance of happiness. For example, we might define happiness as the simultaneous contraction of the *zygomatic major* (which is the muscle that makes your mouth turn up when you smile) and the *orbicularis oculi* (which is the muscle that makes your eyes crinkle when you smile). After defining happiness as a specific set of muscular contractions, we would then need to measure those contractions, and the **electromyograph (EMG)**—which is *a device that measures muscle contractions under the surface of a person's skin*—would do splendidly. Once we have defined happiness and found a way to detect the concrete events that our definition supplies, we are in a position to measure it.

But is this the *right* way to measure happiness? That's hard to say. There are many ways to define the same property and many ways to detect the events that this definition supplies. For instance, we could detect the muscular contractions involved in smiling by using EMG, or we could detect them by asking a human observer to watch a participant's face and tell us how often the participant smiled. We could define happiness in terms of muscular contractions, or we could define it as a person's self-assessment of his or her own emotional state, in which case we could measure it by asking people how happy they feel and recording their answers. With so many options for defining and detecting happiness, how are we to choose among them? As you are about to see, there are many ways to define and detect, but some are much better than others.

"Are you (a) contented, (b) happy, (c) very happy, (d) wildly happy, (e) deliriously happy?"

Validity

Measurement consists of two tasks: *defining,* which is the process by which properties are linked to operational definitions, and *detecting,* which is the process by which operational definitions are linked to measures. If we do either of these tasks badly, then any measurement we make will lack **validity,** which is *the characteristic of an observation that allows one to draw accurate inferences from it.* Because measurement involves precisely two tasks, there are precisely two ways for a measurement to be invalid (see **FIGURE 2.2**). First, a measurement will be invalid when *the operational definition does not adequately define the property,* and second, a measurement will be invalid when *the measure cannot adequately detect the conditions that the operational definition describes.* Let's consider each of these sources of invalidity more closely.

Problems of Defining You can measure a lot of things with a ruler, but happiness isn't one of them because "change in the location of light over time" is not meaningfully related to the emotional experience we call "happiness." We all have some sense of what happiness means, and the distance that a photon travels just isn't it. A good operational definition must have **construct validity,** which is *the tendency for an operational definition and a property to share meaning.* It makes sense to define *wealth* as the amount of money a person has in savings, investments, and real estate because the concrete object we call *money* is meaningfully related to the abstract concept we call *wealth.* It makes no sense to define *wealth* as the number of Junior Mints a person can swallow in one gulp because this ability (as admirable as it may be) has nothing to do with what we mean by the word *wealth.* Some operational definitions are clearly related to their properties, and some are clearly not.

The interesting cases fall between these two extremes. For example, is smiling a valid way to define happiness? Well, this definition certainly has construct validity: We all know from experience that smiling and happiness go together like money and wealth do. But if smiling is a valid definition of happiness, then it should also have **predictive validity,** which is *the tendency for an operational definition to be related to other operational definitions of the same property.* If an operational definition such as smiling is linked to a property such as happiness, then it should also be linked to other operational definitions of the same property. For example, it should be linked to electrical activity in the part of the brain known as the right frontal lobe or to the person's own report of his or her emotional state. If we could demonstrate that people whose right frontal lobes are active and who say, "I sure am happy right now," also tend to smile, then we could be even more certain that smiling is a valid definition of happiness. Predictive validity gets its name from the fact that knowledge of the conditions specified by one operational definition (e.g., knowing whether a person is smiling) should enable us to predict the conditions specified by another operational definition

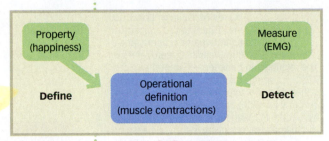

Figure 2.2 Sources of Invalidity The process of *defining* links properties to operational definitions, and the process of *detecting* links operational definitions to measures. Invalidity can result from problems in either of these links.

MEASURE A device that can detect the measurable events to which an operational definition refers.

ELECTROMYOGRAPH (EMG) A device that measures muscle contractions under the surface of a person's skin.

VALIDITY The characteristic of an observation that allows one to draw accurate inferences from it.

CONSTRUCT VALIDITY The tendency for an operational definition and a property to have a clear conceptual relation.

PREDICTIVE VALIDITY The tendency for an operational definition to be related to other operational definitions.

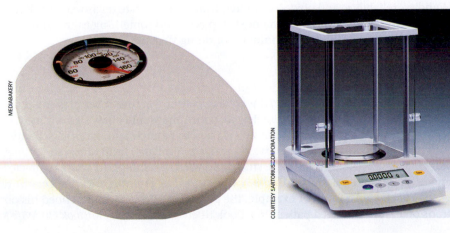

A bathroom scale and a laboratory balance both measure weight, but the balance is more likely to provide exactly the same measurement when it is used to weigh the same object twice (reliability) and more likely to provide different measurements when it is used to weigh two objects that differ by just a fraction of a gram (power). Not surprisingly, the bathroom scale sells for around $30 and the balance for around $3,000. Power and reliability don't come cheap.

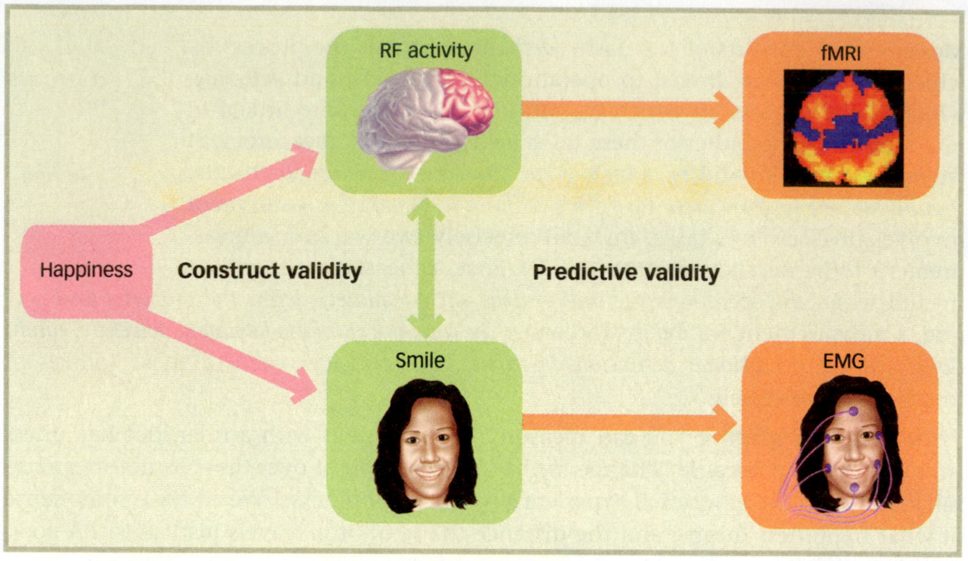

Figure 2.3 Kinds of Validity Construct validity (pink) refers to the conceptual relationship between a property and a measure. Predictive validity (green) refers to the relationship between different measures. In this example, the property called "happiness" is operationally defined as right frontal lobe (RF) activity (which is measured by functional magnetic resonance imaging, or fMRI) and also as smiling (which is measured by facial electromyography, or EMG).

PHOTO COURTESY TAPERT ET AL., 2001.

(e.g., whether the person's right frontal lobe is active or whether the person is claiming to be happy). In short, if we do a good job of defining a property, then our measurement of that property will have validity. **FIGURE 2.3** illustrates the relationship between predictive validity and construct validity.

Problems of Detection Yardsticks made of Jell-O have historically been commercial failures. The stiffness of a yardstick is critical because it means that when we repeatedly use the yardstick to measure an object, we repeatedly get the same result. What's more, anyone else who uses the same yardstick to measure the same object will get the same result we did. **Reliability** is *the tendency for a measure to produce the same result whenever it is used to measure the same thing,* and any measure that lacks this tendency is about as useful as a gelatin ruler. For example, if a person's zygomatic muscle did not move for 10 minutes, we would expect the EMG to produce the same reading for 10 minutes. If the EMG produced different readings from one minute to the next, then it would be an unreliable measure that was detecting differences that weren't really there. A good measure must be reliable. The flip side of reliability is **power**, which is *the tendency for a measure to produce different results when it is used to measure different things.* If a person's zygomatic muscle moved continuously for 10 minutes, we would expect the EMG to produce different readings in those 10 minutes. If the EMG instead produced the same reading from one minute to the next, then it would be a weak or powerless measure that was failing to detect differences that were really there. Reliable and powerful measures are those that detect the conditions specified by an operational definition (a) when they happen and (b) *only* when they happen.

Validity, reliability, and power are prerequisites for accurate measurement. But once you've got a good ruler in hand, the next step is to find something to measure with it. Psychologists have developed techniques for doing that too.

RELIABILITY The tendency for a measure to produce the same result whenever it is used to measure the same thing.

POWER The tendency for a measure to produce different results when it is used to measure different things.

CASE METHOD A method of gathering scientific knowledge by studying a single individual.

POPULATION The complete collection of participants who might possibly be measured.

SAMPLE The partial collection of people who actually were measured in a study.

LAW OF LARGE NUMBERS A statistical law stating that as sample size increases, the attributes of a sample will more closely reflect the attributes of the population from which it was drawn.

Samples

If a pig flew over the White House, it wouldn't matter whether other pigs could do the same trick. The fact that just one pig flew just one time would challenge our most cherished assumptions about animal physiology, aerodynamics, and national security and would thus be an observation well worth making. Similarly, individuals sometimes do remarkable things that deserve close study, and when psychologists study them closely, they are using the **case method,** which is *a method of gathering scientific knowledge by studying a single individual.* For example, the physician Oliver Sacks described his observations of a brain-damaged patient in a book titled *The Man Who Mistook His Wife for a*

Hat, and those observations were worth making because this is a rather unusual mistake for a man to make. As you saw in Chapter 1, people with unusual abilities, unusual experiences, or unusual deficits often provide important insights about human psychology.

But exceptional cases are the exception, and more often than not, psychologists are in the business of observing *un*exceptional people and trying to explain why they think, feel, and act as they do. When psychologists observe ordinary people, they typically observe *many* of them and then try to explain the *average* of those observations rather than explaining each individual observation itself. This simple technique of averaging many observations is one of psychology's most powerful methodological tools.

"This fundamentally changes everything we know about elephants!"

The Law of Large Numbers

If you sat down and started picking cards from a deck, you would expect to pick as many red cards as black cards over the long run. But *only* over the long run. You would not be surprised if you picked just two cards and they both turned out to be red, but you *would* be surprised if you picked just 20 cards and they all turned out to be red. You would be surprised by 20 red cards and not by two red cards because your intuition tells you that when the number of cards you pick is small, you really can't expect your hand to have the same proportion of red and black cards as does the full deck.

Your intuition is exactly right. A **population** is *the complete collection of objects or events that might be measured*, and a **sample** is *the partial collection of objects or events that is measured*. In this case, the full deck is a population, and the cards in your hand are a sample of that population. Your intuition about the cards is captured by the **law of large numbers**, which states that *as sample size increases, the attributes of the sample more closely reflect the attributes of the population from which the sample was drawn*. The law of large numbers suggests that as the size of a sample (that is, the number cards in your hand) increases, the ratio of black to red cards in the sample will more closely approximate the ratio of black to red cards in the population. In plain English, the more cards you pick, the more likely it is that half the cards in your hand will be red and half will be black.

Precisely the same logic informs the methods of psychology. For example, if we wanted to know how happy people are in Florida, we would begin with an operational definition of happiness. For the sake of simplicity, we might define happiness as a person's belief about his or her own emotional state. Then we'd develop a way to measure that belief, for example, by asking the person to make a checkmark on a 10-point rating scale. If we used this measure to measure the happiness of just one Floridian, our lone observation would tell us little about the happiness of the 15 million people who actually live in that state. On the other hand, if we were to measure the happiness of a hundred Floridians, or a thousand Floridians, or even a million Floridians, the average of our measurements would begin to approximate the average happiness of all Floridians. The law of large numbers suggests that as the size of our sample increases, the average happiness of the people in our sample becomes a better approximation of the average happiness of the people in the population. You can prove this to yourself by considering what would happen if you measured the largest possible sample, namely, every Floridian. In that case, the average happiness of your sample and the average happiness of the population would be identical (see the Real World box on the next page).

Measuring the happiness of just one Floridian could provide a misleading estimate of the happiness of the population.

{ THE REAL WORLD } Taking a Chance

A 2002 CBS NEWS POLL FOUND THAT nearly three out of every five Americans believe in extrasensory perception (ESP). Very few psychologists share this belief, and you might wonder why they tend to be such a skeptical lot. As you have seen, psychology's methods often rely on the laws of probability. Some of these laws, such as the law of large numbers, are intuitively obvious, but others are not, and ignorance of the less obvious laws often leads people to "know what isn't so" (Gilovich, 1991).

Consider the case of the amazing coincidence. One night you dream that a panda is piloting an airplane over the Indian Ocean, and the next day you tell a friend, who says, "Wow, I had exactly the same dream last week!" One morning you are humming an old Green Day tune in the shower, and when you get into your car an hour later, the very same song is on the radio. You and your roommate are wondering what kind of pizza to order when suddenly you both open your mouths and say, "Pepperoni and onions," in perfect unison. Coincidences like these feel truly spooky when they happen. How can we possibly explain them as anything other than instances of precognition (knowing the future before it happens) or telepathy (reading another person's thoughts)?

The same question occurred to Nobel Prize–winning physicist Luis Alverez one day when he was reading the newspaper. A particular story got him thinking about an old college friend whom he hadn't seen in

How easy is it to find a coincidence? One of the authors of this textbook was born on November 5. A few minutes of research revealed that jazz pianist Art Tatum (left) died on November 5 and recorded a song called "Paper Moon," while actress Tatum O'Neal (right) was born on November 5 and starred in a movie called Paper Moon. Should we be amazed?

years. A few minutes later, he turned the page and was shocked to see the very same friend's obituary. Was this a case of precognition (he "saw" 2 minutes into his own future) or telepathy (he read the thoughts of someone who was reading the obituary 2 minutes before he did)? Before jumping to such extraordinary conclusions, Alvarez decided to use probability theory to determine just how amazing this coincidence really was.

First he estimated the number of friends that the average person has, and then he estimated how often the average person thinks about each of those friends. With these estimates in hand, Alvarez did a few simple calculations and determined the

likelihood that someone would think about a friend 5 minutes before learning about that friend's death. The odds, it turned out, were astonishingly high. In a country the size of the United States, for example, this amazing coincidence should happen to 10 people every day (Alvarez, 1965). If this seems surprising to you, then know you are not alone. Research has shown that people routinely underestimate the chance likelihood of coincidences (Diaconis & Mosteller, 1989; Falk & McGregor, 1983; Hintzman, Asher, & Stern, 1978). If you want to profit from this fact, you can bet in any group of 24 or more people that at least 2 of them share the same birthday. The odds are in your favor, and the bigger the group, the better the odds. In fact, in a group of 35, the odds are 85%.

So when *should* we be impressed by an amazing coincidence? When it happens more often than we would expect by chance alone. The problem is that we cannot easily calculate the likelihood that a flying panda, a Green Day tune, or a pepperoni-and-onion pizza will come to mind by chance alone. Science deals with events whose chance occurrence can be estimated, and scientists use this estimate to determine when an event really is or is not surprising. In the real world, we often can't make these estimates with any degree of certainty, which is why we can rarely draw legitimate conclusions about the likelihood of everyday coincidences.

ONLY HUMAN

MAYBE THEY COULD PASS A LAW OF LARGE NUMBERS? In 1997, David Cook of Caledonian University in Glasgow, Scotland, told the British Psychological Society's annual conference that his 3-year study shows that politicians have significant behavior patterns in common with criminal psychopaths. Cook said that criminals were relatively easy to analyze but that he did not have as much data as he would like on politicians. "They don't like to be studied," he said.

Averaging

Under the right circumstances, the average of a sample can tell us about the average of a population. But it cannot tell us about the individuals in that population. For example, when psychologists claim that women have better fine motor skills than men (and they do), or that men have better spatial ability than women (and they do), or that children are more suggestible than adults (and they are), or that New Yorkers care more about sex than algebra (well, it seems likely), their claims are not true—and are not *meant* to be true—of every individual in these populations. Rather, when psychologists say that women have better fine motor skills than men, they mean that when the fine motor skills of a large sample of women and men are measured, the average of the women's measurements is reliably higher than the average of the men's.

FIGURE 2.4 illustrates this point with hypothetical observations that are arranged in a pair of **frequency distributions**, which are *graphic representations of the measurements of a sample that are arranged by the number of times each measurement was observed*. These frequency distributions display every possible score on a fine motor skills test on the horizontal axis and display the number of times (or the *frequency* with which) each score was observed among a sample of men and women on the vertical axis. A frequency distribution can have any shape, but it commonly takes

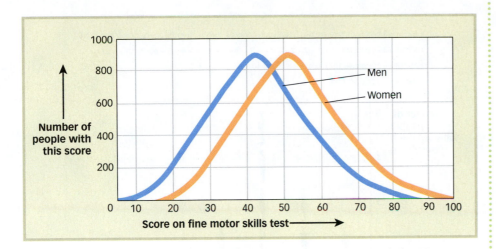

Figure 2.4 **Frequency Distributions**
This graph shows the hypothetical scores of a sample of men and women who took a test of fine motor skills. The scores are represented along the horizontal axis, and the frequency of each score is represented along the vertical axis. As you can see, the average score of women is a bit higher than the average score of men. Both distributions are examples of normal distributions.

the shape known as a **normal distribution** (sometimes also called a *bell curve*). A normal distribution is *a frequency distribution in which most measurments are concentrated around the mean and fall off toward the tails, and the two sides of the distribution are symmetrical.* As you can see in Figure 2.4, normal distributions are *symmetrical* (i.e., the left half is a mirror image of the right half), have a peak in the middle, and trail off at the ends. Most scores can be found toward the center of a normal distribution, with fewer scores at the extremes. In fact, the point at the very center of a normal distribution is where you'll find the average.

A frequency distribution depicts every measurement in a sample and thus provides a full and complete picture of that sample. But like most full and complete pictures, it is a terribly cumbersome way to communicate information. When we ask a friend how she's been, we don't want her to show us a graph depicting her happiness on each day of the previous six months. Rather, we want a brief summary statement that captures the essential information that such a graph would provide—for example, "I'm doing pretty well," or, "I've been having some ups and downs lately." In psychology, brief summary statements that capture the essential information from a frequency distribution are called *descriptive statistics.* There are two important kinds of descriptive statistics:

■ *Descriptions of central tendency* are summary statements about the value of the measurements that lie near the center or midpoint of a frequency distribution. When a friend says that she has been "doing pretty well," she is describing the central tendency (or approximate location of the midpoint) of the frequency distribution of her happiness measurements. The three most common descriptions of central tendency are the **mode** (*the value of the most frequently observed measurement*), the **mean** (*the average value of the measurements*), and the **median** (*the value that is greater than or equal to the values of half the measurements and less than or equal to half the values of the measurements*). In a normal distribution, the mean, median, and mode are all the same value, but when the distribution departs from normality, these three descriptive statistics can differ. **FIGURE 2.5** on the next page shows how each of these descriptive statistics is calculated.

■ *Descriptions of variability* are statements about the extent to which the measurements in a frequency distribution differ from each other. When a friend says that she has been having some "ups and downs" lately, she is offering a brief summary statement that describes how the measurements in the frequency distribution of her happiness scores over the past six months tend to differ from one another. A mathematically simple description of variability is the **range**, which is *the value of the largest measurement minus the value of the smallest measurement.* There are several other common descriptions of variability that are quite mathematically complicated, such as the *variance* and the *standard deviation,* but all such descriptions give us a sense of how similar or different the scores in a distribution tend to be.

FREQUENCY DISTRIBUTION A graphical representation of the measurements of a sample that are arranged by the number of times each measurement was observed.

NORMAL DISTRIBUTION A frequency distribution in which most measurements are concentrated around the mean and fall off toward the tails, and the two sides of the distribution are symmetrical.

MODE The "most frequent" measurement in a frequency distribution.

MEAN The average of the measurements in a frequency distribution.

MEDIAN The "middle" measurement in a frequency distribution. Half the measurements in a frequency distribution are greater than or equal to the median and half are less than or equal to the median.

RANGE The numerical difference between the smallest and largest measurements in a frequency distribution.

Figure 2.5 **Some Descriptive Statistics**
This frequency distribution shows the scores of 15 individuals on a seven-point test. Descriptive statistics include measures of central tendency (such as the mean, median, and mode) and measures of variability (such as the range).

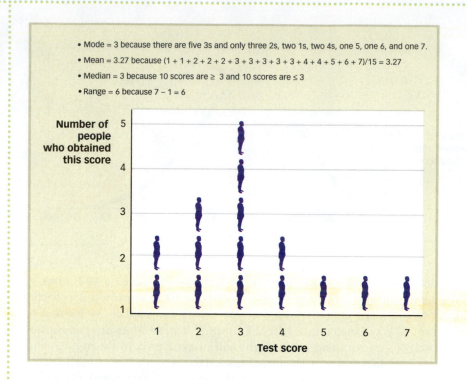

- Mode = 3 because there are five 3s and only three 2s, two 1s, two 4s, one 5, one 6, and one 7.
- Mean = 3.27 because (1 + 1 + 2 + 2 + 2 + 3 + 3 + 3 + 3 + 3 + 4 + 4 + 5 + 6 + 7)/15 = 3.27
- Median = 3 because 10 scores are ≥ 3 and 10 scores are ≤ 3
- Range = 6 because 7 − 1 = 6

As Figure 2.4, shows, the central tendency and the variability of a frequency distribution jointly determine the kinds of conclusions we can draw from it. The mean of the women's scores is higher than the mean of the men's scores, which suggests that women have better fine motor skills than men *on average*. But both frequency distributions also have considerable variability, which is to say that plenty of men scored higher than plenty of women. Indeed, what is true about people on average is almost never true in every case. As you read about studies in other chapters of this book, you will undoubtedly find yourself thinking of exceptions to the conclusions that the researchers have drawn. *But wait a minute,* you may think, *the book says that women have better fine motor skills than men, but Dad is a surgeon and Mom can't even thread a needle. So how can that be right?* If you have this thought, feel free to come back to page 47 and stare at Figure 2.4, which should remind you that a conclusion can be true on average and still allow for exceptions. One *E. coli* bacterium may be pretty much like the next, but no two people are exactly alike, and because people differ, there is almost nothing interesting that is absolutely true of every one of them at all times. Some New Yorkers probably do like algebra better than sex, but this does not change the fact that *on average* they prefer thinking about lovemaking to the quadratic equation. Psychology's empirical methods allow us to observe the differences between individuals, explain those differences, and, if we wish, look beyond those differences to see underlying patterns of similarity.

Now that you understand *why* psychologists measure samples that are drawn from populations, let's look at *how* they actually do this in everyday life.

On average, men have more upper-body strength than women, but there are still many women with more upper-body strength than many men.

Bias

People pick their noses, exceed the speed limit, read each other's mail, and skip over major sections of *War and Peace*, and they are especially likely to do these things when they think no one is looking. It is only natural for people to behave a bit differently when they are in the spotlight of each other's attention, but this fact makes people rather difficult to study because while psychologists are trying to discover how people really *do* behave, people are often trying to behave as they think they *should* behave. **Demand characteristics** are *those aspects of a setting that cause people to behave as they think an observer wants or expects them to behave.* They are called demand characteristics because they seem to "demand" or require that people say and do things that they normally might not. If you have ever been asked the question, "Do you think these jeans make me look fat?" then you have experienced a demand characteristic. Demand characteristics hinder our attempts to measure behavior as it normally unfolds, and psychologists have developed a variety of ways to avoid them.

Avoiding Demand Characteristics

People often behave as they think observers want or expect them to behave, and one way to avoid this problem is to observe people without their knowledge. **Naturalistic observation** is *a technique for gathering scientific knowledge by unobtrusively observing people in their natural environments.* For example, naturalistic observation reveals that the biggest groups tend to leave the smallest tips in restaurants (Freeman, Walker, Borden, & Latané, 1975), that hungry shoppers buy the most impulse items at the grocery store (Gilbert, Gill, & Wilson, 2002), that golfers are most likely to cheat when they play several opponents at once (Erffmeyer, 1984), that men do not usually approach the most beautiful woman at a singles' bar (Glenwick, Jason, & Elman, 1978), and that Olympic athletes smile more when they win the bronze rather than the silver medal (Medvec, Madey, & Gilovich, 1995). All of these conclusions are the result of measurements made by psychologists who observed people who didn't know they were being observed. It is unlikely that any of these things would have happened in exactly the same way if the diners, shoppers, golfers, singles, and athletes had known that they were being scrutinized.

Unfortunately, there are two reasons why naturalistic observation cannot by itself solve the problem of demand characteristics. First, some of the things psychologists want to observe simply don't occur naturally. For example, if we wanted to know whether people who have undergone sensory deprivation perform poorly on motor tasks, we would have to hang around the shopping mall for a very long time before a few dozen blindfolded people with earplugs just happened to wander by and start typing. Second, some of the things that psychologists want to observe can only be gathered from direct interaction with a person—for example, by administering a survey, giving tests, conducting an interview, or hooking someone up to an EEG. If we wanted to know how often someone worried about dying, how accurately they could remember their high school graduation, how quickly they could solve a logic puzzle, or how much electrical activity their brain produced when they felt happy, then simply observing them would not do the trick.

When psychologists cannot avoid demand characteristics by hiding in the bushes, they often avoid them by hiding other things instead. For instance, people are less likely to be influenced by demand characteristics when they cannot be identified as the originators of their actions, and psychologists often take advantage of this fact by allowing people to respond privately (e.g., by having them complete questionnaires when they are alone) or anonymously (e.g., by failing to collect personal information, such as the person's name or address). Another technique that psychologists use to avoid demand characteristics is to measure behaviors that are not susceptible to demand. For instance, behaviors can't be influenced by demand characteristics if they

This bar on 10th Avenue in New York City has a "one-way" mirror in its unisex restroom. Customers see their reflections in the restroom's mirror, and people who are walking down the street see the customers. Are the customers influenced by the fact that pedestrians may be watching them? Hard to say, but one observer did notice a suspiciously "high percentage of people who wash their hands" (Wolf, 2003).

DEMAND CHARACTERISTICS Those aspects of an observational setting that cause people to behave as they think an observer wants or expects them to behave.

NATURALISTIC OBSERVATION A method of gathering scientific knowledge by unobtrusively observing people in their natural environments.

One way to avoid demand characteristics is to measure behaviors that people are unable or unlikely to control, such as facial expressions, reaction times, eye blink rate, and so on. For example, when people feel anxious they tend to involuntarily compress their lips as President George W. Bush did in this 2006 photo taken as he gave a speech in the Rose Garden.

People's expectations can influence their observations. On September 10, 2002, Mr. Gurdeep Wander boarded an airplane with three other dark-skinned men who had no luggage, switched seats, and got up several times to use the restroom. This was enough to convince the pilot to make an emergency landing in Arkansas and have Mr. Wander arrested as a potential terrorist. Mr. Wander is an American citizen who works at Exxon and was on his way to a convention.

aren't under voluntary control. You may not want a psychologist to know that you are feeling excited, but you can't prevent your pupils from dilating when you feel aroused. Behaviors are also unlikely to be influenced by demand characteristics when people don't know that the demand and the behavior are related. You may want a psychologist to believe that you are concentrating on a task, but you probably don't know that your blink rate slows when you are concentrating and thus you won't fake a slow blink.

All of these tricks of the trade are useful, of course, but the very best way to avoid demand characteristics is to keep the people who are being observed (known as *participants*) from knowing the true purpose of the observation. When participants are kept "blind" to the observer's expectations—that is, when they do not know what the observer expects them to do—then they cannot strive to meet those expectations. If you did not know that a psychologist was studying the effects of baroque music on mood, then you would not feel compelled to smile when the psychologist played Bach's *Air on G String*. This is why psychologists often do not reveal the true purpose of a study to the participants until the study is over.

Of course, people are clever and curious, and when psychologists don't tell them the purpose of their observations, participants generally try to figure it out for themselves ("I wonder why the psychologist is playing the violin and watching me"). That's why psychologists sometimes use *cover stories,* or misleading explanations that are meant to keep participants from discerning the true purpose of an observation. For example, if a psychologist wanted to know how baroque music influenced your mood, he or she might tell you that the purpose of the study was to determine how quickly people can do logic puzzles while music plays in the background. (We will discuss the ethical implications of deceiving people later in this chapter.) In addition, the psychologist might use *filler items,* or pointless measures that are meant to mask the true purpose of the observation. So, for example, he or she might ask you a few questions that are relevant to the study ("How happy are you right now?") and a few that are not ("Do you like cats more or less than dogs?"), which would make it difficult for you to guess the purpose of the study from the nature of the questions you were asked. These are just a few of the techniques that psychologists use to avoid demand characteristics.

The Blind Observer

Observers are human beings, and like all human beings, they tend to see what they expect to see. This fact was demonstrated in a classic study in which a group of psychology students were asked to measure the speed with which a rat learned to run through a maze (Rosenthal & Fode, 1963). Some students were told that their rat had been specially bred to be "maze dull" (i.e., slow to learn a maze), and others were told that their rat had been specially bred to be "maze bright" (i.e., quick to learn a maze). Although all the rats were actually the same breed, the students who *thought* they were measuring the speed of a dull rat reported that their rats took longer to learn the maze than did the students who *thought* they were measuring the speed of a bright rat. In other words, the rats seemed to do just what the students who observed them expected them to do.

Why did this happen? First, *expectations can influence observations*. It is easy to make errors when measuring the speed of a rat, and expectations often determine the kinds of errors people make. Does putting one paw over the finish line count as "learning the maze"? If the rat falls asleep, should the stopwatch be left running or should the rat be awakened and given a second chance? If a rat runs a maze in 18.5 seconds, should that number be rounded up or rounded down before it is recorded in the log book? The answers to these questions may depend on whether one thinks the rat is bright or dull. The students who timed the rats probably tried to be honest, vigilant, fair, and objective, but their expectations influenced their observations in subtle ways that they could neither detect nor control. Second, *expectations can influence reality*. Students who expected their rats to learn quickly may have unknowingly done things to help that learning along—for example, by muttering, "Oh no!" when the bright rat turned the wrong way in the maze or by petting the bright rat more affectionately than the dull rat and so on. (We shall discuss these phenomena more extensively in Chapter 16.)

The New York Times

Copyright, 1929, by The New York Times Company.

STOCK PRICES SLUMP $14,000,000,000 IN NATION-WIDE STAMPEDE TO UNLOAD; BANKERS TO SUPPORT MARKET TODAY

PREMIER ISSUES HARD HIT

Unexpected Torrent of Liquidation Again Rocks Markets.

DAY'S SALES 9,212,800

Nearly 3,000,000 Shares Are Traded In Final Hour—The Tickers Lag 167 Minutes.

NEW RALLY SOON BROKEN

Selling by Europeans and "Mob Psychology" Big Factors in Second Big Break.

©THE NEW YORK TIMES

The second hurricane of liquidation within four days hit the stock market yesterday. It came suddenly, and violently, after holders of stocks had been lulled into a sense of security by the rallies of Friday and Saturday. It was a country-wide collapse of open-market security values in which the declines established and the actual losses taken in dollars and cents were probably the most disastrous and far-reaching in the history of the Stock Exchange.

That the storm has now blown itself out, that there will be organized support to put an end to a reaction which has ripped billions of dollars from market values, appeared certain last night from statements by leading bankers.

Although total estimates of the losses on securities are difficult to make, because of the large number of them not listed on any exchange, it was calculated last night that the total shrinkage in American securities on all exchanges yesterday had aggregated some $14,000,000,000, with a decline of about $10,000,000,000 in New York Stock Exchange securities. The figure is necessarily a rough one, but nevertheless gives an idea of the dollars and cents recessions in one of the most extraordinary declines in the history of American markets.

BETTMANN/CORBIS

People's expectations can cause the phenomena they expect. In 1929, investors who expected the stock market to collapse sold their stocks and thereby caused the very crisis they feared. In this photo, panicked citizens stand outside the New York Stock Exchange the day after the crash, which the *New York Times* attributed to "mob psychology."

Observers' expectations, then, can have a powerful influence on both their observations and on the behavior of those whom they observe. Psychologists use many techniques to avoid these influences, and one of the most common is the **double-blind** observation, which is *an observation whose true purpose is hidden from both the observer and the participant*. For example, if the students had not been told which rats were bright and which were dull, then they would not have *had* any expectations about their rats. It is common practice in psychology to keep the observers as blind as the participants. For example, measurements are often made by research assistants who do not know what a particular participant is expected to say or do and who only learn about the nature of the study when it is concluded. Indeed, many modern studies are carried out by the world's blindest experimenter: a computer, which presents information to participants and measures their responses without any expectations whatsoever.

In summary, measurement is a scientific means of observation that involves defining an abstract property in terms of some concrete condition, called an operational definition, and then constructing a device, or a measure, that can detect the conditions that the operational definition specifies. A good operational definition shares meaning with the property (construct validity) and is related to other operational definitions (predictive validity). A good measure detects the conditions specified by the operational definition when those conditions occur (power) and not when they don't (reliability).

Psychologists sometimes use the case method to study single, exceptional individuals, but more often they use samples of many people drawn from a population. The law of large numbers suggests that these samples should be relatively large if they are to reflect accurately the properties of the population from which they were drawn. From samples, psychologists draw conclusions about people on average rather than about individuals. Measurements of a sample can be arranged in a frequency distribution, and descriptive statistics can be used to describe some features of that distribution, such as its central tendency (described by the mean, median, and mode) and its variability (described by the range and the standard deviation).

DOUBLE-BLIND An observation whose true purpose is hidden from the researcher as well as from the participant.

When people know they are being observed, they may behave as they think they should. Demand characteristics are features of a setting that suggest to people that they should behave in a particular way. Psychologists try to reduce or eliminate demand characteristics by observing participants in their natural habitats or by hiding their expectations from the participant. In double-blind observations, they also hide their expectations from the observer, which ensures that observers are not merely seeing what they expect to see and are not inadvertently causing participants to behave as they expect them to behave. ■ ■

The Science of Explanation: Saying Why

The techniques discussed so far allow us to construct valid, reliable, powerful, and unbiased measures of properties such as happiness, to use those instruments to measure the happiness of a sample without demand characteristics, and to draw conclusions about the happiness of a population. Although scientific research always begins with the careful measurement of properties, its ultimate goal is typically the discovery of *causal relationships between properties*. We may want to know if happy people are more altruistic than unhappy people, but what we really want to know is whether their happiness is the *cause* of their altruism. We may want to know if children who are spanked are more likely to become depressed than children who aren't, but what we really want to know is whether being spanked *caused* their depression. These are the kinds of questions that even the most careful measurements cannot answer. Measurements can tell us how *much* happiness, altruism, spanking, and depression occur in a particular sample, but they cannot tell us (a) whether these properties are related and (b) whether their relationship is causal. As you will see, scientists have developed some clever ways of using measurement to answer these questions.

Correlation

If you insult someone, they probably won't give you the time of day. If you have any doubt about this, you can demonstrate it by standing on a street corner, insulting a few people as they walk by ("Hello, you stupid ugly freak . . ."), not insulting others ("Hello . . ."), and then asking everyone for the time of day (". . . could you please tell me what time it is?"). If you did this, the results of your investigation would probably look a lot like those shown in **TABLE 2.1.** Specifically, every person who was not insulted would give you the time of day, and every person who was insulted would refuse. Results such as these would probably convince you that being insulted *causes* people to refuse requests from the people who insulted them. You would conclude that two events—being insulted by someone and refusing to do that person a favor—have a causal relationship. But on what basis did you draw that conclusion? How did you manage to use measurement to tell you not only about *how much* insulting and refusing had occurred, but also about the *relationship* between insulting and refusing?

Patterns of Variation

Measurements can only tell us about properties of objects and events, but we can learn about the relationships between objects and events by comparing the *patterns of variation in a series of measurements*. Consider what actually happened when you performed your hypothetical study of insults and requests.

Table 2.1	Hypothetical Data of the Relationship between Insults and Favors

Participant	Treatment	Response
1	Insulted	Refused
2	Insulted	Refused
3	Not insulted	Agreed
4	Not insulted	Agreed
5	Insulted	Refused
6	Insulted	Refused
7	Not insulted	Agreed
8	Not insulted	Agreed
9	Insulted	Refused
10	Insulted	Refused
11	Not insulted	Agreed
12	Not insulted	Agreed
13	Insulted	Refused
14	Insulted	Refused
15	Not insulted	Agreed
16	Not insulted	Agreed
17	Insulted	Refused
18	Insulted	Refused
19	Not insulted	Agreed
20	Not insulted	Agreed

- First, you carefully measured a pair of **variables**, which are *properties whose values can vary across individuals or over time.* (When you took your first algebra course you were probably horrified to learn that everything you'd been taught in grade school about the distinction between letters and numbers was a lie, that mathematical equations could contain *X*s and *Y*s as well as 7s and 4s, and that the letters are called *variables* because they can have different values under different circumstances. Same idea here.) You measured one variable whose value could vary from *not insulted* to *insulted,* and you measured a second variable whose value could vary from *refused* to *agreed.*
- Second, you did this again. And then again. And then again. That is, you made a *series* of measurements rather than making just one.
- Third and finally, you tried to discern a pattern in your series of measurements. If you look at the second column of Table 2.1, you will see that it contains values that vary as your eyes move down the column. That column has a particular *pattern of variation.* If you compare the third column with the second, you will notice that the patterns of variation in the two columns are synchronized. This synchrony is known as a *pattern of covariation* or a **correlation** (as in "co-relation"). Two variables are said to "covary" or to "be correlated" when *variations in the value of one variable are synchronized with variations in the value of the other.* As the table shows, whenever the value in the second column varies from *not insulted* to *insulted,* the value in the third column varies from *agreed* to *refused.*

By looking for synchronized patterns of variation, we can use measurement to discover the relationships between variables. Indeed, this is the only way anyone has *ever* discovered the relationship between variables, which is why most of the facts you know about the world can be thought of as correlations. For example, you know that adults are generally taller than children, but this is just a shorthand way of saying that as the value of *age* varies from *young* to *old,* the value of *height* varies from *short* to *tall.* You know that people who eat a pound of spinach every day generally live longer than people who eat a pound of bacon every day, but this is just a shorthand way of saying that as the value of *daily food intake* varies from *spinach* to *bacon,* the value of *longevity* varies from *high* to *low.* As these statements suggest, correlations are the fundamental building blocks of knowledge.

But correlations do more than just describe the past. They also allow us to predict the future. How long will a person live if she eats a pound of bacon every day? Probably not as long as she would have lived if she'd instead eaten a pound of spinach every day. How tall will Walter be on his next birthday? Probably taller if he is turning 21 than if he is turning 2. Both of these are questions about events that have not yet happened, and their answers are predictions based on correlations. When two variables

When children line up by age, they also tend to line up by height. The pattern of variation in age (from youngest to oldest) is synchronized with the pattern of variation in height (from shortest to tallest).

VARIABLE A property whose value can vary or change.

CORRELATION The "co-relationship" or pattern of covariation between two variables, each of which has been measured several times.

are correlated, knowledge of the value of one variable (daily food intake or age) allows us to make predictions about the value of the other variable (longevity or height). Indeed, every time we suspect something ("I think it's going to rain soon"), worry about something ("The psych exam will probably be tough"), or feel excited about something ("Greg's party should be wild"), we are using the value of one variable to predict the value of another variable with which it is correlated.

Every correlation can be described in two equally reasonable ways. A positive correlation describes a relationship between two variables in "more-more" or "less-less" terms. When we say that *more spinach* is associated with *more longevity* or that *less spinach* is associated with *less longevity,* we are describing a positive correlation. A negative correlation describes a relationship between two variables in "more-less" or "less-more" terms. When we say that *more bacon* is associated with *less longevity* or that *less bacon* is associated with *more longevity,* we are describing a negative correlation. How we choose to describe any particular correlation is usually just a matter of simplicity and convenience.

Measuring Correlation

The hypothetical variables shown in Table 2.1 are perfectly correlated; that is, each and every time *not insulted* changes to *insulted, agreed* also changes to *refused,* and there are no exceptions to this rule. This perfect correlation allows you to make an extremely confident prediction about how pedestrians will respond to a request after being insulted. But perfect correlations are so rare in everyday life that we had to make up a hypothetical study just to show you one. There actually is a correlation between age and height that allows us to predict that a child will be shorter than an adult, and this prediction will be right more often than it is wrong. But it *will* be wrong in some instances because there are *some* tall kids and *some* short adults. So how much confidence should we have in predictions based on correlations?

Statisticians have developed a way to estimate just how accurate a particular prediction is likely to be by measuring the *strength* of the correlation on which it is based. The **correlation coefficient** is *a measure of the direction and strength of a correlation,* and it is symbolized by the letter *r* (as in "relationship"). Like most measures, the correlation coefficient has a limited range. What does that mean? Well, if you were to measure the number of hours of sunshine per day in your hometown, that measure would have a range of 24 because it could only have a value from 0 to 24. Numbers such as –7 and 36.8 would be meaningless. Similarly, the value of *r* can range from –1 to 1, and numbers outside that range are meaningless. What, then, do the numbers *inside* that range mean?

- When *r* = 1, the relationship between the variables is called a *perfect positive correlation,* which means that every time the value of one variable increases by a certain amount, the value of the second variable also increases by a certain amount, and this happens without exception. If every increase in age of *X* units were associated with an increase in height of *Y* units, then age and height would be perfectly positively correlated.

- When *r* = –1, the relationship between the variables is called a *perfect negative correlation,* which means that as the value of one variable increases by a certain amount, the value of the second variable *decreases* by a certain amount, and this happens without exception. If every increase in age of *X* units were associated with a decrease in height of *Y* units, then age and height would be perfectly negatively correlated.

- When *r* = 0, there is no systematic relationship between the variables, which are said to be *uncorrelated.* This means that the pattern of variation of one variable is not synchronized in any way with the pattern of variation of the other. As the value of one variable increases by a certain amount, the value of the second variable may sometimes increase, sometimes decrease, and sometimes do neither. If increases in age of *X* units were sometimes associated with changes in height of *Y* units and sometimes associated with a change in height of *Z* units, then age and height would be uncorrelated.

The correlations shown in **FIGURE 2.6 a** and **b** are perfect correlations—that is, they show patterns of variation that are perfectly synchronized and without exceptions.

CORRELATION COEFFICIENT A statistical measure of the direction and strength of a correlation, which is signified by the letter *r*.

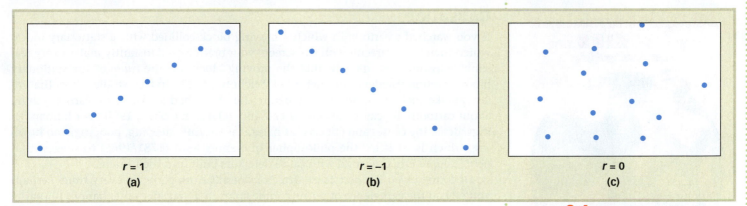

r = 1
(a)

r = –1
(b)

r = 0
(c)

Figure 2.6 Three Kinds of Correlations
This figure illustrates pairs of variables that have (a) a perfect positive correlation ($r = +1$), (b) a perfect negative correlation ($r = -1$), and (c) no correlation ($r = 0$).

Such correlations are extremely rare in real life. It may be true that the more bacon you eat, the fewer years you will live, but it's not as though longevity decreases by exactly 1.23 days for every 100 pounds of bacon you put away annually. Bacon eating and longevity are *negatively* correlated (i.e., as one increases, the other decreases), but they are also *imperfectly* correlated, and thus *r* will lie somewhere between 0 and –1. But where? That depends on how many exceptions there are to the "*X* more pounds of bacon = *Y* fewer years of life" rule. If there are just a few exceptions, then *r* will be much closer to –1 than to 0. But as the number of exceptions increases, then the value of *r* will begin to move toward 0.

FIGURE 2.7 shows four cases in which two variables are positively correlated but have different numbers of exceptions, and as you can see, the number of exceptions changes the value of *r* quite dramatically. Two variables can have a perfect correlation ($r = 1$), a strong correlation (for example, $r = .80$), a moderate correlation (for example, $r = .60$), or a weak correlation (for example, $r = .20$). The correlation coefficient, then, is a measure of both the *direction* and *strength* of the relationship between two variables. The sign of *r* (plus or minus) tells us the direction of the relationship, and the absolute value of *r* (between 0 and 1) tells us about the number of exceptions and hence about how confident we can be when using the correlation to make predictions.

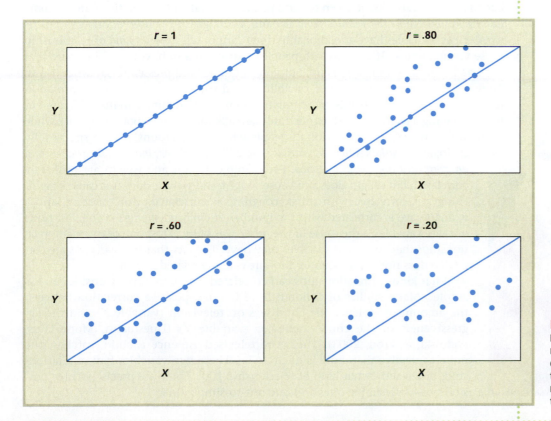

r = 1

r = .80

r = .60

r = .20

Figure 2.7 Positive Correlations of Different Strengths These graphs represent different degrees of positive correlation between two variables. Scores that are on the line adhere strictly to the rule $X = Y$. The more exceptions there are to this rule, the weaker the correlation is.

Although people have smoked tobacco for centuries, only recently has the causal relationship between cigarette smoking and heart and lung disease been detected. By the way, how many physicians said the opposite? And "less irritating" than what?

NATURAL CORRELATION A correlation observed between naturally occurring variables.

A woman's age is correlated with the number of children she has borne, but age does not cause women to become pregnant and pregnancy does not cause women to age.

Causation

If you watched a cartoon in which a moving block collided with a stationary block, which then went careening off the screen, your brain would instantly make a very reasonable assumption, namely, that the moving block was the *cause* of the stationary block's motion (Heider & Simmel, 1944; Michotte, 1963). In fact, studies show that infants make such assumptions long before they have had a chance to learn anything about cartoons, blocks, collisions, or causality (Oakes & Cohen, 1990). For human beings, detecting causes and effects is as natural as sucking, sleeping, pooping, and howling, which is what led the philosopher Immanuel Kant (1781/1965) to suggest that people come into the world with cause detectors built into their brains.

Of course, even the best cause detector doesn't work perfectly every time. Perhaps you've had the experience of putting some coins in an arcade game, happily shooting helicopters or dodging vampires for a minute or so, and then suddenly realizing that you never actually pressed start and that the shooting and dodging you saw on the screen had nothing to do with your nimble handling of the joystick. Mindbugs like this happen all the time (Wegner & Wheatley, 1999). In fact, our brains are so eager to connect causes with effects that they often make connections that aren't really there, which is why astrology continues to be such a popular diversion (Glick, Gottesman, & Jolton, 1989). Conversely, our brains sometimes fail to detect causal relationships that actually do exist. Only in the past century or so have surgeons made it a practice to wash their hands before operating because before that, no one seemed to notice that dirty fingernails were causally related to postsurgical infections. The causal relationships between smoking and lung cancer and between cholesterol and heart disease went undetected for centuries despite the fact that people were smoking tobacco, eating lard, and keeling over with some regularity. The point here is that if we want to discover the causal relationships between variables, then we need more than mere empiricism. What we need is a method for discovering causal relationships. As you're about to see, we've got one.

The Third-Variable Problem

We observe correlations all the time—between automobiles and pollution, between bacon and heart attacks, between sex and pregnancy. **Natural correlations** are *the correlations we observe in the world around us,* and although such observations can tell us *whether* two variables have a relationship, they cannot tell us what *kind* of relationship these variables have. If you saw two people chatting in a pub, you could be sure that they had some kind of relationship, but you would be hard-pressed to say what it was. They could be spouses, classmates, or siblings, and you would need more information (e.g., matching wedding bands, matching textbooks, or matching parents) to figure out which. Having a relationship does not automatically make them spouses because while all spouses have relationships, not all people who have relationships are spouses. By the same logic, *all variables that are causally related are correlated, but not all variables that are correlated are causally related.* For example, height and weight are positively correlated, but height does not cause weight and weight does not cause height. Hunger is correlated with thirst, coughing is correlated with sneezing, and a woman's age is correlated with the number of children she has borne. But none of these variables is the cause of the other. Causality is just one of the many relationships that correlated variables may have. The fact that two variables are correlated does not tell us whether they are causally related as well.

What kinds of relationships can correlated variables have? Consider an example. Many studies of children have found a positive correlation between the amount of violence the child sees on television (variable X) and the aggressiveness of the child's behavior (variable Y) (Huesmann, Moise-Titus, Podolski, & Eron, 2003). The more televised violence a child watches, the more aggressive that child is likely to be. These two variables have a relationship, but exactly what kind of relationship is it? There are precisely three possibilities—two simple ones and one not-so-simple one.

- $X \rightarrow Y$. One simple possibility is that watching televised violence (X) causes aggressiveness (Y). For example, watching televised violence may teach children that aggression is a reasonable way to vent anger and solve problems.
- $Y \rightarrow X$. Another simple possibility is that aggressiveness (Y) causes children to watch televised violence (X). For example, children who are naturally aggressive may enjoy televised violence more and may seek opportunities to watch it.
- $Z \rightarrow X$ and Y. A final and not-so-simple possibility is that a *third variable* (Z) causes children both to

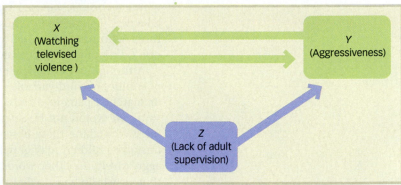

be aggressive (Y) and to watch televised violence (X), neither of which is causally related to the other. For example, lack of adult supervision (Z) may allow children to get away with bullying others and to get away with watching television shows that adults would normally not allow. If so, then watching televised violence (X) and behaving aggressively (Y) may not be causally related to each other at all and may instead be the independent effects of a lack of adult supervision (Z), just as sneezing and coughing may be independent effects of viral infection, height and weight may be independent effects of nutrition, and so on. In other words, the relation between aggressiveness and watching televised violence may be a case of **third-variable correlation**, which means that *two variables are correlated only because each is causally related to a third variable*.

FIGURE 2.8 shows the three possible causes of any correlation. How can we determine by simple observation which of these three possibilities best describes the relationship between televised violence and aggressiveness? We can't. When we observe a natural correlation, *the possibility of third-variable correlation can never be dismissed*. Don't take this claim on faith. Let's try to dismiss the possibility of third-variable correlation and you'll see why such efforts are always doomed to fail.

The most straightforward way to dismiss the possibility that a third variable such as lack of adult supervision (Z) caused children to watch televised violence (X) and behave aggressively (Y) would be to eliminate differences in adult supervision among a group of children and see if the correlation between televised violence and aggressiveness remained. For example, we could observe children in **matched samples**, which is *a technique whereby the participants in two samples are identical in terms of a third variable*. For instance, we could observe only children who are supervised by an adult exactly 87% of the time, thus ensuring that every child who watched a lot of televised violence had exactly the same amount of adult supervision as every child who did not watch a lot of televised violence. Alternatively, we could observe children in **matched pairs**, which is *a technique whereby each participant in one sample is identical to one other participant in another sample in terms of a third variable*. For instance, we could observe children who experience different amounts of adult supervision, but we could make sure that for every child we observe who watches a lot of televised violence and is supervised 24% of the time, we also observe a child who doesn't watch a lot of televised violence and is supervised 24% of the time, thus ensuring that the children who do and do not watch a lot of televised violence have the same amount of adult supervision *on average*. Regardless of

Figure 2.8 Causes of Correlation If X (watching televised violence) and Y (aggressiveness) are correlated, then there are exactly three possible explanations: X causes Y, Y causes X, or Z (some other factor, such as lack of adult supervision) causes both Y and X, neither of which causes the other.

THIRD-VARIABLE CORRELATION
The fact that two variables may be correlated only because they are both caused by a third variable.

MATCHED SAMPLES An observational technique that involves matching the average of the participants in the experimental and control groups in order to eliminate the possibility that a third variable (and not the independent variable) caused changes in the dependent variable.

MATCHED PAIRS An observational technique that involves matching each participant in the experimental group with a specific participant in the control group in order to eliminate the possibility that a third variable (and not the independent variable) caused changes in the dependent variable.

How can third-variable correlation explain the fact that the more tattoos a person has, the more likely he or she is to be involved in a motorcycle accident?

which technique we used, we would know that the children who do and don't watch televised violence have equal amounts of adult supervision on average, and thus if those who watch televised violence are more aggressive on average than those who don't, lack of adult supervision cannot be the cause.

Although both of these techniques can be useful, neither allows us to dismiss the possibility of third-variable correlation. Why? Because even if we use matched samples or matched pairs to dismiss a *particular* third variable (such as lack of adult supervision), we would not be able to dismiss *all* third variables. For example, as soon as we finished making these observations, it might suddenly occur to us that emotionally unstable children may gravitate toward violent television programs and may behave aggressively. In other words, "emotional instability" would be a new third variable that we would have to design new observations to dismiss. Clearly, we could dream up new third variables all day long without ever breaking a sweat, and every time we dreamed one up, we would have to rush out and make a whole new set of observations using matched samples or matched pairs to determine whether *this* third variable was the cause of watching televised violence and of behaving aggressively.

The problem, then, is that there are an infinite number of third variables out there and thus an infinite number of reasons why X and Y might be correlated. Because most of us don't have the time to perform an infinite number of studies with matched samples or matched pairs, we can never be sure that the natural correlation between X and Y is evidence of a causal relationship between them. This problem is so troubling and pervasive that it has its own name (and one that's easy to remember). The **third-variable problem** refers to the fact that *a causal relationship between two variables cannot be inferred from the natural correlation between them because of the ever-present possibility of third-variable correlation*. In other words, if we care about causality, then natural correlations can never tell us what we really want to know.

Experimentation

The third-variable problem prevents us from using natural correlations to learn about causal relationships, and so we have to find another method that will. Let's start by considering once again the source of our trouble. We cannot conclude that watching televised violence causes children to behave aggressively because there is some chance that both behaviors are caused by a third variable, such as lack of adult supervision or emotional instability, and there are so many third variables in the world that we could never do enough studies to dismiss them all. Another way of saying this is that children who do watch and don't watch televised violence differ in countless ways, and any one of these countless differences could be the real cause of their different levels of aggressiveness. This suggests that if we could somehow eliminate *all* of these countless differences at once—somehow find a sample of children who are perfect clones, with identical amounts of adult supervision, identical amounts of emotional stability, identical histories, identical physiologies, identical neighborhoods, siblings, toys, schools, teeth, dreams, and so on—then the natural correlation between watching televised violence and aggressiveness *would* be evidence of a causal relationship. If we could somehow accomplish this amazing feat, we would have a sample of children, some of whom watch televised violence and some of whom don't, but all of whom are identical in terms of *every possible* third variable. If we found that the children in this sample who watched televised violence were more aggressive than those who did not, then watching televised violence would *have to be* the cause of their different levels of aggressiveness because, after all, watching televised violence would be the *only* thing that distinguished the most aggressive children from the least aggressive children.

Finding a sample of clones is, of course, not very realistic. But as it turns out, scientists have another way to eliminate all the countless differences between the people in a sample. An **experiment** is *a technique for establishing the causal relationship between variables*. The best way to understand how experiments accomplish this amazing feat is by examining their two key features: manipulation and randomization.

THIRD-VARIABLE PROBLEM The fact that the causal relationship between two variables cannot be inferred from the correlation between them because of the ever-present possibility of third-variable correlation.

EXPERIMENT A technique for establishing the causal relationship between variables.

Manipulation

The most important thing to know about experiments is that you already know the most important thing about experiments because you've been doing them all your life. Imagine, for instance, what you would do if you were watching television one day when all of a sudden the picture went fuzzy for 10 minutes, then cleared up, then went fuzzy for a few minutes again, and so on. You might suspect that another electronic device, such as your roommate's new cordless telephone, was interfering with the television reception. Your first step would be to observe and measure carefully, noting the clarity of the television picture when your roommate was and was not using his telephone. But even if you observed a natural correlation between television clarity and telephone use, the third-variable problem would prevent you from drawing a causal conclusion. After all, if your roommate was afraid of storms and tended to rush to the phone and call his mommy whenever a cloud passed over the house, then clouds (Z) could be the cause of both the telephone calls (X) and the television interference (Y).

Because you could not draw a causal conclusion from this natural correlation, you would probably try to create an *artificial* correlation by standing in front of the television with the phone in hand, switching it on and off and observing the clarity of the television picture. If you observed that the artificial pattern of variation you created in the telephone (on for 1 second, off for 3 seconds, on for 8 seconds, off for 2 seconds) was nicely synchronized with the pattern of variation in the television (fuzzy for 1 second, fine for 3 seconds, fuzzy for 8 seconds, fine for 2 seconds), then you would instantly conclude that the telephone was the cause of the interference. Standing in front of the TV and turning the phone on and off may seem to show little common sense, but in doing this, you have discovered and used science's most powerful technique for establishing causal relationships: the experiment. Your actions qualify as an experiment because you used **manipulation,** which is *the creation of an artificial pattern of variation in a variable in order to determine its causal powers.*

Manipulation is one of the critical ingredients of an experiment. Up until now, we have approached science like polite dinner guests, taking what we were offered and making the best of it. Nature offered us children who differed in how much televised violence they watched and who differed in how aggressively they behaved, and we dutifully measured the natural patterns of variation in these two variables and computed their correlations. The problem with this approach is that when all was said and done, we still didn't know what we really wanted to know, namely, whether these variables had a causal relationship. No matter how many matched samples or matched pairs we observed, there was always another third variable that we hadn't yet dismissed. Experiments solve this problem. Rather than *measuring* how much televised violence a child watches, *measuring* the child's aggressiveness, and then computing the correlation between these two naturally occurring variables, experiments require that we *manipulate* how much televised violence a child watches in the same way that you manipulated the telephone. In essence, we need to systematically switch the watching of televised violence on and off in a sample of children and then see if aggressiveness goes on and off too.

We might do this by asking some children to participate in an experiment and exposing half of them to 2 hours of televised violence every day for a month while making sure that the other half saw no televised violence at all (see **FIGURE 2.9** on the next page). At the end of a month, we could measure the aggressiveness of the children and compare the measurements across the two groups. When we compared these measurements, we would be computing the correlation between a variable we measured (aggressiveness) and a variable we manipulated (televised violence). Instead of looking for synchrony in the patterns of variation that nature offered us, we would have caused a pattern of variation in one variable, observed a pattern of variation in another, and looked for synchrony between. In so doing, we would have solved the third-variable problem. After all, if we *manipulated* rather than *measured* a child's exposure to televised violence, then we would never have to ask whether a third variable (such as lack of adult supervision) might have caused it. Why? Because we already *know* what caused the child to watch or not watch televised violence. *We* did!

MANIPULATION A characteristic of experimentation in which the researcher artificially creates a pattern of variation in an independent variable in order to determine its causal powers. Manipulation usually results in the creation of an *experimental group* and a *control group*.

Figure 2.9 Manipulation The independent variable is televised violence and the dependent variable is aggressiveness. Manipulation of the independent variable results in an experimental group and a control group. When we compare the behavior of participants in these two groups, we are actually computing the correlation between the independent variable and the dependent variable.

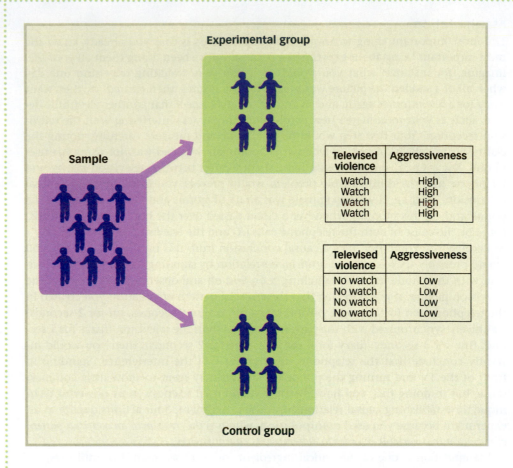

Televised violence	Aggressiveness
Watch	High
Watch	High
Watch	High
Watch	High

Televised violence	Aggressiveness
No watch	Low
No watch	Low
No watch	Low
No watch	Low

INDEPENDENT VARIABLE The variable that is manipulated in an experiment.

EXPERIMENTAL GROUP One of the two groups of participants created by the manipulation of an independent variable in an experiment; the experimental group is exposed to the stimulus being studied and the *control group* is not.

CONTROL GROUP One of the two groups of participants created by the manipulation of an independent variable in an experiment that is not exposed to the stimulus being studied.

DEPENDENT VARIABLE The variable that is measured in a study.

Doing an experiment, then, involves three critical steps (and several technical terms):

■ First, we perform a manipulation. We call *the variable that is manipulated* the **independent variable** because it is under our control, and thus it is "independent" of what the participant says or does. When we manipulate an independent variable (such as watching televised violence), we create at least two groups of participants: an **experimental group**, which is *the group of people who are treated in a particular way,* such as being exposed to televised violence, and a **control group**, which is *the group of people who are not treated in this particular way.*

■ Second, having created a pattern of variation in one variable (televised violence), we now measure the pattern of variation in another variable (aggressiveness). We call *the variable that is measured* the **dependent variable** because its value "depends" on what the participant says or does.

■ Third and finally, we check to see whether the patterns of variation in the dependent and independent variables are synchronized.

When we have manipulated an independent variable, measured a dependent variable, and looked to see whether their patterns of variation are synchronized, we've done one of the two things that experimentation requires. Now let's talk about the second.

Randomization

Manipulation is one of the two critical features of experimentation that allow us to overcome the third-variable problem and establish a causal relationship between an independent and a dependent variable. The second feature is a bit less intuitive but equally important. Imagine that we did the televised violence experiment by finding a sample of children and asking each child whether he or she would like to be in the experimental group or the control group. Imagine that, conveniently enough, half of the children volunteered to watch 2 hours of televised violence every day for a month, and the other half volunteered not to. Imagine that we did as each of the children requested, measured their aggressiveness a month later, and found that the children who watched televised violence were more aggressive than those who did not. Would this experiment allow us to conclude that watching televised violence causes aggressiveness? Definitely not—but *why* not? After all, we switched televised violence on and off and watched to see whether aggressiveness went on and off too. So where did we go wrong?

We went wrong when we let the children decide for themselves how much television they would watch. Many things probably distinguish children who volunteer to watch televised violence from those who don't. For instance, those who volunteer may be older, or stronger, or smarter. Or younger, or weaker, or dumber. Or less often supervised or more emotionally unstable. The list of possible differences goes on and on. The whole point of doing an experiment was to divide children into two groups that differed *in just one way,* namely, in terms of how much televised violence they watched. The moment we allowed the children to select their own groups, the two groups differed in countless ways, and any of those countless differences could have been responsible for differences in their aggressiveness. **Self-selection** is *a problem that occurs when a participant's inclusion in the experimental or control group is determined by the participant.* Just as we cannot allow nature to decide which of the children in our study watches televised violence, we cannot allow the children to decide either. So who decides?

The answer to this question is a bit spooky: *No one decides.* If we want to be sure that there is one and only one difference between the children who do and do not watch televised violence, then their inclusion in these groups must be *randomly determined.* Most of us use the word *random* to mean "without a cause" (as in, "Bill was mad at me today for no reason at all. It was like totally random"). This is precisely how the word should be used, though perhaps without the "like totally" part. If you flipped a coin and a friend asked what had *caused* it to land heads up, you would correctly say that *nothing* had. This is what it means for the outcome of a coin flip to be random. Because the outcome of a coin flip is random, we can put coin flips to work for us to solve the problem that self-selection creates. If we want to be sure that a child's inclusion in the experimental group or the control group was not caused by nature, was not caused by the child, and was not caused by *any* of the infinite number of third variables we could name if we only had the time, then all we have to do is let it be caused by the outcome of a coin flip—which itself has no cause! For example, we could walk up to each child

in our experiment, flip a coin, and, if the coin lands heads up, assign the child to watch 2 hours of televised violence every day for a month. If the coin lands heads down, then we could assign the child to watch no television. **Randomization** is *a procedure that uses random events to ensure that a participant's assignment to the experimental or control group is not determined by any third variable.*

What would happen if we assigned children to groups with a coin flip? As **FIGURE 2.10** on the next page shows, the first thing we would expect is that about half the children would be assigned to watch televised violence and about half would not. That would be convenient. But second—and *much* more importantly—we could expect the experimental group and the control group to have roughly equal numbers of supervised kids and unsupervised kids, roughly equal numbers of

Are you a girl with a Star-Spangled heart?

JOIN THE **WAC** NOW!

THOUSANDS OF ARMY JOBS NEED FILLING!

Women's Army Corps United States Army

LIBRARY OF CONGRESS (LC-USZC4-1653)

Self-selection is a problem in experimentation. For example, we could never draw conclusions about the effects of military service by comparing those who joined to those who didn't because those who do and don't join differ in so many ways.

Figure 2.10 Randomization
Children with adult supervision are shown in orange and without adult supervision are shown in blue. The independent variable is televised violence and the dependent variable is aggressiveness. Randomization ensures that participants in the experimental and control groups are equal on average in terms of all possible third variables. In essence, it ensures that there is no correlation between a third variable and the dependent variable.

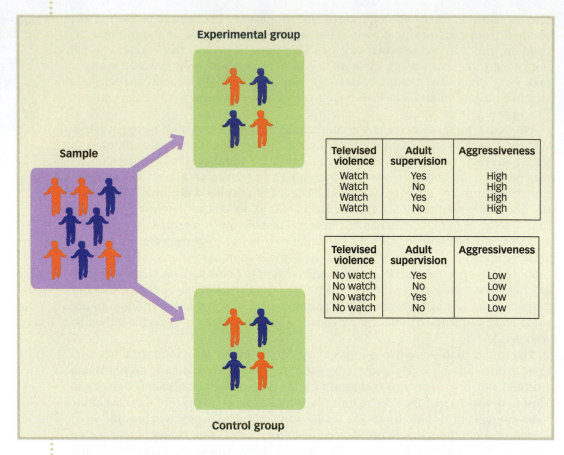

Televised violence	Adult supervision	Aggressiveness
Watch	Yes	High
Watch	No	High
Watch	Yes	High
Watch	No	High

Televised violence	Adult supervision	Aggressiveness
No watch	Yes	Low
No watch	No	Low
No watch	Yes	Low
No watch	No	Low

emotionally stable and unstable kids, roughly equal numbers of big kids and small kids, of active kids, fat kids, tall kids, funny kids, and kids with blue hair named Larry Mc-Sweeny. Indeed, we could expect the two groups to have equal numbers of kids who are anything-you-can-ever-name-and-everything-you-can't! Because the kids in the two groups will be the same on average in terms of height, weight, emotional stability, adult supervision, and every other variable in the known universe except the one we manipulated, we can be sure that the variable we manipulated (televised violence) caused changes in the variable we measured (aggressiveness). Watching televised violence was the only difference between the two groups of children when we started the experiment, and thus it *must* be the cause of the differences in aggressiveness we observed a month later (see the Hot Science box).

Randomization ensures that the participants in the experimental and control groups are, on average, identical in every way except one.

ALAN THORNTON/STONE/GETTY

{ HOT SCIENCE } Establishing Causality in the Brain

SOMETIMES THE BEST WAY TO LEARN about something is to see what happens when it breaks, and the human brain is no exception. Scientists have studied the effects of brain damage for centuries, and those studies reveal a lot about how the brain normally works so well. As you read in Chapter 1, in the middle of the 19th century, a French surgeon named Paul Broca observed that people who had lost their ability to speak often had damage in a particular spot on the left side of their brains. Broca suggested that this region might control speech production but not other functions such as the ability to understand speech. As it turned out, he was right, which is why this brain region is now known as Broca's area.

Scientists have learned a lot about the brain by studying the behavior of people whose brains are defective or have been damaged by accidents. But the problem with studying brain-damaged patients, of course, is the problem with studying any naturally occurring variable: Brain damage may be related to particular patterns of behavior, but that relationship may or may not be causal. Experimentation is the premiere method for establishing causal relationships between variables, but scientists cannot ethically cause brain damage in human beings, and thus they have not been able to establish causal relationships

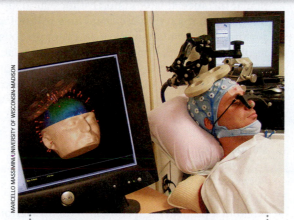

Transcranial magnetic stimulation activates and deactivates regions of the brain with a magnetic pulse, temporarily mimicking brain damage.

between particular kinds of brain damage and particular patterns of behavior.

Until now. Scientists have recently discovered a way to mimic brain damage with a benign technique called *transcranial magnetic stimulation* (or TMS) (Barker, Jalinous, & Freeston, 1985; Hallett, 2000). If you've ever held a magnet under a piece of paper and used it to drag a pin across the paper's surface, you know that magnetic fields can pass through insulating material. The human skull is no exception. TMS delivers a magnetic pulse that passes through the skull and deactivates neurons in the cerebral cortex for a short period. Researchers can direct TMS pulses to particular brain regions—essentially turning them "off"—and then measure temporary changes in the way a person moves, sees, thinks, remembers, speaks, or feels. By manipulating the state of the brain, scientists can perform experiments that establish causal relationships. For example, scientists have recently discovered that magnetic stimulation of the visual cortex temporarily impairs a person's ability to detect the motion of an object without impairing the person's ability to recognize that object (Beckers & Zeki, 1995). This intriguing discovery suggests that motion perception and object recognition are accomplished by different parts of the brain, but moreover, it establishes that the activity of these brain regions *causes* motion perception and object recognition.

For the first time in human history, the causal relationships between particular brain regions and particular behaviors have been unequivocally established. Rather than relying on observational studies of brain-damaged patients or the snapshots provided by MRI or PET scans, researchers can now manipulate brain activity and measure its effects. Studies suggest that TMS has no harmful side effects (Pascual-Leone et al., 1993), and this new tool promises to revolutionize the study of how our brains create our thoughts, feelings, and actions.

Significance

Randomization is a powerful tool, but like a lot of tools, it doesn't work every time you use it. When we randomly assigned children to watch or not watch televised violence, we said that we could expect the two groups to have about equal numbers of supervised and unsupervised kids, rich kids and poor kids, thin kids and fat kids, and so on. The key word in that sentence is *about*. If you were to flip a coin 100 times, you would expect it to land heads up *about* 50 times. But every once in a while, 100 coin flips would produce 80 heads, or 90 heads, or even 100 heads, by sheer chance alone. This would not happen often, of course, but it would happen once in a while. Because random assignment is achieved by using a randomizing device such as a coin, every once in a long while the coin will assign all the unsupervised, emotionally disturbed kids to watch televised violence and all the supervised, emotionally undisturbed kids to watch none. When this happens, we say that random assignment has failed—and when random assignment fails, the third-variable problem rises up out of its grave and comes back to haunt us with a vengeance. When random assignment fails, we cannot conclude that there is a causal relationship between the independent and dependent variables.

How can we tell when random assignment has failed? Unfortunately, we can't tell for sure. But we can calculate the *odds* that random assignment has failed in any particular instance. It isn't important for you to know how to do this calculation, but it is important for you to understand how psychologists interpret its results. Psychologists perform this calculation every time they do an experiment, and they do not accept the results of those experiments unless the calculation tells them that there is less than a 5% chance that random assignment failed. In other words, the calculation must allow the psychologist to be 95% certain that random assignment succeeded before the results of the experiment are accepted. When the odds that random assignment failed are less than 5%, an experimental result is said to be *statistically significant.* You've already learned about a few descriptive statistics, such as the mean, the median, and the standard deviation. A second class of statistics—called *inferential statistics*—tells scientists what kinds of conclusions or inferences they can draw from observed differences between the experimental and control groups. For example, *p* is an inferential statistic that tells psychologists (among other things) the likelihood that random assignment failed in a particular experiment. When psychologists report that $p < .05$, they are saying that according to the inferential statistics they calculated, the odds that random assignment failed are less than 5%, and thus the differences between the experimental and control groups were unlikely to have been caused by a third variable.

Drawing Conclusions

If we were to apply all the techniques we have discussed so far, we could design an experiment that has **internal validity**, which is *the characteristic of an experiment that allows one to draw accurate inferences about the causal relationship between an independent and dependent variable.* When we say that an experiment is internally valid, we mean that everything *inside* the experiment is working exactly as it must in order for us to draw conclusions about causal relationships. Specifically, an experiment is internally valid when

- An independent variable has been effectively manipulated.
- Participants have been randomly assigned to the groups that this manipulation created.
- A dependent variable has been measured in an unbiased way with a valid, powerful, and reliable measure.
- A correlation has been observed between the pattern of variation created in the independent variable and the pattern of variation measured in the dependent variable.

If we do these things, then we may conclude that manipulated changes in the independent variable caused measured changes in the dependent variable. But we may *not* conclude that one abstract property caused another. For example, even the most well-designed and well-executed study on televised violence and aggressiveness would *not* allow us to conclude that watching televised violence causes aggressiveness. Rather, it would allow us to draw the much more limited conclusion that televised violence *as we defined it* caused aggressiveness *as we defined it* in the people *whom we studied.* The phrases "as we defined it" and "whom we studied" represent important restrictions on the kinds of conclusions that scientists may draw, so let's consider each of them in turn.

Representative Variables

When we say that we have established a causal relationship between televised violence and aggressiveness *as we have defined them,* we are acknowledging the fact that operational definitions are never perfectly linked to their properties. You will recall that we can never measure an abstract property such as *aggressiveness* but rather can only measure operational definitions of that property, such as *the number of times a child initiates forceful physical contact with other children on the playground during recess.* Because we cannot measure properties, experiments can never be used to make legitimate claims about them. Experiments allow us to draw conclusions about the causal relationship between the particular operational definitions that we manipulated and measured but not about the abstract properties that these particular operational definitions represent.

INTERNAL VALIDITY The characteristic of an experiment that allows one to draw accurate inferences about the causal relationship between an independent and dependent variable.

Does piercing make a person more or less attractive? The answer, of course, depends entirely on how you operationally define *piercing*.

Like the interstate speed limit, this is one of those rules to which few people pay serious attention. Consider, for example, the current controversy over the effects of violent video games on children. Some people believe that playing violent video games leads children to behave aggressively, others do not, and both claim that scientific experiments support their arguments (Reichhardt, 2003). So who's right? Nobody is, because experiments do not allow us to draw conclusions about abstractions such as *violent video games* and *aggressive behavior*. Rather, they allow us to draw very particular conclusions about how *playing Pac-Man for 2 minutes* or *playing Blood Sport for 10 hours* influences *the tendency to interrupt when others are speaking* or *the tendency to pummel others with blunt objects*. Not surprisingly, experiments on video games and aggression can produce very different results depending on how the independent and dependent variables are operationally defined. Long exposure to a truly violent game will probably produce more aggressive behavior than will brief exposure to a moderately violent game, and exposure to any kind of violent game will probably influence rudeness more easily than it will influence physical aggression.

What, then, is the right way to operationalize such variables? One obvious answer is that experiments should strive for **external validity**, which is *a property of an experiment in which variables have been operationally defined in a normal, typical, or realistic way*. It seems fairly clear that *interrupting* and *pummeling* are not the kinds of aggressive behaviors with which teachers and parents are normally concerned and that most instances of aggression among children lie somewhere between an insult and a chain saw massacre. If the goal of an experiment is to determine whether the kinds of video games that children typically play cause the kinds of aggression in which children typically engage, then external validity is essential.

Indeed, external validity seems like such a good idea that students are often surprised to learn that most psychology experiments are externally *in*valid—and that most psychologists don't mind. The reason for this is that psychologists are rarely trying to learn about the real world by creating tiny replicas of it in their laboratories. Rather, they are usually trying to learn about the real world by using experiments to test theories and hypotheses (Mook, 1983). A **theory** is *a hypothetical account of how and why a phenomenon occurs,* and a **hypothesis** is *a testable prediction made by a theory.* For example, physicists have a theory stating that heat is the result of the rapid movement of molecules. This theory suggests a hypothesis, namely, that if the molecules that constitute an object are slowed, the object should become cooler. Now imagine that a physicist tested this hypothesis by performing an experiment in which a laser was used to slow the movement of the molecules in a rubber ball, whose temperature was then measured. Would we criticize this experiment by saying, "Sorry, but your experiment teaches us nothing about the real world because in the real world, no one actually uses lasers to slow the movement of the molecules in rubber balls"? Let's hope not. The physicist's theory (molecular motion causes heat) led to a hypothesis about

EXTERNAL VALIDITY A characteristic of an experiment in which the independent and dependent variables are operationally defined in a normal, typical, or realistic way.

THEORY A hypothetical account of how and why a phenomenon occurs, usually in the form of a statement about the causal relationship between two or more properties. Theories lead to *hypotheses*.

HYPOTHESIS A specific and testable prediction that is usually derived from a *theory*.

RANDOM SAMPLING A technique for choosing participants that ensures that every member of a population has an equal chance of being included in the sample.

what would happen in the laboratory (slowing the molecules in a rubber ball should cool it), and thus the events that the physicist manipulated and measured in the laboratory served to test the theory.

Similarly, a good theory about the causal relationship between video games and aggression should lead to hypotheses about how people will behave when playing Pac-Man for a few minutes or Blood Sport for many hours. As such, even these unrepresentative forms of video game playing can serve to test the theory. In short, theories allow us to generate hypotheses about what *can* happen, or what *must* happen, or what *will* happen under particular circumstances, and experiments are typically meant to create these circumstances, test the hypotheses, and thereby provide evidence for or against the theories that generated them. Experiments are not meant to be miniature versions of everyday life, and thus external invalidity is not necessarily a problem.

Representative Samples

You will recall that the law of large numbers advises us to measure many people rather than just one or two so that the average behavior of the people in our sample will closely approximate the average behavior of people in the population. But how do we actually *find* the people in our sample? The best way to do this is to use **random sampling**, which is *a technique for choosing participants that ensures that every member of a population has an equal chance of being included in the sample*. When we randomly sample participants from a population, we earn the right to *generalize* from the behavior of the sample to the behavior of the population, that is, to conclude that what we observed in our experiment would also have been observed if we had measured the entire population. You already have good intuitions about the importance of random sampling. For example, if you stopped at a farm stand to buy a bag of cherries and the farmer offered to let you taste a few that he had specially handpicked from the bag, you'd be reluctant to generalize from that nonrandom sample to the population of cherries in the bag. But if the farmer invited you to pull a few cherries from the bag without looking, you'd probably be willing to take those cherries as reasonably representative of the cherry population.

Given the importance of random sampling, you may be surprised to learn that psychologists almost never do it. Indeed, virtually every participant in every psychology experiment you will ever read about was a volunteer, and most were college students who were significantly younger, smarter, healthier, wealthier, and whiter than the average earthling. Psychologists sample their participants the "wrong way" (by nonrandom sampling) because it is just about impossible to do it the "right way" (by random sampling). Even if there were an alphabetized list of all the world's human inhabitants from which we could randomly choose our research participants, the likelihood that we could actually perform experiments on those whom we sampled would be depressingly slim. After all, how would we find the 72-year-old Bedouin woman whose family roams the desert so that we could measure the electrical activity in her brain while she watched cartoons? How would we convince the 3-week-old infant in New Delhi to complete a lengthy questionnaire about his political beliefs? Most psychology experiments are conducted by professors and graduate students at colleges and universities in the Western Hemisphere, and as much as they might like to randomly sample the population of the planet, the practical truth is that they are pretty much stuck studying the folks who volunteer for their studies.

Random sampling is always impractical and usually impossible. And yet, if we don't randomly sample, then we can't automatically generalize from our sample to the population from which it was drawn. So how can we learn *anything* from psychology experiments? Isn't the failure to randomly sample a fatal flaw? No, it's not.

"Hi. You've been randomly selected to participate in a sex survey upstairs in 15 minutes."

Although we can't automatically generalize from nonrandom samples, there are three reasons why this is not a lethal problem for the science of psychology:

■ Sometimes generality does not matter. One flying pig utterly disproves most people's theories of porcine locomotion. Similarly, in psychology it often doesn't matter if *everyone* does something as long as *someone* does it. If playing a violent video game for 1 hour caused a nonrandomly selected group of children to start shoving in the lunch line, then this fact would utterly disprove every theory that claimed that video games cannot cause aggression—and it might even provide important clues about when aggression will and won't occur. An experimental result can be illuminating even when its generality is severely limited.

■ Sometimes generality can be determined. When the generality of an experimental result *is* important, psychologists often perform a new experiment that uses the same procedures on a different sample. For example, if we were to measure how some American children behaved after playing Blood Sport for 2 hours, we could then replicate the experiment with Japanese children, or with teenagers, or with adults. In essence, we could treat the attributes of our sample, such as culture and age, as independent variables and do experiments to determine whether these attributes influenced our dependent variable. If the results of our study were replicated in numerous nonrandom samples, we could be more confident (though never completely confident) that the results would generalize to the population at large.

■ Sometimes generality can be assumed. Instead of asking, "Is there a compelling reason to generalize from a nonrandom sample?" we might just as easily ask, "Is there a compelling reason not to?" For example, few of us would be willing to take an experimental drug that could potentially make us smarter and happier if a nonrandom sample of seven participants took the drug and died a slow, painful death. Indeed, we would probably refuse the drug even if the seven subjects were mice. Although the study used a nonrandom sample of participants who are different from us in many ways, we are willing to generalize from their experience to ours because we know that even mice share enough of our basic biology to make it a good bet that what harms them can harm us too. By this same reasoning, if a psychology experiment demonstrated that some American children behaved violently after playing Blood Sport for 1 hour, we might ask whether there is a compelling reason to suspect that Ecuadorian college students or middle-aged Australians would behave any differently. If we had a reason to suspect they would, then the experimental method would provide a way for us to investigate that possibility.

In summary, to determine whether two variables are causally related, we must first determine whether they are related at all. This can be done by measuring each variable many times and then comparing the patterns of variation within each series of measurements. If the patterns covary, then the variables are correlated. Correlations allow us to predict the value of one variable from knowledge of the value of the other. The direction and strength of a correlation are measured by the correlation coefficient (r).

Even when we observe a correlation between two variables, we can't conclude that they are causally related because there are an infinite number of "third variables" that might be causing them both. Experiments solve this third-variable problem by manipulating an independent variable, randomly assigning participants to the experimental and control groups that this manipulation creates, and measuring a dependent variable. These measurements are then compared across groups. If inferential statistics show that there was less than a 5% chance that random assignment failed, then differences in the measurements across groups are assumed to have been caused by the manipulation.

An internally valid experiment establishes a causal relationship between variables as they were operationally defined and among the participants whom they included. When an experiment mimics the real world—that is, when it is externally valid and when its participants are randomly sampled—we may generalize from its results. But most psychology experiments are not attempts to mimic the real world: They are attempts to test hypotheses and theories. ■ ■

INFORMED CONSENT A written agreement to participate in a study made by a person who has been informed of all the risks that participation may entail.

DEBRIEFING A verbal description of the true nature and purpose of a study that psychologists provide to people after they have participated in the study.

The Ethics of Science:
Saying Please and Thank You

Somewhere along the way, someone probably told you that it isn't nice to treat people like objects. And yet, it may seem that psychologists do just that—creating situations that cause people to feel fearful or sad, to do things that are embarrassing or immoral, and to learn things about themselves that they might not really want to know. Why do psychologists treat people so shabbily? In fact, psychologists go to great lengths to ensure the safety and well-being of their research participants, and they are bound by a code of ethics that is as detailed and demanding as the professional codes that bind physicians, lawyers, and members of the clergy. This code of ethics was formalized by the American Psychological Association in 1958 and offers a number of rules that govern all research conducted with human beings. Here are a few of the most important ones:

■ *Informed consent:* Participants may not take part in a psychological study unless they have given **informed consent,** which is *a written agreement to participate in a study made by an adult who has been informed of all the risks that participation may entail.* This doesn't mean that the person must know everything about the study (the hypothesis), but it does mean that the person must know about anything that might potentially be harmful, painful, embarrassing, or unpleasant. If people cannot give informed consent (perhaps because they are minors or are mentally incapable), then informed consent must be obtained from their legal guardians.

■ *Freedom from coercion:* Psychologists may not coerce participation. Coercion not only means physical and psychological coercion but monetary coercion as well. It is unethical to offer people large amounts of money to persuade them to do something that they might otherwise decline to do. College students may be invited to participate in studies as part of their training in psychology, but they are ordinarily offered the option of learning the same things by other means.

■ *Protection from harm:* Psychologists must take every possible precaution to protect their research participants from physical or psychological harm. If there are two equally effective ways to study something, the psychologist must use the safer method. If no safe method is available, the psychologist may not perform the study.

■ *Risk-benefit analysis:* Although participants may be asked to accept small risks, such as a minor shock or a small embarrassment, they may not even be *asked* to accept large risks, such as severe pain or psychological trauma. Indeed, participants may not be asked to take risks that are greater than those they would ordinarily take in their everyday lives. Furthermore, even when participants are asked to take small risks, the psychologist must first demonstrate that these risks are outweighed by the social benefits of the new knowledge that might be gained from the study.

■ *Debriefing:* Although psychologists need not divulge everything about a study before a person participates, they must divulge it after the person participates. If a participant is deceived in any way before or during a study, the psychologist must provide a **debriefing,** which is *a verbal description of the true nature and purpose of a study.* If the participant was changed in any way (e.g., made to feel sad), the psychologist must attempt to undo that change (e.g., ask the person to do a task that will make them happy) and restore the participant to the state he or she was in before the study.

These rules require that psychologists show extraordinary concern for their participants' welfare, but how are they enforced? Almost all psychology studies are done by psychologists who work at colleges and universities. These institutions have institutional review boards (IRBs) that are composed of instructors and researchers, university staff, and laypeople from the community (e.g., business leaders or members of the clergy). A psychologist may conduct a study only after the IRB has reviewed and approved it. As you can imagine, the code of ethics and the procedure for approval are so strict that many studies simply cannot be performed anywhere, by anyone, at any

"I don't usually volunteer for experiments, but I'm kind of a puzzle freak."

time. For example, psychologists have long wondered how growing up without exposure to language affects a person's subsequent ability to speak and think, but they cannot ethically manipulate such a variable in an experiment. As such, they must be content to study the natural correlations between variables such as language exposure and speaking ability, and they must forever forgo the possibility of firmly establishing causal relationships between these variables. There are many questions that psychologists will never be able to answer definitively because doing so would require unethical experimentation. This is an unavoidable consequence of studying creatures who have fundamental human rights.

Of course, not all research participants have human rights because not all research participants are human. Some are chimpanzees, rats, pigeons, or other nonhuman animals. How does the ethical code of the psychologist apply to nonhuman participants? The question of "animal rights" is one of the most hotly debated issues of our time, and people on opposite sides of the debate rarely have much good to say about each other. And yet, consider three points on which every reasonable person would agree:

- A very small percentage of psychological experiments are performed on nonhuman animals, and a very small percentage of these experiments cause discomfort or death.
- Nonhuman animals deserve good care, should never be subjected to more discomfort than is absolutely necessary, and should be protected by federal and institutional guidelines.
- Some experiments on nonhuman animals have had tremendous benefits for human beings, and many have not.

None of these points is in dispute among thoughtful advocates of different positions, so what exactly is the controversy? The controversy lies in the answer to a single question: Is it morally acceptable to force nonhuman animals to pay certain costs so that human animals can reap uncertain benefits? Most people eat animals, which is to say that most people believe it is morally acceptable to profit at the expense of a nonhuman animal. A small but significant minority of people disagree. Although there are compelling arguments to be made on both sides of this moral dilemma, it is clearly just that—a *moral* dilemma and not a scientific controversy that one can hope to answer with evidence and facts. Anyone who has ever loved a pet can empathize with the plight of the nonhuman animal that is being forced to participate in an experiment, feel pain, or even die when it would clearly prefer not to. Anyone who has ever loved a person with a debilitating illness can understand the desire of researchers to develop drugs and medical procedures by doing to nonhuman animals the same things that farmers and animal trainers do every day. Do animals have rights, and if so, do they ever outweigh the rights of people? This is a difficult question with which individuals and societies are currently wrestling. For now, at least, there is no easy answer.

 ONLY HUMAN

THE WELL-BEING OF PARTICIPANTS ALWAYS COMES FIRST! In 1997 in Mill Valley, California, 10th-grade student Ari Hoffman won first place in the Marin County science fair for doing a study that found that exposure to radiation decreased the offspring of fruit flies. However, he was quickly disqualified for cruelty when it was learned that about 35 of his 200 flies died during the 3-month experiment. Hoffman was disappointed because he had used extraordinary efforts to keep the flies alive, for example, by maintaining a tropical temperature for his flies during the entire experiment.

PAUL McERLANE/REUTERS/CORBIS

Some people consider it unethical to use animals for clothing or research. Others see an important distinction between these two purposes.

In summary, psychologists are acutely aware of the responsibilities that come with conducting research with human and nonhuman animals. Care and consideration are taken to make sure that human research participants give their informed and voluntary consent to participate in studies that pose minimal or no risk. Similar principles guide the humane treatment of nonhuman research subjects. Enforcement of these principles by federal, institutional, and professional governing agencies ensures that the research process is a meaningful one that can lead to significant increases in knowledge. ■ ■

Where Do You Stand?

The Morality of Immoral Experiments

Is it wrong to benefit from someone else's wrongdoing? Although this may seem like an abstract question for moral philosophers, it is a very real question that scientists must ask when they consider the results of unethical experiments. During World War II, Nazi doctors conducted barbaric medical studies on prisoners in concentration camps. They placed prisoners in decompression chambers and then dissected their living brains in order to determine how altitude affects pilots. They irradiated and chemically mutilated the reproductive organs of men and women in order to find inexpensive methods for the mass sterilization of "racially inferior" people. They infected prisoners with streptococcus and tetanus in order to devise treatments for soldiers who had been exposed to these bacteria. And in one of the most horrible experiments, prisoners were immersed in tanks of ice water so that the doctors could discover how long pilots would survive if they bailed out over the North Sea. The prisoners were frozen, thawed, and frozen again until they died. During these experiments, the doctors carefully recorded the prisoners' physiological responses.

These experiments were crimes, hideous beyond all imagining. But the records of these experiments remain, and in some cases they provide valuable information that could never be obtained ethically. For example, because researchers cannot perform controlled studies that would expose volunteers to dangerously cold temperatures, there is still controversy among doctors about the best treatment for hypothermia. In 1988, Dr. Robert Pozos, a physiologist at the University of Minnesota Medical School, who had spent a lifetime studying hypothermia, came across an unpublished report written in 1945 titled "The Treatment of Shock from Prolonged Exposure to Cold, Especially in Water." The report described the results of the horrible freezing experiments performed on prisoners at the Dachau concentration camp, and it suggested that contrary to the conventional medical wisdom, rapid rewarming (rather than slow rewarming) might be the best way to treat hypothermia.

Should the Nazi medical studies have been published so that modern doctors might more effectively treat hypothermia? Many scientists and ethicists thought they should. "The prevention of a death outweighs the protection of a memory. The victims' dignity was irrevocably lost in vats of freezing liquid forty years ago. Nothing can change that," argued bioethicist Arthur Caplan. Others disagreed. "I don't see how any credence can be given to the work of unethical investigators," wrote Dr. Arnold Relman, editor of the *New England Journal of Medicine*. "It goes to legitimizing the evil done," added Abraham Foxman, national director of the Anti-Defamation League (Siegel, 1988). The debate about this issue rages on (Caplan, 1992). If we use data that were obtained unethically, are we rewarding those who collected it and legitimizing their actions? Or can we condemn such investigations but still learn from them? Where do you stand?

Chapter Review

Empiricism: How to Know Things

- Empiricism involves using observation to gain knowledge about the world.
- Because casual observation is prone to error, sciences have methods for observation. These methods are unusually sophisticated in psychology because people are unusually complex, variable, and reactive.

The Science of Observation: Saying What

- Observation begins with measurement. Researchers generate operational definitions of the properties they wish to measure and develop measures to detect the conditions that those definitions specify.
- Measures must be valid, reliable, and powerful. Validity refers to the relationship between the operational definition

and the property (construct validity) and between the operational definition and other operational definitions (predictive validity). Reliability refers to the consistency of a measure, and power refers to the measure's ability to detect differences that do exist and not to detect differences that don't exist.

- Although interesting individuals provide useful information, most measurement is performed on large samples of participants. Larger samples better reflect the characteristics of the population.

- Measurements taken from a sample can be depicted in a frequency distribution, which can be described by various descriptive statistics such as the mean, median, mode, and range.

- Researchers use cover stories and filler items to avoid creating demand characteristics that influence the behavior of participants. They also use double-blind procedures so that the experimenter's expectations do not influence the participant's behavior or the measurement thereof.

The Science of Explanation: Saying Why

- Psychologists are interested in observing and explaining relationships between variables.

- Correlation refers to a relationship signified by synchronization in the patterns of variation of two variables. The correlation coefficient (r) is a statistic that describes both the strength and direction of that relationship.

- Two variables can be correlated for any one of three reasons: $X \rightarrow Y$, $Y \rightarrow X$, or $Z \rightarrow X$ and Y.

- Experimentation can determine for which of these three reasons a pair of variables is correlated. It involves the manipulation of an independent variable (which results in an experimental group and a control group) and the measurement of a dependent variable. It requires that participants be randomly assigned to groups.

- Experiments allow one to conclude that changes in an independent variable caused changes in a dependent variable if (a) inferential statistics show that random assignment was unlikely to have failed and (b) the experiment is internally valid.

- Because psychologists rarely sample their participants randomly, most psychology experiments lack external validity. This is rarely a problem because experiments are meant to test theories and not to mimic real-world events.

The Ethics of Science: Saying Please and Thank You

- Psychologists adhere to a strict code of ethics. People must give their informed consent to participate in any study, they must do so free of coercion, they must be protected from physical and psychological harm, the benefits of the research must outweigh the risks, and participants must be debriefed at the conclusion of the research.

- Institutional review boards must approve all research before it is conducted.

- The treatment of animals is governed by strict rules developed by professional organizations, governmental bodies, and university committees.

Key Terms

empiricism (p. 40)
method (p. 40)
operational definition (p. 41)
measure (p. 42)
electromyograph (EMG) (p. 42)
validity (p. 43)
construct validity (p. 43)
predictive validity (p. 43)
reliability (p. 44)
power (p. 44)
case method (p. 44)
population (p. 45)

sample (p. 45)
law of large numbers (p. 45)
frequency distribution (p. 46)
normal distribution (p. 47)
mode (p. 47)
mean (p. 47)
median (p. 47)
range (p. 47)
demand characteristics (p. 49)
naturalistic observation (p. 49)
double blind (p. 51)

variable (p. 53)
correlation (p. 53)
correlation coefficient (p. 54)
natural correlation (p. 56)
third-variable correlation (p. 57)
matched samples (p. 57)
matched pairs (p. 57)
third-variable problem (p. 58)
experiment (p. 58)
manipulation (p. 59)
independent variable (p. 60)

experimental group (p. 60)
control group (p. 60)
dependent variable (p. 60)
self-selection (p. 61)
randomization (p. 61)
internal validity (p. 64)
external validity (p. 65)
theory (p. 65)
hypothesis (p. 65)
random sampling (p. 66)
informed consent (p. 68)
debriefing (p. 68)

Recommended Readings

Bennett, D. J. (1998). *Randomness*. Cambridge: Harvard University Press. A mathematician discusses probability theory and games of chance.

Miller, A. J. (1986). *The obedience experiments: A case study of controversy in social science*. New York: Praeger. An examination of the most controversial psychology experiment ever conducted: Stanley Milgram's study of obedience.

Pelham, B. W., & Blanton, H. (2003). *Conducting research in psychology: Measuring the weight of smoke* (2nd ed.). Pacific Grove, CA: Thomson Wadsworth. A concise, scholarly, and entertaining look at the process of doing psychological research.

Sobel, D. (1995). *Longitude: The true story of a lone genius who solved the greatest scientific problem of his time*. New York: Walker. In the 18th century, thousands of people died at sea because no one knew how to measure longitude. This is the story of the man who solved the problem that stumped geniuses from Newton to Galileo.

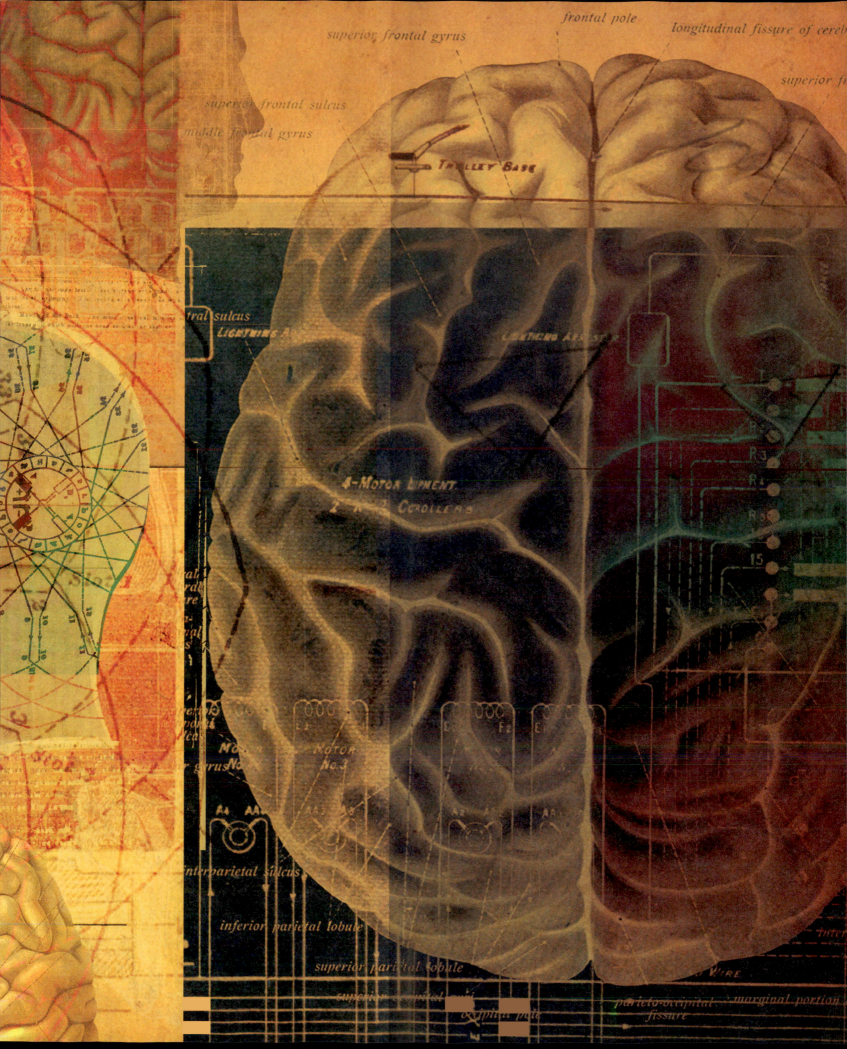

3

Neuroscience and Behavior

Neurons: The Origin of Behavior
Components of the Neuron
Major Types of Neurons
HOT SCIENCE Mirror, Mirror, in My Brain

Electric Signaling: Communicating Information within a Neuron
The Resting Potential: The Origin of the Neuron's Electrical Properties
The Action Potential: Sending Signals over Long Distances

Chemical Signaling: Synaptic Transmission between Neurons
Types of Neurotransmitters
How Drugs Mimic Neurotransmitters

The Organization of the Nervous System
Divisions of the Nervous System
Components of the Central Nervous System
Exploring the Brain
HOT SCIENCE Thought Control
THE REAL WORLD Brain Plasticity and Sensations in Phantom Limbs

The Development and Evolution of Nervous Systems
Prenatal Development of the Central Nervous System
Evolutionary Development of the Central Nervous System
Genes and the Environment

Investigating the Brain
Learning about Brain Organization by Studying the Damaged Brain
Listening to the Brain: Single Neurons and the EEG
Brain Imaging: Watching the Brain in Action
WHERE DO YOU STAND? Brain Death

TWO PATIENTS WERE ADMITTED TO A hospital emergency room late one evening, complaining of problems with their vision. One patient was a 17-year-old named David, and the other was a 75-year-old named Betty. David saw people who weren't there and Betty didn't recognize her own husband, but these weren't problems with their eyes: They were disorders of their brains.

David was brought in by some fellow members of his gang. They told the doctors that David was usually cool and composed, but he had become frantic, believing he kept seeing members of a rival gang sneaking up on him. At first David's friends listened to his warnings and searched for their rivals. After repeated scares and false alarms, they decided David was seeing shadows and thinking they were enemies. The persistence of these phantom sightings worried David—he thought something was wrong with his vision. His friends thought he had gone crazy.

The doctors didn't find any problems with David's eyes. Instead, they discovered he was suffering from hallucinations—a side effect of abusing methamphetamine (McKetin et al., 2006). David's prolonged crystal meth habit altered the normal functioning of some chemicals in his brain, distorting his perception of reality and "fooling" his brain into perceiving things that were not actually there. After he stopped taking the drug, the hallucinations disappeared and David was back to his normal calm self.

The second patient, Betty, had fainted earlier in the day. After she was revived, Betty no longer recognized her husband, George. Disturbed by this, George called their adult sons, who immediately came over to their house. She didn't recognize her two sons either, but otherwise Betty seemed normal. She insisted it was just a problem with her eyes and had the family bring her to the emergency room for examination.

The doctor who examined Betty's eyes found her vision to be perfectly normal. She could recognize colors and identify common objects, even at a distance. Nonetheless, she was unable to recognize her closest family members or to identify her doctor, whom she had known for 30 years. A brain scan showed that Betty had suffered a stroke that damaged a small area on the right side of her brain. Doctors diagnosed Betty with a rare disorder called *prosopagnosia*, which is an inability to recognize familiar faces (Duchaine et al., 2006; Yin, 1970)—a result of the brain damage caused by her stroke.

David and Betty both complained of problems with their vision, but their symptoms were actually caused by disorders in the brain. David's problem resulted from a malfunction in the brain's system for passing chemical messages between cells. Betty's problem resulted from damage to an area of the brain that integrates and interprets visual information. Our ability to perceive the world around us and recognize familiar people depends not only on information we take in through our senses but, perhaps more importantly, on the interpretation of this information performed by the brain.

NEURONS Cells in the nervous system that communicate with one another to perform information-processing tasks.

CELL BODY The part of a neuron that coordinates information-processing tasks and keeps the cell alive.

DENDRITES The part of a neuron that receives information from other neurons and relays it to the cell body.

AXON The part of a neuron that transmits information to other neurons, muscles, or glands.

In this chapter, we'll consider how the brain works, what happens when it doesn't, and how both states of affairs determine behavior. First we'll introduce you to the basic unit of information processing in the brain, the neuron. The electrical and chemical activities of neurons are the starting point of all behavior, thought, and emotion. Next we'll consider the anatomy of the brain, including its overall organization, key structures that perform different functions, and the brain's evolutionary development. Finally, we'll discuss methods that allow us to study the brain and clarify our understanding of how it works. These include methods that examine the damaged brain and methods for scanning the living and healthy brain.

Neurons: The Origin of Behavior

An estimated 1 billion people watched the final game of the 2006 World Cup. That's a whole lot of people, but to put it in perspective, it's still only 16% of the estimated 6.5 billion people currently living on Earth. A more impressive number might be the 30 billion viewers who tuned in to watch any of the World Cup action over the course of the tournament. But a really, really big number is inside your skull right now, helping you make sense of these big numbers you're reading about. There are approximately *100 billion* cells in your brain that perform a variety of tasks to allow you to function as a human being.

Humans have thoughts, feelings, and behaviors that are often accompanied by visible signals. For example, anticipating seeing a friend waiting up the block for you in the movie ticket line may elicit a range of behaviors. An observer might see a smile on your face or notice how fast you are walking; internally, you might mentally rehearse what you'll say to your friend and feel a surge of happiness as you approach her. But all those visible and experiential signs are produced by an underlying invisible physical component coordinated by the activity of your brain cells. The anticipation you have, the happiness you feel, and the speed of your feet are the result of information processing in your brain. In a way, all of your thoughts, feelings, and behaviors spring from cells in the brain that take in information and produce some kind of output.

The 100 billion cells that perform this function trillions of times a day are called neurons. **Neurons** are *cells in the nervous system that communicate with one another to perform information-processing tasks.* In this section, we'll look at how neurons were discovered, what their components are, and how they are specialized for different types of information processing.

During the 1800s, scientists began to turn their attention from studying the mechanics of limbs, lungs, and livers to studying the harder-to-observe workings of the brain. Philosophers wrote poetically about an "enchanted loom" that mysteriously wove a tapestry of behavior, and many scientists confirmed the metaphor (Corsi, 1991). To these scientists, the brain looked as though it were composed of a continuously connected lattice of fine threads, leading to the conclusion that it was one big woven web of material. However, in the late 1880s, a Spanish physician named Santiago Ramón y Cajal (1852–1934) tried a new technique for staining neurons in the brain (DeFelipe & Jones, 1988). The stain highlighted the appearance of entire cells, revealing that they came in different shapes and sizes (see **FIGURE 3.1**). Using this

Santiago Ramón y Cajal (1852–1934) discovered the structure of neurons by using a staining technique that allowed a clear view of the cells. He was awarded the Nobel Prize in Physiology in 1906.

SCIENCE SOURCE/PHOTO RESEARCHERS

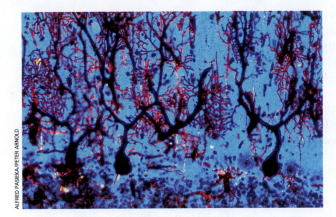

Figure 3.1 **Golgi-Stained Neurons** Santiago Ramón y Cajal used a Golgi stain to highlight the appearance of neurons. These are Purkinje cells from the cerebellum, known for the elaborate branching of their dendrites.

ALFRED PASIEKA/PETER ARNOLD

technique, Cajal was the first to see that each neuron was composed of a body with many threads extending outward toward other neurons. Surprisingly, he also saw that the threads of each neuron did not actually touch other neurons. Cajal believed that neurons are the information-processing units of the brain and that even though he saw gaps between neurons, they had to communicate in some way (Rapport, 2005).

Components of the Neuron

Cajal discovered that neurons are complex structures composed of three basic parts: the cell body, the dendrites, and the axon (see **FIGURE 3.2**). Like cells in all organs of the body, neurons have a **cell body** (also called the *soma*), the largest component of the neuron that *coordinates the information-processing tasks and keeps the cell alive*. Functions such as protein synthesis, energy production, and metabolism take place here. The cell body contains a *nucleus*; this structure houses chromosomes that contain your DNA, or the genetic blueprint of who you are. The cell body is surrounded by a porous cell membrane that allows molecules to flow into and out of the cell.

Unlike other cells in the body, neurons have two types of specialized extensions of the cell membrane that allow them to communicate: dendrites and axons. **Dendrites** *receive information from other neurons and relay it to the cell body*. The term *dendrite* comes from the Greek word for "tree"; indeed, most neurons have many dendrites that look like tree branches.

The **axon** *transmits information to other neurons, muscles, or glands*. Each neuron has a single axon that sometimes can be very long, even stretching up to a meter from the base of the spinal cord down to the big toe.

Figure 3.2 **Components of a Neuron** A neuron is made up of three parts: a cell body that houses the chromosomes with the organism's DNA and maintains the health of the cell, dendrites that receive information from other neurons, and an axon that transmits information to other neurons, muscles, and glands.

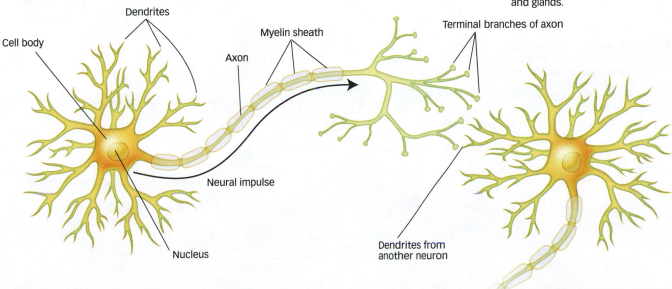

Dendrites

Cell body

Myelin sheath

Axon

Terminal branches of axon

Neural impulse

Nucleus

Dendrites from another neuron

MYELIN SHEATH An insulating layer of fatty material.

GLIAL CELLS Support cells found in the nervous system.

SYNAPSE The junction or region between the axon of one neuron and the dendrites or cell body of another.

In many neurons, the axon is covered by a **myelin sheath**, *an insulating layer of fatty material*. The myelin sheath is composed of **glial cells**, which are *support cells found in the nervous system*. Although there are 100 billion neurons busily processing information in your brain, there are 10 to 50 times that many glial cells serving a variety of functions. Some glial cells digest parts of dead neurons, others provide physical and nutritional support for neurons, and others form myelin to help the axon transmit information more efficiently. Imagine for a minute the pipes coming from the water heater in the basement, leading upstairs to heat a house. When those pipes are wrapped in insulation, they usually perform their task more efficiently: The water inside stays hotter, the heater works more effectively, and so on. Myelin performs this same function for an axon: An axon insulated with myelin can more efficiently transmit signals to other neurons, organs, or muscles.

In fact, in *demyelinating diseases*, such as multiple sclerosis, the myelin sheath deteriorates, causing a slowdown in the transmission of information from one neuron to another (Schwartz & Westbrook, 2000). This leads to a variety of problems, including loss of feeling in the limbs, partial blindness, and difficulties in coordinated movement. In multiple sclerosis there are often cycles of myelin loss and subsequent recovery.

As you'll remember, Cajal observed that the dendrites and axons of neurons do not actually touch each other. There's a small gap between the axon of one neuron and the dendrites or cell body of another. This gap is part of the **synapse**: *the junction or region between the axon of one neuron and the dendrites or cell body of another* (see **FIGURE 3.3**). Many of the 100 billion neurons in your brain have a few thousand synaptic junctions, so it should come as no shock that most adults have between 100 trillion and 500 trillion synapses. As you'll read shortly, the transmission of information across the synapse is fundamental to communication between neurons, a process that allows us to think, feel, and behave.

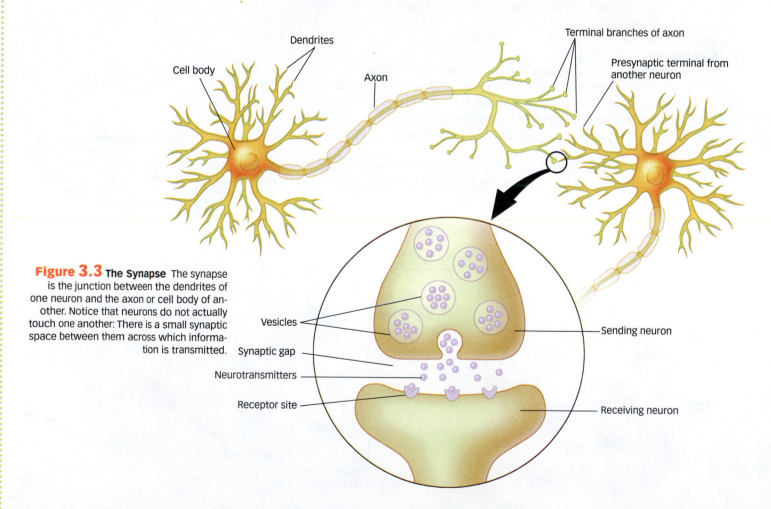

Figure 3.3 **The Synapse** The synapse is the junction between the dendrites of one neuron and the axon or cell body of another. Notice that neurons do not actually touch one another: There is a small synaptic space between them across which information is transmitted.

Major Types of Neurons

There are three major types of neurons, each performing a distinct function: sensory neurons, motor neurons, and interneurons. **Sensory neurons** *receive information from the external world and convey this information to the brain via the spinal cord*. Sensory neurons have specialized endings on their dendrites that receive signals for light, sound, touch, taste, and smell. For example, in our eyes, sensory neurons' endings are sensitive to light. **Motor neurons** *carry signals from the spinal cord to the muscles to produce movement*. These neurons often have long axons that can stretch to muscles at our extremities. However, most of the nervous system is composed of the third type of neuron, **interneurons**, which *connect sensory neurons, motor neurons, or other interneurons*. Some interneurons carry information from sensory neurons into the nervous system, others carry information from the nervous system to motor neurons, and still others perform a variety of information-processing functions within the nervous system. Interneurons work together in small circuits to perform simple tasks, such as identifying the location of a sensory signal, and much more complicated ones, such as recognizing a familiar face. (See the Hot Science box on the next page for a discussion of a sophisticated type of neuron discovered only recently.)

Besides specialization for sensory, motor, or connective functions, neurons are also somewhat specialized depending on their location (see **FIGURE 3.4**). For example, *Purkinje cells* are a type of interneuron that carries information from the cerebellum to the rest of the brain and spinal cord. These neurons have dense, elaborate dendrites

SENSORY NEURONS Neurons that receive information from the external world and convey this information to the brain via the spinal cord.

MOTOR NEURONS Neurons that carry signals from the spinal cord to the muscles to produce movement.

INTERNEURONS Neurons that connect sensory neurons, motor neurons, or other interneurons.

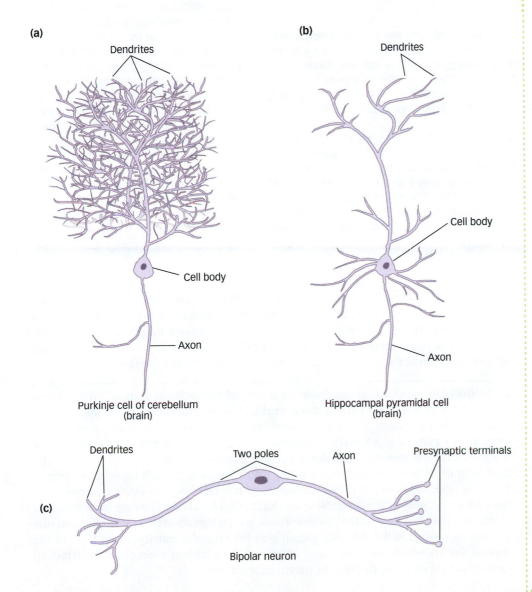

Figure 3.4 Types of Neurons Neurons have a cell body, an axon, and at least one dendrite. The size and shape of neurons vary considerably, however. (a) The Purkinje cell has an elaborate treelike assemblage of dendrites. (b) Pyramidal cells have a triangular cell body and a single, long dendrite with many smaller dendrites. (c) Bipolar cells have only one dendrite and a single axon.

{ HOT SCIENCE } Mirror, Mirror, in My Brain

YOU'VE NO DOUBT HEARD THE EXPRESSION, "Monkey see, monkey do." In fact, you may have taunted a sibling or playmate with that line more than once in your life. You probably didn't realize that you were *that close* to making one of the major discoveries in neuroscience when you uttered those prophetic words!

One of the most exciting recent advances in neuroscience is the discovery of the mirror-neuron system. Mirror neurons are found in the frontal lobe (near the motor cortex) and in the parietal lobe (Rizzolatti & Craighero, 2004). They have been identified in birds, monkeys, and humans, and their name reflects the function they serve. Mirror neurons are active when an animal performs a behavior, such as reaching for or manipulating an object. However, mirror neurons are also activated whenever another animal *observes* this animal performing the behavior. In other words, mirror neurons are active both in the animal reaching for the food and in the animal observing this behavior. This kind of mirroring—one monkey sees, one monkey does, but both monkeys' mirror neurons fire—holds intriguing implications for understanding the brain's role in complex social behavior.

A recent study on mirror neurons used fMRI to monitor the brains of humans as they watched each of three presentations (Iacoboni et al., 2005). Sometimes participants saw a hand making grasping motions but without a context; they just saw a hand moving in midair with no "props" or background.

When one animal observes another engaging in a particular behavior, some of the same neurons become active in the observer as well as in the animal exhibiting the behavior. These mirror neurons, documented in monkeys, birds, and humans, seem to play an important role in social behavior.

Sometimes they saw only the context: coffee cups or scrubbing sponges but no hands making motions to go with them. Other times they saw hand motions in two different contexts, either grasping and moving a coffee cup to drink or cleaning dishes with a sponge.

When actions were embedded in a context, such as in the last set of presentations, the participants' mirror neurons responded more strongly than in either of the other two conditions. This suggests that the same set of neurons involved in action recognition are also involved in understanding the intentions of others. Mirror neurons are active when watching someone perform a behavior, such as grasping in midair. But they are more highly activated when that behavior has some purpose or context, such as grasping a cup to take a drink. Recognizing another person's intentions means that the observer has inferred something about that person's goals, wants, or wishes ("Oh, she must be thirsty"). These fMRI results suggest that this kind of recognition occurs effortlessly at a neural level.

Why is this interesting? Admittedly, there is much work to be done to fully understand the function, scope, and purpose of mirror neurons. However, these results suggest a possible inborn neural basis for empathy. Grasping the intentions of another person—indeed, having your brain respond in kind as another person acts—is critical to smooth social interaction. It allows us to understand other people's possible motivations and anticipate their future actions. In fact, these are the kinds of skills that people suffering from autism severely lack. Autism is a developmental disorder characterized by impoverished social interactions and communication skills (Frith, 2001). Psychologists who study autism focus on trying to understand the nature of the disorder and devise ways to help autistic people cope with and function in human society. Research on mirror neurons may offer one avenue for better understanding the origin and prognosis of this disorder (Iacoboni & Dapretto, 2006).

that resemble bushes. *Pyramidal cells*, found in the cerebral cortex, have a triangular cell body and a single long dendrite among many smaller dendrites. *Bipolar cells*, a type of sensory neuron found in the retinas of the eye, have a single axon and a single dendrite. The brain processes different types of information, so a substantial amount of specialization at the cellular level has evolved to handle these tasks.

In summary, neurons are the building blocks of the nervous system. They process information received from the outside world, they communicate with one another, and they send messages to the body's muscles and organs. Neurons are composed of three major parts: the cell body, dendrites, and the axon. The cell body contains the nucleus, which houses the organism's genetic material. Dendrites receive sensory signals from other neurons and transmit this information to the cell body. Each neuron has only one axon, which carries signals from the cell body to other neurons or to muscles and organs in the body. Neurons don't actually touch: They are separated by a small gap, which is part of the synapse across which signals are transmitted from one neuron to another. Glial cells provide support for neurons, usually in the form of the myelin sheath, which coats the axon to facilitate the transmission of information. In demyelinating diseases, the myelin sheath deteriorates.

Neurons are differentiated according to the functions they perform. The three major types of neurons include sensory neurons, motor neurons, and interneurons. Examples of sensory neurons and interneurons are, respectively, bipolar neurons and Purkinje and pyramidal cells. ■ ■

Electric Signaling: Communicating Information within a Neuron

Understanding how neurons process information is key to appreciating how the brain works, that is, how these tiny cells make it possible for us to think, feel, and act. The communication of information within and between neurons proceeds in two stages—*conduction* and *transmission*. The first stage is the conduction of an electric signal over relatively long distances within neurons, from the dendrites, to the cell body, then throughout the axon. The second stage is the transmission of electric signals between neurons over the synapse. Together, these stages are what scientists generally refer to as the *electrochemical action* of neurons.

The Resting Potential: The Origin of the Neuron's Electrical Properties

As you'll recall, the neuron's cell membrane is porous: It allows small electrically charged molecules, called *ions,* to flow in and out of the cell. If you imagine using a strainer while you're preparing spaghetti, you'll get the idea. The mesh of the strainer cradles your yummy dinner, but water can still seep in and out of it. Just as the flow of water out of a strainer enhances the quality of pasta, the flow of molecules across a cell membrane enhances the transmission of information in the nervous system.

Neurons have a natural electric charge called the **resting potential**, which is *the difference in electric charge between the inside and outside of a neuron's cell membrane* (Kandel, 2000). The resting potential is similar to the difference between the "+" and "−" poles of a battery. Biologists discovered the resting potential in the 1930s while studying marine invertebrates—sea creatures that lack a spine, such as clams, squid, and lobsters (Stevens, 1971). They found that large squids have giant axons that connect the brain to muscles in the tail. These axons have a very large diameter, about 100 times bigger than the largest axons in humans, making it easier to explore their electrical properties. In the summer of 1939, British biologists Alan Hodgkin and Andrew Huxley inserted a thin wire into the squid axon so that it touched the jellylike fluid inside. Then they placed another wire just outside the axon in the watery fluid that surrounds it. They found a substantial difference between the electric charges inside and outside the axon, which they called the resting potential. They measured the resting potential at about −70 millivolts, or roughly 1/200 of the charge of an AA battery.

The resting potential arises from the difference in concentrations of ions inside and outside the neuron's cell membrane. Ions can carry a positive (+) or a negative (−) charge. In the resting state, there is a high concentration of a positively charged ion, potassium (K^+), inside the neuron, compared to the relatively low concentration of K^+ outside the neuron. Raising the concentration of K^+ in the fluid outside the neuron to match the concentration of K^+ inside the neuron causes the resting potential to disappear. This simple test confirms that differences in K^+ concentration are the basis of the resting potential (Dowling, 1992).

The concentration of K^+ inside and outside an axon is controlled by channels in the axon membrane that allow molecules to flow in and out of the neuron. In the resting state, the channels that allow K^+ molecules to flow freely across the cell membrane are open, while channels that allow the flow of other molecules are generally closed. There is a naturally higher concentration of K^+ molecules *inside* the neuron, so some K^+ molecules move out of the neuron through the open channels, leaving the inside of the neuron with a charge of about −70 millivolts relative to the outside (see **FIGURE 3.5** on the next page).

RESTING POTENTIAL The difference in electric charge between the inside and outside of a neuron's cell membrane.

Biologists Alan Hodgkin and Andrew Huxley worked with the giant squid's axon because it is 100 times larger than the biggest axon in humans and discovered the neuron's resting potential.

AP PHOTO/EFE

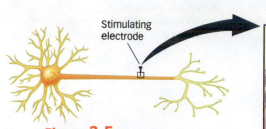

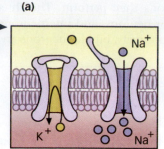 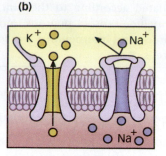 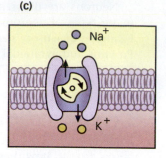

(a)   (b)   (c)

Figure 3.5 **The Action Potential**
(a) Electric stimulation of the neuron shuts down the K⁺ channels and opens the Na⁺ channels, allowing Na⁺ to enter the axon. The increase of Na⁺ inside the neuron results in an action potential. (b) In the refractory period after the action potential, the channels return to their original state, allowing K⁺ to flow out of the axon. This leaves an abundance of K⁺ outside and Na⁺ inside the cell. (c) A chemical pump then reverses the ion balance of ions by moving Na⁺ out of the axon and K⁺ into the axon. The neuron can now generate another action potential.

As an example of this process, imagine a field trip to the zoo. Many zoos have turnstiles that allow only one person at a time to enter. The most eager children rush through the turnstiles to see the lions and tigers and bears, while parents hover outside, deciding where to meet later and who's got the sunscreen. With many children on one side of the turnstile, a greater concentration of parents is left on the opposite side. This is like the many small K⁺ ions that move outside the neuron, leaving some large negatively charged molecules inside the neuron, which produces a resting potential across the cell membrane.

The Action Potential: Sending Signals over Long Distances

The neuron maintains its resting potential most of the time. However, the biologists working with the squid's giant axon noticed that they could produce a signal by stimulating the axon with a brief electric shock, which resulted in the conduction of a large electric impulse down the length of the axon (Hausser, 2000; Hodgkin & Huxley, 1939). This electric impulse is called an **action potential**, which is *an electric signal that is conducted along the length of a neuron's axon to the synapse* (see Figure 3.5). The action potential occurs only when the electric shock reaches a certain level, or *threshold*. When the shock was below this threshold, the researchers recorded only tiny signals, which dissipated rapidly. When the shock reached the threshold, a much larger signal, the action potential, was observed. Interestingly, increases in the electric shock above the threshold did *not* increase the strength of the action potential. The action potential is *all or none*: Electric stimulation below the threshold fails to produce an action potential, whereas electric stimulation at or above the threshold always produces the action potential. The action potential always occurs with exactly the same characteristics and at the same magnitude regardless of whether when the stimulus is at or above the threshold.

The biologists working with the giant squid axon observed another surprising property of the action potential: They measured it at a charge of about +40 millivolts, which is well above zero. This suggests that the mechanism driving the action potential could not simply be the loss of the –70 millivolt resting potential because this would have only brought the charge back to zero. So why does the action potential reach a value above zero?

The action potential occurs when there is a change in the state of the axon's membrane channels. Remember, during the resting potential, only the K⁺ channels are open. However, when an electric charge is raised to the threshold value, the K⁺ channels briefly shut down, and other channels that allow the flow of a *positively* charged ion, sodium (Na⁺), are opened. Na⁺ is typically much more concentrated outside the axon than inside. When the Na⁺ channels open, those positively charged ions flow inside, increasing the positive charge inside the axon relative to that outside. This flow of Na⁺ into the axon pushes the action potential to its maximum value of +40 millivolts.

After the action potential reaches its maximum, the membrane channels return to their original state, and K⁺ flows out until the axon returns to its resting potential. This leaves a lot of extra Na⁺ ions inside the axon and a lot of extra K⁺ ions outside the

ACTION POTENTIAL An electric signal that is conducted along an axon to a synapse.

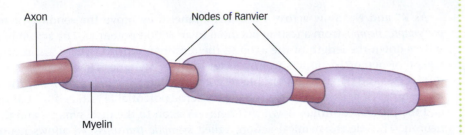

Axon   **Nodes of Ranvier**

Myelin

axon. During this period where the ions are imbalanced, the neuron cannot initiate another action potential, so it is said to be in a **refractory period**, *the time following an action potential during which a new action potential cannot be initiated*. The imbalance in ions eventually is reversed by an active chemical "pump" in the cell membrane that moves Na^+ outside the axon and moves K^+ inside the axon.

Earlier, we describe how the action potential occurs at one point in the neuron. But how does this electric charge move down the axon? When an action potential is generated at the beginning of the axon, it spreads a short distance, which generates an action potential at a nearby location on the axon (see Figure 3.5). That action potential also spreads, initiating an action potential at another nearby location, and so on, thus transmitting the charge down the length of the axon. This simple mechanism ensures that the action potential travels the full length of the axon and that it achieves its full intensity at each step, regardless of the distance traveled.

The myelin sheath, which is made up of glial cells that coat and insulate the axon, facilitates the transmission of the action potential. Myelin doesn't cover the entire axon; rather, it clumps around the axon with little break points between clumps, looking kind of like sausage links. These breakpoints are called the *nodes of Ranvier*, after French pathologist Louis-Antoine Ranvier, who discovered them (see **FIGURE 3.6**). When an electric current passes down the length of a myelinated axon, the charge "jumps" from node to node rather than having to traverse the entire axon. This jumping is called *saltatory conduction*, and it helps speed the flow of information down the axon.

In summary, the neuron's resting potential is due to differences in the K^+ concentrations inside and outside the cell membrane. If electric signals reach a threshold, this initiates an action potential, an all-or-none signal that moves down the entire length of the axon. The action potential occurs when sodium channels in the axon membrane open and potassium channels close, allowing the Na^+ ions to flow inside the axon. After the action potential has reached its maximum, the sodium channels close and the potassium channels open, allowing K^+ to flow out of the axon, returning the neuron to its resting potential. For a brief refractory period, the action potential cannot be re-initiated. Once it is initiated, the action potential spreads down the axon, jumping across the nodes of Ranvier to the synapse. ■ ■

Chemical Signaling: Synaptic Transmission between Neurons

When the action potential reaches the end of an axon, you might think that it stops there. After all, the synaptic space between neurons means that the axon of one neuron and the neighboring neuron's dendrites do not actually touch one another. However, the electric charge of the action potential takes a form that can cross the relatively small synaptic gap by relying on a bit of chemistry. We'll look at that process of information transmission between neurons in this section.

Axons usually end in **terminal buttons**, which are *knoblike structures that branch out from an axon*. A terminal button is filled with tiny *vesicles*, or "bags," that contain **neurotransmitters**, *chemicals that transmit information across the synapse to a receiving neuron's dendrites*. The dendrites of the receiving neuron contain **receptors**, *parts of the cell membrane that receive neurotransmitters and initiate a new electric signal*.

REFRACTORY PERIOD The time following an action potential during which a new action potential cannot be initiated.

TERMINAL BUTTONS Knoblike structures that branch out from an axon.

NEUROTRANSMITTERS Chemicals that transmit information across the synapse to a receiving neuron's dendrites.

RECEPTORS Parts of the cell membrane that receive the neurotransmitter and initiate a new electric signal.

As K$^+$ and Na$^+$ flow across a cell membrane, they move the sending neuron, or *presynaptic neuron*, from a resting potential to an action potential. The action potential travels down the length of the axon to the terminal buttons, where it stimulates the release of neurotransmitters from vesicles into the synapse. These neurotransmitters float across the synapse and bind to receptor sites on a nearby dendrite of the receiving neuron, or *postsynaptic neuron*. A new electric potential is initiated in that neuron, and the process continues down that neuron's axon to the next synapse and the next neuron. This electrochemical action, called *synaptic transmission*, allows neurons to communicate with one another and ultimately underlies your thoughts, emotions, and behavior (see **FIGURE 3.7**).

Now that you understand the basic process of how information moves from one neuron to another, let's refine things a bit. You'll recall that a given neuron may make a few thousand synaptic connections with other neurons, so how would the dendrites know which of the neurotransmitters flooding into the synapse to receive and which to ignore? One answer is that neurons tend to form pathways in the brain that are characterized by specific types of neurotransmitters; one neurotransmitter might be prevalent in one part of the brain, whereas a different neurotransmitter might be prevalent in a different part of the brain.

A second answer is that neurotransmitters and receptor sites act like a lock-and-key system. Just as a particular key will only fit in a particular lock, so too will only some neurotransmitters bind to specific receptor sites on a dendrite. The molecular structure of the neurotransmitter must "fit" the molecular structure of the receptor site.

A second reasonable question is what happens to the neurotransmitters left in the synapse after the chemical message is relayed to the postsynaptic neuron. Something must make neurotransmitters stop acting on neurons; otherwise, there'd be no end to the signals that they send. Neurotransmitters leave the synapse through three processes. First, *reuptake* occurs when neurotransmitters are reabsorbed by the terminal buttons of the presynaptic neuron's axon. Second, neurotransmitters can be destroyed by enzymes in the synapse in a process called *enzyme deactivation*; specific enzymes

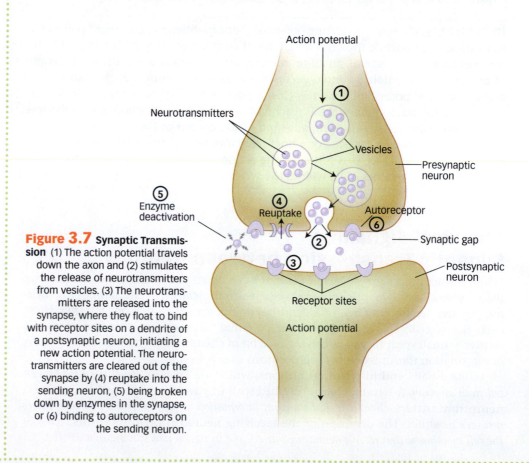

Figure 3.7 Synaptic Transmission (1) The action potential travels down the axon and (2) stimulates the release of neurotransmitters from vesicles. (3) The neurotransmitters are released into the synapse, where they float to bind with receptor sites on a dendrite of a postsynaptic neuron, initiating a new action potential. The neurotransmitters are cleared out of the synapse by (4) reuptake into the sending neuron, (5) being broken down by enzymes in the synapse, or (6) binding to autoreceptors on the sending neuron.

break down specific neurotransmitters. Finally, neurotransmitters can bind to the receptor sites called *autoreceptors* on the presynaptic neurons. Autoreceptors detect how much of a neurotransmitter has been released into a synapse and signal the neuron to stop releasing the neurotransmitter when an excess is present.

Finally, you might wonder how many types of neurotransmitters are floating across synapses in your brain right now, helping you to understand all this information about neurotransmitters. For quite some time, scientists thought that only five neurotransmitters contributed to information-processing activities in the brain. Today we know that some 60 chemicals play a role in transmitting information throughout the brain and body and that they differentially affect thought, feeling, and behavior. Let's look more closely at some neurotransmitters and the jobs they do.

Types of Neurotransmitters

Remember David, the gang member who saw phantom rivals threatening him? The methamphetamine he took altered the function of several neurotransmitters in his brain, which caused his hallucinations. In this case, the actions of chemical messengers at the level of the neurons produced pronounced startling effects in David's behavior. David saw things that weren't there, felt fear that wasn't warranted, and acted oddly without explanation, all of which was eventually traced back to an imbalance in his neurotransmitters. To understand how something like this takes place, let's take a closer look at the major types of neurotransmitters and the tasks they perform (see **TABLE 3.1**).

Acetylcholine (Ach), *a neurotransmitter involved in a number of functions, including voluntary motor control*, was one of the first neurotransmitters discovered. Acetylcholine is found in neurons of the brain and in the synapses where axons connect to muscles and body organs, such as the heart. Acetylcholine activates muscles to initiate motor behavior, but it also contributes to the regulation of attention, learning, sleeping, dreaming, and memory (Gais & Born, 2004; Hasselmo, 2006; Wrenn et al., 2006). These are rather broad effects on a variety of important behaviors, but here are some specific examples. Alzheimer's disease, a medical condition involving severe memory impairments, is associated with the deterioration of Ach-producing neurons. As another example, nicotine excites Ach receptors in the brain, which helps explain why people who wear a nicotine patch often report vivid dreams and why recent ex-smokers often have difficulties thinking or concentrating.

ACETYLCHOLINE (ACH) A neurotransmitter involved in a number of functions, including voluntary motor control.

Table 3.1	Neurotransmitters and Their Functions	
Neurotransmitter	**Function**	**Examples of Malfunctions**
Acetylcholine (Ach)	Enables muscle action; regulates attention, learning, memory, sleeping, and dreaming	With Alzheimer's disease, Ach-producing neurons deteriorate.
Dopamine	Influences movement, motivation, emotional pleasure, and arousal	High levels of dopamine are linked to schizophrenia. Lower levels of dopamine produce the tremors and decreased mobility of Parkinson's disease.
Glutamate	A major excitatory neurotransmitter involved in learning and memory	Oversupply can overstimulate the brain, producing migraines or seizures.
GABA (gamma-aminobutyric acid)	The primary inhibitory neurotransmitter	Undersupply linked to seizures, tremors, and insomnia.
Norepinephrine	Helps control mood and arousal	Undersupply can depress mood.
Serotonin	Regulates hunger, sleep, arousal, and aggressive behavior	Undersupply linked to depression; Prozac and some other antidepressant drugs raise serotonin levels.
Endorphins	Act within the pain pathways and emotion centers of the brain	Lack of endorphins could lower pain threshold or reduce the ability to self-soothe.

DOPAMINE A neurotransmitter that regulates motor behavior, motivation, pleasure, and emotional arousal.

GLUTAMATE A major excitatory neurotransmitter involved in information transmission throughout the brain.

GABA (GAMMA-AMINOBUTYRIC ACID) The primary inhibitory neurotransmitter in the brain.

NOREPINEPHRINE A neurotransmitter that influences mood and arousal.

SEROTONIN A neurotransmitter that is involved in the regulation of sleep and wakefulness, eating, and aggressive behavior.

ENDORPHINS Chemicals that act within the pain pathways and emotion centers of the brain.

When athletes engage in extreme sports, such as rock climbing, they may experience subjective highs that result from the release of endorphins—chemical messengers acting in emotion and pain centers that elevate mood and dull the experience of pain.

© MARC CHAUVIN

Like acetylcholine, other neurotransmitters in the brain affect a range of behaviors. **Dopamine** is *a neurotransmitter that regulates motor behavior, motivation, pleasure, and emotional arousal*. Because of its role in basic motivated behaviors, such as seeking pleasure or associating actions with rewards, dopamine is involved in regulating some critical human activities. For example, higher levels of dopamine are usually associated with positive emotions. But dopamine can produce different effects in different brain pathways because the effect of any neurotransmitter depends on the type of receptor site it fits. For example, dopamine release in some pathways of the brain plays a role in drug addiction (Baler & Volkow, 2006), whereas in other pathways high levels of dopamine have been linked to schizophrenia (Winterer & Weinberger, 2004); in still other pathways, dopamine contributes to decision making, attention, or movement (Tamminga, 2006). As you can see, the level of the neurotransmitter is not as crucial as the location of the receptor sites it unlocks and the associated processes it triggers.

Neurotransmitters can excite or inhibit synaptic transmission, thereby profoundly changing behavior. **Glutamate** is *a major excitatory neurotransmitter involved in information transmission throughout the brain*. This means that glutamate enhances the transmission of information. Glutamate is used by interneurons; hence, it plays an important role in all kinds of information processing. However, glutamate is especially crucial to learning and the formation of memories (Schmitt et al., 2004). **GABA (gamma-aminobutyric acid)**, in contrast, is *the primary inhibitory neurotransmitter in the brain*. Inhibitory neurotransmitters stop the firing of neurons, an activity that also contributes to the function of the organism. GABA works throughout the brain, and without it, the excitation of synapses could proceed unchecked, sending messages through the brain in a crescendoing circuit (Trevelyan et al., 2006). Thus, it makes sense that drugs that enhance GABA are used as anticonvulsants to combat seizures and are also being explored as treatments for conditions such as anxiety (Post, 2004).

Norepinephrine, *a neurotransmitter that influences mood and arousal*, is particularly involved in states of vigilance, or a heightened awareness of dangers in the environment (Ressler & Nemeroff, 1999). Similarly, **serotonin** is *involved in the regulation of sleep and wakefulness, eating, and aggressive behavior* (Kroeze & Roth, 1998). For example, because both neurotransmitters affect mood and arousal, low levels of each have been implicated in mood disorders (Tamminga et al., 2002). Remember, though, that as with dopamine, the actions of these neurotransmitters depend on the receptor sites they unlock and the pathways where they are used, as shown in Figure 3.7.

Another class of chemical messengers is the **endorphins**, *chemicals that act within the pain pathways and emotion centers of the brain* (Keefe, Lumley, Anderson, Lynch, & Carson, 2001). The term *endorphin* is a contraction of *end*ogenous m*orphine*, and that's a pretty apt description. Morphine is a synthetic drug that has a calming and pleasurable effect; an endorphin is an internally produced substance that has similar properties, such as dulling the experience of pain and elevating moods. The "runner's high" experienced by many athletes as they push their bodies to painful limits of endurance can be explained by the release of endorphins in the brain.

Each of these neurotransmitters affects thought, feeling, and behavior in different ways, so normal functioning involves a delicate balance of each. Even a slight imbalance—too much of one neurotransmitter or not enough of another—can dramatically affect behavior. These imbalances sometimes occur naturally: The brain doesn't produce enough serotonin, for example, which contributes to depressed or anxious moods. Other times a person may actively seek to cause imbalances. People who smoke, drink alcohol, or take drugs, legal or not, are altering the balance of neurotransmitters in their brains. The drug LSD, for example, is structurally very similar to serotonin, so it binds very easily with serotonin receptors in the brain, producing similar effects on thoughts, feelings, or behavior. In the next section, we'll look at how some drugs are able to "trick" receptor sites in just this way.

How Drugs Mimic Neurotransmitters

Many drugs that affect the nervous system operate by increasing, interfering with, or mimicking the manufacture or function of neurotransmitters (Cooper, Bloom, & Roth, 2003; Sarter, 2006). **Agonists** are *drugs that increase the action of a neurotransmitter.* **Antagonists** are *drugs that block the function of a neurotransmitter.* Some drugs alter a step in the production or release of the neurotransmitter, whereas others have a chemical structure so similar to a neurotransmitter that the drug is able to bind to that neuron's receptor. If, by binding to a receptor, a drug activates the neurotransmitter, it is an agonist; if it blocks the action of the neurotransmitter, it is an antagonist (see **FIGURE 3.8**).

Many drugs have been developed to mimic or block the actions of certain neurotransmitters (Barchas, Berger, Ciranello, & Elliot, 1980). For example, a drug called L-dopa has been developed to treat Parkinson's disease, a movement disorder involving the loss of neurons that use the neurotransmitter dopamine. Dopamine is created in neurons by a modification of a common molecule called L-dopa. Ingesting L-dopa will elevate the amount of L-dopa in the brain and spur the surviving neurons to produce more dopamine. In other words, L-dopa acts as an agonist for dopamine. The use of L-dopa has become a major success in the alleviation of Parkinson's disease symptoms (Muenter & Tyce, 1971).

Some unexpected evidence also highlights the central role of dopamine in regulating movement and motor performance. In 1982, six people ranging in age from 25 to 45 from the San Francisco Bay area were admitted to emergency rooms with a bizarre set of symptoms: paralysis, drooling, and an inability to speak (Langston, 1995). A diagnosis of advanced Parkinson's disease was made, as these symptoms are consistent with

AGONISTS Drugs that increase the action of a neurotransmitter.

ANTAGONISTS Drugs that block the function of a neurotransmitter.

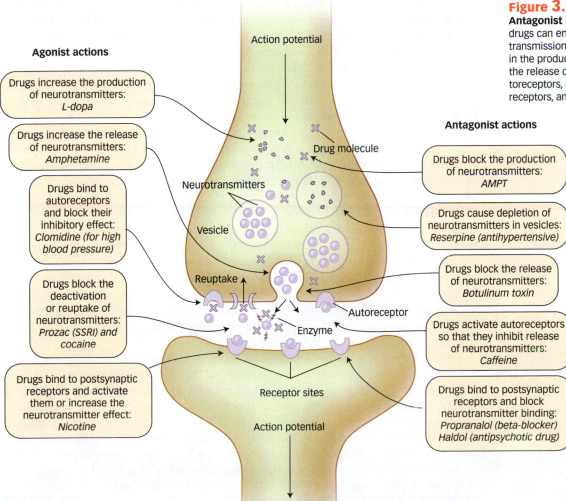

Figure 3.8 The Actions of Agonist and Antagonist Drugs Agonist and antagonist drugs can enhance or interfere with synaptic transmission at every point in the process: in the production of neurotransmitters, in the release of neurotransmitters, at the autoreceptors, in reuptake, in the postsynaptic receptors, and in the synapse itself.

MARK WILSON/GETTY IMAGES

PLINIO LEPRI/AP PHOTO

RICARDO MAZALAN/AP PHOTO

Many people suffer from Parkinson's disease, including these well-known personalities: former world heavyweight boxing champion Muhammad Ali; actor Michael J. Fox; the late Pope John Paul II; and, at least according to a diagnosis offered by the CIA, Cuban leader Fidel Castro. The greater visibility of these famous figures has brought with it a greater awareness of the disease and, perhaps, greater efforts directed toward finding a cure.

the later stages of this degenerative disease. It was unusual for six fairly young people to come down with advanced Parkinson's at the same time in the same geographical area. Indeed, none of the patients had Parkinson's, but they were all heroin addicts.

These patients thought they were ingesting a synthetic form of heroin (called MPPP), but instead they ingested a close derivative called MPTP, which unfortunately had the effects of destroying dopamine-producing neurons in an area of the brain crucial for motor performance. Hence, these "frozen addicts" exhibited paralysis and masklike expressions. The patients experienced a remarkable recovery after they were given L-dopa. In fact, it was later discovered that chemists who had worked with MPTP early in their careers later developed Parkinson's disease. Just as L-dopa acts as an agonist by enhancing the production of dopamine, drugs such as MPTP act as antagonists by destroying dopamine-producing neurons.

Like MPTP, other street drugs can alter neurotransmitter function. Amphetamine, for example, is a popular drug that stimulates the release of norepinephrine and dopamine. In addition, both amphetamine and cocaine prevent the reuptake of norepinephrine and dopamine. The combination of increased release of norepinephrine and dopamine and prevention of their reuptake floods the synapse with those neurotransmitters, resulting in increased activation of their receptors. Both of these drugs therefore are strong agonists, although the psychological effects of the two drugs differ somewhat because of subtle distinctions in where and how they act on the brain. Norepinephrine and dopamine play a critical role in mood control, such that increases in either neurotransmitter result in euphoria, wakefulness, and a burst of energy. However, norepinephrine also increases heart rate. An overdose of amphetamine or cocaine can cause the heart to contract so rapidly that heartbeats do not last long enough to pump blood effectively, leading to fainting and sometimes to death.

Prozac, a drug commonly used to treat depression, is another example of a neurotransmitter agonist. Prozac blocks the reuptake of the neurotransmitter *serotonin*, making it part of a category of drugs called *selective serotonin reuptake inhibitors*, or *SSRIs* (Wong, Bymaster, & Engelman, 1995). Patients suffering from clinical depression typically have reduced levels of serotonin in their brains. By blocking reuptake, more of the neurotransmitter remains in the synapse longer and produces greater activation of serotonin receptors. Serotonin elevates mood, which can help relieve depression.

An antagonist with important medical implications is a drug called *propranolol*, one of a class of drugs called *beta-blockers* that obstruct a receptor site for norepinephrine in the heart. Because norepinephrine cannot bind to these receptors, heart rate slows down, which is helpful for disorders in which the heart beats too fast or irregularly.

Beta-blockers are also prescribed to reduce the agitation, racing heart, and nervousness associated with stage fright (Mills & Dimsdale, 1991).

As you've read, many drugs alter the actions of neurotransmitters. Think back to David: His paranoid hallucinations were induced by his crystal meth habit. The actions of methamphetamine involve a complex interaction at the neuron's synapses—it affects pathways for dopamine, serotonin, and norepinephrine—making it difficult to interpret exactly how it works. But the combination of its agonist and antagonist effects alters the functions of neurotransmitters that help us perceive and interpret visual images. In David's case, it led to hallucinations that called his eyesight, and his sanity, into question.

In summary, the action potential triggers synaptic transmission through the release of neurotransmitters from the terminal buttons of the sending neuron's axon. The neurotransmitter travels across the synapse to bind with receptors in the receiving neuron's dendrite, completing the transmission of the message. Neurotransmitters bind to dendrites based on existing pathways in the brain and specific receptor sites for neurotransmitters. Neurotransmitters leave the synapse through reuptake, through enzyme deactivation, and by binding to autoreceptors. Some of the major neurotransmitters are acetylcholine (Ach), dopamine, glutamate, GABA, norepinephrine, serotonin, and endorphins. Drugs can affect behavior by acting as agonists, that is, facilitating or increasing the actions of neurotransmitters, or as antagonists by blocking the action of neurotransmitters. ■ ■

The Organization of the Nervous System

Our glimpse into the microscopic world of neurons reveals a lot about their structure and how they communicate with one another. It's quite impressive that billions of tiny engines cause our thoughts, feelings, and behaviors. Nonetheless, billions of anything working in isolation suggests a lot of potential but not much direction. Neurons work by forming circuits and pathways in the brain, which in turn influence circuits and pathways in other areas of the body. Without this kind of organization and delegation, neurons would be churning away with little purpose. Neurons are the building blocks that form *nerves*, or bundles of axons and the glial cells that support them. The **nervous system** *is an interacting network of neurons that conveys electrochemical information throughout the body.* In this section, we'll look at the major divisions of the nervous system, focusing particularly on structures in the brain and their specific functions.

Divisions of the Nervous System

There are two major divisions of the nervous system: the central nervous system and the peripheral nervous system (see **FIGURE 3.9** on the next page). The **central nervous system (CNS)** *is composed of the brain and spinal cord.* The central nervous system receives sensory information from the external world, processes and coordinates this information, and sends commands to the skeletal and muscular systems for action. At the top of the CNS rests the brain, which contains structures that support the most complex perceptual, motor, emotional, and cognitive functions of the nervous system. The spinal cord branches down from the brain; nerves that process sensory information and relay commands to the body connect to the spinal cord.

The **peripheral nervous system (PNS)** *connects the central nervous system to the body's organs and muscles.* The peripheral nervous system is itself composed of two major subdivisions, the somatic nervous system and the autonomic nervous system. The **somatic nervous system** *is a set of nerves that conveys information into and out of the central nervous system.* Humans have conscious control over this system and use it to perceive, think, and coordinate their behaviors. For example, directing your hand to reach out and pick up a coffee cup involves the elegantly orchestrated activities of the somatic nervous system: Information from the receptors in your eyes travels to your brain, registering that a cup is on the table; signals from your brain travel to the

NERVOUS SYSTEM An interacting network of neurons that conveys electrochemical information throughout the body.

CENTRAL NERVOUS SYSTEM (CNS) The part of the nervous system that is composed of the brain and spinal cord.

PERIPHERAL NERVOUS SYSTEM (PNS) The part of the nervous system that connects the central nervous system to the body's organs and muscles.

SOMATIC NERVOUS SYSTEM A set of nerves that conveys information into and out of the central nervous system.

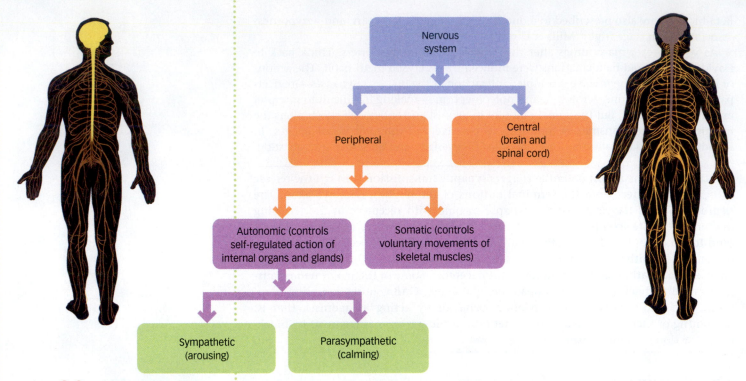

Figure 3.9 The Human Nervous System
The nervous system is organized into the peripheral and central nervous systems. The peripheral nervous system is further divided into the automatic and somatic nervous systems.

AUTONOMIC NERVOUS SYSTEM (ANS) A set of nerves that carries involuntary and automatic commands that control blood vessels, body organs, and glands.

SYMPATHETIC NERVOUS SYSTEM A set of nerves that prepares the body for action in threatening situations.

PARASYMPATHETIC NERVOUS SYSTEM A set of nerves that helps the body return to a normal resting state.

muscles in your arm and hand; feedback from those muscles tells your brain that the cup has been grasped; and so on. The somatic nervous system is kind of an "information superhighway," linking the external world of experience with the internal world of the central nervous system.

In contrast, the **autonomic nervous system (ANS)** is *a set of nerves that carries involuntary and automatic commands that control blood vessels, body organs, and glands*. As suggested by its name, this system works on its own to regulate bodily systems, largely outside of conscious control. The ANS has two major subdivisions, the sympathetic nervous system and the parasympathetic nervous system. Each exerts a different type of control on the body. The **sympathetic nervous system** is *a set of nerves that prepares the body for action in threatening situations* (see **FIGURE 3.10**). The nerves in the sympathetic nervous system emanate from the top and bottom of the spinal cord and connect to a variety of organs, such as the eyes, salivary glands, heart and lungs, digestive organs, and sex organs. The sympathetic nervous system coordinates the control of these organs so that the body can take action by fleeing the threatening situation or preparing to face it and fight.

For example, imagine that you hear footsteps behind you in a dark alley. You feel frightened and turn to see someone approaching you from behind. Your sympathetic nervous system kicks into action at this point: It dilates your pupils to let in more light, increases your heart rate and respiration to pump more oxygen to muscles, diverts blood flow to your brain and muscles, and activates sweat glands to cool your body. To conserve energy, the sympathetic nervous system inhibits salivation and bowel movements, suppresses the body's immune responses, and suppresses responses to pain and injury. The sum total of these fast, automatic responses is that they increase the likelihood that you can escape.

The **parasympathetic nervous system** *helps the body return to a normal resting state*. When you're five blocks away from your would-be attacker, your body doesn't need to remain on red alert. Now the parasympathetic nervous system kicks in to reverse the effects of the sympathetic nervous system and return your body to its normal state. The parasympathetic nervous system generally mirrors the connections of the sympathetic nervous system. For example, the parasympathetic nervous system

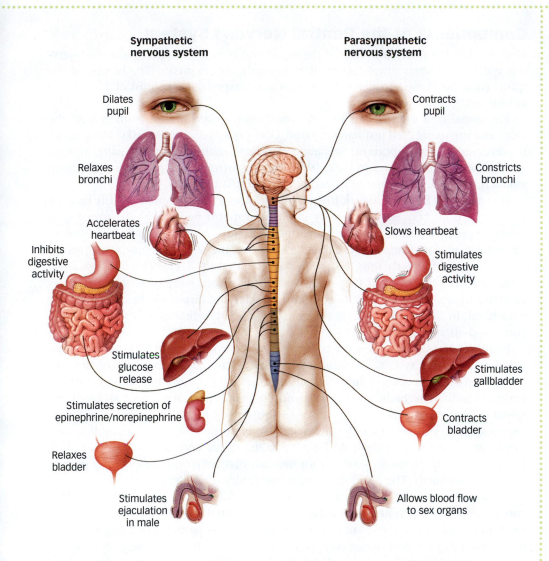

Sympathetic nervous system

Dilates pupil

Relaxes bronchi

Accelerates heartbeat

Inhibits digestive activity

Stimulates glucose release

Stimulates secretion of epinephrine/norepinephrine

Relaxes bladder

Stimulates ejaculation in male

Parasympathetic nervous system

Contracts pupil

Constricts bronchi

Slows heartbeat

Stimulates digestive activity

Stimulates gallbladder

Contracts bladder

Allows blood flow to sex organs

Figure 3.10 Sympathetic and Parasympathetic Systems The autonomic nervous system is composed of two subsystems that complement each other. Activation of the sympathetic system serves several aspects of arousal, whereas the parasympathetic nervous system returns the body to its normal resting state.

constricts your pupils, slows your heart rate and respiration, diverts blood flow to your digestive system, and decreases activity in your sweat glands.

As you might imagine, the sympathetic and parasympathetic nervous systems coordinate to control many bodily functions. One example is sexual behavior. In men, the parasympathetic nervous system engorges the blood vessels of the penis to produce an erection, but the sympathetic nervous system is responsible for ejaculation. In women, the parasympathetic nervous system produces vaginal lubrication, but the sympathetic nervous system underlies orgasm. In both men and women, a successful sexual experience depends on a delicate balance of these two systems; in fact, anxiety about sexual performance can disrupt this balance. For example, sympathetic nervous system activation caused by anxiety can lead to premature ejaculation in males and lack of lubrication in females.

Let's return briefly to an earlier point. Without some kind of coordinated effort, billions and billions of neurons would simply produce trillions and trillions of independent processes. The nervous system has evolved so that the sympathetic and parasympathetic nervous systems work in concert, which in turn allows the autonomic nervous system to function rather effortlessly and, in coordination with the somatic nervous system, allows information to be gathered from the external world. This information travels through the peripheral nervous system and is eventually sent to the brain via the spinal cord, where it can be sorted, interpreted, processed, and acted on. Like the organizational chart of a complex corporation, the organization of the human nervous system is a triumph of delegation of responsibilities.

SPINAL REFLEXES Simple pathways in the nervous system that rapidly generate muscle contractions.

Components of the Central Nervous System

Compared to the many divisions of the peripheral nervous system, the central nervous system may seem simple. After all, it has only two elements: The brain and the spinal cord. But those two elements are ultimately responsible for most of what we do as humans.

The spinal cord often seems like the brain's poor relation: The brain gets all the glory and the spinal cord just hangs around, doing relatively simple tasks. Those tasks, however, are pretty important: keeping you breathing, responding to pain, moving your muscles, allowing you to walk. What's more, without the spinal cord, the brain would not be able to put any of its higher processing into action.

For some very basic behaviors, the spinal cord doesn't need input from the brain at all. Connections between the sensory inputs and motor neurons in the spinal cord mediate **spinal reflexes,** *simple pathways in the nervous system that rapidly generate muscle contractions*. For example, if you touch a hot stove, the sensory neurons that register pain send inputs directly into the spinal cord (see **FIGURE 3.11**). Through just a few synaptic connections within the spinal cord, interneurons relay these sensory inputs to motor neurons that connect to your arm muscles and direct you to quickly retract your hand. In other words, you don't need a whole lot of brainpower to rapidly pull your hand off a hot stove!

More elaborate tasks require the collaboration of the spinal cord and the brain. The peripheral nervous system communicates with the central nervous system through nerves that conduct sensory information into the brain, carry commands out of the brain, or both. The brain sends commands for voluntary movement through the spinal cord to motor neurons, whose axons project out to skeletal muscles and send the message to contract. (See the Hot Science box on page 92 for a description of a novel type of movement control.) Damage to the spinal cord severs the connection from the brain to the sensory and motor neurons that are essential to sensory perception and movement. The location of the spinal injury often determines the extent of the abilities that are lost. As you can see in **FIGURE 3.12,** different regions of the spinal cord control different systems of the body. Patients with damage at a particular level of the spinal cord lose sensation of touch and pain in body parts below the level of the injury as well as a loss of motor control of the muscles in the same areas. A spinal injury higher up the cord usually predicts a much poorer prognosis, such as quadriplegia (the loss of sensation and motor control over all limbs), breathing through a respirator, and lifelong immobility.

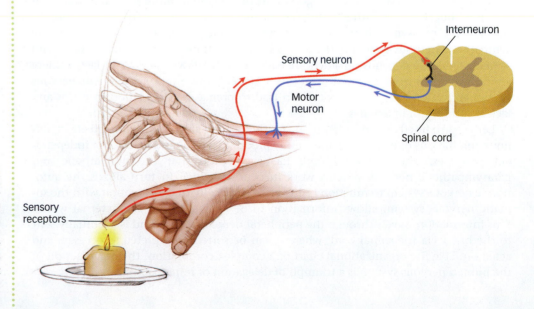

Figure 3.11 **The Pain Withdrawal Reflex** Many actions of the central nervous system don't require the brain's input. For example, withdrawing from pain is a reflexive activity controlled by the spinal cord. Painful sensations (such as a pin jabbing your finger) travel directly to the spinal cord via sensory neurons, which then issue an immediate command to motor neurons to retract the hand.

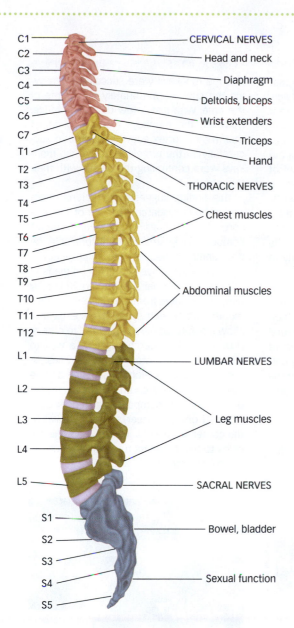

C1 ——— CERVICAL NERVES
C2 ——— Head and neck
C3
C4 ——— Diaphragm
C5 ——— Deltoids, biceps
C6 ——— Wrist extenders
C7 ——— Triceps
T1 ——— Hand
T2
T3 ——— THORACIC NERVES
T4
T5 ——— Chest muscles
T6
T7
T8
T9
T10 ——— Abdominal muscles
T11
T12
L1 ——— LUMBAR NERVES
L2
L3 ——— Leg muscles
L4
L5 ——— SACRAL NERVES
S1
S2 ——— Bowel, bladder
S3
S4 ——— Sexual function
S5

Figure 3.12 **Regions of the Spinal Cord** The spinal cord is divided into four main sections, each of which controls different parts of the body. Damage higher on the spinal cord usually portends greater impairment.

The late actor Christopher Reeve, shown on the left as Superman in 1984 and on the right in 2004, severely damaged his spinal cord in a horseback riding accident in 1995. Reeve worked tirelessly to advocate for greater funding of stem cell research, which could potentially provide enormous breakthroughs for the treatment of spinal cord injuries.

The late actor Christopher Reeve, who starred as Superman in four Superman movies, damaged his spinal cord in a horseback riding accident in 1995, resulting in loss of sensation and motor control in all of his body parts below the neck. Despite great efforts over several years, Reeve made only modest gains in his motor control and sensation, highlighting the extent to which we depend on communication from the brain through the spinal cord to the body and showing how difficult it is to compensate for the loss of these connections (Edgerton et al., 2004). Sadly, Christopher Reeve died at age 52 in 2004 from complications due to his paralysis.

Exploring the Brain

The human brain is really not much to look at. It's about 3 pounds of slightly slimy, pinkish grayish stuff that sits there like a lump. You already know,

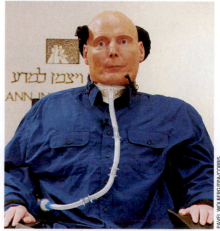

CANNON/THE KOBAL COLLECTION

PAVEL WOLBERG/EPA/CORBIS

{ HOT SCIENCE } Thought Control

IN THE STEVEN SPIELBERG REMAKE OF THE movie *War of the Worlds,* small, squishy aliens control gigantic robots to wreak havoc on humankind. You've probably seen more than one science-fiction movie with that kind of theme: An intruder from another planet steers a monstrous machine through downtown San Francisco or an evil scientist uses brain waves to direct a malevolent robot's actions. You've probably also watched with a fair amount of disbelief. After all, how can a slimy alien or scrawny inventor control that much machinery to do that much damage?

Recently, some *good* scientists have been bringing that science-fiction fantasy closer to reality. Experiments with monkeys provide evidence that mechanical devices can be controlled by thoughts alone. Researchers at Duke University implanted multiple wires into the monkeys' motor cortices (Carmena et al., 2003; Nicolelis, 2001). They then trained the monkeys to move a joystick that controlled a cursor on a computer screen. On each trial, a small target would appear on the screen, and whenever the monkey moved the cursor

from an arbitrary starting position to that target, it was rewarded with fruit juice. After the monkeys had learned the task well, the researchers recorded the action potentials from the motor cortex neurons. Using the activity patterns of many neurons, they created a computer model of the neural activity that corresponded to different directions of joystick movements. Then they disconnected the joystick from the computer and instead connected the signals that their model extracted from the monkey's motor cortex activity directly to the computer.

Now when the monkeys attempted to perform the task, physically manipulating the joystick had no effect. However, their motor cortex cells still produced the neural firings that corresponded to the movement of the joystick, and now these activity patterns directly moved the cursor. At first the motor cortex activity was somewhat crude,

and the monkeys were successful in moving the cursor appropriately only some of the time. With just a few days of practice, however, the monkeys learned to adjust their motor cortex activity patterns to successfully hit the targets. It is as if the monkeys were controlling the cursor with their thoughts.

This finding suggests an exciting direction in brain research. The use of multiple cortical recordings and state-of-the-art computer programs could, in principle, be developed for people with spinal injuries. Great advances have already been made in this area: Wheelchairs can be controlled by puffs of air blown from a paralyzed person's mouth, and speech synthesizers exist that allow a paralyzed person to "talk" to others. However, this research suggests a way to eliminate those intermediary devices. A person's thoughts alone might one day be able to effectively control the movements of a wheelchair, compose e-mail messages to loved ones, or steer a vehicle down to the corner store. Let's just hope no one decides to use thoughts to control a murderous robot instead.

Monkey Using a Joystick to Control a Cursor (a) The monkey with electrodes implanted in its motor cortex first learns to move a cursor on a computer screen with a joystick. The electrodes are connected to a device that records activity in the motor cortex cells produced when the monkey moves the cursor. After the monkey learns to control the cursor with the joystick, it is disconnected and the activity patterns in the monkey's motor cortex move the cursor to the target. (b) One of the tasks in which the monkey moves the cursor to the green target that appears at random on the screen.

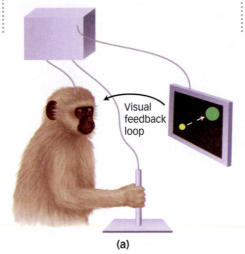

Data acquisition box

Visual feedback loop

(a)

(b)

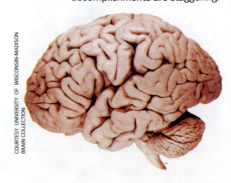

The human brain weighs only 3 pounds and isn't much to look at, but its accomplishments are staggering.

of course, that the neurons and glial cells that make up that lump are busy humming away, giving you consciousness, feelings, and potentially brilliant ideas. But to find out which neurons in which parts of the brain control which functions, scientists first had to divide and conquer: that is, find a way of describing the brain that allows researchers to communicate with one another.

There are several ways that neuroscientists divide up the brain. It can be helpful to talk about areas of the brain from "bottom to top," noting how the different regions are specialized for different kinds of tasks. In general, simpler functions are performed at the "lower levels" of the brain, whereas more complex functions are performed at successively "higher" levels (see **FIGURE 3.13**). As you'll see shortly, the brain can also be approached in a "side-by-side" fashion: although each side of the brain is roughly analogous, one half of the brain specializes in some tasks that the other half doesn't.

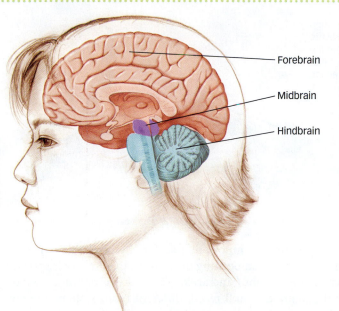

Figure 3.13 **The Major Divisions of the Brain** The brain can be organized into three parts, moving from the bottom to the top, from simpler functions to the more complex: the hindbrain, the midbrain, and the forebrain.

Forebrain

Midbrain

Hindbrain

HINDBRAIN An area of the brain that coordinates information coming into and out of the spinal cord.

MEDULLA An extension of the spinal cord into the skull that coordinates heart rate, circulation, and respiration.

RETICULAR FORMATION A brain structure that regulates sleep, wakefulness, and levels of arousal.

CEREBELLUM A large structure of the hindbrain that controls fine motor skills.

Although these divisions make it easier to understand areas of the brain and their functions, keep in mind that none of these structures or areas in the brain can act alone: They are all part of one big, interacting, interdependent whole.

Let's look first at the divisions of the brain and the responsibilities of each part, moving from the bottom to the top. Using this view, we can divide the brain into three parts: the hindbrain, the midbrain, and the forebrain (see Figure 3.13).

The Hindbrain

If you follow the spinal cord from your tailbone to where it enters your skull, you'll find it difficult to determine where your spinal cord ends and your brain begins. That's because the spinal cord is continuous with the **hindbrain**, *an area of the brain that co-ordinates information coming into and out of the spinal cord*. The hindbrain is sometimes called the *brain stem*; indeed, it looks like a stalk on which the rest of the brain sits. The hindbrain controls the most basic functions of life: respiration, alertness, and motor skills. There are three anatomical structures that make up the hindbrain: the medulla, the cerebellum, and the pons (see **FIGURE 3.14**).

The **medulla** is *an extension of the spinal cord into the skull that coordinates heart rate, circulation, and respiration*. Inside the medulla is a small cluster of neurons called the **reticular formation**, which *regulates sleep, wakefulness, and levels of arousal*. Damage to this tiny area of the brain can produce dramatically large consequences for behavior. For example, in one early experiment, researchers stimulated the reticular formation of a sleeping cat. This caused the animal to awaken almost instantaneously and remain alert. Conversely, severing the connections between the reticular formation and the rest of the brain caused the animal to lapse into an irreversible coma (Moruzzi & Magoun, 1949). The reticular formation maintains the same delicate balance between alertness and unconsciousness in humans. In fact, many general anesthetics work by reducing activity in the reticular formation, rendering the patient unconscious.

Behind the medulla is the **cerebellum**, *a large structure of the hindbrain that controls fine motor skills*. *Cerebellum* is Latin for "little brain," and the structure does look like a small replica of the brain. The cerebellum orchestrates the proper sequence of movements when we ride a bike, play the piano, or maintain balance while walking and running. The cerebellum contains a layer of *Purkinje cells*, the elaborate, treelike neurons you read about earlier in the chapter. Purkinje cells are some of the largest neurons in the brain, and they are the sole output for motor coordination originating in the cerebellum and spreading to the rest of the brain.

Damage to the cerebellum produces impairments in coordination and balance, although not the paralysis or immobility you might think would be associated with a

Figure 3.14 **The Hindbrain** The hindbrain coordinates information coming into and out of the spinal cord and controls the basic functions of life. It includes the medulla, the reticular formation, the cerebellum, and the pons.

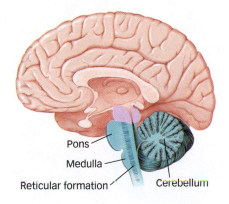

Pons

Medulla

Reticular formation

Cerebellum

PONS A brain structure that relays information from the cerebellum to the rest of the brain.

TECTUM A part of the midbrain that orients an organism in the environment.

TEGMENTUM A part of the midbrain that is involved in movement and arousal.

Olympic medalist Apolo Anton Ohno relies on his cerebellum to execute graceful, coordinated motions on the ice. The cerebellum, part of the hindbrain, helps direct the smooth action of a variety of motor behaviors.

AP PHOTO/KEVORK DJANSEZIAN

motor control center. This highlights an important role for the cerebellum: It contributes to the "fine tuning" of behavior, smoothing our actions to allow their graceful execution rather than initiating the actions (Smetacek, 2002). The initiation of behavior involves other areas of the brain; as you'll recall, different brain systems interact and are interdependent with one another.

The last major area of the hindbrain is the **pons**, *a structure that relays information from the cerebellum to the rest of the brain. Pons* means "bridge" in Latin. Although the detailed functions of the pons remain poorly understood, it essentially acts as a "relay station" or bridge between the cerebellum and other structures in the brain.

The Midbrain

Sitting on top of the hindbrain is the *midbrain*, which is relatively small in humans. As you can see in **FIGURE 3.15,** the midbrain contains two main structures: the tectum and the tegmentum. The **tectum** *orients an organism in the environment*. The tectum receives stimulus input from the eyes, ears, and skin and moves the organism in a coordinated way toward the stimulus. For example, when you're studying in a quiet room and you hear a *click* behind and to the right of you, your body will swivel and orient to the direction of the sound; this is your tectum in action.

The **tegmentum** is *involved in movement and arousal*; it also helps to orient an organism toward sensory stimuli. However, parts of the tegmentum are involved in pleasure seeking and motivation. It makes sense, then, that an abundance of dopamine-producing neurons is found in this midbrain structure. You'll recall that dopamine contributes to motor behavior, motivation, and pleasure; all are tasks that the tegmentum coordinates. What's more, another structure of the brain loaded with

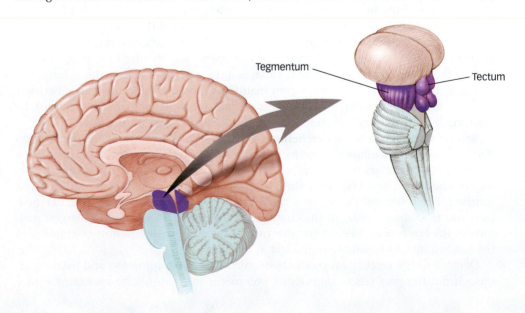

Figure 3.15 The Midbrain The midbrain is important for orientation and movement. It includes structures such as the tectum and tegmentum.

Tegmentum

Tectum

dopamine neurons, the *substantia nigra*, is found in this area. Serotonin, a neurotransmitter that contributes to mood and arousal, is also plentiful in the midbrain. The midbrain may be relatively small, but it is a central location of neurotransmitters involved in arousal, mood, and motivation and the brain structures that rely on them (White, 1996).

You could survive if you had only a hindbrain and a midbrain. The structures in the hindbrain would take care of all the bodily functions necessary to sustain life, and the structures in the midbrain would orient you toward or away from pleasurable or threatening stimuli in the environment. But this wouldn't be much of a life. To understand where the abilities that make us fully human come from, we need to consider the last division of the brain.

The Forebrain

When you appreciate the beauty of a poem, detect the sarcasm in a friend's remark, plan to go skiing next winter, or notice the faint glimmer of sadness on a loved one's face, you are enlisting the forebrain. The *forebrain* is the highest level of the brain—literally and figuratively—and controls complex cognitive, emotional, sensory, and motor functions (see **FIGURE 3.16**). The forebrain itself is divided into two main sections: the cerebral cortex and the subcortical structures. The **cerebral cortex** is *the outermost layer of the brain, visible to the naked eye, and divided into two hemispheres*. We'll have much more to say about these cerebral hemispheres and the functions they serve in a little bit. First we'll examine the **subcortical structures**, *areas of the forebrain housed under the cerebral cortex near the very center of the brain*.

The subcortical structures are nestled deep inside the brain, where they are quite protected. If you imagine sticking an index finger in each of your ears and pushing inward until they touch, that's about where you'd find the thalamus, hypothalamus, pituitary gland, limbic system, and basal ganglia (see **FIGURE 3.17** on the next page). Each of these subcortical structures plays an important role in relaying information throughout the brain, as well as performing specific tasks that allow us to think, feel, and behave as humans.

The **thalamus** *relays and filters information from the senses and transmits the information to the cerebral cortex*. The thalamus receives inputs from all the major senses except smell, which has direct connections to the cerebral cortex. The thalamus acts as a kind of computer server in a networked system, taking in multiple inputs and relaying them to a variety of locations (Guillery & Sherman, 2002). However, unlike the mechanical operations of a computer—"send input A to location B"—the thalamus actively filters sensory information, giving more weight to some inputs and less weight to others. The thalamus also closes the pathways of incoming sensations during sleep, providing a valuable function in *not* allowing information to pass to the rest of the brain.

The **hypothalamus**, located below the thalamus (*hypo-* is Greek for "under"), *regulates body temperature, hunger, thirst, and sexual behavior*. Although the hypothalamus is a tiny area of the brain, clusters of neurons in the hypothalamus oversee a wide range of basic behaviors. For example, the hypothalamus makes sure that body temperature, blood sugar levels, and metabolism are kept within an optimal range for normal human functioning. Lesions to some areas of the hypothalamus result in overeating, whereas lesions to other areas leave an animal with no desire for food at all. Also, when you think about sex, messages from your cerebral cortex are sent to the hypothalamus to trigger the release of hormones. Finally, electric stimulation of the hypothalamus in cats can produce hissing and biting, whereas stimulation of other areas in the hypothalamus can produce what appears to be intense pleasure for an animal (Siegel, Roeling, Gregg, & Kruk, 1999). Researchers James Olds and Peter Milner found that a small electric current delivered to a certain region of a rat's hypothalamus was extremely rewarding for the animal (Olds & Milner, 1954). In fact, when allowed

CEREBRAL CORTEX The outermost layer of the brain, visible to the naked eye and divided into two hemispheres.

SUBCORTICAL STRUCTURES Areas of the forebrain housed under the cerebral cortex near the very center of the brain.

THALAMUS A subcortical structure that relays and filters information from the senses and transmits the information to the cerebral cortex.

HYPOTHALAMUS A subcortical structure that regulates body temperature, hunger, thirst, and sexual behavior.

Figure 3.16 The Forebrain The forebrain is the highest level of the brain and is critical for complex cognitive, emotional, sensory, and motor functions. The forebrain is divided into two parts: the cerebral cortex and the underlying subcortical structures. These include the thalamus, hypothalamus, pituitary gland, amygdala, and hippocampus. The corpus callosum connects the two hemispheres of the brain.

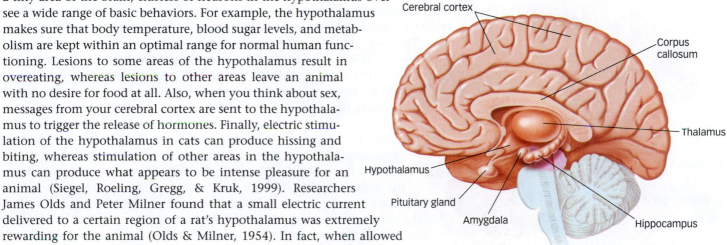

Cerebral cortex

Corpus callosum

Thalamus

Hypothalamus

Pituitary gland

Amygdala

Hippocampus

PITUITARY GLAND The "master gland" of the body's hormone-producing system, which releases hormones that direct the functions of many other glands in the body.

LIMBIC SYSTEM A group of forebrain structures including the hypothalamus, the amygdala, and the hippocampus, which are involved in motivation, emotion, learning, and memory.

HIPPOCAMPUS A structure critical for creating new memories and integrating them into a network of knowledge so that they can be stored indefinitely in other parts of the cerebral cortex.

AMYGDALA A part of the limbic system that plays a central role in many emotional processes, particularly the formation of emotional memories.

BASAL GANGLIA A set of subcortical structures that directs intentional movements.

to press a bar attached to the electrode to initiate their own stimulation, rats would do so several thousand times an hour, often to the point of exhaustion! It's been suggested, then, that the hypothalamus is in charge of the "four Fs" of behavior: (1) fighting, (2) fleeing, (3) feeding, and (4) mating.

Located below the hypothalamus is the **pituitary gland**, *the "master gland" of the body's hormone-producing system, which releases hormones that direct the functions of many other glands in the body*. The hypothalamus sends hormonal signals to the pituitary gland, which in turn sends hormonal signals to other glands to control stress, digestive activities, and reproductive processes. For example, when a baby suckles its mother's breast, sensory neurons in her breast send signals to her hypothalamus, which then signals her pituitary gland to release a hormone called *oxytocin* into the bloodstream (McNeilly, Robinson, Houston, & Howie, 1983). Oxytocin, in turn, stimulates the release of milk from reservoirs in the breast. The pituitary gland is also involved in the response to stress. When we sense a threat, sensory neurons send signals to the hypothalamus, which stimulates the release of adrenocorticotropic hormone (ACTH) from the pituitary gland. ACTH, in turn, stimulates the adrenal glands (above the kidneys) to release hormones that activate the sympathetic nervous system (Selye & Fortier, 1950). As you read earlier in this chapter, the sympathetic nervous system prepares the body to either meet the threat head-on or flee from the situation.

The thalamus, hypothalamus, and pituitary gland, located in the center of the brain, make possible close interaction with several other brain structures: They receive information, process it, and send it back out again. The hypothalamus is part of the **limbic system**, *a group of forebrain structures including the hypothalamus, the amygdala, and the hippocampus, which are involved in motivation, emotion, learning, and memory* (Maclean, 1970; Papez, 1937). The limbic system is found in a bagel-shaped area around the hypothalamus, where the subcortical structures meet the cerebral cortex (see Figure 3.17). The two remaining structures of the limbic system are the hippocampus (from the Latin for "sea horse," due to its shape) and the amygdala (from the Latin for "almond," also due to its shape).

The **hippocampus** is *critical for creating new memories and integrating them into a network of knowledge so that they can be stored indefinitely in other parts of the cerebral cortex*. Patients with damage to the hippocampus can acquire new information and keep it in awareness for a few seconds, but as soon as they are distracted, they forget the information and the experience that produced it (Scoville & Milner, 1957). This kind of disruption is limited to everyday memory for facts and events that we can bring to consciousness; memory of learned habitual routines or emotional reactions remains intact (Squire, Knowlton, & Musen, 1993). As an example, people with damage to the hippocampus can remember how to drive and talk, but they cannot recall where they have recently driven or a conversation they have just had. You will read more about the hippocampus and its role in creating, storing, and combining memories in Chapter 5.

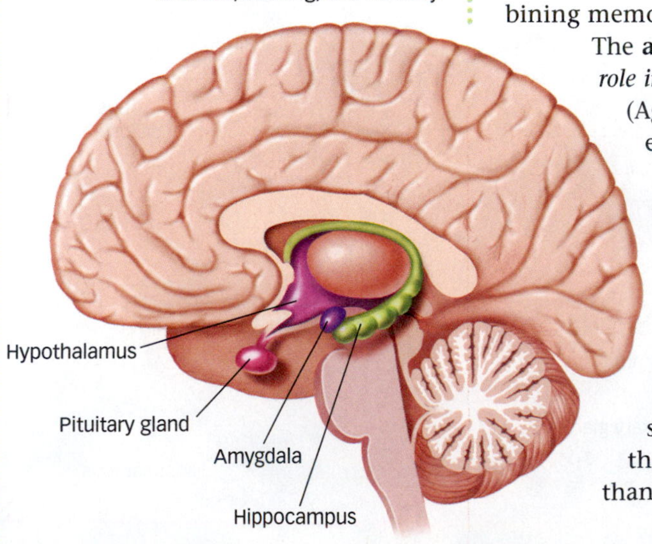

The **amygdala**, *located at the tip of each horn of the hippocampus, plays a central role in many emotional processes, particularly the formation of emotional memories* (Aggleton, 1992). The amygdala attaches significance to previously neutral events that are associated with fear, punishment, or reward (LeDoux, 1992). As an example, think of the last time something scary or unpleasant happened to you: A car came barreling toward you as you started walking into an intersection or a ferocious dog leapt out of an alley as you passed by. Those stimuli—a car or a dog—are fairly neutral; you don't have a panic attack every time you walk by a used car lot. The emotional significance attached to events involving those stimuli is the work of the amygdala. When we are in emotionally arousing situations, the amygdala stimulates the hippocampus to remember many details surrounding the situation (Kensinger & Schacter, 2005). For example, after the terrorist attacks of September 11, 2001, most people recalled much more than the fact that planes crashed into the World Trade Center in New York

Figure 3.17 The Limbic System The limbic system includes the hippocampus and the amygdala, as well as the hypothalamus. These structures are involved in motivation, emotion, learning, and memory.

Hypothalamus

Pituitary gland

Amygdala

Hippocampus

City; the Pentagon in Washington, D.C.; and a field in western Pennsylvania. People who lived through the attacks remember vivid details about where they were, what they were doing, and how they felt when they heard the news, even years later. In particular, the amygdala seems to be especially involved in encoding events as *fearful* (Adolphs et al., 1995). We'll have more to say about the amygdala's role in emotion and motivated behavior in Chapter 10. For now, keep in mind that a group of neurons the size of a lima bean buried deep in your brain help you to laugh, weep, or shriek in fright when the circumstances call for it.

There are several other structures in the subcortical area, but we'll consider just one more. The **basal ganglia** are *a set of subcortical structures that directs intentional movements*. The basal ganglia are located near the thalamus and hypothalamus; they receive input from the cerebral cortex and send outputs to the motor centers in the brain stem (see **FIGURE 3.18**). One part of the basal ganglia, the *striatum*, is involved in the control of posture and movement. Patients who suffer from Parkinson's disease typically show symptoms of uncontrollable shaking and sudden jerks of the limbs and are unable to initiate a sequence of movements to achieve a specific goal. This happens because the dopamine-producing neurons in the substantia nigra (found in the tegmentum of the midbrain) have become damaged (Dauer & Przedborski, 2003). The undersupply of dopamine then affects the striatum in the basal ganglia, which in turn leads to the visible behavioral symptoms of Parkinson's.

So, what's the problem in Parkinson's—the jerky movements, the ineffectiveness of the striatum in directing behavior, the botched interplay of the substantia nigra and the striatum, or the underproduction of dopamine at the neuronal level? The answer is "all of the above." This unfortunate disease provides a nice illustration of two themes regarding the brain and behavior. First, invisible actions at the level of neurons in the brain can produce substantial effects at the level of behavior. Second, the interaction of hindbrain, midbrain, and forebrain structures shows how the various regions are interdependent.

The Cerebral Cortex

Our tour of the brain has taken us from the very small (neurons) to the somewhat bigger (major divisions of the brain) to the very large: the cerebral cortex. The cortex is the highest level of the brain, and it is responsible for the most complex aspects of perception, emotion, movement, and thought (Fuster, 2003). It sits over the rest of the brain, like a mushroom cap shielding the underside and stem, and it is the wrinkled surface you see when looking at the brain with the naked eye.

The smooth surfaces of the cortex—the raised part—are called *gyri* (*gyrus* if you're talking about just one), and the indentations or fissures are called *sulci* (*sulcus* when singular). Sulci and gyri represent a triumph of evolution. The cerebral cortex occupies about 2,500 cubic centimeters of space, or roughly the area of a newspaper page. Fitting that much cortex into a human skull is a tough task. But if you crumple a sheet of newspaper, you'll see that the same surface area now fits compactly into a much smaller space. The cortex, with its wrinkles and folds, holds a lot of brainpower in a relatively small package that fits comfortably inside the human skull (see **FIGURE 3.19**).

The functions of the cerebral cortex can be understood at three levels: the separation of the cortex into two hemispheres, the functions of each hemisphere, and the role of specific cortical areas. The first level of organization divides the cortex into the left and right hemispheres. The two hemispheres are more or less symmetrical in their appearance and, to some extent, in their functions. However, each hemisphere controls the functions of the opposite side of the body. This is called *contralateral control*, meaning that your right cerebral hemisphere perceives stimuli from and controls movements on the left side of your body, whereas your left cerebral hemisphere perceives stimuli from and controls movement on the right side of your body (see **FIGURE 3.20** on the next page).

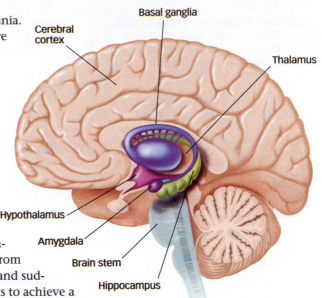

Figure 3.18 **The Basal Ganglia** The basal ganglia are a group of subcortical brain structures that direct intentional movement. They receive input from the cerebral cortex and send output to the motor centers in the brain stem.

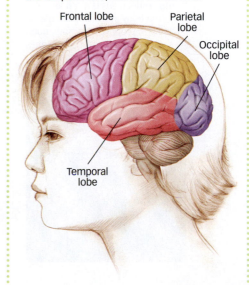

Figure 3.19 **Cerebral Cortex and Lobes** The four major lobes of the cerebral cortex are the occipital lobe, the parietal lobe, the temporal lobe, and the frontal lobe.

CORPUS CALLOSUM A thick band of nerve fibers that connects large areas of the cerebral cortex on each side of the brain and supports communication of information across the hemispheres.

OCCIPITAL LOBE A region of the cerebral cortex that processes visual information.

PARIETAL LOBE A region of the cerebral cortex whose functions include processing information about touch.

Figure 3.20 Cerebral Hemispheres Top view of the brain with part of the right cerebral hemisphere pulled away to expose the corpus callosum.

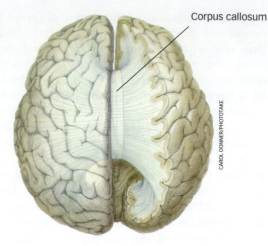

Corpus callosum

CAROL DONNER/PHOTOTAKE

The cerebral hemispheres are connected to each other by *commissures*, bundles of axons that make possible communication between parallel areas of the cortex in each half. The largest of these commissures is the **corpus callosum**, which *connects large areas of the cerebral cortex on each side of the brain and supports communication of information across the hemispheres*. This means that information received in the right hemisphere, for example, can pass across the corpus callosum and be registered, virtually instantaneously, in the left hemisphere.

The second level of organization in the cerebral cortex distinguishes the functions of the different regions within each hemisphere of the brain. Each hemisphere of the cerebral cortex is divided into four areas or *lobes*: From back to front, these are the occipital lobe, the parietal lobe, the temporal lobe, and the frontal lobe, as shown in Figure 3.19. We'll examine the functions of these lobes in more detail later, noting how scientists have used a variety of techniques to understand the operations of the brain. For now, here's a brief overview of the main functions of each lobe.

The **occipital lobe**, located at the back of the cerebral cortex, *processes visual information*. Sensory receptors in the eyes send information to the thalamus, which in turn sends information to the primary areas of the occipital lobe, where simple features of the stimulus are extracted. These features are then processed into a more complex "map" of the stimulus onto the occipital cortex, leading to comprehension of what's being seen. As you might imagine, damage to the primary visual areas of the occipital lobe can leave a person with partial or complete blindness. Information still enters the eyes, which work just fine. But without the ability to process and make sense of the information at the level of the cerebral cortex, the information is as good as lost (Zeki, 2001).

The homunculus is a rendering of the body in which each part is shown in proportion to how much of the somatosensory cortex is devoted to it.

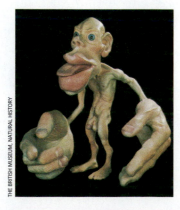

THE BRITISH MUSEUM, NATURAL HISTORY

The **parietal lobe**, located in front of the occipital lobe, carries out functions that include *processing information about touch*. The parietal lobe contains the *somatosensory cortex*, a strip of brain tissue running from the top of the brain down to the sides (see **FIGURE 3.21**). Within each hemisphere, the somatosensory cortex represents the skin areas on the contralateral surface of the body. Each part of the somatosensory cortex maps onto a particular part of the body. If a body area is more sensitive, a larger part of the somatosensory cortex is devoted to it. For example, the part of the somatosensory cortex that corresponds to the lips and tongue is larger than the area corresponding to the feet. The somatosensory cortex can be illustrated as a distorted figure, called a *homunculus* ("little man"), in which the body parts are rendered according to how much of the somatosensory cortex is devoted to them (Penfield & Rasmussen, 1950).

Directly in front of the somatosensory cortex, in the frontal lobe, is a parallel strip of brain tissue called the *motor cortex*. Like the somatosensory cortex, different parts of the motor cortex correspond to different body parts. The motor cortex initiates voluntary movements and sends messages to the basal ganglia, cerebellum, and spinal cord. The motor and somatosensory cortices, then, are like sending and receiving areas of the cerebral cortex, taking in information and sending out commands as the case might be.

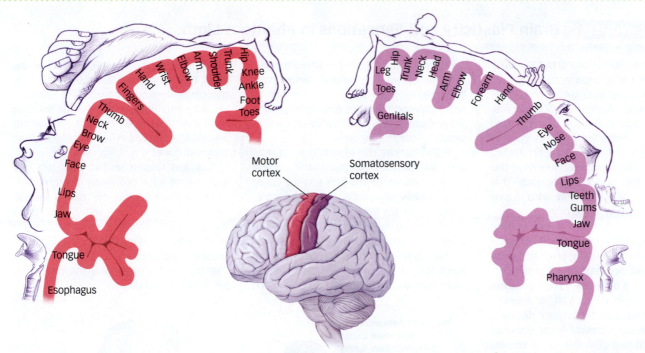

Motor cortex

Somatosensory cortex

Figure 3.21 **Somatosensory and Motor Cortices** The motor cortex, a strip of brain tissue in the frontal lobe, represents and controls different skin and body areas on the contralateral side of the body. Directly behind the motor cortex, in the parietal lobe, lies the somatosensory cortex. Like the motor cortex, the somatosensory cortex represents skin areas of particular parts on the contralateral side of the body.

The **temporal lobe**, located on the lower side of each hemisphere, is *responsible for hearing and language*. The *primary auditory cortex* in the temporal lobe is analogous to the somatosensory cortex in the parietal lobe and the primary visual areas of the occipital lobe—it receives sensory information from the ears based on the frequencies of sounds. Secondary areas of the temporal lobe then process the information into meaningful units, such as speech and words. The temporal lobe also houses the visual association areas that interpret the meaning of visual stimuli and help us recognize common objects in the environment (Martin, 2007).

The **frontal lobe**, which sits behind the forehead, has *specialized areas for movement, abstract thinking, planning, memory, and judgment*. As you just read, it contains the motor cortex, which coordinates movements of muscle groups throughout the body. Other areas in the frontal lobe coordinate thought processes that help us manipulate information and retrieve memories, which we can use to plan our behaviors and interact socially with others. In short, the frontal cortex allows us to do the kind of thinking, imagining, planning, and anticipating that sets humans apart from most other species (Stuss & Benson, 1986).

The third level of organization in the cerebral cortex involves the representation of information within specific lobes in the cortex. There is a hierarchy of processing stages from primary areas that handle fine details of information all the way up to **association areas**, which are *composed of neurons that help provide sense and meaning to information registered in the cortex*. For example, neurons in the primary visual cortex are highly specialized—some detect features of the environment that are in a horizontal orientation, others detect movement, and still others process information about human versus nonhuman forms. The association areas of the occipital lobe interpret the information extracted by these primary areas—shape, motion, and so on—to make sense of what's being perceived; in this case, perhaps a large cat leaping toward your face. Similarly, neurons in the primary auditory cortex register sound frequencies, but it's the association areas of the temporal lobe that allow you to turn those noises into the meaning of your friend screaming, "Look out for the cat!!" Association areas, then, help stitch together the threads of information in the various parts of the cortex to produce a meaningful understanding of what's being registered in the brain. Neurons in the association areas are usually less specialized and more flexible than neurons in the primary areas. As such, they can be shaped by learning and experience to do their job more effectively. This kind of shaping of neurons by environmental forces allows the brain flexibility, or "plasticity," our next topic.

TEMPORAL LOBE A region of the cerebral cortex responsible for hearing and language.

FRONTAL LOBE A region of the cerebral cortex that has specialized areas for movement, abstract thinking, planning, memory, and judgment.

ASSOCIATION AREAS Areas of the cerebral cortex that are composed of neurons that help provide sense and meaning to information registered in the cortex.

{ THE REAL WORLD } Brain Plasticity and Sensations in Phantom Limbs

LONG AFTER A LIMB IS AMPUTATED, MANY patients continue to experience sensations where the missing limb would be, a phenomenon called *phantom limb syndrome.* Patients can feel their missing limbs moving, even in coordinated gestures such as shaking hands. Some even report feeling pain in their phantom limbs. Why does this happen? Some evidence suggests that phantom limb syndrome may arise in part because of plasticity in the brain.

Researchers stimulated the skin surface in various regions around the face, torso, and arms while monitoring brain activity in amputees and non-amputated volunteers (Ramachandran & Blakeslee, 1998; Ramachandran, Rodgers-Ramachandran, & Stewart, 1992). Brain-imaging techniques displayed the somatosensory cortical areas activated when the skin was stimulated. This allowed the researchers to map how touch is represented in the somatosensory cortex for different areas of the body. For example, when the face was touched, the researchers could determine which areas in the somatosensory cortex were most active; when the torso was stimulated, they could see which areas responded; and so on.

Brain scans of the amputees revealed that stimulating areas of the face and upper arm activated an area in the somatosensory cortex that previously would have been activated by a now-missing hand. The face and arm were represented in the somatosensory

cortex in an area adjacent to where the person's hand—now amputated—would have been represented. Stimulating the face or arm produced phantom limb sensations in the amputees; they reported "feeling" a sensation in their missing limbs.

Brain plasticity can explain these results (Pascual-Leone et al., 2005). The cortical representations for the face and the upper arm normally lie on either side of the representation for the hand. The somatosensory areas for the face and upper arm were larger in amputees and had taken over the part of the cortex normally representing the hand. Indeed, the new face and arm representations were now contiguous with each

other, filling in the space occupied by the hand representation. Some of these new mappings were quite concise. For example, in some amputees, when specific areas of the facial skin were activated, the patient reported sensations in just *one finger* of the phantom hand!

This and related research suggest one explanation for a previously poorly understood phenomenon. How can a person "feel" something that isn't there? Brain plasticity, an adaptive process through which the brain reorganizes itself, offers an answer (Flor, Nikolajsen, & Jensen, 2006). The brain established new mappings that led to novel sensations.

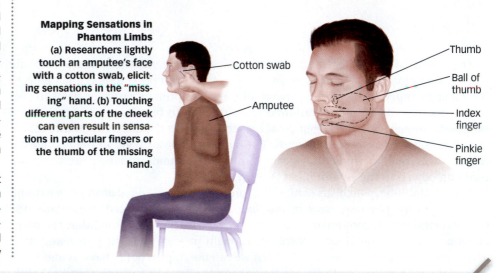

Mapping Sensations in Phantom Limbs (a) Researchers lightly touch an amputee's face with a cotton swab, eliciting sensations in the "missing" hand. (b) Touching different parts of the cheek can even result in sensations in particular fingers or the thumb of the missing hand.

Cotton swab

Amputee

Thumb

Ball of thumb

Index finger

Pinkie finger

Brain Plasticity

The cerebral cortex may seem like a fixed structure, one big sheet of neurons designed to help us make sense of our external world. Remarkably, though, sensory cortices are not fixed. They can adapt to changes in sensory inputs, a quality researchers call *plasticity* (i.e., "the ability to be molded"). As an example, if you lose your middle finger in an accident, the part of the somatosensory area that represents that finger is initially unresponsive (Kaas, 1991). After all, there's no longer any sensory input going from that location to that part of the brain. You might expect the "left middle finger neurons" of the somatosensory cortex to wither away. However, over time, that area in the somatosensory cortex becomes responsive to stimulation of the fingers *adjacent* to the missing finger. The brain is plastic: Functions that were assigned to certain areas of the brain may be capable of being reassigned to other areas of the brain to accommodate changing input from the environment. This suggests that sensory inputs "compete" for representation in each cortical area. (See the Real World box for a striking illustration of "phantom limbs.")

Plasticity doesn't only occur to compensate for missing digits or limbs, however. An extraordinary amount of stimulation of one finger can result in that finger "taking over" the representation of the part of the cortex that usually represents other, adjacent fingers (Merzenich, Recanzone, Jenkins, & Grajski, 1990). For example, concert pianists have highly developed cortical areas for finger control: The continued input from the fingers commands a larger area of representation in the somatosensory cortices in the brain. Similar findings have been obtained with quilters (who may have highly developed areas for the thumb and forefinger, which are critical to their profession) and taxi drivers (who have overdeveloped brain areas in the hippocampus that are used during spatial navigation; Maguire, Woollett, & Spiers, 2006).

In summary, neurons make up nerves, which in turn form the human nervous system. The nervous system is divided into the peripheral and the central nervous system. The peripheral nervous system connects the central nervous system with the rest of the body, and it is itself divided into the somatic nervous system and the autonomic nervous system. The somatic nervous system, which conveys information into and out of the central nervous system, controls voluntary muscles, whereas the autonomic nervous system automatically controls the body's organs. The autonomic nervous system is further divided into the sympathetic and parasympathetic nervous systems, which complement each other in their effects on the body. The sympathetic nervous system prepares the body for action in threatening situations, and the parasympathetic nervous system returns it to its normal state.

The central nervous system is composed of the spinal cord and the brain. The spinal cord can mediate some basic behaviors such as spinal reflexes without input from the brain. The brain can be divided into the hindbrain, midbrain, and forebrain. The hindbrain generally coordinates information coming into and out of the spinal cord with structures such as the medulla, the reticular formation, the cerebellum, and the pons. These structures respectively coordinate breathing and heart rate, regulate sleep and arousal levels, coordinate fine motor skills, and communicate this information to the cortex. The midbrain, with the help of structures such as the tectum and tegmentum, generally coordinates functions such as orientation to the environment and movement and arousal toward sensory stimuli. The forebrain generally coordinates higher-level functions, such as perceiving, feeling, and thinking. The forebrain houses subcortical structures, such as the thalamus, hypothalamus, limbic system (including the hippocampus and amygdala), and basal ganglia; all these structures perform a variety of functions related to motivation and emotion. The cerebral cortex, composed of two hemispheres with four lobes each (occipital, parietal, temporal, and frontal) performs tasks that help make us fully human: thinking, planning, judging, perceiving, and behaving purposefully and voluntarily. Finally, neurons in the brain can be shaped by experience and the environment, making the human brain amazingly plastic. ■ ■

The Development and Evolution of Nervous Systems

Other ways to understand the organization of the nervous system are to consider its development in the uterus and its evolution over time. The first approach reveals how the nervous system develops and changes within each member of a species, whereas the second approach reveals how the nervous system in humans evolved and adapted from other species. Both approaches help us understand how the human brain came to be the way it is, which is surprisingly imperfect. Far from being a single, elegant machine—the enchanted loom the philosophers wrote so poetically about—the human brain is instead a system composed of many distinct components that have been added at different times during the course of evolution. The human species has retained what worked best in earlier versions of the brain, then added bits and pieces to get us to our present state through evolution. We'll look at that process after we first consider how an individual nervous system develops.

Figure 3.22 Prenatal Brain Development The more primitive parts of the brain, the hindbrain and midbrain, develop first, followed by successively higher levels. The cerebral cortex with its characteristic fissures doesn't develop until the middle of the pregnancy. The cerebral hemispheres undergo most of their development in the final trimester.

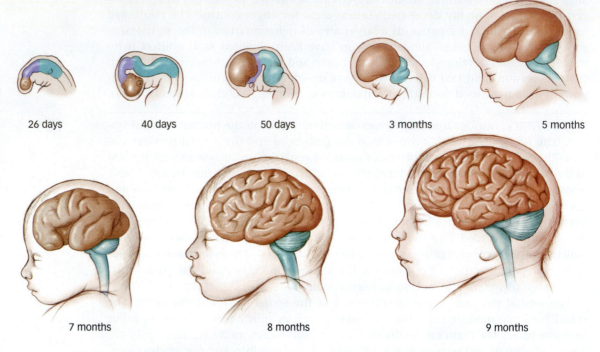

26 days   40 days   50 days   3 months   5 months

7 months   8 months   9 months

Prenatal Development of the Central Nervous System

The nervous system is the first major bodily system to take form in an embryo (Moore, 1977). It begins to develop within the third week after fertilization, when the embryo is still in the shape of a sphere. Initially, a ridge forms on one side of the sphere and then builds up at its edges to become a deep groove. The ridges fold together and fuse to enclose the groove, forming a structure called the *neural tube*. The tail end of the neural tube will remain a tube, and as the embryo grows larger, it forms the basis of the spinal cord. The tube expands at the opposite end, so that by the fourth week the three basic levels of the brain are visible; during the fifth week, the forebrain and hindbrain further differentiate into subdivisions. During the seventh week and later, the forebrain expands considerably to form the cerebral hemispheres.

As the embryonic brain continues to grow, each subdivision folds onto the next one and begins to form the structures easily visible in the adult brain (see **FIGURE 3.22**): The hindbrain forms the cerebellum and medulla, the midbrain forms the tectum and the tegmentum, and the forebrain subdivides further, separating the thalamus and hypothalamus from the cerebral hemispheres. Over time, the cerebral hemispheres undergo the greatest development, ultimately covering almost all the other subdivisions of the brain.

The *ontogeny* of the brain—how it develops within a given individual—is pretty remarkable. In about half the time it takes you to complete a 15-week semester, the basic structures of the brain are in place and rapidly developing, eventually allowing a newborn to enter the world with a fairly sophisticated set of abilities. In comparison, the *phylogeny* of the brain—how it developed within a particular species—is a much slower process. However, it too has allowed humans to make the most of the available brain structures, enabling us to perform an incredible array of tasks.

Evolutionary Development of the Central Nervous System

The central nervous system evolved from the very simple one found in simple animals to the elaborate nervous system in humans today. Even the simplest animals have sensory neurons and motor neurons for responding to the environment (Shepherd,

1988). For example, single-celled protozoa have molecules in their cell membrane that are sensitive to food in the water. These molecules trigger the movement of tiny threads called *cilia*, which help propel the protozoa toward the food source. The first neurons appeared in simple invertebrates, such as jellyfish; the sensory neurons in the jellyfish's tentacles can feel the touch of a potentially dangerous predator, which prompts the jellyfish to swim to safety. If you're a jellyfish, this simple neural system is sufficient to keep you alive.

The first central nervous system worthy of the name, though, appeared in flatworms. The flatworm has a collection of neurons in the head—a simple kind of brain—that includes sensory neurons for vision and taste and motor neurons that control feeding behavior. Emerging from the brain are a pair of tracts that form a spinal cord. They are connected by *commissures*, neural fibers that cross between the left and right side of the nervous system to allow communication between neurons at symmetrical positions on either side of the body. The tracts are also connected by smaller collections of neurons called *ganglia*, which integrate information and coordinate motor behavior in the body region near each ganglion.

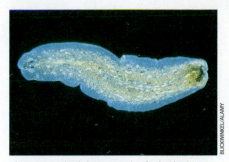

Flatworms don't have much of a brain, but then again, they don't need much of a brain. The rudimentary brain areas found in simple invertebrates eventually evolved into the complex brain structures found in humans.

During the course of evolution, a major split in the organization of the nervous system occurred between invertebrate animals (those without a spinal column) and vertebrate animals (those with a spinal column). The central nervous system of invertebrates continued along the "flatworm plan," but the nervous system in vertebrates changed dramatically.

In all vertebrates, the central nervous system is a single tubular structure, and the brain is a series of expansions of the tube that forms in the embryo. Also, the central nervous system in vertebrates separates sensory and motor processing. Sensory processing occurs mainly in the back of the brain and spinal cord, whereas motor coordination is controlled by the front of the brain and spinal cord, although as you have already seen, there is considerable communication between the sensory and motor areas. Furthermore, the central nervous system is organized into a hierarchy: The lower levels of the brain and spinal cord execute simpler functions, while the higher levels of the nervous system perform more complex functions. As you saw earlier, in humans, reflexes are accomplished in the spinal cord. At the next level, the midbrain executes the more complex task of orienting toward an important stimulus in the environment. Finally, a more complex task, such as imagining what your life will be like 20 years from now, is performed in the forebrain (Addis, Wong, & Schacter, 2007; Szpunar, Watson, & McDermott, 2007).

The forebrain undergoes further evolutionary advances in vertebrates. In lower vertebrate species such as amphibians (frogs and newts), the forebrain consists only of small clusters of neurons at the end of the neural tube. In higher vertebrates, including reptiles, birds, and mammals, the forebrain is much larger, and it evolves in two different patterns. In reptiles and birds, large groups of neurons develop along the inside edge of the neural tube and form the striatum, which controls their most complex behaviors. The neurons on the outside edge of the neural tube develop into paperlike layers that form the cerebral cortex, which is quite small and thin compared to the striatum. Birds, in particular, have almost no cerebral cortex, but their striatum is developed enough to control complex behavioral patterns, including learning, song production, social behavior, and reproductive behavior (Farries, 2004). The striatum is also fairly well developed in mammals, but even more impressive is the cerebral cortex, which develops multiple areas that serve a broad range of higher mental functions. This forebrain development has reached its peak—so far—in humans.

The human brain, then, is not so much one remarkable thing; rather, it is a succession of extensions from a quite serviceable foundation. Like other species, humans have a hindbrain, and like those species, it performs important tasks to keep us alive. For some species, that's sufficient. All flatworms need to do to ensure their species survival is eat, reproduce, and stay alive a reasonable length of time. But as the human brain

"You're making more at this firm than anyone else whose brain is the size of a walnut."

GENE The unit of hereditary transmission.

CHROMOSOMES Strands of DNA wound around each other in a double-helix configuration.

evolved, structures in the midbrain and forebrain developed to handle the increasingly complex demands of the environment. The forebrain of a bullfrog is about as differentiated as it needs to be to survive in a frog's world. The human forebrain, however, shows substantial refinement, which allows for some remarkable, uniquely human abilities: self-awareness, sophisticated language use, social interaction, abstract reasoning, imagining, and empathy, among others.

There is intriguing evidence that the human brain evolved more quickly than the brains of other species (Dorus et al., 2004). Researchers compared the sequences of 200 brain-related genes in mice, rats, monkeys, and humans and discovered a collection of genes that evolved more rapidly among primates. What's more, they found that this evolutionary process was more rapid along the lineage that led to humans. That is, primate brains evolved quickly compared to those of other species, but the brains of the primates who eventually became humans evolved even more rapidly. These results suggest that in addition to the normal adaptations that occur over the process of evolution, the genes for human brains took particular advantage of a variety of mutations (changes in a gene's DNA) along the evolutionary pathway. These results also suggest that the human brain is still evolving—becoming bigger and more adapted to the demands of the environment (Evans et al., 2005; Mekel-Bobrov et al., 2005).

Genes may direct the development of the brain on a large, evolutionary scale, but they also guide the development of an individual and, generally, the development of a species. Let's take a brief look at how genes and the environment contribute to the biological bases of behavior.

Genes and the Environment

You may have heard the phrase "nature vs. nurture," as though these twin influences grapple with each other for supremacy in directing a person's behavior. This suggests that either genetics ("nature") or the environment ("nurture") played a major role in producing particular behaviors, personality traits, psychological disorders, or pretty much any other thing that a human does. The emerging picture from current research is that both nature *and* nurture play a role in directing behavior, and the focus has shifted to examining the relative contributions of each influence rather than the absolute contributions of either influence alone. In short, it's the interaction of genes and environmental influences that determines what humans do (Gottesman & Hanson, 2005; Rutter & Silberg, 2002).

A **gene** is *the unit of hereditary transmission*. Genes are built from strands of DNA (deoxyribonucleic acid) and are organized into large threads called **chromosomes**, which are *strands of DNA wound around each other in a double-helix configuration* (see **FIGURE 3.23**). Chromosomes come in pairs, and humans have 23 pairs each. These pairs of chromosomes are similar but not identical: You inherit one of each pair from your father and one from your mother. There's a twist, however: The selection of *which* of each pair is given to you is random.

Figure 3.23 Genes, Chromosomes, and Their Recombination The cell nucleus houses chromosomes, which are made up of double-helix strands of DNA. Every cell in our bodies has 23 pairs of chromosomes. Genes are segments on a strand of DNA with codes that make us who we are.

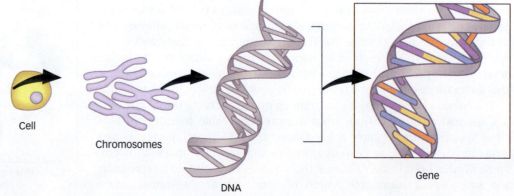

Cell

Chromosomes

DNA

Gene

Perhaps the most striking example of this random distribution is the determination of sex. The chromosomes that determine sex are the X and Y chromosomes; females have two X chromosomes, whereas males have one X and one Y chromosome. You inherited an X chromosome from your mother since she has only X chromosomes to give. Your biological sex, therefore, was determined by whether you received an additional X chromosome or a Y chromosome from your father.

There is considerable variability in the genes that individual offspring receive. Nonetheless, children share a higher proportion of their genes with their parents than with more distant relatives or with nonrelatives. Children share half their genes with each parent, a quarter of their genes with their grandparents, an eighth of their genes with cousins, and so on. The probability of sharing genes is called *degree of relatedness*. The most genetically related people are *monozygotic twins* (also called *identical twins*), who develop from the splitting of a single fertilized egg and therefore share 100% of their genes. *Dizygotic twins* (*fraternal twins*) develop from two separate fertilized eggs and share 50% of their genes, the same as any two siblings born separately.

Many researchers have tried to determine the relative influence of genetics on behavior. One way to do this is to compare a trait shown by monozygotic twins with that same trait among dizygotic twins. This type of research usually enlists twins who were raised in the same household, so that the impact of their environment—their socioeconomic status, access to education, parental child-rearing practices, environmental stressors—remains relatively constant. Finding that monozygotic twins have a higher prevalence of a specific trait suggests a genetic influence (Boomsma, Busjahn, & Peltonen, 2002).

As an example, the likelihood that the dizygotic twin of a person who has schizophrenia (a mental disorder we'll discuss in greater detail in Chapter 13) will *also* develop schizophrenia is 27%. However, this statistic rises to 50% for monozygotic twins. This observation suggests a substantial genetic influence on the likelihood of developing schizophrenia. Monozygotic twins share 100% of their genes, and if one assumes environmental influences are relatively consistent for both members of the twin pair, the 50% likelihood can be traced to genetic factors. That sounds scarily high . . . until you realize that the remaining 50% probability must be due to environmental influences. In short, genetics can contribute to the development, likelihood, or onset of a variety of traits. But a more complete picture of genetic influences on behavior must always take the environmental context into consideration. Genes express themselves within an environment, not in isolation.

Genes set the range of possibilities that can be observed in a population, but the characteristics of any individual within that range are determined by environmental factors and experience. Genetically, it's possible for humans to live comfortably 12,000 feet above sea level. The residents of La Paz, Bolivia, have done so for centuries. But chances are *you* wouldn't enjoy gasping for breath on a daily basis. Your environmental

Monozygotic twins (left) share 100% of their genes in common, while dizygotic twins (right) share 50% of their genes, the same as other siblings. Studies of monozygotic and dizygotic twins help researchers estimate the relative contributions of genes and environmental influences on behavior.

"The title of my science project is 'My Little Brother: Nature or Nurture.'"

experiences have made it unlikely for you to live that way, just as the experience and environment of the citizens of La Paz have made living at high altitude quite acceptable. Genetically, you and the Bolivians come from the same species, but the range of genetic capabilities you share is not expressed in the same way. What's more, neither you nor a Bolivian can breathe underwater in Lake Titicaca, which is also 12,000 feet above sea level. The genetic capabilities that another species might enjoy, such as breathing underwater, are outside the range of *your* possibilities, no matter how much you might desire them.

With these parameters in mind, behavioral geneticists use calculations based on relatedness to compute the heritability of behaviors (Plomin et al., 2001). **Heritability** is *a measure of the variability of behavioral traits among individuals that can be accounted for by genetic factors.* Heritability is calculated as a proportion, and its numerical value (index) ranges from 0 to 1.00. A heritability of 0 means that genes do not contribute to individual differences in the behavioral trait; a heritability of 1.00 means that genes are the *only* reason for the individual differences. As you might guess, scores of 0 or 1.00 occur so infrequently that they serve more as theoretical limits than realistic values; almost nothing in human behavior is completely due to the environment or owed *completely* to genetic inheritance. Scores between 0 and 1.00, then, indicate that individual differences are caused by varying degrees of genetic and environmental contributions—a little stronger influence of genetics here, a little stronger influence of the environment there, but each always within the context of the other.

For human behavior, almost all estimates of heritability are in the moderate range, between .30 and .60. For example, a heritability index of .50 for intelligence indicates that half of the variability in intelligence test scores is attributable to genetic influences and the remaining half is due to environmental influences. Smart parents often (but not always) produce smart children; genetics certainly plays a role. But smart and not-so-smart children attend good or not-so-good schools, practice their piano lessons with more or less regularity, study or not study as hard as they might, have good and not-so-good teachers and role models, and so on. Genetics is only half the story in intelligence. Environmental influences also play a significant role in predicting the basis of intelligence (see Chapter 9).

Heritability has proven to be a theoretically useful and statistically sound concept in helping scientists understand the relative genetic and environmental influences on behavior. However, there are four important points about heritability to bear in mind.

First, remember that *heritability is an abstract concept*: It tells us nothing about the *specific* genes that contribute to a trait. A heritability index of .40 gives us a reasonable approximation of the extent to which genes influence a behavior, but it says nothing about *which* genes are responsible. Flipping that around also illustrates the point. Heritability of .40 means that there's also an "environmentality" of .60 in predicting the behavior in question. Most people would find it extremely difficult, however, to pinpoint what *one exact factor* in the environment contributed to that estimate. With further decoding of the human genome and a greater understanding of each gene's specific roles, scientists someday may be able to isolate the exact genes that contribute to a specific behavior, but they have not yet attained that degree of precision.

Second, *heritability is a population concept*: It tells us nothing about an individual. For example, a .50 heritability of intelligence means that, on average, about 50% of the differences in intellectual performance are attributable to genetic differences among individuals in the population. It does *not* mean that 50% of any given person's intelligence is due to her or his genetic makeup. Heritability provides guidance for understanding differences across individuals in a population rather than abilities within an individual.

Third, *heritability is dependent on the environment*. Just as behavior occurs within certain contexts, so do genetic influences. For example, intelligence isn't an unchanging quality: People are intelligent within a particular learning context, a social setting, a

HERITABILITY A measure of the variability of behavioral traits among individuals that can be accounted for by genetic factors.

family environment, a socioeconomic class, and so on. Heritability, therefore, is meaningful only for the environmental conditions in which it was computed, and heritability estimates may change dramatically under other environmental conditions. At present, heritability estimates for intelligence, to stick with our example, are computed across a range of environments and have a fair amount of stability. But if all the earth's population suddenly had access to better nutrition, higher-quality schooling, and good health care, that change in the environmental context would necessitate a recalculation of heritability within those contexts.

Finally, *heritability is not fate*. It tells us nothing about the degree to which interventions can change a behavioral trait. Heritability is useful for identifying behavioral traits that are influenced by genes, but it is not useful for determining how individuals will respond to particular environmental conditions or treatments.

In summary, examining the development of the nervous system over the life span of an individual—its ontogeny—and across the time within which a species evolves—its phylogeny—presents further opportunities for understanding the human brain. The nervous system is the first system that forms in an embryo, starting as a neural tube, which forms the basis of the spinal cord. The neural tube expands on one end to form the hindbrain, midbrain, and forebrain, each of which folds onto the next structure. Within each of these areas, specific brain structures begin to differentiate. The forebrain shows the greatest differentiation, and in particular, the cerebral cortex is the most developed in humans.

Nervous systems evolved from simple collections of sensory and motor neurons in simple animals, such as flatworms, to elaborate centralized nervous systems found in mammals. The evolution of the human nervous system can be thought of as a process of refining, elaborating, and expanding structures present in other species. In reptiles and birds, the highest processing area is the striatum; in mammals, the highest processing area is the cerebral cortex. The human brain appears to have evolved more quickly compared to other species to become adapted to a more complex environment.

The gene, or the unit of hereditary transmission, is built from strands of DNA in a double-helix formation that is organized into chromosomes. Humans have 23 pairs of chromosomes—half come from each parent. A child shares 50% of his or her genes with each parent. Monozygotic twins share 100% of their genes, while dizygotic twins share 50%, the same as any other siblings. Because of their genetic relatedness, twins are often participants in genetic research.

The study of genetics indicates that both genes and the environment work together to influence behavior. Genes set the range of variation in populations within a given environment, but they do not predict individual characteristics; experience and other environmental factors play a crucial role as well. ■ ■

Investigating the Brain

So far, you've read a great deal about the nervous system: how it's organized, how it works, what its components are, and what those components do. But one question remains largely unanswered—*how* do we know all of this? Anatomists can dissect a human brain and identify its structures, but they cannot determine which structures play a role in producing which behaviors by dissecting a nonliving brain. In this section, we'll look at some of the methods psychologists and neuroscientists have developed for linking brain structures with the thoughts, feelings, and behaviors they direct.

Scientists use a variety of methods to understand how the brain affects behavior. Let's consider three of the main ones: testing people with brain damage and observing their deficits, studying electrical activity in the brain during behavior, and conducting brain scans while people perform various tasks. Studying people with

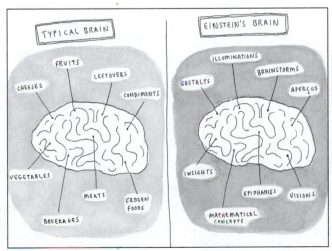

brain damage highlights one of the central themes of this book: To better understand the normal operation of a process, it is instructive to understand what happens when that process fails. Observing the behavioral mindbugs that result from damage to certain areas of the brain enables researchers to identify the functions of those areas. The second approach, studying the brain's electrical activity, has a long history and has produced a wealth of information about which neurons fire when behavior is enacted. The modern extensions of that technique are the various ways that the brain can be scanned, mapped, and coded using a variety of sophisticated instruments, which is the third approach we'll consider. Let's examine each of these ways of investigating the brain.

Learning about Brain Organization by Studying the Damaged Brain

Remember Betty, the 75-year-old grandmother admitted to the emergency room because she couldn't recognize her own husband? She had suffered a stroke from a blood clot that deprived her brain of oxygen and caused the death of neurons in the afflicted area. Betty's stroke affected part of the association area in her temporal lobe, where complex visual objects are identified. Betty's occipital lobe, the main area where visual processing takes place, was unaffected, so Betty could see her husband and two sons, but because of the damage to her temporal lobe, she could not recognize them.

In Betty's case, the damage was small, and no other visual capacities were affected; the brain areas that process simple visual forms, color, motion, and other features were still intact. So, her vision was not affected, but she had lost her ability to identify familiar faces, even her husband's. Betty thought she was having problems with her vision, but her neuropsychologist recognized the symptoms of *agnosia*, a term that means "without knowledge." Betty's case involved a specific version of this affliction called *prosopagnosia*, which means "without knowledge of faces" (Kleinschmidt & Cohen, 2006).

Much research in neuroscience correlates the loss of specific perceptual, motor, emotional, or cognitive functions with specific areas of brain damage (Andrewes, 2001; Kolb & Whishaw, 2003). By studying these mindbugs, neuroscientists can theorize about the functions those brain areas normally perform. The modern history of neuroscience can be dated to the work of Paul Broca (see Chapter 1). In 1861, Broca described a patient who had lost the capacity to produce spoken language (but not the ability to understand language) due to damage in a small area in the left frontal lobe. In 1874, Carl Wernicke (1848–1905) described a patient with an impairment in language comprehension (but not the ability to produce speech) associated with damage to an area in the upper-left temporal lobe. These areas were named, respectively, *Broca's area* and *Wernicke's area,* and they provided the earliest evidence that the brain locations for speech production and speech comprehension are separate and that for most people, the left hemisphere is critical to producing and understanding language (Young, 1990).

The Emotional Functions of the Frontal Lobes

As you've already seen, the human frontal lobes are a remarkable evolutionary achievement. However, psychology's first glimpse at some functions of the frontal lobes came from a rather unremarkable fellow; so unremarkable, in fact, that a single event in his life defined his place in the annals of psychology's history (Macmillan, 2000).

Phineas Gage was a muscular 25-year-old boss of the Rutland and Burlington Railroad excavating crew. On September 13, 1848, in Cavendish, Vermont, he was packing an explosive charge into a crevice in a rock when disaster struck. Here is an account of the event in the words of John M. Harlow, the physician who examined him:

> The powder and fuse had been adjusted in the hole, and he was in the act of "tamping it in," as it is called. . . . While doing this, his attention was attracted by his men in the pit behind him. Averting his head and looking over his right shoulder, at the same instant dropping the iron upon the charge, it struck fire upon the rock, and the

explosion followed, which projected the iron obliquely upwards . . . passing completely through his head, and high into the air, falling to the ground several [meters] behind him, where it was afterwards picked up by his men, smeared with blood and brain (Harlow, 1848).

In short, Phineas Gage had a 3-foot, 13-pound iron rod propelled through his head at high speed. As **FIGURE 3.24** shows, the rod entered through his lower left jaw and exited through the middle top of his head. Gruesome but unremarkable; industrial accidents unfortunately happen quite often.

The remarkable part of this story is that Gage lived to tell the tale. After the accident, Gage sat up, climbed in the back of a wagon, and journeyed to town to seek medical treatment. He lived for another 12 years, residing in various parts of the United States and abroad and even joining P. T. Barnum's museum of oddities for a brief stint. He died in 1860 after a series of seizures, whereupon his skull and the iron rod were donated to the Warren Anatomical Museum of the Harvard University Medical School, where they are still displayed today.

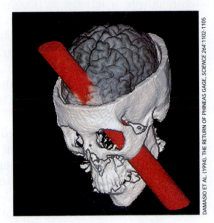

Before the accident, Gage had been mild mannered, quiet, conscientious, and a hard worker. After the accident, however, Gage's personality underwent a significant change. He became irritable, irresponsible, indecisive, and given to profanity. The sad decline of Gage's personality and emotional life nonetheless provided an unexpected benefit to psychology. His case study was the first to allow researchers to investigate the hypothesis that the frontal lobe is involved in emotion regulation, planning, and decision making. Furthermore, because the connections between the frontal lobe and the subcortical structures of the limbic system were affected, scientists were able to better understand how the amygdala, hippocampus, and related brain structures interacted with the cerebral cortex (Damasio, 2005).

The Distinct Roles of the Left and Right Hemispheres

You'll recall that the cerebral cortex is divided into two hemispheres, although typically the two hemispheres act as one integrated unit. Sometimes, though, disorders can threaten the ability of the brain to function, and the only way to stop them is with radical methods. This is sometimes the case with patients who suffer from severe, intractable epilepsy. Seizures that begin in one hemisphere cross the corpus callosum (the thick band of nerve fibers that allows the two hemispheres to communicate) to the opposite hemisphere and start a feedback loop that results in a kind of firestorm in the brain.

To alleviate the severity of the seizures, surgeons can sever the corpus callosum in a procedure called a *split-brain procedure*. This meant that a seizure that starts in one hemisphere is isolated in that hemisphere since there is no longer a connection to the other side. This procedure helps the patients with epilepsy but also produces some unusual, if not unpredictable, behaviors.

Nobel laureate Roger Sperry (1913–94) and his colleagues designed several experiments that investigated the behaviors of split-brain patients and in the process revealed a great deal about the independent functions of the left and right hemispheres (Sperry, 1964). Normally, any information that initially enters the left hemisphere is also registered in the right hemisphere and vice versa: The information comes in and travels across the corpus callosum, and both hemispheres understand what's going on. But in a split-brain patient, information entering one hemisphere stays there. Without an intact corpus callosum,

Figure 3.24 Phineas Gage Phineas Gage's traumatic accident allowed researchers to investigate the functions of the frontal lobe and its connections with emotion centers in the subcortical structures. The likely path of the metal rod through Gage's skull is reconstructed here.

ONLY HUMAN

DO-IT-YOURSELF ANATOMY LESSON
1995—Troy Harding, 19, was released from a Portland, Oregon, hospital 3 weeks after he turned around abruptly when talking to friends and walked into the radio antenna of his car. The antenna went up his nose almost four inches, pierced his sinus, and entered his brain, coming to rest in his pituitary gland.

Roger Wolcott Sperry (1913–94) received the Nobel Prize in Physiology in 1981 for his pioneering work investigating the independent functions of the cerebral hemispheres.

there's no way for that information to reach the other hemisphere. Sperry and his colleagues used this understanding of lateralized perception in a series of experiments. For example, they had patients look at a spot in the center of a screen and then projected a stimulus on one side of the screen, isolating the stimulus to one hemisphere.

The hemispheres themselves are specialized for different kinds of tasks. You just learned about Broca and Wernicke's areas, which revealed that language processing is a left-hemisphere activity. So imagine that some information came into the left hemisphere of a split-brain patient, and she was asked to verbally describe what it was. No problem: The left hemisphere has the information, it's the "speaking" hemisphere, so the patient should have no difficulty verbally describing what she saw. But suppose the patient was asked to reach behind a screen with her left hand and pick up the object she just saw. Remember that the hemispheres exert contralateral control over the body, meaning that the left hand is controlled by the right hemisphere. But this patient's right hemisphere has no clue what the object was because that information was received in the left hemisphere and was unable to travel to the right hemisphere! So, even though the split-brain patient saw the object and could verbally describe it, she would be unable to use the right hemisphere to perform other tasks regarding that object, such as correctly selecting it from a group with her left hand (see **FIGURE 3.25**).

Of course, information presented to the right hemisphere would produce complementary deficits. In this case, a patient might be presented with a familiar object in her left hand (such as a key), be able to demonstrate that she knew what it was (by twisting and turning the key in midair), yet be unable to verbally describe what she was holding. In this case, the information in the right hemisphere is unable to travel to the left hemisphere, which controls the production of speech.

Furthermore, suppose a split-brain person was shown the unusual face in **FIGURE 3.26**. This is called a *chimeric face*, and it is assembled from half-face components of the full faces also shown in the figure. When asked to indicate which face was presented, a split-brain person would indicate that she saw *both* faces because information about the face on the left is recorded in the right hemisphere and information about the face on the right is recorded in the left hemisphere (Levy, Trevarthen, & Sperry, 1972).

These split-brain studies reveal that the two hemispheres perform different functions and can work together seamlessly as long as the corpus callosum is intact. Without a way to transmit information from one hemisphere to the other, information gets "stuck" in the hemisphere it initially entered and we become acutely aware of

Figure 3.25 Split-Brain Experiment When a split-brain patient is presented with the picture of a ring on the right and that of a key on the left side of a screen, she can verbalize *ring*, but not *key* because the left hemisphere "sees" the ring and language is usually located in the left hemisphere. This patient would be able to choose a key with her left hand from a set of objects behind a screen. She would not, however, be able to pick out a ring with her right hand since what the left hemisphere "sees" is not communicated to the right side of her body.

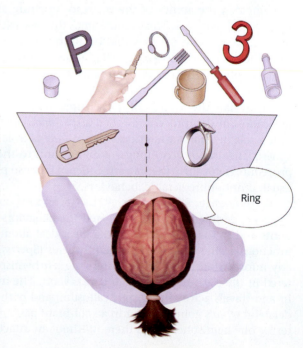

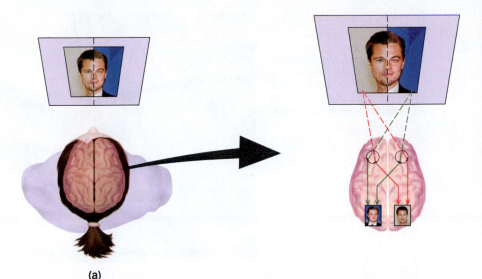

Figure 3.26 Chimeric Faces and the Split Brain (a) When a split-brain patient views a chimeric face of Brad Pitt and Leonardo DiCaprio, her left hemisphere is aware only of Leonardo DiCaprio and her right hemisphere sees only Brad Pitt. (b) When asked who she sees, the patient answers, "Leonardo DiCaprio," because speech is controlled by the left hemisphere. (c) When asked to point to the face she saw with her left hand, she points to Brad Pitt because her right hemisphere is only aware of the left half of the picture.
PHOTO OF BRAD PITT: AP PHOTO/ALEX BRANDON; PHOTO OF LEONARDO DICAPRIO: AP PHOTO/TAMMIE ARROYO

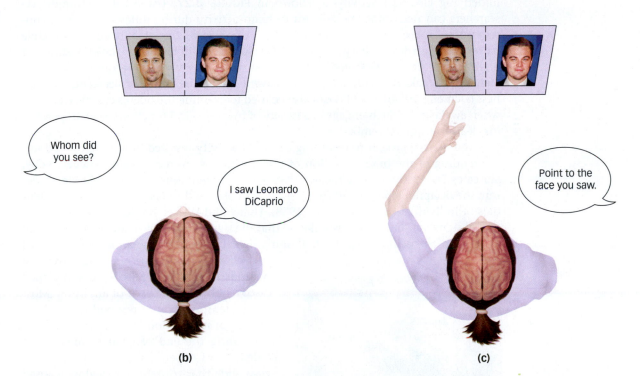

the different functions of each hemisphere. Of course, a split-brain patient can adapt to this by simply moving her eyes a little so that the same information independently enters both hemispheres. Split-brain studies have continued over the past few decades and continue to play an important role in shaping our understanding of how the brain works (Gazzaniga, 2006).

Listening to the Brain: Single Neurons and the EEG

A second approach to studying the link between brain structures and behavior involves recording the pattern of electrical activity of neurons. An **electroencephalogram (EEG)** is *a device used to record electrical activity in the brain*. Typically electrodes are placed on the outside of the head, and even though the source of electrical activity in synapses and action potentials is far removed from these wires, the electric signals can be amplified several thousand times by the EEG. This provides a visual record of the

ELECTROENCEPHALOGRAM (EEG)
A device used to record electrical activity in the brain.

Figure 3.27 EEG The electroencephalogram (EEG) records electrical activity in the brain. Many states of consciousness, such as wakefulness and stages of sleep, are characterized by particular types of brainwaves.

AJPHOTO/PHOTO RESEARCHERS

underlying electrical activity, as shown in **FIGURE 3.27**. Using this technique, researchers can determine the amount of brain activity during different states of consciousness. For example, as you'll read in Chapter 8, the brain shows distinctive patterns of electrical activity when awake versus asleep; in fact, there are even different brain-wave patterns associated with different stages of sleep. EEG recordings allow researchers to make these fundamental discoveries about the nature of sleep and wakefulness (Dement, 1974). The EEG can also be used to examine the brain's electrical activity when awake individuals engage in a variety of psychological functions, such as perceiving, learning, and remembering.

A different approach to recording electrical activity resulted in a more refined understanding of the brain's division of responsibilities, even at a cellular level. Nobel laureates David Hubel and Torsten Wiesel used a technique that inserted electrodes into the occipital lobes of anesthetized cats and observed the patterns of action potentials of individual neurons (Hubel, 1988). Hubel and Wiesel amplified the action potential signals through a loudspeaker so that the signals could be heard as clicks as well as seen on an oscilloscope. While flashing lights in front of the animal's eye, Hubel and Wiesel recorded the resulting activity of neurons in the occipital cortex. What they discovered was not much of anything: Most of the neurons did not respond to this kind of general stimulation.

Nearing the end of what seemed like a failed set of experiments, they projected a glass slide that contained a shadow (caused by the edge of the slide) to show an image in front of the cat's eyes, reasoning that the flaw wouldn't make much difference to the already unimpressive experimental outcomes. Instead, they heard a brisk flurry of clicks as the neurons in the cat's occipital lobe fired away! They discovered that neurons in the primary visual cortex are activated whenever a contrast between light and dark occurs in part of the visual field, seen particularly well when the visual stimulus was a thick line of light against a dark background. In this case, the shadow caused

David Hubel (left, b. 1926) and Torsten Wiesel (right, b. 1924) received the Nobel Prize in Physiology in 1981 for their work on mapping the visual cortex.

AP PHOTO

by the edge of the slide provided the kind of contrast that prompted particular neurons to respond. They then found that each neuron responded vigorously only when presented with a contrasting edge at a particular orientation. Since then, many studies have shown that neurons in the primary visual cortex represent particular features of visual stimuli, such as contrast, shape, and color (Zeki, 1993).

These neurons in the visual cortex are known as *feature detectors* because they selectively respond to certain aspects of a visual image. For example, some neurons fire only when detecting a vertical line in the middle of the visual field, other neurons fire when a line at a 45-degree angle is perceived, and still others in response to wider lines, horizontal lines, lines in the periphery of the visual field, and so on (Livingstone & Hubel, 1988). The discovery of this specialized function for neurons was a huge leap forward in our understanding of how the visual cortex works. Feature detectors identify basic dimensions of a stimulus ("slanted line . . . other slanted line . . . horizontal line"); those dimensions are then combined during a later stage of visual processing to allow recognition and perception of a stimulus ("oh, it's a letter *A*").

Other studies have identified a variety of features that are detected by sensory neurons. For example, some visual processing neurons in the temporal lobe are activated only when detecting faces (Kanwisher, 2000; Perrett, Rolls, & Caan, 1982). These neurons lie in the same area of the temporal cortex that was damaged in Betty's stroke. Neurons in this area are specialized for processing faces; damage to this area results in an inability to perceive faces. These complementary observations—showing that the type of function that is lost or altered when a brain area is damaged corresponds to the kind of information processed by neurons in that cortical area—provide the most compelling evidence linking the brain to behavior.

Brain Imaging: Watching the Brain in Action

The third major way that neuroscientists can peer into the workings of the human brain has only become possible within the past several decades. EEG readouts give an overall picture of a person's level of consciousness, and single-cell recordings shed light on the actions of particular clumps of neurons. The ideal of neuroscience, however, has been the ability to see the brain in operation while behavior is being enacted. This goal has been steadily achieved thanks to a wide range of *neuroimaging techniques* that use advanced technology to create images of the living, healthy brain (Posner & Raichle, 1994; Raichle & Mintun, 2006).

One of the first neuroimaging techniques developed was the *computerized axial tomography (CT) scan.* In a CT scan, a scanner rotates a device around a person's head and takes a series of x-ray photographs from different angles. Computer programs then combine these images to provide views from any angle. CT scans show different densities of tissue in the brain. For example, the higher-density skull looks white on a CT scan, the cortex shows up as gray, and the least dense fissures and ventricles in the brain look dark (see **FIGURE 3.28** on the next page). CT scans are used to locate lesions or tumors, which typically appear darker since they are less dense than the cortex.

Magnetic resonance imaging (MRI) involves applying brief but powerful magnetic pulses to the head and recording how these pulses are absorbed throughout the brain. For very short periods, these magnetic pulses cause molecules in the brain tissue to twist slightly and then relax, which releases a small

off the mark .com   by Mark Parisi

I THINK WE MAY HAVE FOUND *THE CAUSE OF YOUR* SUDDEN MEMORY LOSS . . .

© MARK PARISI/ATLANTIC FEATURE SYNDICATE

offthemark.com

ONLY HUMAN

JUST LET US KNOW IF YOU EXPERIENCE ANY DISCOMFORT . . . 1996—Employees of the Advanced Medical Imaging clinic in Newburgh, New York, forgot that Brenda Revella, 42, was in the claustrophobia-inducing MRI machine when they locked up for the night. (The patient lies in a tube 27 inches wide with the top of the tube only 4 inches from his or her face.) Revella managed to wiggle out 3 hours later.

Figure 3.28 Structural Imaging Techniques (CT and MRI) CT (left) and MRI (right) scans are used to provide information about the structure of the brain and can help to spot tumors and other kinds of damage. Each scan shown here provides a snapshot of a single slice in the brain. Note that the MRI scan provides a clearer, higher resolution image than the CT scan (see the text for further discussion of how these images are constructed and what they depict).

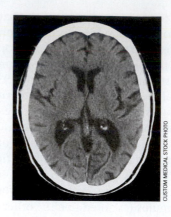
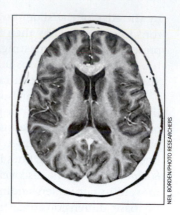

CUSTOM MEDICAL STOCK PHOTO

NEIL BORDEN/PHOTO RESEARCHERS

amount of energy. Differently charged molecules respond differently to the magnetic pulses, so the energy signals reveal brain structures with different molecular compositions. Magnetic resonance imaging produces pictures of soft tissue at a better resolution than a CT scan, as you can see in Figure 3.28. These techniques give psychologists a clearer picture of the structure of the brain and can help localize brain damage (as when someone suffers a stroke), but they reveal nothing about the functions of the brain.

Two newer techniques show researchers much more than just the structure of the brain. *Functional-brain-imaging* techniques allow us to actually watch the brain in action. These techniques rely on the fact that activated brain areas demand more energy for their neurons to work. This energy is supplied through increased blood flow to the activated areas. Functional-imaging techniques can detect such changes in blood flow. In *positron emission tomography (PET),* a harmless radioactive substance is injected into a person's bloodstream. Then the brain is scanned by radiation detectors as the person performs perceptual or cognitive tasks, such as reading or speaking. Areas of the brain that are activated during these tasks demand more energy and greater blood flow, resulting in a higher amount of the radioactivity in that region. The radiation detectors record the level of radioactivity in each region, producing a computerized image of the activated areas (see **FIGURE 3.29**). Note that PET scans differ from CT scans and MRIs in that the image produced shows activity in the brain while the person performs certain tasks. So, for example, a PET scan of a person speaking would show activation in Broca's area in the left frontal lobe.

For psychologists, the most widely used functional-brain-imaging technique nowadays is *functional magnetic resonance imaging (fMRI),* which detects the twisting of hemoglobin molecules in the blood when they are exposed to magnetic pulses. Hemoglobin is the molecule in the blood that carries oxygen to our tissues, including the brain. When active neurons demand more energy and blood flow, oxygenated hemoglobin concentrates in the active areas. fMRI detects the oxygenated hemoglobin and provides a picture of the level of activation in each brain area (see Figure 3.29). Just as MRI was a major advance over CT scans, *functional* MRI represents a similar leap in our ability to record the brain's activity during behavior. Both fMRI and PET allow researchers to localize changes in the brain very accurately. However, fMRI has a couple of advantages over PET. First, fMRI does not require any exposure to a radioactive substance. Second, fMRI can localize changes in brain activity across briefer periods than PET, which makes it more useful for analyzing psychological processes that occur extremely quickly, such as reading a word or recognizing a face. With PET, researchers often have to use experimental designs different from those they would use in the psychological laboratory in order to adapt to the limitations of PET technology. With fMRI, researchers can design experiments that more closely resemble the ones they carry out in the psychological laboratory.

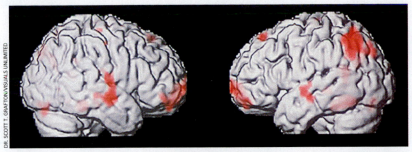

Gesture preparation

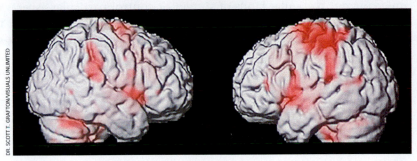

Gesture production

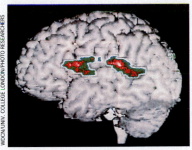

Figure 3.29 Functional-Imaging Techniques (PET fMRI) PET and fMRI scans provide information about the functions of the brain by revealing which brain areas become more or less active in different conditions. The PET scan (directly above) shows areas in the left hemisphere (Broca's area, left; lower parietal-upper temporal area, right) that become active when people hold in mind a string of letters for a few seconds. The fMRI scans (all views to the left) show several different regions in both hemispheres that become active when someone is thinking about a gesture (top) and when performing a gesture (bottom).

PET and fMRI provide remarkable insights into the types of information processing that take place in specific areas of the brain. For example, when a person performs a simple perceptual task, such as looking at a circular checkerboard, the primary visual areas are activated. As you have read, when the checkerboard is presented to the left visual field, the right visual cortex shows activation, and when the checkerboard is presented to the right visual field, the left visual cortex shows activation (Fox et al., 1986). Similarly, when people look at faces, fMRI reveals strong activity in a region in the visual association cortex called the *fusiform gyrus* (Kanwisher, McDermott, & Chun, 1997). When this structure is damaged, people experience problems with recognizing faces, as Betty did in the opening vignette. Finally, when people perform a task that engages emotional processing, for example, looking at sad pictures, researchers observe significant activation in the amygdala, which you learned earlier is linked with emotional arousal (Phelps, 2006). There is also increased activation in parts of the frontal lobe that are involved in emotional regulation, in fact, in the same areas that were most likely damaged in the case of Phineas Gage (Wang et al., 2005).

As you may have noticed, then, the most modern brain-imaging techniques confirm what studies of brain damage from over 100 years ago suspected. When Broca and Wernicke reached their conclusions about language production and language comprehension, they had little more to go on than some isolated cases and good hunches. PET scans have since confirmed that different areas of the brain are activated when a person is listening to spoken language, reading words on a screen, saying words out loud, or thinking of related words. This suggests that different parts of the brain are activated during these related but distinct functions. Similarly, it was pretty clear to the physician who examined Phineas Gage that the location of Gage's injuries played a major role in his drastic change in personality and emotionality. fMRI scans have since confirmed that the frontal lobe plays a central role in regulating emotion. It's always nice when independent methods—in these instances, very old case studies and very recent technology—arrive at the same conclusions. As you'll also see at various points in the text, brain-imaging techniques such as fMRI are also revealing new and surprising findings, such as the insights described in the Where Do You Stand? box. Although the human brain still holds many mysteries, researchers are developing increasingly sophisticated ways of unraveling them.

In summary, there are three major approaches to studying the link between the brain and behavior. Neuroscientists observe how perceptual, motor, intellectual, and emotional capacities are affected following brain damage. By carefully relating specific psychological and behavioral disruptions to damage in particular areas of the brain, researchers can better understand how the brain area normally plays a role in producing those behaviors. A second approach looks at global electrical activity in the brain and the activity patterns of single neurons. The patterns of electrical activity in large brain areas can be examined from outside the skull using the electroencephalograph (EEG). Single-cell recordings taken from specific neurons can be linked to specific perceptual or behavioral events, suggesting that those neurons represent particular kinds of stimuli or control particular aspects of behavior. With brain imaging, the third major approach, researchers can scan the brain as people perform different perceptual or intellectual tasks. Correlating energy consumption in particular brain areas with specific cognitive and behavioral events suggests that those brain areas are involved in specific types of perceptual, motor, cognitive, or emotional processing. ■ ■

Where Do You Stand?

Brain Death

A story shrouded in mystery follows the memory of Andreas Vesalius (1514–64), a Belgian physician regarded as one of the founders of modern anatomy. According to the story, Vesalius conducted an autopsy in 1564 in front of a large crowd in Madrid, Spain. When the cadaver's chest was opened, the audience saw that the man's heart was still beating! The possibility that the patient was still alive created a scandal that forced Vesalius to leave Spain, where he was serving as the imperial physician at the time. He died during his exodus in a shipwreck, on a pilgrimage to Jerusalem under the pressures of the Spanish Inquisition.

We may never know whether this story is accurate. However, it raises a question related to the brain and behavior that is still fiercely debated today. In Vesalius's time, if a patient didn't appear to be breathing, was generally unresponsive, or gave no strong evidence of a heartbeat, the person could safely be considered dead (despite the occasional misdiagnosis). Modern resuscitative techniques can keep the heart, lungs, and other organs functioning for days, months, or even years, so physicians have identified measures of brain function that allow them to decide more definitively when someone is dead.

In 1981, the President's Commission for the Study of Ethical Problems in Medicine and Biomedical and Behavioral Research defined brain death as the *irreversible loss of all functions of the brain*. Contrary to what you may think, brain death is not the same as being in a coma or being unresponsive to stimulation. Indeed, even a flat-line EEG does not indicate that all brain functions have stopped; the reticular formation in the hindbrain, which generates spontaneous respiration and heartbeat, may still be active.

Brain death came to the forefront of national attention during March 2005 in the case of Terri Schiavo, a woman who had been kept alive on a respirator for nearly 15 years in a Florida nursing home. She died on March 31, 2005, after the feeding tube that sustained her was removed. A person like Schiavo is commonly referred to as brain dead, but such an individual is more accurately described as being in a *persistent vegetative state*. In fact, people in a persistent vegetative state are still considered to be alive by some. Respiration is controlled by structures in the hindbrain, such as the medulla, and will continue as long as this area is intact. A heartbeat does not require input from any area of the brain, so the heart will continue to beat as long it continues to receive oxygen, either by intact respiration or if the patient is artificially ventilated. Also, a patient who is brain dead may continue to have muscle spasms, twitches, or even sit up. This so-called *Lazarus reflex* is coordinated solely by the spinal cord.

Terri Schiavo's parents thought she had a substantial level of voluntary consciousness; they felt that she appeared to smile, cry, and turn toward the source of a voice. Terri's parents hired physicians who claimed that she had a primitive type of consciousness. However, neurologists who specialize in these cases emphasized that these responses could be automatic reflexes supported by circuits in the thalamus and midbrain. These neurologists considered Schiavo to be in a persistent vegetative state; they failed to see conclusive evidence of consciousness or voluntary behavior.

Terri's husband, Michael, agreed with the neurologists and asked the courts to remove the feeding tube that kept her alive, a decision a Florida court accepted. Nonetheless, Florida governor Jeb Bush decreed in 2003 that doctors retain Terri's feeding tube and continue to provide medical care. Eventually, the court again ordered her feeding tube removed, and this time it was not replaced, resulting in her death.

Where do you stand on this issue? Should Terri Schiavo have been kept alive indefinitely? The definition of brain death includes the term "irreversible," suggesting that as long as *any* component of the brain can still function—with or without the aid of a machine—the person should be considered alive. But does a persistent vegetative state qualify as "life"? Is a simple consensus of qualified professionals—doctors, nurses, social workers, specialists—sufficient to decide whether someone is "still living" or at least "still living enough" to maintain whatever treatments may be in place? How should the wishes of family members be considered? For that matter, should the wishes of lawmakers and politicians play a role at all? What is your position on these questions of the brain and the ultimate behavior: staying alive?

After you've considered your answers to these questions, consider this: A recent study found evidence that a person diagnosed as being in a vegetative state showed intentional mental activity (Owen et al., 2006). Researchers used fMRI to observe the patterns of brain activity in a 25-year-old woman with severe brain injuries as the result of a traffic accident. When the researchers spoke ambiguous sentences ("The creak came from a beam in the ceiling") and unambiguous sentences ("There was milk and sugar in his coffee"), fMRI revealed that the activated areas in the woman's brain were comparable to those areas activated in the brains of normal volunteers. What's more, when the woman was instructed to imagine playing a game of tennis and then imagine walking through the rooms of her house, the areas of her brain that showed activity were again indistinguishable from those brain areas in normal, healthy volunteers.

The researchers suggest that these findings are evidence for, at least, conscious understanding of spoken commands and, at best, a degree of intentionality in an otherwise vegetative person. The patient's brain activity while "playing tennis" and "walking through her house" revealed that she could both understand the researchers' instructions and willfully complete them. Unfortunately, it's too early to tell how these and other research findings may impact decisions regarding the brain and when life ends (Laureys, Giacino, Schiff, Schabus, Power, 2006).

Chapter Review

Neurons: The Origin of Behavior

- Neurons are the information processing elements of the nervous system. They are composed of three main elements: the cell body, dendrites, and the axon. The cell body contains the nucleus and the machinery necessary for cell metabolism. Multiple dendrites receive signals from other neurons, whereas axons conduct a signal to the synapse.

- The synapse is a junction between neurons. Electrochemical "messages" cross the synapse to allow neurons to communicate with one another.

- Glial cells serve a support function in the nervous system. As one example, glial cells form a myelin sheath, which is insulating material that speeds the transmission of information down an axon.

- There are three main types of neurons. Sensory neurons receive information from the external world and convey this information to the brain via the spinal cord. Motor neurons carry signals from the spinal cord to the muscles to produce movement. Interneurons connect sensory neurons, motor neurons, or other interneurons.

Electric Signaling: Communicating Information within a Neuron

- Neurons have a resting potential that is created by the balance of electrical forces on charged molecules that can pass through the cell membrane. In particular, there is a high concentration of potassium ions inside the neuron, relative to outside the neuron.

- At the start of an axon, electric potentials build to produce a depolarization that is above threshold, which is called an action potential. Action potentials fire in a consistent "all-or-none" fashion and are conducted down the entire length of the axon.

In myelinated axons, the electric signal "jumps" from breakpoint to breakpoint in the myelin sheath.

Chemical Signaling: Synaptic Transmission between Neurons

- When an action potential arrives at the end of an axon, it stimulates the release of neurotransmitters, which are stored in terminal buttons in the axon. The neurotransmitter enters the synapse and then attaches to the dendrite of the receiving cell.

- Neurotransmitters and receptor sites operate in a lock-and-key fashion; only certain neurotransmitters can be taken up by certain receptors.

- An overflow of neurotransmitters in the synapse can be dealt with in one of three ways: reuptake, enzyme deactivation, or the action of autoreceptors.

- Some of the major neurotransmitters are acetylcholine, norepinephrine, serotonin, dopamine, glutamate, and GABA.

- Many drugs work by facilitating or interfering with a step in the cycle of a neurotransmitter. Drugs that enhance or mimic neurotransmitters are called agonists, whereas those that block neurotransmitters are called antagonists.

The Organization of the Nervous System

- The nervous system is divided into the central nervous system, which is composed of the brain and spinal cord, and the peripheral nervous system, which is composed of the somatic nervous system and the autonomic nervous system. The somatic nervous system receives sensory information and controls the contractions of voluntary muscles. The autonomic nervous system controls the body's organs.

- The autonomic nervous system is divided further into the sympathetic nervous system that prepares the body for action in threatening circumstances and the parasympathetic nervous system that helps return the body to its normal resting state.

- The spinal cord controls basic reflexes and helps transmit information to and from the brain. Injuries to the spinal cord often result in varying degrees of paralysis or other incapacities.

- The brain can be conceptually divided into three main sections: the hindbrain, the midbrain, and the forebrain.

- The hindbrain is responsible for life-sustaining functions, such as respiration and consciousness, and contains the medulla, pons, and cerebellum. The midbrain contains the tectum and the tegmentum, which help to orient an organism in the environment.

- The forebrain is divided into the cerebral cortex and subcortical structures. The subcortical structures include the thalamus, hypothalamus, pituitary gland, hippocampus, amygdala, and basal ganglia. The motivational and emotional functions of some of the subcortical structures are interrelated, suggesting they could be grouped into an overall organization called the limbic system.

- The cerebral cortex is divided into two hemispheres that exert contralateral control over the body. The cortex can also be divided into lobes: occipital, temporal, parietal, and frontal. Each lobe coordinates different kinds of behaviors.

- Association areas are parts of the cortex that perform higher-level operations. There is also evidence of brain plasticity, or the ability of the brain to reassign functions to other brain areas.

The Development and Evolution of Nervous Systems

- The nervous system initially develops as a neural tube in the embryo. Over time, the tube enlarges at one end to form the hindbrain, midbrain, and forebrain.

- From an evolutionary perspective, the human brain represents successive developments from previous models. In reptiles and birds, the highest processing area of the brain is the striatum. In mammals, the highest processing area is the cerebral cortex. The structures and functions of the hindbrain and midbrain seen in other species are retained in humans. There is also some evidence that the human forebrain evolved at a comparatively faster rate, compared to other mammals.

- Both genes and environmental factors exert influence on people's behaviors. Genes set the range of possible behaviors within a given environment, but they do not predict individual characteristics.

- Heritability is a measure of the variability in behavioral traits that can be accounted for by genetic variation. Despite its utility, there are several cautions to interpreting heritability.

Investigating the Brain

- The field of neuroscience investigates the links between the brain and behavior. Three main approaches to this topic are studies of brain damage, electrical recording of brain activity, and imaging techniques of the brain in action.

- Careful case studies of people with brain damage allow researchers to piece together the normal functioning of the brain. When an area is damaged and a specific deficit results, investigators can work backward to discover the likely responsibilities of that brain area. Functions such as speech, language use, emotionality, decision making, and the independent nature of the cerebral hemispheres benefited from this approach.

  An electroencephalograph (EEG) lets researchers measure the overall electrical activity of the brain. However, more recent techniques such as CT scans, MRI, PET, and fMRI provide an increasingly sophisticated way of observing how the brain responds when a variety of tasks are performed.

Key Terms

neurons (p. 74)
cell body (p. 75)
dendrites (p. 75)
axon (p. 75)
myelin sheath (p. 76)
glial cell (p. 76)
synapse (p. 76)
sensory neurons (p. 77)
motor neurons (p. 77)
interneurons (p. 77)
resting potential (p. 79)
action potential (p. 80)
refractory period (p. 81)
terminal buttons (p. 81)
neurotransmitters (p. 81)
receptors (p. 81)
acetylcholine (Ach) (p. 83)

dopamine (p. 84)
glutamate (p. 84)
GABA (gamma-aminobutyric acid) (p. 84)
norepinephrine (p. 84)
serotonin (p. 84)
endorphins (p. 84)
agonists (p. 85)
antagonists (p. 85)
nervous system (p. 87)
central nervous system (CNS) (p. 87)
peripheral nervous system (PNS) (p. 87)
somatic nervous system (p. 87)
autonomic nervous system (ANS) (p. 88)

sympathetic nervous system (p. 88)
parasympathetic nervous system (p. 88)
spinal reflexes (p. 90)
hindbrain (p. 93)
medulla (p. 93)
reticular formation (p. 93)
cerebellum (p. 93)
pons (p. 94)
tectum (p. 94)
tegmentum (p. 94)
cerebral cortex (p. 95)
subcortical structures (p. 95)
thalamus (p. 95)
hypothalamus (p. 95)
pituitary gland (p. 96)

limbic system (p. 96)
hippocampus (p. 96)
amygdala (p. 96)
basal ganglia (p. 97)
corpus callosum (p. 98)
occipital lobe (p. 98)
parietal lobe (p. 98)
temporal lobe (p. 99)
frontal lobe (p. 99)
association areas (p. 99)
gene (p. 104)
chromosomes (p. 104)
heritability (p. 106)
electroencephalograph (EEG) (p. 111)

Recommended Readings

Damasio, A. (2005). *Descartes' error: Emotion, reason, and the human brain*. New York: Penguin. Emotion and reason seem like competing forces in directing our behavior: One force wants to feel good, while the other wants to think things through. Antonio Damasio, a distinguished neuroscientist, considers how emotion and reason relate to each other and how both cooperate to allow the brain to function efficiently.

Diamond, M., & Schiebel, A. B. (1986). *The human brain coloring book*. New York: Collins. Marian Diamond is a professor of anatomy; who better to assemble a book on the structure of the brain? This is a fun way to quiz yourself on the various parts of the brain and a good reason to break out your crayons.

Johnson, S. (2004). *Mind wide open: Your brain and the neuroscience of everyday life*. New York: Scribner. Steven Johnson is a science writer who synthesizes scholarly research for a popular audience. In this book, he explores a range of findings related to neuroscience, including techniques for studying the brain (such as MRI), the purposes and functions of brain structures (such as the amygdala), and the meaning behind what the brain does and why it does it.

LeDoux, J. (2002). *The synaptic self: How our brains become who we are*. New York: Viking. Joseph LeDoux is a neuroscientist who studies how cortical and subcortical structures direct behavior. In this book, he takes us on a journey from a basic understanding of what neurons are to a proposal that our synaptic connections make us who we are: Personality, self, and related concepts stem from the interwoven connections that make up our brains.

Ramachandran, V. S., & Blakeslee, S. (1998). *Phantoms in the brain: Probing the mysteries of the human mind*. New York: Morrow. Vilayanur Ramachandran is a leading theorist in understanding how the brain produces the mind. Susan Blakeslee is a *New York Times* science writer. Together they explore the sometimes bizarre world of the usual and not-so-usual workings of the brain. This book is a good survey of several topics discussed in the current chapter and a nice introduction to some related ideas.

4

Sensation and Perception

The Doorway to Psychology
Psychophysics
Measuring Thresholds
Signal Detection
Sensory Adaptation
THE REAL WORLD Multitasking

Vision: More Than Meets the Eye
Sensing Light
Perceiving Color
The Visual Brain
Recognizing Objects by Sight
Perceiving Depth and Size
Perceiving Motion

Audition: More Than Meets the Ear
Sensing Sound
The Human Ear
Perceiving Pitch
HOT SCIENCE Cochlear Implants
Localizing Sound Sources

The Body Senses: More Than Skin Deep
Touch
Pain
Body Position, Movement, and Balance

The Chemical Senses: Adding Flavor
Smell
Taste
THE REAL WORLD Supertasters
WHERE DO YOU STAND?
Perception and Persuasion

N is sort of . . . rubbery . . . smooth, L is sort of the consistency of watery paint . . . Letters also have vague personalities, but not as strongly as numerals do.

—Julieta

The letter A is blue, B is red, C is kind of a light gray, D is orange. . . .

—Karen

I hear a note by one of the fellows in the band and it's one color. I hear the same note played by someone else and it's a different color. When I hear sustained musical tones, I see just about the same colors that you do, but I see them in textures.

—Jazz musician Duke Ellington (George, 1981, p. 226)

Basically, I taste words.

—Amelia

THESE COMMENTS ARE NOT FROM A recent meeting of the Slightly Odd Society. They're the remarks of otherwise perfectly normal people describing what seem to be perfectly bizarre experiences except to them—they think these experiences are quite commonplace and genuine. After all, if you can't trust Duke Ellington, an internationally acclaimed jazz composer and bandleader, who can you trust? Perhaps Stevie Wonder? Eddie Van Halen? Vladimir Nabokov, the author of *Lolita*? Franz Liszt, the classical composer? Richard Feynman, the Nobel Prize–winning physicist? Take your pick because these and many other notable people have at least one thing in common: Their perceptual worlds seem to be quite different from most of ours.

What do these people have in common? Duke Ellington, Stevie Wonder, Eddie Van Halen, and Franz Liszt are all musicians, but Richard Feynman was a physicist. All of these people are men, but that has little to do with it. Some are living; some are dead. In fact, all of these people have fairly well-documented experiences of synesthesia, the experience of one sense that is evoked by a different sense.

Duke Ellington

Stevie Wonder

Eddie Van Halen

Franz Liszt

Richard Feynman

SYNESTHESIA The perceptual experience of one sense that is evoked by another sense.

These unusual perceptual events are varieties of **synesthesia**, *the perceptual experience of one sense that is evoked by another sense* (Hubbard & Ramachandran, 2003). For some synesthetes, musical notes evoke the visual sensation of color. Other people with synesthesia see printed letters (**FIGURE 4.1**) or numbers in specific, consistent colors (always seeing the digit 2 as pink and 3 as green, for example). Still others experience specific tastes when certain sounds are heard.

For those of us who don't experience synesthesia, the prospect of tasting sounds or hearing colors may seem unbelievable or the product of some hallucinogenic experience. Indeed, for many years scientists dismissed synesthesia either as a rare curiosity or a case of outright faking. But recent research indicates that synesthesia is far more common than previously believed. Synesthesia was once thought to occur in as few as one in every 25,000 people, but it is now clear that some forms of synesthesia are not as rare as others and may be found in as many as one in every 100 people (Hubbard & Ramachandran, 2005). The experience of seeing colors evoked by sounds or of seeing letters in specific colors is much more common among synesthetes than, say, a smell evoked by touching a certain shape.

Recent research has documented the psychological and neurobiological reality of synesthesia. For example, a synesthete who sees the digits 2 and 4 as pink and 3 as green will find it easier to pick out a 2 among a bunch of 3s than among a bunch of 4s, whereas a nonsynesthete will perform these two tasks equally well (Palmieri, Ingersoll, & Stone, 2002). Brain-imaging studies also show that in some synesthetes, areas of the brain involved in processing colors are more active when they hear words that evoke color than when they hear tones that don't evoke color; no such differences are seen among people in a control group (Nunn, Gregory, & Brammer, 2002).

So, synesthesia is neither an isolated curiosity nor the result of faking. In fact, it may indicate that in some people, the brain is "wired" differently than in most, so that brain regions for different sensory modalities cross-activate one another (Ramachandran & Hubbard, 2003). Whatever the ultimate explanations for these fascinating phenomena, this recent wave of research shows that synesthesia is a mindbug that can shed new light on how the brain is organized and how we sense and perceive the world.

In this chapter we'll explore key insights into the nature of sensation and perception. These experiences are basic to survival and reproduction; we wouldn't last long without the ability to accurately make sense of the world around us. Indeed, research on sensation and perception is the basis for much of psychology, a pathway toward understanding more complex cognition and behavior such as memory, emotion, motivation, or decision making. Yet sensation and perception also sometimes reveal mindbugs, ranging from the complexities of synesthesia to various kinds of perceptual illusions that you might see at a science fair or in a novelty shop. These mindbugs are reminders that the act of perceiving the world is not as simple or straightforward as it might seem.

We'll look at how physical energy in the world around us is encoded by our senses, sent to the brain, and enters conscious awareness. Vision is predominant among our

Figure 4.1 Synesthesia Most of us see letters printed in black as they appear in (a). Some people with synesthesia link their perceptions of letters with certain colors and perceive letters as printed in different colors, as shown in (b). In synesthesia, brain regions for different sensory modalities cross-activate one another.

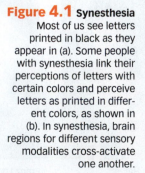

(a) Usual appearance

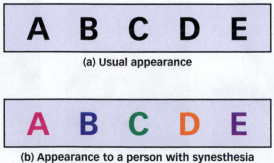

(b) Appearance to a person with synesthesia

senses; correspondingly, we'll devote a fair amount of space to understanding how the visual system works. Then we'll discuss how we perceive sound waves as words or music or noise, followed by the body senses, emphasizing touch, pain, and balance. We'll end with the chemical senses of smell and taste, which together allow you to savor the foods you eat. But before doing any of that, we will provide a foundation for examining all of the sensory systems by reviewing how psychologists measure sensation and perception in the first place.

The Doorway to Psychology

From the vantage point of our own consciousness, sensation and perception appear to be one seamless event. Information comes in from the outside world, gets registered and interpreted, and triggers some kind of action: no breaks, no balks, just one continuous process. Psychologists know, however, that sensation and perception are two separate activities.

Sensation is *simple awareness due to the stimulation of a sense organ*. It is the basic registration of light, sound, pressure, odor, or taste as parts of your body interact with the physical world. After a sensation registers in your central nervous system, **perception** takes place at the level of your brain: It is *the organization, identification, and interpretation of a sensation in order to form a mental representation*. As an example, your eyes are coursing across these sentences right now. The sensory receptors in your eyeballs are registering different patterns of light reflecting off the page. Your brain, however, is integrating and processing that light information into the meaningful perception of words, such as "meaningful," "perception," and "words." Your eyes—the sensory organ—aren't really seeing words; they're simply encoding different shapes and patterns of ink on a page. Your brain—the perceptual organ—is transforming those shapes into a coherent mental representation of words and concepts.

If all of this sounds a little peculiar, it's because from the vantage point of your conscious experience, it *seems* as if you're reading words directly; again, sensation and perception feel like one single event. If you think of the discussion of brain damage in Chapter 3, however, you'll recall that sometimes a person's eyes can work just fine, yet the individual is still "blind" to faces she has seen for many years. Damage to the visual-processing centers in the brain can interfere with the interpretation of information coming from the eyes: The senses are intact, but perceptual ability is compromised. Sensation and perception are related—but separate—events.

We all know that sensory events involve vision, hearing, touch, taste, and smell. Arguably, we possess several more senses besides these five. Touch, for example, encompasses distinct body senses, including sensitivity to pain and temperature, joint position and balance, and even the state of the gut—perhaps to sense nausea via the autonomic nervous system. Despite the variety of our senses, they all depend on the process of **transduction**, which occurs *when many sensors in the body convert physical signals from the environment into neural signals sent to the central nervous system*.

In vision, light reflected from surfaces provides the eyes with information about the shape, color, and position of objects. In audition, vibrations (from vocal cords or a guitar string, perhaps) cause changes in air pressure that propagate through space to a listener's ears. In touch, the pressure of a surface against the skin signals its shape, texture, and temperature. In taste and smell, molecules dispersed in the air or dissolved in saliva reveal the identity of substances that we may or may not want to eat. In each case physical energy from the world is converted to neural energy inside the central nervous system. We've already seen that synesthetes experience a mixing of these perceptions; however, even during synesthesia the processes of transduction that begin those perceptions are the same. Despite "hearing colors," your eyes simply can't transduce sound waves, no matter how long you stare at your stereo speakers!

SENSATION Simple awareness due to the stimulation of a sense organ.

PERCEPTION The organization, identification, and interpretation of a sensation in order to form a mental representation.

TRANSDUCTION What takes place when many sensors in the body convert physical signals from the environment into neural signals sent to the central nervous system.

Psychophysics

It's intriguing to consider the possibility that our basic perceptions of sights or sounds might differ fundamentally from those of other people. One reason we find synesthetes fascinating is because their perceptual experiences are so different from most of ours. But we won't get very far in understanding such differences by simply relying on casual self-reports. As you learned in Chapter 2, to understand a behavior researchers must first *operationalize* it, and that involves finding a reliable way to measure it.

Any type of scientific investigation requires objective measurements. Measuring the physical energy of a stimulus, such as the color and brightness of a light, is easy enough: You can probably buy the necessary instruments online to do that yourself. But how do you quantify a person's private, subjective *perception* of that light? It's one thing to know that a flashlight produces "100 candlepower" or gives off "8,000 lumens," but it's another matter entirely to measure a person's psychological experience of that light energy.

The structuralists, led by Wilhelm Wundt and Edward Titchener, tried using introspection to measure perceptual experiences (see Chapter 1). They failed miserably at this task. After all, you can describe your experience to another person in words, but that person cannot know directly what you perceive when you look at a sunset. You both may call the sunset "orange" and "beautiful," but neither of you can directly perceive the other's experience of the same event. Evoked memories and emotions intertwine with what you are hearing, seeing, and smelling, making your perception of an event—and therefore your experience of that event—unique.

Given that perception is different for each of us, how could we ever hope to measure it? This question was answered in the mid-1800s by the German scientist and philosopher Gustav Fechner (1801–87). Fechner was originally trained as a physicist but developed strong interests in philosophy and psychology, especially the study of perception. He began conducting informal studies of visual perception on himself during the 1830s. However, he got a bit carried away with his research and temporarily blinded himself while staring at the sun for a prolonged time. Fechner's eyes became so sensitive to light that he had to bandage them before leaving the house, and they bothered him the rest of his life. Limited in his abilities, Fechner took on extra work to help support his family, such as translating works from French to German and even writing much of an encyclopedia of household knowledge (Watson, 1978). His workload and eye problems resulted in a psychological breakdown and severe depression, leading him to resign his professorship at the University of Leipzig and go into seclusion.

Although this was a difficult period in his life, it was of great importance to psychology. In his isolation, Fechner was free to think deeply about the issues that interested him the most, especially how it might be possible to link psychology and physics. His efforts led him to develop an approach to measuring sensation and perception called **psychophysics**: *methods that measure the strength of a stimulus and the observer's sensitivity to that stimulus* (Fechner, 1860). In a typical psychophysics experiment, researchers ask people to make a simple judgment—whether or not they saw a flash of light, for example. The psychophysicist then relates the measured stimulus, such as the brightness of the light flash, to each observer's yes-or-no response.

Measuring Thresholds

Psychophysicists begin the measurement process with a single sensory signal to determine precisely how much physical energy is required to evoke a sensation in an observer.

Absolute Threshold

The simplest quantitative measurement in psychophysics is the **absolute threshold,** *the minimal intensity needed to just barely detect a stimulus*. A *threshold* is a boundary. The doorway that separates the inside from the outside of a house is a threshold, as is the

PSYCHOPHYSICS Methods that measure the strength of a stimulus and the observer's sensitivity to that stimulus.

ABSOLUTE THRESHOLD The minimal intensity needed to just barely detect a stimulus.

Table **4.1**	Approximate Sensory Thresholds
Sense	**Absolute Threshold**
Vision	A candle flame 30 miles away on a clear, dark night
Hearing	A clock's tick 20 feet away when all is quiet
Touch	A fly's wing touching the cheek from 1 centimeter away
Smell	A single drop of perfume diffused through an area equivalent to the volume of six rooms
Taste	A teaspoon of sugar dissolved in two gallons of water

Source: Adapted from Galanter (1962).

boundary between two psychological states ("awareness" and "unawareness," for example). In finding the absolute threshold for sensation, the two states in question are *sensing* and *not sensing* some stimulus. **TABLE 4.1** lists the approximate sensory thresholds for each of the five senses.

To measure the absolute threshold for detecting a sound, for example, an observer sits in a soundproof room wearing headphones linked to a computer. The experimenter presents a pure tone (the sort of sound made by striking a tuning fork) using the computer to vary the loudness or the length of time each tone lasts and recording how often the observer reports hearing that tone under each condition. The outcome of such an experiment is graphed in **FIGURE 4.2**. Notice from the shape of the curve that the transition from *not hearing* to *hearing* is gradual rather than abrupt. Investigators typically define the absolute threshold as the loudness required for the listener to say she or he has heard the tone on 50% of the trials.

If we repeat this experiment for many different tones, we can observe and record the thresholds for tones ranging from very low pitch to very high. It turns out that people tend to be most sensitive to the range of tones corresponding to human conversation. If the tone is low enough, such as the lowest note on a pipe organ, most humans cannot hear it at all; we can only feel it. If the tone is high enough, we likewise cannot hear it, but dogs and many other animals can.

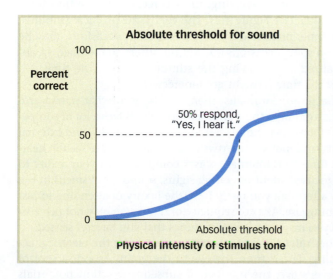

Figure 4.2 Absolute Threshold Some of us are more sensitive than others, and we may even detect sensory stimulation below our own absolute threshold. Absolute threshold is graphed here as the point where the increasing intensity of the stimulus enables an observer to detect it on 50% of the trials. As its intensity gradually increases, we detect the stimulation more frequently.

JUST NOTICEABLE DIFFERENCE (JND) The minimal change in a stimulus that can just barely be detected.

WEBER'S LAW The just noticeable difference of a stimulus is a constant proportion despite variations in intensity.

Difference Thresholds

The absolute threshold is useful for assessing how sensitive we are to faint stimuli, but most everyday perception involves detecting differences among stimuli that are well above the absolute threshold. Most people are pretty adept at noticing that a couch is red, but they're likely to want to know if the couch is redder than the drapes they're considering. Similarly, parents can usually detect their own infant's cry from the cries of other babies, but it's probably more useful to be able to differentiate the "I'm hungry" cry from the "I'm cranky" cry from the "something is biting my toes" cry. In short, the human perceptual system excels at detecting *changes* in stimulation rather than the simple onset or offset of stimulation.

As a way of measuring this difference threshold, Fechner proposed the **just noticeable difference**, or **JND**, *the minimal change in a stimulus that can just barely be detected*. The JND is not a fixed quantity; rather, it depends on how intense the stimuli being measured are and on the particular sense being measured. Consider measuring the JND for a bright light. An observer in a dark room is shown a light of fixed intensity, called the *standard* (S), next to a comparison light that is slightly brighter or dimmer than the standard. When S is very dim, observers can see even a very small difference in brightness between the two lights: The JND is small. But if S is bright, a much larger increment is needed to detect the difference: The JND is larger.

In fact, the just noticeable difference can be calculated for each sense. It is roughly proportional to the magnitude of the standard stimulus. This relationship was first noticed in 1834 by a German physiologist named Ernst Weber, who taught at the University of Leipzig around the time that Fechner was a student there and likely influenced Fechner's thinking (Watson, 1978). Fechner applied Weber's insight directly to psychophysics, resulting in a formal relationship called **Weber's law**, which states that *the just noticeable difference of a stimulus is a constant proportion despite variations in intensity*. As an example, the JND for weight is about 2%. If you picked up a one-ounce envelope, then a two-ounce envelope, you'd probably notice the difference between them. But if you picked up a five-pound package, then a five-pound, one-ounce package, you'd probably detect no difference at all between them. In fact, you'd probably need about a five-and-a-half-pound package to detect a JND. When calculating a difference threshold, it is the proportion between stimuli that is important; the measured size of the difference, whether in brightness, loudness, or weight, is irrelevant.

Signal Detection

Measuring absolute and difference thresholds requires a critical assumption: that a threshold exists! But much of what scientists know about biology suggests that such a discrete, all-or-none change in the brain is unlikely. Humans don't suddenly and rapidly switch between perceiving and not perceiving; in fact, recall that the transition from *not sensing* to *sensing* is gradual (see Figure 4.2). The very same physical stimulus, such as a dim light or a quiet tone, presented on several different occasions, may be perceived by the same person on some occasions but not on others. Remember, an absolute threshold is operationalized as perceiving the stimulus 50% of the time . . . which means the other 50% of the time it might go undetected.

Our accurate perception of a sensory stimulus, then, can be somewhat haphazard. Whether in the psychophysics lab or out in the world, sensory signals face a lot of competition, or *noise,* which refers to all the other stimuli coming from the internal and external environment. Memories, moods, and motives intertwine with what you are seeing, hearing, and smelling at any given time. This internal "noise" competes with your ability to detect a stimulus with perfect, focused attention. Other sights, sounds, and smells in the world at large also compete for attention; you rarely have the luxury of attending to just one stimulus apart from everything else. As a consequence of noise, you may not perceive everything that you sense, and you may even perceive things that you haven't sensed.

To see how these mismatches might happen, imagine measuring the electrical activity of a single neuron sending signals from the eye to the brain. As a dim spot of light is flashed onto an observer's eye, the number of subsequent action potentials fluctuates from one presentation to the next even when the light is exactly the same brightness each time. Occasionally, the neuron might fire even if no light is presented—a *spontaneous action potential* has occurred. Sensory systems are noisy; when the signals are very small, dim, or quiet, the senses provide only a "fuzzy" indicator of the state of the world.

This variability among neural responses helps explain why Figure 4.2 shows a gradual rise in the likelihood of hearing a tone. For a fixed tone intensity, the evoked neural response varies a little from one presentation to the next. On some presentations, the auditory neurons' responses will be a bit greater than average, and the listener will be more likely to detect the tone. On other presentations, the neural response will, by chance, be a bit less than average, and the listener will be less likely to detect the tone. On still other occasions, the neurons might produce spontaneous action potentials, leading the observer to claim that a tone was heard when none was presented.

Given the variability in neural responses, observers are faced with a decision. If they say, "Yes, I heard a tone," anytime there is any activity in the auditory system, they will often respond "yes" when no tone is presented. So observers might adopt a more conservative response criterion, deciding to say, "Yes, I heard a tone," only when the sensory experience is quite obvious. The problem now is that an observer will often miss fainter tones that were actually presented. Think of the last time you had a hearing test. You no doubt missed some of the quiet beeps that were presented, but you also probably said you heard beeps that weren't really there.

An approach to psychophysics called **signal detection theory** holds that *the response to a stimulus depends both on a person's sensitivity to the stimulus in the presence of noise and on a person's response criterion.* That is, observers consider the sensory evidence evoked by the stimulus and compare it to an internal decision criterion (Green & Swets, 1966; Macmillan & Creelman, 2005). If the sensory evidence exceeds the criterion, the observer responds by saying, "Yes, I detected the stimulus," and if it falls short of the criterion, the observer responds by saying, "No, I did not detect the stimulus."

Signal detection theory allows researchers to quantify an observer's response in the presence of noise. In a signal detection experiment, a stimulus, such as a dim light, is randomly presented or not. If you've ever taken an eye exam that checks your peripheral vision, you have an idea about this kind of setup: Lights of varying intensity are flashed at various places in the visual field, and your task is to respond anytime you see one. Observers in a signal detection experiment must decide whether they saw the light or not, leading to the four possible outcomes shown in **FIGURE 4.3a**. If the light is presented and the observer correctly responds, "Yes," the outcome is a *hit*. If the light is presented and the observer says, "No," the result is a *miss*. However, if the light is *not* presented and the observer nonetheless says it was, a *false alarm* has occurred. Finally, if the light is *not* presented and the observer responds, "No," a *correct rejection* has occurred: The observer accurately detected the absence of the stimulus.

Observers can adopt a very liberal response criterion, saying, "Yes," at the slightest hint of evidence for the stimulus (see **FIGURE 4.3b**). Notice that this strategy will produce a lot of hits but also a lot of false alarms. Conversely, adopting a very conservative criterion—saying, "Yes," only when the stimulus is clear, strong, and unambiguous—should minimize the rate of false alarms but increase the proportion of misses (see **FIGURE 4.3c**).

SIGNAL DETECTION THEORY An observation that the response to a stimulus depends both on a person's sensitivity to the stimulus in the presence of noise and on a person's response criterion.

Figure 4.3 **Signal Detection Criteria** Sensation depends not only on our sensitivity to stimulation but also on how we make decisions. Of the four possible outcomes on the grid in (a), we may correctly report the presence (a hit) or absence (correct rejection) of a stimulus, fail to detect it (a miss), or say we detect it when it's not there (false alarm). People may be equally sensitive to stimulation but adopt very different decision criteria. Those who tend to say they detect a signal produce many false alarms as well as many hits (b). Those who tend to say they detect no signal minimize false alarms but often miss the stimulus (c). Decision criteria have wide application in areas as diverse as drug trials and dating.

	Yes	No
Light presented	Hit	Miss
Light not presented	False alarm	Correct rejection

(a) Possible outcomes on each trial

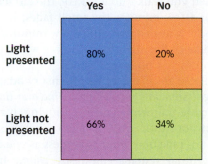

	Yes	No
Light presented	80%	20%
Light not presented	66%	34%

(b) Purely liberal criterion response

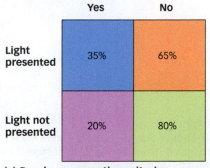

	Yes	No
Light presented	35%	65%
Light not presented	20%	80%

(c) Purely conservative criterion response

Signal detection theory is a more sophisticated approach than was used in the early days of establishing absolute thresholds. Back then, it might have been assumed that everyone (or at least a majority of observers) heard a tone or saw a flickering candle flame with equal facility. Signal detection theory, in contrast, explicitly takes into account observers' response tendencies, such as liberally saying, "Yes," or reserving identifications only for obvious instances of the stimulus. It's interesting, then, to learn that the ideas behind signal detection theory were developed first by none other than Fechner (1860). It's not clear why such important ideas were not grasped by later psychologists who appreciated other aspects of Fechner's work, but it's possible that most of those researchers lacked the mathematical training required to appreciate Fechner's insights (Link, 1994). In short, Fechner anticipated long ago that both the characteristics of the stimulus *and* the characteristics of the observer need to be taken into account, producing a better understanding of the perceptual process.

Signal detection theory proposes a way to measure *perceptual sensitivity*—how effectively the perceptual system represents sensory events—separately from the observer's decision-making strategy. Two observers with opposite decision criteria and correspondingly distinct hit rates and false alarm rates may exhibit similar levels of sensitivity. That is, even though one person says, "Yes," much more often than another, both may be equally accurate in distinguishing between the presence or absence of a stimulus. Even though the purely conservative and liberal strategies represent two poles on a long continuum of possible decision criteria, signal detection theory has practical applications at home, school, work, and even while driving.

For example, a radiologist may have to decide whether a mammogram shows that a patient has breast cancer. The radiologist knows that certain features, such as a mass of a particular size and shape, are associated with the presence of cancer. But noncancerous features can have a very similar appearance to cancerous ones. The radiologist may decide on a strictly liberal criterion and check every possible case of cancer with a biopsy. As shown in Figure 4.3b, this decision strategy minimizes the possibility of missing a true cancer but leads to many false alarms. A strictly conservative criterion will cut down on false alarms but will miss some treatable cancers (see Figure 4.3c).

As another example, imagine that police are on the lookout for a suspected felon who they have reason to believe will be at a crowded soccer match. Although the law enforcement agency provided a fairly good description—6'0", sandy brown hair, beard, glasses—there are still thousands of people to scan. Rounding up all men between 5'5" and 6'5" would probably produce a hit (the felon is caught) but at the expense of an extraordinary number of false alarms (many innocent people are detained and questioned).

These different types of errors have to be weighed against one another in setting the decision criterion. Signal detection theory offers a practical way to choose among criteria that permit decision makers to take into account the consequences of hits, misses, false alarms, and correct rejections (McFall & Treat, 1999; Swets, Dawes, & Monahan, 2000). (For an example of a common everyday task that can interfere with signal detection, see The Real World box on the next page.)

Sensory Adaptation

When you walk into a bakery, the aroma of freshly baked bread overwhelms you, but after a few minutes the smell fades. If you dive into cold water, the temperature is shocking at first, but after a few minutes you get used to it. When you wake up in the middle of the night for a drink of water, the bathroom light blinds you, but after a few minutes you no longer squint.

These are all examples of **sensory adaptation,** the observation that *sensitivity to prolonged stimulation tends to decline over time as an organism adapts to current conditions.* Imagine that while you are studying in a quiet room, your neighbor in the apartment next door turns on the stereo. That gets your attention, but after a few minutes the sounds fade from your awareness as you continue your studies. But remember that our perceptual systems emphasize *change* in responding to sensory events: When the music stops, you notice.

SENSORY ADAPTATION Sensitivity to prolonged stimulation tends to decline over time as an organism adapts to current conditions.

{ THE REAL WORLD } Multitasking

BY ONE ESTIMATE, USING A CELL PHONE while driving makes having an accident four times more likely (McEvoy et al., 2005). In response to highway safety experts and statistics such as this, state legislatures are passing laws that restrict, and sometimes ban, using mobile phones while driving. You might think that's a fine idea . . . for everyone else on the road. But surely *you* can manage to punch in a number on a phone, carry on a conversation, or maybe even text-message while simultaneously driving in a safe and courteous manner. Right?

In a word, *wrong*. The issue here is *selective attention*, or perceiving only what's currently relevant to you. Try this. Without moving a muscle, think about the pressure of your skin against your chair right now. Effortlessly you shifted your attention to allow a sensory signal to enter your awareness. This simple shift shows that your perception of the world depends both on what sensory signals are present and on your choice of which signals to attend to and which to ignore. Perception is an active, moment-to-moment exploration for relevant or interesting information, not a passive receptacle for whatever happens to come along.

Talking on a cell phone while driving demands that you juggle two independent sources of sensory input—vision and audition—at the same time. Normally this kind of *multitasking* works rather well. It's only when you need to react suddenly that your driving performance may suffer. Researchers

Shifting Attention Participants received fMRI scans as they performed tasks that required them to shift their attention between visual and auditory information. (a) When focusing on auditory information, a region in the superior (upper) temporal lobe involved in auditory processing showed increased activity (yellow/orange). (b) In striking contrast, a visual region, the fusiform gyrus, showed decreased activity when participants focused on auditory information (blue).

have tested experienced drivers in a highly realistic driving simulator, measuring their response times to brake lights and stop signs while they listened to the radio or carried on phone conversations about a political issue, among other tasks (Strayer, Drews, & Johnston, 2003).

These experienced drivers reacted significantly slower during phone conversations than during the other tasks. This is because a phone conversation requires memory retrieval, deliberation, and planning what to say and often carries an emotional stake in the conversation topic. Tasks such as listening to the radio require far less attention or none at all.

The tested drivers became so engaged in their conversations that their minds no longer seemed to be in the car. Their slower braking response translated into an increased stopping distance that, depending on the driver's speed, would have resulted in a rear-end collision. Whether the phone was handheld or hands free made little difference. This suggests that laws requiring drivers to use hands-free phones may have little effect on reducing accidents.

Other researchers have measured brain activity using fMRI while people were shifting attention between visual and auditory information. The strength of visual and auditory brain activity was affected: When attention was directed to audition, activity in visual areas decreased compared to when attention was directed to vision (Shomstein & Yantis, 2004). It was as if the participants could adjust a mental "volume knob" to regulate the flow of incoming information according to which task they were attending to at the moment.

So how well do we multitask in several thousand pounds of metal hurtling down the highway? Experienced drivers can handle divided attention to a degree, yet most of us have to acknowledge that we have had close calls due to driving while distracted. Unless you have two heads with one brain each—one to talk and one to concentrate on driving—you might do well to keep your eyes on the road and not on the phone.

Sensory adaptation is a useful process for most organisms. Imagine what your sensory and perceptual world would be like without it. When you put on your jeans in the morning, the feeling of rough cloth against your bare skin would be as noticeable hours later as it was in the first few minutes. The stink of garbage in your apartment when you first walk in would never dissipate. If you had to constantly be aware of how your tongue feels while it is resting in your mouth, you'd be driven to distraction. Our perceptual systems respond more strongly to changes in stimulation rather than to constant stimulation. A stimulus that doesn't change usually doesn't require any action; your car probably emits a certain hum all the time that you've gotten used to. But a change in stimulation often signals a need for action. If your car starts making different kinds of noises, you're not only more likely to notice them, but you're also more likely to do something about it.

In summary, sensation and perception are critical to survival. Sensation is the simple awareness that results from stimulation of a sense organ, whereas perception organizes, identifies, and interprets sensation at the level of the brain. All sensory modalities depend on the process of transduction, which converts physical signals from the environment into neural signals carried by sensory neurons into the central nervous system. In the 19th century, researchers developed psychophysics, an approach to studying perception that measures the strength of a stimulus and an observer's sensitivity to that

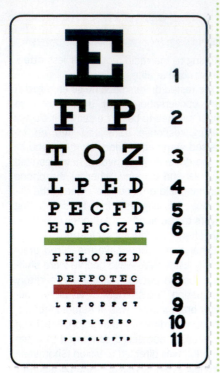

The Snellen chart is commonly used to measure visual acuity. Chances are good you've seen one yourself on more than one occasion.

stimulus. Psychophysicists have developed procedures for measuring an observer's absolute threshold, or the smallest intensity needed to just barely detect a stimulus, and the just noticeable difference (JND), or the smallest change in a stimulus that can just barely be detected. Signal detection theory allows researchers to distinguish between an observer's perceptual sensitivity to a stimulus and criteria for making decisions about the stimulus. Sensory adaptation occurs because sensitivity to lengthy stimulation tends to decline over time. ■ ■

Vision: More Than Meets the Eye

You might be proud of your 20/20 vision, even if it is corrected by glasses or contact lenses. *20/20* refers to a measurement associated with a Snellen chart, named after Hermann Snellen (1834–1908), the Dutch ophthalmologist who developed it as a means of assessing **visual acuity**, *the ability to see fine detail;* it is the smallest line of letters that a typical person can read from a distance of 20 feet. But if you dropped into the Birds of Prey Ophthalmologic Office, your visual pride would wither. Hawks, eagles, owls, and other raptors have much greater visual acuity than humans; in many cases, about eight times greater, or the equivalent of 20/2 vision. That's handy if you want to spot a mouse from a mile away, but if you simply need to see where your roommate left the big bag of Fritos, you can probably live with the fact that no one ever calls you "Ol' Eagle Eye."

Although you won't win any I Spy contests against a hawk, your sophisticated visual system has evolved to transduce visual energy in the world into neural signals in the brain. Humans have sensory receptors in their eyes that respond to wavelengths of light energy. When we look at people, places, and things, patterns of light and color give us information about where one surface stops and another begins. The array of light reflected from those surfaces preserves their shapes and enables us to form a mental representation of a scene (Rodieck, 1998). Understanding vision, then, starts with understanding light.

Sensing Light

Visible light is simply the portion of the electromagnetic spectrum that we can see, and it is an extremely small slice. You can think about light as waves of energy. Like ocean waves, light waves vary in height and in the distance between their peaks, or *wavelengths,* as **TABLE 4.2** shows.

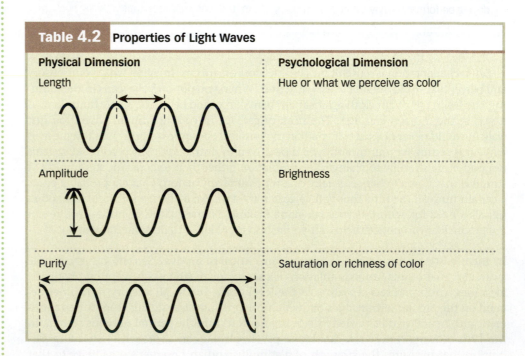

Table 4.2	Properties of Light Waves	
Physical Dimension	**Psychological Dimension**
Length	Hue or what we perceive as color
Amplitude	Brightness
Purity	Saturation or richness of color

VISUAL ACUITY The ability to see fine detail.

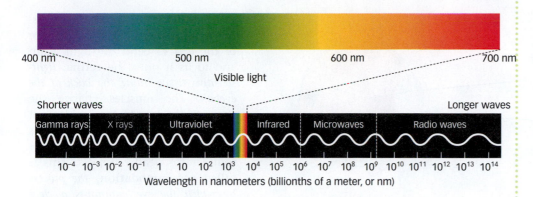

Figure 4.4 **Electromagnetic Spectrum**
The sliver of light waves visible to humans as a rainbow of colors from violet-blue to red is bounded on the short end by ultraviolet rays, which honeybees can see, and on the long end by infrared waves, upon which night-vision equipment operates. Someone wearing night-vision goggles, for example, can detect another person's body heat in complete darkness. Light waves are minute, but the scale along the bottom of this chart offers a glimpse of their varying lengths, measured in nanometers (nm; 1 nm = 1 billionth of a meter).

There are three properties of light waves, each of which has a physical dimension that produces a corresponding psychological dimension. The *length* of a light wave determines its hue, or what humans perceive as color. The intensity or *amplitude* of a light wave—how high the peaks are—determines what we perceive as the brightness of light. The third property is *purity,* or the number of wavelengths that make up the light. Purity corresponds to what humans perceive as saturation, or the richness of colors (see **FIGURE 4.4**). In other words, light doesn't need a human to have the properties it does: Length, amplitude, and purity are properties of the light waves themselves. What humans perceive from those properties are color, brightness, and saturation.

To understand how the properties of waves affect how we sense light, it's helpful to understand how our eyes detect light in the first place.

The Human Eye

FIGURE 4.5 shows the human eye in cross-section. Light that reaches the eyes passes first through a clear, smooth outer tissue called the *cornea,* which bends the light wave and sends it through the *pupil,* a hole in the colored part of the eye. This colored part is the *iris,* which is a translucent, doughnut-shaped muscle that controls the size of the pupil and hence the amount of light that can enter the eye.

When you move from the dim illumination of a movie theater into the bright sunshine outside, your irises contract, reducing the size of the pupils and the amount of light passing through them. You may still have to shade your eyes until their light-sensitive cells adapt to the brighter light level. This process is a type of sensory adaptation called *light adaptation.*

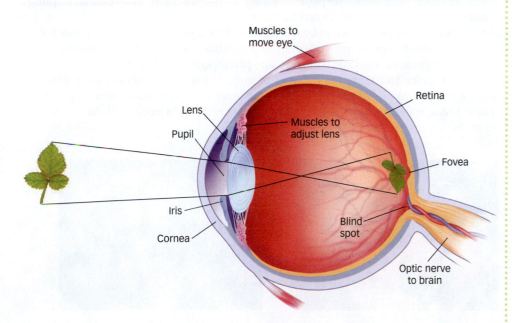

Figure 4.5 **Anatomy of the Human Eye**
Light reflected from a surface enters the eye via the transparent cornea, bending to pass through the pupil at the center of the colored iris. Behind the iris, the thickness and shape of the lens adjust to focus the light on the retina, where the image appears upside down and backward. Basically, this is how a camera lens works. Light-sensitive receptor cells in the retinal surface, excited or inhibited by spots of light, influence the specialized neurons that convey nerve impulses to the brain's visual centers through their axons, which make up the optic nerve.

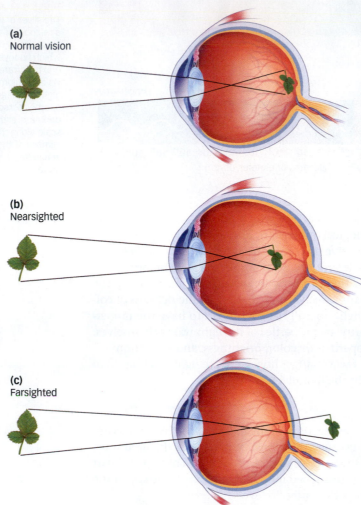

Figure 4.6 Accommodation Inside the eye, the lens changes shape to focus nearby or faraway objects on the retina. (a) People with normal vision focus the image on the retina at the back of the eye, both for near and far objects. (b) Nearsighted people see clearly what's nearby, but distant objects are blurry because light from them is focused in front of the retina, a condition called myopia. (c) Farsighted people have the opposite problem: Distant objects are clear, but those nearby are blurry because their point of focus falls beyond the surface of the retina, a condition called hyperopia.

(a) Normal vision

(b) Nearsighted

(c) Farsighted

Immediately behind the iris, muscles inside the eye control the shape of the *lens* to bend the light again and focus it onto the **retina**, *light-sensitive tissue lining the back of the eyeball*. The muscles change the shape of the lens to focus objects at different distances, making the lens flatter for objects that are far away or rounder for nearby objects. This is called **accommodation**, *the process by which the eye maintains a clear image on the retina*. **FIGURE 4.6a** shows how accommodation works.

If your eyeballs are a little too long or a little too short, the lens will not focus images properly on the retina. If the eyeball is too long, images are focused in front of the retina, leading to nearsightedness (*myopia*), which is shown in **FIGURE 4.6b**. If the eyeball is too short, images are focused behind the retina, and the result is farsightedness (*hyperopia*), as shown in **FIGURE 4.6c**. Eyeglasses, contact lenses, and surgical procedures can correct either condition. For example, eyeglasses and contacts both provide an additional lens to help focus light more appropriately, and procedures such as LASIK physically reshape the eye's existing lens.

RETINA Light-sensitive tissue lining the back of the eyeball.

ACCOMMODATION The process by which the eye maintains a clear image on the retina.

CONES Photoreceptors that detect color, operate under normal daylight conditions, and allow us to focus on fine detail.

RODS Photoreceptors that become active only under low-light conditions for night vision.

Phototransduction in the Retina

The retina is the interface between the world of light outside the body and the world of vision inside the central nervous system. Two types of *photoreceptor cells* in the retina contain light-sensitive pigments that transduce light into neural impulses. **Cones** *detect color, operate under normal daylight conditions, and allow us to focus on fine detail*. **Rods** *become active only under low-light conditions for night vision* (see **FIGURE 4.7**).

Rods are much more sensitive photoreceptors than cones, but this sensitivity comes at a cost. Because all rods contain the same photopigment, they provide no information about color and sense only shades of gray. Think about this the next time you wake up in the middle of the night and make your way to the bathroom for a drink of water. Using only the moonlight from the window to light your way, do you see the room in color or in shades of gray?

The full-color image on the left is what you'd see when your rods and cones were fully at work. The grayscale image on the right is what you'd see if only your rods were functioning.

Figure 4.7 Close-up of the Retina The surface of the retina is composed of photoreceptor cells, the rods and cones, beneath a layer of transparent neurons, the bipolar and retinal ganglion cells, connected in sequence. Viewed close up in this cross-sectional diagram is the area of greatest visual acuity, the fovea, where most color-sensitive cones are concentrated, allowing us to see fine detail as well as color. Rods, the predominant photoreceptors activated in low-light conditions, are distributed everywhere else on the retina.

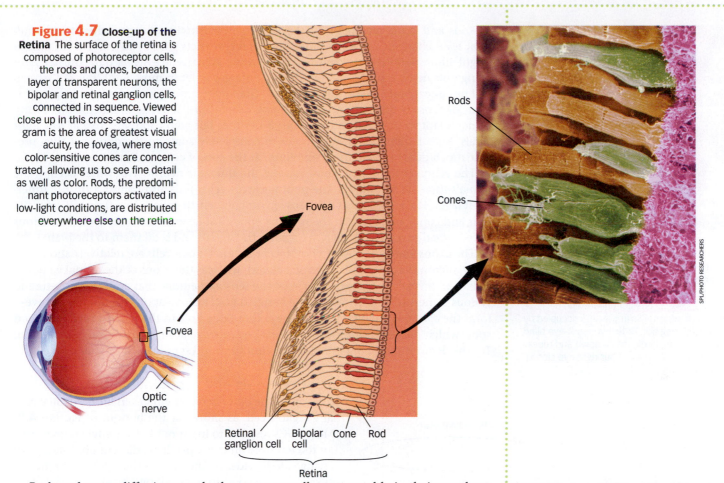

Rods

Cones

Fovea

Fovea

Optic nerve

Retinal ganglion cell   Bipolar cell   Cone   Rod

Retina

SPL/PHOTO RESEARCHERS

Rods and cones differ in several other ways as well, most notably in their numbers. About 120 million rods are distributed more or less evenly around each retina except in the very center, the **fovea**, *an area of the retina where vision is the clearest and there are no rods at all.* The absence of rods in the fovea decreases the sharpness of vision in reduced light, but it can be overcome. For example, when amateur astronomers view dim stars through their telescopes at night, they know to look a little off to the side of the target so that the image will fall not on the rod-free fovea but on some other part of the retina that contains many highly sensitive rods.

In contrast to rods, each retina contains only about 6 million cones, which are densely packed in the fovea and much more sparsely distributed over the rest of the retina, as you can see in Figure 4.7. The high concentration of cones in the fovea directly affects visual acuity and explains why objects off to the side, in your *peripheral vision,* aren't so clear. The light reflecting from those peripheral objects has a difficult time landing in the fovea, making the resulting image less clear. The more fine detail encoded and represented in the visual system, the clearer the perceived image. The process is analogous to the quality of photographs taken with a six-megapixel digital camera versus a two-megapixel camera.

FOVEA An area of the retina where vision is the clearest and there are no rods at all.

COURTESY OF DAVE ETCHELLS

COURTESY OF DAVE ETCHELLS

The image on the left was taken at a higher resolution than the image on the right. The difference in quality is analogous to light falling on the fovea versus not.

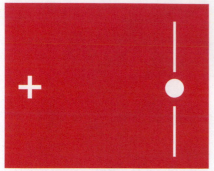

Figure 4.8 Blind Spot Demonstration
To find your blind spot, close your left eye and stare at the cross with your right eye. Hold the book six to 12 inches (15 to 30 centimeters) away from your eyes and move it slowly toward and away from you until the dot disappears. The dot is now in your blind spot and so is not visible. At this point the vertical lines may appear as one continuous line because the visual system fills in the area occupied by the missing dot. To test your left-eye blind spot, turn the book upside down and repeat with your right eye closed.

Rods and cones also differ in the way their sensitivity changes when the overall light level changes. Remember that the pupil constricts when you move from dim to bright illumination. Now consider the reverse: When you enter a dark theater after being outside on a sunny day, your pupil enlarges to let in more light, but at first you will be almost blind to the seating layout. Gradually, however, your vision adapts. This form of sensory adaptation is called *dark adaptation* (Hecht & Mandelbaum, 1938). Cones adapt to the dark within about 8 minutes but aren't too sensitive at low light levels. Rods require about 30 minutes to completely adapt to the dark, but they provide much better sensitivity in dim light, at the cost of color vision.

The retina is thick with cells. Among the different neuron types that occupy the retina's three distinct layers, the photoreceptor cells (rods and cones) form the innermost layer. The middle layer contains *bipolar cells,* which collect neural signals from the rods and cones and transmit them to the outermost layer of the retina, where neurons called *retinal ganglion cells* (RGCs) organize the signals and send them to the brain.

The axons and dendrites of photoreceptors and bipolar cells are relatively short (just a few microns long, or millionths of a meter), whereas the axons of the retinal ganglion cells span several centimeters. RGCs are the sensory neurons that connect the retina to various centers within the brain. The bundled RGC axons—about 1.5 million per eye—form the *optic nerve,* which leaves the eye through a hole in the retina called the **blind spot**, which *contains neither rods nor cones and therefore has no mechanism to sense light.* Try the demonstration in **FIGURE 4.8** to find the blind spot in each of your own eyes.

Receptive Fields and Lateral Inhibition

Each axon in the optic nerve originates in an individual retinal ganglion cell, as shown at the bottom of **FIGURE 4.9**. Most RGCs respond to input not from a single retinal cone or rod but from an entire patch of adjacent photoreceptors lying side by side, or laterally, in the retina. A particular RGC will respond to light falling anywhere within that small patch, which is called its **receptive field**, *the region of the sensory surface that, when stimulated, causes a change in the firing rate of that neuron.* Although we'll focus on vision here, the general concept of receptive fields applies to all sensory systems. For example, the cells that connect to the touch centers of the brain have receptive fields, which are the part of the skin that, when stimulated, causes that cell's response to change in some way.

Within a receptive field, neighboring photoreceptors respond to stimulation differently: Some cells are excited, whereas some are inhibited. These opposing responses interact, which means that the signals they send through the bipolar cells to the RGC are based on differing levels of receptor activation, a process called *lateral inhibition.* Moving from top to bottom in Figure 4.9, a spot of light that covers any or all of the cones will activate one or more bipolar cells, which in turn causes the ganglion cell to change the rate at which it sends action potentials.

A given RGC responds to a spot of light projected anywhere within a small, roughly circular patch of retina (Kuffler, 1953). Most receptive fields contain either a central excitatory zone surrounded by a doughnut-shaped inhibitory zone, which is called an *on-center cell,* or a central inhibitory zone surrounded by an excitatory zone, which is called an *off-center cell* (see **FIGURE 4.10**). The doughnut-shaped regions represent patches of retina, as if the top of the diagram in Figure 4.9 were tilted forward so we could look at the cones end-on.

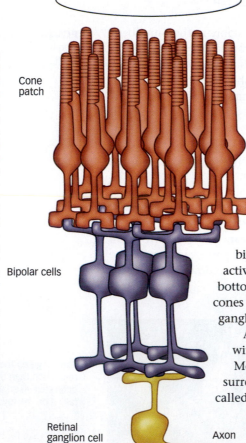

Figure 4.9 Receptive Field of a Retinal Ganglion Cell The axon of a retinal ganglion cell, shown at the bottom of the figure, joins with all other RGC axons to form the optic nerve. Moving back toward the surface of the retina in this side view, each RGC connects to a cluster of five or six bipolar cells. The responses conveyed to the ganglion cell by each bipolar cell depend on the combination of excitatory or inhibitory signals transduced by the larger group of photoreceptors connected to that bipolar cell. The entire grouping, from photoreceptors to RGC, forms a receptive field, shown at the top of the figure. The RGC responds to a spot of light falling on any or all of the photoreceptors within its receptive field as a result of lateral inhibition.

Receptive field

Cone patch

To retina

Bipolar cells

Retinal ganglion cell

Axon

To optic nerve

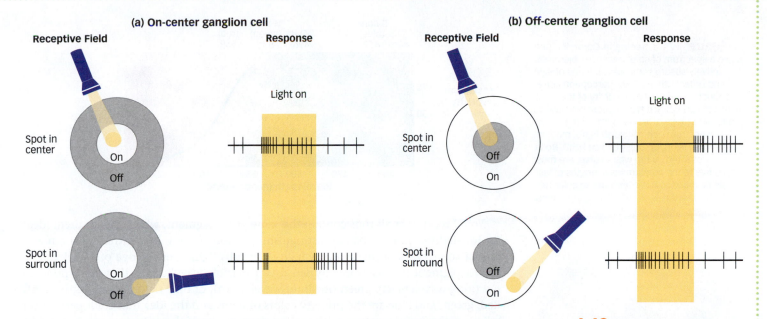

(a) On-center ganglion cell

Receptive Field

Response

Spot in center

On
Off

Light on

Spot in surround

On
Off

(b) Off-center ganglion cell

Receptive Field

Response

Spot in center

Off
On

Light on

Spot in surround

Off
On

Figure 4.10 RGC Receptive Fields Viewed End-on Imagine that you're looking down on the receptive field represented at the top of Figure 4.9. (a) An on-center ganglion cell increases its firing rate when the receptive field is stimulated by light in the central area but decreases its firing rate when the light strikes the surrounding area. Both neural response levels are shown in the right column. (b) The off-center ganglion cell decreases its firing rate when its receptive field is stimulated by light in the central area but increases its firing rate when the light strikes the surrounding area. Both responses are shown at the right.

Think about the response of an on-center retinal ganglion cell when its receptive field is stimulated with spots of light of different sizes (**FIGURE 4.10a**). A small spot shining on the central excitatory zone increases the RGC's firing rate. When the spot exactly fills the excitatory zone, it elicits the strongest response, whereas light falling on the surrounding inhibitory zone elicits the weakest response or none at all. The response of an off-center cell, shown in **FIGURE 4.10b**, is just the opposite. A small spot shining on the central inhibitory zone elicits a weak response, and a spot shining on the surrounding excitatory zone elicits a strong response in the RGC.

If a spot of light "spills over" into the inhibitory zone of either receptive-field type, the cell's response decreases somewhat, and if the entire receptive field is stimulated, excitatory and inhibitory activations cancel out due to lateral inhibition and the RGC's response will look similar to its response in the dark. Why would the RGC respond the same way to a uniformly bright field as to a uniformly dark field? The answer is related to the idea of difference thresholds: The visual system encodes *differences* in brightness or color. In other words, the RGC is a kind of "spot detector," recording the relative changes in excitation and inhibition of receptive fields.

Lateral inhibition reveals how the visual system begins to encode the spatial structure of a scene and not merely the point-by-point light intensity sensed at each location in the retina. The retina is organized in this way to detect edges—abrupt transitions from light to dark or vice versa. Edges are of supreme importance in vision. They define the shapes of objects, and anything that highlights such boundaries improves our ability to see an object's shape, particularly in low-light situations.

Perceiving Color

We thrill to the burst of colors during a fireworks display, "ooh" and "aah" at nature's palette during sunset, and marvel at the vibrant hues of a peacock's tail feathers. Color indeed adds zest to the visual world, but it also offers fundamental clues to an object's identity. A black banana or blue lips are color-coded calls to action—to avoid or sound the alarm, as the case might be.

Seeing Color

Sir Isaac Newton pointed out around 1670 that color is not something "in" light. In fact, color is nothing but our perception of light's wavelength (see **FIGURE 4.11** on page 136). We perceive the shortest visible wavelengths as deep purple. As wavelengths increase, the color perceived changes gradually and continuously to blue, then green, yellow, orange, and, with the longest visible wavelengths, red. This rainbow of hues and accompanying wavelengths is called the *visible spectrum,* illustrated in Figure 4.11.

BLIND SPOT An area of the retina that contains neither rods nor cones and therefore has no mechanism to sense light.

RECEPTIVE FIELD The region of the sensory surface that, when stimulated, causes a change in the firing rate of that neuron.

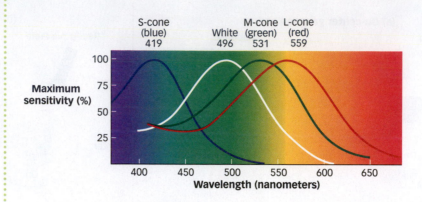

Figure 4.11 **Seeing in Color** We perceive a spectrum of color because objects selectively absorb some wavelengths of light and reflect others. Color perception corresponds to the summed activity of the three types of cones. Each type is most sensitive to a narrow range of wavelengths in the visible spectrum—short (bluish light), medium (greenish light), or long (reddish light). Rods, represented by the white curve, are most sensitive to the medium wavelengths of visible light but do not contribute to color perception.

You'll recall that all rods contain the same photopigment, which makes them ideal for low-light vision but bad at distinguishing colors. Cones, by contrast, contain any one of three types of pigment. Each cone absorbs light over a range of wavelengths, but its pigment type is especially sensitive to visible wavelengths that correspond to red (long-wavelength), green (medium-wavelength), or blue (short-wavelength) light. Red, green, and blue are the primary colors of light, and the idea that color perception relies on three components in the retina dates to the 19th century, when it was first proposed by the English scientist Thomas Young (1773–1829). Young produced staggering accomplishments—he was a practicing physician and a distinguished physicist, and in his spare time he contributed to solving the mystery of the Rosetta stone (a tablet that allowed archeologists to translate Egyptian hieroglyphics to Greek, a language they actually understood!). He knew so much about so many topics that a recent biographer called him "the last man who knew everything" (Robinson, 2006). Happily for psychology, Young had some pretty good ideas abut how color vision works. But it was the great German scientist Hermann von Helmholtz (1821–94) who more fully developed Young's idea that color perception results from different combinations of the three basic elements in the retina that respond to the wavelengths corresponding to the three primary colors of light. This insight has several implications and applications.

For example, lighting designers add primary colors of light together, such as shining red and green spotlights on a surface to create a yellow light, as shown in **FIGURE 4.12a.** Notice that in the center of the figure, where the red, green, and blue lights overlap, the surface looks white. This demonstrates that a white surface really is reflecting all visible wavelengths of light. Increasing light to create color in this way is called *additive color mixing*.

Centuries before Newton first experimented with light, Renaissance painters in Italy had learned that they could re-create any color found in nature simply by mixing only three colors: red, blue, and yellow. You may have discovered this process for

Figure 4.12 **Color Mixing** The millions of shades of color that humans can perceive are products not only of a light's wavelength but also of the mixture of wavelengths a stimulus absorbs or reflects. We see a ripe banana as yellow because the banana skin reflects the light waves that we perceive as yellow but absorbs the wavelengths that we perceive as shades of blue to green and those that make us see red. (a) Additive color mixing works by increasing the reflected wavelengths—by adding light to stimulate the red, blue, or green photopigments in the cones. When all visible wavelengths are present, we see white. (b) Subtractive color mixing removes wavelengths, thus absorbing light waves we see as red, blue, or yellow. When all visible wavelengths are absorbed, we see black.

(a) Additive color mixing (red, blue, green)

(b) Subtractive color mixing (red, blue, yellow)

yourself by mixing paints. This *subtractive color mixing* works by removing light from the mix, such as when you combine yellow and red to make orange or blue and yellow to make green, shown in Figure 4.12b. The darker the color, the less light it contains, which is why black surfaces reflect no light.

When you perceive color, then, the cone receptors in your retina encode the wavelengths of light reflected from a surface. But color processing in the human visual system occurs in two stages. The first stage—encoding—occurs in the retina, whereas the second stage—processing—requires the brain (Gegenfurtner & Kiper, 2003).

Trichromatic Color Representation in the Cones

Light striking the retina causes a specific pattern of response in the three cone types (Schnapf, Kraft, & Baylor, 1987). One type responds best to short-wavelength (bluish) light, the second type to medium-wavelength (greenish) light, and the third type to long-wavelength (reddish) light. Researchers refer to them as S-cones, M-cones, and L-cones, respectively (see Figure 4.11).

This **trichromatic color representation** means that *the pattern of responding across the three types of cones provides a unique code for each color.* Researchers can "read out" the wavelength of the light entering the eye by working backward from the relative firing rates of the three types of cones. A genetic disorder in which one of the cone types is missing—and, in some very rare cases, two or all three—causes a *color deficiency.* This trait is sex-linked, affecting men much more often than women.

Color deficiency is often referred to as *color blindness,* but in fact, people missing only one type of cone can still distinguish many colors, just not as many as someone who has the full complement of three cone types. Like synesthetes, people whose vision is color deficient often do not realize that they experience color differently from others.

Trichromatic color representation is well established as the first step of encoding color in the visual system (Abromov & Gordon, 1994). Sensory adaptation helps to explain the second step.

Color-Opponent Representation into the Brain

Recall that sensory adaptation occurs because our sensitivity to prolonged stimulation tends to decline over time. Just like the rest of your body, cones need an occasional break too. Staring too long at one color fatigues the cones that respond to that color, producing a form of sensory adaptation called *color afterimage.* To demonstrate this effect for yourself, follow these instructions for **FIGURE 4.13**:

- Stare at the small cross between the two color patches for about 1 minute. Try to keep your eyes as still as possible.
- After a minute, look at the lower cross. You should see a vivid color aftereffect that lasts for a minute or more. Pay particular attention to the colors in the afterimage.

Were you puzzled that the red patch produces a green afterimage and the green patch produces a red afterimage? This result may seem like nothing more than a curious mindbug, but in fact it reveals something important about color perception. The explanation stems from the second stage of color representation, the **color-opponent system**, where *pairs of visual neurons work in opposition;* red-sensitive cells against green-sensitive (as in Figure 4.13) and blue-sensitive cells against yellow-sensitive (Hurvich & Jameson, 1957). How do opponent pairs of *four* colors make sense if we have just *three* cone types?

It may be that opponent pairs evolved to enhance color perception by taking advantage of excitatory and inhibitory stimulation. Red-green cells are excited (they increase their firing rates) in response to wavelengths corresponding to red and inhibited (they decrease their firing rates) in response to wavelengths corresponding to green. Blue-yellow cells increase their firing rate in response to blue wavelengths (excitatory) and decrease their firing rate in response to yellow wavelengths (inhibitory). The color pairs are linked to each other as opposites.

TRICHROMATIC COLOR REPRESENTATION The pattern of responding across the three types of cones that provides a unique code for each color.

COLOR-OPPONENT SYSTEM Pairs of visual neurons that work in opposition.

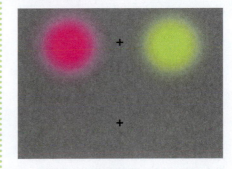

Figure 4.13 Color Afterimage Demonstration Follow the accompanying instructions in the text, and sensory adaptation will do the rest. When the afterimage fades, you can get back to reading the chapter.

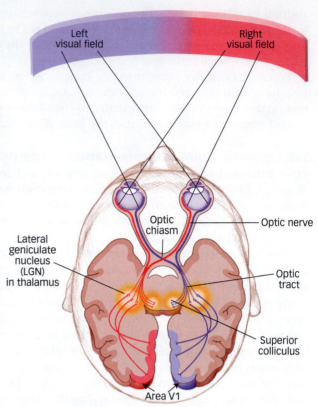

Figure 4.14 Visual Pathway from Eye through Brain Objects in the right visual field stimulate the left half of each retina, and objects in the left visual field stimulate the right half of each retina. The optic nerves, one exiting each eye, are formed by the axons of retinal ganglion cells emerging from the retina. Just before they enter the brain at the optic chiasm, about half the nerve fibers from each eye cross. The left half of each optic nerve, representing the *right* visual field, runs through the brain's left hemisphere via the thalamus, and the right halves, representing the *left* visual field, travel this route through the right hemisphere. So information from the right visual field ends up in the left hemisphere and information from the left visual field ends up in the right hemisphere.

The color-opponent system explains color aftereffects. When you view a color, let's say, green, the cones that respond most strongly to green become fatigued over time. Fatigue leads to an imbalance in the inputs to the red-green color-opponent neurons, beginning with the retinal ganglion cells: The weakened signal from the green-responsive cones leads to an overall response that emphasizes red. A similar explanation can be made for other color aftereffects; find a bright blue circle of color and get ready to make your roommate see yellow spots!

Working together, the trichromatic and color-opponent systems begin the process of color perception. S-, M-, and L-cones connect to color-opponent RGCs with excitatory and/or inhibitory connections that produce the color-opponent response. Color-opponent, excitatory-inhibitory processes then continue down the visual pathways to the brain, first to neurons in the thalamus and then to the occipital cortex, as mapped in **FIGURE 4.14** (De Valois, Abramov, & Jacobs, 1966).

The Visual Brain

A great deal of visual processing takes place within the retina itself, including the encoding of simple features such as spots of light, edges, and color. More complex aspects of vision, however, require more powerful processing, and that enlists the brain.

Streams of action potentials containing information encoded by the retina travel to the brain along the optic nerve. Half of the axons in the optic nerve that leave each eye come from retinal ganglion cells that code information in the right visual field, whereas the other half code information in the left visual field. These two nerve bundles link to the left and right hemispheres of the brain, respectively (see Figure 4.14). The optic nerve travels from each eye to the *lateral geniculate nucleus* (*LGN*), located in the thalamus. As you will recall from Chapter 3, the thalamus receives inputs from all of the senses except smell. From there the visual signal travels to the back of the brain, to a location called **area V1**, the *part of the occipital lobe that contains the primary visual cortex*. Here the information is systematically mapped into a representation of the visual scene. There are about 30 to 50 brain areas specialized for vision, located mainly in the occipital lobe at the back of the brain and in the temporal lobes on the sides of the brain (Orban, Van Essen, & Vanduffel, 2004; Van Essen, Anderson, & Felleman, 1992).

AREA V1 The part of the occipital lobe that contains the primary visual cortex.

Neural Systems for Perceiving Shape

One of the most important functions of vision involves perceiving the shapes of objects; our day-to-day lives would be a mess if we couldn't distinguish individual shapes from one another. Imagine not being able to reliably differentiate between a warm doughnut with glazed icing and a straight stalk of celery and you'll get the idea; breakfast could become a traumatic experience if you couldn't distinguish shapes. Perceiving shape depends on the location and orientation of an object's edges. It is not surprising, then, that area V1 is specialized for encoding edge orientation.

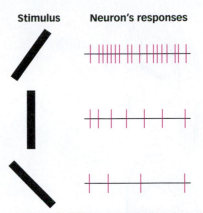

FIRTZ GORO, LIFE MAGAZINE, 1971 TIME WARNER, INC.

As you read in Chapter 3, neurons in the visual cortex selectively respond to bars and edges in specific orientations in space (Hubel & Weisel, 1962, 1998). In effect, area V1 contains populations of neurons, each "tuned" to respond to edges oriented at each position in the visual field. This means that some neurons fire when an object in a vertical orientation is perceived, other neurons fire when an object in a horizontal orientation is perceived, still other neurons fire when objects in a diagonal orientation of 45 degrees are perceived, and so on (see **FIGURE 4.15**). The outcome of the coordinated response of all these feature detectors contributes to a sophisticated visual system that can detect where a doughnut ends and celery begins.

Figure 4.15 **Single Neuron Feature Detectors** Area V1 contains neurons that respond to specific orientations of edges. Here a single neuron's responses are recorded (at right) as the monkey views bars at different orientations (left). This neuron fires continuously when the bar is pointing to the right at 45 degrees, less often when it is vertical, and not at all when it is pointing to the left at 45 degrees.

Pathways for What, Where, and How

In Chapter 2 you learned how brain researchers have used transcranial magnetic stimulation (TMS) to demonstrate that a person who can recognize what an object is may not be able to perceive that the object is moving. This observation implies that one brain system identifies people and things and another tracks their movements, or guides our movements in relation to them. Two functionally distinct pathways, or *visual streams,* project from the occipital cortex to visual areas in other parts of the brain (see **FIGURE 4.16**):

- The *ventral* ("below") *stream* travels across the occipital lobe into the lower levels of the temporal lobes and includes brain areas that represent an object's shape and identity—in other words, what it is. The damage caused by Betty's stroke that you read about in Chapter 3 interrupted this "what pathway" (Tanaka, 1996). As a result, Betty could not recognize familiar faces even though she could still see them.
- The *dorsal* ("above") *stream* travels up from the occipital lobe to the parietal lobes (including some of the middle and upper levels of the temporal lobes), connecting with brain areas that identify the location and motion of an object—in other words, where it is. Because the dorsal stream allows us to perceive spatial relations, researchers originally dubbed it the "where pathway" (Ungerleider & Mishkin, 1982).

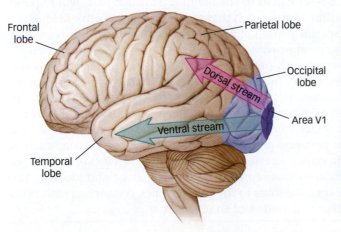

Figure 4.16 **Visual Streaming** One interconnected visual system forms a pathway that courses from the occipital visual regions into the lower temporal lobe. This ventral pathway enables us to identify what we see. Another interconnected pathway travels from the occipital lobe through the upper regions of the temporal lobe into the parietal regions. This dorsal pathway allows us to locate objects, to track their movements, and to move in relation to them.

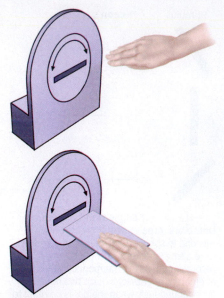

Figure 4.17 **Testing Visual Form Agnosia** When researchers asked patient D. F. to orient her hand to match the angle of the slot in the testing apparatus, as shown at the top, she was unable to comply. Asked to insert a card into the slot at various angles, as shown at the bottom, however, D. F. accomplished the task virtually to perfection.

More recently, neuroscientists have argued that because the dorsal stream is crucial for guiding movements, such as aiming, reaching, or tracking with the eyes, the "where pathway" should more appropriately be called the "how pathway" (Milner & Goodale, 1995).

Some of the most dramatic evidence for two distinct visual streams comes from studying the mindbugs that result from brain injury. A patient known as D. F. suffered permanent brain damage following exposure to toxic levels of carbon monoxide (Goodale, Milner, Jakobson, & Carey, 1991). A large region of the lateral occipital cortex was destroyed, an area in the ventral stream that is very active when people recognize objects. D. F.'s ability to recognize objects by sight was greatly impaired, although her ability to recognize objects by touch was normal. This suggests that the *visual representation* of objects, and not D. F.'s *memory* for objects, was damaged. Like Betty's inability to recognize familiar faces, D. F.'s brain damage belongs to a category called **visual-form agnosia**, *the inability to recognize objects by sight* (Goodale & Milner, 1992, 2004).

Oddly, although D. F. could not recognize objects visually, she could accurately *guide* her actions by sight. D. F. was shown a display board with a slot in it, as in **FIGURE 4.17.** The researchers could adjust the orientation of the slot. In one version of the task, shown at the top in the figure, they asked D. F. to report the orientation of the slot by holding her hand up at the same angle as the slot. D. F. performed very poorly at this task, almost randomly, suggesting that she did not have a reliable representation of visual orientation.

In another version of the task, shown at the bottom in Figure 4.17, D. F. was asked to insert a flat block into the slot, as if she were posting a letter into a mail slot. Now she performed the task almost perfectly! The paradox is that D. F.'s explicit or conscious understanding of what she was seeing was greatly impaired, but her ability to use this very same information nonconsciously to guide her movements remained intact. When D. F. was scanned with fMRI, researchers found that she showed normal activation of regions within the dorsal stream during guided movement (James et al., 2003).

Other patients with brain damage to the parietal section of the dorsal stream have difficulty using vision to guide their reaching and grasping movements, a condition termed *optic ataxia* (Perenin & Vighetto, 1988). However, these patients' ventral streams are intact, meaning they recognize what objects are. We can conclude from these two patterns of impairment that the ventral and dorsal visual streams are functionally distinct; it is possible to damage one while leaving the other intact.

In summary, light initially passes through several layers in the eye, with the retina linking the world of light outside and the world of visual perception inside the central nervous system. Two types of photoreceptor cells in the retina transduce light into neural impulses: cones, which operate under normal daylight conditions and sense color, and rods, which are active only under low-light conditions for night vision.

The retina contains several layers, and the outermost consists of retinal ganglion cells (RGCs) that collect and send signals to the brain. A particular RGC will respond to light falling anywhere within a small patch that constitutes its receptive field. Light striking the retina causes a specific pattern of response in each of three cone types that are critical to color perception: short-wavelength (bluish) light, medium-wavelength (greenish) light, and long-wavelength (reddish) light. The overall pattern of response across the three cone types results in a unique code for each color, known as its trichromatic color representation. Information encoded by the retina travels to the brain along the optic nerve, which connects to the lateral geniculate nucleus in the thalamus and then to the primary visual cortex, area V1, in the occipital lobe.

Two functionally distinct pathways project from the occipital lobe to visual areas in other parts of the brain. The ventral stream travels into the lower levels of the temporal lobes and includes brain areas that represent an object's shape and identity. The dorsal stream goes from the occipital lobes to the parietal lobes, connecting with brain areas that identify the location and motion of an object. ■ ■

VISUAL-FORM AGNOSIA The inability to recognize objects by sight.

Recognizing Objects by Sight

Take a quick look at the letters in the accompanying illustration. Even though they're quite different from one another, you probably effortlessly recognized them as all being examples of the letter *G*. Now consider the same kind of demonstration using your best friend's face. Your friend might have long hair, but one day she decides to get it cut dramatically short. Even though your friend now looks strikingly different, you still recognize that person with ease. Add glasses. A dye job, producing reddish hair. Maybe your friend grows a beard or mustache. Or he uses colored contact lenses. Perhaps she gets piercings to accommodate a nose ring. Any or all of these elements have the effect of producing a distinctly different-looking face, yet just like the variability in *G*s you somehow are able to extract the underlying features of the face that allow you to accurately identify your friend.

This thought exercise may seem trivial, but it's no small perceptual feat. If the visual system were somehow stumped each time a minor variation occurred in an object being perceived, the inefficiency of it all would be overwhelming. We'd have to effortfully process information just to perceive our friend as the same person from one meeting to another, not to mention laboring through the process of knowing when a *G* is really a *G*. In general, though, object recognition proceeds fairly smoothly, in large part due to the operation of the feature detectors we discussed earlier.

How do feature detectors help the visual system get from a spatial array of light hitting the eye to the accurate perception of an object, such as your friend's face? Some researchers argue for a *modular view:* that specialized brain areas, or modules, detect and represent faces or houses or even body parts. Using fMRI to examine visual processing in healthy young adults, researchers found a subregion in the temporal lobe that responds selectively to faces compared to just about any other object category, while a nearby area responds selectively to buildings and landscapes (Kanwisher, McDermott, & Chun, 1997). This view suggests we not only have feature detectors to aid in visual perception but also "face detectors," "building detectors," and possibly other types of neurons specialized for particular types of object perception (Kanwisher & Yovel, 2006).

Psychologists and researchers who argue for a more *distributed representation* of object categories challenge the modular view. Researchers have shown that although a subregion in the temporal lobes does respond more to faces than to any other category, parts of the brain outside this area may also be involved in face recognition. In this view, it is the pattern of activity across multiple brain regions that identifies any viewed object, including faces (Haxby et al., 2001). Each of these views explains some data better than the other one, and researchers are continuing to debate their relative merits.

Representing Objects and Faces in the Brain

Investigations of how the brain responds to complex objects and to faces began in the 1980s with experiments using primates as research subjects. Researchers recorded from single cells in the temporal lobes of macaque monkeys and found that different neurons respond selectively to different object shapes (Tanaka, 1996). Other investigators found neurons that respond best to other monkey faces or to human faces.

In the mid-1990s, neuroscientists began using fMRI to investigate whether specialized neurons like these operate in the human brain. They showed healthy participants photographs of faces, houses, and other object categories—shoes, tools, or dogs, for example. During the past decade, fMRI studies have revealed that some brain regions in the occipital and temporal lobes do respond selectively to specific object categories (Downing, Chan, Peelen, Dodds, & Kanwisher, 2006).

Another perspective on this issue is provided by experiments designed to measure precisely where seizures originate; these experiments have provided insights on how single neurons in the human brain respond to objects and faces (Quiroga, Reddy, Kreiman, Koch, & Fried, 2005). Electrodes were placed in the temporal lobes of people who suffer from epilepsy. Then the volunteers were shown photographs of faces and objects as the researchers recorded their neural responses. The researchers found that neurons in the temporal lobe respond to specific objects viewed from multiple angles and to people wearing different clothing and facial expressions and photographed

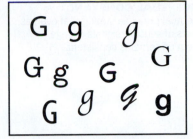

A quick glance and you recognize all these letters as *G*, but their varying sizes, shapes, angles, and orientations ought to make this recognition task difficult. What is it about the process of object recognition that allows us to perform this task effortlessly?

PERCEPTUAL CONSTANCY A perceptual principle stating that even as aspects of sensory signals change, perception remains consistent.

from various angles. In some cases, the neurons also respond to the words for the objects they prefer. For example, a neuron that responded to photographs of the Sydney Opera House also responded when the words *Sydney Opera* were displayed but not when the words *Eiffel Tower* were displayed (Quiroga et al., 2005).

Taken together, these experiments demonstrate the principle of **perceptual constancy**: *Even as aspects of sensory signals change, perception remains consistent.* Think back once again to our discussion of difference thresholds early in this chapter. Our perceptual systems are sensitive to relative differences in changing stimulation and make allowances for varying sensory input. This general principle helps explain why you still recognize your friend despite changes in hair color or style or the addition of facial jewelry. It's not as though your visual perceptual system responds to a change with, "Here's a new and unfamiliar face to perceive." Rather, it's as though it responds with, "Interesting . . . here's a deviation from the way this face usually looks." Perception is sensitive to changes in stimuli, but perceptual constancies allow us to notice the differences in the first place.

Principles of Perceptual Organization

Before object recognition can even kick in, the visual system must perform another important task: to group the image regions that belong together into a representation of an object. The idea that we tend to perceive a unified, whole object rather than a collection of separate parts is the foundation of Gestalt psychology, which you read about in Chapter 1. Gestalt principles characterize many aspects of human perception. Among the foremost are the Gestalt *perceptual grouping rules,* which govern how the features and regions of things fit together (Koffka, 1935). Here's a sampling:

- *Simplicity:* A basic rule in science is that the simplest explanation is usually the best. This is the idea behind the Gestalt grouping rule of *Pragnanz,* which translates as "good form." When confronted with two or more possible interpretations of an object's shape, the visual system tends to select the simplest or most likely interpretation (see **FIGURE 4.18a**).
- *Closure:* We tend to fill in missing elements of a visual scene, allowing us to perceive edges that are separated by gaps as belonging to complete objects (see **FIGURE 4.18b**).
- *Continuity:* Edges or contours that have the same orientation have what the Gestaltists called "good continuation," and we tend to group them together perceptually (see **FIGURE 4.18c**).
- *Similarity:* Regions that are similar in color, lightness, shape, or texture are perceived a belonging to the same object (see **FIGURE 4.18d**).
- *Proximity:* Objects that are close together tend to be grouped together (see **FIGURE 4.18e**).
- *Common fate:* Elements of a visual image that move together are perceived as parts of a single moving object (see **FIGURE 4.18f**).

Figure 4.18 Perceptual Grouping Rules Principles first identified by Gestalt psychologists and now supported by experimental evidence demonstrate that the brain is predisposed to impose order on incoming sensations. One neural strategy for perception involves responding to patterns among stimuli and grouping like patterns together.

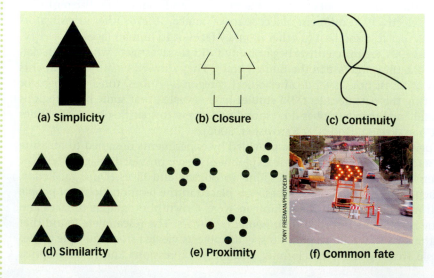

(a) Simplicity (b) Closure (c) Continuity

(d) Similarity (e) Proximity (f) Common fate

Separating Figure from Ground

Perceptual grouping is a powerful aid to our ability to recognize objects by sight. Grouping involves visually separating an object from its surroundings. In Gestalt terms, this means identifying a *figure* apart from the (back)*ground* in which it resides. For example, the words on this page are perceived as figural: They stand out from the ground of the sheet of paper on which they're printed. Similarly, your instructor is perceived as the figure against the backdrop of all the other elements in your class-room. You certainly can perceive these elements differently, of course: The words *and* the paper are all part of a thing called "a page," and your instructor *and* the classroom can all be perceived as "your learning environment." Typically, though, our perceptual systems focus attention on some objects as distinct from their environments.

Size provides one clue to what's figure and what's ground: Smaller regions are likely to be figures, such as tiny letters on a big paper. Movement also helps: Your instructor is (we hope) a dynamic lecturer, moving around in a static environment. Another crit-ical step toward object recognition is *edge assignment*. Given an edge, or boundary, be-tween figure and ground, which region does that edge belong to? If the edge belongs to the figure, it helps define the object's shape, and the background continues behind the edge. Sometimes, though, it's not easy to tell which is which.

Edgar Rubin (1886–1951), a Danish psychologist, capitalized on this ambiguity in developing a famous illusion called the *Rubin vase* or, more generally, a *reversible figure-ground relationship*. You can view this "face-vase" illusion in **FIGURE 4.19** in two ways, either as a vase on a black background or as a pair of silhouettes facing each other. Your visual system settles on one or the other interpretation and fluctuates between them every few seconds. This happens because the edge that would normally separate figure from ground is really part of neither: It equally defines the contours of the vase as it does the contours of the faces. Evidence from fMRIs shows, quite nicely, that when people are seeing the Rubin image as a face, there is greater activity in the face-selective region of the temporal lobe we discussed earlier than when they are seeing it as a vase (Hasson, Hendler, Bashat, & Malach, 2001).

Theories of Object Recognition

Researchers have proposed two broad explanations of object recognition, one based on the object as a whole and the other on its parts. Each set of theories has strengths and weaknesses, making object recognition an active area of study in psychology.

According to *image-based object recognition* theories, an object you have seen before is stored in memory as a **template**, *a mental representation that can be directly compared to a viewed shape in the retinal image* (Tarr & Vuong, 2002). Shape templates are stored along with name, category, and other associations to that object. Your memory com-pares its templates to the current retinal image and selects the template that most closely matches the current image. For example, supermarket scanners use a form of template matching to identify the bar codes on grocery labels.

Image-based theories are widely accepted, yet they do not explain everything about object recognition. For one thing, the time it takes to recognize a familiar object does not depend on its current orientation relative to the object's standard orientation: You can quickly recognize that a cup is a cup even when it is tilted on its side. Correctly matching images to templates suggests that you'd have to have one template for cups in a normal orientation, another template for cups on their side, another for cups upside down, and so on. This makes for an unwieldy and inefficient system and therefore one that is unlikely to be effective, yet seeing a cup on its side rarely perplexes anyone for long. Another limitation is that image-based theories cannot account for objects you have never seen before. How can you correctly identify an object by matching it to a template if you don't have a template because you've never seen the object before? This roundabout reasoning suggests that people would be mystified when encountering un-familiar objects, yet actually we make sense of even unfamiliar objects quite readily.

Parts-based object recognition theories propose instead that the brain deconstructs viewed objects into a collection of parts (Marr & Nishihara, 1978). One important

Figure 4.19 Ambiguous Edges Here's how Rubin's classic reversible figure-ground illusion works: Fixate your eyes on the center of the image, and your perception will alternate between a vase and facing silhouettes, even as the sensory stimulation remains constant.

TEMPLATE A mental representation that can be directly compared to a viewed shape in the retinal image.

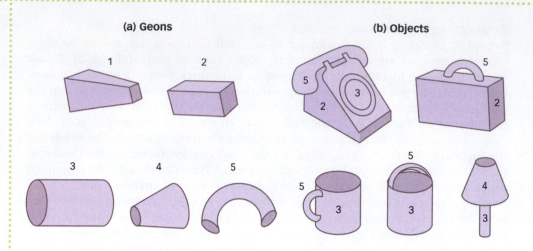

(a) Geons **(b) Objects**

Figure 4.20 **An Alphabet of Geometric Elements** Parts-based theory holds that objects such as those shown in (b) are made up of simpler three-dimensional components called geons, shown in (a), much as letters combine to form different words.

parts-based theory contends that objects are stored in memory as structural descriptions: mental inventories of object parts along with the spatial relations among those parts (Biederman, 1987). The parts inventories act as a sort of "alphabet" of geometric elements called *geons* that can be combined to make objects, just as letters are combined to form words (see **FIGURE 4.20**). For example, elements such as *curved, cylindrical,* or *pointy* might be indexed in an inventory, along with their relations to each other. In parts-based theories, object recognition constructs an image into its visible parts, notes the spatial relations among these parts, and then compares this structural description to inventories stored in memory (see Figure 4.20).

Like image-based theories, parts-based object recognition has major limitations. Most importantly, it allows for object recognition only at the level of categories and not at the level of the individual object. Parts-based theories offer an explanation for recognizing an object such as a face, for example, but are less effective at explaining how you distinguish between your best friend's face and a stranger's face.

As you can see, there are strengths and weaknesses of both image-based and parts-based explanations of object recognition. Researchers are developing hybrid theories that attempt to exploit the strengths of each approach (Peissig & Tarr, 2007).

Perceiving Depth and Size

You've probably never appreciated the mundane benefits of knowing where you are at any given time. If you've ever been in an unfamiliar environment, though, the benefits of knowing what's around you become readily apparent. Think of being in a house of mirrors: Is the exit to your left or to your right, or are you completely turned around? Imagine being in a new shopping mall: Was Abercrombie and Fitch on the top floor of the west wing, or was that American Eagle? Are those your friends over there at the food court or just some people who look like them? Knowing what's around you is important. Knowing where each object is located is important too. Whether one object is above, below, or to the left or right of another is first encoded in the retinal image.

Objects in the world are arranged in three dimensions—length, width, and depth—but the retinal image contains only two dimensions, length and width. How does the brain process a flat, two-dimensional retinal image so that we perceive the depth of an object and how far away it is? The answer lies in a collection of *depth cues* that change as you move through space. Monocular, binocular, and motion-based depth cues all help visual perception (Howard, 2002).

Monocular Depth Cues

If you had to wear an eye patch for a few hours each day, perhaps in your role as Salty the Pirate at the local fast-food joint, you might predict you'd have a difficult time perceiving things. After all, there must be a good reason for having two eyes! However,

Figure 4.21 Familiar Size and Relative Size When you view images of people, such as the men in the left-hand photo, or of things you know well, the object you perceive as smaller appears farther away. With a little image manipulation, you can see in the right-hand photo that the relative size difference projected on your retinas is far greater than you perceive. The image of the man in the blue vest is exactly the same size in both photos.

some aspects of visual perception involve **monocular depth cues,** *aspects of a scene that yield information about depth when viewed with only one eye.* These cues rely on the relationship between distance and size. Even with one eye closed, the retinal image of an object you're focused on grows smaller as that object moves farther away and larger as it moves closer. Our brains routinely use these differences in retinal image size, or *relative size,* to perceive distance.

This works particularly well in a monocular depth cue called *familiar size.* Most adults, for example, fall within a familiar range of heights (perhaps five to seven feet tall), so retinal image size alone is usually a reliable cue to how far away they are. Our visual system automatically corrects for size differences and attributes them to differences in distance. **FIGURE 4.21** demonstrates how strong this mental correction for familiar size is.

Monocular cues are often called *pictorial depth cues* because they are present even in two-dimensional paintings, photographs, and videos where the third dimension of depth is not really there. In addition to relative size and familiar size, there are several more monocular depth cues, such as

> I have no depth perception. Is there a cop standing on the corner, or do you have a tiny person in your hair?

- *Linear perspective,* which describes the phenomenon that parallel lines seem to converge as they recede into the distance (see **FIGURE 4.22a** on the next page).
- *Texture gradient,* which arises when you view a more or less uniformly patterned surface because the size of the pattern elements, as well as the distance between them, grows smaller as the surface recedes from the observer (see **FIGURE 4.22b**).
- *Interposition,* which occurs when one object partly blocks another (see **FIGURE 4.22c**). You can infer that the block*ing* object is closer than the block*ed* object. However, interposition by itself cannot provide information about how far apart the two objects are.
- *Relative height in the image* depends on your field of vision (see **FIGURE 4.22d**). Objects that are closer to you are lower in your visual field, while faraway objects are higher.

MONOCULAR DEPTH CUES Aspects of a scene that yield information about depth when viewed with only one eye.

BINOCULAR DISPARITY The difference in the retinal images of the two eyes that provides information about depth.

MOTION PARALLAX A depth cue based on the movement of the head over time.

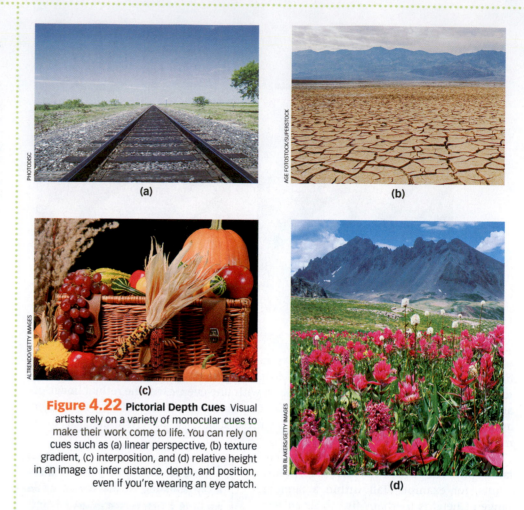

Figure 4.22 Pictorial Depth Cues Visual artists rely on a variety of monocular cues to make their work come to life. You can rely on cues such as (a) linear perspective, (b) texture gradient, (c) interposition, and (d) relative height in an image to infer distance, depth, and position, even if you're wearing an eye patch.

Binocular Depth Cues

Portraying pirates is not a hot occupation, mainly because two eyes are better than one, especially when it comes to depth perception. *Binocular depth cues* exist because we have stereoscopic vision: Having space between our eyes means that each eye registers a slightly different view of the world.

Hold your right index finger up about two feet in front of your face, close one eye, and look at your finger. Now alternate, opening and closing each eye rapidly. Your finger appears to jump back and forth as you do this.

The difference in these two views provides direct and compelling information about depth. The closer the object you're looking at, the greater the **binocular disparity**, *the difference in the retinal images of the two eyes that provides information about depth.* Your brain computes the disparity between the two retinal images to perceive how far away objects are, as shown in **FIGURE 4.23**. Viewed from above in the figure, the images of the more distant square and the closer circle each fall at different points on each retina.

Binocular disparity as a cue to depth perception was first discussed by Sir Charles Wheatstone in 1838. Wheatstone went on to invent the stereoscope, essentially a holder for a pair of photographs or drawings taken from two horizontally displaced locations (Wheatstone did not lack for

Figure 4.23 Binocular Disparity We see the world in three dimensions because our eyes are a distance apart and the image of an object falls on the retinas of each eye at a slightly different place. In this two-object scene, the images of the square and the circle fall on different points of the retina in each eye. The disparity in the positions of the circle's retinal images provides a compelling cue to depth.

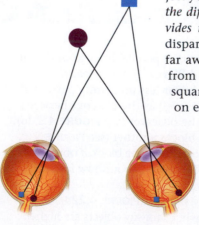

The View-Master has been a popular toy for decades. It is based on the principle of binocular disparity: Two images taken from slightly different angles produce a stereoscopic effect.

original ideas—he also invented the accordion and an early telegraph and coined the term *microphone*). When viewed, one by each eye, the pairs of images evoked a vivid sense of depth. The View-Master toy is the modern successor to Wheatstone's invention, and 3-D movies are based on this same idea.

Motion-Based Depth Cues

When you're riding in a car, bus, or train, the scene changes systematically and continuously. Nearby objects appear to zip by quickly, but faraway objects appear to move slowly or not at all. This phenomenon is called **motion parallax,** *a depth cue based on the movement of the head over time*. The speed and direction of the images on your retina depend on where you are looking and on how far away the objects you see are.

The depth perception you experience from motion parallax is essentially the same as that provided by binocular disparity. Both involve mentally comparing retinal image information from multiple viewpoints. In the case of binocular disparity, two slightly different viewpoints are sampled simultaneously by the two eyes. In motion parallax, the two viewpoints are sampled in succession, over time.

As you move forward through a scene, the motion cues to depth behave a little differently: As objects get closer, their image sizes on the retina increase, and their contours move outward on the retina, toward the side. *Optic flow,* the pattern of motion that accompanies an observer's forward movement through a scene, is a form of motion parallax. At any given point, the scene ahead moves outward from the point toward which the observer is moving. This kind of motion parallax is therefore useful for navigation while walking, driving, or landing an airplane.

If you have ever watched an old episode of Star Trek, you will recognize as optic flow the visual effect on the view screen when the spaceship jumps to warp speed. Trails of starlight out ahead expand outward from a central point. Back on Earth, you can see this effect when you look out the windshield as you drive through a snowstorm at night. As your headlights illuminate the onrushing snowflakes, the flakes at the center are farthest away (near the horizon) and the flakes on the periphery are closest to you.

Illusions of Depth and Size

We all are vulnerable to *illusions,* which, as you'll remember from Chapter 1, are errors of perception, memory, or judgment in which subjective experience differs from objective reality (Wade, 2005). These mindbugs inspired the Gestalt psychologists, whose contributions continue to influence research on object perception. Recall the Mueller-Lyer illusion from Chapter 1 (see Figure 1.3). Even though the horizontal lines in that figure are exactly the same length, the top horizontal line looks longer than the bottom one. That's because you don't perceive the horizontal lines in isolation: Your perception of them is related to and influenced by the surrounding vertical lines.

 **ONLY HUMAN**

I KNOW IT'S AROUND HERE SOMEPLACE. . . A 44-year-old man was arrested for DUI in Australia's Northern Territory after he asked a police officer how to get to the hard-to-miss Uluru (Ayers Rock, the huge, 1,000-foot-high rock formation that appears red in sunlight), which was about 300 feet in front of him, illuminated in his headlights.

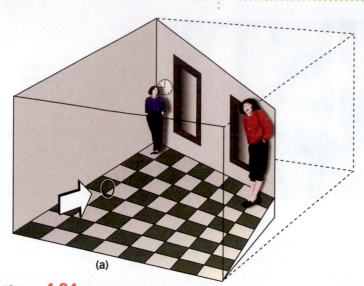

(a)

(b)

PHIL SCHERMEISTER/CORBIS

Figure 4.24 **The Amazing Ames Room** (a) A diagram showing the actual proportions of the Ames room reveals its secrets. The sides of the room form a trapezoid with parallel sides but a back wall that's way off square. The uneven floor makes the room's height in the far back corner shorter than the other. Add misleading cues such as specially designed windows and flooring and position the room's occupants in each far corner and you're ready to lure an unsuspecting observer. (b) Looking into the Ames room through the viewing port with only one eye, the observer infers a normal size-distance relationship—that both girls are the same distance away. But the different image sizes they project on the retina leads the viewer to conclude, based on the monocular cue of familiar size, that one girl is very small and the other very large.

The moon at the horizon appears to be much larger than when it is high in the sky. This illusion happens because of visual cues at the horizon such as buildings and trees.

DAVID NUNUK/PHOTO RESEARCHERS

The relation between size and distance has been used to create elaborate illusions that depend on fooling the visual system about how far away objects are. All these illusions depend on the same principle: When you view two objects that project the same retinal image size, the object you perceive as farther away will be perceived as larger.

One of the most famous illusions is the *Ames room,* constructed by the American ophthalmologist Adelbert Ames in 1946. The room is trapezoidal in shape rather than square: Only two sides are parallel (see **FIGURE 4.24a**). A person standing in one corner of an Ames room is physically twice as far away from the viewer as a person standing in the other corner. But when viewed with one eye through the small peephole placed in one wall, the Ames room looks square because the shapes of the windows and the flooring tiles are carefully crafted to *look* square from the viewing port (Ittelson, 1952).

The visual system perceives the far wall as perpendicular to the line of sight so that people standing at different positions along that wall appear to be at the same distance, and the viewer's judgments of their sizes are based directly on retinal image size. As a result, a person standing in the right corner appears to be much larger than a person standing in the left corner (see **FIGURE 4.24b**).

The *moon illusion* is another case where incorrectly perceived distance affects the perception of size (Hershenson, 1989). The full moon often appears much larger when it is near the horizon than when it is directly overhead. In fact, the moon projects identical retinal image sizes in both positions. What accounts for this compelling mindbug? When the moon is near the horizon, it appears farther away because many features—hills, trees, buildings—intervene between the viewer and the moon. Nothing intervenes when the moon is directly overhead, so it appears smaller.

Perceiving Motion

You should now have a good sense of how we see what and where objects are, a process made substantially easier when the objects stay in one place. But real life, of course, is full of moving targets; objects change position over time. To sense motion, the visual system must encode information about both space and time. The simplest case to consider is an observer who does not move trying to perceive an object that does.

As an object moves across an observer's stationary visual field, it first stimulates one location on the retina, and then a little later it stimulates another location on the retina. Neural circuits in the brain can detect this change in position over time and respond to specific speeds and directions of motion (Emerson, Bergen, & Adelson, 1992). A region in the middle of the temporal lobe referred to as *MT* ((part of the dorsal stream we discussed earlier) is specialized for the visual perception of motion (Born & Bradley, 2005; Newsome & Paré, 1988), and brain damage in this area leads to a deficit in normal motion perception (Zihl, von Cramon, & Mai, 1983).

Of course, in the real world, rarely are you a stationary observer. As you move around, your head and eyes move all the time, and motion perception is not as simple. The motion-perception system must take into account the position and movement of your eyes, and ultimately of your head and body, in order to perceive the motions of objects correctly and allow you to approach or avoid them. The brain accomplishes this by monitoring your eye and head movements and "subtracting" them from the motion in the retinal image.

Motion perception, like color perception, operates in part on opponent processes and is subject to sensory adaptation. A motion aftereffect called the *waterfall illusion* is analogous to color aftereffects. If you stare at the downward rush of a waterfall for several seconds, you'll experience an upward motion aftereffect when you then look at stationary objects near the waterfall such as trees or rocks. What's going on here?

The process is similar to seeing green after staring at a patch of red. Motion-sensitive neurons are connected to motion detector cells in the brain that encode motion in opposite directions. A sense of motion comes from the difference in the strength of these two opposing sensors. If one set of motion detector cells is fatigued through adaptation to motion in one direction, then the opposing sensor will take over. The net result is that motion is perceived in the opposite direction. Evidence from fMRIs indicates that when people experience the waterfall illusion while viewing a stationary stimulus, there is increased activity in region MT, which plays a key role in motion perception (Tootell et al., 1995).

The movement of objects in the world is not the only event that can evoke the perception of motion. The successively flashing lights of a Las Vegas casino sign can evoke a strong sense of motion, exactly the sort of illusion that inspired Max Wertheimer to investigate the *phi phenomenon*, discussed in Chapter 1. Recall, too, the Gestalt grouping rule of *common fate:* People perceive a series of flashing lights as a whole, moving object (see Figure 4.18f). This *perception of movement as a result of alternating signals appearing in rapid succession in different locations* is called **apparent motion**.

Video technology and animation depend on apparent motion. A sequence of still images sample the continuous motion in the original scene. In the case of motion pictures, the sampling rate is 24 frames per second (fps). A slower sampling rate would produce a much choppier sense of motion; a faster sampling rate would be a waste of resources because we would not perceive the motion as any smoother than it appears at 24 fps.

In summary, some regions in the occipital and temporal lobes respond selectively to specific object categories, supporting the modular view that specialized brain areas represent particular classes of objects. The principle of perceptual constancy holds that even as sensory signals change, perception remains consistent. Gestalt principles of perceptual grouping, such as simplicity, closure, and continuity, govern how the features and regions of things fit together. Depth perception depends on monocular cues, such as familiar size and linear perspective; binocular cues, such as retinal disparity; and motion-based cues, such as motion parallax, which is based on the movement of the head over time. We experience a sense of motion through the differences in the strengths of output from motion-sensitive neurons. These processes can give rise to illusions such as apparent motion. ■ ■

APPARENT MOTION The perception of movement as a result of alternating signals appearing in rapid succession in different locations.

Audition: More Than Meets the Ear

Vision is based on the spatial pattern of light waves on the retina. The sense of hearing, by contrast, is all about *sound waves*—changes in air pressure unfolding over time. Plenty of things produce sound waves: the collision of a tree hitting the forest floor, the impact of two hands clapping, the vibration of vocal cords during a stirring speech, the resonance of a bass guitar string during a thrash metal concert. Except for synesthetes who "hear colors," understanding most people's auditory experience requires understanding how we transform changes in air pressure into perceived sounds.

Sensing Sound

Plucking a guitar string or striking a tuning fork produces a *pure tone*, a simple sound wave that first increases air pressure and then creates a relative vacuum. This cycle repeats hundreds or thousands of times per second as sound waves propagate outward in all directions from the source.

Just as there are three dimensions of light waves corresponding to three dimensions of visual perception, so too there are three physical dimensions of a sound wave. Frequency, amplitude, and complexity determine what we hear as the pitch, loudness, and quality of a sound (see **TABLE 4.3**).

The *frequency* of the sound wave, or its wavelength, depends on how often the peak in air pressure passes the ear or a microphone, measured in cycles per second, or hertz (abbreviated Hz). Changes in the physical frequency of a sound wave are perceived by humans as changes in **pitch**, *how high or low a sound is.*

The *amplitude* of a sound wave refers to its height, relative to the threshold for human hearing (which is set at zero decibels, or dBs). Amplitude corresponds to **loudness**, or *a sound's intensity*. To give you an idea of amplitude and intensity, the rustling of leaves in a soft breeze is about 20 dB, normal conversation is measured at about 40 dB, shouting

Motorhead is the loudest band in the world. Oddly, front man Lemmy Kilmister reports little hearing loss despite more than 30 years of standing in front of a huge stack of amplifiers. Most of the rest of us would suffer severe damage to our hearing under such circumstances.

ZUMA PRESS/NEWSCOM

PITCH How high or low a sound is.

LOUDNESS A sound's intensity.

TIMBRE A listener's experience of sound quality or resonance.

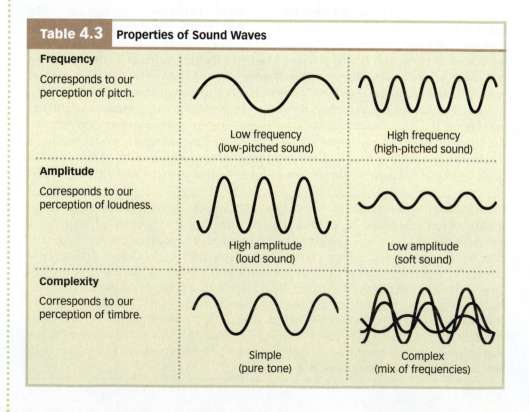

Table 4.3	Properties of Sound Waves	
Frequency Corresponds to our perception of pitch.	Low frequency (low-pitched sound)	High frequency (high-pitched sound)
Amplitude Corresponds to our perception of loudness.	High amplitude (loud sound)	Low amplitude (soft sound)
Complexity Corresponds to our perception of timbre.	Simple (pure tone)	Complex (mix of frequencies)

produces 70 dB, a Slayer concert is about 130 decibels, and the sound of the space shuttle taking off one mile away registers at 160 dB or more. That's loud enough to cause permanent damage to the auditory system and is well above the pain threshold; in fact, any sounds above 85 decibels can be enough to cause hearing damage, depending on the length and type of exposure.

Differences in the *complexity* of sound waves, or their mix of frequencies, correspond to **timbre**, *a listener's experience of sound quality or resonance*. Timbre (pronounced "TAM-ber") offers us information about the nature of sound. The same note played at the same loudness produces a perceptually different experience depending on whether it was played on a flute versus a trumpet, a phenomenon due entirely to timbre. Many "natural" sounds also illustrate the complexity of wavelengths, such as the sound of bees buzzing, the tonalities of speech, or the babbling of a brook. Unlike the purity of a tuning fork's hum, the drone of cicadas is a clamor of overlapping sound frequencies.

Of the three dimensions of sound waves, frequency provides most of the information we need to identify sounds. Amplitude and complexity contribute texture to our auditory perceptions, but it is frequency that carries their meaning. Sound-wave frequencies blend together to create countless sounds, just as different wavelengths of light blend to create the richly colored world we see.

Moreover, sound-wave frequency is as important for audition as spatial perception is for vision. Changes in frequency over time allow us to identify the location of sounds, an ability that can be crucial to survival and also allow us to understand speech and appreciate music, skills that are valuable to our cultural survival. The focus in our discussion of hearing, then, is on how the auditory system encodes and represents sound-wave frequency (Kubovy, 1981).

"The ringing in your ears—I think I can help."

The Human Ear

How does the auditory system convert sound waves into neural signals? The process is very different from the visual system, which is not surprising, given that light is a form of electromagnetic radiation whereas sound is a physical change in air pressure over time: Different forms of energy suggest different processes of transduction. The human ear is divided into three distinct parts, as shown in **FIGURE 4.25.** The *outer ear* collects sound waves and funnels them toward the *middle ear,* which transmits the vibrations to the *inner ear,* embedded in the skull, where they are transduced into neural impulses.

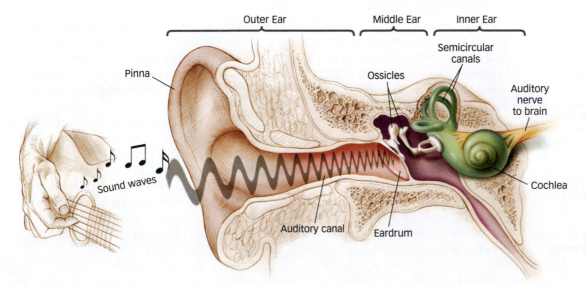

Figure 4.25 Anatomy of the Human Ear The pinna funnels sound waves into the auditory canal to vibrate the eardrum at a rate that corresponds to the sound's frequency. In the middle ear, the ossicles pick up the eardrum vibrations, amplify them, and pass them along by vibrating a membrane at the surface of the fluid-filled cochlea in the inner ear. Here fluid carries the wave energy to the auditory receptors that transduce it into electrochemical activity, exciting the neurons that form the auditory nerve, leading to the brain.

Figure 4.26 **Auditory Transduction** Inside the cochlea, shown here as though it were uncoiling, the basilar membrane undulates in response to wave energy in the cochlear fluid. Waves of differing frequencies ripple varying locations along the membrane, from low frequencies at its tip to high frequencies at the base, and bend the embedded hair cell receptors at those locations. The hair-cell motion generates impulses in the auditory neurons, whose axons form the auditory nerve that emerges from the cochlea.

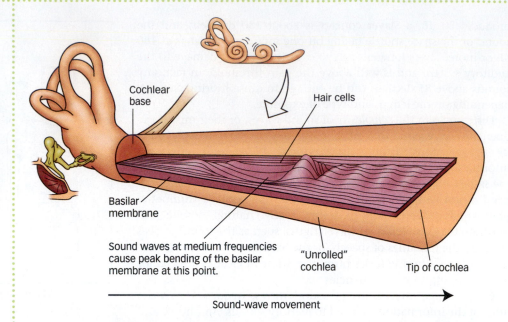

Cochlear base

Hair cells

Basilar membrane

Sound waves at medium frequencies cause peak bending of the basilar membrane at this point.

"Unrolled" cochlea

Tip of cochlea

Sound-wave movement

The outer ear consists of the visible part on the outside of the head (called the *pinna*); the auditory canal; and the eardrum, an airtight flap of skin that vibrates in response to sound waves gathered by the pinna and channeled into the canal. The middle ear, a tiny, air-filled chamber behind the eardrum, contains the three smallest bones in the body, called *ossicles*. Named for their appearance as hammer, anvil, and stirrup, the ossicles fit together into a lever that mechanically transmits and intensifies vibrations from the eardrum to the inner ear.

The inner ear contains the spiral-shaped **cochlea** (Latin for "snail"), *a fluid-filled tube that is the organ of auditory transduction*. The cochlea is divided along its length by the **basilar membrane**, *a structure in the inner ear that undulates when vibrations from the ossicles reach the cochlear fluid* (see **FIGURE 4.26**). Its wavelike movement stimulates thousands of tiny **hair cells**, *specialized auditory receptor neurons embedded in the basilar membrane*. The hair cells then release neurotransmitter molecules, initiating a neural signal in the auditory nerve that travels to the brain. You might not want to think that the whispered "I love you" that sends chills up your spine got a kick start from lots of little hair cells wiggling around, but the mechanics of hearing are what they are!

Perceiving Pitch

From the inner ear, action potentials in the auditory nerve travel to the thalamus and ultimately to the contralateral ("opposite side"; see Chapter 3) hemisphere of the cerebral cortex. This is called **area A1**, *a portion of the temporal lobe that contains the primary auditory cortex* (see **FIGURE 4.27**). For most of us, the auditory areas in the left hemisphere analyze sounds related to language and those in the right hemisphere specialize in rhythmic sounds and music.

Neurons in area A1 respond well to simple tones, and successive auditory areas in the brain process sounds of increasing complexity (Schreiner, Read, & Sutter, 2000). Like area V1 in the visual cortex, area A1 has a topographic organization: Similar frequencies activate neurons in adjacent locations (see Figure 4.27, inset). A young adult with normal hearing ideally can detect sounds between about 20 and 20,000 Hz, although the ability to hear at the upper range decreases with age; an upper limit of about 16,000 Hz may be more realistic. The human ear is most sensitive to frequencies around 1,000 to 3,500 Hz. But how is the frequency of a sound wave encoded in a neural signal?

COCHLEA A fluid-filled tube that is the organ of auditory transduction.

BASILAR MEMBRANE A structure in the inner ear that undulates when vibrations from the ossicles reach the cochlear fluid.

HAIR CELLS Specialized auditory receptor neurons embedded in the basilar membrane.

AREA A1 A portion of the temporal lobe that contains the primary auditory cortex.

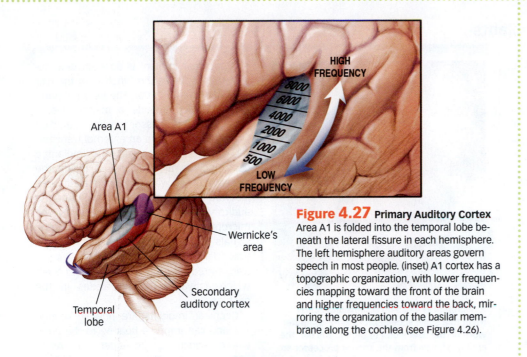

Area A1

Wernicke's
area

Secondary
auditory cortex

Temporal
lobe

HIGH
FREQUENCY

8000
6000
4000
2000
1000
500

LOW
FREQUENCY

Figure 4.27 Primary Auditory Cortex
Area A1 is folded into the temporal lobe beneath the lateral fissure in each hemisphere.
The left hemisphere auditory areas govern
speech in most people. (inset) A1 cortex has a
topographic organization, with lower frequencies mapping toward the front of the brain
and higher frequencies toward the back, mirroring the organization of the basilar membrane along the cochlea (see Figure 4.26).

Our ears have evolved two mechanisms to encode sound-wave frequency, one for
high frequencies and one for low frequencies. The **place code**, used mainly for high
frequencies, is active when *the cochlea encodes different frequencies at different locations
along the basilar membrane*. In a series of experiments carried out from the 1930s to the
1950s, Nobel laureate Georg von Békésy (1899–1972) used a microscope to observe the
basilar membrane in the inner ear of cadavers that had been donated for medical research (Békésy, 1960). Békésy found that the movement of the basilar membrane resembles a traveling wave (see Figure 4.26). The wave's shape depends on the frequency
of the stimulating pitch. When the frequency is low, the wide, floppy tip (*apex*) of the
basilar membrane moves the most; when the frequency is high, the narrow, stiff end
(*base*) of the membrane moves the most.

The movement of the basilar membrane causes hair cells to bend, initiating a
neural signal in the auditory nerve. Axons fire the strongest in the hair cells along
the area of the basilar membrane that moves the most; in other words, the place of
activation on the basilar membrane contributes to the perception of sound. The
place code works best for relatively high frequencies that resonate at the basilar
membrane's base and less well for low frequencies that resonate at the tip because
low frequencies produce a broad traveling wave and therefore an imprecise frequency code.

A complementary process handles lower frequencies. A **temporal code** *registers low
frequencies via the firing rate of action potentials entering the auditory nerve*. Action potentials from the hair cells are synchronized in time with the peaks of the incoming
sound waves (Johnson, 1980). If you imagine the rhythmic *boom-boom-boom* of a bass
drum, you can probably also imagine the *fire-fire-fire* of action potentials corresponding to the beats. This process provides the brain with very precise information about
pitch that supplements the information provided by the place code.

However, individual neurons can produce action potentials at a maximum rate of
only about 1,000 spikes per second, so the temporal code does not work as well as the
place code for high frequencies. (Imagine if the action potential has to fire in time
with the *rat-a-tat-a-tat-a-tat* of a snare drum roll!) Like trichromatic representation and
opponent processes in color processing, the place code and the temporal code work
together to cover the entire range of pitches that people can hear. (For research on
how to combat hearing loss, see the Hot Science box on the next page.)

PLACE CODE The cochlea encodes
different frequencies at different locations
along the basilar membrane.

TEMPORAL CODE The cochlea
registers low frequencies via the firing rate
of action potentials entering the auditory
nerve.

{ HOT SCIENCE } Cochlear Implants

TEN DAYS AFTER NATALIE WAS BORN, SHE developed a persistent, high fever. Her pediatrician's diagnosis was meningitis, an inflammation of the lining around the brain and spinal cord. Natalie spent several weeks in the hospital, at times close to death. Finally, the fever broke and Natalie seemed to recover fully.

During the next several months, Natalie's parents grew increasingly concerned because she was not responding to sound. They took her to a pediatric audiologist for assessment and learned that the meningitis had damaged the hair cells in Natalie's cochleas. The damage was irreversible.

Broadly speaking, hearing loss has two main causes. *Conductive hearing loss* arises because the eardrum or ossicles are damaged to the point that they cannot conduct sound waves effectively to the cochlea. The cochlea itself, however, is normal, making this a kind of "mechanical problem" with the moving parts of the ear: the hammer, anvil, stirrup, or eardrum. In many cases, medication or surgery can correct the problem. Sound amplification from a hearing aid also can improve hearing through conduction via the bones around the ear directly to the cochlea.

Sensorineural hearing loss is caused by damage to the cochlea, the hair cells, or the auditory nerve. This was Natalie's affliction, rare in an infant but commonly experienced

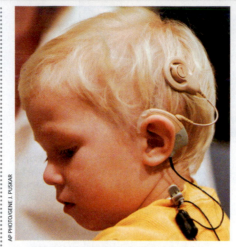

AP PHOTO/GENE J. PUSKAR

A microphone picks up sounds and sends them to a small speech-processing computer worn on the user's belt or behind the ear. The electric signals from the speech processor are transmitted to an implanted receiver, which sends the signals via electrodes to the cochlea, where the signals directly stimulate the auditory nerve.

by people as they grow older. Sensorineural hearing loss can be heightened in people regularly exposed to high noise levels (such as rock musicians or jet mechanics). Simply amplifying the sound does not help because the hair cells can no longer transduce sound waves. In these cases a *cochlear implant* may offer some relief.

A cochlear implant is an electronic device that replaces the function of the hair cells (Waltzman, 2006). The external parts of the device include a microphone, a small speech processor the size of an iPod (worn on a belt), and an external transmitter worn behind the ear. The implanted parts include a receiver just inside the skull and a thin wire containing electrodes inserted into the cochlea to stimulate the auditory nerve. Sound picked up by the microphone is transformed into electric signals by the speech processor, which is essentially a small computer. The signal is transmitted to the implanted receiver, which activates the electrodes in the cochlea.

Cochlear implants are now in routine use and can improve hearing to the point where speech can be understood. As of 2006, some 60,000 people worldwide have received cochlear implants. Young infants like Natalie, who have not yet learned to speak, are especially vulnerable because they may miss the critical period for language learning (see Chapter 7). Without auditory feedback during this time, normal speech is nearly impossible to achieve. Efforts are under way to introduce cochlear implants to children as early as 12 months or younger to maximize their chances of normal language development (DesJardin, Eisenberg, & Hodapp, 2006).

Localizing Sound Sources

Just as the differing positions of our eyes give us stereoscopic vision, the placement of our ears on opposite sides of the head give us stereophonic hearing. The sound arriving at the ear closer to the sound source is louder than the sound in the farther ear, mainly because the listener's head partially blocks sound energy. This loudness difference decreases as the sound source moves from a position directly to one side (maximal difference) to straight ahead (no difference).

Another cue to a sound's location arises from timing: Sound waves arrive a little sooner at the near ear than at the far ear. The timing difference can be as brief as a few microseconds, but together with the intensity difference, it is sufficient to allow us to perceive the location of a sound. When the sound source is ambiguous, you may find yourself turning your head from side to side to localize it. By doing this, you are changing the relative intensity and timing of sound waves arriving in your ears and collecting better information about the likely source of the sound.

In summary, perceiving sound depends on three physical dimensions of a sound wave: The frequency of the sound wave determines the pitch; the amplitude determines the loudness; and differences in the complexity, or mix, of frequencies determines the sound quality or timbre. Auditory perception begins in the ear, which consists of an outer ear that funnels sound waves toward the middle ear, which in turn sends the vibrations to the inner ear, which contains the cochlea. Action potentials from the inner ear travel along an auditory pathway through the thalamus to the contralateral primary auditory cortex, area A1, in the temporal lobe. Auditory perception depends on both a place code and a temporal code, which together cover the full range of pitches that people can hear. Our ability to localize sound sources depends critically on the placement of our ears on opposite sides of the head. ■ ■

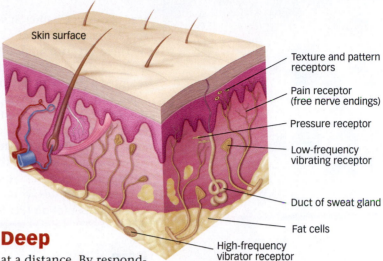

Skin surface

Texture and pattern receptors

Pain receptor (free nerve endings)

Pressure receptor

Low-frequency vibrating receptor

Duct of sweat gland

Fat cells

High-frequency vibrator receptor

The Body Senses: More Than Skin Deep

Vision and audition provide information about the world at a distance. By responding to light and sound energy in the environment, these "distance" senses allow us to identify and locate the objects and people around us. In comparison, the body senses, also called *somatosenses* (*soma* from the Greek for "body"), are up close and personal. **Haptic perception** results from our *active exploration of the environment by touching and grasping objects with our hands*. We use sensory receptors in our muscles, tendons, and joints as well as a variety of receptors in our skin to get a feel for the world around us (see **FIGURE 4.28**).

Figure 4.28 Touch Receptors Specialized sensory neurons form distinct groups of haptic receptors that detect pressure, temperature, and vibrations against the skin. Touch receptors respond to stimulation within their receptive fields, and their long axons enter the brain via the spinal or cranial nerves. Pain receptors populate all body tissues that feel pain: They are distributed around bones and within muscles and internal organs as well as under the skin surface. Both types of pain receptors—the fibers that transmit immediate, sharp pain sensations quickly and those that signal slow, dull pain that lasts and lasts—are free nerve endings.

This rather unimposing geodesic dome sits on the floor of the Exploratorium, a world-renowned science museum in San Francisco. Called the Tactile Dome, it was created in 1971 by August Coppola (brother of director Francis Ford Coppola and father of actor Nicholas Cage) and Carl Day, who wanted to create an environment in which only haptic perception could be used. The inside of the dome is pitch black; visitors must crawl, wiggle, slide, and otherwise navigate the unfamiliar terrain using only their sense of touch. How would you feel being in that environment for an hour or so?

©EXPLORATORIUM

Touch

Four types of receptors located under the skin's surface enable us to sense pressure, texture, pattern, or vibration against the skin (see Figure 4.28). The receptive fields of these specialized cells work together to provide a rich tactile (from Latin, "to touch") experience when you explore an object by feeling it or attempt to grasp it. In addition, *thermoreceptors,* nerve fibers that sense cold and warmth, respond when your skin temperature changes. All these sensations blend seamlessly together in perception, of course, but detailed physiological studies have successfully isolated the parts of the touch system (Johnson, 2002).

Touch begins with the transduction of skin sensations into neural signals. Like cells in the retina of each eye, touch receptors have receptive fields with central excitatory zones surrounded by doughnut-shaped inhibitory zones that, when stimulated, cause that cell's response to change. The representation of touch in the brain follows a topographic scheme, much as vision and hearing do. Think back to the homunculus you

HAPTIC PERCEPTION The active exploration of the environment by touching and grasping objects with our hands.

read about in Chapter 3; you'll recall that different locations on the body project sensory signals to different locations in the somatosensory cortex in the parietal lobe.

There are two important principles regarding the neural representation of the body's surface. First, there is contralateral organization: The left half of the body is represented in the right half of the brain and vice versa. Second, just as more of the visual brain is devoted to foveal vision where acuity is greatest, more of the tactile brain is devoted to parts of the skin surface that have greater spatial resolution. Regions such as the fingertips and lips are very good at discriminating fine spatial detail, whereas areas such as the lower back are quite poor at that task. These perceptual abilities are a natural consequence of the fact that the fingertips and lips have a relatively dense arrangement of touch receptors and a large topographical representation in the somatosensory cortex; comparatively, the lower back, hips, and calves have a relatively small representation (Penfield & Rasmussen, 1950).

Pain

Although pain is arguably the least pleasant of sensations, this aspect of touch is among the most important for survival: Pain indicates damage or potential damage to the body. The possibility of a life free from pain might seem appealing, but without the ability to feel pain, we might ignore infections, broken bones, or serious burns. Congenital insensitivity to pain, a rare inherited disorder that specifically impairs pain perception, is more of a curse than a blessing: Children who experience this disorder often mutilate themselves (biting into their tongues, for example, or gouging their skin while scratching) and are at increased risk of dying during childhood (Nagasako, Oaklander, & Dworkin, 2003).

Tissue damage is transduced by pain receptors, the free nerve endings shown in Figure 4.28. Researchers have distinguished between fast-acting *A-delta fibers,* which transmit the initial sharp pain one might feel right away from a sudden injury, and slower *C fibers,* which transmit the longer-lasting, duller pain that persists after the initial injury. If you were running barefoot outside and stubbed your toe against a rock, you would first feel a sudden stinging pain transmitted by A-delta fibers that would die down quickly, only to be replaced by the throbbing but longer-lasting pain carried by C fibers. Both the A-delta and C fibers are impaired in cases of congenital insensitivity to pain, which is one reason why the disorder can be life threatening.

As you'll remember from Chapter 3, the pain withdrawal reflex is coordinated by the spinal cord. No brainpower is required when you touch a hot stove; you retract your hand almost instantaneously. But neural signals for pain—such as wrenching your elbow as you brace yourself from falling—travel to two distinct areas in the brain and evoke two distinct psychological experiences (Treede, Kenshalo, Gracely, & Jones, 1999). One pain pathway sends signals to the somatosensory cortex, identifying where the pain is occurring and what sort of pain it is (sharp, burning, dull). The second pain pathway sends signals to the motivational and emotional centers of the brain, such as the hypothalamus and amygdala, and to the frontal lobe. This is the aspect of pain that is unpleasant and motivates us to escape from or relieve the pain.

Pain typically feels as if it comes from the site of the tissue damage that caused it. If you burn your finger, you will perceive the pain as originating there. But we have pain receptors in many areas besides the skin—around bones and within muscles and internal organs as well. When pain originates internally, in a body organ, for example, we actually feel it on the surface of the body. This kind of **referred pain** occurs when *sensory information from internal and external areas converge on the same nerve cells in the spinal cord.* One common example is a heart attack: Victims often feel pain radiating from the left arm rather than from inside the chest.

Pain intensity cannot always be predicted solely from the extent of the injury that causes the pain (Keefe, Abernathy, & Campbell, 2005). For example, *turf toe* sounds like the mildest of ailments; it is pain at the base of the big toe as a result of bending or pushing off repeatedly, as a runner or football player might do during a sporting

REFERRED PAIN Feeling of pain when sensory information from internal and external areas converge on the same nerve cells in the spinal cord.

GATE-CONTROL THEORY A theory of pain perception based on the idea that signals arriving from pain receptors in the body can be stopped, or *gated,* by interneurons in the spinal cord via feedback from two directions.

event. This small-sounding injury in a small area of the body can nonetheless sideline an athlete for a month with considerable pain. On the other hand, you've probably heard a story or two about someone treading bone-chilling water for hours on end, or dragging their shattered legs a mile down a country road to seek help after a tractor accident, or performing some other incredible feat despite searing pain and extensive tissue damage. Pain type and pain intensity show a less-than-perfect correlation, a fact that has researchers intrigued.

Some recent evidence indicates subjective pain intensity may differ among ethnic groups. A study that examined responses to various kinds of experimentally induced pain, including heat pain and cold pain, found that compared to White young adults, Black young adults had a lower tolerance for several kinds of pain and rated the same pain stimuli as more intense and unpleasant (Campbell, Edward, & Fillingim, 2005).

How do psychologists account for this puzzling variability in pain perception? According to **gate-control theory**, *signals arriving from pain receptors in the body can be stopped, or gated, by interneurons in the spinal cord via feedback from two directions* (Melzack & Wall, 1965). Pain can be gated by the skin receptors, for example by rubbing the affected area. Rubbing your stubbed toe activates neurons that "close the gate" to stop pain signals from traveling to the brain. Pain can also be gated from the brain by modulating the activity of pain-transmission neurons. This neural feedback is elicited not by the pain itself, but rather by activity deep within the thalamus.

The neural feedback comes from a region in the midbrain called the *periaqueductal gray* (PAG). Under extreme conditions, such as high stress, naturally occurring endorphins can activate the PAG to send inhibitory signals to neurons in the spinal cord that then suppress pain signals to the brain, thereby modulating the experience of pain. The PAG is also activated through the action of opiate drugs, such as morphine.

A different kind of feedback signal can *increase* the sensation of pain. This system is activated by events such as infection and learned danger signals. When we are quite ill, what might otherwise be experienced as mild discomfort can feel quite painful. This pain facilitation signal presumably evolved to motivate people who are ill to rest and avoid strenuous activity, allowing their energy to be devoted to healing.

Gate-control theory offers strong evidence that perception is a two-way street. The senses feed information, such as pain sensations, to the brain, a pattern termed *bottom-up control* by perceptual psychologists. The brain processes this sensory data into perceptual information at successive levels to support movement, object recognition, and eventually more complex cognitive tasks, such as memory and planning. But there is ample evidence that the brain exerts plenty of control over what we sense as well. Visual illusions and the Gestalt principles of filling in, shaping up, and rounding out what isn't really there provide some examples. This kind of *top-down control* also explains the descending pain pathway initiated in the midbrain.

Body Position, Movement, and Balance

It may sound odd, but one aspect of sensation and perception is knowing where parts of your body are at any given moment. It's not as though your arm sneaks out of the bedroom window at night to meet some friends. Your body needs some way to sense its position in physical space other than moving your eyes to constantly visually check the location of your limbs. Sensations related to position, movement, and balance depend on stimulation produced within our bodies. Receptors in the muscles, tendons, and joints signal the position of the body in space, whereas information about balance and head movement originates in the inner ear.

Sensory receptors provide the information we need to perceive the position and movement of our limbs, head, and body. These receptors also provide feedback about whether we are performing a desired movement correctly and how resistance from held objects may be influencing the movement. For example, when you swing a baseball bat, the weight of the bat affects how your muscles move your arm as well as the change in sensation when the bat hits the ball. Muscle, joint, and tendon

MALCOM DALY

In 2003, Aron Ralston was hiking in a remote canyon in Utah when tragedy struck. A 1,000-pound boulder pinned him in a three-foot-wide space for 5 days, eventually leaving him no choice but to amputate his own arm with a pocketknife. He then applied a tourniquet, rappelled down the canyon, and hiked out to safety. These and similar stories illustrate that the extent of an injury is not perfectly correlated with the amount of pain felt. Although self-amputation is undoubtedly excruciating, luckily in this case it was not debilitating.

AP PHOTO/RICK RYCROFT

Hitting a ball with a bat or racket provides feedback as to where your arms and body are in space as well as how the resistance of these objects affects your movement and balance. Successful athletes, such as Serena Williams, have particularly well-developed body senses.

feedback about how your arms actually moved can be used to improve performance through learning.

Maintaining balance depends primarily on the **vestibular system**, *the three fluid-filled semicircular canals and adjacent organs located next to the cochlea in each inner ear* (see Figure 4.25). The semicircular canals are arranged in three perpendicular orientations and studded with hair cells that detect movement of the fluid when the head moves or accelerates. This detected motion enables us to maintain our balance, or the position of our bodies relative to gravity. The movements of the hair cells encode these somatic sensations (Lackner & DiZio, 2005).

Vision also helps us keep our balance. If you see that you are swaying relative to a vertical orientation, such as the contours of a room, you move your legs and feet to keep from falling over. Psychologists have experimented with this visual aspect of balance by placing people in rooms that can be tilted forward and backward (Bertenthal, Rose, & Bai, 1997; Lee & Aronson, 1974). If the room tilts enough—particularly when small children are tested—people will topple over as they try to compensate for what their visual system is telling them. When a mismatch between the information provided by visual cues and vestibular feedback occurs, motion sickness can result. Remember this discrepancy the next time you try reading in the backseat of a moving car!

In summary, touch is represented in the brain according to a topographic scheme in which locations on the body project sensory signals to locations in the somatosensory cortex, a part of the parietal lobe. The experience of pain depends on signals that travel along two distinct pathways. One sends signals to the somatosensory cortex to indicate the location and type of pain, and another sends signals to the emotional centers of the brain that result in unpleasant feelings that we wish to escape. The experience of pain varies across individuals, which is explained by bottom-up and top-down aspects of gate-control theory. Balance and acceleration depend primarily on the vestibular system but are also influenced by vision. ■ ■ ■

The Chemical Senses: Adding Flavor

Somatosensation is all about physical changes in or on the body: Vision and audition sense energetic states of the world—light and sound waves—and touch is activated by physical changes in or on the body surface. The last set of senses we'll consider shares a chemical basis to combine aspects of distance and proximity. The chemical senses of *olfaction* (smell) and *gustation* (taste) respond to the molecular structure of substances floating into the nasal cavity as you inhale or dissolving in saliva. Smell and taste combine to produce the perceptual experience we call *flavor*.

Smell

Olfaction is the least understood sense and the only one directly connected to the forebrain, with pathways into the frontal lobe, amygdala, and other forebrain structures (recall from Chapter 3 that the other senses connect first to the thalamus). This mapping indicates that smell has a close relationship with areas involved in emotional and social behavior. Smell seems to have evolved in animals as a signaling sense for the familiar—a friendly creature, an edible food, or a sexually receptive mate.

Countless substances release odors into the air, and some of their *odorant molecules* make their way into our noses, drifting in on the air we breathe. Situated along the top of the nasal cavity shown in **FIGURE 4.29** is a mucous membrane called the *olfactory epithelium*, which contains about 10 million **olfactory receptor neurons (ORNs)**, *receptor cells that initiate the sense of smell*. Odorant molecules bind to sites on these specialized receptors, and if enough bindings occur, the ORNs send action potentials into the olfactory nerve (Dalton, 2003).

VESTIBULAR SYSTEM The three fluid-filled semicircular canals and adjacent organs located next to the cochlea in each inner ear.

OLFACTORY RECEPTOR NEURONS (ORNS) Receptor cells that initiate the sense of smell.

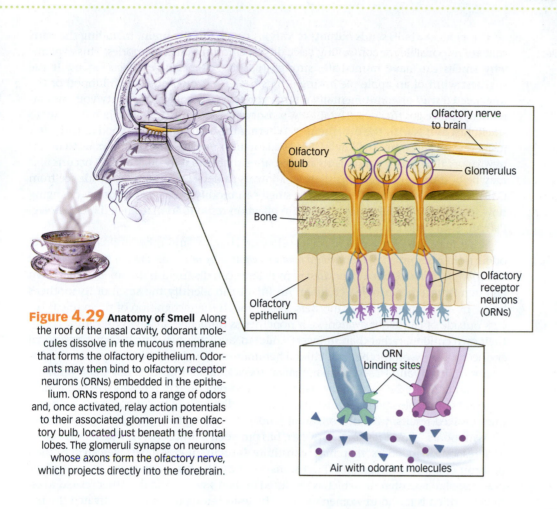

Figure 4.29 **Anatomy of Smell** Along the roof of the nasal cavity, odorant molecules dissolve in the mucous membrane that forms the olfactory epithelium. Odorants may then bind to olfactory receptor neurons (ORNs) embedded in the epithelium. ORNs respond to a range of odors and, once activated, relay action potentials to their associated glomeruli in the olfactory bulb, located just beneath the frontal lobes. The glomeruli synapse on neurons whose axons form the olfactory nerve, which projects directly into the forebrain.

Each olfactory neuron has receptors that bind to some odorants but not to others, as if the receptor is a lock and the odorant is the key (see Figure 4.29). Groups of ORNs send their axons from the olfactory epithelium into the **olfactory bulb,** *a brain structure located above the nasal cavity beneath the frontal lobes.* Humans possess about 350 different ORN types that permit us to discriminate among some 10,000 different odorants through the unique patterns of neural activity each odorant evokes. This setup is similar to our ability to see a vast range of colors based on only a small number of retinal cell types or to feel a range of skin sensations based on only a handful of touch receptor cell types.

The axons of all ORNs of a particular type converge at a site called a *glomerulus* within the olfactory bulb; thus, humans have about 350 glomeruli. Different odorant molecules produce varied patterns of activity (Rubin & Katz, 1999). A given odorant may strongly activate some glomeruli, moderately activate others, and have little effect on still others. The genetic basis for this olfactory coding was worked out in large part by Linda Buck and Richard Axel (1991), who were awarded the Nobel Prize in 2004 for their efforts.

Some dogs have as many as 100 times more ORNs than humans do, producing a correspondingly sharpened ability to detect and discriminate among millions of odors. Nevertheless, humans are sensitive to the smells of some substances in extremely small concentrations. For example, a chemical compound that is added to natural gas to help detect gas leaks can be sensed at a concentration of just 0.0003 parts per million. By contrast, acetone (nail polish remover), something most people regard as pungent, can be detected only if its concentration is 15 parts per million or greater.

OLFACTORY BULB A brain structure located above the nasal cavity beneath the frontal lobes.

PHEROMONES Biochemical odorants emitted by other members of their species that can affect an animal's behavior or physiology.

The olfactory bulb sends outputs to various centers in the brain, including the parts that are responsible for controlling basic drives, emotions, and memories. This explains why smells can have immediate, strongly positive or negative effects on us. If the slightest whiff of an apple pie baking brings back fond memories of childhood or the unexpected sniff of vomit mentally returns you to a particularly bad party you once attended, you've got the idea. Thankfully, sensory adaptation is at work when it comes to smell, just as it is with the other senses. Whether the associations are good or bad, after just a few minutes the smell fades. Smell adaptation makes sense: It allows us to detect new odors that may require us to act, but after that initial evaluation has occurred, it may be best to reduce our sensitivity to allow us to detect other smells. Evidence from fMRIs indicates that experience with a smell can modify odor perception by changing how specific parts of the brain involved in olfaction respond to that smell (Li, Lexenberg, Parrish, & Gottfried, 2006).

Smell may also play a role in social behavior. Humans and other animals can detect odors from **pheromones**, *biochemical odorants emitted by other members of their species that can affect the animal's behavior or physiology*. Parents can distinguish the smell of their own children from other people's children. An infant can identify the smell of its mother's breast from the smell of other mothers. Even though the recognition of these smells occurs outside of conscious awareness, it nonetheless influences behavior: Parents pick up their own children rather than strangers' children, and breast feeding becomes a personal connection between mother and child. Pheromones also play a role in reproductive behavior in insects and in several mammalian species, including mice, dogs, and primates (Brennan & Zufall, 2006). Can the same thing be said of human reproductive behavior?

Studies of people's preference for the odors of individuals of the opposite sex have produced mixed results, with no consistent tendency for people to prefer them over other pleasant odors. Recent research, however, has provided a link between sexual orientation and responses to odors that may constitute human pheromones. Researchers used positron emission tomography (PET) scans to study the brain's response to two odors, one related to testosterone, which is produced in men's sweat, and the other related to estrogen, which is found in women's urine. The testosterone-based odor activated the hypothalamus (a part of the brain that controls sexual behavior; see Chapter 3) in heterosexual women but not heterosexual men, whereas the estrogen-based odor activated the hypothalamus in heterosexual men but not women. Strikingly, homosexual men responded to the two chemicals in the same way as women did: The hypothalamus was activated by the testosterone- but not estrogen-based odor (Savic, Berglund, & Lindstrom, 2005; see **FIGURE 4.30**). Other common odors unrelated to sexual arousal were processed similarly by all three groups. A follow-up study with lesbian women showed that their responses to the testosterone- and estrogen-based odors were largely similar to those of heterosexual men (Berglund, Lindstrom, & Savic, 2006). Taken together, the two studies suggest that some human pheromones are related to sexual orientation.

Other evidence also indicates that pheromones can affect human physiology. Women who live in close proximity for extended periods—living together in a college dormitory, for example—tend to synchronize menstrual periods. To test the hypothesis that this synchrony might be mediated by pheromones, a group of women wore cotton pads in their armpits to collect sweat (McClintock, 1971). The secretions were

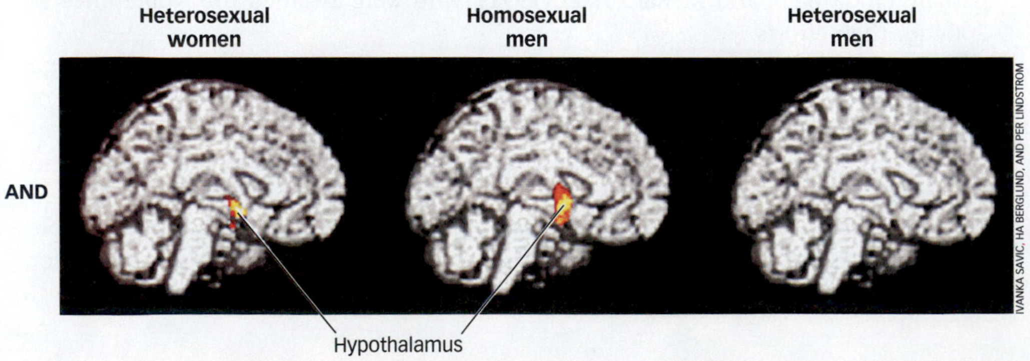

Figure 4.30 **Smell and Social Behavior** In a PET study, heterosexual women, homosexual men, and heterosexual men were scanned as they were presented with each of several odors. During the presentation of a testosterone-based odor (referred to in the figure as AND), there was significant activation in the hypothalamus for heterosexual women (left) and homosexual men (center) but not for heterosexual men (right) (Savic et al., 2005).

Heterosexual women   Homosexual men   Heterosexual men

AND

Hypothalamus

IVANKA SAVIC, HA BERGLUND, AND PER LINDSTROM

transferred to the upper lip (under the nose) of women with whom they had no other contact. This procedure did indeed cause the menstrual cycles of the pairs to synchronize over time, although the mechanism remains a mystery. It does not appear to involve any conscious awareness of the smell: The recipient women in these studies reported that they could not discriminate between the smell of the pads worn by the donor women from pads that had not been treated. Nonetheless, the introduction of these pheromones contributed to the regulation of the women's bodily states.

Taste

One of the primary responsibilities of the chemical sense of taste is identifying things that are bad for you—as in "poisonous and lethal." Many poisons are bitter, and we avoid eating things that nauseate us for good reason, so taste aversions have a clear adaptive significance. Some aspects of taste perception are genetic, such as an aversion to extreme bitterness, and some are learned, such as an aversion to a particular food that once caused nausea. In either case, the direct contact between a tongue and possible foods allows us to anticipate whether something will be harmful or palatable.

The tongue is covered with thousands of small bumps, called *papillae*, which are easily visible to the naked eye. Within each papilla are hundreds of **taste buds**, *the organ of taste transduction* (see **FIGURE 4.31**). Most of our mouths contain between 5,000 and 10,000 taste buds fairly evenly distributed over the tongue, roof of the mouth, and upper throat (Bartoshuk & Beauchamp, 1994; Halpern, 2002). Each taste bud contains 50 to 100 taste receptor cells. Taste perception fades with age: On average, people lose half their taste receptors by the time they turn 20. This may help to explain why young children seem to be "fussy eaters," since their greater number of taste buds brings with it a greater range of taste sensations. (For a striking example of extreme taste sensitivity, see The Real World box on the next page.)

The human eye contains millions of rods and cones, the human nose contains some 350 different types of olfactory receptors, but the taste system contains just five main types of taste receptors, corresponding to five primary taste sensations: salt, sour, bitter, sweet, and umami (savory). The first four are quite familiar, but *umami* may not be. In fact, perception researchers are still debating its existence. The umami receptor was discovered by Japanese scientists who attributed it to the tastes evoked by foods containing a high concentration of protein, such as meats and cheeses (Yamaguchi, 1998). If you're a meat eater and you savor the feel of a steak topped with butter or a cheeseburger as it sits in your mouth, you've got an idea of the umami sensation.

Each taste bud contains several types of taste receptor cells whose tips, called *microvilli*, react with *tastant molecules* in food. Salt taste receptors are most strongly activated by sodium chloride—table salt. Sour receptor cells respond to acids, such as vinegar or lime juice. Bitter and sweet taste receptors are more complex. Some 50 to 80 distinct binding sites in bitter receptors are activated by an equal number of different

TASTE BUDS The organ of taste transduction.

Figure 4.31 A **Taste Bud** (a) Taste buds stud the bumps (papillae) on your tongue, shown here, as well as the back, sides, and roof of the mouth. (b) Each taste bud contains a range of receptor cells that respond to varying chemical components of foods called tastants. Tastant molecules dissolve in saliva and stimulate the microvilli that form the tips of the taste receptor cells. (c) Each taste bud contacts the branch of a cranial nerve at its base.

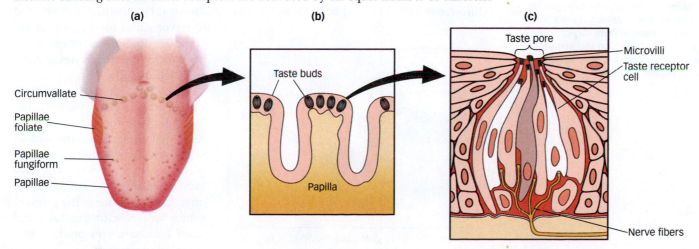

(a) (b) (c)

Circumvallate

Papillae foliate

Papillae fungiform

Papillae

Taste buds

Papilla

Taste pore

Microvilli

Taste receptor cell

Nerve fibers

{ THE REAL WORLD } Supertasters

WE ALL KNOW FUSSY EATERS. CHILDREN who don't like to eat their vegetables quickly come to mind. Even some adults shun dark green vegetables such as Brussels sprouts, kale, and broccoli throughout their lifetimes. If you enjoy these vegetables, such taste preferences may seem a little irrational.

But what if different people actually experience the taste of broccoli differently; not like the lie your parents told you—"It tastes like ice cream!"—but in a qualitatively different way from other folks? About 50% of people report a mildly bitter taste in caffeine, saccharine, certain green vegetables, and other substances, while roughly 25% report no bitter taste. Members of the first group are called *tasters* and members of the second group are called *nontasters*. The remaining 25% of people are *supertasters*, who report that such substances, especially dark green vegetables, are extremely bitter, to the point of being inedible.

There's an evolutionary rationale for this. Aversion to bitter tastes is present at birth; not too surprising, since bitter-tasting substances often are poisons. However, many foods that taste bitter—those dark green veggies included—are beneficial in promoting health and protecting us from disease. Ironically, the very evolutionary mechanism that may keep you from poisoning yourself

Fussy eater or just too many taste buds? Our taste perception declines with age: We lose about half of our taste receptors by the time we're 20 years old. That can make childhood either a time of savory delight or a sensory overload of taste.

may also keep you from ingesting some of the most healthy food available.

There are substantial individual differences in taste preference as well. For example, not everyone has taste receptors for bitter sensations, based on their genetics (Bartoshuk, Duffy, & Miller, 1994). As another example, people from Asia, Africa, and South America are more likely to be supertasters than are others. Women's sensitivity to bitter tastes tends to intensify during pregnancy but to diminish after menopause. Children start out as tasters or supertasters, which could help explain their early tendency toward fussiness in food preference. However, some children grow up to become nontasters.

Supertasters also experience other flavors differently from nontasters. Supertasters get more "burn" from chili peppers and more creaminess from fats and thickeners in food than others do. They also experience oral pain more intensely than nontasters (Bartoshuk, 2000). Because supertasters tend to avoid fruits and vegetables that contain tastes they experience as extremely bitter, they may be at increased health risk for diseases such as colon cancer. On the other hand, because they also tend to avoid fatty, creamy foods, they tend to be thinner and may have decreased risk of cardiovascular disease (Bartoshuk, 2000).

The difference between the experiences of nontasters and supertasters can be compared to the difference in experiences among people with normal color vision and those with genetic color deficiencies, where at least one of the three cone types is missing. In each case, personal perceptual experiences differ in ways that may be impossible for others to grasp. A color-deficient supertaster, in fact, has probably learned to avoid the gray broccoli.

ONLY HUMAN

I LOVE THE TASTE OF ASPHALT IN THE MORNING In April 2006, Jim Werych of the Wednesday Night Classics car club in Brookfield, Wisconsin, ritually dragged his tongue, in a deep lick, across Lisbon Road (with traffic stopped in both directions) to verify, and proclaim, that the streets are free of winter salt and thus safe for the club's delicate classics.

bitter-tasting chemicals. Sweet receptor cells likewise can be activated by a wide range of substances in addition to sugars.

Although umami receptor cells are the least well understood, researchers are honing in on their key features (Chandrashekar, Hoon, Ryba, & Zuker, 2006). They respond most strongly to glutamate, an amino acid in many protein-containing foods. Recall from Chapter 3, glutamate acts as a neurotransmitter; in fact, it's a major excitatory neurotransmitter. The food additive *monosodium glutamate* (MSG), which is often used to flavor Asian foods, particularly activates umami receptors. Some people develop headaches or allergic reactions after eating MSG.

Of course, the variety of taste experiences greatly exceeds the five basic receptors discussed here. Any food molecules dissolved in saliva evoke specific, combined patterns of activity in the five taste receptor types. Although we often think of taste as the primary source for flavor, in fact, taste and smell collaborate to produce this complex perception.

"We would like to be genetically modified to taste like Brussels sprouts."

As any wine connoisseur will attest, the full experience of a wine's flavor cannot be appreciated without a finely trained sense of smell. Odorants from substances outside your mouth enter the nasal cavity via the nostrils, and odorants in the mouth enter through the back of the throat. This is why wine aficionados are taught to pull air in over wine held in the mouth: It allows the wine's odorant molecules to enter the nasal cavity through this "back door."

You can easily demonstrate the contribution of smell to flavor by tasting a few different foods while holding your nose, preventing the olfactory system from detecting their odors. If you have a head cold, you probably already know how this turns out. Your favorite spicy burrito or zesty pasta probably tastes as bland as can be.

In summary, our experience of smell, or olfaction, is associated with odorant molecules binding to sites on specialized olfactory receptors, which converge at the glomerulus within the olfactory bulb. The olfactory bulb in turn sends signals to parts of the brain that control drives, emotions, and memories, which helps to explain why smells can have immediate and powerful effects on us. Smell is also involved in social behavior, as illustrated by pheromones, which are related to reproductive behavior and sexual responses in several species. Sensations of taste depend on taste buds, which are distributed across the tongue, roof of the mouth, and upper throat and on taste receptors that correspond to the five primary taste sensations of salt, sour, bitter, sweet, and umami.

VICTORIA SNOWBER/GETTY

Together, taste and smell produce what we perceive as flavor. This is why smelling the "bouquet" of a wine is an essential part of the wine-tasting ritual. Without smell, it would be difficult to taste subtle differences between wines.

Where Do You Stand?

Perception and Persuasion

In the 1950s, movie theater owners experimented with a new and controversial marketing technique: subliminal advertising. They screened films into which studios had spliced single frames containing photographs of popcorn and soda or word images such as *I'm thirsty*. At normal projection speed, these images were too brief for moviegoers to perceive consciously, but theater owners hoped that projecting the messages would register with viewers and thus increase concession sales during intermissions. However, scientific evidence for this kind of subliminal persuasion has been mixed at best.

These days, marketers advocate a more subtle form of advertising known as *sensory branding* (Lindstrom, 2005). The idea is to exploit all the senses to promote a product or a brand. We're used to seeing advertisements that feature exciting, provocative, or sexual images to sell products. In television commercials these images are accompanied by popular music that advertisers hope will evoke an overall mood favorable to the product. The notion is that the sight and sound of exciting things will become associated with what might be an otherwise drab product.

But sensory branding goes beyond sight and sound by enlisting smell, taste, and touch as well as vision and hearing. You probably recognize the distinctive aroma of a newly opened can of Play-Doh or a fresh box of Crayola crayons. Their scents are unmistakable, but they're also somewhat inadvertent: Play-Doh was first sold in 1956 and Crayola crayons appeared in 1903, both long before there was any thought given to marketing as a total sensory experience.

Sensory branding is a much more intentional approach to marketing. That new-car smell you anticipate while you take a test drive? Actually, it's a manufactured fragrance sprayed into the car, carefully tested to evoke positive feelings among potential buyers. Bang and Olufsen, a Danish high-end stereo manufacturer, carefully designed its remote control units to have a certain distinctive "feel" in a user's hand. Singapore Airlines, which has consistently been rated "the world's best airline," has actually patented the smell of their airplane cabins (it's called Stefan Floridian Waters).

Another form of advertising that has grown dramatically in recent years is product placement: Companies pay to have their products appear prominently in motion pictures and television productions. Do you notice when the star of a film drinks a can of a well-known beverage or drives a particular model of automobile in a car chase? Although viewers may not notice or even be aware of the product, advertisers believe that product placement benefits their bottom lines.

Video technology has advanced even to the point where products can be placed in motion pictures after the fact. Princeton Video, using its L-VIS (live-video insertion) system, placed a Snackwell's cookie box on the kitchen counter of a Bewitched rerun from the 1960s, long before the Snackwell's brand existed (Wenner, 2004)! Currently, there's a wave of interest in developing product placement advertising for multiplayer online games, even to the extent that ads can be tailored to specific users based on their preferences and previous buying habits.

Is there any harm in marketing that bombards the senses or even sneaks through to perception undetected? Advertising is a business, and like any business it is fueled by innovation in search of a profit. Perhaps these recent trends are simply the next clever step to get potential buyers to pay attention to a product message. On the other hand, is there a point when "enough is enough"? Do you want to live in a world where every sensory event is trademarked, patented, or test-marketed before reaching your perceptual system? Does the phrase, "Today's sunset was brought to you by the makers of . . ." cause you alarm? Where do you stand?

Chapter Review

The Doorway to Psychology

- Sensation and perception are separate events that, from the vantage point of the perceiver, feel like one single process. Sensation is simple awareness due to the stimulation of a sense organ, whereas perception is a brain activity that organizes, identifies, and interprets a sensation in order to form a mental representation.

- Transduction is the process that converts physical energy in the world into neural signals in the central nervous system. All senses rely on transduction, although the types of energy being sensed differ (e.g., light waves for vision, sound waves for audition).

- Psychophysics was a field of study during the mid- to late-1800s that sought to understand the link between properties of a physical stimulus and people's psychological reactions to them.

- Psychophysics researchers developed the idea of an absolute threshold, the minimal intensity needed to just barely detect a stimulus, and the difference threshold, the minimal change in a stimulus that can just barely be detected. The difference threshold is also referred to as the just noticeable difference (JND). Signal detection theory represents a refinement of these basic approaches and takes into account a perceived hit, miss, false alarm, and correct rejection rates.

- Sensory adaptation occurs when sensitivity to prolonged stimulation tends to decline over time as an organism adapts to current conditions. This adaptive process illustrates that the perceptual system is more sensitive to changes in stimulation than to constant levels of stimulation.

Vision: More Than Meets the Eye

- Vision takes place when light waves are transduced by cells in the eye. Light waves have the properties of length, amplitude, and purity. These physical properties are perceived as color, brightness, and saturation, respectively.

- Light enters the eye through the cornea and pupil, landing on the retina, tissue that lines the back of each eyeball. The retina is composed of three layers of cells: photoreceptors, bipolar cells, and retinal ganglion cells (RGCs). Photoreceptors take the form of rods and cones; rods are specialized for low-light vision, whereas cones are specialized for color vision.

- The optic nerve is composed of bundled axons from the retinal ganglion cells; it leaves the eye via the blind spot at the back of each eyeball. Retinal ganglion cells have a receptive field that responds to light falling anywhere in it; some responses are excitatory, whereas others are inhibitory.

- Cones specialized to sense red, green, or blue wavelengths begin the process of color vision. Combinations of these cones firing produces the spectrum of colors we can see. Cones also operate in red-green and blue-yellow opponent combinations to contribute to color vision. Both additive and subtractive color mixing determine how shades of color can be produced.

- The optic nerve makes its way through various parts of the brain to terminate in area V1, the primary visual cortex, located in the occipital lobe. There specialized neurons respond to the sensation of bars and edges in different orientations. The ventral stream leaves the occipital cortex to provide a "what" visual pathway to other parts of the brain. The dorsal stream provides a "where" and "how" pathway.

- Both the modular view and the distributed representation view offer explanations of how we perceive and recognize objects in the world. At a minimum, humans show a great deal of perceptual constancy: Even as aspects of sensory signals change, perception remains consistent. We are rarely misled to think that distant objects are actually tiny, that the moon increases in physical size as it rises, or that a friend who grew a mustache is a totally different person.

- Gestalt psychologists delineated basic perceptual principles long ago, such as simplicity, closure, continuity, and proximity. Gestalt psychologists also observed that we tend to perceive figures set against some kind of background. Many visual illusions capitalize on perceptual ambiguities related to these principles.

- Both template-matching and parts-based explanations of object recognition have strengths and weaknesses. Neither account fully captures how humans correctly and efficiently perceive objects in their environment.

- Monocular, binocular, and motion-based cues all enable us to perceive size and depth, although we sometimes fall prey to visual illusions. Humans are also quite adept at perceiving motion through a variety of mechanisms.

Audition: More Than Meets the Ear

- Hearing takes place when sound waves are transduced by receptors in the ear. Sound waves have the properties of frequency, amplitude, and complexity. These physical properties are perceived as pitch, loudness, and timbre.

- There are three parts of the human ear: the outer ear, the middle ear, and the inner ear. The outer ear channels sound waves toward the middle ear, where tiny bones (called ossicles) mechanically transmit and intensify vibrations from the eardrum to the inner ear.

- The inner ear contains the cochlea, which is divided along its length by the basilar membrane. The undulation of the basilar membrane stimulates thousands of tiny hair cells, specialized auditory receptor neurons embedded in the basilar membrane. The hair cells then release neurotransmitter molecules, initiating a neural signal in the auditory nerve.

- Both a place code and a temporal code are involved in transducing sound frequencies. A place code is used for high-frequency sounds, whereas a temporal code is used for low-frequency sounds. Auditory signals travel to area A1, the primary auditory cortex in the temporal lobe.

- The placement of the ears on the head enables us to localize sounds in the environment.

The Body Senses: More Than Skin Deep

- Haptic perception involves the active exploration of the environment through touching and grasping. Four types of specialized receptor cells are located under the surface of the skin to transduce pressure, texture, pattern, or vibration. There are also receptor cells for sensing temperature and pain.

- The somatosensory strip is organized like a homunculus; areas of the body that are more sensitive occupy a greater area in the somatosensory strip. For example, fingertips have a greater representation than do the calves of the legs.
- Pain is a useful body sense; without it, we might quickly succumb to the effects of unnoticed wounds. A-delta fibers and C fibers are two types of pathways by which pain signals reach the brain.
- Gate-control theory proposes both a bottom-up and a top-down way of controlling pain signals in the body. This helps to account for individual differences in the experience of pain.
- Body position and movement are regulated by receptors located in the muscles, joints, and tendons. Balance is regulated by the semicircular canals in the inner ear and to some extent by visual cues.

The Chemical Senses: Adding Flavor

- Smell and taste are both chemical senses; smell occurs when molecules enter the nose, and taste occurs when molecules are dissolved in saliva. Smell and taste combine to produce the experience of flavor.
- The olfactory epithelium, located at the top of the nasal cavity, contains about 10 million olfactory receptor neurons (ORNs). Each olfactory neuron has receptors that operate like a lock and key with odorant molecules. Groups of ORNs send their axons to a glomerulus within the olfactory bulb.
- Pheromones are biochemical odorants that affect behavior and physiology. There is mixed evidence that pheromones affect some aspects of human sexual behavior.
- The tongue is covered with papillae, which contain taste buds, the organs of taste transduction. Each taste bud contains taste receptor cells that respond to either salty, sweet, bitter, sour, or umami taste sensations. Umami refers to the savoriness of foods.
- Both taste and smell contribute to the perception of flavor. Odorants from food enter the nasal cavity both through the nose and through the back of the mouth. Plugging your nose while you eat can make palatable foods taste bland or make unpalatable foods taste acceptable.

Key Terms

synesthesia (p. 122)
sensation (p. 123)
perception (p. 123)
transduction (p. 123)
psychophysics (p. 124)
absolute threshold (p. 124)
just noticeable difference (JND) (p. 126)
Weber's law (p. 126)
signal detection theory (p. 127)
sensory adaptation (p. 128)
visual acuity (p. 130)
retina (p. 132)
accommodation (p. 132)
cones (p. 132)
rods (p. 132)
fovea (p. 133)
blind spot (p. 134)
receptive field (p. 134)
trichromatic color representation (p. 137)
color-opponent system (p. 137)
area V1 (p. 138)
visual-form agnosia (p. 140)
perceptual constancy (p. 142)
template (p. 143)
monocular depth cues (p. 145)
binocular disparity (p. 146)
motion parallax (p. 147)
apparent motion (p. 149)
pitch (p. 150)
loudness (p. 150)
timbre (p. 151)
cochlea (p. 152)
basilar membrane (p. 152)
hair cells (p. 152)
area A1 (p. 152)
place code (p. 153)
temporal code (p. 153)
haptic perception (p. 155)
referred pain (p. 156)
gate-control theory (p. 157)
vestibular system (p. 158)
olfactory receptor neurons (ORNs) (p. 158)
olfactory bulb (p. 159)
pheromones (p. 160)
taste buds (p. 161)

Recommended Readings

Cytowic, R. (2003). *The man who tasted shapes.* Cambridge: MIT Press. Richard Cytowic is a neurologist and author who offers insights on synesthesia. Interspersed with first-person accounts of synesthetic experiences are Cytowic's views on how and why the brain developed as it did and the implications of that evolutionary process for the mind, behavior, and social interaction.

Enns, J. T. (2004). *The thinking eye, the seeing brain.* New York: Norton. James Enns offers a tour through the visual system, focusing both on sensations in the eye and perception in the brain. This is a fine summary of the key points mentioned in the current chapter and a nice starting point for branching out to other topics in the science of vision.

Goodale, M., & Milner, D. (2004). *Sight unseen.* Oxford: Oxford University Press. Melvyn Goodale and David Milner explore conscious and unconscious vision in this intriguing book. Their arguments from studies of brain damage and neuroscience lead to the proposal of dual systems in visual perception.

Illusions

http://www.philomel.com/phantom_words/description.html

http://www.faculty.ucr.edu/~rosenblu/VSMcGurk.html

http://www.psychologie.tu-dresden.de/i1/kaw/diverses%20 Material/www.illusionworks.com/html/hall_of_illusions.html

Visual illusions trick the eye and the brain, and they're admittedly fun to demonstrate and intriguing in their operation. However, there are other types of sensory and perceptual illusions that you may find interesting. Visit some of these websites for demonstrations and more information.

5

Memory

Encoding: Transforming Perceptions into Memories
Elaborative Encoding
Visual Imagery Encoding
Organizational Encoding

Storage: Maintaining Memories over Time
Sensory Storage
Short-Term Storage and Working Memory
Long-Term Storage
Memories in the Brain
HOT SCIENCE A Memory Drug?

Retrieval: Bringing Memories to Mind
Retrieval Cues: Reinstating the Past
Separating the Components of Retrieval

Multiple Forms of Memory: How the Past Returns
Implicit and Explicit Memory
Semantic and Episodic Memory

Memory Failures: The Seven Sins of Memory
Transience
Absentmindedness
Blocking
Memory Misattribution
THE REAL WORLD Deadly Misattributions
Suggestibility
Bias
Persistence
Are the Seven Sins Vices or Virtues?
WHERE DO YOU STAND? The Mystery of Childhood Amnesia

A POPULAR PHRASE HAS IT, "IF YOU CAN remember the '60s, then you weren't there." Let's meet a man who *can* remember the '60s even though he *was* there. But that's not what makes his story interesting.

In the late 1960s, many young people decided to turn on, tune in, and drop out. Greg was one of those people. He quit school; let his hair grow to his shoulders; tried a variety of soft and not-so-soft drugs; and moved to New York City's Greenwich Village, where his primary occupation seemed to be attending Grateful Dead concerts. But getting high and listening to music didn't prove to be quite as fulfilling as Greg had hoped, and in

1971 he joined the International Society for Krishna Consciousness and moved to their temple in New Orleans. At about that same time, Greg began having trouble with his vision. The trouble worsened, and by the time he sought medical attention, he was completely blind. His doctors discovered a tumor the size of a small orange in Greg's brain, and although they were able to remove it, the damage had already been done. Greg lost his sight, but because the tumor had also destroyed a part of the temporal lobe that is crucial for forming and retaining memories of everyday experience, Greg lost much of his memory as well.

MEMORY The ability to store and retrieve information over time.

In 1977, Greg was admitted to a hospital for patients requiring long-term care. When the neurologist Oliver Sacks interviewed him, Greg had no idea why he was in the hospital but suspected that it might be due to his past drug abuse. Dr. Sacks noticed piles of rock albums in Greg's room and asked him about his interest in music, whereupon Greg launched into a version of his favorite Grateful Dead song, "Tobacco Road," and then shared a vivid memory of a time when he had heard the group perform in New York's Central Park. "When did you hear them in Central Park?" asked Dr. Sacks. "It's been a while, over a year maybe," Greg replied. In fact, the concert had taken place 8 years earlier (Sacks, 1995, p. 48). Dr. Sacks conducted more tests, asking Greg to recall lists of words and simple stories. He noticed that Greg could hold on to the information for a few seconds but that within just a few minutes, he would forget nearly everything he had been told. Greg could sometimes learn songs and jingles if they were repeated over and over, but even when he learned them, he had no recollection of how or when he had done so.

Greg was upset when he was told that his father had died, but then he seemed quickly to forget about it. However, his demeanor changed after he learned of his father's death. He became increasingly sad and no longer wanted to go home for special occasions such as Thanksgiving, although he couldn't say why.

It is sometimes said of middle-aged men with bald spots and ponytails that they are "stuck in the '60s," but for Greg this was literally true. He was unaware that his favorite member of the Grateful Dead, the keyboard player Pigpen, had died in 1973. He knew nothing of President Nixon's visit to China, the death of Janis Joplin, the Arab-Israeli War, or Elvis Presley's divorce. When asked to name the president of the United States (who at that time was Jimmy Carter), he guessed that it was either Lyndon Johnson or John F. Kennedy. When Dr. Sacks gave Greg a hint—"The president's first name is Jimmy"—Greg perked up. "Jimi Hendrix?" he asked hopefully.

After 14 years in the hospital, Dr. Sacks took Greg to a Grateful Dead concert at Madison Square Garden. When the band performed their well-known songs from the 1960s, Greg sang along enthusiastically, but he was puzzled when the band played more recent songs, which he thought sounded "futuristic" and strange. "That was fantastic," Greg told Dr. Sacks as they left the concert. "I will always remember it. I had the time of my life." When Dr. Sacks saw Greg the next morning, he asked him about the Grateful Dead concert. "I love them. I heard them in Central Park and at the Fillmore East," replied Greg, recalling concerts he had seen more than 2 decades ago. "Didn't you just hear them at Madison Square Garden?" asked Dr. Sacks. "No," replied Greg, "I've never been to the Garden" (Sacks, 1995, pp. 76–77).

Memory is *the ability to store and retrieve information over time,* and as Greg's story suggests, it is more than just a handy device that allows us to find our car keys and schedule our dental appointments. In a very real way, our memories define us. Each of us has a unique identity that is intricately tied to the things we have thought, felt, done, and experienced. Memories are the residue of those events, the enduring

Greg's brain damage interfered with his ability to form new memories, so he was able to remember the Grateful Dead only as they sounded and performed in the early 1970s, not as they appeared more recently.

changes that experience makes in our brains and leaves behind when it passes. If an experience passes without leaving a trace, it might just as well not have happened. For Greg, the last 20 years of his life have come and gone without a trace, leaving him forever frozen in 1969. He can revisit old memories, but he cannot make new ones, and so he himself can never change. What he says and does, what he feels and imagines, is there and then gone, like smoke in the wind. As he admitted to Dr. Sacks one day, "It's not much of a life" (Sacks, 1995, p. 68).

Those of us who *can* remember what we did yesterday often fail to appreciate just how complex that act of remembering really is because it occurs so easily. But just consider the role that memory plays in the simplest act, such as arranging to meet a friend at the movies. You must recall your friend's name and telephone number and how to make a call. You must remember what her voice sounds like so that you'll recognize who answers the phone, and you need to remember how to talk to her and how to make sense of the things she says. You need to remember which movies are currently playing, as well as the types of movies that you and your friend enjoy. To find a convenient day and time, you need to remember everything else that is happening in your life as well. Eventually, you will need to remember how to get to the theater, how to drive your car, and what your friend looks like so you can recognize her among the people standing in front of the theater. And finally, you'll have to remember which movie you just saw so that you don't accidentally do this all this over again tomorrow. These are ordinary tasks, tasks so simple that you never give them a second thought. But the fact is that the most sophisticated computer could not even begin to accomplish them as efficiently as any average human.

Because memory is so remarkably complex, it is also remarkably fragile (Schacter, 1996). Every one of us has had the experience of forgetting something we desperately wanted to remember or of remembering something that never really happened. Why does memory serve us so well in some situations and play such cruel tricks on us in other cases? When can we trust our memories and when should we view them skeptically? Is there just one kind of memory, or are there many? These are among the questions that psychologists have asked and answered.

As you've seen in other chapters, the mind's errors and misfires provide key insights into its fundamental nature, and there is no better illustration of these mindbugs than in the realm of memory. Though often fascinating and sometimes frustrating, the mindbugs of memory teach us much about how we remember our pasts and hence about who we are. In this chapter we shall consider the three key functions of memory: **encoding**, *the process by which we transform what we perceive, think, or feel into an enduring memory*; **storage**, *the process of maintaining information in memory over time*; and **retrieval**, *the process of bringing to mind information that has been previously encoded and stored*. We shall then examine several different kinds of memory and focus on the ways in which errors, distortions, and imperfections can reveal the nature of memory itself.

Encoding: Transforming Perceptions into Memories

For at least 2,000 years, people have thought of memory as a recording device, like some sort of video camera that makes exact copies of information that comes in through our senses and then stores those copies for later use. This idea is simple and intuitive. In fact, the only thing wrong with this idea it is that it is thoroughly and completely incorrect. Consider the case of Bubbles P., a professional gambler with no formal education, who spent most of his time shooting craps at local clubs or playing high-stakes poker. If you take the digit memory test shown in **FIGURE 5.1**, you will probably find that you can recall about seven numbers after one look back at the digits. But Bubbles had no difficulty rattling off 20 numbers, in either forward or backward order, after just a single glance (Ceci, DeSimone, & Johnson, 1992). You might conclude that Bubbles must have had a "photographic memory" that allowed him to make an instant copy of the information that he could "look at" later. In fact, that isn't at all how Bubbles accomplished his astounding feats of memory.

ENCODING The process by which we transform what we perceive, think, or feel into an enduring memory.

STORAGE The process of maintaining information in memory over time.

RETRIEVAL The process of bringing to mind information that has been previously encoded and stored.

Figure 5.1 Digit Memory Test How many digits can you remember? Start on the first row and cover the rows below it with a piece of paper. Study the numbers in the row for 1 second and then cover that row back up again. After a couple of seconds, try to repeat the numbers. Then uncover the row to see if you were correct. If so, continue down to the next row, using the same instructions, until you can't recall all the numbers in a row. The number of digits in the last row you can remember correctly is your digit span. Bubbles P. could remember 20 random numbers, or about 5 rows deep. How did you do?

2 8
6 9 1
0 4 7 3
8 7 4 5 4
9 0 2 4 8 1
5 7 4 2 2 9 6
6 4 7 1 9 3 0 4
3 5 6 7 1 8 4 8 5
1 0 2 8 8 3 4 7 2 9
4 7 2 0 8 2 7 4 2 6 4
7 3 1 0 9 3 4 3 5 1 3 8

ELABORATIVE ENCODING The process of actively relating new information to knowledge that is already in memory.

VISUAL IMAGERY ENCODING The process of storing new information by converting it into mental pictures.

To understand how Bubbles did this, we must abandon the notion that memories are copies of sensory experience. On the contrary, memories are made by combining information we *already* have in our brains with new information that comes in through our senses. In this way memory is much less like photography and much more like cooking. Like starting from a recipe but improvising along the way, we add old information to new information, mix, shake, bake, and out pops a memory. Memories are *constructed*, not recorded, and encoding is the process by which we transform what we perceive, think, or feel into an enduring memory. Let's look at three types of encoding processes: elaborative encoding, visual imagery encoding, and organizational encoding.

Elaborative Encoding

Memories are a combination of old and new information, so the nature of any particular memory depends as much on the old information already in our memories as it does on the new information coming in through our senses. In other words, how we remember something depends on how we think about it at the time. In one study, researchers presented participants with a series of words and asked them to make one of three types of judgments (Craik & Tulving, 1975). *Semantic judgments* required the participants to think about the meaning of the words ("Is *hat* a type of clothing?"), *rhyme judgments* required the participants to think about the sound of the words ("Does *hat* rhyme with *cat*?"), and *visual judgments* required the participants to think about the appearance of the words ("Is *HAT* written uppercase or lowercase?"). The type of judgment task influenced how participants thought about each word—what old information they combined with the new—and thus had a powerful impact on their memories (**FIGURE 5.2**). Those participants who made semantic judgments (i.e., had thought about the meaning of the words) had much better memory for the words than did participants who had thought about how the word looked or sounded. The results of these and many other studies have shown that long-term retention is greatly enhanced by **elaborative encoding**, which involves *actively relating new information to knowledge that is already in memory* (Brown & Craik, 2000).

These findings would not have surprised Bubbles P. As a professional gambler, Bubbles found numbers unusually meaningful, and so when he saw a string of digits, he tended to think about their meanings. For example, he might have thought about how they related to his latest bet at the racetrack or to his winnings after a long night at the poker table. Whereas you might try to memorize the string 22061823 by saying it over and over, Bubbles would think about betting $220 at 6 to 1 odds on horse number 8 to place 2nd in the 3rd race. Indeed, when Bubbles was tested with materials other than numbers—faces, words, objects, or locations—his memory performance was no better than average.

You may consciously use Bubbles's strategy when you study for exams ("Well, if Napoleon was born in 1769, that would have made him 7 years old when America declared independence"), but you also use it automatically every day. Have you ever wondered why you can remember 20 experiences (your last summer vacation, your 16th birthday party, your first day at college) but not 20 digits? The reason is that most of the time we think of the meaning behind our experiences, and so we elaboratively encode them without even trying to (Craik & Tulving, 1975). Your 16th birthday party, for example, was probably not just an occasion for cake but rather signaled a transition to being able to drive a car, maybe having a meaningful dating relationship, or buying that electric guitar you never really played after a few months because it was hard to learn. The significance and deeper meaning

Figure 5.2 Levels of Processing Elaborative encoding enhances subsequent retention. Thinking about a word's meaning (making a *semantic judgment*) results in deeper processing—and better memory for the word later—than merely attending to its sound (*rhyme judgment*) or shape (*visual judgment*). (From Craik & Tulving, 1975)

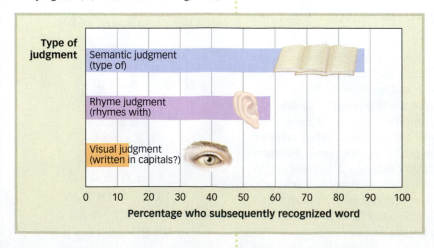

Type of judgment

- Semantic judgment (type of)
- Rhyme judgment (rhymes with)
- Visual judgment (written in capitals?)

0 10 20 30 40 50 60 70 80 90 100
Percentage who subsequently recognized word

attached to the experience of your 16th birthday allowed you to encode that event more readily and thereby commit it to memory. The point is that Bubbles's amazing memory for numbers and your amazing memory for experiences are both due to elaborative encoding and not to some mysterious kind of "photographic memory."

So where does this elaborative encoding take place? What's going on in the brain when this type of information processing occurs? Studies reveal that elaborative encoding is uniquely associated with increased activity in the inner part of the left temporal lobe and the lower left part of the frontal lobe (**FIGURE 5.3a, b**) (Demb et al., 1995; Kapur et al., 1994; Wagner et al., 1998). In fact, the amount of activity in each of these two regions during encoding is directly related to whether people later remember an item. The more activity there is in these areas, the more likely the person will remember the information.

Visual Imagery Encoding

At a banquet in Athens in 477 BC, the Greek poet Simonides regaled his audience with some stand-up poetry. Moments after the emcee announced, "Simonides has left the building!" the banquet hall collapsed and killed all the people inside. Talk about bringing down the house! Simonides was able to name every one of the dead simply by visualizing each chair around the banquet table and recalling the person who had been sitting there. Simonides wasn't the first, but he was among the most proficient, to use **visual imagery encoding**, which involves *storing new information by converting it into mental pictures* (**FIGURE 5.4**).

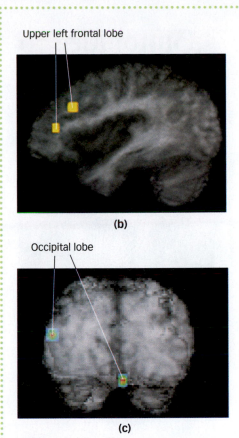

(a)

(b)

(c)

Figure 5.3 **Brain Activity during Different Types of Judgments** fMRI studies reveal that different parts of the brain are active during different types of judgments: (a) During semantic judgments, the lower left frontal lobe is active; (b) during organizational judgments, the upper left frontal lobe is active; and (c) during visual judgments, the occipital lobe is active.

(a) Courtesy of Anthony Wagner; (b) Savage et al., 2001, *Brain, 124*(1), pp. 219–231, Fig. 1c, p. 226. Courtesy of C. R. Savage; (c) Kosslyn et al., *Science, 284*, pp. 167–170, Fig. 2, p. 168. Courtesy of Stephen M. Kosslyn.

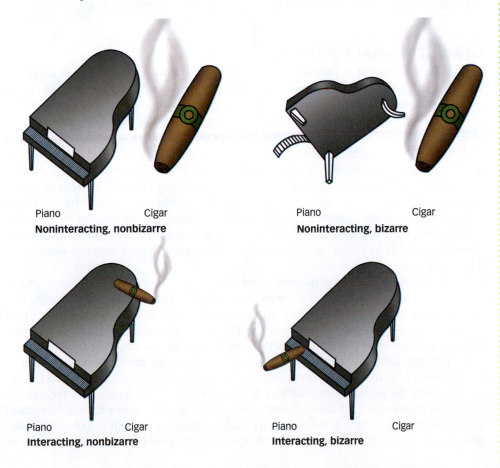

Piano   Cigar
Noninteracting, nonbizarre

Piano   Cigar
Noninteracting, bizarre

Piano   Cigar
Interacting, nonbizarre

Piano   Cigar
Interacting, bizarre

Figure 5.4 **Visual Imagery** One way to better remember something is by relating it to something else using visual imagery. Here it is easier to remember a piano and a cigar when they are interacting than as individual items. This strategy works well, whether the images are bizarre or not (Wollen, Weber, & Lowry, 1972).

No one remembers how the Greek poet Simonides actually looked, but his memory improvement method, which uses visual images to encode new information, has never been forgotten.

COURTESY THE NUREMBERG CHRONICLES, MORSE LIBRARY, BELOIT COLLEGE

If you wanted to use Simonides' method to create an enduring memory, you could simply convert the information that you wanted to remember into a visual image and then "store it" in a familiar location. For instance, if you were going to the grocery store and wanted to remember to buy Coke, popcorn, and cheese dip, you could use the rooms in your house as locations and imagine your living room flooded in Coke, your bedroom pillows stuffed with popcorn, and your bathtub as a greasy pond of cheese dip. When you arrived at the store, you could then take a "mental walk" around your house and "look" into each room to remember the items you needed to purchase. While you're at the store, you might also want to buy a mop to clean up the mess at home.

Numerous experiments have shown that visual imagery encoding can substantially improve memory. In one experiment, participants who studied lists of words by creating visual images of them later recalled twice as many items as participants who just mentally repeated the words (Schnorr & Atkinson, 1969). Another experiment found similar results for people who studied lists composed of concrete words that are easily visualized, such as *tree, battleship,* or *sun,* compared to abstract words, such as *idea, democracy,* or *will* (Paivio, 1969). Why does visual imagery encoding work so well? First, visual imagery encoding does some of the same things that elaborative encoding does: When you create a visual image, you relate incoming information to knowledge already in memory. For example, a visual image of a parked car might help you create a link to your memory of your first kiss.

Second, when you use visual imagery to encode words and other verbal information, you end up with two different mental "placeholders" for the items—a visual one and a verbal one—which gives you more ways to remember them than just a verbal placeholder alone (Paivio, 1971, 1986). How do we know these multiple placeholders are created? As you just read, elaborative encoding seems to activate the frontal and temporal lobes of the brain, but visual imagery encoding activates regions in the occipital lobe (Kosslyn et al., 1993), which as you'll recall from Chapter 3, is the center of visual processing. This finding suggests that people indeed enlist the visual system when forming memories based on mental images (see **FIGURE 5.3c**).

Organizational Encoding

Have you ever ordered dinner with a group of friends and watched in amazement as your server took the order without writing anything down? To find out how this is done, one researcher spent 3 months working in a restaurant where waitresses routinely wrote down orders but then left the check at the customer's table before proceeding to the kitchen and *telling* the cooks what to make (Stevens, 1988). The researcher wired each waitress with a microphone and asked her to think aloud, that is, to say what she was thinking as she walked around all day doing her job. The researcher found that as soon as the waitress left a customer's table, she immediately began *grouping* or *categorizing* the orders into hot drinks, cold drinks, hot foods, and cold foods. The waitresses grouped the items into a sequence that matched the layout of the kitchen, first placing drink orders, then hot food orders, and finally cold food orders. The waitresses remembered their orders by relying on **organizational encoding**, which involves *noticing the relationships among a series of items*.

For example, how easily do you think you could memorize the words *peach, cow, chair, apple, table, cherry, lion, couch, horse, desk*? If you are like most people, this doesn't seem like a particularly easy list to remember. But if you organized the items into three categories—*peach, apple, cherry* and *cow, lion, horse* and *chair, couch, desk*—you would likely have no problems. Studies have shown that instructing people to sort items into categories like this is an effective way to enhance their subsequent recall of those items (Mandler, 1967). Even more complex organizational schemes have been used, such as the hierarchy in **FIGURE 5.5** (Bower et al., 1969). As you can see, people improved their recall of individual items by organizing them into multiple-level categories, all the way from a general category such as *animals,* through intermediate categories such as *birds* and *songbirds,* down to specific examples such as *wren* and *sparrow.*

ORGANIZATIONAL ENCODING The act of categorizing information by noticing the relationships among a series of items.

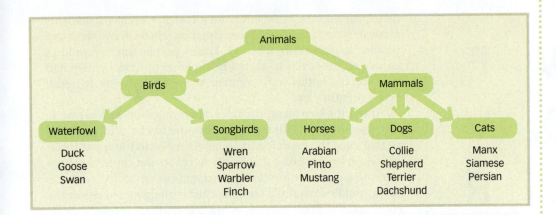

Figure 5.5 **Organizing Words into a Heirarchy** Organizing words into conceptual groups and relating them to one another—such as in this example of a hierarchy—makes it easier to reconstruct the items from memory later (Bower et al., 1969). Keeping track of the 17 items in this example can be facilitated by remembering the hierarchical groupings they fall under.

Organizing by categories encourages you to focus on the similarities among items. But organizational encoding can also take advantage of the differences between items (Hunt & McDaniel, 1993). Look at the following items for a couple of seconds each, and then try to recall them: VRZ, BGR, HPL, WQM, 247, SWY, RNB, PLB. In this list, "247" is the oddball item, and because it stands out from the others, you will probably tend to remember it best—better, in fact, than if it appeared in a list with other numbers (von Restorff, 1933). The relationships between things—how they fit together and how they differ—can help us remember them.

Just as elaborative and visual imagery encoding activate distinct regions of the brain, so too does organizational encoding. As you can see in Figure 5.3b, organizational encoding activates the upper surface of the left frontal lobe (Fletcher, Shallice, & Dolan, 1998; Savage et al., 2001). Different types of encoding strategies appear to rely on different areas of brain activation.

In summary, encoding is the process by which we transform what our senses take in, and what we experience, into a lasting memory. Most instances of spectacular memory performance reflect the skillful use of encoding strategies rather than so-called photographic memory. Memory is influenced by the type of encoding we perform regardless of whether we consciously intend to remember an event or a fact. Elaborative encoding, visual imagery encoding, and organizational encoding all increase memory, but they use different parts of the brain to accomplish that. ■ ■

Storage: Maintaining Memories over Time

Encoding is the process of turning perceptions into memories. But one of the hallmarks of a memory is that you can bring it to mind on Tuesday, not on Wednesday, and then bring it to mind again on Thursday. So where are our memories when we aren't using them? Clearly, those memories are *stored* somewhere in your brain. **Memory storage** is *the process of maintaining information in memory over time.* We can think of a memory store as a place in which memories are kept when we are not consciously experiencing them. The memory store has three major divisions—sensory, short-term, and long-term. As these names suggest, the three divisions are distinguished primarily by the amount of time in which a memory can be kept inside them.

Sensory Storage

The **sensory memory store** is *the place in which sensory information is kept for a few seconds or less.* In a series of classic experiments, research participants were asked to remember rows of letters (Sperling, 1960). In one version of the procedure, participants viewed three rows of four letters each, as shown in **FIGURE 5.6** on the next page. The researcher flashed the letters on a screen for just 1/20th of a second. When asked to

MEMORY STORAGE The process of maintaining information in memory over time.

SENSORY MEMORY STORE The place in which sensory information is kept for a few seconds or less.

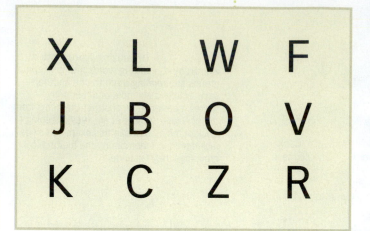

Figure 5.6 **Iconic Memory Test** When a grid of letters is flashed on-screen for only 1/20th of a second, it is difficult to recall individual letters. But if prompted to remember a particular row immediately after the grid is shown, research participants will do so with high accuracy. Sperling used this procedure to demonstrate that although iconic memory stores the whole grid, the information fades away too quickly for a person to recall everything (Sperling, 1960).

remember all 12 of the letters they had just seen, participants recalled fewer than half of them (Sperling, 1960). There were two possible explanations for this: Either people simply couldn't encode all the letters in such a brief period of time, or they had encoded the letters but forgotten them while trying to recall everything they had seen.

To test the two ideas, the researchers relied on a clever trick. Just after the letters disappeared from the screen, a tone sounded that cued the participants to report the letters in a particular row. A *high tone* cued participants to report the contents of the top row, a *medium* tone cued participants to report the contents of the middle row, and a *low* tone cued participants to report the contents of the bottom row. When asked to report only a single row, people recalled almost all of the letters in that row! Because the tone sounded *after* the letters disappeared from the screen, the researchers concluded that people could have recalled the same number of letters from *any* of the rows had they been asked to. Participants had no way of knowing which of the three rows would be cued, so the researchers inferred that virtually all the letters had been encoded. In fact, if the tone was substantially delayed, participants couldn't perform the task; the information had slipped away from their sensory memories. Like the afterimage of a flashlight, the 12 letters flashed on a screen are visual icons, a lingering trace stored in memory for a very short period.

Because we have more than one sense, we have more than one kind of sensory memory. **Iconic memory** is *a fast-decaying store of visual information.* A similar storage area serves as a temporary warehouse for sounds. **Echoic memory** is *a fast-decaying store of auditory information.* When you have difficulty understanding what someone has just said, you probably find yourself replaying the last few words—listening to them echo in your "mind's ear," so to speak. When you do that, you are accessing information that is being held in your echoic memory store. The hallmark of both the iconic and echoic memory stores is that they hold information for a very short time. Iconic memories usually decay in about a second or less, and echoic memories usually decay in about five seconds (Darwin, Turvey, & Crowder, 1972). These two sensory memory stores are a bit like doughnut shops: The products come in, they sit briefly on the shelf, and then they are discarded. If you want one, you have to grab it fast.

Short-Term Storage and Working Memory

A second kind of memory store is the **short-term memory store**, which is *a place where nonsensory information is kept for more than a few seconds but less than a minute.* For example, if someone tells you a telephone number, you can usually wait a few seconds and repeat it back with ease. But if you wait too long, you can't. How long is too long? In a study that examined how long people can hold information in short-term memory, research participants were given consonant strings to remember, such as DBX and HLM. After seeing each string, participants were asked to count backward from 100 by 3s for varying amounts of time and were then asked to recall the strings (Peterson & Peterson, 1959). As shown in **FIGURE 5.7,** memory for the consonant strings declined rapidly, from approximately 80% after a 3-second delay to less than 20% after a 20-second delay.

These results suggest that information can be held in the short-term memory store for about 15 to 20 seconds, but for most of us, that's not nearly long enough. So we use a trick that allows us to get around the natural limitations of our short-term memories. If someone gives us a telephone number and we don't have a pencil, we say it over and over to ourselves until we find one. **Rehearsal** is *the process of keeping information in short-term memory by mentally repeating it.* Why does rehearsal work so well? Because each time you repeat the number, you are putting it back or "reentering" it into short-term memory, thus giving it another 15 to 20 seconds of shelf life.

ICONIC MEMORY A fast-decaying store of visual information.

ECHOIC MEMORY A fast-decaying store of auditory information.

SHORT-TERM MEMORY STORE A place where nonsensory information is kept for more than a few seconds but less than a minute.

REHEARSAL The process of keeping information in short-term memory by mentally repeating it.

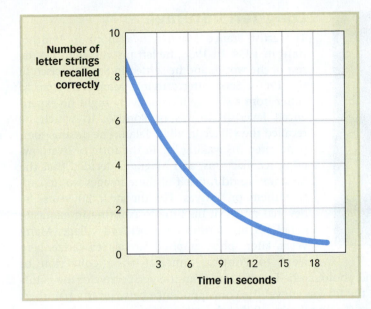

Figure 5.7 The Decline of Short-Term Memory A 1959 experiment showed how quickly short-term memory fades without rehearsal. On a test for memory of three-letter strings, research participants were highly accurate when tested a few seconds after exposure to each string, but if the test was delayed another 15 seconds, people barely recalled the strings at all (Peterson & Peterson, 1959).

Short-term memory is naturally limited in how *long* it can hold information, but it is also naturally limited in how *much* information it can hold. Experiments suggest that most people can keep approximately seven numbers in short-term memory, and if they put more new numbers in, then old numbers begin to fall out (Miller, 1956). It is no accident that telephone numbers were (until recently) limited to seven digits. But there is something puzzling here. If we can keep only seven numbers in short-term memory, then how is it that we can also keep seven words? After all, seven words could easily involve more than 50 letters. The answer is that short-term term memory can hold about seven *meaningful items,* and therefore one way to circumvent its natural limitations is to group several letters into a single meaningful item. **Chunking** involves *combining small pieces of information into larger clusters or chunks.* Short-term memory can hold about seven chunks of information, and although a word may contain more than 10 letters, it is still considered a single chunk (Miller, 1956). Recall the waitresses who organized the customers' orders into groups. These waitresses were essentially chunking the information, thus giving themselves less to remember.

Just as sensory memory can be subdivided into iconic and echoic components, short-term memory can also be conceptualized as having different elements. Short-term memory was originally conceived of as a kind of "place" where information is kept for a limited amount of time. Indeed, the language that researchers use to talk about memory (e.g., *store, storage area*) illustrates that approach. A more dynamic model of a limited-capacity memory system has been developed and refined over the past few decades. **Working memory** refers to *active maintenance of information in short-term storage* (Baddeley & Hitch, 1974). It differs from the traditional view that short-term memory is simply a place to hold information and instead includes the operations and processes we use to work with information in short-term memory.

Working memory includes subsystems that store and manipulate visual images or verbal information. If you wanted to keep the arrangement of pieces on a chessboard in mind as you contemplated your next move, you'd be relying on working memory. Working memory includes the visual representation of the positions of the pieces, your mental manipulation of the possible moves, and your awareness of the flow of information into and out of memory ("Is my time almost up?" "Wait; there's a better move!" "The pawn might work over there."), all stored for a limited amount of time. In short, the working memory model acknowledges both the limited nature of this kind of memory storage and the activities that are commonly associated with it.

CHUNKING Combining small pieces of information into larger clusters or chunks that are more easily held in short-term memory.

WORKING MEMORY Active maintenance of information in short-term storage.

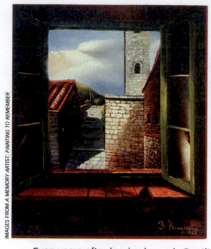 

Even years after leaving home in Pontito, Italy, painter Franco Magnani was able to create a near-perfect reproduction of what he'd seen there. Magnani's painting (left), based on a memory of a place he hadn't seen for years, is remarkably similar to the photograph Susan Schwartzenberg took of the actual scene (right).

 ONLY HUMAN

HELP! I'VE EATEN AND I CAN'T GET HOME! In Oslo, Norway, Jermund Slogstad, 50, was moving into his new apartment when he took a break to get something to eat. He went to a nearby café but forgot to take his wallet, which contained his new address. He was unable to find his way home. "This is embarrassing," he told a newspaper a month later, hoping word of his plight would reach his new landlady, whom he had paid a month's rent in advance.

Long-Term Storage

The artist Franco Magnani was born in Pontito, Italy, in 1934. In 1958, he left his village to see the rest of the world, and he settled in San Francisco in the 1960s. Soon after arriving, Magnani began to suffer from a strange illness. Every night he experienced feverish dreams of Pontito, in which he recalled the village in vivid detail. The dreams soon penetrated his waking life in the form of overpowering recollections, and Magnani decided that the only way to rid himself of these images was to capture them on canvas. For the next 20 years, he devoted much of his time to painting in exquisite detail his memories of his beloved village. Many years later, photographer Susan Schwartzenberg went to Pontito, armed with a collection of Magnani's paintings, and photographed each scene from the perspective of the paintings. As you can see in the images above, the correspondence between the paintings and the photographs was striking (Sacks, 1995; Schacter, 1996).

Many years intervened between Magnani's visual perception and artistic reconstruction of the village, suggesting that very detailed information can sometimes be stored for a very long time. The **long-term memory store** is *a place in which information can be kept for hours, days, weeks, or years*. In contrast to both the sensory and short-term memory stores, the long-term store has no known capacity limits (see **FIGURE 5.8**). For example, most people can recall 10,000 to 15,000 words in their native language, tens of thousands of facts ("Columbus discovered America in 1492" and "3 × 3 = 9"), and an untold number of personal experiences. Just think of all the song lyrics you can recite by heart, and you'll understand that you've got a lot of information tucked away in long-term memory!

Amazingly, people can recall items from the long-term memory store even if they haven't recalled them for years. For example, do you think you would you be able to recognize your classmates if their high school photographs showed up, say, on *America's Most Wanted* 10 years from now? Researchers have found that even 50 years after graduation, people can accurately recognize about 90% of their high school classmates from yearbook photographs (Bahrick, 2000). Although Franco Magnani's memories are impressive, we are all capable of quite remarkable feats of long-term storage.

Not everybody has the ability to put information into the long-term memory store. In 1953, a 27-year-old man, known by the initials HM, suffered from intractable epilepsy (Scoville & Milner, 1957). To prevent further spread of epileptic tissue, HM had parts of his temporal lobes removed, including the hippocampus and some surrounding regions (**FIGURE 5.9**). After the operation, HM could converse easily, use and understand language, and perform well on intelligence tests. Indeed, the only thing

You probably have a pretty good memory for the names and faces of the people who went to your high school. That information got stored in long-term memory, and you will likely still remember most of the people in your high school in 50 years' time.

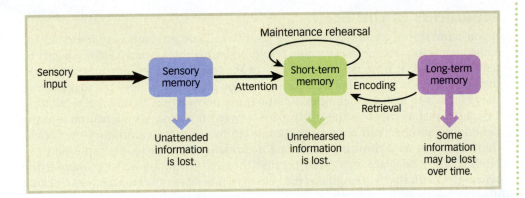

Figure 5.8 The Flow of Information through the Memory System Information moves through several stages of memory as it gets encoded, stored, and made available for later retrieval.

HM could *not* do was remember things that happened to him *after* the operation. For example, he would often forget that he had just eaten a meal or fail to recognize the hospital staff who helped him on a daily basis. Like Greg, who was stuck in the 1960s, HM lacked the ability to hang on to the new memories he created. HM could repeat a telephone number with no difficulty, suggesting that his short-term memory store was just fine (Corkin, 1984, 2002; Hilts, 1995). But after information left the short-term store, it was gone forever. For HM, everything that had ever happened had either happened in the last few moments or prior to 1953.

Studies of HM and others have shown that the hippocampal region of the brain is critical for putting new information into the long-term store. When this region is damaged, patients suffer from a condition known as **anterograde amnesia**, which is *the inability to transfer new information from the short-term store into the long-term store.* Some amnesic patients also suffer from **retrograde amnesia**, which is *the inability to retrieve information that was acquired before a particular date, usually the date of an injury or operation.* Although HM could not store new memories, he was generally able to recall knowledge acquired during adolescence and childhood and could also recall some of his youthful experiences, although his early personal memories lacked detail (Corkin, 2002). The fact that HM had much worse anterograde than retrograde amnesia suggests that the hippocampal region is not the site of long-term memory; indeed, research has shown that different aspects of a single memory are stored in different places in the cortex (Damasio, 1989; Schacter, 1996; Squire & Kandel, 1999). Consider, for example, your memory of the first concert you ever attended. Memories of the band's appearance are probably stored in your visual cortex, perhaps in the occipital lobe or inferior temporal lobe (see Chapters 3 and 4). Memories of the tunes they played are probably stored in your auditory cortex.

If different parts of a memory are stored in different parts of the brain, then why does hippocampal damage cause any kind of amnesia at all? Think about it: If bits and pieces of experience are scattered throughout the cortex, then *something* has to gather them together in order for us to have a single, integrated memory. Psychologists now believe that the hippocampal region serves this function, acting as a kind of "index" that links together all of these otherwise separate bits and pieces so that we remember them as one (Schacter, 1996; Squire, 1992; Teyler & DiScenna, 1986). If you were making a pie, the recipe would serve as an index—it would tell you to retrieve eggs and butter from the refrigerator, flour from the pantry, and rhubarb from the garden and then to mix them all together to produce the pie. But if the hippocampus is a memory index, then why was HM able to recall scenes from his childhood? Good question! It appears that when people recall experiences over and over again, the bits and pieces start to become integrated, and they no longer need the hippocampal index to tie them together. If you made rhubarb pies every day, you wouldn't need a recipe after only a week or so. When the butter came out, so would the eggs. Scientists are still debating the extent to which the hippocampal regions helps us to remember details of our old memories (Bayley et al., 2005; Moscovitch et al., 2006), but the notion of the hippocampus as an index explains why people like HM *cannot* make new memories and why they *can* remember old ones.

LONG-TERM MEMORY STORE A place in which information can be kept for hours, days, weeks, or years.

ANTEROGRADE AMNESIA The inability to transfer new information from the short-term store into the long-term store.

RETROGRADE AMNESIA The inability to retrieve information that was acquired before a particular date, usually the date of an injury or operation.

Figure 5.9 The Hippocampus Patient HM had his hippocampus and adjacent structures of the medial temporal lobe (indicated by the shaded area) surgically removed to stop his epileptic seizures. As a result, he could not remember things that happened after the surgery.

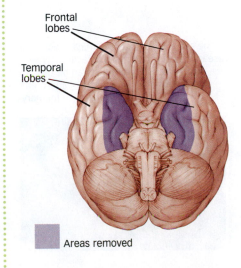

Frontal lobes

Temporal lobes

Areas removed

LONG-TERM POTENTIATION (LTP)
Enhanced neural processing that results from the strengthening of synaptic connections.

NMDA RECEPTOR A hippocampal receptor site that influences the flow of information from one neuron to another across the synapse by controlling the initiation of long-term potentiation.

Memories in the Brain

If you could shrink yourself down to the size of a cell and go wandering around inside someone's brain, where exactly would you look for their memories? You'd probably be tempted to look at their neurons; after all, at the level of the cell, there's really nothing *but* neurons to look at. But that isn't where you'd find them. Research suggests that the best place to look for memories is in the *spaces* between neurons. You'll recall from Chapter 3 that a *synapse* is the small space between the axon of one neuron and the dendrite of another, and neurons communicate by sending neurotransmitters across these synapses. As it turns out, sending a neurotransmitter across a synapse isn't like sending a toy boat across a pond because the act of sending actually *changes* the synapse. Specifically, it strengthens the connection between the two neurons, making it easier for them to transmit to each other the next time. This is why researchers sometimes say, "Cells that fire together wire together" (Hebb, 1949).

The idea that the connections between neurons are strengthened by their communication, thus making communication easier the next time, provides the neurological basis for long-term memory, and much of what we know about this comes from the tiny sea slug *Aplysia*. Having an extremely simple nervous system consisting of only 20,000 neurons (compared to roughly 100 billion in the human brain), *Aplysia* has been attractive to researchers because it is relatively uncomplicated. When an experimenter stimulates *Aplysia*'s tail with a mild electric shock, the slug immediately withdraws its gill, and if the experimenter does it again a moment later, *Aplysia* withdraws its gill even more quickly. If the experimenter comes back an hour later and shocks *Aplysia*, the withdrawal of the gill happens as slowly as it did the first time, as if *Aplysia* can't "remember" what happened an hour earlier (Abel et al., 1995). But if the experimenter shocks *Aplysia* over and over, it does develop an enduring "memory" that can last for days or even weeks. Research suggests that this long-term storage involves the growth of new synaptic connections between neurons (Abel et al., 1995; Squire & Kandel, 1999). So, learning in *Aplysia* is based on changes involving the synapses for both short-term storage (enhanced neurotransmitter release) and long-term storage (growth of new synapses). Any experience that results in memory produces physical changes in the nervous system—even if you're a slug.

If you're something more complex than a slug—say, a mammal or your roommate—a similar process of synaptic strengthening happens in the hippocampus, which we've seen is an area crucial for storing new long-term memories. In the early 1970s, researchers applied a brief electrical stimulus to a neural pathway in a rat's hippocampus (Bliss & Lømo, 1973). They found that the electrical current produced a stronger connection between synapses that lay along the pathway and that the strengthening lasted for hours or even weeks. They called this **long-term potentiation**, more commonly known as **LTP**, which is *enhanced neural processing that results from the strengthening of synaptic connections.* Long-term potentiation has a number of properties that indicate to researchers that it plays an important role in long-term memory storage: It occurs in several pathways within the hippocampus; it can be induced rapidly; and it can last for a long time. In fact, drugs that block LTP can turn rats into rodent versions of patient HM: The animals have great difficulty remembering where they've been recently and become easily lost in a maze (Bliss, 1999; Morris, Anderson, Lynch, & Baudry, 1986).

So how does LTP take place? What's going on in the neurons in the hippocampus to produce these stronger synaptic connections? The primary agent is a neural receptor site called NMDA, known more formally as *N*-methyl-D-aspartate. The **NMDA receptor** *influences the flow of information from one neuron to another across the synapse by controlling the initiation of LTP in most hippocampal pathways* (Bliss, 1999). Here's how it works. The hippocampus contains an abundance of NMDA receptors, more so than in other areas of the brain. This is not surprising because the hippocampus is intimately involved in the formation of long-term memories. But for these NMDA receptors to become activated, two things must happen at roughly the same time. First, the presynaptic, or "sending," neuron releases a neurotransmitter called *glutamate* (a major

The sea slug *Aplysia californica* is useful to researchers because it has an extremely simple nervous system that can be used to investigate the mechanisms of short- and long-term memory.

GERALD & BUFF CORSI/VISUALS UNLIMITED

excitatory neurotransmitter in the brain), which attaches to the NMDA receptor site on the postsynaptic, or "receiving," neuron. Second, excitation takes place in the postsynaptic neuron. Together, these two events initiate LTP, which in turn increases synaptic connections by allowing neurons that fire together to wire together (**FIGURE 5.10**).

Don't get lost wandering around all these neurons . . . in fact, un-shrink yourself from the size of a cell and look at the big picture for a minute. It's easy to say that humans and other animals can form long-term memories. We can tell from a person's behavior that information has been stored and is able to be called up again and acted on. But it's another matter to understand *how* and *why* long-term memories are formed. The neural research on LTP and NMDA receptors helps us link an observable mental phenomenon ("Look! The squirrel remembered where the nuts were! She went right back to the correct tree!") with the biological underpinnings that produce it. More work remains to be done in this area to conclusively show how LTP leads to the formation of long-term memories, but the implications of this line of research are considerable. You can read about some of those implications in the Hot Science box.

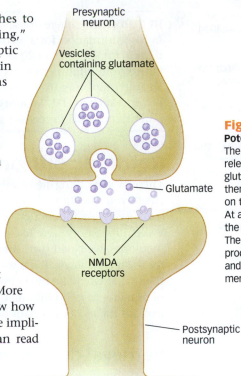

Figure 5.10 Long-Term Potentiation in the Hippocampus The presynaptic neuron (top of figure) releases the neurotransmitter glutamate into the synapse. Glutamate then binds to the NMDA receptor sites on the postsynaptic neuron (bottom). At about the same time, excitation in the postsynaptic neuron takes place. The combined effect of these two processes initiate long-term potentiation and the formation of long-term memories.

{ HOT SCIENCE } A Memory Drug?

IT'S DIFFICULT TO IMAGINE MANY THINGS that people would welcome more than a memory-enhancing drug. A memory enhancer could help eliminate forgetting associated with aging and disease. Furthermore, such a drug could help people remember past experiences more clearly and help us acquire new information more easily for school and at work. As scientists learn more about memory, we are closing in on this tantalizing goal.

Some of the most exciting evidence comes from research that has built on earlier findings linking LTP and memory to identify a gene that improves memory in mice (Tang et al., 1999). The gene makes a protein that assists the NMDA receptor, which plays an important role in long-term memory by helping to initiate LTP. Mice bred to have extra copies of this gene showed more activity in their NMDA receptors, more LTP, and improved performance on several different memory tasks—learning a spatial layout, recognizing familiar objects, and recalling a fear-inducing shock (Tang et al., 1999).

If these basic insights about genes, LTP, and the synaptic basis of memory can be translated to people—and that remains to be seen— they could pave the way for memory-enhancing treatments. Like steroids for bulking up the muscles, these drugs would bulk up memory. As exciting as this may sound, it also raises troubling issues. Consider the potential educational implications of memory-enhancing drugs. If memory enhancers were available, children who used them might be able to acquire and retain extraordinary amounts of information, allowing them to progress far more rapidly in school than they could otherwise. How well could the brain handle such an onslaught of information? What happens to children who don't have access to the latest memory enhancers? Are they left behind in school—and as a result handicapped later in life?

What are the potential implications of memory-enhancing drugs for the workplace? Imagine that you are applying for a job that requires a good memory, such as a manager at a technology company or a sales position that requires remembering customers' names as well as the attributes of different products and services. Would you take a memory-enhancing drug to increase your chances of landing the position? Would people who felt uncomfortable taking such a drug find themselves cut out of lucrative career opportunities?

Memory drugs might also help take the sting out of disturbing memories that we wish we could forget but can't. The 2004 hit movie *Eternal Sunshine of the Spotless Mind* told the story of a young man seeking just such freedom from the painful memories of a romantic breakup. As you will see in the section on persistence later in the chapter, emotionally arousing events often create intrusive memories, and researchers have already muted emotional memories with drugs that block the action of key hormones. Should emergency workers who must confront horrifying accident scenes that can burden them with persisting memories be provided with such drugs? Should such drugs be given to rape victims who can't forget the trauma? Memory drugs might provide some relief to such individuals. But could they also interfere with an individual's ability to assimilate and come to terms with a difficult experience? We may find ourselves struggling with these kinds of questions in the not-too-distant future.

The film *Eternal Sunshine of the Spotless Mind* **builds on the premise that erasing some memories might be a good idea.**

LEE DAVID/FOCUS FEATURES/THE KOBAL COLLECTION

RETRIEVAL CUE External information that is associated with stored information and helps bring it to mind.

ENCODING SPECIFICITY PRINCIPLE The idea that a retrieval cue can serve as an effective reminder when it helps re-create the specific way in which information was initially encoded.

STATE-DEPENDENT RETRIEVAL The tendency for information to be better recalled when the person is in the same state during encoding and retrieval.

TRANSFER-APPROPRIATE PROCESSING The idea that memory is likely to transfer from one situation to another when we process information in a way that is appropriate to the retrieval cues that will be available later.

 **ONLY HUMAN**

PERHAPS BAKERS GET UP A BIT TOO EARLY Burglars broke into the safe in the Wonder-Hostess Thrift Shop bakery in Davenport, Iowa. Police said the burglars had an easy time because the bakery employees could not remember the safe's combination: They had written it out and posted it on the nearby bulletin board.

A particular light, odor, or melody can make a memory reappear vividly, with all its force and its precision, as if a window opened on the past.

CHARLES GULLING/PHOTONICA/GETTY IMAGES

In summary, there are several different types of memory storage: Sensory memory holds information for a second or two; short-term or working memory retains information for about 15 to 20 seconds; and long-term memory stores information for anywhere from minutes to years or decades. The hippocampus and nearby structures play an important role in long-term memory storage, as shown by the severe amnesia of patients such as HM. Memory storage depends on changes in synapses, and long-term potentiation (LTP) increases synaptic connections. ■ ■

Retrieval: Bringing Memories to Mind

There is something fiendishly frustrating about piggy banks. You can put money in them, you can shake them around to assure yourself that the money is there, but you can't easily get the money out, which is why no one carries a piggy bank instead of a wallet. If memory were like a piggy bank, it would be similarly useless. We could make memories, we could store them, and we could even shake our heads around and listen for the telltale jingle. But if we couldn't bring our memories out of storage and use them, then what would be the point of saving them in the first place? Retrieval is the process of bringing to mind information that has been previously encoded and stored, and it is perhaps the most important of all memorial processes (Roediger, 2000; Schacter, 2001a).

Retrieval Cues: Reinstating the Past

When someone asks you to juggle three apples, you know exactly what to do. You keep one apple in the air at all times, you keep your mind focused, you get a good rhythm going, and you hope you can juggle long enough to impress any potential dating partners who might be watching. But what do you do when you try to *remember* how to juggle? The answer is that you probably seek help. One of the best ways to retrieve information from *inside* your head is to encounter information *outside* your head that is somehow connected to it. The information outside your head is called a **retrieval cue**, which is *external information that is associated with stored information and helps bring it to mind.* Retrieval cues can be incredibly effective.

In one experiment, undergraduates studied lists of words, such as *table, peach, bed, apple, chair, grape,* and *desk* (Tulving & Pearlstone, 1966). Later, the students took a test in which they were simply asked to write down all the words from the list that they could remember. The students remembered and wrote and remembered some more, and when they were absolutely sure that they had emptied their memory stores of every last word that was in them, they took another test. This time the experimenter asked them to remember the words on the list, but he provided them with retrieval cues, such as "furniture" or "fruit." The students who were sure that they had done all the remembering they possibly could were suddenly able to remember more words (Tulving & Pearlstone, 1966). These results suggest that information is sometimes *available* in memory even when it is momentarily *inaccessible* and that retrieval cues help us bring inaccessible information to mind. Of course, this is something you already knew. How many times have you said something like, "I *know* who starred in *Charlie and the Chocolate Factory,* but I just can't remember it"? only to have a friend give you a hint ("Wasn't he in *Pirates of the Caribbean*?"), which instantly brings the answer to mind ("Johnny Depp!").

Although hints are a form of retrieval cue, not all retrieval cues come in the form of hints. The **encoding specificity principle** states that *a retrieval cue can serve as an effective reminder when it helps re-create the specific way in which information was initially encoded* (Tulving & Thomson, 1973). In other words, the thoughts or feelings we had at the time we encoded information are associated with the information we encoded, and so those thoughts and feelings can also help us retrieve it. For example, you'd probably expect a fellow student who studied for an exam while drunk to perform poorly, and you would probably be right—but only if he made the mistake of taking the exam while sober! Studies suggest that if the student studied while drunk, he would probably perform poorly the next day, but he'd perform better if he'd had a six-pack instead of Cheerios for breakfast. Why should that be? Because a person's physiological or psychological state at the time of encoding is associated with the information being encoded. If the person's state at the time of retrieval matches the person's state at the time of encoding, the state itself serves as a retrieval cue—a bridge that connects the moment at which we experience something to the moment at which we remember it.

State-dependent retrieval is *the tendency for information to be better recalled when the person is in the same state during encoding and retrieval.* State-dependent retrieval has been documented with both alcohol and marijuana (Eich, 1980; Weissenborn, 2000). Similar effects occur with natural (as opposed to drug-induced) states. For example, retrieving information when you are in a sad or happy mood increases the likelihood that you will retrieve sad or happy episodes (Eich, 1995), which is part of the reason it is so hard to "look on the bright side" when you're feeling low. And by the way, you'd probably do *much* better on an exam if you were alert and sober when you studied and alert and sober when you took the test!

Almost any similarity between the context in which an item is encoded and the context in which it is retrieved can serve as a retrieval cue. For example, in one study divers learned some words on land and some other words underwater; they recalled the words best when they were tested in the same dry or wet environment in which they had initially learned them because the environment itself served as a retrieval cue (Godden & Baddely, 1975). Recovering alcoholics often experience a renewed urge to drink when visiting places in which they once drank because these places serve as retrieval cues. There may even be some wisdom to finding a seat in a classroom, sitting in it every day, and then sitting in it again when you take the test because the feel of the chair and the sights you see may help you remember the information you learned while you sat there. Retrieval cues need not be inner states and they need not be external environments—they can even be thoughts themselves, as when one thought calls to mind another, related thought (Anderson et al., 1976).

Consider just one more unusual consequence of the encoding specificity principle. You learned earlier that making semantic judgments about a word (e.g., "What does *orange* mean?") usually produces more durable memory for the word than does making rhyme judgments (e.g., "What rhymes with *orange*?"). So if you were asked to think of a word that rhymes with *brain* and your friend was asked to think about what *brain* means, we would expect your friend to remember the word better the next day if we simply asked you both, "Hey, what was that word you saw yesterday?" However, if instead of asking that question, we asked you both, "What was that word that rhymed with *train*?" we would expect you to remember it better than your friend did (Fisher & Craik, 1977). This is a fairly astounding finding. Semantic judgments almost always yield better memory than rhyme judgments. But in this case, the typical finding is turned upside down because the retrieval cue matched your encoding context better than it matched your friend's. The principle of **transfer-appropriate processing** states that *memory is likely to transfer from one situation to another when we process information in a way that is appropriate to the retrieval cues that will be available later* (Morris, Bransford, & Franks, 1977; Roediger, Weldon, & Challis, 1989) (**FIGURE 5.11**).

Callahan

"I wonder if you'd mind giving me directions. I've never been sober in this part of town before."

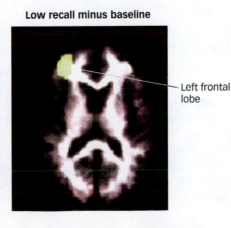

High recall minus baseline

Low recall minus baseline

— Left frontal lobe

Hippocampus —

Figure 5.11 **PET Scans of Successful and Unsuccessful Recall** When people successfully remembered words they saw earlier in an experiment, achieving high levels of recall on a test, the hippocampus showed increased activity. When people tried but failed to recall words they had seen earlier, achieving low levels of recall on a test, the left frontal lobe showed increased activity (Schacter et al., 1996a).

Separating the Components of Retrieval

Finally, let's look at how the process of retrieval works. There is reason to believe that *trying* to recall an incident and *actually* recalling one are fundamentally different processes that occur in different parts of the brain (Moscovitch, 1994; Schacter, 1996). For example, regions within the right frontal lobe show heightened activity when people retrieve information that was presented to them earlier (Shallice et al., 1994; Squire et al., 1992; Tulving et al., 1994), and many psychologists believe that this activity reflects the mental effort that people put forth when they struggle to dredge up the past event (Lepage et al., 2000). However, successfully remembering a past experience tends to be accompanied by activity in the hippocampal region and also in parts of the brain that play a role in processing the sensory features of an experience (Eldridge et al., 2000; Nyberg et al., 1996; Schacter et al., 1996a). For instance, recall of previously heard sounds is accompanied by activity in the auditory cortex (the upper part of the temporal lobe), whereas recall of previously seen pictures is accompanied by activity in the visual cortex (in the occipital lobe) (Wheeler, Petersen, & Buckner, 2000). Although retrieval may seem like a single process, brain studies suggest that separately identifiable processes are at work.

In summary, whether we remember a past experience depends on whether retrieval cues are available to trigger recall. Retrieval cues are effective when they help reinstate how we encoded an experience. Moods and inner states can serve as retrieval cues. Retrieval can be separated into the effort we make while trying to remember what happened in the past and the successful recovery of stored information. Neuroimaging studies suggest that trying to remember activates the right frontal lobe, whereas successful recovery of stored information activates the hippocampus and regions in the brain related to sensory aspects of an experience. ■ ■

Multiple Forms of Memory: How the Past Returns

If someone offered to give you a quick lesson in farming, you'd be suspicious. After all, how could farming be taught in a single lesson when it includes everything from raising sheep to raising barns? True, all these things *are* components of farming, but farming itself is much more than any one of them. The same is true of memory. We say that we cannot remember what happened to us last May 13, we will always remember what happened to Abraham Lincoln in Ford's Theatre on April 14, 1865, we ought to remember that China is bigger than Thailand, we hope to remember that you can't divide anything by zero, and we must remember to take out the trash. Sometimes we even *behave* as though we are remembering things while claiming to remember nothing at all. Although each of these is an example of memory, the diversity of the examples suggests that there must be many different kinds of memory (Eichenbaum & Cohen, 2001; Schacter & Tulving, 1994; Schacter, Wagner, & Buckner, 2000; Squire & Kandel, 1999). Indeed, there are; let's consider some of them.

Implicit and Explicit Memory

Although Greg was forever stranded in the Summer of Love and unable to make new memories, some of the new things that happened to him seemed to leave a mark. For example, Greg did not recall learning that his father had died, but he did seem sad and withdrawn for years after hearing the news. Similarly, HM could not make new memories after his surgery, but if he played a game in which he had to track a moving target, his performance gradually improved with each round (Milner, 1962). Greg could not consciously remember hearing about his father's death, and HM could not consciously remember playing the tracking game, but both showed clear signs of having been permanently changed by experiences that they so rapidly forgot. Research suggests that this

EXPLICIT MEMORY The act of consciously or intentionally retrieving past experiences.

IMPLICIT MEMORY The influence of past experiences on later behavior and performance, even though people are not trying to recollect them and are not aware that they are remembering them.

PROCEDURAL MEMORY The gradual acquisition of skills as a result of practice, or "knowing how," to do things.

nebulous sauerkraut vagueness

is not unusual. For example, when patients with amnesia practice a task, they generally show improvements similar to those of healthy volunteers, despite the fact that they cannot remember ever having performed the task. For instance, to figure out the identities of the mirror-inverted words above, you have to mentally manipulate the spatial positions of the letters until you "see" the word. With practice, most people can read the inverted words faster and faster. But so can people who have amnesia—despite the fact that such patients generally cannot remember having ever seen the words (Cohen & Squire, 1980). Amnesic patients have even proved capable of learning how to program computers despite having no conscious recollection of their training (Glisky, Schacter, & Tulving, 1986)!

The fact that people can be changed by past experiences without having any awareness of those experiences suggests that there must be at least two different kinds of memory. **Explicit memory** occurs *when people consciously or intentionally retrieve past experiences*. Recalling last summer's vacation, incidents from a novel you just read, or facts you studied for a test all involve explicit memory. Indeed, anytime you start a sentence with, "I remember . . ." you are talking about an explicit memory. **Implicit memory** occurs when *past experiences influence later behavior and performance, even though people are not trying to recollect them and are not aware that they are remembering them* (Graf & Schacter, 1985; Schacter, 1987). Implicit memories are not consciously recalled, but their presence is "implied" by our actions. Greg's persistent sadness after his father's death, even though he had no conscious knowledge of the event, is an example of implicit memory. So is HM's improved performance on a tracking task that he didn't consciously remember doing (**FIGURE 5.12**).

All of this makes implicit memory sound mysterious, but really we all have implicit memories. For example, how do you balance on a two-wheeled bicycle? You might be tempted to say, "Gee, I don't know," but if you don't know, why can you do it so easily? Your knowledge of how to balance on a bicycle is a particular kind of implicit memory called **procedural memory**, which refers to *the gradual acquisition of skills as a result of practice, or "knowing how," to do things*. One of the hallmarks of procedural memory is that the things you remember (e.g., how to shift gears in a car, how to play a G chord on the guitar) are automatically translated into actions. All you have to do is will the action and it happens, but it happens because you have implicit memories of how to make it happen. Sometimes you can explain how it is done ("Put one finger on the third fret of the E string, one finger . . .") and sometimes you can't ("Get on the bike and . . . well, uh . . . just balance"). The fact that people who have amnesia can acquire new procedural memories suggests that the hippocampal structures

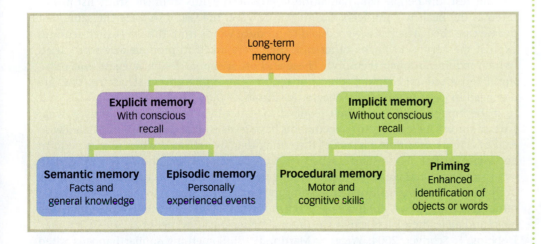

Figure 5.12 Multiple Forms of Memory Explicit and implicit memories are distinct from each other. Thus, a person with amnesia may lose explicit memory yet display implicit memory for material that she or he cannot consciously recall learning.

PRIMING An enhanced ability to think of a stimulus, such as a word or object, as a result of a recent exposure to the stimulus.

SEMANTIC MEMORY A network of associated facts and concepts that make up our general knowledge of the world.

EPISODIC MEMORY The collection of past personal experiences that occurred at a particular time and place.

that are usually damaged in these patients may be necessary for explicit memory, but they aren't needed for implicit procedural memory. In fact, it appears that brain regions outside the hippocampal area (including areas in the motor cortex) are involved in procedural memory. Chapter 6, on learning, discusses this evidence further, where you will also see that procedural memory is crucial for learning various kinds of motor, perceptual, and cognitive skills.

Not all implicit memories are "how to" memories. For example, in one study, participants were asked to memorize a list of words, and for some people, that list included the word *moon* (Nisbett & Wilson, 1977). Later, they were asked to name their favorite brands of several grocery items, including laundry detergent. The results showed that those participants who had earlier memorized the word *moon* were more likely to say that their favorite detergent was Tide, but none of them was aware that the memorization task had influenced their answer. This is an example of **priming**, which refers to *an enhanced ability to think of a stimulus, such as a word or object, as a result of a recent exposure to the stimulus* (Tulving & Schacter, 1990). Just as priming a pump makes water flow more easily, priming the memory system makes some information more accessible.

In one experiment, college students were asked to study a long list of words, including items such as *avocado, mystery, climate, octopus,* and *assassin* (Tulving, Schacter, & Stark, 1982). Later, explicit memory was tested by showing participants some of these words along with new ones they hadn't seen and asking them which words were on the list. To test for priming, participants received word fragments and were asked them to come up with a word that fit the fragment.

Try the test yourself: ch–––nk   o–t–p––   –og–y–––   –l–m–te.

You probably had difficulty coming up with the answers for the first and third fragments (*chipmunk, bogeyman*) but had little problem coming up with answers for the second and fourth (*octopus, climate*). Seeing *octopus* and *climate* on the original list primed your ability to generate them on the fragment completion test. In the experiment, people showed priming for studied words even when they failed to consciously remember that they had seen them earlier.

In a sense, the healthy participants in this study behaved like patients with amnesia. Many experiments have shown that amnesic patients can show substantial priming effects—often as large as healthy, nonamnesic people—even though they have no explicit memory for the items they studied. In one study, researchers showed patients with amnesia and healthy volunteers in the control group a list of words, including *table* and *motel,* and then gave them two different types of tests (Graf, Squire, & Mandler, 1984). One of these tested their explicit memory by providing them with the first three letters of a word (e.g., *tab___*) and asking them to remember a word from the list that began with those letters. On this test, amnesic patients remembered fewer words than the healthy volunteers.

The second test was identical to the first, except that people were given the first three letters of a word and simply asked to write down any word that came to mind. On this test, the people who had amnesia produced words from the study list just as often as the healthy volunteers did. As you can see, the two tests were the same, but in one case the participants were asked to produce words from the list (which requires explicit memory) and in the other case they were asked to produce any word at all (which requires implicit memory). These and other similar results suggest that priming, like procedural memory, does not require the hippocampal structures that are damaged in cases of amnesia (Schacter & Curran, 2000).

If the hippocampal region isn't required for procedural memory and priming, what parts of the brain are involved? Experiments have revealed that priming is associated with *reduced* activity in various regions of the cortex that are activated when people perform an unprimed task. For instance, when research participants are shown the word stem *mot___* or *tab___* and are asked to provide the first word that comes to mind, parts of the occipital lobe involved in visual processing and parts of the frontal lobe involved in word retrieval become active. But if people perform the same task after being primed by seeing *motel* and *table,* there's less activity in these same regions (Buckner et al., 1995; Schacter, Dobbins, & Schnyer, 2004; Wiggs & Martin, 1998). Something similar happens when

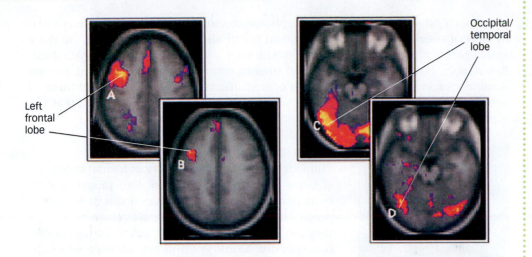

Left frontal lobe

Occipital/temporal lobe

Figure 5.13 **Primed and Unprimed Processing of Stimuli** Priming is associated with reduced levels of activation in the cortex on a number of different tasks. In each pair of fMRIs, the images on the upper left (A, C) show brain regions in the frontal lobe (A) and occipital/temporal lobe (C) that are active during an unprimed task (in this case, providing a word response to a visual word cue). The images on the lower right within each pair (B, D) show reduced activity in the same regions during the primed version of the same task.

D. L. Schacter & R. L. Buckner, 1998, Priming and the Brain, *Neuron, 20,* pp. 185–195.

people see pictures of everyday objects on two different occasions. On the second exposure to a picture, there's less activity in parts of the visual cortex that were activated by seeing the picture initially. Priming seems to make it easier for parts of the cortex that are involved in perceiving a word or object to identify the item after a recent exposure to it. This suggests that the brain "saves" a bit of processing time after priming (**FIGURE** 5.13).

Semantic and Episodic Memory

Consider these two questions: (1) Why do we celebrate on July 4? and (2) what is the most spectacular celebration you've ever seen? Every American knows the answer to the first question (we celebrate the signing of the Declaration of Independence on July 4, 1776), but we all have our own answers to the second. For instance, *you* might remember the time your neighbor bought two shopping bags' worth of illegal fireworks from out of state and shot them off in his backyard, at which point his wife yelled at him for scaring the dog, the police came, and there was a seriously scorched spot on the lawn for the rest of that summer. However, it is unlikely that anyone else (other than the neighbor, the wife, the police, and the dog) has precisely that same memory. Although both of these questions required you to search your long-term memory and explicitly retrieve information that was stored there, one required you to revisit a particular time and place—or episode—from your personal past, and one required you to dredge up a fact that everyone knows and that is not part of your personal autobiography. These memories are called *episodic* and *semantic* memories, respectively (Tulving, 1972, 1983, 1998). **Semantic memory** is *a network of associated facts and concepts that make up our general knowledge of the world*, whereas **episodic memory** is *the collection of past personal experiences that occurred at a particular time and place*.

This contestant on the game show *Who Wants to Be a Millionaire?* is consulting her semantic memory in order to answer the question. The answer is B: Bulgaria.

Episodic Memory in Humans

Episodic memory is special because it is the only form of memory that allows us to engage in "mental time travel," projecting ourselves into the past and revisiting events that have happened to us. This ability allows us to connect our pasts and our presents and construct a cohesive story of our lives. People who have amnesia can usually travel back in time and revisit episodes that occurred before they became amnesiac, but they are unable to revisit episodes that happened later. For example, Greg couldn't travel back to any time after 1969 because that's when he stopped being able to create new episodic memories. But can people with amnesia create new semantic memories?

Researchers have studied three young adults who suffered damage to the hippocampus during birth as a result of difficult deliveries that interrupted the oxygen supply to their brains (the hippocampus is especially sensitive to the lack of oxygen) (Vargha-Khadem et al., 1997). Their parents noticed that the children could not recall what happened during a typical day, had to be constantly reminded of appointments, and often became lost and disoriented. Beth (14 years old), Jon (19 years old), and Kate (22 years old) all showed clear evidence of episodic memory problems on laboratory tests. In view of their hippocampal damage, you might also expect that each of the three would perform poorly in school and might even be classified as learning disabled. Remarkably, however, all three learned to read, write, and spell; developed normal vocabularies; and acquired other kinds of semantic knowledge that allowed them to perform well at school. Based on this evidence, researchers have concluded that the hippocampus is not necessary for acquiring new *semantic* memories.

Clark's nutcracker shows a remarkable ability to remember thousands of seed hiding spots months after storing the seeds. Researchers are debating whether this type of memory indicates an ability for humanlike episodic memory.

Do Animals Have Episodic Memory?

Thinking about episodic memory as mental time travel raises an intriguing question: Can monkeys, rats, birds, or other nonhuman animals revisit their pasts as people do? We know that animals *behave* as though they can retrieve information acquired during specific past episodes. Monkeys act as though they are recalling objects they've seen only once during experimental tests (Zola & Squire, 2000). Rats seem to remember places they've visited recently in a maze (Olton & Samuelson, 1976). And birds that store food (such as Clark's nutcracker) can store as many as 30,000 seeds in 5,000 locations during the fall and then retrieve them all the next spring (Kamil & Jones, 1997; Shettleworth, 1995). But do these smart pet tricks involve the same kind of mental time travel that we all do when we relive the July 4 picnic when Uncle Harry spilled barbecue sauce all over Aunt Norma? Or are the episodic memories of animals more similar to the kinds of memory available to people who have amnesia; for example, are they simply implicit procedural memories?

It's difficult to say. Explicit memory always has a subjective component: When information "comes to mind," it *feels* like something. Animals cannot tell us whether they are having this subjective experience, and we can never tell by watching them whether they are actually having that experience or just behaving as though they are. Some researchers believe that even birds possess abilities closely related to episodic memory. Food-storing scrub jays act as though they can recall what type of food they've stored (a worm or a peanut), where they stored it (on one side of a storage tray or another), and when they stored it (hours or days prior to a test) (Clayton & Dickinson, 1998). Other researchers remain skeptical that demonstrations of highly detailed memories in birds or other animals truly signal the presence of mental time travel (Tulving, 1998). Human episodic memory involves a conscious experience of the self at different points in time. Does a scrub jay project itself backward in time when the bird recalls where and when it stored a worm or a peanut? No one knows for sure. The only reason we are so confident that other *people* engage in mental time travel is that they tell us they do. Because animals can't talk, it seems likely that we will never have a definitive answer to this intriguing question.

In summary, long-term memory consists of several different forms. Explicit memory is the collection of our conscious retrieval of past experiences, whereas implicit memory refers to the unconscious influences of past experiences on later behavior and performance, such as procedural memory and priming. Procedural memory involves the acquisition of skills as a result of practice, and priming is a change in the ability to recognize or identify an object or a word as the result of past exposure to it. People who have amnesia are able to retain implicit memory, including procedural memory and priming, but they lack explicit memory. Episodic memory is the collection of personal experiences from a particular time and place, whereas semantic memory is a networked, general, impersonal knowledge of facts, associations, and concepts. Animals possess extensive memory abilities, but it is still a matter of debate as to whether they can engage in the "mental time travel" characteristic of human episodic memory. ■ ■

Memory Failures: The Seven Sins of Memory

You probably haven't given much thought to breathing today, and the reason is that from the moment you woke up, you've been doing it effortlessly and well. But the moment breathing fails, you are reminded of just how important it is. Memory is like that. Every time we see, think, notice, imagine, or wonder, we are drawing on our ability to use information stored in our brains, but it isn't until this ability fails that we become acutely aware of just how much we should treasure it. Like a lot of human behavior, we can better understand how a process works correctly by examining what happens when it works incorrectly. We've seen in other contexts how an understanding of mindbugs—those foibles and errors of human thought and action—reveals the normal operation of various behaviors. It's useful to think of memory mindbugs as the "seven sins" of memory (Schacter, 1999, 2001b). These "sins" include *transience* (forgetting over time), *absentmindedness* (lapses in attention that result in forgetting), *blocking* (temporary inability to retrieve information), *memory misattribution* (confusing the source of a memory), *suggestibility* (incorporating misleading information into a memory), *bias* (the influence of present knowledge, beliefs, and feelings on recollections of the past), and *persistence* (recalling unwanted memories we would prefer to forget).

Transience

The investigation and eventual impeachment of former president Bill Clinton held the nation spellbound in the late 1990s. Aside from political jockeying and tabloid revelations about Clinton's relationship with White House intern Monica Lewinsky, the investigation also produced a lot of discussion about Clinton's claims to have forgotten a variety of things. Based on his own intuitions about what a person might reasonably be expected to forget, the special prosecutor, Kenneth Starr, decided that Clinton's apparent memory lapses were self-serving conveniences designed to avoid embarrassing admissions.

Starr was especially interested in what Clinton said in January 1998, when he testified in a sexual harassment lawsuit brought against him by Paula Jones (Schacter, 2001b). In that deposition, Clinton discussed a meeting he held 3 weeks earlier with his good friend Vernon Jordan, who had on the same evening met with Lewinsky. She told Jordan that she had received a subpoena from the independent counsel's office to testify in their investigation. Jordan testified that he discussed these matters with Clinton, but the president claimed he did not recall exactly what had happened. But when he testified in the Jones case, about three weeks after that meeting, the president said, "I didn't remember all the details of all this. I didn't remember what—when Vernon talked to me about Monica Lewinsky, whether she talked to him on the telephone or had a meeting, I didn't remember all those details."

Was Clinton's claim to have forgotten a credible one, or was it just the feeble excuse of someone caught in a transparent lie? The culprit in this incident is **transience:** *forgetting what occurs with the passage of time*. Transience occurs during the storage phase of memory, after an experience has been encoded and before it is retrieved. You've already seen the workings of transience—rapid forgetting—in sensory storage and short-term storage. Transience also occurs in long-term storage, as illustrated dramatically by amnesic patients such as Greg and HM. But transience affects all our memories to some extent. To understand transience, we need to address some key questions: How quickly do our memories fade over time? What kinds of information are we most likely to forget as time passes?

The psychological study of transience dates to the late 1870s, when a young German philosopher named Hermann Ebbinghaus measured his own memory for lists of nonsense syllables at different delays after studying them (Ebbinghaus, 1885/1964). The first researcher to study memory, Ebbinghaus charted his recall of nonsense syllables over time, creating the forgetting curve shown in **FIGURE 5.14**. on the next page. Ebbinghaus noted a rapid drop-off in retention during the first few tests, followed by a slower rate of forgetting on later tests—a general pattern confirmed by many subsequent memory

TRANSIENCE Forgetting what occurs with the passage of time.

President Clinton hugs Monica Lewinsky as he greets the crowd at a public appearance. Clinton's claims to have forgotten several incidents related to their affair may be an example of transience.

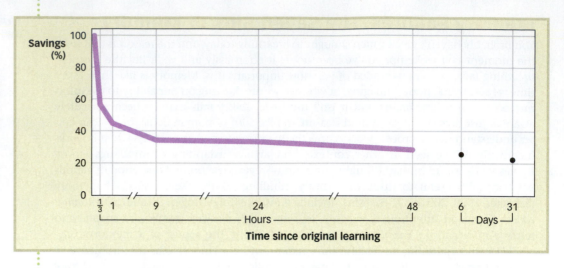

Figure 5.14 **The Curve of Forgetting** Hermann Ebbinghaus measured his retention at various delay intervals after he studied lists of nonsense syllables. Retention was measured in percent savings, that is, the percentage of time needed to relearn the list compared to the time needed to learn it initially.

Hermann Ebbinghaus (1850–1909), a German philosopher and psychologist, conducted some of the first scientific studies of memory. Ebbinghaus trained himself to memorize lists of nonsense syllables, then kept track of how long he could retain the information. Ebbinghaus's research revealed a great deal about the nature of remembering and forgetting.

researchers (Wixted & Ebbesen, 1991). This consistent finding shows that memories don't fade at a constant rate as time passes; most forgetting happens soon after an event occurs, with increasingly less forgetting as more time passes.

Memory doesn't just erode with the passage of time: The quality of our memories also changes. At early time points on the forgetting curve—minutes, hours, and days—memory preserves a relatively detailed record, allowing us to reproduce the past with reasonable if not perfect accuracy. But with the passing of time, we increasingly rely on our general memories for what usually happens and attempt to reconstruct the details by inference and even sheer guesswork. Transience involves a gradual switch from specific to more general memories (Brewer, 1996; Eldridge, Barnard, & Bekerian, 1994; Thompson et al., 1996). These findings illuminate President Clinton's memory lapse. The government attorney might have been appropriately skeptical had Clinton claimed to have entirely forgotten an important meeting with Vernon Jordan three weeks after it happened. But Clinton's confusion about the details of that meeting—whether Lewinsky spoke to Jordan on the telephone or face-to-face—is exactly the sort of confusion that we would expect based on both naturalistic and laboratory studies.

There's an important research basis for these conclusions as well. After Ebbinghaus developed his nonsense syllable task, many researchers thought that was a dandy way of studying memory. By stripping the to-be-remembered information of all meaning, the *process* of remembering and forgetting could be examined, uncontaminated by any meaning associated with the information itself. One researcher who disagreed with that approach did some pioneering work that addresses transience. Sir Frederick Bartlett (1932) asked British research participants to read a brief Native American folktale that had odd imagery and unfamiliar plots in it and then recount it as best they could after 15 minutes and sometimes after longer periods. The readers made interesting but understandable errors, often eliminating details that didn't make sense to them or adding elements to make the story more coherent. As the specifics of the story slipped away, the general meaning of the events stayed in memory but usually with elaborations and embellishments that were consistent with the readers' worldview. Because the story was unfamiliar to the readers, they raided their stores of general information and patched together a reasonable recollection of what *probably* happened.

Why does transience happen? Do details of experience simply disappear or decay as time passes? The simple answer is yes. In a study of memory for Spanish vocabulary acquired by English speakers during high school or college courses, participants were tested for retention of Spanish at different times (ranging from 1 year to 50 years) after the students stopped taking Spanish courses (Bahrick, 1984, 2000). There was a rapid drop-off in memory for the Spanish vocabulary during the first three years after the students' last class, followed by tiny losses in later years. But research suggests that the decay caused by the mere passage of time is not nearly as important as *what* happens as time passes (**FIGURE 5.15**). As time goes by, new experiences occur and new memories are created, and these new memories can interfere with our retrieval of old ones.

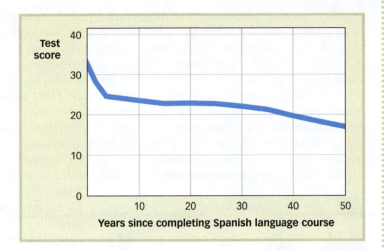

Years since completing Spanish language course

Figure 5.15 **The Decline of Spanish Language Skills** Language skills (measured here as scores on a language exam) decay rapidly for the first few years after instruction ends, followed by a much slower decline over the next few decades. Like many other memories, the knowledge of Spanish is transient unless it is rehearsed or remains actively used (Bahrick, 1984, 2000).

Retroactive interference occurs when *later learning impairs memory for information acquired earlier* (Postman & Underwood, 1973). If you carry out the same activities at work each day, by the time Friday rolls around, it may be difficult to remember what you did on Monday because later activities blend in with earlier ones. **Proactive interference**, in contrast, refers to situations in which *earlier learning impairs memory for information acquired later.* If you use the same parking lot each day at work or school, you've probably gone out to find your car and then stood there confused by the memories of having parked it on previous days.

RETROACTIVE INTERFERENCE Situations in which later learning impairs memory for information acquired earlier.

PROACTIVE INTERFERENCE Situations in which earlier learning impairs memory for information acquired later.

ABSENTMINDEDNESS A lapse in attention that results in memory failure.

Absentmindedness

The great cellist Yo-Yo Ma put his treasured $2.5 million instrument in the trunk of a taxicab in Manhattan and then rode to his destination. After a 10-minute trip, he paid the driver and left the cab, forgetting his cello. Minutes later, Ma realized what he had done and called the police. Fortunately, they tracked down the taxi and recovered the instrument within hours (Finkelstein, 1999). But how had the celebrated cellist forgotten about something so important that had occurred only 10 minutes earlier? Transience is not a likely culprit. If someone had reminded Mr. Ma about his instrument, he surely would have recalled where he had put it. This information had not disappeared from his memory (which is why he was able to tell the police where the cello was). Instead, Yo-Yo Ma was a victim of **absentmindedness**, which is *a lapse in attention that results in memory failure.*

What makes people absentminded? Attention plays a vital role in encoding information into long-term memory. In studies of "divided attention," research partici-pants are given materials to remember, such as a list of words, a story, or a series of pictures. At the same time, they are required to perform an additional task that draws their attention away from the mate-rial. For example, in one study, participants listened to lists of 15 words for a later mem-ory test (Craik et al., 1996). They were allowed to pay full attention to some of the lists, but while they heard other lists, they simultaneously viewed a visual display con-taining four boxes and pressed different keys to indicate where an asterisk was appearing and disappearing. On a later test, participants recalled far fewer words from the list they had heard while their atten-tion was divided.

Yo-Yo Ma with his $2.5 million cello. The famous cellist lost it when he absentmindedly forgot that he'd placed the instrument in a taxi's trunk minutes earlier.

Many everyday instances of absentmindedness probably result from a kind of "divided attention" that occurs frequently in our daily lives. Mentally consumed with planning for a psychology test the next day, you might place your keys in an unusual spot as you are reading over your notes. Because your attention was focused on the test and not your keys, you do not encode where you put the keys. So, you later have no memory of the incident and must frantically search before finding the keys. Attentional lapses that lead to absentminded forgetting are particularly common during routine activities, such as driving or typing, that do not require elaborative encoding. When you first learn to drive a car, you pay careful attention to every step of the activity. As your skill increases with practice, you rely more and more on procedural memory, and less and less attention is required to perform the same tasks (Anderson & Fincham, 1994; Logan,

1988). Most experienced drivers, for example, are familiar with the unsettling experience of cruising along at 65 miles per hour on a six-lane interstate and suddenly realizing that they have no recollection of the road for the past 5 miles. Experienced drivers rely on the well-learned skills that allow them to drive safely even when on "automatic." Absorbed with other concerns, they remember nothing of it, until they face a prosecutor.

Talking on a cell phone while driving is a common occurrence of divided attention in everyday life. This can be dangerous, and an increasing number of states have banned the practice.

What happens in the brain when attention is divided? In one study, volunteers tried to learn a list of word pairs while researchers scanned their brains with positron emission tomography (PET) (Shallice et al., 1994). Some people simultaneously performed a task that took little attention (they moved a bar the same way over and over), whereas other people simultaneously performed a task that took a great deal of attention (they moved a bar over and over but in a novel, unpredictable way each time). The researchers observed less activity in the participants' lower left frontal lobe when their attention was divided. As you saw earlier, greater activity in the lower left frontal region during encoding is associated with better memory. Dividing attention, then, prevents the lower left frontal lobe from playing its normal role in elaborative encoding, and the result is absentminded forgetting.

Neuroimaging evidence also links the lower left frontal lobe with automatic behavior. Researchers performed PET scans while they showed volunteers a series of common nouns and asked them to generate related verbs (Raichle et al., 1994). For example, when shown the noun *dog,* participants might generate the verb *bark* or *walk.* When the volunteers first performed this task, it was associated with extensive activity in the lower left frontal lobe (and many other parts of the brain). This activity probably reflected a kind of elaborative encoding related to thinking about properties of dogs and the kinds of actions they perform. Remembering dog facts requires a bit of mental work. But as the volunteers practiced the task repeatedly with the same nouns and generated the verbs more quickly and automatically, activity in the lower left frontal lobe gradually decreased. This suggests that automatic behaviors, which are the cause of many absentminded errors, are associated with low levels of left prefrontal activity.

Many errors of absentmindedness involve forgetting to carry out actions that we planned to do in the future. You may think of memory as a link to the past, but in everyday life, you rely on memory to deal with the future as much as the past. On any given day, you need to remember the times and places that your classes meet, you need to remember with whom and where you are having lunch, you need to remember which grocery items to pick up for dinner, and you need

"It says, 'Please disregard this reminder if your check is in the mail.'"

to remember which page of this book you were on when you fell asleep. Forgetting these things would leave you uneducated, friendless, hungry, and with an unsettling desire to start reading this book from the beginning. In other words, you have to remember to remember, and this is called **prospective memory**, or *remembering to do things in the future* (Einstein & McDaniel, 1990).

Failures of prospective memory are a major source of absentmindedness. Avoiding these mindbugs often requires having a cue available at the moment you need to remember to carry out an action. For example, air traffic controllers must sometimes postpone an action but remember to carry it out later, such as when they cannot immediately grant a pilot's request to change altitude. In a simulated air traffic control experiment, researchers provided controllers with electronic signals to remind them to carry out a deferred request 1 minute later. The reminders were made available either during the 1-minute waiting period, at the time the controller needed to act on the deferred request, or both. Compared with a condition in which no reminder was provided, controllers' memory for the deferred action improved only when the reminder was available at the time needed for retrieval. Providing the reminder during the waiting period did not help (Vortac, Edwards, and Manning, 1995). An early reminder, then, is no reminder at all.

Blocking

Look at the definitions in **TABLE 5.1** and try to think of the correct word for each one. Chances are that you will recall some of the words and not others. Some of the unrecalled words will cause you to draw a complete blank, but others will feel as though they are "on the tip of your tongue." For example, you may remember the first letter or two

Many people rely on memory aids such as calendars—and, more recently, personal digital assistants (PDAs)—to help them remember to perform a particular activity in the future.

ONLY HUMAN

MONEY TO BURN Chef Albert Grabham of the New House Hotel in Wales hid the restaurant's New Year's Eve earnings in the oven. He failed to remember that when he lit the same oven to prepare New Year's Day lunch.

Table 5.1	**Inducing a Tip-of-the-Tongue Experience**

Instructions

Below are the dictionary definitions of 10 uncommon words. Please look at each definition and try to think of the word it defines. If you can't think of the word but it seems like it's on the "tip of your tongue," try this: Try to guess the first letter of the word, or try to think of one or two words that sound similar to the one you're trying to find. The answers are given below. No peeking!

Definitions

1. A blood feud in which members of the family of a murdered person try to kill the murderer or members of his family.

2. A protecting charm to ward off spirits.

3. A dark, hard, glassy volcanic rock.

4. A person who makes maps.

5. A building used for public worship by Moslems.

6. An Egyptian ornament in the shape of a beetle.

7. The staff of Hermes, symbol of a physician or of the medical corps.

8. A sword with a short curved blade, used by the Turks and Arabs.

9. House of rest for travelers or for the terminally ill, often kept by a religious order.

10. Something out of keeping with the times in which it exists.

Answers: 1. Vendetta, 2. Amulet, 3. Obsidian, 4. Cartographer, 5. Mosque, 6. Scarab, 7. Caduceus, 8. Scimitar, 9. Hospice, 10. Anachronism

PROSPECTIVE MEMORY
Remembering to do things in the future.

of the word and feel certain that it is rolling around in your head *somewhere* but that you just can't retrieve it at the moment. This problem is called **blocking,** which is *a failure to retrieve information that is available in memory even though you are trying to produce it.* The sought-after information has been encoded and stored, and a cue is available that would ordinarily trigger recall of it. The information has not faded from memory, and you aren't forgetting to retrieve it. Rather, you are experiencing a full-blown retrieval failure, which makes this memory mindbug especially frustrating. It seems absolutely clear that you should be able to produce the information you seek, but the fact of the matter is that you can't. How can you know you know something but not know what it is?

The most common type of blocking is known as the **tip-of-the-tongue experience**, which is *the temporary inability to retrieve information that is stored in memory, accompanied by the feeling that you are on the verge of recovering the information.* The tip-of-the-tongue state has been described as "a mild torment, something like [being] on the brink of a sneeze" (Brown & McNeil, 1966, p. 326). Researchers have found that when people are in tip-of-the-tongue states, they often know something about the item they can't recall, such as the meaning of a word. For example, knowing the number of syllables in a blocked word is very common. People frequently know the first letter of the blocked word, less frequently know the final letter, and even less often know the middle letters. During tip-of-the-tongue states, people also frequently come up with words that are related in sound or meaning to the sought-after item. If you blocked on any of the items in Table 5.1, you might have thought of a word that was similar to the one you were seeking even though you were sure that it was not the blocked word itself.

When experimenters induced tip-of-the-tongue states by playing participants theme songs from 1950s and 1960s television shows and asking for the names of the shows, people who were blocked on *The Munsters* often came up with the similarly themed *The Addams Family*. Likewise, some of those who blocked on *Leave It to Beaver* thought of *Dennis the Menace* (Riefer, Kevari, & Kramer, 1995) (**FIGURE 5.16**). If these titles mean anything at all to you, then you are either middle-aged or watching too much *Nick-at-Nite*.

Blocking and tip-of-the-tongue states occur especially often for the names of people and places (Cohen, 1990; Valentine, Brennen, & Brédart, 1996). Why? Because their links to related concepts and knowledge are weaker than for common names. That somebody's last name is Baker doesn't tell us much about the person, but saying that he *is* a baker does. To illustrate this point, researchers showed people pictures of cartoon and comic strip characters, some with descriptive names that highlight key features of the character (e.g., Grumpy, Snow White, Scrooge) and others with arbitrary names (e.g., Aladdin, Mary Poppins, Pinocchio) (Brédart and Valentine, 1998). Even though the two types of names were equally familiar to participants in the experiment, they blocked less often on the descriptive names than on the arbitrary names.

Figure 5.16 **Blocking** Suppose you were asked to name a classic television comedy from hearing the show's theme music. The tip-of-the-tongue experience might cause you to block the Munsters, pictured on the left, for their close counterparts the Addams Family, on the right.

Although it's frustrating when it occurs, blocking is a relatively infrequent event for most of us. However, it occurs more often as we grow older, and it is a very common complaint among people in their sixties and seventies (Burke et al., 1991). Even more striking, some brain-damaged patients live in a nearly perpetual tip-of-the-tongue state. One patient could recall the names of only 2 of 40 famous people when she saw their photographs, compared to 25 out of 40 for healthy volunteers in the control group (Semenza & Zettin, 1989). Yet she could still recall correctly the occupations of 32 of these people—the same number as healthy people could recall. This case and similar ones have given researchers important clues about what parts of the brain are involved in retrieving proper names. Name blocking usually results from damage to parts of the left temporal lobe on the surface of the cortex, most often as a result of a stroke. In fact, studies that show strong activation of regions within the temporal lobe when people recall proper names support this idea (Damasio et al., 1996; Tempini et al., 1998).

Memory Misattribution

Shortly after the devastating 1995 bombing of the federal building in Oklahoma City, police set about searching for two suspects they called John Doe 1 and John Doe 2. John Doe 1 turned out to be Timothy McVeigh, who was quickly apprehended and later convicted of the crime and sentenced to death. The FBI believed that John Doe 2 had accompanied McVeigh when he rented a van from Elliott's Body Shop in Junction City, Kansas, 2 days before the bombing, but the FBI never found John Doe 2. They later learned that John Doe 2 was a product of the memory of Tom Kessinger, a mechanic at Elliott's Body Shop who was present when McVeigh rented the van. He recalled seeing two men that day and described them in great detail. Kessinger's description of John Doe 2, however, is a near perfect fit to a man he encountered at Elliott's Body Shop a day later, when Army Sergeant Michael Hertig and his friend Private Todd Bunting also rented a van in Kessinger's presence. Hertig, like McVeigh, was tall and fair. Bunting was shorter and stockier, was dark haired, wore a blue-and-white cap, and had a tattoo beneath his left sleeve—a match to the description of John Doe 2. Tom Kessinger had confused his recollections of men he had seen on separate days in the same place. He was a victim of **memory misattribution:** *assigning a recollection or an idea to the wrong source* (**FIGURE 5.17**).

Memory misattribution errors are some of the primary causes of eyewitness misidentifications. The memory researcher Donald Thomson was accused of rape based on the victim's detailed recollection of his face, but he was eventually cleared when it turned out he had an airtight alibi. At the time of the rape, Thompson was giving a live television interview on the subject of distorted memories! The victim had been watching the show just before she was assaulted and misattributed her memory of Thomson's face to the rapist (Schacter, 1996; Thomson, 1988).

BLOCKING A failure to retrieve information that is available in memory even though you are trying to produce it.

TIP-OF-THE-TONGUE EXPERIENCE The temporary inability to retrieve information that is stored in memory, accompanied by the feeling that you are on the verge of recovering the information.

MEMORY MISATTRIBUTION Assigning a recollection or an idea to the wrong source.

DAVID GLASS/AP PHOTO

FBI/THE OKLAHOMAN/AP PHOTO

Figure 5.17 **Memory Misattribution** In 1995, the Murrah Federal Building in Oklahoma City was bombed in an act of terrorism. The police sketch shows "John Doe 2," who was originally thought to have been culprit Timothy McVeigh's partner in the bombing. It was later determined that the witness had confused his memories of different men whom he had encountered at Elliott's Body Shop on different days.

Doonesbury

SOURCE MEMORY Recall of when, where, and how information was acquired.

FALSE RECOGNITION A feeling of familiarity about something that hasn't been encountered before.

Part of memory is knowing where our memories came from. This is known as **source memory:** *recall of when, where, and how information was acquired* (Johnson, Hashtroudi, & Lindsay, 1993; Schacter, Harbluk, & McLachlan, 1984). People sometimes correctly recall a fact they learned earlier or accurately recognize a person or object they have seen before but misattribute the source of this knowledge. Experiments have shown, for instance, that people can remember perfectly well that they saw a previously presented face yet misremember the time or place that they saw it, as happened to Tom Kessinger and the rape victim in the Donald Thomson incident (Davies, 1988). Such misattribution could be the cause of déjà vu experiences, where you suddenly feel that you have been in a situation before even though you can't recall any details. A present situation that is similar to a past experience may trigger a general sense of familiarity that is mistakenly attributed to having been in the exact situation previously (Reed, 1988).

Patients with damage to the frontal lobes are especially prone to memory misattribution errors (Schacter et al., 1984; Shimamura & Squire, 1987). This is probably because the frontal lobes play a significant role in effortful retrieval processes, which are required to dredge up the correct source of a memory. These patients sometimes produce bizarre misattributions. In 1991, a British photographer in his mid-40s known as MR was overcome with feelings of familiarity about people he didn't know. He kept asking his wife whether each new passing stranger was "somebody"—a screen actor, television newsperson, or local celebrity. MR's feelings were so intense that he often could not resist approaching strangers and asking whether they were indeed famous celebrities. When given formal tests, MR recognized the faces of actual celebrities as accurately as did healthy volunteers in the control group. But MR also "recognized" more than 75% of unfamiliar faces, whereas healthy controls hardly ever did. Neurological exams revealed that MR suffered from multiple sclerosis, which had caused damage to his frontal lobes (Ward et al., 1999).

Psychologists call the type of memory misattribution made by MR **false recognition**, which is *a feeling of familiarity about something that hasn't been encountered before*. We are all vulnerable to false recognition.

Patient MR probably would have felt that the unfamiliar man on the left is as famous as professional basketball player Shaquille O'Neal (Ward et al., 1999).

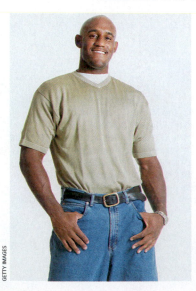

Take the following test and there is a good chance that you will experience false recognition for yourself. First study the two lists of words presented in **TABLE 5.2** by reading each word for about 1 second. When you are done, return to the paragraph you were reading for more instructions, but don't look back at the table!

Now take a recognition test by indicating which of these words—*taste, bread, needle, king, sweet, thread*—appeared on the lists you just studied. If you think that *taste* and *thread* were on the lists you studied, you're right. And if you think that *bread* and *king* weren't on those lists, you're also right. But if you think that *needle* or *sweet* appeared on the lists, you're dead wrong.

Most people make exactly the same mistake, claiming with confidence that they saw *needle* and *sweet* on the list. Experiments have shown that undergraduates claim to recognize *needle* and *sweet* about as often (84%) as they claim to recognize words that really were on the list (86%). (Undergraduates claimed to recognize unrelated words such as *bread* or *king* only 20% of the time.) This type of false recognition occurs because all the words in the lists are associated with *needle* or *sweet*. Seeing each word in the study list activates related words. Because *needle* and *sweet* are related to all of the associates, they become more activated than other words—so highly activated that only minutes later, people swear that they actually studied the words. But they are misattributing a powerful feeling of familiarity to having seen (or heard) the word (Deese, 1959; Roediger & McDermott, 1995, 2000).

Brain scanning studies using PET and fMRI have shown one reason why people are so easily fooled into "remembering" words such as *needle* and *sweet*: Many of the same brain regions are active during false recognition and true recognition, including the hippocampus (Cabeza et al., 2001; Schacter et al., 1996b; Slotnick & Schacter, 2004). However, there are some differences in brain activity. For example, a PET scanning experiment revealed that a part of the auditory cortex (on the surface of the temporal lobe) showed greater activity for words that had actually been heard earlier in the experiment than for associated words such as *needle* or *sweet,* which had not been heard previously (Schacter et al., 1996b). A later fMRI study showed that true recognition of previously studied visual shapes produced more activity in parts of the visual cortex than false recognition of new shapes that looked similar to those previously studied (Slotnick & Schacter, 2004) (**FIGURE 5.18**).

It is possible, however, to reduce or avoid false recognition by presenting distinctive information, such as a picture of *thread*, and encouraging participants to require specific recollections of seeing the picture before they say "yes" on a recognition test (Schacter, Israel, & Racine, 1999). Unfortunately, we do not always demand specific recollections before we say that we encountered a word in an

Table 5.2	False Recognition
Sour	Thread
Candy	Pin
Sugar	Eye
Bitter	Sewing
Good	Sharp
Taste	Point
Tooth	Prick
Nice	Thimble
Honey	Haystack
Soda	Pain
Chocolate	Hurt
Heart	Injection
Cake	Syringe
Tart	Cloth
Pie	Knitting

Figure 5.18 Hippocampal Activity during True and False Recognition Many brain regions show similar activation during true and false recognition, including the hippocampus. The figure shows results from an fMRI study of true and false recognition of visual shapes (Slotnick & Schacter, 2004). (a) A plot showing the activity level in the strength of the fMRI signal from the hippocampus over time. This shows that after a few seconds, there is comparable activation for true recognition of previously studied shapes (red line) and false recognition of similar shapes that were not presented (yellow line). Both true and false recognition show increased hippocampal activity compared with correctly classifying unrelated shapes as new (purple line). (b) A region of the left hippocampus.

(b) Slotnick & Schacter, *Nature Neuroscience,* 2004, 7(61), p. 669.

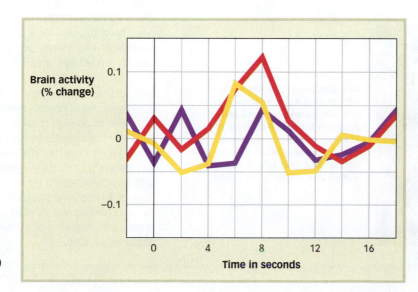

(a)

Brain activity (% change)

Time in seconds

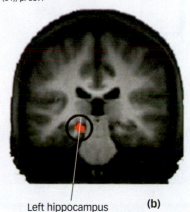

Left hippocampus   (b)

SUGGESTIBILITY The tendency to incorporate misleading information from external sources into personal recollections.

experiment or—more importantly—make a positive identification of a suspect. When people experience a strong sense of familiarity about a person, object, or event but lack specific recollections, a potentially dangerous recipe for memory misattribution is in place. Understanding this point may be a key to reducing the dangerous consequences of misattribution in eyewitness testimony (see the Real World box).

{ THE REAL WORLD } Deadly Misattributions

ON JULY 25, 1984, A 9-YEAR-OLD GIRL WAS found dead in the woods near Baltimore after being brutally beaten and sexually assaulted. A witness identified 23-year-old Kirk Bloodsworth as the killer, based on a sketch police generated from five other witness accounts. Although Bloodsworth passionately maintained his innocence, a jury convicted him of first-degree murder and the judge sentenced him to death. After Bloodsworth spent 2 years on death row, the sentence was reduced to life in prison on an appeal. In 1993, DNA testing revealed that Bloodsworth was not the source of incriminating semen stains in the victim's underwear. He was released from prison after serving 9 years, later received a full pardon, and returned to his quiet life as a crab fisherman (Chebium, 2000; Connors, Lundregan, Miller, & Mc-Ewen, 1997; Wells et al., 1998). In addition to losing nearly a decade of his young adulthood, Bloodsworth's mother did not live to see him freed: She died of a heart attack several months before his release.

Bloodsworth is not alone. The first 40 cases in which DNA evidence led to the release of wrongfully imprisoned individuals revealed that 36 of the convictions—

90%—were based partly or entirely on mistaken eyewitness identification (Wells et al., 1998). Fifty separate eyewitnesses were involved in these cases; they were all confident in their memories but seriously mistaken. These statistics are especially troubling because eyewitness testimony is frequently relied on in the courtroom: Each year more than 75,000 criminal trials are decided on the basis of eyewitness testimony (Ross et al., 1994, p. 918). Why do memory misattribution errors occur, and what can be done to avoid them?

Common lineup identification practices may often promote misattribution because people are encouraged to rely on general familiarity (Wells et al., 1998, 2000). In standard lineup procedures, witnesses are shown several suspects; after seeing all of them, they attempt to identify the culprit. Under these conditions, witnesses tend to rely on "relative judgments": They choose the person who, relative to the others in the lineup, looks most like the suspect. The problem is that even when the suspect is *not in* the lineup, witnesses still tend to choose the person who looks most like the suspect. Witnesses rely on general similarities between a face in a lineup and the

actual culprit, even when they lack specific recollections of the culprit. There are ways to minimize reliance on relative judgments: Ask witnesses to make a "thumbs-up or thumbs-down" decision about each suspect immediately after seeing each face instead of waiting until all suspects' faces have been displayed (Wells et al., 1998, 2000). This procedure encourages people to examine their memories more carefully and evaluate whether the pictured suspect matches the details of their recollections.

One encouraging development is that law enforcement officials are listening to what psychologists have to say about the construction of lineups and other identification procedures that could promote inaccurate identification. In early 1998, then attorney general Janet Reno formed a working group of psychologists, police, and attorneys to develop guidelines for collecting eyewitness evidence. This group eventually published a set of guidelines based on rigorous psychological studies that provide law enforcement officials with specific steps to take when questioning witnesses or constructing lineups in order to reduce the likelihood of eyewitness errors (Wells et al., 2000).

Kirk Bloodsworth spent 9 years behind bars for a crime he didn't commit. He was released after DNA evidence led to the reversal of his conviction based on mistaken eyewitness testimony. Here he holds up the book that tells his story, by author and attorney Tim Junkin.

Suggestibility

On October 4, 1992, an El Al cargo plane crashed into an apartment building in a southern suburb of Amsterdam, killing 39 residents and all four members of the airline crew. The disaster dominated news in the Netherlands for days as people viewed footage of the crash scene and read about the catastrophe. Ten months later, Dutch psychologists asked a simple question of university students: "Did you see the television film of the moment the plane hit the apartment building?" Fifty-five percent answered "yes." In a follow-up study, 66% responded affirmatively (Crombag et al., 1996). The students also recalled details concerning the speed and angle of the plane when it hit the building and what happened to the body of the plane right after the collision. All of this might seem perfectly normal except for one key fact: There was no television film of the moment when the plane actually crashed. The researchers had asked a suggestive question that implied that television film of the crash had been shown. Respondents may have viewed television film of the post-crash scene, and they may have read, imagined, or talked about what might have happened when the plane hit the building, but they most definitely did not see it. The suggestive question led participants to misattribute information from these or other sources to a film that did not exist. **Suggestibility** is the *tendency to incorporate misleading information from external sources into personal recollections.* Suggestibility is closely related to memory misattribution in the sense that converting suggestions into inaccurate memories must involve misattribution. Unlike suggestibility, however, memory misattribution often occurs in the absence of specific suggestions.

Research evidence of suggestibility abounds. For example, in one study, Elizabeth Loftus and her colleagues showed participants a videotape of an automobile accident involving a white sports car (Loftus, 1975; Loftus et al., 1978). Some participants were then asked how fast the car was going when it passed the barn. Nearly 20% of these individuals later recalled seeing a barn in the videotape—even though there was no barn (participants who weren't asked about a barn almost never recalled seeing one). In later experiments, Loftus showed that people who received a misleading suggestion that they had earlier seen a car stop at a yield sign (they had actually seen the car at a stop sign) often claimed later to remember seeing a yield sign. Misleading suggestions do not eliminate the original memory (Berkerian & Bowers, 1983; McCloskey & Zaragoza, 1985). Instead, they cause participants to make source memory errors: They have difficulty recollecting whether they actually saw a yield sign or only learned about it later.

If misleading details can be implanted in people's memories, is it also possible to suggest entire episodes that never occurred? Could you be convinced, for example, that you had once been lost in a shopping mall as a child or spilled a bowl of punch at a wedding—even though these events never actually happened? The answer seems to be "yes" (Loftus, 1993, 2003). In one study, the research participant, a teenager named Chris, was asked by his older brother, Jim, to try to remember the time Chris had been lost in a shopping mall at age 5. He initially recalled nothing, but after several days, Chris produced a detailed recollection of the event. He recalled that he "felt so scared I would never see my family again" and remembered that a kindly old man wearing a flannel shirt found him crying (Loftus, 1993, p. 532). But according to Jim and other family members, Chris was never lost in a shopping mall. Of 24 participants in a larger study on implanted memories, approximately 25% falsely remembered being lost as a child in a shopping mall or in a similar public place (Loftus & Pickrell, 1995).

In 1992, an El Al cargo plane crashed into an apartment building in a suburb of Amsterdam. When Dutch psychologists asked students if they'd seen the television film of the plane crashing, most said they had. In fact, no such footage exists (Crombag, Wagenaar, & Koppen, 1996).

In a classic experiment by Elizabeth Loftus, people were shown a videotape of a car at a stop sign. Those who later received a misleading suggestion that the car had stopped at a yield sign often claimed they had seen the car at a yield sign (Loftus, Miller, & Burns, 1978).

Other researchers have also successfully implanted false memories of childhood experiences in a significant minority of participants (Hyman & Billings, 1998; Hyman & Pentland, 1996). In one study, college students were asked about several childhood events that, according to their parents, actually happened. But they were also asked about an event that never happened. For instance, the students were asked if they remembered a wedding reception they attended when they were 5, running around with some other kids and bumping into a table and spilling the punch bowl on the parents of the bride. Students remembered nearly all of the true events and initially reported no memory for the false events. However, with repeated probing, approximately 20% to 40% of the participants in different experimental conditions eventually came to describe some memory of the false event.

People develop false memories in response to suggestions for some of the same reasons memory misattribution occurs. We do not store all the details of our experiences in memory, making us vulnerable to accepting suggestions about what might have happened or should have happened. In addition, visual imagery plays an important role in constructing false memories (Goff & Roediger, 1998). Asking people to imagine an event like spilling punch all over the bride's parents at a wedding increases the likelihood that they will develop a false memory of it (Hyman & Pentland, 1996).

Imagery also had a dramatic effect on false memories in a study that examined people's earliest recollections. What is the first thing you can recall from childhood? For most of us, first memories date from 3 to 5 years of age. People generally cannot remember incidents that occurred before they were 2 years old, probably because the brain regions necessary for episodic memory are not yet fully mature (Nadel & Zola-Morgan, 1984; Schacter & Moscovitch, 1984). But when researchers introduced a suggestive procedure by asking participants to visualize themselves as toddlers, they got reports of earliest memories as dating to approximately 18 months, well before the presumed end of childhood amnesia (Malinoski & Lynn, 1999; for more on childhood amnesia, see the Where Do You Stand? box on pp. 204–205). In fact, one-third of those exposed to the suggestive procedure reported an earliest recollection from prior to 12 months, whereas nobody did so without visualization suggestions.

So is this what happens when adults suddenly develop memories of childhood events that involve disturbing behavior or even crimes that have gone unpunished? This question was at the center of a controversy that arose during the 1980s and 1990s concerning the accuracy of childhood memories that people recall during psychotherapy. Suggestibility played an important role in the controversy. Diana Halbrooks was a happily married woman from Texas who started psychotherapy in the late 1980s. As her treatment progressed, she began recalling disturbing incidents from her childhood—for example, that her mother had tried to kill her and that her father had abused her sexually. Although her parents denied that these events had ever occurred, her therapist encouraged her to believe in the reality of her memories. Had Halbrooks retrieved terrible memories of events that had actually occurred, or were the memories inaccurate, perhaps the result of suggestive probing during psychotherapy?

In the early 1990s, more and more American families found themselves coping with similar stories. Educated middle-class women (and some men) entered psychotherapy for depression or related problems, only to emerge with recovered memories of previously forgotten childhood sexual abuse, typically perpetrated by fathers and sometimes by mothers. Families and psychologists were split by these controversies. Patients believed their memories were real, and many therapists supported those beliefs, but accused parents contended that the alleged abuses had never happened and that they were instead the products of false memories. A number of prominent memory researchers, as well as some therapists, raised doubts about the accuracy of recovered memories, noting that memory is susceptible to suggestion and distortion (Lindsay & Read, 1994; Loftus, 1993). But others questioned whether people would ever falsely recall such a traumatic event as childhood sexual abuse (Freyd, 1996; Herman, 1992).

Who was right? A few recovered memories of childhood abuse have been corroborated and appear to be accurate (Gleaves, Smith, Butler, & Spiegel, 2004; Pendergrast, 1995). In these cases, individuals who experienced an episode (or episodes) of abuse did not think about the incident until they were reminded of it years later. For example, a Massachusetts man named Frank Fitzpatrick suddenly recalled one day that he had been abused by a priest as a child and later recorded the priest confessing to what he had done (Pendergrast, 1995).

Several kinds of evidence suggest that many recovered memories are inaccurate. First, some people have recovered highly implausible memories of being abused repeatedly during bizarre practices in satanic cults, and yet there is no proof of these practices or even that the cults exist (Pendergrast, 1995; Wright, 1994). Second, a number of the techniques used by psychotherapists to try to pull up forgotten childhood memories are clearly suggestive. A survey of 145 therapists in the United States revealed that approximately 1 in 3 tried to help patients remember childhood sexual abuse by using hypnosis or by encouraging them to imagine incidents that might or might not have actually happened (Poole et al., 1995). Yet imagining past events and hypnosis can help create false memories (Garry, Lindsay, Memor, & Boll, 1996; Hyman & Pentland, 1996; McConkey, Barnier, & Sheehan, 1998).

Finally, a growing number of patients eventually retracted their recovered memories after leaving therapy or returned to their families (McHugh, Lief, Freyd, & Fetkewicz, 2004). This is just what happened to Diana Halbrooks: She stopped therapy and eventually came to realize that the "memories" she had recovered were inaccurate. By the end of the 1990s, the number of new cases of disputed recovered memories of childhood sexual abuse had slowed to a trickle (McHugh et al., 2004). This probably occurred, at least in part, because some of the therapists who had been using suggestive procedures stopped doing so (McNally, 2003).

Bias

In 2000, the outcome of a very close presidential race between George W. Bush and Al Gore was decided by the Supreme Court 5 weeks after the election had taken place. At issue were dangling chads and recounts in Florida, all of which led to a high degree of uncertainty for the candidates and voters alike. Eventually, Al Gore conceded the election on December 15, 2000, sending George Bush to the first of his two terms in office.

The day after the election (when the result was still in doubt), supporters of Bush and Gore were asked to predict how happy they would be after the outcome of the election was determined (Wilson, Meyers, & Gilbert, 2003). These same respondents reported how happy they felt with the outcome on the day after Al Gore conceded. And 4 months later, the participants recalled how happy they had been right after the election was decided. In short, both Bush and Gore supporters predicted their future happiness, reported their current happiness, and recalled their previous happiness with the election outcomes.

Bush supporters, who eventually enjoyed a positive result (their candidate took office), were understandably happy on the day after the Supreme Court's decision. However, their retrospective accounts *over*estimated how happy they were at the time. Conversely, Gore supporters were not pleased with the outcome. But

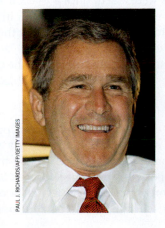
PAUL J. RICHARDS/AFP/GETTY IMAGES

DOUG MILLS/AP PHOTO

How happy do you think you'd be if the candidate you supported won an election? Do you think you'd accurately remember your level of happiness if you recalled it several months later? Chances are good that bias in the memory process would alter your recollection of your previous happiness. Indeed, 4 months after they heard the outcome of the 2000 presidential election, Bush supporters *over*estimated how happy they were, while Gore supporters *under*estimated how happy they were.

BIAS The distorting influences of present knowledge, beliefs, and feelings on recollection of previous experiences.

SHOOT/AGE FOTOSTOCK

The way each member of this happy couple recalls earlier feelings toward the other depends on how each currently views their relationship.

when polled 4 months after the election was decided, Gore supporters *under*estimated how happy they actually were at the time of the result. In both groups, recollections of happiness were at odds with existing reports of their actual happiness at the time (Wilson et al., 2003).

These results illustrate the problem of **bias**, which is *the distorting influences of present knowledge, beliefs, and feelings on recollection of previous experiences.* Sometimes what people remember from their pasts says less about what actually happened than about what they think, feel, or believe now. Both Bush and Gore supporters re-scripted their memories of December 2000 to fit how they felt months afterward. Other researchers have also found that our current moods can bias our recall of past experiences (Bower, 1981; Eich, 1995). So, in addition to helping you recall actual sad memories (as you saw earlier in this chapter), a sad mood can also bias your recollections of experiences that may not have been so sad. Bias can influence memory in three ways: by altering the past to fit the present (*consistency bias*), by exaggerating differences between past and present (*change bias*), and by distorting the past to make us look better (*egocentric bias*).

Consistency Bias

In addition to moods, current knowledge and beliefs can produce biasing effects. Several researchers have described a *consistency bias,* in which people reconstruct the past to fit what they presently know or believe. One researcher asked people in 1973 to rate their attitudes toward a variety of controversial social issues, including legalization of marijuana, women's rights, and aid to minorities (Marcus, 1986). They were asked to make the same rating again in 1982 and also to indicate what their attitudes had been in 1973. Researchers found that participants' recollections of their 1973 attitudes in 1982 were more closely related to what they believed in 1982 than to what they had actually said in 1973.

The consistency bias is often quite striking in romantically involved couples. In a study of dating couples, participants were asked to evaluate themselves, their dating partner, and their relationship twice—first in an initial session and then again 2 months later (McFarland & Ross, 1987). During the second session, participants were also asked to recall their earlier evaluations. Researchers found that participants whose relationships had soured over time recalled their initial evaluations as more negative than they really were. However, when participants reported a positive or deeper relationship in the present, they also recalled having felt more liking or loving in the past.

Change Bias

Just as we sometimes exaggerate the similarity of the past and the present, we sometimes exaggerate the *difference* between what we feel or believe now and what we felt or believed in the past. In other words, *change biases* also occur. For example, most of us would like to believe that our romantic attachments grow stronger over time. In one study, dating couples were asked, once a year for 4 years, to assess the present quality of their relationships and to recall how they felt in past years (Sprecher, 1999). Couples who stayed together for the 4 years recalled that the strength of their love had increased since they last reported on it. Yet their actual ratings at the time did not show any increases in love and attachment. Objectively, the couples did not love each other more today than yesterday. But they did from the subjective perspective of memory.

Egocentric Bias

Sometimes we exaggerate the change between present and past in order make ourselves look good in retrospect, thus revealing a *self-enhancing* or *egocentric bias*. For example, students sometimes remember feeling more anxious before taking an exam than they actually reported at the time (Keuler & Safer, 1998), and blood donors sometimes recall being more nervous about giving blood than they actually were (Breckler, 1994). In both cases, change biases color memory and make people feel that they behaved more bravely or courageously than they actually did. Our memories for grades that we achieved in school also reflect an egocentric bias. Can you recall your grades from high school courses? Do you remember how many As and Ds appeared on your report card? Chances are that you will recall more of the good grades than the bad ones. When college students tried to remember high school grades and their memories were checked against actual transcripts, they were highly accurate for grades of A (89% correct) and extremely inaccurate for grades of D (29% correct) (Bahrick, Hall, & Berger, 1996). The students were remembering the past as they wanted it to be rather than the way it was.

Persistence

The artist Melinda Stickney-Gibson awoke in her Chicago apartment to the smell of smoke. She jumped out of bed and saw black plumes rising through cracks in the floor. Melinda tried to call the fire department, but the phone lines had already burned out. Raging flames had engulfed the entire building, and there was no chance to escape except by jumping from her third-floor window. Shortly after she crashed to the ground, the building exploded into a brilliant fireball. She lost all her possessions and her beloved dog, but she saved her own life. Alas, that life was never the same. Melinda became overwhelmed by memories of the fire and frequently could think of little else. Her paintings, which were previously bright, colorful abstractions, became dark meditations that included only black, orange, and ochre—the colors of the fire. When Melinda sat down in front of a blank canvas to start a new painting, her memories of that awful night intruded. She remembered the incident vividly for years, even after she had recovered physically from the injuries suffered in her fall (Schacter, 1996).

Melinda Stickney-Gibson's experiences illustrate memory's seventh and most deadly sin: **persistence,** or *the intrusive recollection of events that we wish we could forget.* Melinda's experience is far from unique: Persistence frequently occurs after disturbing or traumatic incidents, such as the fire that destroyed her home. Although being able to quickly call up memories is usually considered a good thing, in the case of persistence, that ability mutates into a bedeviling mindbug.

Controlled laboratory studies have revealed that emotional experiences tend to be better remembered than nonemotional ones. For instance, memory for unpleasant pictures, such as mutilated bodies, or pleasant ones, such as attractive men and women, is more accurate than for emotionally neutral pictures, such as household objects (Ochsner, 2000). Emotional arousal seems to focus our attention on the central features of an event. In one experiment, people who viewed an emotionally arousing sequence of slides involving a bloody car accident remembered more of the central themes and fewer peripheral details than people who viewed a nonemotional sequence (Christianson & Loftus, 1987).

Intrusive memories are undesirable consequences of the fact that emotional experiences generally lead to more vivid and enduring recollections than nonemotional experiences do. One line of evidence comes from the study of **flashbulb memories,** which are *detailed recollections of when and where we heard about shocking events.* In one study, all but 1 of 40 people who were questioned about the assassination of President John F. Kennedy in November 1963 reported specific, vivid recollections of when and where they heard the news (Brown & Kulik, 1977). It was as if a mental flashbulb had gone off and recorded the event. Many of us can remember where we were and how we heard about the September 11, 2001, terrorist attack on the World Trade Center and the Pentagon.

Several studies have shown that flashbulb memories are not always entirely accurate, but they are generally better remembered than mundane news events from the same time (Neisser & Harsch, 1992; Larsen, 1992). Enhanced retention of flashbulb memories is partly attributable to the emotional arousal elicited by events such as the

PERSISTENCE The intrusive recollection of events that we wish we could forget.

FLASHBULB MEMORIES Detailed recollections of when and where we heard about shocking events.

Some events are so emotionally charged, such as the Kennedy assassination and the terrorist attack on the World Trade Center, that we form unusually detailed memories of when and where we heard about them. These flashbulb memories generally persist much longer than memories for more ordinary events.

September 11 terrorist attacks and partly attributable to the fact that we tend to talk and think a lot about these experiences. Recall that elaborative encoding enhances memory: When we talk about flashbulb experiences, we elaborate on them and thus further increase their memorability (and decrease their accuracy).

Why do our brains succumb to persistence? A key player in the brain's response to emotional events is a small almond-shaped structure called the amygdala, shown in **FIGURE 5.19.** Buried deep in the inner regions of the temporal lobe, the amygdala is located next to the hippocampus but performs different functions. Damage to the amygdala does not result in a general memory deficit. Patients with amygdala damage, however, do not remember emotional events any better than nonemotional events (Cahill & McGaugh, 1998).

For example, consider what happened when people viewed a series of photographic slides that began with a mother walking her child to school and later included an emotionally arousing event: the child being hit by a car. When tested later, the research participants remembered the arousing event better than the mundane ones. But patients with amygdala damage remembered the mundane and emotionally arousing events equally well (Cahill & McGaugh, 1998). PET and fMRI scans show that when healthy people view a slide sequence that includes an emotionally arousing event, the level of activity in their amygdalas at the time they see it is a good predictor of their subsequent memory for the slide. When there is heightened activity in the amygdala as people watch emotional events, there's a better chance that they will recall those events on a later test (Cahill et al., 1996; Kensinger & Schacter, 2005).

The amygdala influences hormonal systems that kick into high gear when we experience an arousing event. The release of stress-related hormones, such as adrenaline and cortisol, mobilizes the brain and the body in the face of threat or other sources of stress. These hormones also enhance memory for the experience. For instance, administering stress-related hormones heightens a rat's memory for an electrical shock or for places in a maze that it has visited recently (LeDoux, 1996). When the

Figure 5.19 The Amygdala's Influence on Memory The amygdala, located next to the hippocampus, responds strongly to emotional events. Patients with amygdala damage are unable to remember emotional events any better than nonemotional ones (Cahill & McGaugh, 1998).

Hippocampus

Amygdala

amygdala is damaged, it no longer releases the stress-related hormones that enhance memory. When people are given a drug that interferes with the release of stress-related hormones, their memory for the emotional sections of a slide sequence is no better than their memory for the mundane sections. It seems, then, that the amygdala influences memory storage by turning on the hormones that allow us to respond to and vividly remember emotionally arousing events.

Are the Seven Sins Vices or Virtues?

You may have concluded that evolution burdened us with an extremely inefficient memory system that is so prone to error that it often jeopardizes our well-being. Not so. The seven sins are the price we pay for the many benefits that memory provides (Schacter, 2001b). These mindbugs are the occasional result of the normally efficient operation of the human memory system.

Consider the seemingly buggy nature of transience, for example. Wouldn't it be great to remember all the details of every incident in your life, no matter how much time had passed? Not necessarily. It is helpful and sometimes important to forget information that isn't current, like an old phone number. If we didn't gradually forget information over time, our minds would be cluttered with details that we no longer need (Bjork & Bjork, 1988). Information that is used infrequently is less likely to be needed in the future than information that is used more frequently over the same period (Anderson & Schooler, 1991, 2000). Memory, in essence, makes a bet that when we haven't used information recently, we probably won't need it in the future. We win this bet more often than we lose it, making transience an adaptive property of memory. But we are acutely aware of the losses—the frustrations of forgetting—and are never aware of the wins. This is why people are often quick to complain about their memories: The drawbacks of forgetting are painfully evident, but the benefits of forgetting are hidden.

Absentmindedness can also be irritating, but we would be even more irritated without it. Absentminded errors happen in part because events that receive little attention and elaboration when they occur are difficult to recall later. But if all events were registered in elaborate detail, our minds would be cluttered with useless information. This is just what happened in the unusual case of a journalist named Solomon Shereshevskii (Luria, 1968). He formed and retained highly detailed memories of almost everything that happened to him, important or not. Because Shereshevskii's mind was always populated with trivia, he was unable to generalize or function at an abstract level. The struggle to forget plagued him throughout his life, and he used elaborate rituals to try to rid himself of the mass of information competing for space in his mind. The details of past experiences that left Shereshevskii overwhelmed by information are best denied entry to memory in the first place.

Similarly, although blocking is such a frustrating mindbug that we are often tempted to bite the tips of our tongues clean off, it has adaptive features (Bjork & Bjork, 1988). People generally block information that has not been used recently because the odds are that such information will not be needed in the future. In general, blocking helps the memory system to run smoothly and efficiently but occasionally causes embarrassing incidents of retrieval failure.

Memory misattribution and suggestibility both occur because we often fail to recall the details of exactly when and where we saw a face or learned a fact. This is because memory is adapted to retain information that is most likely to be needed in the environment in which it operates. We seldom need to remember all the precise contextual details of every experience. Our memories carefully record such details only when we think they may be needed later, and most of the time we are better off for it. We pay the price, however, when we are required to recollect specific information about an experience that did not elicit any special effort to encode details about its source.

Bias is also a problem, skewing our memories so that we depict ourselves in an overly favorable light. This mindbug may seem self-serving and unduly optimistic, but it can produce the benefit of contributing to our overall sense of contentment. Holding positive illusions about ourselves can lead to greater psychological well-being (Taylor, 1989).

Finally, persistence has both a dark and light side. Although it can cause us to be haunted by traumas that we'd be better off forgetting, overall, it is probably adaptive to remember threatening or traumatic events that could pose a threat to survival. If you could conveniently forget being burned on a hot stove, you might fail to avoid stoves in the future.

In summary, memory's mindbugs can be classified into seven "sins." *Transience* is reflected by a rapid decline in memory followed by more gradual forgetting. With the passing of time, memory switches from detailed to general. Both decay and interference contribute to transience. *Absentmindedness* results from failures of attention, shallow encoding, and the influence of automatic behaviors and is often associated with forgetting to do things in the future. *Blocking* occurs when stored information is temporarily inaccessible, as when information is on the tip of the tongue. *Memory misattribution* happens when we experience a sense of familiarity but don't recall, or mistakenly recall, the specifics of when and where an experience occurred. Misattribution can result in eyewitness misidentification or false recognition. Patients suffering from frontal lobe damage are especially susceptible to false recognition. *Suggestibility* gives rise to implanted memories of small details or entire episodes. Suggestive techniques such as hypnosis or visualization can promote vivid recall of suggested events, and therapists' use of suggestive techniques may be responsible for some patients' false memories of childhood traumas. *Bias* reflects the influence of current knowledge, beliefs, and feelings on memory or past experiences. Bias can lead us to make the past consistent with the present, exaggerate changes between past and present, or remember the past in a way that makes us look good. *Persistence* reflects the fact that emotional arousal generally leads to enhanced memory, whether we want to remember an experience or not. Persistence is partly attributable to the operation of hormonal systems influenced by the amygdala. Although each of the seven sins can cause trouble in our lives, they have an adaptive side as well. You can think of the seven sins as costs we pay for benefits that allow memory to work as well as it does most of the time. ■ ■

Where Do You Stand?

The Mystery of Childhood Amnesia

As you have seen, transience is a pervasive characteristic of memory. Nonetheless, you can easily recall many experiences from different times in your life, such as last summer's job or vacation, the sights and sounds of a favorite concert, or the most exciting sporting event you've ever attended. But there is one period of time from which you likely have few or no memories: the first few years of your life. This lack of memory for our early years is called *childhood amnesia* or *infantile amnesia*.

Psychoanalyst Sigmund Freud was one of the first psychologists to comment on childhood amnesia (see Chapter 1). In 1905, he hood experiences prior to their sixth or eighth

described a "peculiar amnesia which, in the case of most people, though by no means all, hides the earliest beginnings of their childhood up to their sixth or eighth year" (Freud, 1905/1953, p. 174). Freud's assessments of childhood amnesia were based on observations of individual patients from his psychoanalytic practice.

In the 1930s and 1940s, psychologists carried out systematic studies in which they asked large samples of individuals to report their earliest memories with the dates when they occurred. Contrary to Freud's suggestion that most people cannot remember childhood experiences prior to their sixth or eighth

year, these studies revealed that, on average, an individual's earliest memory dates to about 3½ years of age (Dudycha & Dudycha, 1933; Waldfogel, 1948). Later studies suggested that women report slightly earlier first memories (3.07 years of age) than men (3.4 years) (Howes, Siegel, & Brown, 1993).

Try to recall your own earliest memory. As you mentally search for it, you may encounter a problem that has troubled researchers: How do you know the exact time when your recollection took place? Memory for dates is notoriously poor, so it is often difficult to determine precisely when your earliest memory occurred (Friedman,

1993). To address this problem, researchers asked people about memories for events that have clearly definable dates, such as the birth of a younger sibling, the death of a loved one, or a family move (Sheingold & Tenney, 1982; Usher & Neisser, 1993). In one study researchers asked individuals between 4 and 20 years old to recall as much as they could about the birth of a younger sibling (Sheingold & Tenney, 1982). Participants who were at least 3 years old at the time of the birth remembered it in considerable detail, whereas participants who were younger than 3 years old at the time of the birth remembered little or nothing. A more recent study found that individuals can recall events surrounding the birth of a sibling that occurred when they were about 2.4 years old; some people even showed evidence of recall from ages 2.0 to 2.4 years, although these memories were very sketchy (Eacott & Crawley, 1998).

It is difficult to draw firm conclusions from these kinds of studies. On the one hand, they suggest that people can come up with memories from earlier in life than was previously thought. On the other hand, memories of early events may be based on family conversations that took place long after the events occurred. An adult or a child who remembers having ice cream in the hospital as a 3-year-old when his baby sister was born may be recalling what his parents told him after the event. Consistent with this idea, cross-cultural studies have turned up an interesting finding. Individuals from cultures that emphasize talking about the past, such as North American culture, tend to report earlier first memories than individuals from cultures that place less emphasis on talking about the past, such as Korean and other Asian cultures (MacDonald, Uesilana, & Hayne, 2000; Mullen, 1994).

Recent research has examined whether the events that people say they remember from early childhood really are *personal recollections*, which involve conscious re-experiencing of some aspect of the event, or whether people *just know* about these events (perhaps from family photos and discussions), even though they don't truly possess personal recollections (Multhaup, Johnson, & Tetirick, 2005). Several experiments revealed that personal recollections tend to emerge later than memories based on "just knowing," with the transition from mostly "know" memories to mostly "recollect" memories occurring at 4.7 years.

Some events in your personal history are personal recollections. In other words, you actually remember the occurrence of the event. Personal recollections are ones in which you can become consciously aware again of some aspects of the event, of what happened, or of what you experienced at the time. Perhaps you have an image of the event or can re-experience some specific details.

Other events from your past are ones that you know happened but are not personal recollections. In other words, you know the event occurred, but you cannot consciously recollect any aspect of what happened or of what you experienced at the time. Instead, your knowledge of the event is based on an external source of information, perhaps your parents and/or other family members, friends, pictures, photo albums, diaries, or family stories. To find out about your own "recollected" versus "known" memories, complete the items listed below from the 2005 study by Multhaup et al.

Instructions	Event	Recollect	Know	Age	Don't Know
Please label each of the events listed as a personal "recollection" or as an event that you "know" happened but that is not a personal memory. If you neither "recollect" nor "know" the event (perhaps because you never experienced it), please label it as "don't know." For each event you "recollect" or "know," indicate your age at the time the event occurred, as best you can determine, with the year followed by month (e.g., 4.0 is 4 years old exactly, 4.6 is 4½ years old, 4.9 is 4¾, and so forth).	You read your first book with chapters.	❑	❑	❑	❑
	You went to your first sleepover.	❑	❑	❑	❑
	You saw your first movie in a movie theater.	❑	❑	❑	❑
	You took your first swimming lesson.	❑	❑	❑	❑
	You joined your first organized sports team.	❑	❑	❑	❑
	You learned to write in cursive.	❑	❑	❑	❑
	You stopped taking naps.	❑	❑	❑	❑
	You learned to spell your name.	❑	❑	❑	❑
	You went to an amusement park for the first time.	❑	❑	❑	❑
	You were toilet trained.	❑	❑	❑	❑
	Your first permanent tooth came in.	❑	❑	❑	❑
	You learned to ride a bicycle (2 wheels, no training wheels).	❑	❑	❑	❑
	You slept in a bed instead of a crib.	❑	❑	❑	❑

(Items are sampled from experiments 1 and 2 of Multhaup et al., 2005, p. 172.)

Chapter Review

Encoding: Transforming Perceptions into Memories

- Memories are not passive recordings of the world but instead result from combining incoming information with previous experiences. Encoding is the process of linking new and old information.

- Elaborative encoding (actively linking incoming information to existing associations and knowledge), visual imagery encoding (converting incoming information into mental pictures), and organizational encoding (noticing relationships among items you want to encode) all benefit memory.

- Different regions within the frontal lobe play important roles in elaborative encoding and organizational encoding, whereas the visual cortex (occipital lobe) appears to be important for visual imagery encoding.

Storage: Maintaining Memories over Time

- Three major forms of memory storage hold information for different amounts of time: sensory memory (a second or two), short-term or working memory (less than a minute), and long-term memory (minutes, hours, weeks, and years).

- The hippocampus puts information into long-term storage so that it can later be consciously remembered. Amnesic patients with damage to the hippocampal region have little ability to remember their recent experiences.

- Memories are most likely stored in the synapses that connect neurons to one another.

Retrieval: Bringing Memories to Mind

- Recall of past experiences depends critically on retrieval cues, which trigger recall by reinstating what we thought or how we felt during the encoding of an experience.

- Information or experiences we can't recall on our own are sometimes only temporarily inaccessible and can be brought to mind with appropriate retrieval cues.

- Different parts of the brain seem to be activated when we put forth the mental effort to try to call up a past experience and when we actually remember the experience.

Multiple Forms of Memory: How the Past Returns

- Memory can be broadly divided into explicit memory, involving conscious, intentional retrieval of previous experiences, and implicit memory, which is a nonconscious, unintentional form of memory.

- Priming (an enhanced ability to think of a stimulus as a result of recent exposure to the stimulus) and procedural memory (learning skills from practice) both draw on implicit memory.

- Episodic memory (recollection of specific personal experiences) and semantic memory (general knowledge of the world) involve explicit recall information.

Memory Failures: The Seven Sins of Memory

- There are seven major ways in which memory can cause us trouble: transience, absentmindedness, blocking, memory misattribution, suggestibility, bias, and persistence. The first three sins all involve different types of forgetting, the next three involve different types of distortion, and the final sin involves remembering what we wish we could forget.

- Each of the seven sins has adaptive features. The sins are prices we pay for benefits in memory that generally serve us well. Understanding these memory mindbugs helps researchers better understand the normal operations of memory.

Key Terms

Memory (p. 168)
Encoding (p. 169)
Storage (p. 169)
Retrieval (p. 169)
Elaborative encoding (p. 170)
Visual imagery encoding (p. 171)
Organizational encoding (p. 172)
Memory storage (p. 173)
Sensory memory store (p. 173)
Iconic memory (p. 174)
Echoic memory (p. 174)
Short-term memory store (p. 174)

Rehearsal (p. 174)
Chunking (p. 175)
Working memory (p. 175)
Long-term memory store (p. 176)
Anterograde amnesia (p. 177)
Retrograde amnesia (p. 177)
Long-term potentiation (LTP) (p. 178)
NMDA receptor (p. 178)
Retrieval cue (p. 180)
Encoding specificity principle (p. 180)
State-dependent retrieval (p. 181)

Transfer-appropriate processing (p. 181)
Explicit memory (p. 183)
Implicit memory (p. 183)
Procedural memory (p. 183)
Priming (p. 184)
Semantic memory (p. 185)
Episodic memory (p. 185)
Transience (p. 187)
Retroactive interference (p. 189)
Proactive interference (p. 189)
Absentmindedness (p. 189)

Prospective memory (p. 191)
Blocking (p. 192)
Tip-of-the-tongue experience (p. 192)
Memory misattribution (p. 193)
Source memory (p. 194)
False recognition (p. 194)
Suggestibility (p. 197)
Bias (p. 200)
Persistence (p. 201)
Flashbulb memories (p. 201)

Recommended Readings

Brainerd, C. J., & Reyna, V. F. (2005). *The science of false memory.* New York: Oxford University Press. Written by two of the leading researchers into the nature of false memories, this volume provides a readable summary of what we know about false memories and how they differ from true memories.

McNally, R. J. (2003). *Remembering trauma.* Cambridge, MA: Harvard University Press. This is the single most comprehensive source concerning traumatic memories. McNally explains the characteristics and origins of traumatic memories and also provides a useful discussion of the controversy concerning the accuracy of repressed and recovered traumatic memories.

Neisser, U., & Hyman, I. E. (Eds.). (2000). *Memory observed: Remembering in natural contexts.* New York: Worth. A fascinating collection of articles and essays concerned with how people remember and forget in the real world.

Schacter, D. L. (2001). *The seven sins of memory.* New York and Boston: Houghton Mifflin. This book provides a more in-depth treatment of memory's seven sins than that provided in this chapter, including many more examples of how the seven sins affect us in everyday life.

Wearing, D. (2006). *Forever today.* London: Corgi Books. Clive Wearing is a gifted musician who also has the dubious distinction of having one of the most severe cases of amnesia ever documented. His memory lasts for about 7 seconds, making every experience seem new to him. His wife, Deborah, wrote a book about their relationship and the challenges associated with coping with this kind of brain damage.

6

Learning

ADAM AND TERI'S DAUGHTER, CARLY, WAS born at 2:00 p.m. on September 11, 2000. This fact is unremarkable in itself, except that it means Carly celebrated her first birthday on September 11, 2001. The family happened to be living in Boston at the time, and they awoke that morning (on a 1-year-old's early-rising schedule) full of anticipation for a fun-filled day of birthday celebration.

What they got instead was a phone call from a friend in Texas, urging them to turn on the local news. Like many Americans, Adam and Teri watched with sadness and horror as terrorist attacks in New York, Pennsylvania, and the nation's capital took place before their eyes. American Airlines Flight 11, which crashed into the North Tower of the World Trade Center, had originated from Boston that morning, heightening the sense of uncertainty and anxiety that already had begun to define the day. Adam and Teri watched in

shock as United Airlines Flight 175 crashed into the South Tower on live television. As the news reports filtered in throughout the day, each more disturbing than the last, the couple could scarcely avert their eyes from the television, and they ended up having CNN on all day long.

Yet through it all, young Carly played with her presents, blissfully unaware of the events unfolding on the TV screen. One gift, a small yellow soccer goal, turned out to be a favorite. When the ball hit the back of the net, it triggered a voice that yelled, "Goooooaaaalllll!" and then played one of several songs at random. Carly loved to hear the music, and she would repeatedly whack the toy to make it play a song. In a surreal scene, fire, turmoil, and carnage were set to the strains of "John Jacob Jingleheimer Schmidt."

And that's what makes this a story about learning.

Defining Learning: Experience That Causes a Permanent Change
The Case of Habituation
Learning and Behaviorism

Classical Conditioning: One Thing Leads to Another
Pavlov's Experiments on Classical Conditioning
The Basic Principles of Classical Conditioning
THE REAL WORLD Understanding Drug Overdoses
Conditioned Emotional Responses: The Case of Little Albert
A Deeper Understanding of Classical Conditioning
HOT SCIENCE Can Animals Learn Language?

Operant Conditioning: Reinforcements from the Environment
The Early Days: The Law of Effect
Reinforcement, Punishment, and the Development of Operant Conditioning
The Basic Principles of Operant Conditioning
A Deeper Understanding of Operant Conditioning

Observational Learning: Look at Me
Learning without Direct Experience
Observational Learning in Humans
Observational Learning in Animals

Implicit Learning: Under the Wires
Ways to Study Implicit Learning
THE REAL WORLD Can You Sleep on It?
Implicit and Explicit Learning Use Distinct Neural Pathways
WHERE DO YOU STAND? Learning for Rewards or for Its Own Sake?

As baby Carly played with her new soccer goal, television images showed the horrifying events of September 11, 2001. Carly's parents, Adam and Teri, learned an association between the baby's toy and the 9/11 events that lasted for years.

Quite a curious thing happened. As the weeks turned to months and 2001 turned to 2002, the immediate emotional impact of 9/11 faded for Adam. Carly grew and developed, and she continued to love playing with her soccer goal. Each time it played a song, though, Adam felt a chill run through his body and saw images of burning buildings in his mind's eye. It was as though John Jacob Jingleheimer Schmidt was a madman bent on bedeviling his life. Carly is much older now, and her baby toys have been put up on a shelf. But just the sight of that little yellow goal can still bring back a flood of sad memories and call up a welter of unpleasant emotions for her parents.

What's at work here is a type of learning based on association. Adam and Teri came to associate a unique historical tragedy and a child's toy, and as a result, either of the two stimuli produced certain mental and emotional reactions. The fear and sadness that were triggered by watching the events of 9/11 came to be triggered by an innocuous plaything, and it was an effect that lasted for years. In this chapter, we'll consider this type of learning as well as other ways that knowledge is acquired and stored.

Defining Learning: Experience That Causes a Permanent Change

Learning is shorthand for a collection of different techniques, procedures, and outcomes that produce changes in an organism's behavior. Learning psychologists have identified and studied as many as 40 different kinds of learning. However, there is a basic principle at the core of all of them. **Learning** involves *some experience that results in a relatively permanent change in the state of the learner.* This definition emphasizes several key ideas: Learning is based on experience; learning produces changes in the organism; and these changes are relatively permanent. Think back to Adam and Teri's experiences on September 11, 2001—seeing the horrors of 9/11 unfold on their TV screen and hearing Carly's toy changed their response to what had been a harmless child's toy. Furthermore, the association they learned lasted for years.

Learning can be conscious and deliberate or unconscious. For example, memorizing the names of all the U.S. presidents is a conscious and deliberate activity, with an explicit awareness of the learning process as it is taking place. In comparison, the kind of learning that associated Carly's toy with images of horror is much more implicit. Adam and Teri certainly weren't aware of or consciously focused on learning as it was taking place. Some other forms of learning start out explicitly but become more implicit over time. When you first learned to drive a car, for example, you probably devoted a lot of attention to the many movements and sequences that needed to be carried out simultaneously ("step lightly on the accelerator while you push the turn indicator and look in the rearview mirror while you turn the steering wheel"). That complex interplay of motions is now probably quite effortless and automatic for you. Explicit learning has become implicit over time.

These distinctions in learning might remind you of similar distinctions in memory and for good reason. In Chapter 5, you read about the differences between *implicit* and *explicit* memories as well as *procedural, semantic,* and *episodic* memories. Do different forms of learning mirror different types of memory? It's not that simple, but it is true that learning and memory are inextricably linked. Learning produces memories, and conversely, the existence of memories implies that knowledge was acquired, that experience was registered and recorded in the brain, or that learning has taken place.

The Case of Habituation

Adam and Teri's learning is certainly not simple, but let's consider some of the simplest forms of learning. If you've ever lived under the flight path of your local airport, near railroad tracks, or by a busy highway, you probably noticed the deafening roar as a Boeing 737 made its way toward the landing strip, the clatter of a train speeding down the track, or the sound of traffic when you first moved in. You probably also noticed that after a while, the roar wasn't quite so deafening anymore and that eventually you ignored the sounds of the planes, trains, or automobiles in your vicinity.

Habituation is *a general process in which repeated or prolonged exposure to a stimulus results in a gradual reduction in responding.* For example, a car that back-fires unexpectedly as you walk by will produce a startle response: You'll jump back; your eyes will widen; your muscles will tense; and your body will experience an increase in sweating, blood pressure, and alertness. If another car were to backfire a block later, you may show another startle response, but it will be less dramatic and subside more quickly. If a third backfire should occur, you will likely not respond at all. You will have become *habituated* to the sound of a car backfiring.

Habituation is a simple form of learning. An experience results in a change in the state of the learner: In the preceding example, you begin by reacting one way to a stimulus and, with experience, your reactions change. However, this kind of change usually isn't permanent. In most cases of habituation, a person will exhibit the original reaction if enough time has gone by. To continue our example, if another car backfires a week later, you will almost certainly have a full-blown startle response. Similarly, when you return home from a 2-week vacation, the roar of the jets will probably be just as loud as ever.

A simple experiment explored the question of just how robust habituation to a loud sound could be (Leaton, 1976). One group of rats was exposed to several hundred loud tones within a 5-minute span. Another group was exposed to one loud tone each day over an 11-day period. The researchers found that the two groups reacted quite differently. The rats in the first group showed the expected startle response at first, but it quickly gave way to a rather indifferent attitude toward the tones. However, this reaction didn't last. When the tone was presented 24 hours later, the rats showed a full-blown startle response. The rats in the other group, however, showed a slow, continuous decline in the startle response over the entire 11 days of the experiment. The second outcome reflects the basic principle underlying most types of learning—that change in behavior has some permanence to it.

Living near a busy highway can be unpleasant. Most people who live near major highways become habituated to the sound of traffic.

MICHAEL KLINEC/ALAMY

Learning and Behaviorism

As you'll recall from Chapter 1, a sizable chunk of psychology's history was devoted to a single dominant viewpoint. Behaviorism, with its insistence on measuring only observable, quantifiable behavior and its dismissal of mental activity as irrelevant and unknowable, was the major outlook of most psychologists working from the 1930s through the 1950s. This was also the period during which most of the fundamental work on learning theory took place.

You might find the intersection of behaviorism and learning theory a bit surprising. After all, at one level learning seems abstract: Something intangible happens to you, and you think or behave differently thereafter. It seems that you'd need to explain that transformation in terms of a change in mental outlook, the development of a new way of thinking, or any of several other phrases that evoke mental processes that behaviorists do not consider in their learning theories. In fact, most behaviorists argued that the "permanent change in experience" that resulted from learning could be demonstrated equally well in almost any organism: rats, dogs, pigeons, mice, pigs, or humans. From this perspective, behaviorists viewed learning as a purely behavioral, eminently observable activity that did not necessitate any mental activity.

As you'll see shortly, in many ways the behaviorists were right. Much of what we know about how organisms learn comes directly from the behaviorists' observations of behaviors. However, the behaviorists also overstated their case. There are some important cognitive considerations—that is, elements of mental activity—that need to be addressed in order to understand the learning process.

LEARNING Some experience that results in a relatively permanent change in the state of the learner.

HABITUATION A general process in which repeated or prolonged exposure to a stimulus results in a gradual reduction in responding.

CLASSICAL CONDITIONING When a neutral stimulus evokes a response after being paired with a stimulus that naturally evokes a response.

UNCONDITIONED STIMULUS (US) Something that reliably produces a naturally occurring reaction in an organism.

UNCONDITIONED RESPONSE (UR) A reflexive reaction that is reliably elicited by an unconditioned stimulus.

CONDITIONED STIMULUS (CS) A stimulus that is initially neutral and produces no reliable response in an organism.

CONDITIONED RESPONSE (CR) A reaction that resembles an unconditioned response but is produced by a conditioned stimulus.

"Perhaps, Dr. Pavlov, he could be taught to seal envelopes."

Classical Conditioning: One Thing Leads to Another

You'll recall from Chapter 1 that American psychologist John B. Watson kick-started the behaviorist movement, arguing that psychologists should "never use the terms *consciousness, mental states, mind, content, introspectively verifiable, imagery,* and the like" (Watson, 1913, p. 166). Watson's firebrand stance was fueled in large part by the work of a Russian physiologist, Ivan Pavlov (1849–1936).

Pavlov was awarded the Nobel Prize in Physiology in 1904 for his work on the salivation of dogs. Pavlov studied the digestive processes of laboratory animals by surgically implanting test tubes into the cheeks of dogs to measure their salivary responses to different kinds of foods. Serendipitously, however, his explorations into spit and drool revealed the mechanics of one form of learning, which came to be called classical conditioning. **Classical conditioning** occurs *when a neutral stimulus evokes a response after being paired with a stimulus that naturally evokes a response.* In his classic experiments, Pavlov showed that dogs learned to salivate to neutral stimuli such as a bell or a tone after that stimulus had been associated with another stimulus that naturally evokes salivation, such as food.

Pavlov's Experiments on Classical Conditioning

Pavlov's basic experimental setup involved cradling dogs in a harness to administer the foods and to measure the salivary response, as shown in **FIGURE 6.1.** He noticed that dogs that previously had been in the experiment began to produce a kind of "anticipatory" salivary response as soon as they were put in the harness, before any food was presented. Pavlov and his colleagues regarded these responses as annoyances at first because they interfered with collecting naturally occurring salivary secretions. In reality, the dogs were behaving in line with the four basic elements of classical conditioning.

When the dogs were initially presented with a plate of food, they began to salivate. No surprise here—placing food in front of most animals will launch the salivary process. Pavlov called the presentation of food an **unconditioned stimulus (US)**, or *something that reliably produces a naturally occurring reaction in an organism.* He called the dogs' salivation an **unconditioned response (UR)**, or *a reflexive reaction that is reliably elicited by an unconditioned stimulus.* As a shorthand, these elements are often abbreviated US and UR, and the whole thing is quite natural and sensible: Food makes animals salivate.

Pavlov soon discovered that he could make the dogs salivate to stimuli that don't usually make animals salivate, such as the sound of a buzzer. In various experiments, Pavlov paired the presentation of food with the sound of a buzzer, the ticking of a metronome, the humming of a tuning fork, or the flash of a light (Pavlov, 1927). Sure enough, he found that the dogs salivated to the sound of a buzzer, the ticking of a

Figure 6.1 **Pavlov's Apparatus for Studying Classical Conditioning** Pavlov presented auditory stimuli to the animals using a bell or a tuning fork. Visual stimuli could be presented on the screen. The inset shows a close-up of the tube inserted in the dog's salivary gland for collecting saliva.

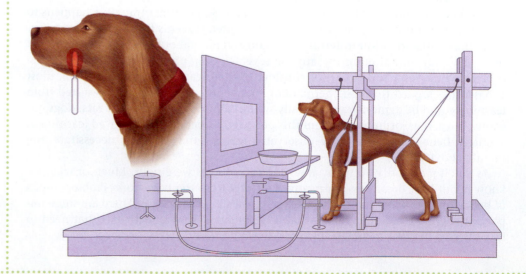

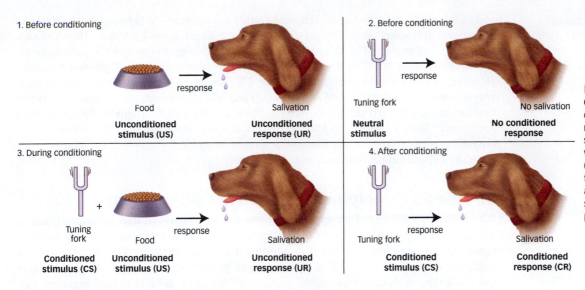

1. Before conditioning

Food
Unconditioned stimulus (US)

response → Salivation
Unconditioned response (UR)

2. Before conditioning

Tuning fork
Neutral stimulus

response → No salivation
No conditioned response

3. During conditioning

Tuning fork   Food
Conditioned stimulus (CS)   **Unconditioned stimulus (US)**

response → Salivation
Unconditioned response (UR)

4. After conditioning

Tuning fork
Conditioned stimulus (CS)

response → Salivation
Conditioned response (CR)

Figure 6.2 **The Elements of Classical Conditioning** In classical conditioning, a previously neutral stimulus (such as the sound of a tuning fork) is paired with an unconditioned stimulus (such as the presentation of food). After several trials associating the two, the conditioned stimulus (the sound) alone can produce a conditioned response.

metronome, the humming of a tuning fork, or the flash of a light, each of which had become a **conditioned stimulus (CS)**, or *a stimulus that is initially neutral and produces no reliable response in an organism* (see **FIGURE 6.2**). When dogs hear the sound of a buzzer in the wild, they're not known to salivate: There's nothing natural or predictable about the sound of a buzzer producing a particular kind of behavior in a dog. However, when the conditioned stimulus (CS), in this case the sound of a buzzer, is paired over time with the unconditioned stimulus (US), or the food, the animal will learn to associate food with the sound and eventually the CS is sufficient to produce a response, or salivation. This response resembles the UR, but Pavlov called it the **conditioned response (CR)**, or *a reaction that resembles an unconditioned response but is produced by a conditioned stimulus*. In this example, the dogs' salivation (CR) was eventually prompted by the sound of the buzzer (CS) alone because the sound of the buzzer and the food (US) had been associated so often in the past. Technically, though, the salivation is not a UR (the naturally occurring, reflexive reaction to the presentation of food) because it is produced instead by the CS (the sound of the buzzer). As you can imagine, a range of stimuli might be used as a CS, and as we noted earlier, several different stimuli became the CS in Pavlov's experiment.

Let's apply these four basic elements of the classical-conditioning process—the US, UR, CS, and CR—to a couple of examples. First, consider your own dog (or cat). You probably think you have the only dog that can tell time because she always knows when dinner's coming and gets prepared, stopping short of pulling up a chair and tucking a napkin into her collar. It's as though she has one eye on the clock every day, waiting for the dinner hour. Sorry to burst your bubble, but your dog is no clock-watching wonder hound. Instead, the presentation of food (the US) has become associated with a complex CS—your getting up, moving into the kitchen, opening the cabinet, working the can opener—such that the CS alone signals to your dog that food is on the way and therefore initiates the CR of her getting ready to eat.

Another example comes from the popular film *Super Size Me* (2004), director Morgan Spurlock's documentary about fast-food consumption and obesity in America. In one scene, Spurlock is lamenting to an interviewee about the perils of childhood obesity and how restaurants seem to lure children with playscapes, Fun Meals, and birthday celebrations. Reflecting the seeming impossibility of steering young children clear of such fast-food attractions, Spurlock jokingly comments that if he had a child, he would punch him each time they passed a McDonald's. This shocking but facetious image is classical conditioning in action. The painful US (a punch) should become associated with a CS (the sight of McDonald's) so that eventually the CS alone produces the CR (feelings of fear and avoidance whenever the restaurant is in view). Even though it might be an effective method to keep kids away from fast food, it's not one that any parent should ever consider.

DENNIS THE MENACE

"I think Mom's using the can opener."

ACQUISITION The phase of classical conditioning when the CS and the US are presented together.

Finally, think back to Adam, Teri, and Carly's experiences on September 11, 2001. As Adam and Teri watched the World Trade Center collapsing on television, they felt sadness, fear, and anxiety. The images of devastation and horror were the US and the negative feelings were the UR: Seeing horrible things usually makes people feel horrible. However, Carly's soccer goal acted as the CS. The toy—and especially, the songs it played—was an initially neutral stimulus that was associated with the US that day. As the horrific images flashed across the screen, "Skip to My Lou," "Twinkle, Twinkle, Little Star," and "She's a Grand Old Flag" provided an endless sound track. As Adam experienced, eventually the CS all by itself—the music played by the toy—was sufficient to produce the CR—feelings of sadness, fear, and anxiety.

The Basic Principles of Classical Conditioning

When Pavlov's findings first appeared in the scientific and popular literature (Pavlov, 1923a, b), they produced a flurry of excitement because psychologists now had demonstrable evidence of how conditioning produced learned behaviors. This was the kind of behaviorist psychology John B. Watson was proposing: An organism experiences events or stimuli that are observable and measurable, and changes in that organism can be directly observed and measured. Dogs learned to salivate to the sound of a buzzer, and there was no need to resort to explanations about why it had happened, what the dog wanted, or how the animal thought about the situation. In other words, there was no need to consider the mind in this classical-conditioning paradigm, which appealed to Watson and the behaviorists. Pavlov also appreciated the significance of his discovery and embarked on a systematic investigation of the mechanisms of classical conditioning. Let's take a closer look at some of these principles. (As the Real World box on the facing page shows, these principles help explain how drug overdoses occur.)

Acquisition

Remember when you first got your dog? Chances are she didn't seem too smart, especially the way she stared at you vacantly as you went into the kitchen, not anticipating that food was on the way. That's because learning through classical conditioning requires some period of association between the CS and US. This period is called **acquisition**, or *the phase of classical conditioning when the CS and the US are presented together*. During the initial phase of classical conditioning, typically there is a gradual increase in learning: It starts low, rises rapidly, and then slowly tapers off, as shown on the left side of **FIGURE 6.3**. Pavlov's dogs gradually increased their amount of salivation over several trials of pairing a tone with the presentation of food, and similarly, your dog eventually learned to associate your kitchen preparations with the subsequent appearance of food. After learning has been established, the CS by itself will reliably elicit the CR.

Figure 6.3 **Acquisition, Extinction, and Spontaneous Recovery** In classical conditioning, the CS is originally neutral and produces no specific response. After several trials pairing the CS with the US, the CS alone comes to elicit the salivary response (the CR). Learning tends to take place fairly rapidly and then levels off as stable responding develops. In extinction, the CR diminishes quickly until it no longer occurs. A rest period, however, is typically followed by spontaneous recovery of the CR. In fact, a well-learned CR may show spontaneous recovery after more than one rest period even though there have been no additional learning trials.

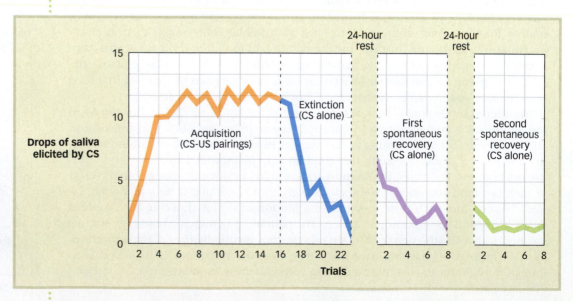

{ THE REAL WORLD } Understanding Drug Overdoses

ALL TOO OFTEN, POLICE ARE CONFRONTED with a perplexing problem: the sudden death of addicts from a drug overdose. These deaths are puzzling for at least three reasons: The victims are often experienced drug users, the dose taken is usually not larger than what they usually take, and the deaths tend to occur in unusual settings. Experienced drug users are just that: experienced! You'd think that if a heroin addict or crack cocaine user were ingesting a typical amount of a substance they'd used many times before, the chances of an overdose would be *lower* than usual.

Classical conditioning provides some insight into how these deaths occur. First, when classical conditioning takes place, the CS is more than a simple bell or tone: It also includes the overall *context* within which the conditioning takes place. Indeed, Pavlov's dogs often began to salivate even as they approached the experimental apparatus. Second, many CRs are compensatory reactions to the US. In some of Pavlov's early experiments, he used a very mild acid solution as the US because it produces large amounts of saliva that dilute the acid in the dog's mouth. When that salivary response is eventually conditioned to the sound of a tone, in a way it represents the remnants of the body's natural reaction to the presentation of the US.

These two finer points of classical conditioning help explain what happens when someone takes a drug such as heroin (Siegel, 1984). When the drug is injected, the entire setting (the drug paraphernalia, the room, the lighting, the addict's usual companions) functions as the CS, and the addict's brain reacts to the heroin by secreting

AP PHOTO/CHRIS GARDNER

Although opium dens and crack houses may be considered blight, it is often safer for addicts to use drugs there. The environment becomes part of the addict's CS, so ironically, busting crack houses may contribute to more deaths from drug overdose when addicts are pushed to use drugs in new situations.

neurotransmitters that counteract its effects. Over time, this protective physiological response becomes part of the CR, and like all CRs, it occurs in the presence of the CS but prior to the actual administration of the drug. These compensatory physiological reactions are also what make drug abusers take increasingly larger doses to achieve the same effect; ultimately, these reactions produce *drug tolerance,* discussed in Chapter 8.

Based on these principles of classical conditioning, taking drugs in a new environment can be fatal for a longtime drug user. If an addict injects the usual dose in a setting that is sufficiently novel or where heroin has never been taken before, the CS is now altered. What's more, the physiological compensatory CR either does not occur or is substantially decreased. As a result, the addict's usual dose becomes an overdose and death often results. This effect has also been shown experimentally: Rats that have had extensive experience with morphine in one setting were much more likely to survive dose increases in that same setting than in a novel one (Siegel, 1976).

The basic principles of classical conditioning help explain this real-world tragedy of drug overdose. Intuitively, addicts may stick with the crack houses, opium dens, or "shooting galleries" with which they're familiar for just this reason.

Second-Order Conditioning

After conditioning has been established, a phenomenon called **second-order conditioning** can be demonstrated: *conditioning where the US is a stimulus that acquired its ability to produce learning from an earlier procedure in which it was used as a CS.* For example, in an early study Pavlov repeatedly paired a new CS, a black square, with the now-reliable tone. After a number of training trials, his dogs produced a salivary response to the black square even though the square itself had never been directly associated with the food. You could do the same thing with your own dog. After she has learned the association between your kitchen noises and the presentation of food, you might try humming a particular tune each time you walk into the kitchen for any reason. After a while you should find that humming the tune by itself causes your dog to salivate.

Psychologists quickly appreciated the applications of second-order conditioning to daily life. For example, it can help explain why some people desire money to the point that they hoard it and value it even more than the objects that it can be used to purchase. Money is initially used to purchase objects that produce gratifying outcomes, such as expensive cars or big-screen televisions. Although money is not directly associated with the thrill of a high-speed drive in a new sports car or the amazing clarity of a high-definition TV, through second-order conditioning money can become linked with these desirable qualities.

SECOND-ORDER CONDITIONING Conditioning where the US is a stimulus that acquired its ability to produce learning from an earlier procedure in which it was used as a CS.

Some people desire money to the extent that they hoard it and value it more than the things it can buy. Multibillionaire technology executives Lawrence Ellison (left) and Paul Allen (right) donated considerably less than 1% of their personal fortunes in 2006, instead hoarding the money for themselves. Such people may be showing the effects of second-order conditioning.

Extinction

After Pavlov and his colleagues had explored the process of acquisition extensively, they turned to the next logical question: What would happen if they continued to present the CS (tone) but stopped presenting the US (food)? Repeatedly presenting the CS without the US produces exactly the result you might imagine. As shown on the right side of the first panel in Figure 6.3, behavior declines abruptly and continues to drop until eventually the dog ceases to salivate to the sound of the tone. This process is called **extinction**, *the gradual elimination of a learned response that occurs when the US is no longer presented*. The term was introduced because the conditioned response is "extinguished" and no longer observed. If you make noises in the kitchen without subsequently presenting a meaty plate of Alpo, eventually your dog will stop salivating or even getting aroused every time you walk into the kitchen.

Spontaneous Recovery

Having established that he could produce learning through conditioning and then extinguish it, Pavlov wondered if this elimination of conditioned behavior was permanent. Is a single session of extinction sufficient to knock out the CR completely, or is there some residual change in the dog's behavior so that the CR might reappear?

To explore this question, Pavlov extinguished the classically conditioned salivation response and then allowed the dogs to have a short rest period. When they were brought back to the lab and presented with the CS again, they displayed **spontaneous recovery**, *the tendency of a learned behavior to recover from extinction after a rest period*. This phenomenon is shown in the middle panel in Figure 6.3. Notice that this recovery takes place even though there have not been any additional associations between the CS and US. Some spontaneous recovery of the conditioned response even takes place in what is essentially a second extinction session after another period of rest (see the right-hand panel in Figure 6.3 on p. 214). Clearly, extinction had not completely wiped out the learning that had been acquired. The ability of the CS to elicit the CR was weakened, but it was not eliminated.

Pavlov proposed that spontaneous recovery came about because the extinction process has two distinct effects. First, it weakened the associations formed during acquisition, and second, it inhibited the conditioned response. If this explanation was correct, how often could spontaneous recovery occur? Is it possible to ever completely extinguish a conditioned response after it was learned? As you see from Figure 6.3, some spontaneous recovery can be seen after a second rest period and, occasionally, a third. Eventually, however, the conditioned response will cease to occur.

But consider this. Even if a sufficient number of extinction trials are conducted so that there is no longer any evidence of spontaneous recovery, can we still conclude that any residual associations have been completely eliminated? The answer is no. If

EXTINCTION The gradual elimination of a learned response that occurs when the US is no longer presented.

SPONTANEOUS RECOVERY The tendency of a learned behavior to recover from extinction after a rest period.

GENERALIZATION A process in which the CR is observed even though the CS is slightly different from the original one used during acquisition.

DISCRIMINATION The capacity to distinguish between similar but distinct stimuli.

the CS-US pairings are introduced again, the animal will show rapid conditioning, much more rapid than during the initial acquisition phase. This effect is known as savings, since it suggests that some underlying neural changes that occurred during the initial learning are "saved" no matter how many extinction trials are conducted.

Generalization

Suppose you decide to break down and buy a new can opener, replacing the crummy one that you've had for years. Let's say the new one makes a slightly different sound. Did you consider your dog at any point in this decision making? After all, Fido had associated the sound of the old can opener with the onset of food, and now you've gone and changed things. Do you think your dog will be stumped, unable to anticipate the presentation of her food? Will a whole new round of conditioning need to be established with this modified CS?

Probably not. It wouldn't be very adaptive for an organism if each little change in the CS-US pairing required an extensive regimen of new learning. Rather, the phenomenon of **generalization** tends to take place, in which *the CR is observed even though the CS is slightly different from the original one used during acquisition*. This means that the conditioning "generalizes" to stimuli that are similar to the CS used during the original training. As you might expect, the more the new stimulus changes, the less conditioned responding is observed. If you replaced the can opener with an electric can opener, your dog would probably show a much weaker conditioned response (Pearce, 1987; Rescorla, 2006).

Some generalization studies used a 1,000-hertz (Hz) tone as the CS during the acquisition phase. The test stimuli used were tones of higher or lower pitches. As you might expect, an animal gives the maximum response to the original stimulus of 1,000 Hz, with a systematic drop-off as the pitch of the replacement stimulus is farther away from the original tone of 1,000 Hz regardless of whether the tone was higher or lower. Interestingly, when the stimulus is one of the octaves of the original stimulus (octaves in music are tones that are direct multiples of each other), either 500 Hz or 2,000 Hz, there is a slight increase in responding. In these cases, the rate of responding is lower than that of the original CS but higher than it is in other cases of dissimilar tones. The animals clearly show that they detect octaves just like we do, and in this case, responding has generalized to those octaves (see **FIGURE 6.4**).

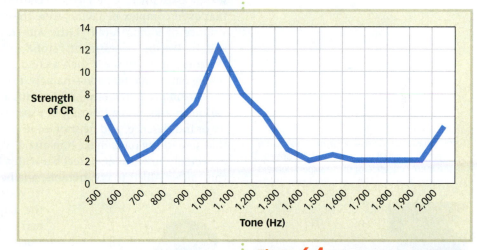

Figure 6.4 Stimulus Generalization In this experiment, an animal was conditioned using a 1,000-Hz tone (the CS) and tested with a variety of tones of higher and lower pitches. As the pitches move farther away from the original CS, the strength of the CR drops off systematically. However, when the tone is an octave of the original (i.e., either 500 or 2,000 Hz), there is an increase in the CR.

Discrimination

When an organism generalizes to a new stimulus, two things are happening. First, by responding to the new stimulus used during generalization testing, the organism demonstrates that it recognizes the similarity between the original CS and the new stimulus. Second, by displaying *diminished* responding to that new stimulus, it also tells us that it notices a difference between the two stimuli. In the second case, the organism shows **discrimination**, or *the capacity to distinguish between similar but distinct stimuli*.

Here's a true story about a talented golden retriever named Splash. Splash was very well trained to perform a number of behaviors when his name was called, as in, "Go, Splash," to fetch a ball. The sound of his name was the CS, and running after a target was the US. Repeated attempts to trick him, by yelling, "Go, Splat!" or, "Go, Crash!" or even, "Go, Spla!" resulted in predictable outcomes. Splash would start to move, but then hesitate, showing that he discriminated between the appropriate stimulus ("Splash!") and the substituted ones ("Splat!").

Conceptually, generalization and discrimination are two sides of the same coin. The more organisms show one, the less they show the other, and training can modify the balance between the two.

Conditioned Emotional Responses: The Case of Little Albert

Before you conclude that classical conditioning is merely a sophisticated way to train your dog, let's revisit the larger principles of Pavlov's work. Classical conditioning demonstrates that durable, substantial changes in behavior can be achieved simply by setting up the proper conditions. By skillfully associating a naturally occurring US with an appropriate CS, an organism can learn to perform a variety of behaviors, often after relatively few acquisition trials. There is no reference to an organism's *wanting* to learn the behavior, *willingness* to do it, *thinking* about the situation, or *reasoning* through the available options. We don't need to consider internal and cognitive explanations to demonstrate the effects of classical conditioning: The stimuli, the eliciting circumstances, and the resulting behavior are there to be observed by one and all.

It was this kind of simplicity that appealed to behaviorists such as John B. Watson. His rallying cry for a behaviorist psychology was based, in large part, on his dissatisfaction with what he saw as mysterious, philosophical, and unverifiable internal explanations for behavior that were being offered by Wundt, Freud, and others during the early days of psychology (see Chapter 1). In fact, Watson and his followers thought that it was possible to develop general explanations of pretty much *any* behavior of *any* organism based on classical-conditioning principles.

As a step in that direction, Watson embarked on a controversial study with his research assistant Rosalie Rayner (Watson & Rayner, 1920). To support his contention that even complex behaviors were the result of conditioning, Watson enlisted the assistance of 9-month-old "Little Albert." Albert was a healthy, well-developed child, and, by Watson's assessment, "stolid and unemotional" (Watson & Rayner, 1920, p. 1). Watson wanted to see if such a child could be classically conditioned to experience a strong emotional reaction—namely, fear.

Watson presented Little Albert with a variety of stimuli: a white rat, a dog, a rabbit, various masks, and a burning newspaper. Albert's reactions in most cases were curiosity or indifference, and he showed no fear of any of the items. Watson also established that something *could* make him afraid. While Albert was watching Rayner, Watson unexpectedly struck a large steel bar with a hammer, producing a loud noise. Predictably, this caused Albert to cry, tremble, and be generally displeased.

Watson and Rayner then led Little Albert through the acquisition phase of classical conditioning. Albert was presented with a white rat. As soon as he reached out to touch it, the steel bar was struck. This pairing occurred again and again over several trials. Eventually, the sight of the rat alone caused Albert to recoil in terror, crying and clamoring to get away from it. In this situation, a US (the loud sound) was paired with a CS (the presence of the rat) such that the CS all by itself was sufficient to produce the CR (a fearful reaction). Little Albert also showed stimulus generalization. The sight of a white rabbit, a seal-fur coat, and a Santa Claus mask produced the same kinds of fear reactions in the infant.

What was Watson's goal in all this? First, he wanted to show that a relatively complex reaction could be conditioned using Pavlovian techniques. Unlike a dog returning a ball or salivating at the

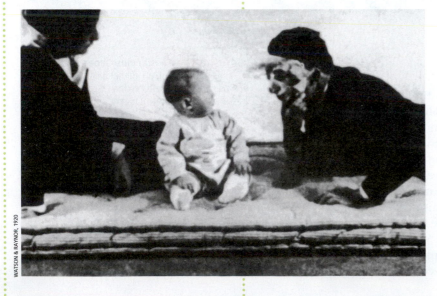

John Watson and Rosalie Rayner show Little Albert an unusual bunny mask. Why doesn't the mere presence of these experimenters serve as a conditioned stimulus in itself?

WATSON & RAYNOR, 1920

sight of food, an organism showing a fearful, anxious, and avoidant response is a bit more sophisticated. Second, he wanted to show that emotional responses such as fear and anxiety could be produced by classical conditioning and therefore need not be the product of deeper unconscious processes or early life experiences as Freud and his followers had argued (see Chapter 1). Instead, Watson proposed that fears could be learned, just like any other behavior. Third, Watson wanted to confirm that conditioning could be applied to humans as well as to other animals. Work with dogs, rats, birds, and other species had shown the utility of classical conditioning as a form of learning, but an application to humans demonstrated the universality of the principles. This bolstered Watson's view that psychology was the study of behavior and that it didn't matter if that behavior was enacted by a dog, a rat, or a little boy.

This study was controversial in its cavalier treatment of a young child, especially given that Watson and Rayner did not follow up with Albert or his mother during the ensuing years (Harris, 1979). Modern ethical guidelines that govern the treatment of research participants make sure that this kind of study could not be conducted today. At the time, however, it was consistent with a behaviorist view of psychology. As Watson (1930) summarized his position several years later:

> Give me a dozen healthy infants, well-formed, and my own specified world to bring them up in and I'll guarantee to take any one at random and train him to become any type of specialist I might select— doctor, lawyer, artist, merchant-chief and, yes, even beggar-man and thief, regardless of his talents, penchants, tendencies, abilities, vocations, and race of his ancestors. (p. 104)

In the very next sentence, Watson added: "I am going beyond my facts and I admit it, but so have the advocates of the contrary and they have been doing it for many thousands of years" (Watson, 1930, p. 104). In short, Watson was promoting a staunch view that learning and the environment were responsible for determining behavior, more so than genetics or personality, as "advocates to the contrary" might have believed at the time. Watson intended his statements to be extreme in order to shake up the young discipline of psychology and highlight the importance of acquired experiences in shaping behavior.

A Deeper Understanding of Classical Conditioning

As a form of learning, classical conditioning could be reliably produced, it had a simple set of principles, and it had applications to real-life situations. In short, classical conditioning offered a good deal of utility for psychologists who sought to understand the mechanisms underlying learning, and it continues to do so today.

Like a lot of strong starters, though, classical conditioning has been subjected to deeper scrutiny in order to understand exactly how, when, and why it works. Let's examine three areas that give us a closer look at the mechanisms of classical conditioning.

The Neural Elements of Classical Conditioning

Pavlov saw his research as providing insights into how the brain works. After all, he was trained in medicine, not psychology, and was a bit surprised when psychologists became excited by his findings. Recent research has clarified some of what Pavlov hoped to understand about conditioning and the brain.

The case of Little Albert and the earlier discussion of Adam, Teri, and Carly share a common theme: They are both examples of fear conditioning. In Chapter 3, you saw that the amygdala plays an important role in the experience of emotion, including fear and anxiety. So, it should come as no surprise that the amygdala, particularly an area known as the *central nucleus*, is also critical for emotional conditioning.

Consider a rat who is conditioned to a series of CS-US pairings where the CS is a tone and the US is a mild electric shock. When rats experience sudden painful stimuli in nature, they show a defensive reaction, known as *freezing*, where they crouch down and sit motionless. In addition, their autonomic nervous systems go to work: Heart rate and blood pressure increase, and various hormones associated with stress are released. When fear conditioning takes place, these two components—one behavioral and one physiological—occur, except that now they are elicited by the CS.

The central nucleus of the amygdala plays a role in producing both of these outcomes through two distinct connections with other parts of the brain. If connections linking the amygdala to a particular part of the midbrain are disrupted, the rat does not exhibit the behavioral freezing response. If the connections between the amygdala and the lateral part of the hypothalamus are severed, the autonomic responses associated with fear cease (LeDoux et al., 1988). Hence, the action of the amygdala is an essential element in fear conditioning, and its links with other areas of the brain are responsible for producing specific features of conditioning. The amygdala is involved in fear conditioning in people as well as rats and other animals (Phelps & LeDoux, 2005).

The Cognitive Elements of Classical Conditioning

Pavlov's work was a behaviorist's dream come true. In this view, conditioning is something that *happens to* a dog, a rat, or a person, apart from what the organism thinks about the conditioning situation. However, eventually someone was bound to ask an important question: *Why didn't Pavlov's dogs salivate to Pavlov?* After all, he was instrumental in the arrival of the CS. If Pavlov delivered the food to the dogs, why didn't they form an association with him? Indeed, if Watson was present whenever the unpleasant US was sounded, why didn't Little Albert come to fear *him?*

Maybe classical conditioning isn't such an unthinking, mechanical process as behaviorists originally had assumed (Rescorla, 1966, 1988). Somehow, Pavlov's dogs were sensitive to the fact that Pavlov was not a *reliable* indicator of the arrival of food. Pavlov was linked with the arrival of food, but he was also linked with other activities that had nothing to do with food, including checking on the apparatus, bringing the dog from the kennel to the laboratory, and standing around and talking with his assistants. These observations suggest that perhaps cognitive components are involved in classical conditioning after all.

Robert Rescorla and Allan Wagner (1972) were the first to theorize that classical conditioning only occurs when an animal has learned to set up an *expectation*. The sound of a tone, because of its systematic pairing with food, served to set up this cognitive state for the laboratory dogs; Pavlov, because of the lack of any reliable link with food, did not. In fact, in situations such as this, many responses are actually being conditioned. When the tone sounds, the dogs also wag their tails, make begging sounds, and look toward the food source (Jenkins et al., 1978). In short, what is really happening is something like the situation shown in **FIGURE 6.5**. (See also the Hot Science box on the facing page, which explains one dog's remarkable learning abilities.)

The *Rescorla-Wagner model* introduced a cognitive component that accounted for a variety of classical-conditioning phenomena that were difficult to understand from a simple behaviorist point of view. For example, the model predicted that conditioning would be easier when the CS was an *unfamiliar* event than when it was familiar. The reason is that familiar events, being familiar, already have expectations associated

Figure 6.5
Expectation in Classical Conditioning In the Rescorla-Wagner model of classical conditioning, a CS serves to set up an expectation. The expectation in turn leads to an array of behaviors associated with the presence of the CS.

Conditioned stimulus (e.g., tone, bell) → Expectation of food →

Salivation

Tail wagging

Looking for food

Begging

DON MASON/CORBIS

{ HOT SCIENCE } Can Animals Learn Language?

THE SOUND TRACK FOR THE CHILDREN'S film *Dr. Doolittle* featured a rousing little ditty called "Talk to the Animals," which crescendoed in the line, "And they could squeak and squawk and speak and talk to us!" Toe-tapping fun for many a 6-year-old, to be sure, but for the rest of us, the idea that an animal can learn a language seems a little dubious.

Nonetheless, a recent study has produced the fascinating finding that Rico, a border collie living in Leipzig, Germany, may have a remarkable word-learning ability (Kaminski, Call, & Fischer, 2004). Rico appears capable of learning new words using a process called *fast mapping,* which refers to the burst of learning that toddlers go though as they acquire the meanings of the tens of thousands of words that will make up their mature vocabulary (see Chapter 7). One way that fast mapping works is by simple association. A child is presented with a new object and told that it's called a "mouse." The child links the sound with the object and the word is learned. A different technique is based on the ability to make inferences. For example, suppose a child already knows the meaning of the words *dog* and *cat.* While on a walk, Dad points to a group of three animals containing a dog and cat and an unknown creature and says, "Oh, look at the duck." The child immediately infers that this new word is the name of the unfamiliar creature.

Psychologists have long known that some animals are capable of the first kind of learning, although their vocabularies tend to be rather limited. Rico, however, has shown that he knows the names of over 200 objects and can fetch any of them on command, a number that is far beyond anything seen before in dogs and matched only by a few rather talented chimps, dolphins, and parrots. Rico, by the way, only understands German, so if you want him to fetch a flower, you must ask him for a *Blume.* However, it is not clear whether Rico really has a cognitive sense that *Blume means* "flower" or whether he simply has learned a simple associative link between the sound and the object and embedded them in a game of go fetch.

One way to answer this question is to see if he can learn by inference, as children do. To test this, a novel item was placed in a room along with nine familiar objects. Rico was then told to fetch using the name of the unknown object. Rico returned with the unfamiliar object on 7 out of 10 trials. Moreover, when he was tested for these newly learned objects 4 weeks later, he was able to pick them out of a display containing 4 well-known objects and 4 objects he had never seen before on 3 of 6 trials. That's a performance level comparable to that of an average 3-year-old child.

Before you trade in your 3-year-old nephew for a border collie, realize that Rico is far from developing into a native German *speaker.* Your nephew at least stands a good chance of developing real language skills someday. Nonetheless, Rico's impressive performance has three implications. First, it indicates that fast mapping may not be a strictly human ability. We're all pretty amazed when toddlers add word after word to their vocabularies in short order and rightly so. But save some of your amazement: Other species may have the same capacity. Second, the results imply that the ability to attach meaning to an arbitrary sound evolved earlier than and independently of the ability to speak. Rico's not going to speak anytime soon, except for maybe a "voof" in response to the familiar, "Speak, boy!" He does, however, have the ability to match meanings with sounds.

Finally, the results suggest that the basic perceptual and cognitive processes that underlie the learning of a language are a good deal older than believed, evolutionarily speaking. Understanding concepts is a building block of learning language, and it's a foundation that Rico sits proudly on.

REUTERS/MANUELA HARTLING/NEWS.COM

Rico—one smart collie.

with them, making new conditioning difficult. For example, Adam didn't recoil in horror every time he saw his daughter Carly, even though she was present during the acquisition phase of 9/11/2001. The familiarity of Carly in multiple contexts made her, thankfully, a poor CS for Adam's fear conditioning. In short, classical conditioning might appear to be a primitive and unthinking process, but it is actually quite sophisticated and incorporates a significant cognitive element.

The Evolutionary Elements of Classical Conditioning

In addition to this cognitive component, evolutionary mechanisms also play an important role in classical conditioning. As you learned in Chapter 1, evolution and natural selection go hand in hand with adaptiveness: Behaviors that are adaptive allow an organism to survive and thrive in its environment. In the case of classical conditioning, psychologists began to appreciate how this type of learning could have adaptive value. Research exploring this adaptiveness has focused on three main areas: conditioned food aversions, conditioned food preferences, and biological preparedness.

Under certain conditions, people may develop food aversions. This serving of hummus looks inviting and probably tastes delicious, but at least one psychologist avoids it like the plague.

Rats can be difficult to poison because of learned taste aversions, which are an evolutionarily adaptive element of classical conditioning. Here a worker tries his best in the sewers of France.

Food aversions can occur for quite sensible reasons, as when Aunt Dolly offers you her famous eel-and-kidney pie and you politely decline. Food aversions can also be classically conditioned. A psychology professor was once on a job interview in Southern California, and his hosts took him to lunch at a Middle Eastern restaurant. Suffering from a case of bad hummus, he was up all night long. Needless to say, he was in pretty rough shape the following day, and he didn't get the job offer.

This colleague developed a lifelong aversion to hummus. Why would one bad incident taint food preferences in such a lasting way? On the face of it, this looks like a case of classical conditioning. The hummus was the CS, its apparent toxicity was the US, and the resulting gastric distress was the UR. The UR (the nausea) became linked to the once-neutral CS (the hummus) and became a CR (an aversion to hummus). However, there are several unusual aspects in this case.

For starters, all of the psychologist's hosts also ate the hummus, yet none of them reported feeling ill. It's not clear, then, what the US was; it couldn't have been anything that was actually in the food. What's more, the time between the hummus and the distress was several hours; usually a response follows a stimulus fairly quickly. Most baffling, this aversion was cemented with a single acquisition trial. Usually it takes several pairings of a CS and US to establish learning.

These peculiarities are not so peculiar from an evolutionary perspective. What seems like a mindbug is actually the manifestation of an adaptive process. Any species that forages or consumes a variety of foods needs to develop a mechanism by which it can learn to avoid any food that once made it ill. To have adaptive value, this mechanism should have several properties.

First, there should be rapid learning that occurs in perhaps one or two trials. If learning takes more trials than this, the animal could die from eating a toxic substance. Second, conditioning should be able to take place over very long intervals, perhaps up to several hours. Toxic substances often don't cause illness immediately, so the organism would need to form an association between food and the illness over a longer term. Third, the organism should develop the aversion to the smell or taste of the food rather than its ingestion. It's more adaptive to reject a potentially toxic substance based on smell alone than it is to ingest it. Finally, learned aversions should occur more often with novel foods than familiar ones. It is not adaptive for an animal to develop an aversion to everything it has eaten on the particular day it got sick. Our psychologist friend didn't develop an aversion to the Coke he drank with lunch or the scrambled eggs he had for breakfast that day; however, the sight and smell of hummus do make him uneasy.

John Garcia and his colleagues illustrated the adaptiveness of classical conditioning in a series of studies with rats (Garcia & Koelling, 1966). They used a variety of CSs (visual, auditory, tactile, taste, and smell) and several different USs (injection of a toxic substance, radiation) that caused nausea and vomiting hours later. The researchers found weak or no conditioning when the CS was a visual, auditory, or tactile stimulus, but a strong food aversion developed with stimuli that have a distinct taste and smell. In one experiment, they presented water accompanied by bright lights and tinkling sounds as the CS, and little or no conditioned aversion was observed. However, if the CS was water laced with a harmless but distinctly flavored novel substance (such as strawberry), the researchers found a strong aversion to the smell and taste of strawberries. Moreover, if the CS was a familiar food that the animal had eaten before, the aversion was much less likely to develop. Other researchers have shown that these food aversions can be acquired even when the organism is unconscious. Rats that were administered a toxic substance while under total anesthesia developed a taste aversion to foods they had eaten earlier when awake (Rabin & Rabin, 1984).

This research had an interesting application. It led to the development of a technique for dealing with an unanticipated side effect of radiation and chemotherapy: Cancer patients who experience nausea from their treatments often develop aversions to foods they ate before the therapy. Broberg and Bernstein (1987) reasoned that, if the findings with rats generalized to humans, a simple technique should minimize the negative consequences of this effect. They gave their patients an unusual food (coconut or root-beer-flavored candy) at the end of the last meal before undergoing treatment. Sure enough, the conditioned food aversions that the patients developed were overwhelmingly for one of the unusual flavors and not for any of the other foods in the meal. Other than any root beer or coconut fanatics among the sample, patients were spared developing aversions to more common foods that they are more likely to eat. Understanding the basis of mindbugs can have practical as well as theoretical value.

Other research has revealed a parallel mechanism, one that allows organisms to learn to *prefer* particular substances over others (Sclafani, 1995). In one study, rats were given flavored water (e.g., cherry). As they drank, a nutritive substance (such as sucrose) was delivered directly into their stomachs. On other occasions, another flavor (e.g., orange) was used, but it was paired with the delivery of water to their stomachs. After only a few trials, the rats developed a strong preference for the flavor paired with sucrose over that paired with water. The effect also occurs with substances other than sucrose: Recent work shows that conditioned food preferences can be produced by sources of fat, such as corn oil and safflower oil (Ackroff, Lucas, & Sclafani, 2005).

Studies such as these suggest that evolution has provided each species with a kind of **biological preparedness**, *a propensity for learning particular kinds of associations over others,* so that some behaviors are relatively easy to condition in some species but not others. For example, the taste and smell stimuli that produce food aversions in rats do not work with most species of birds. Birds depend primarily on visual cues for finding food and are relatively insensitive to taste and smell. However, as you might guess, it is relatively easy to produce a food aversion in birds using an unfamiliar visual stimulus as the CS, such as a brightly colored food (Wilcoxon, Dragoin, & Kral, 1971). Indeed, most researchers agree that conditioning works best with stimuli that are biologically relevant to the organism (Domjan, 2005).

Humans also have biological predispositions for conditioning, as in the case of phobias. As you'll see in Chapter 13, phobias are strong, irrational, emotional reactions to some stimulus or situation. Early behaviorists, such as Watson, viewed them as the result of simple classical conditioning: A CS is paired with a threatening US and that's that. However, research on learned aversions and preferences suggests that his perspective may have been a bit naive. Humans do indeed suffer from a variety of phobias, but not all phobias occur with the same frequency: Some phobias are common, whereas others are quite rare, and some are relatively mild, whereas others can be debilitating. Virtually everyone has cut himself or herself with a kitchen knife, yet phobias associated with knives are so rare that they are almost nonexistent. But fear of the dark and fear of heights are common and often show up in individuals who have never had any particularly unpleasant experiences associated with the dark or with heights.

Humans have a biological preparedness to develop phobias of situations that, in our evolutionary past, were potentially dangerous to survival (Ohman & Mineka, 2001). A species that is relatively physically vulnerable and has poor night vision needs to be wary of predators that lurk in the night. A species that spends a good bit of time in trees will live longer if it develops a healthy appreciation of the dangers of falling. Hence, we are biologically prepared for easy classical conditioning to fear circumstances such as darkness or heights that, ironically, are no longer as life threatening as they were for our ancestors.

In summary, classical conditioning can be thought of as an exercise in pairing a neutral stimulus with a meaningful event or stimulus. Ivan Pavlov's initial work paired a neutral tone (a conditioned stimulus) with a meaningful act: the presentation of food to a hungry animal (an unconditioned stimulus). As he and others demonstrated, the pairing of a CS and US during the acquisition phase of classical conditioning eventually allows the CS all by itself to elicit a response called a conditioned response (CR).

Classical conditioning was embraced by behaviorists such as John B. Watson, who viewed it as providing a foundation for a model of human behavior. As a behaviorist, Watson believed that no higher-level functions, such as thinking or awareness, needed

BIOLOGICAL PREPAREDNESS A propensity for learning particular kinds of associations over others.

Some phobias in humans might be the result of biological predispositions. Fear of the dark is one example. In fact, part of the synopsis for this horror movie states "*Fear of the Dark* is a tightly woven tale that taps into our universal fear of what lies hidden in the dark. It's what scares you the most."

to be invoked to understand behavior. As later researchers showed, however, the underlying mechanism of classical conditioning turned out to be more complex (and more interesting) than the simple association between a CS and a US. As Pavlov assumed, the brain is involved in many types of conditioning, as in the case of fear conditioning and the action of the amygdala. Researchers discovered that even simple species set up expectations and are sensitive to the degree to which the CS functions as a genuine predictor of the US, indicating that classical conditioning involves some degree of cognition. The evolutionary aspects of classical conditioning show that each species is biologically predisposed to acquire particular CS-US associations based on its evolutionary history. In short, classical conditioning is not an arbitrary mechanism that merely forms associations. Rather, it is a sophisticated mechanism that evolved precisely because it has adaptive value. ■ ■

Operant Conditioning: Reinforcements from the Environment

The learned behaviors you've seen so far share a common feature: They all occurred beyond the voluntary control of the organism. Most animals don't voluntarily salivate or feel spasms of anxiety; rather, these animals exhibit these responses involuntarily during the conditioning process. In fact, these reflexlike behaviors make up only a small portion of our behavioral repertoires. The remainder are behaviors that we voluntarily perform, behaviors that modify and change the environment around us. The study of classical conditioning is the study of behaviors that are *reactive*. We turn now to a different form of learning: **operant conditioning**, *a type of learning in which the consequences of an organism's behavior determine whether it will be repeated in the future.* The study of operant conditioning is the exploration of behaviors that are *active*.

The Early Days: The Law of Effect

The study of how active behavior affects the environment began at about the same time as classical conditioning. In fact, Edward L. Thorndike (1874–1949) first examined active behaviors back in the 1890s, before Pavlov published his findings. Thorndike's research focused on *instrumental behaviors,* that is, behavior that required an organism to *do* something, solve a problem, or otherwise manipulate elements of its environment (Thorndike, 1898). For example, Thorndike completed several experiments using a puzzle box, which was a wooden crate with a door that would open when a concealed lever was moved in the right way (see **FIGURE 6.6**). A hungry cat

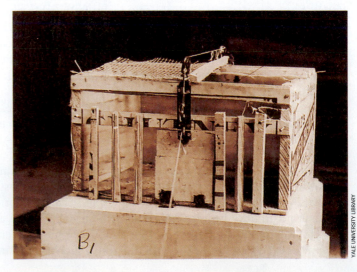

Figure 6.6 Thorndike's Puzzle Box In Thorndike's original experiments, food was placed just outside the door of the puzzle box, where the cat could see it. If the cat triggered the appropriate lever, it would open the door and let the cat out.

YALE UNIVERSITY LIBRARY

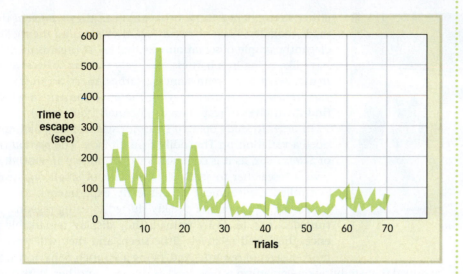

Figure 6.7 **The Law of Effect**
Thorndike's cats displayed trial-and-error be-havior when trying to escape from the puzzle box. They made lots of irrelevant movements and actions until, over time, they discovered the solution. Once they figured out what be-havior was instrumental in opening the latch, they stopped all other ineffective behaviors and escaped from the box faster and faster.

placed in a puzzle box would try various behaviors to get out—scratching at the door, meowing loudly, sniffing the inside of the box, putting its paw through the open-ings—but only one behavior opened the door and led to food: tripping the lever in just the right way. After this happened, Thorndike placed the cat back in the box for another round. Don't get the wrong idea. Thorndike probably *really liked* cats. Far from teasing them, he was after an important behavioral principle.

Fairly quickly, the cats became quite skilled at triggering the lever for their release. Notice what's going on. At first, the cat enacts any number of likely (but ultimately in-effective) behaviors, but only one behavior leads to freedom and food. That behavior is *instrumental* for the cat in achieving the desired outcome: escape from the box and access to food. Over time, the ineffective behaviors become less and less frequent, and the one instrumental behavior (going right for the latch) becomes more frequent (see **FIGURE 6.7**). From these observations, Thorndike developed the **law of effect**, which states that *behaviors that are followed by a "satisfying state of affairs" tend to be repeated and those that produce an "unpleasant state of affairs" are less likely to be repeated.*

The circumstances that Thorndike used to study learning were very different from those in studies of classical conditioning. Remember that in classical-conditioning ex-periments, the US occurred on every training trial no matter what the animal did. Pavlov delivered food to the dog whether it salivated or not. But in Thorndike's work, the behavior of the animal determined what happened next. If the behavior was "cor-rect" (i.e., the latch was triggered), the animal was rewarded with food. Incorrect be-haviors produced no results and the animal was stuck in the box until it performed the correct behavior. Although different from classical conditioning, Thorndike's work resonated with most behaviorists at the time: It was still observable, quantifiable, and free from explanations involving the mind (Galef, 1998).

Oddly, John B. Watson, the founder of behaviorism, originally rejected Thorndike's ideas about the potential of rewards to influence behavior. Watson thought this was some kind of magic, possibly akin to some cognitive explanation of "wanting" or "will-ing" to perform a behavior. It took a different kind of behaviorist promoting a different kind of behaviorism to develop Thorndike's ideas into a unified explanation of learning.

Reinforcement, Punishment, and the Development of Operant Conditioning

Several decades after Thorndike's work, B. F. Skinner (1904–90) coined the term **operant behavior** to refer to *behavior that an organism produces that has some impact on the environment.* In Skinner's system, all of these emitted behaviors "operated" on the en-vironment in some manner, and the environment responded by providing events that

OPERANT CONDITIONING A type of learning in which the consequences of an organism's behavior determine whether it will be repeated in the future.

LAW OF EFFECT The principle that be-haviors that are followed by a "satisfying state of affairs" tend to be repeated and those that produce an "unpleasant state of affairs" are less likely to be repeated.

OPERANT BEHAVIOR Behavior that an organism produces that has some impact on the environment.

WALTER DAWN/PHOTO RESEARCHERS

Figure 6.8 **Skinner Box** In a typical Skinner box, or *operant conditioning chamber,* a rat, pigeon, or other suitably sized animal is placed in this environment and observed during learning trials that use operant conditioning principles.

either strengthened those behaviors (i.e., they *reinforced* them) or made them less likely to occur (i.e., they *punished* them). Skinner's elegantly simple observation was that most organisms do *not* behave like a dog in a harness, passively waiting to receive food no matter what the circumstances. Rather, most organisms are like cats in a box, actively engaging the environment in which they find themselves to reap rewards (Skinner, 1938, 1953).

In order to study operant behavior scientifically, Skinner developed a variation on Thorndike's puzzle box. The *operant chamber,* or *Skinner box,* as it is commonly called, shown in **FIGURE 6.8**, allows a researcher to study the behavior of small organisms in a controlled environment. In his early experiments, Skinner preferred using rats, but he quickly shifted to using pigeons. Pigeons turned out to be easily trained; they display remarkable persistence, they need relatively little sleep, and they will work for the most meager of rewards. And, being a staunch behaviorist, Skinner assumed that studying one organism was as good as studying another. With a focus on behavior and no recourse for mental processes to get in the way, Skinner could easily conduct research with participants that were readily available and easy to manage.

Skinner's approach to the study of learning focused on *reinforcement* and *punishment.* These terms, which have commonsense connotations, turned out to be rather difficult to define. For example, some people love roller coasters, whereas others find them horrifying; the chance to go on one will be reinforcing for one group but punishing for another. Dogs can be trained with praise and a good belly rub—procedures that are nearly useless for most cats. Skinner settled on a "neutral" definition that would characterize each term by its effect on behavior. Therefore, a **reinforcer** is *any stimulus or event that functions to increase the likelihood of the behavior that led to it,* whereas a **punisher** is *any stimulus or event that functions to decrease the likelihood of the behavior that led to it.*

Whether a particular stimulus acts as a reinforcer or punisher depends in part on whether it increases or decreases the likelihood of a behavior. Presenting food is usually reinforcing, producing an increase in the behavior that led to it; removing food is often punishing, leading to a decrease in the behavior. Turning on an electric shock is typically punishing (the behavior that led to it); turning it off is rewarding (and increases the behavior that led to it).

To keep these possibilities distinct, Skinner used the term *positive* for situations in which a stimulus was presented and *negative* for situations in which it was removed. Consequently, there is *positive reinforcement* (where something desirable is presented) and *negative reinforcement* (where something undesirable is removed), as well as *positive punishment* (where something unpleasant is administered) and *negative punishment* (where something desirable is removed). Here the words *positive* and *negative* mean, respectively,

REINFORCER Any stimulus or event that functions to increase the likelihood of the behavior that led to it.

PUNISHER Any stimulus or event that functions to decrease the likelihood of the behavior that led to it.

B.F. SKINNER FOUNDATION

B. F. Skinner with some of his many research participants.

Table 6.1	Reinforcement and Punishment	
	Increases the Likelihood of Behavior	Decreases the Likelihood of Behavior
Stimulus is presented	Positive reinforcement	Positive punishment
Stimulus is removed	Negative reinforcement	Negative punishment

Negative reinforcement involves the removal of something undesirable from the environment. When Daddy stops the car, he gets a reward: His little monster stops screaming. However, from the perspective of the child, this is positive reinforcement. The child's tantrum results in something positive added to the environment—stopping for a snack.

something that is *added* or something that is *taken away*. As you can see from **TABLE 6.1**, positive and negative reinforcement increase the likelihood of the behavior and positive and negative punishment decrease the likelihood of the behavior.

These distinctions can be confusing at first; after all, "negative reinforcement" and "punishment" both sound like they should be "bad" and produce the same type of behavior. There are a couple of ways to keep track of these distinctions. First, remember that *positive* and *negative* simply mean *presentation* or *removal,* and the terms don't necessarily mean "good" or "bad" as they do in everyday speech. Negative reinforcement, for example, involves something pleasant; it's the *removal* of something unpleasant, like a shock, and the absence of a shock is indeed pleasant.

Second, bear in mind that reinforcement is generally more effective than punishment in promoting learning. There are many reasons (Gershoff, 2002), but one reason is this: Punishment signals that an unacceptable behavior has occurred, but it doesn't specify what should be done instead. Spanking a young child for starting to run into a busy street certainly stops the behavior—which, in this case, is probably a good idea. But it doesn't promote any kind of learning about the *desired* behavior. Should the child never venture into a street, wait for an adult, hold someone's hand, walk slowly into the busy street, or what? A more effective strategy would be to skillfully administer reinforcement for desired behaviors. Each time the child waits for an adult and holds that person's hand, for example, reinforcement would be given, perhaps in the form of verbal praise ("That's the right thing to do!"), a warm smile, a big hug, or the presentation of some other stimulus that the child finds desirable. Remember the law of effect: The intended behavior of waiting for an adult should become more frequent, and unwanted behaviors such as running into the street should decrease.

Primary and Secondary Reinforcement and Punishment

Reinforcers and punishers often gain their functions from basic biological mechanisms. A pigeon who pecks at a target in a Skinner box is usually reinforced with food pellets, just as an animal who learns to escape a mild electric shock has avoided the punishment of tingly paws. Food, comfort, shelter, or warmth are examples of *primary reinforcers* because they help satisfy biological needs. However, the vast majority of reinforcers or punishers in our daily lives have little to do with biology: Handshakes, verbal approval, an encouraging grin, a bronze trophy, or money all serve powerful reinforcing functions, yet none of them taste very good or help keep you warm at night. The point is, we learn to perform a lot of behaviors based on reinforcements that have little or nothing to do with biological satisfaction.

These *secondary reinforcers* derive their effectiveness from their associations with primary reinforcers through classical conditioning. For

"Oh, not bad. The light comes on, I press the bar, they write me a check. How about you?"

Secondary reinforcers often aren't valuable in themselves. After all, money is just pieces of paper—as illustrated by this virtually worthless currency that was used during the German hyperinflation in 1923. The reinforcing quality of secondary reinforcers derives from their association with primary reinforcers.

example, money starts out as a neutral CS that, through its association with primary USs like acquiring food or shelter, takes on a conditioned emotional element. Flashing lights, originally a neutral CS, acquire powerful negative elements through association with a speeding ticket and a fine. Under normal circumstances, as long as the CS-US link is maintained, the secondary reinforcers and punishers can be used to modify and control behavior. If the links are broken (that is, an extinction procedure is introduced), they typically lose these functions. Money that is no longer backed by a solvent government quickly loses its reinforcing capacity and becomes worth no more than the paper it is printed on.

The Neutrality of Reinforcers

Some reinforcers are more effective than others, but this is not always easy to discern. However, as David Premack (1962) pointed out, there is a simple and practical way to check. The *Premack principle* states that discerning which of two activities someone would rather engage in means that the preferred activity can be used to reinforce a nonpreferred one. For example, many children prefer to spend more time watching TV than doing their homework. As many parents have discovered, the preferred activity can be a useful reinforcer for the performance of the nonpreferred activity: No TV until the homework's done! Of course, this reinforcement will not work for all children. There are some who prefer doing their homework to watching TV; for these children, the effectiveness of the reinforcers will be reversed. In short, it's important to establish a hierarchy of behaviors for an individual in order to determine which kinds of events might be maximally reinforcing.

The Premack principle makes it clear why Skinner's neutral definitions of reinforcement and punishment make sense. A stimulus or event will be *relatively* reinforcing based on a host of factors, many of which are specific to the individual. What's more, the effectiveness of particular stimuli can be manipulated. For example, it seems pretty obvious that water can be used to reinforce a thirsty rat for running in an exercise wheel. However, the relationship between these two activities can be reversed. Depriving a rat of exercise for several days but allowing it free access to water creates a situation in which the rat will now drink in order to be given the opportunity to spend time running in the wheel.

Some Limiting Conditions of Reinforcement

Any card-carrying behaviorist during the 1930s through 1960s would tell you that providing rewards for performing a behavior should make that behavior more likely to occur again in the future. Unfortunately, this isn't always the case, and sometimes the presentation of rewards can cause the exact opposite effect: a decrease in performing the behavior. This mindbug occurs because extrinsic reinforcement—rewards that come from external sources—doesn't always capture the reasons why people engage in behavior in the first place. Many times people engage in activities for intrinsic rewards, such as the pure pleasure of simply doing the behavior.

The **overjustification effect**, *when external rewards can undermine the intrinsic satisfaction of performing a behavior,* captures this mind-bug for examination. In one study nursery school children were given colored pens and paper and were asked to draw whatever they wanted (Lepper & Greene, 1978). For a young child, this is a pretty satisfying event: The pleasures of drawing and creative expression are rewarding all by themselves. Some children, though, received a "Good Player Award" for their efforts at artwork, whereas other children did not. As you may have guessed, the Good Players spent more time at the task than the other children. As you may not have guessed, when the experimenters stopped handing out the Good Player certificates to the first group, the amount of time the children spent drawing dropped significantly below that of the group that never received any external reinforcements.

This was a case of *over*justification, or too much reinforcement. The children who received the extrinsic reinforcement of the certificate came to view their task as one that gets rewards. The children who didn't receive the extrinsic reinforcement continued to perform the task for its own sake. When the extrinsic rewards were later removed, children in the first group found little reason to continue engaging in the task. Other researchers have found that when people are paid for tasks such as writing poetry, drawing, or finding solutions to economic and business problems, they tend to produce *less* creative solutions when monetary rewards are offered (Amabile, 1996). You can weigh in on these issues in the Where Do You Stand? box at the end of this chapter.

Drawing pictures is fun. Drawing pictures for external rewards might, oddly enough, make drawing pictures seem like much less fun.

The Basic Principles of Operant Conditioning

After establishing how reinforcement and punishment produced learned behavior, Skinner and other scientists began to expand the parameters of operant conditioning. This took the form of investigating some phenomena that were well known in classical conditioning (such as discrimination, generalization, and extinction) as well as some practical applications, such as how best to administer reinforcement or how to produce complex learned behaviors in an organism. Let's look at some of these basic principles of operant conditioning.

Discrimination, Generalization, and the Importance of Context

Here are some things you probably haven't given much thought to: We all take off our clothes at least once a day, but usually not in public. We scream at rock concerts but not in libraries. We say, "Please pass the gravy," at the dinner table but not in a classroom. Although these observations may seem like nothing more than common sense, Thorndike was the first to recognize the underlying message: Learning takes place *in contexts,* not in the free range of any plausible situation. As Skinner rephrased it later, most behavior is under *stimulus control,* which develops when a particular response only occurs when the appropriate stimulus is present.

It's easy to demonstrate this simple truth. If a pigeon is reinforced for pecking a key whenever a particular tone is sounded but never reinforced if the tone is absent, that tone will quickly become a *discriminative stimulus,* or a stimulus that is associated with reinforcement for key pecking in that situation. Pigeons, reinforced under these conditions, will quickly learn to engage in vigorous key pressing whenever the tone sounds but cease if it is turned off. The tone sets the occasion for the pigeon to emit the operant response, much like being at a rock concert sets the occasion for your loud, raucous behavior.

Stimulus control, perhaps not surprisingly, shows both discrimination and generalization effects similar to those we saw with classical conditioning. To demonstrate this, researchers used either a painting by the French Impressionist Claude Monet or one of Pablo Picasso's paintings from his Cubist period for the discriminative stimulus

OVERJUSTIFICATION EFFECT
Circumstances when external rewards can undermine the intrinsic satisfaction of performing a behavior.

In research on stimulus control, participants trained with Picasso paintings, such as the one on the left, responded to other paintings by Picasso or even to paintings by other Cubists. Participants trained with Monet paintings, such as the one on the right, responded to other paintings by Monet or by other French Impressionists. Interestingly, the participants in this study were pigeons.

TATE GALLERY, LONDON/ART RESOURCE, NY

TATE GALLERY, LONDON/ART RESOURCE, NY

(Watanabe, Sakamoto, & Wakita, 1995). Participants in the experiment were only reinforced if they responded when the appropriate painting was present. After training, the participants discriminated appropriately; those trained with the Monet painting responded when other paintings by Monet were presented and those trained with a Picasso painting reacted when other Cubist paintings by Picasso were shown. And as you might expect, Monet-trained participants did not react to Picassos and Picasso-trained participants did not respond to Monets. What's more, the research participants showed that they could generalize *across* painters as long as they were from the same artistic tradition. Those trained with Monet responded appropriately when shown paintings by Auguste Renoir (another French Impressionist), and the Picasso-trained participants responded to artwork by Cubist painter Henri Matisse, despite never having seen these paintings before. If these results don't seem particularly startling to you, it might help to know that the research participants were pigeons who were trained to key-peck to these various works of art. Stimulus control, and its ability to foster stimulus discrimination and stimulus generalization, is effective even if the stimulus has no meaning to the respondent.

Extinction

As in classical conditioning, operant behavior undergoes extinction when the reinforcements stop. Pigeons cease pecking at a key if food is no longer presented following the behavior. You wouldn't put more money into a vending machine if it failed to give you its promised candy bar or soda. Warm smiles that are greeted with scowls and frowns will quickly disappear. On the surface, extinction of operant behavior looks like that of classical conditioning: The response rate drops off fairly rapidly and, if a rest period is provided, spontaneous recovery is typically seen.

However, there is an important difference. In classical conditioning, the US occurs on every trial no matter what the organism does. In operant conditioning, the reinforcements only occur when the proper response has been made, and they don't always occur even then. Not every trip into the forest produces nuts for a squirrel, auto salespeople don't sell to everyone who takes a test drive, and researchers run many experiments that do not work out and never get published. Yet these behaviors don't weaken and gradually extinguish. In fact, they typically become stronger and more resilient. Curiously, then, extinction is a bit more complicated in operant conditioning than in classical conditioning because it depends in part on how often reinforcement is received. In fact, this principle is an important cornerstone of operant conditioning that we'll examine next.

FIXED INTERVAL SCHEDULE (FI)
An operant conditioning principle in which reinforcements are presented at fixed time periods, provided that the appropriate response is made.

VARIABLE INTERVAL SCHEDULE (VI) An operant conditioning principle in which behavior is reinforced based on an average time that has expired since the last reinforcement.

Schedules of Reinforcement

Skinner was intrigued by the apparent paradox surrounding extinction, and in his autobiography, he described how he began studying it (Skinner, 1979). He was laboriously rolling ground rat meal and water to make food pellets to reinforce the rats in his early experiments. It occurred to him that perhaps he could save time and effort by not giving his rats a pellet for every bar press but instead delivering food on some intermittent schedule. The results of this hunch were dramatic. Not only did the rats continue bar pressing but they also shifted the rate and pattern of bar pressing depending on the timing and frequency of the presentation of the reinforcers. Unlike classical conditioning, where the sheer *number* of learning trials was important, in operant conditioning the *pattern* with which reinforcements appeared was crucial.

Skinner explored dozens of what came to be known as *schedules of reinforcement* (Ferster & Skinner, 1957) (see **FIGURE 6.9**). The two most important are *interval schedules,* based on the time intervals between reinforcements, and *ratio schedules,* based on the ratio of responses to reinforcements.

Under a **fixed interval schedule (FI),** *reinforcements are presented at fixed time periods, provided that the appropriate response is made.* For example, on a 2-minute fixed interval schedule, a response will be reinforced, but only after 2 minutes have expired since the last reinforcement. Rats and pigeons in Skinner boxes produce predictable patterns of behavior under these schedules. They show little responding right after the presentation of reinforcement, but as the next time interval draws to a close, they show a burst of responding. If this pattern seems odd to you, consider that virtually every undergraduate has behaved exactly like this. They do relatively little work until just before the upcoming exam, then engage in a burst of reading and studying.

Under a **variable interval schedule (VI),** a *behavior is reinforced based on an average time that has expired since the last reinforcement.* For example, on a 2-minute variable interval schedule, responses will be reinforced every 2 minutes *on average* but not after each 2-minute period. Variable interval schedules typically produce steady, consistent responding because the time until the next reinforcement is less predictable. Variable interval schedules are not encountered that often in real life, although one example might be radio promotional giveaways. A radio station might advertise that they give

Students cramming for an exam often show the same kind of behavior as pigeons being reinforced under a fixed interval schedule.

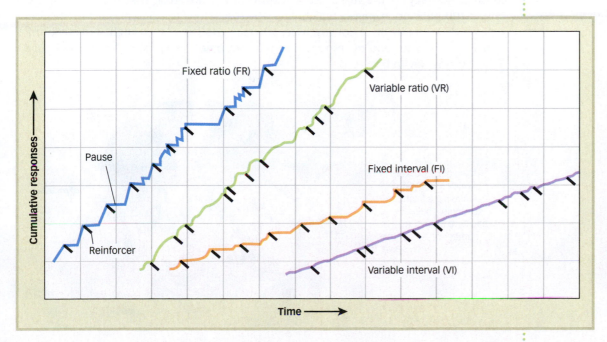

Figure 6.9 Reinforcement Schedules Different schedules of reinforcement produce different rates of responding. These lines represent the amount of responding that occurs under each type of reinforcement. The black slash marks indicate when reinforcement was administered. Notice that ratio schedules tend to produce higher rates of responding than do interval schedules, as shown by the steeper lines for fixed ratio and variable ratio reinforcement.

Radio station promotions and giveaways often follow a variable interval schedule of reinforcement.

away concert tickets every hour, which is true, but the DJs are likely to say, "Sometime this hour, I'll be giving away a pair of tickets to see the Arctic Monkeys in concert!" which is also true. The reinforcement—getting the tickets—might average out to once an hour across the span of the broadcasting day, but the presentation of the reinforcement is variable: It might come early in the 10:00 o'clock hour, later in the 11:00 o'clock hour, immediately into the 12:00 o'clock hour, and so on.

Both fixed interval schedules and variable interval schedules tend to produce slow, methodical responding because the reinforcements follow a time scale that is independent of how many responses occur. It doesn't matter if a rat on a fixed interval schedule presses a bar 1 time during a 2-minute period or 100 times: The reinforcing food pellet won't drop out of the shoot until 2 minutes have elapsed, regardless of the number of responses.

Under a **fixed ratio schedule (FR)**, *reinforcement is delivered after a specific number of responses have been made.* One schedule might present reinforcement after every fourth response, a different schedule might present reinforcement after every 20 responses; the special case of presenting reinforcement after *each* response is called *continuous reinforcement,* and it's what drove Skinner to investigate these schedules in the first place. Notice that in each example, the ratio of reinforcements to responses, once set, remains fixed.

There are many situations in which people, sometimes unknowingly, find themselves being reinforced on a fixed ratio schedule: Book clubs often give you a "freebie" after a set number of regular purchases, pieceworkers get paid after making a fixed number of products, and some credit card companies return to their customers a percent of the amount charged. When a fixed ratio schedule is operating, it is possible, in principle, to know exactly when the next reinforcer is due. A laundry pieceworker on a 10-response fixed ratio schedule who has just washed and ironed the ninth shirt knows that payment is coming after the next shirt is done.

Under a **variable ratio schedule (VR)**, *the delivery of reinforcement is based on a particular average number of responses.* For example, if a laundry worker was following a 10-response variable ratio schedule instead of a fixed ratio schedule, she or he would still be paid, on average, for every 10 shirts washed and ironed but not for *each* 10th shirt. Most people who work in sales find themselves operating under variable ratio schedules. Real estate brokers won't sell every house they show but will establish an average ratio of houses shown to houses sold. Slot machines in a modern casino pay off on variable ratio schedules that are determined by the random number generator that controls the play of the machines. A casino might advertise that they pay off on "every 100 pulls on average," which could be true. However, one player might hit a jackpot after 3 pulls on a slot machine, whereas another player might not hit until after 80 pulls. The ratio of responses to reinforcements is variable, which probably helps casinos stay in business.

These pieceworkers in a textile factory get paid following a fixed ratio schedule: They receive payment after some set number of shirts have been sewn.

All ratio schedules encourage high and consistent rates of responding because the number of rewards received is directly related to the number of responses made. Unlike a rat following a fixed interval schedule, where food is delivered at a specified time regardless of the number of responses, rats following a ratio schedule should respond quickly and often. Not surprisingly, variable ratio schedules produce slightly higher rates of responding than fixed ratio schedules primarily because the organism never knows when the next reinforcement is going to appear. What's more, the higher the ratio, the higher the response rate tends to be; a 20-response variable ratio schedule will produce considerably more responding than a 2-response variable ratio schedule. All of these schedules of reinforcement provide **intermittent reinforcement**, *when only some of the responses made are followed by reinforcement.* They all produce behavior that is much more resistant to extinction than a continuous reinforcement schedule. One way to think about this effect is to recognize that the more irregular and intermittent a schedule is, the more difficult it becomes for an organism to detect when it has actually been placed on extinction.

For example, if you've just put a dollar into a soda machine that, unbeknownst to you, is broken, no soda comes out. Because you're used to getting your sodas on a continuous reinforcement schedule—one dollar produces one soda—this abrupt change in the environment is easily noticed and you are unlikely to put additional money into the machine: You'd quickly show extinction. However, if you've put your dollar into a slot machine that, unbeknownst to you, is broken, do you stop after one or two plays? Almost certainly not. If you're a regular slot player, you're used to going for many plays in a row without winning anything, so it's difficult to tell that anything is out of the ordinary. Under conditions of intermittent reinforcement, all organisms will show considerable resistance to extinction and continue for many trials before they stop responding. The effect has even been observed in infants (Weir et al., 2005).

This relationship between intermittent reinforcement schedules and the robustness of the behavior they produce is called the **intermittent-reinforcement effect**, *the fact that operant behaviors that are maintained under intermittent reinforcement schedules resist extinction better than those maintained under continuous reinforcement.* In one extreme case, Skinner gradually extended a variable ratio schedule until he managed to get a pigeon to make an astonishing 10,000 pecks at an illuminated key for one food reinforcer! Behavior maintained under a schedule like this is virtually immune to extinction.

Shaping through Successive Approximations

Have you ever been to AquaLand and wondered how the dolphins learn to jump up in the air, twist around, splash back down, do a somersault, and then jump through a hoop, all in one smooth motion? Well, they don't. Wait—of course they do; you've seen them. It's just that they don't learn to do all those complex aquabatics in *one* smooth motion. Rather, elements of their behavior get shaped over time until the final product looks like one smooth motion.

Skinner noted that the trial-by-trial experiments of Pavlov and Thorndike were rather artificial. Behavior rarely occurs in fixed frameworks where a stimulus is presented and then an organism has to engage in some activity or another. We are continuously acting and behaving, and the world around us reacts in response to our actions. Most of our behaviors, then, are the result of **shaping**, or *learning that results from the*

COURTESY OF HTTP://PHILIP-GREENSPUN.COM

Slot machines in casinos pay out following a variable ratio schedule. This helps explain why some gamblers feel incredibly lucky, whereas others (like this chap) can't believe they can play a machine for so long without winning a thing.

FIXED RATIO SCHEDULE (FR) An operant conditioning principle in which reinforcement is delivered after a specific number of responses have been made.

VARIABLE RATIO SCHEDULE (VR) An operant conditioning principle in which the delivery of reinforcement is based on a particular average number of responses.

INTERMITTENT REINFORCEMENT An operant conditioning principle in which only some of the responses made are followed by reinforcement.

INTERMITTENT-REINFORCEMENT EFFECT The fact that operant behaviors that are maintained under intermittent reinforcement schedules resist extinction better than those maintained under continuous reinforcement.

SHAPING Learning that results from the reinforcement of successive approximations to a final desired behavior.

Training animals by shaping their behavior through successive approximations can result in some extraordinary feats, such as this tiger's daring jump through fire during the Hangzhou Sapphire Circus in China.

CHINA PHOTOS/GETTY IMAGES

reinforcement of successive approximations to a final desired behavior. The outcomes of one set of behaviors shape the next set of behaviors, whose outcomes shape the next set of behaviors, and so on.

To illustrate the effects of shaping, Skinner noted that if you put a rat in a Skinner box and wait for it to press the bar, you could end up waiting a very long time: Bar pressing just isn't very high in a rat's natural hierarchy of responses. However, it is relatively easy to "shape" bar pressing. Watch the rat closely: If it turns in the direction of the bar, deliver a food reward. This will reinforce turning toward the bar, making such a movement more likely. Now wait for the rat to take a step toward the bar before delivering

B. F. Skinner shaping a dog named Agnes. In the span of 20 minutes, Skinner was able to use reinforcement of successive approximations to shape Agnes's behavior. The result was a pretty neat trick: to wander in, stand on hind legs, and jump.

1 Minute

4 Minutes

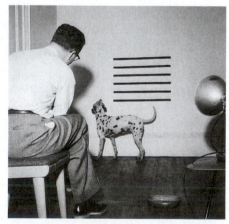

8 Minutes

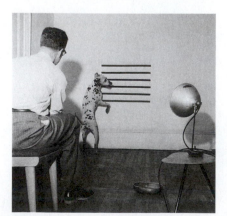

12 Minutes

16 Minutes

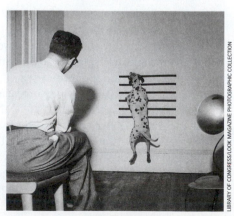

20 Minutes

LIBRARY OF CONGRESS/LOOK MAGAZINE PHOTOGRAPHIC COLLECTION

food; this will reinforce moving toward the bar. After the rat walks closer to the bar, wait until it touches the bar before presenting the food. Notice that none of these behaviors is the final desired behavior—reliably pressing the bar. Rather, each behavior is a *successive approximation* to the final product, or a behavior that gets incrementally closer to the overall desired behavior. In the dolphin example—and indeed, in many instances of animal training in which relatively simple animals seem to perform astoundingly complex behaviors—you can think through how each smaller behavior is reinforced until the overall sequence of behavior gets performed reliably.

Superstitious Behavior

Everything we've discussed so far suggests that one of the keys to establishing reliable operant behavior is the correlation between an organism's response and the occurrence of reinforcement. In the case of continuous reinforcement, when every response is followed by the presentation of a reinforcer, there is a one-to-one, or perfect, correlation. In the case of intermittent reinforcement, the correlation is weaker (i.e., not every response is met with the delivery of reinforcement), but it's not zero. As you read in Chapter 2, however, just because two things are correlated (that is, they tend to occur together in time and space) doesn't imply that there is causality (that is, the presence of one reliably causes the other to occur).

Skinner (1947) designed an experiment that illustrates this distinction. He put several pigeons in Skinner boxes, set the food dispenser to deliver food every 15 seconds, and left the birds to their own devices. Later he returned and found the birds engaging in odd, idiosyncratic behaviors, such as pecking aimlessly in a corner or turning in circles. He referred to these behaviors as "superstitious" and offered a behaviorist analysis of their occurrence. The pigeons, he argued, were simply repeating behaviors that had been accidentally reinforced. A pigeon that just happened to have pecked randomly in the corner when the food showed up had connected the delivery of food to that behavior. Because this pecking behavior was "reinforced" by the delivery of food, the pigeon was likely to repeat it. Now pecking in the corner was more likely to occur, and it was more likely to be reinforced 15 seconds later when the food appeared again.

For each pigeon, the behavior reinforced would most likely be whatever the pigeon happened to be doing when the food was first delivered. Skinner's pigeons acted as though there was a causal relationship between their behaviors and the appearance of food when it was merely an accidental correlation. Superstitious behavior is not limited to pigeons, of course. Baseball players who enjoy several home runs on a day when they happened to have not showered are likely to continue that tradition, laboring under the belief that the accidental correlation between poor personal hygiene and a good day at bat is somehow causal. This "stench causes home runs" hypothesis is just one of many examples of human superstitions (Gilbert, Brown, Pihel, & Wilson, 2000; Radford & Radford, 1949).

 **ONLY HUMAN**

SHAPING YES, WRITING NO 1991—Last summer, a class of 25 psychology students at Kalamazoo College in Michigan trained 14 rats as part of a class project in lieu of writing term papers. Among the tricks the rats mastered were the broad jump, tightrope walking, and playing soccer.

People believe in many different superstitions and engage in all kinds of superstitious behaviors. Many major league baseball players, for example, maintain a superstition of not stepping on the baselines when they enter or leave the field, as illustrated by Baltimore Orioles pitcher Daniel Cabrera. Skinner thought superstitions resulted from the unintended reinforcement of inconsequential behavior.

AP PHOTO/CHRIS GARDNER

A Deeper Understanding of Operant Conditioning

Like classical conditioning, operant conditioning also quickly proved powerful. It's difficult to argue this fact when a rat learns to perform relatively complex behaviors after only 20 minutes of practice, prompted by little more than the skillful presentation of rat chow. The results are evident: "Learning" in its most fundamental sense is a change in behavior brought about by experience. In this case, the rat didn't perform the task at first, and then, after a little training, it learned to perform the task very well indeed. Case closed.

Well, case closed to the satisfaction of behaviorists. Like the behaviorism of John Watson, the behaviorism of B. F. Skinner didn't include the mind in its analysis of an organism's actions. Skinner was satisfied to observe an organism perform the behavior; he didn't look for a deeper explanation of mental processes (Skinner, 1950). In this view, an organism behaved in a certain way as a response to stimuli in the environment, not because there was any wanting, wishing, or willing by the animal in question. However, some research on operant conditioning digs deeper into the underlying mechanisms that produce the familiar outcomes of reinforcement. Let's examine three elements that expand our view of operant conditioning beyond strict behaviorism: the neural, cognitive, and evolutionary elements of operant conditioning.

The Neural Elements of Operant Conditioning

Soon after psychologists came to appreciate the range and variety of things that could function as reinforcers, they began looking for underlying brain mechanisms that might account for these effects. The first hint of how specific brain structures might contribute to the process of reinforcement came from the discovery of what came to be called *pleasure centers*. James Olds and his associates inserted tiny electrodes into different parts of a rat's brain and allowed the animal to control electric stimulation of its own brain by pressing a bar. They discovered that some brain areas, particularly those in the limbic system (see Chapter 3), produced what appeared to be intensely positive experiences: The rats would press the bar repeatedly to stimulate these structures. The researchers observed that these rats would ignore food, water, and other life-sustaining necessities for hours on end simply to receive stimulation directly in the brain. They then called these parts of the brain "pleasure centers" (Olds, 1956) (see **FIGURE 6.10**).

Based on this research, researchers implanted stimulating electrodes into the brains of patients who suffered from disorders such as intractable epilepsy in the hope that they could be used to develop new therapeutic techniques. In a number of cases, these patients did indeed experience a distinct sense of pleasure, most often when the electrodes were placed in limbic areas. Some patients reported feelings that were sexual in nature, but most merely responded that they "felt good" in some vague sense. These studies have been abandoned for various reasons ranging from questions about their ethics to failures to find any particularly useful therapeutic applications (Valenstein, 1973, 1986).

In the years since these early studies, researchers have identified a number of structures and pathways in the brain that deliver rewards through stimulation (Wise, 1989, 2005). The neurons in the *medial forebrain bundle*, a pathway that meanders its way from the midbrain through the *hypothalamus* into the *nucleus accumbens*, are the most susceptible to stimulation that produces pleasure. This is not surprising as psychologists have identified this bundle of cells as crucial to behaviors that clearly involve pleasure, such as eating, drinking, and engaging in sexual activity. Second, the neurons all along this pathway and especially those in the nucleus accumbens itself are all *dopaminergic*; that is, they secrete the neurotransmitter *dopamine*. Remember from Chapter 3 that higher levels of dopamine in the brain are usually associated with positive emotions.

Figure 6.10 Pleasure Centers in the Brain The nucleus accumbens, medial forebrain bundle, and hypothalamus are all major pleasure centers in the brain.

Nucleus accumbens

Hypothalamus

Pituitary gland

Medial forebrain bundle

Amygdala

Hippocampus

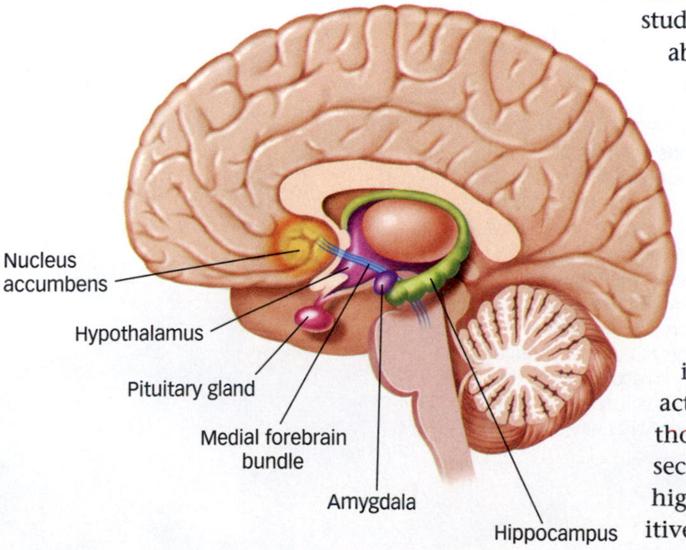

Researchers have found good support for this "reward center." First, as you've just seen, rats will work to stimulate this pathway at the expense of other basic needs (Olds & Fobes, 1981). However, if drugs that block the action of dopamine are administered to the rats, they cease stimulating the pleasure centers (Stellar, Kelley, & Corbett, 1983). Second, drugs such as cocaine, amphetamine, and opiates activate these pathways and centers (Moghaddam & Bunney, 1989), but dopamine-blocking drugs dramatically diminish their reinforcing effects (White & Milner, 1992). Third, fMRI studies (see Chapter 3) show increased activity in the nucleus accumbens in heterosexual men looking at pictures of attractive women (Aharon et al., 2001) and in individuals who believe they are about to receive money (Knutson, Adams, Fong, & Hommer, 2001). Finally, rats given primary reinforcers such as food or water or who are allowed to engage in sexual activity show increased dopamine secretion in the nucleus accumbens—but only if the rats are hungry, thirsty, or sexually aroused (Damsma, Pfaus, Wenkstern, Phillips, & Fibiger, 1992). This last finding is exactly what we might expect given our earlier discussion of the complexities of reinforcement. After all, food tastes a lot better when we are hungry and sexual activity is more pleasurable when we are aroused. These biological structures underlying rewards and reinforcements probably evolved to ensure that species engaged in activities that helped survival and reproduction.

The Cognitive Elements of Operant Conditioning

In Skinner's day, most operant-conditioning researchers argued for a strict behaviorist interpretation of learning. All they required was a complete description of the stimuli, the subsequent response, and the associations between them. As you've already seen, in the case of classical conditioning, this strict behaviorist model was enhanced by considering the role of cognitive activities in learning. Several lines of research suggest that considering the role of cognition can better explain operant conditioning.

Edward Chace Tolman (1886–1959) was the strongest early advocate of a cognitive approach to operant learning. Tolman was dissatisfied with the simple stimulus-response (S-R) approach to understanding learning, arguing that there was more to learning than just knowing the circumstances in the environment (the properties of the stimulus) and being able to observe a particular outcome (the reinforced response). Instead, Tolman proposed that an animal established a means-ends relationship. That is, the conditioning experience produced knowledge or a belief that, in this particular situation, a specific reward (the end state) will appear if a specific response (the means to that end) is made.

Tolman's means-ends relationship may remind you of another paradigm you've read about in this chapter—the Rescorla-Wagner model of classical conditioning. Rescorla argued that the CS functions by setting up an expectation about the arrival of a US—and "expectations" are most certainly mental states. In both Rescorla and Tolman's theories, the stimulus does not directly evoke a response; rather, it establishes an internal cognitive state, which then produces the behavior. These cognitive theories of learning focus less on the S-R connection and more on what happens in the organism's mind when faced with the stimulus. In contrast to staunch S-R behaviorists, cognitively oriented psychologists such as Tolman are more concerned with what goes on between the S and the R.

Early studies with rats and mazes supported the influence of cognition on operant conditioning. Rats that had learned to run through a maze for a small reward ran much faster when they were switched to a larger reward; in fact, they ran faster than a comparable group that had always had the large reward (Crespi, 1942). Similarly, rats that were switched from the large reward to the small one ran slower than those who always had the smaller rewards. In both cases, the rats acted as though they had a pretty good idea

BANCROFT LIBRARY/UNIVERSITY OF CALIFORNIA, BERKELEY

Edward Chace Tolman advocated a cognitive approach to operant learning and provided evidence that in maze learning experiments, rats develop a mental picture of the maze, which he called a cognitive map.

LATENT LEARNING A condition in which something is learned but it is not manifested as a behavioral change until sometime in the future.

COGNITIVE MAP A mental representation of the physical features of the environment.

about what to expect at the end of the maze. Their behavior revealed a cognitive element: The rats appeared to be either excited or annoyed about changes in the reward and seemed to make corresponding changes in their behavior.

During the 1930s and 1940s, Tolman and his students conducted studies that focused on *latent learning* and *cognitive maps,* two phenomena that strongly suggest that simple stimulus-response interpretations of operant learning behavior are inadequate.

In **latent learning,** *something is learned but it is not manifested as a behavioral change until sometime in the future.* Latent learning can easily be established in rats and occurs without any obvious reinforcement, a finding that posed a direct challenge to the then-dominant behaviorist position that all learning required some form of reinforcement (Tolman & Honzik, 1930a).

Tolman gave three groups of rats access to a complex maze every day for over 2 weeks. The control group never received any reinforcement for navigating the maze. They were simply allowed to run around until they reached the goal box at the end of the maze. In **FIGURE 6.11** you can see that over the 2 weeks of the study, this group (in green) got a little better at finding their way through the maze but not by much. A second group of rats received regular reinforcements; when they reached the goal box, they found a small food reward there. Not surprisingly, these rats showed clear learning, as can be seen in blue in Figure 6.11. A third group was treated exactly like the control group for the first 10 days and then rewarded for the last 7 days. This group's behavior (in orange) was quite striking. For the first 10 days, they behaved like the rats in the control group. However, during the final 7 days, they behaved a lot like the rats in the second group that had been reinforced every day. Clearly, the rats in this third group had learned a lot about the maze and the location of the goal box during those first 10 days even though they had not received any reinforcements for their behavior. In other words, they showed evidence of latent learning.

These results suggested to Tolman that beyond simply learning "start here, end here," his rats had developed a sophisticated mental picture of the maze. Tolman called this a **cognitive map**, or *a mental representation of the physical features of the environment.* Beyond simply learning "start here, end here," Tolman thought that the rats had developed a mental picture of the maze, more along the lines of "make two lefts, then a right, then a quick left at the corner." He devised several experiments to test this idea (Tolman & Honzik, 1930b; Tolman, Ritchie, & Kalish, 1946).

One simple experiment provided support for Tolman's theories and wreaked havoc with the noncognitive explanations offered by staunch behaviorists. Tolman trained a group of rats in the maze shown in **FIGURE 6.12a**. As you can see, rats run down a straightaway, take a left, a right, a long right, and then end up in the goal box at the end of the maze. Because we're looking at it from above, we can see that the rat's position at the end of the maze, relative to the starting point, is "diagonal to the upper

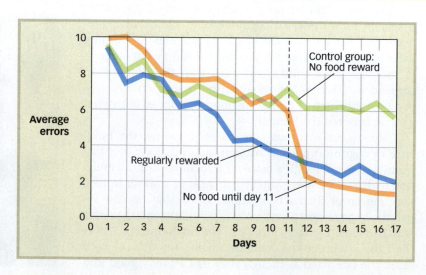

Figure 6.11 **Latent Learning** Rats in a control group that never received any reinforcement (in green) improved at finding their way through the maze over 17 days but not by much. Rats that received regular reinforcements (in blue) showed fairly clear learning; their error rate decreased steadily over time. Rats in the latent learning group (in orange) were treated exactly like the control group rats for the first 10 days and then like the regularly rewarded group for the last 7 days. Their dramatic improvement on day 12 shows that these rats had learned a lot about the maze and the location of the goal box even though they had never received reinforcements. Notice also that on the last 7 days, these latent learners actually seem to make *fewer* errors than their regularly rewarded counterparts.

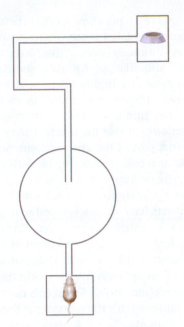

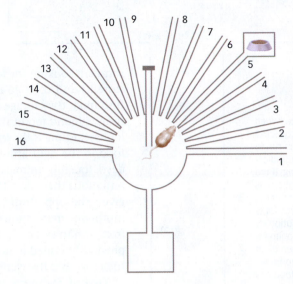

(a) Apparatus used in preliminary training

(b) Apparatus used in test trial

Figure 6.12 Cognitive Maps
(a) Rats trained to run from a start box to a goal box in the maze on the left mastered the task quite readily. When these rats were then placed in the maze on the right (b), in which the main straightaway had been blocked, they did something unusual. Rather than simply backtrack and try the next closest runway (i.e., those labeled 8 or 9 in the figure), which would be predicted by stimulus generalization, the rats typically chose runway 5, which led most directly to where the goal box had been during their training. The rats had formed a cognitive map of their environment and so knew where they needed to end up, spatially, compared to where they began.

right." Of course, all the rat in the maze sees are the next set of walls and turns until it eventually reaches the goal box. Nonetheless, rats learned to navigate this maze without error or hesitation after about four nights. Clever rats. But they were more clever than you think.

After they had mastered the maze, Tolman changed things around a bit and put them in the maze shown in Figure 6.12b. The goal box was still in the same place relative to the start box. However, many alternative paths now spoked off the main platform, and the main straightaway that the rats had learned to use was blocked. Most behaviorists would predict that the rats in this situation—running down a familiar path only to find it blocked—would show stimulus generalization and pick the next closest path, such as one immediately adjacent to the straightaway. This was not what Tolman observed. When faced with the blocked path, the rats instead ran all the way down the path that led directly to the goal box. The rats had formed a sophisticated cognitive map of their environment and behaved in a way that suggested they were successfully following that map after the conditions had changed. Latent learning and cognitive maps suggest that operant conditioning involves much more than an animal responding to a stimulus. Tolman's experiments strongly suggest that there is a cognitive component, even in rats, to operant learning.

The Evolutionary Elements of Operant Conditioning

As you'll recall, classical conditioning has an adaptive value that has been fine-tuned by evolution. Not surprisingly, we can also view operant conditioning from an evolutionary perspective. This viewpoint grew out of a set of curious observations from the early days of conditioning experiments. Several behaviorists who were using simple T mazes like the one shown in **FIGURE 6.13** to study learning in rats discovered that if a rat found food in one arm of the maze on the first trial of the day, it typically ran down the *other* arm on the very next trial. A staunch behaviorist wouldn't expect the rats to behave this way. After all, the rats in these experiments were hungry and they had just been reinforced for turning in a particular direction. According to operant conditioning, this should *increase* the likelihood of turning in that same direction, not reduce it. With additional trials the rats eventually learned to go to the arm with the food, but they had to learn to overcome this initial tendency to go "the wrong way." How can we explain this mindbug?

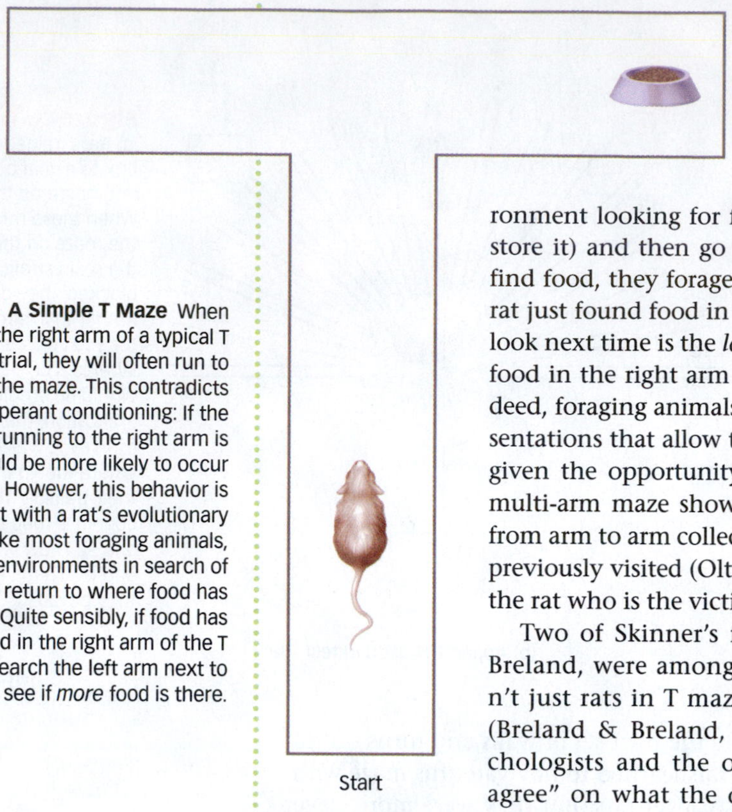

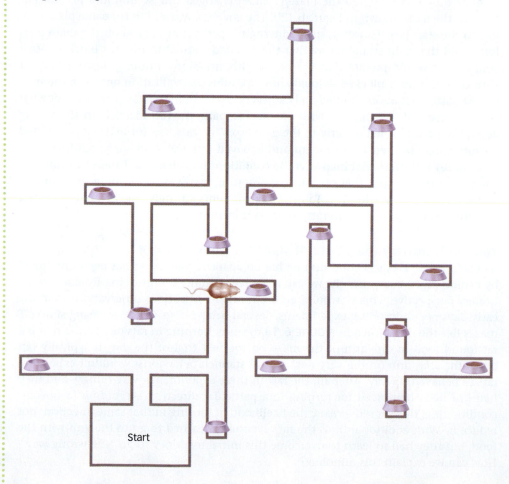

Figure 6.13 **A Simple T Maze** When rats find food in the right arm of a typical T maze, on the next trial, they will often run to the *left* arm of the maze. This contradicts basic principles of operant conditioning: If the behavior of running to the right arm is reinforced, it should be more likely to occur again in the future. However, this behavior is perfectly consistent with a rat's evolutionary preparedness. Like most foraging animals, rats explore their environments in search of food and seldom return to where food has already been found. Quite sensibly, if food has already been found in the right arm of the T maze, the rat will search the left arm next to see if *more* food is there.

Start

What was puzzling from a behaviorist perspective makes sense when viewed from an evolutionary perspective. Rats are foragers, and like all foraging species, they have evolved a highly adaptive strategy for survival. They move around in their environment looking for food. If they find it somewhere, they eat it (or store it) and then go look somewhere else for more. If they do not find food, they forage in another part of the environment. So, if the rat just found food in the *right* arm of a T maze, the obvious place to look next time is the *left* arm. The rat knows that there isn't any more food in the right arm because it just ate the food it found there! Indeed, foraging animals such as rats have well-developed spatial representations that allow them to search their environment efficiently. If given the opportunity to explore a complex environment like the multi-arm maze shown in **FIGURE 6.14**, rats will systematically go from arm to arm collecting food, rarely returning to an arm they have previously visited (Olton & Samuelson, 1976). So, in this case it's not the rat who is the victim of a mindbug; it's the behaviorist theorist!

Two of Skinner's former students, Keller Breland and Marian Breland, were among the first researchers to discover that it wasn't just rats in T mazes that presented a problem for behaviorists (Breland & Breland, 1961). The Brelands pointed out that psychologists and the organisms they study often seemed to "disagree" on what the organisms should be doing. Their argument was simple: When this kind of dispute develops, the animals are always right, and the psychologists had better rethink their theories.

Figure 6.14 **A Complex T Maze** Like many other foraging species, rats placed in a complex T maze such as this one show evidence of their evolutionary preparedness. These rats will systematically travel from arm to arm in search of food, never returning to arms they have already visited.

Start

The Brelands, who made a career out of training animals for commercials and movies, often used pigs because pigs are surprisingly good at learning all sorts of tricks. However, they discovered that it was extremely difficult to teach a pig the simple task of dropping coins in a box. Instead of depositing the coins, the pigs persisted in rooting with them as if they were digging them up in soil, tossing them in the air with their snouts and pushing them around. The Brelands tried to train raccoons at the same task, with different but equally dismal results. The raccoons spent their time rubbing the coins between their paws instead of dropping them in the box.

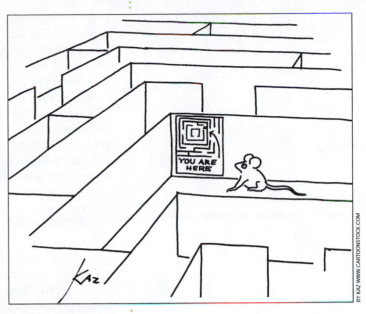

Having learned the association between the coins and food, the animals began to treat the coins as stand-ins for food. Pigs are biologically predisposed to root out their food, and raccoons have evolved to clean their food by rubbing it with their paws. That is exactly what each species of animal did with the coins.

The Brelands' work shows that each species, including humans, is biologically predisposed to learn some things more readily than others and to respond to stimuli in ways that are consistent with its evolutionary history (Gallistel, 2000). Such adaptive behaviors, however, evolved over extraordinarily long periods and in particular environmental contexts. If those circumstances change, some of the behavioral mechanisms that support learning can lead an organism astray. Raccoons that associated coins with food failed to follow the simple route to obtaining food by dropping the coins in the box; "nature" took over and they wasted time rubbing the coins together. The point is that although much of every organism's behavior results from predispositions sharpened by evolutionary mechanisms, these mechanisms sometimes can have ironic consequences.

A clever series of studies showed how evolved predispositions to learn can backfire on an animal (Thomas, 1981). Rats were placed in a Skinner box and the timer was set to deliver food every 20 seconds, no matter what the rats did. (You'll recall that this is a fixed interval schedule of reinforcement.) In fact, if they just lay around doing absolutely nothing, they were guaranteed to get three food pellets every minute. However, the feeding mechanism was rigged so that if a rat actually *did* press the bar before the full 20 seconds was up, a food pellet would be delivered immediately. Aside from not having to wait for their first pellet, the rats gained nothing else from these preemptive bar presses; they still had to wait for the 20-second period to elapse before they could get the next pellet. Because the feedings were controlled in this manner, in

The misbehavior of organisms: Pigs are biologically predisposed to root out their food, just as raccoons are predisposed to wash their food. Trying to train either species to behave differently can prove to be an exercise in futility.

any 1-hour session exactly 180 food pellets were delivered, and nothing the rats did could increase that amount. In short, bar pressing was absolutely useless in the long run. Nevertheless, over several hours of training, the rats increased bar pressing from an average of 0 presses per minute to nearly 30. The rats learned that there was an association between bar pressing and food, even though this association was worthless in terms of the number of reinforcements delivered.

A second experiment showed just how counterproductive this tendency to find associations can be. In this experiment, everything was kept the same except for one important modification. Now those preemptive bar presses that made food immediately available had a severe negative consequence. If a rat pressed the bar, it got food right away, but it was docked food in the next 20-second interval, whether it pressed the bar during this period or not. In other words, a rat that pressed the bar regularly would lose out on every other reinforcement. It could only get a food pellet half the time, and its overall rations would be cut in half, reduced from 3 pellets every minute to an average of only 1.5 pellets. Yet the association between the bar press and the immediate delivery of food was sufficiently strong that the rats still showed systematic increases in bar pressing, some of them averaging over 25 bar presses a minute.

These rats showed the perils of impatience. By opting for immediate rewards, they ended up losing out in the long run. What seems to be a perverse mindbug is a consequence of the usually adaptive tendency to discover the associations between events in the environment. In this case, acting too readily on the association between bar pressing and food delivery backfired as a long-term adaptive strategy.

In summary, operant conditioning, as developed by B. F. Skinner, is a process by which behaviors are reinforced and therefore become more likely to occur, where complex behaviors are shaped through reinforcement, and where the contingencies between actions and outcomes are critical in determining how an organism's behaviors will be displayed. Like Watson, Skinner tried to explain behavior without considering cognitive or evolutionary mechanisms. However, as with classical conditioning, this approach turned out to have serious shortcomings. Operant conditioning has clear cognitive components: Organisms behave as though they have expectations about the outcomes of their actions and adjust their actions accordingly. Moreover, the associative mechanisms that underlie operant conditioning have their roots in evolutionary biology. Some things are relatively easily learned and others are difficult; the history of the species is usually the best clue as to which will be which. ■ ■

Observational Learning: Look at Me

The guiding principle of operant conditioning is that reinforcement determines future behavior. That tenet fit well with behaviorism's insistence on observable action as the appropriate level of explanation and the behaviorists' reluctance to consider what was going on in the mind. As we've already seen, however, cognition helps explain why operant conditioning doesn't always happen as behaviorists would expect. The next section looks at learning by keeping one's eyes and ears open to the surrounding environment and further chips away at strict behaviorist doctrine.

Learning without Direct Experience

Consider this story about 4-year-old Rodney and his 2-year-old sister, Margie. Their parents had always told them to keep away from the stove, and that's good advice for any child and many an adult. Being a mischievous imp, however, Rodney decided one day to heat up a burner, place his hand over it, and slowly press down . . . until the singeing of his flesh led him to recoil, shrieking in pain. Rodney was just fine—more scared than hurt, really—and no one hearing this story doubts that he learned something important that day. But no one doubts that little Margie, who stood by watching each of these events unfold, *also* learned the same lesson. Rodney's story is a behaviorist's textbook example: The administration of punishment led to a learned change in his behavior. But how can we explain Margie's learning? She received neither punishment nor reinforcement—indeed, she didn't even have direct experience with the wicked appliance—yet it's arguable that she's just as likely to keep her hands away from stoves in the future as Rodney is.

Margie's is a case of **observational learning**, in which *learning takes place by watching the actions of others.* Observational learning challenges behaviorism's reinforcement-based explanations of classical and operant conditioning, but there is no doubt that this type of learning produces changes in behavior. In all societies, appropriate social behavior is passed on from generation to generation largely through observation (Bandura, 1965). The rituals and behaviors that are a part of our culture are acquired by each new generation, not only through deliberate training of the young but also through young people observing the patterns of behaviors of their elders. Tasks such as using chopsticks or learning to operate a TV's remote control are more easily acquired if we watch these activities being carried out before we try ourselves. Even complex motor tasks, such as performing surgery, are learned in part through extensive observation and imitation of models. And anyone who is about to undergo surgery is grateful for observational learning. Just the thought of a generation of surgeons acquiring their surgical techniques using the trial-and-error techniques studied by Thorndike or the shaping of successive approximations that captivated Skinner would make any of us very nervous.

Observational learning plays an important role in surgical training, as illustrated by the medical students observing famed German surgeon Vincenz Czerny (beard and white gown) perform stomach surgery in 1901 at a San Francisco hospital.

STANLEY B. BURNS, MD & THE BURNS ARCHIVE N.Y./PHOTO RESEARCHERS

Observational Learning in Humans

In a series of studies that have become landmarks in psychology, Albert Bandura and his colleagues investigated the parameters of observational learning (Bandura, Ross, & Ross, 1961). The researchers escorted individual preschoolers into a play area, where they found a number of desirable toys that they could play with: stickers, ink stamps, crayons, all things that 4-year-olds typically like. An adult *model,* someone whose behavior might serve as a guide for others, was then led into the room and seated in the opposite corner, where there were several adult toys. There were Tinkertoys, a small mallet, and a Bobo doll, which is a large inflatable plastic toy with a weighted bottom that allows it to bounce back upright when knocked down. The adult played quietly for a bit but then started aggressing toward the Bobo doll, knocking it down, jumping on it, hitting it with the mallet, kicking it around the room, and yelling "Pow!" and "Kick him!" When the children who observed these actions were later allowed to play with a variety of toys, including a child-size Bobo doll, they were more than twice as likely to interact with it in an aggressive manner as a group of children who hadn't observed the aggressive model.

OBSERVATIONAL LEARNING A condition in which learning takes place by watching the actions of others.

ALBERT BANDURA, DEPT. OF PSYCHOLOGY, STAMFORD UNIVERSITY

Figure 6.15 **Beating Up Bobo** Children who were exposed to an adult model who behaved aggressively toward a Bobo doll were likely to behave aggressively themselves. This behavior occurred in the absence of any direct reinforcement. Observational learning was responsible for producing the children's behaviors.

So what? Kids like to break stuff, and after all, Bobo dolls are made to be punched. Although that's true, as **FIGURE 6.15** shows, the degree of imitation that the children showed was startling. In fact, the adult model purposely used novel behaviors such as hitting the doll with a mallet or throwing it up in the air so that the researchers could distinguish aggressive acts that were clearly the result of observational learning. The children in these studies also showed that they were sensitive to the consequences of the actions they observed. When they saw the adult models being punished for behaving aggressively, the children showed considerably less aggression. When the children observed a model being rewarded and praised for aggressive behavior, they displayed an increase in aggression (Bandura, Ross, & Ross, 1963).

The observational learning seen in Bandura's studies has implications for social learning, cultural transmission of norms and values, and psychotherapy, as well as moral and ethical issues (Bandura, 1977, 1994). For example, a recent review of the literature on the effects of viewing violence on subsequent behavior concluded that viewing media violence has both immediate and long-term effects in increasing the likelihood of aggressive and violent behavior among youth (Anderson et al., 2003). This conclusion speaks volumes about the impact of violence and aggression as presented on TV, in movies, and in video games on our society, but it is hardly surprising in light of Bandura's pioneering research more than 40 years earlier.

Video games have become a must-have device in many households. Research on observational learning suggests that seeing violent images—in video games, on television, or in movies—can increase the likelihood of enacting violent behavior.

ALEX SEGRE/ALAMY

Observational Learning in Animals

Humans aren't the only creatures capable of learning through observing. A wide variety of species learns by observing. In one study, for example, pigeons watched other pigeons get reinforced for either pecking at the feeder or stepping on a bar. When placed in the box later, the pigeons tended to use whatever technique they had observed other pigeons using earlier (Zentall, Sutton, & Sherburne, 1996).

In an interesting series of studies, researchers showed that laboratory-raised rhesus monkeys that had never seen a snake would develop a fear of snakes simply by observing the fear reactions of other monkeys (Cook & Mineka, 1990; Mineka & Cook, 1988). In fact, the fear reactions of these lab-raised monkeys were so authentic and pronounced that they could function as models for still *other* lab-raised monkeys, creating a kind of observational learning "chain." These results also support our earlier discussion of how each species has evolved particular biological predispositions for specific behaviors. Virtually every rhesus monkey raised in the wild has a fear of snakes, which strongly suggests that such a fear is one of this species' predispositions. This research also helps to explain why some phobias that humans suffer from, such as a fear of heights (acrophobia) or enclosed spaces (claustrophobia), are so common, even in people who have never had unpleasant experiences in these contexts (Mineka & Ohman, 2002). The fears may emerge not from specific conditioning experiences but from observing and learning from the reactions of others.

Observational learning may involve a neural component as well. As you read in Chapter 3, *mirror neurons* are a type of cell found in the brains of primates (including humans). Mirror neurons fire when an animal performs an action, such as when a monkey reaches for a food item. More importantly, however, mirror neurons also fire when an animal watches someone *else* perform the same specific task (Rizzolatti & Craighero, 2004). Although this "someone else" is usually a fellow member of the same species, some research suggests that mirror neurons in monkeys also fire when they observe humans performing an action (Fogassi et al., 2005). For example, monkeys' mirror neurons fired when they observed humans grasping for a piece of food, either to eat it or to place it in a container.

Mirror neurons, then, may play a critical role in the imitation of behavior as well as the prediction of future behavior (Rizzolatti, 2004). If the neurons fire when another organism is seen performing an action, it could indicate an awareness of intentionality, or that the animal is anticipating a likely course of future actions. Both of these elements—rote imitation of well-understood behaviors and an awareness of how behavior is likely to unfold—contribute to observational learning.

ONLY HUMAN

IF ONLY WE COULD MODEL THIS BEHAVIOR AT HOME A female chimpanzee, Judy, escaped at the Little Rock, Arkansas, zoo in January and as she moved about was observed entering a bathroom, grabbing a brush, and cleaning a toilet. She also wrung out a sponge and cleaned off a refrigerator, according to an Associated Press report.

In summary, classical and operant conditioning are forms of learning that are best understood as having cognitive and functional components that are the result of evolutionary processes. The same is true for observational learning. The cognitive component is fairly clear; the very process itself is based on cognitive mechanisms such as attention, perception, memory, or reasoning. But observational learning also has roots in evolutionary biology and for the most basic of reasons: It has survival value. Observational learning is an important process by which species gather information about the world around them. Shaping by successive approximations can be slow and tedious, and trial-and-error learning often results in many errors before learning is complete. However, when one organism patterns its actions on another organism's successful behaviors, learning is speeded up and potentially dangerous errors are prevented. What's more, such observational learning can save an organism from situations that might prove harmful. Learning by observing another individual successfully negotiate a dangerous environment, deciding not to eat a food that has made others ill, or avoiding conflicts with those who have been seen to vanquish all their opponents are all behavioral advantages that can save an organism considerable pain . . . or even its life. ■ ■

Implicit Learning: Under the Wires

So far, we have covered a lot of what is known about learning with only the briefest consideration of *awareness* in the learning process. You may remember we distinguished between explicit learning and implicit learning at the beginning of the chapter. People often know that they are learning, are aware of what they're learning, and can describe what they know about a topic. If you have learned something concrete, such as doing arithmetic or typing on a computer keyboard, you know that you know it and you know *what* it is you know.

But did Pavlov's dogs *know* that they had been conditioned to salivate to a bell? Did Adam and Teri in our opening vignette understand that they had learned to associate their child's toy with an emotional event? Were Bandura's young research participants aware that the adult model was affecting their behavior? Would their behavior have been any different if they were? It certainly makes sense to ask whether these basic learning processes in humans require an awareness on the part of the learner. Perhaps some permanent changes in experience can be acquired without the benefit of awareness.

Researchers began to investigate how children learned such complex behaviors as language and social conduct (Reber, 1967). Most children, by the time they are 6 or 7 years old, are linguistically and socially fairly sophisticated. Yet most children reach this state with very little explicit awareness that they have learned something and with equally little awareness of what it was they have actually learned.

This simple observation poses theoretical challenges to traditional learning theories. As you'll recall from Chapter 1, linguist Noam Chomsky challenged behaviorist explanations of complex processes such as language acquisition and socialization (Chomsky, 1959). Learning to speak and understand English, for example, involves more than acquiring a series of stimulus-response associations or reinforcing successive approximations to grammatical sentences. Using a language is a creative process. Virtually every sentence we speak, hear, write, or read is new. You understand this sentence that you are now reading, although this is almost certainly the first time you have encountered these words in this particular order. In fact, virtually every sentence in this textbook is new to you, yet you understand them with little difficulty. Behaviorism cannot account for this kind of abstract process, so how can we tackle this problem?

For starters, it's safe to assume that people are sensitive to the patterns of events that occur in the world around them. Most people don't stumble through life thoroughly unaware of what's going on. Okay, maybe your roommate does. But people usually are attuned to linguistic, social, emotional, or sensorimotor events in the world around them so much so that they gradually build up internal representations of those patterns that were acquired without explicit awareness. This process is often called **implicit learning**, or *learning that takes place largely independent of awareness of both the process and the products of information acquisition*. As an example, although children are often given explicit rules of social conduct ("Don't chew with your mouth open"), they learn how to behave in a civilized way through experience. They're probably not aware of when or how they learned a particular course of action and may not even be able to state the general principle underlying their behavior. Yet most kids have learned not to eat with their feet, to listen when they are spoken to, and not to kick the dog. Implicit learning is knowledge that sneaks in "under the wires."

Ways to Study Implicit Learning

Early studies of implicit learning showed research participants 15 or 20 letter strings and asked them to memorize them. The letter strings, which at first glance look like nonsense syllables, were actually formed using a complex set of rules called an *artificial grammar* (see **FIGURE 6.16**). Participants were not told anything about the rules, but with experience, they gradually developed a vague, intuitive sense of the "correctness" of particular letter groupings. These letter groups became familiar to the participants, and they processed these letter groupings more rapidly and efficiently than the "incorrect" letter groupings (Reber, 1967, 1996).

IMPLICIT LEARNING Learning that takes place largely independent of awareness of both the process and the products of information acquisition.

Take a look at the letter strings shown in Figure 6.16. The ones on the left are "correct" and follow the rules of the artificial grammar; the ones on the right all violated the rules. The differences are pretty subtle, and if you haven't been through the learning phase of the experiment, both sets look a lot alike. In fact, each nongrammatical string only has a single letter violation. Research participants are asked to classify new letter strings based on whether they follow the rules of the grammar. People turn out to be quite good at this task (usually they get between 60 and 70 percent correct), but they are unable to provide much in the way of explicit awareness of the rules and regularities that they are using. The experience is like when you come across a sentence with a grammatical error—you are immediately aware that something is wrong and you can certainly make the sentence grammatical. But unless you are a trained linguist, you'll probably find it difficult to articulate which rules of English grammar were violated or which rules you used to repair the sentence.

Other studies of implicit learning have used a *serial reaction time* task (Nissen & Bullemer, 1987). Here research participants are presented with five small boxes on a computer screen. Each box lights up briefly, and when it does, the person is asked to press the button that is just underneath that box as quickly as possible. Immediately after the button is pressed, a different box lights up, the person has to press the corresponding button, and so on. As with the artificial grammar task, the sequence of lights appears to be random, but in fact it follows a pattern. Research participants eventually get faster with practice as they learn to anticipate which box is most likely to light up next. If the sequence is changed or the patterns are modified, people's reaction times slow down, indicating that they were actually learning the sequence and not simply learning to press buttons quickly.

In these experiments, people are not looking for rules or patterns; they are "blind" to the goals of the experiments. The participants' learning takes place outside of their awareness. These studies establish implicit learning as a distinct form of learning (Stadler & Frensch, 1998).

Implicit learning has some characteristics that distinguish it from explicit learning. For example, when asked to carry out implicit tasks, people differ relatively little from one another, but on explicit tasks, such as conscious problem solving, they show large individual-to-individual differences (Reber, Walkenfeld, & Hernstadt, 1991). Implicit learning also seems to be unrelated to IQ: People with high scores on standard intelligence tests are no better at implicit-learning tasks, on average, than those whose scores are more modest (Reber & Allen, 2000). Implicit learning changes little across the life span. Researchers discovered well-developed implicit learning of complex, rule-governed auditory patterns in 8-month-old infants (Saffran, Aslin, & Newport, 1996). Infants heard streams of speech that contained experimenter-defined nonsense words. For example, the infants might hear a sequence such as "bidakupadotigolabu-bidaku," which contains the nonsense word *bida*. The infants weren't given any explicit clues as to which sounds were "words" and which were not, but after several repetitions, the infants showed signs that they had learned the novel words. Infants tend to prefer novel information, and they spent more time listening to novel nonsense words that had not been presented earlier than to the nonsense words such as *bida* that had been presented. Remarkably, the infants in this study were as good at learning these sequences as college students. At the other end of the life span, researchers have found that implicit-learning abilities extend well into old age and that they decline more slowly than explicit-learning abilities (Howard & Howard, 1997).

Implicit learning is remarkably resistant to various disorders that are known to affect explicit learning. A group of patients suffering from various psychoses were so severely impaired that they could not solve simple problems that college students had little difficulty with. Yet these patients were able to solve an artificial grammar learning task about as well as college students (Abrams & Reber, 1988). Other studies have found that profoundly amnesic patients not only show normal implicit memories but also display virtually normal implicit learning of artificial grammar (Knowlton,

Grammatical Strings	Nongrammatical Strings
VXJJ	VXTJJ
XXVT	XVTVVJ
VJTVXJ	VJTTVTV
VJTVTV	VJTXXVJ
XXXXVX	XXXVTJJ

Figure 6.16 **Artificial Grammar and Implicit Learning** These are examples of letter strings formed by an artificial grammar. Research participants are exposed to the rules of the grammar and are later tested on new letter strings. Participants show reliable accuracy at distinguishing the valid, grammatical strings from the invalid, nongrammatical strings even though they usually can't explicitly state the rule they are following when making such judgments. Using an artificial grammar is one way of studying implicit learning (Reber, 1996).

{ THE REAL WORLD } Can You Sleep on It?

FOR A LOT OF PEOPLE, SLEEP SEEMS LIKE A waste of time. After all, you don't *do* anything important—like reading comic books, watching TV, or maybe finishing homework—for 5 to 10 hours every night. It's true that your television watching is cut drastically by needing to sleep (a good reason to get yourself a DVR), but it's not true that sleep is a waste of time. In fact, some scientists have proposed that sleep plays a role in learning.

There are two theories for sleep learning. The first theory is that a person can learn something while asleep. Imagine that you settle down for the night with a CD player next to your pillow playing the basic principles of chemistry. When you wake in the morning, you now know more than you ever wanted to about covalent and ionic bonds simply by having it processed by your sleeping brain. The second theory is that while a person is asleep, information that person has experienced during the day is processed and coded by the brain, thereby strengthening learning. Both of these are fascinating scientific hypotheses; if either is true, they would tell us a great deal about how the brain goes about acquiring knowledge.

Unfortunately, the first proposal doesn't hold up since it has proven difficult to document actual learning while people are asleep. When people report some success in using sleep-learning programs (and they occasionally do), it is because they recall items that were playing during the short periods of wakefulness that occur during sleep. You'd be well advised to resist buying any of the various sleep-learning programs touted in magazines and on the Internet. You should also start going to your chemistry class more often.

Researchers have been able to find support for the second hypothesis. As you learned in Chapter 5, experiences that become part of our permanent memories are those that undergo a variety of neurological modifications, and there are good reasons for believing that many of these changes take place during sleep. For example, researchers asked participants to complete a task that involved learning a series of digits presented as stimulus-response sequences but didn't tell them that the series of digits followed a complex rule. Participants exhibited implicit learning—they got faster as they practiced the task—but only about 25% of

them showed awareness of the rule. However, after a night's sleep, nearly 60% of the participants discovered the rule! It wasn't just the passage of time that caused this dramatic increase in learning and insight. Participants in the control group, who stayed awake for the same 8 hours after learning, showed a rate of insight comparable to that shown by the original data; that is, only about 25% of them discovered the rule. It also didn't matter what time of day these events took place. Eight hours awake during the day produced the same outcomes as 8 hours awake during the night (Wagner, Gais, Haider, Verleiger, & Born, 2004). These striking results suggest that sleep can promote the restructuring of knowledge, providing the backdrop for what later appear as sudden and spontaneous insights.

Overall, the latest research shows that sleep plays an important role in promoting learning. From a practical perspective, it is probably a good idea to make sure that you get a full night's sleep after you've engaged in practice or studied novel information. From a theoretical perspective, psychologists now need to develop better theories of exactly how sleep enhances learning.

Ramus, & Squire, 1992). In fact, these patients made accurate judgments about novel letter strings even though they had essentially no explicit memory of having been in the learning phase of the experiment! (The Real World box above discusses research indicating that implicit learning can occur even during sleep.)

Implicit and Explicit Learning Use Distinct Neural Pathways

The fact that patients suffering from psychoses or amnesia show implicit learning strongly suggests that the brain structures that underlie implicit leaning are distinct from those that underlie explicit learning. What's more, it appears that distinct regions of the brain may be activated depending on how people approach a task.

Researchers found that distinct parts of the brain are activated when people approach a learning task in either an implicit or an explicit manner (Reber, Gitelman, Parrish, & Mesulam, 2003). Participants completed a simple pattern perception procedure. During the initial phase of the study, everyone saw a series of dot patterns, each of which looked like an array of stars in the night sky. Actually, all the stimuli were constructed to conform to an underlying prototypical dot pattern. The dots, however, varied so much that it was virtually impossible for a viewer to guess that they all had this common structure. Before the experiment began, half of the participants were told about the existence of the prototype; in other words, they were given instructions that encouraged explicit processing. The others were given standard implicit-learning instructions: They were told nothing other than to attend to the dot patterns.

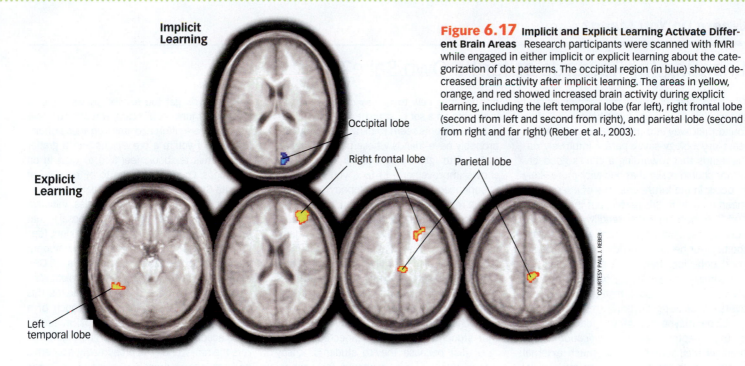

Implicit Learning

Explicit Learning

Occipital lobe

Right frontal lobe

Parietal lobe

Left temporal lobe

COURTESY PAUL J. REBER

Figure 6.17 **Implicit and Explicit Learning Activate Different Brain Areas** Research participants were scanned with fMRI while engaged in either implicit or explicit learning about the categorization of dot patterns. The occipital region (in blue) showed decreased brain activity after implicit learning. The areas in yellow, orange, and red showed increased brain activity during explicit learning, including the left temporal lobe (far left), right frontal lobe (second from left and second from right), and parietal lobe (second from right and far right) (Reber et al., 2003).

The participants were then scanned as they made decisions about new dot patterns, attempting to categorize them into those that conformed to the prototype and those that did not. Interestingly, both groups performed equally well on this task, correctly classifying about 65% of the new dot patterns. However, the brain scans revealed that the two groups were making these decisions using very different parts of their brains (see **FIGURE 6.17**). Participants who were given the explicit instructions showed *increased* brain activity in the prefrontal cortex, parietal cortex, hippocampus, and a variety of other areas known to be associated with the processing of explicit memories. Those given the implicit instructions showed *decreased* brain activation primarily in the occipital region, which is involved in visual processing. This finding suggests that participants recruited distinct brain structures in different ways depending on whether they were approaching the task using explicit or implicit learning.

In summary, implicit learning is a process that detects, learns, and stores patterns without the application of explicit awareness on the part of the learner. Complex behaviors, such as language use or socialization, can be learned through this implicit process. Tasks that have been used to document implicit learning include artificial grammar and serial reaction time tasks. Implicit and explicit learning differ from each other in a number ways: There are fewer individual differences in implicit than explicit learning, psychotic and amnesic patients with explicit-learning problems can exhibit intact implicit learning, and neuroimaging studies indicate that implicit and explicit learning recruit distinct brain structures, sometimes in different ways. ■ ■

Where Do You Stand?

Learning for Rewards or for Its Own Sake?

The principles of operant conditioning and the merits of reinforcement have more than found their way into mainstream culture. The least psychology-savvy parent intuitively understands that rewarding a child's good behavior should make that behavior more likely to occur in the future; the "law of effect" may mean nothing to this parent, but the principle and the outcome are readily appreciated nonetheless. And what parent wouldn't want the best for her or his child? If reward shapes good behavior, then more reward must be the pathway to exemplary behavior, often in the form of good grades, high test scores, and overall clean living. So, bring on the rewards!

Maybe, maybe not. As you learned earlier in this chapter, the *overjustification effect* predicts that sometimes too much external reinforcement for performing an intrinsically rewarding task can undermine future performance. Rewarding a child for getting good grades or high test scores might backfire: The child may come to see the behavior as directed toward the attainment of rewards rather than for its own satisfying outcomes. In short, learning should be fun for its own sake,

not because new toys, new clothes, or cash are riding on a set of straight A's.

Many parents seem to think differently. You probably have friends whose parents shower them with gifts whenever a report card shows improvement; in fact, you may have experienced this yourself. Nobody objects to a little recognition now and then, and it's nice to know that others appreciate your hard work. In fact, if you'd like to know the many, many others who'll appreciate your hard work, pay a visit to www.rewardsforgrades.com. It's a website that lists organizations that will give students external reinforcements for good grades, high test scores, perfect school attendance, and other behaviors that students are usually expected to produce just because they're students. Krispy Kreme offers a free doughnut for each A, Blockbuster gives free kids' movie rentals, Chick-fil-A rewards honor roll membership and perfect attendance with free kids' meals, and Limited Too offers a $5 discount on merchandise if you present a report card "with passing grades" (which, in many school districts, might mean all D's).

Before you get too excited by visions of a "grades for junk food" scam, you should know that there are often age limits on these offers. However, if you're a precocious fourth grader reading this textbook, feel free to cash in on the goods. Or if you happen to be enrolled at Wichita State University, you already might be familiar with the Cash for Grades initiative (www.cashforgrades.com). The proposal is that an 8%-per-credit-hour increase to student fees would be used to then reward good student performance: $624 to a student with a 3.5 GPA at the end of a semester, $804 for straight A's.

Where do you stand on this issue? Is this much ado about nothing or too much of a good thing? Some proponents of rewarding good academic performance argue that it mirrors the real world that, presumably, academic performance is preparing students to enter. After all, in most jobs, better performance is reinforced with better salaries, so why not model that in the school system? On the other hand, shouldn't the search for knowledge be reward enough? Is the subtle shift away from wanting to learn for its own sake to wanting to learn for a doughnut harmful in the long run?

Chapter Review

Defining Learning: Experience That Causes a Permanent Change

- Learning refers to any of several processes that produce relatively permanent changes in an organism's behavior.

- Habituation is a process by which an organism changes the way it reacts to external stimuli. Short-term habituation is distinguished from learning because the changes are not long lasting; long-term habituation is generally regarded as learning.

Classical Conditioning: One Thing Leads to Another

- Classical conditioning is a kind of learning in which a reflexlike reaction (conditioned response) becomes associated with a previously neutral stimulus (conditioned stimulus).

- Stimulus generalization occurs if a CS that is similar to the one used in the original training is introduced. Stimulus discrimination is the flip side of generalization.

- Extinction of a learned response will occur if the CS is presented repeatedly without being followed by the US. Spontaneous recovery occurs if an organism is allowed a rest period following extinction.

- Classical conditioning originally was viewed as an automatic and mechanical process. However, it was soon discovered that neural, cognitive, and evolutionary elements were involved in the process.

Operant Conditioning: Reinforcements from the Environment

- Operant conditioning is a kind of learning in which behaviors are shaped by reinforcement.

- Whereas classical conditioning involves reflexlike behaviors elicited from an organism, operant conditioning deals with overt, controlled, and emitted behaviors.

- Reinforcement is any operation that functions to increase the likelihood of the behavior that led to it. Punishment functions to decrease the likelihood of the behavior.

- Like classical conditioning, operant conditioning shows acquisition, generalization, discrimination, and extinction. The schedule with which reinforcements are delivered has a dramatic effect on how well an operant behavior is learned and how resistant it is to extinction.

- Like classical conditioning, operant conditioning is better understood by taking into account underlying neural, cognitive, and evolutionary components.
- Latent learning and the development of cognitive maps in animals clearly implicate cognitive factors underlying operant learning. The evolutionary histories of individual species promote different patterns of operant learning.

Observational Learning: Look at Me

- Learning can take place through the observation of others and does not necessarily require that the acquired behaviors be performed and reinforced. Observational learning does not simply result in imitation; it can also show creative elements. A child who sees an adult behave in a gentle manner with a toy will often show a variety of gentle reactions, including ones that were not exhibited by the adult model.
- Observational learning occurs in various animal species, including pigeons and monkeys. At a neural level, mirror cells are implicated in the imitation and expectation of behavior.

Implicit Learning: Under the Wires

- Implicit learning takes place largely in the absence of awareness of either the actual learning or the knowledge of what was learned. Infants show intact implicit learning long before they develop conscious awareness. Various patient populations, such as psychotics and those with severe neurological disorders, show virtually normal implicit learning.
- Implicit learning is mediated by areas in the brain that are distinct from those activated during explicit learning. The brain structures that regulate the implicit-learning system evolved much earlier than those that regulate explicit processing.

Key Terms

learning (p. 210)

habituation (p. 211)

classical conditioning (p. 212)

unconditioned stimulus (US) (p. 212)

unconditioned response (UR) (p. 212)

conditioned stimulus (CS) (p. 213)

conditioned response (CR) (p. 213)

acquisition (p. 214)

second-order conditioning (p. 215)

extinction (p. 216)

spontaneous recovery (p. 216)

generalization (p. 217)

discrimination (p. 217)

biological preparedness (p. 223)

operant conditioning (p. 224)

law of effect (p. 225)

operant behavior (p. 225)

reinforcer (p. 226)

punisher (p. 226)

overjustification effect (p. 229)

fixed interval schedule (FI) (p. 231)

variable interval schedule (VI) (p. 231)

fixed ratio schedule (FR) (p. 232)

variable ratio schedule (VR) (p. 232)

intermittent reinforcement (p. 233)

intermittent-reinforcement effect (p. 233)

shaping (p. 233)

latent learning (p. 238)

cognitive map (p. 238)

observational learning (p. 243)

implicit learning (p. 246)

Recommended Readings

Animal Training at SeaWorld. http://www.seaworld.org/animal-info/info-books/training/how-animals-learn.htm. This website offers a glimpse at the operant conditioning techniques used to train Shamu, porpoises, and the occasional squid or two. There are solid, research-based discussions of the principles of reinforcement, observational learning, and other concepts in this chapter.

Bandura, A. (1986). *Social foundations of thought and action: A social cognitive theory.* Englewood Cliffs, NJ: Prentice Hall. This book is a classic statement of Albert Bandura's ideas on the origins of human functioning. Drawing from the beginnings of observational learning, Bandura sketches an elegant and comprehensive theory of how behavior develops and the determinants that shape it.

Buckley, K. W. (1989). *Mechanical man: John Broadus Watson and the beginnings of behaviorism.* New York: Guilford Press. There are many biographies of Watson available; Kerry Buckley's one of the best. Buckley is a historian specializing in the history of psychology, and he has published numerous scholarly works on Watson's life and ideas.

Hartley, M., & Commire, A. (1990). *Breaking the silence.* New York: Putnam Group. Mariette Hartley is a well-known television actress and the granddaughter of John B. Watson. Her autobiography focuses on . . . well, *her* life, mainly. But there are some references to Watson and what it's like growing up as a relative of a controversial figure.

Skinner, B. F. (1971). *Beyond freedom and dignity.* New York: Bantam Books. This book, reprinted by Hackett Publishing in 2002, is largely considered Skinner's definitive statement on humankind and its behavior. Skinner argues that most of society's problems can be better addressed by reshaping the environment following the principles of operant conditioning. Outmoded concepts such as "freedom" and "human dignity" should be abandoned in favor of developing more effective cultural practices. A controversial book when it first appeared, it remains so today.

Todes, D. P. (2000). *Pavlov: Exploring the animal machine.* New York: Oxford University Press. This overview of Pavlov's life and work is part of the Oxford Portraits in Science series, a set of titles that provide easy access to information about key scientists in all disciplines. This title should provide a bit more background about Pavlov's discoveries and the events in his life that helped shape his work.

7

Language and Thought

Language and Communication: Nothing's More Personal
The Complex Structure of Human Language
Language Development
Theories of Language Development
The Neurological Specialization That Allows Language to Develop
Can Other Species Learn Human Language?
THE REAL WORLD Does Bilingualism Interfere with Cognitive Development?
Language and Thought: How Are They Related?

Concepts and Categories: How We Think
The Organization of Concepts and Category-Specific Deficits
Psychological Theories of Concepts and Categories

Judging, Valuing, and Deciding: Sometimes We're Logical, Sometimes Not
Decision Making: Rational, Optimal, and Otherwise
HOT SCIENCE The Neuroscience of Risky Decision Making
Other Approaches to Human Decision Making

Problem Solving: Working It Out
Means-Ends Analysis
Analogical Problem Solving
Creativity and Insight

Transforming Information: How We Reach Conclusions
WHERE DO YOU STAND? Choosing a Mate

AN ENGLISH BOY NAMED CHRISTOPHER showed an amazing talent for languages. By the age of 6, he had learned French from his sister's schoolbooks; he acquired Greek from a textbook in only 3 months. His talent was so prodigious that grown-up Christopher could converse fluently in 16 languages. When tested on English-French translations, he scored as well as a native French speaker. Presented with a made-up language, he figured out the complex rules easily, even though advanced language students found them virtually impossible to decipher (Smith & Tsimpli, 1995).

If you've concluded that Christopher is extremely smart, perhaps even a genius, you're wrong. Instead, he's a savant with highly limited cognitive abilities. His scores on standard intelligence tests are far below normal. He fails simple cognitive tests that 4-year-old children pass with ease, and he cannot even learn the rules for simple games like tic-tac-toe. Despite his dazzling talent, Christopher lives in a halfway house because he does not have the cognitive capacity to make decisions, reason, or solve problems in a way that would allow him to live independently.

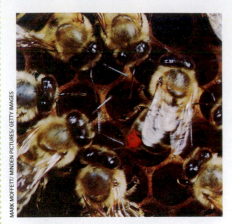

Honeybees communicate with each other about the location of food by doing a waggle dance that indicates the direction and distance of food from the hive.

Christopher's strengths and weaknesses offer compelling evidence that cognition is composed of distinct abilities. People who learn languages with lightning speed are not necessarily gifted at decision making or problem solving. People who excel at reasoning may have no special ability to master languages. In this chapter, you will learn about several higher cognitive functions that distinguish us as humans: acquiring and using language, forming concepts and categories, making decisions, solving problems, and reasoning. We excel at these skills compared with other animals, and they help define who we are as a species.

Language and Communication: Nothing's More Personal

Language is *a system for communicating with others using signals that convey meaning and are combined according to rules of grammar.* Language allows individuals to exchange information about the world, coordinate group action, and form strong social bonds. Most social species have systems of communication that allow them to transmit messages to each other. Honeybees communicate the location of food sources by means of a "waggle dance" that indicates both the direction and distance of the food source from the hive (Kirchner & Towne, 1994; Von Frisch, 1974). Vervet monkeys have three different warning calls that uniquely signal the presence of their main predators: a leopard, an eagle, and a snake (Cheney & Seyfarth, 1990). A leopard call provokes them to climb higher into a tree; an eagle call makes them look up into the sky. Each different warning call conveys a particular meaning and functions like a word in a simple language.

In this section, we'll examine the elements of human language that contribute to its complex structure, the ease with which we acquire language despite this complexity, and how both biological and environmental influences shape language acquisition and use. We'll also look at startling disorders that reveal how language is organized in the brain and at researchers' attempts to teach apes human language. Finally, we'll consider the long-standing puzzle of how language and thought are related.

The Complex Structure of Human Language

Human language may have evolved from signaling systems used by other species. However, three striking differences distinguish human language from vervet monkey yelps, for example. First, the complex structure of human language distinguishes it from simpler signaling systems. Most humans can express a wider range of ideas and concepts than are found in the communications of other species. Second, humans use words to refer to intangible things, such as *unicorn* or *democracy*. These words could not have originated as simple alarm calls. Third, we use language to name, categorize, and describe things to ourselves when we think, which influences how knowledge is organized in our brains. It's doubtful that honeybees consciously think, *I'll fly north today to find more honey so the queen will be impressed!*

Compared with other forms of communication, human language is a relatively recent evolutionary phenomenon, emerging as a spoken system no more than 1 to 3 million years ago and as a written system as little as 6,000 years ago. There are approximately 4,000 human languages, which linguists have grouped into about 50 language families (Nadasdy, 1995). Despite their differences, all of these languages share a basic structure involving a set of sounds and rules for combining those sounds to produce meanings.

Basic Characteristics

The smallest unit of sound that is recognizable as speech rather than as random noise is the **phoneme**. These building blocks of spoken language differ in how they are produced. For example, when you say *ba,* your vocal cords start to vibrate as soon as you begin the sound, but when you say *pa,* there is a 60-millisecond lag between the time you start the *p* sound and the time your vocal cords start to vibrate. *B* and *p* are classified as separate phonemes in English because they differ in the way they are produced by the human speaker.

LANGUAGE A system for communicating with others using signals that convey meaning and are combined according to rules of grammar.

PHONEME The smallest unit of sound that is recognizable as speech rather than as random noise.

PHONOLOGICAL RULES A set of rules that indicate how phonemes can be combined to produce speech sounds.

MORPHEMES The smallest meaningful units of language.

GRAMMAR A set of rules that specify how the units of language can be combined to produce meaningful messages.

MORPHOLOGICAL RULES A set of rules that indicate how morphemes can be combined to form words.

SYNTACTICAL RULES A set of rules that indicate how words can be combined to form phrases and sentences.

Different languages use between 12 and 85 phonemes; English has about 40 (Miller, 1994). What makes something a phoneme rather than noise depends on its use as a speech signal, not on its physical properties. For example, the language spoken by the !Kung population of Namibia and Angola includes a clicking sound, a phoneme that does not appear in English.

Every language has **phonological rules** that *indicate how phonemes can be combined to produce speech sounds*. For example, the initial sound *ts* is acceptable in German but not in English. Typically, people learn these phonological rules without instruction, and if the rules are violated, the resulting speech sounds so odd that we describe it as speaking with an accent. As you'll see in a little while, infants are born with the ability to distinguish among phonemes, and learning rules for combining them occurs automatically as long as infants hear language spoken around them.

Phonemes are combined to make **morphemes,** *the smallest meaningful units of language* (see **FIGURE 7.1**). For example, your brain recognizes the *pə* sound you make at the beginning of *pat* as a speech *sound,* but it carries no particular meaning. The morpheme *pat,* on the other hand, is recognized as an element of speech that carries meaning.

All languages have a **grammar,** *a set of rules that specify how the units of language can be combined to produce meaningful messages.* These rules generally fall into two categories: rules of morphology and rules of syntax. **Morphological rules** *indicate how morphemes can be combined to form words.* Some morphemes—content morphemes and function morphemes—can stand alone as words. *Content morphemes* refer to things and events (e.g., "cat," "dog," "take"). *Function morphemes* serve grammatical functions, such as tying sentences together ("and," "or," "but") or indicating time ("when"). About half of the morphemes in human languages are function morphemes, and it is the function morphemes that make human language grammatically complex enough to permit us to express abstract ideas rather than simply to verbally point to real objects in the here and now.

Content and function morphemes can be combined and recombined to form an infinite number of new sentences, which are governed by syntax. **Syntactical rules** *indicate how words can be combined to form phrases and sentences.* A simple syntactical rule in English is that every sentence must contain one or more nouns, which may be combined with adjectives or articles to create noun phrases (see **FIGURE 7.2**). A sentence also must contain one or more verbs, which may be combined with adverbs or articles to create verb phrases. The utterance "dogs bark" is a full sentence because it contains

Figure 7.1 Units of Language A sentence—the largest unit of language—can be broken down into progressively smaller units: phrases, morphemes, and phonemes. In all languages, phonemes and morphemes form words, which can be combined into phrases and ultimately into sentences.

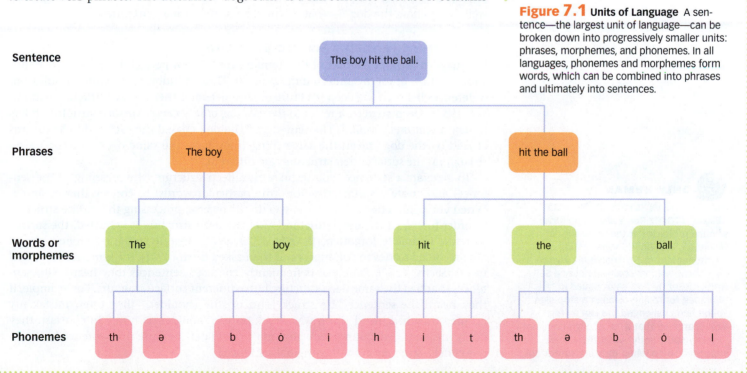

Figure 7.2 Syntactical Rules
Syntactical rules indicate how words can be combined to form sentences. Every sentence must contain one or more nouns, which may be combined with adjectives or articles to create a noun phrase. A sentence also must contain one or more verbs, which may be combined with noun phrases, adverbs, or articles to create a verb phrase.

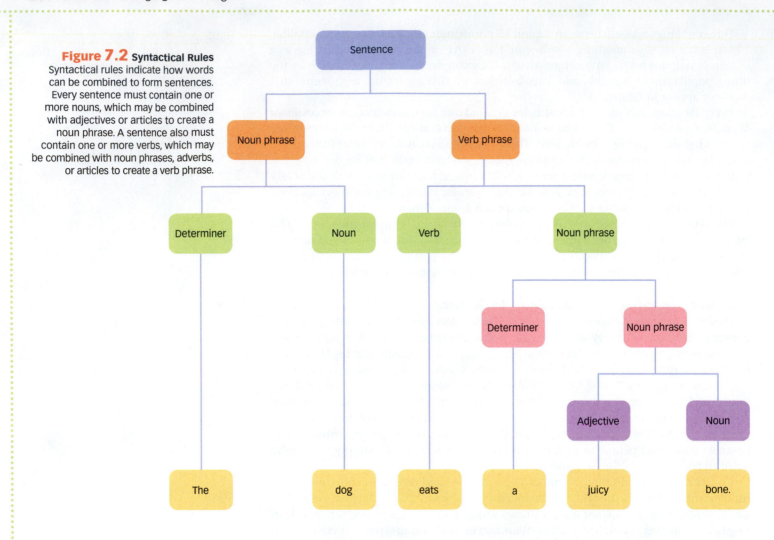

both a noun phrase and a verb phrase. The utterance "the big gray dog over by the building" is not a sentence because there is no verb phrase, only a very long noun phrase. If someone uttered that phrase to you, you'd find yourself wondering, "Yes, well, what about the dog?"—that is, you'd be waiting for a verb phrase.

Deep Structure versus Surface Structure

Language, like other features of the human mind, is not perfect. Everyday experience shows us how often misunderstandings occur. These mindbugs sometimes result from differences between the deep structure of sentences and their surface structure (Chomsky, 1957). **Deep structure** refers to *the meaning of a sentence*. **Surface structure** refers to *how a sentence is worded*. The sentences "The dog chased the cat" and "The cat was chased by the dog" mean the same thing (they have the same deep structure) even though on the surface their structures are different.

To generate a sentence, you begin with a deep structure (the meaning of the sentence) and create a surface structure (the particular words) to convey that meaning. When you comprehend a sentence, you do the reverse, processing the surface structure in order to extract the deep structure. After the deep structure is extracted, the surface structure is usually forgotten (Jarvella, 1970, 1971). In one study, researchers played tape-recorded stories to volunteers and then asked them to pick the sentences they had heard (Sachs, 1967). Participants frequently confused sentences they heard with sentences that had the same deep structure but a different surface structure. For example, if they heard the sentence "He struck John on the shoulder," they often mistakenly claimed they had heard "John was struck on the shoulder by him." In contrast, they rarely misidentified "John struck him on the shoulder" because this sentence has a different deep structure from the original sentence.

ONLY HUMAN

DID YOU MEAN "STOP" OR "REALLY, REALLY STOP"? Rod Yellon, a political science professor at the University of Manitoba, was fined for protesting a postponement of the trial in his 4-year-long constitutional challenge over a $25 traffic ticket he had been issued in Winnipeg for rolling through a stop sign. Yellon had challenged the law as too vague, arguing that a "stop" sign does not "specify sufficiently" what drivers are supposed to do when they encounter one.

Language Development

Language is a complex cognitive skill, yet we learn to speak and understand with little effort. We can carry on complex conversations with playmates and family before we begin school. Let's look at how children master the complexity of language despite having very little formal training.

Three characteristics of language development are worth bearing in mind. First, children learn language at an astonishingly rapid rate. The average 1-year-old has a vocabulary of 10 words. This tiny vocabulary expands to over *10,000* words in the next 4 years, requiring the child to learn, on average, about six or seven new words *every day*. Second, children make few errors while learning to speak, and the errors they do make usually respect grammatical rules. This is an extraordinary feat. There are over 3 *million* ways to rearrange the words in any 10-word sentence, but only a few of these arrangements will be both grammatically correct and meaningful (Bickerton, 1990). Third, children's *passive mastery* of language develops faster than their *active mastery*. At every stage of language development, children understand language better than they speak.

Distinguishing Speech Sounds

At birth, infants can distinguish among all of the contrasting sounds that occur in all human languages. Within the first 6 months of life, they lose this ability, and, like their parents, can only distinguish among the contrasting sounds in the language they hear being spoken around them. For example, two distinct sounds in English are the *l* sound and the *r* sound, as in *lead* and *read*. These sounds are not distinguished in Japanese; instead, the *l* and *r* sounds fall within the same phoneme. Japanese adults cannot hear the difference between these two phonemes, but American adults can distinguish between them easily—and so can Japanese infants.

In one study, researchers constructed a tape of a voice saying "la-la-la" or "ra-ra-ra" repeatedly (Eimas et al., 1971). They rigged a pacifier so that whenever an infant sucked on it, a tape player that broadcasted the "la-la" tape was activated. When the *la-la* sound began playing in response to their sucking, the babies were delighted and kept sucking on the pacifier to keep the *la-la* sound playing. After a while, they began to lose interest, and sucking frequency declined to about half of its initial rate. At this point, the experimenters switched the tape so that the voice now said "ra-ra-ra" repeatedly. The Japanese infants began sucking again with vigor, indicating that they could hear the difference between the old, boring *la* sound and the new, interesting *ra* sound.

These kinds of studies help explain why it is so difficult to learn a second language as an adult. You might not be able to even *hear* some of the speech sounds that carry crucial information in the language you want to learn, much less pronounce them properly. In a very real sense, your brain has become too specialized for your native language!

Infants can distinguish among speech sounds, but they cannot produce them reliably, relying mostly on cooing, cries, laughs, and other vocalizations to communicate.

DEEP STRUCTURE The meaning of a sentence.

SURFACE STRUCTURE How a sentence is worded.

In this videotaped test, the baby watches an animated toy animal while a single speech sound is repeated. After a few repetitions, the sound changes and then the display changes, and then they both change again. If the baby switches her attention when the sound changes, she is anticipating the new display, which demonstrates that she can discriminate between the sounds.

COURTESY DR. PATRICIA K. KUHL, UW INSTITUTE FOR LEARNING AND BRAIN SCIENCES

Between the ages of about 4 and 6 months, they begin to babble speech sounds. Regardless of the language they hear spoken, all infants go through the same babbling sequence. For example, *d* and *t* appear in infant babbling before *m* and *n*. Even deaf babies babble sounds they've never heard, and they do so in the same order as hearing babies do (Ollers & Eilers, 1988). This is evidence that babies aren't simply imitating the sounds they hear and suggests that babbling is a natural part of the language development process. Deaf babies don't babble as much, however, and their babbling is delayed relative to hearing babies (11 months rather than 6).

In order for vocal babbling to continue, however, babies must be able to hear themselves. In fact, delayed babbling or the cessation of babbling merits testing for possible hearing difficulties. Babbling problems can lead to speech impairments, but they do not necessarily prevent language acquisition. Deaf infants whose parents communicate using American Sign Language (ASL) begin to babble with their hands at the same age that hearing children begin to babble vocally—between 4 and 6 months (Petitto & Marentette, 1991). Their babbling consists of sign language syllables that are the fundamental components of ASL.

Language Milestones

At about 10 to 12 months of age, babies begin to utter (or sign) their first words. By 18 months, they can say about 50 words and can understand several times more than that. Toddlers generally learn nouns before verbs, and the nouns they learn first are names for everyday, concrete objects (e.g., chair, table, milk) (see **TABLE 7.1**). At about this time, their vocabularies undergo explosive growth. By the time the average child begins school, a vocabulary of 10,000 words is not unusual. By fifth grade, the average child knows the meanings of 40,000 words. By college, the average student's vocabulary is about 200,000 words. **Fast mapping**, in which *children map a word onto an underlying concept after only a single exposure,* enables them to learn at this rapid pace (Mervis & Bertrand, 1994). This astonishingly easy process contrasts dramatically with the effort required later to learn other concepts and skills, such as arithmetic or writing.

Around 24 months, children begin to form two-word sentences, such as "more milk" or "throw ball." Such sentences are referred to as **telegraphic speech** because they are *devoid of function morphemes and consist mostly of content words.* Yet despite the absence of function words, such as prepositions or articles, these two-word sentences tend to be grammatical; the words are ordered in a manner consistent with the syntactical rules of the language children are learning to speak. So, for example, toddlers will

Table 7.1	Language Milestones
Average Age	**Language Milestones**
0–4 months	Can tell the difference between speech sounds (phonemes). Cooing, especially in response to speech.
4–6 months	Babbles consonants.
6–10 months	Understands some words and simple requests.
10–12 months	Begins to use single words.
12–18 months	Vocabulary of 30–50 words (simple nouns, adjectives, and action words).
18–24 months	Two-word phrases ordered according to the syntactic rules. Vocabulary of 50–200 words. Understands rules.
24–36 months	Vocabulary of about 1,000 words. Production of phrases and incomplete sentences.
36–60 months	Vocabulary grows to more than 10,000 words; production of full sentences; mastery of grammatical morphemes (such as *-ed* for past tense) and function words (such as *the, and, but*). Can form questions and negations.

say "throw ball" rather than "ball throw" when they want you to throw the ball to them and "more milk" rather than "milk more" when they want you to give them more milk. With these seemingly primitive expressions, 2-year-olds show that they have already acquired an appreciation of the syntactical rules of the language they are learning.

The Emergence of Grammatical Rules

Evidence of the ease with which children acquire grammatical rules comes from some interesting developmental mindbugs: errors that children make while forming sentences. If you listen to average 2- or 3-year-old children speaking, you may notice that they use the correct past-tense versions of common verbs, as in the expressions "I ran" and "You ate." By the age of 4 or 5, the same children will be using incorrect forms of these verbs, saying such things as "I runned" or "You eated"—forms most children are unlikely to have ever heard (Prasada & Pinker, 1993). The reason is that very young children memorize the particular sounds (i.e., words) that express what they want to communicate. But as children acquire the grammatical rules of their language, they tend to *overgeneralize*. For example, if a child overgeneralizes the rule that past tense is indicated by *-ed,* then *run* becomes *runned* or even *ranned* instead of *ran.*

These errors show that language acquisition is not simply a matter of imitating adult speech. Instead, children acquire grammatical rules by listening to the speech around them and using the rules to create verbal forms they've never heard. They manage this without explicit awareness of the grammatical rules they've learned. In fact, few children or adults can articulate the grammatical rules of their native language, yet the speech they produce obeys these rules.

By about 3 years of age, children begin to generate complete simple sentences that include function words (e.g., "Give me *the* ball" and "That belongs *to* me"). The sentences increase in complexity over the next 2 years. By 4 to 5 years of age, many aspects of the language acquisition process are complete. As children continue to mature, their language skills become more refined, with added appreciation of subtler communicative uses of language, such as humor, sarcasm, or irony.

Theories of Language Development

We know a good deal about how language develops, but the underlying acquisition processes have been the subject of considerable controversy and (at times) angry exchanges among theoreticians. The study of language and cognition underwent an enormous change in the 1950s, when linguist Noam Chomsky published a blistering reply to B. F. Skinner's behaviorist explanation of language learning. As you learned in Chapter 1, Skinner used principles of reinforcement to argue that we learn language the way he thought we learn everything—through imitation, instruction, and trial-and-error learning. According to Chomsky, however, language-learning capacities are built into the brain, which is specialized to rapidly acquire language through simple exposure to speech. Let's look at each theory and then examine more recent accounts of language development.

Behaviorist Explanations

According to behaviorists, children acquire language through simple principles of operant conditioning, which you learned about in Chapter 6 (Skinner, 1957). As infants mature, they begin to vocalize. Those vocalizations that are not reinforced gradually diminish, and those that are reinforced remain in the developing child's repertoire. So, for example, when an infant gurgles "prah," most parents are pretty indifferent. However, a sound that even remotely resembles "da-da" is likely to be reinforced with smiles, whoops, and cackles of "Gooooood baaaaaby!" by doting parents. Maturing children also imitate the speech patterns they hear. Then parents or other adults shape those speech patterns by reinforcing those that are grammatical and ignoring or punishing those that are ungrammatical. "I no want milk" is likely to be squelched by

FAST MAPPING The fact that children can map a word onto an underlying concept after only a single exposure.

TELEGRAPHIC SPEECH Speech that is devoid of function morphemes and consists mostly of content words.

NATIVIST THEORY The view that language development is best explained as an innate, biological capacity.

LANGUAGE ACQUISITION DEVICE (LAD) A collection of processes that facilitate language learning.

GENETIC DYSPHASIA A syndrome characterized by an inability to learn the grammatical structure of language despite having otherwise normal intelligence.

parental clucks and titters, whereas "No milk for me, thanks" will probably be reinforced. According to Skinner, then, we learn to talk in the same way we learn any other skill: through reinforcement, shaping, extinction, and the other basic principles of operant conditioning.

The behavioral explanation is attractive because it offers a simple account of language development, but the theory cannot account for many fundamental characteristics of language development (Chomsky, 1986; Pinker, 1994; Pinker & Bloom, 1990).

- First, parents don't spend much time teaching their children to speak grammatically. In one well-documented study, researchers found that parents typically respond more to the truth content of their children's statements than to the grammar (Brown & Hanlon, 1970). So, for example, when a child expresses a sentiment such as "Nobody like me," his or her mother will respond with something like "Why do you think that?" or "I like you!" rather than "Now, listen carefully and repeat after me: Nobody likes me."

- Second, children generate many more grammatical sentences than they ever hear. This shows that children don't just imitate; they learn the rules for generating sentences. You'll recall that the same deep structure can generate a multitude of surface structures. It's highly unlikely that each of those separate surface structures was heard, reinforced, and learned by the developing child and much more likely that children simply acquire the ability to generate grammatical sentences.

- Third, as you read earlier in this chapter, the errors children make when learning to speak tend to be overgeneralizations of grammatical rules. The behaviorist explanation would not predict these overgeneralizations if children were learning through trial and error or simply imitating what they hear. That is, it would be difficult to overgeneralize if language development consisted solely of reinforced individual sentences or phrases.

Nativist Explanations

Contrary to Skinner's behaviorist theory of language acquisition, Chomsky and others have argued that humans have a particular ability for language that is separate from general intelligence. This **nativist theory** holds that *language development is best explained as an innate, biological capacity.* According to Chomsky, the human brain is equipped with a **language acquisition device (LAD)**–*a collection of processes that facilitate language learning.* Language processes naturally emerge as the infant matures, provided the infant receives adequate input to maintain the acquisition process.

Christopher's story is consistent with the nativist view of language development—his genius for language acquisition, despite his low overall intelligence, indicates that language capacity can be distinct from other mental capacities. Other individuals show the opposite pattern: People with normal or near-normal intelligence can find certain aspects of human language difficult or impossible to learn. This condition is known **genetic dysphasia**, *a syndrome characterized by an inability to learn the grammatical structure of language despite having otherwise normal intelligence.* Genetic dysphasia tends to run in families, and a single dominant gene has been implicated in its transmission (Gopnik, 1990a, 1990b). Consider some sentences generated by children with the disorder:

She remembered when she hurts herself the other day.

Carol is cry in the church.

Notice that the ideas these children are trying to communicate are intelligent. The problem lies in their inability to grasp syntactical rules (see Figure 7.2). Individuals with the disorder cannot correctly complete the following simple sentences, which requires a rudimentary grasp of past tense and pluralization rules:

Here is a "wug." Here are two of them. There are two ____.

Here is a man who likes to "rick." Yesterday he did the same thing. Yesterday he ____.

"Got idea. Talk better. Combine words. Make sentences."

© SIDNEY HARRIS

Average 4-year-old children can successfully complete these sentences, yet adults with genetic dysphasia may find them difficult or impossible (see **FIGURE 7.3**). Their problems with grammatical rules persist even if they receive special language training. When asked to describe what she did over the weekend, one child wrote "On Saturday I watch TV." Her teacher corrected the sentence to "On Saturday, I watch*ed* TV," drawing attention to the *-ed* rule for describing past events. The following week, the child was asked to write another account of what she did over the weekend. She wrote "On Saturday I wash myself and I watched TV and I went to bed." Notice that although she had memorized the past tense forms *watched* and *went,* she could not generalize the rule to form the past tense of another word (*washed*).

As predicted by the nativist view, studies of people with genetic dysphasia suggest that normal children learn the grammatical rules of human language with ease in part because they are " wired" to do so. This biological predisposition to acquire language explains why newborn infants can make contrasts among phonemes that occur in all human languages—even phonemes they've never heard spoken. If we learned language through imitation, as behaviorists theorized, infants would only distinguish the phonemes they'd actually heard. The nativist theory also explains why deaf babies babble speech sounds they have never heard and why the pattern of language development is similar in children throughout the world. These characteristics of language development are just what would be expected if our biological heritage provided us with the broad mechanics of human language.

Also consistent with the nativist view is evidence that language can be acquired only during a restricted period of development, as has been observed with songbirds. If young songbirds are prevented from hearing adult birds sing during a particular period in their early lives, they do not learn to sing. A similar mechanism seems to affect human language learning, as illustrated by the tragic case of Genie (Curtiss, 1977). At the age of 20 months, Genie was tied to a chair by her parents and kept in virtual isolation. Her father forbade Genie's mother and brother to speak to her, and he himself only growled and barked at her. She remained in this brutal state until the age of 13, when her partially blind mother left home with her following an argument with Genie's father. Genie's life improved substantially, and she received years of language instruction. But it was too late. Her language skills remained extremely primitive. She developed a basic vocabulary and could communicate her ideas, but she could not grasp the grammatical rules of English.

In contrast, Isabelle—a child who also suffered social isolation and silence but only until the age of 6—required a year of language training to learn to speak normally (Brown, 1958; Davis, 1947). Similar cases have been reported, with a common theme: Once puberty is reached, acquiring language becomes extremely difficult (Brown, 1958). Data from studies of language acquisition in immigrants support this conclusion. In one study, researchers found that the proficiency with which immigrants spoke English depended not on how long they'd lived in the United States, but on their age at immigration (Johnson & Newport, 1989). Those who arrived as children were the most proficient, whereas among those who immigrated after puberty, proficiency showed a significant decline regardless of the number of years in their new country. Given these data, it is unfortunate that most U.S. schools do not offer other languages until middle school or high school.

This is a wug.

Figure 7.3 An **Item from the Wug Test** The test was designed as a way to explore whether children can utilize rules for forming plurals and past tense in words they've never heard.

Now there is another one. There are two of them. There are two _____.

Immigrants who learn English as a second language are more proficient if they start to learn English before puberty rather than after.

MICHAEL NEWMAN / PHOTOEDIT

A group of deaf children in Nicaragua created their own sign language, complete with grammatical rules, without receiving formal instruction. The language has evolved and matured over the past 25 years.

SUSAN MEISELAS/MAGNUM

Interactionist Explanations

Nativist theories are often criticized because they do not explain *how* language develops; they merely explain why. A complete theory of language acquisition requires an explanation of the processes by which the innate, biological capacity for language combines with environmental experience. This is just what interactionist accounts of language acquisition do. Interactionists point out that parents tailor their verbal interactions with children in ways that simplify the language acquisition process: They speak slowly, enunciate clearly, and use simpler sentences than they do when speaking with adults (Bruner, 1983; Farrar, 1990). This observation supports the interactionist notion that although infants are born with an innate ability to acquire language, social interactions play a crucial role in language.

Further evidence of the interaction of biology and experience comes from a fascinating study of deaf children's creation of a new language (Senghas, Kita, & Ozyurek, 2004). Prior to about 1980, deaf children in Nicaragua stayed at home and usually had little contact with other deaf individuals. In 1981, some deaf children began to attend a new vocational school. At first, the school did not teach a formal sign language, and none of the children had learned to sign at home, but the children gradually began to communicate using hand signals that they invented.

Over the past 25 years, their sign language has developed considerably, and researchers have studied this new language for the telltale characteristics of languages that have evolved over much longer periods. For instance, mature languages typically break down experience into separate components. When we describe something in motion, such as a rock rolling down a hill, our language separates the type of movement (rolling) and the direction of movement (down). If we simply made a gesture, however, we would use a single continuous downward movement to indicate this motion. This is exactly what the first children to develop the Nicaraguan sign language did. But younger groups of children, who have developed the sign language further, use separate signs to describe the direction and the type of movement—a defining characteristic of mature languages. That the younger children did not merely copy the signs from the older users suggests that a predisposition exists to use language to dissect our experiences. Thus, their acts of creation nicely illustrate the interplay of nativism (the predisposition to use language) and experience (growing up in an insulated deaf culture).

Figure 7.4 Broca's and Wernicke's Areas Neuroscientists study people with brain damage in order to better understand how the brain normally operates. When Broca's area is damaged, patients have a hard time producing sentences. When Wernicke's area is damaged, patients can produce sentences, but they tend to be meaningless.

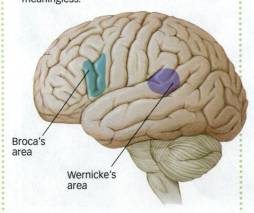

Broca's area

Wernicke's area

The Neurological Specialization That Allows Language to Develop

As the brain matures, specialization of specific neurological structures takes place, and this allows language to develop. In early infancy, language processing is distributed across many areas of the brain. But language processing gradually becomes more and more concentrated in two areas, sometimes referred to as the language centers of the brain. The first, *Broca's area,* is located in the left frontal cortex; it is involved in the production of the sequential patterns in vocal and sign languages (see **FIGURE 7.4**). The second, *Wernicke's area,* located in the left temporal cortex, is involved in language comprehension (whether spoken or signed). As the brain matures, these areas become increasingly specialized for language, so much so that damage to them results in a serious condition called **aphasia,** defined as *difficulty in producing or comprehending language.*

As you saw in Chapter 1, Broca's area is named after French physician Paul Broca, who first reported on speech problems resulting from damage to a specific areas of the left frontal cortex (Broca, 1861, 1863). Patients with this damage understand language relatively well, although they have increasing comprehension difficulty as grammatical structures get more complex. But their real struggle is with speech production: Typically, they speak in short, staccato phrases that consist mostly of content morphemes (e.g., *cat, dog*). Function morphemes (e.g., *and, but*) are usually missing and grammatical structure is impaired. A person with the condition might say something like "Ah, Monday, uh, Casey park. Two, uh, friends, and, uh, 30 minutes."

German neurologist Carl Wernicke first described the area that bears his name after observing speech difficulty in patients who had sustained damage to the left posterior temporal cortex (Wernicke, 1874). Patients with *Wernicke's aphasia* differ from those with Broca's aphasia in two ways: They can produce grammatical speech, but it tends to be meaningless, and they have considerable difficulty comprehending language. A patient suffering from Wernicke's aphasia might say something like "I feel very well. In other words, I used to be able to work cigarettes. I don't know how. Things I couldn't hear from are here."

In normal language processing, Wernicke's area is highly active when we make judgments about word meaning, and damage to this area impairs comprehension of spoken and signed language although the ability to identify nonlanguage sounds is unimpaired. For example, Japanese can be written using symbols that, like the English alphabet, represent speech sounds, or by using pictographs that, like Chinese pictographs, represent ideas. Japanese patients who suffer from Wernicke's aphasia encounter difficulties in writing and understanding the symbols that represent speech sounds but not pictographs.

In normal language development, Broca's area and Wernicke's area become specialized for processing and producing language as long as the developing child is exposed to spoken or signed language. (See The Real World box on the next page for research on how bilingualism affects the brain.) As the cases of Genie and Isabelle show, there is a critical period during which this specialization occurs, and if the developing brain does not receive adequate language input, this process can be permanently disrupted.

Can Other Species Learn Human Language?

The human vocal tract and the extremely nimble human hand are better suited to human language than are the throats and paws of other species. Nonetheless, attempts have been made to teach nonhuman animals, particularly apes, to communicate using human language.

Early attempts to teach apes to speak failed dismally because their vocal tracts cannot accommodate the sounds used in human languages (Hayes & Hayes, 1951). Later attempts to teach apes human language have met with more success—including teaching them to use American Sign Language and computer-monitored keyboards that display geometric symbols that represent words. Allen and Beatrix Gardner were the first to use ASL with apes (Gardner & Gardner, 1969). The Gardners worked with a young female chimpanzee named Washoe as though she were a deaf child, signing to her regularly, rewarding her correct efforts at signing, and assisting her acquisition of signs by manipulating her hands in a process referred to as "molding." In 4 years, Washoe learned approximately 160 words and could construct simple sentences, such as "More fruit." She also formed novel word constructions such as "water bird" for "duck." After a fight with a Rhesus monkey, she signed "dirty monkey!" This constituted a creative use of the term because she had only been taught the use of "dirty" to refer to soiled objects.

Other chimpanzees were immersed in ASL in a similar fashion, and Washoe and her companions were soon signing to each other, creating a learning environment conducive to language acquisition. One of Washoe's cohorts, a chimpanzee named Lucy, learned to sign "drink fruit" for watermelon. When Washoe's second infant died, her caretakers arranged for her to adopt an infant chimpanzee named Loulis. In a few months, young Loulis, who was not exposed to human signers, learned 68 signs simply by watching Washoe communicate with the other chimpanzees. People who have observed these interactions and are themselves fluent in ASL report little difficulty in following the conversations (Fouts & Bodamer, 1987). One such observer, a *New York Times*

APHASIA Difficulty in producing or comprehending language.

Allen and Beatrix Gardner used sign language to teach the female chimpanzee Washoe about 160 words. Washoe could also construct simple sentences and combine words in novel ways.

{ THE REAL WORLD } Does Bilingualism Interfere with Cognitive Development?

Question: What do you call someone who speaks more than one language?

Answer: A polyglot.

Question: What do you call someone who speaks only one language?

Answer: An American.

IN MOST OF THE WORLD, BILINGUALISM IS the norm, not the exception. In fact, nearly half of the world's population grows up speaking more than one language (Bialystok & Hakuta, 1994; Hakuta, 1986, 1999). Despite this, bilingualism is the source of considerable controversy in the American educational system. In recent years, many states have passed laws and many courts have issued rulings outlawing bilingual educational environments, and well-meaning authorities have discouraged parents from raising their children bilingually. These well-intentioned actions have been based on the assumption that bilingualism slows or interferes with normal cognitive development. Because much of our conceptual learning occurs verbally, the fear is that communicating with

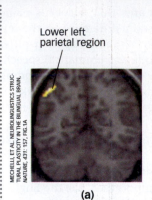

In the United States, we are used to seeing street signs in English only, but in many countries multiple languages are used.

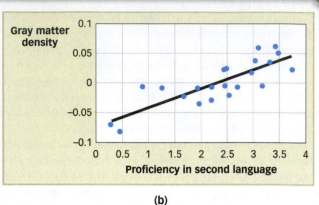

(a)

(b)

Bilingualism Alters Brain Structure Learning a second language early in life increases the density of gray matter in the brain. (a) A view of the lower left parietal region; has denser gray matter in bilinguals relative to monolinguals. (b) As proficiency in a second language increases, so does the density of gray matter in the lower parietal region. People who acquired a second language earlier in life were also found to have denser gray matter in this region. Interestingly, this area corresponds to the same area that is activated during verbal fluency tasks.
Mechelli et al., 2004.

children in more than one language might hinder the proper acquisition and retrieval of crucial conceptual knowledge as well as slow the development of language skills. Is there any evidence for these assumptions?

Early studies of bilingual children seemed to support this assumption. When compared with monolingual children, bilingual children performed more slowly when processing language, and their IQ scores were lower. A reexamination of these studies, however, revealed several crucial flaws. First, the tests were given in English even when that was not the child's primary language. Second, the bilingual participants were often first- or second-generation immigrants whose parents were not proficient in English. Finally, the bilingual children came from lower socioeconomic backgrounds than the monolingual children (Andrews, 1982).

Later studies controlled for these factors, revealing a very different picture of bilingual children's cognitive skills. The available evidence concerning language acquisition indicates that bilingual and monolingual children do not differ significantly in the course and rate of their language development (Nicoladis & Genesee, 1997). In fact, middle-class participants who are fluent in two languages have been found to score higher than monolingual participants on measures of cognitive functioning, including cognitive flexibility and analytic reasoning (Bialystok, 1999; Campbell & Sais, 1995). These studies did reveal one slight disadvantage, however: Bilinguals process language more slowly than monolinguals and can sometimes take longer to formulate sentences (Taylor & Lambert, 1990).

Recent research on the brains of bilingual individuals indicates that learning a second language produces lasting changes in a part of the left parietal lobe that is involved in language (Mechelli et al., 2004). The gray matter in this region is denser in bilinguals than in monolinguals, and the increased density is most pronounced in those individuals who are most proficient in using their second language. Thus, rather than impairing language development specifically or cognitive development more broadly, learning a second language seems to increase the ability of the left parietal lobe to handle linguistic demands.

reporter who spent some time with Washoe, reported "Suddenly I realized I was conversing with a member of another species in my native tongue."

To give you some idea of what chimp communication is like, take a look at the three sets of sentences shown in **FIGURE 7.5,** read the caption, think about it, then continue reading the text.

Set 1	Set 2	Set 3
Big train; Red book.	Drink red; Comb black.	Want milk.
Walk street; Go store.	Clothes Mrs. G.; You hat.	Mike paint.
Put book; Hit ball.	Go in; Look out.	At school, wash face.

Figure 7.5 Differing Language Skills
These sets of sentences were each produced by 13-year-old Genie, who was deprived of social contact during her upbringing; a normal 2-year-old toddler; or a chimpanzee who was taught sign language. Can you guess which speaker produced which set of sentences? Make your guesses before continuing to read the text.

The first set consists of the two-word sentences of a normal toddler. Washoe produced the second set and 13-year-old Genie, the third set. All are grammatical; they follow the rules of English, and so we can easily understand what is being communicated. What is striking—particularly in the case of 13-year-old Genie—is the lack of grammatical complexity in the sentences. Rather than saying "At school, I washed my face," or "Mike is painting," Genie's expressions lack function morphemes (like *-ed* in the past tense), determiners, and so on. The ability to produce grammatically complex sentences appears to depend on having particular neural circuitry. This circuitry seems to be lacking in chimps, takes time to develop in humans, and can be disrupted by extreme environmental deprivation during critical periods (Maynard-Smith & Szathmary, 1995).

Other researchers have taught bonobo chimpanzees to communicate using a geometric keyboard system (Savage-Rumbaugh, Shanker, & Taylor, 1998). Their star pupil, Kanzi, learned the keyboard system by watching researchers try to teach his mother. Like Loulis, young Kanzi picked up the language relatively easily (his mother never did learn the system), suggesting that like humans, birds, and other species, apes experience a critical period for acquiring communicative systems.

Kanzi has learned hundreds of words and has combined them to form thousands of word combinations. Also like human children, his passive mastery of language appears to exceed his ability to produce language. In one study, researchers tested 9-year-old Kanzi's understanding of 660 spoken sentences. The grammatically complex sentences asked him to perform simple actions, such as "Go get the balloon that's in the microwave" and "Pour the Perrier into the Coke." Some sentences were also potentially misleading, such as "Get the pine needles that are in the refrigerator," when there were pine needles in clear view on the floor. Impressively, Kanzi correctly carried out 72% of the 660 requests (Savage-Rumbaugh & Lewin, 1996).

These results indicate that apes can acquire sizable vocabularies, string words together to form short sentences, and process sentences that are grammatically complex. Their skills are especially impressive because human language is hardly their normal means of communication. Research with apes also suggests that the neurological "wiring" that allows us to learn language overlaps to some degree with theirs (and perhaps with other species').

Kanzi, a young male chimpanzee, learned hundreds of words and word combinations through a keyboard system as he watched researchers try to teach his mother.

"He says he wants a lawyer."

Equally informative are the limitations apes exhibit when learning, comprehending, and using human language. The first limitation is the size of the vocabularies they acquire. As mentioned, Washoe's and Kanzi's vocabularies number in the hundreds, but an average 4-year-old human child has a vocabulary of approximately 10,000 words. The second limitation is the type of words they can master, primarily names for concrete objects and simple actions. Apes (and several other species) have the ability to map arbitrary sounds or symbols onto objects and actions, but learning, say, the meaning of the word *economics* would be difficult for Washoe or Kanzi. In other words, apes can learn signs for concepts they understand, but their conceptual repertoire is smaller and simpler than humans.

The third and perhaps most important limitation is the complexity of grammar that apes can use and comprehend. Apes can string signs together, but their constructions rarely exceed three or four words, and when they do, they are rarely grammatical. For example, the gorilla Koko once signed "Stomach me you orange juice" out of concern for her caretaker, who was complaining of a stomachache. Koko apparently thought giving her orange juice would help. This communication shows compassion and intelligence on Koko's part but difficulty with the grammatical complexity of ASL. Comparing the grammatical structures produced by apes with those produced by human children highlights the complexity of human language as well as the ease and speed with which we generate and comprehend it.

Language and Thought: How Are They Related?

Language is such a dominant feature of our mental world that it is tempting to equate language with thought. Some theorists have even argued that language is simply a means of expressing thought. The **linguistic relativity hypothesis** maintains that *language shapes the nature of thought*. This idea was championed by Benjamin Whorf, an engineer who studied language in his spare time and was especially interested in Native American languages (1956). The most frequently cited example of linguistic relativity comes from the Inuit in Canada. Their language has many different terms for frozen white flakes of precipitation, for which we use the word *snow*. Whorf believed that because they have so many terms for snow, the Inuit perceive and think about snow differently than do English speakers.

Whorf has been criticized for the anecdotal nature of his observations (Pinker, 1994), and some controlled research has cast doubt on Whorf's hypothesis. Eleanor Rosch (1973) studied the Dani, an isolated agricultural tribe living in New Guinea. They have only two terms for colors that roughly refer to "dark" and "light." If Whorf's hypothesis were correct, you would expect the Dani to have problems perceiving and learning different shades of color. But in Rosch's experiments, they learned shades of color just as well as people who have many more color terms in their first language.

LINGUISTIC RELATIVITY HYPOTHESIS The proposal that language shapes the nature of thought.

The Inuit in Canada use many different terms for snow, leading Benjamin Whorf to propose that they think about snow differently than do English speakers.

More recent evidence shows that language may influence color processing (Roberson, Davidoff, Davies, & Shapiro, 2004). Researchers compared English children with African children from a cattle-herding tribe in Namibia known as the Himba. The English have 11 basic color terms, but the Himba, who are largely isolated from the outside world, have only five. For example, they use the term *serandu* to refer to what English speakers would call red, pink, or orange.

Researchers showed a series of colored tiles to each child and then asked the child to choose that color from an array of 22 different colors. The youngest children, both English and Himba, who knew few or no color names, tended to confuse similar colors. But as the children grew and acquired more names for colors, their choices increasingly reflected the color terms they had learned. English children made fewer errors matching tiles that had English color names; Himba children made fewer errors for tiles with color names in Himba. These results support the linguistic relativity hypothesis: Language may influence thought.

In another study supporting Whorf's hypothesis, researchers looked at the way people think about time. In English, we often use spatial terms: We look *forward* to a promising future or move a meeting *back* to fit our schedule. We also use these terms to describe horizontal spatial relations, such as taking three steps *forward* or two steps *back* (Boroditsky, 2001). In contrast, speakers of Mandarin (Chinese) often describe time using terms that refer to a vertical spatial dimension: Earlier events are referred to as "up," and later events as "down." To test the effect of this difference, researchers showed English speakers and Mandarin speakers either a horizontal or vertical display of objects and then asked them to make a judgment involving time, such as whether March comes before April (Boroditsky, 2001). English speakers were faster to make the time judgments after seeing a horizontal display, whereas for Mandarin speakers the opposite was true. When English speakers learned to use Mandarin spatial terms, their time judgments were also faster after seeing the vertical display! This result nicely shows a direct influence of language on thought. Bear in mind, though, that either thought or language abilities can be severely impaired while the capacity for the other is spared, as illustrated by the dramatic case of Christopher that you read earlier.

In summary, human language is characterized by a complex organization—from phonemes to morphemes to phrases and finally sentences. Each of these levels of human language is constructed and understood according to grammatical rules, none of which are ever taught explicitly. Instead, children appear to be biologically predisposed to process language in ways that allow them to extract these grammatical rules from the language they hear, a predisposition that takes the form of neurological specialization. Our abilities to produce and comprehend language depend on distinct regions of the brain, with Broca's area critical for language production and Wernicke's area critical for comprehension. Nonhuman primates can learn new vocabulary and construct simple sentences, but there are significant limitations on the size of their vocabularies and the grammatical complexity they can handle. Recent studies on color processing and time judgments point to an influence of language on thought. However, it is also clear that language and thought are to some extent separate. ■ ■

Concepts and Categories: How We Think

Concept refers to a *mental representation that groups or categorizes shared features of related objects, events, or other stimuli.* A concept is an abstract representation, description, or definition that serves to designate a class or category of things. For example, your concept of a chair might include such features as sturdiness, relative flatness, an object that you can sit on. That set of attributes defines a category of objects in the world—desk chairs, recliner chairs, flat rocks, bar stools, and so on—that can all be described in that way.

CONCEPT A mental representation that groups or categorizes shared features of related objects, events, or other stimuli.

CATEGORY-SPECIFIC DEFICIT A neurological syndrome that is characterized by an inability to recognize objects that belong to a particular category while leaving the ability to recognize objects outside the category undisturbed.

Concepts are fundamental to our ability to think and make sense of the world. As with other aspects of cognition, we can gain insight into how concepts are organized by looking at some instances in which they are rather disorganized. We'll encounter some mindbugs in the form of unusual disorders that help us understand how concepts are organized in the brain. We'll also compare various theories that explain the organization of concepts and then consider studies of children that demonstrate how we acquire concepts.

The Organization of Concepts and Category-Specific Deficits

Over 20 years ago, two neuropsychologists described a mindbug resulting from brain injury that had major implications for understanding how concepts are organized (Warrington & McCarthy, 1983). Their patient could not recognize a variety of human-made objects or retrieve any information about them, but his knowledge of living things and foods was perfectly normal. In the following year, the two neuropsychologists reported four patients who exhibited the reverse pattern: They could recognize information about human-made objects, but their ability to recognize information about living things and foods was severely impaired (Warrington & Shallice, 1984). Since the publication of these pioneering studies, over 100 similar cases have been reported (Martin & Caramazza, 2003). The syndrome is called **category-specific deficit**, *an inability to recognize objects that belong to a particular category while leaving the ability to recognize objects outside the category undisturbed.*

Category-specific deficits like these have been observed even when the brain trauma that produces them occurs shortly after birth. Two researchers reported the case of Adam, a 16-year-old boy who suffered a stroke a day after he was born (Farah & Rabinowitz, 2003). Adam has severe difficulty recognizing faces and other biological objects. When shown a picture of a cherry, he identified it as "a Chinese yo-yo." When shown a picture of a mouse, he identified it as an owl. He made errors like these on 79% of the animal pictures and 54% of the plant pictures he was shown. In contrast, he made only 15% errors when identifying pictures of nonliving things, such as spatulas, brooms, and cigars. The fact that 16-year-old Adam exhibited category-specific deficits despite suffering his stroke when he was only 1 day old strongly suggests that the brain is "prewired" to organize perceptual and sensory inputs into broad-based categories, such as living and nonliving things.

The type of category-specific deficit suffered depends on where the brain is damaged. Deficits usually result when an individual suffers a stroke or other trauma to areas in the left hemisphere of the cerebral cortex (Martin & Caramazza, 2003). Damage to the front part of the left temporal lobe results in difficulty identifying humans, damage to the lower left temporal lobe results in difficulty identifying animals, and damage to the region where the temporal lobe meets the occipital and parietal lobes impairs the ability to retrieve names of tools (Damasio, Grabowski, Tranel, Hichwa, & Damasio, 1996). Similarly, when healthy people undertake the same task, imaging studies have demonstrated that the same regions of the brain are more active during naming of tools than animals and vice versa, as shown in **FIGURE 7.6** (Martin & Chao, 2001).

Cases of category-specific deficit provide new insights into how the brain organizes our concepts about the world, classifying them into categories based on shared similarities. Our category for "dog" may be something like "small, four-footed animal with fur that wags its tail and barks." Our category for "bird" may be something like "small, winged, beaked creature that

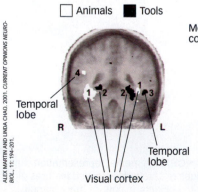

Figure 7.6 Brain Areas Involved in Category-Specific Processing Participants were asked to silently name pictures of animals and tools while they were scanned with fMRI. The fMRIs revealed greater activity in the areas in white when participants named animals, and areas in black showed greater activity when participants named tools. Specific regions indicated by numbers include areas within the visual cortex (1, 2), parts of the temporal lobe (3, 4), and the motor cortex (5). Note that the images are left/right reversed.

☐ Animals ■ Tools

Motor cortex

Temporal lobe

Visual cortex

Temporal lobe

Visual cortex

Temporal lobe

ALEX MARTIN AND LINDA CHAO. 2001. *CURRENT OPINIONS NEUROBIOL.,* 11: 194–201.

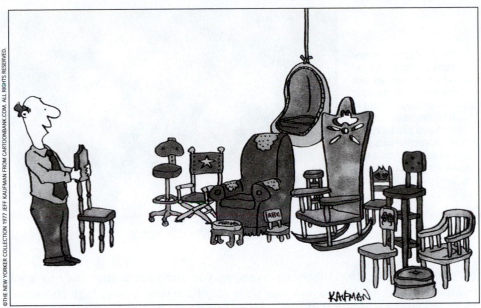

"Attention, everyone! I'd like to introduce the newest member of our family."

flies." We form these categories in large part by noticing similarities among objects and events that we experience in everyday life. A stroke or trauma that damaged the particular place in your brain that stores your "dog" category would wipe out your ability to recognize dogs or remember anything about them.

Psychological Theories of Concepts and Categories

Psychologists have investigated the nature of human concepts, how they are acquired, and how they are used to make decisions and guide actions. Early psychological theories described concepts as rules that specify the necessary and sufficient conditions for membership in a particular category. A necessary condition is something that must be true of the object in order for it to belong to the category. A sufficient condition is something that, if it is true of the object, proves that it belongs to the category. For example, suppose you came upon an unfamiliar animal and you were trying to determine whether it was a dog. It is necessary that the creature be a mammal; otherwise it doesn't belong to the category "dog" because all dogs are mammals. "Mammal" is therefore a necessary condition for membership in the category "dog." Suppose someone told you that the creature was a German shepherd and you know that a German shepherd is a type of dog. "German shepherd" is a sufficient condition for membership in the category "dog." If you know that the creature is a German shepherd, this is sufficient to categorize it as a dog.

Most natural categories, however, cannot be so easily defined in terms of this classical approach of necessary and sufficient conditions. For example, what is your definition of "dog"? Can you come up with a rule of "dogship" that includes all dogs and excludes all nondogs? Most people can't, but they still use the term *dog* intelligently, easily classifying objects as dogs or nondogs. Several theories seek to explain how people perform these acts of categorization.

Family Resemblance Theory

Eleanor Rosch put aside necessity and sufficiency to develop a theory of concepts based on **family resemblance**—that is, *features that appear to be characteristic of category members but may not be possessed by every member* (Rosch, 1973, 1975; Rosch & Mervis,

FAMILY RESEMBLANCE THEORY
Members of a category have features that appear to be characteristic of category members but may not be possessed by every member.

There is family resemblance between family members despite the fact that there is no defining feature that they all have in common. Instead, there are shared common features. Someone who also shares some of those features may be categorized as belonging to the family.

1975; Wittgenstein, 1953/1999). For example, you and your brother may have your mother's eyes, although you and your sister may have your father's high cheekbones. There is a strong family resemblance between you, your parents, and your siblings despite the fact that there is no necessarily defining feature that you all have in common. Similarly, many members of the "bird" category have feathers and wings, so these are the characteristic features. Anything that has these features is likely to be classified as a bird because of this "family resemblance" to other members of the bird category. **FIGURE 7.7** illustrates family resemblance theory.

Figure 7.7 Family Resemblance Theory The family resemblance here is unmistakable, even though no two Smith brothers share all the family features. The prototype is brother 9. He has it all: brown hair, large ears, large nose, mustache, and glasses.

PROTOTYPE The "best" or "most typical member" of a category.

Prototype Theory

Building on the idea of family re-semblance, Rosch also proposed that psychological categories (those that we form naturally) are best described as organized around a **prototype**, which is *the "best" or "most typical member"* of the category. A prototype possesses most (or all) of the most characteristic features of the category. For North Americans, the pro-totype of the bird category would be something like a wren: a small ani-

Properties	Generic bird	Wren	Blue heron	Golden eagle	Domestic goose	Penguin
Flies regularly	✔	✔	✔	✔		
Sings	✔	✔	✔			
Lays eggs	✔	✔	✔	✔	✔	✔
Is small	✔	✔				
Nests in trees	✔	✔				

mal with feathers and wings that flies through the air, lays eggs, and migrates (see **FIGURE 7.8**). If you lived in Antarctica, your prototype of a bird might be a penguin: a small ani-mal that has flippers, swims, and lays eggs.

According to *prototype theory,* if your prototypical bird is a robin, then a canary would be considered a better example of a bird than would an ostrich because a canary has more features in common with a robin than an ostrich does. People make category judgments by comparing new instances to the category's prototype. This contrasts with the classical approach to concepts in which something either is or is not an example of a concept (i.e., it either does or does not belong in the category "dog" or "bird").

Several lines of research support prototype theory. In one set of studies, researchers asked people to list the attributes of several category members (Rosch & Mervis, 1975) (see **FIGURE 7.9**). For example, "apple," "coconut," and "orange" are members of the category "fruit." Attributes are characteristic features, such as "red," "round," and "juicy" for "apple"; "brown," "round," and "hairy" for "coconut; and "orange," "round," and "juicy" for "orange."

The researchers then calculated a family resemblance score for each category mem-ber, which reflected the number of attributes a member had that were shared by other members of the category. In our example, "apple" and "orange" have two attributes that are shared by other members of the category ("round" and "juicy"), so they would each receive a family resemblance score of 2. "Coconut," on the other hand, has only one attribute in common with the other members ("round"), so it would re-ceive a family resemblance score of 1.

Figure 7.8 Critical Features of a Category We tend to think of a generic bird as possessing a number of critical features, but not every bird possesses all of those features. In North America, a wren is a "better exam-ple" of a bird than a penguin or an ostrich.

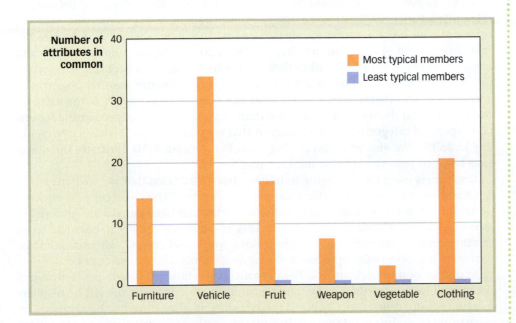

Figure 7.9 Prototype Theory Category members that have many features in com-mon with other members are rated as more typical of the category than are members that share few common features.
After Rosch & Mervis, 1975.

"Don't panic. It's only a prototype."

Another group of people was then asked to rate how typical of the category each member was on a scale of 1 to 7, with higher scores representing greater typicality. These ratings were highly correlated with family resemblance scores. The items that were rated as highly typical had many attributes in common with other members of the category, whereas items that were rated as atypical had few. For example, "apple" and "peach" were rated as typical members of the category "fruit," whereas "coconut" and "fig" were rated as atypical. Similarly, "robin" and "bluebird" received high typicality ratings for the category "bird," whereas "chicken" and "ostrich" were rated as atypical.

According to prototype theory, results such as these show that our concepts are organized in terms of typicality and shared features and not simply in terms of rules defining necessary and sufficient conditions. Participants in these studies knew that, for example, chickens and robins are both birds, but their mental concept "bird" is organized according to shared features, not according to purely logical definition.

Exemplar Theory

In contrast to prototype theory, **exemplar theory** holds that *we make category judgments by comparing a new instance with stored memories for other instances of the category* (Medin & Schaffer, 1978). Imagine that you're out walking in the woods, and from the corner of your eye you spot a four-legged animal that might be a wolf or coyote but that reminds you of your cousin's German shepherd. You figure it must be a dog and continue to enjoy your walk rather than fleeing in a panic. You probably categorized this new animal as a dog because it bore a striking resemblance to other dogs you've encountered; in other words, it was a good example (or an *exemplar*) of the category "dog." Exemplar theory does a better job than prototype theory in accounting for certain aspects of categorization, especially in that we recall not only what a *prototypical* dog looks like but also what *specific* dogs look like. **FIGURE 7.10** illustrates the difference between prototype theory and exemplar theory.

Researchers using neuroimaging techniques have concluded that we use both prototypes and exemplars when forming concepts and categories. The visual cortex is involved in forming prototypes, whereas the prefrontal cortex and basal ganglia are involved in learning exemplars (Ashby & Ell, 2001). This evidence suggests that exemplar-based learning involves analysis and decision making (prefrontal cortex), whereas prototype formation is a more holistic process involving image processing (visual cortex).

In one set of studies (Marsolek, 1995), participants classified prototypes faster when the stimuli were presented to the right visual field, meaning that the left hemisphere received the input first (see Chapter 3 for a discussion of how the two hemispheres receive input from the outside world). In contrast, participants classified previously seen

EXEMPLAR THEORY A theory of categorization that argues that we make category judgments by comparing a new instance with stored memories for other instances of the category.

Exemplars

Prototype

Exemplar Theory

Prototype Theory

New stimulus

Figure 7.10 **Prototype Theory and Exemplar Theory** According to prototype theory, we classify new objects by comparing them to the "prototype" (or most typical) member of a category. According to exemplar theory, we classify new objects by comparing them to all category members.

exemplars faster when images were presented to the left visual field (meaning that the right hemisphere received the input first). These results suggest that the left hemisphere is primarily involved in forming prototypes and the right hemisphere is mainly active in recognizing exemplars.

In summary, we organize knowledge about objects, events, or other stimuli by creating concepts, prototypes, and exemplars. Studies of people with cognitive deficits have shown that the brain organizes concepts into distinct categories, such as living things and human-made things. We acquire concepts using three theories: family resemblance theory, which states that items in the same category share certain features, if not all; prototype theory, which uses the most "typical" member of a category to assess new items; and exemplar theory, which states that we compare new items with stored memories of other members of the category. Finally, studies have shown that prototypes and exemplars are processed in different parts of the brain. ■ ■

Judging, Valuing, and Deciding: Sometimes We're Logical, Sometimes Not

We use categories and concepts to guide the hundreds of decisions and judgments we make during the course of an average day. Some decisions are easy—what to wear, what to eat for breakfast, and whether to walk, ride a bicycle, or drive to class—and

AP PHOTO/MARK DUNCAN

Elizabeth Edwards, wife of Democratic presidential candidate John Edwards, spoke about her battle with recurring breast cancer at a campaign stop in March 2007. Diagnosis of breast cancer can be tricky. A group of 100 physicians were asked to predict the incidence of breast cancer among women who test positive for breast cancer on mammogram screening tests. Ninety-five of the 100 physicians estimated the probability of breast cancer after a positive mammogram to be about 75%! The correct answer was 8%.

Eddy, 1982.

People don't always make rational choices. When a lottery jackpot is larger than usual, more people will buy lottery tickets, thinking that they might well "win big." However, more people buying lottery tickets reduces the likelihood probability of any one person's winning the lottery. Ironically, people have a better chance at winning a lottery with a relatively small jackpot.

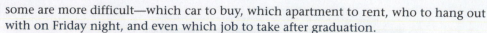

BILL GREENBLATT/NEWSMAKERS/GETTY IMAGES

some are more difficult—which car to buy, which apartment to rent, who to hang out with on Friday night, and even which job to take after graduation.

Decision making, like other cognitive activities, is vulnerable to mindbugs—many of little consequence. Had you really thought through your decision to go out with Marge, you might instead have called Emily, who's a lot more fun, but all in all, your decision about the evening was okay. The same kinds of slips in the decision-making process can have tragic results, however. Consider the actual case of a well-meaning surgeon who advised many of his female patients to undergo a mastectomy in order to avoid developing breast cancer. A newspaper article described his "pioneering" approach (Dawes, 1986). During a 2-year period, this doctor convinced 90 "high-risk" women without cancer to sacrifice their breasts "in a heroic exchange for the certainty of saving their lives and protecting their loved ones from suffering and loss" (Gigerenzer, 2002, p. 82). Unfortunately, the physician did not interpret the statistical data on breast cancer properly. If he had, he would have found that the vast majority of these women (85 out of 90, to be exact) were not expected to develop breast cancer at all (Gigerenzer, 2002).

Although extreme, this case is not unusual. In one experiment, 100 physicians were asked to predict the incidence of breast cancer among women whose mammogram screening tests showed possible evidence of breast cancer. The physicians were told to take into consideration the rarity of breast cancer (1% of the population at the time the study was done) and radiologists' record in diagnosing the condition (correctly recognized only 79% of the time and falsely diagnosed almost 10% of the time). Of the 100 physicians, 95 estimated the probability that cancer was present to be about 75%! The correct answer was 8%. The physicians apparently experienced difficulty taking so much information into account when making their decision (Eddy, 1982). Similar dismal results have been reported with a number of medical screening tests (Hoffrage & Gigerenzer, 1996; Windeler & Kobberling, 1986).

Before you conclude that humans are poorly equipped to make important decisions, note that our success rate often depends on the nature of the task. We excel at some cognitive tasks, such as estimating *frequency,* or simply the number of times something will happen. In contrast, we perform poorly on tasks that require us to think in terms of *probabilities,* or the likelihood that something will happen, as in the medical examples just discussed. Even with probabilities, however, performance varies depending on how the problem is described. Let's find out why this is so.

Decision Making: Rational, Optimal, and Otherwise

Economists contend that if we are rational and are free to make our own decisions, we will behave as predicted by **rational choice theory:** *We make decisions by determining how likely something is to happen, judging the value of the outcome, and then multiplying the two* (Edwards, 1955). This means that our judgments will vary depending on the value we assign to the possible outcomes. Suppose, for example, you were asked to choose between a 10% opportunity to gain $500 and a 20% chance of gaining $2,000. The rational person would choose the second alternative because the expected payoff is $400 ($2,000 × 20%), whereas the first offers an expected gain of only $50 ($500 × 10%). Selecting the option with the highest expected value seems so straightforward that many economists accepted the basic ideas in rational choice theory. But how well does this theory describe decision making in our everyday lives? In many cases, the answer is "not very well."

As you learned earlier in the chapter, humans easily recognize recurring patterns, group events and objects into categories based on similarity, and classify new events and objects by deciding how similar they are to categories that have already been learned. However, these strengths of human decision making can turn into weaknesses when certain tasks inadvertently activate these skills. In other words, the same principles that allow cognition to occur easily and accurately can pop up as mindbugs to bedevil our decision making.

Judging Frequencies and Probabilities

Consider the following list of words:

> *block table block pen telephone block disk glass table block telephone block watch table candy*

You probably noticed that the words *block* and *table* occurred more frequently than the other words did. In fact, studies have shown that people are quite good at estimating the frequency with which things occur. How many times did the word *block* occur in the above list? Chances are, you guessed the correct answer of five, or something pretty close to five. You probably also remember *block* and *table* better than the other words: More frequently presented items are generally easier to remember than less frequently presented ones. Adults judge frequency accurately and nearly automatically, and young children perform just as well on similar tasks. All of this suggests that this type of processing is "natural" and easy for most humans to accomplish (Barsalou & Ross, 1986; Gallistel & Gelman, 1992; Hasher & Zacks, 1984).

This skill matters quite a bit when it comes to decision making. As you'll remember, physicians performed dismally when they were asked to estimate the true probability of breast cancer among women who showed possible evidence of the disease. However, dramatically different results were obtained when the study was repeated using *frequency* information instead of *probability* information. Stating the problem as "10 out of every 1,000 women actually have breast cancer" instead of "1% of women actually have breast cancer" led 46% of the physicians to derive the right answer, compared to only 8% who came up with right answer when the problem was presented using probabilities (Hoffrage & Gigerenzer, 1998). This finding suggests at a minimum that when seeking advice—even from a highly skilled decision maker—make sure that your problem is described using frequencies rather than probabilities.

Availability Bias

Take a look at the list of names in **FIGURE 7.11.**

Now look away from the book and estimate the number of male names and female names in the figure. Did you notice that some of the women on the list are famous and none of the men are? Was your estimate off because you thought the list contained more women's than men's names (Tversky & Kahneman, 1973, 1974)? The reverse would have been true if you had looked at a list with the names of famous men and unknown women because people typically fall prey to a mindbug called the **availability bias,** in which *items that are more readily available in memory are judged as having occurred more frequently.*

The availability bias affects our estimates because memory strength and frequency of occurrence are directly related. Frequently occurring items are remembered more easily than *in*frequently occurring items, so you naturally conclude that items for which you have better memory must also have been more frequent. Unfortunately, better memory in this case was not due to greater *frequency,* but to greater *familiarity.*

Shortcuts such as the availability bias are sometimes referred to as **heuristics:** *fast and efficient strategies that may facilitate decision making but do not guarantee that a solution will be reached.* Heuristics are mental shortcuts, or "rules of thumb," that are often—but not always—effective when approaching a problem (Swinkels, 2003). In contrast, an **algorithm** is *a well-defined sequence of procedures or rules that guarantees a solution to a problem.* Consider, for example, two approaches to finding a misplaced object: (1) You try to remember the last time the object was in your possession; (2) you follow a set of directions that identify its location—for example, your roommate sheepishly telling you to walk over to the bookcase near the door and look in the yellow coffee cup, where she put your car keys when straightening up the room.

The first procedure is an intelligent heuristic that may be successful, but you could continue searching your memory until you finally run out of time or patience. The second strategy is a series of well-defined steps that, if properly executed, will guarantee a solution.

ONLY HUMAN

NOW, LET ME CALCULATE HOW LIKELY IT IS WE'LL WALK AWAY FROM THIS. . . . Some of the 280 survivors (out of 340) of a Dutch charter plane that crashed in a wind gust in the resort town of Faro, Portugal, gathered to tell their stories to reporters. Wim Kodman, 27, who is a botanist, said he was trying to calm a friend during the wind turbulence by appealing to logic. Said Kodman, "I told him, 'I'm a scientist; we're objective.' I told him a crash was improbable. I was trying to remember the exact probability when we smashed into the ground."

Figure 7.11 **Availability Bias** Looking at this list of names, estimate the number of women's and men's names.

Jennifer Aniston	Robert Kingston
Judy Smith	Gilbert Chapman
Frank Carson	Gwyneth Paltrow
Elizabeth Taylor	Martin Mitchell
Daniel Hunt	Thomas Hughes
Henry Vaughan	Michael Drayton
Agatha Christie	Julia Roberts
Arthur Hutchinson	Hillary Clinton
Jennifer Lopez	Jack Lindsay
Allan Nevins	Richard Gilder
Jane Austen	George Nathan
Joseph Litton	Britney Spears

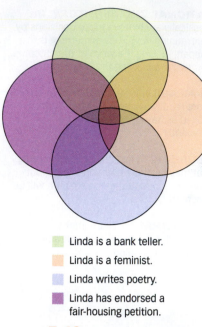

- Linda is a bank teller.
- Linda is a feminist.
- Linda writes poetry.
- Linda has endorsed a fair-housing petition.

Figure 7.12 **The Conjunction Fallacy** People often think that with each additional bit of information, the probability that all the facts are simultaneously true of a person increases. In fact, the probability decreases dramatically. Notice how the intersection of all these possibilities is much smaller than the area of any one possibility alone.

CONJUNCTION FALLACY When people think that two events are more likely to occur together than either individual event.

The Conjunction Fallacy

The availability bias illustrates a potential source of error in human cognition. Unfortunately, it's not the only one.

Consider the following description:

Linda is 31 years old, single, outspoken, and very bright. In college, she majored in philosophy. As a student, she was deeply concerned with issues of discrimination and social justice and also participated in antinuclear demonstrations.

Which state of affairs is more probable?

a. Linda is a bank teller.
b. Linda is a bank teller and is active in the feminist movement.

In one study, 89% of participants rated option b as more probable than option a (Tversky & Kahneman, 1983), although that's logically impossible. Let's say there's a 20% chance that Linda is a bank teller; after all, there are plenty of occupations she might hold. Independently, let's say there's also a 20% chance that she's active in the feminist movement; she probably has lots of interests. The joint probability that *both* things are true simultaneously is the product of their separate probabilities. In other words, the 20% chance that she's a teller multiplied by the 20% chance that she's in the feminist movement produces a 4% chance that both things are true at the same time ($.20 \times .20 = .04$, or 4%). The combined probability of events is always less than the independent probability of each event; therefore, it's always *more* probable that any one state of affairs is true than is a set of events simultaneously.

This mindbug is called the **conjunction fallacy** because *people think that two events are more likely to occur together than either individual event.* The fallacy is that with more and more pieces of information, people think there's a higher probability that all are true. Actually, the probability diminishes rapidly. Based on her description, do you think Linda also voted for the liberal candidate in the last election? Do you think she also writes poetry? Do you think she's also signed her name to fair-housing petitions? With each additional bit of information, you probably think you're getting a better and better description of Linda, but as you can see in **FIGURE 7.12,** the likelihood of all those events being true *at the same time* is very small.

Representativeness Heuristic

Think about the following situation:

A panel of psychologists wrote 100 descriptions based on interviews with engineers and lawyers. THE DESCRIPTIONS CAME FROM 70 ENGINEERS AND 30 LAWYERS. You will be shown a random selection of these descriptions. Read each and then pause and decide if it is more likely that the person is an engineer or a lawyer. Note your decision and read on.

1. Jack enjoys reading books on social and political issues. During the interview, he displayed particular skill at argument.
2. Tom is a loner who enjoys working on mathematical puzzles during his spare time. During the interview, his speech remained fairly abstract and his emotions were well controlled.
3. Harry is a bright man and an avid racquetball player. During the interview, he asked many insightful questions and was very well spoken.

Research participants were shown a series of descriptions like these and asked after each one to judge the likelihood that the person described was a lawyer or an engineer (Kahneman & Tversky, 1973). Remember, of the descriptions, 70 were engineers and 30 were lawyers. If participants took this proportion into consideration, their judgments should have reflected the fact that there were more than twice as many engineers as lawyers. But a mindbug was operating: Researchers found that people didn't use this information and based their judgments solely on how closely the description matched their concepts of lawyers and engineers. So, the majority of participants thought descriptions such as 1 were more likely to be lawyers, those like 2 were more likely to be engineers, and those like 3 could be either.

Consider participants' judgments about Harry. His description doesn't sound like a lawyer's or an engineer's, so most people said he was *equally likely* to hold either occupation. But the pool contains more than twice as many engineers as lawyers, so it is far *more* likely that he is an engineer. People seem to ignore information about *base rate*, or the existing probability of an event, basing their judgments on similarities to categories. Researchers call this the **representativeness heuristic**—*making a probability judgment by comparing an object or event to a prototype of the object or event* (Kahneman & Tversky, 1973). Thus, the probability judgments were skewed toward the participants' prototypes of lawyer and engineer. The greater the similarity, the more likely they were judged to be members of that category despite the existence of much more useful base rates.

Mindbugs such as availability, representativeness, or the conjunction fallacy highlight both the strengths and weakness of the way we think. We are very good at forming categories based on prototypes and making classification judgments on the basis of similarity to prototypes. Judging probabilities is not our strong suit. As we saw earlier in this chapter, the human brain easily processes frequency information, and decision-making performance can usually be improved if probability problems are reframed using frequencies.

Framing Effects

You've seen that according to rational choice theory, our judgments will vary depending on the value we place on the expected outcome. So how effective are we at assigning value to our choices? Not surprisingly, a mindbug can affect this situation. Studies show that **framing effects**, which occur when *people give different answers to the same problem depending on how the problem is phrased (or framed)*, can influence the assignment of value.

For example, if people are told that a particular drug has a 70% effectiveness rate, they're usually pretty impressed: 70% of the time the drug cures what ails you sounds like a good deal. Tell them instead that a drug has a 30% failure rate—30% of the time it does no good—and they typically perceive it as risky, potentially harmful, something to be avoided. Notice that the information is the same: A 70% effectiveness rate means that 30% of the time, it's ineffective. The way the information is framed, however, leads to substantially different conclusions (Tversky & Kahneman, 1981).

One of the most striking framing effects is the **sunk-cost fallacy**, which occurs when *people make decisions about a current situation based on what they have previously invested in the situation.* Imagine waiting in line for 3 hours, paying $100 for a ticket to the Warped Tour to see your favorite bands, and waking on the day of the outdoor concert to find that it's bitterly cold and rainy. If you go, you'll feel miserable. But you go anyway, reasoning that the $100 you paid for the ticket and the time you spent in line will have been wasted if you stay home.

Notice that you have two choices: (1) spend $100 and stay comfortably at home or (2) spend $100 and endure many uncomfortable hours in the rain. The $100 is gone in either case; it's a sunk cost, irretrievable at the moment of your decision. But the way you framed the problem created a mindbug: Because you invested time and money, you feel obligated to follow through, even though it's something you no longer want. If you can turn off the mindbug and ask, "Would I rather spend $100 to be comfortable or spend it to be miserable?" the smart choice is clear: Stay home and listen to the podcast!

Even the National Basketball Association (NBA) is guilty of a sunk-cost fallacy. Coaches should play their most productive players and keep them on the team longer. But they don't. The most *expensive* players are given more time on court and are kept on the team longer than cheaper players, even if the costly players are not performing up to par (Staw & Hoang, 1995). Coaches act to justify their team's investment in an expensive player rather than recognize the loss. Mindbugs can be costly! (See the Hot Science box on the next page for insights from brain damage into how decisions are made.)

REPRESENTATIVENESS HEURISTIC A mental shortcut that involves making a probability judgment by comparing an object or event to a prototype of the object or event.

FRAMING EFFECTS When people give different answers to the same problem depending on how the problem is phrased (or framed).

SUNK-COST FALLACY A framing effect in which people make decisions about a current situation based on what they have previously invested in the situation.

Worth the cost? Sports teams sometimes try to justify their investment in an expensive player who is underperforming, an example of a sunk-cost effect. Adrian Beltre is a highly paid baseball player, but his performance has not always lived up to his salary.

{ HOT SCIENCE } The Neuroscience of Risky Decision Making

A PATIENT IDENTIFIED AS "Elliot" (whom you met briefly in Chapter 1) was a successful businessman, husband, and father prior to developing a brain tumor. After surgery, his intellectual abilities seemed intact, but he was unable to differentiate between important and unimportant activities and would spend hours at mundane tasks. He lost his job and got involved in several risky financial ventures that bankrupted him. He had no difficulty discussing what had happened, but his descriptions were so detached and dispassionate that it seemed as though his abstract intellectual functions had become dissociated from his social and emotional abilities.

Research confirms that this interpretation of Elliot's downfall is right on track. In one study, researchers looked at how healthy volunteers differed from people with prefrontal lobe damage on a risky decision-making task (Bechara et al., 1994, 1997). Four decks of cards were placed facedown, and participants were required to make 100 selections of cards that specified an amount of play money they could win or lose. Two of the decks usually provided large payoffs or large losses, whereas the other two provided smaller payoffs and losses. While playing the game, the participants' galvanic skin responses (GSR) were recorded to measure heightened emotional reactions.

The performance of players with prefrontal lobe damage mirrored Elliot's real-life problems: They selected cards equally from the riskier and the safer decks, leading most to eventually go bankrupt. At first, the healthy volunteers also selected from each deck equally, but they gradually shifted to choosing primarily from the safer decks. This difference in strategy occurred even though both groups showed strong emotional reactions to big gains and losses, as measured by their comparable GSR scores.

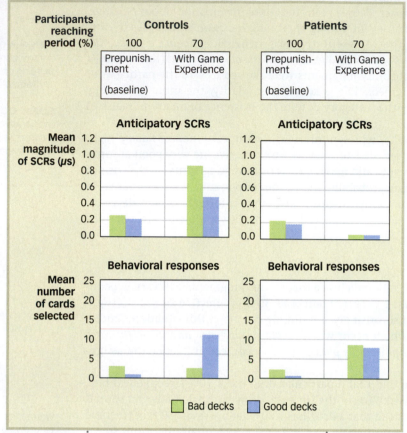

In a study of risky decision making, researchers compared healthy controls' choices to those made by people with damage to the prefrontal cortex. Participants played a game in which they selected a card from one of four decks. Two of the decks were made up of riskier cards, that is, cards that provided large payoffs or large losses. The other two contained "safer" cards—those with much smaller payoffs and losses. At the beginning of the game, both groups chose cards from the two decks with equal frequency. Over the course of the game, the healthy controls avoided the bad decks and they showed large emotional responses (SCRs, or skin conductance responses) when they even considered choosing a card from a "risky" deck. Patients with prefrontal brain damage, on the other hand, continued to choose cards from the two decks with equal frequency and showed no evidence of emotional learning. These participants eventually went bankrupt. After Bechara et al., 1997.

The two groups differed in one important way. As the game progressed, the healthy participants began to show anticipatory emotional reactions when they even *considered* choosing a card from the risky deck.

Their GSR scores jumped dramatically even before they were able to say that some decks were riskier than others (Bechara et al., 1997). The patients with prefrontal damage didn't show these anticipatory feelings when they were thinking about selecting a card from the risky deck. Apparently their emotional reactions did not guide their thinking, and so they continued to make risky decisions, as shown in the accompanying figure.

Further studies of these patients suggest that their risky decision making grows out of insensitivity to the future consequences of their behavior. Unable to think beyond immediate consequences, they could not shift their choices in response to a rising rate of losses or a declining rate of rewards (Bechara, Tranel, & Damasio, 2000). Interestingly, substance-dependent individuals, such as alcoholics and cocaine addicts, act the same way. Most perform as poorly on the gambling task as do patients with prefrontal damage. In fact, their scores can be predicted on the basis of a combination of such factors as years of substance abuse, duration of current abstinence, and number of relapses and times in treatment (Bechara et al., 2001).

Taken together, these studies suggest several conclusions. First, in addition to other physiological consequences, substance dependence may impair prefrontal cortical functions to an extent comparable with other forms of brain damage. Second, these impairments can have dramatic consequences for decision making. Robbed of the ability to take into account the future consequences of their behavior, substance abusers may persist in risky and ineffective actions. And finally, knowing what to do—making a rational, reasonable choice—and how we feel about it—experiencing the joy or dread associated with the decision—are two separate cognitive events.

Other Approaches to Human Decision Making

As you have seen, everyday decision making seems riddled with errors and shortcomings. Our decisions vary wildly depending on how a problem is presented (e.g., frequencies versus probabilities or framed in terms of losses rather than savings), and we seem to be prone to fallacies, such as the sunk-cost fallacy or the conjunction fallacy. Psychologists have developed several explanations for why everyday decision making suffers from these failings. We'll review two of the most influential theories—prospect theory and the frequency format hypothesis.

Prospect Theory

According to a totally rational model of inference, people should make decisions that maximize value; in other words, they should seek to increase what psychologists and economists call *expected utility*. We face decisions like this everyday. If you are making a decision that involves money and money is what you value, then you should choose the outcome that is likely to bring you the most money. When deciding which of two apartments to rent, you'd compare the monthly expenses for each and choose the one that leaves more money in your pocket.

As you have seen, however, people often make decisions that are inconsistent with this simple principle. The question is, why? To explain these effects, Amos Tversky and Daniel Kahneman (1992) developed **prospect theory**, which argues that *people choose to take on risk when evaluating potential losses and avoid risks when evaluating potential gains*. These decision processes take place in two phases.

- First, people simplify available information. So, in a task like choosing an apartment, they tend to ignore a lot of potentially useful information because apartments differ in so many ways (the closeness of restaurants, the presence of a swimming pool, the color of the carpet, and so forth). Comparing each apartment on each factor is simply too much work; focusing only on differences that matter is more efficient.

- In the second phase, people choose the prospect that they believe offers the best value. This value is personal and may differ from an objective measure of "best value." For example, you might choose the apartment with higher rent because you can walk to eight great bars and restaurants.

Prospect theory makes other assumptions that account for people's choice patterns. One assumption, called the *certainty* effect, suggests that when making decisions, people give greater weight to outcomes that are a sure thing. When deciding between playing a lottery with an 80% chance of winning $4,000 or receiving $3,000 outright, most people choose the $3,000, even though the expected value of the first choice is $200 more ($4,000 × 80% = $3,200)! Apparently, people weigh certainty much more heavily than expected payoffs when making choices.

Prospect theory also assumes that in evaluating choices, people compare them to a reference point. For example, suppose you're still torn between two apartments. The $400 monthly rent for apartment A is discounted $10 if you pay before the fifth of the month. A $10 surcharge is tacked onto the $390 per month rent for apartment B if you pay after the fifth of the month. Although the apartments are objectively identical in terms of cost, different reference points may make apartment A seem psychologically more appealing than B. The reference point for apartment A is $400, and the offer describes a change in terms of a potential gain (money saved), whereas the reference point for B is $390, and the change involves a potential loss (money penalized).

Prospect theory also assumes that people are more willing to take risks to avoid losses than to achieve gains. Given a choice between a definite $300 rebate on your first month's rent or spinning a wheel that offers an 80% chance of getting a $400 rebate, you'll most likely choose the lower sure payoff over the higher potential payoff ($400 × 80% = $320). However, given a choice between a sure fine of $300 for damaging an apartment or a spinning of a wheel that has an 80% chance of a $400 fine, most

PROSPECT THEORY Proposes that people choose to take on risk when evaluating potential losses and avoid risks when evaluating potential gains.

FREQUENCY FORMAT HYPOTHESIS
The proposal that our minds evolved to notice how frequently things occur, not how likely they are to occur.

people will choose the higher potential loss over the sure loss. This asymmetry in risk preferences shows that we are willing to take on risk if we think it will ward off a loss, but we're risk-averse if we expect to lose some benefits.

Frequency Format Hypothesis

According to the **frequency format hypothesis**, *our minds evolved to notice how frequently things occur, not how likely they are to occur* (Gigerenzer, 1996; Gigerenzer & Hoffrage, 1995). Thus, we interpret, process, and manipulate information about frequency with comparative ease because that's the way quantitative information usually occurs in natural circumstances. For example, the 20 men, 15 women, 5 dogs, 13 cars, and 2 bicycle accidents you encountered on the way to class came in the form of frequencies, not probabilities or percentages. Probabilities and percentages are, evolutionarily speaking, recent developments, emerging in the mid-seventeenth century (Hacking, 1975). Millennia passed before humans developed these cultural notions, and years of schooling are needed to competently use them as everyday cognitive tools. Thus, our susceptibility to mindbugs when dealing with probabilities is not surprising.

In contrast, people can track frequencies virtually effortlessly and flawlessly (Hasher & Zacks, 1984). We are also remarkably good at recognizing how often two events occur together (Mandel & Lehman, 1998; Spellman, 1996; Waldmann, 2000). Infants as young as 6 months of age can tell the difference between displays that differ in the number of items present (Starkey, Spelke, & Gelman, 1983, 1990). Frequency monitoring is a basic biological capacity rather than a skill learned through formal instruction. According to the frequency format hypothesis, presenting statistical information in frequency format rather than probability format results in improved performance because it capitalizes on our evolutionary strengths (Gigerenzer & Hoffrage, 1995; Hertwig & Gigerenzer, 1999).

In summary, human decision making often departs from a completely rational process, and the mindbugs that accompany this departure tell us a lot about how the human mind works. The values we place on outcomes weigh so heavily in our judgments that they sometimes overshadow objective evidence. When people are asked to make probability judgments, they will turn the problem into something they know how to solve, such as judging memory strength, judging similarity to prototypes, or estimating frequencies. This can lead to errors of judgment. When a problem fits their mental algorithms, people show considerable skill at making appropriate judgments. In making a judgment about the probability of an event, performance can vary dramatically. Because we feel that avoiding losses is more important than achieving gains, framing effects can affect our choices. Emotional information also strongly influences our decision making, even when we are not aware of it. Although this mindbug can lead us astray, it often is crucial for making decisions in everyday life. ■ ■

Even though it may not be easy to put together this Lego model, having instructions for assembly makes it a well-defined problem.

CORBIS COLLECTION/ALAMY

Problem Solving: Working It Out

You have a problem when you find yourself in a place where you don't want to be. In such circumstances, you try to find a way to change the situation so that you end up in a situation you *do* want. Let's say that it's the night before a test, and you are trying to study but just can't settle down and focus on the material. This is a situation you don't want. So, you try to think of ways to help yourself focus. You might begin with the material that most interests you or provide yourself with rewards, such as a music break or trip to the refrigerator. If these activities enable you to get down to work, your problem is solved.

Two major types of problems complicate our daily lives. The first and most frequent is the *ill-defined problem*, one that does not have a clear goal or well-defined solution paths. Your study block is an ill-defined problem: Your goal isn't clearly defined (i.e., "somehow get focused"), and the solution path for achieving the goal is even less clear (i.e., there are many ways to gain focus). Most everyday problems—being a "better person," finding that "special someone," achieving "success"—are ill defined. In contrast, a *well-defined problem* is one with clearly specified goals and clearly defined solution paths. Examples include following a clear set of directions to get to school, solving simple algebra problems, or playing a game of chess.

Means-Ends Analysis

In 1945, a German psychologist named Karl Duncker reported some important studies of the problem-solving process. He presented people with ill-defined problems and asked them to "think aloud" while solving them (Duncker, 1945). Based on what people said about how they solve problems, Duncker described problem solving in terms of **means-ends analysis**, which is *a process of searching for the means or steps to reduce the differences between the current situation and the desired goal.* This process usually took the following steps:

1. Analyze the goal state (i.e., the desired outcome you want to attain).
2. Analyze the current state (i.e., your starting point, or the current situation).
3. List the differences between the current state and the goal state.
4. Reduce the list of differences by
   - Direct means (a procedure that solves the problem without intermediate steps).
   - Generating a subgoal (an intermediate step on the way to solving the problem).
   - Finding a similar problem that has a known solution.

Consider, for example, one of Duncker's problems:

A patient has an inoperable tumor in his abdomen. The tumor is inoperable because it is surrounded by healthy but fragile tissue that would be severely damaged during surgery. How can the patient be saved?

The *goal state* is a patient without the tumor and with undamaged surrounding tissue. The *current state* is a patient with an inoperable tumor surrounded by fragile tissue. The *difference* between these two states is the tumor. A *direct means solution* would be to destroy the tumor with x rays, but the required x-ray dose would destroy the fragile surrounding tissue and possibly kill the patient. A *subgoal* would be to modify the x-ray machine to deliver a weaker dose. After this subgoal is achieved, a direct means solution could be to deliver the weaker dose to the patient's abdomen. But this solution won't work either: The weaker dose wouldn't damage the healthy tissue but also wouldn't kill the tumor.

So, what to do? Find a similar problem that has a known solution. Let's see how this can be done.

Analogical Problem Solving

When we engage in **analogical problem solving**, we attempt to *solve a problem by finding a similar problem with a known solution and applying that solution to the current problem.* Consider the following story:

An island surrounded by bridges is the site of an enemy fortress. The massive fortification is so strongly defended that only a very large army could overtake it. Unfortunately, the bridges would collapse under the weight of such a huge force. So, a clever general divides the army into several smaller units and sends the units over different bridges, timing the crossings so that the many streams of soldiers converge on the fortress at the same time and the fortress is taken.

Does this story suggest a solution to the tumor problem? It should. Removing a tumor and attacking a fortress are very different problems, but the two problems are analogous because they share a common structure: The *goal state* is a conquered fortress and with undamaged surrounding bridges. The *current state* is an occupied fortress surrounded by fragile bridges. The *difference* between the two states is the occupying

MEANS-ENDS ANALYSIS A process of searching for the means or steps to reduce differences between the current situation and the desired goal.

ANALOGICAL PROBLEM SOLVING Solving a problem by finding a similar problem with a known solution and applying that solution to the current problem.

Figure 7.13 Analogical Problem Solving Just as smaller, lighter battalions can reach the fortress without damaging the bridges, so can many small x-ray doses get to the tumor without harming the delicate surrounding tissue. In both cases, the additive strength achieves the objective.

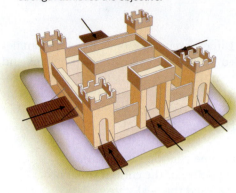

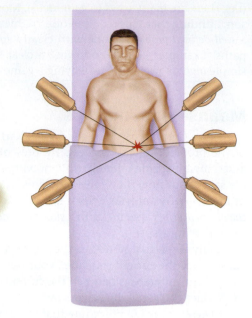

enemy. The *solution* is to divide the required force into smaller units that are light enough to spare the fragile bridges and send them down the bridges simultaneously so that they converge on the fortress. The combined units will form an army strong enough to take the fortress (see **FIGURE 7.13**).

This analogous problem of the island fortress suggests the following direct-means solution to the tumor problem:

> Surround the patient with x-ray machines and simultaneously send weaker doses that converge on the tumor. The combined strength of the weaker x-ray doses will be sufficient to destroy the tumor, but the individual doses will be weak enough to spare the surrounding healthy tissue.

Did this solution occur to you after reading the fortress story? In studies that have used the tumor problem, only 10% of participants spontaneously generated the correct solution. This percentage rose to 30% if participants read the island fortress problem or other analogous story. However, the success climbed dramatically to 75% among participants who had a chance to read more than one analogous problem or were given a deliberate hint to use the solution to the fortress story (Gick & Holyoak, 1980).

Why was the fortress problem so ineffective by itself? Apparently problem solving among novices is strongly affected by superficial similarities between problems, and the analogy between the tumor and fortress problems lies deep in their structure (Catrambone, 2002). In a set of studies demonstrating this mindbug, a researcher used examples to demonstrate solutions to mathematics problems. When participants tried to solve new problems, they often spontaneously reminded themselves of instructional examples that had the same cover story as the problem they were trying to solve—regardless of whether the mathematical structures were the same. For example, they made remarks such as, "Oh, yeah, another pizza problem," rather than, "Oh, yeah, another convergence problem" (Ross, 1984).

Creativity and Insight

Analogical problem solving shows us that successfully solving a problem often depends on learning the principles underlying a particular type of problem and also that solving lots of problems improves our ability to recognize certain problem types and generate effective solutions. Some problem solving, however, seems to involve brilliant flashes of insight and creative solutions that have never before been tried. Creative and insightful solutions often rely on restructuring a problem so that it turns into a problem you already know how to solve.

**ONLY HUMAN**

HMMM . . . WHY DOESN'T THIS HAVE ANY INSTRUCTIONS PRINTED ON IT? George Gibbs, 23, of Columbus, Ohio, suffered second- and third-degree burns on his head. He had diagnosed his car's problem as a frozen fuel line, which he thought he could correct by running warm gasoline through it. Accordingly, he tried to heat a two-gallon can of gasoline on a gas stove.

Genius and Insight

Consider the exceptional mind of the mathematician Friedrich Gauss (1777–1855). One day, Gauss's elementary school teacher asked the class to add up the numbers 1 through 10. While his classmates laboriously worked their sums, Gauss had a flash of insight that caused the answer to occur to him immediately.

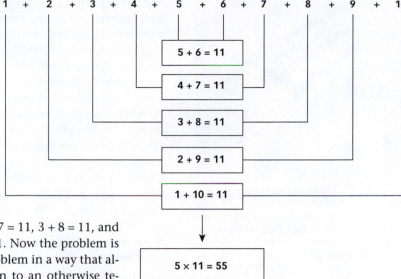

Gauss imagined the numbers 1 through 10 as weights lined up on a balance beam, as shown in **FIGURE 7.14**. Starting at the left, each "weight" increases by 1. In order for the beam to balance, each weight on the left must be paired with a weight on the right. You can see this by starting at the middle and noticing that $5 + 6 = 11$, then moving outward, $4 + 7 = 11$, $3 + 8 = 11$, and so on. This produces five number pairs that add up to 11. Now the problem is easy. Multiply. Gauss's genius lay in restructuring the problem in a way that allowed him to notice a very simple and elegant solution to an otherwise tedious task—a procedure, by the way, that generalizes to series of any length.

According to Gestalt psychologists, insights such as these reflect a spontaneous restructuring of a problem. A sudden flash of insight contrasts with incremental problem-solving procedures in which one gradually gets closer and closer to a solution. Early researchers studying insight found that people were more likely to solve a non-insight problem if they felt they were gradually getting "warmer" (incrementally closer to the solution). But whether someone felt "warm" did not predict the likelihood of their solving an insight problem (Metcalfe & Wiebe, 1987). The solution for an insight problem seemed to appear out of the blue, regardless of what the participant felt.

Later research, however, suggests that sudden insightful solutions may actually result from unconscious incremental processes (Bowers et al., 1990). In one study, research participants were shown paired, three-word series like those in **FIGURE 7.15**

Figure 7.14 Genius and Insight Young Friedrich Gauss imagined the scheme shown here and quickly reduced a laborious addition problem to an easy multiplication task. Gauss's early insight led him to realize later an intriguing truth: This simple solution generalizes to number series of any length. After Wertheimer, 1945/1982.

Coherent	Incoherent
Playing	Still
Credit	Pages
Report	Music
Blank	Light
White	Folk
Lines	Head
ticket	Town
Shop	Root
Broker	Car
Magic	House
Plush	Lion
Floor	Butter
Base	Swan
Snow	Army
Dance	Mask
Gold	Noise
Stool	Foam
Tender	Shade

Solutions: Card, paper, pawn, carpet, ball, bar

Figure 7.15 Insightful Solutions Are Really Incremental Participants were asked to find a fourth word that was associated with the other three words in each series. Even if they couldn't find a solution, they could reliably choose which series of three words were solvable and which were not. Try to solve these. After Bowers et al., 1990.

and asked to find a fourth word that was associated with the three words in each series. However, only one series in each pair had a common associate. Solvable series were termed *coherent,* whereas those with no solution were called *incoherent.*

Even if participants couldn't find a solution, they could reliably decide, more than by chance alone, which of the pairs was coherent. However, if insightful solutions actually occur in a sudden, all-or-nothing manner, their performance should have been no better than chance. Thus, the findings suggest that even insightful problem solving is an incremental process—one that occurs outside of conscious awareness. The process works something like this: The pattern of clues that constitute a problem unconsciously activates relevant information in memory. Activation then spreads through the memory network, recruiting additional relevant information (Bowers, Regehr, Balthazard, & Parker, 1990). When sufficient information has been activated, it crosses the threshold of awareness and we experience a sudden flash of insight into the problem's solution.

Finding a connection between the words *strawberry* and *traffic* might take some time, even for someone motivated to figure out how they are related. But if the word *strawberry* activates *jam* in long-term memory (see Chapter 5) and the activation spreads from *strawberry* to *traffic,* the solution to the puzzle may suddenly spring into awareness without the thinker knowing how it got there. What would seems like an all-or-nothing, sudden insight would really result from an incremental process that consists of activation spreading through memory, adding new information as more knowledge is activated.

Functional Fixedness

If insight is a simple incremental process, why isn't its occurrence more frequent? In the research discussed previously, participants produced insightful solutions only 25% of the time. Insight is rare because problem solving (like decision making) suffers from framing effects. In problem solving, framing tends to limit the types of solutions that occur to us.

Functional fixedness—*the tendency to perceive the functions of objects as fixed*—is a mindbug that constricts our thinking. Look at **FIGURES 7.16** and **7.17** and see if you can solve the problems before reading on. In Figure 7.16, your task is to illuminate a dark room using the following objects: some thumbtacks, a box of matches,

Figure 7.16 Functional Fixedness and the Candle Problem How can you use these objects—a box of matches, thumbtacks, and a candle—to mount the candle on the wall so that it illuminates the room? Give this problem some thought before you check the answer in Figure 7.19 on page 286.

Figure 7.17 Functional Fixedness and the String Problem The strings hung from hooks on either side of the ceiling are long enough to be tied together, but they are positioned too far apart to reach one while holding on to the other. Using the tools shown on the table, how can you accomplish the task? Compare your answer to that in Figure 7.20 on page 286.

and a candle. In **FIGURES 7.17**, you're holding a string hanging from the ceiling and without letting go of it and using the items on the table, you're expected to reach another string too far away to grasp.

Difficulty solving these problems derives from our tendency to think of the objects only in terms of their normal, typical, or "fixed," functions. We don't think to use the matchbox for a candleholder because boxes typically hold matches, not candles. Similarly, using the hammer as a pendulum weight doesn't spring to mind because hammers are typically used to pound things. Did functional fixedness prevent you from solving these problems? (The solutions are shown in Figures 7.19 and 7.20.)

Sometimes framing limits our ability to generate a solution. Before reading on, look at **FIGURE 7.18**. Without lifting your pencil from the page, try to connect all nine dots with only four straight lines.

To solve this problem, you must allow the lines you draw to extend outside the imaginary box that surrounds the dots (see Figure 7.21). This constraint does not reside in the problem but in the mind of the problem solver. Despite the apparent sudden flash of insight that seems to yield a solution to problems of this type, research indicates that the thought processes people use when solving even this type of insight problem are best described as an incremental, means-ends analysis (MacGregor, Ormerod, & Chronicle, 2001).

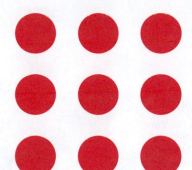

Figure 7.18 **The Nine-Dot Problem** Connect all nine dots with four straight lines without lifting your pencil from the paper. Compare your answer to those in Figure 7.21 on page 287.

In summary, like concept formation and decision making, problem solving is a process in which new inputs (in this case, problems) are interpreted in terms of old knowledge. Problems may be ill defined or well defined, leading to more or less obvious solutions. The solutions we generate depend as much on the organization of our knowledge as they do on the objective characteristics of the problems. Means-end analysis and analogical problem solving offer pathways to effective solutions, although we often frame things in terms of what we already know and already understand. Sometimes, as in the case of functional fixedness, that knowledge can restrict our problem-solving processes, making it difficult to find solutions that should be easy to find. ■ ■

Transforming Information: How We Reach Conclusions

Reasoning is *a mental activity that consists of organizing information or beliefs into a series of steps to reach conclusions.* Not surprisingly, sometimes our reasoning seems sensible and straightforward, and other times it seems a little off. Consider some reasons offered by people who filed actual insurance accident claims (www.swapmeetdave.com):

- "I left for work this morning at 7:00 a.m. as usual when I collided straight into a bus. The bus was 5 minutes early."
- "Coming home, I drove into the wrong house and collided with a tree I don't have."
- "My car was legally parked as it backed into another vehicle."
- "The indirect cause of the accident was a little guy in a small car with a big mouth."
- "Windshield broke. Cause unknown. Probably voodoo."

When people like these hapless drivers argue with you in a way that seems inconsistent or poorly thought out, you may accuse them of being "illogical." Logic is a system of rules that specifies which conclusions follow from a set of statements. To put it another way, if you know that a given set of statements is true, logic will tell you which other statements *must* also be true. If the statement "Jack and Jill

FUNCTIONAL FIXEDNESS The tendency to perceive the functions of objects as fixed.

REASONING A mental activity that consists of organizing information or beliefs into a series of steps to reach conclusions.

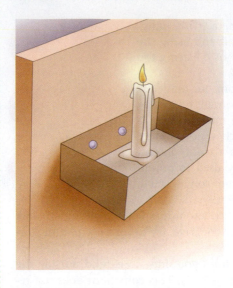

Figure 7.19 The Solution to the Candle Problem What makes this problem difficult is that the usual function of the box (to hold matches) interferes with recognizing that it can be tacked to the wall to serve as a candleholder.

went up the hill" is true, then according to the rules of logic, the statement "Jill went up the hill" must also be true. To accept the truth of the first statement while denying the truth of the second statement would be a contradiction. Logic is a tool for evaluating reasoning, but it should not be confused with the process of reasoning itself. Equating logic and reasoning would be like equating carpenter's tools (logic) with building a house (reasoning).

Earlier in the chapter, we discussed decision making, which often depends on reasoning with probabilities. Practical reasoning and theoretical reasoning also allow us to make decisions (Walton, 1990). **Practical reasoning** is *figuring out what to do, or reasoning directed toward action.* Means-ends analysis is one kind of practical reasoning. An example is figuring out how to get to a concert across town if you don't have a car. In contrast, **theoretical reasoning** (sometimes also called *discursive reasoning*) is *reasoning directed toward arriving at a belief.* We use theoretical reasoning when we try to determine which beliefs follow logically from other beliefs.

Suppose you asked your friend Bruce to take you to a concert, and he said that his car wasn't working. You'd undoubtedly find another way to get to the concert. If you then spied him drive into the concert parking lot, you might reason: "Bruce told me his car wasn't working. He just drove into the parking lot. If his car wasn't working, he couldn't drive it here. So, either he suddenly fixed it, or he was lying to me. If he was lying to me, he's not much of a friend." Notice the absence of an action-oriented goal. Theoretical reasoning is just a series of inferences concluding in a belief—in this case, about your so-called friend's unfriendliness!

If you concluded from these examples that we are equally adept at both types of reasoning, experimental evidence suggests you're wrong. People generally find figuring out what to do easier than deciding which beliefs follow logically from other beliefs. In

Figure 7.20 The Solution to the String Problem The usual function of the hammer (to pound things) interferes with recognizing that it can also serve as a weighted pendulum to swing the string into the person's grasp.

cross-cultural studies, this tendency to respond practically when theoretical reasoning is sought has been demonstrated in individuals without schooling. Consider, for example, this dialogue between a Nigerian rice farmer, a member of the preliterate Kpelle people, and an American researcher (Scribner, 1975, p. 155):

Experimenter: All Kpelle men are rice farmers. Mr. Smith (this is a Western name) is not a rice farmer. Is he a Kpelle man?

Participant: I don't know the man in person. I have not laid eyes on the man himself.

Experimenter: Just think about the statement.

Participant: If I know him in person, I can answer that question, but since I do not know him in person, I cannot answer that question.

Experimenter: Try and answer from your Kpelle sense.

Participant: If you know a person, if a question comes up about him, you are able to answer. But if you do not know a person, if a question comes up about him, it's hard for you to answer it.

As this excerpt shows, the participant does not seem to understand that the problem can be resolved with theoretical reasoning. Instead, he is concerned with retrieving and verifying facts, a strategy that does not work for this type of task.

A very different picture emerges when members of preliterate cultures are given tasks that require practical reasoning. One well-known study of rural Kenyans illustrates a typical result (Harkness, Edwards, & Super, 1981). The problem describes a dilemma in which a boy must decide whether to obey his father and give the family some of the money he has earned, even though his father previously promised that the boy could keep it all. After hearing the dilemma, the participants were asked what the boy should do. Here is a typical response from a villager:

A child has to give you what you ask for just in the same way as when he asks for anything you give it to him. Why then should he be selfish with what he has? A parent loves his child and maybe the son refused without knowing the need of helping his father . . . . By showing respect to one another, friendship between us is assured, and as a result this will increase the prosperity of our family.

This preliterate individual had little difficulty understanding this practical problem. His response is intelligent, insightful, and well reasoned. A principal finding from this kind of cross-cultural research is that the appearance of competency on reasoning tests depends more on whether the task makes sense to participants than on their problem-solving ability.

Educated individuals in industrial societies are prone to similar failures in reasoning. Psychological studies have identified a mindbug called the **belief bias**, in which *people's judgments about whether to accept conclusions depend more on how believable the conclusions are than on whether the arguments are logically valid* (Evans, Barston, & Pollard, 1983).

For example, in **syllogistic reasoning**, we assess *whether a conclusion follows from two statements that we assume to be true*. Consider the two following syllogisms, evaluate the argument, and ask yourself whether or not the conclusions must be true if the statements are true:

Syllogism 1

Statement 1: No cigarettes are inexpensive.

Statement 2: Some addictive things are inexpensive.

Conclusion: Some addictive things are not cigarettes.

Syllogism 2

Statement 1: No addictive things are inexpensive.

Statement 2: Some cigarettes are inexpensive.

Conclusion: Some cigarettes are not addictive.

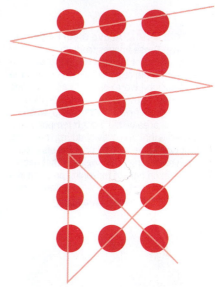

Figure 7.21 Two Solutions to the Nine-Dot Problem Solving this problem requires "thinking outside the box," that is, going outside the imaginary box implied by the dot arrangement. The limiting box isn't really there; it is imposed by the problem solver's perceptual set.

PRACTICAL REASONING Figuring out what to do, or reasoning directed toward action.

THEORETICAL REASONING Reasoning directed toward arriving at a belief.

BELIEF BIAS People's judgments about whether to accept conclusions depend more on how believable the conclusions are than on whether the arguments are logically valid.

SYLLOGISTIC REASONING Determining whether a conclusion follows from two statements that are assumed to be true.

Figure 7.22 Active Brain Regions in Reasoning These images from an fMRI study show that different types of reasoning activate different brain regions. (a) Areas within the parietal lobe were especially active during logical reasoning that is not influenced by prior beliefs (belief-neutral reasoning), whereas (b) an area within the left temporal lobe showed enhanced activity during reasoning that was influenced by prior beliefs (belief-laden reasoning). This suggests that people approach each type of reasoning problem in a different way.
Goel and Dolan, 2003.

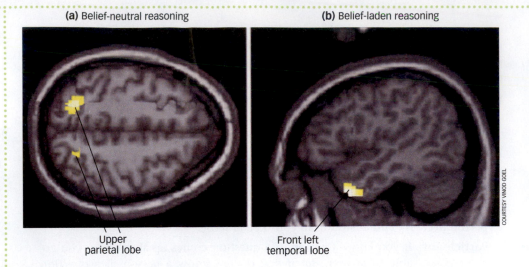

(a) Belief-neutral reasoning   **(b)** Belief-laden reasoning

Upper parietal lobe

Front left temporal lobe

COURTESY VINOD GOEL

If you're like most people, you probably concluded that the reasoning is valid in syllogism 1 but flawed in syllogism 2. Indeed, researchers found that nearly 100% of participants accepted the first conclusion as valid, but fewer than half accepted the second (Evans, Barston, & Pollard, 1983). But notice that the syllogisms are in exactly the same form. This form of syllogism is valid, so both conclusions are valid. Evidently, the believability of the conclusions influences people's judgments.

Research using fMRI provides novel insights into belief biases on reasoning tasks. In *belief-laden* trials, participants were scanned while they reasoned about syllogisms that could be influenced by knowledge affecting the believability of the conclusions. In *belief-neutral* trials, syllogisms contained obscure terms whose meaning was unknown to participants, as in the following example:

Syllogism 3

Statement 1: No codes are highly complex.

Statement 2: Some quipu are highly complex.

Conclusion: No quipu are codes.

Belief-neutral reasoning activated different brain regions than did belief-laden reasoning (as shown in **FIGURE 7.22**). Activity in a part of the left temporal lobe involved in retrieving and selecting facts from long-term memory increased during belief-laden reasoning. In contrast, that part of the brain showed little activity and parts of the parietal lobe involved in mathematical reasoning and spatial representation showed greater activity during belief-neutral reasoning (Goel & Dolan, 2003). This evidence suggests that participants took different approaches to the two types of reasoning tasks, relying on previously encoded memories in belief-laden reasoning and on more abstract thought processes in belief-neutral reasoning.

In summary, the success of human reasoning depends on the content of the argument or scenario under consideration. People seem to excel at practical reasoning while stumbling when theoretical reasoning requires evaluation of the truth of a set of arguments. Belief bias describes a mindbug that distorts judgments about conclusions of arguments, causing people to focus on the believability of the conclusions rather than on the logical connections between the premises. Neuroimaging provides evidence that different brain regions are associated with different types of reasoning. We can see here and elsewhere in the chapter that some of the same strategies that earlier helped us to understand perception, memory, and learning—carefully examining mindbugs and trying to integrate information about the brain into our psychological analyses—are equally helpful in understanding thought and language. ■ ■

Where Do You Stand?

Choosing a Mate

Perhaps the most important decision that we make as adults is who to marry. Your spouse is a partner in all of your most valued and intimate human activities: bearing and raising children, acquiring and sharing wealth, and providing emotional sustenance. If divorce rates are considered, however, it appears that we are not very good at making this type of decision. According to the National Center for Health Statistics, 43 percent of first marriages in the United States end in separation or divorce within 15 years (Bramlett & Mosher, 2001). Projections indicate that the proportion could be as high as 50% for people now in their early 40s (Kreider & Fields, 2002).

Why is choosing a mate such a difficult decision? It may be that mate choice constitutes the ultimate "ill-defined" problem. There are no clearly specified decision-making procedures that will ensure a satisfactory outcome. The desired goal itself (the "perfect spouse" or "perfect marriage") may be difficult to specify precisely, may change as a function of age, and perhaps most importantly may be defined differently by the two parties involved. A large body of research indicates that men and women value different characteristics in prospective mates.

Research by more than 50 scientists studying more than 10,000 individuals inhabiting 33 countries shows that women prefer male mates who possess good financial prospects, favorable social status, and ambition, while men prefer female mates who possess physical attractiveness and good health (Buss et al., 1990; Buss, 1994).

The most frequent explanation for this virtually universal sex-linked difference is that men and women, with respect to reproductive success, have confronted different adaptive problems over evolutionary history (Buss, 1994; Buss & Schmitt, 1993). The different adaptive problems between the genders concerns parental investment, which researchers define as any investment of time, energy, or risk that an animal makes to enhance the survival and eventual reproduction of an offspring (Krebs & Davies 1991; Trivers, 1972a). Among mammals, females typically invest more in childbearing and child-rearing than males do. Females carry the offspring within their bodies, undergo the risks of childbirth, nurse the infant, and care for their offspring until they are old enough to care for themselves. The reproductive cost for females is therefore greater than for males. This means that reproductive success in females is limited by access to resources, while reproductive success in males is limited by access to potential mates.

Where do you stand on the issue of choosing a mate? Do you think that we should take this type of evolutionary analysis seriously? If so, does this mean that we are "prisoners of biology"? We don't think so—while we are affected by our evolutionary history, we are not constrained by it. For example, one study found that Hungarian women did not seek mates with resources as frequently as females in other nations (Bereczkei, Vorgos, Gal, & Bernath, 1997). Since the collapse of communism in Hungary, there are still relatively few men with an income sufficient enough to maintain a family. The researchers speculate that, because of this, females in this culture have shifted their attention to cues other than those referring to resources when seeking mates, such as physical attractiveness or compatibility of values (Bereczkei et al., 1997). Understanding mating decisions clearly requires us to take into account social and cultural factors as well as cognitive and evolutionary ones.

Chapter Review

Language and Communication: Nothing's More Personal

- Human language is characterized by a complex organization, from phonemes to morphemes to phrases and finally to sentences. Each level of human language is constructed and understood according to grammatical rules, none of which are taught explicitly.

- Children appear to be biologically predisposed to process language in ways that allow them to extract grammatical rules from the language they hear. This *language acquisition device* emerges as a child matures.

- Some areas of the human brain are specialized for language processing. For example, Broca's area is specialized for language production and Wernicke's area is specialized for language comprehension.

- Apes can learn new vocabulary and construct simple sentences but compared with humans are limited in terms of vocabulary and grammatical complexity.

- According to the linguistic relativity hypothesis, language may influence thought. Research also reveals that thought influences language.

Concepts and Categories: How We Think

- We store our knowledge in three main ways—our experiences in terms of individual memories, generalizations that take the form of prototypes, and factual information that is codified in terms of rules.

- The brain organizes concepts into distinct categories, such as living things and human-made things. We rely on family resemblance, prototypes, and exemplars to categorize and keep track of our knowledge about the world.

- We use concepts and categories to solve problems, make inferences, and guide judgments.

Judging, Valuing, and Deciding: Sometimes We're Logical, Sometimes Not

- Human decision making often departs from a strictly rational model of inference. Numerous processes interject themselves to make decision making less than perfect.

- We excel at estimating frequencies, defining categories, and making similarity judgments, but we do not make probability judgments very well. The frequency format hypothesis suggests that evolution might have played a role in our superior frequency estimates.

- Human decision-making performance varies dramatically depending on whether or not the task is presented in a format that fits our mental algorithms.

- Many decision-making tasks require evaluating the probability of events as well as their value to us. Evaluating value is crucial for making the kinds of decisions that we normally encounter in everyday life, but it is also vulnerable to errors.

- Errors in decision making often take the form of biases and heuristic reasoning. For example, the availability bias, the conjunction fallacy, and the representativeness heuristic all illustrate potential pitfalls in judgment.

- Decision making can vary depending on how the decision is framed. For example, framing influences our feelings toward avoiding losses versus achieving gains. Prospect theory was developed in part to account for these tendencies.

- Emotional information strongly influences our decision making even when we are not aware of it.

Problem Solving: Working It Out

- Problem solving is a process in which new information is interpreted in terms of old knowledge. The solutions we generate often depend on the organization of our knowledge as well as the objective characteristics of the problems. Problems can be either ill defined or well defined.

- There are several effective approaches to problem solving. Means-ends analysis is a process of moving a current state more in line with a desired end state. In analogical problem solving, we attempt to solve a problem by finding a similar problem with a known solution and applying that solution to the current problem.

- Creative and insightful solutions often involve "restructuring" a problem so that it turns into a problem for which a solution procedure is already known.

Transforming Information: How We Reach Conclusions

- The success of human reasoning depends on the content of the argument or scenario under consideration.

- Our reasoning performance varies as a function of the kinds of task we are required to do. We perform better on tasks that require practical reasoning than we do on tasks that require theoretical reasoning.

Key Terms

language (p. 254)

phoneme (p. 254)

phonological rules (p. 255)

morphemes (p. 255)

grammar (p. 255)

morphological rules (p. 255)

syntactical rules (p. 255)

deep structure (p. 256)

surface structure (p. 256)

fast mapping (p. 258)

telegraphic speech (p. 258)

nativist theory (p. 260)

language acquisition device (LAD) (p. 260)

genetic dysphasia (p. 260)

aphasia (p. 262)

linguistic relativity hypothesis (p. 266)

concept (p. 267)

category-specific deficit (p. 268)

family resemblance theory (p. 269)

prototype (p. 271)

exemplar theory (p. 272)

rational choice theory (p. 274)

availability bias (p. 275)

heuristic (p. 275)

algorithm (p. 275)

conjunction fallacy (p. 276)

representativeness heuristic (p. 277)

framing effects (p. 277)

sunk-cost fallacy (p. 277)

prospect theory (p. 279)

frequency format hypothesis (p. 280)

means-ends analysis (p. 281)

analogical problem solving (p. 281)

functional fixedness (p. 284)

reasoning (p. 285)

practical reasoning (p. 286)

theoretical reasoning (p. 286)

belief bias (p. 287)

syllogistic reasoning (p. 287)

Recommended Readings

Belsky, G., & Gilovich, T. (2000). *Why smart people make big money mistakes—and how to correct them: Lessons from the new science of behavioral economics.* New York: Fireside. Belsky is a financial journalist and Gilovich is a Cornell psychology professor. The intersection of their talents produced this fine summary of research on human decision making, with special emphasis on the practicalities of money management.

Cummins, D. D., & Allen, C. A. (2000). *The evolution of mind.* New York: Oxford University Press. This anthology contains entertaining and informative papers written by psychologists, anthropologists, ethologists, and philosophers that utilize new ideas about biological functions to illuminate puzzling questions of human cognitive evolution.

Dawes, R. M. (2001). *Everyday irrationality: How pseudo scientists, lunatics, and the rest of us systematically fail to think rationally.* Boulder, CO: Westview Press. An informal and humorous commentary on our society based on rigorous psychological research undertaken by Daniel Kahneman, Amos Tversky, Richard Thaler, and other pioneering researchers of human cognition.

Leighton, J. P., & Sternberg, R. J. (Eds.). (2003). *The nature of reasoning.* Cambridge, MA: Cambridge University Press. This handy collection of current theory and research on the psychology of reasoning not only presents the state of the science but also charts new directions. This is a comprehensive account of what is known about reasoning in psychology and cognitive science.

Pinker, S. (1994). *The language instinct.* New York: Morrow. A provocative, entertaining, and skillfully written book on language and language development by a professor who specializes in language research.

8

Consciousness

Conscious and Unconscious: The Mind's Eye, Open and Closed
The Mysteries of Consciousness
The Nature of Consciousness
The Unconscious Mind
HOT SCIENCE How Smart Is the Unconscious Mind?

Sleep and Dreaming: Good Night, Mind
Sleep
Dreams
HOT SCIENCE Dreaming and the Brain

Drugs and Consciousness: Artificial Inspiration
Drug Use and Abuse
Types of Psychoactive Drugs
THE REAL WORLD Drugs and the Regulation of Consciousness

Hypnosis: Open to Suggestion
Induction and Susceptibility
Hypnotic Effects

Meditation and Religious Experiences: Higher Consciousness
Meditation
Ecstatic Religious Experiences
WHERE DO YOU STAND?
Between NORML and MADD: What Is Acceptable Drug Use?

UNCONSCIOUSNESS IS SOMETHING YOU don't really appreciate until you need it. Belle Riskin needed it one day on an operating table, when she awoke just as doctors were pushing a breathing tube down her throat. She felt she was choking, but she couldn't see, breathe, scream, or move. Unable even to blink an eye, she couldn't signal to the surgeons that she was conscious. "I was terrified. Why is this happening to me? Why can't I feel my arms? I could feel my heart pounding in my head. It was like being buried alive, but with somebody shoving something down your throat," she explained later. "I knew I was conscious, that something was going on during the surgery. I had just enough awareness to know I was being intubated" (Groves, 2004).

How could this happen? Anesthesia for surgery is supposed to leave the patient unconscious, "feeling no pain," and yet in this case—and in about one in a thousand other operations (Sandin et al., 2000)—the patient regains consciousness at some point and even remembers the experience. Some patients remember pain; others remember the clink of surgical instruments in a pan or the conversations of doctors and nurses. There may be lingering memories of being pushed, pulled, cut, or stitched. This is *not* how modern surgery is supposed to go, but the problem arises because muscle-relaxing drugs are used to keep the patient from moving involuntarily and making unhelpful contributions

to the operation. Then, when the drugs that are given to induce unconsciousness fail to do the job, the patient with extremely relaxed muscles is unable to show or tell doctors that there is a problem.

Waking up in surgery sounds pretty rough all by itself, but this could cause additional complications. The conscious patient could become alarmed and emotional during the operation, spiking blood pressure and heart rate to dangerous levels. Awareness also might lead to later emotional problems. Fortunately, new methods of monitoring wakefulness by measuring the electrical activity of the brain are being developed. One system uses sensors attached to the person's head and gives readings on a scale from 0 (no electrical activity signaling consciousness in the brain) to 100 (fully alert), providing a kind of "consciousness meter." Anesthesiologists

When it's time for surgery, it's great to be unconscious.

CONSCIOUSNESS The person's subjective experience of the world and the mind.

CARTESIAN THEATER (after philosopher René Descartes) A mental screen or stage on which things appear to be presented for viewing by the mind's eye.

using this index deliver anesthetics to keep the patient in the recommended range of 40 to 65 for general anesthesia during surgery; they have found that this system reduces postsurgical reports of consciousness and memory for the surgical experience (Sigl & Chamoun, 1994). One of these devices in the operating room might have helped Belle Riskin settle into the unconsciousness she so dearly needed.

Most of the time, of course, consciousness is something we cherish. How else could we experience a favorite work of art; the mellow strains of an oldie on the radio; the taste of a sweet, juicy peach; or the touch of a loved one's hand? **Consciousness** is *a person's subjective experience of the world and the mind*. Although you might think of consciousness as simply "being awake," the defining feature of consciousness is *experience,* which you have when you're not awake but experiencing a vivid dream. Conscious experience is essential to what it means to be human. The anesthesiologist's dilemma in trying to monitor Belle Riskin's consciousness is a stark reminder, though, that it is impossible for one person to experience another's consciousness. Your consciousness is utterly private, a

world of personal experience that only you can know.

How can this private world be studied? One way to explore consciousness is to examine it directly, trying to understand what it is like, how it seems to be created, how it works, and how it compares with the mind's *un*conscious processes. We'll begin with this direct approach, looking at the mysteries of consciousness and its known properties. Another way to explore consciousness is to examine its altered states, in other words, the cases in which the experience of being human departs from normal, everyday waking. We will probe these changes, beginning with the major alterations that happen during sleep, when waking consciousness steals away only to be replaced by the surreal form of consciousness experienced in dreams. Then we'll look into how we alter our consciousness through intoxication with alcohol and other drugs, and other changes in consciousness that occur during hypnosis and meditation. Like the traveler who learns the meaning of *home* by roaming far away, we can learn the meaning of consciousness by exploring its exotic variations.

Conscious and Unconscious: The Mind's Eye, Open and Closed

What does it feel like to be you right now? It probably feels as though you are somewhere inside your head, looking out at the world through your eyes. You can feel your hands on this book, perhaps, and notice the position of your body or the sounds in the room when you orient yourself toward them. If you shut your eyes, you may be able to imagine things in your mind, even though all the while thoughts and feelings come and go, passing through your imagination. The philosopher Daniel Dennett called this "place in your head" where "you" are the **Cartesian Theater** (after philosopher René Descartes), *a mental screen or stage on which things appear to be presented for viewing by your mind's eye* (Dennett, 1991). But where are "you," really? And how is it that this theater of consciousness gives you a view of some things in your world and your mind but not others? The Cartesian Theater unfortunately isn't available on DVD, making it difficult to share exactly what's on our mental screen with our friends, a researcher, or even ourselves in precisely the same way a second time. As you'll recall from Chapter 1, Wilhelm Wundt encountered similar problems when studying consciousness in the earliest days of psychology. We'll look at the difficulty of studying consciousness directly but also move along to examine the nature of consciousness (what it is that can be seen in this mental theater) and then explore the unconscious mind (what is *not* visible to the mind's eye).

"We keep this section closed off."

The Mysteries of Consciousness

Other sciences, such as physics, chemistry, and biology, have the great luxury of studying *objects*, things that we all can see. Psychology studies objects too, looking at people and their brains and behaviors, but it has the unique challenge of also trying to make sense of *subjects*. A physicist is not concerned with what it is like to be a neutron, but psychologists hope to understand what it is like to be a human, that is, grasping the subjective perspectives of the people that they study. Psychologists hope to include an understanding of **phenomenology**, *how things seem to the conscious person,* in their understanding of mind and behavior. After all, consciousness is an extraordinary human property that could well be unique to us. But including phenomenology in psychology brings up mysteries pondered by great thinkers almost since the beginning of thinking. Let's look at two of the more vexing mysteries of consciousness: the problem of other minds and the mind/body problem.

The Problem of Other Minds

One great mystery is called the **problem of other minds**, *the fundamental difficulty we have in perceiving the consciousness of others*. How do you know that anyone else is conscious? They tell you that they are conscious, of course, and are often willing to describe in depth how they feel, how they think, what they are experiencing, and how good or how bad it all is. But perhaps they are just *saying* these things. There is no clear way to distinguish a conscious person from someone who might do and say all the same things as a conscious person but who is *not* conscious. Philosophers have called this hypothetical nonconscious person a "zombie," in reference to the living-yet-dead creatures of horror films (Chalmers, 1996). A philosopher's zombie could talk about experiences ("The lights are so bright!") and even seem to react to them (wincing and turning away) but might not be having any inner experience at all. No one knows whether there could be such a zombie, but then again, because of the problem of other minds, none of us will ever know for sure that another person is *not* a zombie.

Even the "consciousness meter" used by anesthesiologists falls short. It certainly doesn't give the anesthesiologist any special insight into what it is like to be the patient on the operating table; it only predicts whether patients will *say* they were conscious. We simply lack the ability to directly perceive the consciousness of others. In short, you are the only thing in the universe you will ever truly know what it is like to be.

The problem of other minds also means there is no way you can tell if another person's experience of anything is at all like yours. Although you know what the color red looks like to you, for instance, you cannot know whether it looks the same to other people. Maybe they're seeing what you see as blue and just *calling* it red in a consistent way. If their inner experience "looks" blue, but they say it looks hot and is the color of a tomato, you'll never be able to tell that their experience differs from yours. Of course, most people have come to trust each other in describing their inner lives, reaching the general assumption that other human minds are pretty much like their own. But they don't know this for a fact, and they can't know it directly.

The problem of other minds is not just a matter of how we perceive people. In an essay asking, What is it like to be a bat?, philosopher Thomas Nagel (1974) wondered

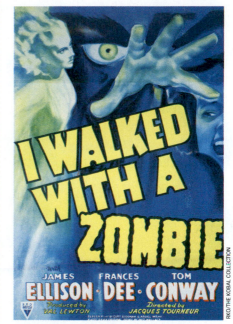

How would you know if you walked with a zombie? Could you perceive its lack of consciousness?

Does a computer have a mind? Champion chess player Gary Kasparov may have thought so as he played against the computer X3D Fritz during a virtual reality match in New York, Tuesday, November 18, 2003. After the third game in a four-game match, Kasparov and computer were tied one-and-a-half games each.

Noreldo, the mental marvel, reads the mind of his cat, Ned.

what it's like flying around in a dark cave, sensing the walls through the echoes made by your ultrasonic screeches. Would your experience of the cave include visual images, or sounds, or something else entirely? It's difficult to imagine; we're not bats. And if bat consciousness is hard to imagine, what about all the other animals? When a puppy looks up at you with those warm brown eyes, seemingly saying, "I love you and everything you stand for," you can't really know what it's like in there—so your appreciation of the puppy's mind reflects what's going on in *your* head more than in the puppy's. The perception of other minds is in fact something that happens in the mind of the perceiver.

How do people perceive other minds? Researchers conducting a large online survey asked people to compare the minds of 13 different targets, such as a baby, chimp, robot, man, and woman, on 18 different mental capacities, such as feeling pain, pleasure, hunger, and consciousness (see **FIGURE 8.1**) (Gray, Gray, & Wegner, 2007). Respondents who were judging the mental capacity to feel pain, for example, compared pairs of targets: Is a frog or a dog more able to feel pain? Is a baby or a robot more able to feel pain? Is a 7-week-old fetus or a man in a persistent vegetative state more able to feel pain? When the researchers examined all the comparisons on the different mental capacities with the computational technique of factor analysis (see Chapter 9), they found two dimensions of mind perception. People judge minds according to the capacity for *experience* (such as the ability to feel pain, pleasure, hunger, consciousness, anger, or fear) and the capacity for *agency* (such as the ability for self-control, planning, memory, or thought). As shown in Figure 8.1, respondents rated some targets as having little experience or agency (the dead person), others as having experiences but little agency (the baby), and yet others as having both experience and agency (adult humans). Still others were perceived to have agency without experiences (the robot, God). The perception of minds, then, involves more than just whether something has a mind. People appreciate that minds both have experiences and act as agents that perform actions.

Ultimately, the problem of other minds is a problem for psychological science. As you'll remember from Chapter 2, the scientific method requires that any observation made by one scientist should, in principle, be available for observation by any other scientist. But if other minds aren't observable, how can consciousness be a topic of scientific study? One radical solution is to eliminate consciousness from psychology entirely and follow the other sciences into total objectivity by renouncing the study of *anything* mental. This was the solution offered by behaviorism, and it turned out to have its own shortcomings, as you saw in Chapter 1. Despite the problem of other minds, modern psychology has embraced the study of consciousness. The astonishing richness of mental life simply cannot be ignored.

Figure 8.1 Dimensions of Mind Perception When participants judged the mental capacities of 13 targets, two dimensions of mind perception were discovered (Gray et al., 2007). Participants perceived minds as varying in the capacity for experience (such as abilities to feel pain or pleasure) and in the capacity for agency (such as abilities to plan or exert self-control). They perceived normal adult humans (male, female, or "you," the respondent) to have minds on both dimensions, whereas other targets were perceived to have reduced experience or agency. The man in a persistent vegetative state ("PVS man"), for example, was judged to have only some experience and very little agency.

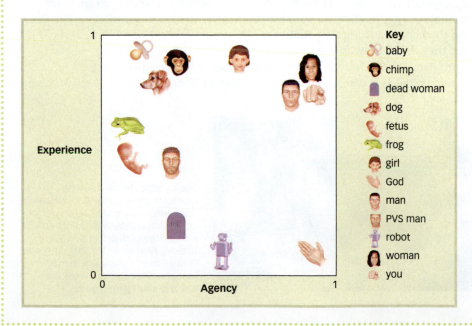

The Mind/Body Problem

Another mystery of consciousness is the **mind/body problem,** *the issue of how the mind is related to the brain and body.* French philosopher and mathematician René Descartes (1596–1650) is famous, among other things, for proposing that mind and body are made of different substances. As you read in Chapter 1, Descartes believed that the human body is a machine made of physical matter but that the human mind or soul is a separate entity made of a "thinking substance." He proposed that the mind has its effects on the brain and body through the pineal gland, a small structure located near the center of the brain. It has the appealing property of being unitary, whereas the rest of the brain is split into right and left halves (see **FIGURE 8.2**). In fact, the pineal gland is not even a nerve structure but rather is an endocrine gland quite poorly equipped to serve as a center of human consciousness.

But Descartes was right in pointing out the difficulty of reconciling the physical body with the mind. Most psychologists assume that mental events are intimately tied to brain events, such that every thought, perception, or feeling is associated with a particular pattern of activation of neurons in the brain (see Chapter 3). Thinking about a particular duck, for instance, occurs with a unique array of neural connections and activations. If the neurons repeat that pattern, then you must be thinking of the duck; conversely, if you think of the duck, the brain activity occurs in that pattern. Far from the tiny connection between mind and brain in the pineal gland that was proposed by Descartes, instead the mind and brain are connected everywhere to each other! In other words, "the mind is what the brain does" (Minsky, 1986, p. 287). Studies of the brain structures associated with conscious thinking in particular (as opposed to all the other mental efforts that go on in the background of the mind) suggest that conscious thought is supported widely in the brain by many different structures (Koch, 2004).

One telling set of studies, however, suggests that the brain's activities *precede* the activities of the conscious mind. The electrical activity in the brains of volunteers was measured using sensors placed on their scalps as they repeatedly decided when to move a hand (Libet, 1985). Participants were also asked to indicate exactly when they consciously chose to move by reporting the position of a dot moving rapidly around the face of a clock just at the point of the decision (**FIGURE 8.3a**). As a rule, the brain begins to show electrical activity around half a second before a voluntary action (535 milliseconds, to be exact). This makes sense since brain activity certainly seems to be necessary to get an action started.

What this experiment revealed, though, was that the brain also started to show electrical activity before the person's conscious decision to move. As shown in **FIGURE 8.3b**, these studies found that the brain becomes active more than 300 milliseconds before participants report that they are consciously trying to move. The feeling that you are consciously willing your actions, it seems, may be a result rather than a cause of your brain activity. Although your personal intuition is that you *think* of an action and *then* do it, these experiments suggest that your brain is getting started before *either* the thinking or the doing, preparing the way for both thought and action. Quite simply, it may appear to us that our minds are leading our brains and bodies, but the order of events may be the other way around (Wegner, 2002).

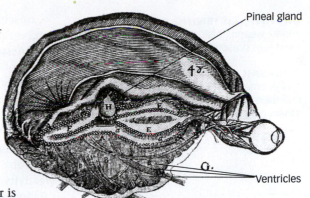

Pineal gland

Ventricles

Figure 8.2 **Seat of the Soul** Descartes imagined that the seat of the soul—and consciousness—might reside in the pineal gland located in the ventricles of the brain. This original drawing from Descartes (1662) shows the pineal gland (H) nicely situated for a soul, right in the middle of the brain.

MIND/BODY PROBLEM The issue of how the mind is related to the brain and body.

Figure 8.3 **The Timing of Conscious Will** (a) In Benjamin Libet's experiments, the participant was asked to move fingers at will while simultaneously watching a dot move around the face of a clock to mark the moment at which the action was consciously willed. Meanwhile, EEG sensors timed the onset of brain activation and EMG sensors timed the muscle movement. (b) The experiment showed that brain activity (EEG) precedes the willed movement of the finger (EMG) but that the reported time of consciously willing the finger to move follows the brain activity.

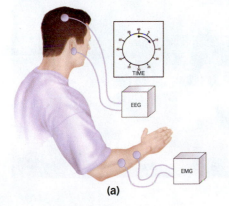

(a)

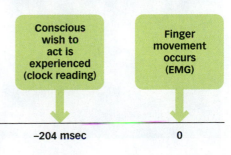

Time → **−535 msec** | Brain activity begins (EEG)

−204 msec | Conscious wish to act is experienced (clock reading)

0 | Finger movement occurs (EMG)

(b)

DICHOTIC LISTENING A task in which people wearing headphones hear different messages presented to each ear.

COCKTAIL PARTY PHENOMENON A phenomenon in which people tune in one message even while they filter out others nearby.

Consciousness has its mysteries, but psychologists like a challenge. Although researchers may not be able to see the consciousness of others or know exactly how consciousness arises from the brain, this does not prevent them from collecting people's reports of conscious experiences and learning how these reports reveal the nature of consciousness. We'll consider that topic next.

The Nature of Consciousness

How would you describe your own consciousness? Researchers examining people's descriptions suggest that consciousness has four basic properties—intentionality, unity, selectivity, and transience of consciousness—that it occurs on different levels, and that it includes a range of different contents. Let's examine each of these points in turn.

Four Basic Properties

Consciousness is always *about* something. Philosophers call this first property the *intentionality of consciousness,* the quality of being directed toward an object. Psychologists, in turn, have tried to measure the relationship between consciousness and its objects, examining the size and duration of the relationship. How long can consciousness be directed toward an object, and how many objects can it take on at one time? Researchers have found that conscious attention is limited. Despite all the lush detail you see in your mind's eye, the kaleidoscope of sights and sounds and feelings and thoughts, the object of your consciousness at any one moment is just a small part of all of this (see **FIGURE 8.4**). To describe how this limitation works, psychologists refer to three other properties of consciousness: unity, selectivity, and transience.

The *unity of consciousness* is its resistance to division. This property becomes clear when you try to attend to more than one thing at a time. You may wishfully think that you can study and watch TV simultaneously, for example, but research suggests not. One study had research participants divide their attention by reacting to two games superimposed on a television screen (see **FIGURE 8.5**). They had to push one button when one person slapped another's hands in the first game and push another button when a ball was passed in the second game. The participants were easily able to follow one game at a time, but their performance took a nosedive when they tried to follow both simultaneously. Their error rate when attending to the two tasks was eight times greater than when attending to either task alone (Neisser & Becklen, 1975). Your attempts to study, in other words, could seriously interfere with a full appreciation of your TV show.

The *selectivity of consciousness* is its capacity to include some objects and not others. This property is shown through studies of **dichotic listening**, *in which people wearing headphones are presented with different messages in each ear.* Research participants were instructed to repeat aloud the words they heard in one ear while a different message

Figure 8.4 Bellotto's Dresden and Close-up The people on the bridge in the distance look very finely detailed in *View of Dresden with the Frauenkirche at Left*, by Bernardo Bellotto (1720–80) (left). However, when you examine the detail closely (right), you find that the people are made of brushstrokes merely *suggesting* people—an arm here, a torso there. Consciousness produces a similar impression of "filling in," as it seems to consist of extreme detail even in areas that are peripheral (Dennett, 1991).

NORTH CAROLINA MUSEUM OF ART/CORBIS

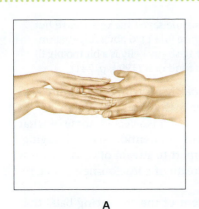
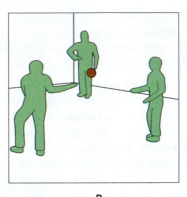
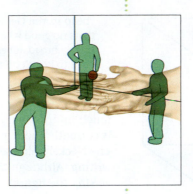

A   B   C

Figure 8.5 Divided Attention Research participants presented with two different games (A and B) could easily follow each game separately. When participants tried to follow the action in the two different games simultaneously (C), they performed remarkably poorly (Neisser & Becklen, 1975).

was presented to the other ear (Cherry, 1953). As a result of focusing on the words they were supposed to repeat, participants noticed little of the second message, often not even realizing that at some point it changed from English to German! So, consciousness *filters out* some information. At the same time, participants did notice when the voice in the unattended ear changed from a male's to a female's, suggesting that the selectivity of consciousness can also work to *tune in* other information.

How does consciousness decide what to filter in and what to tune out? The conscious system is most inclined to select information of special interest to the person. For example, in what has come to be known as the **cocktail party phenomenon,** *people tune in one message even while they filter out others nearby.* In the dichotic listening situation, for example, research participants are especially likely to notice if their own name is spoken into the unattended ear (Moray, 1959). Perhaps you too have noticed how abruptly your attention is diverted from whatever conversation you are having when someone else within earshot at the party mentions your name. Selectivity is not only a property of waking consciousness, however; the mind works this way in other states. People are more sensitive to their own name than others' names, for example, even during sleep (Oswald, Taylor, & Triesman, 1960). This is why when you are trying to wake someone up, it is best to use the person's name (particularly if you want to sleep with that person again).

A final basic property is the *transience of consciousness,* or its tendency to change. Consciousness wiggles and fidgets like that toddler in the seat behind you on the airplane. The mind wanders not just sometimes, but incessantly, from one "right now" to the next "right now" and then on to the next (Wegner, 1997). William James, whom you met way back in Chapter 1, famously described consciousness as a stream: "Consciousness . . . does not appear to itself chopped up in bits. Such words as 'chain' or 'train' do not describe it. . . . It is nothing jointed; it flows. A 'river' or a 'stream' are the metaphors by which it is most naturally described" (James, 1890, Vol. 1, p. 239). Books written in the "stream of consciousness" style, such as James Joyce's *Ulysses,* illustrate the whirling, chaotic, and constantly changing flow of consciousness. Here's an excerpt:

> I wished I could have picked every morsel of that chicken out of my fingers it was so tasty and browned and as tender as anything only for I didn't want to eat everything on my plate those forks and fishslicers were hallmarked silver too I wish I had some I could easily have slipped a couple into my muff when I was playing with them then always hanging out of them for money in a restaurant for the bit you put down your throat we have to be thankful for our mangy cup of tea itself as a great compliment to be noticed the way the world is divided in any case if its going to go on I want at least two other good chemises for one thing and but I dont know what kind of drawers he likes none at all I think didn't he say yes and half the girls in Gibraltar never wore them either naked as God made them that Andalusian singing her Manola she didn't make much secret of what she hadnt yes and the second pair of silkette stockings is laddered after one days wear I could have brought them back to Lewers this morning and kicked up a row and made that one change them only not to upset myself and run the risk of walking into him and ruining the whole thing and one of those kidfitting corsets Id want advertised

Participants in a dichotic listening experiment hear different messages played to the right and left ear and may be asked to "shadow" one of the messages by repeating it aloud.

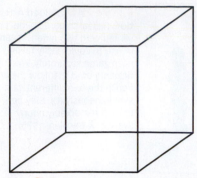

Figure 8.6 **The Necker Cube** This cube has the property of reversible perspective in that you can bring one or the other of its two square faces to the front in your mind's eye. Although it may take awhile to reverse the figure at first, once people have learned to do it, they can reverse it regularly, about once every 3 seconds (Gomez et al., 1995). The stream of consciousness flows even when the target is a constant object.

cheap in the Gentlewoman with elastic gores on the hips he saved the one I have but thats no good what did they say they give a delightful figure line 11/6 obviating that unsightly broad appearance across the lower back to reduce flesh my belly is a bit too big Ill have to knock off the stout at dinner or am I getting too fond of it (1994, p. 741)

The stream of consciousness may flow in this way partly because of the limited capacity of working memory. Remember from Chapter 5 that you can hold only so much information in your mind, so when more information is selected, some of what is currently there must disappear. As a result, your focus of attention keeps changing. The Necker cube (see **FIGURE 8.6**) is the visual counterpart to stream of consciousness writing. Although the cube is a constant object, the stream of consciousness flows, reversing the figure.

The basic properties of consciousness are reminiscent of the "bouncing ball" that moves from word to word when the lyrics of a sing-along tune are shown on a karaoke machine. The ball always bounces on something (intentionality), there is only one ball (unity), the ball selects one target and not others (selectivity), and the ball keeps bouncing all the time (transience).

Levels of Consciousness

Consciousness can also be understood as having levels, ranging from minimal consciousness to full consciousness to self-consciousness. These levels of consciousness would probably all register as "conscious" on that wakefulness meter for surgery patients you read about at the beginning of the chapter. The levels of consciousness that psychologists distinguish are not a matter of degree of overall brain activity but instead involve different qualities of awareness of the world and of the self.

In its minimal form, consciousness is just a connection between the person and the world. When you sense the sun coming in through the window, for example, you might turn toward the light. Such **minimal consciousness** is *consciousness that occurs when the mind inputs sensations and may output behavior* (Armstrong, 1980). This level of consciousness is a kind of sensory awareness and responsiveness, something that could even happen when someone pokes you during sleep and you turn over. Something seems to register in your mind, at least in the sense that you experience it, but you may not think at all about having had the experience. It could be that animals or, for that matter, even plants can have this minimal level of consciousness. But because of the problem of other minds and the notorious reluctance of animals and plants to talk to us, we can't know for sure that they *experience* the things that make them respond. At least in the case of humans, we can safely assume that there is something it "feels like" to be them and that when they're awake, they are at least minimally conscious.

Human consciousness is often more than this, of course, but what exactly gets added? Consider the glorious feeling of waking up on a spring morning as rays of sun stream across your pillow. It's not just that you are having this experience; being fully conscious means that you are also *aware* that you are having this experience. The critical ingredient that accompanies **full consciousness** is that you *know and are able to report your mental state*. That's a subtle distinction; being fully conscious means that you are aware of having a mental state while you are experiencing the mental state itself.

MINIMAL CONSCIOUSNESS A low-level kind of sensory awareness and responsiveness that occurs when the mind inputs sensations and may output behavior.

FULL CONSCIOUSNESS Consciousness in which you know and are able to report your mental state.

SELF-CONSCIOUSNESS A distinct level of consciousness in which the person's attention is drawn to the self as an object.

It's easy to zone out while reading: Your eyes continue to follow the print, but you're not processing the content and your mind has drifted elsewhere. Hello? Are you still paying attention while you're reading this?

When you have a hurt leg and mindlessly rub it, for instance, your pain may be minimally conscious. After all, you seem to be experiencing pain because you are indeed rubbing your leg. It is only when you realize that it hurts, though, that the pain becomes fully conscious. Full consciousness involves not only thinking about things but also thinking about the fact that you are thinking about things (Jaynes, 1976).

Full consciousness fluctuates over time, coming and going throughout the day. You've no doubt had experiences of reading and suddenly realizing that you have "zoned out" and are not processing what you read. When people are asked to report each time they zone out during reading, they report doing this every few minutes. Even then, when an experimenter asks these people at other random points in their reading whether they are zoned out at that moment, they are sometimes caught in the state of having "zoned out" even before they've noticed it (Schooler, Reichle, & Halpern, 2001). It's at just this point—when you are zoned out but don't know it—that you seem to be unaware of your own mental state. You are minimally conscious of wherever your mind has wandered, and you return with a jolt into the full consciousness that your mind had drifted away. Thinking about thinking allows you to realize that you weren't thinking about what you wanted to be thinking.

Full consciousness involves a certain consciousness of oneself; the person notices the self in a particular mental state ("Here I am, reading this sentence"). However, this is not quite the same thing as *self*-consciousness. Sometimes consciousness is entirely flooded with the self ("Gosh, I'm such a good reader!"), focusing on the self to the exclusion of almost everything else. William James (1890) and other theorists have suggested that **self-consciousness** is yet another distinct level of consciousness in which *the person's attention is drawn to the self as an object.* Most people report experiencing such self-consciousness when they are embarrassed; when they find themselves the focus of attention in a group; when someone focuses a camera on them; or when they are deeply introspective about their thoughts, feelings, or personal qualities.

Self-consciousness brings with it a tendency to evaluate yourself and notice your shortcomings. Looking in a mirror, for example, is all it takes to make people evaluate themselves—thinking not just about their looks but also about whether they are good or bad in other ways. People go out of their way to avoid mirrors when they've done something they are ashamed of (Duval & Wicklund, 1972). Self-consciousness can certainly spoil a good mood, so much so that a tendency to be chronically self-conscious is associated with depression (Pyszczynski, Holt, & Greenberg, 1987). However, because it makes people self-critical, the self-consciousness that results when people see their own mirror images can make them briefly more helpful, more cooperative, and less aggressive (Gibbons, 1990). Perhaps everyone would be a bit more civilized if mirrors were held up for them to see themselves as objects of their own scrutiny.

Most animals can't follow this path to civilization. The typical dog, cat, or bird seems mystified by a mirror, ignoring it or acting as though there is some other critter back there. However, chimpanzees that have spent time with mirrors sometimes behave in ways that suggest they recognize themselves in a mirror. To examine this, researchers painted an odorless red dye over the eyebrow of an anesthetized chimp and then watched when the awakened chimp was presented with a mirror (Gallup, 1977). If the chimp interpreted the mirror image as a representation of some other chimp with an unusual approach to cosmetics, we would expect it just to look at the mirror or perhaps to reach toward it. But the chimp reached toward its *own eye* as it looked into the mirror—not the mirror image—suggesting that it recognized the image as a reflection of itself.

Versions of this experiment have now been repeated with many different animals (Gallup, 1997), and it turns out that like humans, animals such as chimpanzees and orangutans, possibly dolphins (Reiss & Marino, 2001), and maybe even elephants (Plotnik, de Waal, & Reiss, 2006) recognize their own mirror images. Dogs, cats, birds, monkeys, and gorillas have been tested and don't seem to know they are looking at themselves. Even humans don't have self-recognition right away. Infants don't recognize themselves in mirrors until they've reached about 18 months of age (Lewis & Brooks-Gunn, 1979). The experience of self-consciousness, as measured by self-recognition in mirrors, is limited to a few animals and to humans only after a certain stage of development.

Self-consciousness is a curse and a blessing. Looking in a mirror can make people evaluate themselves on deeper attributes such as honesty as well as superficial ones such as looks.

A chimpanzee tried to wipe off the red dye on its eyebrow in the Gallup experiment. This suggests that some animals recognize themselves in the mirror.

Dilbert

Conscious Contents

What's on your mind? For that matter, what's on everybody's mind? The contents of consciousness are, of course, as rich and varied as human experience itself. But there are some common themes in the topics that occupy consciousness and in the form that consciousness seems to take as different contents come to mind.

One way to learn what is on people's minds is to ask them, and much research has called on people simply to *think aloud.* A more systematic approach is the *experience sampling technique,* in which people are asked to report their conscious experiences at particular times. Equipped with electronic beepers, for example, participants are asked to record their current thoughts when beeped at random times throughout the day (Csikszentmihalyi & Larson, 1987). Experience sampling studies show that consciousness is dominated by the immediate environment, what is seen, felt, heard, tasted, and smelled—all are at the forefront of the mind. Much of consciousness beyond this orientation to the environment turns to the person's *current concerns,* or what the person is thinking about repeatedly (Klinger, 1975). **TABLE 8.1** shows the results of a Minnesota study where 175 college students were asked to report their current concerns (Goetzman, Hughes, & Klinger, 1994). The researchers sorted the concerns into the categories shown in the table. Keep in mind that these concerns are ones the students didn't mind reporting to psychologists; their private preoccupations may have been different and probably far more interesting.

Think for a moment about your own current concerns. What topics have been on your mind the most in the past day or two? Your mental "to do" list may include things you want to get, keep, avoid, work on, remember, and so on (Little, 1993). Items on the list often pop into mind, sometimes even with an emotional punch

Table 8.1	What's on Your Mind? College Students' Current Concerns	
Current Concern Category	**Example**	**Frequency of Students Who Mentioned the Concern**
Family	Gain better relations with immediate family	40%
Roommate	Change attitude or behavior of roommate	29%
Household	Clean room	52%
Friends	Make new friends	42%
Dating	Desire to date a certain person	24%
Sexual intimacy	Abstaining from sex	16%
Health	Diet and exercise	85%
Employment	Get a summer job	33%
Education	Go to graduate school	43%
Social activities	Gain acceptance into a campus organization	34%
Religious	Attend church more	51%
Financial	Pay rent or bills	8%
Government	Change government policy	14%

("The test in this class is tomorrow!"). People in one study had their skin conductance level (SCL) measured to assess their emotional responses (Nikula, Klinger, & Larson-Gutman, 1993). SCL sensors attached to their fingers indicated when their skin became moist—a good indication that they were thinking about something distressing. Once in a while, SCL would rise spontaneously, and at these times the researchers quizzed the participants about their conscious thoughts. These emotional moments, compared to those when SCL was normal, often corresponded with a current concern popping into mind. Thoughts that are not emotional all by themselves can still come to mind with an emotional bang when they are topics of our current concern.

Current concerns do not seem all that concerning, however, during *daydreaming,* a state of consciousness in which a seemingly purposeless flow of thoughts comes to mind. When thoughts drift along this way, it may seem as if you are just wasting time. However, psychologists have long suspected that daydreams reflect the mind's attempts to deal with difficult projects and problems. A computer program designed to simulate daydreams, for example, works on the basis of this assumption to produce passages that resemble human daydreams (Mueller, 1990). The program draws on the idea that people learn from past experiences by "replaying" them in daydreams, that they discover creative approaches to the future by imaging fanciful scenarios, and that all this helps them to control and channel their emotions.

In one case, the Daydreamer program was given the information that it had been turned down for a date by a famous Hollywood actress and then was allowed to "daydream" in response. In a daydream, it imagined that going out with the actress would have been a hassle because of the reporters; this daydream helped rationalize the failure and make it less disappointing. Another daydream by the program envisioned a new way of asking her out, one that would have secured her phone number so she could have been approached again later on; this response created new information that would be helpful in similar situations in the future. Human daydreams and fantasies, like these computer-simulated versions, may be more useful than they appear at first glance.

The current concerns that populate consciousness can sometimes get the upper hand, transforming daydreams or everyday thoughts into rumination and worry. Thoughts that return again and again, or problem-solving attempts that never seem to succeed, can come to dominate consciousness. When this happens, people may exert **mental control**, *the attempt to change conscious states of mind.* For example, someone troubled by a recurring worry about the future ("What if I can't get a decent job when I graduate?") might choose to try not to think about this because it causes too much anxiety and uncertainty. Whenever this thought comes to mind, the person engages in **thought suppression**, the *conscious avoidance of a thought.* This may seem like a perfectly sensible strategy because it eliminates the worry and allows the person to move on to think about something else.

Or does it? The great Russian novelist Fyodor Dostoevsky (1863–1955) remarked on the difficulty of thought suppression: "Try to pose for yourself this task: not to think of a polar bear, and you will see that the cursed thing will come to mind every minute." Inspired by this observation, Daniel Wegner and his colleagues gave people this exact task in the laboratory (1987). Participants were asked to try not to think about a white bear for 5 minutes while they recorded all their thoughts aloud into a tape recorder. In addition, they were asked to ring a bell if the thought of a white bear came to mind. On average, they mentioned the white bear or rang the bell (indicating the thought) more than once per minute. Thought suppression simply didn't work and instead produced a flurry of returns of the unwanted thought. What's more, when some research participants later were specifically asked to change tasks and deliberately *think* about a white bear, they became oddly preoccupied with it. A graph of their bell rings in **FIGURE 8.7** on the next page shows that these participants had the white bear come to mind far more often than did people who had only been asked to think about the bear from the outset, with no prior suppression. This **rebound effect of thought suppression**, *the tendency of a thought to return to consciousness with greater frequency following suppression,* suggests that attempts at mental control may be difficult indeed. The act of trying to suppress a thought may itself cause that thought to return to consciousness in a robust way.

MENTAL CONTROL The attempt to change conscious states of mind.

THOUGHT SUPPRESSION The conscious avoidance of a thought.

REBOUND EFFECT OF THOUGHT SUPPRESSION The tendency of a thought to return to consciousness with greater frequency following suppression.

"Are you not thinking what I'm not thinking?"

Figure 8.7 **Rebound Effect** Research participants were first asked to try not to think about a white bear, and then they were asked to think about it and to ring a bell whenever it came to mind. Compared to those who were simply asked to think about a bear without prior suppression, those people who *first* suppressed the thought showed a rebound of increased thinking (Wegner et al., 1987).

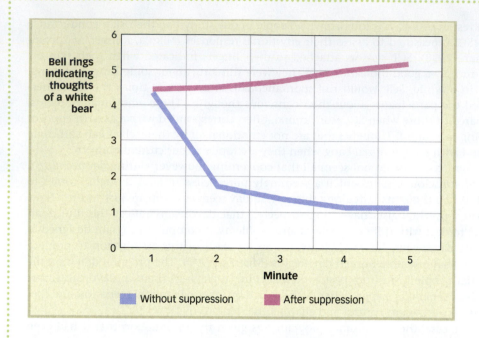

Bell rings indicating thoughts of a white bear

Minute

■ Without suppression ■ After suppression

As with thought suppression, other attempts to "steer" consciousness in any direction can result in mental states that are precisely the opposite of those desired. How ironic: Trying to consciously achieve one task may produce precisely the opposite outcome! These ironic effects seem most likely to occur when the person is distracted or under stress. People who are distracted while they are trying to get into a good mood, for example, tend to become sad (Wegner, Erber, & Zanakos, 1993), and those who are distracted while trying to relax actually become more anxious than those who are not trying to relax (Wegner, Broome, & Blumberg, 1997). Likewise, an attempt not to overshoot a golf putt, undertaken during distraction, often yields the unwanted overshot (Wegner, Ansfield, & Pilloff, 1998). The theory of **ironic processes of mental control** proposes that such *ironic errors occur because the mental process that monitors errors can itself produce them* (Wegner, 1994). In the attempt not to think of a white bear, for instance, a small part of the mind is ironically *searching* for the white bear.

This ironic-monitoring process is not present in consciousness. After all, trying *not* to think of something would be useless if monitoring the progress of suppression required keeping that target in consciousness. For example, if trying not to think of a white bear meant that you consciously kept repeating to yourself, "No white bear! No white bear!" then you've failed before you've begun: That thought is present in consciousness even as you strive to eliminate it. Rather, the ironic monitor is a process of the mind that works *outside* of consciousness, making us sensitive to all the things we do not want to think, feel, or do so that we can notice and consciously take steps to regain control if these things come back to mind. The person trying not to think about a white bear, for

IRONIC PROCESSES OF MENTAL CONTROL Mental processes that can produce ironic errors because monitoring for errors can itself produce them.

DYNAMIC UNCONSCIOUS An active system encompassing a lifetime of hidden memories, the person's deepest instincts and desires, and the person's inner struggle to control these forces.

REPRESSION A mental process that removes unacceptable thoughts and memories from consciousness.

Go ahead, look away from the book for a minute and try not to think about a white bear.

example, would unconsciously monitor any signs of the thought and so be prompted to try consciously to think of something else if it returns. As this unconscious monitoring whirs along in the background, it unfortunately increases the person's sensitivity to the very thought that is unwanted. Ironic processes are mental functions that are needed for effective mental control—they help in the process of banishing a thought from consciousness—but they can sometimes yield the very failure they seem designed to overcome. Ironic processes of mental control are among the mindbugs that the study of psychology holds up for examination. And because ironic processes occur outside of consciousness, they remind us, too, that much of the mind's machinery may be hidden from our view, lying outside the fringes of our experience.

The Unconscious Mind

Many mental processes are unconscious, in the sense that they occur without our experience of them. When we speak, for instance, "We are not really conscious either of the search for words, or of putting the words together into phrases, or of putting the phrases into sentences. . . . [The] actual process of thinking . . . is not conscious at all . . . only its preparation, its materials, and its end result are consciously perceived" (Jaynes, 1976). Just to put the role of consciousness in perspective, think for a moment about the mental processes involved in simple addition. What happens in consciousness between hearing a problem ("What's 4 plus 5?") and thinking of the answer ("9")? Probably nothing—the answer just appears in the mind. But this is a piece of calculation that must take at least a bit of thinking. After all, at a very young age you may have had to solve such problems by counting on your fingers. Now that you don't have to do that anymore (. . . right?), the answer seems to pop into your head automatically, by virtue of a process that doesn't require you to be aware of any underlying steps, and, for that matter, doesn't even *allow* you to be aware of the steps. The answer just suddenly appears.

In the early part of the 20th century, when structuralist psychologists, such as Wilhelm Wundt, believed that introspection was the best method of research (see Chapter 1), research volunteers trained in describing their thoughts tried to discern what happens in such cases—when a simple problem brings to mind a simple answer (e.g., Watt, 1905). They drew the same blank you probably did. Nothing conscious seems to bridge this gap, but the answer comes from somewhere, and this emptiness points to the unconscious mind. To explore these hidden recesses, we can look at the classical theory of the unconscious introduced by Sigmund Freud and then at the modern cognitive psychology of unconscious mental processes.

Freudian Unconscious

The true champion of the unconscious mind was Sigmund Freud. As you read in Chapter 1, Freud's psychoanalytic theory viewed conscious thought as the surface of a much deeper mind made up of unconscious processes. Far more than just a collection of hidden processes, Freud described a **dynamic unconscious**—*an active system encompassing a lifetime of hidden memories, the person's deepest instincts and desires, and the person's inner struggle to control these forces.* The dynamic unconscious might contain hidden sexual thoughts about one's parents, for example, or destructive urges aimed at a helpless infant—the kinds of thoughts people keep secret from others and may not even acknowledge to themselves. According to Freud's theory, the unconscious is a force to be held in check by **repression**, *a mental process that removes unacceptable thoughts and memories from consciousness and keeps them in the unconscious.* Without repression, a person might think, do, or say every unconscious impulse or animal urge, no matter how selfish or immoral. With repression, these desires are held in the recesses of the dynamic unconscious.

Freud looked for evidence of the unconscious mind in speech errors and lapses of consciousness, or what are commonly called "Freudian slips." Forgetting the name of someone you dislike, for example, is a mindbug that seems to have special meaning. Freud believed that errors are not random and instead have some surplus meaning that may appear to have been created by an intelligent unconscious mind, even though the person consciously disavows them. For example, when Condoleezza Rice, serving as the National Security Advisor for President George W. Bush, was addressing an audience at a Washington, DC, dinner party, she reportedly said, "As I was telling my husba—" before breaking off and correcting herself: "As I was telling President Bush . . . ." Although no one seriously believes the single Rice and married Bush are an "item," you can almost hear her dynamic unconscious trumpeting the psychological intimacy they enjoy.

One experiment revealed that slips of speech can indeed be prompted by a person's pressing concerns (Motley & Baars, 1979). Research participants in one group were told they might receive minor electric shocks, whereas those in another group heard no mention of this. Each person was then asked to read quickly through a series of word pairs, including *shad bock*. Those in the group warned about shock more often slipped in pronouncing this pair, blurting out *bad shock*.

Unlike errors created in experiments such as this one, many of the meaningful errors Freud attributed to the dynamic unconscious were not predicted in advance and so seem to depend on clever after-the-fact interpretations. That's not so good. Suggesting a pattern to a series of random events is quite clever, but it's not the same as scientifically predicting and explaining when and why an event should happen. Anyone can offer a reasonable, compelling explanation for an event after it has already happened, but the true work of science is to offer testable hypotheses that are evaluated based on reliable evidence. Freud's book *The Psychopathology of Everyday Life* (Freud, 1901/1938) suggests not so much that the dynamic unconscious produces errors but that Freud himself was a master at finding meaning in errors that might otherwise have seemed random. Condi Rice's curious slip about being married to President Bush may have been a random error, only meaningful in the minds of news commentators who found it amusing and worthy of explanation.

Cognitive Unconscious

Modern psychologists share Freud's interest in the impact of unconscious mental processes on consciousness and on behavior. However, rather than Freud's vision of the unconscious as a teeming menagerie of animal urges and repressed thoughts, the current study of the unconscious mind views it as the factory that builds the products of conscious thought and behavior (Kihlstrom, 1987; Wilson, 2002). The **cognitive unconscious** includes *all the mental processes that are not experienced by the person but that give rise to the person's thoughts, choices, emotions, and behavior* (see the Hot Science box on the facing page).

One indication of the cognitive unconscious at work is when the person's thought or behavior is changed by exposure to information outside of consciousness. This happens in **subliminal perception**, when *thought or behavior are influenced by stimuli that a person cannot consciously report perceiving*. Worries about the potential of subliminal influence were first provoked in 1957, when a marketer, James Vicary, claimed he had increased concession sales at a New Jersey theater by flashing the words "Eat Popcorn" and "Drink Coke" briefly on-screen during movies. It turns out his story was a hoax, and many attempts to increase sales using similar methods have failed. But the very idea of influencing behavior outside of consciousness created a wave of alarm about insidious "subliminal persuasion" that still concerns people (Epley, Savitsky, & Kachelski, 1999; Pratkanis, 1992).

Subliminal perception does occur, but the degree of influence it has on behavior is not very large (Dijksterhuis, Aarts, & Smith, 2005). One set of studies examined whether beverage choices could be influenced by brief visual exposures to thirst-related words (Strahan, Spencer, & Zanna, 2002). Research volunteers were asked to perform a computer task that involved deciding whether each of 26 letter strings was a word or not. This ensured that they would be looking intently at the screen when, just before each letter string appeared, a target was shown that could not be consciously perceived: A word was flashed for 16 milliseconds just off the center of the screen, followed by a row of *x*'s in that spot to mask any visual memory of the word. For half the participants, this subliminal word was thirst related (such as *thirst* and *dry*) and for the other half it was unrelated (such as *pirate* and *won*). When the volunteers afterward were

COGNITIVE UNCONSCIOUS The mental processes that give rise to the person's thoughts, choices, emotions, and behavior even though they are not experienced by the person.

SUBLIMINAL PERCEPTION A thought or behavior that is influenced by stimuli that a person cannot consciously report perceiving.

How Smart Is the Unconscious Mind?

A BASKETBALL PLAYER ON A HOT STREAK IS sometimes described as "unconscious," in the sense that the play is so good that the player doesn't even seem to be thinking about it. Although a truly unconscious player might be a serious liability for the team, lying there on the floor and all, a player whose *moves* appear to be unconscious is usually an asset. No doubt you trust the talents of your unconscious mind as well. When you type, for example, your unconscious mind takes care of remembering what finger movements stand for what letters on your keyboard so you only have to worry consciously about what to write. Your unconscious mind knows, too, that when you extend your arm out in front of you, your body must lean backward just slightly to balance the movement, or you would fall over forward. The unconscious mind can be a kind of "mental butler," taking over background tasks that are too tedious, subtle, or bothersome for consciousness to trifle with (Bargh & Chartrand, 1999; Bower, 1999).

Psychologists have long debated just how smart this mental butler might be. Freud attributed great intelligence to the unconscious, believing that it harbors complex motives and inner conflicts and that it expresses these in an astonishing array of thoughts and emotions, as well as psychological disorders (see Chapter 12). Contemporary cognitive psychologists wonder whether the unconscious is so smart, however, and point out that some unconscious processes even seem downright stupid (Loftus & Klinger, 1992). For example, the unconscious processes that underlie the perception of subliminal visual stimuli do not seem able to understand the combined meaning of word pairs, although they can understand single words. To the *conscious* mind, for example, a word pair such as *enemy loses* is somewhat positive—it is good to have your enemy lose. However, subliminal presentations of this word pair make people think of negative things, as though the unconscious mind is simply adding together the unpleasantness of the single words *enemy* and *loses* (Greenwald, 1992). Perhaps the mental butler is not all that bright.

New research suggests, however, that at least in some cases the unconscious mind makes better decisions than the conscious mind. Participants in an experiment were asked to choose which of three hypothetical people they would prefer to have as a roommate (Dijksterhuis, 2004). Each candidate was described with 12 attributes, so the participants saw lots of information—36 items such as "Roommate A has fun friends," "Roommate B is messy," "Roommate C has a

Choosing a roommate can be like playing the lottery: Sometimes you win, many times you lose.

good CD collection," and so on, each item presented for just 2 seconds on a computer screen. The research participants weren't told that the information was rigged to make one roommate a good choice (eight positive qualities, four negative), another one a fair choice (six positive qualities, six negative), and the third a poor choice (four positive qualities, eight negative). You may have guessed that people would pick up on this, and you're right—many did—preferring the good choice to the fair choice and the fair choice to the poor choice.

The participants were divided into three groups, and each group was instructed to arrive at the best decision using a different method. One group of people was prompted to make a *conscious decision;* after seeing the information they were given 4 minutes to think about what their answer should be. A second group was given no time at all to make a wise decision; this *immediate decision* group was asked for their answer as soon as the information display was over. Finally, the third group was encouraged to reach an *unconscious decision*. This group was allowed the same 4 minutes of time

after the display ended to give their answer (as the conscious group had been given), but during this interval their conscious minds were occupied with solving a set of anagrams (for example, what word can be made from the letters *icpeb?*). They were distracted from thinking consciously about what to do. And by the way, the anagram spells *bicep.*

As you can see in the figure below, the unconscious decision group showed a stronger preference for the good roommate than did the immediate decision or conscious decision groups. Unconscious minds seemed *better able* than conscious minds to sort out the information and arrive at the best choice. Dijksterhuis found in other studies that people making unconscious decisions remember the information about their choice alternatives in a more organized way than do those making conscious or hurried decisions, which may be why the unconscious decision is a better one. In some cases, consciousness can even hurt by drawing attention to idiosyncratic ideas and taking attention away from your "gut feeling" (Wilson & Schooler, 1991). This may be why you sometimes end up more satisfied with decisions you make after just "letting it happen" than with the decisions you consciously agonize over.

Should all decisions be made unconsciously? It is important to remember that even gut feelings can be wrong. After all, an unconscious mind that can't appreciate when an "enemy loses" may not always be a wise leader. On balance, this new research on the apparent intelligence of unconscious decisions suggests simply that devoting more time and thought to a decision is no guarantee that the smartest choice will be made.

People making roommate decisions who had some time for unconscious deliberation chose better roommates than those who thought about the choice consciously or those who made snap decisions (Dijksterhuis, 2004).

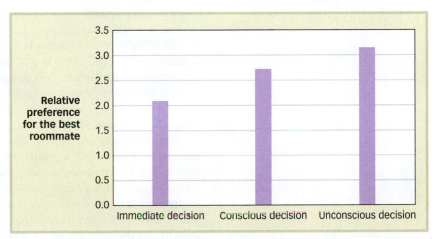

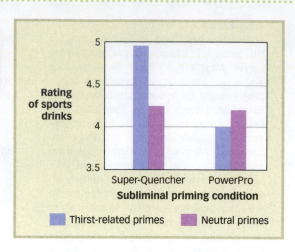

Figure 8.8 Subliminal Influence
Preference for a thirst-quenching beverage, "Super-Quencher," increased relative to another sports drink, "PowerPro," among people subliminally primed with thirst words (Strahan et al., 2002).

Rating of sports drinks

Subliminal priming condition

◼ Thirst-related primes   ◼ Neutral primes

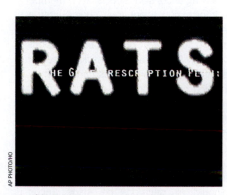

President George W. Bush denied that Republican Party commercials used subliminal messages (which he called "subliminable") after Democrats complained that the word *RATS* subtly flashed on-screen in a TV spot criticizing his opponent Al Gore in the 2000 election. "One frame out of 900 hardly makes a conspiracy," he said in the ad's defense—although the ad was pulled off the air.

given a choice of free coupons toward the purchase of possible new sports beverages *Super-Quencher* ("the best thirst-quenching beverage ever developed") and *PowerPro* ("the best electrolyte-restoring beverage ever developed"), those who had been subliminally exposed to thirst words more often chose Super-Quencher (see **FIGURE 8.8**).

There are two important footnotes to this research. First, the influence of the subliminal persuasion was primarily found for people who reported already being thirsty when the experiment started. The subliminal exposure to thirst words had little effect on people who didn't feel thirsty, suggesting that Vicary's "Drink Coke" campaign, even if it had actually happened, would not have drawn people out to the lobby unless they were already inclined to go. Second, the researchers also conducted a study in which other participants were shown the target words at a slower speed (300 milliseconds) so the words could be seen and consciously recognized. Their conscious perception of the thirst words had effects just like subliminal perception. Subliminal influences might be worrisome because they can change behavior without our conscious awareness but not because they are more powerful in comparison to conscious influences.

Unconscious influences on behavior are not limited to cases of subliminal persuasion—they can happen when you are merely reminded of an idea in passing. For example, the thought of getting old can make a person walk more slowly. John Bargh and his colleagues discovered this by having college students complete a survey that called for them to make sentences with various words (1996). The students were not informed that most of the words were commonly associated with aging (Florida, gray, wrinkled), and even afterward they didn't report being aware of this trend. In this case, the "aging" idea wasn't presented subliminally, just not very noticeably. As these research participants left the experiment, they were clocked as they walked down the hall. Compared with those not exposed to the aging-related words, these people walked more slowly! Just as with subliminal perception, a passing exposure to ideas can influence actions without conscious awareness.

In summary, consciousness is a mystery of psychology because other people's minds cannot be perceived directly and because the relationship between mind and body is perplexing. Nonetheless, people's reports of their consciousness can be studied, and these reveal basic properties such as intentionality, unity, selectivity, and transience. Consciousness also can be understood in terms of levels—minimal consciousness, full consciousness, and self-consciousness—and can be investigated for contents such as current concerns, daydreams, and unwanted thoughts. There are mental processes that are not conscious as well, and there are two main views of these. Unconscious processes are sometimes understood as expressions of the Freudian dynamic unconscious but are more commonly viewed as processes of the cognitive unconscious that create and influence our conscious thoughts and behaviors. The cognitive unconscious is at work when subliminal perception influences a person's thought or behavior without the person's awareness. ◼ ◼

Sleep and Dreaming: Good Night, Mind

What's it like to be asleep? Sometimes it's like nothing at all. Sleep can produce a state of unconsciousness in which the mind and brain apparently turn off the functions that create experience: The Cartesian Theater is closed. But this is an oversimplification because the theater actually seems to reopen during the night for special shows of bizarre cult films—in other words, dreams. Dream consciousness involves a transformation of experience that is so radical it is commonly considered an **altered state of consciousness**—*a form of experience that departs significantly from the normal subjective experience of the world and the mind.* Such altered states can be accompanied by changes in thinking, disturbances in the sense of time, feelings of the loss of control, changes in emotional expression, alterations in body image and sense of self, perceptual distortions, and changes in meaning or significance (Ludwig, 1966). The world of sleep and dreams, then, provides two unique perspectives on consciousness: a view of the mind without consciousness and a view of consciousness in an altered state.

Sleep

Consider a typical night. As you begin to fall asleep, the busy, task-oriented thoughts of the waking mind are replaced by wandering thoughts and images, odd juxtapositions, some of them almost dreamlike. This presleep consciousness is called the *hypnagogic state.* On some rare nights you might experience a *hypnic jerk,* a sudden quiver or sensation of dropping, as though missing a step on a staircase. (No one is quite sure why these happen, but there is no truth to the theory that you are actually levitating and then fall.) Eventually, your presence of mind goes away entirely. Time and experience stop, you are unconscious, and in fact there seems to be no "you" there to have experiences. But then come dreams, whole vistas of a vivid and surrealistic consciousness you just don't get during the day, a set of experiences that occur with the odd prerequisite that there is nothing "out there" you are actually experiencing. More patches of unconsciousness may occur, with more dreams here and there. And finally, the glimmerings of waking consciousness return again in a foggy and imprecise form as you enter postsleep consciousness (the *hypnopompic state*) and then awake, often with bad hair.

Sleep Cycle

The sequence of events that occurs during a night of sleep is part of one of the major rhythms of human life, the cycle of sleep and waking. This **circadian rhythm** is *a naturally occurring 24-hour cycle*—from the Latin *circa,* "about," and *dies,* "day." Even people who are sequestered in underground buildings without clocks ("time-free environments") and are allowed to sleep when they want to tend to have a rest-activity cycle of about 25.1 hours (Aschoff, 1965). This slight deviation from 24 hours is not easily explained (Lavie, 2001), but it seems to underlie the tendency many people have to want to stay up a little later each night and wake up a little later each day. We're 25.1-hour people living in a 24-hour world.

ALTERED STATES OF CONSCIOUSNESS Forms of experience that depart from the normal subjective experience of the world and the mind.

CIRCADIAN RHYTHM A naturally occurring 24-hour cycle.

MOORE: ALBERT JOSEPH/BIRMINGHAM MUSEUMS AND ART GALLERY/
THE BRIDGEMAN ART LIBRARY

Dreamers, by Albert Joseph Moore (1879/1882). Without measuring REM sleep, it's hard to know whether Moore's "Dreamers" are actually dreaming.

REM SLEEP A stage of sleep characterized by rapid eye movements and a high level of brain activity.

ELECTROOCULOGRAPH (EOG) An instrument that measures eye movements.

The sleep cycle is far more than a simple on/off routine, however, as many bodily and psychological processes ebb and flow in this rhythm. In 1929 researchers made EEG (electroencephalograph) recordings of the human brain for the first time (Berger, 1929; see Chapter 3). Before this, many people had offered descriptions of their nighttime experiences, and researchers knew that there are deeper and lighter periods of sleep, as well as dream periods. But no one had been able to measure much of anything about sleep without waking up the sleeper and ruining it. The EEG recordings revealed a regular pattern of changes in electrical activity in the brain accompanying the circadian cycle. During waking, these changes involve alternation between high-frequency activity (called *beta waves*) during alertness and lower-frequency activity (*alpha waves*) during relaxation.

The largest changes in EEG occur during sleep. These changes show a regular pattern over the course of the night that allowed sleep researchers to identify five sleep stages (see **FIGURE 8.9**). In the first stage of sleep, the EEG moves to frequency patterns even lower than alpha waves (*theta waves*). In the second stage of sleep, these patterns are interrupted by short bursts of activity called *sleep spindles* and *K complexes,* and the sleeper becomes somewhat more difficult to awaken. The deepest stages of sleep are 3 and 4, known as slow-wave sleep, in which the EEG patterns show activity called *delta waves.*

During the fifth sleep stage, **REM sleep**, *a stage of sleep characterized by rapid eye movements and a high level of brain activity,* EEG patterns become high-frequency saw-tooth waves, similar to beta waves, suggesting that the mind at this time is as active

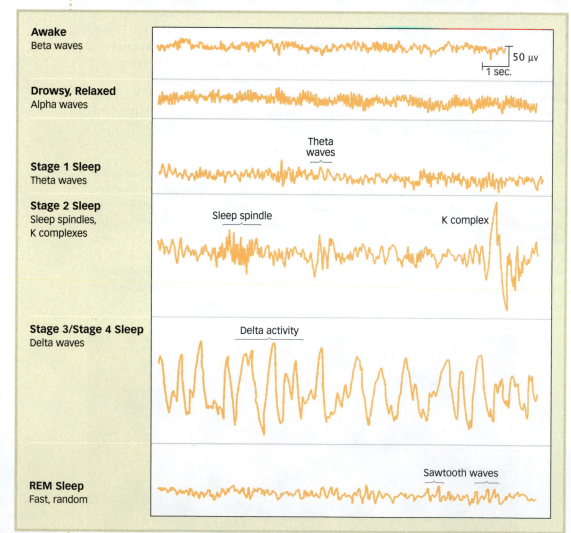

Awake
Beta waves

50 μv
1 sec.

Drowsy, Relaxed
Alpha waves

Stage 1 Sleep
Theta waves

Theta waves

Stage 2 Sleep
Sleep spindles, K complexes

Sleep spindle

K complex

Stage 3/Stage 4 Sleep
Delta waves

Delta activity

REM Sleep
Fast, random

Sawtooth waves

Figure 8.9 **EEG Patterns during the Stages of Sleep** The waking brain shows high-frequency beta wave activity, which changes during drowsiness and relaxation to lower-frequency alpha waves. Stage 1 sleep shows lower-frequency theta waves, which are accompanied in Stage 2 by irregular patterns called sleep spindles and K complexes. Stages 3 and 4 are marked by the lowest frequencies, delta waves. During REM sleep, EEG patterns return to higher-frequency sawtooth waves that resemble the beta waves of waking.

as it is during waking (see Figure 8.9). Using an **electrooculograph (EOG)**, *a device to measure eye movements,* during sleep, researchers found that sleepers wakened during REM periods reported having dreams much more often than those wakened during non-REM periods (Aserinsky & Kleitman, 1953). During REM sleep, the pulse quickens, blood pressure rises, and there are telltale signs of sexual arousal. At the same time, measurements of muscle movements indicate that the sleeper is very still, except for a rapid side-to-side movement of the eyes. (Watch someone sleeping and you may be able to see the REMs through their closed eyelids. Be careful doing this with strangers down at the bus depot.)

Although many people believe that they don't dream much (if at all), some 80% of people awakened during REM sleep report dreams. If you've ever wondered whether dreams actually take place in an instant or whether they take as long to happen as the events they portray might take, the analysis of REM sleep offers an answer. Sleep researchers William Dement and Nathaniel Kleitman (1957) woke volunteers either 5 minutes or 15 minutes after the onset of REM sleep and asked them to judge, on the basis of the events in the remembered dream, how long they had been dreaming. Sleepers in 92 of 111 cases were correct, suggesting that dreaming occurs in "real time." The discovery of REM sleep has offered many insights into dreaming, but not all dreams occur in REM periods. Some dreams are also reported in other sleep stages (non-REM sleep, also called *NREM sleep*) but not as many—and the dreams that occur at these times are described as less wild than REM dreams and more like normal thinking.

Putting EEG and REM data together produces a picture of how a typical night's sleep progresses through cycles of sleep stages (see **FIGURE 8.10**). In the first hour of the night, you fall all the way from waking to the fourth and deepest stage of sleep, the stage marked by delta waves. These slow waves indicate a general synchronization of neural firing, as though the brain is doing one thing at this time rather than many—the neuronal equivalent of "the wave" moving through the crowd at a stadium, as lots of individuals move together in synchrony. You then return to lighter sleep stages, eventually reaching REM and dreamland. Note that although REM sleep is lighter than that of lower stages, it is deep enough that you may be difficult to awaken. You then continue to cycle between REM and slow-wave sleep stages every 90 minutes or so throughout the night. Periods of REM last longer as the night goes on, and lighter sleep stages predominate between these periods, with the deeper slow-wave stages 3 and 4 disappearing halfway through the night. Although you're either unconscious or dream-conscious at the time, your brain and mind cycle through a remarkable array of different states each time you have a night's sleep.

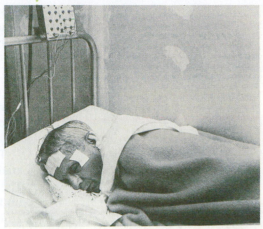

REM sleep discoverer Nathaniel Kleitman as a participant in his own sleep experiment with REM and EEG measurement electrodes in place.

WILLIAM VANDIVERT

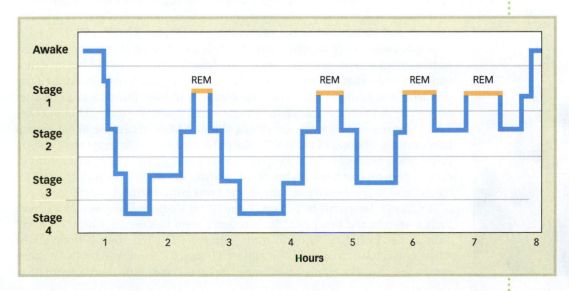

Figure 8.10 Stages of Sleep during the Night Over the course of the typical night, sleep cycles into deeper stages early on and then more shallow stages later. REM periods become longer in later cycles, and the deeper slow-wave sleep of stages 3 and 4 disappears halfway through the night.

Sleep Needs and Deprivation

How much do people sleep? The answer depends on the age of the sleeper (Dement, 1999). Newborns will sleep 6 to 8 times in 24 hours, often totaling more than 16 hours. Their napping cycle gets consolidated into "sleeping through the night," usually sometime between 9 and 18 months, but sometimes even later. The typical 6-year-old child might need 11 or 12 hours of sleep, and the progression to less sleep then continues into adulthood, when the average is about 7 to 7½ hours per night. With aging, people can get along with even a bit less sleep than that. Over a whole lifetime, we get about 1 hour of sleep for every 2 hours we are awake.

This is a lot of sleeping, and you might wonder whether less than this might be tolerable. Rather than sleeping our lives away, perhaps we can stay awake and enjoy life. The world record for staying awake belongs to Randy Gardner, who at age 17 stayed up for 264 hours and 12 minutes in 1965 for a science project. Randy was followed around for much of the 11 days and nights by sleep researchers, who noted that he seemed remarkably chipper and easy to keep awake during the day—but that he struggled mightily at night, when fighting drowsiness required heroic measures. Along with the researchers, he spent the last night in a penny arcade playing hundreds of games on a baseball machine. He won easily, suggesting that even extreme sleep deprivation is not entirely debilitating or that sleep researchers are lousy at arcade games. The main symptom of his deprivation was sleepiness, along with a couple of minor hallucinatory experiences. When Randy finally did go to sleep, he slept only 14 hours and 40 minutes and awakened essentially recovered (Dement, 1978).

Feats like this one suggest that sleep might be expendable. This is the theory behind the classic "all-nighter" that you may have tried on the way to a rough exam. But it turns out that this theory is mistaken. Robert Stickgold and his colleagues (2000b) found that when people learning a difficult perceptual task are kept up all night after they finished practicing the task, their learning of the task is wiped out. Even after two nights of catch-up sleep, they show little indication of their initial training on the task. Sleep following learning appears to be essential for memory consolidation (see Chapter 5). It is as though memories normally deteriorate unless sleep occurs to help keep them in place. Studying all night may help you cram for the exam, but it won't make the material stick—which pretty much defeats the whole point.

Sleep turns out to be a necessity rather than a luxury in other ways as well. At the extreme, sleep loss can be fatal. When rats are forced to break Randy Gardner's human waking record and stay awake even longer, they have trouble regulating their body temperature and lose weight although they eat much more than normal. Their bodily systems break down and they die, on average, in 21 days (Rechsthaffen et al., 1983). Shakespeare called sleep "nature's soft nurse," and it is clear that even for healthy young humans, a few hours of sleep deprivation each night can have a cumulative detrimental effect: reducing mental acuity and reaction time, increasing irritability and depression, and increasing the risk of accidents and injury (Coren, 1997).

Sleep deprivation can often be diagnosed without the help of any psychologists or brain-scanning equipment.

SONDA DAWES/THE IMAGE WORKS

Some studies have deprived people of different sleep stages selectively by waking them whenever certain stages are detected. Studies of REM sleep deprivation indicate that this part of sleep is important psychologically, as memory problems and excessive aggression are observed in both humans and rats after only a few days of being wakened whenever REM activity starts (Ellman et al., 1991). The brain must value something about REM sleep because REM deprivation causes a rebound of more REM sleep the next night (Brunner et al., 1990). Deprivation from slow-wave sleep (in stages 3 and 4), in turn, has more physical effects, with just a few nights of deprivation leaving people feeling tired, fatigued, and hypersensitive to muscle and bone pain (Lentz et al., 1999).

It's clearly dangerous to neglect the need for sleep. But why would we have such a need in the first place? Insects don't seem to sleep, but most "higher" animals do, including fish and birds. Giraffes sleep less than 2 hours daily, whereas brown bats snooze for almost 20 hours. These variations in sleep needs, and the very existence of a need, are hard to explain. Is the restoration that happens during the unconsciousness of sleep something that simply can't be achieved during consciousness? Sleep is, after all, potentially costly in the course of evolution. The sleeping animal is easy prey, so the habit of sleep would not seem to have developed so widely across species unless it had significant benefits that made up for this vulnerability. Theories of sleep have not yet determined why the brain and body have evolved to need these recurring episodes of unconsciousness.

Sleep Disorders

In answer to the question, "Did you sleep well?" comedian Stephen Wright said, "No, I made a couple of mistakes." Sleeping well is something everyone would love to do, but for many people, sleep disorders are mindbugs that can get in the way. Disorders that plague sleep include insomnia, sleep apnea, somnambulism, narcolepsy, sleep paralysis, nightmares, and night terrors. Perhaps the most common sleep disorder is **insomnia**, *difficulty in falling asleep or staying asleep*. About 15% of adults complain of severe or frequent insomnia, and another 15% report having mild or occasional insomnia (Bootzin, Manber, Perlis, Salvio, & Wyatt, 1993). Although people often overestimate their insomnia, the distress caused even by the perception of insomnia can be significant. There are many causes of insomnia, including anxiety associated with stressful life events, so insomnia may sometimes be a sign of other emotional difficulties.

Insomnia can be exacerbated by worry about insomnia (Borkevec, 1982). No doubt you've experienced some nights on which sleeping was a high priority, such as before a class presentation or an important interview, and you've found that you were unable to fall asleep and may have even stayed up later than usual. In this situation, sleeping seems to be an emergency, and every wish to sleep takes you further from that goal. The desire to sleep initiates an ironic process of mental control—a heightened sensitivity to signs of sleeplessness—and this sensitivity interferes with sleep. In fact, participants in an experiment who were instructed to go to sleep quickly became hypersensitive and had more difficulty sleeping than those who were not instructed to hurry (Ansfield, Wegner, & Bowser, 1996). The paradoxical solution for insomnia in some cases, then, may be to give up the pursuit of sleep and instead find something else to do.

Giving up on trying so hard to sleep is probably better than another common remedy—the use of sleeping pills. Although sedatives can be useful for brief sleep problems associated with emotional events, their long-term use is not effective. To begin with, most sleeping pills are addictive. People become dependent on the pills to sleep and may need to increase the dose over time to achieve the same effect. Even in short-term use, sedatives can interfere with the normal sleep cycle. Although they promote sleep, they reduce the proportion of time spent in REM and slow-wave sleep (Nishino, Mignot, & Dement, 1995), robbing people of dreams and their deepest sleep stages. As a result, the quality of sleep achieved with pills may not be as high as without, and there may be side effects such as grogginess and irritability during the day. Finally, stopping the treatment suddenly can produce insomnia that is worse than before.

Sleep apnea is *a disorder in which the person stops breathing for brief periods while asleep*. A person with apnea usually snores, as apnea involves an involuntary obstruction of the breathing passage. When episodes of apnea occur for over 10 seconds at a time and recur many times during the night, they may cause many awakenings and sleep loss or insomnia. Apnea occurs most often in middle-age overweight men (Partinen, 1994) and may go undiagnosed because it is not easy for the sleeper to notice. Bed partners may be the ones who finally get tired of the snoring and noisy gasping for air when the sleeper's breathing restarts, or the sleeper may eventually seek treatment because of excessive sleepiness during the day. Therapies involving weight loss, drugs, or surgery may solve the problem.

Another sleep disorder is **somnambulism**, commonly called sleepwalking, which occurs when *a person arises and walks around while asleep*. Sleepwalking is more common in children, peaking around the age of 11 or 12, with as many as 25% of children experiencing at least one episode (Empson, 1984). Sleepwalking tends to happen early

INSOMNIA Difficulty in falling asleep or staying asleep.

SLEEP APNEA A disorder in which the person stops breathing for brief periods while asleep.

SOMNAMBULISM (sleepwalking) Occurs when the person arises and walks around while asleep.

NARCOLEPSY A disorder in which sudden sleep attacks occur in the middle of waking activities.

SLEEP PARALYSIS The experience of waking up unable to move.

NIGHT TERRORS (or sleep terrors) Abrupt awakenings with panic and intense emotional arousal.

in the night, usually in slow-wave sleep, and sleepwalkers may awaken during their walk or return to bed without waking, in which case they will probably not remember the episode in the morning. The sleepwalker's eyes are usually open in a glassy stare, although walking with hands outstretched is uncommon except in cartoons. Sleepwalking is not usually linked to any additional problems and is only problematic in that sleepwalkers can hurt themselves. People who walk while they are sleeping do not tend to be very coordinated and can trip over furniture or fall down stairs. Contrary to popular belief, it is safe to wake sleepwalkers or lead them back to bed.

There are other sleep disorders that are less common. **Narcolepsy** is *a disorder in which sudden sleep attacks occur in the middle of waking activities.* Narcolepsy involves the intrusion of a dreaming state of sleep (with REM) into waking and is often accompanied by unrelenting excessive sleepiness and uncontrollable sleep attacks lasting from 30 seconds to 30 minutes. This disorder appears to have a genetic basis, as it runs in families, and can be treated effectively with medication. **Sleep paralysis** is *the experience of waking up unable to move* and is sometimes associated with narcolepsy. This eerie experience usually lasts only a few moments, happens in hypnagogic or hypnopompic sleep, and may occur with an experience of pressure on the chest (Hishakawa, 1976). **Night terrors** (or sleep terrors) are *abrupt awakenings with panic and intense emotional arousal.* These terrors, which occur mainly in boys ages 3 to 7, happen most often in NREM sleep early in the sleep cycle and do not usually have dream content the sleeper can report.

To sum up, there is a lot going on when we close our eyes for the night. Humans follow a pretty regular sleep cycle, going through five stages of NREM and REM sleep during the night. Disruptions to that cycle, either from sleep deprivation or sleep disorders, can produce consequences for waking consciousness. But something else happens during a night's sleep that affects our consciousness, both while asleep and when we wake up. It's dreaming, and we'll look at what psychologists know about dreams next.

Dreams

Pioneering sleep researcher William C. Dement (1959) said, "Dreaming permits each and every one of us to be quietly and safely insane every night of our lives." Indeed, dreams do seem to have a touch of insanity about them. We experience crazy things in dreams, but even more bizarre is the fact that we are the writers, producers, and directors of the crazy things we experience. Just what are these experiences, and how can the experiences be explained?

Dream Consciousness

Dreams depart dramatically from reality. You may dream of being naked in public, of falling from a great height, of sleeping through an important appointment, of your teeth being loose and falling out, of being chased, or even of flying (Holloway, 2001). These things don't happen much in reality unless you have a very bad life.

The quality of consciousness in dreaming is also altered significantly from waking consciousness. There are five major characteristics of dream consciousness that distinguish it from the waking state (Hobson, 1988). For one, we intensely feel *emotion,* whether it is bliss or terror or love or awe. Second, dream *thought* is illogical: The continuities of time, place, and person don't apply. You may find you are in one place and then another, for example, without any travel in between—or people may change identity from one dream scene to the next. Third, *sensation* is fully formed and meaningful; visual sensation is predominant, and you may also deeply experience sound, touch, and movement (although pain is very uncommon). A fourth aspect of dreaming is *uncritical acceptance,* as though the images and events were perfectly normal rather than bizarre. A final feature of dreaming is the *difficulty of remembering* the dream after it is over. People often remember dreams only if they are awakened during the dream and even then may lose recall for the dream within just a few minutes of waking. If waking memory were this bad, you'd be standing around half naked in the street much of the time, having forgotten your destination, clothes, and probably your lunch money.

Maxine

Some of the most memorable dreams are nightmares, as these frightening dreams often wake up the dreamer. One set of daily dream logs from college undergraduates suggested that the average student has about 24 nightmares per year (Wood & Bootzin, 1990), although some people may have them as often as every night. Children have more nightmares than adults, and people who have experienced traumatic events are inclined to have nightmares that relive those events. Following the 1989 earthquake in the San Francisco Bay Area, for example, college students who had experienced the quake reported more nightmares than those who had not and often reported that the dreams were about the quake (Wood et al., 1992). This effect of trauma may not only produce dreams of the traumatic event: When police officers experience "critical incidents" of conflict and danger, they tend to have more nightmares in general (Neylan et al., 2002).

Not all of our dreams are fantastic and surreal, however. We also dream about mundane topics that reflect prior waking experiences or "day residue." Current conscious concerns pop up (Nikles et al., 1998), along with images from the recent past. A dream may even incorporate sensations experienced during sleep, as when sleepers in one study were led to dream of water when drops were sprayed on their faces during REM sleep (Dement & Wolpert, 1958). The day residue does not usually include episodic memories, that is, complete daytime events replayed in the mind. Rather, dreams that reflect the day's experience tend to single out sensory experiences or objects from waking life. After watching a badminton tournament one evening, for example, you might dream about shuttlecocks darting through the air. One study had research participants play the computer game Tetris and found that participants often reported dreaming about the Tetris geometrical figures falling down—even though they seldom reported dreams about being in the experiment or playing the game (Stickgold et al., 2001). Even severely amnesic patients who couldn't recall playing the game at all reported Tetris-like images appearing in their dreams (Stickgold et al., 2000b). The content of dreams takes snapshots from the day rather than retelling the stories of what you have done or seen. This means that dreams often come without clear plots or storylines, and so they may not make a lot of sense.

Dream Theories

Dreams are puzzles that cry out to be solved. How could you *not* want to make sense out of these experiences—although dreams are fantastic and confusing, they are emotionally riveting, filled with vivid images from your own life, and they seem very real. The search for dream meaning goes all the way back to biblical figures, who interpreted dreams and looked for prophecies in them. In the Old Testament, the prophet Daniel (a favorite of the authors of this book) curried favor with King Nebuchadnezzar of Babylon by interpreting the king's dream. The question of what dreams mean has been burning since antiquity, mainly because the meaning of dreams is usually far from obvious.

The Nightmare, by Henry Fuseli (1790). Fuseli depicts not only a mare in this painting but also an incubus—an imp perched on the dreamer's chest that is traditionally associated with especially horrifying nightmares.

{ HOT SCIENCE } Dreaming and the Brain

WHAT HAPPENS IN THE BRAIN WHEN WE dream? Several studies have made fMRI scans of people's brains during sleep, focusing on the areas of the brain that show changes in activation during REM periods. These studies show that the brain changes that occur during REM sleep correspond clearly with certain alterations of consciousness that occur in dreaming. The figure to the right shows some of the patterns of activation and deactivation found in the dreaming brain (Schwartz & Maquet, 2002).

One notable feature that distinguishes dreams from waking consciousness, for instance, is their scariness. Nightmares by definition are terrifying, but even your common, run-of-the-mill dream is often populated with anxiety-producing images (Neilson, Deslauriers, & Baylor, 1991). There are heights to look down from, dangerous people lurking, the occasional monster, lots of minor worries, and at least once in a while that major exam you've forgotten about until you walk into class. These thoughts suggest that the brain areas responsible for fear or emotion somehow work overtime in dreams, and it turns out that this is clearly visible in fMRI scans. The amygdala is involved in responses to threatening or stressful events, and indeed the amygdala is quite active during REM sleep.

The typical dream is also a visual wonderland, with visual events present in almost all dreams. However, there are fewer auditory sensations, even fewer tactile sensations, and almost no smells or tastes. This dream "picture show" doesn't involve actual perception, of course, just the imagination of visual events. It turns out that the areas of the brain responsible for visual perception are *not* activated during dreaming, whereas the visual association areas in the occipital lobe that are responsible for visual imagery *do* show activation (Braun et al., 1998), as shown in the figure. Your brain is smart enough to realize that it's not really seeing bizarre images but acts instead as though it's imagining bizarre images.

During REM, the prefrontal cortex shows relatively less arousal than it usually does during waking consciousness. What does this mean for the dreamer? As a rule, the prefrontal areas are associated with planning

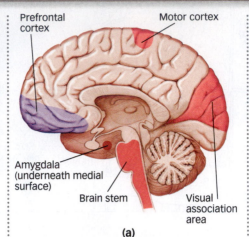

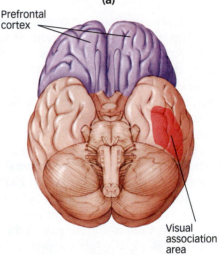

Brain activation and deactivation during REM sleep. Brain areas shaded red are activated during REM sleep; those shaded blue are deactivated. (a) The medial view shows the activation of the amygdala, the visual association areas, the motor cortex, and the brain stem and the deactivation of the prefrontal cortex. (b) The ventral view shows the activation of other visual association areas and the deactivation of the prefrontal cortex (Schwartz & Maquet, 2002).

and executing actions, and often dreams seem to be unplanned and rambling. Perhaps this is why dreams often don't have very sensible storylines—they've been scripted by an author whose ability to plan is inactive.

Another odd fact of dreaming is that while the eyes are moving rapidly, the body is otherwise very still. During REM sleep, the motor cortex is activated, but spinal neurons running through the brain stem inhibit the expression of this motor activation (Lai & Siegal, 1999). This turns out to be a useful property of brain activation in dreaming; otherwise, you might get up and act out every dream! In fact, when this inhibitory area is lesioned in cats, they become highly active during REM sleep (Jouvet & Mounier, 1961). People who are thrashing around during sleep are probably not dreaming. If they were dreaming, they'd be very still. The brain specifically inhibits movement during dreams, perhaps to keep us from hurting ourselves.

Brain scans may also someday help solve the intriguing question of whether people can be aware that they are dreaming. Some people claim that they only become aware they have been dreaming when they wake up and realize "it was all a dream." The dream state in this case seems to be like the waking state of minimal consciousness, in that the person is not aware of being in the mental state. Other individuals report, however, that they sometimes know they are dreaming while the dream is ongoing— they experience the dream equivalent of full consciousness. Such *lucid dreaming*, the awareness of dreaming during the dream, has been described often (LaBerge & Rheingold, 1990) but is still a matter of controversy because evidence of such dreams comes only from these descriptions reported by the dreamers. One goal of brain imaging research is to examine how the brain may be involved in the creation of such elusive states of mind. Researchers have not yet established whether there are differences in brain activation between minimal consciousness and full consciousness during waking, but perhaps if they do, brain research can corroborate the reports of lucid dreamers.

At present, studies of the activities of the dreaming brain yield a picture of dreaming as a unique state of mind. The brain's activities in dreaming underlie extensive visual activity, reductions of other sensations, increased sensitivity to emotions such as fear, lessened capacities for planning, and the prevention of movement.

In the first psychological theory of dreams, Freud (1900/1965) proposed that dreams are confusing and obscure because the dynamic unconscious creates them precisely *to be* confusing and obscure. According to Freud's theory, dreams represent wishes, and some of these wishes are so unacceptable, taboo, and anxiety producing that the mind can only express them in disguised form. Freud believed that many of the most unacceptable wishes are sexual, so he interpreted a dream of a train going into a tunnel as symbolic of sexual intercourse. According to Freud, the **manifest content** of a dream, *a dream's apparent topic or superficial meaning,* is a smoke screen for its **latent content,** *a dream's true underlying meaning.* For example, a dream about a tree burning down in the park across the street from where a friend once lived (the manifest content) might represent a camouflaged wish for the death of the friend (the latent content). In this case, wishing for the death of a friend is unacceptable, so it is disguised as a tree on fire. The problem with this approach is that there are an infinite number of potential interpretations of any dream and finding the correct one is a matter of guesswork—and of convincing the dreamer that one interpretation is superior to the others.

Although dreams may not represent elaborately hidden wishes, there is evidence that they do feature the return of suppressed thoughts. Researchers asked volunteers to think of a personal acquaintance and then to spend 5 minutes before going to bed writing down whatever came to mind (Wegner, Wenzlaff, & Kozak, 2004). Some participants were asked to suppress thoughts of this person as they wrote, others were asked to focus on thoughts of the person, and yet others were asked just to write freely about anything. The next morning, participants wrote dream reports. Overall, all participants mentioned dreaming more about the person they had named than about other people. But they most often dreamed of the person they named if they were in the group that had been assigned to suppress thoughts of the person the night before. This finding suggests that Freud was right to suspect that dreams harbor unwanted thoughts. Perhaps this is why actors dream of forgetting their lines, travelers dream of getting lost, and football players dream of fumbling the ball.

Another key theory of dreaming is the **activation-synthesis model** (Hobson & McCarley, 1977). This theory proposes that *dreams are produced when the mind attempts to make sense of random neural activity that occurs in the brain during sleep.* During waking consciousness, the mind is devoted to interpreting lots of information that arrives through the senses. You figure out that the odd noise you're hearing during class is your cell phone vibrating, for example, or you realize that the strange smell in the hall outside your room must be from burned popcorn. In the dream state, the mind doesn't have access to external sensations, but it keeps on doing what it usually does: interpreting information. Because that information now comes from neural activations that occur without the continuity provided by the perception of reality, the brain's interpretive mechanisms can run free (see the Hot Science box on the facing page). This might be why, for example, a person in a dream can sometimes change into someone else. There is no actual person being perceived to help the mind keep a stable view. In the mind's effort to perceive and give meaning to brain activation, the person you view in a dream about a grocery store might seem to be a clerk but then change to be your favorite teacher when the dream scene moves to your school. The great interest people have in interpreting their dreams the next morning may be an extension of the interpretive activity they've been doing all night.

The Freudian theory and the activation-synthesis theory differ in the significance they place on the meaning of dreams. In Freud's theory, dreams begin with meaning, whereas in the activation-synthesis theory, dreams begin randomly—but meaning can be added as the mind lends interpretations in the process of dreaming. Dream research has not yet sorted out whether one of these theories or yet another might be the best account of the meaning of dreams.

In summary, sleep and dreaming present a view of the mind with an altered state of consciousness. EEG and EOG measures have revealed that during a night's sleep, the brain passes through a five-stage sleep cycle, moving in and out of lighter sleep stages, from slow-wave sleep stages to the REM sleep stage, in which most dreaming occurs.

MANIFEST CONTENT A dream's apparent topic or superficial meaning.

LATENT CONTENT A dream's true underlying meaning.

ACTIVATION-SYNTHESIS MODEL The theory that dreams are produced when the brain attempts to make sense of activations that occur randomly during sleep.

BRENT MADISON

The seat of consciousness.

Sleep needs decrease over the life span, but deprivation from sleep and dreams has psychological and physical costs. Sleep can be disrupted through disorders that include insomnia, sleep apnea, somnambulism, narcolepsy, sleep paralysis, and night terrors. Dreaming is an altered state of consciousness in which the dreamer uncritically accepts changes in emotion, thought, and sensation but poorly remembers the dream on awakening. Dream consciousness is paralleled by changes in brain activation, and theories of dreaming include Freud's psychoanalytic theory and more current views such as the activation-synthesis model. ■ ■

Drugs and Consciousness: Artificial Inspiration

The author of the anti-utopian novel *Brave New World,* Aldous Huxley, once wrote of his experiences with the drug mescaline. His essay "The Doors of Perception" described the intense experience that accompanied his departure from normal consciousness. He described "a world where everything shone with the Inner Light, and was infinite in its significance. The legs, for example, of [a] chair—how miraculous their tubularity, how supernatural their polished smoothness! I spent several minutes—or was it several centuries?—not merely gazing at those bamboo legs, but actually *being* them" (Huxley, 1954).

Being the legs of a chair? This is better than being a seat cushion, but it still sounds like an odd experience. Still, many people seek out such experiences, often through using drugs. **Psychoactive drugs** are *chemicals that influence consciousness or behavior by altering the brain's chemical message system.* As you read in Chapter 3, information is communicated in the brain through neurotransmitters that convey neural impulses to neighboring neurons. Some of the most common neurotransmitters are serotonin, dopamine, gamma aminobutyric acid (GABA), and acetylcholine. Drugs alter these neural connections by preventing the bonding of neurotransmitters to sites in the postsynaptic neuron or by inhibiting the reuptake of or enhancing the bonding and transmission of neurotransmitters. Different drugs can intensify or dull transmission patterns, creating changes in brain electrical activity that mimic natural operations of the brain. For example, a drug such as Valium (benzodiazepine) induces sleep but prevents dreaming and so creates a state similar to slow-wave sleep, that is, what the brain naturally develops several times each night. Other drugs prompt patterns of brain activity that do not occur naturally, however, and their influence on consciousness can be dramatic. Like Huxley experiencing himself becoming the legs of a chair, people using drugs can have experiences unlike any they might find in normal waking consciousness or even in dreams. To understand these altered states, let's explore how people use and abuse drugs and examine the major categories of psychoactive drugs.

Drug Use and Abuse

Why do children sometimes spin around until they get dizzy and fall to the ground? There is something strangely attractive about states of consciousness that depart from the norm, and people throughout history have sought out these altered states by dancing, fasting, chanting, meditating, and ingesting a bizarre assortment of chemicals to intoxicate themselves (Tart, 1969). People pursue altered consciousness even when there are costs, from the nausea that accompanies dizziness to the life-wrecking obsession with a drug that can come with addiction. In this regard, the pursuit of altered consciousness can be a malicious mindbug.

Often, drug-induced changes in consciousness begin as pleasant and spark an initial attraction. Researchers have measured the attractiveness of psychoactive drugs by seeing how much laboratory animals will work to get them. In one study researchers allowed rats to intravenously administer cocaine to themselves by pressing a lever (Bozarth & Wise, 1985). Rats given free access to cocaine increased their use over the course of the 30-day study. They not only continued to self-administer at a high rate but also occasionally binged to the point of giving themselves convulsions. They stopped grooming themselves and eating until they lost on average almost a third of their body weight. About 90% of the rats died by the end of the study.

Rats are not tiny little humans, of course, so such research is not a firm basis for understanding human responses to cocaine. But these results do make it clear that cocaine is addictive and that the results of such addiction can be dire. Studies of self-administration of drugs in laboratory animals show that animals will work to obtain not only cocaine but also alcohol, amphetamines, barbiturates, caffeine, opiates (such as morphine and heroin), nicotine, phenylcycladine (PCP), MDMA (ecstasy), and THC (tetrahydrocannabinol, the active ingredient in marijuana). There are some psychoactive drugs that animals won't work for (such as mescaline or the antipsychotic drug phenothiazine), suggesting that these drugs have less potential for causing addiction (Bozarth, 1987).

People usually do not become addicted to a psychoactive drug the first time they use it. They may experiment a few times, then try again, and eventually find that their tendency to use the drug increases over time due to several factors, such as drug tolerance, physical dependence, and psychological dependence. **Drug tolerance** is *the tendency for larger drug doses to be required over time to achieve the same effect.* Physicians who prescribe morphine to control pain in their patients are faced with tolerance problems because steadily greater amounts of the drug may be needed to dampen the same pain. With increased tolerance comes the danger of drug overdose; recreational users find they need to use more and more of a drug to produce the same high. But then, if a new batch of heroin or cocaine is more concentrated than usual, the "normal" amount the user takes to achieve the same high can be fatal.

Self-administration of addictive drugs can also be prompted by withdrawal symptoms, which result when the drug is abruptly discontinued. Some withdrawal symptoms signal *physical dependence,* when pain, convulsions, hallucinations, or other unpleasant symptoms accompany withdrawal. People who suffer from physical dependence seek to continue drug use to avoid getting physically ill. A common example is the "caffeine headache" some people complain of when they haven't had their daily jolt of java. Other withdrawal symptoms result from *psychological dependence,* a strong desire to return to the drug even when physical withdrawal symptoms are gone. Drugs can create an emotional need over time that continues to prey on the mind, particularly in circumstances that are reminders of the drug. Some ex-smokers report longing wistfully for an after-dinner smoke, for example, even years after they've successfully quit the habit.

Drug addiction reveals a human mindbug: our inability to look past the immediate consequences of our behavior. Although we would like to think that our behavior is guided by a rational analysis of future consequences, more typically occasions when we "play first, pay later" lead directly to "let's just play a lot right now." There is something intensely inviting about the prospect of a soon-to-be-had pleasure and something pale, hazy, and distant about the costs this act might bring at some future time. For example, given the choice of receiving $1 today or $2 a week later, most people will take the $1 today. However, if the same choice is to be made for some date a year in the future (when the immediate pleasure of today's windfall is not so strong), people choose to wait and get the $2 (Ainslie, 2001). The immediate satisfaction associated with taking most drugs may outweigh a rational analysis of the later consequences that can result from taking those drugs, such as drug addiction.

The psychological and social problems stemming from addiction are major. For many people, drug addiction becomes a way of life, and for some, it is a cause of death. Like the cocaine-addicted rats in the study noted earlier (Bozarth & Wise, 1985), some people become so attached to a drug that their lives are ruled by it. However, this is not always the end of the story. This ending is most well known because the addict becomes a recurrent, visible social problem, "publicized" through repeated crime and repeated appearances in prisons and treatment programs. But a life of addiction is not the only possible endpoint of drug use. Stanley Schachter (1982) suggested that the visibility of addiction is misleading and that in fact many people overcome addictions. He found that 64% of a sample of people who had a history of cigarette smoking had quit successfully, although many had to try again and again to achieve their success. One study of soldiers who became addicted to heroin in Vietnam found that 3 years after

PSYCHOACTIVE DRUG A chemical that influences consciousness or behavior by altering the brain's chemical message system.

DRUG TOLERANCE The tendency for larger doses of a drug to be required over time to achieve the same effect.

The antique espresso machine, a sight that warms the hearts of caffeine lovers around the world.

JOHN LANDER/ALAMY

DEPRESSANTS Substances that reduce the activity of the central nervous system.

People will often endure significant inconveniences to maintain their addictions.

their return, only 12% remained addicted (Robins et al., 1980). The return to the attractions and obligations of normal life, as well as the absence of the familiar places and faces associated with their old drug habit, made it possible for returning soldiers to successfully quit. Although addiction is dangerous, it may not be incurable.

It may not be accurate to view all recreational drug use under the umbrella of "addiction." Many people at this point in the history of Western society, for example, would not call the repeated use of caffeine an addiction, and some do not label the use of alcohol, tobacco, or marijuana in this way. In other times and places, however, each of these has been considered a terrifying addiction worthy of prohibition and public censure. In the early 17th century, for example, tobacco use was punishable by death in Germany, by castration in Russia, and by decapitation in China (Corti, 1931). Not a good time to be traveling around waving a cigar. By contrast, cocaine, heroin, marijuana, and amphetamines have each been popular and even recommended as medicines at several points throughout history, each without any stigma of addiction attached (Inciardi, 2001).

Although addiction has a certain meaning here and now, this meaning is open to interpretation (Cherry, Dillon, & Rugh, 2002). Indeed, the concept of addiction has been extended to many human pursuits, giving rise to such terms as "sex addict," "gambling addict," "workaholic," and, of course, "chocoholic." Societies react differently at different times, with some uses of drugs ignored, other uses encouraged, others simply taxed, and yet others subjected to intense prohibition (see the Real World box on pp. 324–325). Rather than viewing *all* drug use as a problem, it is important to consider the costs and benefits of such use and to establish ways to help people choose behaviors that are informed by this knowledge (Parrott, Morinan, Moss, & Scholey, 2004).

"Hi, my name is Barry, and I check my E-mail two to three hundred times a day."

Types of Psychoactive Drugs

Four in five North Americans use caffeine in some form every day, but not all psychoactive drugs are this familiar. To learn how both the well-known and lesser-known drugs influence the mind, let's consider several broad categories of drugs: depressants, stimulants, narcotics, hallucinogens, and marijuana. **TABLE 8.2** summarizes what is known about the potential dangers of these different types of drugs.

| Table 8.2 | Dangers of Drugs | | |

	Dangers		
	Overdose	**Physical Dependence**	**Psychological Dependence**
Drug	**(Can taking too much cause death or injury?)**	**(Will stopping use make you sick?)**	**(Will you crave it when you stop using it?)**
Depressants			
Alcohol	X	X	X
Barbiturates/benzodiazepines	X	X	X
Toxic inhalants	X	X	X
Stimulants			
Amphetamines	X	X	X
MDMA (Ecstasy)	X		?
Cocaine	X	X	X
Narcotics (opium, heroin, morphine, methadone, codeine)	X	X	X
Hallucinogens (LSD, mescaline, psilocybin, PCP, ketamine)	X		?
Marijuana			?

Depressants

Depressants are *substances that reduce the activity of the central nervous system.* The most commonly used depressant is alcohol, and others include barbiturates, benzodiazepines, and toxic inhalants (such as glue or gasoline). Depressants have a sedative or calming effect, tend to induce sleep in high doses, and can arrest breathing in extremely high doses. Depressants can produce both physical and psychological dependence.

Alcohol

Alcohol is "king of the depressants," with its worldwide use beginning in prehistory, its easy availability in most cultures, and its widespread acceptance as a socially approved substance. Fifty-two percent of Americans over 12 years of age report having had a drink in the past month, and 15% have binged on alcohol (over five drinks in succession) in that time. Young adults (ages 18 to 25) have even higher rates, with 60% reporting a drink last month and 31% reporting a binge (*Health, United States,* 2001; National Center for Health Statistics, 2001).

Alcohol's initial effects, euphoria and reduced anxiety, feel pretty positive. As it is consumed in greater quantities, drunkenness results, bringing slowed reactions, slurred speech, poor judgment, and other reductions in the effectiveness of thought and action. The exact way in which alcohol influences neural mechanisms is still not understood, but like other depressants, alcohol increases activity of the neurotransmitter GABA (De Witte, 1996). As you read in Chapter 3, GABA normally inhibits the transmission of neural impulses, so one effect of alcohol is as a disinhibitor—a chemical that lets transmissions occur that otherwise would be held in check. But there are many contradictions. Some people using alcohol become loud and aggressive, others become emotional and weepy, others become sullen, and still others turn giddy—and the same person can experience each of these effects in different circumstances. How can one drug do this? Two theories have been offered to account for these variable effects: *expectancy theory* and *alcohol myopia.*

Expectancy theory suggests that *alcohol effects are produced by people's expectations of how alcohol will influence them in particular situations* (Marlatt & Rohsenow, 1980). So,

EXPECTANCY THEORY The idea that alcohol effects can be produced by people's expectations of how alcohol will influence them in particular situations.

"Hey, what is this stuff? It makes everything I think seem profound."

for instance, if you've watched friends or family drink at weddings and notice that this often produces hilarity and gregariousness, you could well experience these effects yourself should you drink alcohol on a similarly festive occasion. Seeing people getting drunk and fighting in bars, in turn, might lead to aggression after drinking.

The expectancy theory has been tested in studies that examine the effects of actual alcohol ingestion independent of the *perception* of alcohol ingestion. In experiments using a **balanced placebo design**, *behavior is observed following the presence or absence of an actual stimulus and also following the presence or absence of a placebo stimulus*. In such a study, participants are given drinks containing alcohol or a substitute liquid, and some people in each group are led to believe they had alcohol and others are led to believe they did not. People told they are drinking alcohol when they are not, for instance, might get a touch of vodka on the plastic lid of a cup to give it the right odor when the drink inside is merely tonic water. These experiments often show that the belief that one has had alcohol can influence behavior as strongly as the ingestion of alcohol itself (Goldman, Brown, & Christiansen, 1987). You may have seen people at parties getting rowdy after only one beer—perhaps because they expected this effect rather than because the beer actually had this influence.

Another approach to the varied effects of alcohol is the theory of **alcohol myopia**, which proposes that *alcohol hampers attention, leading people to respond in simple ways to complex situations* (Steele & Josephs, 1990). This theory recognizes that life is filled with complicated pushes and pulls, and our behavior is often a balancing act. Imagine that you are really attracted to someone who is dating your friend. Do you make your feelings known or focus on your friendship? The myopia theory holds that when you drink alcohol, your fine judgment is impaired. It becomes hard to appreciate the subtlety of these different options, and the inappropriate response is to veer full tilt one way or the other. So, alcohol might lead you to make a wild pass at your friend's date or perhaps just cry in your beer over your timidity—depending on which way you happened to tilt in your myopic state.

In one study on the alcohol myopia theory, men, half of whom were drinking alcohol, watched a video showing an unfriendly woman and then were asked how acceptable it would be for a man to act sexually aggressive toward a woman (Johnson, Noel, & Sutter-Hernandez, 2000). The unfriendly woman seemed to remind them that sex was out of the question, and indeed, men who were drinking alcohol and had seen this video were no more likely to think sexual advances were acceptable than men who were sober. However, when the same question was asked of a group of men who had seen a video of a *friendly* woman, those who were drinking were more inclined to recommend sexual overtures than those who were not, even when these overtures might be unwanted. Apparently, alcohol makes the complicated decisions involved in relationships seem simple ("Gee, she was so friendly")—and potentially open to serious misjudgments.

Both the expectancy and myopia theories suggest that people using alcohol will often go to extremes. In fact, it seems that drinking is a major contributing factor to social problems that result from extreme behavior. Drinking while driving is a main cause of auto accidents, for example, contributing to 39% of crash fatalities in 1997 (National Center for Injury Prevention and Control, 2001–2002). A survey of undergraduates revealed that alcohol contributes to as many as 90% of rapes and 95% of violent crimes on campus (Wechsler et al., 1994). Of the binge drinkers in the student sample, 41% reported that they had had unplanned sex due to drinking, and 22% said their drinking led to unprotected sex.

Barbiturates, Benzodiazepines, and Toxic Inhalants

Compared to alcohol, the other depressants are much less popular but still are widely used and abused. Barbiturates such as Seconal or Nembutal are prescribed as sleep aids and as anesthetics before surgery. Benzodiazepines such as Valium and Xanax are also called minor tranquilizers and are prescribed as antianxiety drugs. These drugs are prescribed by physicians to treat anxiety or sleep problems, but they are dangerous when

BALANCED PLACEBO DESIGN A study design in which behavior is observed following the presence or absence of an actual stimulus and also following the presence or absence of a placebo stimulus.

ALCOHOL MYOPIA A condition that results when alcohol hampers attention, leading people to respond in simple ways to complex situations.

used in combination with alcohol. Physical dependence is possible since withdrawal from long-term use can produce severe symptoms (including convulsions), and psychological dependence is common as well. Finally, toxic inhalants are perhaps the most alarming substances in this category. These drugs are easily accessible even to children in the vapors of glue, gasoline, or propane. Sniffing or "huffing" these vapors can promote temporary effects that resemble drunkenness, but overdoses are sometimes lethal, and continued use holds the potential for permanent brain damage (Fornazzari, Wilkinson, Kapur, & Carler, 1983).

Stimulants

The **stimulants** are *substances that excite the central nervous system, heightening arousal and activity levels*. They include caffeine, amphetamines, nicotine, cocaine, and ecstasy (MDMA) and sometimes have a legitimate pharmaceutical purpose. Amphetamines (also called "speed"), for example, were originally prepared for medicinal uses and as diet drugs; however, amphetamines such as Methedrine and Dexedrine are widely abused, causing insomnia, aggression, and paranoia with long-term use. Stimulants increase the levels of dopamine and norepinephrine in the brain, thereby inducing higher levels of activity in the brain circuits that depend on these neurotransmitters. As a result, they increase alertness and energy in the user, often producing a euphoric sense of confidence and a kind of agitated motivation to get things done. All stimulants produce physical and psychological dependence, and their withdrawal symptoms involve depressive effects such as fatigue and negative emotions.

Ecstasy is an amphetamine derivative also known as MDMA, "X," or "e." It is a stimulant, but it has added effects somewhat like those of hallucinogens (we'll talk about those shortly). Ecstasy is particularly known for making users feel empathic and close to those around them. It is used often as a party drug to enhance the group feeling at dances or raves, but it has unpleasant side effects such as causing jaw clenching and interfering with the regulation of body temperature. The rave culture has popularized pacifiers and juices as remedies for these problems, but users remain highly susceptible to heatstroke and exhaustion. Although ecstasy is not as likely as some other drugs to cause physical or psychological dependence, it nonetheless can lead to some dependence. What's more, the impurities sometimes found in "street" pills are also dangerous (Parrott, 2001). Ecstasy's potentially toxic effect on serotonin-activated neurons in the human brain is under intense debate, and a good deal of research attention is being devoted to studying the effects of this drug on humans.

Cocaine is derived from leaves of the coca plant, which has been cultivated by indigenous peoples of the Andes for millennia and chewed as a medication. Yes, the urban legend is true: *Coca-Cola* contained cocaine until 1903 and still may use coca leaves (with cocaine removed) as a flavoring—although the company's not telling (*Pepsi-Cola* never contained cocaine and is probably made from something brown).

STIMULANTS Substances that excite the central nervous system, heightening arousal and activity levels.

DANNY LEHMANN/CORBIS

Coca-Cola has been a popular product for more than 100 years. In the early days, one of the fatigue-relieving ingredients was a small amount of cocaine.

{ THE REAL WORLD } Drugs and the Regulation of Consciousness

WHY DOES EVERYONE HAVE AN OPINION about drug use? Given that it's not possible to perceive what happens in anyone else's mind (that pesky "other minds" mystery of consciousness), why does it matter so much to us what people do to their own consciousness? Is consciousness something that governments should be able to legislate—or should people be free to choose their own conscious states (McWilliams, 1993)? After all, how can a "free society" justify regulating what people do inside their own heads?

Individuals and governments alike answer these questions by pointing to the costs of drug addiction, both to the addict and to the society that must "carry" unproductive people, pay for their welfare, and often even take care of their children. Drug users appear to be troublemakers and criminals, the culprits behind all those "drug-related" shootings, knifings, robberies, and petty thefts you see in the news day after day. It makes sense that their behavior appears to be caused by drug use, and you might even be able to understand the frustration that led Darryl Gates, then chief of the Los Angeles Police Department, to remark to the U.S. Senate Judiciary Committee in 1990 that "casual drug users should be taken out and shot." Although most government officials are more compassionate than this, widespread anger about the drug problem has surfaced in the form of the "War on Drugs," a federal

LIBRARY OF CONGRESS

HAGLEY MUSEUM AND LIBRARY

Prohibition was an attempt to legislate self-control that eventually produced so many problems that people campaigned in the streets to repeal the law.

government program that has focused on drug use as a criminal offense and has attempted to stop drug use through the imprisonment of users.

Social commentators such as economist Milton Friedman and psychiatrist Thomas Szasz believe that the War on Drugs is much like the era of Prohibition, the federal government's 1920–33 ban on alcohol (Trebach & Zeese, 1992). This famous experiment failed because the harm produced by the policy outweighed the damage produced by legal alcohol consumption. Illegal alcohol became wildly expensive, and the promise of large profits led to the rapid growth of organized criminal suppliers, an entire criminal subculture complete with gang killings and turf wars over distribution rights. With the huge jump in organized crime came a parallel wave of crime by "users"—illegal alcohol was so expensive that people who were dependent on it begged, stole, or sold anything to get money to buy it.

The current War on Drugs has led to the same buildup of criminal supply systems, along with an increase in crimes committed by users to get drug money—and an unprecedented increase in the incarceration of drug offenders. From 1990 to 1999, for example, the number of drug offenders in state and federal prisons increased from 179,070 to 319,560—a jump of 78% (Bureau of Justice Statistics, 2001)—not because of a measurable increase in drug use, but because of the rapidly increasing use of

Sigmund Freud tried cocaine and wrote effusively about it for a while. Cocaine (usually snorted) and crack cocaine (smoked) produce exhilaration and euphoria and are seriously addictive, both for humans and the rats you read about earlier in this chapter. Withdrawal takes the form of an unpleasant "crash," cravings are common, and antisocial effects like those generated by amphetamines—aggressiveness and paranoia—are frequent with long-term use. Although cocaine has enjoyed popularity as a "party drug," its extraordinary potential to create dependence should be taken very seriously.

Narcotics

Opium, which comes from poppy seeds, and its derivatives heroin, morphine, methadone, and codeine (as well as prescription drugs such as Demerol and Oxycontin) are known as **narcotics** or **opiates**, *drugs derived from opium that are capable of relieving pain*. Narcotics induce a feeling of well-being and relaxation that is enjoyable but can also induce stupor and lethargy. The addictive properties of narcotics are powerful, and long-term use produces both tolerance and dependence. Because these

NARCOTICS or **OPIATES** Highly addictive drugs derived from opium that relieve pain.

imprisonment for drug offenses. Many people who are being prevented from ruining their lives with drugs are instead having their lives ruined by prison. These observations bring up the question of whether it is the drug use that causes social problems or the *prohibition* of drug use that causes these problems.

What should be done? One possibility is the **harm reduction approach,** *a response to high-risk behaviors that focuses on reducing the harm such behaviors have on people's lives* (Marlatt, 1998). This approach (which originated in the Netherlands and England) focuses on reducing drug harm rather than reducing drug use. Harm reduction involves tactics such as providing intravenous drug users with sterile syringes to help them avoid contracting HIV and other infections from shared needles. Harm reduction may even involve providing drugs for addicts to reduce the risks of poisoning and overdose they face when they get impure drugs of unknown dosage from criminal suppliers. A harm reduction idea for alcoholics, in turn, is to allow moderate drinking; the demand to be cold sober may keep many alcoholics on the street and away from any treatment at all (Marlatt et al., 1993). Harm reduction strategies may not always find public support because they challenge the popular idea that the solution to drug and alcohol problems must always be prohibition: stopping use entirely.

The mistaken belief in prohibition is fueled, in part, by the worry that drug use turns people into criminals and causes psy-

In the Netherlands, marijuana use is not prosecuted. The drug is sold in "coffee shops" to those over 18.

chological disorders. A key study that followed 101 children as they grew from the age of 3 to 18 did not confirm this theory (Shedler & Block, 1990). Personality assessments given to participants showed that those who were frequent drug users at 18 indeed were the most irresponsible, inconsiderate, irritable, rebellious, low in self-esteem, and so on. However, the adjustment problems of the frequent users were *already present* in early childhood, long before they started using drugs. Some other factor (a poor family environment as a child, perhaps) caused both their adjustment problems *and* their frequent drug use. As you read in Chapter 2, in this case, a third variable was at work in producing a correlation. It may be that allowing some limited forms of drug use—and instead focusing greater attention on reducing harm—would not create the problems we fear.

Harm reduction seems to be working in the Netherlands. The Netherlands Ministry of Justice (1999) reported that the decriminalization of marijuana there in 1979 has not led to increased use and that the use of other drugs remains at a level far below that of other European countries and the United States. Conversely, in the United States, the War on Drugs seems to have had little real impact. A comparison of drug users in Amsterdam and San Francisco revealed that the city in which marijuana is criminalized—San Francisco—had higher rates of drug use for both marijuana and other drugs (Reinarman, Cohen, & Kaal, 2004). Separating the markets in which people buy marijuana and alcohol from those in which they get "hard" drugs such as heroin, cocaine, or methamphetamine may create a social barrier that reduces interest in the hard drugs. There may be solutions that involve reasonable responses to drugs, a middle ground between prohibition and deregulation, as a way of reducing harm. Perhaps we can eliminate some casualties in the War on Drugs by fighting drug harm rather than heaping further harm on drug users. Regulating consciousness may be less important for society than reducing the harm that is caused when individuals try to regulate their own consciousness through drug use.

HARM REDUCTION APPROACH A response to high-risk behaviors that focuses on reducing the harm such behaviors have on people's lives.

drugs are often administered with hypodermic syringes, they also introduce the danger of diseases such as HIV when users share syringes. Unfortunately, these drugs are especially alluring because they are external mimics of the brain's own internal relaxation and well-being system.

The brain produces **endorphins** or **endogenous opiates,** which are *neurotransmitters that are closely related to opiates.* Endorphins play a role in how the brain copes internally with pain and stress. These substances reduce the experience of pain naturally. When you exercise for a while and start to feel your muscles burning, for example, you may also find that there comes a time when the pain eases—sometimes even *during* the exercise. Endorphins are secreted in the pituitary gland and other brain sites as a response to injury or exertion, creating a kind of natural remedy (like the so-called runner's high) that subsequently reduces pain and increases feelings of well-being. When people use narcotics, the brain's endorphin receptors are artificially flooded, however, reducing receptor effectiveness and possibly also depressing the production of endorphins. When external administration of narcotics stops, withdrawal symptoms are likely to occur.

ENDORPHINS or **ENDOGENOUS OPIATES** Neurotransmitters that have a similar structure to opiates and that appear to play a role in how the brain copes internally with pain and stress.

Psychedelic art and music of the 1960s were inspired by some visual and auditory effects of drugs such as LSD.

HALLUCINOGENS Drugs that alter sensation and perception and often cause visual and auditory hallucinations.

MARIJUANA The leaves and buds of the hemp plant.

HYPNOSIS An altered state of consciousness characterized by suggestibility and the feeling that one's actions are occurring involuntarily.

 ONLY HUMAN

JUSTICE FOR ALL? In Salt Lake City, Federal Judge Paul G. Cassell, remarking that mandatory minimum-sentencing laws gave him no choice, sent a 25-year-old, small-quantity marijuana dealer to prison for 55 years (because he had a gun during two of the transactions). Two hours before that, in a crime Cassell described as far more serious but not subject to the same mandatory sentencing minimums, he sentenced a man to 22 years in prison for beating an elderly woman to death with a log (Berman, 2005).

Hallucinogens

The drugs that produce the most extreme alterations of consciousness are the **hallucinogens**, *drugs that alter sensation and perception, often causing hallucinations*. These include LSD (lysergic acid diethylamide), or acid; mescaline; psilocybin; PCP (phencyclidine); and ketamine (an animal anesthetic). Some of these drugs are derived from plants (mescaline from peyote cactus, psilocybin or "shrooms" from mushrooms) and have been used by people since ancient times. For example, the ingestion of peyote plays a prominent role in some Native American religious practices. The other hallucinogens are largely synthetic. LSD was first made by chemist Albert Hofman in 1938, leading to a rash of experimentation that influenced popular culture in the 1960s. Timothy Leary, at the time a Harvard psychology professor, championed the use of LSD to "turn on, tune in, and drop out"; the Beatles sang of *L*ucy in the *s*ky with *d*iamonds (denying, of course, that this might be a reference to LSD); and the wave of interest led many people to experiment with hallucinogens.

The experiment was not a great success. These drugs produce profound changes in perception. Sensations may seem unusually intense, objects may seem to move or change, patterns or colors may appear, and these perceptions may be accompanied by exaggerated emotions ranging from blissful transcendence to abject terror. These are the "I've-become-the-legs-of-a-chair!" drugs. But the effects of hallucinogens are dramatic and unpredictable, creating a psychological roller-coaster ride that some people find intriguing but others find deeply disturbing. Hallucinogens are the main class of drugs that animals *won't* work to self-administer, so it is not surprising that in humans these drugs are unlikely to be addictive. Hallucinogens do not induce significant tolerance or dependence, and overdose deaths are rare. Although hallucinogens still enjoy a marginal popularity with people interested in experimenting with their perceptions, they have been more a cultural trend than a dangerous attraction.

Marijuana

The *leaves and buds of the hemp plant* contain THC, the active ingredient in **marijuana**. When smoked or eaten, either as is or in concentrated form as *hashish,* this drug produces an intoxication that is mildly hallucinogenic. Users describe the experience as euphoric, with heightened senses of sight and sound and the perception of a rush of ideas. Marijuana affects judgment and short-term memory and impairs motor skills and coordination— making driving a car or operating heavy equipment a poor choice during its use ("Where did I leave the darn bulldozer?"). Researchers have found that receptors in the brain that respond to THC (Stephens, 1999) are normally activated by a neurotransmitter called *anandamide* that is naturally produced in the brain (Wiley, 1999). Anandamide is involved in the regulation of mood, memory, appetite, and pain perception and has been found temporarily to stimulate overeating in laboratory animals, much as marijuana does in humans (Williams & Kirkham, 1999). Some chemicals found in dark chocolate also mimic anandamide, although very weakly, perhaps accounting for the well-being some people claim they enjoy after a "dose" of chocolate.

The addiction potential of marijuana is not strong, as tolerance does not seem to develop, and physical withdrawal symptoms are minimal. Psychological dependence is possible, however, and some people do become chronic users. Marijuana use has been widespread throughout the world for recorded history, both as a medicine for pain and/or nausea and as a recreational drug, but its use remains controversial. States such as California and Oregon have passed legislation favoring medical uses, as has British Columbia in Canada, but the U.S. federal government classifies marijuana as a "Schedule I Controlled Substance," recognizing no medical use and maintaining that marijuana has the same high potential for abuse as heroin. All told, it seems that the greatest danger of marijuana is that its use is illegal.

In summary, psychoactive drugs influence consciousness by altering the brain's chemical messaging system and intensifying or dulling the effects of neurotransmitters. The altered consciousness brought about by drug use is attractive to many people, but in many cases drugs cause serious harm. Drug tolerance can result in overdose, and physical and psychological dependence can lead to addiction. Although people can sometimes overcome addiction, it is a serious human weakness that reveals the difficulty people have in acting with their best long-term interests in mind. The most commonly used and abused psychoactive drugs include depressants, stimulants, narcotics, hallucinogens, and marijuana. The varying effects of alcohol, a depressant, are explained by theories of alcohol expectancy and alcohol myopia. Each of the major classes of psychoactive drugs was developed for medical, social, or religious reasons, but each has different effects and presents a different array of dangers. ■ ■

Hypnosis: Open to Suggestion

You may have never been hypnotized, but you have probably heard or read about it. Its wonders are often described with an air of amazement, and demonstrations of stage hypnosis make it seem very powerful and mysterious. When you think of hypnosis, you may envision people down on all fours acting like farm animals or perhaps "regressing" to early childhood and talking in childlike voices. Some of what you might think is true, but many of the common beliefs about hypnosis are false. **Hypnosis** is *an altered state of consciousness characterized by suggestibility and the feeling that one's actions are occurring involuntarily.* In other words, it is mainly a state of mind in which people follow instructions readily and feel that their actions are things that are happening to them rather than things they are doing (Lynn, Rhue, & Weekes, 1990).

As you gaze at this magazine cover, you are getting sleepy . . . very sleepy. . . .

Induction and Susceptibility

How do people get hypnotized? An early form of hypnotic induction is credited to Franz Anton Mesmer (1734–1815), a physician working in Paris. He attempted to cure people of illness through contact with what he called "animal magnetism." He introduced patients to his theory that a force could be generated from water and iron to rejuvenate their health and then proceeded to get them involved in several curious rituals. Patients held on to iron rods immersed in a large water tub, sometimes with their waists loosely tied to the tub with rope, and were asked to sit quietly while Mesmer passed his hands lightly over their bodies (Gauld, 1992). These theatrical gestures led many patients to believe that their ailments were cured. Some patients reported miraculous cures of chronic stomach problems, headaches, paralysis, and even blindness, and those whose cures were less dramatic still often agreed that they too felt better for all this. *Mesmerism* became a major sensation. Although Mesmer's theory was eventually discredited and he was dismissed as a charlatan (it turned out that none of the water tubs or paraphernalia were even needed for the effect), his technique of influencing people developed into what is now called hypnosis.

The essence of Mesmer's technique was persuading people that his actions would influence them. In a modern hypnotic induction, many people already know enough about hypnosis to suspect that something the hypnotist does might indeed have an effect on them. To induce hypnosis, then, a hypnotist may ask the person to be hypnotized to sit quietly and focus on some item (such as a spot on the wall) and then suggest to the person what effects hypnosis will have (for example, "Your eyelids are slowly closing" or "Your arms are getting heavy"). Modern hypnosis shares a common theme with mesmerism: In both cases, the hypnotist and participant engage in a social interaction in which the participants are led to expect that certain things will happen to them that are outside of their conscious will (Wegner, 2002).

The induction of hypnosis usually involves a number of different "suggestions," ideas the hypnotist mentions to the volunteer about what the volunteer will do. Some of

Stage hypnotists often perform an induction on a whole audience and then bring some of the more susceptible members onstage for further demonstrations. This hypnotist seems to think it is entertaining to see people slump over.

these ideas seem to cause the actions—just thinking about their eyelids slowly closing, for instance, may make many people shut their eyes briefly or at least blink. Just as you may find yawning contagious when you think about someone else yawning, many different behaviors can be made more common just by concentrating on them. In hypnosis, a series of behavior suggestions can induce in some people a state of mind that makes them susceptible to even very unusual suggestions, such as getting down on all fours and sniffing in the corner.

Not everyone is equally hypnotizable. Susceptibility varies greatly, such that some hypnotic "virtuosos" are strongly influenced, most people are only moderately influenced, and some people are entirely unaffected. Susceptibility is not easily predicted by a person's personality traits, so tests of hypnotic susceptibility are made up of a series of suggestions in a standard hypnotic induction. One of the best indicators of a person's susceptibility is the person's own judgment. So, if you think you might be hypnotizable, you may well be (Hilgard, 1965). People with active, vivid imaginations, or who are easily absorbed in activities such as watching a movie, are also somewhat more prone to be good candidates for hypnosis (Sheehan, 1979; Tellegen & Atkinson, 1974).

Hypnotic Effects

From watching stage hypnotism, you might think that the major effect of hypnosis is making people do peculiar things. In fact, there are some impressive demonstrations. At the 1849 festivities for Prince Albert of England's birthday, for example, a hypnotized guest was asked to ignore any loud noises and then didn't even flinch when a pistol was fired near his face. The real effects of hypnosis are often clouded, however, by extravagant claims—that hypnotized people can perform extraordinary physical stunts, for example, or that they can remember things they have forgotten in normal consciousness.

Hypnotists often claim that their volunteers can perform great feats not possible when the volunteers are fully conscious. One of the claims for superhuman strength involves asking a hypnotized person to become "stiff as a board" and lie unsupported with shoulders on one chair and feet on another. However, many people can do this without hypnosis. Similarly, the claim that people will perform extreme actions when hypnotized fails to take into account that people will also perform these actions when they are simply under a lot of social pressure. Some early studies reported, for instance,

An 1849 demonstration of hypnosis at the festivities for Prince Albert's birthday. A pistol is discharged near the face of a young man in a trance, and he does not even flinch.

A hypnotist stands on a subject who has been rendered "stiff as a board" by hypnosis.

HULTON-DEUTSCH COLLECTION/CORBIS

that hypnotized people could be led to throw what they thought was a flask of acid in an experimenter's face (Rowland, 1939; Young, 1948). In further examinations of this phenomenon, participants who were not hypnotized were asked to *simulate* being hypnotized (Orne & Evans, 1965). They were instructed to be so convincing in faking their hypnosis that they would fool the experimenter. These people, just like the hypnotized participants, threw what they thought was acid in the experimenter's face! Clearly, hypnotic induction was not a necessary requirement to produce this behavior in the research participants.

Other strong claims for hypnosis have arisen because of the extraordinary agreeableness of many hypnotized people. When a susceptible person under hypnosis is asked to go back in time to childhood, for example, the person may become remarkably childlike, even to the point of babbling like an infant or breaking down in tears. One young man whose first language was Japanese but who was raised speaking English from the age of 8 reverted to Japanese spontaneously when under hypnosis; it was suggested that he was only 3 years old (Hilgard, 1986). Such cases have made psychologists wonder whether there is true "hypnotic age regression" or whether such cases are matters of playacting. (After all, does the hypnotized person who barks like a dog actually *become* a dog?) It turns out that the mental abilities of adults who have been age-regressed in hypnosis do not truly revert to early developmental stages or show childlike ways of thinking (Nash, 1987).

Hypnosis also has been touted as a cure for lost memory. The claim that hypnosis helps people to unearth memories that they are not able to retrieve in normal consciousness, however, seems to have surfaced because hypnotized people often make up memories to satisfy the hypnotist's suggestions. For example, Paul Ingram, a sheriff's deputy accused of sexual abuse by his daughters in the 1980s, was asked by interrogators in session after session to relax and imagine having committed the crimes. He emerged from these sessions having confessed to dozens of horrendous acts of "satanic ritual abuse." These confessions were called into question, however, when independent investigator Richard Ofshe used the same technique to ask Ingram about a crime that Ofshe had simply made up out of thin air, something of which Ingram had never been accused. Ingram produced a three-page handwritten confession, complete with dialogue (Ofshe, 1992). Still, prosecutors in the case accepted Ingram's guilty plea, and he was only released in 2003 after a public outcry and years of work on his defense. After a person claims to remember something, even under hypnosis, it is difficult to convince others that the memory was false (Loftus & Ketchum, 1994).

POSTHYPNOTIC AMNESIA The failure to retrieve memories following hypnotic suggestions to forget.

HYPNOTIC ANALGESIA The reduction of pain through hypnosis in people who are susceptible to hypnosis.

Hypnosis can also undermine memory. People susceptible to hypnosis can be led to experience **posthypnotic amnesia**, *the failure to retrieve memories following hypnotic suggestions to forget.* Ernest Hilgard (1986) taught a hypnotized person the populations of some remote cities, for example, and then suggested that he forget the study session. The person was quite surprised after the session at being able to give the census figures correctly. (Asked how he knew the answers, the individual decided he might have learned them from a TV program.) Such amnesia can then be reversed in subsequent hypnosis.

However, research does *not* find that people can retrieve through hypnosis memories that were not originally lost through hypnosis. Instead, hypnotized people try to report memories in line with the hypnotist's questioning. In one study, 27 hypnotizable research volunteers were given suggestions during hypnosis that they had been awakened by loud noises in the night a week before. After hypnosis, 13 of them—roughly 50%—reported that they had been awakened by loud noises (Laurence & Perry, 1983). Hypnosis does not enhance the accuracy of memory and instead only increases the person's *confidence* in false memory reports (Kihlstrom, 1985).

Although all the preceding claims for hypnosis are somewhat debatable, one well-established effect is **hypnotic analgesia**, *the reduction of pain through hypnosis in people who are hypnotically susceptible.* For example, one study (see **FIGURE 8.11**) found that for pain induced in volunteers in the laboratory, hypnosis was more effective than morphine, diazepam (Valium), aspirin, acupuncture, or placebos (Stern et al., 1977). For people who are hypnotically susceptible, hypnosis can be used to control pain in surgeries and dental procedures, in some cases more effectively than any form of anesthesia (Druckman & Bjork, 1994; Kihlstrom, 1985). Evidence for pain control supports the idea that hypnosis is a different state of consciousness and not entirely a matter of skillful role-playing on the part of highly motivated people.

The conscious state of hypnosis is accompanied by unique patterns of brain activation. In one study, researchers prescreened highly hypnotizable people for their ability to hallucinate during hypnosis (Szechtman et al., 1998). After a standard hypnotic induction, these participants were tested in a PET (positron emission tomography) scanner while performing each of three tasks: perception, imagination, and hypnotic hallucination. For the perception task, participants heard a recording of the sentence "The man did not speak often, but when he did, it was worth hearing what he had to say." For the imagination task, they were asked to imagine hearing this line again. For the hypnotic hallucination task, they listened as the hypnotist suggested that the tape was playing once more (although it was not). The researchers expected this last suggestion to prompt an auditory hallucination of the line, and participants indeed reported thinking they heard it.

Figure 8.11 **Hypnotic Analgesia** The degree of pain reduction reported by people using different techniques for the treatment of laboratory-induced pain. Hypnosis wins. From Stern et al., 1977.

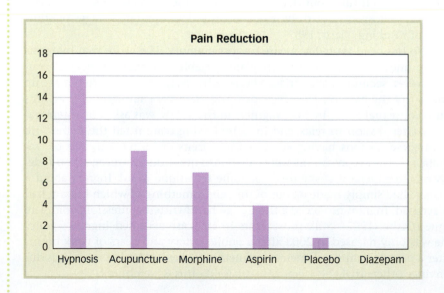

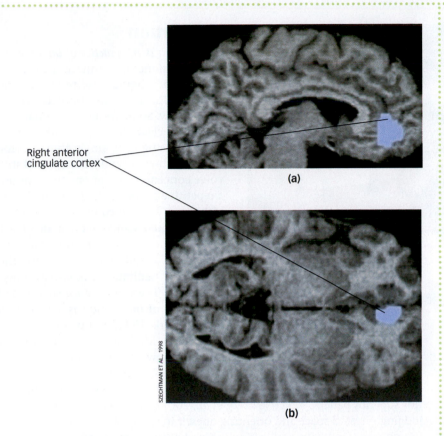

Right anterior
cingulate cortex

(a)

SZECHTMAN ET AL., 1998

(b)

Figure 8.12 **Brain Activity during Hypnosis** Researchers found right anterior cingulate cortex activation in hypnotized research participants both when they were hearing a target sentence and when they were following the suggestion to hallucinate the sentence. The right anterior cingulate cortex is involved in the regulation of attention. The brain is viewed here in two cross-sectional scans: (a) upright and (b) horizontal.

The PET scan revealed that the right anterior cingulate cortex, an area involved in the regulation of attention, was just as active while the participants were hallucinating as when they were actually hearing the line. However, there was less activation in this brain area when participants were merely imagining the sentence. **FIGURE 8.12** shows where the right anterior cingulate area was activated in the hypnotizable participants both during hearing and hallucinating. This pattern of activation was not found in people who were not highly hypnotizable. The researchers concluded that hypnosis stimulated the brain to register the hallucinated voice as real rather than as imagined.

In summary, although there are many claims for hypnosis that overstate its effects, this altered state of consciousness characterized by suggestibility does have a range of real effects on individuals who are susceptible. Inductions of hypnosis can create the experience that one's actions are occurring involuntarily, influence memory reports, lead people to experience posthypnotic amnesia, create analgesia, and even change brain activations in ways that suggest that hypnotic experiences are more than imagination. ■ ■

Meditation and Religious Experiences: Higher Consciousness

Some altered states of consciousness occur without hypnosis, without drugs, and without other external aids. In fact, the altered states of consciousness that occur naturally or through special practices such as meditation can provide some of the best moments in life. Abraham Maslow (1962) described these "peak experiences" as special states of mind in which you feel fully alive and glad to be human. Sometimes these come from simple pleasures—a breathtaking sunset or a magical moment of personal creativity—and other times they can arise through meditative or religious experiences.

Meditation can confer physical and psychological benefits on its practitioners—but research has not yet determined how it might work.

Meditation

Meditation is *the practice of intentional contemplation.* Techniques of meditation are associated with a variety of religious traditions and are also practiced outside religious contexts. The techniques vary widely. Some forms of meditation call for attempts to clear the mind of thought, others involve focusing on a single thought (for example, thinking about a candle flame), and still others involve concentration on breathing or on a mantra, a repetitive sound such as *om*. At a minimum, the techniques have in common a period of quiet.

Why would someone meditate? The time spent meditating can be restful and revitalizing, and according to meditation enthusiasts, the repeated practice of meditation can enhance psychological well-being. The evidence for such long-term positive effects of meditation is controversial (Druckman & Bjork, 1994), but meditation does produce temporarily altered patterns of brain activation. Meditation influences EEG recordings of brain waves, usually producing patterns known as *alpha waves* that are associated with relaxation (Dillbeck & Orme-Johnson, 1987). A brain-scanning study of Buddhist practitioners during meditation found especially low levels of activation in the posterior superior parietal lobe (Newberg et al., 2001). This area is normally associated with judging physical space and orienting oneself in space—knowing angles, distances, and the physical landscape and distinguishing between the self and other objects in space. When this area is deactivated during meditation, its normal function of locating the self in space may subside to yield an experience of immersion and a loss of self.

Ecstatic Religious Experiences

In some religious traditions, people describe personal experiences of altered consciousness—feelings of ecstasy, rapture, conversion, or mystical union. Members of a religious group may "speak in tongues," or the celebrants may go into trances, report seeing visions, or feel as though they are possessed by spirits. These altered states may happen during prayer or worship or without any special religious activity. Over 40% of one sample of Americans reported having a profound experience of this kind at least once in their lives (Greeley, 1975), and altered states of consciousness of one sort or another are associated with religious practices around the world (Bourguignon, 1968).

Whirling dervishes of the Mevlevi order of Sufism perform the Sema, a spiritual ceremony that aids in their quest for divine illumination.

MEDITATION The practice of intentional contemplation.

Like meditation, certain brain activation patterns are associated with ecstatic religious experiences. Some people who experience religious fervor show the same type of brain activation that occurs in some cases of epilepsy. Several prophets, saints, and founders of religions have been documented as having epilepsy—Joan of Arc, for example, had symptoms of epilepsy accompanying the religious visions that inspired her and her followers (Saver & Rabin, 1997). People asked to describe what it is like to have a seizure, in turn, sometimes report feeling what they call a religious "aura." One patient described his seizures as consisting of feelings of incredible contentment, detachment, and fulfillment, accompanied by the visualization of a bright light and soft music; sometimes he also saw a bearded man he assumed was Jesus Christ (Morgan, 1990). Surgery to remove a tumor in the patient's right anterior temporal lobe eliminated the seizures but also stopped his religious ecstasies. Cases such as this suggest the right anterior temporal lobe might be involved when people without epilepsy experience profound religious feelings. The special moments of connection that people feel with God or the universe may depend on the way in which brain activation promotes a religious state of consciousness.

The states of religious ecstasy and meditation are just two of the intriguing varieties of experience that consciousness makes available to us. Our consciousness ranges from the normal everyday awareness of walking, thinking, or gazing at a picture to an array of states that are far from normal or every day—sleep, dreams, drug intoxication, hypnosis, and beyond. These states of mind stand as a reminder that the human mind is not just something that students of psychology can look at and study. The mind is something each of us looks *through* at the world and at ourselves.

In summary, meditation and religious ecstasy can be understood as altered states of consciousness. Meditation involves contemplation that may focus on a specific thought, sound, or action (such as breathing) or may be an attempt to avoid any focus. The practice of meditation promotes relaxation in the short term, but the long-term benefits claimed by enthusiasts have not been established. Ecstatic religious experiences may have a basis in the same brain region—the right anterior temporal lobe—associated with some forms of epilepsy. ■ ■

Where Do You Stand?

Between NORML and MADD: What Is Acceptable Drug Use?

Where is the line between drug use and abuse, between acceptable chemical alteration of consciousness and over-the-top drug-crazed insanity? Some people think that the line is drawn too strictly—organizations such as NORML (National Organization for the Reform of Marijuana Laws) lobby for the legalization of marijuana. Others think the line is too loose—MADD (Mothers Against Drunk Driving) asks bars and restaurants to end "happy hours" that promote alcohol consumption. At the extremes, some people advocate the legalization of cocaine and heroin (for instance, Jenny Tonge, member of the British Parliament), and others propose to fight caffeine addiction (for example, Rosemarie Ives, mayor of Redmond, Washington). Where do you stand?

It may not be entirely clear where you stand after all because you may not have thought this through. Drug use is a controversial topic, and whenever it comes up, you may find yourself face-to-face with people who have very strong opinions. Talking with some people about drugs and alcohol may feel like talking with interrogators under a bright light down at the police station, and you may find yourself taking sides that do not reflect how you really feel. On the other hand, people you know who drink or use drugs may make you feel like a stick-in-the-mud if you don't always approve of what they're doing. Where do you stand? Should people be legally allowed to use psychoactive drugs and if yes, which ones? What about alcohol? Should there be restrictions on when or where these substances are used? For a legal drug, how old should a person be to use it?

Chapter Review

Conscious and Unconscious: The Mind's Eye, Open and Closed

- Consciousness is a mystery of psychology because other people's minds cannot be perceived directly and also because the relationship between mind and body is perplexing.

- Consciousness is intentional, unified, and selective but transient and can be viewed as having levels of minimal consciousness, full consciousness, and self-consciousness. The contents of the stream of consciousness include current concerns, daydreams, and unwanted thoughts.

- Unconscious processes are sometimes understood as expressions of the Freudian dynamic unconscious but are more commonly seen as processes of the cognitive unconscious that create and influence conscious thoughts and behaviors.

Sleep and Dreaming: Good Night, Mind

- The sleep cycle involves a regular pattern of sleep and dreaming that creates altered states of consciousness. Humans progress through stages of NREM and REM sleep throughout the night.

- There are several sleep disorders that influence the quality of both sleep and dreams, including insomnia, sleep apnea, somnambulism, narcolepsy, sleep paralysis, nightmares, and night terrors.

- Sleep deprivation and dream deprivation are both detrimental to psychological effectiveness and physical health.

- The contents of dreams are related to waking life and can be understood by examining the areas of the brain that are activated when people dream. Different theories about why dreams occur and their potential meanings have been proposed. Older views focus on symbolism and the unconscious, whereas more recent accounts approach dreaming as an aspect of normal brain activity.

Drugs and Consciousness: Artificial Inspiration

- Psychoactive drugs influence consciousness and sometimes produce addiction. Addiction to drugs involves drug tolerance and drug withdrawal, which may include both physical and psychological dependence.

- Specific effects on consciousness and behavior occur with different classes of psychoactive drugs. These classes include depressants, stimulants, narcotics, hallucinogens, and marijuana.

- Depressants are substances that reduce the activity of the central nervous system, producing a sedative or calming effect. Examples of depressants are alcohol, barbiturates, benzodiazepines, and toxic inhalants. Stimulants are substances that excite the nervous system and include caffeine, amphetamines, nicotine, cocaine, and ecstasy (MDMA).

- Narcotics are highly addictive drugs derived from opium, such as heroin, morphine, methadone, and codeine. Hallucinogens produce altered sensations and perceptions. Examples include LSD, psilocybin, mescaline, PCP, and ketamine.

- Marijuana, the leaves and buds of the hemp plant, produces heightened sensations but impairs memory and motor skills.

Hypnosis: Open to Suggestion

- Inductions of hypnosis can alter consciousness in people who are susceptible, making them feel that their actions are occurring involuntarily and leading them to follow the hypnotist's suggestions.

- Hypnosis can cause amnesia and lead people to make up memories but is useful as an analgesic for pain.

Meditation and Religious Experiences: Higher Consciousness

- Changes in consciousness away from the normal state may be attained through meditation, yielding short-term relaxation but no clearly measured long-term effects.

- Religious experiences are sometimes associated with brain regions that are also affected by epilepsy.

Key Terms

consciousness (p. 294)

Cartesian Theater (p. 294)

phenomenology (p. 295)

problem of other minds (p. 295)

mind/body problem (p. 297)

dichotic listening (p. 298)

cocktail party phenomenon (p. 299)

minimal consciousness (p. 300)

full consciousness (p. 300)

self-consciousness (p. 301)

mental control (p. 303)

thought suppression (p. 303)

rebound effect of thought suppression (p. 303)

ironic processes of mental control (p. 304)

dynamic unconscious (p. 305)

repression (p. 305)

cognitive unconscious (p. 306)

subliminal perception (p. 306)

altered state of consciousness (p. 309)

circadian rhythm (p. 309)

REM sleep (p. 310)

electrooculograph (EOG) (p. 311)

insomnia (p. 313)

sleep apnea (p. 313)

somnambulism (p. 313)

narcolepsy (p. 314)

sleep paralysis (p. 314)

night terrors (p. 314)

manifest content (p. 317)

latent content (p. 317)

activation-synthesis model (p. 317)

psychoactive drugs (p. 318)

drug tolerance (p. 319)

depressants (p. 321)

expectancy theory (p. 321)

balanced placebo design (p. 322)

alcohol myopia (p. 322)

stimulants (p. 323)

narcotics or opiates (p. 324)

harm reduction approach (p. 325)

endorphins or endogenous opiates (p. 325)

hallucinogens (p. 326)

marijuana (p. 326)

hypnosis (p. 327)

posthypnotic amnesia (p. 330)

hypnotic analgesia (p. 330)

meditation (p. 332)

Recommended Readings

Blackmore, S. (2004). *Consciousness: An introduction.* New York: Oxford University Press. Susan Blackmore is the sort of writer whom you might expect would show up every few weeks with her hair freshly dyed in a new pattern of rainbow colors, and in fact this is exactly what she does. Her book blends philosophy, psychology, and neuroscience in a clear, enjoyable, and colorfully written introduction to the field of consciousness.

Hobson, A. (1988). *The dreaming brain.* New York: Basic Books. This book's subtitle is "How the Brain Creates Both the Sense and the Nonsense of Dreams." Hobson examines the history of dream theories, including psychoanalytic theory, and then provides his own "activation synthesis" hypothesis—that dreaming is the brain's way of making sense of its own nighttime activations.

Wegner, D. M. (1994). *White bears and other unwanted thoughts: Suppression, obsession, and the psychology of mental control.* New York: Guilford Press. Why it is that we have so much trouble controlling our own minds? This book describes the initial experiments in which people were asked to try to stop thinking about a white bear—and found they could not.

Wegner, D. M. (2002). *The illusion of conscious will.* Cambridge: MIT Press. This book describes how it is that we come to believe that we consciously will our own actions and examines along the way such anomalies as phantom limbs, Ouija board spelling, spirit possession, and hypnosis.

Zeman, A. (2002). *Consciousness: A user's guide.* New Haven, CT: Yale University Press. The author is a neurologist, and his wide-ranging interests in everything from Shakespeare to the architecture of the brain make for exhilaratingly broad reading—and a high-level introduction to the science of consciousness.

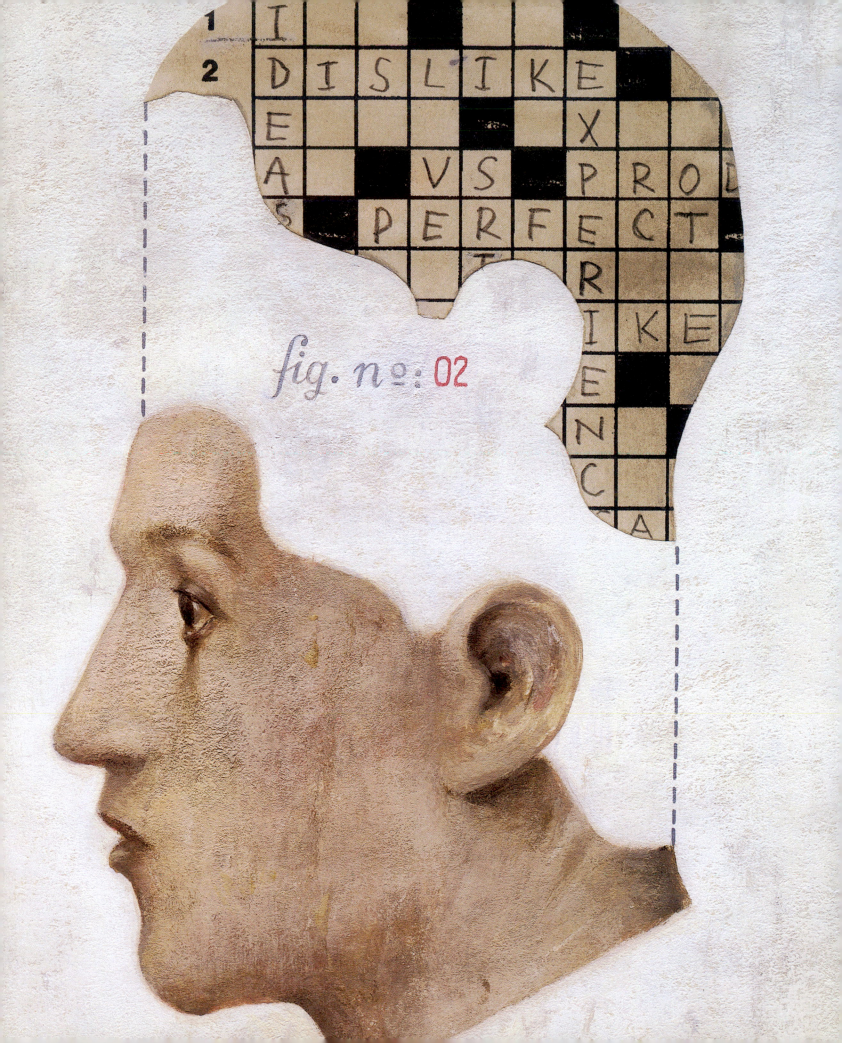

fig. nº: 02

9

Intelligence

The Measurement of Intelligence: Highly Classified
The Intelligence Quotient
The Logic of Intelligence Testing
Consequential Behaviors
THE REAL WORLD Look Smart

The Nature of Intelligence: Pluribus or Unum?
General and Specific Abilities
The Middle-Level Abilities

The Origins of Intelligence: From SES to DNA
Intelligence and Genes
Intelligence and Groups

The Future of Intelligence: Wising Up
Changing Intelligence
Improving Intelligence
HOT SCIENCE The Plot Thickens
WHERE DO YOU STAND? Making Kids Smart or Making Smart Kids?

WHEN ANNE McGARRAH DIED IN 2006 AT the age of 57, she had lived more years than she could count. That's because Anne couldn't count at all. Like most people with Williams syndrome, she couldn't add three and seven, couldn't make change for a dollar, and couldn't distinguish right from left. Indeed, her retardation was so severe that she was unable to care for herself or hold a full-time job. So what did she do with her time?

"I love to read. Biographies, fiction, novels, different articles in newspapers, articles in magazines, just about anything. I just read a book about a young girl—she was born in Scotland—and her family who lived on a farm. . . . I love listening to music. I like a little bit of Beethoven, but I specifically like Mozart and Chopin and Bach. I like the way they develop their music—it's very light, it's very airy, and it's very cheerful music. I find Beethoven depressing." (Finn, 1991, p. 54)

People with Williams syndrome have a distinct "elfin" facial appearance characterized by a wide mouth, a prominent lower lip, small evenly spaced teeth, a sunken nasal bridge, and blue eyes with a starry pattern.

Although people with Williams syndrome are often unable to tie their own shoes or make their own beds, they typically have gifts for speech and music that anyone might envy. Williams syndrome is caused by the absence of 20 genes on chromosome 7, and no one knows why this tiny genetic glitch so profoundly impairs a person's cognitive abilities and yet spares his or her capacity for music and language.

Was Anne McGarrah intelligent? That's a difficult question. It seems odd to say that someone is intelligent when she can't do simple addition, but it seems equally odd to say that someone is unintelligent when she can articulate the difference between baroque counterpoint and 19th-century romanticism. In a world of Albert Einsteins and Homer Simpsons, we'd have no trouble distinguishing the geniuses from the dullards. But ours is a world of people like Anne McGarrah and people like us—people who are sometimes brilliant, typically competent, and occasionally dimmer than broccoli. Such complexity forces us to ask hard questions. What exactly is intelligence? How can it be measured? Where does it come from? Can it be improved? Psychologists have been asking such questions for more than a century, and in this chapter we will discuss the progress they've made in answering them.

We will first discuss how intelligence is measured and then discuss what intelligence is. If this seems backward to you, then you are very intelligent. It *is* backward. But for the best of reasons and the worst of reasons, psychologists attempted to measure intelligence long before they knew what it was. As you'll see, the attempt to measure intelligence is what ultimately forced psychologists to ask and answer the deeper questions about its nature.

The Measurement of Intelligence: Highly Classified

Few things are more dangerous than a man with a mission. In the 1920s, psychologist Henry Goddard administered intelligence tests to arriving immigrants at Ellis Island and concluded that the overwhelming majority of Jews, Hungarians, Italians, and Russians were "feebleminded." Goddard also used his tests to identify feebleminded American families (whom, he claimed, were largely responsible for the nation's social problems) and suggested that the government should segregate them in isolated colonies and "take away from these people the power of procreation" (Goddard, 1913, p. 107). The United States subsequently passed laws restricting the immigration of people from Southern and Eastern Europe, and 27 states passed laws requiring the sterilization of "mental defectives."

When immigrants arrived at Ellis Island in the 1920s they were given intelligence tests, which supposedly revealed that Jews, Hungarians, Italians, and Russians were "feebleminded."

From Goddard's day to our own, intelligence tests have been used to rationalize prejudice and legitimate discrimination against people of different races, religions, and nationalities, and while intelligence testing has achieved many notable successes, its history is marred by more than its share of fraud and disgrace (Chorover, 1980; Lewontin, Rose, & Kamin, 1984). The fact that intelligence tests have occasionally been used to further detestable ends is especially ironic because, as we are about to see, such tests were originally developed for a noble purpose: to help the poorest schoolchildren prosper, learn, and grow.

The Intelligence Quotient

At the end of the 19th century, France instituted a sweeping set of education reforms that made a primary school education available to children of every social class, and suddenly French classrooms were filled with a heterogeneous mix of children who differed dramatically in their readiness to learn. The French government called on psychologist Alfred Binet and physician Theophile Simon to develop a test that would allow educators to develop remedial programs for those children who lagged behind their peers. "Before these children could be educated," Binet (1909) wrote, "they had to be selected. How could this be done?"

Alfred Binet (left, 1857–1911) and Theodore Simon (right, 1872–1961) developed the first intelligence test to identify children who needed remedial education.

Binet and Simon worried that if teachers were allowed to do the selecting, then the remedial classrooms would be filled with poor children, and if parents were allowed to do the selecting, then the remedial classrooms would be empty. So they set out to develop an objective test that would provide an unbiased measure of a child's ability. They began, sensibly enough, by looking for tasks that the best students in a class could perform and that the worst students could not—in other words, tasks that could distinguish the best and worst students in a current class and could be used to predict a future child's success in school. The tasks they tried included solving logic problems; remembering words; copying pictures; distinguishing edible and inedible foods; making rhymes; and answering questions such as, "When anyone has offended you and asks you to excuse him, what ought you to do?" Binet and Simon settled on 30 of these tasks and assembled them into a test that they claimed could measure a child's "natural intelligence." What did they mean by that phrase?

> We here separate natural intelligence and instruction . . . by disregarding, insofar as possible, the degree of instruction which the subject possesses. . . . We give him nothing to read, nothing to write, and submit him to no test in which he might succeed by means of rote learning. In fact, we do not even notice his inability to read if a case occurs. It is simply the level of his natural intelligence that is taken into account. (Binet, 1905)

Binet and Simon designed their test to measure a child's *aptitude* for learning independent of the child's prior educational *achievement*, and it was in this sense that they called theirs a test of "natural intelligence." They suggested that teachers could use their test to estimate a child's "mental level" simply by computing the average test score of children in different age groups and then finding the age group whose average test score was most like that of the child's. For example, a child who was 10 years old but whose score was about the same as the score of the average 8-year-old was considered to have the mental level of an 8-year-old and thus to need remedial education.

German psychologist William Stern (1914) suggested that this mental level could be thought of as a child's *mental age* and that the best way to determine whether a child was developing normally was to examine the ratio of the child's mental age to the child's physical age. American psychologist Lewis Terman (1916) formalized this comparison with the intelligence quotient or **ratio IQ**, which is *a statistic obtained by dividing a person's mental age by the person's physical age and then multiplying the quotient by 100.* Thus, a 10-year-old child whose test score was about the same as the average 10-year-old child's test score would have a ratio IQ of 100 because $(10/10) \times 100 = 100$. But a 10-year-old child whose test score was about the same as the average 8-year-old child's test score would have a ratio IQ of 80 because $(8/10) \times 100 = 80$.

RATIO IQ A statistic obtained by dividing a person's mental age by the person's physical age and then multiplying the quotient by 100 (see *deviation IQ*).

William Stern (left, 1871–1938) and Lewis Terman (right, 1877–1956) devised the idea of the intelligence quotient. The abbreviation *IQ* has become a common synonym for intelligence.

DEVIATION IQ A statistic obtained by dividing a person's test score by the average test score of people in the same age group and then multiplying the quotient by 100 (see *ratio IQ*).

The ratio of a person's mental and physical ages seems like a handy way to talk about his or her intelligence—until you actually stop and think about it. For example, a 6-year-old who performs like the average 12-year-old will have a ratio IQ of 200. That makes a certain amount of sense because a 6-year-old who can do algebra is pretty darn smart. But a 30-year-old who performs like the average 60-year-old will also have a ratio IQ of 200. That doesn't make much sense because it means that a perfectly ordinary 30-year-old need only maintain his or her mental abilities for a few decades to be labeled a genius.

As a result of anomalies such as this, researchers devised a new measure called the **deviation IQ**, which is *a statistic obtained by dividing a person's test score by the average test score of people in the same age group and then multiplying the quotient by 100*. According to this formula, a person who scored the same as the average person his or her age would have a deviation IQ of 100. The good thing about the deviation IQ is that a 30-year-old cannot become a genius simply by getting older. The bad thing about the deviation IQ is that it does not allow comparisons between people of different ages. A 5-year-old and a 65-year-old might both have a deviation IQ of 120 because they both outscored their peers, but this does not mean that they are equally intelligent. To solve this problem, modern researchers compute the ratio IQ for children and the deviation IQ for adults. **FIGURE 9.1** shows the percentage of people who typically score at each level of IQ on a standard intelligence test.

 **ONLY HUMAN**

THE FAILURE OF PRACTICAL INTELLIGENCE In 1993, police charged Vernon Edsel Brooks of Raleigh, North Carolina, with robbing a Radio Shack. Although Brooks had been smart enough to take the surveillance camera with him when he fled, he neglected to take the recorder to which it was attached.

Figure 9.1 The Normal Curve of Intelligence Deviation IQ scores produce a normal curve. This chart shows the percentage of people who score in each range of IQ.

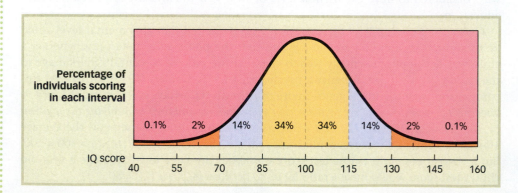

Percentage of individuals scoring in each interval

0.1% 2% 14% 34% 34% 14% 2% 0.1%

IQ score

40 55 70 85 100 115 130 145 160

The Logic of Intelligence Testing

Binet and Simon's test did a good job of predicting a child's performance in school, and intelligence is surely one of the factors that contributes to that performance. But surely there are others. Affability, motivation, intact hearing, doting parents—all of these seem likely to influence a child's scholastic performance. Binet and Simon's test identified students who were likely to perform poorly in school, but was it a test of intelligence?

As you learned in Chapter 2, psychological research typically involves generating an operational definition of a hypothetical property that one wishes to measure. For instance, if we wanted to study aggressiveness in children, we might operationally define it as "shoving others." We might then measure aggressiveness by following a small group of children around for a week and noting how many times they shoved. Of course, that kind of measurement takes such a long time that it wouldn't be practical to do with a large group of children, so we might instead develop a set of questions ("Do you believe that most people need a good kick in the shins from time to time?") or a set of tasks ("How quickly can you decapitate this doll?") that are easy to administer and the answers to which are known to be highly correlated with shoving.

We could then easily give this set of questions and tasks—which we could call a *test*—to a large group of children. But would it be an "aggressiveness test"? Strictly speaking, no. It would be a measure of *responses* ("Yes, I think most people do need a good kick in the shins from time to time") that are known to be correlated with *consequential behaviors* (shoving) that are thought to be correlated with a *hypothetical property* (aggressiveness). Our test would be quite useful for identifying bullies before they bloodied their peers, but it would not be a test of aggressiveness because the correlation between the responses and the consequential behaviors would be imperfect (e.g., some children will say that others need a good kick in the shins but then not actually do it), and the correlation between the consequential behaviors and the property would be imperfect too (e.g., some children may shove because they are nearsighted or clumsy).

What's true of aggressiveness tests is also true of intelligence tests. **FIGURE 9.2** illustrates the distinction between *responses, consequential behaviors,* and *hypothetical properties* and shows how an intelligence test is built. We begin with the assumption that a hypothetical property called intelligence enables people to perform a wide variety of consequential behaviors such as getting good grades in school, becoming a group leader, earning a large income, finding the best route to the gym, or inventing a greaseless burrito. Measuring how well people perform each of these consequential behaviors would, of course, be highly impractical, so we instead devise an easily administered set of tasks (e.g., a geometric puzzle) and questions (e.g., "*Butterfly* is to *caterpillar* as *woman* is to ____") whose performance is known to be correlated with those behaviors. Now, instead of measuring the consequential behaviors (which is difficult to do), we can simply give people our test (which is easy to do). We could certainly call this "an intelligence test" as long as we understood that what we mean by that phrase is "a measurement of responses that are imperfectly correlated with consequential behaviors that are imperfectly correlated with intelligence." In other words, intelligence tests do not "measure" intelligence in the same way that thermometers measure temperature. Rather, they measure the ability to answer questions and perform tasks that are highly correlated with the ability to get good grades, solve real-world problems, and so on.

Finding such questions and tasks isn't easy, and since Binet and Simon's day, psychologists have worked hard to construct intelligence tests that can predict a person's ability to perform the consequential behaviors that intelligence should make possible. Today the most widely used intelligence tests are the *Stanford-Binet* (a test that is based on Binet and Simon's original test but that has

Is a Rubik's Cube an intelligence test? Intelligence is a hypothetical property that makes possible consequential behavior such as school achievement and job performance, and people who can perform such behaviors can often solve puzzles like this one.

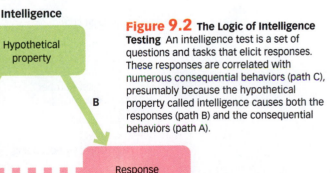

Figure 9.2 The Logic of Intelligence Testing An intelligence test is a set of questions and tasks that elicit responses. These responses are correlated with numerous consequential behaviors (path C), presumably because the hypothetical property called intelligence causes both the responses (path B) and the consequential behaviors (path A).

Intelligence
Hypothetical property

A   B

Consequential behavior — C — Response

**Grades in school
Job performance
Income
Health, etc.**

Questions and tasks

been modified and updated many times, most notably by Lewis Terman and his colleagues at Stanford University) and the *WAIS* (the Wechsler Adult Intelligence Scale). Both tests require respondents to answer a variety of questions and solve a variety of problems. For example, the WAIS's 13 subtests involve seeing similarities and differences, drawing inferences, working out and applying rules, remembering and manipulating material, constructing shapes, articulating the meaning of words, recalling general knowledge, explaining practical actions in everyday life, working with numbers, attending to details, and so forth. Only 3 of the 13 tests require the examinee to write anything down, and none requires writing words. Some sample problems are shown in **TABLE 9.1.**

Table 9.1	The Wechsler Adult Intelligence Scale III
WAIS-III Subtest	**Mental Activity Assessed**
Vocabulary	The test taker is asked to tell the examiner what certain words mean. For example, *chair* (easy), *hesitant* (medium), *presumptuous* (hard). There are 33 words in all.
Similarities	The test taker says what two words have in common. For example: In what way are an apple and a pear alike? In what way are a painting and a symphony alike? There are 19 such questions.
Information	There are 28 general knowledge questions. These cover people, places, and events. For example: How many days are in a week? What is the capital of France? Name three oceans. Who wrote *The Inferno*?
Comprehension	These are questions about everyday life problems, aspects of society, and proverbs. For example: "Tell me some reasons why we put food in a refrigerator." "Why do people require driving licenses?" What does it mean to say "a bird in the hand is worth two in the bush"?
Picture completion	The test taker is asked to spot the missing element in a series of more than 20 color drawings. For example: Spokes might be missing from one wheel in a picture of a bicycle; in a picture of a person, the person's jacket could be missing a buttonhole.
Block design	The test taker is shown two-dimensional patterns made up of red and white squares and triangles. He or she has to reproduce these patterns using cubes with red and white faces.
Matrix reasoning	The test taker is asked to add a missing element to a pattern so that it progresses logically.
Picture arrangement	The test taker is given a series of cartoon drawings and asked to put them in an order that tells a logical story.
Arithmetic	The test taker attempts to solve 20 mental arithmetic problems, progressing from easy to difficult ones.
Digit span	The test taker repeats a sequence of numbers to the examiner. Sequences run from two to nine numbers in length. In the second part of this test, the sequences must be repeated in reversed order. An easy example is to repeat 3-7-4. A harder one is 3-9-1-7-4-5-3-9.
Letter-number sequencing	The examiner reads a series of alternate letters and numbers. The test taker is asked to repeat them, putting the numbers first and in numerical order, followed by the letters in alphabetical order. For example, he or she would repeat "W-4-G-8-L-3" as "3-4-8-G-L-W."
Digit symbol coding	The test taker writes down the number that corresponds to a code for a given symbol (for example, a cross, a circle, and an upside-down T) and does as many as he or she can in 90 seconds.
Symbol search	The test taker indicates whether one of a pair of abstract symbols is contained in a list of abstract symbols. There are many of these lists, and the test taker does as many as he or she can in 2 minutes.

Consequential Behaviors

What are the consequential behaviors that scores on these tests predict? Binet and Simon would be pleased to know that intelligence tests predict school performance better than they predict just about anything else. The correlation between a person's score on a standard intelligence test and his or her academic performance is roughly $r = .5$ across a wide range of people and situations. An intelligence test score is also the best predictor of the number of years of education an individual will receive, which is in part why these scores also predict a person's occupational status and income. For example, a person's score on an intelligence test taken in early adulthood correlates about $r = .4$ with the person's later occupational status (Jencks, 1979). One study of brothers found that the brother who exceeded his sibling by 15 IQ points had, on average, about 17% greater annual earnings. **FIGURE 9.3** shows the average weekly income of people who have equal amounts of education but different intelligence test scores. There is also a strong correlation between the average intelligence score of a nation and its overall economic status (Lynn & Vanhanen, 2002). Clearly, it pays to be smart.

Some psychologists have pointed out that prestigious occupations with high salaries typically require professional degrees and that professional schools typically use test scores as one of their criteria for admission, which means that intelligence test scores may *predict* occupational success in part because they *influence* it. Although this is probably true, it is also true that intelligence test scores predict outcomes that they cannot possibly influence, such as how likely teenagers are to commit crimes and how long adults will live, neither of which is determined by a college admissions committee (Gottfredson & Deary, 2004; Whalley & Deary, 2001).

Indeed, a reanalysis of the data from thousands of studies revealed that intelligence test scores are among the best predictors of how well employees perform in their jobs (Hunter & Hunter, 1984), and job performance correlates more highly with intelligence ($r = .53$) than with factors such as performance during a job interview ($r = .14$) or education ($r = .10$). The conclusion to be drawn from almost a century of research on the topic is that "for hiring employees without previous experience in the job, the most valid measure of future performance and learning is general mental ability" (Schmidt & Hunter, 1998, p. 252). Because these tests are such good predictors of job performance, the cost of *not* using them in the United States would equal total corporate profits, or 20% of the federal budget (Hunter & Hunter, 1984).

But intelligence scores don't just predict success at school and work. Intelligence scores also do a reasonably good job of predicting a wide variety of behaviors that most of us think of as "smart" (see The Real World Box on page 345). One study identified 320 people with extremely high intelligence test scores at age 13 and followed them for 10 years (Lubinski et al., 2001). Not only were they 50 times more likely than the general population to get graduate degrees and 500 times more likely than the general population to obtain a perfect score on the Graduate Record Examination, but also, at a time when fewer than a quarter of their peers had completed an undergraduate degree, they had already published scientific studies in peer-reviewed journals and stories in leading literary magazines, obtained prestigious scholastic fellowships, written operas, developed successful commercial products, and obtained patents. Clearly,

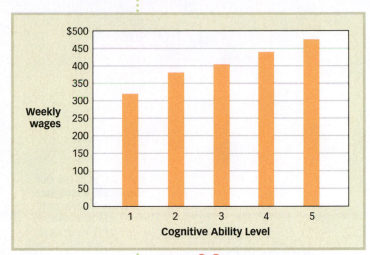

Figure 9.3 Income and Intelligence When amount of education is held constant, people's cognitive abilities still predict their incomes.
Adapted from Ceci & Williams (1997).

Intelligence is highly correlated with income. *Jeopardy* contestant Ken Jennings finally lost on September 7, 2004, after becoming the biggest money winner in TV game show history at the time, earning $2,520,700 over a 74-game run.

JEOPARDY PRODUCTIONS VIA GETTY IMAGES

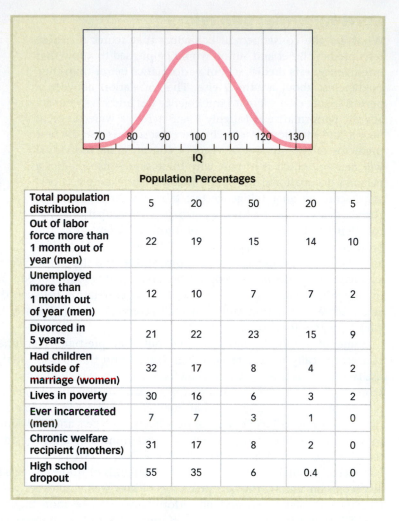

IQ

Population Percentages

	70	80	90	100	110	120	130
Total population distribution	5		20	50	20		5
Out of labor force more than 1 month out of year (men)	22		19	15	14		10
Unemployed more than 1 month out of year (men)	12		10	7	7		2
Divorced in 5 years	21		22	23	15		9
Had children outside of marriage (women)	32		17	8	4		2
Lives in poverty	30		16	6	3		2
Ever incarcerated (men)	7		7	3	1		0
Chronic welfare recipient (mothers)	31		17	8	2		0
High school dropout	55		35	6	0.4		0

Figure 9.4 Life Outcomes and Intelligence
People with lower intelligence test scores typically have poorer life outcomes. This chart shows the percentage of people at different levels of IQ who experience the negative life outcomes listed in the leftmost column.
Adapted from Gottfredson (1998).

intelligence scores predict many of the behaviors that we would expect intelligent people to perform (see **FIGURE 9.4**).

Moreover, intelligence test scores predict very basic responses that cannot possibly be influenced by the scores themselves. For instance, when people are briefly exposed to a pair of vertical lines and are asked to determine which is longer, people with high intelligence test scores have considerably shorter "inspection times," which is defined as the minimum duration of exposure necessary to get the answer right (Deary & Stough, 1996; Grudnick & Kranzler, 2001; Nettleback & Lally, 1976). The same is true when people attempt to distinguish between colors or between tones (Acton & Schroeder, 2001). People with high intelligence test scores also have faster and less variable reaction times to almost any kind of stimulus (Deary, Der, & Ford, 2001).

In summary, early intelligence tests were designed to predict a child's scholastic performance but were eventually used to calculate an *intelligence quotient* either as a ratio of the person's mental to physical age or a deviation of the person's test score from the average score of his or her peers. Intelligence is a hypothetical property that cannot be directly measured, so intelligence tests measure responses (to questions and on tasks) that are known to be correlated with consequential behaviors that are thought to be made possible by intelligence. These consequential behaviors include academic performance, job performance, health, and wealth, all of which are enhanced by intelligence. ■ ■

{ THE REAL WORLD } Look Smart

YOUR INTERVIEW IS IN 30 MINUTES. YOU'VE checked your hair twice, eaten your weight in breath mints, combed your resume for typos, and rehearsed your answers to all the standard questions. Now you have to dazzle them with your intelligence whether you've got it or not. Because intelligence is one of the most valued of all human traits, we are often in the business of trying to make others think we're smart regardless of whether that's true. So we make clever jokes and drop the names of some of the longer books we've read in the hope that prospective employers, prospective dates, prospective customers, and prospective in-laws will be appropriately impressed.

But are we doing the right things, and if so, are we getting the credit we deserve? Research shows that ordinary people are, in fact, reasonably good judges of other people's intelligence (Borkenau & Liebler, 1995). For example, observers can look at a pair of photographs and reliably determine which of the two people in them is smarter (Zebrowitz et al., 2002). When observers watch 1-minute videotapes of different people engaged in social interactions, they can accurately estimate which person has the highest IQ—even if they see the videos without sound (Murphy, Hall, & Colvin, 2003).

People base their judgments of intelligence on a wide range of cues, from physical features (being tall and attractive) to dress (being well groomed and wearing glasses) to behavior (walking and talking quickly). And yet, none of these cues is actually a reliable indicator of a person's intelligence. The reason why people are such good judges of intelligence is that in addition to all these useless cues, they also take into account one very useful cue: eye gaze. As it turns out, intelligent people hold the gaze of their conversation partners both when they are speaking and when they are listening, and observers know this, which is what enables them to accurately estimate a person's intelligence despite their mythical beliefs about the informational value of spectacles and neckties (Murphy et al., 2003). All of this is especially true when the observers are women (who tend to be better judges of intelligence) and the people being observed are men (whose intelligence tends to be easier to judge).

The bottom line? Breath mints are fine and a little gel on the cowlick certainly can't hurt, but when you get to the interview, don't forget to stare.

The Nature of Intelligence: Pluribus or Unum?

During the 1990s, Michael Jordan won the National Basketball Association's Most Valuable Player award five times, led the Chicago Bulls to six league championships, and had the highest regular season scoring average in the history of the game. The Associated Press named him the second-greatest athlete of the century, and ESPN named him the first. So when Jordan quit professional basketball in 1993 to join professional baseball, he was as surprised as anyone to find that he—well, there's really no way to say this nicely—sucked. One of his teammates lamented that Jordan "couldn't hit a curveball with an ironing board," and a major-league manager called him "a disgrace to the game" (Wulf, 1994). Given his lackluster performance, it's no wonder that Jordan gave up baseball after just one season and returned to basketball, where he led his team to three consecutive championships.

Michael Jordan's brilliance on the basketball court and his mediocrity on the baseball field proved beyond all doubt that these two sports require different abilities that are not necessarily possessed by the same individual. But if basketball and baseball require different abilities, then what does it mean to say that someone is the greatest athlete of the century? Is *athleticism* a meaningless abstraction? The science of intelligence has grappled with a similar question for more than a hundred years. As we have seen, intelligence test scores predict consequential behaviors that hint at the existence of a hypothetical property called intelligence. But is there really such a property, or is intelligence just a meaningless abstraction?

EUGENE GARCIA/AFP/GETTY IMAGES

Michael Jordan was an extraordinary basketball player and a mediocre baseball player. So was he or wasn't he a great athlete?

General and Specific Abilities

Charles Spearman was a student of Wilhelm Wundt (who founded the first experimental psychology laboratory), and he set out to answer precisely this question. Spearman invented a technique known as **factor analysis**, which is *a statistical technique that explains a large number of correlations in terms of a small number of underlying factors.* (We'll get into a bit more detail about this in the next section.) Although Spearman's technique was complex, his reasoning was simple: If there really is a single, general

FACTOR ANALYSIS A statistical technique that explains a large number of correlations in terms of a small number of underlying factors.

Charles Spearman (left, 1863–1945) discovered that people who did well on one ability test tended to do well on another, which he attributed to a hypothetical property called general intelligence, or *g*. Louis Thurstone (right, 1887–1955) disagreed with Spearman's interpretation of the data and believed that people had several primary mental abilities and not a single ability called general intelligence.

ability called intelligence that enables people to perform a variety of intelligent behaviors, then those who have this ability should do well at just about everything and those who lack it should do well at just about nothing. In other words, if intelligence is a single, general ability, then there should be a very strong, positive correlation between people's performances on all kinds of tests.

To find out if there was, Spearman (1904) measured how well school-age children could discriminate small differences in color, auditory pitch, and weight, and he then correlated these scores with the children's grades in different academic subjects as well as with their teachers' estimates of their intellectual ability. His research revealed two things. First, it revealed that most of these measures were indeed positively correlated: Children who scored high on one measure—for example, distinguishing the musical note C-sharp from D—tended to score high on the other measures—for example, solving algebraic equations. Some psychologists have called this finding "the most replicated result in all of psychology" (Deary, 2000, p. 6). Second, Spearman's research revealed that although different measures were positively correlated, they were not perfectly correlated: The child who had the very highest score on one measure didn't necessarily have the very highest score on *every* measure. Spearman combined these two facts into a **two-factor theory of intelligence**, which suggested that *every task requires a combination of a general ability* (g) *and skills that are specific to the task* (s).

As sensible as Spearman's conclusions were, not everyone agreed with them. Louis Thurstone (1938) noticed that while scores on most tests were indeed positively correlated, scores on verbal tests were more highly correlated with scores on other verbal tests than they were with scores on perceptual tests. Thurstone took this "clustering of correlations" to mean that there was actually no such thing as *g* and that there were instead a few stable and independent mental abilities such as perceptual ability, verbal ability, and numerical ability, which he called the *primary mental abilities*. These primary mental abilities were neither general like *g* (for example, a person might have strong verbal abilities and weak numerical abilities) nor specific like *s* (for example, a person who had strong verbal abilities tended both to speak and read well). In essence, Thurstone argued that just as we have games called *baseball* and *basketball* but no game called *athletics,* so we have abilities such as verbal ability and perceptual ability but no general ability called intelligence. **TABLE 9.2** shows the primary mental abilities that Thurstone identified.

The debate among Spearman, Thurstone, and other mathematical giants was quite technical, and it raged for half a century as psychologists hotly debated the existence

TWO-FACTOR THEORY OF INTELLIGENCE Spearman's theory suggesting that every task requires a combination of a general ability (which he called *g*) and skills that are specific to the task (which he called *s*).

Table 9.2	Thurstone's Primary Mental Abilities
Primary Mental Ability	**Description**
Word fluency	Ability to solve anagrams and to find rhymes, etc.
Verbal comprehension	Ability to understand words and sentences
Number	Ability to make mental and other numerical computations
Space	Ability to visualize a complex shape in various orientations
Memory	Ability to recall verbal material, learn pairs of unrelated words, etc.
Perceptual speed	Ability to detect visual details quickly
Reasoning	Ability to induce a general rule from a few instances

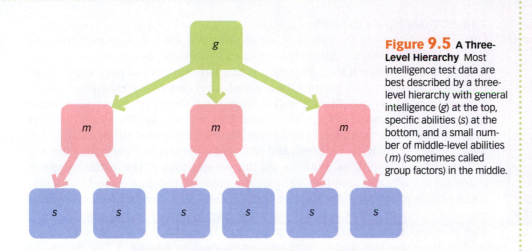

Figure 9.5 **A Three-Level Hierarchy** Most intelligence test data are best described by a three-level hierarchy with general intelligence (*g*) at the top, specific abilities (*s*) at the bottom, and a small number of middle-level abilities (*m*) (sometimes called group factors) in the middle.

of *g*. But in the 1980s, a new mathematical technique called *confirmatory factor analysis* brought the debate to a quiet close by revealing that both Spearman and Thurstone had each been right in his own way. Specifically, this new technique showed that the correlations between scores on different mental ability tests are best described by a three-level hierarchy (see **FIGURE 9.5**) with a *general factor* (like Spearman's *g*) at the top, *specific factors* (like Spearman's *s*) at the bottom, and a set of factors called *group factors* (like Thurstone's *primary mental abilities*) in the middle (Gustafsson, 1984). A re-analysis of massive amounts of data collected over 60 years from more than 130,000 healthy adults, schoolchildren, infants, college students, people with learning disabilities, and people with mental and physical illnesses has shown that almost every study done over the past half century results in a three-level hierarchy of this kind (Carroll, 1993). This hierarchy suggests that people have a very general ability called intelligence, which is made up of a small set of independent subabilities, which are made up of a large set of specific abilities that are unique to particular tasks. Although this resolution to a hundred years of disagreement is not particularly exciting, it has the compensatory benefit of being true.

The Middle-Level Abilities

Michael Jordan played basketball much better than baseball, but he played both sports much better than most people can. His specific abilities allowed him to be more successful at one sport than another, but his general ability allowed him to outperform 99.9% of the world's population on both the court and the field. It is easy to see that Michael Jordan had both specific abilities (dribbling) and a general ability (athleticism), but it is not so easy to say precisely what his middle-level abilities were. Should we draw a distinction between speed and power, between guile and patience, or between the ability to work with a team or perform as an individual? Should we describe his athleticism as a function of 3 middle-level abilities or 4? Or 6? Or 92?

Similar questions arise when we consider intelligence. Most psychologists agree that there are very specific mental abilities as well as a very general mental ability and that one of the important challenges is to describe the broad domains of ability that lie between them. Some psychologists have taken a *bottom-up approach* to this problem by starting with people's responses on intelligence tests and then looking to see what kinds of independent clusters these responses form. Other psychologists have taken a *top-down approach* to this problem by starting with a broad survey of human abilities and then looking to see which of these abilities intelligence tests measure—or fail to measure. These approaches have led to rather different suggestions about the best way to describe the middle-level abilities that constitute intelligence.

PHILIPPE HUGUEN/AFP/GETTY IMAGES

Fluid and crystallized intelligence may have different neural substrates, which may explain why Alzheimer's disease impairs fluid intelligence more strongly than crystallized intelligence.

The Bottom-Up Approach

One way to determine the nature of the middle-level abilities is to start with the data and work our way up. Just as Spearman and Thurstone did, we could compute the correlations between the performances of a large number of people on a large number of tests and then see how those correlations cluster. For example, imagine that we tested how quickly and well a large group of people could (a) balance teacups, (b) understand Shakespeare, (c) swat flies, and (d) sum the whole numbers between one and a thousand. Now imagine that we computed the correlation between scores on each of these tests and observed a pattern of correlations like the one shown in **FIGURE 9.6a.** What would this pattern tell us? This pattern suggests that a person who can swat flies well can also balance teacups well and that a person who can understand Shakespeare well can also sum numbers well but that a person who can swat flies well and balance teacups well may or may not be able to sum numbers or understand Shakespeare well. From this pattern, we could conclude that there are two middle-level abilities (shown in **FIGURE 9.6b**), which we might call "physical coordination" (the ability that allows people to swat flies and balance teacups well) and "academic skill" (the ability that allows people to understand Shakespeare and sum numbers well). This pattern suggests that different specific abilities such as fly swatting and teacup balancing are made possible by a single middle-level ability and that this middle-level ability is unrelated to the other middle-level ability, which makes possible number summing and Shakespeare understanding. As this example reveals, simply by examining the pattern of correlations between different tests, we can divine the nature and number of the middle-level abilities.

In the real world, of course, there are more than four tests. So what kinds of patterns do we observe when we calculate the correlations between the tests of mental ability that psychologists actually use? This is precisely what psychologist John Carroll set out to discover in his landmark analysis of intelligence test scores from nearly 500 studies conducted over a half century (Carroll, 1993). Carroll found that the pattern of correlations among these tests suggested the existence of eight independent middle-level abilities: *memory and learning, visual perception, auditory perception, retrieval ability, cognitive speediness, processing speed, crystallized intelligence,* and *fluid intelligence.* Although most of the abilities on this list are self-explanatory, the last two are not. **Fluid intelligence** is *the ability to process information,* and **crystallized intelligence** is *the accuracy and amount of information available for processing* (Horn & Cattell, 1966). If we think of the brain as a machine that uses old information ("Some spiders don't spin webs" and "All spiders eat insects") as raw material to produce new information ("That means some spiders must stalk their prey rather than trapping them"), then fluid intelligence refers to the way the machine runs and crystallized intelligence refers to the information it uses and produces (Salthouse, 2000). Whereas crystallized intelligence

Figure 9.6 Patterns of Correlation Can Reveal Middle-Level Abilities The pattern of correlations shown in (a) suggests that these four specific abilities can be thought of as instances of the two middle-level abilities — physical coordination and academic skill—shown in (b).

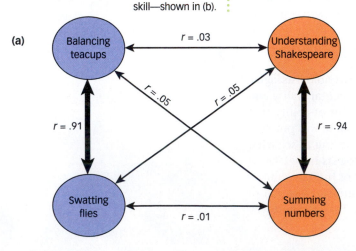

(a)

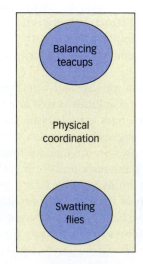

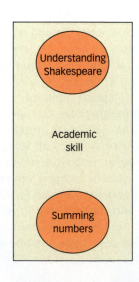

(b)

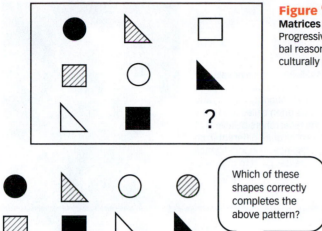

Figure 9.7 Raven's Progressive Matrices Test This item from the Raven's Progressive Matrices Test measures nonverbal reasoning abilities and is unlikely to be culturally biased.

Which of these shapes correctly completes the above pattern?

FLUID INTELLIGENCE The ability to process information (see *crystallized intelligence*).

CRYSTALLIZED INTELLIGENCE The accuracy and amount of information available for processing (see *fluid intelligence*).

is generally assessed by tests of vocabulary, factual information, and so on, fluid intelligence is generally assessed by tests that pose novel, abstract problems that must be solved under time pressure, such as the Raven's Progressive Matrices Test, shown in **FIGURE 9.7**.

The Top-Down Approach

The bottom-up approach attempts to discover the middle-level abilities by analyzing people's responses to questions on intelligence tests. The good thing about this approach is that its conclusions are based on hard evidence. But the bad thing about this approach is that it is incapable of discovering any middle-level ability that intelligence tests fail to measure. For example, no intelligence test asks people to find three new uses for an origami bird or to answer the question, "What is the question you thought you'd be asked but weren't?" As a result, the scores from these tests may be incapable of revealing a middle-level ability such as creativity. Are there middle-level abilities to which the bottom-up approach is blind?

Psychologist Robert Sternberg believes there are. He suggests that there are three kinds of intelligence, which he calls *analytic intelligence, creative intelligence*, and *practical intelligence*. Analytical intelligence is the ability to identify and define problems and to find strategies for solving them. Creative intelligence is the ability to generate solutions that other people do not. Practical intelligence is the ability to apply and implement these solutions in everyday settings. According to Sternberg, standard intelligence tests typically confront people with clearly defined problems that have one right answer and then supply all the information needed to solve them. These kinds of problems require (and thus serve to measure) analytic intelligence. But everyday life confronts people with situations in which they must formulate the problem, find the information needed to solve it, and then choose among multiple acceptable solutions. These situations require (and thus serve to measure) practical intelligence. Some studies suggest that these different kinds of intelligence are independent. For example, workers at milk-processing plants develop complex strategies for efficiently combining partially filled cases of milk, and not only do they outperform highly educated white-collar workers, but their performance is also unrelated to their scores on intelligence tests, suggesting that practical and analytic intelligence are not the same thing (Scribner, 1984). Sternberg has argued that tests of practical intelligence are better than tests of analytic intelligence at predicting a person's job performance, though such claims have been severely criticized (Brody, 2003; Gottfredson, 2003).

"I don't have to be smart, because someday I'll just hire lots of smart people to work for me."

Philip K. Dick (1928–82), whose novels and stories were the basis of hit movies such as *Bladerunner, Total Recall, Minority Report,* and *A Scanner Darkly,* was often called a "literary genius." Some researchers believe that "creative intelligence" is quite different from the "analytic intelligence" that intelligence tests are designed to measure.

COURTESY OF ISA DICK-HACKETT/COURTESY OF THE PHILIP K. DICK TRUST

SELFE, L. NADIA: A CASE OF EXTRAORDINARY DRAWING ABILITY IN CHILDREN. LONDON: ACADEMIC PRESS, 1977 © ELSEVIER PRESS.

The 5-year-old who drew the picture on the left is a savant—a "low-functioning" autistic child with a mental age of about 3 years. The picture on the right was drawn by a normal 5–year-old.

FROM THE COLLECTION OF ELLEN WINNER

ONLY HUMAN

DON'T TELL PEOPLE THEIR IQ UNLESS THEY ASK In 1997, Daniel Long was fired from his job as a greeter at a Wal-Mart in Des Moines, Iowa, because he told a customer that she had to be "smarter than the cart" to get two of them unstuck.

PRODIGY A person of normal intelligence who has an extraordinary ability.

SAVANT A person of low intelligence who has an extraordinary ability.

INTELLIGENCE A hypothetical mental ability that enables people to direct their thinking, adapt to their circumstances, and learn from their experiences.

Psychologist Howard Gardner also believes that standard intelligence tests fail to measure some important human abilities. His observations of ordinary people, people with brain damage, **prodigies** (*people of normal intelligence who have an extraordinary ability*), and **savants** (*people of low intelligence who have an extraordinary ability*) led him to conclude that there are eight distinct kinds of intelligence: *linguistic, logical-mathematical, spatial, musical, bodily-kinesthetic, interpersonal, intrapersonal,* and *naturalistic.* Although there are few data to confirm the existence or independence of these eight abilities, Gardner's suggestions are intriguing. Moreover, he argues that standard intelligence tests measure only the first three of these abilities because they are the abilities most valued by Western culture but that other cultures may conceive of intelligence differently. For instance, the Confucian tradition emphasizes the ability to behave properly, the Taoist tradition emphasizes humility and self-knowledge, and the Buddhist tradition emphasizes determination and mental effort (Yang & Sternberg, 1997). Westerners regard people as intelligent when they speak quickly and often, but Africans regard people as intelligent when they are deliberate and quiet (Irvine, 1978). Unlike Western societies, many African and Asian societies conceive of intelligence as including social responsibility and cooperativeness (Azuma & Kashiwagi, 1987; Serpell, 1974; White & Kirkpatrick, 1985), and the word for *intelligence* in Zimbabwe, *ngware,* means to be wise in social relationships.

Definitions of intelligence may even differ within a culture: Californians of Latino ancestry are more likely to equate intelligence with social competence while

Californians of Asian ancestry are more likely to equate it with cognitive skill (Okagaki & Sternberg, 1993). Some researchers take all this to mean that different cultures have radically different conceptualizations of intelligence, but others are convinced that what appear to be differences in the conceptualization of intelligence are really just differences in language. They argue that every culture values the ability to solve important problems and that what really distinguishes cultures is the *kind* of problems that is considered to be important.

Where does all this leave us? About 15 years ago, 52 experts on the topic came together to see if they could put an end to this century-long debate by agreeing on a standard definition of intelligence (Gottfredson, 1997). They concluded that intelligence is . . .

> a very general mental capability that, among other things, involves the ability to reason, plan, solve problems, think abstractly, comprehend complex ideas, learn quickly, and learn from experience. It is not merely book learning, a narrow academic skill, or test-taking smarts. Rather, it reflects a broader and deeper capability for comprehending our surroundings—"catching on," "making sense" of things, or "figuring out" what to do. (p. 13)

We may then (at long last) define **intelligence** as *a hypothetical mental ability that enables people to direct their thinking, adapt to their circumstances, and learn from their experiences.* Although this definition is not particularly crisp, it does seem to capture the basic themes that characterize both the scientist's and the layperson's conception of intelligence.

Unlike Americans, Africans describe people as intelligent when they are deliberate and quiet. *Thought is hallowed in the lean oil of solitude,* wrote Nigerian poet Wole Soyinka, who won the Nobel Prize in Literature in 1986.

In summary, a person's score on one test of mental ability is likely to be highly (but not perfectly) correlated with his or her score on another. This led Charles Spearman to suggest that performances require both *g* (general intelligence) and *s* (specific abilities). Modern research reveals that between *g* and *s* are several middle-level abilities. The bottom-up approach suggests that there are eight of them, but the top-down approach suggests that there may be middle-level abilities that intelligence tests don't measure. Cultures may disagree about what constitutes intelligence, but Western scientists agree that it involves reasoning, planning, solving problems, thinking abstractly, comprehending complex ideas, and learning quickly from experience. ■ ■

The Origins of Intelligence: From SES to DNA

Stanford professor Lewis Terman improved on Binet and Simon's work and produced the intelligence test now known as the Stanford-Binet. Among the things his test revealed was that Whites performed much better than non-Whites. "Are the inferior races really inferior, or are they merely unfortunate in their lack of opportunity to learn?" he asked, and then answered unequivocally: "Their dullness seems to be racial, or at least inherent in the family stocks from which they come." He went on to suggest that "children of this group should be segregated into separate classes . . . [because] they cannot master abstractions but they can often be made into efficient workers" (Terman, 1916).

A century later, these sentences make us cringe, and it is difficult to decide which of Terman's suggestions is the most repugnant. Is it the suggestion that a person's intelligence is a product of his or her genes? Is it the suggestion that members of some racial groups score better than others on intelligence tests? Or is it the suggestion that the groups that score best do so because they are genetically superior? If all of these suggestions seem repugnant to you, then you may be surprised to learn that the first and second suggestions are now widely accepted as facts by most scientists. Intelligence *is* influenced by genes and some groups *do* perform better than others on intelligence tests. However, the last of Terman's suggestions—that genes *cause* some groups to outperform others—is not a fact. Indeed, it is a highly provocative claim that has been the subject of both passionate and acrimonious debate. Let's examine all three suggestions and see what the facts really are.

Sir Francis Galton (1822–1911) studied the physical and psychological traits that appeared to run in families. In his book *Hereditary Genius,* he concluded that intelligence was largely inherited.

IDENTICAL TWINS (also called MONOZYGOTIC TWINS) Twins who develop from the splitting of a single egg that was fertilized by a single sperm (see *fraternal twins*).

FRATERNAL TWINS (also called DIZYGOTIC TWINS) Twins who develop from two different eggs that were fertilized by two different sperm (see *identical twins*).

Small genetic differences can make a big difference. A single gene on chromosome 15 determines whether a dog will be too small for your pocket or too large for your garage.

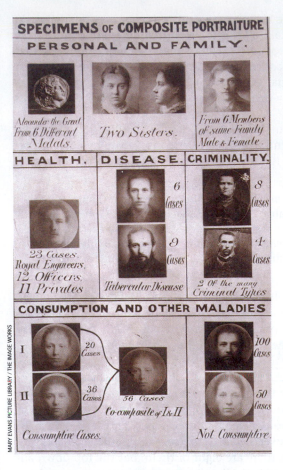

Intelligence and Genes

The notion that all people are not born equal is at least two millennia old. In *The Republic,* the philosopher Plato suggested that some people are naturally constituted to rule, others to be soldiers, and others to be tradesmen. But it wasn't until late in the 19th century that this suggestion became the subject of scientific inquiry. Sir Francis Galton was a half cousin of Charles Darwin, and his contributions to science range from meteorology to fingerprinting. Late in life, Galton (1869) became interested in the origins of intelligence. He did careful genealogical studies of eminent families, and he collected measurements that ranged from head size to the ability to discriminate tones from over 12,000 people. As the title of his book *Hereditary Genius* suggests, he concluded that intelligence was inherited. Was he right? Intelligence is clearly a function of how and how well the brain works, and given that brains are designed by genes, it would be rather remarkable if genes *didn't* play a role in determining a person's intelligence. Indeed, what separates you from a person with Williams syndrome is a mere 20 genes on a single chromosome!

The importance of genes is easy to see when we compare the intelligence test scores of people who do and do not share genes. For example, brothers and sisters share genes, and thus we should expect the intelligence test scores of siblings to be much more similar than the intelligence test scores of unrelated people. And they are—by a country mile. But there is a problem with this kind of comparison, which is that siblings share many things other than genes. For instance, siblings typically grow up in the same house, go to the same schools, read many of the same books, and have many of the same friends. Thus, the similarity of their intelligence test scores may reflect the similarity of their genes or it may reflect the similarity of their experiences. To solve this problem, psychologists have studied the similarity of the intelligence test scores of people who share genes but not experiences, who share experiences but not genes, or who share both.

Identical twins (also called *monozygotic twins*) are *twins who develop from the splitting of a single egg that was fertilized by a single sperm,* and **fraternal twins** (also called *dizygotic twins*) are *twins who develop from two different eggs that were fertilized by two different sperm.* Identical twins are genetic copies of each other, whereas fraternal twins are merely siblings who happened to have spent 9 months together in their mother's womb. Identical twins share 100% of their genes, and fraternal twins (like all siblings who have the same biological mother and father) share on average 50% of their genes. Studies show that the intelligence test scores of identical twins are correlated about $r = .86$ when the twins are raised in the same household and about $r = .78$ when they are raised in different households (for example, when they are adopted by different families). As you'll notice from **TABLE 9.3,** identical twins who are raised apart have more similar intelligence scores than do fraternal twins who are raised together.

| Table 9.3 | Intelligence Test Correlations between People with Different Relationships |

Relationship	Shared Home?	% Shared Genes	Correlation between Intelligence Test Scores (*r*)
Twins			
Identical twins (*n* = 4,672)	Yes	100%	.86
Identical twins (*n* = 93)	No	100%	.78
Fraternal twins (*n* = 5,533)	Yes	50%	.60
Parents and Children			
Parent-biological child (*n* = 8,433)	Yes	50%	.42
Parent-biological child (*n* = 720)	No	50%	.24
Nonbiological parent-adopted child (*n* = 1,491)	Yes	0%	.19
Siblings			
Biological siblings (2 parents in common) (*n* = 26,473)	Yes	50%	.47
Nonbiological siblings (no parents in common) (*n* = 714)	Yes	0%	.32
Biological siblings (2 parents in common) (*n* = 203)	No	50%	.24

Source: Plomin et al., 2001a, p. 168.

In other words, people who share all their genes have extremely similar intelligence test scores regardless of whether they share experiences. Indeed, the correlation between the intelligence test scores of identical twins who have never met is about the same as the correlation between the intelligence test scores of a single person who has taken the test twice! By comparison, the intelligence test scores of unrelated people raised in the same household (for example, two siblings, one or both of whom were adopted) are correlated about *r* = .32 (Bouchard & McGue, 1981). These patterns of correlation clearly suggest that genes play an important role in determining intelligence. Of course, Table 9.3 shows that shared environments play a role too. Genetic influence can be seen by noting that identical twins raised apart are more similar than fraternal twins raised together, but environmental influence can be seen by noting that unrelated siblings raised together are more similar than related siblings raised apart.

Exactly how powerful is the effect of genes on intelligence? The **heritability coefficient** (commonly denoted as h^2) is *a statistic that describes the proportion of the difference between people's scores that can be explained by differences in their genetic*

HERITABILITY COEFFICIENT A statistic (commonly denoted as h^2) that describes the proportion of the difference between people's scores that can be explained by differences in their genetic makeup.

Identical twins (such as hockey players Daniel and Henrik Sedin) share 100% of their genes. Fraternal twins (such as swimmer Susie Maroney and her brother, Sean) share about 50% of their genes, as do nontwin siblings (such as tennis players Serena and Venus Williams).

Figure 9.8 How to Ask a Dumb Question These four rectangles differ in size. How much of the difference in their sizes is due to differences in their widths and how much is due to differences in their heights? Answer: 100% and 0%, respectively. Now, how much of rectangle A's size is due to width and how much is due to height? Answer: That's a dumb question.

makeup. When the data from numerous studies of children and adults are analyzed together, the heritability of intelligence is roughly .5, which is to say that about 50% of the difference between people's intelligence test scores is due to genetic differences between them (Plomin & Spinath, 2004). This fact may tempt you to conclude that half your intelligence is due to your genes and half is due to your experiences, but that's not right. To understand why, consider the rectangles in **FIGURE 9.8.**

These rectangles clearly differ in size. If you were asked to say what percentage of the difference in their sizes is due to differences in their heights and what percentage is due to differences in their widths, you would quickly and correctly say that 100% of the difference in their sizes is due to differences in their widths and 0% is due to differences in their heights (which are, after all, identical). Good answer. Now, if you were asked to say how much of the size of rectangle A was due to its height and how much was due to its width, you would quickly and correctly say, "That's a dumb question." And it is a dumb question because the size of a single rectangle cannot be due more (or less) to height than to width. Only the *differences* in the sizes of rectangles can.

Similarly, if you measured the intelligence of all the people in your psychology class and were then asked to say what percentage of the difference in their intelligences was due to differences in their genes and what percentage was due to differences in their experiences, you would quickly and correctly say that about half was due to each. That's what the heritability coefficient of .5 suggests. If you were next asked to say how much of a particular classmate's intelligence is due to her genes and how much is due to her experiences, you would (we hope) quickly and correctly say, "That's a dumb question." It is a dumb question because the intelligence of a single person cannot be due more (or less) to genes than to experience.

The heritability coefficient tell us why people in a particular group differ from one another, and thus its value can change depending on the particular group of people we measure. For example, the heritability of intelligence among wealthy children is about .72 and among poor children about .10 (Turkheimer, Haley, Waldron, D'Onofrio, & Gottesman, 2003). How can that be? Well, if we assume that wealthy children have fairly similar environments—that is, if they all have nice homes with books, plenty of free time, ample nutrition, and so on—then all the differences in their intelligence must be due to the one and only factor that distinguishes them from each other, namely, their genes. Conversely, if we assume that poor children have fairly different environments—that is, some have books and free time and ample nutrition while others have some or none of these—then the difference in their intelligences may be due to either of the factors that distinguish them, namely, their genes and their environments. The heritability coefficient can also depend on the age of the people being measured and is typically larger among adults than among children (see **FIGURE 9.9**), which suggests that the environments of any pair of 65-year-olds tend to be more similar than the environments of any pair of 3-year-olds. In short, when people have identical experiences, then the difference in their intelligences must be due to the difference in their genes, and when people have identical genes, then the difference in their intelligences must be due to the difference in their experiences. It may seem paradoxical, but in a science-fictional world of perfect clones, the heritability of intelligence (and of everything else) would be zero.

A river separates one of the richest and one of the poorest neighborhoods in Bombay, India. Research suggests that intelligence is more heritable in wealthy than poor neighborhoods.

© VIVIANE MOOS/CORBIS

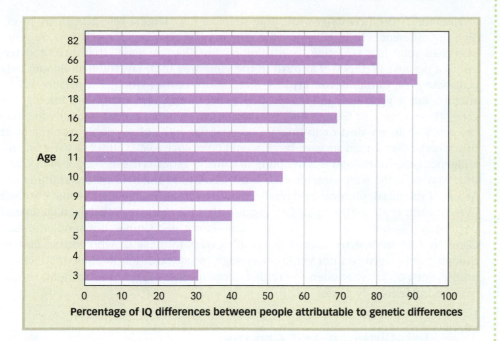

Figure 9.9 **Age and Heritability of Intelligence** The heritability of intelligence generally increases with the age of the sample measured.

The chart shows Age (vertical axis) versus Percentage of IQ differences between people attributable to genetic differences (horizontal axis, 0 to 100). Ages listed: 82, 66, 65, 18, 16, 12, 11, 10, 9, 7, 5, 4, 3.

Does this imply that in a science-fictional world of individuals who lived in exactly the same kinds of houses and received exactly the same kinds of meals, educations, parental care, and so on, the heritability coefficient would be 1? Not likely. Two unrelated people who live in the same household will have *some* but not *all* of their experiences in common. The **shared environment** refers to *those environmental factors that are experienced by all relevant members of a household*. For example, siblings raised in the same household have about the same level of affluence, the same number and type of books, the same diet, and so on. The **nonshared environment** refers to *those environmental factors that are not experienced by all relevant members of a household*. Siblings raised in the same household may have very different friends and teachers and may contract different illnesses. Being raised in the same household is only a rough measure of the similarity of two people's experiences (Turkheimer & Waldron, 2000). As psychologist Eric Turkheimer (2000, p. 162) notes, "The appropriate conclusion [to draw from twin studies] is not so much that the family environment does not matter for development, but rather that the part of the family environment that is shared by siblings does not matter. What does matter is the individual environments of children, their peers, and the aspects of their parenting that they do not share."

SHARED ENVIRONMENT Those environmental factors that are experienced by all relevant members of a household (see *nonshared environment*).

NONSHARED ENVIRONMENT Those environmental factors that are not experienced by all relevant members of a household (see *shared environment*).

Contrary to what you might think, as siblings get older, their intelligence test scores become *more* similar, not less.

Heritability coefficients give us some sense of how large a role genes play in explaining differences in intelligence. But whether large or small, exactly *how* do genes play their role? It is tempting to imagine an "intelligence gene" that directly determines a person's brainpower at birth in the same way that, say, the hemoglobin beta gene found on chromosome 11p15.4 directly determines whether a person will be anemic. But a gene that influences intelligence is not necessarily an "intelligence gene" (Posthuma & de Geus, 2006). For instance, a gene that caused someone to enjoy the smell of library dust or to interact successfully with other people would almost surely make that person smarter, but it would be strange to call either of these an "intelligence gene." Although it is tempting to think of genes as the direct causes of traits, they may actually exert some of their most powerful influences by determining the nature of the social, physical, and intellectual environments in which people live their lives (Plomin et al., 2001a). This fact suggests that the distinction between genes and environments—between nature and nurture—is not just simple, but simpleminded. Genes and environments interact in complex ways to make us who we are, and although psychologists do not yet know enough to say exactly how these interactions unfold, they do know enough to say that Terman's first suggestion was right: Intelligence is influenced by genes.

"I don't know anything about the bell curve, but I say heredity is everything."

Intelligence and Groups

But what of Terman's second suggestion? Are some groups of people more intelligent than others? We should all hope so. If atomic scientists and neurosurgeons aren't a little bit smarter than other people, then those of us who live near nuclear power plants or need spinal cord surgery have a lot to worry about. Between-group differences in intelligence are not inherently troubling. No one is troubled by the possibility that Nobel laureates are on average more intelligent than shoe salesmen, and that includes the shoe salesmen. But most of us are extremely troubled by the possibility that people of one gender, race, or nationality are more intelligent than people of another because intelligence is a valuable commodity and it just doesn't seem fair for a few groups to corner the market by accidents of birth or geography. But fair or not, some groups do routinely outscore others on intelligence tests. For example, Asians routinely outscore Whites, who routinely outscore Latinos, who routinely outscore Blacks (Neisser et al., 1996; Rushton, 1995). Women routinely outscore men on tests that require rapid access to and use of semantic information, production and comprehension of complex prose, fine motor skills, and perceptual speed of verbal intelligence, but men routinely outscore women on tests

Research suggests that men tend to outperform women in abstract mathematical and scientific domains and women tend to outperform men on production and comprehension of complex prose. Sonya Kovalevsky (1850–91), who was regarded as one of the greatest mathematicians of her time, wrote: *It seems to me that the poet must see what others do not see, must look deeper than others look. And the mathematician must do the same thing. As for myself, all my life I have been unable to decide for which I had the greater inclination, mathematics or literature.*

that require transformations in visual or spatial memory, certain motor skills, spatiotemporal responding, and fluid reasoning in abstract mathematical and scientific domains (Halpern, 1997). Indeed, group differences in performance on intelligence tests "are among the most thoroughly documented findings in psychology"(Suzuki & Valencia, 1997, p. 1104). Although the average difference between groups is considerably less than the average difference within groups, Terman's second suggestion was clearly right: Some groups really do perform better than others on intelligence tests. The important questions that follow from this fact are (a) do group differences in intelligence test scores reflect group differences in actual intelligence, and (b) if so, what causes these group differences?

Group Differences in Scores

As mentioned earlier, intelligence tests are imperfect measures of the hypothetical property called intelligence. Do those imperfections create an advantage for one group over another? There is little doubt that the earliest intelligence tests were culturally biased—that is, they asked questions whose answers were more likely to be known by members of one culture (usually White Europeans) than another. When Binet and Simon asked students, "When anyone has offended you and asks you to excuse him, what ought you to do?" they were looking for answers such as, "Accept the apology graciously." The answer, "Demand three goats," would have been counted as wrong. But intelligence tests have come a long way in a century, and one would have to look awfully hard to find questions on a modern intelligence test that have a clear cultural bias (Suzuki & Valencia, 1997). Moreover, group differences emerge even on those portions of intelligence tests that measure nonverbal skills, such as the Raven's Progressive Matrices Test (see Figure 9.7). In short, culturally biased tests are very unlikely to explain group differences in intelligence test scores.

But even when test *questions* are unbiased, testing *situations* may not be. For example, African American students perform more poorly on tests if they are asked to report their race at the top of the answer sheet because doing so causes them to feel anxious about confirming racial stereotypes and this anxiety naturally interferes with their test performance (Steele & Aronson, 1995). European American students do not show the same effect when asked to report their race. When Asian American women are reminded of their gender, they perform unusually poorly on tests of mathematical skill, presumably because they are aware of stereotypes suggesting that women can't do math. But when the same women are instead reminded of their ethnicity, they perform unusually well on the same tests, presumably because they are aware of stereotypes suggesting that Asians are especially good at math (Shih, Pittinsky, & Ambady,

MICHAEL J. DOOLITTLE/THE IMAGE WORKS

Can anxiety over racial and gender stereotypes affect individual student performance? Studies show that if these students are asked to list their ethnicities prior to taking the exam, the African-American students will score poorer and the Asian-American students will score higher than if neither group was asked to list their ethnicity. Interestingly, if Asian-American women are asked to list their gender instead of their race, the opposite occurs and the women will perform unusually poorer than expected on math tests. What can these studies teach us about standardized testing?

1999). Indeed, simply reading an essay suggesting that mathematical ability is strongly influenced by genes causes women to perform more poorly on subsequent tests of mathematical skill (Dar-Nimrod & Heine, 2006)! Findings such as these remind us that the situation in which intelligence tests are administered can affect members of different groups differently and may cause group differences in performance that do not reflect group differences in intelligence.

Group Differences in Intelligence

Situational biases may explain some of the between-group difference in intelligence test scores but surely not all. If we assume that some of these differences reflect real differences in the abilities that intelligence tests measure, then what could account for these ability differences? The obvious candidates are genes and experiences. Although scientists do not yet know enough about the complex interaction of these two candidates to say which is the more important determinant of between-group differences, this much is clear: Different groups *may* have different genes that influence intelligence, but they *definitely* have different experiences that influence intelligence. For example, in America, the average Black child has lower socioeconomic status (SES) than the average White child. Black children come from families with less income; attend worse schools; and have lower birth weights, poorer diets, higher rates of chronic illness, lower rates of treatment, and so on (Acevedo-Garcia, McArdle, Osysuk, Lefkowitz, & Kringold, 2007; National Center for Health Statistics, 2004). All of these factors can affect intelligence. Indeed, for almost a century socioeconomic status has proved to be a better predictor than ethnicity of a child's intelligence test performance. As one researcher wrote in 1921, "There is more likeness between children of the same social status but different race than children of the same race but of different social status" (Arlitt, 1921, p. 183). Everyone agrees that *some* percentage of the between-group difference in intelligence is accounted for by experiential differences, and the only question is whether *any* of the between-group difference in intelligence is accounted for by genetic differences.

Some scientists believe that the answer to this question is yes, and others believe the answer is no. Perhaps because the question is so technically difficult to answer or perhaps because the answer has such important social and political repercussions, there is as yet no consensus among those who have carefully studied the data. To draw firm conclusions about genetic causes of between-group differences will require (a) the identification of a gene or gene complex whose presence is strongly correlated with performance on intelligence tests and (b) the demonstration that this gene or gene complex is more prevalent in one group than another. Such findings are critical to establishing the role of genes in producing between-group differences.

For example, scientists know that Eastern European Jews are more likely than others to carry a mutant gene that produces Tay-Sachs disease. Evidence clearly shows that between-group differences in susceptibility to Tay-Sachs are genetic in origin, and it is the kind of evidence that is currently lacking in the debate on genetic causes of between-group differences in intelligence. So far, investigators have explored only a small portion of the human genome and have found no replicable, significant associations between particular genes and intelligence (Plomin et al., 2001b). The molecular genetic investigation of intelligence has just begun, of course, but until such evidence is found or found lacking, we can expect the debate about genetic causes of between-group differences in intelligence to continue without a convincing resolution. When the American Psychological Association appointed a special task force to summarize what is known about the cause of the difference between the intelligence test scores of Black and White Americans, they concluded: "Culturally based explanations of the Black/White IQ differential have been proposed; some are plausible, but so far none has been conclusively supported. There is even less empirical support for a genetic interpretation. In short, no adequate explanation of the differential between the IQ means of Blacks and Whites is presently available" (Neisser et al., 1996, p. 97). Such is the state of the art.

In summary, genes exert a significant influence on intelligence. The heritability coefficient (h^2) tells us what percent of the difference between the intelligence scores of different people is attributable to differences in their genes, and this statistic changes depending on the socioeconomic level and age of the people being measured. Genes may directly influence intelligence, but they may also influence it by determining the environments to which people are drawn and by which they are shaped. Some groups of people have lower average intelligence test scores than others. Part of the difference between groups is clearly attributable to environmental factors, and it is not yet known whether some of the difference is also attributable to genetic factors. ■ ■

Genetic does not mean "unchangeable." In the 19th century, Dutch men such as Vincent van Gogh were renowned for being short. Today the average Dutch man is 6 feet tall.

The Future of Intelligence: Wising Up

Americans believe that every individual should have an equal chance to succeed in life, and one of the reasons we bristle when we hear about genetic influences on intelligence is that we mistakenly believe that our genes are our destinies—that "genetic" is a synonym for "unchangeable." In fact, traits that are influenced by genes are almost always modifiable. The Dutch were renowned for being short in the 19th century but are now the second-tallest people in the world, and most scientists attribute their dramatic and rapid change in height to changes in diet. Yes, height is a highly heritable trait. But genes do not dictate a person's precise height so much as they dictate the range of heights that a person may achieve (Scarr & McCartney, 1983). "Genes do not fix behavior, rather they establish a range of possible reactions to the range of possible experiences that environments can provide" (Weinberg, 1989, p. 101).

Changing Intelligence

So is intelligence like height in this regard? Alfred Binet (1909) thought so:

> A few modern philosophers . . . assert that an individual's intelligence is a fixed quantity that cannot be increased. We must protest and react against this brutal pessimism. . . . With practice, training, and above all method, we manage to increase our attention, our memory, our judgment, and literally to become more intelligent than we were before.

Was Binet right? Can intelligence change? Yes—it can and it does. For example, **TABLE 9.4** shows the results of six longitudinal studies in which the same people were given intelligence tests many years apart. The relatively large correlations between the pairs of tests tell us that the people who got the best (or worst) scores

Table 9.4	The Stability of Intelligence Test Scores over Time		
Study	Mean Initial Age (Years)	Mean Follow-up Age (Years)	Correlation (*r*)
1	2	9	.56
2	14	42	.68
3	19	61	.78
4	25	65	.78
5	30	43	.64–.79
6	50	70	.90

Source: Adapted from Deary, Whalley, Lemon, Crawford, Starr, 2000.

Although their school was burned by attackers in 2006, the students at the Girls High School of Mondrawet in Afghanistan continue to attend. Studies show that education increases intelligence.

when the test was administered the first time tended to get the best (or worst) scores when it was administered the second time. In other words, an individual's *relative intelligence* is likely to be stable over time, and the people who are the most intelligent at age 11 are likely to be the most intelligent at age 80 (Deary et al., 2000; Deary et al., 2004; Deary et al., 2006). On the other hand, an individual's *absolute intelligence* typically changes over the course of his or her lifetime (Owens, 1966; Schaie, 1996, 2005; Schwartzman, Gold, & Andres, 1987). How can a person's relative intelligence remain stable if his or her absolute intelligence changes? Well, the shortest person in your first-grade class was probably not the tallest person in your high school class, which is to say that the relative heights of your classmates probably stayed about the same as they aged. On the other hand, everyone got taller (we hope) between first and twelfth grade, which is to say that everyone's absolute height changed. Intelligence is like that. Not only does it change over the life span but it also changes in some domains more than others. For example, on tests that measure vocabulary, general information, and verbal reasoning, people show little change from the ages of 18 to 70, but on tests that are timed, have abstract material, involve making new memories, or require reasoning about spatial relationships, most people show marked declines in performance as they age (Avolio & Waldman, 1994; Lindenberger & Baltes, 1997; Salthouse, 2001). Furthermore, there is increasing evidence of an age-related decline in general intelligence (Salthouse, 1996a; Salthouse, 2000), which may be due to a slowing of the brain's processing speed (Salthouse, 1996b; Zimprich & Martin, 2002).

Perhaps it is some consolation that while intelligence tends to decrease across the life span, it tends to increase across generations. The *Flynn effect* refers to the accidental discovery by political scientist James Flynn that the average intelligence test score has been rising by about 0.3% every year, which is to say that the average person today scores about 15 IQ points higher than the average person did 50 years ago (Dickens & Flynn, 2001; Flynn, 1984). Researchers have attributed the effect to better nutrition, better parenting, better schooling, better test-taking ability, and the visual and spatial demands of television and video games (Neisser, 1998). But other researchers (and that includes James Flynn) are not convinced that the statistical trend represents a real change in intelligence (Holloway, 1999). (See the Hot Science box.)

Improving Intelligence

Intelligence waxes and wanes naturally. But what about intentional efforts to improve it? Modern education is an attempt to do just that on a mass scale, and the correlation between the amount of formal education a person receives and his or her intelligence is quite high—somewhere in the range of *r* = .55 to .90 (Ceci, 1991; Neisser et al.,

{ HOT SCIENCE } The Plot Thickens

FRANCIS GALTON STARTED IT ALL BY measuring the circumference of people's heads, and ever since then, scientists have been trying to determine whether brain size is correlated with intelligence. Because head size is such a poor proxy for brain size, it has only been in recent years—with the advent of advanced neuroimaging techniques—that this question has been clearly answered. And the answer is yes: People with larger brains do tend to be slightly more intelligent than people with smaller brains (McDaniel, 2005). But new data suggest that the relationship between the brain's structure and function is a lot more complicated—and a lot more interesting—than "bigger is better."

Using magnetic resonance imaging, a team of researchers from the National Institute of Mental Health and McGill University (Shaw et al., 2006) gave standard intelligence tests to more than 300 healthy children and then divided them into three groups: average intelligence (IQ = 83–108), high intelligence (IQ = 109–120), and superior

intelligence (IQ > 120). They then scanned the children's brains at different times over the course of several years and measured the thickness of their cerebral cortices. (As the cortex matures, it thickens, so thickness is an indicator of growth and development.) What they found surprised them: The children in the superior intelligence group showed a *delayed* but *extended* growth spurt in the cerebral cortex. In other words, children in the superior intelligence group had *thinner*—that is, *less* mature—cerebral cortices than their peers early on. Then, around age 7, their cortices began to thicken, peaking at about the age of 13. In contrast, cortical thickness peaked between 7 and 9 years of age in the other two groups of children. The most pronounced differences in cortical development were in the prefrontal cortex, which is generally thought to be the seat of abstract thinking.

The prefrontal cortex of children with superior intelligence seems to begin its development later but keep at it longer. Why would this pattern of development be as-

sociated with superior intelligence? The researchers could only guess: "The prolonged phase of prefrontal cortical gain in the most intelligent might afford an even more extended 'critical' period for the development of high-level cognitive cortical circuits" (Shaw et al., 2006, p. 678). In other words, slow-maturing brains may have more time to do the things that eventually make them smart—whatever those things may be. Perhaps intelligence, like good wine, is something that can't be rushed.

These brain maps show the difference between the group of children with superior intelligence and the other groups. Purple and blue regions indicate parts of the cortex that were thinner in the superior intelligence group, and red, yellow, and green regions indicate parts of the cortex that were thicker in this group. The superior intelligence group had a thinner prefrontal cortex at age 7 (purple and blue regions) but later experienced a rapid increase in cortical thickness (red, green, and yellow regions) that peaked at age 13 and waned in late adolescence.

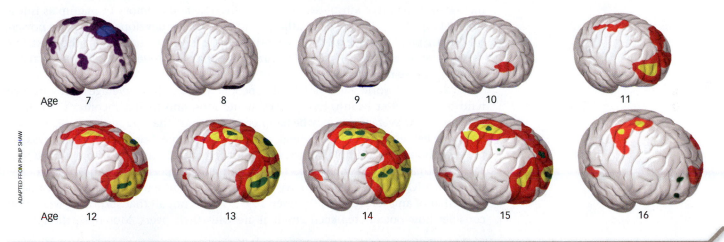

ADAPTED FROM PHILIP SHAW

Age 7   8   9   10   11

Age 12   13   14   15   16

1996). But is this correlation so high because smart people tend to stay in school or because school makes people smart? The answer, it seems, is both. More intelligent people are indeed more likely to stay in high school and go on to college, but it also appears that staying in school can itself increase IQ (Ceci & Williams, 1997, p. 1052). Although psychologists cannot ethically perform experiments to determine whether education increases intelligence because doing so would entail depriving some people of education, there are naturally occurring data that support this claim.

For instance, the intelligence of schoolchildren declines during the summer, and these declines are most pronounced for children whose summers are spent on the least academically oriented activities (Hayes & Grether, 1983; Heyns, 1978). Furthermore, children born in the first 9 months of a calendar year typically start school an entire year earlier than those born in the last 3 months of the same year, and sure enough, students with late birthdays tend to have lower intelligence test scores than students with early birthdays (Baltes & Reinert, 1969). (By the way, the authors of this book who were born in February and March find this much easier to believe than does the author born in November, but perhaps that's because he's not as smart as they are.) Does this mean that anyone can be a genius with enough education? Unfortunately not. Educational programs can reliably increase intelligence, but studies suggest that such programs usually have only a minor impact, tend to enhance test-taking ability more than cognitive ability, and have effects that dwindle and vanish within a few years (Perkins & Grotzer, 1997). In other words, educational programs appear to produce increases in intelligence that are smaller, narrower, and shorter-lived than we might wish.

Education is a moderately effective way to increase intelligence, but it is also expensive and time consuming. Not surprisingly, then, scientists are looking for cheaper, quicker, and more effective ways to boost the national IQ. *Cognitive enhancers* are drugs that produce improvements in the psychological processes that underlie intelligent behavior, such as memory, attention, and executive function. For example, conventional stimulants such as methylphenidate, or Ritalin (Elliott et al., 1997; Halliday et al., 1994; McKetin, Ward, Catts, Matlick, & Bell, 1999), can enhance cognitive performance, which is why there has been an alarming increase in their abuse by healthy students over the past few years. Cognitive performance can also be enhanced by a new class of drugs called ampakines, which boost the activity of the neurotransmitter glutamate (Ingvar et al., 1997). For example, modafinil is a dopamine reuptake inhibitor that has been shown to improve short-term memory and planning abilities in healthy, young volunteers (Turner et al., 2003).

Scientists have also successfully manipulated the genes that guide hippocampal development and created a strain of "smart mice" that have extraordinary memory and learning abilities, leading researchers to conclude that "genetic enhancement of mental and cognitive attributes such as intelligence and memory in mammals is feasible" (Tang et al., 1999, p. 64). Although no one has yet developed a safe and powerful "smart pill," many experts believe that this is likely to happen in the next few years (Farah et al., 2004; Rose, 2002; Turner & Sahakian, 2006). Clearly, we are about to enter a brave new world.

What kind of world will it be? Because people who are above average in intelligence tend to have better health, longer lives, better jobs, and higher incomes than those who are below average, we may be tempted to conclude that the more intelligence we have, the better off we are. In general, this is probably true, but there are some reasons to be cautious. For example, although moderately gifted children (those with IQs of 130 to 150) are as well adjusted as their less intelligent peers, profoundly gifted children (with IQs of 180 or more) have a rate of social and emotional problems that is twice that of an average child (Winner, 1997). This is not all that surprising when you consider how out of step such children are with their peers. Moreover, the gifts of

Dr. Joseph Tsien is one of the scientists who genetically engineered Droogie, the "smart mouse."

PEDRICK LAURA/CORBIS SYGMA

childhood do not necessarily ripen into the fruits of adulthood. Profoundly gifted children are no more likely than moderately intelligent children to become major contributors to the fields in which they work (Richert, 1997; Terman & Oden, 1959). No one knows why this is. Perhaps there is a natural limit on how much intelligence can influence life outcomes, or perhaps the educational system fails to help profoundly gifted children make the best use of their talents (Robinson & Clinkenbeard, 1998).

In any case, it is interesting to note that gifted children are rarely gifted in all departments. Rather, they tend to have very specialized gifts. For example, more than 95% of gifted children show a sharp disparity between their mathematical and verbal abilities (Achter, Lubinski, & Benbow, 1996), suggesting that those who are exceptionally talented in one domain are not quite so talented in the other. Indeed, as the study of savants shows, children can be profoundly gifted in one area and severely challenged in another (Fiering & Taft, 1985; Reis, Neu, & McGuire, 1995; Richert, 1997; Yewchuk, 1985). Some research suggests that what really distinguishes gifted children is the sheer amount of time they spend engaged in their domain of excellence (Ericsson & Charness, 1999). The essence of nature's "gift" may be the capacity for passionate devotion to a single activity.

In summary, intelligence tends to decrease over the life span and increase across generations. Education increases intelligence, but its impact is smaller, narrower, and shorter-lived than we might wish. Cognitive enhancers can also increase intelligence, though it is not clear by how much. People who are extremely intelligent are not necessarily happier, and their gifts tend to be highly specialized. ■ ■

Where Do You Stand?

Making Kids Smart or Making Smart Kids?

Once upon a time, babies were a surprise. Until the day they were born, no one knew if Mom would deliver a girl, a boy, or perhaps one of each. Advances in medicine such as amniocentesis and ultrasound technology have allowed parents to look inside the womb and learn about the gender and health of their fetuses long before they meet them. Now parents can do more than just look. For example, IVF (in vitro fertilization) involves creating dozens of human embryos in the laboratory, using PGD (pre-implantation genetic diagnosis) to determine which have genetic abnormalities, and then implanting only the normal embryos in a woman's womb. Gene therapy involves replacing the faulty sections of an embryo's DNA with healthy sections. These and other techniques may (or may soon) be used to reduce a couple's chances of having a child with a devastating illness such as Tay-Sachs, early-onset Alzheimer's, sickle-cell disease, hemophilia, neurofibromatosis, muscular dystrophy, and Fanconi's anemia. But in the not-too-distant future they may also enable a couple to increase the odds that their baby will have the traits they value—such as intelligence.

If in the coming years scientists find genes or gene complexes that are directly related to intelligence, IVF and gene therapy will provide methods of increasing a couple's chances of having an intelligent—and perhaps even an extraordinarily intelligent—child. Those who oppose the selection or manipulation of embryos fear that there is no bright line that separates repairing or selecting genes that cause disease and repairing or de-selecting genes that cause normal intelligence. "Today it's early-onset Alzheimer's" that we use PGD to avoid, said Jeffrey Kahn, director of the University of Minnesota's Center for Bioethics. "Tomorrow it could easily be intelligence, or a good piano player or many other things we might be able to identify the genetic factors for" (Tanner, February 7, 2002). This could ultimately lead to a lot of interesting people never being born. As Shannon Brownlee (2002) of the New America Foundation noted, "Today,

Tom Sawyer and Huck Finn would have been diagnosed with attention-deficit disorder and medicated. Tomorrow, they might not be allowed out of the petri dish."

People on the other side of this debate wonder what the fuss is about. After all, couples are already selecting their offspring for high IQ by mating with the smartest people they can find. And once their babies are born, most parents will work hard to enhance their children's intelligence by giving them everything from carrots to cello lessons. Science writer Ron Bailey predicted that "parents will someday use PGD to screen embryos for desirable traits such as tougher immune systems, stronger bodies, and smarter brains. What horrors do such designer babies face? Longer, healthier, smarter, and perhaps even happier lives? It is hard to see any ethical problem with that" (Bailey, 2002).

Should parents be allowed to use PGD or gene therapy to increase the intelligence of their children? Where do you stand?

Chapter Review

The Measurement of Intelligence: Highly Classified

- Early intelligence tests were designed to predict a child's scholastic performance but were eventually used to calculate an intelligence quotient either as a ratio of the person's mental to physical age or a deviation of the person's test score from the average score of his or her peers.

- Intelligence is a hypothetical property that cannot be directly measured, so intelligence tests measure responses (to questions and on tasks) that are known to be correlated with consequential behaviors that are thought to be made possible by intelligence.

- These consequential behaviors include academic performance, job performance, health, and wealth, all of which are enhanced by intelligence.

The Nature of Intelligence: Pluribus or Unum?

- A person's score on one test of mental ability is likely to be highly (but not perfectly) correlated with his or her score on another. This led Charles Spearman to suggest that performances require both g (general intelligence) and s (specific abilities).

- Modern research reveals that between g and s are several middle-level abilities. The bottom-up approach suggests that there are eight of them, but the top-down approach suggests that there may be middle-level abilities that intelligence tests don't measure.

- Cultures may disagree about what constitutes intelligence, but Western scientists agree that it involves reasoning, planning, solving problems, thinking abstractly, comprehending complex ideas, and learning quickly from experience.

The Origins of Intelligence: From SES to DNA

- Genes exert a significant influence on intelligence. The heritability coefficient (h^2) tells us what percent of the difference between the intelligence scores of different people is attributable to differences in their genes, and this statistic changes depending on the socioeconomic level and age of the people being measured.

- Genes may directly influence intelligence, but they may also influence it by determining the environments to which people are drawn and by which they are shaped.

- Some groups of people have lower average intelligence test scores than others. Part of the difference between groups is clearly attributable to environmental factors, and it is not yet known whether some of the difference is also attributable to genetic factors.

The Future of Intelligence: Wising Up

- Intelligence tends to decrease over the life span and increase across generations.

- Education increases intelligence, but its impact is smaller, narrower, and shorter-lived than we might wish.

- Cognitive enhancers can also increase intelligence, though it is not clear by how much.

- People who are extremely intelligent are not necessarily happier, and their gifts tend to be highly specialized.

Key Terms

ratio IQ (p. 339)

deviation IQ (p. 340)

factor analysis (p. 345)

two-factor theory of intelligence (p. 346)

fluid intelligence (p. 348)

crystallized intelligence (p. 348)

prodigies (p. 350)

savants (p. 350)

intelligence (p. 351)

identical twins (p. 352)

fraternal twins (p. 352)

heritability coefficient (p. 353)

shared environment (p. 355)

nonshared environment (p. 355)

Recommended Readings

Deary, I. J. (2001). *Intelligence: A very short introduction*. Oxford, UK: Oxford University Press. This is a short, accessible, and lively introduction to many of the important issues in the study of intelligence by one of the leading scientists in the area. Each chapter deals with a different topic, such as whether there are several different types of intelligence, whether intelligence differences are caused by genes or the environment, the biological basis of intelligence differences, and whether intelligence declines or increases as we grow older.

Herrnstein, R. J., & Murray, C. (1994). *The bell curve*. New York: Free Press. *National Review* wrote, "Our intellectual landscape has been disrupted by the equivalent of an earthquake." And it was true. *The Bell Curve* was one of the most controversial books of the second half of the 20th century. It examined the influence of intelligence on life outcomes and discussed the stratification of American society on the basis of intelligence differences. But what made it so controversial was its claim that group differences in intelligence are largely genetic. Find out for yourself what the debate was about.

Mackintosh, N. J. (1998). *IQ and human intelligence.* Oxford, UK: Oxford University Press. This book provides an authoritative overview of the main issues surrounding the modern development of IQ tests, the heritability of intelligence, theories of intelligence, environmental effects on IQ, factor analysis, relationship of cognitive psychology to measuring IQ, and intelligence in the social context. The clear, accessible style and numerous explanatory boxes make this an ideal text for advanced undergraduate and graduate students in psychology.

Miller, G. (2000). *The mating mind.* London: Heinemann. Here is something different! Geoffrey Miller argues that intelligent behaviors are mating signals and that people who demonstrate their cognitive accomplishments are advertising their sexiness. The *New York Times* called it "ingenious stuff . . . a welcome change from a lot of evolutionary psychology."

Neisser, U., et al. (1996). Intelligence: Knowns and Unknowns. *American Psychologist, 51,* 77–101. After the controversy surrounding *The Bell Curve,* the American Psychological Association put together this task force to report clearly and fairly what was known, and not yet known, about human intelligence differences.

10

Emotion and Motivation

Emotional Experience: The Feeling Machine
  What Is Emotion?
  The Emotional Body
  The Emotional Brain
  The Regulation of Emotion

Emotional Communication: Msgs w/o Wrds
  HOT SCIENCE The Pleasures of Uncertainty
  Communicative Expression
  THE REAL WORLD That's Gross!
  Deceptive Expression

Motivation: Getting Moved
  The Function of Emotion
  The Conceptualization of Motivation
  Eating and Mating
  Kinds of Motivation
  WHERE DO YOU STAND? Here Comes the Bribe

"WHY? WHY? WHY? WHY? THAT'S THE question I think everyone is asking."

At 6:02 p.m. on October 2, 2002, James Martin was walking across the Shoppers Food Warehouse parking lot in Wheaton, Maryland, with a bag of groceries in his arms. He'd left his office at the usual time that evening and stopped at the grocery store to pick up a few things for the youth group at his church. His wife, Billie, and their 11-year-old son, Ben, were waiting for him at home, but their wait would be in vain. As Martin approached his truck, there was a sudden, loud pop, and a bullet from a Bushmaster XM15 semiautomatic rifle severed his spinal cord and perforated his aorta. He crumpled to the pavement and bled to death.

James Martin was the first, but he would not be the last. The next day, in a period of less than 90 minutes, James Buchanan was shot while mowing the lawn, Premkumar Walekar was shot while pumping gas, Sarah Ramos was shot while sitting at a bus stop, Lori Ann Lewis-Rivera was shot while vacuuming her car, and Pascal Charlot was shot while taking a walk. In the days that followed, there were more shootings and more deaths. The serial killer whom the media called the "Beltway Sniper" seemed to select his victims at random and shoot them from afar, leaving authorities to guess at his motive. "The thrill of the kill," speculated one FBI agent. "Playing God. Having the power over these individuals. Life and death. That's a real heady rush" (Horwitz & Ruane, 2003). The sniper's motive seemed to become clear when authorities received a note demanding that they pay him $10 million to stop killing people. The note provided clues that led police to 42-year-old John Allen Muhammad and 17-year-old Lee Boyd Malvo, who were arrested in a blue Chevrolet Caprice whose trunk had been modified to serve as a sniper's perch.

STEVE HELBER/AP/GETTY IMAGES

AP PHOTO/SUSAN WALSH, FILE

What motivated John Allen Muhammad (left) and Lee Boyd Malvo (right), to spend 22 days killing people at random?

Why did two men ride around in a car for 22 days, slaughtering innocent people at random? Authorities discovered that the plot to extort money had been hatched only *after* the men had killed most of their victims. Prosecutors claimed that, in fact, Muhammad had come to Maryland to kill his ex-wife and that when he was unable to locate her, he went mad and "began shooting people around her" (Ahlers, 2003). Muhammad's attorney argued that his client was a troubled veteran for whom "something went terribly wrong. He came back from Desert Storm a different man" (Sipe, 2006). A psychologist described Muhammad as a "very, very angry individual," but added, "Of course there are a lot of angry people who don't explode. So there must have been something in his social interaction—in his marriage or his military career—that pulled the trigger" (Leonard, 2002).

The teenage Malvo claimed that he had not wanted to kill anyone and that he participated in the slaughter in order to please Muhammad, whom he called "Father." Not everyone believed that the two men were motivated by greed, by rage, or by filial loyalty. "Muhammad might have seen himself as a foot soldier in the jihad against the United States and he took up arms to terrorize Americans," wrote one commentator (Pipes, 2002). "In a society that celebrates celebrity above all, they were seeking to enter the Hall of Fame in the only category where they stood a chance, as criminals and serial killers," wrote another (Buchanan, 2002).

"**W**hy? Why? Why? Why? That's the question I think everyone is asking," said Malvo's brother (Pipes, 2002). And indeed it was. Serial killers fascinate us—not because of a morbid curiosity, but because we are fascinated by people whose motives we can't fathom and whose emotions we can't comprehend. What led Muhammad to select another human being at random and put a bullet through his heart? What compelled Malvo to take aim at a pregnant woman simply because his surrogate father asked him to? How could these men have pulled the triggers of their rifles; watched helpless men, women, and children fall to the ground; and then driven away calmly? How could they not have felt sadness, remorse, or disgust? The behaviors in question are mercifully rare, but the questions themselves are not. When we ask why people feel and act as they do, we are asking questions about their emotions and motivations. As you will see, emotions and motivations are intimately connected, and understanding their connection allows us to answer the "Why?" question that everyone is asking.

Emotional Experience: The Feeling Machine

Trying to describe love to someone who had never experienced it would be a bit like trying to describe green to someone who was born blind. You could tell them about its sources ("It's that feeling you get when you see your sweetheart across the room") and you could describe its physiological correlates ("It makes your pupils dilate"), but in the end, your descriptions would largely miss the point because the essential feature of love—like the essential feature of all emotions—is the *experience*. It *feels* like something to love, and what it feels like is love's defining attribute.

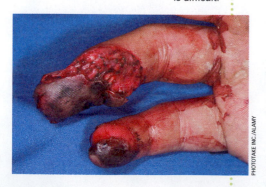

For most people, these pictures evoke emotional experiences. Having these experiences is easy, but describing them is difficult.

What Is Emotion?

What can we do when we want to study something whose defining attribute resists description? Psychologists have developed a clever technique that capitalizes on the fact that while people can't always say what an emotional experience feels like ("Love is . . . um . . . uh . . ."), they can usually say how similar it is to another ("Love is more like happiness than like anger"). By asking people to rate the similarity of dozens of emotional experiences, psychologists have been able to map those experiences using a sophisticated technique known as *multidimensional scaling*. The mathematics behind this technique is complex, but the logic is simple. If you listed the distances between a dozen U.S. cities and then handed the list to a friend and challenged him to draw a map on which every city was the listed distance from every other, your friend would be forced to draw a map of the United States because there is no other map that allows every city to appear at precisely the right distance from every other. Sure, there are lots of ways to draw a map so that San Francisco is 344 miles from Los Angeles, but there is only one way to draw a map so that San Francisco is 344 miles from Los Angeles *and* 1,863 miles from Chicago *and* 2,582 miles from New York, and so on. The point is that a map of the physical landscape can be generated from nothing but a list of distances between cities.

The same logic can be used to generate a map of the emotional landscape. If you listed the similarity of a dozen emotional experiences (giving smaller numbers to those that were conceptually "close" to each other and larger numbers to those that are conceptually "far away" from each other) and then challenged a friend to draw a map on which every experience was the listed "distance" from every other, your friend would draw a map like the one shown in **FIGURE 10.1**. This is the unique map that allows every emotional experience to be precisely the right "distance" from every other.

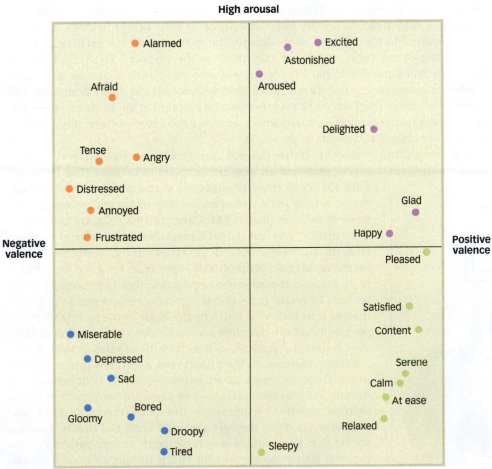

Figure 10.1 **Two Dimensions of Emotion** Just as cities can be mapped by their longitude and latitude, emotions can be mapped by their arousal and valence.

EMOTION A positive or negative experience that is associated with a particular pattern of physiological activity.

JAMES-LANGE THEORY A theory about the relationship between emotional experience and physiological activity suggesting that stimuli trigger activity in the autonomic nervous system, which in turn produces an emotional experience in the brain.

CANNON-BARD THEORY A theory about the relationship between emotional experience and physiological activity suggesting that a stimulus simultaneously triggers activity in the autonomic nervous system and emotional experience in the brain.

TWO-FACTOR THEORY A theory about the relationship between emotional experience and physiological activity suggesting that emotions are inferences about the causes of undifferentiated physiological arousal.

What good is this map? As it turns out, maps don't just show how close things are to each other: They also reveal the *dimensions* on which those things vary. For example, a U.S. map reveals that cities differ on two dimensions called longitude and latitude, and thus every city can be described by its unique coordinates in this two-dimensional space. Similarly, an emotion map reveals that emotional experiences differ on two dimensions that are called *valence* (how positive or negative the experience is) and *arousal* (how active or passive the experience is), and every emotional experience can be described by its unique coordinates in this two-dimensional space (Russell, 1980; Watson & Tellegen, 1985).

This map of emotional experience suggests that any definition of emotion must include two things: first, the fact that emotional experiences are always good or bad, and second, the fact that these experiences are associated with characteristic levels of bodily arousal. As such, **emotion** can be defined as *a positive or negative experience that is associated with a particular pattern of physiological activity*. As you are about to see, the first step in understanding emotion involves understanding how experience and physiological activity are related.

The Emotional Body

You probably think that if you walked into your kitchen right now and saw a bear nosing through the cupboards, you would feel fear, your heart would start to pound, and the muscles in your legs would prepare you for running. Presumably away. But William James and Carl Lange suggested that the events that produce an emotion might actually happen in the opposite order (Lange & James, 1922). The **James-Lange theory** of emotion asserts that *stimuli trigger activity in the autonomic nervous system, which in turn produces an emotional experience in the brain*. In other words, first you see the bear, then your heart starts pounding and your leg muscles contract, and *then* you experience fear, which is simply your experience of your body's activity. As James (1884) wrote, "Bodily changes follow directly the perception of the exciting fact. . . . And feeling of the same changes as they occur *is* the emotion" (pp. 189–190). For James, each unique emotional experience was associated with a unique pattern of "bodily reverberation," and he suggested that without all the heart pounding and muscle clenching, there would be no experience of emotion at all. In short, James saw emotional experience as the consequence—and not the cause—of our physiological reactions to objects and events in the world.

But James's former student, Walter Cannon, disagreed, and together with *his* student, Philip Bard, Cannon proposed an alternative to James's theory. The **Cannon-Bard theory** of emotion suggested that *a stimulus simultaneously triggers activity in the autonomic nervous system and emotional experience in the brain* (Bard, 1934; Cannon, 1927). Canon favored his own theory over the James-Lange theory for several reasons. First, the autonomic nervous system reacts too slowly to account for the rapid onset of emotional experience. For example, a blush is an autonomic response to embarrassment that takes 15 to 30 seconds to occur, and yet one can feel embarrassed long before that, so how could the blush be the cause of the feeling? Second, people often have difficulty accurately detecting changes in their own autonomic activity, such as their heart rates. If people cannot detect increases in their heart rates, then how can they experience those increases as an emotion? Third, if nonemotional stimuli—such as temperature—can cause the same pattern of autonomic activity that emotional stimuli do, then why don't people feel afraid when they get a fever? Fourth and finally, Cannon argued that there simply weren't enough unique patterns of autonomic activity to account for all the unique emotional experiences people have. If many different emotional experiences are

"I never realized they had feelings."

associated with the same pattern of autonomic activity, then how could that pattern of activity be the sole determinant of the emotional experience?

These are all good questions, and about 30 years after Cannon asked them, psychologists Stanley Schachter and Jerome Singer supplied some answers (Schachter & Singer, 1962). James and Lange were right, they claimed, to equate emotion with the perception of one's bodily reactions. Cannon and Bard were also right, they claimed, to note that there are not nearly enough distinct bodily reactions to account for the wide variety of emotions that human beings can experience. Whereas James and Lange had suggested that different emotions are *different experiences* of *different patterns* of bodily activity, Schachter and Singer claimed that different emotions are merely *different interpretations* of *a single pattern* of bodily activity, which they called "undifferentiated physiological arousal" (see **FIGURE 10.2**).

Schachter and Singer's **two-factor theory** of emotion claimed that *emotions are inferences about the causes of undifferentiated physiological arousal.* When you see a bear in your kitchen, your heart begins to pound. Your brain quickly scans the environment, looking for a reasonable explanation for all that pounding, and it finds, of all things, a bear. Having noticed both a bear and a pounding heart, your brain then does what brains do so well: It puts two and two together, makes a logical inference, and interprets your arousal as fear. In other words, when people are physiologically aroused in the presence of something that they think should scare them, they label their arousal as *fear*. But if they have precisely the same bodily response in the presence of something that they think should delight them, they may label that arousal as *excitement*. According to Schachter and Singer, people have the same physiological reaction to all emotional stimuli, but they interpret that reaction differently on different occasions.

To demonstrate their claim, Schachter and Singer gave participants in an experiment an injection of epinephrine, a neurotransmitter that mimics the action of the sympathetic nervous system, causing increases in blood pressure, heart rate, blood flow to the brain, blood sugar levels, and respiration. Some participants were correctly informed that side effects of the injection would include trembling hands, a flushed face, and an increased heart rate. Other participants were incorrectly informed that the side effects of the injection would include numb feet, an itching sensation all over the body, and a slight headache. Next, participants were given the opportunity to interact with one of two people who, unbeknownst to them, were confederates of the experimenter. In one condition of the experiment, the confederate acted giddy, doodling on some paper, crumbling it into a makeshift basketball, constructing paper airplanes, and swinging some hula hoops he found. In the other condition, the confederate acted surly, spending his time grousing and harrumphing his way through a

England's Prince William blushes with embarrassment as he arrives at his hotel and finds a throng of adoring female fans. Because the experience of embarrassment precedes blushing by up to 30 seconds, it is unlikely that blushing is the cause of the experience.

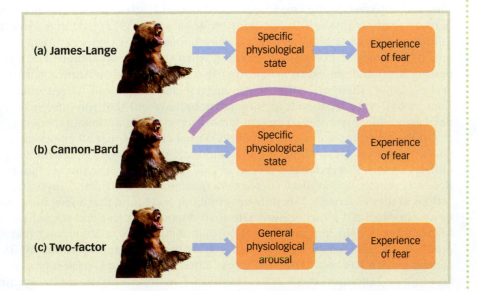

Figure 10.2 Classic Theories of Emotion Classic theories make different claims about the origins of emotion. (a) The James-Lange theory suggests that stimuli trigger specific physiological states, which are then experienced as emotions. (b) The Cannon-Bard theory suggests that stimuli trigger both specific physiological states and emotional experiences independently. (c) The two-factor theory suggests that stimuli trigger general physiological arousal whose cause the brain interprets, and this interpretation leads to emotional experience.

Some of the pioneers of emotion theory are William James, Carl Lange, and Walter Cannon (top row, left to right), and Phillip Bard, Stanley Schachter, and Jerome Singer (bottom row, left to right).

questionnaire before finally ripping up the paper and storming out of the room. Schachter and Singer predicted that participants who were correctly informed about the side effects would correctly interpret their arousal ("I'm feeling a little revved up because of the shot") but that participants who were not correctly informed about the side effects would seek an explanation for their arousal—and that the confederate's behavior would supply it. Specifically, they predicted that when the confederate acted goofy, the misinformed participants would conclude that they were feeling *happy* but that when the confederate acted nasty, they would conclude that they were feeling *angry*. And that's just what happened.

How has the two-factor model fared in the last half century? In one sense, it has fared quite well. Research has shown that when people are aroused, say, by having them ride an exercise bike in the laboratory, they subsequently find attractive people more attractive, annoying people more annoying, and funny cartoons funnier—as if they were interpreting their exercise-induced arousal as attraction, annoyance, and delight, respectively (Byrne, Allgeier, Winslow, & Buckman, 1975; Dutton & Aron, 1974; Zillmann, Katcher, & Milausky, 1972). Indeed, these effects occur even when people merely *think* they're aroused—for example, when they hear an audiotape of a rapidly beating heart and are led to believe that the heartbeat they're hearing is their own (Valins, 1966). These and other studies suggest that people can indeed misattribute their arousal to other stimuli in their environments and that the inferences people draw about the causes of their arousal can influence their emotional experience.

On the other hand, one of the model's central claims is that all emotional experiences derive from the same pattern of bodily activity, namely, undifferentiated physiological arousal. Research has not been so kind to this part of the theory. Paul Ekman, Robert Levenson, and Wallace Friesen (1983) measured participants' physiological reactions as they experienced six different emotions and found that anger, fear, and sadness each produced a higher heart rate than disgust; that fear and disgust produced higher galvanic skin response (sweating) than did sadness or anger; and that anger produced a larger increase in finger temperature than did fear (see **FIGURE 10.3**). This general pattern has been replicated across different age groups, professions, genders, and cultures (Levenson et al., 1991; Levenson, Ekman, & Friesen, 1990; Levenson et

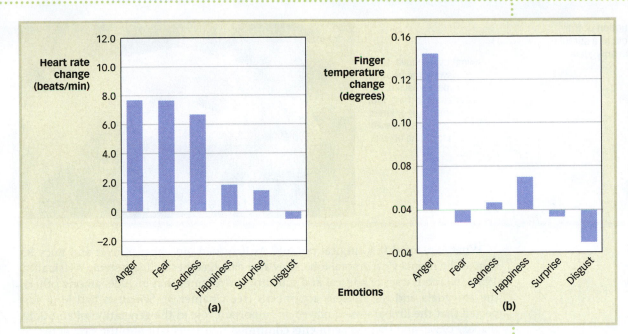

Figure 10.3
Different Physiological Patterns of Emotion Contrary to the claims of the two-factor theory, different emotions do seem to have different underlying patterns of physiological arousal. (a) Anger, fear, and sadness all produce higher heart rates compared to happiness, surprise, and disgust. (b) Anger produces a much larger increase in finger temperature than any other emotion.

al., 1992). In fact, some physiological responses seem unique to specific emotions. For example, a blush is the result of increased blood volume in the subcutaneous capillaries in the face, neck, and chest, and research suggests that people blush when they feel embarrassment but not when they feel any other emotion (Leary et al., 1992). Similarly, certain patterns of activity in the parasympathetic branch of the autonomic nervous system (which is responsible for slowing and calming rather than speeding and exciting) seem uniquely related to prosocial emotions such as compassion (Oately, Keltner, & Jenkins, 2006).

It now appears that James and Lange were right when they suggested that patterns of physiological response are not the same for all emotions. But it appears that Cannon and Bard were right when they suggested that people are not perfectly sensitive to these patterns of response, which is why people must sometimes make inferences about what they are feeling. Our bodily activity and our mental activity are both the causes and the consequences of our emotional experience. The precise nature of their interplay is not yet fully understood, but as you are about to see, much progress has been made over last few decades by following the trail of emotion from the beating heart to the living brain.

The Emotional Brain

Psychologist Heinrich Klüver was curious: Why do monkeys smack their lips after being given hallucinogenic drugs? So on the afternoon of December 7, 1936, he and the physician Paul Bucy removed the temporal lobe of a particularly aggressive rhesus monkey named Aurora and ultimately learned nothing whatsoever about lip smacking. They did, however, produce what Klüver would later call "the most striking behavior changes ever produced by a brain operation in animals" (Klüver, 1951, p. 151). Their surgical experiments revealed that monkeys whose temporal lobes had been removed would eat just about anything and have sex with just about anyone or anything—as though they could no longer distinguish between good and bad food or good and bad mates. But the most striking thing about these monkeys was their extraordinary lack of fear. They were eerily calm when being handled by experimenters or being confronted by snakes, both of which rhesus monkeys typically find alarming (Klüver & Bucy, 1937, 1939). This constellation of behaviors became known as "temporal lobe syndrome" or "Klüver-Bucy syndrome" (though it was later pointed out that the syndrome had been described in 1888 by Brown and Schafer).

APPRAISAL An evaluation of the emotion-relevant aspects of a stimulus that is performed by the amygdala.

Animals with Klüver-Bucy syndrome become hypersexual and will attempt to mate with members of different species and even inanimate objects.

PETER MILLER/PHOTO RESEARCHERS

What explained this surgical taming? As it turned out, when Klüver and Bucy lesioned the monkey's temporal lobe, they also damaged her limbic system (Weiskrantz, 1956), which is a set of cortical and subcortical structures that include, among others, the amygdala and the nucleus accumbens (see Chapter 3). Scientists had long suspected that the limbic system played an important role in the generation of emotions (Papez, 1937), and these experiments confirmed that speculation in the case of fear. A few decades later, psychologists James Olds and Peter Milner implanted electrodes in the brains of rats to see how the rats would respond to direct electrical stimulation of their brains (Olds & Milner, 1954). When Olds and Milner stimulated the rat's limbic system, they found that it quickly returned to whatever part of the cage it had just been in—as though the rat were trying to re-create the circumstances that had led to the electric stimulation. When they allowed the rat to stimulate its own brain by pressing a lever, the rat did so for hours on end, often choosing electric stimulation over food. These studies suggested that the limbic system was also implicated in the experience of emotions such as pleasure.

More recent research has demonstrated that a particular limbic structure—the amygdala—plays a key role in the production of emotion. William James (1884) claimed that "bodily changes follow directly the perception of the exciting fact" (p. 189), which means that some part of the brain decides which facts are exciting. Between the moment that information about an approaching bear enters our eye and the moment our heart starts pounding, our brain has to decide that a bear is something to be afraid of. That decision is called an **appraisal**, which is *an evaluation of the emotion-relevant aspects of a stimulus* (Arnold, 1960; Lazarus, 1984; Roseman, 1984; Roseman & Smith, 2001; Scherer, 1999, 2001), and research suggests that making appraisals is the amygdala's primary job (see **FIGURE 10.4**). For example, in one study,

Figure 10.4 Emotion Recognition and the Amygdala Facial expressions of emotion were morphed into a continuum that ran from happiness to surprise to fear to sadness to disgust to anger and back to happiness. This sequence was shown to a patient with bilateral amygdala damage and to a group of 10 people without brain damage. Although the patient's recognition of happiness, sadness, and surprise was generally in line with that of the undamaged group, her recognition of anger, disgust, and fear was impaired. (Calder et al., 1996)

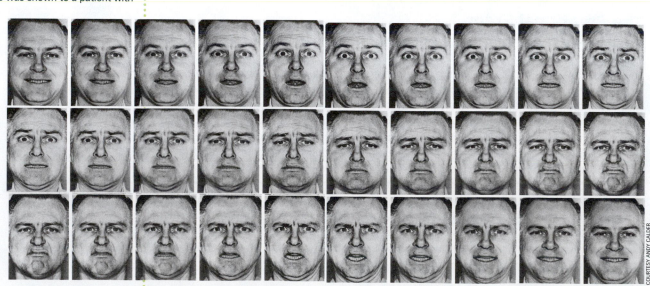

COURTESY ANDY CALDER

researchers performed an operation on monkeys so that information entering the monkey's left eye could be transmitted to the amygdala but information entering the monkey's right eye could not (Downer, 1961). When these monkeys were allowed to see a threatening stimulus with only their left eye, they responded with fear and alarm, but when they were allowed to see the threatening stimulus with only their right eye, they were calm and unruffled. These results suggest that if visual information doesn't reach the amygdala, then its emotional significance cannot be assessed. Klüver and Bucy's monkeys were calm in the presence of a snake because their amygdalae had been damaged, so the sight of a snake was no longer coded as threatening. Research on human beings has reached a similar conclusion. For example, normal people have superior memory for emotionally evocative words such as *death* or *crap,* but people whose amygdalae are damaged (LaBar & Phelps, 1998) or who take drugs that temporarily impair neurotransmission in the amygdala (van Stegeren et al., 1998) do not.

The amygdala's job is to make a very rapid appraisal of a stimulus, and thus it does not require much information (Zajonc, 1980, 1984). When people are shown fearful faces at speeds so fast that they are unaware of having seen them, their amygdalae show increased activity (Whalen et al., 1998). Psychologist Joseph LeDoux (2000) mapped the route that information about a stimulus takes through the brain and found that it is transmitted simultaneously along two distinct routes: the "fast pathway," which goes from the thalamus directly to the amygdala, and the "slow pathway," which goes from the thalamus to the cortex and *then* to the amygdala (see **FIGURE 10.5**). This means that while the cortex is slowly using the information to conduct a full-scale investigation of the stimulus's identity and importance ("This seems to be an animal . . . probably a mammal . . . perhaps a member of the genus *Ursus* . . ."), the amygdala has already received the information directly from the thalamus and is making one very fast and very simple decision: "Is this bad for me?" If the amygdala's answer to that question is "yes," it initiates the neural processes that ultimately produce the bodily reactions and conscious experience that we call fear.

When the cortex finally finishes processing the information, it sends a signal to the amygdala telling it to maintain fear ("We've now analyzed all the data up here, and sure enough, that thing is a bear—and bears bite!") or decrease it ("Relax, it's just some guy in a bear costume"). When people are asked to *experience* emotions such as happiness, sadness, fear, and anger, they show increased activity in the limbic system and decreased activity in the cortex (Damasio et al., 2000), but when people are asked to *inhibit* these emotions, they show increased cortical activity and decreased limbic

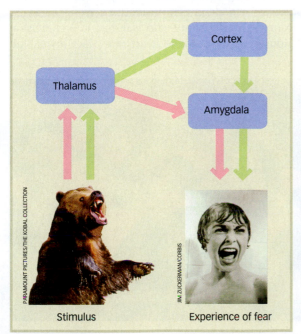

Thalamus

Cortex

Amygdala

Stimulus

Experience of fear

Figure 10.5 The Fast and Slow Pathways of Fear According to Joseph LeDoux, information about a stimulus takes two routes simultaneously: the "fast pathway" (shown in pink), which goes from the thalamus directly to the amygdala, and the "slow pathway" (shown in green), which goes from the thalamus to the cortex and then to the amygdala. Because the amygdala receives information from the thalamus before it receives information from the cortex, people can be afraid of something before they know what it is.

EMOTION REGULATION The use of cognitive and behavioral strategies to influence one's emotional experience.

REAPPRAISAL A strategy that involves changing one's emotional experience by changing the meaning of the emotion-eliciting stimulus.

activity (Ochsner Burge, Gross, & Gabrieli, 2002). In a sense, the amygdala presses the emotional gas pedal and the cortex then hits the brakes. That's why adults with cortical damage and children (whose cortices are not well developed) have difficulty inhibiting their emotions (Stuss & Benson, 1986).

Studies of the brain confirm what psychologists have long suspected: Emotion is a primitive system that prepares us to react rapidly and on the basis of little information to things that are relevant to our survival and well-being. While our newly acquired cortex identifies a stimulus, considers what it knows about it, and carefully plans a response, our ancient limbic system does what it has done so well for all those millennia before the cortex evolved: It makes a split-second decision about the significance of the objects and events in our environment and, when necessary, prepares our hearts and our legs to get our butts out of the woods.

The Regulation of Emotion

No one is agnostic about their own emotional experience. We may not care whether we have cereal or eggs for breakfast, whether we play cricket or cards this afternoon, or whether we spend a few minutes thinking about hedgehogs, earwax, or the War of 1812. But we always care whether we are feeling happy or fearful, angry or relaxed, joyful or disgusted. Because we care so much about our emotional experiences, we take an active role in determining which ones we will have. **Emotion regulation** refers to *the cognitive and behavioral strategies people use to influence their own emotional experience*. Although emotion regulation is typically an attempt to turn negative emotions into positive ones, there are times when people feel a bit too chipper for their own good and seek ways to "cheer down" (Erber, Wegner, & Therriault, 1996; Parrott, 1993). A patient who is feeling depressed may whistle a silly song while waiting for his doctor, and a doctor who is feeling silly may think a few depressing thoughts before entering the room to give the patient bad news. Both are regulating their emotional experience.

Nine out of 10 people report that they attempt to regulate their emotional experience at least once a day (Gross, 1998), and they describe more than a thousand different strategies for doing so (Parkinson & Totterdell, 1999). Some of these are behavioral strategies (e.g., avoiding situations that trigger unwanted emotions, doing distracting activities, or taking drugs) and some are cognitive strategies (e.g., trying not to think about the cause of the unwanted emotion or recruiting memories that trigger the desired emotion). Research suggests that one of the most effective strategies for emotion regulation is **reappraisal**, which involves *changing one's emotional experience by changing the meaning of the emotion-eliciting stimulus*. How people think about an event can determine how they feel about it. For example, participants who watched a circumcision that was described as a joyous religious ritual had slower heart rates, had lower skin

Taking heroin and singing in church would seem to have little in common, but both can be forms of emotion regulation.

conductance levels, and reported less distress than did participants who watched the circumcision but did not hear the same description (Lazarus & Alfert, 1964). Everyone knows that the phrase "Don't forget your umbrella" elicits annoyance when it is construed as nagging and gratitude when it is construed as caring, and we can regulate our emotional experience by construing it in one of these ways rather than the other.

More than two millennia ago, Roman emperor Marcus Aurelius wrote: "If you are distressed by anything external, the pain is not due to the thing itself, but to your estimate of it; and this you have the power to revoke at any moment." But is that true? Do we have the power to change how we think about events in order to change our emotional experiences? Research suggests that to some extent we do. In one study, participants' brains were scanned as they saw photos that induced negative emotions, such as a photo of a woman crying during a funeral. Some participants were then asked to reappraise the picture, for example, by imagining that the woman in the photo was at a wedding rather than a funeral. The results showed that when participants initially saw the photo, their amygdalae became active. But as they reappraised the picture, several key areas of the cortex became active, and moments later, their amygdalae were deactivated (Ochsner et al., 2002). In other words, participants consciously and willfully turned down the activity of their own amygdalae simply by thinking about the photo in a different way.

Studies such as these demonstrate at the neural level what psychologists have observed for centuries at the behavioral level: Because emotions are reactions to the appraisals of an event and not to the event itself, changes in appraisal bring about changes in emotional experience. As you will learn in Chapter 14, therapists often attempt to alleviate depression and distress by helping people find new ways to think about the events that happen to them. Indeed, reappraisal appears to be important for both mental and physical health (Davidson, Putnam, & Larson, 2000), and the inability to reappraise events lies at the heart of psychiatric disorders, such as depression (Gross & Munoz, 1995).

In summary, emotional experiences are difficult to describe, but psychologists have identified their two underlying dimensions: arousal and valence. Psychologists have spent more than a century trying to understand how emotional experience and physiological activity are related. The James-Lange theory suggests that a stimulus causes a physiological reaction, which leads to an emotional experience; the Cannon-Bard theory suggests that a stimulus causes both an emotional experience and a physiological reaction simultaneously; and Schachter and Singer's two-factor theory suggests that a stimulus causes undifferentiated physiological arousal about which people draw inferences. None of these theories is entirely right, but each has elements that are supported by research.

Emotions are produced by the complex interaction of limbic and cortical structures. Information about a stimulus is sent simultaneously to the amygdala (which makes a quick appraisal of the stimulus's goodness or badness) and the cortex (which does a slower and more comprehensive analysis of the stimulus). In some instances, the amygdala will trigger an emotional experience that the cortex later inhibits. People care about their emotional experiences and use many strategies to regulate them. Reappraisal involves changing the way one thinks about an object or event, and it is one of the most effective strategies for emotion regulation (see the Hot Science box on the next page). ■ ■

Emotional Communication: Msgs w/o Wrds

Emotions may be private events, but the "bodily reactions" they produce are not. An **emotional expression** is *an observable sign of an emotional state*, and human beings exhibit many such signs. For example, people's emotional states influence the way they talk—from intonation and inflection to loudness and duration—and research shows

 **ONLY HUMAN**

WHO ENFORCES THE EMOTION REGULATION? In 1991, the mayor of Sund, Norway, proposed a resolution to the town council that banned crankiness and required people to be happy and think positively. The resolution contained an exemption for those who had a good reason to be unhappy.

EMOTIONAL EXPRESSION Any observable sign of an emotional state.

{ HOT SCIENCE } The Pleasures of Uncertainty

WOULD YOU RATHER WIN THE LOTTERY OR become permanently disabled? You probably think that's the easiest question you've ever been asked. After all, isn't it *obvious* that one of these events would make you deliriously happy for years to come and the other would make you hopelessly depressed? Obvious, yes—but not necessarily true. Research shows that just a year after the event, lottery winners and paraplegics are about equally happy (Brickman, Coates, & Janoff-Bulman, 1978). If you find that hard to believe, then you're not alone. Timothy Wilson and Daniel Gilbert have studied **affective forecasting,** which is *the process by which people predict their emotional reactions to future events,* and they've found that people are not particularly good at predicting how they will feel after experiencing positive or negative events (Gilbert, Driver-Linn, & Wilson, 2002; Wilson & Gilbert, 2003). People routinely overestimate the joy of falling in love and the pain of falling out of it, the thrill of winning a football game and the agony of losing one, the delight of getting promoted and the distress of getting fired—and many other good and bad events (Gilbert, Pirel, Wilson, Blumberg, & Wheatley, 1998; Wilson Wheatley, Meyers, Gilbert, & Axsom, 2000). The fact is that you could know exactly what your future will hold and still not know how much you're going to like it when you get there.

Why are we so poor at forecasting our emotional reactions to future events? One reason is that most of us have a poor understanding of how our own emotions work. For example, imagine that you are studying in the library when a fellow student walks up to you, hands you a card that has a dollar coin attached to it, and then walks away. If you received the card shown on the left, how happy do you think you'd be 20 minutes later? Okay, how about if you received the card on the right?

Most people believe that getting a dollar from a stranger would make them feel happy, but they don't think it matters whether the card is the one on the left or the right. But most people are wrong. When researchers actually did this experiment, they found that people were happier if they had received the card on the left than if they had received the card on the right (Wilson, Centerbar, Kerner, & Gilbert, 2005).

Why? Although both cards contain declarative statements such as, "We like to promote random acts of kindness," the card on the right also contains questions to which those declarative statements are the answers. The card on the right provides no extra information, but because it uses a question-and-answer format, it makes people *feel* as though they understand why the experimenter gave them the card ("Aha, now I see—that guy is from the Smile Society, and the reason he does this is to promote acts of kindness"). One of the basic laws of emotion is that people have stronger emotional reactions to events whose causes they don't understand ("Yikes! What was that thumping noise?") than to events whose causes they do understand ("The washing machine is making that thumping noise again"). Because the card on the right makes us feel that we understand *why* the stranger walked up to us and gave us a dollar, our emotional reaction to that event subsides more quickly. But most people don't know about this law of emotion, and thus they can't accurately predict their own reactions to explained and unexplained events.

Indeed, people typically *prefer* to have an explanation than to remain in mystery, and thus they may choose things that undermine their own happiness. In one study, participants were college students who were linked to an Internet chat room where they had conversations with several other students (Wilson et al., 2005). After a little while, the experimenter asked everyone in the chat room to send a private e-mail message to the person whom they liked best explaining why they liked that person so much. What participants didn't know was that all the "other students" with whom

they were chatting were actually confederates of the experimenter. As soon as the participants sent off their e-mail messages, they received e-mail messages from *every one* of the "other students" explaining why the other student had chosen the participant as the person they liked most. In one condition of the study, every e-mail message was clearly identified so that the participant could tell which of the other students had sent it. In another condition of the experiment, the e-mail messages were anonymous so that the participant couldn't tell which student had sent which message. The results revealed two things. First, participants were happier when they could *not* identify the sender of the messages than when they could. Because unexplained events produce more intense and enduring emotions, the students who were "in the dark" about this happy event were happier for longer. Second, when a new group of participants were asked whether they would prefer to be able to identify the sender of each e-mail or to be kept in the dark, every one of them said they would prefer to know the sender's identity.

Studies such as these suggest that most people don't know enough about the nature of their own emotions to predict how happy they will be in different situations or to choose the situations that will make them happiest. Our emotional blind spots, it seems, can make us strangers to ourselves (Gilbert, 2006; Wilson, 2002).

AFFECTIVE FORECASTING The process by which people predict their emotional reactions to future events.

that listeners can infer a speaker's emotional state from vocal cues alone with better-than-chance accuracy (though vocal signs of anger, happiness, and sadness are somewhat easier to recognize than are vocal signs of fear and disgust; Banse & Scherer, 1996; Frick, 1985). The voice is not the only clue to a person's emotional state. In fact, observers can often estimate a person's emotional state from the direction of the person's gaze, gait, posture, and even from a person's touch (Dittrich, Troscianko, Lea, & Morgan, 1996; Keltner & Shiota, 2003; Wallbott, 1998). In some sense, we are walking, talking advertisements for what's going on inside us.

No part of the body is more exquisitely designed for communicating emotion than the face. Underneath every face lie 43 muscles that are capable of creating more than 10,000 unique configurations, which enables a face to convey information about its owner's emotional state with an astonishing degree of subtlety and specificity (Ekman, 1965). Psychologists Paul Ekman and Wallace Friesen (1978) spent years cataloguing the muscle movements of which the human face is capable. They isolated 46 unique movements, which they called *action units,* and they gave each one a number and a memorable name, such as "cheek puffer" and "dimpler" and "nasolabial deepener" (all of which, oddly enough, are also the names of heavy metal bands). Research has shown that combinations of these action units are reliably related to specific emotional states (Davidson, Ekman, Savon, Senulis, & Friesen, 1990). For example, when someone feels happy, the movements of the *zygomatic major* (a muscle that pulls the lip corners up) and the *obicularis oculi* (a muscle that crinkles the outside edges of the eyes) produce a unique facial expression that psychologists describe as "action units 6 and 12" and that the rest of us simply call smiling (Ekman & Friesen, 1982; Frank, Ekman, & Friesen, 1993; Steiner, 1986).

Communicative Expression

Why are our emotions written all over our faces? In 1872, Charles Darwin published a book titled *The Expression of the Emotions in Man and Animals,* in which he speculated about the evolutionary significance of emotional expression (Darwin, 1998). Darwin noticed that people and animals seem to share certain facial and postural expressions, and he suggested that these expressions are a means by which organisms communicate information about their internal states to each other. If a dominant animal can bare its teeth and communicate the message "I am angry at you" and if a subordinate animal can lower its head and communicate the message "I am afraid of you," then the two may be able to establish a pecking order without actually spilling blood. Emotional expressions are a convenient way for one animal to let another animal know how it is feeling and hence how it is prepared to act. In this sense, emotional expressions are a bit like the words or phrases of a nonverbal language.

The Universality of Expression

Of course, a language only works if everybody speaks the same one, and that fact led Darwin to develop the **universality hypothesis**, which suggests that *emotional expressions have the same meaning for everyone.* In other words, everyone expresses happiness

UNIVERSALITY HYPOTHESIS The hypothesis that emotional expressions have the same meaning for everyone.

Some animals looking soothed, angry, and sulky, according to Charles Darwin.

FROM DARWIN, C. (1872). THE EXPRESSION OF THE EMOTIONS IN MAN AND ANIMALS. LONDON: MURRAY. COURTESY OF UNIVERSITY OF CAMBRIDGE, DARWIN-ONLINE.ORG.UK

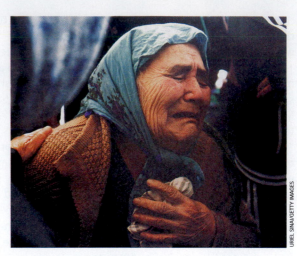

An Israeli woman cries at the funeral of a relative who was killed in a suicide attack in 2005. The universality hypothesis suggests that any human being who looks at this picture will know what she is feeling.

URIEL SINAI/GETTY IMAGES

with a smile and everyone understands that a smile signifies happiness. Two lines of evidence suggest that Darwin was largely correct. First, people are quite accurate at judging the emotional expressions of members of other cultures (Boucher & Carlson, 1980; Ekman & Friesen, 1971; Ekman et al., 1987; Elfenbein & Ambady, 2002; Frank & Stennet, 2001; Haidt & Keltner, 1999; Izard, 1971; McAndrew, 1986; Shimoda, Argyle, & Ricci-Bitt, 1978). Not only do Chileans, Americans, and Japanese all recognize a smile as a sign of happiness and a frown as a sign of sadness, but so do members of preliterate cultures. In the 1950s, researchers showed photographs of people expressing anger, disgust, fear, happiness, sadness, and surprise to members of the South Fore, a people who lived a Stone Age existence in the highlands of Papua New Guinea and who had had little contact with the outside world. The researchers discovered that the Fore could recognize the emotional expressions of Americans about as accurately as Americans could and vice versa. The one striking exception to this rule was that the Fore had trouble distinguishing expressions of surprise from expressions of fear, perhaps because for people who live in the wild, surprises are rarely pleasant.

The second line of evidence in favor of the universality hypothesis is that people who have never seen a human face make the same facial expressions as those who have. For instance, congenitally blind people make all the facial expressions associated with the basic emotions, and though their expressions are not quite as recognizable as those made by sighted individuals, the underlying action of the facial muscles is quite similar (Galati, Scherer, & Ricci-Bitt, 1997). Two-day-old infants (who have had virtually no exposure to human faces) react to sweet tastes with a smile and to bitter tastes with an expression of disgust (Steiner, 1973, 1979). In short, a good deal of evidence suggests that the facial displays of at least six emotions—anger, disgust, fear, happiness, sadness, and surprise—are universal. Recent evidence suggests that some other emotions, such as embarrassment, amusement, guilt, or shame, may have a universal pattern of facial expression as well (Keltner, 1995; Keltner & Buswell, 1996; Keltner & Haidt, 1999; Keltner & Harker, 1998).

The Cause and Effect of Expression

Why do so many people seem to express so many emotions in the same ways? After all, people in different cultures don't speak the same languages, so why do they smile the same smiles and frown the same frowns? The answer is that words are *symbols* and facial expressions are *signs*. Symbols are arbitrary designations that have no causal relationship with the things they symbolize. We English speakers use the word *cat* to indicate a particular animal, but there is nothing about felines that actually causes this particular sound to pop out of our mouths, and we aren't

Why is Stevie Wonder smiling? Perhaps it's the 22 Grammy awards he's won since 1974. Research shows that people who are born blind express emotion on their faces in the same ways that sighted people do.

EVERETT KENNEDY BROWN/EPA/CORBIS

On September 19, 1982, Scott Fahlman posted a message to an Internet user's group that read, "I propose the following character sequence for joke markers: :-) Read it sideways." And so the emoticon was born. Fahlman's smile (above left) is a sign of happiness, whereas his emoticon is a symbol.

COURTESY OF SCOTT FAHLMAN

FACIAL FEEDBACK HYPOTHESIS
The hypothesis that emotional expressions can cause the emotional experiences they signify.

surprised when other human beings make different sounds—such as *popoki* or *gatto*—to indicate the same thing. Facial expressions, on the other hand, are not arbitrary symbols of emotion. They are signs of emotion, and signs are *caused* by the things they signify. The feeling of happiness *causes* the contraction of the zygomatic major and thus its contraction is a sign of that feeling in the same way a footprint in the snow is a sign that someone walked there.

Although emotional experiences cause emotional expressions, there are instances in which the causal path runs in the other direction. The **facial feedback hypothesis** (Adelmann & Zajonc, 1989; Izard, 1971; Tomkins, 1981) suggests that *emotional expressions can cause the emotional experiences they signify.* For instance, people feel happier when they are asked to make the sound of a long *e* or to hold a pencil in their teeth (both of which cause contraction of the zygomatic major) than when they are asked to make the sound of a long *u* or to hold a pencil in their lips (Strack, Martin, & Stepper, 1988; Zajonc, 1989) (see **FIGURE 10.6**). Some researchers believe that this happens because the muscle contractions of a smile change the temperature of the brain, which in turn brings about a pleasant affective state (Zajonc, 1989). Others believe that the smile and the feeling of happiness become so strongly associated through experience that one always brings about the other. Although no one is sure why it happens, smiling does seem to be a cheap cure for the blues.

The fact that emotional expressions can cause the emotional experiences they signify may help explain why people are generally so good at recognizing the emotional expressions of others. Some studies suggest that observers unconsciously mimic the body postures and facial expressions of the people they are watching (Chartrand & Bargh, 1999; Dimberg, 1982). When we see someone lean forward and smile, we lean very slightly and slightly contract our zygomatic major. What purpose does this subtle mimicry serve? If making a facial expression brings about the feeling it signifies, then one can tell what others are feeling simply by imitating

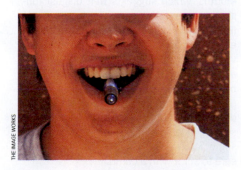
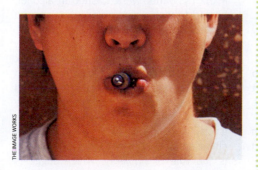

THE IMAGE WORKS
THE IMAGE WORKS

Figure 10.6 The Facial Feedback Hypothesis Research shows that people who hold a pen in their teeth feel happier than those who hold a pen in their lips. Holding a pen in the teeth contracts the zygomatic major muscles of the face in the same way a smile does.

their expressions and thereby experiencing their feelings oneself (Lipps, 1907). If this is actually what happens, then we would expect people who have trouble experiencing emotions to have trouble recognizing the emotional expressions of others. In fact, people with amygdala damage are typically quite poor at recognizing facial expressions of fear and anger (Adolphs, Russell, & Tranel, 1999), and this is especially true if their brain damage was sustained early in life (Adolphs, Cahill, Schol, & Babinsky, 1997). Similarly, people who are low in empathy find it difficult to know what others are feeling, and research shows that they are less likely to mimic the facial expressions of those with whom they interact (Sonnby-Borgstrom, Jonsson, & Svensson, 2003). All of this suggests that our emotional expressions play an important role in both sending and receiving information (see the Real World box).

{ THE REAL WORLD } That's Gross!

IF YOU WANT TO FEEL ONE OF THE MOST powerful, most irrational, and most poorly understood of all emotions, just spit in a glass of water. Then drink it. Despite the fact that the spit is yours and despite the fact that it was in your mouth just a moment ago, you will probably experience disgust.

Psychologist Paul Rozin has spent a lifetime disgusting people in order to understand the nature of this emotion, which is produced by the prospect of incorporating an offensive substance into one's body (Rozin & Fallon, 1987). The disgust reaction is characterized by feelings of nausea, a facial expression marked by distinct actions of the nose and mouth, and an etymology meaning "bad taste" (Rozin, Haidt, & McCauley, 1999). In this sense, disgust is a kind of defensive response that ensures that improper substances do not enter our bodies through our mouths, noses, or other orifices. For Americans, these improper substances include certain animals (such as rats and roaches), certain body products (such as vomit, feces, or blood), and certain foods (such as dog meat). The thought of eating a sumptuous meal of stewed monkey brains or of biting into an apple teeming with maggots makes most Americans feel nauseated, despite the fact that people in many other countries find both dishes quite palatable. Things that remind us of our animal nature, such as poor hygiene (body odor), inappropriate sex (i.e., with animals or family members), body boundary violations (open sores, amputated limbs), or contact with death (touching a corpse, watching an autopsy) also elicit disgust (Rozin & Fallon, 1987; Rozin et al., 1999). We like to distance ourselves from the rest of the animal kingdom, so reminders of our own animal origins, from belching to blood to barbarity, get tagged as disgusting.

COURTESY ALAN SWINKELS

San Francisco's Exploratorium features an exhibit on disgust that invites visitors to drink clean water from a toilet. Casual observation suggests that 5-year-olds are generally willing and 55-year-olds are not.

Disgust plays an important role, but it can be quite irrational, and its irrationality seems to follow two rules. The first is the rule of *contagion,* which suggests that any two things that were once in contact will continue to share their properties. So, for example, would you be willing to lick raisins off a flyswatter? Of course not. The flyswatter may have invisible traces of roach legs and fly guts on it, and those things can make you sick. Okay, then, what if the flyswatter were washed in alcohol, heated to within a degree of melting, and cooled to within a degree of breaking, making it the most sterile and hygienic thing in your entire house? Would you lick raisins off it then? Most people still say no (Rozin, Millman, & Nemeroff, 1986b). And the reason is that the swatter once touched a bug and thus it will forever have a disgusting "buginess" that cannot be cleansed away. The second irrational rule is the rule of *similarity,* which suggests

that things that share appearances also share properties. If someone whipped up a batch of fudge that was shaped to look convincingly like dog poop, chances are you'd turn down the opportunity to sample it. Fudge is fudge, of course, and its shape shouldn't matter, but most people still balk at this proposition (Rozin et al., 1986b)—most people, that is, except children. Children under 2 years of age will readily put any number of disgusting things in their mouths, which suggests that disgust (unlike many emotions) develops late in life (Rozin et al., 1986a). A 4-year-old will avoid eating human hair because it doesn't taste very good, but a 10-year-old child will avoid eating it because . . . well, it's haaaaaaaaair—and that's gross!

If you want to observe the irrationality of disgust for yourself, just offer your friends some guacamole in a disposable diaper or some lemonade in a bedpan. And make sure to stir it with a comb.

Deceptive Expression

Given how important emotional expressions are, it's no wonder that people have learned to use them to their advantage. Because you can control most of the muscles in your face, you don't have to display the emotion you are actually feeling or actually feel the emotion you are displaying. When your roommate makes a sarcastic remark about your haircut, you may make the facial expression for contempt (accompanied, perhaps, by a reinforcing hand gesture), but when your boss makes the same remark, you probably swallow hard and display a pained smile. Your expressions are moderated by your knowledge that it is permissible to show contempt for your peers but not for your superiors. **Display rules** are *norms for the control of emotional expression* (Ekman, 1972; Ekman & Friesen, 1968), and following them requires using several techniques:

- *Intensification* involves exaggerating the expression of one's emotion, as when a person pretends to be more surprised by a gift than she really is.
- *Deintensification* involves muting the expression of one's emotion, as when the loser of a contest tries to look less distressed than he really is.
- *Masking* involves expressing one emotion while feeling another, as when a poker player tries to look distressed rather than delighted as she examines a hand with four aces.
- *Neutralizing* involves feeling an emotion but displaying no expression, as when judges try not to betray their leanings while lawyers make their arguments.

Although people in different cultures all use the same techniques, they use them in the service of different display rules. For example, in one study, Japanese and American college students watched an unpleasant film of car accidents and amputations (Ekman, 1972; Friesen, 1972). When the students didn't know that the experimenters were observing them, Japanese and American students made similar expressions of disgust, but when they realized that they were being observed, the Japanese students (but not the American students) masked their disgust with pleasant expressions. In many Asian societies, there is a strong cultural norm against displaying negative emotions in the presence of a respected person, and people in these societies may mask or neutralize their expressions. The fact that different cultures have different display rules may also help explain the fact that people are better at recognizing the facial expressions of people from their own cultures (Elfenbein & Ambady, 2002).

Our attempts to obey our culture's display rules don't always work out so well. Darwin (1898/1998) noted that "those muscles of the face which are least obedient to the will, will sometimes alone betray a slight and passing emotion" (p. 79). Despite our best attempts to smile bravely when we receive a poor grade on an exam or appear concerned when a friend receives the same, our voices, bodies, and faces are "leaky" instruments that may betray our emotional states even when we don't want them to. Four sets of features can allow a careful observer to tell whether our emotional expression is sincere (Ekman, 2003a):

- *Morphology:* Certain facial muscles tend to resist conscious control, and for a trained observer, these so-called *reliable muscles* are quite revealing. For example, the zygomatic major raises the corners of the mouth, and this happens when people smile spontaneously or when they force themselves to smile. But only a genuine, spontaneous smile engages the obicularis oculi, which crinkles the corners of the eyes (see **FIGURE 10.7**.

Can you tell what this woman is feeling? She hopes not. Helen Duann is a champion poker player who knows how to keep a "poker face," which is a neutral expression that provides little information about her emotional state.

DISPLAY RULES Norms for the control of emotional expression.

Figure 10.7 Genuine and Fake Smiles Both spontaneous smiles (left) and voluntary smiles (right) raise the corners of the mouth, but only a spontaneous smile crinkles the corners of the eye.

- *Symmetry:* Sincere expressions are a bit more symmetrical than insincere expressions. A slightly lopsided smile is less likely to be genuine than is a perfectly even one.

- *Duration:* Sincere expressions tend to last between a half second and 5 seconds, and expressions that last for shorter or longer periods are more likely to be insincere.

- *Temporal patterning:* Sincere expressions appear and disappear smoothly over a few seconds, whereas insincere expressions tend to have more abrupt onsets and offsets.

Our emotions don't just leak on our faces: They leak all over the place. Research has shown that many aspects of our verbal and nonverbal behavior are altered when we tell a lie (DePaulo et al., 2003). For example, liars speak more slowly, take longer to respond to questions, and respond in less detail than do those who are telling the truth. Liars are also less fluent, less engaging, more uncertain, more tense, and less pleasant than truth tellers. Oddly enough, one of the telltale signs of a liar is that his or her performances tend to be just a bit too good: Liars' speech lacks the imperfections of truthful speech, such as superfluous details ("I noticed that the robber was wearing the same shoes that I saw on sale last week at Bloomingdale's and I found myself wondering what he paid for them"), spontaneous corrections ("He was six feet tall . . . well, no, actually more like six-two"), and expressions of self-doubt ("I think he had blue eyes, but I'm really not sure").

Given the reliable differences between sincere and insincere expressions, you might think that people would be quite good at telling one from the other. In fact, studies show that human lie detection ability is fairly awful. In studies in which a score of 100% represents perfect accuracy and a score of 50% represents pure chance, some trained professionals can attain scores of 80% (Ekman & O'Sullivan, 1991; Ekman, O'Sullivan, & Frank, 1999) (see **FIGURE 10.8**). But under most conditions, most people score barely better than chance (DePaulo, Stone, & Lassiter, 1985; Ekman, 1992; Zuckerman, DePaulo, & Rosenthal, 1981; Zuckerman & Driver, 1985). One reason for this is

Figure 10.8 Jobs and Lie Detection Most people are poor lie detectors, but some professionals aren't so bad. In tasks in which merely guessing would produce an accuracy rate of 50%, federal officers are 73% accurate. No one knows if the training for such jobs improves people's lie detection ability or if people who happen to be good lie detectors tend to get such jobs. (Ekman & O'Sullivan, 1991; Ekman, O'Sullivan & Frank, 1999).

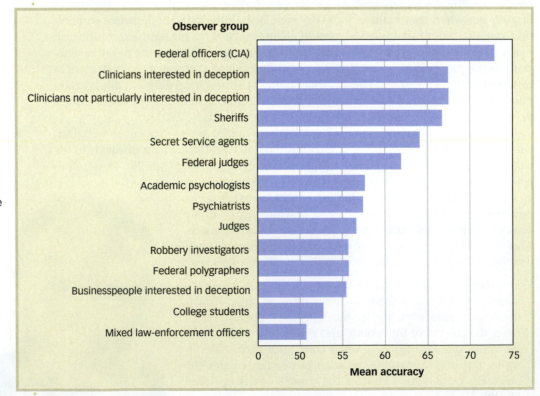

that people have a strong bias toward believing that others are sincere. In everyday life, most people are sincere most of the time, so it makes sense that we are predisposed to believe what we see and hear. This may explain why people tend to mistake liars for truth tellers but not the other way around (Gilbert, 1991). A second reason why people are such poor lie detectors is that they don't seem to know which pieces of information to attend to and which to ignore. People seem to think that certain things—such as whether a person speaks quickly or averts her gaze—are associated with lying when, in fact, they are not, and people seem to think that certain other things—such as talking too little or repeating words—are not associated with lying when, in fact, they are. These instances of myth and ignorance may explain why the correlation between a person's ability to detect lies and the person's confidence in that ability is essentially zero (DePaulo, Charlton, Cooper, Lindsay, & Muhlenbruck, 1997).

When people can't do something well (e.g., adding numbers or picking up 10-ton rocks), they typically turn the job over to machines (see **FIGURE 10.9**). Can machines detect lies better than we can? The answer is yes, but that's not saying much. The most widely used lie detection machine is the *polygraph,* which measures a variety of physiological responses that are associated with stress, which people often feel when they are afraid of being caught in a lie. In fact, the machine is so widely used by governments and businesses that the National Research Council recently met to consider all the scientific evidence on its validity. After much study, they concluded that the polygraph can indeed detect lies at a rate that is significantly better than chance (National Research Council, 2003). However, they also concluded that "almost a century of research in scientific psychology and physiology provides little basis for the expectation that a polygraph test could have extremely high accuracy" (p. 212).

The council went on to note the dangers of using a test that has the polygraph's error rate. Imagine, for example, that in a group of 10,000 people, 10 are terrorists and that when hooked up to a polygraph, all 10,000 people proclaim their innocence.

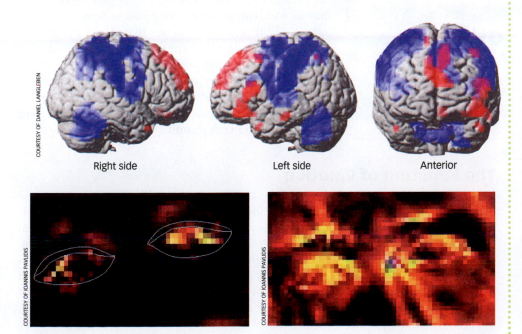

COURTESY OF DANIEL LANGLEBEN

Right side   Left side   Anterior

COURTESY OF IOANNIS PAVLIDIS

Figure 10.9 **Lie Detection Machines**
Some researchers hope to replace the polygraph with more accurate machines, such as those that measure changes in blood flow in the brain and the face. As the top panel shows, some areas of the brain are more active when people tell lies than when they tell the truth (shown in red), and some are more active when people tell the truth than when they tell lies (shown in blue) (Langleben et al., 2005). The bottom panel shows images taken by a thermal camera that detects the heat caused by blood flow to different parts of the face. The images show a person's face before (left) and after (right) telling a lie (Pavlidus, Eberhardt, & Levine, 2002). Although neither of these new techniques is extremely accurate, that could soon change.

Given the machine's error rate, a polygraph operator who caught 8 of the 10 terrorists would also "catch" 1,598 innocent people. If the operator were willing to use more stringent criteria for guilt, he could reduce the number of innocent people he caught to 39—but then he'd only catch 2 of the 10 terrorists! Furthermore, these numbers assume that the terrorists don't know how to fool the polygraph, which is something that people can, in fact, be trained to do. The council warned: "Given its level of accuracy, achieving a high probability of identifying individuals who pose major security risks in a population with a very low proportion of such individuals would require setting the test to be so sensitive that hundreds, or even thousands, of innocent individuals would be implicated for every major security violator correctly identified" (p. 6). In short, neither people nor machines are particularly good at lie detection, which is why lying continues to be a staple of human social interaction.

In summary, the voice, the body, and the face all communicate information about a person's emotional state. Darwin suggested that these emotional expressions are the same for all people and are universally understood, and research suggests that this is generally true. Emotional expressions are caused by the emotions they signify, but they can also cause those emotions. Emotional mimicry allows people to experience and hence identify the emotions of others.

Not all emotional expressions are sincere because people use display rules to help them decide which emotions to express. Cultures have different display rules, but people obey them by using the same set of techniques. There are reliable differences between sincere and insincere emotional expressions, just as there are reliable differences between truthful and untruthful utterances, but people are generally poor at determining when an expression or an utterance is sincere. Although machines such as the polygraph can make this determination with better-than-chance accuracy, their error rates are dangerously high. ■ ■

Motivation: Getting Moved

You now know something about how emotions are produced, experienced, and communicated. But what in the world are they *for*? Emotions have several functions, and one of the most important is that they motivate behavior. **Motivation** refers to *the purpose for or cause of an action,* and it is no coincidence that the words *emotion* and *motivation* share a common linguistic root that means "to move." We act because our emotions move us to do so, and they move us in two different ways: First, emotions provide us with *information* about the world, and second, emotions are the *objectives* toward which we strive. Let's examine each of these in turn.

The Function of Emotion

In the film *Invasion of the Body Snatchers,* a young couple suspects that most of the people they know have been kidnapped by aliens and replaced with replicas. This bizarre belief is the trope of many sci-fi movies, but it is also the primary symptom of Capgras syndrome (see **FIGURE 10.10**). People who suffer from this syndrome typically believe that one or more of their family members are imposters. As one Capgras sufferer told her doctor, "He looks exactly like my father, but he really isn't. He's a nice guy, but he isn't my father. . . . Maybe my father employed him to take care of me, paid him some money so he could pay my bills" (Hirstein & Ramachandran, 1997, p. 438). The patient's father had not been body-snatched, of course, nor had he hired his own stand-in. Rather, the patient had sustained damage to the neural

MOTIVATION The purpose for or cause of an action.

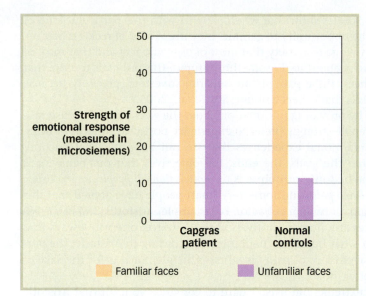

Figure 10.10 Capgras Syndrome This graph shows the emotional responses (as measured by skin conductance) of a patient with Capgras syndrome and a group of control participants to a set of familiar and unfamiliar faces. Although the controls have stronger emotional responses to the familiar than to the unfamiliar faces, the Capgras patient has similar emotional responses to both. (Hirstein & Ramachandran, 1997)

connections between her temporal lobe (where people's faces are identified) and her limbic system (where emotions are generated). As a result, when she saw her father's face, she could easily recognize it, but because this information was not transmitted to her limbic system, she didn't feel the warm emotions that her father's face once produced. Her father "looked right" but didn't "feel right," and so she concluded that the man before her was an imposter.

The patient's conclusions were wrong, of course, but her logic was sound. The patient used her emotional experience as information about the world, and studies show that most of us do the same thing. For example, people report being more satisfied with their lives in general when they are asked the question on a sunny day rather than a rainy day. Why? Because people feel happier on sunny days, and they use their happiness as information about the quality of their lives (Schwarz & Clore, 1983). People who are in good moods believe that they have a higher probability of winning a lottery than do people who are in bad moods. Why? Because people use their moods as information about the likelihood of succeeding at a task (Isen & Patrick, 1983). We all know that satisfying lives and bright futures make us feel good—so when we feel good, we naturally conclude that our lives must be satisfying and our futures must be bright. Because the world influences our emotions, our emotions provide information about the world (Schwarz, Mannheim, & Clore, 1988).

Indeed, without this information, we wouldn't know what to do next. When neurologist Antonio Damasio was asked to examine a patient with an unusual form of brain damage, he asked the patient to choose between two dates for an appointment. As Damasio (1994) later noted:

> For the better part of a half-hour, the patient enumerated reasons for and against each of the two dates: Previous engagements, proximity to other engagements, possible meteorological conditions, virtually anything that one could reasonably think about concerning a simple date. . . . He was walking us through a tiresome cost-benefit analysis, an endless outlining and fruitless comparison of options and possible consequences. (p. 193)

The patient's inability to make a simple decision was not due to any impairment of his ability to think or reason. On the contrary, he could think and reason all too well. What he couldn't do was feel. The patient's injury had left him unable to experience emotion, and thus when he entertained one option ("If I come next Tuesday, I'll have to cancel my lunch with Fred"), he didn't feel any better or any worse than when he entertained another ("If I come next Wednesday, I'll have to get up early to catch the bus"). And because he *felt* nothing when he thought about an option, he couldn't

HEDONIC PRINCIPLE The notion that all people are motivated to experience pleasure and avoid pain.

decide which was better. Studies show that when patients with this particular kind of brain damage are given the opportunity to gamble, they make a lot of reckless bets because they don't feel the twinge of anxiety that most of us would feel and that most of us would take to mean we're about to do something stupid. (It's only fair to note that under certain circumstances, these patients are superior investors, precisely because they are willing to take risks that others will not; Shiv et al., 2005.)

Emotions motivate us by providing information about the world, but they also motivate us more directly. People strongly prefer to experience positive rather than negative emotions, and the emotional experiences that we call happiness, satisfaction, pleasure, and joy are often the goals, the ends, the objectives that our behavior is meant to accomplish. The **hedonic principle** is *the notion that all people are motivated to experience pleasure and avoid pain,* and some very smart people have argued that this single principle can explain all human behavior. For example, Aristotle (350 BC/1998) observed that if one traces any human motivation to its source, one will always find the desire for pleasure, or what he called "happiness." According to Aristotle, the pursuit of pleasure and the avoidance of pain "is a first principle, for it is for the sake of this that we all do all that we do."

This may sound a bit extreme, but it isn't hard to convince yourself that Aristotle was on to something. If a friend asked you why you went to the mall, you might explain that you wanted to buy a new pair of mittens. If your friend then asked why you wanted to buy a new pair of mittens, you might explain that you wanted to keep your hands warm. If your friend then asked why you wanted to keep your hands warm, you might explain that warm hands are a pleasure and cold hands are a pain. Each of these motivations rests on another, and thus each of your answers would make sense.

But if your friend then asked you why you wanted to experience pleasure instead of pain, you'd find yourself tongue-tied. There is no answer to this question because there is no other motivation on which the desire for pleasure rests. The desire for pleasure is at the bottom of the pile—it holds everything else up and nothing lies beneath it. We want many other things, of course, from peace and prosperity to health and security, but the reason we want these things is that they (like new mittens) help us experience pleasure and avoid pain. As Aristotle's teacher, Plato (380 BC/1956), asked about all the many things that human beings call *good:* "Are these things good for any other reason except that they end in pleasure, and get rid of and avert pain? Are you looking to any other standard but pleasure and pain when you call them good?" Plato was suggesting that pleasure doesn't just matter to us—it is what *mattering* means.

According to the hedonic principle, then, our emotional experience can be thought of as a gauge that ranges from bad to good, and our primary motivation—perhaps even our *sole* motivation—is to keep the needle on the gauge as close to *g* as possible. Even when we voluntarily do things that tilt the needle in the opposite direction, such as letting the dentist drill our teeth or waking up early for a boring class, we are doing these things because we believe that they will nudge the needle toward *g* in the future and keep it there longer.

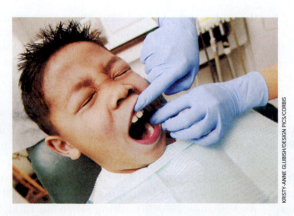

Many people voluntarily do things that cause them pain. According to the hedonic principle, people would not visit the dentist unless the pain of having dental work was ultimately outweighed by the pleasure of having had it done.

KRISTY-ANNE GLUBISH/DESIGN PICS/CORBIS

The Conceptualization of Motivation

The hedonic principle sets the stage for an understanding of motivation but leaves many questions unanswered. For example, if our primary motivation is to keep the needle on *g,* so to speak, then which things push the needle in that direction and which things push it away? And where do these things get the power to push our needle around, and exactly how do they do the pushing? The answers to such questions lie in two concepts that have played an unusually important role in the history of psychology: *instincts* and *drives.*

Instincts

When a newborn baby is given a drop of sugar water, it smiles, but when it is given a check for $10,000, it acts like it couldn't care less. By the time the baby gets into college, these responses pretty much reverse. It seems clear that nature endows us with certain motivations and that experience endows us with others. Almost a century ago, William McDougall (1908) argued that "observation of animals of any one species shows that all members of the species seek and strive toward a limited number of goals of certain types . . . and all members of the species seek these goals independently of example and of prior experience of attainment of them. . . . We are justified, then, in inferring that each member of the species inherits the tendencies of the species to seek goals of these several types" (p. 458). William James (1890) called the inherited tendency to seek a particular goal an *instinct,* which he defined as "the faculty of acting in such a way as to produce certain ends, without foresight of the ends, and without previous education in the performance" (p. 383). According to both McDougall and James, nature hardwired penguins, parrots, puppies, and people to want certain things without training and to execute the behaviors that produce these things without thinking. They and other psychologists of their time tried to make a list of what those things were.

Unfortunately, they were quite successful, and in just a few decades the list of instincts they generated had grown preposterously long, coming to include some rather exotic entries such as "the instinct to be secretive" and "the instinct to grind one's teeth" (both of which were contributed by James himself). In his 1924 survey of the burgeoning literature on instinct, sociologist Luther Bernard counted 5,759 instincts and concluded that after three decades of list making, the term seemed to be suffering from "a great variety of usage and the almost universal lack of critical standards" (Bernard, 1924, p. 21). Furthermore, to explain the fact that people befriend each other by claiming that people have an "affiliation instinct" didn't seem like much of an explanation at all. When Aristotle explained the downhill movement of water and the upward movement of fire by claiming that the former had "gravity" and the latter had "levity," it didn't take long for his fellow philosophers to catch on to the fact that Aristotle had merely named these tendencies and not really explained them. Psychologists worried that instincts were explanatory tautologies of Aristotelian proportion (Ayres, 1921; Dunlap, 1919; Field, 1921).

By 1930, the concept of instinct had taken "a sharp turn toward obscurity" (Herrnstein, 1972, p. 23). Yes, the concept was somewhat vague and vacuous, but that wasn't its real problem. Its real problem was that it flew in the face of American psychology's newest and most unstoppable force: behaviorism. Behaviorists rejected the concept of instinct on two grounds. First, they believed that behavior should be explained by the external stimuli that evoke it and not by reference to the hypothetical internal states on which it depends. John Watson (1913) had written that "the time seems to have come when psychology must discard all reference to consciousness" (p. 163), and behaviorists saw instincts as just the sort of unnecessary "internal talk" that Watson forbade. Second, behaviorists wanted nothing to do with the notion of inherited behavior because for them all complex behavior was learned. Because instincts were inherited tendencies that resided inside the organism, behaviorists considered them doubly repugnant.

All animals are born with both the motivation and the ability to perform certain complex behaviors. Spiders don't teach their offspring how to build elaborate webs, but their offspring build them nonetheless.

All mammals experience sex drives and hunger drives. This one seems to experience Sunday drives as well.

Drives

But within a few decades, some of Watson's younger followers began to realize that the strict prohibition against the mention of internal states made certain phenomena difficult to explain. For example, if all behavior is a response to an external stimulus, then why does a rat that is sitting still in its cage at 9:00 a.m. start wandering around and looking for food by noon? Nothing in the cage has changed, so why has the rat's behavior changed? What visible, measurable external stimulus is the wandering rat responding to? The obvious answer (obvious, at least, to any ordinary person) is that the rat is responding to something inside itself, which meant that one should look inside the rat if one wanted to explain its wandering. Because the right answer obviously had something to do with internal states and because Watson had forbidden behaviorists to talk about internal states, his young followers—the "new behaviorists"—had to use code words. The code word chosen by their leader, B. F. Skinner (1932a, 1932b), was *drive.*

The new behaviorists began by noting that bodies are like thermostats. When thermostats detect that the room is too cold, they send signals that initiate corrective actions such as turning on a furnace. Similarly, when bodies detect that they are underfed, they send signals that initiate corrective actions such as eating. **Homeostasis** is *the tendency for a system to take action to keep itself in a particular state,* and two of the new behaviorists, Clark Hull and Kenneth Spence, suggested that rats, people, and thermostats are all homeostatic mechanisms. To survive, an organism needs to maintain precise levels of nutrition, warmth, and so on, and when these levels depart from an optimal point, the organism receives a signal to take corrective action. That signal is called a **drive**, which is *an internal state generated by departures from physiological optimality.* According to Hull and Spence, it isn't food per se that organisms find rewarding; it is the reduction of the drive for food. Hunger is a drive, a drive is an internal state, and when organisms eat, they are attempting to change their internal state. It is important to understand that behaviorists had to use a great many words in order to avoid using the forbidden ones. So if "an internal state whose amelioration is rewarding" sounds suspiciously like a "bad feeling" to you, then join the club.

Eating and Mating

The words *instinct* and *drive* are no longer widely used in psychology, but the concepts remain part of the modern conception of motivation. The concept of instinct reminds us that nature endows organisms with a tendency to seek certain things, and the concept of drive reminds us that this seeking is initiated by an internal state. Psychologist William McDougall (1930) called the study of motivation "hormic psychology," which is a term derived from the Greek word for "urge," and people clearly have urges—some of which they acquire through experience and some of which they do not—that motivate them to take action. What kinds of urges do we have, and what kinds of actions do we take to satisfy them?

Abraham Maslow (1954) attempted to organize the list of human urges—or, as he called them, *needs*—in a meaningful way (see **FIGURE 10.11**). He noted that some needs (such as the need to eat) must be satisfied before others (such as the need to mate), and he built a hierarchy of needs that had the strongest and most immediate needs at the bottom and the weakest and most deferrable needs at the top. Maslow suggested that as a rule, people will not experience a need until all the needs below it are met. So when people are hungry or thirsty or exhausted, they will not seek intellectual fulfillment or moral clarity, which is to say that philosophy is a luxury of the well fed. Although many aspects of Maslow's theory failed to win empirical support (e.g., a person on a hunger strike may value her principles more than her physical needs; see

HOMEOSTASIS The tendency for a system to take action to keep itself in a particular state.

DRIVE An internal state generated by departures from physiological optimality.

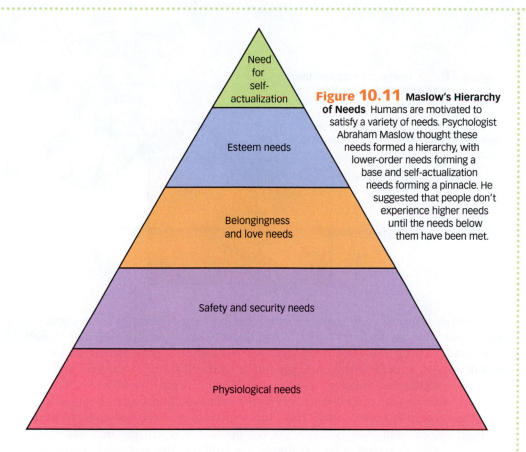

Figure 10.11 Maslow's Hierarchy of Needs Humans are motivated to satisfy a variety of needs. Psychologist Abraham Maslow thought these needs formed a hierarchy, with lower-order needs forming a base and self-actualization needs forming a pinnacle. He suggested that people don't experience higher needs until the needs below them have been met.

Wahba & Bridwell, 1976), the idea that some needs take precedence over others is clearly right. And although there are exceptions, those that typically take precedence are those that we share with other mammals and that are related to our common biology. Two of these needs—the need to eat and the need to mate—are among the most powerful and well studied, so let's see how they work.

The Hunger Signal

Hunger tells an organism to eat. But how does hunger arise? At every moment, your body is sending signals to your brain about its current energy state. If your body needs energy, it sends an *orexigenic* signal to tell your brain to switch hunger on, and if your body has sufficient energy, it sends an *anorexigenic* signal to tell your brain to switch hunger off (Gropp et al., 2005). No one knows precisely what these signals are or how they are sent and received, but research has identified a variety of candidates. For example, *leptin* is a chemical secreted by fat cells, and it appears to be an anorexigenic signal that tells the brain to switch hunger off. *Ghrelin* is a chemical that is produced in the stomach, and it appears to be an orexigenic signal that tells the brain to switch hunger on (Inui, 2001; Nakazato et al., 2001). Blood concentrations of ghrelin increase just before eating and decrease as eating proceeds (Cummings et al., 2001), and when people are injected with ghrelin, they become intensely hungry and eat about 30% more than usual (Wren et al., 2001). These are just two of the chemical messengers that tell the brain when to switch hunger on or off. Some researchers believe that there is no general state called hunger but rather that there are many different hungers, each of which is a response to a unique nutritional deficit and each of which is switched on by a unique chemical messenger (Rozin & Kalat, 1971). For example, rats that are deprived of protein will turn down fats and carbohydrates and specifically seek proteins, suggesting that they are experiencing a specific "protein hunger" and not a general hunger (Rozin, 1968).

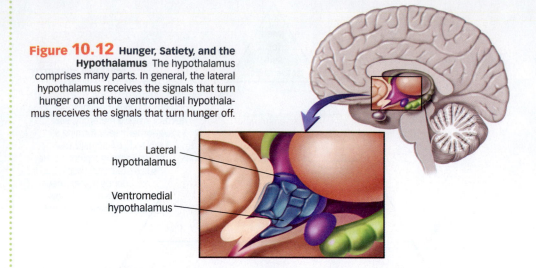

Figure 10.12 Hunger, Satiety, and the Hypothalamus The hypothalamus comprises many parts. In general, the lateral hypothalamus receives the signals that turn hunger on and the ventromedial hypothalamus receives the signals that turn hunger off.

Lateral hypothalamus

Ventromedial hypothalamus

Whether hunger is one signal or many, the primary receiver of these signals is the hypothalamus. Different parts of the hypothalamus receive different signals (see **FIGURE 10.12**). The *lateral hypothalamus* receives orexigenic signals, and when it is destroyed, animals sitting in a cage full of food will starve themselves to death. The *ventromedial hypothalamus* receives anorexigenic signals, and when it is destroyed, animals will gorge themselves to the point of illness and obesity (Miller, 1960; Steinbaum & Miller, 1965). These two structures were once thought to be the "hunger center" and "satiety center" of the brain, but recent research has shown that this view is far too simple. For example, some studies suggest that damage to the ventromedial hypothalamus causes animals to eat because it increases insulin production, which causes a larger percentage of the animal's meal to be turned into fat. This means that a smaller percentage of the animal's meal is available to meet its immediate energy needs, and thus the animal must eat more to compensate (Woods et al., 1998). It is tempting to think of different brain areas as hunger and satiety centers, but as psychologist Douglas Mook (1996) noted, "A map of the brain will not look like a map of Europe: Spain for satiety, France for feeding, Denmark for drinking. It will look more like a map of the Los Angeles freeway system, with routes diverging, converging, and crossing over, and many different destinations even for those all traveling the same route at the moment" (p. 98). Hypothalamic structures play an important role in turning hunger on and off, but the way they execute these functions is complex and poorly understood (Stellar & Stellar, 1985).

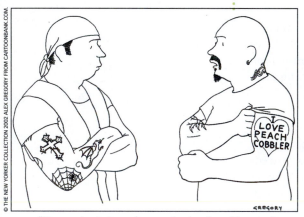

"Never get a tattoo when you're drunk and hungry."

Eating Problems

Feelings of hunger tell us when to eat and when to stop. But for the 10 to 30 million Americans who have eating disorders, eating is a much more complicated affair (Hoek & van Hoeken, 2003). For instance, **bulimia nervosa** is *a disorder characterized by binge eating followed by purging*. Bulimics typically ingest large quantities of food in a relatively short period and then take laxatives or induce vomiting to purge the food from their bodies. Bulimics are caught in a cycle: They eat to ameliorate negative emotions such as sadness and anxiety, but then concern about weight gain leads them to experience negative emotions such as guilt and self-loathing, and these emotions then lead them to purge.

Anorexia nervosa is *a disorder characterized by an intense fear of being fat and severe restriction of food intake*. Anorexics tend to have a distorted body image that leads them to believe they are fat when they are actually emaciated, and they tend to be high-achieving perfectionists who see their severe control of eating as a triumph of will over

BULIMIA NERVOSA An eating disorder characterized by binge eating followed by purging.

ANOREXIA NERVOSA An eating disorder characterized by an intense fear of being fat and severe restriction of food intake.

impulse. Contrary to what you might expect, anorexics have extremely *high* levels of ghrelin in their blood, which suggests that their bodies are trying desperately to switch hunger on, but that hunger's call is being suppressed, ignored, or overridden (Ariyasu et al., 2001). Like most eating disorders, anorexia strikes more women than men, and 40% of newly identified cases of anorexia are among females who are 15 to 19 years old. Anorexics believe that thinness equals beauty, and it isn't hard to understand why. The average American woman is 5'4" tall and weighs 140 pounds, but the average American fashion model is 5'11" tall and weighs 117 pounds. Indeed, most college-age women want to be thinner than they are (Rozin, Trachtenberg, & Cohen, 2001), and nearly one in five reports being *embarrassed* to buy a chocolate bar (Rozin, Bauer, & Catanese, 2003).

Bulimia and anorexia are problems for many people. But America's most pernicious and pervasive eating-related problem is obesity, which is defined as having a body mass index of 30 or greater. **TABLE 10.1** allows you to compute your body mass index, and the odds are that you won't like what you learn. Approximately 3 million Americans die each year from obesity-related illnesses (Allison, Fontaine, Manson, Stevens, & VanItallie, 1999), and that number is growing fast. Obese people are viewed negatively by others, have lower self-esteem, and have a lower quality of life (Hebl & Heatherton, 1997; Kolotkin, Meter, & Williams, 2001). Indeed, the stigma of obesity is so powerful that average-weight people are viewed negatively if they even have a relationship with someone who is obese (Hebl & Mannix, 2003).

Obesity can result from biochemical abnormalities, and it seems to have a strong genetic component, but overeating is often a part of its cause. If the brain has a complex system of on and off switches that regulate hunger, why does anyone overeat? Hunger is just one of the reasons why people eat—and not always the most important one. For example, whether a person eats depends on their knowledge of when they last ate, which is why amnesiacs will happily eat a second lunch shortly after finishing an unremembered first one (Rozin, Dow, Moscovitch, & Rajaram, 1998). People often eat to reduce negative emotions such as sadness or anxiety, and they often eat out of habit ("It's noon") or obligation ("Everyone else is ordering lunch"), all of which can cause people to eat more than they should.

Although people who suffer from anorexia are dangerously thin, they typically see themselves as fat. Sixteen-year-old Hannah Hartney has been suffering from anorexia since she was 9 years old.

| Table 10.1 | Body Mass Index Table |

	Normal							Overweight				Obese										Extreme Obesity														
BMI	19	20	21	22	23	24	25	26	27	28	29	30	31	32	33	34	35	36	37	38	39	40	41	42	43	44	45	46	47	48	49	50	51	52	53	54
Height (Inches)															Body Weight (pounds)																					
58	91	96	100	105	110	115	119	124	129	134	138	143	148	153	158	162	167	172	177	181	186	191	196	201	205	210	215	220	224	229	234	239	244	248	253	258
59	94	99	104	109	114	119	124	128	133	138	143	148	153	158	163	169	173	178	183	188	193	198	203	308	212	217	222	227	232	237	242	247	252	257	262	267
60	97	102	107	112	116	123	128	133	138	143	148	153	156	163	168	174	179	184	189	194	199	204	209	215	220	225	230	235	240	245	250	256	261	266	271	278
61	100	108	111	116	122	127	132	137	143	148	153	156	164	169	174	180	186	190	195	201	206	211	217	222	227	232	238	243	248	254	259	264	269	275	280	285
62	104	109	115	120	126	131	138	142	147	153	158	164	169	175	180	186	191	196	202	207	213	218	224	229	235	240	248	251	258	262	267	273	278	264	289	295
63	107	113	118	124	130	135	141	148	152	158	163	169	175	180	188	191	197	203	208	214	220	225	231	237	242	248	254	260	265	270	278	282	287	293	299	304
64	110	118	122	128	134	140	145	151	157	163	169	174	180	188	192	197	204	209	215	221	227	232	238	244	250	258	262	267	273	279	285	291	298	302	308	314
65	114	120	128	132	138	144	150	156	162	168	174	180	186	192	193	204	210	218	222	228	234	240	246	252	258	264	270	278	282	288	294	300	308	312	318	324
66	118	124	130	138	142	148	155	161	167	173	179	186	192	198	204	210	216	223	229	235	241	247	253	260	266	272	278	284	291	297	303	309	315	322	328	334
67	121	127	134	140	146	153	159	166	172	178	185	191	198	204	211	217	223	230	238	242	249	256	261	268	274	280	287	293	299	308	312	319	325	331	338	344
68	125	131	138	144	151	158	164	171	177	184	190	197	203	210	216	223	230	236	243	249	256	262	269	278	282	289	295	302	303	315	322	328	335	341	348	354
69	128	135	142	149	155	162	169	178	182	189	195	203	209	218	223	230	236	243	250	257	263	270	277	284	291	297	304	311	318	324	331	338	345	351	358	365
70	132	139	146	153	160	167	174	181	188	195	202	209	216	222	229	236	243	250	257	264	271	278	285	292	299	308	313	320	327	334	341	348	355	362	369	378
71	138	143	150	157	166	172	179	186	193	200	208	215	222	229	235	243	250	257	265	272	279	288	293	301	308	315	322	329	338	343	351	358	365	372	379	388
72	140	147	154	162	169	177	184	191	199	208	213	221	228	235	242	250	258	265	272	279	287	294	302	309	316	324	331	338	346	353	361	368	375	383	390	397
73	144	151	159	166	174	182	189	197	204	212	219	227	236	242	250	257	266	272	280	288	295	302	310	318	326	333	340	348	355	363	371	378	388	393	401	408
74	148	155	163	171	179	186	194	202	210	218	225	233	241	249	258	264	272	280	287	295	303	311	319	328	334	342	350	358	365	373	381	389	398	404	412	420
75	152	160	166	178	184	192	200	208	216	224	232	240	248	256	264	272	279	287	295	303	311	319	327	335	343	351	359	367	375	383	391	399	407	415	423	431
76	158	164	172	180	189	197	205	213	221	230	238	246	254	263	271	279	287	295	304	312	320	328	338	344	353	361	369	377	385	394	402	410	418	428	436	443

Source: Adapted from National Institutes of Health, 1998, *Clinical Guidelines on the Identification, Evaluation, and Treatment of Overweight and Obesity in Adults: The Evidence Report.* This and other information about overweight and obesity can be found at www.nhlbi.nih.gov/guidelines/obesity/ob_home.htm.

Prejudice against obese people is powerful and widespread. In this photo, members of the self-proclaimed "Bod Squad" protest against weight loss surgery in front of a San Francisco hospital.

Moreover, nature seems to have designed us for overeating. For most of our evolutionary history, the kinds and amounts of food available to people made it rather unlikely that anyone would eat too much, and the main food-related problem facing our ancestors was starvation. Their brains and bodies evolved two strategies to avoid it. First, they developed a strong attraction to foods that provide large amounts of energy per bite—in other words, foods that are calorically rich—which is why most of us prefer hamburgers and milk shakes to celery and water. Second, they developed an ability to store excess food energy in the form of fat, which enabled them to eat more than they needed when food was plentiful and then live off their reserves when food was scarce. We are beautifully engineered for a world in which food is generally low cal and scarce, and the problem is that we don't live in that world anymore. Rather, most of us live in a world in which the calorie-laden miracles of modern technology—from chocolate cupcakes to sausage pizzas—are inexpensive and readily available.

It is all too easy to overeat and become overweight or obese, and it is all too difficult to reverse course. The human body resists weight loss in two ways. First, when we gain weight, we experience an increase in both the size and the number of fat cells in our bodies (usually in our abdomens if we are male and in our thighs and buttocks if we are female). But when we lose weight, we experience a decrease in the size of our fat cells but no decrease in their number. Once our bodies have added a fat cell, that cell is pretty much there to stay. It may become thinner when we diet, but it is unlikely to die. Second, our bodies respond to dieting by decreasing our **metabolism**, which is *the rate at which energy is used*. When our bodies sense that we are living through a famine (which is what they conclude when we refuse to feed them), they find more efficient ways to turn food into fat—a great trick for our ancestors but a real nuisance for us. Indeed, when rats are overfed, then put on diets, then overfed again and put on diets again, they gain weight faster and lose it more slowly the second time around, which suggests that with each round of dieting, their bodies become increasingly efficient at converting food to fat (Brownell, Greenwood, Stellar, & Shrager, 1986). The bottom line is that avoiding obesity is much easier than overcoming it.

Sexual Interest

Essayist Florence King (1990) once remarked, "I've had sex and I've had food, and I'd rather eat." Indeed, food motivates us more strongly than sex because food is essential to our survival. But sex is essential to our DNA's survival, and thus evolution has ensured that a healthy desire for sex is wired deep into the brain of every mammal. In

METABOLISM The rate at which energy is used by the body.

some ways, that wiring scheme is simple: Glands secrete hormones, which travel through the blood to the brain and stimulate sexual desire. But which hormones, which parts of the brain, and what triggers the launch in the first place?

A hormone called dihydroepiandosterone (DHEA) seems to be involved in the initial onset of sexual desire. Both males and females begin producing this slow-acting hormone at about the age of 6, which may explain why boys and girls both experience their initial sexual interest at about the age of 10 despite the fact that boys reach puberty much later than girls. Two other hormones have more gender-specific effects. Both males and females produce testosterone and estrogen, but males produce more of the former and females produce more of the latter. As you will learn in Chapter 11, these two hormones are largely responsible for the physical and psychological changes that characterize puberty. But are they also responsible for the waxing and waning of sexual desire in adults? The answer appears to be yes—as long as those adults are rats. Testosterone increases the sexual desire of male rats by acting on a particular area of the hypothalamus, and estrogen increases the sexual desire of female rats by acting on a different area of the hypothalamus. Lesions to these areas reduce sexual motivation in the respective genders, and when testosterone or estrogen is applied to these areas, sexual motivation increases. In short, testosterone regulates sexual desire in male rats and estrogen regulates both sexual desire and fertility in female rats.

The story for human beings is far more interesting. The females of most mammalian species—for example, dogs, cats, and rats—have little or no interest in sex except when their estrogen levels are high, which happens when they are ovulating (i.e., when they are "in estrus" or "in heat"). In other words, estrogen regulates both ovulation and sexual interest in these mammals. But female human beings—like female monkeys and apes—can be interested in sex at any point in their monthly cycles. Although the level of estrogen in a woman's body changes dramatically over the course of her monthly menstrual cycle, studies suggest that sexual desire changes little if at all. Somewhere in the course of our evolution, it seems, women's sexual interest became independent of their ovulation. Some theorists have speculated that the advantage of this independence was that it made it more difficult for males to know whether a female was in the fertile phase of her monthly cycle. Male mammals often guard their mates jealously when their mates are ovulating but go off in search of other females when their mates are not. If a male cannot use his mate's sexual receptivity to tell when she is ovulating, then he has no choice but to stay around and guard her all the time. For females who are trying to keep their mates at home so that they will contribute to the rearing of children, sexual interest that is continuous and independent of fertility may be an excellent strategy.

If estrogen is not the hormonal basis of women's sex drives, then what is? Two pieces of evidence suggests that the answer is testosterone—the same hormone that drives male sexuality. First, when women are given testosterone, their sex drives increase. Second, men naturally have more testosterone than women do, and they clearly have a stronger sex drive. Men are more likely than women to think about sex, have sexual fantasies, seek sex and sexual variety (whether positions or partners), masturbate, want sex at an early point in a relationship, sacrifice other things for sex, have permissive attitudes toward sex, and complain about low sex drive in their partners. Indeed, a group of researchers summarized decades of research on sex drive by concluding that "by all measures, men have a stronger sex drive than women . . . [and] there were no measures that showed women having stronger sex drives than men" (Baumeister, Cantanese, & Vohs, 2001, pp. 263–264). All of this suggests that testosterone may be the hormonal basis of sex drive in both men and women.

"Come back, young man. He needs a booster shot."

The red coloration on the female gelada's chest indicates she is in estrus and thus amenable to sex. The sexual interest of female human beings is not limited to a particular time in their monthly cycle, and they do not clearly advertise their fertility.

Sexual Activity

Men and women may have different levels of sexual drive, but their physiological responses during sex are fairly similar. Prior to the 1960s, data on human sexual behavior consisted primarily of people's answers to questions about their sex lives—and you may have noticed that this is a topic about which people don't always tell the truth. William Masters and Virginia Johnson changed all that by conducting groundbreaking studies in which they actually measured the physical responses of many hundreds of volunteers as they masturbated or had sex in the laboratory (Masters & Johnson, 1966). Their work led to many discoveries, including a better understanding of the **human sexual response cycle**, which refers to *the stages of physiological arousal during sexual activity* (see **FIGURE 10.13**). Human sexual response has four phases:

■ During the *excitement phase,* muscle tension and blood flow increase in and around the sexual organs, heart and respiration rates increase, and blood pressure rises. Both men and women may experience erect nipples and a "sex flush" on the skin of the upper body and face. A man's penis typically becomes erect or partially erect and his testicles draw upward, while a woman's vagina typically becomes lubricated and her clitoris becomes swollen.

■ During the *plateau phase,* heart rate and muscle tension increase further. A man's urinary bladder closes to prevent urine from mixing with semen, and muscles at the base of his penis begin a steady rhythmic contraction. A man's Cowper gland may secrete a small amount of lubricating fluid (which often contains enough sperm to cause pregnancy). A woman's clitoris may withdraw slightly, and her vagina may become more lubricated. Her outer vagina may swell, and her muscles may tighten and reduce the diameter of the opening of the vagina.

■ During the *orgasm* phase, breathing becomes extremely rapid and the pelvic muscles begin a series of rhythmic contractions. Both men and women experience quick cycles of muscle contraction of the anus and lower pelvic muscles, and women often experience uterine and vaginal contractions as well. During this phase, men ejaculate about 2 to 5 milliliters of semen (depending on how long it has been since their last orgasm and how long they were aroused prior to ejaculation). Ninety-five percent of heterosexual men and 69% of heterosexual women reported having an orgasm during their last sexual encounter (Richters, de Visser, Rissel, & Smith, 2006), though it is worth noting that roughly 15% of women never experience orgasm, less than half experience orgasm from intercourse alone, and roughly half report having "faked" an orgasm at least once (Wiederman, 1997). The frequency with which women have orgasms seems to have a relatively large genetic component (Dawood et al., 2005). When men and women do have orgasms, they typically experience them as intensely pleasurable, and although many of us assume that these pleasurable experiences are different for men and for women, studies suggest that they are similar (Mah & Binik, 2002). Indeed, when gynecologists, psychologists, and medical students read people's descriptions of their orgasmic experiences, they cannot reliably tell whether those descriptions were written by men or by women (Vance & Wagner, 1976).

■ During the *resolution phase,* muscles relax, blood pressure drops, and the body returns to its resting state. Most men and women experience a *refractory period,* during which further stimulation does not produce excitement. This period may last from minutes to days and is typically longer for men than for women.

Men and women are similar in their responses during sexual activity, and they are also similar in their reasons for engaging in sexual activity in the first place. Sex is necessary for reproduction, of course, but the vast majority of sexual acts are performed for other reasons, which include experiencing pleasure, coping with negative emotions, increasing emotional intimacy between partners, pleasing one's partner, impressing one's friends, and reassuring oneself of one's own attractiveness (Cooper, Shapiro, & Powers, 1998). Both women and men report that their primary motivation for having sex is to create intimacy with their partners. Women are less likely than

HUMAN SEXUAL RESPONSE CYCLE The stages of physiological arousal during sexual activity.

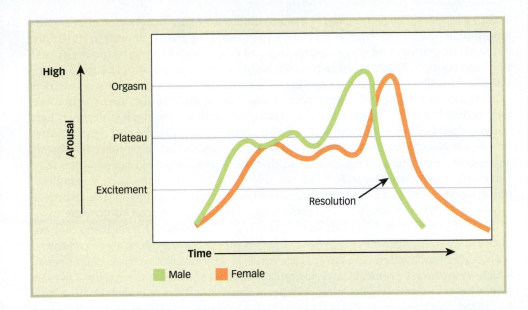

Figure 10.13 **The Human Sexual Response Cycle** The pattern of the sexual response cycle is quite similar for men and for women. Both men and women go through the excitement, plateau, orgasm, and resolutions phases, though the timing of their response may differ.

men to have sex to impress their friends, and men become less likely to have sex for this reason as they get older. Interestingly, as they age, both men and women are more likely to have sex for pleasure but no less likely to have sex to reassure themselves of their attractiveness. It is worth noting that not all sex is motivated by one of these reasons: About half of college-age women and a quarter of college-age men report having unwanted sexual activity in a dating relationship (O'Sullivan & Allegeier, 1998). We will have much more to say about sexual attraction and relationships in Chapter 16.

Kinds of Motivation

Without Carolus Linnaeus, there would be no *Homo sapiens*. Linnaeus was the eighteenth-century Swedish naturalist who developed the classification system, or "taxonomy," by which all living things are described. For example, he decided that your genus would be called *Homo* and your species would be called *sapiens,* and his organizational scheme made modern biology possible. Eating and mating are two things that human beings are strongly motivated to do—but what are the others, and how do they relate to each other? Alas, there is no widely accepted taxonomy of human motivations, which has made it difficult for psychologists to develop theories about where motivations come from and how they operate. Nonetheless, psychologists have made initial progress by identifying several of the dimensions on which motivations differ.

Intrinsic vs. Extrinsic

Taking a psychology exam is not like eating a french fry. One makes you tired and the other makes you fat, one requires that you move your lips and one requires that you don't, and so on. But the key difference between these activities is that one is a means to an end and one is an end in itself. An **extrinsic motivation** is *a motivation to take actions that lead to reward.* When we floss our teeth so we can avoid gum disease (and get dates), when we work hard for money so we can pay our rent (and get dates), and when we take an exam so we can get a college degree (and get money to get dates), we are extrinsically motivated. None of these things directly brings pleasure, but all may lead to pleasure in the long run. An **intrinsic motivation** is *a motivation to take actions that are themselves rewarding.* When we eat a french fry because it tastes good, exercise because it feels good, or listen to music because it sounds good, we are intrinsically motivated. These activities don't have to *have* a payoff because they *are* a payoff.

Extrinsic motivation gets a bad rap. Americans tend to believe that people should "follow their hearts" and "do what they love," and we feel sorry for or disdainful of students who choose courses just to please their parents and parents who choose jobs just

EXTRINSIC MOTIVATION A motivation to take actions that are not themselves rewarding but that lead to reward.

INTRINSIC MOTIVATION A motivation to take actions that are themselves rewarding.

CONSCIOUS MOTIVATION A motivation of which one is aware.

UNCONSCIOUS MOTIVATION A motivation of which one is not aware.

NEED FOR ACHIEVEMENT The motivation to solve worthwhile problems.

to earn a lot of money. But the fact is that our ability to engage in behaviors that are unrewarding in the present because we believe they will bring greater rewards in the future is one of our species' most significant talents, and no other species can do it quite as well as we can (Gilbert, 2006). In research on the ability to delay gratification, people are typically faced with a choice between getting something they want right now (e.g., a scoop of ice cream) or waiting and getting more of what they want later (e.g., two scoops of ice cream). Waiting for ice cream is a lot like taking an exam or flossing: It isn't much fun, but you do it because you know you will reap greater rewards in the end. Studies show that 4-year-old children who can delay gratification are judged to be more intelligent and socially competent 10 years later and that they have higher SAT scores when they enter college (Mischel, Shoda, & Rodriguez, 1989). In fact, the ability to delay gratification is a better predictor of a child's grades in school than is the child's IQ (Duckworth & Seligman, 2005). Apparently there is something to be said for extrinsic motivation.

There is a lot to be said for intrinsic motivation too. People work harder when they are intrinsically motivated, they enjoy what they do more, and they do it more creatively. Both kinds of motivation have advantages, which is why many of us try to build lives in which we are both intrinsically and extrinsically motivated by the same activity—lives in which we are paid the big bucks for doing exactly what we like to do best. Who hasn't fantasized about becoming a professional artist, a professional athlete, or a professional chocolatier? Alas, research suggests that it is difficult to eat your chocolate and have it too because extrinsic rewards can undermine intrinsic rewards (Deci, Koestner, & Ryan, 1999; Henderlong & Lepper, 2002). For example, in one study, college students who were intrinsically interested in a puzzle were either paid to complete it or completed it for free, and those who were paid were less likely to play with the puzzle later on (Deci, 1971). In a similar study, children who enjoyed drawing with Magic Markers were either promised or not promised an award for using them, and those who were promised the award were less likely to use the markers later (Lepper, Greene, & Nisbett, 1973). It appears that under some circumstances, people take rewards to indicate that an activity isn't inherently pleasurable ("If they had to pay me to do that puzzle, it couldn't have been a very fun one") and thus rewards can cause people to lose their intrinsic motivation.

Just as rewards can undermine intrinsic motivation, punishments can create it. In one study, children who had no intrinsic interest in playing with a toy suddenly gained an interest when the experimenter threatened to punish them if they touched it (Aronson, 1963). College students who had no intrinsic motivation to cheat on a test were more likely to do so if the experimenter explicitly warned against it (Wilson & Lassiter, 1982). Threats can suggest that a forbidden activity is desirable, and they can also have the paradoxical consequence of promoting the very behaviors they are meant to discourage. For example, when a group of day-care centers got fed up with parents who arrived late to pick up their children, some of them instituted a financial penalty for tardiness. As **FIGURE 10.14** shows, the financial penalty caused an *increase*

Figure 10.14 **When Threats Backfire** Threats can cause behaviors that were once intrinsically motivated to become extrinsically motivated. Day-care centers that instituted fines for late-arriving parents saw an increase in the number of parents who arrived late.

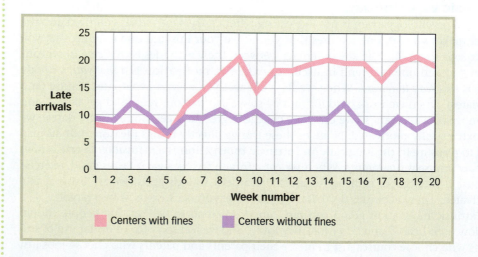

in late arrivals (Gneezy & Rustichini, 2000). Why? Because parents are intrinsically motivated to fetch their kids and they generally do their best to be on time. But when the day-care centers imposed a fine for late arrival, the parents became extrinsically motivated to fetch their children—and because the fine wasn't particularly large, they decided to pay a small financial penalty in order to leave their children in day care for an extra hour. When threats and rewards change intrinsic motivation into extrinsic motivation, unexpected consequences can follow.

Will this child enjoy swimming when he grows up? Studies suggest that extrinsic motivators, such as money, can undermine a person's intrinsic interest in performing activities such as swimming.

Conscious vs. Unconscious

When prizewinning artists or scientists are asked to explain their achievements, they typically say things like "I wanted to liberate color from form" or "I wanted to cure diabetes." They almost never say, "I wanted to exceed my father's accomplishments, thereby proving to my mother that I was worthy of her love." A **conscious motivation** is *a motivation of which one is aware,* and an **unconscious motivation** is *a motivation of which one is not aware.* Freud believed that people have unconscious motivations, but do they? In one sense, this is a trivial question. As you learned in Chapter 8, people often can't identify the reasons for or causes of their own behavior, and in this sense, people clearly have motivations of which they are unaware. We may avoid movies that star a particular actor without also knowing that the reason why we can't stand his face is that he resembles our eighth-grade algebra teacher.

But some psychologists have suggested that people have unconscious motivations that are anything but trivial. For example, David McClelland and John Atkinson argued that people vary in their **need for achievement**—which is *the motivation to solve worthwhile problems* (McClelland et al., 1953). They argued that this basic motivation is unconscious and thus must be measured with special techniques such as the *Thematic Apperception Test,* which presents people with a series of drawings and asks them to tell stories about them. The amount of "achievement-related imagery" in the person's story ostensibly reveals the person's unconscious need for achievement. (You'll learn more about these sorts of tests in Chapter 14.) Although there has been much controversy about the validity and reliability of measures such as these (Lilienfeld, Wood, & Garb, 2000; Tuerlinckx, De Boeck, & Lens, 2002), research shows that a person's responses on this test reliably predict the person's behavior in certain circumstances. For example, they can predict a child's grades in school (Khalid, 1991). Research also suggests that this motivation can be "primed" in much the same way that thoughts and feelings can be primed. For example, when words such as *achievement* are presented on a computer screen so rapidly that people cannot consciously perceive them, those people will work especially hard to solve a puzzle (Bargh, Gollwitzer, Lee-Chai, Barndollar, & Trötschel, 2001) and will feel especially unhappy if they fail (Chartrand & Kay, in press).

Some of our motivations are conscious and some are not. So which are which? A person who is shopping for mittens may be simultaneously motivated to increase her happiness, to keep her hands warm, and to find the mitten aisle in the store. Which of these motives will she be aware of? You'll notice that some of these motivations are quite general (increasing happiness) and some are quite specific (looking for mittens). Robin Vallacher and Daniel Wegner have suggested that people tend to be aware of their general motivations unless the complexities of executing an action force them to become aware of their specific motivations (Vallacher & Wegner, 1985, 1987). For example, if a person is changing a lightbulb and is asked about her motivation, she may say something like, "I'm helping my dad out." But the moment the lightbulb gets stuck, her answer will change to, "I'm trying to get these threads aligned." The person

 ONLY HUMAN

ACHIEVEMENT MOTIVATION GONE WILD
Vitaly Klimakhin dropped out of high school in 1991 to become a writer, and over a period of 107 days, he turned out a book that consisted entirely of the word *Ford* written 400,000 times. Klimakhin explained, "For a time, I would get up every morning and think, 'I've got to stop doing this before I lose my mind.' But ultimately my determination to finish won out."

APPROACH MOTIVATION A motivation to experience positive outcomes.

AVOIDANCE MOTIVATION A motivation not to experience negative outcomes.

has both motivations, of course, but she is conscious of her more general motivation when her action is easy and of her more specific motivation when her action is difficult. In one experiment, participants drank coffee either from a normal mug or from a mug that had a heavy weight attached to the bottom, which made the mug difficult to manipulate. When asked what they were doing, those who were drinking from the normal mug explained that they were "satisfying my needs," whereas those who were drinking from the weighted mug explained that they were "swallowing" (Wegner Vallacher, Macomber, Wood, & Arps, 1984).

Approach vs. Avoidance

The poet James Thurber (1956) wrote: "All men should strive to learn before they die / what they are running from, and to, and why." The hedonic principle describes two conceptually distinct motivations: a motivation to "run to" pleasure and a motivation to "run from" pain. These correspond to what psychologists call an **approach motivation**, which is *a motivation to experience a positive outcome,* and an **avoidance motivation**, which is *a motivation not to experience a negative outcome.* Although pleasure and pain seem like two sides of the same coin, they are independent phenomena that occur in different parts of the brain (Davidson et al., 1990), so it's not surprising that the motivation to experience positive emotions and the motivation not to experience negative emotions behave a bit differently.

For example, research suggests that, all else being equal, avoidance motivations tend to be more powerful than approach motivations. As you learned in Chapter 4, most people will turn down a chance to bet on a coin flip that would pay them $10 if it came up heads but would require them to pay $8 if it came up tails because they believe that the pain of losing $8 will be more intense than the pleasure of winning $10 (Kahneman & Tversky, 1979). Because people expect losses to have more powerful emotional consequences than equal-size gains, they will take more risks to avoid a loss than to achieve a gain. When participants are told that a disease is expected to kill 600 people and that one vaccine will definitely save 400 people, whereas another has a one-third chance of saving 600 people and a two-thirds chance of saving no one, they typically say that the government should play it safe and use the first vaccine. But when people are told that one vaccine will definitely allow 200 people to die, whereas the other has a one-third chance of letting no one die and a two-thirds chance of letting 600 people die, they say that the government should gamble and use the second vaccine (Tversky & Kahneman, 1981). If you whip out your calculator, you will quickly see that these are just two ways of describing the same thing—and yet when the vaccines are described in terms of the number of lives lost instead of the number of lives gained, most people are ready to take a big risk in order to avoid the horrible loss of 600 human lives.

Although avoidance motivation tends to be stronger than approach motivation overall, there are people for whom this is more or less true. For instance, people with a high need for achievement tend to be somewhat more motivated by their hope for success, whereas people with a low need for achievement tend to be somewhat more motivated by their fear of failure. This causes the "highs" to set reasonable goals that maximize their chances of achieving a worthwhile, meaningful success, and it causes "lows" to set goals that are either too easy (which ensures their success) or too difficult (which provides an excuse for their failure). When participants in one study were invited to play a game in which they had to toss a ring onto a pole and were allowed to stand as close to the pole as they wished, participants who had a high need for achievement tended to stand an intermediate distance from the pole—close enough to make success a good possibility, but far enough to make success worthwhile. Participants who were low in the need for achievement, on the other hand, were more likely to stand very close to the pole or very far from it (Atkinson & Litwin, 1960).

In another study, participants were given an anagram task. Some were told that they would be paid $4 for the experiment, but they could earn an extra dollar by finding 90% or more of all the possible words. Others were told that they that they would

People are motivated to avoid losses and achieve gains, but whether an outcome is seen as a loss or a gain often depends on how it is described. Smart retailers refer to price discrepancies such as this one as a "cash discount" rather than a "credit card surcharge."

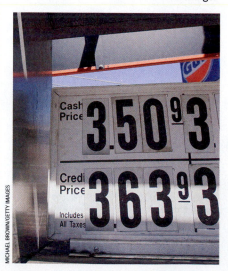

MICHAEL BROWN/GETTY IMAGES

be paid $5 for the experiment, but they could avoid losing a dollar by not missing more than 10% of all the possible words. People who had a "promotion focus"—which is a tendency to think in terms of achieving gains—performed better in the first case than in the second. But people who had a "prevention focus"—which is a tendency to think in terms of avoiding losses—performed better in the second case than in the first (Shah, Higgins, & Friedman, 1998).

In summary, emotions motivate us indirectly by providing information about the world, but they also motivate us directly. The hedonic principle suggests that people approach pleasure and avoid pain and that this basic motivation underlies all others. All organisms are born with some motivations and acquire others through experience.

When the body experiences a deficit, we experience a drive to remedy it. Biological drives such as eating and mating generally take precedence over others. Hunger is the result of a complex system of physiological processes, and problems with this system can lead to eating disorders and obesity, both of which are very difficult to overcome. With regard to sexual drives, men and women tend to be more similar than different. Both genders experience the same sequence of physiological arousal, engage in sex for most of the same reasons, and have sex drives that are regulated by testosterone.

People have many motivations that can be classified in many ways. Intrinsic motivations can be undermined by extrinsic rewards and punishments. People tend to be aware of their more general motivations unless difficulty with the production of action forces them to be aware of their more specific motivations. Avoidance motivations are generally more powerful than approach motivations, but this is more true for some people than for others. ■ ■

Where Do You Stand?

Here Comes the Bribe

Americans prize their right to vote. They talk about it, they sing about it, and they die for it. They just don't use it very much.

The U.S. Census Bureau estimates that about 60% of American citizens who are eligible to vote in a presidential election actually do so, and the numbers are significantly lower for "off-year" elections. Everyone seems to agree that this is a problem, including the people who don't vote, so what can be done? Government officials and social scientists have investigated numerous ways to increase voter turnout, and some of their efforts have had modest effects, but none has come close to solving the problem. And yet not all countries have this problem. Belgium, for instance, has a voter turnout rate close to 100% because for the better part of a century, failing to vote in Belgium has been illegal. (If you failed to vote in Belgium, don't worry; this only applies to Belgians.) Belgians who fail to vote may be fined, and if they fail to vote several times in a row, they may be "legally disenfranchised," which makes it difficult for them to get a job. Although some people have suggested that America should join the long list of countries that have compulsory voting, Americans generally don't like the threat of punishment.

But they sure do love the possibility of reward—and that's what led Arizona ophthalmologist Mark Osterloh to propose the Arizona Voter Reward Act, which would have awarded $1 million to a randomly selected voter in every election. As soon as Osterloh announced his idea, principled people lined up against it. "People should not go vote because they might win a lottery," said Curtis Gans, the director of the Center for the Study of the American Electorate in Washington. "We need to rekindle the religion of civic duty, and that is a hard job, but we should not make voting crassly commercial" (Archibold, 2006). An editorial in the *Yuma Sun* stated: "A jackpot is not the right motivator for voting. . . . People should vote because they want to and because they think it is important. . . . Bribing people to vote is a superficial approach that will have no beneficial outcome to the process, except to make some people feel good that the turnout numbers are higher" (Editorial, 2006). Nonetheless, 185,902 of Osterloh's fellow Arizonans thought his idea had merit, and they signed their names to get his measure on the ballot.

In November 2006, Arizonans defeated the measure by a sound margin, but Osterloh wasn't dejected. "I believe somebody is eventually going to bring this back and get this approved somewhere around the world, and it's going to spread," he said days after the election. "If anybody has a better idea of how to get people to vote, let me know and I will support it" (Rotstein, 2006).

Should our government motivate people to vote with extrinsic rewards or punishments? We know where Arizonans stand on this issue. How about you?

Chapter Review

Emotional Experience: The Feeling Machine

- Emotional experiences are difficult to describe, but psychologists have identified their two underlying dimensions: arousal and valence.

- Psychologists have spent more than a century trying to understand how emotional experience and physiological activity are related. The James-Lange theory suggests that a stimulus causes a physiological reaction, which leads to an emotional experience; the Cannon-Bard theory suggests that a stimulus causes both an emotional experience and a physiological reaction simultaneously; and Schachter and Singer's two-factor theory suggests that a stimulus causes undifferentiated physiological arousal about which people draw inferences.

- Emotions are produced by the complex interaction of limbic and cortical structures. Information about a stimulus is sent simultaneously to the amygdala (which makes a quick appraisal of the stimulus's goodness or badness) and the cortex (which does a slower and more comprehensive analysis of the stimulus). In some instances, the amygdala will trigger an emotional experience that the cortex later inhibits.

- People care about their emotional experiences and use many strategies to regulate them. Reappraisal involves changing the way one thinks about an object or event, and it is one of the most effective strategies for emotion regulation.

Emotional Communication: Msgs w/o Wrds

- Darwin suggested that emotional expressions are the same for all people and are universally understood, and research suggests that this is generally true.

- Emotional expressions are caused by the emotions they signify, but they can also cause those emotions.

- Emotional mimicry allows people to experience and hence identify the emotions of others.

- Not all emotional expressions are sincere because people use display rules to help them decide which emotions to express. Cultures have different display rules, but people obey them by using the same set of techniques.

- There are reliable differences between sincere and insincere emotional expressions, just as there are reliable differences between truthful and untruthful utterances, but people are generally poor at determining when an expression or an utterance is sincere. Although machines such as the polygraph can make this determination with better-than-chance accuracy, their error rates are dangerously high.

Motivation: Getting Moved

- Emotions motivate us indirectly by providing information about the world, but they also motivate us directly. The hedonic principle suggests that people approach pleasure and avoid pain and that this basic motivation underlies all others.

- All organisms are born with some motivations and acquire others through experience.

- When the body experiences a deficit, we experience a drive to remedy it. Biological drives such as eating and mating generally take precedence over others.

- Hunger is the result of a complex system of physiological processes, and problems with this system can lead to eating disorders and obesity, both of which are very difficult to overcome.

- With regard to sexual drives, men and women tend to be more similar than different. Both genders experience the same sequence of physiological arousal, engage in sex for most of the same reasons, and have sex drives that are regulated by testosterone.

- Intrinsic motivations can be undermined by extrinsic rewards and punishments.

- People tend to be aware of their more general motivations unless difficulty with the production of action forces them to be aware of their more specific motivations.

- Avoidance motivations are generally more powerful than approach motivations, but this is more true for some people than for others.

Key Terms

emotion (p. 370)
James-Lange theory (p. 370)
Cannon-Bard theory (p. 370)
two-factor theory (p. 371)
appraisal (p. 374)
emotion regulation (p. 376)
reappraisal (p. 376)
emotional expression (p. 377)

affective forecasting (p, 378)
universality hypothesis (p. 379)
facial feedback hypothesis (p. 381)
display rules (p. 383)
motivation (p. 386)
hedonic principle (p. 388)
homeostasis (p. 390)

drive (p. 390)
bulimia nervosa (p. 392)
anorexia nervosa (p. 392)
metabolism (p. 394)
human sexual response cycle (p. 396)
extrinsic motivation (p. 397)
intrinsic motivation (p. 397)

conscious motivation (p. 399)
unconscious motivation (p. 399)
need for achievement (p. 399)
approach motivation (p. 400)
avoidance motivation (p. 400)

Recommended Readings

Ekman, P. (2003b). *Emotions revealed: Recognizing faces and feelings to improve communication and emotional life.* New York: Times Books. Psychologist Paul Ekman explains the roots of our emotions and their expressions and answers such questions as: How does our body signal to others whether we are slightly sad or anguished, peeved or enraged? Can we learn to distinguish between a polite smile and the genuine thing? Can we ever truly control our emotions? A fascinating and fun book, packed with unique exercises and photographs.

Gilbert, D. T. (2006). *Stumbling on happiness.* New York: Knopf. In this award-winning international best seller, psychologist Daniel Gilbert examines our uniquely human ability to imagine the future and predict how much we will like it when we get there. *New Scientist* described it as "a witty, insightful and superbly entertaining trek through the foibles of human imagination."

LeDoux, J. (1996). *The emotional brain: The mysterious underpinnings of emotional life.* New York: Simon & Schuster. Neuroscientist Joseph LeDoux explains how the human brain processes information and generates emotions. The amygdala, he argues, processes information more quickly than other parts of the brain, thus allowing a rapid "fear response" that can save our lives before other parts of the brain have had a chance to react. Amazon.com called it "a compelling read about the mysteries of emotions and the workings of the brain."

11

Development

Prenatality: A Womb with a View
Prenatal Development
Prenatal Environment

Infancy and Childhood: Becoming a Person
Perceptual and Motor Development
Cognitive Development
Social Development
HOT SCIENCE An Accountant in the Crib?
Moral Development
THE REAL WORLD The Truth about Day Care

Adolescence: Minding the Gap
The Protraction of Adolescence
Sexuality
Parents and Peers

Adulthood: The Short Happy Future
Changing Abilities
Changing Orientations
Changing Roles
WHERE DO YOU STAND?
Licensing Parents

HIS MOTHER CALLED HIM ADI AND showered him with affection, but his father was not so kind. As his sister later recalled, "Adi challenged my father to extreme harshness and got his sound thrashing every day. . . . How often on the other hand did my mother caress him and try to obtain with her kindness where the father could not succeed with harshness." Although his father wanted him to become a civil servant, Adi's true love was art, and his mother quietly encouraged that gentler interest. Adi was just 18 years old when his mother was diagnosed with terminal cancer, and he was heartbroken when she died. Even her physician remarked that "in all my career, I have never seen anyone so prostrate with grief."

But Adi had little time for grieving. As he wrote, "Poverty and hard reality compelled me to make a quick decision. I was faced with the problem of somehow making my own living." Adi resolved to make his living as an artist. He moved to the city and applied to art school, but he was flatly rejected. Motherless and penniless, Adi wandered the city streets for 5 long years, sleeping on park benches, living in homeless shelters, and eating in soup kitchens, all the while trying desperately to sell his sketches and watercolors. Ten years later, Adi had achieved the fame he so desired, and today his paintings are sought by collectors, who pay significant sums to acquire them.

The largest collection of Adi's work is owned by the U.S. government, which keeps them locked in a room in Washington, D.C., and never allows them to be displayed. The curator of the collection, Marylou Gjernes, once remarked, "I often looked at them and wondered, 'What if? What if he had been accepted into art school? Would World War II have happened?'" Why would the curator ask such a question? Because while the artist's mother called him Adi, the rest of us know him as Adolph Hitler.

One of Adi's paintings, *The Church of Preux-Au-Bois,* sold at auction in 2006 for just under $20,000.

BARRY BATCHELOR/EMPICS/LANDOV

DEVELOPMENTAL PSYCHOLOGY
The study of continuity and change across the life span.

ZYGOTE A single cell that contains chromosomes from both a sperm and an egg.

GERMINAL STAGE The 2-week period of prenatal development that begins at conception.

EMBRYONIC STAGE The period of prenatal development that lasts from the second week until about the eighth week.

From infancy to childhood to adolescence to adulthood, people exhibit both continuity and change.

DANIEL GILBERT

Why is it so difficult to imagine the greatest mass murderer of the 20th century as a gentle child who loved to draw, as a compassionate adolescent who cared for his ailing mother, or as a dedicated young adult who suffered cold and hunger for the sake of beauty? After all, none of us began as the people we are now, and few of us will end up that way. From birth to infancy, from childhood to adolescence, from young adulthood to old age, one of the most obvious facts about human beings is that they change over time. Their development includes both dramatic transformations and striking consistencies in the way they look, think, feel, and act. **Developmental psychology** is *the study of continuity and change across the life span,* and every human being exhibits both. In the last century, psychologists have made some remarkable discoveries about how we acquire our first understanding of ourselves and our worlds; about what we seem to know at birth, what we must learn along the way, and what we never seem to get quite right; about the emotional bonds between us and our parents and then, later, between us and our children; about how we develop our sense of right and wrong; and about the radical transformations of adolescence, the subtle transformations of adulthood, and the surprising delights of old age.

Prenatality: A Womb with a View

You probably calculate your age by counting your birthdays, but the fact is that when you were born, you were already 9 months old. The *prenatal stage* of development ends with birth, but it begins 9 months earlier when about 200 million sperm begin a hazardous journey from a woman's vagina, through her uterus, and on to her fallopian tubes. Many of these sperm have defects that prevent them from swimming vigorously enough to make progress, and others get stuck in the spermatazoidal equivalent of a traffic jam in which too many sperm are on the same road, headed in the same direction at the same time. Of those that manage to make their way through the uterus, many take a wrong turn and end up in the fallopian tube that does not contain an egg. A mere 200 or so of the original 200 million sperm (or 0.0001%) manage to find the right fallopian tube and get close enough to an egg to release digestive enzymes that erode the egg's protective outer layer. As soon as one of these sperm manages to penetrate the coating, the egg quickly releases a chemical that seals the coating and keeps all the remaining sperm from entering. (Think of them as silver medalists.) After triumphing over massive odds, the one successful sperm sheds its tail and fertilizes the egg. In about 12 hours, the nuclei of the sperm and the egg merge, and the prenatal development of a unique human being begins.

Prenatal Development

The fertilized egg is called a **zygote**, which is *a single cell that contains chromosomes from both a sperm and an egg*. From the first moment of its existence, a zygote has one thing in common with the person it will ultimately become: gender. Each human sperm cell and each human egg cell contains 23 *chromosomes* that contain *genes,* which provide the blueprint for all biological development. Some sperm carry an X chromosome, and others carry a Y chromosome. If the egg is fertilized by a sperm that carries a Y chromosome, then the zygote is male; if the egg is fertilized by a sperm that carries an X chromosome, the zygote is female.

The 2-week period that begins at conception is known as the **germinal stage**, and it is during this stage that the one-celled zygote begins to divide—into two cells which divide into four, which divide into eight, and so on. By the time of birth, the zygote has divided into trillions of cells, each of which contains exactly one set of 23 chromosomes from the sperm and one set of 23 chromosomes from the egg. During the germinal stage, the zygote migrates back down the fallopian tube and implants itself in the wall of the uterus. This is a difficult journey, and about half of all zygotes do not complete it, either because they are defective or because they implant themselves in an inhospitable part of the uterus. Male zygotes are especially unlikely to complete this journey, and no one understands why, though some suggest that it's because male zygotes are especially unwilling to stop and ask for directions.

When the zygote implants itself on the uterine wall, a new stage of development begins. The **embryonic stage** is *a period that lasts from the second week until about the eighth week* (see **FIGURE 11.1**). During this stage, the zygote continues to divide and its cells begin to differentiate. The zygote at this stage is known as an *embryo,* and although it is just an inch long, it already has a beating heart and other body parts, such as arms and legs. Embryos that have one X chromosome and one Y chromosome begin to produce a hormone called testosterone, which masculinizes their reproductive organs, and embryos that have two X chromosomes do not. Without testosterone, the embryo continues developing as a female. In a sense, then, males are a specialized form of females.

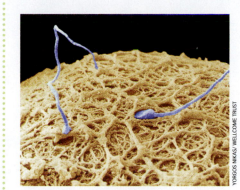

This electron micrograph shows a false-color image of several human sperm, one of which is fertilizing an egg.

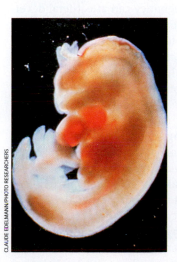
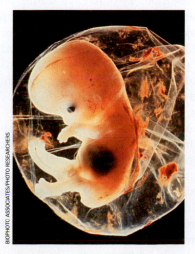
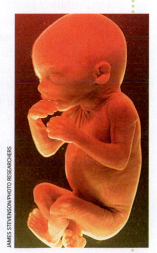

Figure 11.1 Prenatal Development Human beings undergo amazing development in the 9 months of prenatal development. These images show an embryo at 30 days, an embryo at 8 to 9 weeks, and a fetus at 5 months.

The **fetal stage** is *a period that lasts from the ninth week until birth.* The embryo at this stage is known as a *fetus,* and it has a skeleton and muscles that make it capable of movement. During the last 3 months of the fetal stage, the size of the fetus increases rapidly. It develops a layer of insulating fat beneath its skin, and its digestive and respiratory systems mature. Because the brain is the most complex organ in the body, it is also the most sensitive structure to develop during the prenatal stage. The cells that ultimately become the brain divide very quickly around the third and fourth week of life, and this process is more or less complete by 6 months. Then two things must happen. First, when brain cells are manufactured, they consist mainly of a cell body, and it is only after they have migrated toward a specific area of the brain that their axons and dendrites (which permit communication with other brain cells) are generated. Second, a process known as **myelination**—which is *the formation of a fatty sheath around the axons of a brain cell*—begins. Just as plastic sheathing insulates a wire, myelin insulates a brain cell and prevents the leakage of neural signals that travel along the axon. The process of myelination does not occur at a constant rate across all areas. For example, the spinal cord and the brain stem have more myelin than the cerebral cortex itself, and the myelination of the cortex continues into adulthood.

Although the brain undergoes rapid and complex growth during the fetal period, at birth it is nowhere near its adult size. Whereas a newborn chimp's brain is nearly 60% of its adult size, a newborn human's brain is only 25% of its adult size, which is to say that 75% of the brain's development occurs outside the womb. Why are human beings born with such underdeveloped brains when other primates are not? There are at least two reasons. First, the human brain has nearly tripled in size in just 2 million years of evolution, and bigger brains require bigger heads to house them. If a newborn's head were closer to its adult size, the baby could not pass through its mother's birth canal. Second, one of our species' greatest talents is its ability to adapt to a wide range of novel environments that differ in terms of climate, social structure, and so on. Rather than arriving in the world with a fully developed brain that may or may not meet the requirements of its environment, human beings arrive with brains that do much of their developing *within* the very environments in which they will function. The fact that our underdeveloped brains are specifically shaped by the unique social and physical environment into which we are born allows us to be exceptionally adaptable.

Prenatal Environment

It is natural to assume that genes influence development from the moment of conception and that the environment influences development from the moment of birth. But that's not so. The womb is an environment that influences development in a multitude of ways. For example, the *placenta* is the organ that physically links the bloodstreams of the mother and the developing embryo or fetus and permits the exchange of materials. As such, the foods a woman eats during pregnancy can affect fetal development. Toward the end of World War II, the Nazis imposed a food embargo on large Dutch cities, and many pregnant women suffered severe food deprivation. Subsequent research on their children's development demonstrated that food deprivation during the first 6 months of pregnancy caused the children to have both physical problems (Stein et al., 1975) and psychological problems, most notably an increased likelihood of schizophrenia and antisocial personality disorder (Neugebauer, Hoek, & Susser, 1999; Susser, Brown, & Matte, 1999).

These effects are not unique to food. Almost anything that a woman eats, drinks, inhales, injects, or otherwise comes into contact with can pass through the placenta and affect the development of her fetus. *Agents that damage the process of development* are called **teratogens**, which literally means "monster makers." Teratogens include environmental poisons such as lead in the water, paint dust in the air, or mercury in fish, but they also include common substances such as tobacco and alcohol. **Fetal alcohol syndrome** is *a developmental disorder that stems from heavy alcohol use by the mother during pregnancy,* and it increases the risk of birth defects, especially with respect to the shape and size of the head and the structure of the brain. Children with fetal alcohol

FETAL STAGE The period of prenatal development that lasts from the ninth week until birth.

MYELINATION The formation of a fatty sheath around the axons of a brain cell.

TERATOGENS Agents that damage the process of development, such as drugs and viruses.

FETAL ALCOHOL SYNDROME A developmental disorder that stems from heavy alcohol use by the mother during pregnancy.

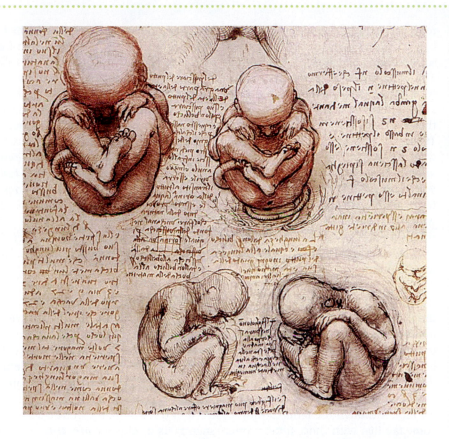

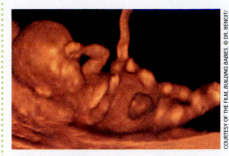

In 1510, Leonardo da Vinci imagined what a fetus looked like (left). As you can see from the modern sonogram above, his renderings were remarkably accurate.

syndrome frequently exhibit mental retardation and have more problems with academic achievement than other children (Carmichael Olson et al., 1997; Streissguth et al., 1999). Similarly, babies whose mothers smoke tobacco have lower birth weights (Horta et al., 1997) and are more likely to have perceptual and attentional problems in childhood (Fried & Watkinson, 2000). Even secondhand smoke can lead to reduced birth weight and deficits in attention and learning (Makin, Fried, & Watkinson, 1991; Windham, Eaton, & Hopkins, 1999). The effect of teratogens generally depends on the developmental stage at which they are encountered. The embryo is more vulnerable to teratogens than is the fetus, but structures such as the central nervous system are vulnerable throughout the entire prenatal period. As far as scientists can tell, there are no "safe amounts" of alcohol and tobacco for pregnant women.

The prenatal environment is rich with chemicals, but it is also rich with information. Unlike an automobile, which operates only after it has been fully assembled, the human brain functions even as it is being built, and research shows that the developing

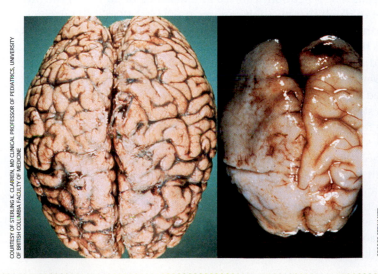

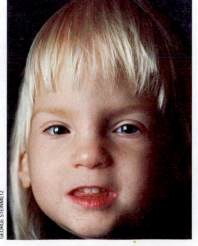

The panel on the far left shows the brains of a normal 6-week-old child (left) and a 6-week-old child born with fetal alcohol syndrome (FAS) (right). The child in the photo has the telltale facial features associated with FAS: short eye openings, a flat midface, an indistinct or flat ridge under the nose, and a thin upper lip. Children with FAS may also have tiny folds of tissue along the eye opening, a low nasal bridge, an underdeveloped jaw, and minor ear anomalies.

INFANCY The stage of development that begins at birth and lasts between 18 and 24 months.

MOTOR DEVELOPMENT The emergence of the ability to execute physical action.

REFLEXES Specific patterns of motor response that are triggered by specific patterns of sensory stimulation.

CEPHALOCAUDAL RULE The "top-to-bottom" rule that describes the tendency for motor skills to emerge in sequence from the head to the feet.

PROXIMODISTAL RULE The "inside-to-outside" rule that describes the tendency for motor skills to emerge in sequence from the center to the periphery.

fetus can sense stimulation—and can learn. Wombs are dark because only the brightest light can filter through the mother's abdomen, but they are not quiet. High-frequency sounds tend to be muffled, but low-frequency sounds penetrate the mother's abdomen. The fetus can hear its mother's heartbeat and the gastrointestinal sounds associated with her digestion, but most importantly, it can hear its mother's voice. Newborns who are just 2 hours old will suck a nipple more vigorously when they hear the sound of their mother's voice than when they hear the voice of a female stranger (Querleu et al., 1984), which suggests that they became familiar with their mothers' voice while they were developing inside her. Experiments confirm this. In one study, researchers arranged for some women to read aloud a short passage from *The Cat in the Hat* repeatedly during the last 6 weeks of pregnancy. Once the babies were born, the researchers tested their reactions to passages from *The Cat in the Hat* as well as other stories. Babies whose mothers had read aloud reacted to the passage from *The Cat in the Hat* differently than they reacted to an unfamiliar passage, whereas infants whose mothers had not read aloud reacted to both passages similarly (DeCasper & Spence, 1986). Clearly, the fetus is listening.

In summary, developmental psychology studies continuity and change across the life span. The prenatal stage of development begins when a sperm fertilizes an egg, producing a zygote. The zygote, which contains chromosomes from both the egg and the sperm, develops into an embryo at 2 weeks and then a fetus at 8 weeks. The fetal environment has important physical and psychological influences on the fetus. In addition to the food a pregnant woman eats, teratogens, or agents that impair fetal development, can affect the fetus. Some of the most common teratogens are tobacco and alcohol. Although the fetus cannot see much in the womb, it can hear sounds and become familiar with those it hears often, such as its mother's voice. ■ ■

Infancy and Childhood: Becoming a Person

Newborns may appear to be capable of little more than squalling and squirming, but in the last decade, researchers have discovered that they are actually more sophisticated than anyone suspected. **Infancy** is *the stage of development that begins at birth and lasts between 18 and 24 months,* and as you will see, much more happens during this stage than meets the untrained eye.

Perceptual and Motor Development

New parents like to stand around the crib and make goofy faces at the baby because they think the baby will be amused. In fact, newborns have a rather limited range of vision. The level of detail that a newborn can see at a distance of 20 feet is roughly equivalent to the level of detail that an adult can see at 600 feet (Banks & Salapatek, 1983). On the other hand, when visual stimuli are close enough to be seen, newborns are quite responsive to them. Studies show that newborns can follow a moving stimulus with their eyes and that they can distinguish stimuli they have seen before from those they have not. Newborns in one study were shown a circle with diagonal stripes, and they initially stared at it for quite some time. But as the circle was presented again and again, the infants stared less and less each time. Recall from Chapter 6 that *habituation* is the tendency for organisms to respond less intensely to a stimulus as the frequency of exposure to that stimulus increases, and babies habituate just like the rest of us do. So what happened when the researchers rotated the circle 90 degrees? The newborns once again began staring intently, which indicates that they noticed the change in the circle's orientation (Slater, Morison, & Somers, 1988).

Interestingly, newborns seem to be especially attuned to social stimuli. For example, newborns in one study were shown a blank disk, a disk with scrambled facial features, or a disk with a regular face. When the disk was moved across their fields of vision, the newborns tracked the disk by moving both their heads and their eyes. Moreover, they

ONLY HUMAN

NO OFFENSE TAKEN In December 1996, officials at the Wellington City Art Gallery in New Zealand denied entry to a 9-day-old baby whose mother sought to buy a ticket. Director Paula Savage said she was strictly enforcing the gallery's policy of not permitting minors to see the sexually explicit work of controversial photographer Robert Mapplethorpe.

tracked the disk with the regular face longer than they tracked the other disks (Johnson et al., 1991). But newborns don't merely track social stimuli with their eyes; they respond to them in other surprising ways. Researchers in one study stood close to some newborns while sticking out their tongues and stood close to other newborns while pursing their lips. Newborns in the first group stuck out their own tongues more often than those in the second group did, and newborns in the second group pursed their lips more often than those in the first group did (Meltzoff & Moore, 1977). Indeed, newborns have been shown to mimic facial expressions in their very first *hour* of life (Reissland, 1988).

Although infants can use their eyes right away, they must spend considerably more time learning how to use most of their other parts. **Motor development** is *the emergence of the ability to execute physical actions* such as reaching, grasping, crawling, and walking. Infants are born with a small set of **reflexes**, which are *specific patterns of motor response that are triggered by specific patterns of sensory stimulation*. For example, the *rooting reflex* is the tendency for infants to move their mouths toward any object that touches their cheek, and the *sucking reflex* is the tendency to suck any object that enters their mouths. These two reflexes allow newborns to find their mother's nipple and begin feeding—a behavior so vitally important that nature took no chances and hardwired it into every one of us. Interestingly, these and other reflexes that are present at birth seem to disappear in the first few months as children learn to execute more sophisticated motor behavior.

The development of these more sophisticated behaviors tends to obey two general rules. The first is the **cephalocaudal rule** (or the "top-to-bottom" rule), which describes *the tendency for motor skills to emerge in sequence from the head to the feet*. Infants tend to gain control over their heads first, their arms and trunks next, and their legs last. A young baby who is placed on her stomach may lift her head and may even lift her chest by using her arms for support, but she typically has little control over her legs. The second rule is the **proximodistal rule** (or the "inside-to-outside" rule), which describes *the tendency for motor skills to emerge in sequence from the center to the periphery*. Babies learn to control their trunks before their elbows and knees, and they learn to control their elbows and knees before their hands and feet (see **FIGURE 11.2**).

Infants mimic the facial expressions of adults. And vice versa.

GERI ENGBERG/THE IMAGE WORKS

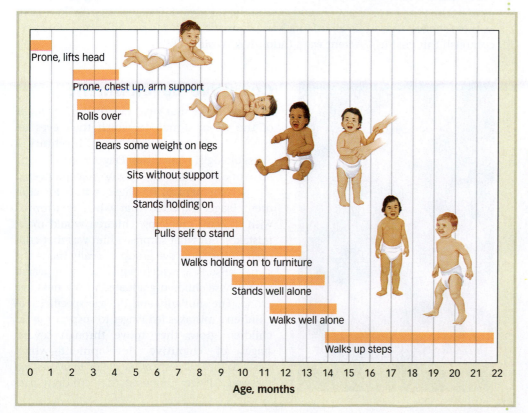

Figure 11.2 **Motor Development** Infants learn to control their bodies from head to feet and from center to periphery. These skills emerge in a strict sequence.

COGNITIVE DEVELOPMENT The emergence of the ability to understand the world.

SENSORIMOTOR STAGE A stage of development that begins at birth and lasts through infancy in which infants acquire information about the world by sensing it and moving around within it.

SCHEMAS Theories about or models of the way the world works.

ASSIMILATION The process by which infants apply their schemas in novel situations.

ACCOMMODATION The process by which infants revise their schemas in light of new information.

OBJECT PERMANENCE The idea that objects continue to exist even when they are not visible.

Some children develop motor skills earlier than others.

QILAI SHEN/PANOS PICTURES

Motor skills generally emerge in an orderly sequence that corresponds to these rules, but they do not emerge on a strict timetable. Rather, the timing of these skills is influenced by many factors, such as the baby's incentive for reaching, body weight, muscular development, and general level of activity. In one study, babies who had visually stimulating mobiles hanging above their cribs began reaching for objects 6 weeks earlier than babies who did not (White & Held, 1966). Furthermore, different infants seem to acquire the same skill in different ways. One study examined how children learn to reach by closely following the development of four infants (Thelen et al., 1993). Two of the infants were especially energetic and initially produced large circular movements of both arms. To reach accurately, these infants had to learn to dampen these large circular movements by holding their arms rigid at the elbow and swiping at an object. The other two infants were less energetic and did not produce large, circular movements. Thus, their first step in learning to reach involved learning to lift their arms against the force of gravity and extend them forward. Detailed observations such as these suggest that while all infants learn skills such as reaching, different infants accomplish this goal in different ways (Adolph & Avoilio, 2000).

Jean Piaget (1896–1980) is widely considered to be the father of modern developmental psychology.

FARRELL GREHAN/CORBIS

Cognitive Development

Infants can see. But what exactly do they make of the visual stimuli to which their eyes respond? In the first half of the 20th century, a Swiss biologist named Jean Piaget was following up work by Alfred Binet, who had pioneered the development of intelligence tests for children. Piaget expected that when confronted with difficult problems, children would make mistakes. But what surprised him was that children in the same age group typically made the same mistakes, which virtually disappeared when these children graduated to the next age group. The similarity and the age specificity of children's mistakes led Piaget to suspect that as children grow, they move through several stages of **cognitive development**—which refers to *the emergence of the ability to understand the world*. Piaget proposed that children pass

Table **11.1**	Piaget's Four Stages of Cognitive Development
Stage	**Characteristics**
Sensorimotor (Birth–2 years)	Infant experiences world through movement and senses, develops schemas, begins to act intentionally, and shows evidence of understanding object permanence.
Preoperational (2–6 years)	Child acquires motor skills but does not understand conservation of physical properties. Child begins this stage by thinking egocentrically but ends with a basic understanding of other minds.
Concrete operational (6–11 years)	Child can think logically about physical objects and events and understands conservation of physical properties.
Formal operational (11 years and up)	Child can think logically about abstract propositions and hypotheticals.

through four sequential stages, which he called the *sensorimotor* stage, the *preoperational* stage, the *concrete operational* stage, and the *formal operational* stage (Piaget, 1954a) (see **TABLE 11.1**).

Discovering Our Worlds

The first of Piaget's four stages is the **sensorimotor stage**, which is *a stage of development that begins at birth and lasts through infancy.* As the word *sensorimotor* suggests, infants at this stage use their ability to *sense* (perceptual development) and their ability to *move* (motor development) to acquire information about the world in which they live (cognitive development). By actively exploring their environments with their eyes, mouths, and fingers, infants begin to construct **schemas**, which can be thought of as *theories about or models of the way the world works.*

As every scientist knows, the key advantage of having a theory is that one can use it to predict and control what will happen in novel situations. If an infant learns that tugging at a stuffed animal causes the toy to come closer, then that observation is incorporated into the infant's theory about how physical objects behave, and the infant can later use that theory when he or she wants a different object to come closer, such as a rattle or a ball. Piaget called this process **assimilation**, which occurs when *infants apply their schemas in novel situations.* Of course, if the infant tugs the tail of the family cat, the cat is likely to sprint in the opposite direction. Infants' theories about the world ("Things come closer if I pull them") are occasionally disconfirmed, and thus infants must occasionally adjust their schemas in light of their new experiences ("Aha! *Inanimate* things come closer when I pull them"). Piaget called this process **accommodation**, which occurs when *infants revise their schemas in light of new information.* Piaget believed that cognitive development was an ongoing process in which infants develop, apply, and adjust their schemas as they build an understanding of the world.

What kinds of schemas do infants develop, apply, and adjust? Piaget suggested that infants do not have—and hence must acquire—some very basic understandings about the physical world. For example, when you put a pair of socks away, you know that the socks exist even after you close the drawer, and you would be quite surprised if you opened the drawer a moment later and found it empty. But according to Piaget, this would not surprise an infant because infants do not have a theory of **object permanence**, which is *the idea that objects continue to exist even when they are not visible.* Piaget noted that in the first few months of life, infants act as though objects stop existing the moment they are out of sight. For instance, he observed that a 2-month-old infant will track a moving object with her eyes, but once the object leaves her visual field, she will not search for it.

During the sensorimotor stage, infants explore with their hands and mouths, learning important lessons about the physical world such as, "If you whack guacamole hard enough, you can actually wear it as a hat."

"You mustn't pull the cat's tail so hard it tugs the head inside, sweetie!"

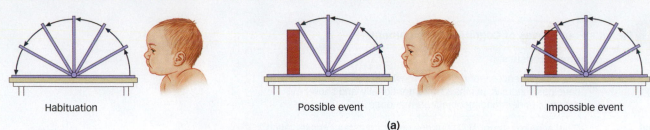

Habituation   Possible event   Impossible event

(a)

Figure 11.3 **The Possible and the Impossible Event** (a) In the habituation trials, infants watched a drawbridge flip back and forth with nothing in its path until they grew bored. Then a box was placed behind the drawbridge and the infants were shown one of two events: In the possible event, the box kept the drawbridge from flipping all the way over; in the impossible event, it did not. (b) The graph shows the infants' "looking time" during the habituation and the test trials. During the test trials, their interest was reawakened by the impossible event but not by the possible event (Baillargeon, Spelke, & Wasserman, 1985).

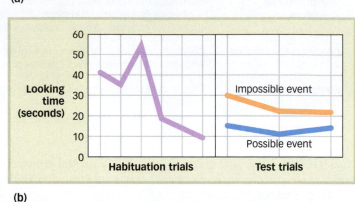

(b)

Was Piaget right? As it turns out, searching for unseen objects requires motor skills that infants may not have, and recent research suggests that when infants are tested in other ways, they demonstrate a sense of object permanence much earlier than Piaget realized. For instance, in one study, infants were shown a miniature drawbridge that flipped up and down. Once the babies got used to this, they watched as a box was placed behind the drawbridge—in its path but out of their sight. Some infants then saw a *possible* event: The drawbridge began to flip and then suddenly stopped, as if impeded by the box that the infants could not see. Other infants saw an *impossible* event: The drawbridge began to flip and then continued, as if unimpeded by the box (see **FIGURE 11.3**). What did infants do? Four-month-old infants stared longer at the impossible event than at the possible event, suggesting that they were puzzled by it (Baillargeon, Spelke, & Wasserman, 1985). The only thing that made the event impossible, of course, was the presence of an unseen box. The fact that the infants were puzzled by the impossible event suggests that they knew the box existed even when they could not see it (Fantz, 1964).

Studies such as these suggest that infants do have some understanding of object permanence. For example, what do infants see when they look at the line labeled A in **FIGURE 11.4**? Adults see a continuous blue line that is being obstructed by the solid orange block in front of it. Do infants see line A as continuous and obstructed, or do they see it as two blue objects on either side of an orange object? Studies show that when infants are allowed to become familiar with line A, they are subsequently more surprised by line C than by line B—despite the fact that line C actually *looks* more like line A than does line B (Kellman & Spelke, 1983). This suggests that infants see line A as a continuous line. Clearly, infants do not think of the world only in terms of its visible parts, and at some level they must "know" that when objects are out of sight (because they are partially obstructed), they continue to exist. Although infants seem to have a better understanding of the physical world than Piaget claimed, it is still not clear just how much they know or how and when they come to know it. As Piaget (1977/1927) wrote: "The child's first year of life is unfortunately still an abyss of mysteries for the psychologist. If only we could know what is going on in a baby's mind while observing him in action, we could certainly understand everything there is to psychology."

Figure 11.4 **Object Permanence** Do infants see line A as continuous or broken? Infants who are shown line A are subsequently more interested when they are shown line C than line B. This indicates that they consider C more novel than B, which suggests that the infants saw line A as continuous and not broken (Kellman & Spelke, 1983).

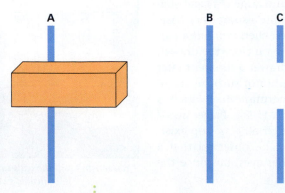

Discovering Our Minds

The long period following infancy is called **childhood,** which is *the stage of development that begins at about 18 to 24 months and lasts until adolescence, which begins between 11 and 14 years.* One of the most important things children learn how to do during this stage is what psychologists call "concrete operations." What does this mean? When you first learned to do arithmetic, you began by learning about *things* called numbers, and then you learned how to *operate* on those things by adding, dividing, subtracting, and multiplying them. Piaget suggested that cognitive development during childhood is a bit like that. Infants learn about physical *things,* but children learn how those things can be *operated* on or transformed. For example, we all know that ice melts into water, which evaporates as steam; that a red apple can look gray in low light; and that the weight of a pizza remains the same no matter how many slices we cut it into. But we all know these things because we are adults, and studies suggest that young children don't share our understanding and that older children do.

According to Piaget, childhood consists of two stages. The first is a **preoperational stage,** which is *the stage of development that begins at about 2 years and ends at about 6 years,* during which the child cannot perform concrete operations. Next is the **concrete operational stage,** which is *the stage of development that begins at about 6 years and ends at about 11 years,* during which the child can perform concrete operations. In one study, Piaget showed children a row of cups and asked them to place an egg in each. Preoperational children were able to do this, and afterward they readily agreed that there were just as many eggs as there were cups. Then Piaget removed the eggs and spread them out in a long line that extended beyond the row of cups. Preoperational children incorrectly claimed that there were now more eggs than cups, pointing out that the row of eggs was longer than the row of cups and hence there must be more of them. Concrete-operational children, on the other hand, correctly reported that the number of eggs did not change when they were spread out in a longer line. They understood that *quantity* is a property of a set of objects that does not change when an operation such as *spreading out* alters the set's appearance (Piaget, 1954b). Piaget called this insight **conservation,** which is *the notion that the quantitative properties of an object are invariant despite changes in the object's appearance.*

Why don't preoperational children seem to grasp the notion of conservation? Piaget suggested that children have several tendencies that explain their mistakes. For instance, *centration* is the tendency to focus on just one property of an object to the exclusion of all others. Whereas adults can consider several properties at once, children focus on the length of the line of eggs without simultaneously considering the amount of space between each egg. Piaget also suggested that children fail to think about *reversibility.* That is, they do not consider the fact that the operation that made the line of eggs longer could be reversed: The eggs could be repositioned more closely together, and the line would become shorter. But errors such as these may be manifestations of a more basic problem. One reason why preoperational children do not fully grasp the notion of conservation is that they do not fully grasp the fact that they have *minds* and that these minds contain *mental representations* of the world.

As adults, we all grasp this fact, which is why we distinguish between the subjective and the objective, between appearances and realities, between things in the mind and things in the world. We realize that things aren't always as they seem—that a wagon can *be* red but *look* gray at dusk, a highway can *be* dry but *look* wet in the heat. We make a distinction between the way things *are* and the way we *see* them. But preoperational children don't make this distinction so easily. When something *looks* gray or wet, they tend to assume it *is* gray or wet. As children develop, they begin to realize that the way

CHILDHOOD The stage of development that begins at about 18 to 24 months and lasts until adolescence.

PREOPERATIONAL STAGE The stage of development that begins at about 2 years and ends at about 6 years, in which children have a preliminary understanding of the physical world.

CONCRETE OPERATIONAL STAGE The stage of development that begins at about 6 years and ends at about 11 years, in which children acquire a basic understanding of the physical world and a preliminary understanding of their own and others' minds.

CONSERVATION The notion that the quantitative properties of an object are invariant despite changes in the object's appearance.

 ONLY HUMAN

VOTE EARLY, VOTE OFTEN In August 1991, the government of Finland proposed having a referendum on the age at which children should start school and suggested that children as young as 5 should be allowed to vote on the measure. The "preliterate" voters would be presented three drawings of birthday cakes with 5, 6, and 7 candles and would be asked to circle one of them.

LAURA DWIGHT/PHOTOEDIT

When preoperational children are shown two equal-size glasses filled with equal amounts of liquid, they correctly say that neither glass "has more." But when the contents of one glass are poured into a taller, thinner glass, they incorrectly say that the taller glass now "has more." Concrete operational children don't make this mistake because they recognize that operations such as pouring change the appearance of the liquid but not its actual volume.

At the preoperational stage, children generally do not distinguish between the way things look and the way things are. They do not realize that when a friendly adult wears a scary mask, he is still a friendly adult.

the world *appears* is not necessarily the way the world really *is*. Once children understand that brains represent—and hence can misrepresent—objects in the world, they are in a better position to solve a variety of problems that require them to ignore an object's subjective appearance while attempting to understand its objective properties.

For instance, concrete operational children can understand that when a ball of clay is rolled, stretched, or flattened, it is still the same amount of clay despite the fact that it looks larger in one form than another. They can understand that when water is poured from a short, wide beaker into a tall, thin cylinder, it is still the same amount of water despite the fact that the water level in the cylinder is higher. They can understand that when a sponge is painted gray to look like a rock, it is still a sponge despite its mineral appearance. Once children can make a distinction between objects and their mental representation of objects, between an object's properties and an object's appearance, they can begin to understand that some operations change what an object *looks* like without changing what the object *is* like.

Children at the concrete operational stage can solve a variety of physical problems. But it isn't until they move on to the **formal operational stage**, which is *the stage of development that begins around the age of 11 and lasts through adulthood,* that they can solve nonphysical problems with similar ease. Childhood ends when formal operations begin, and people who move on to this stage (and Piaget believed that some people never did) are able to reason systematically about abstract concepts such as *liberty* and *love* and about events that *will* happen, that *might have* happened, and that *never* happened. At the concrete operational stage, children realize that their minds contain mental representations that *refer* to things in the world, but at the formal operational stage, they realize that some of their mental representations have no physical referents at all. There are no tangible objects in the world to which words such as *freedom* or *mortality* refer, and yet people at the formal operational stage can think and reason about such concepts in a systematic way. The ability to generate, consider, reason about, or otherwise operate on these nonreferential abstractions is the hallmark of formal operations.

Discovering Other Minds

As children develop, they discover their own minds. They also discover the minds of others. Because preoperational children don't fully grasp the fact that they have minds that mentally represent objects, they also don't fully grasp the fact that other people have minds that may mentally represent the same objects in different ways. Hence, they generally expect others to see the world as they do. **Egocentrism** is *the failure to understand that the world appears differently to different observers.* When 3-year-old children are asked what a person on the opposite side of a table is seeing, they typically claim that the other person sees what they see.

Just as 3-year-old children have trouble understanding that others may not see what they see, so too do they have trouble understanding that others may not know what they know. In one study using the *false belief test,* children saw a puppet named Maxi deposit some chocolate in a cupboard and then leave the room. A second puppet arrived a moment later, found the chocolate, and moved it to a different cupboard. The children were then asked where Maxi would look for the chocolate when he returned—in the first cupboard where he had initially put it or in the second cupboard where the children knew it was currently. Most 5-year-olds realized that Maxi would search the first cupboard because, after all, Maxi had not seen the chocolate being moved. But 3-year-olds typically claimed that Maxi would look in the second cupboard because, after all, that's where *the children* knew the chocolate really was (Wimmer & Perner, 1983). Children all over the world pass and fail the false belief test at about the same age (Callaghan et al., 2005; see **FIGURE 11.5**). One curious finding is that 4-year-olds are more likely to pass the false belief task if the person whose beliefs they are being asked about is their own twin (Cassidy et al., 2005).

FORMAL OPERATIONAL STAGE The stage of development that begins around the age of 11 and lasts through adulthood, in which children gain a deeper understanding of their own and others' minds and learn to reason abstractly.

EGOCENTRISM The failure to understand that the world appears differently to different observers.

THEORY OF MIND The idea that human behavior is guided by mental representation, which gives rise to the realization that the world is not always the way it looks and that different people see it differently.

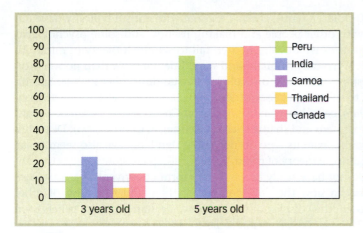

Figure **11.5** The False
Belief Test across Cultures
A very small percentage of
3-year-old children and a
very large percentage of
5-year-old children give the
correct response in the false
belief test. Research shows
that this transition happens
at about the same time in a
wide variety of cultures
(Callaghan et al., 2005).

Egocentrism colors children's understandings of others, and it can also color their understanding of themselves. Researchers showed young children an M&M's box and then opened it, revealing that it contained pencils instead of candy. Then the researchers closed the box and asked, "When I first showed you the box all closed up like this, what did you think was inside?" Although most 5-year-olds said, "M&M's," most 3-year-olds said, "Pencils" (Gopnik & Astington, 1988). For the 3-year-old child, a past self is like another person, and thus the past self must have known then what the child knows now. Only when the child understands the concept of mental representation can she understand that different people—including herself at different times—sometimes have different beliefs. Although we all ultimately achieve this insight, research suggests that even adults have trouble believing that others see the world differently than they do (Gilovich, Kruger, & Savitsky, 1999; Royzman, Cassidy, & Baron, 2003). It seems that egocentrism goes away, but that it doesn't go very far.

Different people have different perceptions and beliefs. They also have different desires and emotions. Do children understand that these aspects of other people's mental lives may also differ from their own? Surprisingly, even very young children (who cannot understand that others have different perceptions or beliefs) seem to understand that other people have different desires. For example, a 2-year-old who likes dogs can understand that other children don't and can correctly predict that other children will avoid dogs that the child herself would approach. When 18-month-old toddlers see an adult express disgust while eating a food that the toddlers enjoy, they hand the adult a different food, as if they understand that different people have different tastes (Repacholi & Gopnik, 1997). On the other hand, children take quite a long time to understand that other people may have emotional reactions unlike their own. When 5-year-olds hear a story in which Little Red Riding Hood knocks on her grandmother's door, unaware that a wolf is inside waiting to devour her, they realize that Little Red Riding Hood does not know what they know. Nonetheless, they expect Little Red Riding Hood to feel afraid (Bradmetz & Schneider, 2004; DeRosnay et al., 2004; Harris et al., 1989). It is only at about 6 years of age that children come to understand that because they and others have different knowledge, they and others may also experience different emotions in the same situation.

Clearly, children have a whole lot to learn about how the mind works—and most of them eventually do. The vast majority of children ultimately come to understand that they and others have minds and that these minds represent the world in different ways. Once children understand these things, they are said to have acquired a **theory of mind**, which is *the idea that human behavior is guided by mental representations*. But two groups of children lag far behind their peers in acquiring this understanding. *Autism* is a relatively rare disorder that affects

Because children are egocentric, they think that others see what they see. When small children are told to hide, they sometimes cover their eyes. Because they cannot see themselves, they think that others can't see them either.

"You're five. How could you possibly understand the problems of a five-and-a-half-year-old?"

Daniel Tammet is an autistic man who cannot drive a car or tell left from right. But he recently broke a European record by spending 5 hours, 9 minutes, and 24 seconds reciting the first 22,514 digits of pi from memory. "I just wanted to show people that disability needn't get in the way," he said (Johnson, 2005). Although only 10% of autistic people have extraordinary abilities such as this, they are 10 times more likely to have such abilities than are nonautistic people. No one knows why.

Prior to the 18th century, children were thought of as "faulty small adults" and were typically portrayed with adult features, proportions, gestures, and dress. But modern research reveals that children and adults are remarkably different and that they think about the world in fundamentally different ways. These two boys are George Villiers, Second Duke of Buckingham, and his brother, Lord Francis Villiers, painted by Van Dyke in 1635.

approximately 1 in 2,500 children (Frith, 2003). Children with autism typically have difficulty communicating with other people and making friends, and some psychologists have suggested that this is because autistic children fail to acquire a theory of mind. Although autistic children are typically normal—and sometimes far *better* than normal—on most intellectual dimensions, they have difficulty understanding other people. Specifically, they do not seem to understand that other people can have false beliefs (Baron-Cohen, Leslie, & Frith, 1985), belief-based emotions (Baron-Cohen, 1991), or self-conscious emotions such as embarrassment and shame (Heerey, Keltner, & Capps, 2003). Deaf children who are born to hearing parents who do not know sign language also seem to lag behind their peers in acquiring a theory of mind. These children are slow to learn to communicate because they do not have ready access to any form of conventional language, and this restriction seems to slow the development of their understanding of other minds. Like autistic children, they display difficulties in understanding false beliefs even at 5 or 6 years of age (DeVilliers, 2005; Peterson & Siegal, 1999).

Some autistic and deaf children display a marked departure from the standard timetable for understanding other minds. But even among children with no obvious disabilities, there is considerable variability in the rate at which a theory of mind is acquired. What causes this variability? A variety of factors have been examined, including the number of siblings that a child has, the frequency with which the child engages in pretend play, whether the child has an imaginary companion, and the socioeconomic status of the child's family. Of all the factors researchers have studied, language seems to be the most important (Astington & Baird, 2005). Children's language skills are an excellent predictor of how well they perform on false belief tests (such as the one in which Maxi looks for chocolate), and for both normal and autistic children, the likelihood of correctly completing this test increases with verbal ability (Happe, 1995).

The way that caregivers talk to children is also a good predictor of their success at these tests. Children whose caregivers frequently talk about thoughts and feelings tend to be good at understanding beliefs and belief-based emotions. Some psychologists speculate that children benefit from hearing psychological words such as *want, think, know,* and *sad;* others suggest that children benefit from the grammatically complex sentences that typically contain these psychological words; and some believe that caregivers who use psychological words are also more effective in getting children to reflect on mental states. Whatever the explanation, it is clear that language—and especially language about thoughts and feelings—is an important tool for helping children make sense of their own and others' minds (Harris, de Rosnay, & Pons, 2005).

Cognitive development—from the sensorimotor stage to formal operations—is a complex journey, and Piaget's ideas about it were nothing less than groundbreaking. Although many of these ideas have held up quite well, in the last few decades, psychologists have discovered two important ways in which his claims must be qualified. First, Piaget thought that children graduated from one stage to another in the same way that they graduated from kindergarten to first grade: A child is in kindergarten *or* first grade, he is never in both, and there is a particular moment of transition to which everyone can point. Modern psychologists see development as a more continuous and less steplike progression than Piaget believed. Children who are transitioning between stages may perform more mature behaviors one day and less mature behaviors the next. Cognitive development is more like the change of seasons than it is like graduation: The days get colder as summer turns to fall, but there are always a few cool days in August and a few warm days in October.

There is a second way in which Piaget's claims must be qualified. Piaget specified the ages at which these steplike transitions occurred, but modern experiments reveal that children generally acquire many of the abilities that Piaget described much *earlier* than he realized. For example, Piaget suggested that infants had no sense of object permanence because they did not actively search for objects that were moved out of their sight. But when researchers use experimental procedures that allow infants to "show what they know," even 4-month-olds display a sense of object permanence. Every year, it seems, research lowers the age at which babies can demonstrate their ability to perform sophisticated cognitive tasks.

Discovering Our Cultures

What causes children to develop a theory of mind? Do they inexorably move from one stage to another in the same way that a caterpillar metamorphoses into a butterfly? Piaget thought that children were born curious and that their cognitive development unfolded as a result of their interaction with objects in the world, such as eggs, clay, sponges, and cats. He saw the child as a lone scientist who made observations, developed theories, and then revised those theories in light of new observations. And yet, most scientists don't start from scratch. Rather, they receive training from more experienced scientists and they inherit the theories and methods of their disciplines. According to Russian psychologist Lev Vygotsky, children do much the same thing. Vygotsky was born in 1896, the same year as Piaget, but unlike Piaget, he believed that cognitive development was largely the result of the child's interaction with members of his or her own culture rather than his or her interaction with objects. Vygotsky noted that *cultural tools,* such as language and counting systems, exert a strong influence on cognitive development. Language systems and counting systems are not merely ways for children to *express* their thoughts; they are ways for children to *have* thoughts, which is why children can perform certain tasks only if they are allowed to talk to themselves.

For example, in English, the numbers beyond 20 are named by a decade (twenty) that is followed by a digit (one) and their names follow a logical pattern (twenty-one, twenty-two, twenty-three, etc.). In Chinese, the numbers from 11 to 19 are similarly constructed (ten-one, ten-two, ten-three . . .). But in English, the names of the numbers between 11 and 19 either reverse the order of the decade and the digit (sixteen, seventeen) or are entirely arbitrary (eleven, twelve). The difference in the regularity of these two systems makes a big difference to the children who must learn them. It is obvious to a Chinese child that 12—which is called "ten-two"—can be decomposed into 10 and 2, but it is not so obvious to an American child, who calls the number "twelve" (see **FIGURE 11.6** on the next page. In one study, children from many countries were asked to hand an experimenter a certain number of bricks. Some of the bricks were single, and some were glued together in strips of 10. When Asian children were asked to hand the experimenter 26 bricks, they tended to hand over two strips of 10 plus six singles. Non-Asian children tended to use the clumsier strategy of counting out 26 single bricks (Miura et al., 1994). Results such as these suggest that the regularity of the counting system that children inherit can promote or discourage their discovery of the fact that two-digit numbers can be decomposed.

Vygotsky believed that at any age, a child was capable of acquiring a wide—but nonetheless bounded—range of skills, and he called this range the child's *zone of proximal development.* He suggested that children who interacted with teachers tended to acquire skills toward the top of this range, whereas children who did not tended to acquire skills toward the bottom. Parents seem to have an intuitive understanding of the zone of proximal development: They tend to direct their instruction toward the upper end of a child's range of skills, and as the child becomes more competent, they encourage the child to think about problems at higher levels. Of course, the ability to learn from others requires fundamental communicative skills that take time to develop. At a bare minimum, communication requires that two people focus on the same topic and on each other's responses to it. Babies may look at an adult's eyes, but it isn't until around 9 to 15 months that infants begin looking at the point in space to which an adult's eyes are directed, a phenomenon known as *joint attention.* (Interestingly, following a human being's gaze is something that dogs can do but monkeys can't.) At about the same time, infants also begin looking at adults to gauge their reactions, a phenomenon known as *social referencing.* These two emerging tendencies prepare the infant to learn from more skilled members of its species (see the Hot Science box on page 421).

Lev Vygotsky (pictured here with his daughter) was a Soviet developmental psychologist whose theories emphasized the role that social life—rather than individual experience—plays in cognitive development.

Children are not lone explorers who discover the world for themselves but members of families, communities, and societies that teach them much of what they need to know.

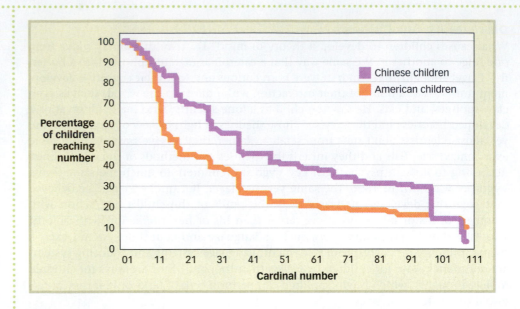

Figure 11.6 Twelve or Two-Teen? As this graph shows, the percentage of American children who can count through the cardinal numbers drops off suddenly when they hit the number 11, whereas the percentage of Chinese children shows a more gradual decline (Miller, Smith, & Zhu, 1995).

Social Development

Unlike the infants of many other species, human infants cannot survive without caregivers. But what exactly do caregivers provide? The obvious answers are warmth, safety, and food, and those obvious answers are right. But caregivers also provide something else that is every bit as essential to an infant's development.

During World War II, psychologists studied infants who were living in orphanages while awaiting adoption. Although these children were warm, safe, and well fed, many were physically and developmentally retarded, and nearly two out of five died before they could be adopted (Spitz, 1949). Shortly thereafter, psychologist Harry Harlow (1958; Harlow & Harlow, 1965) discovered that baby rhesus monkeys that were warm, safe, and well fed but were allowed no social contact for the first 6 months of their lives developed a variety of pathologies. They compulsively rocked back and forth while biting themselves, and when they were finally introduced to other monkeys, they avoided them entirely. The socially isolated monkeys turned out to be incapable of communicating with or learning from others of their kind, and when the females matured and became mothers, they ignored, rejected, and sometimes even attacked their own babies. Harlow also discovered that when socially isolated monkeys were put in a cage with two "artificial mothers"—one that was made of wire and dispensed food and one that was made of cloth and dispensed no food—they spent most of their time clinging to the soft cloth mother despite the fact that the wire mother was the source of their nourishment. Clearly, both human and simian infants require something more from their caregivers than mere sustenance. But what?

Harlow's monkeys preferred the comfort and warmth of a terry-cloth mother (right) to the wire mother (left) even when the wire mother was associated with food.

{ HOT SCIENCE } An Accountant in the Crib?

1. Object placed in case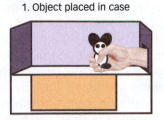

2. Screen comes up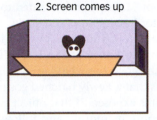

3. Second object added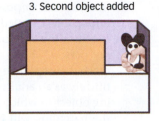

4. Hand leaves empty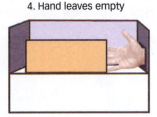

Then either: possible outcome

5. Screen drops...

revealing two objects

or: impossible outcome

5. Screen drops...

revealing one object

AS FAR AS ANYONE CAN TELL, INFANTS can't do calculus. But if Karen Wynn of Yale University is right, they can count. In a recent experiment in her laboratory, infants watched as an experimenter placed a mouse doll at the center of a small stage. A screen then came up to hide the doll. Next, infants watched as an experimenter holding another mouse doll placed her hand behind the screen and then withdrew her empty hand a moment later, strongly implying that the second mouse doll had been deposited behind the screen alongside the first one. Finally, the screen was removed and infants saw one of two outcomes. Infants who saw a *possible* outcome saw two mouse dolls sitting on the stage, but infants who saw an *impossible* outcome saw just one mouse doll sitting on the stage. The experimenters measured how long the infants stared at the stage and found that infants looked longer at the one mouse doll than at the two

mouse dolls. This suggests that the infants were keeping track of the *number* of mouse dolls that were—or at least that should have been—behind the screen (Wynn, 1992).

Does this mean that counting is an innate ability? Not necessarily. Peter Gordon of Columbia University recently made an expedition to Amazonia to investigate the numerical abilities of members of the Pirahã tribe. The Pirahã are a community of hunter-gatherers who live along the banks of the Maici River in the lowland Amazonia region of Brazil, and they have an extremely simple counting system that consists of just three terms: *one, two,* and *many.* Gordon asked members of the Pirahã community to perform a "copying task" in which he laid out a certain number of ground nuts in a cluster and asked the participants to lay out the same number of a different object, such as batteries, in a line. As you can see from the accompanying figure, when there were

When infants were presented with two outcomes—possible and impossible—they stared longer at the impossible event than at the possible event. This suggests that the infants were keeping track of the number of objects and that they were surprised by the disappearance of the added object (Wynn, 1992).

just one or two ground nuts in the cluster, participants responded quite accurately by laying out the same number of batteries. But once the number exceeded two, their accuracy declined rapidly, and by the time the cluster contained nine ground nuts, participants couldn't do the task at all (Gordon, 2004). These findings suggest that counting systems do not merely *express* our ability to count, they create it—just as Vygotsky surmised. The ability to distinguish between *one, two,* and *many* may arise early and on its own, as Wynn's experiments suggest. But the ability to differentiate the different varieties of *many* seems to require a cultural tool.

(a)

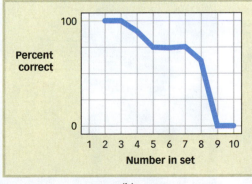

(b)

Counting abilities seem to be determined in part by culture. (a) Members of the Pirahã tribe were asked to perform the copying task. (b) The participants were very accurate with one or two items, but their accuracy declined rapidly after two items, and they couldn't do the task at all with nine or more items (Gordon, 2004).

ATTACHMENT The emotional bond that forms between newborns and their primary caregivers.

STRANGE SITUATION A behavioral test developed by Mary Ainsworth that is used to determine a child's attachment style.

Becoming Attached

When Konrad Lorenz was a child, he wanted to be a goose. As he explained in his Nobel Prize acceptance speech, "I yearned to become a wild goose and, on realizing that this was impossible, I desperately wanted to *have* one and, when this also proved impossible, I settled for having domestic ducks. . . . From a neighbour, I got a one day old duckling and found, to my intense joy, that it transferred its following response to my person." Every farmer knows that a baby duck or goose will normally follow its mother everywhere she goes, but what Lorenz discovered as a child (and proved scientifically as an adult) is that a newly hatched gosling will faithfully follow the first moving object to which it is exposed. If that object is a human being or a tennis ball, then the hatchling will ignore its mother and follow the object instead. Lorenz theorized that the first moving object a hatchling saw was somehow *imprinted* on its bird brain as "the thing I must always stay near" (Lorenz, 1952).

Psychiatrist John Bowlby was fascinated by this work as well as by the studies of rhesus monkeys reared in isolation and children in orphanages, and he sought to understand how human infants form attachments to their caregivers (Bowlby, 1969, 1973, 1980). Bowlby began by noting that from the moment they are born, goslings waddle after their mothers and monkeys cling to their mothers' furry chests because the newborns of both species must stay close to their caregivers to survive. Human babies, he suggested, have a similar need, but they are much less physically developed than goslings or monkeys and hence cannot waddle or cling. Because they cannot stay close to their caregivers, human babies pursue a different strategy: They do things that cause their caregivers to stay close to them. When a baby cries, gurgles, coos, makes eye contact, or smiles, most adults reflexively move toward the baby, and Bowlby claimed that this is *why* the baby emits these "come hither" signals.

Bowlby claimed that babies begin their lives by sending these signals to anyone within range to receive them, but during their first 6 months, they begin to keep a mental tally of who responds most often and most promptly, and they soon begin to target their signals to the best responder or *primary caregiver.* This person quickly becomes the emotional center of the infant's universe. Infants feel secure in the primary caregiver's presence and will happily crawl around, exploring their environments with their eyes, ears, fingers, and mouths. But if their primary caregiver gets too far away, infants begin to feel insecure, and like the imprinted gosling, they take action to decrease the distance between themselves and their primary caregiver, perhaps by crawling toward their caregiver or by crying until their caregiver moves toward them. Indeed, anything that threatens the infant's sense of security—for example, the sudden appearance of a stranger in the room—will cause the infant to move closer to the caregiver. In Bowlby's view, infants are a bit like runners in a baseball game who feel secure when they are touching the base but who become increasingly anxious and insecure as they step farther and farther away from it. Bowlby believed that all of this happens because evolution has equipped human infants with a social reflex that is every bit as basic as the physical reflexes that cause them to suck and to grasp. Human infants are predisposed to form an **attachment**—that is, *an emotional bond*—with a primary caregiver.

Given the fundamental importance of attachment, it is not surprising that infants who are deprived of the opportunity to become attached suffer a variety of social and emotional deficits (O'Connor & Ruter, 2000; Rutter, O'Connor, & the English and Romanian Adoptees Study Team,

Like goslings, human babies need to stay close to their mothers to survive. Unlike goslings, human babies know how to get their mothers to come to them rather than the other way around.

2004). Furthermore, even when attachment does happen, it can happen in ways that are more or less successful (Ainsworth et al., 1978). Psychologist Mary Ainsworth developed what has come to be known as the **strange situation**, which is *a behavioral test used to determine a child's attachment style.* The test involves bringing a child and his or her primary caregiver (usually the child's mother) to a laboratory room and then staging a series of episodes that range from abandonment (in which the primary caregiver briefly leaves the room) to reunion (in which the primary caregiver returns) as well as several interactions with a stranger, both in the absence and in the presence of the primary caregiver. Impartial observers watch the infant (usually via a hidden camera) and code his or her reactions to these potentially stressful events. Research shows that infants' reactions tend to fit one of four attachment styles: *secure, avoidant, ambivalent,* or *disorganized.*

- Roughly 60% of American infants display a *secure* attachment style. If these infants are distressed when their caregiver leaves the room, they go to her promptly when she returns and are quickly calmed by her proximity. If they are not distressed when their caregiver leaves the room, they acknowledge her return with a glance or a greeting. These infants seem to regard their caregiver as a *secure base* from which to explore their environments (Waters & Cummings, 2000).

- Roughly 20% of American infants display an *avoidant* attachment style (sometimes called an *insecure-avoidant* style). These infants are generally not distressed when their caregiver leaves the room, and they generally do not acknowledge her when she returns.

- Roughly 15% of American infants display an *ambivalent* attachment style (sometimes called an *insecure-resistant* style). These infants are almost always distressed when their caregiver leaves the room, and they go to her promptly when she returns. But then they rebuff their caregiver's attempt to calm them, arching their backs and squirming to get away when their caregiver tries to comfort them.

- Roughly 5% or fewer of American infants display a *disorganized* attachment style. These infants show no consistent pattern of responses. They may or may not be distressed when their caregiver leaves, they may or may not go to her when she returns, and their reactions are often contradictory. For example, they may look fearful as they approach their caregiver, they may be calm when she leaves and then suddenly become angry, or they may simply freeze and appear confused or disoriented.

Research has shown that a child's behavior in the strange situation correlates fairly well with his or her behavior at home (Solomon & George, 1999) and in the laboratory (see **FIGURE 11.7**). Nonetheless, as with any typology, this one should be interpreted cautiously. For instance, it is not unusual for a child's attachment style to change over time (Lamb, Sternberg, & Prodromidis, 1992). And while some aspects of attachment styles appear to be stable across cultures (secure attachment is the most common style in just about every country that has ever been studied; van Ijzendoorn & Kroonenberg, 1988), other aspects of attachment styles vary across cultures. For example, German children (whose parents tend to foster independence) are more likely to have avoidant than ambivalent attachment styles, whereas Japanese children (whose mothers typically stay home and do not leave them in the care of others) are more likely to have ambivalent than avoidant attachment styles (Takahashi, 1986). No one is sure why there are differences across time and cultures, but the fact that such differences occur suggests that attachment styles should not be viewed either as sharply defined categories or as immutable characteristics of the child.

It doesn't take a psychologist to see that this child is securely attached.

JEFF GREENBERG/OMNI PHOTO

Figure 11.7 Attachment Style and Memory We often remember best those events that fit with our view of the world. Researchers assessed 1-year-old children's attachment styles with the strange situation test. Two years later, the same group of children were shown a puppet show in which some happy events (e.g., the puppet got a present) or unhappy events (e.g., the puppet spilled his juice) occurred. Securely attached children later remembered more of the happy events than the unhappy ones, but insecurely attached children showed the opposite pattern (Belsky, Spritz, & Crnic, 1996).

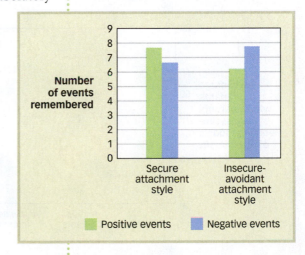

INTERNAL WORKING MODEL OF ATTACHMENT A set of expectations about how the primary caregiver will respond when the child feels insecure.

TEMPERAMENTS Characteristic patterns of emotional reactivity.

Working Models

Why do different infants have different attachment styles? The capacity for attachment may be innate, but the quality of that attachment is influenced by the child, the primary caregiver, and their interaction. Infants seem to keep track of the responsiveness of their primary caregiver and use this information to create an **internal working model of attachment**, which is *a set of expectations about how the primary caregiver will respond when the child feels insecure.* Infants with different attachment styles appear to have different working models. Specifically, infants with a secure attachment style seem to be certain that their primary caregiver will respond, infants with an avoidant attachment style seem to be certain that their primary caregiver will not respond, and infants with an ambivalent attachment style seem to be uncertain about whether their primary caregiver will respond. Infants with a disorganized attachment style seem to be confused about their caregivers, which has led some psychologists to speculate that this style primarily characterizes children who have been abused (Carolson, 1998; Cicchetti & Toth, 1998).

If different working models cause infants to have different attachment styles, then what causes infants to have different working models? Attachment is an interaction between two people, and thus both of them—the primary caregiver and the child—play a role in determining the nature of the child's working model (see **FIGURE 11.8**). Different children are born with different **temperaments**, or *characteristic patterns of emotional reactivity* (Thomas & Chess, 1977). Whether measured by parents' reports or by physiological indices such as heart rate or cerebral blood flow, very young children vary in their tendency toward fearfulness, irritability, activity, positive affect, and other emotional traits (Rothbart & Bates, 1998). These differences are usually stable over time. For example, infants who react fearfully to novel stimuli—such as sudden movements, loud sounds, or unfamiliar people—tend to be more subdued, less social, and less positive at 4 years old (Kagan, 1997). Children who are negative and impulsive as youngsters tend to have behavioral and adjustment problems in adolescence and poorer relationships in adulthood (Caspi et al., 1995). These differences in temperament seem to emerge from stable differences in biology. For example, 10% to 15% of infants have highly reactive limbic systems that produce an "inhibited" temperament. These infants thrash and cry when shown a new toy or a new person; they grow into children who tend to avoid novel people, objects, and situations; and they ultimately become quiet, cautious, and sometimes shy adults (Schwartz et al., 2003). These studies suggest that from the earliest moments of life, some infants are prone to feel insecure when their primary caregiver leaves a room and are inconsolable when she returns.

But all is not writ in stone. A caregiver's behavior also has an important influence on the infant's working model and attachment style. Studies have shown that mothers of securely attached infants tend to be especially sensitive to signs of their child's emotional state, especially good at detecting their infant's "request" for reassurance, and especially responsive to that request (Ainsworth et al., 1978; De Wolff & van Ijzendoorn, 1997). Mothers of infants with an ambivalent attachment style tend to respond inconsistently, only sometimes attending to their infants when they show signs of distress. Mothers of infants with an avoidant attachment style are typically indifferent to their child's need for reassurance and may even reject their attempts at physical closeness (Isabelle, 1993).

Research suggests that differences in how mothers respond are probably due in large measure to differences in their ability to read their infant's emotional state. Mothers who are highly sensitive to these signs are almost twice as likely to have a securely attached child as are mothers who are less sensitive (van Ijzendoorn &

Figure 11.8 Parents' Attachment Styles Affect Their Children's Attachment Styles Studies suggest that securely attached infants tend to have parents who have secure working models of attachment (van IJzendoorn, 1995).

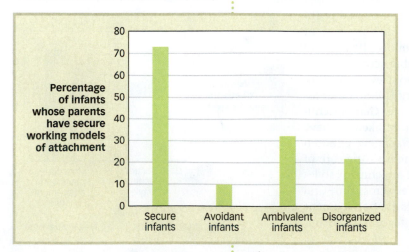

Sagi, 1999). Although such data are merely correlational, there is reason to suspect that a mother's sensitivity and responsiveness *cause* the infant's attachment style. Researchers studied a group of young mothers whose babies were particularly irritable or difficult. When the babies were about 6 months old, half the mothers participated in a training program designed to sensitize them to their babies' emotional signals and to encourage them to be more responsive. The results showed that when the children were 18 months, 24 months, and 3 years old, those whose mothers had received the training were more likely to have a secure attachment style than were those whose mothers did not (van den Boon, 1994, 1995). Another study found that when mothers think of their babies as unique individuals with emotional lives and not just as creatures with urgent physical needs, their infants end up more securely attached (Meins, 2003; Meins et al., 2001).

Does a baby's attachment style have any influence on his or her subsequent development? The jury is still out on that question. Children who were securely attached as infants do better than children who were not securely attached on a wide variety of measures, from the quality of their social relationships (Schneider, Atkinson, & Tardif, 2001; Steele et al., 1999; Vondra et al., 2001) to their academic achievement (Jacobson & Hoffman, 1997). Some psychologists have suggested that this is because children apply the working models they developed as infants to their later relationships with teachers and friends, which is to say that attachment style causes securely attached infants to become more successful children and adults (Sroufe, Egeland, & Kruetzer, 1990). But other psychologists argue that attachment style is correlated with later success only because both of these are caused by the same environment, which is to say that sensitive and responsive caregivers are causes of both the infant's attachment style and the child's subsequent success (Lamb et al., 1985). Because the data on the long-term consequences of attachment style are necessarily correlational, this debate will not be easily resolved. But it is not unreasonable to suspect that both of these arguments are right to some extent (see the Real World box on the next page).

Moral Development

From the moment of birth, human beings can make one distinction quickly and well, and that's the distinction between pleasure and pain. Before babies hit their very first diapers, they can tell when something feels good, they can tell when something feels bad, and they strongly prefer the former to the latter. But as they mature, they begin to notice that their pleasures ("Throwing food is fun") are often someone else's pains ("Throwing food makes Mom mad"), which means that doing what they please doesn't always please others. This is a problem. Human beings need each other to survive and thrive, and when people make others feel bad, then others tend to avoid them, exclude them, or retaliate against them. We are social animals, and it is in our own selfish interests to learn how to balance our needs and the needs of others. We do this by developing a new distinction—the distinction between right and wrong. Although philosophers have been debating the meanings of these words for millennia, it is clear that morality is primarily an interpersonal concept. Stealing, lying, and cheating are wrong because they benefit the person who does them at the expense of those to whom they are done. "Bad behavior" usually involves the gratification of our own desires at the expense of someone else's, and most moral systems are a set of recommendations for balancing different people's competing needs.

How do children learn to decide what is right and what is wrong?

SUPERSTOCK

IN 1975, ABOUT 37% OF MARRIED AMERICAN women with children under age 6 worked outside the home. In 1998, that figure had risen to 64%. So what are working parents doing with their children? The vast majority of working parents entrust their children's care to someone else for some part of the day, and that someone else is often a day-care provider. While liberals applaud the economic liberation of women, conservatives lament the emotional toll that they believe day care takes on children. According to feminist author Gloria Steinem (1970), "The most damaged children were not those whose mothers worked, but those whose mothers preferred to work but stayed home out of the role-playing desire to be a 'good mother.'" Conservative commentator Phyllis Schlafly (2001) argued that "the day-care issue strikes at the heart of feminist ideology that it is oppression of women for society to expect mothers to care for their own children."

It is the job of pundits to create more heat than light. But scientists at the National Institute for Child Health and Development have been trying to do just the opposite by conducting a large-scale study of the effects of day care on approximately 1,300 children living in a wide variety of settings in North America. What have they found? So far, the results of the study suggest that day care has little effect on the quality of the attachment that children establish with their primary caregivers. While the attachment styles of infants and toddlers are strongly influenced by their mother's sensitivity and responsiveness, they are generally not influenced by the quality, amount, age of entry, stability, or

Would these children in day care be better off at home with their mothers?

© ELLEN B. SENISI/THE IMAGE WORKS

type of day care they receive (NICHD Early Child Care Research Network, 1997). The scientific coordinator of the study explained, "We're finding again and again that child care is not the source of worry that existed when we started the study" (Shapiro, 2005). In fact, the few negative effects of child care that the study *did* find tended to be quite minor.

But the results were not all good news. Although day care had no large, direct effects on children's attachments, there was evidence of a subtle interaction between a child's experience at home and at day care. Specifically, 15-month-old infants were likely to be insecurely attached if their mothers were low in sensitivity *and* the infants (a) attended a poor quality day care, (b) spent more than 10 hours a week in day care, or (c) had more than one day-care arrangement. This suggests that day care

does not increase the risk of emotional insecurity in and of itself but that certain kinds of day care can do so when combined with the stress of having a mother who is unresponsive and insensitive. A similar effect was observed among toddlers who were 24 and 36 months old (NICHD Early Child Care Research Network, 1999). It is also important to note that while the quality of day care does not have a powerful influence on emotional attachment, it does influence a child's cognitive and social competence (NICHD Early Child Care Research Network, 2002).

In short, the best evidence to date suggests that day care does not put children at risk, but that *bad* day care puts *some* children at risk. This may not be the all-or-none conclusion that spinmeisters on both the left and right want to hear, but it has the redeeming quality of being true.

Knowing What's Right

How do children think about right and wrong? Piaget spent time playing marbles with children and quizzing them about how they came to know the rules of the game and what they thought should happen to children who broke them. By listening carefully to what children said, Piaget noticed that their moral thinking changed systematically over time in three important ways (Piaget, 1932/1965):

■ First, Piaget noticed that children's moral thinking tends to shift *from realism to relativism.* Very young children regard moral rules as real, inviolable truths about the world that (like most truths) are communicated to them by authorities such as teachers and parents. For the young child, right and wrong are like day and night—they exist in the world and do not depend on what people think or say. That's why young children generally don't believe that a bad action, such as hitting someone, can be good even if everyone agreed to allow it. As they mature, children begin to realize that some moral rules (e.g., wives should obey their husbands) are inventions and not discoveries and that groups of people can therefore agree to adopt them, change them, or abandon them entirely.

■ Second, Piaget noticed that children's moral thinking tends to shift *from prescriptions to principles*. Young children think of moral rules as guidelines for specific actions in specific situations ("Children should take turns playing marbles"). As they mature, children come to see that rules are expressions of more general principles, such as fairness and equity, which means that rules can be abandoned or modified when they fail to serve the general principle ("If a child missed his turn, then it would be fair to give him two turns").

■ Third and finally, Piaget noticed that children's moral thinking tends to shift *from consequences to intentions*. For the young child, an unintentional action that causes great harm seems "more wrong" than an intentional action that causes slight harm because young children tend to judge the morality of an action by its consequences rather than by what the actor intended (cf. Yuill & Perner, 1988). As they mature, children begin to see that the morality of an action is critically dependent on the actor's state of mind.

Piaget thought of moral reasoning as a skill, and he believed that its development was closely tied to other cognitive skills, such as the ability to think abstractly, to take another's perspective, and so on.

Psychologist Lawrence Kohlberg picked up where Piaget left off and offered a more detailed theory of the development of moral reasoning (Kohlberg, 1963, 1986). According to Kohlberg, moral reasoning proceeds through three stages (each of which has two substages that we won't discuss here). Kohlberg based his theory on people's responses to a series of moral dilemmas such as this one:

> A woman was near death from a special kind of cancer. There was one drug that the doctors thought might save her. It was a form of radium that a druggist in the same town had recently discovered. The drug was expensive to make, but the druggist was charging ten times what the drug cost him to make. He paid $200 for the radium and charged $2,000 for a small dose of the drug. The sick woman's husband, Heinz, went to everyone he knew to borrow the money, but he could only get together about $1,000, which is half of what it cost. He told the druggist that his wife was dying and asked him to sell it cheaper or let him pay later. But the druggist said: "No, I discovered the drug and I'm going to make money from it." So Heinz got desperate and broke into the man's store to steal the drug for his wife. Should the husband have done that?

On the basis of their responses, Kohlberg concluded that most children are at the **preconventional stage**, *a stage of moral development in which the morality of an action is primarily determined by its consequences for the actor*. Immoral actions are those for which one is punished, and the appropriate resolution to any moral dilemma is to choose the behavior with the least likelihood of punishment. For example, children at this stage often base their moral judgment of Heinz on the relative costs of one decision ("It would be bad if he got blamed for his wife's death") and another ("It would be bad if he went to jail for stealing").

Kohlberg argued that at about the time of adolescence, children move to the **conventional stage**, which is *a stage of moral development in which the morality of an action is primarily determined by the extent to which it conforms to social rules*. Children at this stage believe that everyone should uphold the generally accepted norms of their cultures, obey the laws of society, and fulfill their civic duties and familial obligations. They believe that Heinz must weigh the dishonor he will bring upon himself and his family by stealing (i.e., breaking a law) against the guilt he will feel if he allows his wife to die (i.e., failing to fulfill a duty). Children at this stage are concerned not just about spankings and prison sentences but also about the approval and opprobrium of others. Immoral actions are those for which one is condemned.

Finally, Kohlberg believed that some adults move to the **postconventional stage**, which is *a stage of moral development at which the morality of an action is determined by a set of general principles that reflect core values*, such as the right to life, liberty, and the pursuit of happiness. When a behavior violates these principles, it is immoral, and if a law requires these principles to be violated, then it should be disobeyed. For a person

PRECONVENTIONAL STAGE A stage of moral development in which the morality of an action is primarily determined by its consequences for the actor.

CONVENTIONAL STAGE A stage of moral development in which the morality of an action is primarily determined by the extent to which it conforms to social rules.

POSTCONVENTIONAL STAGE A stage of moral development at which the morality of an action is determined by a set of general principles that reflect core values.

During World War II, Lawrence Kohlberg served on a carrier ship, where he helped Jews escape from Europe by hiding them in banana crates. He spent his life trying to understand how people determine what is right and what is wrong.

who has reached the postconventional stage, a woman's life is always more important than a shopkeeper's profits and so stealing the drug is not only a moral behavior, it is a moral obligation. Kohlberg believed that people must go through these stages in this order because each requires a more sophisticated set of cognitive skills than the one before it. He also believed that different people take different amounts of time to move through them and that many people never reach the last one.

Research supports Kohlberg's general claim that moral reasoning shifts from an emphasis on punishment to an emphasis on social rules and finally to an emphasis on ethical principles (Walker, 1988). But research also suggests that these stages are not quite as discrete as Kohlberg thought. For instance, a single person may use preconventional, conventional, and postconventional thinking in different circumstances, which suggests that the developing person does not "reach a stage" so much as he "acquires a skill" that he may or may not use on a particular occasion.

The use of the male pronoun here is intentional. Because Kohlberg developed his theory by studying a sample of American boys, some critics have suggested that it does not describe the development of moral thinking in girls (Gilligan, 1982) or in non-Westerners (Simpson, 1974). The first of these criticisms has received little scientific support (Jaffee & Hyde, 2000; Turiel, 1998), but the second is well taken. For example, some non-Western societies value obedience and community over liberty and individuality, and thus the moral reasoning of people in those societies may appear to reflect a conventional devotion to social norms when it actually reflects a postconventional consideration of ethical principles. Other critics have noted that while a child's level of moral reasoning is generally correlated with his or her own moral behavior (Blasi, 1980), that correlation is not particularly strong. This is particularly true when the moral behavior involves doing a good deed rather than refraining from doing a bad deed (Haidt, 2001; Thoma et al., 1999). These critics suggest that how people reason about morality may be interesting in the abstract, but it has little to do with how people actually behave in their everyday lives. So if moral reasoning doesn't determine moral behavior, then what does?

Feeling What's Right

Research on moral reasoning portrays children as little jurists who use rational analysis—sometimes simple and sometimes sophisticated—to distinguish between right and wrong. But moral dilemmas don't just make us think. They also make us *feel*. Consider two scenarios (see **FIGURE 11.9**).

> You are standing on a bridge. Below you can see a runaway trolley hurtling down the track toward five people who will be killed if it remains on its present course. You are sure that you can save these people by flipping a lever that will switch the trolley onto a different track, where it will kill just one person instead of five. Is it morally permissible to divert the trolley and prevent five deaths at the cost of one?

Now consider a slightly different version of this problem:

> You and a large man are standing on a bridge. Below you can see a runaway trolley hurtling down the track toward five people who will be killed if it remains on its present course. You are sure that you can save these people by pushing the large man onto the track, where his body will be caught up in the trolley's wheels and stop it before it kills the five people. Is it morally permissible to push the large man and thus prevent five deaths at the cost of one?

If you are like most people, you believe that it is morally permissible to sacrifice one person for the sake of five in the first case but not in the second case. And if you are like most people, you can't say why. Indeed, you probably didn't reach this conclusion by moral reasoning at all. Rather, you had a negative emotional reaction to the mere thought of pushing another human being into the path of an oncoming trolley, and that reaction was sufficient to convince you that pushing him would be wrong. You may have come up with a few good arguments to support this position, but those arguments probably followed rather than preceded your conclusion (Greene et al., 2001).

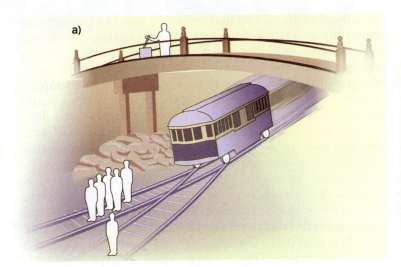

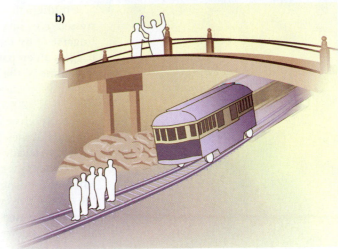

The way people respond to cases such as these has convinced some psychologists that moral judgments are the consequences—and not the causes—of emotional reactions (Haidt, 2001). According to this *moral intuitionist* perspective, we have evolved to react emotionally to a small family of events that are particularly relevant to reproduction and survival, and we have developed the distinction between right and wrong as a way of labeling and explaining these emotional reactions. For instance, most of us think that incest disgusts us because we consider it wrong. But another possibility is that we consider it wrong because it disgusts us. Incest is a poor method for producing genetically viable offspring, and thus nature may have selected for people who are disgusted by it. Our reasoning about the immorality of incest may follow from that disgust rather than cause it. Some research supports the moral intuitionist perspective. In one experiment, participants were hypnotized and told that whenever they heard the word *take,* they would experience "a brief pang of disgust . . . a sickening feeling in your stomach." After they came out of the hypnotic state, the participants were asked to rate the morality of several actions, ranging from incest to bribery. When the description of the action contained the word *take,* participants rated the action as less moral, suggesting that their feelings were guiding—rather than being guided by—their moral reasoning (Wheatley & Haidt, 2005).

According to the moral intuitionist perspective, the reason most people consider it permissible to stop a trolley by pulling a switch but not by pushing someone onto the tracks is that people have negative emotional reactions to other people's physical pain (Greene et al., 2001). This aversion to others' suffering begins early in childhood. When adults in one study pretended to hit their thumbs with a hammer, even very young children seemed alarmed and attempted to comfort them (Zahn-Waxler et al., 1992). These efforts are occasionally clumsy or inappropriate—for example, a toddler may offer a distressed adult a teddy bear—but they suggest that children are moved by other people's pain. Indeed, even very young children distinguish between actions that are wrong because they violate a social rule and actions that are wrong because they cause suffering. When asked whether it would be okay to leave toys on the floor in a school that allowed such behavior, young children tend to say it would. But when asked whether it would be okay to hit another child in a school that allowed such behavior, young children tend to say it would not (Smetana, 1981; Smetana & Braeges, 1990). Indeed, young children say that hitting is wrong even if an adult instructs someone to do it (Laupa & Turiel, 1986).

Figure 11.9 The Trolley Problem Why does it seem permisssble to trade one life for five lives by pulling a switch but not by pushing a man from a bridge? Research suggests that the scenario shown in (b) elicits a more negative emotional response than does the scenario shown in (a), and this emotional response may be the basis for our moral intuitions.

Most people are upset by the suffering of others, and research suggests that even young children have this response, which may be the basis of their emerging morality.

Children clearly think about transgressions that cause others to be observably distressed (e.g., hitting) differently from transgressions that do not (e.g., eating with one's fingers). Why might that be? One possibility is that observing distress automatically triggers an empathic reaction in the brain of the observer. Recent research has shown that some of the brain regions that are activated when people experience an unpleasant emotion are also activated when people see someone else experience that emotion (Carr et al., 2003). (See the discussion of mirror neurons in Chapter 3.) In one study, women received a shock or watched their romantic partners receive a shock on different parts of their bodies. The regions of the women's brains that processed information about the location of the shock were activated only when the women experienced the shock themselves, but the regions that processed emotional information were activated whether the women received the shock or observed it (Singer et al., 2004). Similarly, the emotion-relevant brain regions that are activated when a person smells a foul odor are also activated when the person sees someone else smelling the foul odor (Wicker et al., 2003). Studies such as these suggest that our brains respond to other people's *expressions* of distress by creating within us the *experience* of distress, and this mechanism may have evolved because it allows us to know instantly what others are feeling. The fact that we can actually *feel* another person's distress may explain why even a small child who is incapable of sophisticated moral reasoning still considers it wrong to inflict distress on others.

In summary, infants have a limited range of vision, but they can see and remember objects that appear within it. They learn to control their bodies from the top down and from the center out. Infants slowly develop theories about how the world works. Piaget believed that these theories developed through four stages, in which children learn basic facts about the world, such as the fact that objects continue to exist even when they are out of sight, and the fact that objects have enduring properties that are not changed by superficial transformations. Children also learn that their minds represent objects, hence objects may not be as they appear, and others may not see them as the child does. Cognitive development also comes about through social interactions in which children are given tools for understanding that have been developed over millennia by members of their cultures.

At a very early age, human beings develop strong emotional ties to their primary caregivers. The quality of these ties is determined both by the caregiver's behavior and the child's temperament. People get along with each other by learning and obeying moral principles. Children's reasoning about right and wrong is initially based on an action's consequences, but as they mature, children begin to consider the actor's intentions as well as the extent to which the action obeys abstract moral principles. Moral intuitions may also be derived from one's emotional reactions to events, such as the suffering of others. ■ ■

ADOLESCENCE The period of development that begins with the onset of sexual maturity (about 11 to 14 years of age) and lasts until the beginning of adulthood (about 18 to 21 years of age).

PUBERTY The bodily changes associated with sexual maturity.

PRIMARY SEX CHARACTERISTICS Bodily structures that are directly involved in reproduction.

SECONDARY SEX CHARACTERISTICS Bodily structures that change dramatically with sexual maturity but that are not directly involved in reproduction.

Adolescence: Minding the Gap

Between childhood and adulthood is an extended developmental stage that may not qualify for a hood of its own but that is clearly distinct from the stages that come before and after. **Adolescence** is *the period of development that begins with the onset of sexual maturity (about 11 to 14 years of age) and lasts until the beginning of adulthood (about 18 to 21 years of age)*. Unlike the transition from embryo to fetus or from infant to child, this transition is both sudden and clearly marked. In just 3 or 4 years, the average adolescent gains about 40 pounds and grows about 10 inches. Girls' growth rates begin to accelerate around the age of 10, and they reach their full heights at around 15½ years. Boys experience an equivalent growth spurt about 2 years later and reach their full heights at around 17½ years. The growth spurt signals the onset of **puberty**, which refers to *the bodily changes associated with sexual maturity*. These changes involve

primary sex characteristics, which are *bodily structures that are directly involved in reproduction,* for example, the onset of menstruation in girls and the enlargement of the testes, scrotum, and penis and the emergence of the capacity for ejaculation in boys. They also involve **secondary sex characteristics**, which are *bodily structures that change dramatically with sexual maturity but that are not directly involved in reproduction,* for example, the enlargement of the breasts and the widening of the hips in girls and the appearance of facial hair, pubic hair, underarm hair, and the lowering of the voice in both genders. This pattern of changes is caused by increased production of sex-specific hormones: estrogen in girls and testosterone in boys.

Just as the body changes during adolescence, so too does the brain. For example, there is a marked increase in the growth rate of tissue connecting different regions of the brain just before puberty (Thompson et al., 2000). Between the ages of 6 and 13, the connections between the temporal lobe (the brain region specialized for language) and the parietal lobe (the brain region specialized for understanding spatial relations) multiply rapidly and then stop—just about the time that the critical period for learning a language ends (see **FIGURE 11.10**). But the most intriguing set of changes associated with adolescence occurs in the prefrontal cortex. An infant's brain forms many more new synapses than it actually needs, and by the time a child is 2 years old, she has about 15,000 synapses per neuron—which is twice as many as the average adult (Huttenlocher, 1979). This early period of synaptic proliferation is followed by a period of synaptic pruning in which those connections that are not frequently used are eliminated. This is a clever system that allows our brain's wiring to be determined both by our genes and our experiences: Our genes "offer" a very large set of synaptic connections to the environment, which then "chooses" which ones to keep. Scientists used to think that this process ended early in life, but recent evidence suggests that the prefrontal cortex undergoes a second wave of synaptic proliferation just before puberty and a second round of synaptic pruning during adolescence (Giedd et al., 1999). Clearly, the adolescent brain is a work in progress.

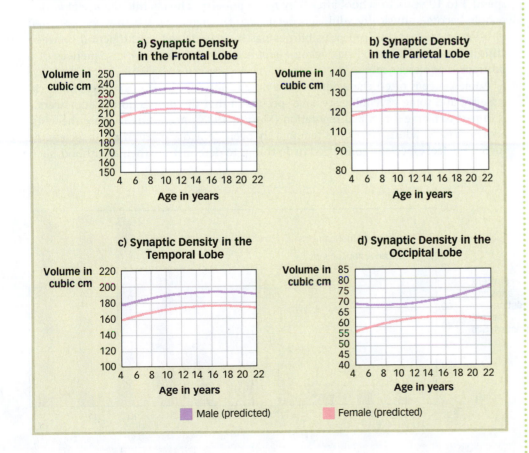

Figure 11.10 Your Brain on Puberty The development of neurons peaks in the frontal and parietal lobes at about age 12 (a, b), in the temporal lobe at about age 16 (c), and continues to increase in the occipital lobe through age 20 (d).

Early puberty is big news.

The Protraction of Adolescence

Although the onset of puberty is largely determined by a genetic program (no one reaches puberty at 2 or 72), there is considerable variation across individuals (e.g., people tend to reach puberty at about the same age as their same-sexed parent did) and across cultures (e.g., African American girls tend to reach puberty before European American girls do) (see **FIGURE 11.11**). There is also considerable variation across generations (Malina, Bouchard, & Beunen, 1988). For example, in Scandinavia, the United Kingdom, and the United States, the age of first menstruation was between 16 and 17 years in the 19th century but was approximately 13 years in 1960. Currently, about a third of all boys in the United States show some signs of genital maturity by the age of 9 (Reiter & Lee, 2001). The decrease in the age of the onset of puberty is due at least in part to changes in the environment (Ellis & Garber, 2000). For example, both body fat and stress hormones hasten the onset of puberty (Kim & Smith, 1998), and there is reason to suspect that both factors have increased over the last century in the industrialized world.

The increasingly early onset of puberty has important psychological consequences. Just two centuries ago, the gap between childhood and adulthood was relatively brief because people became physically adult at roughly the same time that they were ready to accept adult roles in society, and these roles did not normally require them to have extensive schooling. But in modern societies, people typically spend 3 to 10 years in school after they reach puberty. Thus, while the age at which people become physically adult has decreased, the age at which they are prepared or allowed take on adult responsibilities has increased, and so the period between childhood and adulthood has become *protracted*. What are the consequences of a protracted adolescence?

Adolescence is often characterized as a time of internal turmoil and external recklessness, and some psychologists have speculated that the protraction of adolescence is in part to blame for its bad reputation (Moffitt, 1993). According to these theorists, adolescents are adults who have temporarily been denied a place in adult society. As such, they feel especially compelled to do things to demonstrate their adulthood, such

Figure 11.11 Secondary Sexual Characteristics The graph shows the percentage of girls in each age group who show breast and/or pubic hair development. These characteristics appear earlier in African American than European American girls. There is no evidence that African American boys mature earlier than European American boys (Herman-Giddens et al., 1997).

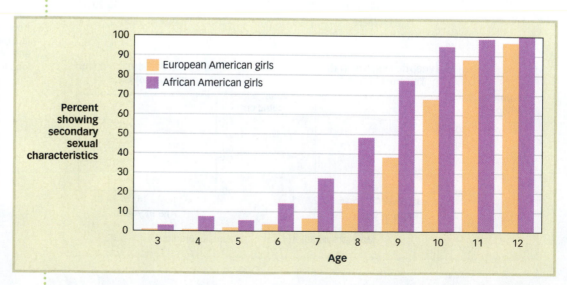

as smoking, drinking, using drugs, having sex, and committing crimes. In addition, because they cannot partake in adult culture, they must establish their own subculture with unique rites and rituals. In a sense, adolescents are people who are forced to live in the gap between two worlds, and the so-called storm and stress of adolescence may be understood in part as a consequence of this dilemma.

The only thing wrong with this explanation is that the storm and stress of adolescence is not quite as intense as all those coming-of-age movies would have us believe (Steinberg & Morris, 2001). Research suggests that the "moody adolescent" who is a victim of "raging hormones" is largely a myth. In fact, adolescents are no moodier than children (Buchanan, Eccles, & Becker, 1992), and fluctuations in their hormone levels have only a tiny impact on their moods (Brooks-Gunn, Graber, & Paikoff, 1994). The common stereotype of adolescents as "reckless rebels" is also more than a little misleading. The vast majority of adolescents do dabble in misbehavior but don't actually major in it. For example, most adolescents in the United States get drunk at least once before they graduate from high school, but few develop drinking problems or allow alcohol to impair their academic success or personal relationships (Hughs, Power, & Francis, 1992; Johnston, Bachman, & O'Malley, 1997). Adolescents tend to experiment, but their experiments appear to have few long-term consequences, and most adolescents who try drugs or break the law end up becoming sober, law-abiding adults (Steinberg, 1999). In short, adolescence is not a terribly troubled time for most people, and adolescents typically "age out" of the troubles they get themselves into (Sampson & Laub, 1995).

Although many adolescents experiment with various forms of reckless behavior, few continue to behave recklessly as adults.

Some cultures skip adolescence entirely. When a Krobo female menstruates for the first time, older women take her into seclusion for 2 weeks and teach her about sex, birth control, and marriage. Afterward, a public ceremony called the durbar is held, and the young female who that morning was regarded as a child is thereafter regarded as an adult.

Sexuality

The most visible sign of adolescence is the rapid and striking physical metamorphosis that turns boys into men and girls into women. These dramatic physical changes are not merely decorative. Along with all this new sexual equipment comes a new and increasingly sharp interest in sex itself.

Sexual Awakening

Boys and girls report the onset of sexual interest at about the same time despite the fact that many of the physical changes associated with puberty have an earlier onset in girls. This suggests that *adrenal androgen* (a hormone whose production increases at about the same time in boys and girls) may play a key role in the onset of sexual

KAREN KASMAUSKI/CORBIS

Sex education does not increase the likelihood that teenagers will have sex, but it does decrease the likelihood that they will have babies. Teenage mothers and their children fare quite poorly on most measures of success and well-being.

interest (McClintock & Herdt, 1996). Of course, sexual interest does not automatically translate into sexual activity because every human culture has strict rules about when and with whom people may have sex. For example, while some Middle Eastern cultures prohibit adolescent women from having any contact with males outside their family circle, more than 65% of American women report having had sexual intercourse by age 18 and 90% by age 21 (Hogan, Sun, & Cornwell, 2000). Clearly, religious traditions and social norms play a leading role in determining when and how sexual interest will be expressed in behavior.

When sexual activity does begin, it usually follows a script, and many features of this script appear to be standard across cultures. For example, in most cultures kissing precedes fondling, which precedes genital contact (Michael, 1994). But one feature of the sexual script that differs drastically among cultures is the use of contraception. Although about a quarter of U.S. teenagers have had four or more sexual partners by their senior year in high school, only about half report using a condom during their last intercourse (CDC, June 28, 2002). The United States has one of the highest rates of teen pregnancy of all modern industrialized nations (Darroch et al., 2001)—twice the rate of Great Britain and seven times the rate of Denmark and the Netherlands (Coley & Chase-Landale, 1998).

Although American adolescents aren't more sexually active than Western European adolescents (Darroch et al., 2001), American parents are less comfortable with sex education than are Western European parents. In the United States, most parents do not talk to their children extensively about sex (Ansuini, Fiddler-Woite, & Woite, 1996), and if they do, they tend to start too late because they drastically underestimate the age at which their children are having sex (Jaccard, Dittus, & Gordon, 1998) (see **FIGURE 11.12**). Sex education in schools is often absent, sketchy, or based on the goal of abstinence rather than pregnancy prevention. Although studies show that sex education does not (as some American parents fear) increase the likelihood that adolescents will engage in sexual activity (Satcher, 2001), less than half of all sex education courses in public schools teach the correct use of condoms (CDC, August 18, 2000), and about a third of all school districts in the United States require an "abstinence only" approach (Gold & Nash, 2001). Abortion, AIDS, and other sexually transmitted diseases are just some of the unfortunate consequences of sexual ignorance. Teenage pregnancy is another, and it is troubling for many reasons, not the least of which is that teenage mothers fare more poorly than teenage women without children on almost every measure of academic and economic achievement, and their children fare more poorly on most measures of educational success and emotional well-being than do the children of older mothers (Olausson et al., 2001).

Figure 11.12 Parental Misconceptions about Teenage Sex When American parents talk to teens about sex, it is often too little and too late. Research shows that American teens have sex earlier than their parents think they do (Jaccard et al., 1998).

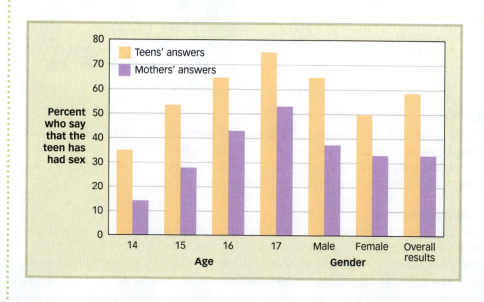

Sexual Orientation

Puberty is not an easy time for anyone, but it is especially difficult for some. Boys who reach puberty later than their peers often find this period especially stressful because immature boys may be less athletic and may feel less "manly" than their peers (Petersen, 1985). Among girls, it is those who reach puberty earlier than their peers who are most likely to experience a variety of negative consequences ranging from distress (Peskin, 1973) to delinquency (Caspi, 1991). Early-maturing girls don't have as much time as their peers do to develop the skills necessary to cope with adolescence (Petersen and Grockett, 1985), but because they appear to be mature, others expect them to act like adults. Early-maturing girls also tend to receive attention from older males, who may lead them into a variety of unhealthy activities (Ge, Conger, & Elder, 1996). Some research suggests that the timing of puberty has a greater influence on emotional and behavioral problems than does the occurrence of puberty itself (Buchanan et al., 1992).

For some adolescents, puberty is additionally complicated by the fact that they are attracted to members of the same sex. Not only does this make them different from the vast majority of their peers, but with few exceptions, human cultures tend to disapprove of homosexual behavior and react to it with responses that range from snickering to beheading (see **FIGURE 11.13**). In a recent survey, 50% of Americans agreed with the statement "homosexuality can never be justified," and America is more accepting of homosexuality than most other nations. In Nigeria and Kenya, for example, 98% agreed with that statement (Pew Research Center for People and the Press, 2006). It is little wonder that while 2% to 10% of adults classify themselves as homosexual, only 0.5% of young teenagers are willing to do the same (Garofalo et al., 1999).

What determines whether a person is sexually oriented toward the same or the opposite sex? In the past, psychologists believed that a person's sexual orientation depended entirely on their upbringing. For example, psychoanalytic theorists suggested that boys who grow up with a domineering mother and a submissive father are less likely to identify with their father and are thereby more likely to become homosexual. However, scientific research has failed to identify *any* aspect of parenting that has a significant impact on sexual orientation (Bell, Weinberg, & Hammersmith, 1981), and indeed, children raised by homosexual couples and heterosexual couples are equally likely to become heterosexual adults (Patterson, 1995). There is also little support for the idea that a person's early sexual encounters have a lasting impact on his or her sexual orientation (Bohan, 1996).

On the other hand, there is considerable evidence to suggest that genetics plays a role in determining sexual orientation. Gay men and lesbians tend to have a larger proportion of gay and lesbian siblings than do heterosexuals (Bailey et al., 1999). Furthermore, the identical twin of a gay man (with whom he shares 100% of his genes) has a 50% chance of being homosexual, whereas the fraternal twin or nontwin brother of a gay man (with whom he shares 50% of his genes) has only a 15% chance (Bailey & Pillard, 1991; Gladue, 1994). A similar pattern has emerged in studies of women (Bailey et al., 1993). In addition, some evidence suggests that the fetal environment may play a role in determining sexual orientation and that high levels of androgens predispose the fetus—whether male or female—later to develop a sexual preference for women (Ellis & Ames, 1987; Meyer-Bahlberg et al., 1995).

Of course, biology cannot be the sole determinant of a person's sexual orientation because, as these figures indicate, homosexual men and women often have twins who are genetically identical, who shared their fetal environment, and who are heterosexual nonetheless. Although gay or bisexual males who acknowledge their sexual orientations claim to have become aware of feelings of attraction toward other males at around the age of 8 and feel that they have "always been gay" (Savin-Williams, 1998), a sizable minority of lesbian women report that they were initially heterosexual and became lesbian only in midlife after experiencing an attraction to another woman (Schneider, 2001). This fact fits with the claim that women's sexuality is more plastic—

Figure 11.13 Heterosexuals' Attitudes toward Homosexuals It isn't surprising that homosexual adolescents are reluctant to reveal their sexual orientations. As a recent public opinion survey shows, a sizable percentage of heterosexual men and women say that they feel "somewhat or very uncomfortable" being around a gay man or a lesbian (Herek, 2002).

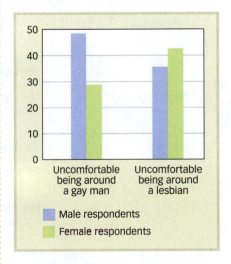

that is, it can be oriented and reoriented more easily—than men's (Baumeister, 2004). On the other hand, this difference may be due to the somewhat greater acceptance of female homosexuality than of male homosexuality in Western societies. Although the science of sexual orientation is still young and fraught with conflicting findings, one fact is clear: Sexual orientation is not a simple matter of choice.

Parents and Peers

"Who am I?" is a question asked both by amnesiacs and adolescents, but they ask it for different reasons. Adolescents can typically remember their names and mailing addresses, but they are much less sure about what they want, what they believe, and what they *should* want and believe. The child's view of herself and her world is tightly tied to the views of her parents, but puberty creates a new set of needs that begins to snip away at these bonds by orienting the adolescent toward peers rather than parents. The psychologist Erik Erikson characterized each stage of life by the major task confronting the individual at that stage, and he suggested that the major task of adolescence was the development of an adult identity (see **TABLE 11.2**). Whereas children define themselves almost entirely in terms of their relationships with parents and siblings, adolescence marks a shift in emphasis from family relations to peer relations.

Two things can make this shift difficult. First, children cannot choose their parents, but adolescents can choose their peers. As such, adolescents have the power to shape themselves by joining groups that will lead them to develop new values, attitudes, beliefs, and perspectives. In a sense, the adolescent has the opportunity to invent the adult he or she will soon become, and the responsibility this opportunity entails can be overwhelming. Second, as adolescents strive for greater autonomy, their parents naturally rebel. For instance, parents and adolescents tend to disagree about the age at which certain adult behaviors, such as staying out late or having sex, become permissible, and you don't need a psychologist to tell you

"So I blame you for everything—whose fault is that?"

Table 11.2	Erikson's Stages of Human Development			
Stage	**Ages**	**Crisis**	**Key Event**	**Positive Resolution**
1. Oral-sensory	Birth to 12 to 18 months	Trust vs. mistrust	Feeding	Child develops a belief that the environment can be counted on to meet his or her basic physiological and social needs.
2. Muscular-anal	18 months to 3 years	Autonomy vs. shame/doubt	Toilet training	Child learns what he/she can control and develops a sense of free will and corresponding sense of regret and sorrow for inappropriate use of self-control.
3. Locomotor,	3 to 6 years	Initiative vs. guilt	Independence	Child learns to begin action, to explore, to imagine, and to feel remorse for actions.
4. Latency	6 to 12 years	Industry vs. inferiority	School	Child learns to do things well or correctly in comparison to a standard or to others.
5. Adolescence	12 to 18 years	Identity vs. role confusion	Peer relationships	Adolescent develops a sense of self in relationship to others and to own internal thoughts and desires.
6. Young adulthood	19 to 40 years	Intimacy vs. isolation	Love relationships	Person develops the ability to give and receive love; begins to make long-term commitment to relationships.
7. Middle adulthood	40 to 65 years	Generativity vs. stagnation	Parenting	Person develops interest in guiding the development of the next generation.
8. Maturity	65 to death	Ego integrity vs. despair	Reflection on and acceptance of one's life	Person develops a sense of acceptance of life as it was lived and the importance of the people and relationships that individual developed over the life span.

which position each party tends to hold (Holmbeck & O'Donnell, 1991). Because adolescents and parents often have different ideas about who should control the adolescent's behavior, their relationships may become more conflictive and less close and their interactions briefer and less frequent (Larson & Richards, 1991).

But these conflicts and tensions are not as dramatic, pervasive, and inevitable as many seem to believe. For example, adolescents tend to have aspirations and values that are quite similar to those of their parents (Elder & Conger, 2000), and familial bickering tends to be about much smaller issues, such as dress and language, which explains why teenagers argue more with their mothers (who are typically in charge of such issues) than with their fathers (Caspi et al., 1993). Furthermore, in cultures that emphasize the importance of duty and obligation, parents and adolescents may show few if any signs of tension and conflict (Greenfield et al., 2003).

As adolescents pull away from their parents, they move toward their peers. Studies show that across a wide variety of cultures, historical epochs, and even species, peer relations evolve in a similar way (Dunphy, 1963; Weisfeld, 1999). Young adolescents initially form groups or "cliques" (Brown, Mory, & Kinney, 1994) with others of their gender, many of whom were friends during childhood. Next, male cliques and female cliques begin to meet in public places, such as town squares or shopping malls, and they begin to interact—but only in groups and only in public. After a few years, the older members of these single-sex cliques "peel off" and form smaller, mixed-sex cliques, which may assemble in private as well as in public but usually assemble as a group. Finally, couples (typically a male and a female) "peel off" from the small mixed-sex clique and begin romantic relationships.

Studies show that throughout adolescence, people spend increasing amounts of time with opposite-sex peers while maintaining the amount of time they spend with same-sex peers (Richards et al., 1998), and they accomplish this by spending less time with their parents (Larson & Richards, 1991). Although peers exert considerable influence on the adolescent's beliefs and behaviors—both for better and for worse—this influence generally occurs because adolescents respect, admire, and like their peers and not because their peers pressure them (Susman et al., 1994). Acceptance by peers is of tremendous importance to adolescents, and those who are rejected by their peers tend to be withdrawn, lonely, and depressed (Pope & Bierman, 1999). Fortunately for those of us who were seventh-grade nerds, individuals who are unpopular in early adolescence can become popular in later adolescence as their peers become less rigid and more tolerant (Kinney, 1993).

© PURESTOCK/ALAMY

Adolescents form same-sex cliques that meet opposite-sex cliques in public places. Eventually, these people will form mixed-sex cliques, pair off into romantic relationships, get married, and have children who will take their places at the mall.

In summary, adolescence is a stage of development that is distinct from those that come before and after it. It begins with a growth spurt and with puberty, the onset of sexual maturity of the human body. Puberty is occurring earlier than ever before, and the entrance of young people into adult society is occurring later. During this "in-between stage," adolescents are somewhat more prone to do things that are risky or illegal, but they rarely inflict serious or enduring harm on themselves or others. During adolescence, sexual interest intensifies, and in some cultures, sexual activity begins. Sexual activity typically follows a script, many aspects of which are standard across cultures. Although most people are attracted to members of the opposite sex, some are not, and research suggests that biology plays a key role in determining a person's sexual orientation. As adolescents seek to develop their adult identities, they seek increasing autonomy from their parents and become more peer-oriented, forming single-sex cliques, followed by mixed-sex cliques, and finally pairing off as couples. ■ ■

Adulthood: The Short Happy Future

It takes fewer than 7,000 days for a single-celled zygote to become a registered voter. The speed with which this radical transformation happens is astonishing, which is why we see our baby cousin or teenage nephew at the annual family reunion and feel compelled to say things like "Just *look* at you!" On the other hand, middle-aged uncles usually elicit remarks more along the lines of, "You haven't changed a bit." Indeed, the rate of observable physical change slows considerably in **adulthood**, which is *the stage of development that begins around 18 to 21 years and ends at death,* and this is all the more remarkable when you consider the fact that adulthood lasts about three times longer than all the previous stages combined. Because observable change slows from a gallop to a crawl, we sometimes have the sense that adulthood is a destination to which development delivers us and that once we've arrived, our journey is complete. But that's not so. Although they are more gradual and less noticeable, many physical, cognitive, and emotional changes take place between our first legal beer and our last legal breath.

Changing Abilities

The physical transformations that take place during adulthood can be characterized succinctly: Things quickly get worse slowly. In other words, our physical decline begins painfully early but is mercifully gradual. The early 20s are the peak years for health, stamina, vigor, and prowess, and because our psychology is so closely tied to our biology, these are also the years during which most of our cognitive abilities are at their sharpest. At this very moment you see further, hear better, remember more, and weigh less than you ever will again. Enjoy it. This glorious moment at life's summit will last for a few dozen more months—and then, somewhere between the ages of 26 and 30, you will begin the slow and steady decline that does not end until you do. A mere 10 or 15 years after puberty, your body will begin to deteriorate in almost every way: Your muscles will be replaced by fat, your skin will become less elastic, your hair will thin and your bones will weaken, your sensory abilities will become less acute, and your brain cells will die at an accelerated rate. If you are a woman, your ovaries will stop producing eggs and you will become infertile; if you are a man, your erections will be fewer and further between. Indeed, other than being more resistant to colds and less sensitive to pain, older bodies just don't work as well as younger ones do.

Although these physical changes happen slowly, as they accumulate they begin to have measurable psychological consequences (see **FIGURE 11.14**). For instance, as your brain ages, your prefrontal cortex and its associated subcortical connections will deteriorate more quickly than will the other areas of your brain (Raz, 2000). Recall from Chapter 3 that your prefrontal cortex is responsible for *controlled processing*, which means that you will experience the most noticeable cognitive decline on tasks that require effort, initiative, or strategy. For instance, we all know that memory worsens with age, but not all memory worsens at the same rate. Older adults show a much more pronounced decline on tests of working memory (the ability to hold information "in mind") than on tests of long-term memory (the ability to retrieve information), a much more pronounced decline on tests of episodic memory (the ability to remember particular past events) than on tests of semantic memory (the ability to remember general information such as the meanings of words), and a much more pronounced decline on tests of retrieval (the ability to "go find" information in memory) than on tests of recognition (the ability to decide whether information was encountered before).

And yet, while the cognitive machinery gets rustier with age, research suggests that the operators of that machinery often compensate by using it more skillfully. Although older chess players *remember* chess positions more poorly than younger players do, they *play* as well as younger players because they search the board more efficiently (Charness, 1981). Although older typists *react* more slowly than younger typists do, they *type* as quickly and accurately as younger typists because they are better at anticipating the

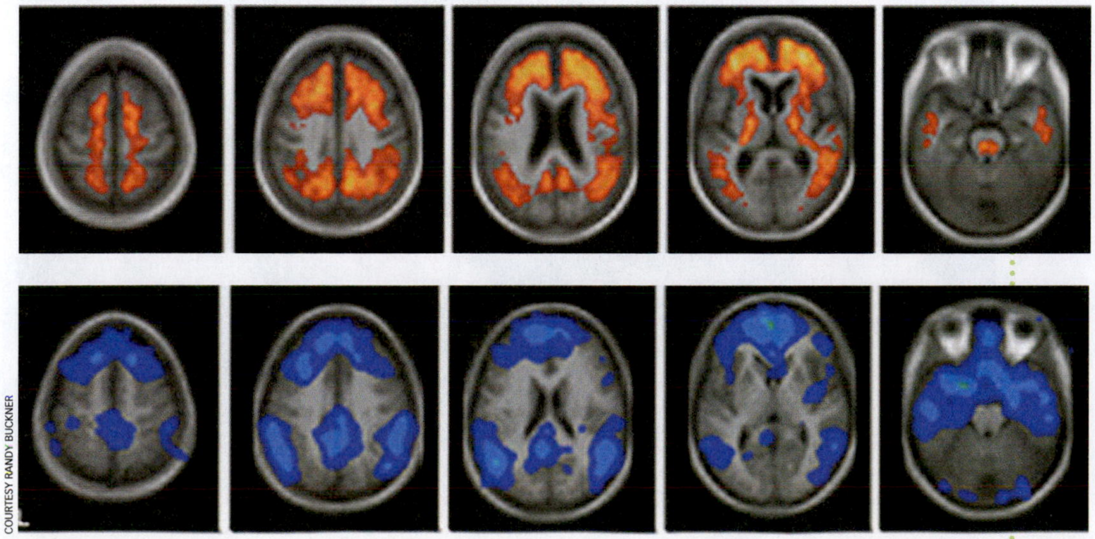

Figure 11.14 Alzheimer's and Daydreaming Alzheimer's disease affects as many as 4.5 million older Americans, who suffer severe impairments of language, thought, and memory. The disease is characterized by the formation of abnormal clumps of a material called "amyloid plaque." Interestingly, these plaques seem to develop in the very regions of the brain that are active when healthy people are musing, daydreaming, or letting their minds wander. The lower panel shows brain activity among healthy young adults who are daydreaming. The upper panel shows the location of amyloid plaques in older adults who have Alzheimer's disease. The regions include the medial and lateral posterior parietal regions, posterior cingulate, retrosplenial cortex, and frontal cortex along the midline. This fact has led some scientists to suggest that Alzheimer's disease may be the result of high metabolic activity over the course of a lifetime—in a sense, the everyday wear and tear caused by daydreaming (Buckner et al., 2005).

Although young chess players can remember the positions of pieces better than older players can, older players search the board more efficiently.

next word (Salthouse, 1984). Years of experience often allow people to develop strategies in their special domains of expertise that can compensate for cognitive decline (Bäckman & Dixon, 1992; Salthouse, 1987). Older airline pilots are considerably worse than younger pilots when it comes to keeping a list of words in short-term memory, but this age difference disappears when those words are the "heading commands" that pilots receive from the control tower every day (Morrow et al., 1994). This pattern of errors suggests that older adults are somehow compensating for age-related declines in memory and attention.

How do older adults implement these compensatory strategies? When a younger person tries to keep verbal information in working memory, his left prefrontal cortex is more strongly activated than the right, and when he tries to keep spatial information in working memory, his right prefrontal cortex is more strongly activated than the left (Smith & Jonides, 1997). But this *bilateral asymmetry* is not seen among older adults, and some scientists take this to mean that older brains compensate for the declining abilities of one neural structure by calling on other neural structures to help out (Cabeza, 2002; see **FIGURE 11.15**). The young brain can be characterized as a group of specialists, but as these specialists becomes older and less able, they begin to work together on tasks that each once handled independently. In short, the machinery of body and brain do break down with age, but a seasoned driver in an old jalopy can often hold his own against a rookie in a hot rod.

Figure 11.15 Bilaterality in Older and Younger Brains Across a variety of tasks, older adult brains show bilateral activation and young adult brains show unilateral activation. One possible explanation for this is that older brains compensate for the declining abilities of one neural structure by calling on other neural structures for help (Cabeza, 2002).

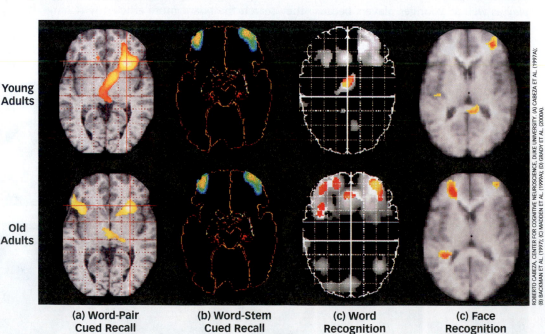

Young Adults

Old Adults

(a) Word-Pair Cued Recall (b) Word-Stem Cued Recall (c) Word Recognition (c) Face Recognition

Changing Orientations

One reason why Grandpa can't find his car keys is that his prefrontal cortex doesn't function like it used to. But another reason is that the location of car keys just isn't the sort of thing that grandpas spend their precious time memorizing. According to *socioemotional selectivity theory* (Carstensen & Turk-Charles, 1994), younger adults are generally oriented toward the acquisition of information that will be useful to them in the future (e.g., reading the newspaper), whereas older adults are generally oriented toward information that brings emotional satisfaction in the present (e.g., reading novels). Because young people have such long futures, they *invest* their time attending to, thinking about, and remembering potentially *useful information* that may serve them well in the many days to come. But older people have shorter futures and so they *spend* their time attending to, thinking about, and remembering *positive information* that serves them well in the moment (see **FIGURE 11.16**). As people age, they spend less time thinking about the future, but contrary to our stereotypes of the elderly, they do not spend more time thinking about the past (Carstensen, Isaacowitz, & Charles, 1999). Rather, they spend more time thinking about the present. Research suggests that the shortening of the future is indeed the cause of this basic change in our orientation toward information, which also occurs among younger people who learn that they have a terminal illness (Carstensen & Fredrickson, 1998).

Some of the declines in the cognitive performance of older adults may have less to do with changes in their brains and more to do with changes in their orientation (Hess, 2005). For example, older people do considerably worse than younger people when they are asked to remember a series of unpleasant faces, but they do only slightly worse when they are asked to remember a series of pleasant faces (Mather & Carstensen, 2003). Apparently, older adults find it difficult to attend to information that doesn't make them happy, and so they perform poorly on many standard memory tasks, which rarely include photos of their grandchildren. Perhaps it is not surprising, then, that people remember their lives more positively as they age (Kennedy, Mather, & Carstensen, 2004).

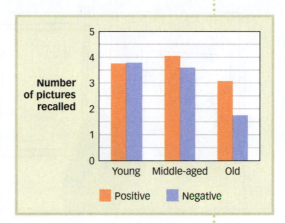

Figure 11.16 Memory for Pictures Memory declines with age in general, but the ability to remember negative information—such as unpleasant pictures—declines much more quickly than the ability to remember positive information (Carstensen et al., 2000).

As people age, they prefer to spend time with family and a few close friends rather than large circles of acquaintances. Some grandfathers will even dress like ducks to impress important members of their small social networks.

"Two Stones tickets, please, senior discount."

This change in orientation toward information influences much more than memory. Not only are older adults less likely than younger adults to attend to or remember negative information but they are also less likely to be emotionally influenced by it. Whereas younger adults show activation of the amygdala when they see both pleasant and unpleasant pictures, older adults show greater activation when they see pleasant pictures than when they see unpleasant pictures (Mather et al., 2004). Studies also reveal that as people age, they tend to experience far fewer negative emotions and more complex emotions (Carstensen et al., 2000; Charles, Reynolds, & Gatz, 2001, see **FIGURE 11.17**; Mroczek & Spiro, 2005). What's more, older people seem better able than younger people to sustain their positive emotional experiences and to curtail their negative ones (Lawton et al., 1992).

The change in our orientation toward information also influences our activities. Psychologists have long known that social networks get smaller as people age, and they have assumed that this happens because friends die at an accelerating rate. Some of this shrinkage is indeed due to loss, but it now appears that much of it is a matter of choice. Because a shortened future orients people toward emotionally satisfying rather than intellectually profitable information, older adults become more selective about their interaction partners, choosing to spend time with family and a few close friends rather than with a large circle of acquaintances. One study followed a group of people from the 1930s to the 1990s and found that their rate of interaction with acquaintances declined from early to middle adulthood, but their rate of interaction with spouses, parents, and siblings stayed stable or increased (Carstensen, 1992). A study of older adults who ranged in age from 69 to 104 found that the oldest adults had fewer peripheral social partners than the younger adults did, but they had just as many emotionally close partners whom they identified as member of their "inner circle" (Lang & Carstensen, 1994). Apparently, "Let's go meet some new people" just isn't something that most 60-year-olds tend to say. In a recent survey, 38% of people over 65 described themselves as very happy, but only 28% of 18- to 29-year-olds said

Figure 11.17 Happiness and Age
Despite what our youth-oriented culture would have you believe, people's overall happiness generally increases with age. As this graph shows, people experience a small decrease in positive affect beginning around age 55, but this is more than compensated for by the large decrease in negative affect that begins around the age of 15 and continues through middle age. (Charles, Reynolds, & Gatz, 2001).

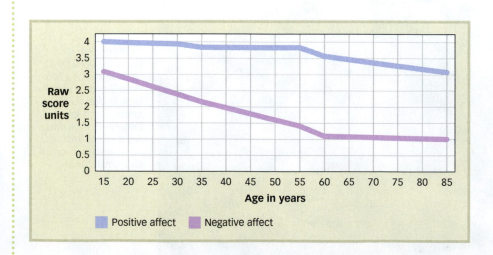

the same (Pew Research Center for the People & the Press, 1997). Although Western culture values youth (which is why Westerners spend billions of dollars every year trying to prolong it), research suggests that one of the best ways to increase one's share of happiness in life is simply to get older. The machinery may not work as well, but the passengers seem to enjoy the ride more.

Changing Roles

The psychological separation from parents that begins in adolescence becomes a physical separation in adulthood. In virtually all human societies, young adults leave home, get married, and have children of their own. They may stay at home until the day of their wedding or they may live on their own for years, but by and large, most human beings eventually leave one family and start another. Marriage and parenthood are two of the most significant aspects of adult life, and you will probably experience both of them. Census statistics suggest that if you are a college-age American, you are likely to get married at around the age of 27, have approximately 1.8 children, and consider both your partner and your children to be your greatest sources of joy. Indeed, in a recent survey, a whopping 93% of American mothers said that their children were a source of happiness all or most of the time (Pew Research Center, 1997).

But do marriage and children really make us happy? Research has consistently shown that married people live longer (see **FIGURE 11.18**), have more frequent sex (and enjoy that sex more), and earn several times as much money as unmarried people do (Waite, 1995). Given these differences, it is no surprise that married people consistently report being happier than unmarried people—whether those

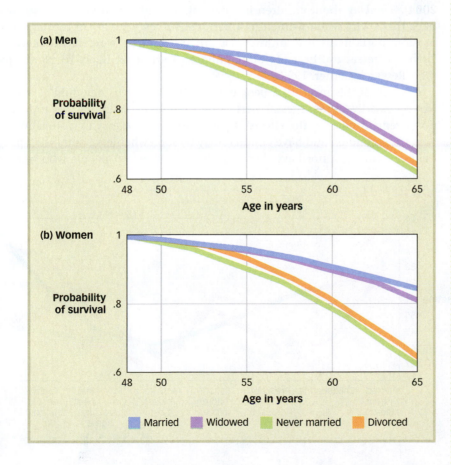

Figure 11.18 Till Death Do Us Part
Married people live longer than unmarried people, and this is true of both men and women. But while widowed men die as young as never-married and divorced men do (a), widowed women live longer than never-married or divorced women do (b). In other words, the loss of a wife is always bad, but the loss of a husband is only bad if he's still alive! (Lillard and Waite, 1995).

unmarried people are single, widowed, divorced, or cohabiting (Johnson & Wu, 2002). That's why many researchers consider marriage one of the best investments a person can make in their own happiness. But other researchers suggest that married people may be happier because happy people may be more likely to get married and that marriage may be the consequence—and not the cause—of happiness (Lucas et al., 2003). The general consensus among scientists seems to be that both of these positions are right: Even before marriage, people who end up married tend to be happier than those who never marry, but marriage does seem to confer further benefits.

Children are another story. In general, research suggests that children decrease rather than increase their parents' happiness (DiTella, MacCulloch, & Oswald, 2003). For example, parents typically report lower marital satisfaction than do non-parents—and the more children they have, the less satisfaction they report (Twenge, Campbell, & Foster, 2003). Studies of marital satisfaction at different points in the life span reveal an interesting pattern of peaks and valleys: Marital satisfaction starts out high, plummets at about the time that the children are in diapers, begins to recover, plummets again when the children are in adolescence, and returns to its premarital levels only when children leave home (see **FIGURE 11.19**). Given that mothers typically do much more child care than fathers, it is not surprising that the negative impact of parenthood is stronger for women than for men. Women with young children are especially likely to experience role conflicts ("How am I supposed to manage being a full-time lawyer and a full-time mother?") and restrictions of freedom ("I never get to play tennis anymore"). A study that measured the moment-to-moment happiness of American women as they went about their daily activities found that women were less happy when taking care of their children than when eating, exercising, shopping, napping, or watching television and only slightly happier than when they were doing housework (Kahneman et al., 2004). *Thinking* about children is a delight, but *raising* children is hard work. Perhaps that's why when women in a national survey were asked to name a mother's most important quality, mothers of grown children were most likely to name "love," whereas mothers of young children were most likely to name "patience" (Pew Research Center, 1997).

Does all of this mean that people would be happier if they didn't have children? Not necessarily. Because researchers cannot randomly assign people to be parents or nonparents, studies of the effects of parenthood are necessarily correlational. People who want children and have children may be somewhat less happy than people who neither want them nor have them, but it is possible that people who want children

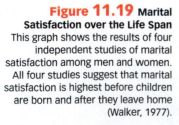

Figure 11.19 Marital Satisfaction over the Life Span This graph shows the results of four independent studies of marital satisfaction among men and women. All four studies suggest that marital satisfaction is highest before children are born and after they leave home (Walker, 1977).

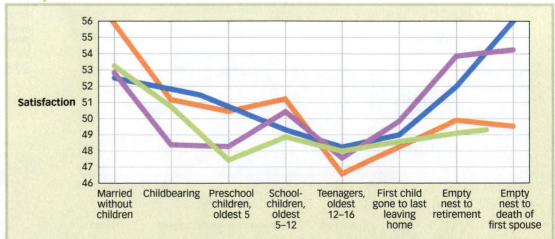

would be even less happy if they didn't have them. What seems clear is that raising children is a challenging job that most people find to be meaningful and rewarding—especially when it's over.

In summary, older adults show declines in working memory, episodic memory, and retrieval tasks, but they often develop strategies to compensate. Gradual physical decline begins early in adulthood and has clear psychological consequences, some of which are offset by increases in skill and expertise. Older people are more oriented toward emotionally satisfying information, which influences their basic cognitive performance, the size and structure of their social networks, and their general happiness. For most people, adulthood means leaving home, getting married, and having children. People who get married are typically happier, but children and the responsibilities that parenthood entails present a significant challenge, especially for women. ■ ■

Where Do You Stand?

Licensing Parents

Common law states that "when practice of a profession or calling requires special knowledge or skill and intimately affects public health, morals, order or safety, or general welfare, legislature may prescribe reasonable qualifications for persons desiring to pursue such professions or calling and require them to demonstrate possession of such qualifications by examination." Most of us would probably agree that this is reasonable and that people who want to operate automobiles, use firearms, pilot airplanes, or perform surgeries should be required to demonstrate their proficiency and obtain a license. After all, if people were allowed to practice law or build bridges without first demonstrating their knowledge and skill, the public welfare would be gravely compromised.

So why not apply this logic to parenting? Why not outlaw reproduction by citizens who can't qualify for a parenting license? Because this suggestion sounds so outrageous, you may be surprised to learn that it has become the subject of serious debate among ethicists who are trying to decide how best to balance the interests of parents against the damage that bad parenting can do (Tittle, 2004; Warnock, 2003). The arguments *against* parental licensing are all too

obvious: People have a fundamental right to reproduce; people have different definitions of "good parenting"; a licensing system would invite abuse by governments that want to limit the reproduction of citizens who have the wrong genes, the wrong skin color, or the wrong political beliefs. Americans are naturally suspicious of governmental intrusion into private affairs, and what could be more private than the decision to have a child?

For most people, parental licensing is a ridiculous and dangerous idea. And yet some of the arguments in its favor are not easily dismissed. Consider a few:

- Bad flossing is a private affair. Bad parenting is not. Every one of us pays the price when parents abuse, neglect, or fail to educate their children. Bad parents impose significant social and economic burdens on the rest of society—not to mention on their own children. Society has a clear interest in *preventing* (and not just punishing) abusive and negligent parenting.
- Licensing is not meant to prevent potentially bad parents from having children—it is meant to make potentially bad parents into good ones. Driver's education turns potentially bad drivers into

good ones, but most people wouldn't sign up for such training if they didn't have to in order to qualify for a driver's license. Licensing would motivate people to learn the things that every parent should know.

- If we demand that people meet certain standards before they are allowed to *adopt* children, then why should we not demand that they meet the same standards before being allowed to *bear* children? Are our biological children worth less than our adopted ones?
- All licensing systems are open to abuse. But is there any reason to believe that this one would be more open to abuse than others? And are the costs of abuse clearly greater than the costs of having no licensing system at all?

Anyone who has read George Orwell's *1984* or Aldous Huxley's *Brave New World* will find the notion of parental licensing more than a little frightening. And yet the arguments in favor of it cannot be dismissed without a counterargument. Bad parenting can have devastating consequences for children and for society, and we should all be concerned about it. Is parental licensing the right solution, or is it a bad answer to a good question? Where do you stand?

Chapter Review

Prenatality: A Womb with a View

- Life begins when a sperm and egg produce a zygote. The zygote develops into an embryo and then a fetus, and all are impacted by the environment of the womb.

Infancy and Childhood: Becoming a Person

- When infants are born, they have limited motor skills and must learn how to control their own bodies. This doesn't take them nearly as long as it takes them to learn about the physical and psychological worlds. Jean Piaget believed that children do this in stages and that among the things they learn are that objects continue to exist even when they are out of sight, that objects have enduring properties that are not changed by superficial transformations, and that their minds represent objects.

- Cognitive development occurs in part as a result of social interaction in which adults provide tools for understanding. At an early age, people develop strong emotional ties to their primary caregivers, and they learn to get along with one another by obeying moral rules. People's reasoning about right and wrong undergoes striking transformations as they grow.

Adolescence: Minding the Gap

- Adolescence occurs earlier and lasts longer than ever before, but adolescents are not as moody and rebellious as many people think. Adolescence marks the beginning of sexual maturity, the intensification of sexual interest, and for some, the onset of sexual activity.

- Biology plays an important role in determining whether adolescents are attracted to members of the same or the opposite sex.

- Adolescents develop adult identities by seeking autonomy from their parents and becoming more peer oriented.

Adulthood: The Short Happy Future

- For most people, adulthood means leaving home, getting married, and having children.

- As people age, they show physical and psychological declines that may be offset by compensatory strategies. They also tend to concentrate on people and things that make them happy.

Key Terms

developmental psychology (p. 406)

zygote (p. 407)

germinal stage (p. 407)

embryonic stage (p. 407)

fetal stage (p. 408)

myelination (p. 408)

teratogens (p. 408)

fetal alcohol syndrome (p. 408)

infancy (p. 410)

motor development (p. 411)

reflexes (p. 411)

cephalocaudal rule (p. 411)

proximodistal rule (p. 411)

cognitive development (p. 412)

sensorimotor stage (p. 413)

schemas (p. 413)

assimilation (p. 413)

accommodation (p. 413)

object permanence (p. 413)

childhood (p. 415)

preoperational stage (p. 415)

concrete operational stage (p. 415)

conservation (p. 415)

formal operational stage (p. 416)

egocentrism (p. 416)

theory of mind (p. 417)

attachment (p. 421)

strange situation (p. 423)

internal working model of attachment (p. 424)

temperaments (p. 424)

preconventional stage (p. 427)

conventional stage (p. 427)

postconventional stage (p. 427)

adolescence (p. 430)

puberty (p. 430)

primary sex characteristics (p. 431)

secondary sex characteristics (p. 431)

adulthood (p. 438)

Recommended Readings

Bloom, P. (2004). *Descartes' baby: How the science of child development explains what makes us human.* New York: Basic Books. Most of us feel that we are a mind that inhabits a body. But why? Why have people traditionally thought of their bodies as mere vehicles for something immaterial—a mind, a psyche, or a soul? In this fascinating book full of great insights and startling examples, Paul Bloom suggests that infants naturally divide the world into the physical and the mental and that this early distinction gives rise to our dualist intuitions.

DeLoache, J. S., & Gottlieb, A. (2000). *A world of babies: Imagined childcare guides for seven societies.* Cambridge: Cambridge University Press. Judy DeLoache and Alma Gottlieb

explore cultural differences in child-rearing practices in seven cultures in this book. Written as a series of fictional child-care manuals in the style of *Dr. Spock's Baby and Child Care,* the authors use factual information from real sources as well as research by psychologists, anthropologists, and historians.

Gopnik, A., Meltzoff, A., & Kuhl, P. (1999). *The scientist in the crib: What early learning tells us about the mind.* New York: HarperCollins. Developmental scientists Alison Gopnik, Andrew Meltzoff, and Patricia Kuhl present decades of research on cognitive development that reveals what infants know and how they learn about people, objects, and language. The authors suggest that babies are born knowing a lot more than previously thought by psychologists such as Piaget, and they describe their own and other developmentalists' research in this accessible book.

The Up Series: *Seven up, 7 plus seven, 21 up, 28 up, 35 up, 42 up, 49 up.* (1964–2005). A remarkable series of seven documentary films follows the lives of 14 British people from age 7 to (so far) age 49. (*Seven Up* was directed by Paul Almond, while the other films were directed by Michael Apted.) In 1964, specific participants were selected to represent the range of socioeconomic backgrounds in England. The filmmakers wanted to explore the idea that people's futures were predetermined by their place in British society and all that comes with it, such as attendance at elite universities and entry into the business and financial world. Over the course of four decades, this proved to be true for some of the participants, but others from both upper and middle classes diverged from the paths expected for their lives. *56 Up* will be filmed in 2011 or 2012.

12

Personality

Personality: What It Is and How It Is Measured
  Describing and Explaining Personality
  Measuring Personality

The Trait Approach: Identifying Patterns of Behavior
  Traits as Behavioral Dispositions and Motives
  The Search for Core Traits
  Traits as Biological Building Blocks
  THE REAL WORLD Do Different Genders Lead to Different Personalities?

The Psychodynamic Approach: Forces That Lie beneath Awareness
  Unconscious Motives
  The Structure of the Mind: Id, Ego, and Superego
  Dealing with Inner Conflict
  Psychosexual Stages and the Development of Personality

The Humanistic-Existential Approach: Personality as Choice
  Human Needs and Self-actualization
  Conditions for Growth
  Personality as Existence

The Social Cognitive Approach: Personalities in Situations
  Consistency of Personality across Situations
  Personal Constructs
  Personal Goals and Expectancies

The Self: Personality in the Mirror
  Self-concept
  Self-esteem
  HOT SCIENCE Implicit Egotism: Liking Ourselves without Knowing It
  WHERE DO YOU STAND? Personality Testing for Fun and Profit

EDITH PIAF, A CABARET STAR WITH A haunting voice, was the top French singer during the 1940s and 1950s. Her songs ached with desolation and lost love, echoing her own life—a tragic story of addictions and fleeting relationships. She became close to many men, but each new love was undone by her compulsive promiscuity. Her only child, fathered by a delivery boy she met at age 16, died in infancy. Her lovers included a brutal pimp, a nightclub owner who contributed the stage name *Piaf* (Parisian slang for "sparrow"), and, as her fame grew, a succession of would-be singers who hoped to gain by association with her. She fell into alcoholism and, after a car accident, became addicted to morphine—once even stepping offstage during a show to inject herself through her skirt and hose. Her legendary vulnerability and diminutive 4'8" stature clashed with the great strength in her stage presence and the raw emotional power of her music. Her songs "La vie en rose," "Milord," and "Non, je ne regrette rien" (No regrets) became anthems of Paris and of France.

How can we account for this unique personality? What could make someone so magnetic and yet so self-destructive—so strong and yet so weak? We could look to her parents: Edith's mother was an alcoholic street singer known for prostitution at carnivals and circuses. She neglected her infant daughter and after 2 months abandoned her

to the father, a Parisian street acrobat. Edith's father was more loving but also failed her, sending her to be raised by his mother, who ran a brothel in Normandy. Life at the brothel was not especially wholesome and inspirational either. Three-year-old Edith briefly became blind, and when her sight returned, she surely saw much that shaped her personality. In her autobiography, she wrote, "This upbringing had not made me very sentimental . . . I thought that when a boy signaled to a girl, the girl should never refuse. I thought women should behave like that" (Piaf, 2004, p. 62).

Still regarded as one of France's greatest popular singers, Edith Piaf's strength was in the passionate power of her voice. The complexities of her tragic life offer avenues for exploring the nature of personality.

The forces that create any one personality are always something of a mystery. Your personality is different from anyone else's and expresses itself pretty consistently across settings—at home, in the classroom, and elsewhere. You pay attention to others' personality differences when you choose your friends and when dealing with difficult people. But how and why do people differ psychologically? By studying many unique individuals, psychologists seek to gather enough information to scientifically answer these, the central questions of personality psychology. Edith Piaf, always one for a quirky quote, once observed, "Your whole personality is in your nose" (Piaf, 2004, p. 66). There's more to it than that.

Personality is *an individual's characteristic style of behaving, thinking, and feeling.* Piaf's addictions to alcohol and morphine, her belief that sex should be undertaken with almost anyone who asked for it, and her melodramatic style of song and life were all parts of her personality. In this chapter, we will explore personality, first by looking at what it is and how it is measured and then by focusing on each of four main approaches to understanding personality—trait-biological, psychodynamic, humanistic-existential, and social cognitive. (Psychologists have personalities too, so their different approaches, even to the topic of personality, shouldn't be that surprising.) At the end of the chapter, we will discuss the psychology of self to see how our views of what we are like can shape and define our personality.

Personality: What It Is and How It Is Measured

If someone said, "You have no personality," how would you feel? Like a cookie-cutter person, a grayish lump, probably boring to boot, who should go out and get a personality as soon as possible? People don't usually strive for a personality; one seems to develop naturally as we travel through life. As psychologists have tried to understand the process of personality development, they have pondered questions of description (How do people differ?), explanation (Why do people differ?), and the more quantitative question of measurement (How can personality be assessed?).

Describing and Explaining Personality

Like early biology studies, the descriptive aspect of personality psychology is taxonomic in approach. The first biologists earnestly attempted to classify all plants and animals—whether lichens or ants or fossilized skunks. Similarly, personality psychologists began by labeling and describing different personalities. And just as biology came of age with Darwin's theory of evolution, which *explained* how differences among species arose, the maturing study of personality has also developed explanations of the basis for psychological differences among people.

What People Are Like

Most personality psychologists focus on specific, psychologically meaningful individual differences—characteristics such as honesty or anxiousness or moodiness. Still, personality is often in the eye of the beholder. When one person describes another as "a conceited jerk," for example, you may wonder whether you have just learned more about the describer or the person being described. Interestingly, studies that ask acquaintances to describe each other find a high degree of similarity among any one individual's descriptions of many different people ("Jason thinks that Bob is considerate, Jeff is kind, and Gina is nice to others"). In contrast, resemblance is quite low when many people describe one person ("Bob thinks Jason is smart, Jeff thinks he is competitive, and Gina thinks he has a good sense of humor") (Dornbusch et al., 1965). As you will see, theorists also differ in their views on the characteristics of personality worth describing.

PERSONALITY An individual's characteristic style of behaving, thinking, and feeling.

How would you describe each of these personalities?

Why People Are the Way They Are

What drove Edith Piaf to embrace men, alcohol, and morphine? What made the "sparrow" fly from nest to nest? In general, explanations of personality differences are concerned with (1) *prior events* that can shape an individual's personality or (2) *anticipated events* that might motivate the person to reveal particular personality characteristics. In a biological and chemical prior event, Edith received genes from her parents that may have led her to a life of addiction and broken loves. Researchers interested in events that happen prior to our behavior delve into our subconscious and into our circumstances and interpersonal surroundings as well as studying our biology and brains.

Edith expected that she would find love through sexual relationships and happiness in drugs and alcohol, and those motives also might explain her behavior. The consideration of *anticipated events* emphasizes the person's own perspective and often seems intimate and personal in its reflection of the person's inner life—hopes, fears, and aspirations. Of course, our understanding of the puzzle that was Edith Piaf's life—or the life of any ordinary woman or man—also depends on insights into the interaction between the past and future: We need to know how her history may have shaped her motivations. If we were to ask Edith why she so often found herself desiring immediate sexual liaisons without wondering about the future of her relationships, she might have offered motivational explanations, pointing to what she wanted and what she loved to do. But she was also aware of the forces that prompted these desires and would often admit that her behavior seemed to be a product of forces beyond her control. Personality psychologists study questions of how our personalities are determined both by the forces in our minds and in our personal history of heredity and environment and by the choices we make and the goals we seek.

Measuring Personality

Of all the things psychologists have set out to measure, personality must be one of the toughest. How do you capture the uniqueness of a person—like a moonbeam in a jar? Different traditions have tended to favor different measurement techniques. The general personality measures can be classified broadly into personality inventories and projective techniques.

Personality Inventories

To learn about an individual's personality, you could follow the person around and, clipboard in hand, record every single thing the person does, says, thinks, and feels—including how long this goes on before the person calls the police. Some observations might involve your own impressions ("Day 5: seems to be getting irritable"); others would involve objectively observable events that anyone could verify ("Day 7: grabbed my pencil and broke it in half, then bit my hand").

Table 12.1	Sensation-Seeking Scale
Circle One	**Sample Items**
T F	I enjoy getting into new situations where you can't predict how things will turn out.
T F	I'll try anything once.
T F	I sometimes do "crazy" things just for fun.
T F	I like to explore a strange city or section of town by myself, even if it means getting lost.

Source: Zuckerman et al., 1964.

Psychologists have figured out ways to obtain objective data on personality without driving their subjects to distraction. The most popular technique is the **self-report**—*a series of answers to a questionnaire that asks people to indicate the extent to which sets of statements or adjectives accurately describe their own behavior or mental state.* The respondent typically produces a self-description by circling a number on a scale or indicating whether an item is true or false. The researcher then combines the answers to get a general sense of the individual's personality with respect to a particular domain. **TABLE 12.1** shows several items from a self-report test of sensation seeking, the tendency to seek out new and exciting sensations (Zuckerman et al., 1964). In this case, the respondent is asked to indicate whether each statement is true or false. A person with high levels of sensation seeking would mark most of these statements "true."

Perhaps the best-known self-report measure is the **Minnesota Multiphasic Personality Inventory (MMPI)**, *a well-researched, clincal questionnaire used to assess personality and psychological problems.* The MMPI consists of more than 500 descriptive statements—for example, "I often feel like breaking things," "I think the world is a dangerous place," and "I'm good at socializing"—to which the respondent answers "true," "false," or "cannot say," depending on whether or not the item applies to him or her. Its 10 main subscales measure different personality characteristics, which are thought to represent personality difficulties when demonstrated to an extreme degree (Hathaway & McKinley, 1951). Like many early psychological tests, the original items were generated by studying how specific groups of people as compared to the general population completed a variety of items and then creating the scales from the items that these groups answered differently.

In addition to assessing tendencies toward clinical problems—for example, depression, hypochondria, anxiety, paranoia, and unconventional ideas or bizarre thoughts and beliefs—the MMPI measures some relatively general personality characteristics, such as degree of masculine and feminine gender role identification, sociability versus social inhibition, and impulsivity. The MMPI also includes *validity scales* that assess a person's attitudes toward test taking and any tendency to try to distort the results by faking answers.

Personality inventories such as the MMPI are easy to administer: Just give someone a pencil and away they go. The person's scores can be calculated by a computer and compared with the average ratings of thousands of other test takers. Because no interpretation of the responses is needed, biases are minimized. Of course, an accurate reading of personality will only occur if people provide honest responses—especially about characteristics that might be unflattering—and if they don't always agree or always disagree—a phenomenon known as *response style*. The validity scales help detect these problems but cannot take them away altogether.

Another drawback is related to the actual characteristics being measured. Certain personality factors may function largely outside of consciousness, and so asking people to tell us about them makes little sense. For example, would someone know if he or she was conceited? A truly self-centered person would probably not even know it. Despite potential drawbacks, however, personality inventories remain an efficient and effective means of testing, classifying, and researching a wide range of personality characteristics.

Projective Techniques

The second major class of tools for evaluating personality, the **projective techniques**, consist of *a standard series of ambiguous stimuli designed to elicit unique responses that reveal inner aspects of an individual's personality.* The developers of projective tests assumed that people will project personality factors that are out of awareness—wishes, concerns, impulses, and ways of seeing the world—onto ambiguous stimuli and will not censor these responses. As an example of such projection, consider the game of cloud watching. If you and a friend were looking at the sky one day and she suddenly

SELF-REPORT A series of answers to a questionnaire that asks people to indicate the extent to which sets of statements or adjectives accurately describe their own behavior or mental state.

MINNESOTA MULTIPHASIC PERSONALITY INVENTORY (MMPI) A well-researched, clinical questionnaire used to assess personality and psychological problems.

PROJECTIVE TECHNIQUES A standard series of ambiguous stimuli designed to elicit unique responses that reveal inner aspects of an individual's personality.

RORSCHACH INKBLOT TEST A projective personality test in which individual interpretations of the meaning of a set of unstructured inkblots are analyzed to identify a respondent's inner feelings and interpret his or her personality structure.

THEMATIC APPERCEPTION TEST (TAT) A projective personality test in which respondents reveal underlying motives, concerns, and the way they see the social world through the stories they make up about ambiguous pictures of people.

became seriously upset because one cloud looked to her like a flesh-eating monster, her response would reveal a lot more about her inner conflicts than her explicit answer to a direct question about the kind of things that frighten her.

Probably the best-known and mostly widely used technique is the **Rorschach Inkblot Test,** *a projective personality test in which individual interpretations of the meaning of a set of unstructured inkblots are analyzed to identify a respondent's inner feelings and interpret his or her personality structure.* Swiss psychiatrist Hermann Rorschach devised the test in 1918 by pouring ink on paper and folding the pages in half (Ellenberger, 1954). The Rorschach responses are scored according to complicated systems (derived in part from research with patients) that classify *what* is seen (content), *where* it is seen (location), and *why* it is seen that way (determinants). For example, a person who never makes use of the color in some of the blots may be thought to have a restricted and inhibited emotional style (Klopfer & Kelley, 1942). Someone who is unable to see obvious items (such as the birds or people most people see when they look at an image similar to the one shown in **FIGURE 12.1**) when he or she responds to a blot may be described as having difficulty perceiving the world as others do and as seeing things according to his or her unique perspective (Exner, 1993; Rapaport, 1946).

Can psychologists using the Rorschach test discover aspects of personality that are usually hidden, even from the person taking the test? Critics argue that although the Rorschach captures some of the more complex and private aspects of personality, the test is open to the subjective interpretation and theoretic biases of the examiner. In fact, to have value, a test of personality should permit prediction of a person's behavior, but evidence is sparse that Rorschach test scores have such predictive value (Dawes, 1994; Fowler, 1985; Wood, Nezworski, Lilienfeld, & Garb, 2003; Wood, Nezworski, & Stejskal, 1996). Many psychologists still use the technique, but it is losing its popularity (Garb, 1999; Widiger, 2001).

In the early 1930s, American psychologist Henry Murray introduced the **Thematic Apperception Test (TAT),** *a projective personality test in which respondents reveal underlying motives, concerns, and the way they see the social world through the stories they make up about ambiguous pictures of people.* To get a sense of the test, look at **FIGURE 12.2**. Who are those people, and what are they doing and thinking? What led them to this moment, and what will happen next? Different people tell very different stories about this image, as they do about the standard images in the TAT set. In creating the stories, the test taker is thought to identify with the main characters and to project his or her view of others and the world onto the other details in the drawing. Psychologists who use the TAT look for repeated themes and their relationship across a large number of cards, typically 10.

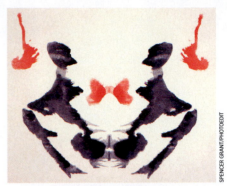

Figure 12.1 **Sample Rorschach Inkblot** Test takers are shown a card such as this sample and asked, "What might this be?" What they perceive, where they see it, and why it looks that way are assumed to reflect unconscious aspects of their personality. (Behn-Rorschach Test, Verlag Hans Huber, Bern, Switzerland, 1941.)

 **ONLY HUMAN**

RORSCHACH TEST WITH TOMATO SAUCE? 1991—In March, motorists in Stone Mountain, Georgia, reported seeing the image of Christ in a forkful of spaghetti on a Pizza Hut billboard. One woman said the image caused her to abandon plans to quit her church choir.

Figure 12.2 **Sample TAT Card** Test takers are shown cards with ambiguous scenes such as this sample and are asked to tell a story about what is happening in the picture. The main themes of the story, the thoughts and feelings of the characters, and how the story develops and resolves are considered useful indices of unconscious aspects of an individual's personality. (Murray, 1943.)

Many of the TAT drawings tend to elicit a consistent set of themes, such as successes and failures, competition and jealousy, conflict with parents and siblings, feelings about intimate relationships, aggression and sexuality. The sample card shown in Figure 12.2 tends to elicit themes regarding mother-daughter relationships, aging, and concerns regarding femininity and women's roles (Murray, 1943). Here is one young woman's response to the drawing—one that seems to reveal her own personal internal situation and a conflict between her wish for independence and fear that this is wrong and is punishable by a tragic loss: "The old lady in the background seems angry and thinks the younger one is making a big mistake. Maybe they're related. . . . Everything the young woman does is wrong in her mother's eyes. The daughter just wants to get away and live her own life but is too guilty to leave her mother's side, thinking it will hurt her. In the end, hmm? The girl does leave and the mother dies."

Projective tests remain controversial in psychology. Although a TAT story about church choir members all being naked under their robes may *seem* revealing, the examiner must always add an interpretation (Was this about church, about sex, about trying to be funny or creative or oddball?), and that interpretation could well be the scorer's *own* projection into the mind of the test taker. Thus, despite the rich picture of a personality and the insights into an individual's motives that these tests offer, they should be understood primarily as a way in which a psychologist can get to know someone personally and intuitively (McClelland et al., 1953). When measured by rigorous scientific criteria, the TAT, like the Rorschach and other projective tests, has not been found to be reliable or valid in predicting behavior (Lilienfeld, Lynn, & Lohr, 2003).

In summary, a person's characteristic style of behaving, thinking, and feeling is what psychologists call personality. Among the key questions for personality psychologists are the following: How best to describe personality? How best to explain how personalities come about? And how do we measure personality? Psychologists have developed a number of measurement instruments to assess personality. Two general classes of personality tests are personality inventories, such as the MMPI, and projective techniques, such as the Rorschach Inkblot Test and the TAT. ■ ■

The Trait Approach: Identifying Patterns of Behavior

Imagine writing a story about the people you know. To capture their special qualities, you might describe their traits: Lulu is *friendly, aggressive,* and *domineering;* Seth is *flaky, humorous,* and *superficial.* With a dictionary and a free afternoon, you might even be able to describe Gino as *perspicacious, flagitious,* and *callipygian.* The trait approach to personality uses such trait terms to characterize differences among individuals. In attempting to create manageable and meaningful sets of descriptors, trait theorists face two significant challenges: narrowing down the almost infinite set of adjectives and answering the more basic question of why people have particular traits—whether they arise from biological or hereditary foundations.

Traits as Behavioral Dispositions and Motives

Gordon Allport (1937), one of the first trait theorists, proposed that personality can best be understood as a combination of traits. A **trait** is *a relatively stable disposition to behave in a particular and consistent way.* For example, a person who keeps his books organized alphabetically in bookshelves, hangs his clothing neatly in the closet, knows the schedule for the local bus, keeps a clear agenda in a daily planner, and lists birthdays of friends and family in his calendar can be said to have the trait of *orderliness.* This trait consistently manifests itself in a variety of settings.

The "orderliness" trait, of course, describes a person but doesn't explain his or her behavior. *Why* does the person behave in this way? There are two basic ways in which a

TRAIT A relatively stable disposition to behave in a particular and consistent way.

A closet isn't just a place for clothes. In some cases, it's a personality test.

trait might serve as an explanation—the trait may be a preexisting disposition of the person that causes the person's behavior, or it may be a motivation that guides the person's behavior. Allport saw traits as preexisting dispositions, causes of behavior that reliably trigger the behavior. The person's orderliness, for example, is an inner property of the person that will cause the person to straighten things up and be tidy in a wide array of situations. Not surprisingly, Henry Murray's interest in motivation led him to suggest instead that traits reflect needs or desires. Just as a hunger motive might explain someone's many trips to the snack bar, a need for orderliness might explain the neat closet, organized calendar, and familiarity with the bus schedule (Murray & Kluckhohn, 1953). As a rule, researchers examining traits as causes have used personality inventories to measure them, whereas those examining traits as motives have more often used projective tests.

What kinds of personality traits have been studied? Among the hundreds of traits that researchers have described and measured is right-wing *authoritarianism,* or the tendency toward political conservatism, obedience to authority, and conformity. In the 1940s, this characteristic drew the attention of researchers who were trying to understand what made people support the rise of Nazi Germany and fascism after World War II (Adorno et al., 1950). Although research on the personality traits that lead to political conservatism continues (Jost, Glaser, Kruglanski, & Sullaway, 2003), the topic became less focal for researchers once World War II receded into history. Examples of other traits that have come into vogue over the years include cognitive complexity, defensiveness, hypnotizability, sensation seeking, and optimism. As with television shows and hairstyles, fashions in trait dimensions come and go over time.

By most accounts, Kim Jong II of North Korea is a despotic ruler who starves his people, insists on worshipful loyalty, and puts the world on edge by testing nuclear weapons. Why would anyone want to follow such a dictator? The study of the authoritarian personality was inspired by the idea that some people might follow most anyone because their personalities make them adhere to hierarchies of authority, submitting to those above them and dominating those below.

BIG FIVE The traits of the five-factor model: conscientiousness, agreeableness, neuroticism, openness to experience, and extraversion.

The Search for Core Traits

Picking a fashionable trait and studying it in depth doesn't get us very far in the search for the core of human character—for the basic set of traits that define how humans differ from one another. How have researchers tried to discover such core traits?

Classification Using Language

The study of core traits began with an exploration of how personality is represented in the store of wisdom we call language. Generation after generation, people have described people with words, so early psychologists proposed that core traits could be discerned by finding the main themes in all the adjectives used to describe personality. In one such analysis, a painstaking count of relevant words in a dictionary of English resulted in a list of over 18,000 potential traits (Allport and Odbert, 1936)!

Although narrowing down such a list isn't too difficult because so many words are synonyms—for example, *giving, generous,* and *bighearted* all mean more or less the same thing—still, the process is too subjective to permit development of a true set of core of traits. Just looking at traitlike words that seemed to represent motives, for example, led Murray (1938) to propose over 40 basic motivations in addition to the need for orderliness. Further, similarity in meaning may not be the only basis for relationships among traits. Adjectives that describe certain behaviors tend to be associated with one another even though they do not mean the same thing—for example, it's hard to imagine a *calm* person who is not also *even-tempered*—even though the words describe different personality characteristics. As you can see in **FIGURE 12.3** behavioral tendencies might be related in a hierarchical pattern.

More recently, researchers have used the computational procedure called *factor analysis,* described in Chapter 9, which sorts trait terms into a small number of underlying dimensions, or "factors," based on how people use the traits to rate themselves.

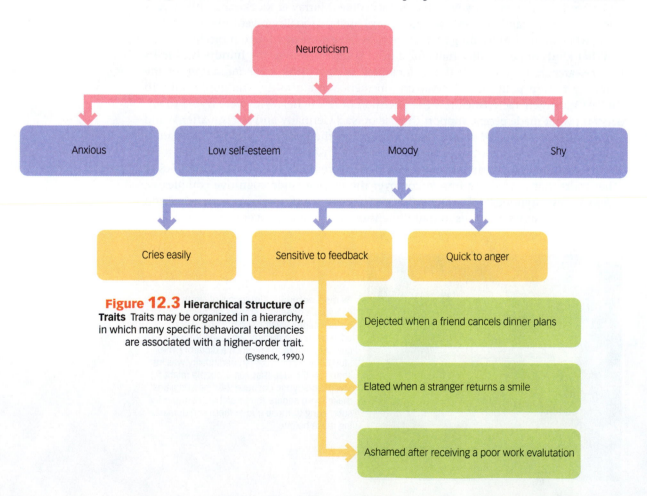

Figure 12.3 Hierarchical Structure of Traits Traits may be organized in a hierarchy, in which many specific behavioral tendencies are associated with a higher-order trait. (Eysenck, 1990.)

Neuroticism

Anxious | Low self-esteem | Moody | Shy

Cries easily | Sensitive to feedback | Quick to anger

Dejected when a friend cancels dinner plans

Elated when a stranger returns a smile

Ashamed after receiving a poor work evaluation

In a typical study using factor analysis, hundreds of people rate themselves on hundreds of adjectives, indicating how accurately each one describes their personality. The researcher then calculates the patterns to determine similarities in the raters' usage—whether, for example, people who describe themselves as *responsible* also describe themselves as *careful* but not *negligent* or *careless*. Factor analysis can also reveal which adjectives are unrelated. For example, if people who describe themselves as *responsible* are neither more nor less likely to describe themselves as *creative* or *innovative,* the factor analysis would reveal that responsibility and creativity/innovation represent different factors. Each factor is typically presented as a continuum, ranging from one extreme trait, such as responsible, to its opposite, in this case, careless.

Different factor analysis techniques have yielded different views of personality structure. Raymond Cattell (1950) proposed a 16-factor theory of personality, whereas others have found his scheme too complex and have argued for theories with far fewer basic dimensions. Hans Eysenck (1967) took the opposite tack and developed a model of personality with only two (later expanded to three) major traits.

Eysenck's factor analysis identified one dimension that distinguished people who are sociable and active (extraverts) from those who are relatively introspective and quiet (introverts). His analysis also identified a second dimension ranging from the tendency to be very neurotic or emotionally unstable to the tendency to be more emotionally stable. He believed that many behavioral tendencies could be understood in terms of their relation to these core traits. **FIGURE 12.4** suggests that these two dimensions may not be an oversimplified view—the two central dimensions seem to capture and characterize a much larger number of specific traits.

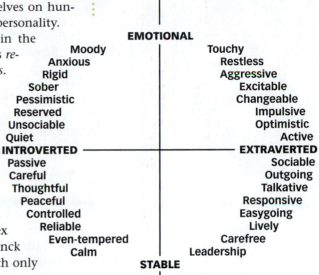

Figure 12.4 **Eysenck's Depiction of Trait Dimensions** The trait dimensions shown here can be combined to describe a great deal of the variability in human personality. If you look at the adjectives between any two of the four possible points on the grid, you'll see an interesting range of possible surface characteristics.

(Eysenck & Eysenck, 1985.)

The Big Five Dimensions of Personality

Today many factor analysis researchers agree that personality is best captured by 5 factors rather than 2, 3, 16, 40, or 18,000 (John & Srivastava, 1999; McCrae & Costa, 1999). The **Big Five**, as they are affectionately called, are *the traits of the five-factor model: conscientiousness, agreeableness, neuroticism, openness to experience, and extraversion* (see **TABLE 12.2**). The five-factor model, which overlaps with the pioneering work of Cattell and Eysenck, is now widely preferred for several reasons. First, modern factor analysis techniques confirm that this set of five factors strikes the right balance between accounting for as much variation in personality as possible while avoiding overlapping traits. Second, in a large number of studies using different kinds of data—people's descriptions of their own personalities, other people's descriptions of their personalities, interviewer checklists, and behavioral observation—the same five factors have emerged. Third, and perhaps most important, the basic five-factor structure seems to show up across a wide range of participants, including children, adults in other cultures, and even among those who use other languages, suggesting that the Big Five may be universal (John & Srivastava, 1999).

In fact, the Big Five dimensions are so "universal" that they show up even when people are asked to evaluate the traits of complete strangers (Passini & Norman, 1966). This finding suggests that these dimensions of personality might reside "in the eye of the beholder"—categories that people use to evaluate others regardless of how well they know them. However, it's not all perception. The reality of these traits has been clearly established in research showing that self-reports on the Big Five are associated with predictable patterns of behavior and social outcomes. People identified as high in extraversion, for example, tend to choose to spend time with lots of other people and are more likely to look people in the eye than introverts. People high in

Table 12.2	The Big Five Factor Model	
Conscientiousness	organized········disorganized careful·············careless self-disciplined·····weak-willed	
Agreeableness	softhearted··········ruthless trusting···········suspicious helpful·········uncooperative	
Neuroticism	worried·················calm insecure·············secure self-pitying········self-satisfied	
Openness to experience	imaginative······down-to-earth variety··············routine independent·······conforming	
Extraversion	social·············retiring fun loving···········sober affectionate·········reserved	

Source: McCrae & Costa, 1999, 1990.

conscientiousness generally perform well at work and tend to live longer. People low on conscientiousness and low in agreeableness are more likely than average to be juvenile delinquents (John & Srivastava, 1999).

Research on the Big Five has shown that people's personalities tend to remain stable through their lifetime, scores at one time in life correlating strongly with scores at later dates, even later decades (Caspi, Roberts, & Shiner, 2005). Some variability is typical in childhood, with less in adolescence and then greater stability in adulthood. As William James put it: "It is well for the world that in most of us, by the age of thirty, the character has set like plaster, and will never soften again" (James, 1890, p. 121).

Traits as Biological Building Blocks

Can we explain *why* a person has a stable set of personality traits? Many trait theorists have argued that immutable brain and biological processes produce the remarkable stability of traits over the life span. Allport viewed traits as characteristics of the brain that influence the way people respond to their environment. And as you will see, Eysenck searched for a connection between his trait dimensions and specific individual differences in the workings of the brain.

Brain damage certainly can produce personality change, as the classic case of Phineas Gage so vividly demonstrates (see Chapter 3). You may recall that after the blasting accident that blew a steel rod through his frontal lobes, Gage showed a dramatic loss of social appropriateness and conscientiousness (Damasio, 1994). In fact, when someone experiences a profound change in personality, testing often reveals the presence of such brain pathologies as Alzheimer's disease, stroke, or brain tumor (Feinberg, 2001). The administration of antidepressant medication and other pharmaceutical treatments that change brain chemistry can also trigger personality changes, making people, for example, somewhat more extraverted and less neurotic (Bagby, Levitan, Kennedy, Levitt, & Joffe, 1999; Knutson et al., 1998).

Genes, Traits, and Personality

Some of the most compelling evidence for the importance of biological factors in personality comes from the domain of behavioral genetics. Like researchers studying genetic influences on intelligence (see Chapter 9), personality psychologists have looked at correlations between the traits in monozygotic, or identical, twins who share the same genes and dizygotic, or fraternal, twins (who on average share only half of their genes). The evidence has been generally consistent: In one review of studies involving over 24,000 twin pairs, for example, identical twins proved markedly more similar to each other in personality than did fraternal twins (Loehlin, 1992).

Simply put, the more genes you have in common with someone, the more similar your personalities are likely to be. Genetics seems to influence most personality traits, and current estimates place the average genetic component of personality in the range of .40 to .60. These heritability coefficients, as you learned in Chapter 9, indicate that roughly half the variability among individuals results from genetic factors (Bouchard & Loehlin, 2001). Genetic factors do not account for everything, certainly—the remaining half of the variability in personality remains to be explained by differences in life experiences and other factors—but they appear to be remarkably influential (see also the Real World box). Studies of twins suggest that the extent to which the Big Five traits derive from genetic differences ranges from .35 to .49 (see **TABLE 12.3**).

Table **12.3**	Heritability Estimates for the Big Five Personality Traits
Trait Dimension	**Heritability**
Conscientiousness	.38
Agreeableness	.35
Neuroticism	.41
Openness	.45
Extraversion	.49

Source: Loehlin, 1992.

{ THE REAL WORLD } Do Different Genders Lead to Different Personalities?

DOES A PERSON'S GENDER TELL US anything meaningful about how he or she thinks, feels, and responds? Personality psychologists have struggled with such questions for decades. Do you think there is a typical "female" personality or a typical "male" personality?

Researchers have found some reliable differences between men and women with respect to their self-reported traits, attitudes, and behaviors (Feingold, 1994). Some of these findings conform to North American stereotypes of "masculine" and "feminine." For example, researchers have found women to be more verbally expressive, more sensitive to nonverbal cues, and more nurturing than are men. And although men are more physically aggressive than women, women appear to engage in more social relationship aggression (e.g., ignoring someone) than do men (Eagly & Steffen, 1986). Other gender differences include more assertiveness, slightly higher self-esteem, a more casual approach to sex, and greater sensation seeking in men compared with women. On the Big Five, women have been found to be higher on agreeableness and neuroticism than men, but the genders do not differ in openness to experience. On a variety of other personality characteristics, including helpfulness and sexual desire, men and women on average show no reliable differences.

What do gender differences actually mean? Keep in mind that even statistically significant differences reflect *average group* differences. Men and women are far more alike than they are different, and on an individual level, knowledge of group differences may have little value in predicting whether, for example, your girlfriend will be agreeable and nurturing or your boyfriend will be a sensation seeker. If you base your assessment of people on stereotypes of men's and women's personalities rather than learning about each individual, you will frequently be incorrect.

Sex differences in personality can be a hot button topic. For example, the former president of Harvard University, Lawrence Summers, was criticized widely for remarking that women might not have the "intrinsic aptitude" to pursue careers in science—criticism so fierce that it culminated in his resignation. Many people assume, as did Summers, that if men and women are found to differ on a given psychological characteristic, the reason must be biological. And although biology does play a significant role in shaping personality, there is certainly a lot

GIFT OF JEAN AND FRANCIS MARSHALL/BERKELEY ART MUSEUM/PACIFIC FILM ARCHIVE

Cultures differ in their appreciation of male and female characteristics, but the Hindu deity Ardhanarishwara represents the value of combining both parts of human nature. Male on one side and female on the other, this god is symbolic of the dual nature of the sacred. The only real problem with such side-by-side androgyny comes in finding clothes to fit.

more to being female or male than having a Y or a second X chromosome. Indeed, the evidence for the biological underpinnings of observed personality differences between men and women, such as a possible link between hormones and gender differences in aggression, is as yet inconclusive (Inoff-Germain et al., 1988).

The debate about the origins of gender differences in personality often involves contrasting an evolutionary biological perspective with a social cognitive perspective known as *social role theory*. The evolutionary perspective holds that men and women have evolved different personality characteristics in part because their reproductive success depends on different behaviors. For instance, aggressiveness in men may have an adaptive value in intimidating sexual rivals; women who are agreeable and

nurturing may have evolved to protect and ensure the survival of their offspring (Campbell, 1999) as well as to secure a reliable mate and provider (Buss, 1989).

According to social role theory, personality characteristics and behavioral differences between men and women result from cultural standards and expectations that assign them—socially permissible jobs, activities, and family positions (Eagly & Wood, 1999). Because of their physical size and their freedom from childbearing, men historically took roles of greater power—roles that in postindustrial society don't necessarily require physical strength. These differences then snowball, with men generally taking roles that require assertiveness and aggression (e.g., executive, school principal, surgeon) and women pursuing roles that emphasize greater supportiveness and nurturance (e.g., nurse, day-care worker, teacher).

Regardless of the source of gender differences in personality, the degree to which people identify personally with masculine and feminine stereotypes may tell us about important personality differences between individuals. Sandra Bem (1974) designed a scale, the Bem Sex Role Inventory, that assesses the degree of identification with stereotypically masculine and feminine traits. Bem suggested that psychologically *androgynous* people—those who adopt the "best of both worlds," identifying both with positive feminine traits (such as kindness) and positive masculine traits (such as assertiveness)—might be better adjusted than are people who identify strongly with only one sex role. Research shows that this is particularly true for women, perhaps because many of the traits stereotypically associated with masculinity (such as assertiveness and achievement) are related to psychological health (Cook, 1985).

Bem Sex Role Inventory Sample Items

Respondents taking the Bem Sex Role Inventory rate themselves on each of the items without seeing the gender categorization. Then the scale is scored for masculinity (use of stereotypically masculine items), femininity (use of stereotypically feminine items), and androgyny (the tendency to use both the stereotypically masculine and feminine adjectives to describe oneself) (Bem, 1974).

Masculine items:
    Self-reliant
    Defends own beliefs
    Independent
    Assertive
    Forceful

Feminine items:
    Yielding
    Affectionate
    Flatterable
    Sympathetic
    Sensitive to the needs of others

MONTY MARION/STAR PHOTO

University of Texas graduate student Bryan McCann, member of the Campaign to End the Death Penalty, marches with fellow protestors down Congress Avenue in Austin to call for an end to capital punishment. Many of our opinions and attitudes, such as our view of capital punishment, appear to be shaped by our genes—so odds are that this protest is something his family would approve.

As in the study of intelligence, potential confounding factors must be ruled out to ensure that effects are truly due to genetics and not to environmental experiences. Are identical twins treated more similarly, and do they have a greater *shared environment* than fraternal twins? As children, were they dressed in the same snappy outfits and placed on the same Little League teams, and could this somehow have produced similarities in their personalities? Studies of identical twins reared far apart in adoptive families—an experience that pretty much eliminates the potential effect of shared environmental factors—suggest that shared environments have little impact: Reared-apart identical twins end up at least as similar in personality as those who grow up together (McGue & Bouchard, 1998; Tellegen et al., 1988).

Indeed, one provocative, related finding is that such shared environmental factors as parental divorce or parenting style may have little direct impact on personality (Plomin & Caspi, 1999). According to these researchers, simply growing up in the same family does not make people very similar: In fact, when two siblings are similar, this is thought to be primarily due to genetic similarities.

Researchers have also assessed specific behavioral and attitude similarities in twins, and the evidence for heritability in these studies is often striking. When 3,000 pairs of identical and fraternal twins were asked their opinions on political and social issues, such as the death penalty, censorship, and nudist camps, significantly high heritability estimates were obtained for these and many other attitudes—for example, the score for views on the death penalty was approximately .50 (Martin et al., 1986). A specific gene directly responsible for attitudes on the death penalty or any other specific behavior or attitude is extremely unlikely. Rather, a set of genes—or, more likely, many sets of genes interacting—may produce a specific physiological characteristic such as a tendency to have a strong fear reaction in anticipation of punishment. This biological factor may then shape the person's belief about a range of social issues, perhaps including whether the fear of punishment is effective in deterring criminal behavior (Tesser, 1993).

Do Animals Have Personalities?

Another source of evidence for the biological basis of human personality comes from the study of nonhuman animals. Any dog owner, zookeeper, or cattle farmer can tell you that individual animals have characteristic patterns of behavior. One Missouri woman who reportedly enjoyed raising chickens in her suburban home said that "the best part" was "knowing them as individuals" (Tucker, 2003). As far as we know, this pet owner did not give her feathered companions a personality test, though researcher Sam Gosling (1998) used this approach in a study of a group of spotted hyenas. Well, not exactly. He recruited four human observers to use personality scales to rate the different hyenas in the group. When he examined ratings on the scales, he found five dimensions, of which three closely resembled the Big Five traits of neuroticism (i.e., fearfulness, emotional reactivity), openness to experience (i.e., curiosity), and agreeableness (i.e., absence of aggression).

In similar studies of guppies and octopi, individual differences in traits resembling extraversion and neuroticism were reliably observed (Gosling & John, 1999). In each study, researchers identified particular behaviors that they felt reflected each trait based on their observation of the animals' normal repertoire of activities. Octopi, for example, seldom get invited out to parties, and so they cannot be assessed for their socializing tendencies ("He was all hands!"), but they do vary in terms of whether they prefer to eat in the safety of their den or are willing to venture out at feeding time, and so a behavior that corresponds to extraversion can reasonably be assessed (Gosling & John, 1999). Because different observers seem to agree on where an animal falls on a given dimension, the findings do not simply reflect a particular observer's imagination or tendency to *anthropomorphize*, that is, to attribute human characteristics to nonhuman animals. Such findings of cross-species commonality in behavioral styles help support the idea that there are biological mechanisms that underlie personality traits shared by many species.

From an evolutionary perspective, differences in personality reflect alternative adaptations that species—human and nonhuman—have evolved to deal with the challenges of survival and reproduction. For example, if you were to hang around a bar for an evening or two, you would soon see that humans have evolved more than one way to attract and keep a mate. People who are extraverted would probably show off to attract attention, whereas you'd be likely to see people high in agreeableness displaying affection and nurturance (Buss, 1996). Both approaches might work well to attract mates and reproduce successfully—depending on the environment. Through this process of natural selection, those characteristics that have proved successful in our evolutionary struggle for survival have been passed on to future generations.

How would you rate this chicken? Is it antagonistic or agreeable? Neurotic or emotionally stable? Researchers have found that even animals appear to have personalities. Or should they be called animalities?

Traits in the Brain

But what neurophysiological mechanisms influence the development of personality traits? Let's look at some of the current thinking on this topic, focusing on the extraversion-introversion dimension. In his personality model, Eysenck (1967) speculated that extraversion and introversion might arise from individual differences in alertness. Extraverts may need to seek out social interaction, parties, and even mayhem in the attempt to achieve full mental stimulation, whereas introverts may avoid these situations because they are so sensitive that such stimulation is unpleasant.

Eysenck argued that differences in levels of cortical arousal underlie differences between extraverts and introverts. Extraverts pursue stimulation because their *reticular formation*—the part of the brain that regulates arousal, or alertness (as described in Chapter 3)—is not easily stimulated. To achieve greater cortical arousal and feel fully alert, Eysenck argued, extraverts are drawn to activities such as listening to loud music and having a lot of social contact. In contrast, introverts may prefer reading or quiet activities because their cortex is very easily stimulated to a point higher than optimal.

Introverts and extraverts may seek different levels of social stimulation. This young man's apparent shyness may be due to the reactivity of his nervous system to stimulation.

Behavioral and physiological research generally supports Eysenck's view. When introverts and extraverts are presented with a range of intense stimuli, introverts respond more strongly, including salivating more when a drop of lemon juice is placed on their tongues and reacting more negatively to electric shocks or loud noises (Bartol & Costello, 1976; Stelmack, 1990). This reactivity has an impact on the ability to concentrate: Extraverts tend to perform well at tasks that are done in a noisy, arousing context—such as bartending or teaching—whereas introverts are better at tasks that require concentration in tranquil contexts—such as the work of a librarian or nighttime security guard (Geen, 1984; Lieberman & Rosenthal, 2001; Matthews & Gilliland, 1999).

In a refined version of Eysenck's ideas about arousability, Jeffrey Gray (1970) proposed that the dimensions of extraversion/introversion and neuroticism reflect two basic brain systems. The *behavioral activation system* (*BAS*), essentially a "go" system, activates approach behavior in response to the anticipation of reward. The *behavioral inhibition system* (*BIS*), a "stop" system, inhibits behavior in response to stimuli signaling punishment.

According to Gray, individual differences in the reactivity of these systems may underlie Eysenck's two personality dimensions. People with a highly reactive BAS may actively engage the environment, seeking social reinforcement in a highly extraverted manner. People with a highly reactive BIS, on the other hand, might tend toward neuroticism and emotional instability, anxiously focusing on the possibility of negative outcomes and perceiving the world as threatening. In Gray's analysis, each person might have some combination of these two tendencies—so each person's level of extraversion and neuroticism is produced by the activity of specific brain systems.

In summary, the trait approach tries to identify personality dimensions that can be used to characterize individuals' behavior. Researchers have attempted to boil down the potentially huge array of things people do, think, and feel into some core personality dimensions. Many personality psychologists currently focus on the Big Five personality factors: *conscientiousness, agreeableness, neuroticism, openness to experience,* and *extraversion.* The emphasis in these theories is on broad personality dispositions that are relatively consistent across situations. To address the question of explanation, trait theorists often adopt a biological perspective, construing personality as largely the result of brain mechanisms and processes that are inborn. ■ ■

The Psychodynamic Approach: Forces That Lie beneath Awareness

If you have ever mailed off a check unsigned, locked your car door with the keys still in the ignition, or called someone by the wrong name, you probably dismissed your error as a mere annoyance—maybe the result of distraction or insufficient sleep. Sigmund Freud did not ignore such subtle errors, what he called the "psychopathologies of everyday life." Instead, he built a theory on them.

Rather than trying to understand personality in terms of broad theories for describing individual differences, Freud looked for personality in the details—the meanings and insights revealed by careful analysis of the tiniest blemishes in a person's thought and behavior. Working with patients who came to him with disorders that did not seem to have any physical basis, he began by interpreting the origins of their common mindbugs, errors that have come to be called "Freudian slips." To understand this perennially controversial theory, let's explore how Freud and his followers viewed unconscious motivation, the structure of the mind, psychological defenses, and personality development.

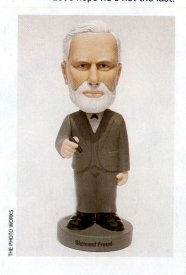

Sigmund Freud was the first psychology theorist to be honored with his own bobble-head doll. Let's hope he's not the last.

THE PHOTO WORKS

Unconscious Motives

Freud used the term *psychoanalysis* to refer both to his theory of personality and his method of treating patients. Freud's ideas were the first of many theories building on his basic idea that personality is a mystery to the person who "owns" it because we can't know our own deepest motives. The theories of Freud and his followers, such as Carl Jung, Alfred Adler, and Karen Horney (discussed in Chapter 14), are referred to as the **psychodynamic approach**. According to this approach, *personality is formed by needs, strivings, and desires largely operating outside of awareness—motives that can produce emotional disorders.*

Mindbugs offer glimpses into these hidden motives. Imagine if you forget your best friend's birthday: Her complaint about your slip—"You don't care enough to remember!"—might offer you real insight into the current state of your relationship. Psychodynamic explanations assume that the motives that guide even the smallest nuances of our behavior develop in our early relationships and conflicts with caregivers. Thus, a psychodynamic interpretation of Edith Piaf's tangled path through life might attribute her problems to her tragic abandonment in childhood and her early experiences in a brothel, which shaped her basic desires in ways that were beyond her awareness.

As you'll recall from Chapter 8, Freud made a strong distinction between the conscious and unconscious mind. He distinguished three different levels of mental life: conscious, preconscious, and unconscious. *Conscious* aspects of mental life are those in awareness at any given moment, but there are a range of *preconscious* mental contents as well—aspects of mental life that are outside awareness but that could easily enter consciousness. The tune of the national anthem, for example, may not have been running through your mind just now, but you probably can bring it to mind easily. Although psychologists today might call such items unconscious—because they are, after all, not currently being experienced—Freud reserved the term *unconscious* for the special part of the mind that has great psychological significance. In fact, he spoke of "*the* unconscious" as though it were an agent or a force. Psychologists call this construct the **dynamic unconscious**—*an active system encompassing a lifetime of hidden memories, the person's deepest instincts and desires, and the person's inner struggle to control these forces.* The dynamic unconscious, unlike the national anthem, is not something you can easily bring to mind; nevertheless, proponents of the theory believe that it is the level that most strongly influences personality.

The power of the unconscious comes from its early origins—experiences that shaped the mind before a person could even put thoughts and feelings into words—and from its contents, which are embarrassing, unspeakable, and even frightening because they operate without any control by consciousness. Imagine having violent competitive feelings toward your father ("I wish I could beat the old man at something, or just beat him up") or a death wish toward a sibling ("It would be so great if my snotty sister just fell down a well"). Whew! Impulses like that are assumed to remain in the unconscious because such powerful forces would be too much for consciousness to bear.

In Freud's psychoanalytic psychotherapy, the process of revealing the unconscious is the main focus of therapy. Freud assumed that insight into the unconscious can never be gained directly, however, because conscious self-reports could never tap the cloaked and censored depths of the unconscious. Psychologists who adopt the psychodynamic approach use projective tests such as the Rorschach Inkblot Test and the TAT in hope of discerning unconscious themes and issues that can be examined in therapy. As you will see in Chapter 14, psychoanalytic psychotherapy makes use of a number of indirect techniques (such as dream interpretation and word association) as a means of undressing—er, *assessing*—the workings of the unconscious mind.

PSYCHODYNAMIC APPROACH An approach that regards personality as formed by needs, strivings, and desires, largely operating outside of awareness—motives that can also produce emotional disorders.

DYNAMIC UNCONSCIOUS An active system encompassing a lifetime of hidden memories, the person's deepest instincts and desires, and the person's inner struggle to control these forces.

Cigar, pencil, skyscraper, hammer . . . zeppelin? Freud believed that the id represents its wishes in terms of symbols. He would probably have been delighted with the symbolic objects in this photo.

©International Film Service, Inc., New York

U. S. ARMY BALLOON AND HANGER.

LAKE COUNTY MUSEUM/CORBIS

ID The part of the mind containing the drives present at birth; it is the source of our bodily needs, wants, desires, and impulses, particularly our sexual and aggressive drives.

PLEASURE PRINCIPLE The psychic force that motivates the tendency to seek immediate gratification of any impulse.

EGO The component of personality, developed through contact with the external world, that enables us to deal with life's practical demands.

REALITY PRINCIPLE The regulating mechanism that enables the individual to delay gratifying immediate needs and function effectively in the real world.

SUPEREGO The mental system that reflects the internalization of cultural rules, mainly learned as parents exercise their authority.

The Structure of the Mind: Id, Ego, and Superego

To explain the emotional difficulties that beset his patients, Freud proposed that the mind consists of three independent, interacting, and often conflicting systems—the id, the ego, and the superego.

The most basic system, the **id**, is *the part of the mind containing the drives present at birth; it is the source of our bodily needs, wants, desires, and impulses, particularly our sexual and aggressive drives.* Freud believed that the id reflects our "true psychic reality" before the impact of the outside world with all of its restraints. The id operates according to the **pleasure principle**, *the psychic force that motivates the tendency to seek immediate gratification of any impulse.* If governed by the id alone, you would never be able to tolerate the buildup of hunger while waiting to be served at a restaurant but would simply grab food from tables nearby.

All that the id can do is wish. To deal with reality, a second system emerges from the id during the first 6 to 8 months of life. The **ego** is *the component of personality, developed through contact with the external world, that enables us to deal with life's practical demands.* The ego operates according to the **reality principle**, *the regulating mechanism that enables the individual to delay gratifying immediate needs and function effectively in the real world.* The ego can be thought of as the "self," with functions such as logical thought, problem solving, creativity, attention, and decision making. The ego helps you resist the impulse to snatch others' food and also finds the restaurant and pays the check. In doing this work, however, it serves the id: The excellent meal in the company of friends is a pleasure that gratifies its desires.

The final system of the mind to emerge (between the ages of 3 and 6) is the **superego**, *the mental system that reflects the internalization of cultural rules, mainly learned as parents exercise their authority.* The superego consists of a set of guidelines, internal standards, and other codes of conduct that regulate and control our behaviors, thoughts, and fantasies. It acts as a kind of conscience, punishing us when it finds we are doing or thinking something wrong (by producing guilt or other painful feelings) and rewarding us (with feelings of pride or self-congratulation) for living up to ideal standards.

Like the id, the superego's hold on reality is tenuous: It is not equipped to differentiate between a thought or fantasy and actual behavior in the real world and will punish or reward regardless of whether we actually do something (bad or good) or merely think about it. For the superego, simply coveting your dinner partner's cheesecake is the equivalent of having grabbed it and wolfed it down. A really strict superego might dole out an appropriate punishment for such imagined gluttony—a wave of guilt or even a stomachache.

The id, ego, and superego go to Hollywood. Freud's themes of the wild id, the gray flannel ego, and the superego saying "no" show up in the movies, just as they do in life.

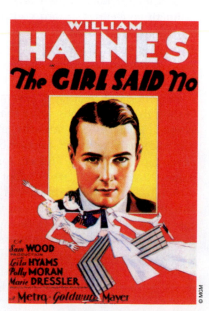

Dealing with Inner Conflict

According to Freud, the relative strength of the interactions among the three systems of mind—that is, which system is usually dominant—determines an individual's basic personality structure. The id force of personal needs, the superego force of social pressures to quell those needs, and the ego force of reality's demands together create constant controversy, almost like a puppet theater or a bad play.

Imagine how these inner agents might have fought for their own interests in Edith Piaf's mind. Her autobiography (2004) reveals an id that was working overtime to generate desires—to take many lovers and to follow every wish to indulge in alcohol and morphine. Her superego was weak and unable to resist these impulses ("All I've ever done all my life is disobey") and instead could only generate feelings of worthlessness following her transgressions: "I am stupid. I always told you I was. I hate myself, and I have no confidence in myself whatsoever." For a woman whose famous songs include one called "No Regrets," she appeared to have many. Her ego, saddled with the job of dealing with reality while her superego lost battle after battle to her id, must have been worried about what would become of her. In her words, "God, am I scared! I don't know why, but I'm terrified. I know something's going to happen to me. I don't know what, but I feel it will be something awful, something irreparable."

Anxiety. Plain and simple.

Anxiety as a Driving Force

According to Freud, the dynamics between the id, ego, and superego are largely governed by *anxiety,* an unpleasant feeling that arises when unwanted thoughts or feelings occur—such as when the id seeks a gratification that the ego thinks will lead to real-world dangers or the superego sees as eliciting punishment. He considered anxiety to be a primary emotional reaction that, from an evolutionary standpoint, has adaptive value as a signal that something is wrong. In contrast to the fear that can be created by specific threats in the outside world (say, a cement truck thundering toward you), anxiety more often arises when the threats are ambiguous or even the product of imagination. A person who thinks about making a nasty remark to a roommate, for example, might feel anxiety about angering the roommate or guilt about hurting the roommate's feelings, all without an actual external threat in sight.

The degree to which the ego anticipates danger depends on the person's early childhood experiences with the id's basic drive states. For example, someone who was harshly punished for shows of anger or aggression as a child might feel anxious over any upsurge of aggression in adulthood, even if that aggression is appropriate and understandable. Without any actual looming cement truck in sight, inner struggles can create profound anxiety.

Defense Mechanisms

When the ego receives an "alert signal" in the form of anxiety, it launches into a defensive position in an attempt to ward off the anxiety. According to Freud, it first tries *repression,* which, as you read in Chapter 8, is a mental process that removes painful experiences and unacceptable impulses from the conscious mind. Repression is sometimes referred to as "motivated forgetting." Indeed, neuroscientific evidence on the repression of memories reveals that this form of mental control may involve decreased activation of the hippocampus—a region (as discussed in Chapter 5) that is central to memory (Anderson et al., 2004) (see **FIGURE 12.5**).

Repression may not be adequate to keep unacceptable drives from entering consciousness. When such material begins to surface, the ego can employ

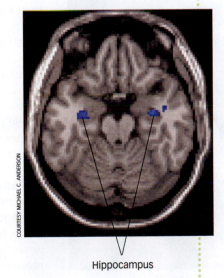

Figure 12.5 Decreased Hippocampal Activity during Memory Suppression fMRI scans of people intentionally trying to forget a list of words reveal reduced activation (shown in blue) in the left and right hippocampal areas.
(From Anderson et al., 2004.)

Hippocampus

DEFENSE MECHANISMS Unconscious coping mechanisms that reduce anxiety generated by threats from unacceptable impulses.

RATIONALIZATION A defense mechanism that involves supplying a reasonable-sounding explanation for unacceptable feelings and behavior to conceal (mostly from oneself) one's underlying motives or feelings.

REACTION FORMATION A defense mechanism that involves unconsciously replacing threatening inner wishes and fantasies with an exaggerated version of their opposite.

PROJECTION A defense mechanism that involves attributing one's own threatening feelings, motives, or impulses to another person or group.

REGRESSION A defense mechanism in which the ego deals with internal conflict and perceived threat by reverting to an immature behavior or earlier stage of development.

DISPLACEMENT A defense mechanism that involves shifting unacceptable wishes or drives to a neutral or less-threatening alternative.

IDENTIFICATION A defense mechanism that helps deal with feelings of threat and anxiety by enabling us unconsciously to take on the characteristics of another person who seems more powerful or better able to cope.

SUBLIMATION A defense mechanism that involves channeling unacceptable sexual or aggressive drives into socially acceptable and culturally enhancing activities.

The youngest daughter of Sigmund Freud, Anna Freud (1895–1982), was a psychodynamic theorist who made many contributions to psychoanalysis. She is particularly well known for advancing the understanding of psychological defense mechanisms. This photo was taken in 1914.

FREUD MUSEUM, LONDON

other means of self-deception, called **defense mechanisms**, which are *unconscious coping mechanisms that reduce anxiety generated by threats from unacceptable impulses.* Anna Freud (1936), Freud's daughter and a psychodynamic theorist, identified a number of defense mechanisms and detailed how they operate. Let's look at a few of the most common.

Rationalization is *a defense mechanism that involves supplying a reasonable-sounding explanation for unacceptable feelings and behavior to conceal (mostly from oneself) one's underlying motives or feelings.* For example, someone who drops a class after having failed an exam might tell herself that she is quitting because poor ventilation in the classroom made it impossible to concentrate. In rationalization, we tell ourselves a "likely story" to explain our behavior instead of facing its real but less comfortable meaning.

Reaction formation is *a defense mechanism that involves unconsciously replacing threatening inner wishes and fantasies with an exaggerated version of their opposite.* Examples include being excessively nice to someone you dislike, finding yourself very worried and protective about a person you have thoughts of hurting, or being cold and indifferent toward someone to whom you are strongly attracted. As with all defenses, reaction formation doesn't always do a good job at concealing the underlying intention from others. For instance, a child with strong ambivalent feelings toward her new brother may literally try to smother him with hugs and cuddles, loving him almost to death!

Through reaction formation, a person defends against underlying feelings, such as covering hostility with an exaggerated display of affection. Maybe there's more to this sibling squeeze than love?

MYLIFE PHOTOS/ALAMY

A revealing example of reaction formation was discovered in research on men who report *homophobia*—the dread of gay men and lesbians (Adams, Wright, & Lohr, 1996). Homophobic participants, heterosexual men who agreed with statements such as "I would feel nervous being with a group of homosexuals," and a comparison group of nonhomophobic men were shown videos of sexual activity, including heterosexual, gay male, and lesbian segments. Each man's sexual arousal was then assessed by means of a device that measures penile tumescence. Curiously, the homophobic men showed greater arousal to the male homosexual images than did men in a control group. The psychoanalytic interpretation seems clear: Men troubled by their own homosexual arousal formed opposite reactions to this unacceptable feeling, turning their unwanted attraction into "dread."

Projection is *a defense mechanism that involves attributing one's own threatening feelings, motives, or impulses to another person or group.* In one study, people were asked to try to suppress thoughts about recent feedback suggesting that they had undesirable personal traits (such as rigidity or dishonesty). When they were later asked to judge others' personality characteristics, their ratings were more negative than were those of a comparison group who had not been asked to suppress thoughts of their faults (Newman, Baumeister, & Duff, 1995). Projection offers comfort: It's not so bad to have unacceptable qualities if someone else has them too!

Regression is *a defense mechanism in which the ego deals with internal conflict and perceived threat by reverting to an immature behavior or earlier stage of development,* a time when things felt safer and more secure. Examples of regression include the use of baby talk or whining in a child (or adult) who has already mastered appropriate speech or a return to thumb sucking, teddy bear cuddling, or watching cartoons in response to something distressing.

Displacement is *a defense mechanism that involves shifting unacceptable wishes or drives to a neutral or less threatening alternative.* Displacement should be familiar to you if you've ever slammed a door, or thrown a textbook across a room, or yelled at your roommate or your cat when you were really angry at your boss.

Identification is *a defense mechanism that helps deal with feelings of threat and anxiety by enabling us unconsciously to take on the characteristics of another person who seems more powerful or better able to cope.* This sometimes involves the phenomenon known as *identification with the aggressor,* in which anxiety is reduced by becoming like the person posing the threat. A child whose parent bullies or severely punishes her may later take on the characteristics of that parent and begin bullying others.

Sublimation is *a defense mechanism that involves channeling unacceptable sexual or aggressive drives into socially acceptable and culturally enhancing activities.* Freud considered sublimation crucial to the development and maintenance of civilization and culture. Football, rugby, and other contact sports, for example, may be construed as culturally sanctioned and valued activities that channel our aggressive drives. Art, music, poetry, and dance may also be considered vehicles that transform and channel id impulses—both sexual and aggressive—into valued activities of benefit to society. Indeed, according to Freud, one of the beauties of sublimation is that at some level the drive is satisfied and discharged while not being too threatening for the ego or superego.

Defense mechanisms are useful mindbugs: They help us overcome anxiety and engage effectively with the outside world. The ego's capacity to use defense mechanisms in a healthy and flexible fashion may depend on the nature of early experiences with caregivers, the defense mechanisms they used, and possibly some biological and temperamental factors as well (McWilliams, 1994). Our characteristic style of defense becomes our signature in dealing with the world—and an essential aspect of our personality.

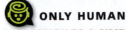 **ONLY HUMAN**

REGRESSION TO A SIMPLER TIME 1994—In November, Lance A. Binkowski, 20, was charged with reckless endangerment in Brookfield, Wisconsin, when he ran from police. Officers had been called after Binkowski had pounded on the back door of a day-care center while dressed in a large sleeper with built-in feet, with a pacifier in his mouth and clutching a teddy bear and a diaper bag. According to the police chief, Binkowski intended no harm to the children but "had his own personal reasons" for being there.

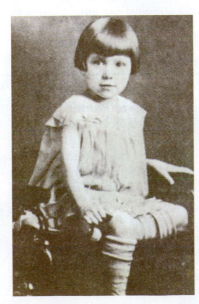

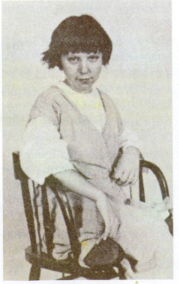

The young woman shown in the photograph on the left grew up under harsh circumstances: family strife, instability, and substance abuse, among other horrors. At age 17, she discovered a photograph of herself taken when she was 5 years old (middle) after which she adopted the look and mannerisms of a 5-year-old child. The image on the right shows the same woman after regression. (Masserman, 1961.)

PSYCHOSEXUAL STAGES Distinct early life stages through which personality is formed as children experience sexual pleasures from specific body areas and caregivers redirect or interfere with those pleasures.

FIXATION A phenomenon in which a person's pleasure-seeking drives become psychologically stuck, or arrested, at a particular psychosexual stage.

ORAL STAGE The first psychosexual stage, in which experience centers on the pleasures and frustrations associated with the mouth, sucking, and being fed.

ANAL STAGE The second psychosexual stage, which is dominated by the pleasures and frustrations associated with the anus, retention and expulsion of feces and urine, and toilet training.

PHALLIC STAGE The third psychosexual stage, during which experience is dominated by the pleasure, conflict, and frustration associated with the phallic-genital region as well as powerful incestuous feelings of love, hate, jealousy, and conflict.

OEDIPUS CONFLICT A developmental experience in which a child's conflicting feelings toward the opposite-sex parent is (usually) resolved by identifying with the same-sex parent.

LATENCY STAGE The fourth psychosexual stage, in which the primary focus is on the further development of intellectual, creative, interpersonal, and athletic skills.

Psychosexual Stages and the Development of Personality

Freud had a great talent for coming up with troubling, highly controversial ideas. People in Victorian society did not openly discuss how much fun it is to suck on things, or the frustrations of their own toilet training, or their childhood sexual desire for their mother. Some people today dismiss this aspect of psychoanalytic theory as just plain rude—but like others who have encountered these ideas, you may find yourself wondering whether your own strong reaction is a signal of how important his observations may be. Many consider Freud's views on personality development to be fanciful, and they are no longer widely held because little research evidence supports them; nevertheless, people find this part of his legacy oddly fascinating.

Freud believed that a person's basic personality is formed before 6 years of age during a series of sensitive periods, or life stages, when experiences influence all that will follow. Freud called these periods **psychosexual stages**, defined as *distinct early life stages through which personality is formed as children experience sexual pleasures from specific body areas and caregivers redirect or interfere with those pleasures*. He argued that as a result of adult interference with pleasure-seeking energies, the child experiences conflict. At each stage, a different bodily region, or *erotogenic* zone, dominates the child's subjective experience—for example, during the oral stage, pleasure centers on the mouth. Each region represents a battleground between the child's id impulses and the adult external world. **TABLE 12.4** provides a summary of the psychosexual stages.

Problems and conflicts encountered at any psychosexual stage, Freud believed, will influence personality in adulthood. Conflict resulting from a person's being deprived or, paradoxically, overindulged at a given stage could result in that *person's pleasure-seeking drives become stuck, or arrested, at that psychosexual stage*—a phenomenon Freud called **fixation**. Freud described particular personality traits as being derived from fixations at the different psychosexual stages. Here's how he explained the effects of fixation.

In the first year and a half of life, the infant is in the **oral stage**, *during which experience centers on the pleasures and frustrations associated with the mouth, sucking, and being fed*. Infants who are deprived of pleasurable feeding or indulgently overfed may develop an oral personality—that is, their lives will center on issues related to fullness and emptiness and what they can "take in" from others and the environment. When angry, such people may express themselves with "biting" sarcasm and "mouth off" at others—referred to as *oral aggression*. Personality traits associated with the oral stage include depression, lack of trust, envy, and demandingness.

Between 2 and 3 years of age, the child moves on to the **anal stage**, *during which experience is dominated by the pleasures and frustrations associated with the anus, retention*

Table 12.4	The Psychosexual Stages				
Stage	**Oral**	**Anal**	**Phallic**	**Latency**	**Genital**
Age	0–18 months	2–3 years	3–5 years	5–13 years	Adulthood
Erotogenic zone	Mouth	Anus/urethra	Penis/clitoris	—	Penis/vagina
Areas of conflict with caregiver	Feeding, weaning	Toileting	Masturbation (Oedipus conflict)	—	Adult responsibilities
Associated personality features	Talkative, dependent, addictive, needy	Orderly, controlling, disorganized, sloppy	Flirtatious, vain, jealous, competitive	—	Authentic investments in love and work; capacity for healthy adult relationships

and expulsion of feces and urine, and toilet training. From the toddler's perspective, the soiling of one's diapers is a wonderful convenience that can feel pretty good. But sooner or later caregivers begin to disagree, and their opinions are voiced more strongly as the child gets older. Individuals who have had difficulty negotiating this conflict may develop a rigid personality and remain preoccupied with issues of control of others and of themselves and their emotions. They may be preoccupied with their possessions, money, issues of submission and rebellion, and concerns about cleanliness versus messiness.

Between the ages of 3 and 5 years, the child is in the **phallic stage**, *during which experience is dominated by the pleasure, conflict, and frustration associated with the phallic-genital region as well as coping with powerful incestuous feelings of love, hate, jealousy, and conflict.* In part, parental concerns about the child's developing awareness of the genital region set off the conflict: The child may touch his or her genitals in public or explore masturbation and may be curious about the parent's genitals.

During the phallic stage, boys are said to struggle with a tumultuous emotional experience that Freud called the Oedipus conflict. According to Freud, the **Oedipus conflict** is *a developmental experience in which a child's conflicting feelings toward the opposite-sex parent is (usually) resolved by identifying with the same-sex parent.* The name for this conflict is derived from the ancient Greek myth of Oedipus (as recounted in the play *Oedipus Rex,* by Sophocles). The myth depicts a young man, Oedipus, who unknowingly kills his father and ends up marrying his mother. Oedipus eventually learns the nature of his transgressions, is overcome with such shame and guilt that he blinds himself, and then is exiled from his home. Freud alludes to this myth as a metaphor for the painful struggles children go through as they experience both loving and hostile feelings toward their parents during development.

Freud viewed growing up with a mother and father as a passionate experience through which we try to secure our place in relation with others, develop autonomy, and learn the most basic rules of social life. As children reach the age of 4 or 5, they start to wonder about their love affair with Mommy, noticing she has positive feelings for someone else (Daddy). In dealing with this love triangle and balancing the wish for an exclusive loving relationship with one parent against the possibility of jeopardizing the relationship with the other, the child comes to realize that he or she is the odd one out. Although boys and girls experience and resolve this conflict differently, Freud believed that both must give up their Oedipal desires if they are to be able to move on and build a life with a partner in the future. The anxiety engendered by this conflict, he believed, is controlled through repression (of the sexual longings) and identification (with the same-sex parent), and this marks the final development of the superego—the internal representation of parental authority.

The personality styles that can arise from fixation at this stage involve morality and sex-role identity. Individuals who get stuck in the phallic period and are unable to resolve the Oedipus conflict tend to be unusually preoccupied with issues of seduction, jealousy, competition, power, and authority. For men, this may include issues of competitiveness, being macho and powerful, and overvaluing success and potency. In women, Freud thought, difficulties at this stage may result in exaggerated expressions of femininity: seductiveness, flirtatiousness, and jealousy.

A more relaxed period in which children are no longer struggling with the power of their sexual and aggressive drives follows the intensity of the Oedipal conflict. Between the ages of 5 and 13 children experience the **latency stage**, *in which the primary focus is on the further development of intellectual, creative, interpersonal, and athletic skills.* Because Freud believed that the most significant aspects of personality development occur during the first three psychosexual stages (before the age of 5 years), psychodynamic psychologists do not speak of fixation at the latency period. Simply making it to the latency period relatively undisturbed by conflicts of the earlier stages is a sign of healthy personality development.

One of the id's desires is to make a fine mess—a desire that is often frustrated early in life, perhaps during the anal stage. Famous painter Jackson Pollack found a way to make extraordinarily fine messes—behavior that at some level all of us envy.

According to the psychodynamic approach, at 4 or 5 years of age children are in the throes of the Oedipus conflict. At this time, children experience intense feelings of love, hate, jealousy, and anxiety related to their longings toward their parents and the wish for an exclusive love relationship with their fathers or mothers.

"Don't worry—it's just a phase."

At puberty and thereafter, the fifth and final stage of personality development occurs. This, the **genital stage**, is *the time for the coming together of the mature adult personality with a capacity to love, work, and relate to others in a mutually satisfying and reciprocal manner.* The degree to which the individual is encumbered by unresolved conflicts at the earlier stages will impact whether he or she will be able to achieve a genital level of development. Freud believed that people who are fixated in a prior stage fail in developing healthy adult sexuality and a well-adjusted adult personality.

What should we make of all this? On the one hand, the psychoanalytic theory of psychosexual stages offers an intriguing picture of early family relationships and the extent to which they allow the child to satisfy basic needs and wishes. The theory picks up on themes that seem to ring true in many cases—you may very well know people who seem to be "oral" or "anal," for example, or who have issues about sexuality that seem to have had a great influence on their personalities. The idea that people must negotiate a way to experience the pleasures of the body in a social world does seem wise. This observation has been a key focus of the many psychodynamic theories that have been offered since Freud's death (e.g., Adler, 1927; Erickson, 1959; Horney, 1937; Sullivan, 1953) and even now continues to provide a rich model of personality (Andersen & Berk, 1998; Westen, 1991).

Critics argue, however, that psychodynamic explanations are too complex and tend to focus on after-the-fact interpretation rather than testable prediction. Describing a person fixated at the oral stage as "biting," for example, seems just so much wordplay—not the basis of a scientific theory. And, for example, the control issues that preoccupy an adult with a so-called anal character might reflect an inborn headstrong and controlling temperament and have nothing to do with a parental style of toilet training. The psychosexual stage theory offers a compelling set of story plots for interpreting lives once they have unfolded but has not generated the kinds of clear-cut predictions that inspire research.

In summary, Freud believed that personality results from a complex interplay of biology and environmental experience that creates the person's unconscious motives. The psychodynamic approach sees the mind as consisting of the interacting systems of id, ego, and superego, which are aimed at satisfying our drives while dealing with reality and our internalized standards of conduct. He explained personality in terms of the sexual and aggressive forces that drive us, our characteristic ways of using defense mechanisms to deal with anxiety, and the degree to which we are able to move through a series of developmental psychosexual stages relatively unhindered. ■ ■

The Humanistic-Existential Approach: Personality as Choice

In the 1950s and 1960s, psychologists began to try to understand personality from a viewpoint quite different from trait theory's biological determinism and Freud's focus on unconscious drives from unresolved child experiences. These new humanistic and existential theorists turned attention to how humans make *healthy choices* that create their personalities.

Proponents of the new approach argued that the ability to consider the future is a core aspect of the human experience that elevates us above our animal nature, giving us the freedom to choose our actions through the exercise of will. Humanistic psychologists emphasized a positive, optimistic view of human nature that highlights people's inherent goodness and their potential for personal growth. Existentialist psychologists focused on the individual as a responsible agent who is free to create and live his or her life while negotiating the issue of meaning and the reality of death. The humanistic-existential approach integrates these insights with a focus on how a personality can become optimal.

GENITAL STAGE The final psychosexual stage, a time for the coming together of the mature adult personality with a capacity to love, work, and relate to others in a mutually satisfying and reciprocal manner.

SELF-ACTUALIZING TENDENCY The human motive toward realizing our inner potential.

UNCONDITIONAL POSITIVE REGARD An attitude of nonjudgmental acceptance toward another person.

Human Needs and Self-actualization

Humanists see the **self-actualizing tendency,** *the human motive toward realizing our inner potential,* as a major factor in personality. The pursuit of knowledge, the expression of one's creativity, the quest for spiritual enlightenment, and the desire to give to society are all examples of self-actualization. Abraham Maslow (1970), a noted humanistic theorist, outlined the steps that people take as they move toward self-actualization. As you saw in Chapter 10, Maslow proposed a *hierarchy of needs,* a model of essential human needs arranged according to their priority, in which basic physiological and safety needs must be satisfied before a person can afford to focus on higher-level psychological needs. Only when these basic needs are satisfied can you pursue higher needs, culminating in *self-actualization*—the need to be good, to be fully alive, and to find meaning in life.

Maslow observed that when people are fully engaged in self-actualizing activities, they occasionally have *peak experiences.* As discussed in Chapter 8, such experiences are altered states of consciousness in which the person loses sense of time and feels in touch with a higher aspect of human existence. Mihaly Csikszentmihalyi (1990) found that engagement in tasks that exactly match one's abilities creates a mental state of energized focus that he called *flow* (see **FIGURE 12.6**). Tasks that are below our abilities cause boredom, those that are too challenging cause anxiety, and those that are "just right" lead to the experience of flow. If you know how to play the piano, for example, and are playing a Chopin prelude that you know well enough that it just matches your abilities, you are likely to experience this optimal state. People report being happier at these times than at any other times. Humanists believe that such peak experiences, or states of flow, reflect the realization of one's human potential and represent the height of personality development.

Figure 12.6 Flow Experience It feels good to do things that challenge your abilities but that don't challenge them too much. Csikszentmihalyi (1990) described this feeling between boredom and anxiety as the "flow experience."

Conditions for Growth

Humanist psychologists explain individual personality differences as arising from the various ways that the environment facilitates—or blocks—attempts to satisfy psychological needs. Like a wilting plant deprived of water, sunshine, and nutrients, an individual growing up in an arid social environment can fail to develop his or her unique potential. For example, someone with the inherent potential to be a great scientist, artist, parent, or teacher might never realize these talents if his or her energies and resources are instead directed toward meeting basic needs of security, belongingness, and the like.

Noted humanist psychotherapist Carl Rogers believed that healthy personality development requires **unconditional positive regard,** *an attitude of nonjudgmental acceptance toward another person* (Rogers, 1951). In particular, he argued, children must be shown that they are loved and valued and that this positive regard will not be withdrawn regardless of how the child behaves (even if the behavior itself is not accepted or valued). He believed that unconditional positive regard is necessary for people to experience the fullness of their being and their inherent goodness and to develop their potentials and accept what they cannot become. In particular, positive regard is crucial for the development of an authentic self that can be in genuine contact with others. Research indicates that when people shape their lives around goals that do not match their true nature and capabilities, they are less likely to be happy than those whose lives and goals do match (Ryan & Deci, 2000).

CHARLES QUIGG/AMHERST COLLEGE PUBLIC AFFAIRS

In the seminar States of Poverty at Amherst College, student Tony Jack asked, "Has anyone here ever actually *seen* a food stamp?" Tony had seen food stamps and more and would never have been able to afford an elite education if Amherst hadn't provided extra help with a full scholarship and a start-up grant and job. Tony was provided with conditions for growth—and graduated with honors in May 2007.

EXISTENTIAL APPROACH A school of thought that regards personality as governed by an individual's ongoing choices and decisions in the context of the realities of life and death.

Personality as Existence

Existentialists agree with humanists about many of the features of personality but focus on challenges to the human condition that are more profound than the lack of a nurturing environment. Rollo May (1983) and Victor Frankl (2000), for example, argued that specific aspects of the human condition, such as awareness of our own existence and the ability to make choices about how to behave, have a double-edged quality: They bring an extraordinary richness and dignity to human life, but they also force us to confront realities that are difficult to face, such as the prospect of our own death. The **existential approach** *regards personality as governed by an individual's ongoing choices and decisions in the context of the realities of life and death.*

According to the existential perspective, the difficulties we face in finding meaning in life and in accepting the responsibility of making free choices provoke a type of anxiety existentialists call *angst* (the anxiety of fully being). You may have experienced angst if you've ever contemplated the way even a small decision can alter your life course. Deciding what to study, when to move to a new city, or whether to cross the street at a particular moment can forever change your whole life path—and your personality. The human ability to consider limitless numbers of goals and actions is exhilarating, but it can also open the door to profound questions such as, "Why am I here?" and, "What is the meaning of my life?"

Thinking about the meaning of existence also can evoke an awareness of its opposite—the potential for nonexistence and death. According to the existentialists, as we think about the inevitability of death, the resulting angst, terror, and fear (or *dread*) can lead us to experience the heaviness of any given moment. What, then, should we do with each moment? What is the purpose of living if life as we know it will end one day, perhaps even today? Alternatively, does life have more meaning given that it is so temporary? The existentialists believe that we inevitably ask these questions when we are truly in touch with our human experience. "Everything has been figured out except how to live," said existential philosopher Jean-Paul Sartre.

Existential theorists do not suggest that people consider these profound existential issues on a day-to-day and moment-to-moment basis. Rather than ruminate about death and meaning, people typically pursue superficial answers that help them deal with the angst and dread they experience, and the defenses they construct form the basis of their personalities (Binswanger, 1958; May, 1983).

Unfortunately, security-providing defense mechanisms can be self-defeating and stifle the potential for personal growth. The pursuit of superficial relationships can make possible the avoidance of real intimacy. A fortress of consumer goods can provide a false sense of security. Immersion in drugs or addictive behaviors such as compulsive web browsing, video gaming, or television watching can numb the mind to existential realities. More commonly, people find security from existential dread by devoting themselves to upholding the values and standards of their culture or families, seldom questioning whether these values fit with their own views. Studies of *mortality salience* have shown that people defend themselves in this way when they have been guided to think even briefly about their own death (Pyszczynski, Solomon, & Greenberg, 2003). As compared with people who are merely thinking about an unpleasant experience such as dental pain, those for whom mortality is salient become unusually protective of their family, culture, country, and religion. Mortality salience has been found to prompt people to condemn critics of their government, recommend tougher sentences for lawbreakers, disparage members of other religious faiths, express prejudice toward other races and ethnicities, and become defensive of their own worldviews. Perhaps this phenomenon

Expressions of patriotism blossomed for months after the terrorist attacks of September 11, 2001.

explains why millions of Americans responded to the terror of the 9/11 attacks by rushing to buy and display their own American flag.

If defenses are so thin and pointless, how do you deal with existence? For existentialists, the solution is to face the issues square on and learn to accept and tolerate the pain of existence. Indeed, being fully human means confronting existential realities rather than denying them or embracing comforting illusions. This requires the courage to accept the inherent anxiety and the dread of nonbeing that is part of being alive. Such courage may be facilitated by developing supportive relationships with others who can supply unconditional positive regard. There's something about being loved that helps take away the angst.

In summary, the humanistic-existential approach to personality grew out of philosophical traditions that are very much at odds with most of the assumptions of the trait and psychoanalytic approaches. The humanists see personality as directed by an inherent striving toward self-actualization and the development of our unique human potentials. They see people as basically good and, if provided with unconditional positive regard, naturally predisposed toward seeking self-actualization. Existentialists focus on angst and dread and the defensive response people often have to these very human experiences. ■ ■

The Social Cognitive Approach: Personalities in Situations

What is it like to be a person? The social cognitive approach to personality explores what it is like to be the person who tries to understand what to do in life's many encounters with people, events, and situations. The **social cognitive approach** *views personality in terms of how the person thinks about the situations encountered in daily life and behaves in response to them.* Bringing together insights from social psychology, cognitive psychology, and learning theory, this approach emphasizes how the person experiences and construes situations (Bandura, 1986; Mischel & Shoda, 1999; Ross & Nisbett, 1991; Wegner & Gilbert, 2000).

The idea that situations cause behavior became clear in basic studies of learning. Consider how the late B. F. Skinner, the strict behaviorist and observer of rats and pigeons (see Chapter 6), would explain your behavior right now. If you have been reinforced in the past by getting good grades when studying only the night before an exam, he would have predicted that you are in fact reading these words for the first time the night before the test! If you have been reinforced for studying well in advance, he

SOCIAL COGNITIVE APPROACH An approach that views personality in terms of how the person thinks about the situations encountered in daily life and behaves in response to them.

would have predicted that you are reading this chapter with plenty of time to spare. For a behaviorist, then, differences in behavior patterns reflect differences in how the behaviors have been rewarded in past situations.

Researchers in social cognition agree that the situation and learning history are key determinants of behavior, but they go much further than Skinner would have in looking inside the psychological "black box" of the mind to examine the thoughts and feelings that come between the situation and the person's response to it. Because human "situations" and "reinforcements" are radically open to interpretation, social cognitive psychologists focus on how people *perceive* their environments. People think about their goals, the consequences of their behavior, and how they might achieve certain things in different situations (Lewin, 1951). The social cognitive approach looks at how personality and situation interact to cause behavior, how personality contributes to the way people construct situations in their own minds, and how people's goals and expectancies influence their responses to situations.

Consistency of Personality across Situations

Although social cognitive psychologists attribute behavior both to the individual's personality and to his or her situation, situation can often trump personality. For example, a person would have to be pretty strange to act exactly the same way at a memorial service and a toga party. In their belief that the strong push and pull of situations can influence almost everyone, social cognitive psychologists are somewhat at odds with the basic assumptions of classic personality psychology—that is, that personality characteristics (such as traits, needs, unconscious drives) cause people to behave in the same way across situations and over time. At the core of the social cognitive approach is a natural puzzle, the **person-situation controversy**, which focuses on *the question of whether behavior is caused more by personality or by situational factors.*

This controversy began in earnest when Walter Mischel (1968) argued that measured personality traits often do a poor job of predicting individuals' behavior. Mischel reviewed decades of research that compared scores on standard personality tests with actual behavior, looking at evidence from studies asking questions such as, "Does a person with a high score on a test of introversion actually spend more time alone than someone with a low score?" Mischel's disturbing conclusion: The average correlation between trait and behavior is only about .30. This is certainly better than zero (i.e., chance) but not very good when you remember that a perfect prediction is represented by a correlation of 1.0.

Mischel also noted that knowing how a person will behave in one situation is not particularly helpful in predicting the person's behavior in another situation. For example, in classic studies Hartshorne and May (1928) assessed children's honesty by examining their willingness to cheat on a test and found that such dishonesty was not consistent from one situation to another. The assessment of a child's trait of honesty in a cheating situation was of almost no use in predicting whether the child would act honestly in a different situation—such as when given the opportunity to steal money. Mischel proposed that measured traits do not predict behaviors very well because behaviors are determined more by situational factors than personality theorists were willing to acknowledge.

Is there no personality, then? Do we all just do what situations require? The person-situation controversy has inspired many studies in the years since Mischel's critique, and it turns out that information about both personality and situation are necessary to predict behavior. Although people may not necessarily act the same way across situations, they often do act in a similar manner within the same type of situation (Mischel & Shoda, 1999). A person who is outgoing at parties but

Is this student, cheating on a test, more likely than others to steal candy or lie to her grandmother? Social cognitive research indicates that behavior in one situation does not necessarily predict behavior in a different situation.

withdrawn at the office would be difficult to characterize as an extravert or an introvert, but if he is *always* outgoing at parties and *always* withdrawn at the office, personality consistency within situations has been demonstrated.

Among the children in Hartshorne and May's studies, cheating versus not cheating on a test was actually a fairly good predictor of cheating on a test later—as long as the situation was similar (Hartshorne & May, 1928). Personality consistency, then, appears to be a matter of when and where a certain kind of behavior tends to be shown. Social cognitive theorists believe these patterns of personality consistency in response to situations arise from the way different people construe situations and from the ways different people pursue goals within situations.

Personal Constructs

How can we understand differences in the way situations are interpreted? Recall our notion of personality often existing "in the eye of the beholder." Situations may exist "in the eye of the beholder" as well. One person's gold mine may be another person's hole in the dirt. George Kelly (1955) long ago realized that these differences in perspective could be used to understand the *perceiver's* personality. He suggested that people view the social world from differing perspectives and that these different views arise through the application of **personal constructs**, *dimensions people use in making sense of their experiences.* Consider, for example, different individuals' personal constructs of a clown: One person may see him as a source of fun, another as a tragic figure, and yet another as so frightening that the circus is off-limits.

Here's how Kelly assessed personal constructs about social relationships: He'd ask people to (1) list the people in their life, (2) consider three of the people and state a way in which two of them were similar to each other and different from the third, and (3) repeat this for other triads of people to produce a list of the dimensions used to classify friends and family. One respondent might focus on the degree to which people (self included) are lazy or hardworking, for example; someone else might attend to the degree to which people are sociable or unfriendly.

Kelly proposed that different personal constructs (*construals*) are the key to personality differences—that is, that different construals lead to disparate behaviors. Taking a long break from work for a leisurely lunch might seem lazy to you. To your friend, the break might seem an ideal opportunity for catching up with friends, so he will wonder why you always choose to eat at your desk. Social cognitive theory explains different responses to situations with the idea that people see things in different ways.

PERSON-SITUATION CONTROVERSY The question of whether behavior is caused more by personality or by situational factors.

PERSONAL CONSTRUCTS Dimensions people use in making sense of their experiences.

Are two of these people taller and one shorter? Are two bareheaded while one wears a hood? Or are two the daughters and one the mom? George Kelly held that the personal constructs we use to distinguish among people in our lives are basic elements of our own personalities.

OUTCOME EXPECTANCIES A person's assumptions about the likely consequences of a future behavior.

LOCUS OF CONTROL A person's tendency to perceive the control of rewards as internal to the self or external in the environment.

Personal Goals and Expectancies

Social cognitive theories also recognize that a person's unique perspective on situations is reflected in his or her personal goals, which are often conscious. In fact, people can usually tell you their goals, whether they are to "find a date for this weekend," "get a good grade in psych," "establish a fulfilling career," or just "get this darn bag of chips open." These goals often reflect the tasks that are appropriate to the person's situation and in a larger sense fit the person's role and stage of life (Cantor, 1990; Klinger, 1977; Little, 1983; Vallacher & Wegner, 1985). For instance, common goals for adolescents include being popular, achieving greater independence from parents and family, and getting into their first-choice college. Common goals for adults include developing a meaningful career, finding a mate, securing financial stability, and starting a family.

People translate goals into behavior in part through **outcome expectancies**, *a person's assumptions about the likely consequences of a future behavior.* Just as a laboratory rat learns that pressing a bar releases a food pellet, we learn that "if I am friendly toward people, they will be friendly in return" or "if I ask people to pull my finger, they will withdraw from me." So we learn to perform behaviors that we expect will have the outcome of moving us closer to our goals. Outcome expectancies are learned through direct experience, both bitter and sweet, and through merely observing other people's actions and their consequences.

Outcome expectancies combine with a person's goals to produce the person's characteristic style of behavior. An individual with the goal of making friends and the expectancy that being kind will produce warmth in return is likely to behave very differently from an individual whose goal is to achieve fame at any cost and who believes that shameless self-promotion is the route to fame. We do not all want the same things from life, clearly, and our personalities largely reflect the goals we pursue and the expectancies we have about the best ways to pursue them.

People differ in their generalized expectancy for achieving goals. Some people seem to feel that they are fully in control of what happens to them in life, whereas others feel that the world doles out rewards and punishments to them irrespective of their actions. Julian Rotter (1966) developed a questionnaire (see **TABLE 12.5**) to measure *a person's tendency to perceive the control of rewards as internal to the self or external in the environment*, a disposition he called **locus of control**. People whose answers suggest that they believe they control their own destiny are said to have an *internal* locus of control, whereas those who believe that outcomes are random, determined by luck, or controlled by other people are described as having an *external* locus of control. These beliefs translate into individual differences in emotion and behavior. For example, people with an internal locus of control tend to be less anxious, achieve more, and cope better with stress than do people with an external orientation (Lefcourt, 1982). To get a sense of your standing on this trait dimension, choose one of the options for each of the sample items from the locus-of-control scale in Table 12.5.

Table 12.5	Rotter's Locus-of-Control Scale

For each pair of items, choose the option that most closely reflects your personal belief. Then turn the book upside down to see if you have more of an internal or external locus of control.

1. a. Many of the unhappy things in people's lives are partly due to bad luck.
   b. People's misfortunes result from the mistakes they make.

2. a. I have often found that what is going to happen will happen.
   b. Trusting to fate has never turned out as well for me as making a decision to take a definite course of action.

3. a. Becoming a success is a matter of hard work; luck has little or nothing to do with it.
   b. Getting a good job depends mainly on being in the right place at the right time.

4. a. When I make plans, I am almost certain that I can make them work.
   b. It is not always wise to plan too far ahead because many things turn out to be a matter of good or bad fortune anyhow.

Source: Rotter, 1966.

Answer: A more internal locus of control would be reflected in choosing options 1b, 2b, 3a, and 4a.

In summary, the social cognitive approach focuses on personality as arising from individuals' behavior in situations. Rather than assuming that people have broad dispositions that are consistent across situations, the social cognitive approach describes the consistency of behavior observed in particular situations. Situations and persons mean different things to different people, as suggested by Kelly's personal construct theory, and people may differ as well in the conscious goals they seek and expectations they have about how their behavior can enable them to reach their goals in different situations. In taking the perspective of the individual who is trying to negotiate the complexities of the world, the social cognitive approach to personality emphasizes how the person sees things and what the person wants in each situation. ■ ■

The Self: Personality in the Mirror

Imagine that you wake up tomorrow morning, drag yourself into the bathroom, look into the mirror, and don't recognize the face looking back at you. This was the plight of a patient studied by neurologist Todd Feinberg (2001). The woman, married for 30 years and the mother of two grown children, one day began to respond to her mirror image as if it were a different person. She talked to and challenged the person in the mirror. When there was no response, she tried to attack it as if it were an intruder. Her husband, shaken by this bizarre behavior, brought her to the neurologist, who was gradually able to convince her that the image in the mirror was in fact herself.

Most of us are pretty familiar with the face that looks back at us from every mirror. We developed the ability to recognize ourselves in mirrors by 18 months of age (as discussed in Chapter 8), and we share this skill with chimps and other apes who have been raised in the presence of mirrors. Self-recognition in mirrors signals our amazing capacity for reflexive thinking, for directing attention to our own thoughts, feelings, and actions—

What do these self-portraits of Frida Kahlo, M. C. Escher, Norman Rockwell, Salvador Dalí, Wanda Wulz, and Jean-Michel Basquiat reveal about each artist's self-concept?

SELF-CONCEPT A person's explicit knowledge of his or her own behaviors, traits, and other personal characteristics.

an ability that enables us to construct ideas about our own personality. Unlike a cow, which will never know that it has a poor sense of humor, or a cat, which will never know that it is awfully friendly (for a cat), humans have rich and detailed self-knowledge.

Admittedly, none of us know all there is to know about our own personality (or psychodynamic psychologists would be out of work). But we do have enough self-knowledge to reliably respond to personality inventories and report on our traits and behaviors. These observations draw on what we think about ourselves—our *self-concept*—and on how we feel about ourselves—our *self-esteem*. Self-concept and self-esteem are critically important facets of personality, not just because they reveal how people see their own personalities, but because they also guide how people think others will see them.

Self-concept

In his renowned psychology textbook, William James (1890) included a theory of self in which he pointed to the self's two facets, the *I* and the *Me*. The *I* is the self that thinks, experiences, and acts in the world; it is the self as a *knower*. The *Me* is the self that is an object in the world; it is the self that is *known*. The *I* is much like consciousness, then, a perspective on all of experience (see Chapter 8), but the *Me* is less mysterious: It is just a concept of a person.

If asked to describe your *Me*, you might mention your physical characteristics (male or female, tall or short, dark-skinned or light), your activities (listening to hip-hop, alternative rock, jazz, or classical music), your personality traits (extraverted or introverted, agreeable or independent), or your social roles (student, son or daughter, member of a hiking club, manager of a noodle factory). These features make up the **self-concept**, *a person's explicit knowledge of his or her own behaviors, traits, and other personal characteristics.* A person's self-concept is an organized body of knowledge that develops from social experiences and has a profound effect on a person's behavior throughout life.

Self-concept Organization

Almost everyone has a place for memorabilia, a drawer or box somewhere that holds all those sentimental keepsakes—photos, yearbooks, cards and letters, maybe that scrap of the old security blanket—all memories of "life as *Me*." Perhaps you've wanted to organize these things sometime but have never gotten around to it. Fortunately, the knowledge of ourselves that we store in our *autobiographical memory* seems to be organized naturally in two ways—as narratives about episodes in our lives and in terms of traits (as would be suggested by the distinction between episodic and semantic memory discussed in Chapter 5).

A key element in personality involves the stories, myths, and fairy tales we tell ourselves about our lives. Are you living the story of the prince or princess in a castle— or are you the troll in the woods?

HIDEO KURIHARA/ALAMY

The aspect of the self-concept that is a *self-narrative*—a story that we tell about ourselves—can be brief or very lengthy. Your life story could start with your birth and upbringing, describe a series of defining moments, and end where you are today. You could select specific events and experiences, goals and life tasks, and memories of places and people that have influenced you. Self-narrative organizes the highlights (and low blows) of your life into a story in which you are the leading character and binds them together into your self-concept (McAdams, 1993). Psychodynamic and humanistic-existential psychologists suggest that people's self-narratives reflect their fantasies and thoughts about core motives and approaches to existence.

Self-concept is also organized in a more abstract way, in terms of personality traits. Just as you can judge an object on its attributes ("Is this apple green?"), you are able to judge yourself on any number of traits—whether you are considerate or smart or lazy or active or, for that matter, green—and do so quite reliably, making the same rating on multiple occasions. Hazel Markus (1977) observed that each person finds certain unique personality traits particularly important for conceptualizing the self. One person might define herself as independent, for example, whereas another might not care much about her level of independence but instead emphasize her sense of style. Markus called the traits people use to define themselves *self-schemas,* emphasizing that they draw information about the self into a coherent scheme. In one study, Markus (1977) asked people to indicate whether they had a trait by pressing response buttons marked "me" or "not me." She found that participants' judgment reaction times were faster for self-schemas than for other traits. It's as though some facets of the self-concept have almost a "knee-jerk" quality—letting us tell quickly who we are and who we are not.

Research also shows that the traits people use to judge the self tend to stick in memory. When people make judgments of themselves on traits, they later recall the traits better than when they judge other people on the same traits (Rogers, Kuiper, & Kirker, 1977). For example, answering a question such as, "Are you generous?"—no matter what your answer—is likely to enhance your memory for the trait generous. In studies of this effect of *self-relevance* on memory, researchers using imaging technologies have found that the simple activity of making judgments about the trait self-concept is accompanied by activation of the medial prefrontal cortex (MPFC)—a brain area involved in understanding people (Mitchell, Heatherton, & Macrae, 2002). This activation is stronger, however, when people are judging their own standing on traits (see **FIGURE 12.7**) than when they are judging the standing of someone else (Kelley et al., 2002). Such stronger activation, then, is linked with better memory for the traits being judged (Macrae, Moran, Heatherton, Banfield, & Kelley, 2004). Studies have not been entirely conclusive about which brain areas are most involved in the processing of self-information (Morin, 2002), but they do show that memory for traits is strengthened when the MPFC is activated during self-judgments.

How do our behavior self-narratives and trait self-concepts compare? These two methods of self-conceptualization don't always match up. You may think of yourself as an honest person, for example, but also recall that time you nabbed a handful of change from your parents' dresser and conveniently forgot to replace it. The traits we use to describe ourselves are generalizations, and not every episode in our life stories may fit. In fact, research suggests that the stores of knowledge about our behaviors and traits are not very well integrated (Kihlstrom & Klein, 1994). In people who develop amnesia, for example, memory for behaviors can be lost even though the trait self-concept remains stable (Klein, 2004). People can have a pretty strong sense of who they are even though they may not remember a single example of when they acted that way.

Causes and Effects of Self-concept

How do self-concepts arise, and how do they affect us? In some sense, you learn more about yourself every day. People tell you that you were a jerk last night, for instance, or that you're looking good today. Although we can gain self-knowledge in private moments of insight, we more often arrive at our self-concepts through interacting with others. Young children in particular receive plenty of feedback from their parents, teachers, siblings, and friends about their characteristics, and this helps them to form an idea of who they are. Even adults would find it difficult to hold a view of the self as "kind" or "smart" if no one else ever shared this impression. The sense of self, then, is largely developed and maintained in relationships with others.

Over the course of a lifetime, however, we become less and less impressed with what others have to say about us. Social theorist George Herbert Mead (1934) observed that all the things people have said about us accumulate after a while into what we see as a kind of consensus held by the "generalized other." We typically adopt this general view of ourselves that is as stable as our concept of anything at all and hold on to it

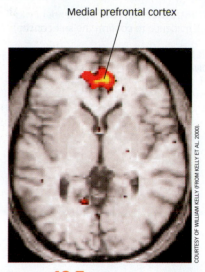

Medial prefrontal cortex

COURTESY OF WILLIAM KELLY (FROM KELLY ET AL. 2000).

Figure 12.7 **Self-concept in the Brain** fMRI scans reveal that the medial prefrontal cortex (MPFC) is activated (shown here in red and yellow) when people make judgments of whether they possess certain personality traits compared to judging whether the traits apply to someone else.
(From Kelley et al., 2002.)

SELF-VERIFICATION The tendency to seek evidence to confirm the self-concept.

SELF-ESTEEM The extent to which an individual likes, values, and accepts the self.

stubbornly. As a result, the person who says you're a jerk may upset you momentarily—but you bounce back, secure in the knowledge that you're not truly a jerk And just as we might argue vehemently with someone who tried to tell us a refrigerator is a pair of underpants or that up is actually down and to the left, we are likely to defend our self-concept against anyone whose view of us departs from our own.

Because it is so stable, a major effect of the self-concept is to promote consistency in behavior across situations (Lecky, 1945). As existential theorists emphasize, people derive a comforting sense of familiarity and stability from knowing who they are. We tend to engage in what William Swann (1983) called **self-verification**, *the tendency to seek evidence to confirm the self-concept,* and we find it disconcerting if someone sees us quite differently from the way we see ourselves. In one study, Swann (1983) gave people who considered themselves submissive feedback that they seemed very dominant and forceful. Rather than accepting this discrepant information, they went out of their way to act in an extremely submissive manner. Our tendency to project into the world our concept of the self contributes to personality coherence. This talent for self-reflection enables the personality to become self-sustaining.

Self-esteem

When you think about yourself, do you feel good and worthy? Do you like yourself, or do you feel bad and have negative, self-critical thoughts? **Self-esteem** is *the extent to which an individual likes, values, and accepts the self.* Thousands of studies have examined differences between people with high self-esteem (who generally like themselves) and those with relatively low self-esteem (who are less keen on, and may actively dislike, themselves). Researchers who study self-esteem typically ask participants to fill out a self-esteem questionnaire, such as one shown in **TABLE 12.6** (Rosenberg, 1965). This widely used measure of self-esteem asks people to evaluate themselves in terms of each statement. People who strongly agree with the positive statements about themselves and strongly disagree with the negative statements are considered to have high self-esteem.

Table 12.6	Rosenberg Self-Esteem Scale			
Consider each statement and circle SA for strongly agree, A for agree, D for disagree, and SD for strongly disagree.				
1. On the whole, I am satisfied with myself.	SA	A	D	SD
2. At times, I think I am no good at all.	SA	A	D	SD
3. I feel that I have a number of good qualities.	SA	A	D	SD
4. I am able to do things as well as most other people.	SA	A	D	SD
5. I feel I do not have much to be proud of.	SA	A	D	SD
6. I certainly feel useless at times.	SA	A	D	SD
7. I feel that I'm a person of worth, at least on an equal plane with others.	SA	A	D	SD
8. I wish I could have more respect for myself.	SA	A	D	SD
9. All in all, I am inclined to feel that I am a failure.	SA	A	D	SD
10. I take a positive attitude toward myself.	SA	A	D	SD

Source: Rosenberg, 1965.

Scoring: For items 1, 3, 4, 7, and 10, SA = 3, A = 2, D = 1, SD = 0; for items 2, 5, 6, 8, and 9, the scoring is reversed, with SA = 0, A = 1, D = 2, SD = 3. The higher the total score, the higher one's self-esteem.

Although some personality psychologists have argued that self-esteem determines virtually everything about a person's life—from the tendency to engage in criminal activity and violence to professional success—evidence has accumulated that the benefits of high self-esteem are less striking and all-encompassing but still significant. In general, compared with people with low self-esteem, those with high self-esteem tend to live happier and healthier lives, cope better with stress, and be more likely to persist at difficult tasks. In contrast, individuals with low self-esteem are more likely—for example—to perceive rejection in ambiguous feedback from others and develop eating disorders than those with high self-esteem (Baumeister, Campbell, Krueger, & Vohs, 2003). How does this aspect of personality develop, and why does everyone—whether high or low in self-esteem—seem to *want* high self-esteem?

Sources of Self-esteem

Some psychologists contend that high self-esteem arises primarily from being accepted and valued by significant others (Brown, 1993). Others focus on the influence of specific self-evaluations, judgments about one's value or competence in specific domains such as appearance, athletics, or scholastics. People's overall self-esteem is most likely the result of a combination of these factors, including both the security of feeling accepted and the satisfaction of positive self-regard. But these sources of self-esteem do not directly influence how we evaluate ourselves. Instead, feedback we receive about ourselves differs in its impact depending on whom we choose for comparisons, the unconscious perspectives we take on ourselves, and our personal belief in whether the feedback actually matters for who we are.

Consider first how comparisons can influence self-esteem. As an example, James (1890) noted that an accomplished athlete who is the second best in the world should feel pretty proud, but this athlete might not if the standard of comparison involves being best in the world. In fact, athletes in the 1992 Olympics who had won silver medals looked less happy during the medal ceremony than those who had won bronze (Medvec, Madey, & Gilovich, 1995). Following pioneering work by humanist Carl Rogers (1957), researchers have investigated the way people compare themselves to standards and how that makes them feel. If the actual self is seen as falling short of the ideal self—the person that they would like to be—people tend to feel sad or dejected; when they become aware that the actual self is inconsistent with the self they have a duty to be, they are likely to feel anxious or agitated (Higgins, 1987).

Silver medalist Duje Draganja of Croatia, gold medalist G. Hall Jr. of the United States, and bronze medalist Roland Schoeman of South Africa show off their medals following their 50-meter swimming final. Notice the expression on Draganja's face compared to those of the gold and bronze medalists.

Fleeting thoughts of authorities can influence self-esteem. Catholic girls shown subliminal photos of Pope John Paul II experienced reduced self-esteem.

Unconscious perspectives we take on feedback can also affect our sense of self-worth. In one study, researchers looked at the effect of an authority figure's disapproval on self-esteem. They examined the self-esteem of young, Catholic, female participants who had read an article from *Cosmopolitan* that described a woman's sexual dream (in PG-13 language) and who had either seen a photo of a disapproving-looking pope or a photo of an unfamiliar disapproving person. The photos were shown subliminally—that is, in such brief flashes that the women could not consciously recognize whom they had seen. In self-ratings made afterward, the women in the disapproving-pope group showed a marked reduction in self-esteem compared with the other women: They rated themselves as less competent, more anxious, and less moral. In the words of the researchers, self-esteem can be influenced when an important authority figure is "watching you from the back of your mind" (Baldwin, Carrell, & Lopez, 1989, p. 435).

Feedback can have different effects on self-esteem depending on its connection to the self-concept. Not surprisingly, overall self-esteem has been found to be affected most by self-evaluations in domains that we consider most important: One person's self-worth might be entirely contingent on, for example, how well she does in school, whereas another's self-worth might be based on his physical attractiveness (Crocker & Wolfe, 2001; Pelham, 1985). To fully understand the impact of feedback on any individual, however, we also need to know whether his or her self-worth is *entirely* contingent on domain-specific self-evaluations and so fluctuates in response to evaluative feedback and performance outcomes or if the person has a core sense of self-acceptance that gives a feeling of worth even in the face of significant failures (Kernis, 2003; Ryan & Deci, 2000). Overall, then, the comparisons we make, the unconscious perspectives we take, and the ways in which we attach our self-esteem to specific features of our self-concept can influence the impact on self-esteem of social feedback and success or failure in life tasks (see the Hot Science box).

The Desire for Self-esteem

What's so great about self-esteem? Why do people want to see themselves in a positive light and avoid seeing themselves negatively? The key theories on the benefits of self-esteem focus on status, belonging, and security.

Does self-esteem feel good because it reflects our degree of social dominance or status? People with high self-esteem seem to carry themselves in a way that is similar to high-status animals of other social species. Dominant male gorillas, for example, appear confident and comfortable and not anxious or withdrawn. Perhaps high self-esteem in humans reflects high social status or suggests that the person is worthy of respect, and this perception triggers natural affective responses (Barkow, 1980; Maslow, 1937).

High self-esteem in humans may reflect the same sort of social status and respect that dominant male gorillas enjoy.

{ HOT SCIENCE } Implicit Egotism: Liking Ourselves without Knowing It

WHAT'S YOUR FAVORITE LETTER OF THE alphabet? About 30% of people answer by picking what just happens to be the first letter of their first name. Could this choice indicate that some people think so highly of themselves that they base judgments of seemingly unrelated topics on how much it reminds them of themselves?

This *name-letter effect* was discovered some years ago (Nuttin, 1985), but only recently have researchers gone on to discover how broad the egotistic bias in preferences can be. Brett Pelham and his colleagues have found subtle yet systematic biases toward this effect when people choose their home cities, streets, and even occupations (Pelham, Mirenberg, & Jones, 2002). When the researchers examined the rolls of people moving into several southern states, for example, they found people named George were more likely than those with other names to move to Georgia. The same was true for Florences (Florida), Kenneths (Kentucky), and Louises (Louisiana). You can guess where the Virginias tended to relocate. People whose last name is Street seem biased toward addresses ending in *street,* whereas Lanes like lanes. The name effect seems to work for occupations as well: Slightly more people named Dennis and Denise chose dentistry and Lauras and Lawrences chose law compared with other occupations. Although the biases are small (if your name is Wally, you don't *have* to move to Walla Walla), they are consistent across many tests of the hypothesis.

These biases have been called expressions of *Implicit egotism* because people are

HEIDI CODY/HEIDICODY.COM

What's your favorite letter?

not typically aware that they are influenced by the wonderful sound of their own names (Pelham, Carvallo, & Jones, 2005). When Buffy moves to Buffalo, she is not likely to volunteer that she did so because it matched her name. Yet people who show this egotistic bias in one way also tend to show it in others: People who strongly prefer their own name letter also are likely to pick their birth date as their favorite number (Koole, Dijksterhuis, & van Knippenberg, 2001). And people who like their name letter were also found to evaluate themselves positively on self-ratings of personality traits. This was especially true when the self-ratings were made in response to instructions to work *quickly.* The people who preferred their name letter made snap judgments of themselves that leaned in a positive direction—suggesting that their special self-appreciation was an automatic response.

At some level, of course, a bit of egotism is probably good for us. It's sad to meet someone who hates her own name or whose snap judgment of self is, "I'm worthless." Yet in another sense, implicit egotism is a curiously subtle mindbug—a tendency to make biased judgments of what we will do and where we will go in life just because we happen to have a certain name. Yes, the bias is only a small one. But your authors wonder: Could we have found better people to work with had we not fallen prey to this bias in our choice of colleagues?

Could the desire for self-esteem come from a basic need to belong or be related to others? Evolutionary theory holds that early humans who managed to survive to pass on their genes were those able to maintain good relations with others rather than being cast out to fend for themselves. Clearly, belonging to groups is adaptive, as is knowing whether you are accepted. Thus, self-esteem could be a kind of *sociometer,* an inner gauge of how much a person feels included by others at any given moment (Leary & Baumeister, 2000). According to evolutionary theory, then, we seek higher self-esteem because we have evolved to seek out belongingness in our families, work groups, and culture, and higher self-esteem indicates that we are being accepted.

The idea that self-esteem is a matter of security is consistent with the existential and psychodynamic approaches to personality. The studies of "mortality salience" discussed earlier suggest that the source of distress underlying negative self-esteem is ultimately the fear of death (Solomon, Greenberg, & Pyszczynski, 1991). In this view,

SELF-SERVING BIAS People's tendency to take credit for their successes but downplay responsibility for their failures.

NARCISSISM A trait that reflects a grandiose view of the self combined with a tendency to seek admiration from and exploit others.

ONLY HUMAN

SPECIAL, SO VERY SPECIAL 2003—Furious at a rush-hour accident that blocked traffic in the Boston suburb of Weymouth, motorist (and software engineer) Anna Gitlin, 25, went ballistic at a police officer and then allegedly bumped him with her car, screaming, "I don't care who [expletive deleted by the *Boston Globe*] died. I'm more important."

humans find it anxiety provoking, in fact terrifying, to contemplate their own mortality, and so they try to defend against this awareness by immersing themselves in activities (such as earning money or dressing up to appear attractive) that their culture defines as meaningful and valuable. The desire for self-esteem is a need to find value in ourselves as a way of escaping the anxiety associated with recognizing our mortality. The higher our self-esteem, the less anxious we feel with the knowledge that someday we will no longer exist.

Whatever the reason that low self-esteem feels so bad and high self-esteem feels so good, people are generally motivated to see themselves positively. In fact, we often process information in a biased manner in order to feel good about the self. Research on the **self-serving bias** shows that *people tend to take credit for their successes but downplay responsibility for their failures.* You may have noticed this tendency in yourself, particularly in terms of the attributions you make about exams when you get a good grade ("I studied really intensely, and I'm good at that subject") or a bad grade ("The test was ridiculously tricky and the professor is a nimnutz").

On the whole, most people satisfy the desire for high self-esteem and maintain a reasonably positive view of self by engaging in the self-serving bias. In fact, if people are asked to rate themselves across a range of characteristics, they tend to see themselves as better than the average person in most domains (Alicke et al., 1995). For example, 90 percent of drivers describe their driving skills as better than average, and 86 percent of workers rate their performance on the job as above average. Even among university professors, 94 percent feel they are above average in teaching ability compared with other professors (Cross, 1977). These kinds of judgments simply cannot be accurate, statistically speaking, since the average of a group of people has to be the average, not better than average! This mindbug may be adaptive, however. People who do not engage in this self-serving bias to boost their self-esteem tend to be more at risk for depression, anxiety, and related health problems (Taylor & Brown, 1988).

On the other hand, a few people take positive self-esteem to the extreme. Unfortunately, seeing yourself as way, way better than average—a trait called **narcissism**, *a grandiose view of the self combined with a tendency to seek admiration from and exploit others*—brings some costs. In fact, at its extreme, narcissism is considered a personality disorder (see Chapter 13). Research has documented disadvantages of an overinflated view of self, most of which arise from the need to defend that grandiose view at all costs. For example, when highly narcissistic individuals in one study were given feedback that someone thought poorly of them, their aggressiveness increased as did their willingness to deliver loud blasts of noise to punish the person who had insulted them (Bushman & Baumeister, 1998).

The self is the part of personality that the person knows and can report about. Some of the personality measures we have seen in this chapter—such as personality inventories

"I got into the stupidest thing with my reflection this morning."

based on self-reports—are really no different from measures of self-concept. Both depend on the person's perceptions and memories of the self's behavior and traits. But personality runs deeper than this as well. The unconscious forces identified in psychodynamic approaches provide themes for behavior, and sources of mental disorder, that are not accessible for self-report. The humanistic and existential approaches remind us of the profound concerns we humans face and the difficulties we may have in understanding all the forces that shape our self-views. Finally, in emphasizing how personality shapes our perceptions of social life, the social cognitive approach brings the self back to center stage. The self, after all, is the hub of each person's social world.

In summary, the self-concept is a person's knowledge of his or her behaviors, traits, and other characteristics. The content of the self-concept ranges from episodic memories of behavior and larger self-narratives to specific beliefs about personality traits. The trait self-concept incorporates important dimensions called self-schemas, and neurological evidence suggests that processing of information about one's self-concept activates the medial prefrontal cortex. People's self-concept develops through social feedback, and they often act to try to verify these views, which promotes consistency in behavior across different situations. Self-esteem is a person's evaluation of self and is correlated with other indicators of well-being. Sources of self-esteem include secure acceptance from others as well as evaluations of the self derived from comparing against standards. Several theories have been proposed to explain the positive feelings associated with positive self-evaluations, including locating these feelings in perceptions of status, or belonging, or of being symbolically protected against mortality. People often cling to positive self-evaluations by engaging in the self-serving bias to boost their self-esteem. The trait of narcissism involves defensively clinging to an overly positive view of self, which can sometimes produce negative social behavior. ■ ■

Where Do You Stand?

Personality Testing for Fun and Profit

Many people enjoy filling out personality tests. In fact, dozens of websites, magazine articles, and popular books offer personality tests to complete as well as handy summaries of test scores. Google *personality test* and you'll see. Unfortunately, many personality tests are no more than a collection of questions someone has put together to offer entertainment to test takers. These tests yield a sense of self-insight that is no more valid than what you might get from the random "wisdom" of a fortune cookie or your daily horoscope.

The personality tests discussed in this chapter are more valid, of course: They have been developed and refined to offer reliable predictions of a person's tendencies. Still, the validity of many personality tests, particularly the projective tests, remains controversial, and critics question whether personality tests should be used for serious purposes.

Would one or more personality tests help you decide what career path to follow after college? Research findings have demonstrated correlations between personality dimensions and certain work-related indicators. In research on the Big Five, for example, people who are high in extraversion have been found to do well in sales and management positions. And as you might expect, people scoring high in conscientiousness tend to get better job performance ratings, while people high in agreeableness and low in neuroticism do well in jobs that require working in groups (John & Srivastava, 1999).

In fact, business, government, and the military often use personality tests in hiring. And vocational counselors use the Myers-Briggs Type Indicator personality test (which primarily assesses the individual's standing on the extraversion/introversion personality dimension) to direct people toward occupations that match their strengths. Although such tests have been criticized for their flimsy theoretical and research foundations (Paul, 2004), businesses have not abandoned them.

The possibility also exists that such tests might be someday used to predict whether criminals behind bars have been rehabilitated or might return to crime if released. If tests could be developed that would predict with certainty whether a person would be likely to commit a violent crime or become a terrorist or a sexual predator, do you think such tests should be used to make decisions about people's lives?

Think of all you have learned about the different approaches to personality, the strengths and weaknesses of different kinds of tests, the person-situation controversy, and the fact that personality measures do correlate significantly (although not perfectly) with a person's behaviors. Are personality tests useful for making decisions about people now? If such tests were perfected, should they be used in the future? Where do you stand?

Chapter Review

Personality: What It Is and How It Is Measured

- Personality psychologists seek ways to describe and also explain individuals' styles of behaving, thinking, and feeling.
- Personality inventories, such as the MMPI and other self-report questionnaires, can be used to assess people's views of themselves and their own personality characteristics.
- Projective techniques, such as the Rorschach Test and the Thematic Apperception Test, can be used to assess aspects of people's personalities of which they may be unaware and that are difficult to access through self-report.

The Trait Approach: Identifying Patterns of Behavior

- Most contemporary trait psychologists are interested in the study of the Big Five: conscientiousness, agreeableness, neuroticism, openness, and extraversion.
- Trait psychologists often look to biological factors to explain the existence of traits.
- Behavioral genetic research and studies of animal behavior generally support the biological underpinning of traits.
- Traits are thought to arise from neuropsychological factors such as the arousability of the cortex.

The Psychodynamic Approach: Forces That Lie beneath Awareness

- Psychodynamic theories hold that behavior is shaped by motivations operating outside of consciousness.
- Freud's model of the structure of the mind includes the id, ego, and superego systems.
- People use a variety of defense mechanisms to deal with anxiety and mental conflict.
- People can become fixated at a specific developmental stage, which then shapes their adult personality.
- Early childhood experiences play a significant role in the formation of personality.

The Humanistic-Existential Approach: Personality as Choice

- Human behavior is motivated by the tendency to actualize our inherent potentials.
- Humans have a hierarchically organized set of basic psychological needs.
- People require unconditional positive regard for optimal personality development and growth.
- Human existence includes feelings of angst and dread, which people often defend against by restricting the range of their experience.
- Authentic existence involves facing the realities of life, and the accompanying angst and dread, with courage.

The Social Cognitive Approach: Personalities in Situations

- Behavior is determined not only by personality but also by how people respond to the situations they encounter.
- Different people make sense of their experiences in different ways, and this shapes their personalities.
- Core elements of personality involve goals and expectancies about the likelihood of goal attainment.

The Self: Personality in the Mirror

- The human capacity for self-reflection allows people to form a self-concept and develop a characteristic level of self-esteem.
- The self-concept includes both self-narratives that represent behavior and self-schemas that represent personality traits.
- The medial prefrontal cortex is implicated in memory for the trait self-concept.
- People's feelings of self-esteem are influenced by feedback about the self that is filtered by processes of self-evaluation.
- Most people tend to see themselves as better than average.
- Narcissism is the trait of excessive high self-esteem.

Key Terms

personality (p. 450)
self-report (p. 452)
Minnesota Multiphasic Personality Inventory (MMPI) (p. 452)
projective techniques (p. 452)
Rorschach Inkblot Test (p. 453)
Thematic Apperception Test (TAT) (p. 453)
trait (p. 454)
Big Five (p. 457)
psychodynamic approach (p. 463)

dynamic unconscious (p. 463)
id (p. 464)
pleasure principle (p. 464)
ego (p. 464)
reality principle (p. 464)
superego (p. 464)
defense mechanisms (p. 466)
rationalization (p. 466)
reaction formation (p. 466)
projection (p. 466)
regression (p. 467)
displacement (p. 467)
identification (p. 467)

sublimation (p. 467)
psychosexual stages (p. 468)
fixation (p. 468)
oral stage (p. 468)
anal stage (p. 468)
phallic stage (p. 469)
Oedipus conflict (p. 469)
latency stage (p. 469)
genital stage (p. 470)
self-actualizing tendency (p. 471)
unconditional positive regard (p. 471)

existential approach (p. 472)
social cognitive approach (p. 473)
person-situation controversy (p. 474)
personal constructs (p. 475)
outcome expectancies (p. 476)
locus of control (p. 476)
self-concept (p. 478)
self-verification (p. 480)
self-esteem (p. 480)
self-serving bias (p. 484)
narcissism (p. 484)

Recommended Readings

Feinberg, T. E. (2001). *Altered egos: How the brain creates the self.* New York: Oxford University Press. A fascinating review of the links between the brain and the experience of the self. This book covers issues of consciousness, identity, and the self and examines how people with various forms of brain injury develop changes in awareness of self, mind, and body.

Freud, S. (1952). *A general introduction to psychoanalysis.* New York: Pocket Books. Sigmund Freud's own introduction to psychoanalytic theory. This version is among the most readable and concise, with a wide array of examples.

Paul, A. M. (2004). *The cult of personality testing.* New York: Free Press. A critique of personality testing, this book examines how tests can be unreliable and invalid and asks whether employers, therapists, or courts should trust personality test results.

Rogers, C. R. (1961). *On becoming a person.* Boston: Houghton Mifflin. The essential text on Carl Rogers's humanistic theory. It provides a very readable and personal exploration of humanistic ideas as applied to psychotherapy, human relations, and life in general.

13

Psychological Disorders

Identifying Psychological Disorders: What Is Abnormal?
Defining the Boundaries of Normality
Classification of Psychological Disorders
Classification and Causation
THE REAL WORLD Cultural Variants of Abnormal Behavior
Consequences of Labeling

Anxiety Disorders: When Fears Take Over
Generalized Anxiety Disorder
Phobic Disorders
Panic Disorder
Obsessive-Compulsive Disorder

Dissociative Disorders: Going to Pieces
Dissociative Identity Disorder
Dissociative Amnesia and Dissociative Fugue

Mood Disorders: At the Mercy of Emotions
Depressive Disorders
Bipolar Disorder
THE REAL WORLD Suicide Risk and Prevention

Schizophrenia: Losing the Grasp on Reality
Symptoms and Types of Schizophrenia
Biological Factors
Psychological Factors

Personality Disorders: Going to Extremes
Types of Personality Disorders
Antisocial Personality Disorder
HOT SCIENCE Positive Psychology: Exterminating the Mindbugs
WHERE DO YOU STAND? Normal or Abnormal

VIRGINIA WOOLF LEFT HER WALKING STICK on the bank of the river, put a large stone in the pocket of her coat, and made her way into the water. Her body was found 3 weeks later. She had written to her husband: "Dearest, I feel certain I am going mad again. . . . And I shan't recover this time. I begin to hear voices, and I can't concentrate. So I am doing what seems the best thing to do" (Dally, 1999, p. 182). Thus, near Rodmell, Sussex, England, on March 28, 1941, life ended for the prolific novelist and essayist, central figure of the avant-garde literary salon known as the Bloomsbury Group, influential feminist—and unfortunate victim of lifelong "breakdowns," with swings in mood between wretched depression and manic excitement.

The madness afflicting Woolf is now known as bipolar disorder. At one extreme were her episodes of depression—sullen, despondent, her creativity at a halt, she was sometimes bedridden for months by her illness. These periods alternated with mania, when, as her husband, Leonard, recounted, "She talked almost without stopping for 2 or 3 days, paying no attention to anyone in the room or anything said to her." Her language "became completely incoherent, a mere jumble of dissociated words." At the height of her spells, birds spoke to her in Greek, her dead mother reappeared and scolded her, and voices commanded her to "do wild things." She refused to eat, wrote pages of nonsense, and launched tirades of abuse at her husband and her companions (Dally, 1999, p. 240).

Between these phases, Woolf somehow managed a brilliant literary life. Her Victorian family had seen no reason for a woman to attend university, but the absence of schooling did not prevent her from becoming the extraordinary intellectual figure celebrated in the title of Edward Albee's play *Who's Afraid of Virginia Woolf?* (1962). All told, she produced nine novels, a play, five volumes of essays, and more than 14 volumes of diaries and letters. Her novels broke away from traditions of strict plot and setting to explore the inner lives and musings of her characters, and her observations revealed a keen appreciation of her own experience of psychological disorder. In a letter to a friend, she remarked, "As an experience, madness is terrific . . . and not to be sniffed at, and in its lava I still find most of the things I write about" (Dally, 1999, p. 240). The price that Woolf paid for her genius, of course, was a dear one, and her husband and companions shared the burden of dealing with her disorder. Disorders of the mind can create immense pain.

English novelist and critic Virginia Woolf (1882–1941), 1902. Her lifelong affliction with bipolar disorder ended in suicide, but the manic phases of her illness helped to fuel her prolific writing.

GEORGE C. BERESFORD/HULTON ARCHIVE/GETTY IMAGES

ymptoms reflecting abnormalities of the mind, called *psychological,* or *mental, disorders,* are hard to define and explain. Psychiatrists and psychologists agree that a psychological disorder is not, say, extreme anxiety before a chemistry test or deep sadness at the death of a beloved pet. To qualify as a mental disorder, thoughts, feelings, and emotions must be persistent, harmful to the person experiencing them, and uncontrollable. Approximately 40% of people will develop some type of mental disorder during the course of their lives—at a substantial cost in health, productivity, and happiness (Kessler et al., 1994; Narrow et al., 2002; Regier et al., 1993; Robins & Regier, 1991). Data compiled by the Global Burden of Disease study reveal that after cardiovascular disease, mental disorders are the second-greatest contributor to a loss of years of healthy life (Murray & Lopez, 1996). Problems of the head are nearly as great a plague on humanity as problems of the heart.

Psychologists who study mental disorders seek to uncover ways to understand, treat, and prevent such human misery. And because the mindbugs they uncover reveal the mind's limits and functions, the study of mental disorders offers insights into the nature of normal mental functioning. This chapter goes deeper into the study of mindbugs than does any other chapter of the book because it is devoted to the psychological problems that are so persistent and intense that they interfere with people's lives. In discovering what goes wrong in psychological disorder, we learn what the mind must do in order to run trouble free. As Virginia Woolf's emotional roller coaster makes clear, for example, the normal mind must regulate its moods to maintain emotional stability.

The study of psychological disorders can be unsettling because you may well see yourself mirrored in the various conditions. Like medical students who come to worry about their own symptoms with each new disease they examine, students of abnormal psychology can catch their own version of "medical students' disease," noticing personal oddities as they read about the peculiarities of others (Woods, Natterson, & Silverman, 1966). Is your late-night frenzy to finish an assignment a kind of mania? Is your fear of snakes a phobia? Does forgetting where you left your keys qualify you for diagnosis with a dissociative disorder? Please relax. You may not always avoid self-diagnosis, but you're not alone. Studying mental disorders heightens everyone's sensitivity to his or her own eccentricities. In fact, you would be "abnormal" if studying mental disorders *didn't* make you reflect on yourself.

In this chapter, we first consider the question: What is abnormal? Virginia Woolf's bouts of depression and mania and her eventual suicide certainly seem abnormal, but at times, she was fine. The enormously complicated human mind can produce behaviors, thoughts, and emotions that change radically from moment to moment. How do psychologists decide that a particular mind is disordered? We will examine the key factors that must be weighed in making such a decision. Our exploration of psychological disorders will then focus on each of several major forms of mental disorder, including anxiety disorders, dissociative disorders, mood disorders, schizophrenia, and personality disorders. As we view each of these problems, we will look at how they can influence the person's thought and behavior and at what is known about their prevalence and their causes.

Identifying Psychological Disorders: What Is Abnormal?

The idea of a *psychological disorder* is a relatively recent invention, historically speaking. People who act strangely or report bizarre thoughts or emotions have been known since ancient times, but their difficulties were often understood in the context of religion or the supernatural. In some cultures and religious traditions, madness is still interpreted as possession by animal spirits or demons, as enchantment by a witch or

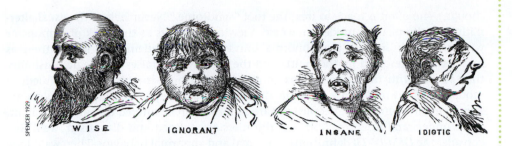

SPENCER 1929

WISE   IGNORANT   INSANE   IDIOTIC

According to the theory of "physiognomy," mental disorders could be diagnosed from facial features. This fanciful theory is now discredited as superstition but was popular from antiquity until the early 20th century.

shaman, or as God's punishment for wrongdoing. In many societies, including our own, people with mental abnormalities have commonly been treated as criminals—punished, imprisoned, or put to death for their "crime" of deviating from the normal. Madness has been feared and ridiculed, and people with mental problems have often been victims of grave maltreatment. Over the past 200 years, these ways of looking at psychological abnormalities have largely been replaced in industrialized areas of the world by a **medical model**, *the conceptualization of psychological abnormalities as diseases that, like biological diseases, have symptoms and causes and possible cures.*

Treating abnormal behavior in the way we treat illness suggests that a first step is to determine the nature of the problem through *diagnosis*. In diagnosis, clinicians seek to determine the nature of the patient's mental disease by assessing *symptoms*—behaviors, thoughts, and emotions suggestive of an underlying abnormal *syndrome*, a coherent cluster of symptoms usually due to a single cause. So, for example, just as a fever, sniffles, and cough are symptoms of a cold, wild behavior, refusal to eat, and tirades of abuse may point to an episode of the syndrome called *mania*.

To facilitate diagnosis, psychologists have generally adopted an approach developed by psychiatrists—the physicians concerned with treatment of mental disorders—who use a system for classifying disorders that is published in the *Diagnostic and Statistical Manual of Mental Disorders (Fourth Edition, Text Revision)*, or *DSM-IV-TR* (American Psychiatric Association, 2000). The *DSM-IV-TR* is *a classification system that describes the features used to diagnose each recognized mental disorder and indicates how the disorder can be distinguished from other, similar problems.* Each disorder is named and classified as though it were a distinct illness.

As useful as the medical model can be, it should nonetheless be viewed with some skepticism. Every action or thought suggestive of abnormality cannot be traced to an underlying disease (American Psychiatric Association, 2000; Keisler, 1999; Persons, 1986). And, as you will discover in Chapter 14, some of the most successful treatments for abnormal behavior or thought focus on simply eliminating the behavior or

MEDICAL MODEL The conceptualization of psychological abnormalities as diseases that, like biological diseases, have symptoms and causes and possible cures.

DSM-IV-TR (Diagnostic and Statistical Manual of Mental Disorders [Fourth Edition, Text Revision].) A classification system that describes the features used to diagnose each recognized mental disorder and indicates how the disorder can be distinguished from other, similar problems.

ARCHIVO ICONOGRAFICO, S.A./CORBIS

Interior of a madhouse, Francisco de Goya (1746–1828), 1815–19. Early treatment of mental disorders amounted to little more than imprisonment.

thought—no effort is made to treat the root "syndrome." Nevertheless, the usual alternatives to the medical model are worse. Viewing disorders as the work of demons or witchcraft or sin suggests that abnormal minds must be condemned. Viewing them as matters to be resolved by the courts and the legal system raises the tragic possibility that people with mental problems should be punished. In this light, the medical model offers a wonderfully humane alternative: Because psychological disorders are seen as medical problems, people who are suffering can be offered care and treatment.

To understand how psychological disorders are defined and diagnosed, we'll first consider the *DSM-IV-TR* definitions of normal and abnormal behavior. Then we'll look at how mental disorders are categorized into groups, how the causes and cures of disorders are viewed in the medical model, and what consequences can occur—for better or for worse—when such disorders are diagnosed.

Defining the Boundaries of Normality

The 2001 film *A Beautiful Mind* tells the story of John Nash, the brilliant, quirky Nobel Prize–winning mathematician, as he gradually develops schizophrenia. The movie conveys his passage into psychological disorder very subtly, making it difficult for the viewer to realize that he has lost touch with reality until his abnormality suddenly looms. In case you haven't seen it, we'll only say that Nash's transition is startling and the film is well worth the rental fee. Mental disorders do not always announce themselves with a cinematic flourish, however, so it is helpful to understand how to draw this line. What makes a mind disordered?

A major misconception is the idea that a mental disorder can be defined entirely in terms of deviation from the average, the typical, or "healthy." Yes, people who have mental disorders may behave, think, or experience emotions in unusual ways, but simple departure from the norm can't be the whole picture, or we'd rapidly be diagnosing mental disorders in the most creative and visionary people. Sorry, Einstein, that theory's kind of weird. Ugh, Picasso, those paintings don't seem normal. And if deviation were the only sign of mental disorder, people who experience events that force them to be deviant—such as extremely stressful or bizarre situations that require unusual responses—would also be diagnosable. If you scream bloody murder and become wildly agitated when someone runs toward you carrying a homemade bomb, does that mean that *you* have the mental disorder?

Russell Crowe as mathematician John Nash in *A Beautiful Mind.* The border between normal and abnormal was not clear when Nash first developed symptoms of schizophrenia.

The *DSM-IV-TR* definition takes these concerns into account by focusing on three key elements that must be present for a cluster of symptoms to qualify as a potential mental disorder:

- A disorder is manifested in symptoms that involve *disturbances in behavior, thoughts, or emotions.*
- The symptoms are associated with significant *personal distress or impairment.*
- The symptoms stem from an *internal dysfunction* (biological, psychological, or both).

So, for example, if someone seems elated and this "emotional disturbance" doesn't distress her or impair her job or life, then her behavior doesn't fit the criteria. Another example: Personal distress caused by the loss of a loved one is not indicative of a mental disorder because bereavement is a normal, expected response that does not originate from internal dysfunction. Similarly, political dissidence and social deviance are not necessarily signs of mental disorder unless they arise from some internal dysfunction that also causes personal distress or impairment. Actually, of course, the person who *doesn't* react violently to a bomb-wielding stranger might be the one with a mental disorder. As carefully qualified as it is, however, the classification system is far from perfect (Widiger & Sankis, 2000). For example, posttraumatic stress disorder (discussed in Chapter 15) is included in the *DSM-IV-TR,* implying that its source is internal, but the condition is defined as resulting from a severe (external) traumatic event (Kutchins & Kirk, 1997).

Thus, the three elements can serve only as general guidelines because mental disorders are so complex, assume so many different forms, and present with varying levels of severity and symptoms. When Virginia Woolf eventually became suicidal, for example, she suffered the ultimate impairment, and a diagnosis of depression was certainly warranted. But what of Woolf's periods of calm between mania and depression, when she felt no pain and was writing away merrily? Did she then have a mental disorder?

As these questions make clear, determining the degree to which a person has a mental disorder is always difficult: Mental disorder exists along a continuum from normal to abnormal without a bright line of separation. The *DSM-IV-TR* recognizes this explicitly by recommending that diagnosis include a *global assessment of functioning,* a 0 to 100 rating of the person, with more severe disorders indicated by lower numbers and more effective functioning by higher numbers (see **TABLE 13.1** on the next page). In addition to this general assessment, the *DSM-IV-TR* includes a system for the classification of disorders into different categories.

Social disorder isn't mental disorder. Violence erupted in central Paris in March 2006 as rioters took over the protest march about a controversial labor law, hurling rocks and bottles at police and lighting cars and shops ablaze. Rioting might seem disordered on the surface, but the *DSM-IV-TR* definition of mental disorders rules out political dissidence and social deviance.

AXELLE DE RUSSE/ABACAUSA/NEWSCOM/KCP

| Table **13.1** | Global Assessment of Functioning (GAF) Scale |

Code	Description
100 91	**Superior functioning in a wide range of activities; life's problems never seem to get out of hand; the individual is sought out by others because of his or her many positive qualities. No symptoms.**
90 81	**Absent or minimal symptoms** (e.g., mild anxiety before an exam), **good functioning in all areas, interested and involved in a wide range of activities, socially effective, generally satisfied with life, no more than everyday problems or concerns** (e.g., an occasional argument with family members).
80 71	**If symptoms are present, they are transient and expectable reactions to psychosocial stressors** (e.g., difficulty concentrating after family argument); **the individual experiences no more than slight impairment in social, occupational, or school functioning** (e.g., temporarily falling behind in schoolwork).
70 61	**Some mild symptoms** (e.g., depressed mood and mild insomnia) **OR some difficulty in social, occupational, or school functioning** (e.g., occasional truancy or theft within the household), **but the individual generally functions pretty well and is able to have some meaningful interpersonal relationships.**
60 51	**Moderate symptoms** (e.g., flat affect and circumstantial speech, occasional panic attacks) **OR moderate difficulty in social, occupational, or school functioning** (e.g., few friends, conflicts with peers or co-workers).
50 41	**Serious symptoms** (e.g., suicidal ideation, severe obsessional rituals, frequent shoplifting) **OR any serious impairment in social, occupational, or school functioning** (e.g., no friends, unable to keep a job).
40 31	**Some impairment in reality testing or communication** (e.g., speech is at times illogical, obscure, or irrelevant) **OR major impairment in several areas, such as work or school, family relations, judgment, thinking, or mood** (e.g., depressed adult avoids friends, neglects family, and is unable to work; child frequently beats up younger children, is defiant at home, and is failing at school).
30 21	**Behavior is considerably influenced by delusions or hallucinations OR serious impairment in communication or judgment** (e.g., sometimes incoherent, acts grossly inappropriately, suicidal preoccupation) **OR inability to function in almost all areas** (e.g., stays in bed all day; no job, home, or friends).
20 11	**Some danger of hurting self or others** (e.g., suicide attempts without clear expectation of death; frequently violent; manic excitement) **OR occasionally fails to maintain minimal personal hygiene** (e.g., smears feces) **OR gross impairment in communication** (e.g., largely incoherent or mute).
10 1	**Persistent danger of severely hurting self or others** (e.g., recurrent violence) **OR persistent inability to maintain minimal personal hygiene OR serious suicidal act with clear expectation of death.**

Source: From the *DSM-IV-TR* (American Psychiatric Association, 2000).

Classification of Psychological Disorders

The *DSM-IV* classification system did not drop out of the sky fully formed; it has evolved as the fields of psychology and psychiatry have developed—and the revision process continues to this day. In the early 20th century, for example, European and North American clinicians typically divided disorders into two categories: *neurosis,* a condition that involves anxiety but in which the person is still in touch with reality, and *psychosis,* a condition in which the person experiences serious distortions of perception and thought that weaken his or her grasp on reality. Although many disorders fit these categories (obsessive-compulsive disorder as neurosis, for example, and schizophrenia as a form of psychosis), no consensus existed on the qualities present in the categories. The terms were mainly used to describe relative severity.

In 1952, in recognition of the need to have a consensual diagnostic system for therapists and researchers, the first version of the *Diagnostic and Statistical Manual of Mental Disorders (DSM)* was published, followed by a revision in 1968 *(DSM-II)*. These early versions provided a common language for talking about disorders, but the diagnostic criteria were still often vague and based on tenuous theoretical assumptions. For example, the *DSM-II* contained a description of *neurosis* that was based only on Freudian psychodynamic theory (discussed in Chapter 12). The definition was clear in specifying that "anxiety is the chief characteristic of the neuroses." However, it then went on to say that the anxiety "may be felt and expressed directly, or it may be controlled unconsciously and automatically by conversion, displacement, and various other psychological mechanisms" (p. 39). Even for an expert in Freudian theory, this definition is open to many interpretations. It suggests that the anxiety might or might not be felt and could be transformed into just about any sort of physical symptom (through conversion) or psychological symptom (through displacement)—and that any of these symptoms would count as neurosis. On the basis of this definition, everyone in the world is neurotic.

Not surprisingly, the early versions of the *DSM* led to unreliable diagnoses. As we explained in Chapter 2, unreliability of measurement leads to confusion about what is being measured. Clinicians using this system could come up with wildly different diagnoses of a particular cluster of symptoms, and so they still had to use their own judgment in deciding whether treatments were necessary and whether the treatments had helped the person, hurt the person, or had no effect.

To address the problem of reliability and promote better agreement among diagnosticians, developers of succeeding editions of the *DSM* have tried to define mental disorders as objectively as possible. Controversial, subjective theoretical concepts have been replaced with behavioral terms that allow clinicians to observe objectively and assess the frequency of disorders. The term *neurosis*, for example, has been replaced by a more concretely described classification called *anxiety disorders*, each of which is defined in terms of observable features such as excessive anxiety in general, excessive anxiety in a particular setting, and the like.

The major mental disorders distinguished in the *DSM-IV-TR* are shown in **TABLE 13.2** on the next page. Because the mind can go awry in such a remarkably large number of ways, however, the path to reliable diagnosis remains thorny. In general, the *DSM-IV-TR* produces better diagnostic reliability than did earlier versions, but critics argue that considerable room for improvement remains. Numerous diagnostic categories continue to depend on interpretation-based criteria rather than on observable behavior, and diagnosis continues to focus on patient self-reports (which are susceptible to censorship and distortion). Levels of agreement among different diagnosticians can vary depending on the diagnostic category (Bertelsen, 1999; Nathan & Lagenbucher, 1999). Agreement among diagnosticians on, say, whether a patient has schizophrenia may even depend on the clinic setting. Such disagreement may not reflect differences in the prevalence of schizophrenia in various localities but rather in the array of symptoms that the clinicians were trained to expect in people with the disease (Keller et al., 1995).

"First off, you're not a nut. You're a legume."

Table 13.2 | **Main *DSM-IV-TR* Categories of Mental Disorders**

1. **Disorders usually first diagnosed in infancy, childhood, or early adolescence:** These include mental retardation, bed-wetting, etc.

2. **Delirium, dementia, amnestic, and other cognitive disorders:** These are disorders of thinking caused by Alzheimer's, human immunodeficiency virus (HIV) and acquired immunodeficiency syndrome (AIDS), Parkinson's disease, etc.

3. **Mental disorders due to a general medical condition not elsewhere classified:** These include problems caused by physical deterioration of the brain due to disease, drug use, etc.

4. **Substance-related disorders:** These problems are caused by dependence on alcohol, cocaine, tobacco, and so forth (see Chapter 8).

5. **Schizophrenia and other psychotic disorders:** This is a group of disorders characterized by major disturbances in perception, language and thought, emotion, and behavior (this chapter).

6. **Mood disorders:** These are problems associated with severe disturbances of mood, such as depression, mania, or alternating episodes of both (this chapter).

7. **Anxiety disorders:** These include problems associated with severe anxiety, such as phobias and obsessive-compulsive disorder (this chapter), and posttraumatic stress disorder (see Chapter 15).

8. **Somatoform disorders:** These are problems related to unusual preoccupation with physical health or physical symptoms with no physical cause (see Chapter 15).

9. **Factitious disorders:** These are disorders that the individual adopts to satisfy some economic or psychological need (see Chapter 15).

10. **Dissociative disorder:** In these types of disorders, the normal integration of consciousness, memory, or identity is suddenly and temporarily altered, such as amnesia and dissociative identity disorder (this chapter).

11. **Sexual and gender identity disorders:** These include problems related to unsatisfactory sexual activity, finding unusual objects or situations arousing, gender identity problems, and so forth.

12. **Eating disorders:** These are problems related to food, such as anorexia nervosa and bulimia nervosa (see Chapter 10).

13. **Sleep disorders:** These include serious disturbances of sleep, such as insomnia, sleep terrors, or hypersomnia (see Chapter 8).

14. **Impulse control disorder not elsewhere classified:** These problems include kleptomania, pathological gambling, and pyromania.

15. **Adjustment disorders:** These problems are related to specific stressors such as divorce, family discord, and economic concern.

16. **Personality disorders:** These problems are related to lifelong behavior patterns such as self-centeredness, overdependency, and antisocial behaviors (this chapter).

17. **Other conditions that may be a focus of clinical attention:** These include problems related to physical or sexual abuse, relational problems, and occupational problems.

Source: From the *DSM-IV-TR* (American Psychiatric Association, 2000).

Diagnostic difficulty is further increased when a person suffers from more than one disorder. As shown in **FIGURE 13.1**, for example, people with depression (a mood disorder) often have secondary diagnoses of anxiety disorders. *The co-occurrence of two or more disorders in a single individual* is referred to as **comorbidity** and is relatively common in patients seen within the *DSM* diagnostic system (Kessler et al., 1994). Comorbidity raises a host of confusing possibilities: A person could be depressed because a

COMORBIDITY The co-occurrence of two or more disorders in a single individual.

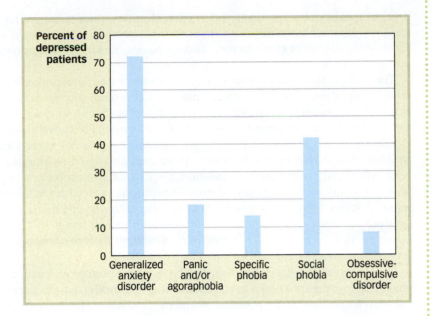

Figure 13.1 Comorbidity of Depression and Anxiety Disorders The comorbidity of depression and anxiety disorders is substantial. Of 102 patients whose primary diagnosis was depression (major depressive disorder or dysthymia), large percentages also had a secondary diagnosis of one or more anxiety disorders. (Brown, Campbell, Lehman, Grisham, & Mancill, 2001.)

phobia makes social situations impossible, or the person could be phobic about showing a despairing mood in public, or the disorders could be unrelated but co-occurring. Diagnosticians try hard to solve the problem of comorbidity because understanding the underlying basis for a person's disorder may suggest methods of treatment.

Classification and Causation

The medical model suggests that knowing a person's diagnosis is useful because any given category of mental illness is likely to have a distinctive cause. In other words, just as different viruses, or bacteria, or types of trauma, or genetic weakness cause different physical illnesses, so a specifiable pattern of causes (or *etiology*) may exist for different mental disorders. The medical model also suggests that each category of mental disorder is likely to have a common *prognosis*, a typical course over time and susceptibility to treatment and cure. Unfortunately, this basic medical model is usually an oversimplification—it is rarely useful to focus on a *single cause* that is *internal* to the person and that suggests a *single cure*.

"Mad Hatter syndrome," first described in the 1800s in workers who used a mercury compound in making felt hats, was one of those rare single-cause disorders. The symptoms: trembling, loss of memory and coordination, slurred speech, depression, and anxiety. The cause: mercury poisoning. The cure: getting out of the hat business. Things are seldom so simple, however, and a full explanation of all the different ways in which the mind can become disordered needs to take into account multiple levels of causation.

An integrated perspective that incorporates biological, psychological, and environmental factors offers the most comprehensive and useful framework for understanding most mental disorders. On the biological side, the focus is on genetic influences, biochemical imbalances, and structural abnormalities of the brain. The psychological perspective focuses on maladaptive learning and coping, cognitive biases, dysfunctional attitudes, and interpersonal problems. Environmental factors include poor socialization, stressful life circumstances, and cultural and social inequities. The complexity of causation suggests that different individuals can experience a similar mental disorder (e.g., depression) for different reasons. A person might fall into depression as a result of biological causes (e.g., genetics, hormones),

The Mad Hatter in *Alice in Wonderland* was Lewis Carroll's portrayal of a mental disorder common among hatmakers in the 1800s. Hatters could become "mad as a hatter" because they unwittingly exposed themselves to a mercury compound with serious side effects when they processed fur into felt for hats.

DIATHESIS-STRESS MODEL Suggests that a person may be predisposed for a mental disorder that remains unexpressed until triggered by stress.

psychological causes (e.g., faulty beliefs, hopelessness, poor strategies for coping with loss), environmental causes (e.g., stress or loneliness), or (more likely) as a result of some combination of these factors. And, of course, multiple causes pretty much rule out single cures.

The notion that causes of disorders are always internal can also lead to another error—that of overlooking external causes. What would be your reaction to a classmate who appeared one day with a bucket on her head and sat quietly through a lecture except for an occasional, mellow, bell-like cough? Pretty weird, you'd probably think. And you'd wonder: A stunt to get attention? A protest? Some kind of demonstration dreamed up by the professor? Does she actually think this is cool? Despite your consideration of external pressures (politics or the professor's request), you'd probably wind up focusing on internal dispositions (a need for attention or a poor sense of style). When trying to understand the behavior of others, people typically overlook external causes and focus on characteristics internal to the person. Such blindness to external causes is a common mindbug called the *fundamental attribution error* (discussed in Chapter 16).

The observation that most disorders have both internal *and* external causes has given rise to a theory known as the **diathesis-stress model**, which suggests that *a person may be predisposed for a mental disorder that remains unexpressed until triggered by stress.* The diathesis is the internal predisposition, and the stress is the external trigger. For example, most people were able to cope with their strong emotional reactions to the terrorist attack of September 11, 2001. However, for some who had a predisposition to negative emotions or were already contending with major life stressors, the horror of the events may have overwhelmed their ability to cope, thereby precipitating a mental disorder.

A diathesis can be inherited. Like mental abilities (see Chapter 9) and personality traits (see Chapter 12), mental disorders vary in their *heritability*. However, inherent in the notion that stressful conditions are necessary for the disorder to manifest itself is the assumption that heritability is not destiny. A person who inherits a diathesis may never encounter the precipitating stress, whereas someone with little genetic propensity to a disorder may come to suffer from it given the right pattern of stress. The relationship between diathesis and stress can snowball—growing over time because an initial vulnerability becomes more severe as the individual reacts to the stress. Imagine Maria, for example, who has a genetic predisposition to be introverted and sensitive to social rejection and who is snubbed at a party by someone she thought was her friend. She might start avoiding this "friend" and others to prevent another rejection. Over time, Maria gets a reputation as a loner and is shunned again and again. She has the same reaction each time and eventually becomes so withdrawn that depression and anxiety result. Diathesis and stress can work together subtly over time, making it a challenge to pick apart etiological factors.

The tendency to oversimplify mental disorders by attributing them to single, internal causes is nowhere more evident than in the interpretation of the role of the brain in mental disorders. Brain scans of people with and without disorders can give rise to

Feeling lonely and depressed? Join the society of loners!

an unusually strong impression that psychological problems are internal—after all, there it is!—and perhaps also permanent, inevitable, and even untreatable. It's as if tracing a disorder to a patient's brain renders him or her immune from other influences. For example, discovering that the brains of individuals with depression show unique patterns of activation (discussed later in this chapter) may make it difficult to appreciate external causes of this disorder. Falling prey to this kind of mindbug is about as useful as assuming that, having learned about the role of the olfactory area of the brain in perceiving the fragrance of the rose, we no longer need any roses! Brain influences and processes are fundamentally important for knowing the full story of mental disorders but are not the only chapter in that story (see the Real World box on the facing page).

{ THE REAL WORLD } Cultural Variants of Abnormal Behavior

PEOPLE DRESS DIFFERENTLY IN DIFFERENT parts of the world, they eat differently, they speak differently—and it turns out they can have different mental disorders as well. Cultural and societal factors can play an important role in the development and expression of abnormal behavior. Consider *anorexia nervosa,* an eating disorder that primarily afflicts young women, which is characterized by intense fear of gaining weight, and often leads to extreme weight loss (discussed in Chapter 10). This disorder is far more prevalent in industrialized societies, where models and movie stars who attain unrealistic thinness represent the feminine ideal, than in nonindustrialized countries, where a heavier, more rounded body type is considered beautiful (Hsu, 1990). This cultural difference is even "catching," as Middle Eastern and Asian women have been found to increase their risk for anorexia when they move to Western countries to live or study (Mumford, Whitehouse, & Platts, 1991; Nasser, 1986).

Looking at cross-cultural differences reveals how different socialization practices can foster different psychological problems and how cultural expectations shape our perceptions of those problems. For example, in Western societies, depression and anxiety are frequent reactions to stressful life experiences. However, in China, the effects of stress are more likely to be manifested in physical problems, such as fatigue, weakness, and other bodily complaints (Kleinman, 1986, 1988). Such differences suggest that it is a mistake to presume that the *DSM-IV-TR* is universal across cultures. Psychologists need to tailor their diagnoses to accommodate culture-specific issues that may contribute to clients' problems. Indeed, evidence is mounting that treatment is more effective when therapists are knowledgeable about their clients' cultures (Sue et al., 1991; Tharp, 1991; Yeh, Takeuchi, & Sue, 1994).

To aid researchers and therapists in their quest to understand the relevance of cultural factors to mental health, the *DSM-IV-TR* includes a description of various "culture-bound syndromes." Culture-bound syndromes are not official diagnostic categories, but some of them share elements with standard *DSM-IV-TR* diagnoses. Here's a sample.

- *Ataque de nervios.* A type of distress principally reported among Latinos from the Caribbean but recognized in many Latin American and Latin Mediterranean groups. Commonly reported symptoms include uncontrollable shouting, attacks of crying, trembling, heat in the chest rising into the head, and verbal or physical aggression. Seizurelike or fainting episodes and suicidal gestures are prominent in some attacks but absent in others. *Ataques de nervios* are frequently precipitated by a stressful event relating to the family (e.g., death of a close relative, an accident involving a family member). Victims may experience amnesia for what occurred during the *ataque de nervios* but then typically return rapidly to their usual level of functioning.

- Ghost sickness. A preoccupation with death and the dead (sometimes associated with witchcraft) observed among members of many American Indian tribes. Various symptoms can be attributed to ghost sickness, including bad dreams, weakness, feelings of danger, loss of appetite, fainting, dizziness, fear, anxiety, hallucinations, loss of consciousness, confusion, feelings of futility, and a sense of suffocation.

- *Koro.* A term, probably of Malaysian origin, that refers to an episode of sudden and intense anxiety that the penis (or in females, the vulva and nipples) will recede into the body and possibly cause death. The syndrome is reported in South and East Asia, where it is known by a variety of local terms, such as *shuk yang, shook yong,* and *suo yang* (Chinese); *jinjinia bemar* (Assam); or *rok-jooi* (Thailand). At times, *koro* occurs in local epidemics in East Asian areas.

- *Mal de ojo.* A concept widely found in Mediterranean cultures (such as Italy, Spain, Turkey, Morocco, and Israel) and elsewhere in the world (such as Mexico). *Mal de ojo* is a Spanish phrase translated into English as "evil eye" and is believed to result from looking at someone, usually a child, with envy. The target of the envy can develop a variety of symptoms, including fitful sleep, crying without apparent cause, diarrhea, vomiting, and fever.

These and other culture-bound syndromes reveal that disorders of the mind can be more difficult to define than disorders of the body. Unlike a common cold, which has the same symptoms around the world, mental disorders can express themselves differently in different cultures. Many of the major forms of disorder (for example, schizophrenia) do appear to be stable across cultures, however, and the culture-bound disorders should be viewed as exceptional. The medical model doesn't seem to tell the whole story about disorders of the mind, though, because "diseases" that vary between cultures might not be diseases at all and instead may be socially shared ways of expressing and interpreting symptoms.

CHRISTIE'S IMAGES

El Curandero, **Diego Rivera (1886–1957), 1948. In some communities in Mexico, a** *curandero,* **or folk healer, might be sought for treatment of** *mal de ojo.*

Searching for the biological causes of mental disorders in the brain and body also tends to invite a particular error in explanation—the *intervention-causation fallacy*. This fallacy involves the assumption that if a treatment is effective, it must address the cause of the problem. Thus, if a patient responds favorably to drugs or other biological interventions, the cause of the disorder is attributed to biology. Conversely, if a psychological intervention such as psychotherapy alleviates the symptoms, psychological factors are seen as the root of the problem. This may sometimes be true, but it is certainly not a general rule. To get a sense of the error in this logic, imagine that you've spent sleepless night after sleepless night worrying about a loved one who was recently hospitalized with a serious illness. You discover that taking a sleeping medicine before bed helps you sleep. On the basis of your favorable response, should we conclude that your insomnia was caused by a deficiency of sleeping pills—that a part of your brain needed the chemicals in the pills? Of course not. Your anxiety and sleeplessness were due to your loved one's illness, not to the absence of a pill. Be cautious about drawing inferences about causality based on responsiveness to treatment; the cure does not necessarily point to the cause.

The diagnosis and classification of mental disorders is a useful basis for exploring causes and cures of psychological problems. At the same time, these tools make it all too easy to assume that the problems arise from single, internal causes that are inherited and involve brain dysfunction—and that therefore can be dispelled with an intervention that simply eliminates the cause. Psychological problems are usually more challenging and complicated than this ideal model would suggest.

Consequences of Labeling

What would your life be like if your nickname was "Crazy"? On hearing your name, people might treat you as if you were odd, and you might find yourself responding by becoming irritated, sullen, or even downright strange. In the same way, psychiatric labels can have negative consequences despite mental health workers' good intensions when they use them in diagnosis. The labels carry excess baggage in the form of negative stereotypes, and these can create new problems.

The stigma associated with mental disorders may help explain why nearly 70% of people with diagnosable mental disorders do not seek treatment (Kessler et al., 1996; Regier et al., 1993; Sussman, Robins, & Earls, 1987). Many people believe that a mental disorder is a sign of personal weakness or a consequence of wrongdoing (Angermeyer & Matschinger, 1996a). Another widespread belief falsely suggests that psychiatric patients are dangerous (Angermeyer & Matschinger, 1996b; Phelan et al., 2000; Wolff et al., 1996), despite considerable evidence that such people are not violent (Eronen, Angermeyer, & Schulze, 1998; Steadman et al., 1998; Swanson, 1994; Torrey, 1994). In light of these misconceptions, a watchful concern and even avoidance when in the presence of individuals with mental disorders is not surprising (Link et al., 1999). To steer clear of these difficulties, people with mental disorders often try to keep their problems secret.

Unfortunately, educating people about mental disorders does not dispel the stigma borne by those with these diseases (Phelan et al., 1997). In fact, expectations created by psychiatric labels can sometimes even compromise the judgment of mental health professionals (Garb, 1998; Langer & Abelson, 1974; Temerlin & Trousdale, 1969). In the classic demonstration of this phenomenon, American psychologist David Rosenhan and six associates reported to different mental hospitals complaining of "hearing voices"—a symptom sometimes found in people with schizophrenia. Each was admitted to a hospital as a result of this feigned complaint, and each then promptly reported that the symptom had ceased. Many of their fellow patients soon identified them as normal, but hospital staffs were much more reluctant to make this decision. It took an average of 19 days for the false patients to secure their release, with a high of 62 days and a low of 9 days. Even then, they were released with the diagnosis of "schizophrenia in remission"—a sticky label indeed (Rosenhan, 1973).

If psychiatric labeling conjures biases in both the general public and psychiatric hospital staff, does it also adversely affect the self-view of the person who is labeled?

At the extreme, some commentators, such as the sociologist Thomas Scheff (1984), have claimed that labels for mental disorders actually serve to create the disorders. Some evidence for this position exists (see Chapter 14), but few believe that the millions of people worldwide who suffer mental disorders do so merely because they have received diagnoses. More likely is the possibility that the labeled person comes to view the self negatively—not just as mentally disordered but also as hopeless or worthless. People who think poorly of themselves can develop attitudes of defeat and as a result may fail to work toward their own recovery. In one small step toward counteracting such consequences, clinicians have adopted the important practice of applying labels to the disorder and not to the people who have disorders. For example, a patient might be described as "a person with schizophrenia" rather than as "a schizophrenic." You'll note that we follow this model in the text.

"We don't use the word 'crazy' in this office, Mr. Channing. Everywhere else, sure, but not here."

In summary, the study of abnormal psychology follows a medical model in which symptoms are understood to indicate an underlying disorder. To diagnose a disorder, psychiatrists and psychologists use the *DSM-IV-TR*, a classification system that defines a mental disorder as occurring when the person experiences disturbances of thought, emotion, or behavior that produce distress or impairment and that arise from internal sources. The classification system includes a global assessment of functioning and a set of categories of disorder. Comorbidity of disorders is common, and the idea that a disorder has a single, internal cause is often an oversimplification because many disorders arise from multiple causes or as a result of the interaction of diathesis and stress. It is also an error to assume that the intervention that cures a disorder reflects the cause of the disorder. The classification of disorders brings with it the possibility of a significant stigma that can create its own problems. When a person is given a diagnosis, the label can be difficult to overcome because the label changes how the person is perceived by mental health workers, by others, and even by the self. ■ ■

Anxiety Disorders: When Fears Take Over

"Okay, time for a pop quiz that will be half your grade for this class!" If your instructor had actually said that, you would probably have experienced a wave of anxiety and dread. Your reaction would be appropriate and—no matter how intense the feeling—would not be a sign that you have a mental disorder. In fact, situation-related anxiety is normal and can be adaptive—in this case, perhaps by reminding you to keep up with your textbook assignments so you are prepared for pop quizzes. When anxiety arises that is out of proportion to real threats and challenges, however, it is maladaptive: It can take hold of people's lives, stealing their peace of mind and undermining their ability to function normally. Pathological anxiety is expressed as an **anxiety disorder**, *the class of mental disorder in which anxiety is the predominant feature.* People commonly experience more than one type of anxiety disorder at a given time, and there is significant comorbidity between anxiety and depression (Brown & Barlow, 2002). Among the anxiety disorders recognized in the *DSM-IV-TR* are *generalized anxiety disorder, phobic disorders, panic disorder,* and *obsessive-compulsive disorder.*

Generalized Anxiety Disorder

Terry, a 31-year-old man, began to experience debilitating anxiety during his first year as an internal medicine resident. The 36-hour on-call periods were grueling, and he became concerned that he and other interns were making too many errors and oversights. He worried incessantly for a year and finally resigned his position. However, he continued to be plagued with anxiety about making mistakes—self-doubt that extended to his personal relationships. When he eventually sought treatment,

ANXIETY DISORDER The class of mental disorder in which anxiety is the predominant feature.

GENERALIZED ANXIETY DISORDER (GAD) A disorder characterized by chronic excessive worry accompanied by three or more of the following symptoms: restlessness, fatigue, concentration problems, irritability, muscle tension, and sleep disturbance.

he described himself as "worthless" and unable to control his debilitating anxiety, and he complained of headaches and constant fatigue (Vitkus, 1996).

Terry's symptoms are typical of **generalized anxiety disorder (GAD)**—called *generalized* because the unrelenting worries are not focused on any particular threat; they are, in fact, often exaggerated and irrational. In people suffering from GAD, *chronic excessive worry is accompanied by three or more of the following symptoms: restlessness, fatigue, concentration problems, irritability, muscle tension, and sleep disturbance.* The uncontrollable worrying produces a sense of loss of control that can so erode self-confidence that simple decisions seem fraught with dire consequences. For example, Terry needed to buy a new suit for a special occasion but began shaking and sweating when he approached a clothing store because he was afraid of choosing the "wrong" suit. He became so anxious that he could not even enter the store.

About 5% of North Americans are estimated to suffer from GAD at some time in their lives (Kessler et al., 1994). GAD occurs more frequently in lower-socioeconomic groups than in middle- and upper-income groups (Blazer et al., 1991) and is approximately twice as common in women as in men (Eaton, Kessler, Wittchen, & McGee, 1994). Research suggests that both biological and psychological factors contribute to the risk of GAD. Family studies indicate a mild to modest level of heritability (Kendler et al., 1992; Mackinnon & Foley, 1996; Plomin et al., 1997). Although identical twin studies of GAD are rare, some evidence suggests that compared with fraternal twins, identical twins have modestly higher *concordance rates* (the percentage of pairs that share the characteristic) (Hettema, Neale, & Kendler, 2001). Moreover, teasing out environmental versus personality influences on concordance rates is quite difficult.

Some patients with GAD respond to certain prescription drugs, which suggests that neurotransmitter imbalances may play a role in the disorder. The precise nature of this imbalance is not clear, but *benzodiazepines*—a class of sedative drugs discussed in Chapter 8 (e.g., Valium, Librium) that appear to stimulate the neurotransmitter *gamma-aminobutyric acid (GABA)*—can sometimes reduce the symptoms of GAD. However, other drugs that do not directly affect GABA levels (e.g., buspirone and antidepressants such as Prozac) can also be helpful in the treatment of GAD (Gobert, Rivet, Cistarelli, Mellon, & Millan, 1999; Michelson et al., 1999; Roy-Byrne & Cowley, 1998). To complicate matters, these different prescription drugs do not help all patients and, in some cases, can produce serious side effects and dependency.

Psychological explanations focus on anxiety-provoking situations in explaining high levels of GAD. The condition is especially prevalent among people who have low incomes, are living in large cities, or are trapped in environments rendered unpredictable by political and economic strife. The relatively high rates of GAD among

Potential anxiety victims? Generalized anxiety disorder is more common for women and children living below the poverty line than for others.

WOLFGANG SPUNBARG/PHOTO EDIT

women may also be related to stress because women are more likely than men to live in poverty, experience discrimination, or be subjected to sexual or physical abuse (Koss, 1990; Strickland, 1991). Research shows that unpredictable traumatic experiences in childhood increase the risk of developing GAD, and this evidence also supports the idea that stressful experiences play a role (Torgensen, 1986). Moreover, major life changes (new job, new baby, personal loss, physical illness, and so forth) often immediately precede the development of GAD (Blazer, Hughes, & George, 1987). Still, many people who might be expected to develop GAD don't, supporting the diathesis-stress notion that personal vulnerability must also be a key factor in this disorder.

Phobic Disorders

Unlike the generalized anxiety of GAD, anxiety in a phobic disorder is more specific. The *DSM* describes **phobic disorders** as characterized by *marked, persistent, and excessive fear and avoidance of specific objects, activities, or situations.* An individual with a phobic disorder recognizes that the fear is irrational but cannot prevent it from interfering with everyday functioning. Consider Mary, a 47-year-old mother of three, who sought treatment for *claustrophobia*—an intense fear of enclosed spaces. She traced her fear to childhood, when her older siblings would scare her by locking her in closets and confining her under blankets. Her own children grown, she wanted to find a job but could not because of a terror of elevators and other confined places that, she felt, shackled her to her home (Carson, Butcher, & Mineka, 2000). Many people feel anxious in enclosed spaces, but Mary's fears were abnormal and dysfunctional because they were wildly disproportional to any actual risk and because they imposed unwanted restrictions on her life.

A **specific phobia** is *an irrational fear of a particular object or situation that markedly interferes with an individual's ability to function.* Specific phobias fall into five categories: (1) animals (e.g., dogs, cats, rats, snakes, spiders); (2) natural environments (e.g., heights, darkness, water, storms); (3) situations (e.g., bridges, elevators, tunnels, enclosed places); (4) blood, injections, and injury; and (5) other phobias, including illness and death. Most people expect many more categories because they've heard some of the fanciful Greek or Latin terms invented for very specific phobias. One website lists phobias (www.phobialist.com) that include, among others, "kathisophobia" (a fear of sitting down), "homichlophobia" (fear of fog), and "ephebiphobia" (fear of teenagers). The terms sound technical enough to be included in the *DSM*, but you

PHOBIC DISORDERS Disorders characterized by marked, persistent, and excessive fear and avoidance of specific objects, activities, or situations.

SPECIFIC PHOBIA A disorder that involves an irrational fear of a particular object or situation that markedly interferes with an individual's ability to function.

No fear of heights here. Construction workers eat their lunches atop a steel beam 800 feet above ground during the 1932 construction of the RCA Building (now the GE Building) in Rockefeller Center in Manhattan.

BETTMANN/CORBIS

won't find them there. These curious pseudo-medical terms obscure the fact that specific phobias share common symptoms and are merely aimed at different objects. Approximately 11% of people in the United States will develop a specific phobia during their lives and—for unknown reasons—the risk seems to be increasing in younger generations (Magee et al., 1996). With few exceptions (e.g., fear of heights), specific phobias are much more common among women than among men, with a ratio of about 4 to 1 (Kessler et al., 1994; Kessler et al., 1996).

Social phobia involves *an irrational fear of being publicly humiliated or embarrassed.* Social phobia can be restricted to situations such as public speaking, eating in public, or urinating in a public bathroom or generalized to a variety of social situations that involve being observed or interacting with unfamiliar people. Individuals with social phobia try to avoid situations where unfamiliar people might evaluate them, and they experience intense anxiety and distress when public exposure is unavoidable. Social phobia can develop in childhood, but it typically emerges between early adolescence and the age of 25 (Schneier et al., 1992). Many people experience social phobia—about 11% of men and 15% of women qualify for diagnosis at some time in their lives (Kessler et al., 1994). Even higher rates are found among people who are undereducated, have low incomes, or both (Magee et al., 1996).

Why are phobias so common? The high rates of both specific and social phobias suggest a predisposition to be fearful of certain objects and situations. Indeed, most of the situations and objects of people's phobias could pose a real threat—for example, falling from a high place or being attacked by a vicious dog or poisonous snake or spider. Social situations have their own dangers. A roomful of strangers may not attack or bite, but they could form impressions that affect your prospects for friends, jobs, or marriage. And of course, in some very rare cases, they could attack or bite.

Observations such as these are the basis for the **preparedness theory** of phobia, which maintains that *people are instinctively predisposed toward certain fears.* The preparedness theory, proposed by Martin E. P. Seligman (1971), is supported by research showing that both humans and monkeys can quickly be conditioned to have a fear response for stimuli such as snakes and spiders but not for neutral stimuli such as flowers or toy rabbits (Cook & Mineka, 1989; Öhman, Dimberg, & Ost, 1985). Similarly, research on facial expressions has shown that people are more easily conditioned to fear angry facial expressions than other types of expressions (Öhman & Dimberg, 1978; Öhman, Dimberg, & Ost, 1985). Phobias are particularly likely to form for objects that evolution has predisposed us to avoid. This idea is also supported by studies of the heritability of phobias. Family studies of specific phobias indicate greater concordance rates for identical than for fraternal twins (Kendler, Myers, & Prescott, 2002; Kendler et al., 1992; O'Laughlin & Malle, 2002). Other studies have found that over 30% of first-degree relatives (parents, siblings, or children) of patients with specific phobias also have a phobia (Fryer et al., 1990).

Temperament may also play a role in vulnerability to phobias. Researchers have found that infants who display excessive shyness and inhibition are at an increased risk for developing a phobic behavior later in life (Hirschfeld et al., 1992; Morris, 2001; Stein, Chavira, & Jang, 2001). Neurobiological factors may also play a role. Abnormalities in the neurotransmitters serotonin and dopamine are more common in individuals who report phobias than they are among people who don't (Stein, 1998). In addition, individuals with phobias sometimes show abnormally high levels of activity in the amygdala, an area of the brain linked with the development of emotional associations (discussed in Chapter 10 and in Hirschfeld et al., 1992; LeDoux, 1998; Morris, 2001; Ninan, 1999; Stein et al., 2001).

This evidence does not rule out the influence of environments and upbringing on the development of phobic overreactions. As learning theorist John Watson (1924b) demonstrated many years ago, phobias can be classically conditioned (see our Chapter 6 discussion of Little Albert and the white rat). Similarly, the discomfort of a dog bite could create a conditioned association between dogs and pain, resulting in an irrational fear of all dogs. The idea that phobias are learned from emotional experiences with feared objects, however, is not a complete explanation for the occurrence of phobias. Most studies find

SOCIAL PHOBIA A disorder that involves an irrational fear of being publicly humiliated or embarrassed.

PREPAREDNESS THEORY The idea that people are instinctively predisposed toward certain fears.

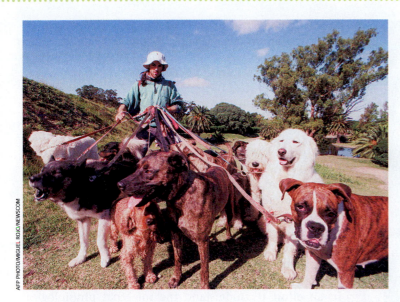

To someone with a phobia of dogs, there are no best friends in this park.

that people with phobias are no more likely than people without phobias to recall personal experiences with the feared object that could have provided the basis for classical conditioning (Craske, 1999; McNally & Steketec, 1985). Moreover, many people are bitten by dogs, but few develop phobias. Despite its shortcomings, however, the idea that this is a matter of learning provides a useful model for therapy (see Chapter 14).

Panic Disorder

If you suddenly found yourself in danger of death, a wave of panic might wash over you. People who suffer panic attacks are frequently overwhelmed by such intense fears and by powerful physical symptoms of anxiety—in the absence of actual danger. Mindy, a 25-year-old art director, had been having panic attacks with increasing frequency, often two or three times a day, when she finally sought help at a clinic. The attacks began with a sudden wave of "horrible fear" that seemed to come out of nowhere, often accompanied by trembling, nausea, and a tightening of the chest. The attacks began when she was in high school and had continued intermittently ever since. During an episode, Mindy feared that she would do something crazy (Spitzer et al., 1994, pp. 201–202).

Mindy's condition, called **panic disorder,** is characterized by *the sudden occurrence of multiple psychological and physiological symptoms that contribute to a feeling of stark terror.* The acute symptoms of a panic attack typically last only a few minutes and include shortness of breath, heart palpitations, sweating, dizziness, depersonalization (a feeling of being detached from one's body) or derealization (a feeling that the external world is strange or unreal), and a fear that one is going crazy or about to die. Not surprisingly, panic attacks often send people rushing to emergency rooms or their physicians' offices for what they believe is either an acute cardiac, respiratory, or neurological episode (Hirschfeld, 1996). Unfortunately, because many of the symptoms mimic various medical disorders, a correct diagnosis may take years in spite of costly medical tests that produce normal results (Hirschfeld, 1996; Katon, 1994). According to the *DSM-IV-TR* diagnostic criteria, a person has panic disorder only on experiencing recurrent unexpected attacks and reporting significant anxiety about having another attack.

A common complication of panic disorder is **agoraphobia,** *extreme fear of venturing into public places.* Many individuals with agoraphobia are not frightened of public places in themselves; instead, they are afraid of having a panic attack in a public place or around strangers who might view them with disdain or fail to help them. In severe cases, people who have panic disorder with agoraphobia are unable to leave home, sometimes for years on end.

PANIC DISORDER A disorder characterized by the sudden occurrence of multiple psychological and physiological symptoms that contribute to a feeling of stark terror.

AGORAPHOBIA An extreme fear of venturing into public places.

In panic disorder with agoraphobia, the fear of having a panic attack in public may prevent the person from going outside.

BOB DAEMMRICH/ THE IMAGE WORKS

Approximately 8% to 12% of the U.S. population reports having an occasional panic attack, typically during a period of intense stress (Norton et al., 1985; Salge, Beck, & Logan, 1988; Telch, Lucas, & Nelson, 1989). An occasional episode is not sufficient for a diagnosis of panic disorder—the individual also has to experience significant dread and anxiety about having another attack. When this criterion is applied, approximately 3.5% of people will have diagnosable panic disorder sometime in their lives, and of those, about three out of seven will also develop agoraphobia (Kessler et al., 1994). Panic disorder is especially prevalent among women, who are twice as likely to be diagnosed with it as are men (Weissman et al., 1997). Family studies suggest a modest hereditary component to panic disorder. If one identical twin has the disorder, the likelihood of the other twin having it is about 30% (Crowe, 1990; Kendler et al., 1995; Torgensen, 1983).

In an effort to understand the role that physiological arousal plays in panic attacks, researchers have compared the responses of experimental participants with and without panic disorder to *sodium lactate,* a chemical that produces rapid, shallow breathing and heart palpitations. Those with panic disorder were found to be acutely sensitive to the drug; within a few minutes after administration, 60% to 90% experienced a panic attack. Participants without the disorder rarely responded to the drug with a panic attack (Liebowitz et al., 1985a; Liebowitz et al., 1985b).

The difference in responses to the chemical may be due to differing interpretations of physiological signs of anxiety—that is, people who experience panic attacks may be hypersensitive to physiological signs of anxiety, which they interpret as having disastrous consequences for their well-being. Supporting this cognitive explanation is research showing that people who are high in anxiety sensitivity (i.e., they believe that bodily arousal and other symptoms of anxiety can have dire consequences) have an elevated risk for experiencing panic attacks (Schmidt, Lerew, & Jackson, 1997; Telch et al., 1989). Thus, panic attacks may be traceable to the fear of fear itself.

Obsessive-Compulsive Disorder

Although anxiety plays a role in obsessive-compulsive disorder, the primary symptoms are unwanted, recurrent thoughts and actions. You've probably had the experience of having something—say, a silly song—pop into your head and "play" over and over, or you've started to do something pointless—like counting ceiling tiles during a boring lecture—and found it hard to stop. In some people, such repetitive thoughts and actions become a serious problem.

Karen, a 34-year-old with four children, sought treatment after several months of experiencing intrusive, repetitive thoughts in which she imagined that one or more of her children was having a serious accident. In addition, an extensive series of protective counting rituals hampered her daily routine. For example, when grocery shopping, Karen had the feeling that if she selected the first item (say, a box of cereal) on a shelf, something terrible would happen to her oldest child. If she selected the second item, some unknown disaster would befall her second child and so on for the four children. The children's ages were also important. The sixth item in a row, for example, was associated with her youngest child, who was 6 years old.

Karen's preoccupation with numbers extended to other activities, most notably the pattern in which she smoked cigarettes and drank coffee. If she had one cigarette, she felt that she had to smoke at least four in a row or one of her children would be harmed in some way. If she drank one cup of coffee, she felt compelled to drink four more to protect her children from harm. She acknowledged that her counting rituals were irrational, but she found that she became extremely anxious when she tried to stop (Oltmanns, Neale, & Davison, 1991).

Karen's symptoms are typical of **obsessive-compulsive disorder (OCD),** in which *repetitive, intrusive thoughts (obsessions) and ritualistic behaviors (compulsions) designed to fend off those thoughts interfere significantly with an individual's functioning.* Anxiety plays a role in this disorder because the obsessive thoughts typically produce anxiety, and the compulsive behaviors are performed to reduce it. It is not uncommon for people to have occasional intrusive thoughts that prompt ritualistic behavior (e.g., double or triple checking to be sure the garage door is closed or the oven is off), but the obsessions and compulsions of OCD are intense, frequent, and experienced as irrational and excessive. Attempts to cope with the obsessive thoughts by trying to suppress or ignore them are of little or no benefit. In fact (as discussed in Chapter 8), thought suppression can backfire, increasing the frequency and intensity of the obsessive thoughts (Wegner, 1989; Wenzlaff & Wegner, 2000).

Approximately 2.5% of people will develop OCD sometime in their lives, with similar rates across different cultures (Gibbs, 1996; Karno & Golding, 1991; Robins & Regier, 1991). Women tend to be more susceptible than men, but the difference is not large (Karno & Golding, 1991). The most common obsessions involve contamination, aggression, death, sex, disease, orderliness, and disfigurement (Jenike, Baer, & Minichiello, 1986; Rachman & DeSilva, 1978). Compulsions typically take the form of cleaning, checking, repeating, ordering/arranging, and counting (Antony, Downie, & Swinson, 1998). Although compulsive behavior is always excessive, it can vary considerably in intensity and frequency. For example, fear of contamination may lead to 15 minutes of hand washing in some individuals, while others may need to spend hours with disinfectants and extremely hot water, scrubbing their hands until they bleed.

The obsessions that plague individuals with OCD typically derive from concerns that could pose a real threat (such as contamination, aggression, disease), which supports preparedness theory. Thinking repeatedly about whether we've left a stove burner on when we leave the house makes sense, after all, if we want to return to a house that is not "well done." The concept of preparedness places OCD in the same evolutionary context as phobias (Marks & Nesse, 1994). However, as with phobias, we need to consider other factors to explain why fears that may have served an evolutionary purpose can become so distorted and maladaptive.

Family studies indicate a moderate genetic heritability for OCD: Identical twins show a higher concordance than do fraternal twins. Relatives of individuals with OCD may not have the disorder themselves, but they are at greater risk for other types of anxiety disorders than are members of the general public (Billet, Richter, & Kennedy, 1998). Researchers have not determined the biological mechanisms that may contribute to OCD, but some evidence implicates heightened neural activity in the caudate nucleus of the brain, a portion of the basal ganglia (discussed in Chapter 3) known to be involved in the initiation of intentional actions (Kronig et al., 1999). Drugs that increase the activity of the neurotransmitter serotonin in the brain can inhibit the activity of the caudate nucleus and relieve some of the symptoms of obsessive-compulsive disorder (Hansen, Hasselbalch, Law, & Bolwig, 2002). However, this finding does not indicate that overactivity of the caudate nucleus is the cause of OCD. It could also be an effect of the disorder: Patients with OCD often respond favorably to psychotherapy and show a corresponding reduction in activity in the caudate nucleus (Baxter et al., 1992).

In summary, people with anxiety disorders have irrational worries and fears that undermine their ability to function normally. The anxiety may be chronic, as in generalized anxiety disorder (GAD), or it may be tied to an object or situation, as in the phobic disorders (specific phobia and social phobia). Phobias typically involve stimuli that humans are evolutionarily prepared to find threatening. People who suffer from panic disorder experience a sudden and intense attack of anxiety that is terrifying and can lead them to become agoraphobic and housebound for fear of public humiliation.

Hand washing is a good idea whether you are an employee or not. But the feeling that one "must wash hands" can come to mind many dozens of times a day in some people with obsessive-compulsive disorder, leading to compulsive washing and even damage to the skin.

 **ONLY HUMAN**

YOU NEVER KNOW WHEN YOU MIGHT NEED ONE OF THESE 1996—In May, Stanford University won the right over the University of California at Berkeley to house the literary legacy of the late Pulitzer- and Oscar-winning writer William Saroyan, apparently because it also agreed to take custody of Saroyan's nonliterary property. Because Saroyan was a compulsive collector, his nonliterary archives include, among other things, hundreds of boxes of rocks, matchbook covers, old newspapers (numbering in the thousands), labels peeled off cans, and a plastic bag filled with about 10,000 rubber bands.

OBSESSIVE-COMPULSIVE DISORDER (OCD) A disorder in which repetitive, intrusive thoughts (obsessions) and ritualistic behaviors (compulsions) designed to fend off those thoughts interfere significantly with an individual's functioning.

People with obsessive-compulsive disorder experience recurring, anxiety-provoking thoughts that compel them to engage in ritualistic, irrational behavior. In general, the anxiety disorders show a moderate level of heritability but appear to be best explained by a combination of biological, psychological, and environmental factors. ■ ■

Dissociative Disorders: Going to Pieces

Can the human mind come apart? Could a person forget who she is one day but remember the next? Mary, a 35-year-old social worker being treated with hypnosis for chronic pain in her forearm, mentioned to her doctor that she often found her car low on fuel in the morning despite her having filled it with gas the day before. Overnight the odometer would gain 50 to 100 miles, even though she had no memory of driving the car.

During one hypnotic session, Mary suddenly blurted out in a strange voice, "It's about time you knew about me." In the new voice, she identified herself as "Marian" and described the drives that she took at night, which were retreats to the nearby hills to "work out problems." Mary knew nothing of "Marian" and her nighttime adventures. Marian was as abrupt and hostile as Mary was compliant and caring. In the course of therapy, six other personalities emerged (including one who claimed to be a 6-year-old child), and considerable tension and disagreement developed among the personalities. On one occasion, one of the personalities threatened suicide and forbade the therapist from discussing it with the other personalities, noting that it would be "a violation of doctor-patient confidentiality" (Spitzer et al., 1994).

Mary suffers from a type of **dissociative disorder**, *a condition in which normal cognitive processes are severely disjointed and fragmented, creating significant disruptions in memory, awareness, or personality that can vary in length from a matter of minutes to many years.* To some extent, a bit of dissociation, or "splitting," of cognitive processes is normal. For example, research on implicit memory shows that we often retain and are influenced by information that we do not consciously remember (discussed in Chapter 5). Moreover, we can engage in more than one activity or mental process while maintaining only dim awareness of the perceptions and decisions that guide other behaviors (such as talking while driving a car). Our ordinary continuity of memory and awareness of our personal identity contrasts with Mary's profound cognitive fragmentation and blindness to her own mental processes and states.

Dissociative Identity Disorder

Dissociative identity disorder (DID) is characterized by *the presence within an individual of two or more distinct identities that at different times take control of the individual's behavior.* The most dramatic form of dissociative disorder, DID has attracted considerable popular attention. When the original personality, or *host personality,* is dominant, the individual often is unaware of the alternate personalities, or *alters* (as in Mary's case). However, the alters typically know about the host personality and about each other. The number of distinct identities can range considerably, with some cases numbering more than a hundred. Sometimes alters share certain characteristics; sometimes they are dissimilar—assuming different vocal patterns, dialects, ages, morals, and even gender identities. No longer called "multiple personality disorder" because the term implies that more than one person is in "residence," the disorder is now conceptualized as involving multiple patterns of thought and behavior, each of which is associated with a different identity.

Prior to 1970, DID was considered rare, with only about 100 cases reported in the professional literature worldwide. However, since that time, the number of reported cases has grown enormously. Recent estimates are that between 0.5% and 1% of the general population suffers from the disorder, with a female to male prevalence of about 9 to 1 (Maldonado & Butler, 1998). Most patients are diagnosed when they are in their 20s or 30s, although the actual age of onset is probably during childhood (Maldonado & Butler, 1998; Putnam et al., 1986).

DISSOCIATIVE DISORDER A condition in which normal cognitive processes are severely disjointed and fragmented, creating significant disruptions in memory, awareness, or personality that can vary in length from a matter of minutes to many years.

DISSOCIATIVE IDENTITY DISORDER (DID) The presence within an individual of two or more distinct identities that at different times take control of the individual's behavior.

Joanne Woodward played Eve White, a woman with dissociative identity disorder, in the 1957 film *The Three Faces of Eve.* This film and others dramatized the disorder and by increasing public awareness stimulated more frequent diagnosis of this problem. It is not clear, though, whether the increased awareness led to greater accuracy in finding cases of the disorder that were already present or if it shaped how people behave (and what therapists tried to find), and so *created* more cases of the disorder.

The strange transition of DID—from a rare disorder to a minor epidemic—has raised concerns that the disorder is a matter of faking or fashion (Spanos, 1994). The most common explanation targets psychotherapists who, though often well meaning, are said to have created the disorder in patients who are vulnerable to their suggestive procedures. Accounts of how therapists treat DID, often using hypnosis, have revealed some cajoling and coaxing of clients into reporting evidence of alternate personalities (Acocella, 1999).

Most patients with DID report a history of severe childhood abuse and trauma (Coons, 1994; Putnam et al., 1986), and that evidence supports a popular explanation rooted in psychodynamic theory. From this viewpoint, the helpless child, confronted with intolerable abuse and trauma, responds with the primitive psychological defense of splitting or dissociating to escape the pain and horror. Because the child cannot escape the situation, she essentially escapes from herself. Once the dissociation takes hold, it can set into motion a psychological process that may lead to the development of multiple identities (Kluft, 1984; Kluft, 1991).

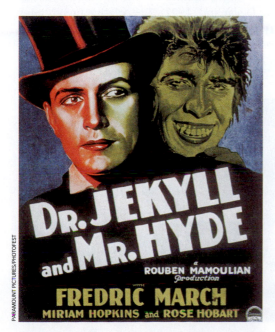

Robert Louis Stevenson's 1886 portrayal of dissociative disorder has become so well known that "Jekyll and Hyde" is popular as a synonym for a radically changing personality. This poster is from a 1931 film version.

 **ONLY HUMAN**

STEP RIGHT UP, LADIES AND GENTLEMEN 1997—In a Virginia case reported in the *Mental Health Law News*, Susanna van de Castle was awarded $350,000 against her psychiatrist-husband, Robert, for malpractice. According to the lawsuit, after having diagnosed her as suffering from multiple personality disorder, he then married her and continued the therapy but also sought deals for a book and a movie about her in addition to staging public lectures (charging admission) in which she was showcased as his subject.

DISSOCIATIVE AMNESIA The sudden loss of memory for significant personal information.

DISSOCIATIVE FUGUE The sudden loss of memory for one's personal history, accompanied by an abrupt departure from home and the assumption of a new identity.

Critics of the psychodynamic explanation of DID have raised the possibility that individuals who exhibit both trauma and DID may be responding to their therapists' expectations that the two are linked (Humphreys & Dennett, 1989; Kluft, 1991; Lalonde et al., 2001). Moreover, in most cases, the determination of childhood trauma is based on self-reported memories, which can be susceptible to errors and distortions (Dorahy, 2001). Curiously, early abuse and trauma are especially prevalent in low-income households, while cases of multiple personality occur almost exclusively among people of middle income (Acocella, 1999). In short, dissociative identity disorder is poorly understood and deep questions exist about what it is, how it arises, and how it can be treated.

Dissociative Amnesia and Dissociative Fugue

Amnesia, The Bourne Identity, Eternal Sunshine of the Spotless Mind, 50 First Dates, Memento, and *The Man without a Past*—these recent movies reveal Hollywood's fascination with forms of dissociative disorder involving memory. The memory oddities invented for film don't always correspond to the real disorders, dissociative amnesia and dissociative fugue. These conditions (by *DSM* definition) cannot result from normal forgetting or brain injury, drugs, or another mental disorder (e.g., posttraumatic stress disorder).

- **Dissociative amnesia** is *the sudden loss of memory for significant personal information.* The memory loss is typically for a traumatic specific event or period of time but can involve extended periods (months or years) of a person's life (Kihlstrom, 2005).
- **Dissociative fugue** involves *the sudden loss of memory for one's personal history, accompanied by an abrupt departure from home and the assumption of a new identity.* The fugue state is usually associated with stressful life circumstances and can be brief or lengthy.

"Burt," a 42-year-old short-order cook in a small town, came to the attention of police when he got into a heated altercation with another man in the diner. When the police took "Burt" to the hospital, they discovered that he had no identification documents and was clueless about his past. While he was in the hospital, the police matched his description to that of Gene Saunders, a resident of a city 200 miles away, who had disappeared a month earlier. When Gene Saunders's wife came to identify him, he denied knowing her and his real identity. Before he disappeared, Gene Saunders had been experiencing considerable difficulties at home and at work and had become withdrawn and irritable. Two days before he left, he had a violent argument with his 18-year-old son, who accused him of being a failure (Spitzer et al., 1994, pp. 254–255).

Both dissociative amnesia and dissociative fugue usually emerge in adulthood and rarely occur after the age of 50 (Sackeim & Devanand, 1991). Dissociative fugue states usually end rather abruptly, and victims typically recover their memories and personal identities. Dissociative amnesia may also be temporary: People have lost significant personal memories and then recovered them later (Brenneis, 2000; Schooler, Bendiksen, & Ambadar, 1997).

Call me "Al." A man identified only by the name "Al" gave a news conference in Denver in 2006 in hopes that someone might be able to tell him more about himself. A victim of a dissociative fugue state, he had no memory of his identity or his life. His fiancée recognized him on TV and confirmed his identity as Jeffrey Alan Ingram, an unemployed machinist from Olympia, Washington.

AP PHOTO/THE DENVER POST, KARL GEHRING

In summary, the dissociative disorders involve severely disjointed and fragmented cognitive processes reflected in significant disruptions in memory, awareness, or personality. People with dissociative identity disorder (DID) shift between two or more identities that are distinctive from each other in terms of personal memories, behavioral characteristics, and attitudes. Previously rare, reported cases of DID have been increasing as the disorder has received more widespread media attention, leading some researchers to believe that it may be overdiagnosed or even created in therapy. Psychodynamic theorists speculate that DID arises when a young person uses psychological detachment as a means of coping with trauma, and this eventually leads to a splitting or dissociation among normally integrated psychological functions. Dissociative amnesia and dissociative fugue involve significant memory loss that is too extensive to be the result of normal forgetting and cannot be attributed to brain injury, drugs, or another mental disorder. Both disorders are believed to be associated with life stresses. In addition to loss of one's personal history, dissociative fugue is accompanied by an abrupt departure from home and the assumption of a new identity. ■ ■ ■

MOOD DISORDERS Mental disorders that have mood disturbance as their predominant feature.

Mood Disorders: At the Mercy of Emotions

You're probably in a mood right now. Maybe you're happy that it's almost time to get a snack or saddened by something you heard on the radio—or you may feel good or bad without having a clue why. As you learned in Chapter 10, moods are relatively long-lasting, nonspecific emotional states—and *nonspecific* means we often may have no idea what has caused a mood. Changing moods lend variety to our experiences, like different-colored lights shining on the stage as we play out our lives. However, for people like Virginia Woolf and others with mood disorders, moods can become so intense that they are pulled or pushed into life-threatening actions. **Mood disorders—** *mental disorders that have mood disturbance as their predominant feature*—take two main forms: depression and bipolar disorder.

Depressive Disorders

Depression is much more than sadness. The experience of R. A., a 58-year-old man who visited his primary-care physician for treatment of his diabetes, is fairly typical. During the visit, he mentioned difficulties falling asleep and staying asleep that left him chronically fatigued. He complained that over the past 6 months, he'd stopped exercising and gained 12 pounds and had lost interest in socializing. Although nothing he normally enjoyed, including sexual activity, could give him pleasure anymore, he denied feeling particularly sad but did say that he had trouble concentrating and was forgetful, irritable, impatient, and frustrated. Although he continued to work, he felt that whatever was happening to him was interfering with his life (Lustman, Caudle, & Clouse, 2002).

Most people occasionally feel depressed, pessimistic, and unmotivated. As comic Emo Philips remarked, "Some mornings, it's just not worth gnawing through the leather straps." But these periods are relatively short-lived and mild compared with R. A.'s sense of hopelessness and weariness and his lack of normal pleasures. Depression is also different from the sorrow and grief that accompany the death of a loved one—a normal, possibly adaptive response to a tragic situation (Bowlby, 1980). Instead, depressive mood disorders are dysfunctional, chronic, and fall outside the range of socially or culturally expected responses.

The Blue Devils. George Cruikshank (1806–77) portrays a depressed man tormented by demons offering him methods of suicide, appearing as bill collectors, and making a funeral procession.

BRIDGEMAN ART LIBRARY

"Waiter! There's a depressed person in my soup."

Major depressive disorder, also known as unipolar depression, is characterized by *a severely depressed mood that lasts 2 or more weeks and is accompanied by feelings of worthlessness and lack of pleasure, lethargy, and sleep and appetite disturbances.* The bodily symptoms in major depression may seem contrary—sleeping too much or sleeping very little, for example, or overeating or failing to eat. Great sadness or despair is not always present, although intrusive thoughts of failure or ending one's life are not uncommon. In a related condition called **dysthymia**, *the same cognitive and bodily problems as in depression are present, but they are less severe and last longer, persisting for at least 2 years.* When both types co-occur, the resulting condition is called **double depression** and is defined as *a moderately depressed mood that persists for at least 2 years and is punctuated by periods of major depression.*

Some people experience *recurrent depressive episodes in a seasonal pattern,* commonly known as **seasonal affective disorder (SAD)**. In most cases, the episodes begin in fall or winter and remit in spring, and this pattern is due to reduced levels of light over the colder seasons (Tam, Lam, & Levitt, 1995). Recurrent summer depressive episodes are not unknown. A winter-related pattern of depression appears to be more prevalent in higher latitudes.

On average, major depression lasts about 6 months (Beck, 1967; Robins & Guze, 1972). However, without treatment, approximately 80% of individuals will experience at least one recurrence of the disorder (Judd, 1997; Mueller et al., 1999). Compared with people who have a single episode, individuals with recurrent depression have more severe symptoms, higher rates of depression in their families, more suicide attempts, and higher rates of divorce (Merikangas, Wicki, & Angst, 1994). The median lifetime risk for depression of about 16% seems to be increasing in younger generations (Lavori et al., 1987; Wittchen, Knauper, & Kessler, 1994). For example, a large international study found evidence of a substantial global increase in the risk for depression across the past century (Cross-National Collaborative Research Group, 1992).

This situation is especially dire for women because they are diagnosed with depression at a rate twice that of men (Kessler et al., 1996; Lavori et al., 1987; Robins et al., 1984; Wittchen et al., 1994). Socioeconomic standing has been invoked as an explanation for women's heightened risk: Their incomes are lower than those of men, and poverty could cause depression. Sex differences in hormones are another possibility: Estrogen, androgen, and progesterone influence depression; some women experience *postpartum depression* (depression following childbirth) due to changing hormone balances.

MAJOR DEPRESSIVE DISORDER A disorder characterized by a severely depressed mood that lasts 2 weeks or more and is accompanied by feelings of worthlessness and lack of pleasure, lethargy, and sleep and appetite disturbances.

DYSTHYMIA A disorder that involves the same symptoms as in depression only less severe, but the symptoms last longer, persisting for at least 2 years.

DOUBLE DEPRESSION A moderately depressed mood that persists for at least 2 years and is punctuated by periods of major depression.

SEASONAL AFFECTIVE DISORDER (SAD) Depression that involves recurrent depressive episodes in a seasonal pattern.

A time for seasonal affective disorder. When the sun goes away, sadness can play.

Susan Nolen-Hoeksema (1987, 1990) has examined the evidence and argues that these causes are not sufficient to explain the size of the sex difference in depression. She believes that the culprit is response style—women's tendency to accept, disclose, and ruminate on their negative emotions in contrast with men's tendency to deny negative emotions and engage in self-distraction such as work and drinking alcohol. Perhaps women's higher rates reflect willingness to face their depression. The search for causes of this disorder in women and men continues and extends to biological and psychological factors.

Actress Brooke Shields experienced severe postpartum depression and wrote a book about it.

Biological Factors

Heritability estimates for major depression typically range from 33% to 45% (Plomin et al., 1997; Wallace, Schnieder, & McGuffin, 2002). However, as with most types of mental disorders, heritability rates vary as a function of severity. For example, a relatively large study of twins found that the concordance rates for severe major depression (defined as three or more episodes) were quite high, with a rate of 59% for identical twins and 30% for fraternal twins (Bertelsen, Harvald, & Hauge, 1977). In contrast, concordance rates for less severe major depression (defined as fewer than three episodes) fell to 33% for identical twins and 14% for fraternal twins. Heritability rates for dysthymia are low and inconsistent (Katz & McGuffin, 1993; Plomin et al., 1997; Roth & Mountjoy, 1997).

Beginning in the 1950s, researchers noticed that drugs that increased levels of the neurotransmitters norepinephrine and serotonin could sometimes reduce depression. This observation suggested that depression might be caused by an absolute or relative depletion of these neurotransmitters and sparked a revolution in the pharmacological treatment of depression (Schildkraut, 1965), leading to the development and widespread use of such popular prescription drugs as Prozac and Zoloft (see Chapter 14). Further research has shown, however, that reduced levels of these neurotransmitters cannot be the whole story. For example, some studies have found *increases* in norepinephrine activity among depressed patients (Thase & Howland, 1995). Moreover, even though the antidepressant medications change neurochemical transmission in less than a day, they typically take at least 2 weeks to relieve depressive symptoms. A biochemical model of depression has yet to be developed that accounts for all the evidence.

Depression may involve diminished activity in the left prefrontal cortex and increased activity in the right prefrontal cortex (see **FIGURE 13.2**)—areas of the brain involved in the processing of emotions (Davidson, 2004; Davidson, Pizzagalli, Nitschke, & Putram, 2002). For example, stroke patients with damage to the left prefrontal cortex often experience higher levels of depression than would otherwise be expected (Robinson & Downhill, 1995). Severely depressed individuals who do not have brain damage often

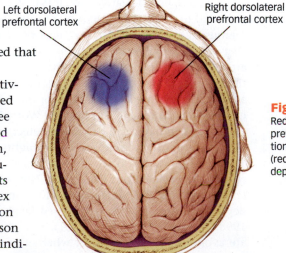

Left dorsolateral prefrontal cortex

Right dorsolateral prefrontal cortex

Figure 13.2 Brain and Depression
Reduced activation in the left dorsolateral prefrontal cortex (blue) and increased activation in the right dorsolateral prefrontal cortex (red) have been found to be linked with depression in several studies.

who do not have brain damage often show diminished activity in the anterior (prefrontal) regions of the cerebral hemispheres—especially on the left side (Thase & Howland, 1995). These abnormal activity patterns may be effects of the mood disturbance, or they may cause people to be more susceptible to depression. The possibility that activity in this brain area does cause depression is supported by the findings that similar types of brain abnormalities occur in patients in remission (Henriques & Davidson, 1990) and in children who are at risk for depression (Tomarken, Simien, & Garber, 1994).

Psychological Factors

If optimists see the world through rose-colored glasses, depressed individuals seem to view it through lenses that are smudged dark gray. Their negative cognitive style is remarkably consistent and, some argue, begins in childhood with experiences that foster pessimism and low self-worth (Blatt & Homann, 1992; Cutler & Nolen-Hoeksema, 1991; Gibb, Alloy, & Tierney, 2001). One of the first theorists to emphasize the role of thought in depression, Aaron Beck (1967), noted that his depressed patients distorted perceptions of their experiences and embraced dysfunctional attitudes that promoted and maintained negative mood states.

Elaborating on this idea, researchers have proposed a theory of depression that emphasizes the role of people's negative inferences about the causes of their experiences (Abramson, Seligman, & Teasdale, 1978). **Helplessness theory** maintains that *individuals who are prone to depression automatically attribute negative experiences to causes that are internal (i.e., their own fault), stable (i.e., unlikely to change), and global (i.e., widespread)*. For example, a student at risk for depression might view a bad grade on a math test as a sign of low intelligence (internal) that will never change (stable) and that will lead to failure in all his or her future endeavors (global). In contrast, a student without this tendency might have the opposite response, attributing the grade to something external (poor teaching), unstable (a missed study session), and/or specific (boring subject).

Supporting the role of thought in depression is a large body of evidence that depressed individuals' judgments, memories, and attributions are negatively biased (Abramson et al., 2002; Blatt & Zuroff, 1992; Coyne & Whiffen, 1995; Wenzlaff & Grozier, 1988). However, in these studies thoughts and judgments were assessed *during* depression, raising the possibility that the biases may be a consequence rather than a cause of the mood disturbance. To demonstrate that negative thoughts contribute to depression, the thoughts must *precede* the development of the disorder. With a few exceptions (Alloy, Jacobson, & Acocella, 1999), research has not detected obvious signs of maladaptive thinking prior to the onset of the depressive mood disturbance (Ingram, Miranda, & Segal, 1998).

Of course, prior negative thoughts may exist in disguised forms as subtle tendencies to attend to negative information or interpret feedback in a negative way. Indeed, numerous studies suggest that people at risk for depression have latent depressive biases that can be activated by negative moods (Ingram et al., 1998). Thus, a gloomy, rainy afternoon could evoke a mood of sadness and isolation, and instead of taking the initiative and calling someone to chat, the person at risk would become dejected. Once activated, these latent biases may contribute to a progressive worsening of mood that can result in depression (see the Real World box on pages 516 and 517).

Negative thinking can be hard to detect in individuals at risk for depression because they are struggling to suppress the thoughts that threaten their emotional well-being. Thought suppression is an effortful process that can be disrupted when cognitive resources are depleted (see Chapter 8). Not surprisingly, then, when cognitive demands arise (time pressures, distraction, stress, and so forth), individuals who are at risk for depression often display heightened levels of negative thinking (Wenzlaff & Bates, 1998; Wenzlaff & Eisenberg, 2001). They may worry about failures, think that people are avoiding them, or wonder whether anything is worthwhile. This breakdown in mental control may explain why stressful life events such as a prolonged illness or the loss of a loved one often precede a descent into depression (Kessler, 1997). Ironically,

HELPLESSNESS THEORY The idea that individuals who are prone to depression automatically attribute negative experiences to causes that are internal (i.e., their own fault), stable (i.e., unlikely to change), and global (i.e., widespread).

Man Ray (1890–1976) offered a caricature of sadness as art in *Tears,* 1930–32.

thought suppression itself may intensify depressive thoughts and ultimately contribute to relapse (Rude et al., 2002; Wenzlaff, 2005; Wenzlaff & Bates, 1998).

Research suggests that people at risk for depression may inadvertently construct their social worlds in ways that contribute to and confirm their negative beliefs. For example, depressed individuals with low self-esteem have been found to seek social feedback that confirms their negative self-views (Giesler, Josephs, & Swann, Jr., 1996; Joiner, Katz, & Lew, 1997; Swann, Wenzlaff, & Tafarodi, 1992). They seek companions who are likely to criticize or belittle them—almost like wearing a sign that says "Kick me hard." Uncertainty about self-worth can also lead individuals at risk for depression to seek excessive reassurance ("Are you really sure it's okay for me to hang out with you guys?"). This behavior can lead to social rejection because others are likely to view it as inappropriate and demanding (Joiner, 2002; Joiner & Metalsky, 1995; Joiner et al., 1999). Thus, depression can be self-perpetuating if people who are depressed behave in ways that prompt depressing reactions from other people.

Bipolar Disorder

If depression is bad, would the opposite be better? Not for Virginia Woolf nor for Julie, a 20-year-old college sophomore. When first seen by a clinician, Julie had gone 5 days without sleep and, like Woolf, was extremely active and expressing bizarre thoughts and ideas. She proclaimed to friends that she did not menstruate because she was "of a third sex, a gender above the two human sexes." She claimed to be a "superwoman," capable of avoiding human sexuality and yet still able to give birth. Preoccupied with the politics of global disarmament, she felt that she had switched souls with the senior senator from her state, had tapped into his thoughts and memories, and could save the world from nuclear destruction. She began to campaign for an elected position in the U.S. government (even though no elections were scheduled at that time). Worried that she would forget some of her thoughts, she had been leaving hundreds of notes about her ideas and activities everywhere, including on the walls and furniture of her dormitory room (Vitkus, 1999).

In addition to her manic episodes, Julie—like Woolf—had a history of depression. The diagnostic label for their constellation of symptoms is **bipolar disorder**—*an unstable emotional condition characterized by cycles of abnormal, persistent high mood (mania) and low mood (depression).* In about two thirds of patients, manic episodes immediately precede or immediately follow depressive episodes (Whybrow, 1997). The depressive phase of bipolar disorder is often clinically indistinguishable from major depression (Perris, 1992). In the manic phase, which must last at least a week to meet *DSM* requirements, mood can be elevated, expansive, or irritable. Other prominent symptoms include grandiosity, decreased need for sleep, talkativeness, racing thoughts, distractibility, and reckless behavior (such as compulsive gambling, sexual indiscretions, and unrestrained spending sprees). Psychotic features such as hallucinations (erroneous perceptions) and delusions (erroneous beliefs) may be present, and so the disorder can be misdiagnosed as schizophrenia.

BIPOLAR DISORDER An unstable emotional condition characterized by cycles of abnormal, persistent high mood (mania) and low mood (depression).

{ THE REAL WORLD } Suicide Risk and Prevention

OVERALL, SUICIDE IS THE 11TH LEADING cause of death in the United States and the third most common form of death among high school and college students (King, 1997). In 2000, 10.6 out of 100,000 Americans died by suicide—a total of 29,350 in the nation that year (National Institute of Mental Health, 2003). Although people have various reasons for taking their own lives, approximately 50% kill themselves during the recovery phase of a depressive episode (Isacsson & Rich, 1997). The lifetime risk of suicide in people with mood disorders is about 4%, compared to a risk of only 0.5% in the general population (Bostwick & Pankratz, 2000). In the United States, women attempt suicide about three to four times more often than men. However, because men typically use more lethal methods than do women (such as guns versus pills), men are three to four times more likely to actually kill themselves than are women (Canetto & Lester, 1995). The tragic effects of suicide extend beyond the loss of life, compounding the grief of families and loved ones who must contend with feelings of abandonment, guilt, shame, and futility.

Researchers have identified a variety of motives for suicide, including a profound sense of alienation, intolerable psychological or physical suffering or both, hopelessness, an escape from feelings of worthlessness, and a desperate cry for help (Baumeister & Tice, 1990; Durkheim, 1951; Joiner, 2006). Suicide rates increase with age, and aging white men are especially at risk (Joiner, 2006; National Institute of Mental Health, 2003). Studies also show an increased risk of suicide among family members with a relative who committed suicide (Kety, 1990; Mann et al., 1999). This elevated risk may be a function of biological factors in depression, or suicide could be contagious, with exposure making it a more salient option during desperate times. Contagious effects are suggested by the occasional "clusters" of suicides in which several people—usually teenagers—attempt to kill themselves following a highly publicized case (Gould, 1990).

The contagion of suicide has been called the "Werther effect" after the rash of suicides that followed the 1774 publication of Goethe's tale of a young romantic who shot himself over a lost love. Werther was wearing a blue coat and yellow vest when he took his life, and so many young men were found dead in similar garb that the book was banned in several countries. In fact, suicide in the United States has been found to increase after nationally televised news or feature stories about suicide (Phillips & Carstensen, 1986), but imitation is not inevitable. When rock musician Kurt Cobain shot himself in 1994, the Werther effect was

DAVID SANGER PHOTOGRAPHY/ALAMY

Over 1,218 people have jumped from the Golden Gate Bridge since its completion in 1937—a jump 98% likely to be fatal. The city of San Francisco continues to debate whether to install a suicide barrier.
(Guthmann, 2005.)

The lifetime risk for bipolar disorder is about 1.3% for both men and women (Wittchen et al., 1994). Bipolar disorder is typically a recurrent condition, with approximately 90% of afflicted people suffering from several episodes over a lifetime (Coryell et al., 1995). About 10% of cases have *rapid cycling bipolar disorder,* characterized by at least four mood episodes (either manic or depressive) every year. Rapid

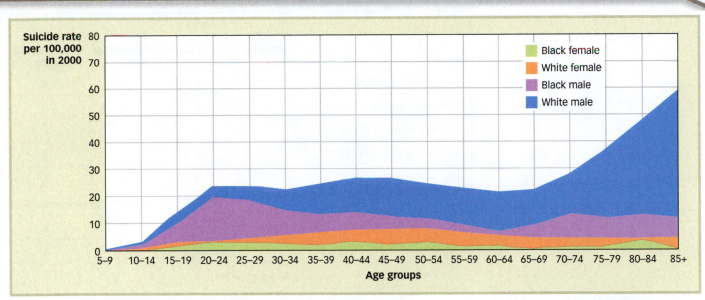

The U.S. suicide rates reveal that men are more likely to commit suicide than women at all ages, that men's likelihood of suicide grows in early adulthood, and that white men remain most suicide prone throughout life—with a spike in the later years.
(From National Institute of Mental Health, 2003.)

not found in his home town of Seattle (Jobes et al., 1996) or in Australia (Martin & Koo, 1997).

How can you tell if someone is at risk for suicide? Unfortunately, definitive prediction is impossible, but a variety of warning signs can suggest an increased risk (Substance Abuse and Mental Health Services Administration, 2005). Any one sign is a cause for concern, and the risk is especially serious when several occur together.

- Talk about suicide. About 90% of people who are suicidal discuss their intentions, so this obvious warning sign should not be dismissed as simply a means of getting attention. Although most people who threaten suicide do not actually attempt it, they are at greater risk than those who do not talk about it.

- An upturn in mood following a prolonged depressive episode. Surprisingly, suicide risk increases at this point. In fact, a sudden lifting of mood may reflect relief at the prospect that suicide will end the emotional suffering.

- A failed love interest, romantic breakup, or loss of a loved one through separation or death.

- A severe, stressful event that is especially shameful or humiliating.

- A family history of suicide, especially of a parent.

- Unusual reckless or risky behavior, seemingly carried out without thinking.

- An unexplained decline in school or workplace performance.

- Withdrawal from friends, family, and regular activities.

- Expressing feelings of being trapped, as though there's "no way out."

- "Cleaning house" by giving away prized possessions.

- Increased alcohol or drug use. Substance abuse is associated with approximately 25% to 50% of suicides and is especially associated with adolescent suicides (Conwell et al., 1996; Woods et al., 1997).

Although discussing suicide with someone possibly at risk might seem to increase actual risk, a caring listener can help put issues in better perspective and reduce feelings of isolation. Anyone who is potentially suicidal should be encouraged to seek professional help. Colleges and universities have student counseling centers, and most cities have suicide prevention centers with 24-hour hotlines and walk-in emergency counseling. The U.S. National Suicide Prevention Lifeline is 1-800-273-TALK.

cycling is more common in women than in men and is sometimes precipitated by taking certain kinds of antidepressant drugs (Liebenluft, 1996; Whybrow, 1997). Unfortunately, bipolar disorder tends to be persistent. In one study, 24% of patients had relapsed within 6 months of recovery from an episode, and 77% had at least one new episode within 4 years of recovery (Coryell et al., 1995).

Table 13.3	Major Twentieth-Century American Poets Born between 1895 and 1935 with Documented Histories of Bipolar Disorder			
Poet	**Pulitzer Prize in Poetry**	**Treated for Major Depressive Illness**	**Treated for Mania**	**Committed Suicide**
Hart Crane (1899–1932)		X	X	X
Theodore Roethke (1908–1963)	X	X	X	
Delmore Schwartz (1913–1966)		X	X	
John Berryman (1914–1972)	X	X	X	X
Randall Jarrell (1914–1965)		X	X	X
Robert Lowell (1917–1977)	X	X	X	
Anne Sexton (1928–1974)	X	X	X	X
Sylvia Plath[a] (1932–1963)	X	X		X

[a]Plath, although not treated for mania, probably had bipolar disorder.
Source: From Goodwin and Jamison (1990).

A significant minority of people with bipolar disorder are highly creative, artistic, or otherwise outstanding in some way. Before the mania becomes too pronounced, the energy, grandiosity, and ambition that it supplies may help people achieve great things. In addition to Virginia Woolf and the poets listed in **TABLE 13.3**, notable individuals thought to have had the disorder include Abraham Lincoln, Ernest Hemingway, Winston Churchill, and Theodore Roosevelt.

Biological Factors

Among the various mental disorders, bipolar disorder has the highest rate of heritability, with concordance as high as 80% for identical twins and 16% for fraternal twins (Bertelsen et al., 1977). Despite considerable effort on the part of researchers, specific genes that contribute to bipolar disorder have not yet been identified (Goodwin & Ghaemi, 1998; Plomin et al., 1997). Close relatives of an individual with bipolar disorder are also at heightened risk for unipolar depression (Bertelsen et al., 1977)—a finding that raises the possibility that the genetic transmission of bipolar disorder is connected to the genetic transmission of unipolar depression. Thus, bipolar disorder may be *polygenic,* arising from the action of many genes in an additive or interactive fashion.

Biochemical imbalances may be involved in bipolar disorder, but specific neurotransmitters have not been identified. Some researchers have suggested that low levels of serotonin and norepinephrine may contribute to the emotional roller coaster that characterizes bipolar disorder (Whybrow, 1997). This notion is not well substantiated and doesn't explain why lithium, a chemical unrelated to these neurotransmitters, often helps stabilize both the depressive and manic symptoms associated with bipolar disorder (see Chapter 14).

Psychological Factors

Stressful life experiences often precede manic and depressive episodes (Ellicot et al., 1990; Hammen, 1995). One study found that severely stressed patients took an average of three times longer to recover from an episode than did patients not affected by stress (Johnson & Miller, 1997). The stress-disorder relationship is not simple, however: High levels of stress have less impact on patients with extroverted personalities than on

Winston Churchill made a pet of his bipolar illness, calling his depression the "black dog" that followed him around.

PHOTODISC

those who are more introverted (Swednsen et al., 1995). Personality characteristics such as neuroticism and conscientiousness have also been found to predict increases in bipolar symptoms over time (Lozano & Johnson, 2001). Finally, patients living with family members who are hostile toward or critical of the patient are more likely to relapse than patients with supportive families (Miklowitz et al., 1988).

In summary, the mood disorders are mental disorders in which a disturbance in mood is the predominant feature. Depressive disorder (or unipolar depression) is characterized by a severely depressed mood lasting at least 2 weeks; symptoms include excessive self-criticism, guilt, difficulty concentrating, suicidal thoughts, sleep and appetite disturbances, and lethargy. Dysthymia, a related disorder, involves less severe symptoms that persist for at least 2 years. For reasons that are not well understood, women are approximately twice as likely as men to suffer from depression. Studies of depression reveal a moderate level of heritability and that it may involve neurotransmitter imbalances, although the exact nature of the imbalance remains unclear. Patterns of negative thinking may also contribute to depression by tainting perceptions and judgments. One such pattern is the tendency to explain personal failures by attributing them to internal, stable, global causes. In addition, depression-prone individuals may inadvertently behave in ways that lead to social rejection, thereby contributing to and confirming a sense of low self-worth.

Bipolar disorder is an unstable emotional condition involving extreme mood swings of depression and mania. The manic phase is characterized by periods of abnormally and persistently elevated, expansive, or irritable mood, lasting at least 1 week. Bipolar disorder has a high rate of heritability, although it is unclear which gene or genes may be responsible for the problem. Patients with bipolar disorder often respond favorably to drug therapy (e.g., lithium), but the precise nature of the drug action is not well understood. Finally, stress and family problems may also contribute to the onset and maintenance of bipolar disorder. ■ ■

Schizophrenia: Losing the Grasp on Reality

Margaret, a 39-year-old mother, believed that God was punishing her for marrying a man she did not love and bringing two children into the world. As her punishment, God had made her and her children immortal so that they would have to suffer in their unhappy home life forever—a realization that came to her one evening when she was washing dishes and saw a fork lying across a knife in the shape of a cross. Margaret found further support for her belief in two pieces of evidence: First, a local station was rerunning old episodes of *The Honeymooners*, a 1950s situation comedy in which the main characters often argue and shout at each other. She saw this as a sign from God that her own marital conflict would go on forever. Second, she believed (falsely) that the pupils of her children's eyes were fixed in size and would neither dilate nor constrict—a sign of their immortality. At home, she would lock herself in her room for hours and sometimes days. The week before her diagnosis, she kept her 7-year-old son home from school so that he could join her and his 4-year-old sister in reading aloud from the Bible (Oltmanns et al., 1991). Margaret was suffering from schizophrenia, one of the most devastating and mystifying of the mental disorders.

Symptoms and Types of Schizophrenia

Schizophrenia is characterized by *the profound disruption of basic psychological processes; a distorted perception of reality; altered or blunted emotion;, and disturbances in thought, motivation, and behavior.* Traditionally, schizophrenia was regarded primarily as a disturbance of thought and perception, in which the sense of reality becomes severely distorted and

SCHIZOPHRENIA A disorder characterized by the profound disruption of basic psychological processes; a distorted perception of reality; altered or blunted emotion; and disturbances in thought, motivation, and behavior.

DELUSION A patently false belief system, often bizarre and grandiose, that is maintained in spite of its irrationality.

HALLUCINATION A false perceptual experience that has a compelling sense of being real despite the absence of external stimulation.

confused. However, this condition is now understood to take different forms affecting a wide range of functions. According to the *DSM-IV-TR*, schizophrenia is diagnosed when two or more of the following symptoms emerge during a continuous period of at least 1 month with signs of the disorder persisting for at least 6 months: *delusion, hallucination, disorganized speech, grossly disorganized behavior* or *catatonic behavior*, and *negative symptoms*. Let's consider each symptom in detail.

■ **Delusion** is *a patently false belief system, often bizarre and grandiose, that is maintained in spite of its irrationality.* For example, an individual with schizophrenia may believe that he or she is Jesus Christ, Napoleon, Joan of Arc, or some other famous person. Such delusions of identity have helped foster the misconception that schizophrenia involves multiple personalities. Unlike dissociative identity disorder, however, adopted identities in schizophrenia do not alternate, exhibit amnesia for one another, or otherwise "split." Delusions of persecution are also common. The patient's belief that the CIA, demons, extraterrestrials, or other malevolent forces are conspiring to harm the patient or control his or her mind may represent an attempt to make sense of the tormenting delusions (Roberts, 1991). People with schizophrenia have little or no insight into their disordered perceptual and thought processes. Because they cannot understand that they have lost control of their own minds, they may develop unusual beliefs and theories that attribute control to external agents.

■ **Hallucination** is *a false perceptual experience that has a compelling sense of being real despite the absence of external stimulation.* The perceptual disturbances associated with schizophrenia can include hearing, seeing, or smelling things that are not there or having tactile sensations in the absence of relevant sensory stimulation. Schizophrenic hallucinations are often auditory—for example, hearing voices that no one else can hear. Among people with schizophrenia, some 65% report hearing voices repeatedly (Frith & Fletcher, 1995). British psychiatrist Henry Maudsley (1886) long ago proposed that these voices are in fact produced in the mind of the schizophrenic individual, and recent research substantiates his idea. In one PET imaging study, auditory hallucinations were accompanied by activation in Broca's area—the part of the brain (as discussed in Chapters 3 and 7) associated with the production of language (McGuire, Shah, & Murray, 1993). Unfortunately, the voices heard in schizophrenia seldom sound like the self or like a kindly uncle offering advice. They command, scold, suggest bizarre actions, or offer snide comments. One patient reported a voice saying, "He's getting up now. He's going to wash. It's about time" (Frith & Fletcher, 1995).

The Clown Voice, 2003. Artist Elizabeth Autumn Daniels writes, "When I was about 17, I started hallucinating and thinking people were out to get me. . . . I thought that people were going to bomb my house. I was hearing 10 voices in my head nonstop. . . . Turns out I am paranoid schizophrenic . . . But finally the past couple of months I have found the right medication. . . . I have been drawing and painting since I was 5 years old. . . . And now it is helping me heal. I drew this because the clown is what I saw when I heard one of the voices in my head. . . ."

- **Disorganized speech** is *a severe disruption of verbal communication in which ideas shift rapidly and incoherently from one to another unrelated topic*. The abnormal speech patterns in schizophrenia reflect difficulties in organizing thoughts and focusing attention. Responses to questions are often irrelevant, ideas are loosely associated, and words are used in peculiar ways. For example, asked by her doctor, "Can you tell me the name of this place?" one patient with schizophrenia responded, "I have not been a drinker for 16 years. I am taking a mental rest after a 'carter' assignment of 'quill.' You know, a 'penwrap.' I had contracts with Warner Brothers Studios and Eugene broke phonograph records but Mike protested. I have been with the police department for 35 years. I am made of flesh and blood—see, Doctor" [pulling up her dress] (Carson et al., 2000, p. 474).

- **Grossly disorganized behavior** is *behavior that is inappropriate for the situation or ineffective in attaining goals, often with specific motor disturbances*. A patient might exhibit constant childlike silliness, improper sexual behavior (such as masturbating in public), disheveled appearance, or loud shouting or swearing. Specific motor disturbances might include strange movements, rigid posturing, odd mannerisms, bizarre grimacing, or hyperactivity. **Catatonic behavior** is *a marked decrease in all movement or an increase in muscular rigidity and overactivity*. Patients with *catatonia* may actively resist movement (when someone is trying to move them) or become completely unresponsive and unaware of their surroundings in a *catatonic stupor*. In addition, patients receiving drug therapy may exhibit motor symptoms (such as rigidity or spasm) as a side effect of the medication. Indeed, the *DSM-IV-TR* has proposed a diagnostic category labeled "medication-induced movement disorders" that identifies motor disturbances arising from the use of medications of the sort commonly used to treat schizophrenia.

- **Negative symptoms** include *emotional and social withdrawal; apathy; poverty of speech; and other indications of the absence or insufficiency of normal behavior, motivation, and emotion*. These symptoms refer to things missing in people with schizophrenia, in contrast to the positive symptoms (such as hallucinations) that appear more in people with schizophrenia than in other people. Negative symptoms may rob people of emotion, for example, leaving them with flat, deadpan responses. Or their ability to act willfully may be reduced, their interest in people or events undermined, or their capacity to focus attention impaired.

The various symptoms of schizophrenia do not all occur in every case. Instead, the disorder can take quite different forms. Recent editions of the *DSM* have identified five subtypes of schizophrenia (see **TABLE 13.4** on the next page). Three of these types—*paranoid*, *catatonic*, and *disorganized*—depend primarily on the relative prominence of various symptoms. The paranoid type involves preoccupation with delusions and hallucinations; the catatonic type involves immobility and stupor or agitated, purposeless motor activity; the disorganized type is often the most severe, featuring disorganized speech and behavior and flat or inappropriate emotion. The *DSM-IV-TR* reserves the *undifferentiated type* for cases that do not neatly fall into these three categories and the *residual type* for individuals who have substantially recovered from at least one schizophrenic episode but still have lingering symptoms.

DISORGANIZED SPEECH A severe disruption of verbal communication in which ideas shift rapidly and incoherently from one to another unrelated topic.

GROSSLY DISORGANIZED BEHAVIOR Behavior that is inappropriate for the situation or ineffective in attaining goals, often with specific motor disturbances.

CATATONIC BEHAVIOR A marked decrease in all movement or an increase in muscular rigidity and overactivity.

NEGATIVE SYMPTOMS Emotional and social withdrawal; apathy; poverty of speech; and other indications of the absence or insufficiency of normal behavior, motivation, and emotion.

A patient suffering from catatonic schizophrenia may assume an unusual posture and fail to move for hours.

Table 13.4	Types of Schizophrenia
Types	**Characteristics**
Paranoid type	Symptoms dominated by absurd, illogical, and changeable delusions, frequently accompanied by vivid hallucinations, with a resulting impairment of critical judgment and erratic, unpredictable, and occasionally dangerous behaviors. In chronic cases, there is usually less disorganization of behavior than in other types of schizophrenia and less extreme withdrawal from social interaction.
Catatonic type	Often characterized by alternating periods of extreme withdrawal and extreme excitement, although in some cases one or the other reaction predominates. In the withdrawal reaction, there is a sudden loss of all animation and a tendency to remain motionless for hours or even days in a single position. The person may undergo an abrupt change, with excitement coming on suddenly; the person may talk or shout incoherently, pace rapidly, and engage in uninhibited, impulsive, and frenzied behavior. In this state, an individual may be dangerous.
Disorganized type	Usually occurs at an earlier age than most other types of schizophrenia and represents a more severe disintegration of the personality. Emotional distortion and blunting typically are manifested in inappropriate laughter and silliness, peculiar mannerisms, and bizarre, often obscene behavior.
Undifferentiated type	A pattern of symptoms in which there is a rapidly changing mixture of all or most of the primary indicators of schizophrenia. Commonly observed are indications of perplexity, confusion, emotional turmoil, delusions, excitement, dreamlike autism, depression, and fear. Most often this picture is seen in patients who are in the process of breaking down and developing schizophrenia. It is also seen, however, when major adjustment demands impinge on a person with an already-established schizophrenic psychosis. In such cases, it frequently foreshadows an impending change to another primary schizophrenic subtype.
Residual type	Mild indication of schizophrenia shown by individuals in remission following a schizophrenic episode.

Schizophrenia occurs in about 1% of the population and is about equally common in men and women (Gottesman, 1991; Jablensky, 1997). The first episode typically occurs during late adolescence or early adulthood (Gottesman, 1991), although females usually have a later onset than do males (Iacono & Beiser, 1992; Marcus et al., 1993). Despite its relatively low frequency, schizophrenia is the primary diagnosis for nearly 40% of all admissions to state and county mental hospitals; it is the second most frequent diagnosis for inpatient psychiatric admission at other types of institutions (Rosenstein, Milazzo-Sayre, & Manderscheid, 1990). The disproportionate rate of hospitalization for schizophrenia is a testament to the devastation it causes in people's lives.

Biological Factors

In 1899, when German psychiatrist Emil Kraepelin first described the syndrome we now know as schizophrenia, he remarked that the disorder was so severe that it suggested "organic," or biological, origins (Kraepelin, 1899). Over the years, accumulating evidence for the role of biology in schizophrenia has come from studies of genetic factors, prenatal and perinatal environments, biochemical factors, and neuroanatomy.

Genetic Factors

Family studies indicate that the closer a person's genetic relatedness to a person with schizophrenia, the greater the likelihood of developing the disorder (Gottesman, 1991). As shown in **FIGURE 13.3**, concordance rates increase dramatically with biological

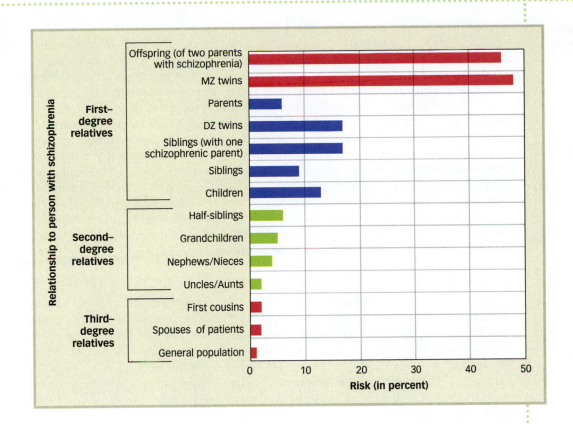

Figure 13.3 **Average Risk of Developing Schizophrenia** The risk of schizophrenia among biological relatives is greater for those with greater degrees of relatedness. An identical (MZ) twin of a twin with schizophrenia has a 48% risk of developing schizophrenia, for example, and offspring of two parents with schizophrenia have a 46% risk of developing the disorder.

(Adapted from Gottesman, 1991.)

relatedness. The rates are estimates and vary considerably from study to study, but almost every study finds the average concordance rates higher for identical twins (48%) than for fraternal twins (17%), which suggests a genetic component for the disorder (Torrey, Bower, Taylor, & Gottesman, 1994).

Prenatal and Perinatal Factors

Although genetics clearly has a strong predisposing role in schizophrenia, considerable evidence suggests that the prenatal and perinatal environments may also affect concordance rates in identical twins (Jurewicz, Owen, & O'Donovan, 2001; Thaker, 2002; Torrey et al., 1994). For example, because approximately 70% of identical twins share the same prenatal blood supply, toxins in the mother's blood could contribute to the high concordance rate. When one twin develops schizophrenia and the other twin does not, birth records often show that the afflicted twin is second born and had a lower birth weight (Wahl, 1976). In addition, people with late winter or early spring birth dates have about a 20% greater risk of schizophrenia than do those born in late summer or early fall (DeLisi, Crow, & Hirsch, 1986), raising the possibility that viral exposure during a critical period for brain development may contribute to the risk of schizophrenia (Rothermundt, Arolt, & Bayer, 2001). Further support for this idea comes from studies showing that maternal influenza in the second trimester of pregnancy is associated with an increased risk of schizophrenia (Wright et al., 1995).

Biochemical Factors

During the 1950s, major tranquilizers were discovered that could reduce the symptoms of schizophrenia by lowering levels of the

"It seems like EVERYONE has some form of schizophrenia these days. Present company excepted, of course."

DOPAMINE HYPOTHESIS The idea that schizophrenia involves an excess of dopamine activity.

neurotransmitter dopamine. The effectiveness of many drugs in alleviating schizophrenic symptoms is related to the drugs' capacity to reduce dopamine in the brain. This finding suggested the **dopamine hypothesis**, the *idea that schizophrenia involves an excess of dopamine activity*. The hypothesis has been invoked to explain why amphetamines, which increase dopamine levels, often aggravate the symptoms of schizophrenia.

If only things were so simple. Considerable evidence suggests that this hypothesis is inadequate (Csermansky & Grace, 1998; Grace & Moore, 1998). For example, many individuals with schizophrenia do not respond favorably to dopamine-blocking drugs (e.g., major tranquilizers), and those who do seldom show a complete remission of symptoms. Moreover, the drugs block dopamine receptors very rapidly, yet individuals with schizophrenia typically do not show a beneficial response for weeks. Finally, research has implicated other neurotransmitters in schizophrenia, suggesting that the disorder may involve a complex interaction among a host of different biochemicals (Benes, 1998; Lewis et al, 1999; Sawa & Snyder, 2002). In sum, the precise role of neurotransmitters in schizophrenia has yet to be determined.

Neuroanatomy

When neuroimaging techniques became available, researchers immediately started looking for distinctive anatomical features of the brain in individuals with schizophrenia. The earliest observations revealed enlargement of the *ventricles,* hollow areas filled with cerebrospinal fluid, lying deep within the core of the brain (see **FIGURE 13.4**) (Johnstone et al., 1976). In some patients—primarily those with chronic, negative symptoms—the ventricles were abnormally enlarged, suggesting a loss of brain tissue mass that could arise from an anomaly in prenatal development (Arnold et al., 1998; Heaton et al., 1994).

Understanding the significance of this brain abnormality for schizophrenia is complicated by several factors, however. First, such enlarged ventricles are found in only a minority of cases of schizophrenia. Second, some individuals who do not have schizophrenia also show evidence of enlarged ventricles. Finally, this type of brain abnormality can be caused by the long-term use of some types of antipsychotic medications commonly prescribed in schizophrenia (Breggin, 1990; Cohen, 1997; Gur et al., 1998).

Recent neuroimaging studies provide evidence of a variety of brain abnormalities in schizophrenia. Paul Thompson and his colleagues (2001) examined changes in the brains of adolescents whose MRI scans could be traced sequentially from the onset of schizophrenia. By morphing the images onto a standardized brain, the researchers were able to detect progressive tissue loss beginning in the parietal lobe and eventually encompassing much of the brain (see **FIGURE 13.5** on the next page). All adolescents

Figure 13.4 **Enlarged Ventricles in Schizophrenia** These MRI scans of monozygotic twins reveal that the twin affected by schizophrenia (a) shows enlarged ventricles (all the central white space) as compared to the unaffected twin (b).
(From Kunugi et al., 2003.)

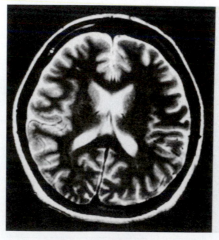
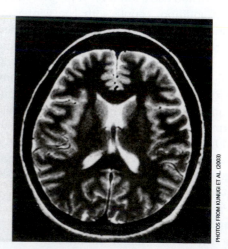

PHOTOS FROM KUNUGI ET AL. (2003)

(a) Twin with schizophrenia   **(b)** Twin without schizophrenia

Side views   Top view

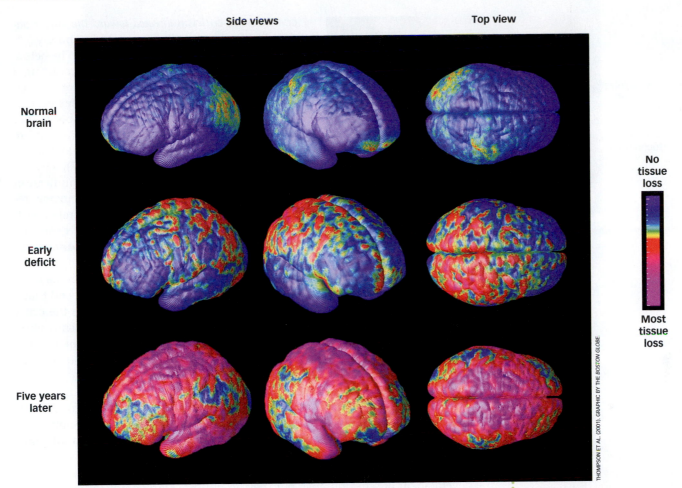

Normal
brain

Early
deficit

Five years
later

No
tissue
loss

Most
tissue
loss

THOMPSON ET AL. (2001). GRAPHIC BY THE *BOSTON GLOBE*

Figure 13.5 **Brain Tissue Loss in Adolescent Schizophrenia** MRI scan composites reveal brain tissue loss in adolescents diagnosed with schizophrenia. Normal brains (top) show minimal loss due to "pruning." Early deficit scans (middle) reveal loss in the parietal areas. Patients at this stage may experience symptoms such as hallucinations or bizarre thoughts. Scans 5 years later (bottom) reveal extensive tissue loss over much of the cortex. Patients at this stage are likely to suffer from delusions, disorganized speech and behavior, and negative symptoms such as social withdrawal.

(From Thompson et al., 2001)

lose some gray matter over time in a kind of normal "pruning" of the brain, but in the case of those developing schizophrenia, the loss was dramatic enough to seem pathological. A variety of specific brain changes found in other studies suggest a clear relationship between biological changes in the brain and the progression of schizophrenia (Shenton, Dickey, Frumin, & McCarley, 2001).

Psychological Factors

With all these potential biological contributors to schizophrenia, you might think there would be few psychological or social causes of the disorder. However, several studies do suggest that the family environment plays a role in the development of and recovery from the condition. One large-scale study compared the risk of schizophrenia in children adopted into healthy families and those adopted into severely disturbed families (Tienari et al., 2004). (Disturbed families were defined as those with extreme conflict, lack of communication, or chaotic relationships.) Among children whose biological mothers had schizophrenia, the disturbed environment increased the likelihood of developing schizophrenia—an outcome that was not found among children who were also reared in disturbed families but whose biological mothers did *not* have schizophrenia. This finding provides support for the diathesis-stress model described earlier.

In a related vein, researchers have found that a certain type of negative communication pattern in families is associated with higher relapse for schizophrenia. The pattern, called **expressed emotion**, involves *emotional overinvolvement* (*intrusiveness*)

EXPRESSED EMOTION Emotional overinvolvement (intrusiveness) and excessive criticism directed toward the former patient by his or her family.

When mothers complain: High levels of expressed emotion in the family predict relapse among patients treated for schizophrenia.

FRANCISCO CRUZ/SUPERSTOCK

and excessive criticism directed toward the former patient by his or her family. The mother who says, "I cry when I think about how you used to be before all this started," for example, is not producing a particularly comforting environment for the patient. Former patients who return to this type of family environment are at a considerably higher risk of relapse than are those who return to more adaptive families (Butzlaff & Hooley, 1998; Hooley & Hiller, 1998; Linszen et al., 1997). The extent to which these negative communication patterns contribute to schizophrenia or merely reflect the turmoil of having a family member with schizophrenia is not clear. For example, expressed emotion seems to rise and fall depending on the disturbed child's current difficulties in the home (Linszen et al., 1997; Scazufca & Kuipers, 1998).

Conclusions about the role of family functioning in the risk of schizophrenia must be tempered by the realization that the studies in this area are correlational and that a basic association between characteristics does not indicate that one causes the other (see Chapter 2). Thus, although dysfunction in families may contribute to schizophrenia, the reverse may also be true. The dysfunctional and bizarre behavior of a family member with schizophrenia may in itself promote dysfunctional communications and interactions among family members.

In summary, schizophrenia is a profound disorder involving hallucinations, disorganized thoughts and behavior, and emotional and social withdrawal. Five subtypes of schizophrenia have been identified: paranoid, catatonic, disorganized, undifferentiated, and residual. Schizophrenia affects only 1% of the population, but it accounts for a disproportionate share of psychiatric hospitalizations. Genetic factors play a role in the development of schizophrenia, but they do not provide a complete account. The first drugs that reduced the availability of dopamine sometimes reduced the symptoms of schizophrenia, suggesting that the disorder involved an excess of dopamine activity. However, recent research suggests that schizophrenia may involve a complex interaction among a variety of neurotransmitters. Neuroimaging studies have found brain abnormalities such as enlarged ventricles in some patients and a general tendency for some loss of gray matter as the disorder develops. Finally, the risk of developing schizophrenia and the likelihood of relapse may be affected by the quality of family communication patterns and relationships. ■ ■

Personality Disorders: Going to Extremes

Think for a minute about high school acquaintances whose personalities made them stand out—not necessarily in a good way. Was there a space ball, for example, a person who didn't seem to make sense, wore strange outfits, sometimes wouldn't respond in conversation—or would respond by bringing up weird things like astrology or mind reading? Or perhaps a drama queen, someone whose theatrics and exaggerated emotions turned everything into a big deal? And don't forget the neat freak, the perfectionist obsessed with control, who had the perfectly organized locker, precisely arranged hair, and sweater with zero lint balls. One way to describe such people is to say they simply have *personalities,* the unique patterns of traits we explored in Chapter 12. But sometimes personal traits can become so rigid and confining that they blend over into mental disorders. **Personality disorders** are *disorders characterized by deeply ingrained, inflexible patterns of thinking, feeling, or relating to others or controlling impulses that cause distress or impaired functioning.* Let's look at the types of personality disorders and then take a closer look at *antisocial personality disorder.*

PERSONALITY DISORDER Disorder characterized by deeply ingrained, inflexible patterns of thinking, feeling, or relating to others or controlling impulses that cause distress or impaired functioning.

Types of Personality Disorders

The *DSM-IV-TR* lists 10 personality disorders (see **TABLE 13.5**). They fall into three clusters—*odd/eccentric, dramatic/erratic,* and *anxious/inhibited.* The high school space ball, for example, could have *schizotypal personality disorder* (odd/eccentric cluster); the drama queen could have *histrionic personality disorder* (dramatic/erratic cluster); the neat freak could have *obsessive-compulsive personality disorder* (anxious/inhibited cluster). In fact, browsing through the list may awaken other high school memories. Don't

Table 13-5	Clusters of Personality Disorders	
Cluster	**Personality Disorder**	**Characteristics**
A. Odd/ Eccentric	Schizotypal	Peculiar or eccentric manners of speaking or dressing. Strange beliefs. "Magical thinking" such as belief in ESP or telepathy. Difficulty forming relationships. May react oddly in conversation, not respond, or talk to self. Speech elaborate or difficult to follow. (Possibly a mild form of schizophrenia.)
	Paranoid	Distrust in others, suspicion that people have sinister motives. Apt to challenge the loyalties of friends and read hostile intentions into others' actions. Prone to anger and aggressive outbursts but otherwise emotionally cold. Often jealous, guarded, secretive, overly serious.
	Schizoid	Extreme introversion and withdrawal from relationships. Prefers to be alone, little interest in others. Humorless, distant, often absorbed with own thoughts and feelings, a daydreamer. Fearful of closeness, with poor social skills, often seen as a "loner."
B. Dramatic/ Erratic	Antisocial	Impoverished moral sense or "conscience." History of deception, crime, legal problems, impulsive and aggressive or violent behavior. Little emotional empathy or remorse for hurting others. Manipulative, careless, callous. At high risk for substance abuse and alcoholism.
	Borderline	Unstable moods and intense, stormy personal relationships. Frequent mood changes and anger, unpredictable impulses. Self-mutilation or suicidal threats or gestures to get attention or manipulate others. Self-image fluctuation and a tendency to see others as "all good" or "all bad."
	Histrionic	Constant attention seeking. Grandiose language, provocative dress, exaggerated illnesses, all to gain attention. Believes that everyone loves them. Emotional, lively, overly dramatic, enthusiastic, and excessively flirtatious. Shallow and labile true emotions. "Onstage."
	Narcissistic	Inflated sense of self-importance, absorbed by fantasies of self and success. Exaggerates own achievement, assumes others will recognize they are superior. Good first impressions but poor longer-term relationships. Exploitative of others.
C. Anxious/ Inhibited	Avoidant	Socially anxious and uncomfortable unless they are confident of being liked. In contrast with schizoid person, yearns for social contact. Fears criticism and worries about being embarrassed in front of others. Avoids social situations due to fear of rejection.
	Dependent	Submissive, dependent, requiring excessive approval, reassurance, and advice. Clings to people and fears losing them. Lacking self-confidence. Uncomfortable when alone. May be devastated by end of close relationship or suicidal if breakup is threatened.
	Obsessive-compulsive	Conscientious, orderly, perfectionist. Excessive need to do everything "right." Inflexibly high standards and caution can interfere with their productivity. Fear of errors can make them strict and controlling. Poor expression of emotions. (*Not* the same as obsessive-compulsive disorder.)

Source: From *DSM-IV-TR* (American Psychiatric Association, 2000).

Teenage drama queen or early signs of histrionic personality disorder?

rush to judgment, however. Most of those kids are probably quite healthy and fall far short of qualifying for a diagnosis—after all, high school can be a rocky time for everyone. The *DSM-IV-TR* even notes that early personality problems often do not persist into adulthood. Still, the array of personality disorders suggests that there are multiple ways an individual's gift of a unique personality could become a burden.

Personality disorders are the most controversial classifications in the *DSM-IV-TR* for several reasons. First, critics question whether having a problem personality is really a disorder. Given that 14.8% of the U.S. population has a personality disorder that fits a *DSM* description (Grant et al., 2004), perhaps it might be better just to admit that a lot of people are difficult and leave it at that. Another question is whether personality problems correspond to "disorders" in that there are distinct *types* or whether such problems might be better understood as extreme values on trait *dimensions* such as the Big Five traits discussed in Chapter 12 (Trull & Durrett, 2005). Finally, definitions of many personality problems share characteristics with the major disorders and may be mild versions of these conditions. Overall, for example, roughly half of people with an anxiety or mood disorder have a comorbid personality disorder (Van Velzen & Emmelkamp, 1996). Research is ongoing on these various questions (Oldham, Skodol, & Bender, 2005).

Many people with personality disorders won't admit to them, and this adds a further diagnostic complication. Personality measurement depends largely on self-reports—a pointless undertaking when self-insight is the exception rather than the rule. Not incidentally, people with exaggerated personalities create problems for themselves, disturb those around them, and often seem blind to the high impact their personalities can have. It's as if their disorder blinds them to their disorder. In people suffering from paranoid personality disorder, for example, suspicion of anyone who accuses them of paranoia is likely; similarly, people with narcissistic personality disorder are likely to see comments on their personality as mere jealousy. It's difficult to see a troubled personality from the inside.

Although some self-report surveys designed to assess personality disorders have proved useful (Clark, 2007), the lack of insight typical of personality disorders renders most instruments untrustworthy. To solve this problem, researchers have turned to *peer nomination* measures, reports by others who know the person. Just like your high school classmates who gossiped about the personality problems of their peers, people in any group seem to develop common conceptions of which members are most troubled or troubling. Research on peer nominations in college sororities and fraternities and in groups of military recruits reveals that groups arrive at remarkably

Military recruits going through basic training develop knowledge of one another's personalities. Their judgments of one another at the end of training—peer nominations—produce valid predictions of who will later receive early discharge from the military.

homogeneous assessments of their personality-disordered members (Oltmanns & Turkheimer, 2006). Through gossip or through personal experience with the "square pegs in round holes," everybody seems to know who is paranoid, dependent, avoidant, or unusual in some other way. Peer nominations using basic reports of the behavior of people in a group can predict which members will have further problems—such as dropping out of college or being discharged early from the military (Fiedler, Oltmanns, & Turkheimer, 2004).

The common feature of personality disorders is a failure to take other people's perspectives, particularly on the self. People with personality disorders often blame others, society, or the universe for their difficulties, distorting their perceptions of the world in a way that makes the personality disorder seem perfectly normal—at least to them. In many of the personality disorders, this blindness perpetuates the disorder and so hurts the person who suffers from it: People with personality disorders are often unhappy or depressed. Antisocial personality disorder, however, is particularly likely to go beyond harm to self and to exact a cost on anyone who knows the person—because the individual with antisocial personality disorder also lacks insight into what it means to hurt others.

Antisocial Personality Disorder

Henri Desiré Landru began using the personal columns to attract a woman "interested in matrimony" in Paris in 1914, and he succeeded in seducing 10 of them. He bilked them of their savings, poisoned them, and cremated them in his stove, also disposing of a boy and two dogs along the way. He recorded his murders in a notebook and maintained a marriage and a mistress all the while. The gruesome actions of serial killers such as Landru leave us frightened and wondering; however, bullies, compulsive liars, and even drivers who regularly speed through a school zone share the same shocking blindness to human pain. The *DSM-IV-TR* suggests that any pattern of extreme disregard for other people should be considered a personality disorder and offers the category **antisocial personality disorder (APD)**, defined as *a pervasive pattern of disregard for and violation of the rights of others that begins in childhood or early adolescence and continues into adulthood.*

Adults with an antisocial personality diagnosis typically have a history of *conduct disorder* before the age of 15—problems such as aggression, destruction of property, rule violations, and deceitfulness, lying, or stealing. Early fire setting and cruelty to animals often predict antisocial tendencies. In adulthood, then, the diagnosis of APD is given to individuals who show three or more of a set of seven diagnostic signs: illegal behavior, deception, impulsivity, physical aggression, recklessness, irresponsibility, and a lack of remorse for wrongdoing. About 3.6% of the general population has antisocial personality disorder, and the rate of occurrence in men is three times the rate in women (Grant et al., 2004).

The terms *sociopath* and *psychopath* describe people with APD who are especially coldhearted, manipulative, and ruthless—yet may be glib and charming (Cleckley, 1976; Hare, 1998). Although psychologists usually try to explain the development of abnormal behavior as a product of childhood experiences or difficult life circumstances, those who work with APD seem less forgiving, often noting the sheer dangerousness of people with this disorder. Many people with APD do commit crimes, and many are caught because of the frequency and flagrancy of their infractions. Among 22,790 prisoners in one study, 47% of the men and 21% of women were diagnosed with antisocial personality disorder (Fazel & Danesh, 2002). Statistics such as these support the notion of a "criminal personality," a person born to be wild.

THREE LIONS/GETTY IMAGES

Henri Desiré Landru (1869–1922), a serial killer who met widows through ads he placed in newspapers' lonely hearts columns. After obtaining enough information to embezzle money from them, he murdered 10 women and the son of one of the women. He was executed for serial murder in 1922.

Positive Psychology: Exterminating the Mindbugs

YOU ARE NOW FAMILIAR WITH SOME OF the most difficult challenges we face—profound, painful mental problems that can cause great unhappiness. Although the downside of human experience has always been part of the domain of psychology, psychologists' interests go beyond the negative aspects of life. Early on, for example, William James (1902) recommended a focus on "healthy mindedness" in contrast to looking only at "sick souls." The desire to look on the sunny side of the mind has popped up often in the history of psychology, and others who have shared this vision include humanistic psychologists such as Abraham Maslow (see Chapter 12) and Carl Rogers (see Chapter 14).

Most recently, the desire to emphasize the positive has surfaced in a flourishing movement known as *positive psychology*—an approach that seeks to understand what makes our lives pleasant, good, and meaningful. Martin E. P. Seligman has championed this movement, organizing the field of positive psychology by suggesting that human happiness and virtue deserve the same careful study usually devoted to mental disorders (and all the other mindbugs). In contrast to the classification of mental disorders in the *DSM,* for example, Seligman and his colleagues (Peterson & Seligman, 2004) introduced a complementary system for classifying, *Character Strengths and Virtues,* the *CSV* (see the accompanying table). These positive qualities of humans are seldom mentioned in the *DSM,* of course, as they show the mind in good order rather than in disorder.

In line with the *CSV* system's positive approach, no individual is expected to have every strength or virtue, and individuals are not supposed to "keep score" by measuring themselves with this list. Rather, the list illustrates our potential to build personal strengths that help to make us happy and human. Listing positive characteristics of people makes for a kind of celebration, an appreciation of what being a person can be.

Virtue	Definition	Specific Strengths
Wisdom and knowledge	Cognitive strengths that entail the acquisition and use of knowledge	Creativity, open-mindedness, curiosity, love of learning, perspective
Courage	Emotional strengths that involve the exercise of will to accomplish goals in the face of opposition, external or internal	Authenticity, bravery, persistence, zest
Humanity	Interpersonal strengths that involve tending and befriending others	Kindness, love, social intelligence
Justice	Civic strengths that underlie healthy community life	Fairness, leadership, teamwork
Temperance	Strengths that protect against excess	Forgiveness, modesty, prudence, self-regulation
Transcendence	Strengths that forge connections to the larger universe and provide meaning	Appreciation of beauty and excellence, gratitude, hope, humor, religiousness

Source: From Peterson and Seligman (2004), *Character Strengths and Virtues.*

Both the early onset of conduct problems and the lack of success in treatment suggest that career criminality has an internal cause (Lykken, 1995). Evidence of brain abnormalities in people with APD is also accumulating (Blair, Peschardt, & Mitchell, 2005). One line of investigation has looked at sensitivity to fear in psychopaths and individuals who show no such psychopathology. For example, criminal psychopaths who are shown negative emotional words such as *hate* or *corpse* exhibit less activity in the amygdala and hippocampus than do noncriminals (Kiehl et al., 2001). The two brain areas are involved in the process of fear conditioning (Patrick, Cuthbert, & Lang, 1994), so their relative inactivity in such studies suggests that psychopaths are less sensitive to fear than are other people. Violent psychopaths can target their aggression toward the self as well as others, often behaving in reckless ways that lead to violent ends. It might seem peaceful to go through life "without fear," but perhaps fear is useful in keeping people from the extremes of antisocial behavior.

The psychological disorders we have examined in this chapter represent a tragic loss of human potential. The contentment, peace, and love that people could be enjoying are crowded out by pain and suffering when the mind goes awry to create disorders (see the Hot Science box above). A scientific approach to mental disorders that

The positive psychology movement has been particularly effective in stimulating research on happiness. Each of us claims to be something of an expert on what will make us happy (Chocolate, please, lots of it, and on the double! No, wait, I'd like servants, that's it—servants! Or should I request world peace? No, no, a speedboat . . .), but it is often surprising just how mistaken we can be about what will bring us the joy we desire (Gilbert, 2006). Research supplies some happy facts:

- Money can buy happiness, but only a little. Wealthy people are only the tiniest bit happier than the average person (Diener, Horwitz, & Emmons, 1985), but extreme poverty is associated with less happiness—particularly in cultures where such poverty is rare (Diener & Biswas-Diener, 2002).

- Friends make you happy. People report that the main source of their happiness is relationships—with their friends, spouses, and children (*Time* poll, 2005). As the old saying goes, people on their deathbed never say, "I should have spent more time at work."

- Some people do "live happily ever after." Married people are happier than singles, especially right after getting married and then again when their children are grown (Coombs, 1991). Their greater happiness may be, however, because they were happier to begin with (Lucas et al., 2003).

- Happiness is born, not made. Twin studies reveal that as much as 50% of variability in happiness is due to genetic factors (Lykken & Tellegen, 1996). Ideally, try to be born happy.

- Happy times may not last. People regularly overestimate the degree to which positive events (such as winning the lottery) will make them happy. They fail to appreciate their own tendency to adjust psychologically to emotional experiences and "get over it," no matter what "it" is (Gilbert, 2006; Wilson & Gilbert, 2003).

- Happiness dispels the blues. Happiness undermines negative emotions such as anger, fear, and sadness, acting to neutralize these feelings and enhance mental health (Fredrickson, 2001).

- Happiness comes from goodness. Doing good deeds or seeing them done can lead to feelings of elevation and happiness (Haidt, 2006).

More happy facts are surfacing every day, as many researchers have joined the movement toward positive psychology (Gable & Haidt, 2005). This movement provides a useful balance to the more common focus of the field on the negative—the disorders, the illusions, the errors, and, yes, the mindbugs. Knowing about mindbugs does aid in understanding how the mind works: As you have seen at many points in the text, you can learn a lot about a mechanism by seeing how it breaks down. All too often, though, the focus in studying psychological disorders and errors can be too gloomy, a constant reminder of the perils of being "only human." Like the good physician who brings to a patient's bedside both an analytical appreciation of the patient's disorder and a warm smile to help the patient through the rough times, the field of psychology must temper the bitter with the sweet. Psychological science can be most effective when it unites the problem-solving approach of studying disorders with the ideals and optimism of studying wellness.

---

views them through a medical model is beginning to sort out their symptoms and causes. As we will see in the next chapter, this approach already offers treatments for some disorders that are remarkably effective and for other disorders offers hope that pain and suffering can be alleviated in the future.

In summary, the personality disorders are deeply ingrained, inflexible patterns of thinking, feeling, relating to others, or controlling impulses that cause distress or impaired functioning. They include three clusters—odd/eccentric, dramatic/erratic, and anxious/inhibited. The classification of these disorders is controversial because they may be no more than extreme examples of normal personality, may represent personality dimensions rather than types of disorder, and are often comorbid with other disorders. One unifying feature of personality disorders is patients' lack of insight into their disorders, so self-report measurement of these disorders is ineffective and peer nomination procedures are more successful. Antisocial personality disorder is associated with a lack of moral emotions and behavior. Those with antisocial personality disorder can be manipulative, dangerous, and reckless, often hurting others and sometimes hurting themselves. "Criminal personalities" are often found in prison populations. ■ ■

Where Do You Stand?

Normal or Abnormal

In the course of learning about mental disorders, you may have found yourself thinking about how they relate to your own experience. On the one hand, imagining the experience of those with anxiety disorders or depression is fairly easy because you know what it feels like to be tense or blue. On the other hand, severe disorders may seem more foreign because they involve extreme distortions of reality reflected by hallucinations and bizarre delusions. But just how unusual are these severe symptoms? In the accompanying table, you will find a list of symptoms that are sometimes considered indications of delusional beliefs (Peters, Joseph, & Garety, 1999). Rate each according to your own judgment of whether the feeling or belief is normal or abnormal.

Some of these symptoms are at least moderately common. In one study of 375 college students, 71% of participants reported hearing brief, occasional hallucinated voices during periods of wakefulness, and 39% had

heard their own thoughts spoken aloud (Linszen et al., 1997; Posey & Losch, 1983). A study of 586 college students found that 30% to 40% had heard voices when no one was present, and of those, almost half heard voices at least once a month (Barrett & Etheridge, 1992). Reports of verbal hallucinations were not associated with measures of overt or incipient psychopathology. Apparently, hallucinatory experiences—at least of an auditory type—may not be as abnormal as you might have guessed.

What about delusional thinking? If beliefs about scientifically unverified, paranormal experiences are any gauge, many people appear to hold some pretty odd notions. For example, in a survey of 60,000 adults, 50% expressed a belief in thought transference between two people, 25% said they believe in ghosts, and 25% in reincarnation (Cox & Cowling, 1989). Formal diagnostic interviews with a cross-section of ordinary U.S. residents revealed that approximately 8%

had delusions that met criteria for paranoia (Eaton et al., 1991). A comparison of the performance on a delusional beliefs questionnaire of healthy individuals and patients with psychotic disorders revealed, not unexpectedly, that the healthy group was less delusional than the psychotic group; however, approximately 10% of the normal group had scores that were higher than the average for the psychotic group (Peters et al., 1999).

So what is normal or abnormal? Where do you stand? Each of us may have some personal quirks that others would surely find abnormal—and we can certainly identify some of the things our friends do as pretty peculiar as well. As we have tried to demonstrate in this chapter, however, questions of what is normal or abnormal hinge more on what causes difficulty in people's lives than on simple counts of what behaviors are common or uncommon.

Instructions

Please rate each of the following statements from 0 (perfectly normal) to 10 (very abnormal). Don't include what might be normal or abnormal under the influence of drugs—consider only a nonintoxicated state of mind.

perfectly normal   very abnormal
0 1 2 3 4 5 6 7 8 9 10

Feeling you are under the control of some force or power other than yourself	0 1 2 3 4 5 6 7 8 9 10
Feeling as if you are a robot or zombie without a will of your own	0 1 2 3 4 5 6 7 8 9 10
Feeling as if you are possessed by someone or something else	0 1 2 3 4 5 6 7 8 9 10
Feeling as if your actions and feelings are not under your control	0 1 2 3 4 5 6 7 8 9 10
Feeling as if someone is playing games with your mind	0 1 2 3 4 5 6 7 8 9 10
Feeling as if people seem to drop hints about you or say things with a double meaning	0 1 2 3 4 5 6 7 8 9 10
Feeling as if things in magazines or on TV were written especially for you	0 1 2 3 4 5 6 7 8 9 10
Thinking that everyone is gossiping about you	0 1 2 3 4 5 6 7 8 9 10
Feeling as if some people are not what they seem to be	0 1 2 3 4 5 6 7 8 9 10
Feeling as if things around you are unreal, as if it was all part of an experiment	0 1 2 3 4 5 6 7 8 9 10
Feeling as if someone is deliberately trying to harm you	0 1 2 3 4 5 6 7 8 9 10
Feeling as if you are being persecuted in some way	0 1 2 3 4 5 6 7 8 9 10
Feeling as if there is a conspiracy against you	0 1 2 3 4 5 6 7 8 9 10

Feeling as if some organization or institution has it in for you	0	1	2	3	4	5	6	7	8	9	10
Feeling as if someone or something is watching you	0	1	2	3	4	5	6	7	8	9	10
Feeling as if you have special abilities or powers	0	1	2	3	4	5	6	7	8	9	10
Feeling as if there is a special mission or purpose to your life	0	1	2	3	4	5	6	7	8	9	10
Feeling as if there is a mysterious power working for the good of the world	0	1	2	3	4	5	6	7	8	9	10
Feeling as if you are destined to be someone very important	0	1	2	3	4	5	6	7	8	9	10
Feeling that you are a very special or unusual person	0	1	2	3	4	5	6	7	8	9	10
Feeling that you are especially close to God	0	1	2	3	4	5	6	7	8	9	10
Thinking that people can communicate telepathically	0	1	2	3	4	5	6	7	8	9	10
Feeling as if electrical devices such as computers can influence the way you think	0	1	2	3	4	5	6	7	8	9	10
Feeling as if there are forces around you that affect you in strange ways	0	1	2	3	4	5	6	7	8	9	10
Feeling as if you have been chosen by God in some way	0	1	2	3	4	5	6	7	8	9	10
Believing in the power of witchcraft, voodoo, or the occult	0	1	2	3	4	5	6	7	8	9	10
Worrying that your partner may be unfaithful	0	1	2	3	4	5	6	7	8	9	10
Thinking that you smell very unusual to other people	0	1	2	3	4	5	6	7	8	9	10
Feeling as if your body is changing in a peculiar way	0	1	2	3	4	5	6	7	8	9	10
Thinking that strangers want to have sex with you	0	1	2	3	4	5	6	7	8	9	10
Feeling you have sinned more than the average person	0	1	2	3	4	5	6	7	8	9	10
Feeling that people look at you oddly because of your appearance	0	1	2	3	4	5	6	7	8	9	10
Feeling as if you had no thoughts in your head at all	0	1	2	3	4	5	6	7	8	9	10
Feeling as if your insides might be rotting	0	1	2	3	4	5	6	7	8	9	10
Feeling as if the world is about to end	0	1	2	3	4	5	6	7	8	9	10
Having your thoughts feel alien to you in some way	0	1	2	3	4	5	6	7	8	9	10

Chapter Review

Identifying Psychological Disorders: What Is Abnormal?

- The study of abnormal behavior not only enhances our understanding of the causes and treatments of mental disorders but also offers insights about normal psychological functioning.
- The reliable identification and classification of mental disorders is essential to the scientific study and treatment of psychological problems.
- Although imperfect, the *DSM* classification system is a noteworthy attempt to identify the key elements of various psychological conditions. Progressive revisions of the *DSM* have led to improvements in reliability, but room for improvement remains.

- Mental disorders are best understood from an integrative perspective that considers a combination of influences, including biological, psychological, and environmental factors.
- The diathesis-stress model proposes that a person may possess a predisposition for a mental disorder that remains unexpressed until it is triggered by stress.
- The social stigma associated with mental disorders can lead to labeling effects that undermine objective judgments and perceptions.

Anxiety Disorders: When Fears Take Over

- Anxiety disorders involve irrational worries and fears that undermine well-being and cause dysfunction.

- The anxiety may be chronic, as in generalized anxiety disorder, or it may be tied to a specific object or situation, as in the phobic disorders.

- In panic disorder, people experience a sudden and intense attack of anxiety that is terrifying and can lead them to become housebound for fear of public humiliation.

- People with obsessive-compulsive disorder experience repetitive, anxiety-provoking thoughts that compel them to engage in ritualistic, irrational behavior.

Dissociative Disorders: Going to Pieces

- The dissociative disorders involve severely disjointed and fragmented cognitive processes reflected in significant disruptions in memory, awareness, or personality.

- People with dissociative identity disorder (DID) shift between two or more identities that are distinct from each other in personal memories, behavioral characteristics, and attitudes. Reported cases of DID have been increasing since the 1970s as the disorder has received more widespread media attention, leading some researchers to believe that it may be overdiagnosed.

- Dissociative amnesia and dissociative fugue involve significant memory loss that is not the result of normal forgetting and cannot be attributed to brain injury, drugs, or another mental disorder. The memory loss is often associated with stressful life circumstances. In addition to a memory loss for one's personal history, dissociative fugue is accompanied by an abrupt departure from home and the assumption of a new identity.

Mood Disorders: At the Mercy of Emotions

- Major depression, also known as unipolar depression, is characterized by a severely depressed mood (lasting at least 2 weeks) that is associated with excessive self-criticism, guilt, concentration difficulties, suicidal thoughts, sleep and appetite disturbances, and lethargy. Approximately twice as many women are diagnosed with depression as are men.

- Dysthymia is a less severe form of depression that persists for at least 2 years.

- Depression shows a moderate level of heritability and may involve neurochemical imbalances. Cognitive biases may also contribute to depression by tainting judgments and perceptions. In addition, depression-prone individuals may inadvertently behave in ways that lead to social rejection, thereby contributing to and confirming a sense of low self-worth.

- Bipolar disorder is an unstable emotional condition involving extreme mood swings of depression and mania. The manic phase is characterized by periods of abnormally and persistently elevated, expansive, or irritable mood.

- Bipolar disorder has a high rate of heritability, although it is unclear which gene or genes may be responsible for the problem. Stress and family problems may also contribute to the onset and maintenance of the disorder.

Schizophrenia: Losing the Grasp on Reality

- Schizophrenia is a profound disorder that can bring hallucinations, delusions, disorganized speech, disorganized or catatonic behavior, and negative symptoms such as motivational deficits. Five subtypes of schizophrenia have been identified: paranoid, catatonic, disorganized, undifferentiated, and residual. Although schizophrenia affects only 1% of the population, it accounts for a disproportionate share of psychiatric hospitalizations.

- Genetic factors play a role in the development of schizophrenia, but they do not provide a complete account. Neuroimaging studies have found brain abnormalities such as enlarged ventricles in some patients and a general tendency for some loss of gray matter as the disorder develops. Drugs that reduce the availability of dopamine sometimes reduce the symptoms of schizophrenia, but research suggests that schizophrenia may involve a complex interaction among a variety of neurotransmitters. The risk of developing schizophrenia and the likelihood of relapse may be affected by the quality of family communication patterns and relationships.

Personality Disorders: Going to Extremes

- Personality disorders are deeply ingrained, inflexible patterns of thinking, feeling, relating to others, or controlling impulses that cause distress or impaired functioning.

- The personality disorders include three clusters—odd/eccentric, dramatic/erratic, and anxious/inhibited. However, the classification of these disorders is controversial because they may be no more than extremes of personality or dimensions rather than types, and they are frequently comorbid with other disorders.

- Patients with personality disorders often lack insight into their disorders. Self-report measurement of these disorders is thus difficult, but peer nomination procedures can be successful.

- Antisocial personality disorder is associated with a lack of moral emotions and behavior. People with antisocial personality disorder can be manipulative, dangerous, and reckless, often hurting others or themselves, and are often found in prison populations.

Key Terms

medical model (p. 491)
DSM-IV-TR (p. 491)
comorbidity (p. 496)
diathesis-stress model (p. 498)
anxiety disorder (p. 501)
generalized anxiety disorder
  (GAD) (p. 502)
phobic disorders (p. 503)
specific phobia (p. 503)
social phobia (p. 504)
preparedness theory (p. 504)

panic disorder (p. 505)
agoraphobia (p. 505)
obsessive-compulsive disorder
  (OCD) (p. 507)
dissociative disorder
  (p. 508)
dissociative identity disorder
  (DID) (p. 508)
dissociative amnesia (p. 510)
dissociative fugue (p. 510)
mood disorders (p. 511)

major depressive disorder
  (p. 512)
dysthymia (p. 512)
double depression (p. 512)
seasonal affective disorder
  (SAD) (p. 512)
helplessness theory (p. 514)
bipolar disorder (p. 515)
schizophrenia (p. 519)
delusion (p. 520)
hallucination (p. 520)

disorganized speech (p. 521)
grossly disorganized behavior
  (p. 521)
catatonic behavior (p. 521)
negative symptoms (p. 521)
dopamine hypothesis (p. 524)
expressed emotion (p. 525)
personality disorders (p. 526)
antisocial personality disorder
  (APD) (p. 529)

Recommended Readings

Jamison, K. R. (1999). *Night falls fast: Understanding suicide.* New York: Random House. Kay Jamison, author of the national best seller *An Unquiet Mind* and a researcher on mood disorders, examines the phenomenon of suicide using data and powerful examples. She discusses factors— biological, psychological, and sociocultural—that contribute to suicide and points out the remarkable lack of attention given to this common killer that claims thousands of lives each year.

Nasar, S. (1998). *A beautiful mind.* New York: Simon & Schuster. The book recounts the story of John Nash, a mathematics prodigy who was awarded the 1993 Nobel Prize in Economics for his influential early contributions but whose work was interrupted for more than 20 years by schizophrenia. The story of his life, his accomplishments, and his struggle with and recovery from schizophrenia are told in moving detail. The book was the basis for the motion picture of the same name.

Rapoport, J. (1989). *The boy who couldn't stop washing: The experience and treatment of obsessive-compulsive disorder.* New York: Penguin. This brief book focuses on obsessive-compulsive disorder, offering both individual stories and general information about the symptoms, causes, and treatment of the disorder. In suggesting drug treatments of the disorder, it focuses on the brain rather than the mind as a cause.

Vonnegut, M. (1976). *The Eden express.* New York: Bantam. The author provides a vivid description of his descent into a psychotic disorder. It is an engaging, thoughtful, poignant, and honest story that provides a rare glimpse into the intriguing and terrifying world of psychosis. Mark Vonnegut— who is the son of famous author Kurt Vonnegut—eventually recovered from his disorder and returned to school, obtaining a degree in medicine.

14

Treatment of Psychological Disorders

THE PLANE WAS STILL AT THE GATE, BUT Lisa was buckled in her seat with her hands tightly squeezing the armrests, her knuckles white. She glanced out the window, swallowed hard, and then stole a look at the people across the aisle. They seemed calm, but she didn't feel calm at all. Her heart was pounding, and then she noticed that the plane was starting to move. She was deathly afraid of flying, but she hoped that this flight might be easier. After all, she wasn't really in a plane. Instead, she was seated in a psychologist's office, wearing virtual reality goggles that projected the sights and sounds of the flight all around her. She was in therapy.

Treatment: Getting Help to Those Who Need It
Why People Need Treatment
Why People Cannot or Will Not Seek Treatment
Approaches to Treatment

Psychological Therapies: Healing the Mind through Interaction
THE REAL WORLD Types of Psychotherapists
Psychodynamic Therapy
Behavioral and Cognitive Therapies
Humanistic and Existential Therapies
Groups in Therapy

Medical and Biological Treatments: Healing the Mind through the Brain
Antipsychotic Medications
THE REAL WORLD Tales from the Madhouse
Antianxiety Medications
Antidepressants and Mood Stabilizers
Herbal and Natural Products
Medications in Perspective
Biological Treatments beyond Medication

Treatment Effectiveness: For Better or for Worse
Evaluating Treatments
Which Treatments Work?
THE REAL WORLD Controversial Treatment: Eye Movement Desensitization and Reprocessing
WHERE DO YOU STAND? Should Drugs Be Used to Prevent Traumatic Memories?

Psychological therapy takes many forms. In this case, Lisa's fear was being treated with a relatively new technique called *virtual reality therapy*. Lisa's fear of flying (sometimes called *aviophobia*) had become a serious personal problem: She had become very unpopular with her husband and children. Exotic family vacations had been postponed again and again, eventually replaced by boring road trips. Lately, she had become exasperated with herself too, and losing a job opportunity because it required occasional air travel had finally convinced her to seek the help of a therapist.

The therapist sat nearby during the virtual flight and described what happened as if it were a real flight. The therapist encouraged Lisa to progress at her own pace through the stages of air travel that made her anxious—sitting on a plane with the engines off, sitting on a plane with the engines on, taxiing on the runway, a smooth takeoff and a smooth flight, a smooth landing, a close pass similar to a missed landing, a rough landing, a turbulent flight, and a rough takeoff. Lisa came back for six sessions over several weeks, and at the end of her virtual travels she reported feeling no anxiety about any of these virtual events. With the therapist's encouragement, she soon took the step of flying in a real plane. This was difficult, but her fear wasn't as strong as it had been, and she was able to succeed. She was finally able to take that family vacation she had put off for so long (Rothbaum et al., 1996).

There are a number of ways to treat most psychological disorders, with the goal of changing a person's thoughts, behaviors, emotions, or coping skills. Treatments requiring a person to wear wraparound video goggles are not yet commonplace, but the variety and ingenuity of goggle-free treatment techniques is remarkable. In this chapter we will explore the most common approaches to psychological treatment. We will examine how psychotherapy for individuals is built on the major theories of the causes and cures of disorders—including psychoanalytic, behavioral, cognitive, and humanistic/existential theories—and explore how psychotherapy can be conducted for people in groups as well. We'll look into medical and biological approaches to treatment that focus on understanding the brain's role in disorders. Finally, we will discuss whether treatment works, as well as how we know that treatment works.

Before examining treatment itself, you might ask yourself why people need to seek treatment in the first place. For example, did Lisa do the right thing in seeing a therapist for her fear of flying rather than simply living with her fear or trying to do something about it on her own? When do people's concerns go from normal and manageable to abnormal and in need of treatment? To answer this question, let's consider when people need to get psychological help.

Virtual reality therapy offers new possibilities for treating people with psychological disorders, especially phobias. Clients can practice engaging in "virtual experiences" before tackling the real-life experiences they fear. On the left is a therapist conducting a virtual flight, on the right, the client's virtual "view" out the "plane" window.

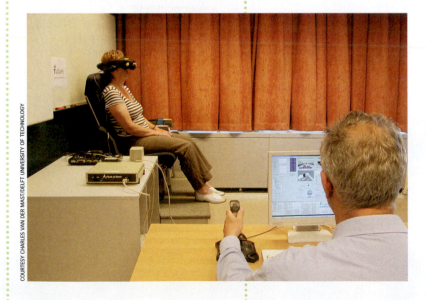

Treatment: Getting Help to Those Who Need It

A physical symptom such as a toothache would send most people to the dentist—a trip that usually results in a successful treatment. The clear source of pain and the obvious solution make for a quick and effective response. In contrast, the path from a mental disorder to a successful treatment is often far less clear. Three major obstacles can prevent successful treatment: People may not recognize that treatment is needed, they may not be able or willing to get treatment, and they may not even know if anything can be done. Let's consider these obstacles one at a time.

Why People Need Treatment

Estimates suggest that almost one in five people suffers from some type of mental disorder (Narrow et al., 2002). As you read in Chapter 13, these disorders have many different symptoms, causes, and consequences. People pursue treatment for many reasons, but most often they are motivated to seek treatment by the personal, social, or financial costs of untreated disorders.

Think about the personal costs if Lisa, our fearful flyer, did not seek treatment or could not get treatment. Yes, she would be unable to take advantage of air travel—but there's more. In the case of a phobia such as fear of flying, her symptoms might worsen without treatment. Some people with aviophobia develop difficulty with simple day-to-day tasks due to a disabling fear of encountering anything that could even remind them of airplanes. Watching an airplane trip on television might be too much to bear, for example, and even the sound of airplane engines flying overhead could be so frightening as to keep the person at home all the time. Every psychological disorder incurs personal costs, and these are often why people pursue treatment.

Beyond the personal costs, the social and financial burdens associated with mental disorders are enormous. For example, people with anxiety disorders report levels of impairment in their daily lives that are comparable to or higher than those of people with chronic medical illnesses, such as multiple sclerosis or end-stage renal disease (Antony et al., 1998). Impairment is widespread, affecting family life, the ability to work, maintenance of friendships, and more. A person with schizophrenia or severe depression may be unable to hold down a job or even get organized enough to collect a welfare check, and people with many disorders stop getting along with family or people who are trying to help. At the extreme, victims of some disorders can become violent and dangerous to themselves or others.

One set of calculations found that the annual financial burden of anxiety disorders alone in the United States was $42.3 billion, or $1,542 per sufferer, including costs of

Cho Seung-Hui slaughtered 32 people at Virginia Tech University in 2007 and then killed himself. He sent an angry, rambling manifesto and videos of himself to the media. Posing with guns, he said, "Jesus was crucifying me. When the time came, I did it. I had no choice. . . .This didn't have to happen." Cho was clearly mentally ill, and effective treatment might have saved these lives.

treatment, diminished productivity, and absenteeism in the workplace (Greenberg et al., 1999). If we add in similar figures for schizophrenia, mood disorders, substance abuse, and all the other psychological problems, the overall costs are astronomical. In addition to the personal benefits of treatment, then, society also stands to benefit from the effective treatment of psychological disorders.

Why People Cannot or Will Not Seek Treatment

Despite the high prevalence of psychological problems in the general population, most people who suffer from such problems do not receive help. One national survey of more than 1,600 adults diagnosed with depression or an anxiety disorder found that only 30% received appropriate treatment for the problem—despite the fact that 83% had seen a health care provider in the previous year (in most cases, a family doctor) (Young et al., 2001). People may fail to get treatment because they don't believe their disorder needs to be treated, because barriers prevent them from gaining access to treatment, or because they don't know enough about treatment to be able to get it.

Recognizing that a disorder needs to be treated is a big first step. Mental illness is often not taken nearly as seriously as physical illness, perhaps because the origin of mental illness is "hidden" and usually cannot be diagnosed by a blood test or x ray. People sometimes assume that depression is similar to normal sadness, for example, or that social anxiety disorder (social phobia) is nothing more than shyness. In reality, depression and social phobia are much more intense than sadness and shyness, and both disorders create much greater interference in a person's life. The stigma of mental illness often includes beliefs that mental problems can be solved by "mind over matter." In other words, some people believe that mental illness is a sign of personal weakness or that people suffering from mental illness are not trying hard enough to help themselves. These beliefs have persisted for centuries, despite efforts to educate the public about mental illness.

There are other barriers to treatment, such as beliefs and circumstances that keep people from getting help. Individuals may believe that they should be able to handle things themselves or that their problems are not as bad as other people's problems, instilling guilt for taking the spot of someone else who "really" needs treatment. Families sometimes discourage their loved ones from seeking help, perhaps because of the stigma associated with mental illness or because of the belief that these things can be better dealt with in the family. For example, a family may not encourage an alcoholic father to seek treatment because the public acknowledgment of his problem is seen as an embarrassment to the family. In other cases, there may be waiting lists or financial obstacles to getting treatment. Barriers may arise from treatment providers or facilities themselves, including such factors as long waiting lists, lack of funding for adequate staffing, or lack of staff education about the most up-to-date treatments.

Even people who acknowledge they have a problem may not know who to see or where to look for services. Like finding a good lawyer or plumber, finding the right psychologist can be more difficult than simply flipping through the yellow pages or searching online. This confusion is understandable given the plethora of different types of treatments available. Cultural and gender factors may also affect who seeks treatment and who does not. A study of college students found that being male predicted negative attitudes toward seeking psychological help, suggesting that men may be less likely than women to seek psychological services (Komiya, 2000). One study found that Asian Canadians failed to get psychological treatment most often because of language difficulties and cultural differences. This population tends to think of mental illness as a physical problem and believe that medical rather than psychological treatments can cure it (Li, 2000).

Many people who have sought and found help do not receive the most effective treatments, which further complicates things. For example, although cognitive and behavioral therapies yield the best results for treating anxiety disorders, most people

There's nothing funny about depression.

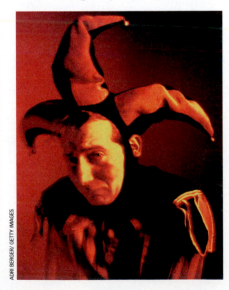

ADRI BERGER/ GETTY IMAGES

do not receive these treatments. In one study, most individuals seeking help in a clinic specializing in anxiety disorders reported having previously received treatments other than cognitive or behavioral therapy for their anxiety problems even though there is little evidence for the effectiveness of these other approaches for anxiety disorders. Only about a third of people reported previously receiving the treatment approaches most strongly supported by prior research (Rowa et al., 2000).

Clearly, before choosing or prescribing a therapy, we need to know what kinds of treatments are available and understand which treatments are best for particular disorders. What types of treatments are there for psychological disorders?

Approaches to Treatment

Treatments can be divided broadly into two kinds—psychotherapy, in which a person interacts with a psychotherapist, and medical or biological treatments, in which the mental disorder is treated with drugs or surgery. In some cases, both psychotherapy *and* biological treatments are used. Lisa's fear of flying, for example, might be treated not only with the virtual reality therapy you read about (a form of psychotherapy) in preparation for the real flight but also with antianxiety medications in the hours before the actual takeoff. For many years, psychotherapy was the main form of treatment for psychological disorders because there were few medical or biological options. The pioneering efforts of Sigmund Freud helped to bring psychotherapy into public view and transform what was once simply "advice giving" into a widely used set of techniques for relief from psychological problems (see Chapter 1). But alongside psychotherapy there have always been folk remedies that depend on biology. As we learn more about the biology and chemistry of the brain, approaches to mental health that begin with the brain are becoming increasingly widespread. We'll discuss each of these approaches to treatment in turn (see the Real World box on the next page).

COURTESY OF MISSOURI STATE ARCHIVES

Patients in steam cabinets, about 1910. Without a clue about how to proceed, early mental health workers gave patients steam baths as a form of treatment for psychological disorders in the forlorn hope that something might work.

In summary, mental illness is often misunderstood, and because of this, it too often goes untreated. Severe emotional suffering can be extremely costly, both with respect to an individual's ability to function and with respect to the social and financial burden mental illness can cause. Indeed, many people who suffer from mental illness do not get the help they need. In some cases, people may be unaware that they have a problem, or they may be too embarrassed to seek help. In other cases, there may be family, financial, or cultural obstacles to getting treatment. Finally, people simply may not know where to turn. Treatments include approaches that focus on the mind through psychotherapy and approaches that focus on the brain and body through medical and biological methods. ■ ■

Psychological Therapies:
Healing the Mind through Interaction

Psychological therapy, or **psychotherapy**, is *an interaction between a therapist and someone suffering from a psychological problem, with the goal of providing support or relief from the problem.* Although there are similarities among all the psychotherapies, each approach is unique in its goals, aims, and methods. Currently there are over 400 different systems of psychotherapy, some of which are well known but many of which are unorthodox and exist on the periphery of treatment (Corsini, 2000).

A survey of 1,000 members of the American Psychological Association Division of Psychotherapy asked participants to describe their main theoretical orientation

PSYCHOTHERAPY An interaction between a therapist and someone suffering from a psychological problem, with the goal of providing support or relief from the problem.

{ THE REAL WORLD } Types of Psychotherapists

WHAT DO YOU DO IF YOU'RE READY TO SEEK the help of a mental health professional? To whom do you turn? Therapists have widely varying backgrounds and training, and this affects the kinds of services they offer. Before you choose a therapist, it is useful to have an understanding of a therapist's background, training, and areas of expertise. There are several major "flavors":

- **Psychologist** A psychologist who practices psychotherapy holds a doctorate with specialization in clinical psychology (a Ph.D. or Psy.D.). This degree takes about 5 years to complete, and the psychologist will have extensive training in therapy, the assessment of psychological disorders, and research. The psychologist will sometimes have a specialty, such as working with adolescents or helping people overcome sleep disorders, and will usually conduct therapy that involves talking. Psychologists must be licensed by the state, and most states require candidates to complete about 2 years of supervised practical training and a competency exam. If you look for a *psychologist* in the yellow pages or through a clinic, you will usually find someone with this background.

- **Psychiatrist** A psychiatrist is a medical doctor who has completed an M.D. with specialized training in assessing and treating mental disorders. Psychiatrists can prescribe medications, and some also practice psychotherapy. General practice physicians can also prescribe medications for mental disorders and often are the first to see people with such disorders because people consult them for a wide range of health problems. However, general practice physicians do not typically receive much training in the diagnosis or treatment of mental disorders, and they do not practice psychotherapy.

- **Social worker** Social workers have a master's degree in social work and have training in working with people in dire life situations such as poverty, homelessness, or family conflict. Clinical or psychiatric social workers also receive special training to help people in these situations who have mental disorders. Social workers often work in government or private social service agencies, and they also may work in hospitals or have a private practice.

- **Counselor** Counselors have a wide range of training. To be a counseling psychologist, for example, requires a doctorate and practical training—the title uses that key term *psychologist* and is regulated by state laws. But states vary in how they define *counselor*. In some cases, a counselor must have a master's degree and extensive training in therapy, whereas in others, this person may have minimal training or relevant education. Counselors who work in schools usually have a master's degree and specific training in counseling in educational settings.

Some people offer therapy under made-up terms that sound professional—"mind/body healing therapist," for example, or "marital adjustment adviser." Often these terms are simply invented to mislead clients and avoid licensing boards, and the "therapist" may have no training or expertise at all. And, of course, there are a few people who claim to be licensed practitioners who are not: Louise Wightman, who had once worked as stripper "Princess Cheyenne" in Boston's Combat Zone, was convicted of fraud in 2007 after conducting psychotherapy as a psychologist with dozens of clients. She claimed she didn't know the Ph.D. degree she had purchased over the Internet was bogus (Associated Press, 2007). People who offer therapy may

Which one? Finding the right psychotherapist can seem like finding the best watermelon: You won't really know until you've had a taste. Shoppers sometimes thump melons on the theory that the sweetest ones sound different, but no one quite knows how a good one will sound. In the case of psychotherapists, fortunately, no thumping is required. You can find out about their qualifications in advance and even talk to several to see which one seems right.

STUART DEE/GETTY IMAGES

be well meaning and even helpful, but they could do harm too. To be safe, it is important to shop wisely for a therapist whose training and credentials reflect expertise and inspire confidence.

How should you shop? One way is to start with people you know—your general practice physician, a school counselor, or a trusted friend or family member who might know of a good therapist. Or you can visit your college clinic or hospital or contact an Internet site of an organization such as the American Psychological Association that offers referrals to licensed mental health care providers. When you do contact someone, they will often be able to provide you with further advice about who would be just the right kind of therapist to consult.

Before you agree to see a therapist for treatment, you should ask questions such as those below to evaluate whether the therapist's style or background is a good match for your problem:

- What type of therapy do you practice?
- What types of problems do you usually treat?
- For how long do you usually see people in therapy?
- Will our work involve "talking" therapy, medications, or both?
- How effective is this type of therapy for the type of problem I'm having?
- What are your fees for therapy, and will health insurance cover them?

Not only will the therapist's answers to these questions tell you about his or her background and experience, but they will also tell you about his or her approach to treating clients. You can then make an informed decision about the type of service you need.

Although you should consider what type of therapist would best fit your needs, the therapist's personality and approach can sometimes be as important as his or her background or training. You should seek out someone who is willing and open to answer questions, who has a clear understanding about the type of problem leading you to seek therapy, and who shows general respect and empathy for you. A therapist is someone you are entrusting with your mental health, and you should only enter into such a relationship when you and the therapist have good rapport.

(Norcross, Hedges, & Castle, 2002; see **FIGURE 14.1**). The most common response, endorsed by over a third of the respondents, was an eclectic or integrative orientation—the use of a mixture of techniques. **Eclectic psychotherapy** involves *drawing on techniques from different forms of therapy, depending on the client and the problem.* For example, an eclectic psychotherapist might use behavioral principles to work on Lisa's fear of flying, humanistic principles to validate her distress over difficult family interactions, and family therapy techniques to change any dysfunctional patterns within her family that were contributing to the problem. We'll discuss the specifics of behavioral, humanistic, and family systems therapies in more detail a bit later. The point here is that most therapists apply an appropriate theoretical perspective that is suited to the problem at hand rather than adhering to a single theoretical perspective for all clients' problems.

Nonetheless, the most common single approach among psychotherapists from the survey was psychodynamic or psychoanalytic therapy, with 29% reporting primary use of this technique, and second was cognitive treatment, used by 16%. Other forms of psychotherapy were used less frequently and appeared to be in decline compared to a similar survey in 1991. Overall, about three quarters of the psychotherapy conducted, as of 2002, was individual psychotherapy, with the remaining treatments involving groups, couples, and families. We will examine each of four major psychotherapies in this section—psychodynamic, behavioral, cognitive, and humanistic/existential—and also explore how psychotherapy techniques are used in groups.

Psychodynamic Therapy

Psychodynamic psychotherapy has its roots in Freud's psychoanalytically oriented theory of personality (see Chapter 12). **Psychodynamic psychotherapies** *explore childhood events and encourage individuals to use this understanding to develop insight into their psychological problems.* There are a number of different psychodynamic therapies that can vary substantially, but they all share the belief that the path to overcoming psychological problems is to develop insight into the unconscious memories, impulses, wishes, and conflicts that are assumed to underlie these problems. Psychodynamic therapies include psychoanalysis and modern psychodynamic therapy, such as interpersonal psychotherapy.

Psychoanalysis

In the late 1800s and early 1900s Sigmund Freud developed *psychoanalysis,* a form of therapy that emphasizes the role of uncovering unconscious desires to develop insight into psychological problems. As you saw in Chapter 12, psychoanalysis assumes that humans are born with aggressive and sexual urges that are repressed during childhood development through the use of defense mechanisms. Psychoanalysts encourage their clients to bring these repressed conflicts into consciousness so that the clients can understand them and reduce their unwanted influences. Psychoanalysts focus a great deal on early childhood events because they believe that urges and conflicts were likely to be repressed during this time.

Freud was trained as a neurologist, but he developed an interest in psychology and psychiatry. He worked with several prominent theorists who were using hypnosis to treat conditions such as dissociative disorders (see Chapter 13) and hysteria (now diagnosed as *conversion disorder;* see Chapter 15). In a few cases, using hypnosis Freud was able to "cure" people who had severe problems such as paralysis in the normal waking state. This cure was highly unreliable, though, and because many people did not respond to hypnosis, Freud eventually abandoned it. He learned through this exploration that the conscious reports of the waking patient ("I can't move my legs") might not be the whole story in psychological disorders (because under hypnosis, the person's legs might move!). As a result, Freud began to experiment with other methods of tapping into the unconscious.

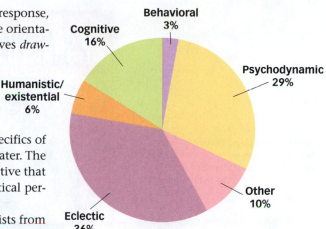

Figure 14.1 **Approaches to Psychotherapy in the 21st Century** This chart shows the percentage of psychologists (from among 1,000 members of the American Psychological Association's Division of Psychotherapy) who have various primary psychotherapy orientations (adapted from Norcross et al., 2002).

ONLY HUMAN

PSYCHO-BEAR-APY? 1994—The Central Park Zoo revealed that it had paid an animal behaviorist $25,000 for psychotherapy for Gus, its 9-year-old polar bear, who was involved in various repetitive behaviors, which the zoo director said could have been a mild neurosis. The behaviorist recommended creating games to make Gus's life less monotonous.

ECLECTIC PSYCHOTHERAPY
Treatment that draws on techniques from different forms of therapy, depending on the client and the problem.

PSYCHODYNAMIC PSYCHOTHERAPIES A general approach to treatment that explores childhood events and encourages individuals to develop insight into their psychological problems.

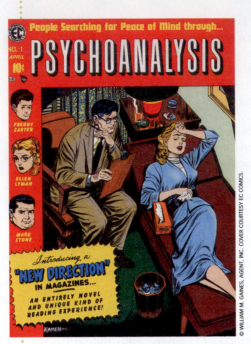

In traditional psychoanalysis, the patient lies on a couch, with the therapist sitting behind, out of the patient's view. This also happens in the comics.

Freud reasoned that unconscious processes can be uncovered when the conscious mind is diverted from controlling the client's thinking. The unconscious is deeply hidden, however, so catching the unconscious at work takes special techniques and typically requires a long time. Traditional psychoanalysis takes place over an average of three to six years, with four or five sessions per week (Ursano & Silberman, 2003). During a session, the client reclines on a couch, facing away from the analyst, and is asked to express whatever thoughts and feelings come to mind. Occasionally, the analyst may comment on some of the information presented by the client, but the analyst does not express his or her values and judgments. The stereotypic image you might have of psychological therapy—a person lying on a couch talking to a person sitting in a chair—springs from this Freudian approach.

How to Develop Insight

The goal of psychoanalysis is for the client to understand the unconscious in a process Freud called developing insight. An example of such insight occurred when Freud (1901/1938) met a young man on a train. The traveler was highly agitated during their conversation, launching into an impassioned speech on politics that he ended forcefully with a quote in Latin from the poet Virgil: *Exoriare aliquis nostria ex ossibus ultor* ("Let someone arise from my bones as an avenger"). A hundred years ago in Austria, Latin poetry was apparently the rage—because Freud knew the phrase. He noticed that the man left out *aliquis* ("someone"). He pursued this omission by asking the man what else this word might mean to him. The man offered associations, mentioning that *aliquis* reminded him of a liquid or fluid and then that it also brought to mind liquidation—a euphemism for killing. After a few more associations, he paused and announced quietly that he knew what all this meant: He was obsessed with an "absent flow of liquid" since he was waiting to hear that day about his girlfriend's pregnancy.

His agitation rapidly subsided after this insight. It was as though his unconscious mind had produced a clue to his agitation—the forgetting of *aliquis*—a clue that he could only recognize consciously through a process of self-discovery. Asking the person to freely associate to an idea is just one such process. Freud's psychoanalytic technique also encourages such insights through dream analysis, interpretation, and the analysis of resistance.

Free association. In free association, the client reports every thought that enters the mind, without censorship or filtering. This strategy allows the stream of consciousness to flow unimpeded. If the client stops, the therapist prompts further associations ("And what does that make you think of?"). Here is an example of a client's free association:

> "I was working on a report when my boss came to talk to me. I was worried I was in trouble, but he said that he was just checking in. (Pause.) I had an old boyfriend who used to say he was 'checking in' on me—he would call at all hours of the day and night. I'm glad I'm not dating him anymore."

The analyst may notice the theme of feeling "watched over" in this free association and would look for further examples of this theme during therapy sessions.

Clients often find the process of free association difficult due to well-ingrained defense mechanisms and **resistance**—*a reluctance to cooperate with treatment for fear of confronting unpleasant unconscious material*. For example, you might find that if you sim-

RESISTANCE A reluctance to cooperate with treatment for fear of confronting unpleasant unconscious material.

ply sit in a room alone and start freely associating out loud, you end up saying some things you'd rather not have come to mind—or at least that you might hesitate to say in public! As a client becomes more trusting and less defended in the context of a good therapeutic relationship, the free association process becomes easier.

Dream analysis. Psychoanalysis treats dreams as metaphors that symbolize unconscious conflicts or wishes. As you learned in Chapter 8, psychoanalysts place great value on the interpretation of dreams in the belief that dreams are disguised clues that the therapist can help the client understand. A psychoanalytic therapy session might begin with an invitation for the client to recount a dream, after which the client might be asked to participate in the interpretation by freely associating to the dream. A client might report that a dream about school and an angry teacher reminded her a bit of her mother. The psychoanalyst might pursue that link by asking the client for more ideas about what this reminder could mean. Rather than taking a dream at face value (the manifest content), the psychoanalyst would seek out its hidden meaning (the latent content) to examine its importance for the client.

"I'll say a normal word, then you say the first sick thing that pops into your head."

Interpretation. This is the process by which the therapist deciphers the meaning (e.g., unconscious impulses or fantasies) underlying what the client says and does. Interpretation is used throughout therapy, during free association, dream analysis, and in other aspects of the treatment. Returning to the example of Lisa, in the opening vignette, a psychoanalyst may interpret her fearful avoidance of flying as a fear of independence, perhaps originating from overprotective parents who discouraged her from leaving home or developing her own ideas and opinions.

During the process of interpretation, the analyst suggests possible meanings to the client, looking for signs that the correct meaning has been discovered. Unfortunately, a correct interpretation is usually not accompanied by giant flashing neon lights. The analyst could overinterpret the client's thoughts and emotions and sometimes even contribute interpretations that are far from the truth. For example, the discovery that a client had a traumatic sexual experience with a visiting relative as a child might seem so important to the analyst that it could come to mind as a way of understanding many of the client's dreams and associations. This particular event actually might *not* be the basis of the client's unconscious conflicts, however, so in this case, the therapist would be directing the client to an insight that is really no insight at all.

Analysis of resistance. In the process of "trying on" different interpretations of the client's thoughts and actions, the analyst may suggest an interpretation that the client finds particularly unacceptable. For example, the therapist might suggest that the client's problem with obsessive health worries could be traced to a childhood rivalry with her mother for her father's love and attention. The client could find the suggestion insulting ("I'd never think of my father *that way*") and fervently resist the interpretation. Curiously, the analyst might interpret this resistance as a signal not that the interpretation is wrong but instead that the interpretation is on the right track. The queen in Shakespeare's *Hamlet* indicated that vigorous resistance to an idea might reveal a person's underlying belief in that idea when she said, "The lady doth protest too much, methinks."

The analysis of even minor forms of resistance (e.g., being late for appointments, shifting the topic of discussion away from a particular idea) can become the basis for further attempts to help the client gain insight. Unfortunately, this strategy also could lead *away* from insight, serving instead as a way for the analyst to exert influence over the client and press for the acceptance of interpretations that the analyst favors. Psychoanalysts hope to guard against such errors of interpretation through rigorous training; analysts themselves undergo psychoanalysis in hopes of overcoming their personal biases.

Sigmund Freud, with his mother, Amalia, on her 90th birthday.

The Process of Transference

Over the course of an intensive and lengthy process of analysis, the client and psychoanalyst often develop a close relationship. Freud noticed this relationship developing in his analyses and was at first troubled by it: Clients would develop an unusually strong attachment to him, almost as though they were viewing him as a parent or lover, and he worried that this could interfere with achieving the goal of insight. Over time, however, he came to believe that the development and resolution of this relationship was a key process of psychoanalysis.

Transference occurs *when the analyst begins to assume a major significance in the client's life and the client reacts to the analyst based on unconscious childhood fantasies.* Successful psychoanalysis involves analyzing the transference so that the client understands this reaction and why it occurs. In fact, insight, the ultimate goal of psychoanalysis, may be enhanced because interpretations of the client's interaction with the therapist also have implications for the client's past and future relationships (Andersen & Berk, 1998).

Beyond Psychoanalysis

Early in the history of psychoanalysis, several of Freud's students broke away from him and developed their own approaches to psychotherapy. Carl Jung (1875–1961) and Alfred Adler (1870–1937) agreed with Freud that insight was a key therapeutic goal but disagreed that insight usually involves unconscious conflicts about sex and aggression (Arlow, 2000). Instead, Jung emphasized what he called the *collective unconscious,* the culturally determined symbols and myths that are shared among all people. Jung held that these widely known ideas about kinds of people, situations, or stories could serve as a basis for interpretation beyond sex or aggression, and his viewpoint is a rich compilation of such ideas. Alfred Adler believed that emotional conflicts are the result of

Psychodynamic therapists Carl Jung (1875–1961), Alfred Adler (1870–1937), Melanie Klein (1882–1960), Karen Horney (1885–1952), Harry Stack Sullivan (1892–1949), and Heinz Kohut (1913–81).

perceptions of inferiority and that psychotherapy should help people overcome problems resulting from inferior social status, sex roles, and discrimination.

Another analyst to break with Freud was Melanie Klein (1882–1960), who believed that primitive fantasies of loss and persecution (for example, worrying about a parent dying or about being bullied) were important factors underlying mental illness. Throughout the first half of the 20th century, other influential theorists pursued the development of psychodynamic theories to include greater focus on the social foundations of psychology. Karen Horney (1885–1952) disagreed with Freud about inherent differences in the psychology of men and women and traced such differences to society and culture rather than biology. Harry Stack Sullivan (1892–1949) emphasized the importance of interpersonal relationships in the formation of emotional problems, and Heinz Kohut (1913–81) expanded psychodynamic psychotherapy by focusing on how the individual forms an understanding of self through relationships with others.

These social themes have been developed most explicitly in **interpersonal psychotherapy (IPT)**, *a form of psychotherapy that focuses on helping clients improve current relationships*. IPT was originally developed as a brief treatment for depression (Weissman, Markowitz, & Klerman, 2000). Its brief duration (12–16 weeks) and focus on improving relationships (rather than on developing insight) set it apart from most other psychodynamic therapies.

Therapists using IPT try to focus treatment on the person's interpersonal behaviors and feelings. They pay particular attention to the client's grief (an exaggerated reaction to the loss of a loved one), role disputes (conflicts with a significant other), role transitions (changes in life status, such as starting a new job, getting married, or retiring), or interpersonal deficits (lack of the necessary skills to start or maintain a relationship). For example, the therapist might help the client deal with grief by encouraging the client to discuss feelings related to the loss and to pursue new interests, activities, and relationships so that he or she can move on (Weissman & Markowitz, 2002). The treatment focuses on interpersonal functioning with the assumption that as interpersonal relations improve, depressive symptoms will subside.

Modern psychodynamic psychotherapies such as IPT differ from classical psychoanalysis in many ways. For starters, the therapist and client typically sit face-to-face. In addition, therapy is less intensive, with meetings often occurring only once a week and the duration of therapy lasting months rather than years. In contrast to classical psychoanalysis, modern psychodynamic therapists are more likely to see relief from symptoms as a reasonable goal for therapy (in addition to the goal of facilitating insight), and they are more likely to offer support or advice in addition to interpretation (Henry et al., 1994). Therapists are also now less likely to interpret a client's statements as a sign of unconscious sexual or aggressive impulses. However, other concepts, such as transference and fostering insight into unconscious processes, remain features of most psychodynamic therapies. Psychodynamic psychotherapy has had an enormous impact on how emotional problems are treated, influencing most subsequent schools of therapy in some form. Freud's couch cast a long shadow.

Behavioral and Cognitive Therapies

Unlike psychodynamic psychotherapy, which emphasizes early developmental processes as the source of psychological dysfunction, cognitive and behavioral treatments emphasize the current factors that contribute to the problem—dysfunctional thoughts and maladaptive behaviors. Cognitive and behavioral therapies have been around for almost half a century, and they continue to increase in popularity. Historically, cognitive and behavioral therapies were considered distinct systems of therapy, and some people continue to follow this distinction, using solely behavioral *or* cognitive techniques. However, many therapists now integrate these approaches into a unified set of procedures known as *cognitive behavioral therapy* (*CBT*). In this section, we will review the origins and techniques of both behavioral and cognitive therapies and explore how these techniques are integrated into CBT.

TRANSFERENCE An event that occurs in psychoanalysis when the analyst begins to assume a major significance in the client's life and the client reacts to the analyst based on unconscious childhood fantasies.

INTERPERSONAL PSYCHOTHERAPY (IPT) A form of psychotherapy that focuses on helping clients improve current relationships.

BEHAVIOR THERAPY A type of therapy that assumes that disordered behavior is learned and that symptom relief is achieved through changing overt maladaptive behaviors into more constructive behaviors.

AVERSION THERAPY A form of behavior therapy that uses positive punishment to reduce the frequency of an undesirable behavior.

Behavior Therapy

The idea of focusing treatment on the client's behavior rather than the client's unconscious was an innovation inspired by behaviorism. As you read in Chapter 1, psychologists' frustration with theories positing "invisible" mental properties that are difficult to test and impossible to observe launched the behaviorist movement. Behaviorists found psychoanalytic ideas particularly hard to test: How do you know that a person has an unconscious conflict, for example, or that insight has occurred? No wonder psychoanalysis takes so long—it's like looking for a shadow in the dark. Behavioral principles, on the other hand, focused solely on symptoms that could be observed (e.g., avoidance of a feared object, such as refusing to get on an airplane). In the 1950s and 1960s, clinical psychologists began to apply learning theory to the treatment of disorders, and this set the stage for the growth of behavior therapy (Eysenck, 1960; Wolpe, 1958). **Behavior therapy** assumes that *disordered behavior is learned and that symptom relief is achieved through changing overt maladaptive behaviors into more constructive behaviors.*

B. F. Skinner first used the term *behavior therapy* to describe how the principles of learning could be used to change problem behaviors in people with schizophrenia (Lindsley, Skinner, & Solomon, 1953). Since then, a variety of behavior therapy techniques have been developed for many disorders. Many of the learning principles you encountered in Chapter 6 have been applied to treatment—including those based on operant conditioning procedures (which focus on reinforcement and punishment) and those based on classical conditioning procedures (which focus on extinction). Behavior therapy techniques can eliminate unwanted behaviors (such as stopping a child from throwing temper tantrums), promote desired behaviors (such as leading a withdrawn patient to participate in social interactions), and reduce unwanted emotional responses (such as helping a phobic patient to stop fearing snakes).

Eliminating unwanted behaviors. What would you do if a 3-year-old boy got into the habit of throwing tantrums at the grocery store? A behavior therapist might look first at what happens before the tantrum: Is the child hungry, did he miss a nap, or is there something he wants? Does the parent usually neglect him during shopping? The therapist would also investigate what happens after the tantrum: Did he get candy to "shut him up"? Did the mortified parent whisk him out to the car and beg him to be quiet? The study of operant conditioning shows that behavior can be predicted by its *antecedents* (the stimuli that occur beforehand) and its *consequences* (the reinforcing or punishing events that follow) and adjusting these might help to change the behavior.

A behavioral therapist might treat this temper tantrum with an analysis of the antecedents, behavior, and consequences of the act.

In fact, a solution might be as easy as A-B-C (antecedent-behavior-consequence). Giving the child more attention in the store beforehand, for example, might prevent the whole incident. If the child throws a tantrum anyway, making the consequences less reinforcing (no candy) and more punishing (a period of time-out in the car while the parent watches from nearby rather than a rush of attention) could eliminate the problem behavior. For people in danger of developing a poor long-term relationship with their child because of frequent tantrums or other problem behaviors, behavior therapy can bring welcome relief and a fresh start. Taking the time to understand a problem behavior in its context can make it less mystifying when it happens—and more open to modification (Tavris, 1989).

Another operant technique for reducing problem behaviors, called **aversion therapy**, involves *using positive punishment to reduce the frequency of an undesirable behavior.* For example, alcoholism is sometimes treated with a drug called disulfiram (Antabuse), which increases the patient's sensitivity to alcohol so that drinking even a small amount leads to a very intense and unpleasant physical reaction such as nausea or headaches. Although aversive therapies are sometimes useful for controlling an unwanted behavior over the short term, in many cases they are not particularly useful for long-term change. In other words, the enticement of an addiction can sometimes be so powerful that a person will tolerate discomfort and illness in order to experience whatever positive benefit the addiction provides.

Promoting desired behaviors. In a psychiatric hospital, patients may sometimes become unresponsive and apathetic, withdrawing from social interaction and failing to participate in treatment programs. A behavior therapy technique sometimes used in such cases is the **token economy**, which involves *giving clients "tokens" for desired behaviors, which they can later trade for rewards.* Tokens for behaviors such as cleaning their rooms, getting exercise, or helping other patients signal positive reinforcement because they can be exchanged for rewards such as time away from the hospital, television privileges, and special foods. Token economies have proven to be effective while the system of rewards is in place, but the learned behaviors are not usually maintained when the reinforcements are discontinued (Glynn, 1990). Similar systems used in classrooms to encourage positive behaviors may work temporarily in school but can undermine students' interest in these behaviors when the reinforcements are no longer available (Lepper & Greene, 1976). A child who is rewarded for controlling his temper in class may become an ogre on the playground when no teacher is present to offer rewards for good behavior.

Reinforcement techniques can sometimes be highly successful in *skills training.* For example, someone with schizophrenia might be taught particular social skills (e.g., how to order a pizza) or skills of daily living (e.g., how to pay an electric bill). Some clients with severe mental illness receive training for particular jobs and supervised job placement as part of treatment, especially if their illness has prevented them from acquiring necessary work experience or skills. Skills such as these can last a lifetime because the reinforcements used by the therapist are later replaced by the rewards of successful skilled behavior ("I got a pizza and the lights are on, so I can see what I'm eating!").

Reducing unwanted emotional responses. One of the most powerful ways to reduce fear is by gradual *exposure* to the feared object or situation, a behavioral method originated by psychiatrist Joseph Wolpe (1958). Wolpe's **exposure therapy** involves *confronting an emotion-arousing stimulus directly and repeatedly, ultimately leading to a decrease in the emotional response.* This technique depends on the processes of habituation and response extinction that were originally discovered in the study of classical conditioning (see Chapter 6). Wolpe called his form of treatment **systematic desensitization**, *a procedure in which a client relaxes all the muscles of his or her body while imagining being in increasingly frightening situations.* For example, a client who fears snakes might first imagine seeing a photo of a snake, followed by imagining seeing a snake that is inside an aquarium, followed eventually by imagining holding a large snake, all while engaging in exercises that relax the muscles of the body. Cognitive behavioral therapists use an exposure hierarchy to expose the client gradually to the feared object or situation. Easier situations are practiced first, and as fear decreases, the client progresses to more difficult or frightening situations (see **TABLE 14.1**).

Systematic desensitization has changed since Wolpe's introduction of the technique (Antony & Swinson, 2000). Exposure is an effective treatment without the relaxation component (Öst et al., 1984), so relaxation is often omitted. Relaxation techniques can be effective all by themselves for treating anxiety and for managing stress more generally (as you'll see in Chapter 15), but they are not essential for desensitization. Wolpe's systematic desensitization also relied strongly on exposure in imagination, but it is now known that *in vivo exposure,* or live exposure, is more effective than imaginary exposure (Emmelkamp & Wessels, 1975; Stern & Marks, 1973). In other words, if a person fears driving, it is better for the person to get behind the wheel of the car and drive than simply to imagine driving. However, imaginary exposure is still recommended in cases where people are so frightened of their thoughts or memories that they can't even bring themselves to attempt live exposure.

TOKEN ECONOMY A form of behavior therapy in which clients are given "tokens" for desired behaviors, which they can later trade for rewards.

EXPOSURE THERAPY An approach to treatment that involves confronting an emotion-arousing stimulus directly and repeatedly, ultimately leading to a decrease in the emotional response.

SYSTEMATIC DESENSITIZATION A procedure in which a client relaxes all the muscles of his or her body while imagining being in increasingly frightening situations.

Table **14.1**	Exposure Hierarchy for Social Phobia
Item	**Fear (0–100)**
1. Have a party and invite everyone from work	99
2. Go to a holiday party for 1 hour without drinking	90
3. Invite Cindy to have dinner and see a movie	85
4. Go for a job interview	80
5. Ask boss for a day off work	65
6. Ask questions in a meeting at work	65
7. Eat lunch with coworkers	60
8. Talk to a stranger on the bus	50
9. Talk to cousin on the telephone for 10 minutes	40
10. Ask for directions at the gas station	35

Exposure therapy is a powerful treatment for overcoming fear. Up to 90% of individuals with animal phobias are able to overcome their fears in as little as one session lasting 2 to 3 hours.

COGNITIVE THERAPY A form of psychotherapy that involves helping a client identify and correct any distorted thinking about self, others, or the world.

Albert Ellis founded rational emotive behavior therapy, a form of cognitive therapy.

The virtual reality therapy that you read about in the chapter-opening vignette involves a kind of systematic desensitization to an imagined stimulus. But as you saw, the imagination is heightened through the use of video and audio simulations, making the entire experience more like a live exposure. Virtual reality programs not only can simulate traveling in an airplane but also can provide exposure for people who fear driving, spiders, snakes, public speaking, heights, or thunderstorms. Clients can be treated for post-traumatic stress disorder (see Chapter 15) through exposure to very specific stimuli—virtual combat in Iraq, for example, or a virtual 9/11-type terrorist attack. One study comparing three sessions of virtual reality exposure to three sessions of live exposure for individuals with a specific phobia of heights found that both treatments were equally effective in reducing participants' fear and that this improvement was maintained when participants were assessed again 6 months later (Emmelkamp et al., 2002).

Exposure can be adapted for particular types of problems. For example, exposure can be combined with *response prevention,* which involves resisting the urge to engage in a compulsive ritual or some other protective behavior. Individuals with obsessive-compulsive disorder who wash their hands many times each day for fear of contamination would be encouraged to touch a feared object like a door handle (exposure) while resisting the urge to wash their hands (response prevention). The exposure helps them extinguish the emotional reaction to the thought of contamination over time, and the response prevention keeps them from performing the ritual behavior that they usually use to neutralize the emotion.

Cognitive Therapy

In the 1960s and 1970s, a number of psychologists and psychiatrists began to enlist cognitive explanations to understand learning-based phenomena. For example, traditional learning theorists might explain a phobia as the outcome of a classical conditioning experience such as being bitten by a dog, where the dog bite leads to the development of a dog phobia through the simple association of the dog with the experience of pain. Cognitive theorists took this simple learning paradigm a step further: They began to emphasize the *meaning* of the event. It might not be the event itself that caused the fear, but rather the individual's beliefs and assumptions about the event and the feared stimulus. In the case of a dog bite, cognitive theorists might focus on a person's new or strengthened belief that dogs are dangerous to explain the fear. Whereas behavior therapy doesn't take into account the person's thoughts and feelings and instead focuses only on the behavior and the situation, cognitive therapy uses the person's reasoning capabilities and rational self-control in the therapy.

Aaron T. Beck, a psychiatrist (b. 1921), and Albert Ellis, a psychologist (1913–2007), are most often credited for founding cognitive treatments. Beck and Ellis felt that the best way to alleviate emotional pain was to help a client change the biased or unrealistic thoughts that were at the core of the client's problems. Beck called his brand of treatment **cognitive therapy,** which focuses on *helping a client identify and correct any distorted thinking about self, others, or the world* (e.g., Beck & Weishaar, 2000). Ellis referred to his treatment as *rational emotive behavior therapy,* in which the therapist points out errors in thinking that the client is making (e.g., Ellis, 2000). Although these therapies share the common belief that psychological problems arise from biased or distorted interpretations of events, they also differ in some ways. Beck's approach is gentler than Ellis's, with the therapist helping the client discover errors in thinking by using pointed questions to guide the client's discovery. Ellis's approach is more direct and forceful, with the therapist actively pointing out flaws in thinking to the client and using humor to identify these flaws.

Cognitive therapies use a principal technique called **cognitive restructuring**, which involves *teaching clients to question the automatic beliefs, assumptions, and predictions that often lead to negative emotions and to replace negative thinking with more realistic and positive beliefs*. Specifically, clients are taught to examine the evidence for and against a particular belief or to be more accepting of outcomes that may be undesirable yet still manageable. For example, a depressed client may believe that she is stupid and will never pass her college courses—all on the basis of one poor grade. In this situation, the therapist would work with the client to examine the validity of this belief. The therapist would consider relevant evidence such as grades on previous exams, performance on other coursework, and examples of intelligence outside of school. It may be that the client has never failed a course before and has achieved good grades in this particular course in the past. In this case, the therapist would encourage the client to consider all this information in determining whether she is truly "stupid."

The goal of cognitive restructuring is *not* to have a client think positively if there is no reason to think positively. If the client really was having trouble in school, it would not be realistic to think that she will easily pass her course. In cases like this, the therapist may instead help the client decide whether doing poorly in one course constitutes being "stupid" and whether there is anything the client can do to better prepare for future exams. **TABLE 14.2** shows a variety of potentially irrational ideas—beliefs and convictions that could be true or that could be false—and so serve to unleash unwanted emotions such as anger, depression, or anxiety. Any of these irrational beliefs can become a mindbug, bedeviling a person with serious emotional problems if left unchallenged.

Some forms of cognitive therapy include techniques for coping with unwanted thoughts and feelings, techniques that resemble meditation (see Chapter 8). Clients may be encouraged to attend to their troubling thoughts or emotions or given meditative techniques that allow them to gain a new focus. One such technique, called **mindfulness meditation**, *teaches an individual to be fully present in each moment; to be aware of his or her thoughts, feelings, and sensations; and to detect symptoms before they become a problem*. Researchers have found mindfulness meditation to be helpful for preventing relapse in depression. In one study, people recovering from depression were about half as likely to relapse during a 60-week assessment period if they received mindfulness-meditation-based cognitive therapy than if they received treatment as usual (Teasdale, Segal, & Williams, 2000).

"Don't make me come over there!"

COGNITIVE RESTRUCTURING A therapeutic approach that teaches clients to question the automatic beliefs, assumptions, and predictions that often lead to negative emotions and to replace negative thinking with more realistic and positive beliefs.

MINDFULNESS MEDITATION A form of cognitive therapy that teaches an individual to be fully present in each moment; to be aware of his or her thoughts, feelings, and sensations; and to detect symptoms before they become a problem.

Western cognitive therapy meets the Eastern Buddhist meditation tradition as Aaron Beck greets his holiness the Dalai Lama at the International Congress for Cognitive Psychotherapy in 2005. Beck's approach to psychotherapy helps people change maladaptive thinking patterns in a direct and rational approach, whereas the practice of Buddhism expressed by the Lama aims to create mental peace through meditation. Here they seem to be amused by each other's choice of clothing.

Table 14.2	Common Irrational Beliefs and the Emotional Responses They Can Cause
Belief	**Emotional Response**
I have to get this done immediately. I must be perfect. Something terrible will happen.	Anxiety, stress
Everyone is watching me. I won't be able to make friends. People know something is wrong with me.	Embarrassment, social anxiety
I'm a loser and will always be a loser. Nobody will ever love me.	Sadness, depression
She did that to me on purpose. He is evil and should be punished. Things ought to be different.	Anger, irritability

COGNITIVE BEHAVIORAL THERAPY (CBT) A blend of cognitive and behavioral therapeutic strategies.

Cognitive Behavioral Therapy

Today, the extent to which therapists use cognitive versus behavioral techniques depends on the individual therapist as well as the type of problem being treated. Most therapists working with anxiety and depression use *a blend of cognitive and behavioral therapeutic strategies,* often referred to as **cognitive behavioral therapy**, or **CBT.** In a way, this technique acknowledges that there may be behaviors that people cannot control through rational thought but also that there are ways of helping people to think more rationally when thought does play a role. Moving beyond its roots in behavior therapy and cognitive therapy, however, cognitive behavior therapy has developed its own unique features. In addition to focusing on dysfunctional thoughts and maladaptive behaviors, CBT is often described as problem focused and action oriented, structured, transparent, and flexible.

Problem focus means that CBT is undertaken for specific problems, and *action orientation* means that CBT tries to solve these problems by encouraging the client to act. Typically, the therapist and client will identify specific goals such as reducing the frequency of panic attacks or returning to work after a bout of depression and then select specific strategies to help meet those goals, thereby decreasing the client's suffering. The client is expected to *do* things, such as practice relaxation exercises or use a diary to monitor relevant symptoms (e.g., the severity of depressed mood, panic attack symptoms). This is in contrast to psychodynamic or other therapies where goals may not be explicitly discussed or agreed on and the client's only necessary action is to attend the therapy session.

Another feature of CBT is that it is *structured*. CBT sessions typically begin with setting an agenda for the meeting and a review of homework from the previous week. For example, the client and therapist may decide at the beginning of the session to discuss a particular incident from the client's week and use this as an example for learning a therapy technique that may be useful, such as keeping a diary. Much of the session focuses on learning new skills or on practicing particular therapy techniques. In the treatment of anxiety, it is not uncommon for the therapist and client to spend the session confronting the client's feared situation, which may include learning-oriented activities such as the client giving a presentation in front of the therapist. Often, each session ends with a homework assignment to be completed before the next session. In contrast, in a psychodynamic therapy session, the client may be asked to simply free-associate for much of the session, with no expectations on what content will be covered.

CBT also contrasts with psychodynamic approaches in its assumptions about what the client can know. CBT is *transparent* in that nothing is withheld from the client. By the end of the course of therapy, most clients have a very good understanding of the treatment they have received as well as the specific techniques that are used to make the desired changes. For example, clients with obsessive-compulsive disorder who fear contamination would feel confident in knowing how to confront feared situations such as public washrooms and why confronting this situation is helpful. Self-help readings are often used to reinforce what is learned in sessions.

Finally, the format of CBT is *flexible*. Usually, CBT is a fairly brief form of therapy, lasting between 10 and 20 sessions, depending on the problem. It may be conducted individually or with groups of clients. The frequency of sessions varies. For example, CBT for obsessive-compulsive disorder has been found to be useful both in a weekly outpatient format over several

"That's Eleanor. She's a fact checker."

The cognitive behavior therapy (CBT) client with obsessive-compulsive disorder who fears contamination in public restrooms might be given "homework" to visit three such restrooms in a week—not necessarily to touch anything, but just to look.

months and in a more intensive format, with daily sessions occurring over 3 weeks. CBT may be conducted outside of the therapist's office. For example, an individual undergoing exposure therapy for a fear of elevators might undergo entire treatment sessions on actual elevators.

Because CBT is based on learning models, it is not surprising that the practice of CBT resembles school. Therapists take the role of teacher, and clients become students. The goal of teaching the client new ways to think and behave is pursued through lessons, homework, and yes, even tests (let's try picking up that snake!). In this way, the CBT model of therapy differs from the more mystical relationship between the therapist and client in psychodynamic psychotherapy, in which the therapist serves almost as a kind of spiritual guide urging the client toward insight.

Humanistic and Existential Therapies

Humanistic and existential therapies emerged in the middle of the 20th century, in part as a reaction to the negative views that psychodynamic psychotherapies hold about human nature. Psychodynamic approaches emphasize unconscious drives toward sex and aggression, as we noted earlier. Humanistic and existential therapies, on the other hand, assume that human nature is generally positive, and they emphasize the natural tendency of each individual to strive for personal improvement. There are many different approaches that fall under the category of humanistic and existential therapies. They share the assumption that psychological problems stem from feelings of alienation and loneliness—and that these feelings can be traced to failures to reach one's potential (in the humanistic approach) or from failures to find meaning in life (in the existential approach). Although interest in humanistic and existential therapies peaked in the 1960s and 1970s, some therapists continue to use these approaches today. This section describes two specific types of therapy that are the most well-known types of this viewpoint—one from a humanistic perspective (person-centered therapy) and one from existential therapy (Gestalt therapy).

Person-Centered Therapy

Person-centered therapy (also known as *client-centered therapy*) *assumes that all individuals have a tendency toward growth and that this growth can be facilitated by acceptance and genuine reactions from the therapist.* Psychologist Carl Rogers (1902–87) developed person-centered therapy in the 1940s and 1950s (Rogers, 1951). Person-centered therapy assumes that each individual is qualified to determine his or her own goals for therapy, such as feeling more confident or making a career decision, and even the frequency and

PERSON-CENTERED THERAPY An approach to therapy that assumes all individuals have a tendency toward growth and that this growth can be facilitated by acceptance and genuine reactions from the therapist.

length of therapy. In this type of *nondirective* treatment, the therapist tends not to provide advice or suggestions about what the client should be doing. Instead, the therapist paraphrases the client's words, mirroring the client's thoughts and sentiments (e.g., "I think I hear you saying . . ."). Person-centered therapists believe that with adequate support, the client will recognize the right things to do.

Rogers encouraged person-centered therapists to demonstrate three basic qualities: congruence, empathy, and unconditional positive regard. *Congruence* refers to openness and honesty in the therapeutic relationship and ensuring that the therapist communicates the same message at all levels. For example, the same message must be communicated in the therapist's words, the therapist's facial expression, and the therapist's body language. Saying, "I think your concerns are valid," while smirking would simply not do. *Empathy* refers to the continuous process of trying to understand the client by getting inside his or her way of thinking, feeling, and understanding the world. Seeing the world from the client's perspective enables the therapist to better appreciate the client's apprehensions, worries, or fears. Finally, the therapist must treat the client with *unconditional positive regard* by providing a nonjudgmental, warm, and accepting environment in which the client can feel safe expressing his or her thoughts and feelings.

Here is an example of what person-centered therapy might sound like for a client who is dealing with conflicted feelings about her daughter being away at college (Raskin & Rogers, 2000).

Client: I'm having a lot of problems dealing with my daughter. She's 20 years old; she's in college; I'm having a lot of trouble letting her go . . . And I have a lot of guilt feelings about her; I have a real need to hang on to her.

Therapist: A need to hang on so you can kind of make up for the things you feel guilty about—is that part of it?

Client: There's a lot of that . . . Also, she's been a real friend to me and filled my life . . . And it's very hard . . . a lot of empty places now that she's not with me.

Therapist: The old vacuum, sort of, when she's not there.

Client: Yes. Yes. I would also like to be the kind of mother that could be strong and say, you know, "Go and have a good life," and this is really hard for me to do.

Therapist: It's very hard to give up something that's been so precious in your life but also something that has caused you pain when you mentioned guilt.

Client: Yeah, and I'm aware that I have some anger toward her that I don't always get what I want. I have needs that are not met. And, uh, I don't feel I have a right to those needs. You know. . . . She's a daughter; she's not my mother—though sometimes I feel as if I'd like her to mother me. . . . It's very difficult for me to ask for that and have a right to it.

Therapist: So it may be unreasonable, but still, when she doesn't meet your needs, it makes you mad.

Client: Yeah, I get very, very angry with her.

From this example you can see that the goal of the exchange was not to uncover repressed conflicts, as in psychodynamic therapy, or to challenge unrealistic thoughts, as in cognitive behavior therapy. Instead, the person-centered therapist tried to understand the client's experience and reflect that experience back to her in a supportive way, encouraging the client's natural tendency toward growth. This style of therapy is a bit reminiscent of psychoanalysis in its way of encouraging the client toward the free expression of thoughts and feelings, although humanistic therapies clearly start from a set of assumptions about human nature that differ diametrically from psychodynamic theories.

Gestalt Therapy

Gestalt therapy was founded by Frederick "Fritz" Perls (1893–1970) and colleagues in the 1940s and 1950s (Perls, Hefferkine, & Goodman, 1951). **Gestalt therapy** *has the goal of helping the client become aware of his or her thoughts, behaviors, experiences, and feelings and to "own" or take responsibility for them.* Gestalt therapists are encouraged to be enthusiastic and warm toward their clients, an approach they share in common with person-centered therapists. To help facilitate the client's awareness, gestalt therapists also reflect back to the client their impressions of the client.

As part of Gestalt therapy, clients are encouraged to imagine that another person is sitting across from them in a chair. The client then moves from chair to chair, role-playing what he or she would say to the imagined person and what that person would answer.

Gestalt therapy emphasizes the experiences and behaviors that are occurring at that particular moment in the therapy session. For example, if a client is talking about something stressful that occurred during the previous week, the therapist might shift the attention to the client's current experience by asking, "How do you feel as you describe what happened to you?" This technique is known as *focusing.* Clients are also encouraged to put their feelings into action. One way to do this is the *empty chair technique,* in which the client imagines that another person (e.g., a spouse, a parent, a coworker) is in an empty chair, sitting directly across from the client. The client then moves from chair to chair, alternating from role playing what he or she would say to the other person and what he or she imagines the other person would respond. In this type of therapy, the goal is to facilitate awareness of the client's thoughts, feelings, behaviors, and experiences in the "here and now." A variety of techniques are used to facilitate awareness, with the assumption that greater honesty and awareness will clear a path to living more fully and meaningfully.

Groups in Therapy

It is natural to think of psychopathology as an illness that affects only the individual. A particular person "is depressed," for example, or "has anxiety." Yet each person lives in a world of other people, and interactions with others may intensify and even create disorders. A depressed person may be lonely after moving away from friends and loved ones, for example, or an anxious person could be worried about pressures from parents. These ideas suggest that people might be able to recover from disorders in the same way they got into them—not just as an individual effort, but through social processes. Indeed, psychotherapy itself is a form of social interaction, an interaction specifically aimed at healing, so therapy conducted in groups of people is really just a further development of the basic idea of therapy.

In this section, we'll look at types of psychotherapy for people in groups. We'll begin with therapies that attempt to treat whole groups—couples and family therapies. Then we'll explore treatment options that expand psychotherapy to include multiple individual participants, often with similar problems—group therapies and self-help and support groups.

Couples and Family Therapy

When a couple is "having problems," neither individual may be suffering from any psychopathology. Rather, it may be the relationship itself that is disordered. *Couples therapy* is when a married, cohabitating, or dating couple is seen together in therapy to work on problems usually arising within the relationship. There are cases when therapy with even larger groups is warranted. An individual may be having a problem—say, an adolescent is abusing alcohol—but the source of the problem is in the individual's relationships with family members; perhaps the mother is herself an alcoholic who subtly encourages the adolescent to drink and the father travels and neglects the family. In this case, it could be useful for the therapist to work with the whole group at once in *family therapy*—psychotherapy involving members of a family.

GESTALT THERAPY An existentialist approach to treatment with the goal of helping the client become aware of his or her thoughts, behaviors, experiences, and feelings and to "own" or take responsibility for them.

Couples therapy is for a relationship in the rough.

THE GRANGER COLLECTION, NEW YORK

The roots of couples and family therapies date back more than 100 years, beginning in the field of social work and related movements (Broderick & Schrader, 1991). Early therapies were educational in nature, often designed to teach individuals (mostly women) about marriage, parenting, and family life (Kaslow & Celano, 1995)—for example, how to take care of domestic responsibilities. These treatments evolved into therapies designed specifically for couples. Today, couples come to therapy for many different reasons, including difficulty communicating (e.g., frequent arguing, lack of communication), sexual dysfunction, marital dissatisfaction, domestic violence, or difficulties dealing with a specific problem impacting the relationship (e.g., when one person in the couple suffers from severe depression).

A traditional use of couples therapy might involve a couple seeking help because they are unhappy with their relationship. In this scenario, both members of the couple are expected to attend therapy sessions and the problem is seen as arising from their interaction rather than from the problems of one half of the couple. For example, it might be that the wife nags the husband, and he withdraws into solitary hobbies and watching sports. She is lonely and unhappy, complaining to him whenever she can about how he avoids her—and he is also deeply dissatisfied, finding every chance he can to escape her bitter complaints by going out to the garage or holing up with the TV in the den. A key part of their misery as a couple, then, might be that each of them sees the problem as something the other person is doing: He sees the problem as her nagging, and she sees the problem as his withdrawal. With both people present, a therapist can gather information from both parties about the nature of the problem as well as observe the couple's actual interactions. In this case, a therapist might be able to help them see the self-defeating cycle of their interaction (see **FIGURE 14.2**). Treatment strategies would target changes in *both* parties, focusing on ways to break their repetitive dysfunctional pattern (Watzlawick, Beavin, & Jackson, 1967).

Couples therapy can also be useful when the relationship itself aids individual therapy for one of the partners. For example, a CBT approach for treating panic disorder with agoraphobia (fear of places that are difficult or embarrassing to escape from in case of a panic attack) has been adapted into a couples-based format (Barlow, O'Brien, & Last, 1984). In this program, treatment includes the standard CBT techniques, such as exposure and cognitive restructuring, except that spouses join the clients in each therapy session and often participate in homework assignments. Spouses are included to help them better understand the nature of the disorder, to train them to be coaches during exposure homework practices, to ensure that they are not doing things to undermine the treatment (such as helping the client to avoid feared situations), and to improve communication in the couple regarding the panic and agoraphobia symptoms. Treatment for agoraphobia and panic disorder that includes spouses has been found more effective than treatment for clients alone (Barlow, O'Brien, & Last, 1984).

In family therapy, the "client" is the entire family rather than one person. The family is thought of as a *system,* so one person's symptoms are really symptoms of the family system as a whole. Family therapists believe that problem behaviors exhibited by a particular family member are the result of a dysfunctional family system. For example, an adolescent girl suffering from bulimia might be treated in therapy with her

GROUP THERAPY Therapy in which multiple participants (who often do not know one another at the outset) work on their individual problems in a group atmosphere.

Figure 14.2 Self-Defeating Interaction Cycle A couple can get caught up in a self-defeating interaction cycle when both partners believe they are acting rationally in response to the other's behavior. There may be no end to the conflict, for example, when a husband withdraws from his wife to avoid her nagging and she nags him for withdrawing (and then he withdraws to avoid her nagging . . . and on and on).

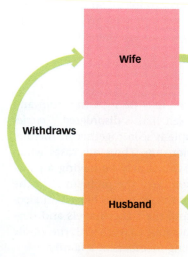

mother, father, and older brother. The therapist would work to understand how the family members relate to one another, how the family is organized, and how it changes over time. In discussions with the family, the therapist might discover that the parents' excessive enthusiasm about her brother's athletic career led the girl to try to gain their approval by controlling her weight to become "beautiful." Both couples and family therapy involve more than one person attending therapy together, and the problems and solutions are seen as arising from the *interaction* of these individuals rather than simply from any one individual.

Families enter therapy for many reasons, sometimes to help particular members and other times because there are problems in one or more of the relationships in the family.

Group Therapy

If individual clients can benefit from talking with a psychotherapist, perhaps they can also benefit from talking with other clients who are talking with the therapist. This is **group therapy**, *a technique in which multiple participants (who often do not know one another at the outset) work on their individual problems in a group atmosphere.* Many psychotherapies (e.g., psychodynamic psychotherapy, CBT, humanistic and existential therapies) have been adapted for groups, although traditional psychoanalysis is a problem because the couch gets so crowded. The therapist in group therapy serves more as a discussion leader than as a personal therapist, conducting the sessions both by talking with individuals and by encouraging them to talk with one another. Group therapy is often used for people who have a common problem, such as substance abuse, but it can also be used for those with differing problems. Group therapy can be helpful for many of the problems targeted by individual therapies, such as anxiety, depression, body image issues, substance abuse, or coping with divorce.

Why do people choose group therapy? One advantage is that groups provide a context in which clients can practice relating to others. People in group therapy have a "built-in" set of peers whom they have to talk to and get along with on a regular basis. This can be especially helpful for clients who are otherwise socially isolated. Second, attending a group with others who have similar problems shows clients that they are not alone in their suffering. Third, group members model appropriate behaviors for one another and share their insights about how to deal with their problems. Beyond these advantages, there is also the practical side: Group treatment is more cost effective than individual therapy, using less therapist time and allowing more people to participate in treatment. Individuals who might not otherwise be able to afford psychotherapy may be able to manage the cost of group therapy.

There are also disadvantages of group therapy over individual therapy. It may be difficult to assemble a group of individuals who have similar needs. This is particularly an issue with CBT, which tends to focus on specific problems such as depression or panic disorder. Group therapy may become a problem if one or more members undermine the treatment of other group members. This can occur if some group members dominate the discussions, threaten other group members, or make others in the group uncomfortable (e.g., attempting to date other members). Finally,

 ONLY HUMAN

HOME ON DERANGE 1993—University of California at Berkeley "environmental psychologist" Clare Cooper Marcus recently started a counseling service for people having difficult relationships with their houses. For $100, she will spend an hour conducting role-playing sessions between the client and his or her house. Dr. Marcus says that having the client voice anxieties to the house, and having the house respond, usually begins relieving the client's stress within the first hour.

"So, does anyone in the group feel like responding to what Richard has just shared with us?"

clients in group therapy get less attention than they might in individual psychotherapy. As a result, those who tend to participate less in the group may not benefit as much as those who participate more.

On balance, group therapy is often a useful format for treating a wide variety of problems, and it has been effectively used with a number of different types of therapy. When group therapy is not available or the person is not ready for this type of intervention, self-help or support groups may be a good alternative.

Self-Help and Support Groups

The costs of health care continue to escalate each year, leading to increasing pressure to find creative ways to improve access to treatment. Self-help and support groups provide help at reasonable or sometimes no cost. Typically, self-help and support groups are discussion or Internet chat groups that focus on a particular disorder or difficult life experience and are often run by peers who have themselves struggled with the same issues. For example, many self-help groups offer support to cancer survivors or to parents of children with autism. There are online support groups for people with mood disorders, eating disorders, substance abuse problems, and self-harming disorders—in fact, for just about every psychological disorder. In addition to being cost effective, self-help and support groups allow people to realize that they are not the only ones with a particular problem and give them the opportunity to offer guidance and support to each other based on personal experiences of success.

In some cases, though, self-help and support groups can do more harm than good. Some members may be disruptive or aggressive or encourage one another to engage in behaviors that are countertherapeutic (e.g., avoiding feared situations or using alcohol to cope). People with moderate problems may be exposed to others with severe problems and may become oversensitized to symptoms they might otherwise have not found disturbing. Because self-help and support groups are usually not led by trained therapists, mechanisms to evaluate these groups or to ensure their quality are rarely in place. Such groups can sometimes evolve into cults with destructive and self-destructive results. The People's Temple in San Francisco that evolved into the Jonestown cult in Guyana—and ended in mass suicide in 1978—began, after all, as a group offering support to people in trouble.

The most famous self-help and support groups are Alcoholics Anonymous (AA), Gamblers Anonymous, and Al-Anon (a program for the family and friends of those with alcohol problems). These groups encourage members to acknowledge their problems, surrender their recovery to a higher power, accept personal flaws, and ultimately lend support to others who may need it. AA was the first such group, founded in Akron, Ohio, in 1935 by men known as Bill W. and Dr. Bob. Both men had struggled with alcoholism and met when Bill W. sought out a fellow alcoholic to help him stay sober on a business trip. His search led him to Dr. Bob, and together they successfully battled their problem drinking. Today, there are more than 2 million AA members in the United States, with 185,000 group meetings that occur around the world (Mack, Franklin, & Frances, 2003).

There are several assumptions underlying the philosophy of AA. Members are taught to view alcoholism as a chronic disease over which they have little control. Self-blame is discouraged, and instead members are prompted to look beyond themselves to get the strength they need. AA is not affiliated

Self-help groups are a cost-effective, time-effective, and treatment-effective solution for dealing with some types of psychological problems.

MANCHAN/GETTY IMAGES

with any particular religious group, but religion and spirituality are strong themes in the program. Members are encouraged to follow "12 steps" to reach the goal of life-long abstinence from all drinking, and the steps include believing in a higher power, practicing prayer and meditation, and making amends for harm to others. Most members attend group meetings several times per week, and between meetings they receive additional support from their "sponsor." AA provides a safe place where people can discuss their problems in an atmosphere of acceptance and understanding. AA is often just one component of a comprehensive treatment for alcohol use disorders, but for many people AA is the only treatment they receive. With this being the case, it is important to know how useful this program is.

Traditionally, AA members have not supported researchers' requests to evaluate the program. A few studies examining the effectiveness of AA have been conducted, and it appears that individuals who participate tend to overcome problem drinking with greater success than those who do not participate in AA (Fiorentine, 1999; Morgenstern et al., 1997). However, several tenets of the AA philosophy are not supported by the research. For example, although AA suggests that the *only* path to recovery is abstinence, a number of studies show that some individuals who abuse alcohol can learn to drink in a controlled, responsible way (Miller, 1978; Sobell & Sobell, 1995). Thus, we know that the general AA program is useful, but questions about which parts of this program are most helpful have yet to be studied.

Considered together, the many social approaches to psychotherapy reveal how important interpersonal relationships are for each of us. It may not always be clear how psychotherapy works, whether one approach is better than another, or what particular theory should be used to understand how problems have developed. What is clear, however, is that social interactions between people—both in individual therapy and in all the different forms of therapy in groups—can be useful in treating psychological disorders.

In summary, there are several major forms of psychotherapy. Freud's psychoanalysis was the initial model for all the psychodynamic therapies, which together emphasize helping clients to gain insight into their unconscious conflicts. Behavior therapy, which applies learning principles to specific behavior problems, and cognitive therapy, which aims at challenging irrational thoughts, have been merged by many therapists into cognitive behavior therapy, or CBT. Humanistic therapies (such as person-centered therapy) and existential approaches (such as Gestalt therapy) focus on helping people to develop a sense of personal worth. Approaches to psychotherapy can also involve more than one person, targeting either group problems or individual problems by involving couples, families, or groups of clients brought together for the purpose of therapy. ■ ■

Medical and Biological Treatments: Healing the Mind through the Brain

Ever since someone discovered that a whack to the head can affect the mind, people have suspected that direct brain interventions might hold the keys to a cure for psychological disorders. There is anthropological evidence, for example, that the occasional human thousands of years ago was "treated" for some malady by the practice of trepanning—drilling a hole in the skull, perhaps in the belief that this would release the evil spirits that people believed were affecting the mind (Alt et al., 1997). Surgery for psychological disorders is a last resort even now, and treatments that focus on the brain usually involve interventions that are less dramatic. The use of drugs to influence the brain was also discovered in prehistory (alcohol, for example, has been around for a long time), and drug treatments have grown in variety and effectiveness to become what is now the most common medical approach in treating psychological disorders.

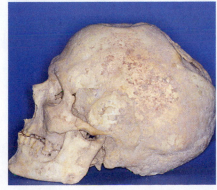

This is a trepanned skull from a Stone Age burial site (about 5900–6200 BC) in the Alsace region of France. Two holes were drilled in the skull and the patient lived afterward—as shown by the regrowth of bone covering the holes (from Alt et al., 1997). Don't try this at home.

DR. KURT W. ALT

ANTIPSYCHOTIC DRUGS
Medications that are used to treat schizophrenia and related psychotic disorders.

PSYCHOPHARMACOLOGY The study of drug effects on psychological states and symptoms.

The fact that the brain can be understood as a biological organ—like the stomach or the elbow—makes it tempting to think of medical and biological treatments as "magic bullets" for mental health, quick fixes that achieve easily what psychotherapy might take a long time to achieve or might never do. Just as taking an aspirin can reduce the pain of tennis elbow, we might assume that medicating the brain could potentially reduce just about any psychological symptom. Perhaps there is a pill to calm obsessive worries about driving a car into oncoming traffic? Or a pill to neutralize the schizophrenic symptom of hearing voices? A pill to stop nail biting? Current knowledge about the brain usually doesn't allow treatments to be so specific. Instead, biological and medical treatments often have broad effects, such as improving a person's mood or making the person more calm. These treatments can reduce the frequency or severity of some symptoms but may not always succeed as magic bullets.

In this section, we will explore the variety of medical and biological treatments currently in use, looking first at medications that broadly target psychosis, anxiety, and depression and then at other biologically based treatments that influence the brain but do not involve drugs.

Antipsychotic Medications

The story of drug treatments for severe psychological disorders starts with a stuffy nose. As you may know, the antihistamines we take for a stuffy nose caused by allergies often have the side effect of inducing drowsiness. French chemist Paul Charpentiere synthesized a drug related to antihistamine from coal tar in 1951, and tests on animals revealed that it had a much stronger sedative effect than antihistamine. Even better, this sedative administered to people with schizophrenia often left them euphoric and docile when they had formerly been agitated and incorrigible (Barondes, 2003). The drug was chlorpromazine (Thorazine), the first in a series of **antipsychotic drugs**, which *treat schizophrenia and related psychotic disorders.*

Through the 1950s and 1960s, related medications such as thioridazine (Mellaril) and haloperidol (Haldol) were introduced and completely changed the way schizophrenia was managed. Before the introduction of the antipsychotic drugs, people with schizophrenia often exhibited bizarre symptoms and were sometimes so disruptive and difficult to manage that the only way to protect them (and other people) was to keep them in asylums. In the period following the introduction of these drugs, the number of people in psychiatric hospitals decreased by more than two thirds (see the Real World box on the facing page). Antipsychotic drugs made possible the deinstitutionalization of hundreds of thousands of people and gave a major boost to the field of **psychopharmacology**, *the study of drug effects on psychological states and symptoms.*

People with schizophrenia are two to three times more likely to smoke tobacco than the average person (Kelly & McCreadie, 2000). There are several explanations being tested for this, including the possibility that people with schizophrenia seek out nicotine to reduce their symptoms. If this is true, their "self-medication" may point the way toward new drug treatments for the disorder that might be more helpful and less harmful than smoking.

ALAIN DAUSSIN/GETTY IMAGES

These antipsychotic medications are believed to block dopamine receptors in parts of the brain such as the mesolimbic area, an area between the tegmentum (in the midbrain) and the limbic system (see Chapter 3). The medication reduces dopamine activity in these areas. As you read in Chapter 13, the effectiveness of schizophrenia medications led to the "dopamine hypothesis," suggesting that schizophrenia may be caused by excess dopamine in the synapse. Research has indeed found that dopamine overactivity in the mesolimbic areas of the brain is related to the more bizarre positive symptoms of schizophrenia, such as hallucinations and delusions (Marangell et al., 2003).

Although antipsychotic drugs work well for positive symptoms, it turns out that negative symptoms such as emotional numbing and social withdrawal may be related to dopamine *under*activity in the mesocortical areas of the brain (connections between parts of the tegmentum and the cortex). This may help explain why antipsychotic medications do not relieve negative symptoms well. Instead of a medication that blocks dopamine receptors, negative symptoms require a medication that *increases* the amount of dopamine available at the synapse. This is a good example of how medical treatments can have broad psychological effects but not target specific psychological symptoms.

{ THE REAL WORLD } Tales from the Madhouse

SOCIETY HAS NEVER QUITE KNOWN WHAT to do with people who have severe mental disorders. For much of recorded history, mentally ill people have been victims of maltreatment, languishing as paupers in the streets or, worse, suffering inhumane conditions in prisons. It was something of a reform, then, when in the 18th century, the few private "madhouses" for the rich became models for the establishment of public asylums in England and France. At the time, no one cared much about any harmful effects of using derogatory terms for the patients of these institutions, so asylums were unashamedly named for their services to "lunatics," "idiots," and "the insane."

In North America, the asylum movement for humane treatment of the mentally ill was fostered initially by Dr. Benjamin Rush (a signer of the Constitution) and later by mental health crusader Dorothea Dix. Dix visited jails and almshouses in Massachusetts and in 1843 reported to the legislature widespread cruelty toward the insane. She witnessed inmates who were in chains, unclothed even in winter, and abused physically and sexually by their keepers. At the Shelburne jail, she recounted finding "a human being, partially extended, cast upon his back amidst a mass of filth. The mistress says 'He's cleaned out now and then; but what's the use for such a creature?'" (Gollaher, 1995). Dix developed a remarkably effective personal campaign across North America and Europe that eventually resulted in the building of hundreds of asylums for the mentally ill.

The creation of asylums encouraged humane treatment but did not guarantee it. London's St. Mary's of Bethlehem Hospital, known for inspiring the term *bedlam,* was typical—even charging visitors to view the inmates as a way of financing the institution. One visitor to this human zoo in 1753 remarked, "To my great surprise, I found at least a hundred people, who, having paid their two pence apiece, were suffered, unattended, to run rioting up and down the wards, making sport and diversion of the miserable inhabitants" (Hitchcock, 2005). To some degree, the abuse of insane inmates by jailers simply was transformed into the abuse of mental patients by asylum workers. For severe disorders, there often was no "treatment" at all, and the focus of the asylum instead was merely on custody (Jones, 1972). Modern exposés of mental hospital life, films such as *Titicut Follies* and *One Flew over the Cuckoo's Nest,* reveal that asylums can be bedlams even in our ostensibly enlightened times.

These weaknesses of the asylum movement eventually led to another revolution in mental health treatment—the deinstitutionalization movement of the 1960s. Drugs were being discovered that helped people to manage their disorders and live outside hospitals. With the funding of a "community mental health" initiative by the Kennedy administration, dozens of mental hospitals across the United States were closed, and meanwhile, thousands of patients were trained to shop, cook, take public transportation, and otherwise deal with living outside the hospital. Former asylum patients were returned to their families or placed in foster homes or group apartments, but in too many cases they were simply released with nowhere to go. Treatment of all but the most untreatable patients was managed through community mental health centers—support units to provide emergency inpatient care as needed but mainly supplying outpatient treatment and assistance in community living (Levine, 1981).

Dorothea Dix (1802–77) was a pioneer in the reform of treatment for the mentally ill.

Has this experiment worked? The jury is still out because many problems remain. Treatment for some severe disorders has improved since deinstitutionalization began. The basic drugs that helped people to manage their lives outside mental hospitals have been refined and improved. But federal funding of the network of community mental health centers was abandoned by the Reagan administration in the 1980s, and state-funded programs and private managed care providers have not made up the difference (Cutler, Bevilacqua, & McFarland, 2003). So, on the one hand, the current approach of deinstitutionalization has increased the autonomy of people with severe mental illnesses, allowing them greater freedom from asylums. But on the other hand, this approach puts many of these people on the streets, where they remain homeless, poor, vulnerable, and sometimes dangerous. It is not clear that in several hundred years real progress has been made.

Missouri State Lunatic Asylum. This asylum represents a somewhat idyllic image of treatment for psychological disorders. Life inside the asylum often presented quite a different reality.

ANTIANXIETY MEDICATIONS Drugs that help reduce a person's experience of fear or anxiety.

After the introduction of antipsychotic medications, there was little change in the available treatments for schizophrenia for more than a quarter of a century. However, in the 1990s, a new class of antipsychotic drugs was introduced. These newer drugs, which include clozapine (Clozaril), risperidone (Risperidal), and olanzepine (Zyprexa), have become known as *atypical antipsychotics* (the older drugs are now often referred to as *conventional* or *typical* antipsychotics). Unlike the older antipsychotic medications, these newer drugs appear to affect both the dopamine and serotonin systems, blocking both types of receptors. The ability to block serotonin receptors appears to be a useful addition since enhanced serotonin activity in the brain has been implicated in some of the core difficulties in schizophrenia, such as cognitive and perceptual disruptions, as well as mood disturbances. This may explain why atypical antipsychotics work at least as well as older drugs for the positive symptoms of schizophrenia but also work fairly well for negative symptoms (Bradford, Stroup, & Lieberman, 2002).

Like most medications, antipsychotic drugs have side effects. The side effects can be sufficiently unpleasant that some people "go off their meds," preferring their symptoms to the drug. One side effect that often occurs with long-term use is *tardive dyskinesia,* a condition of involuntary movements of the face, mouth, and extremities. In fact, patients often need to take another medication to treat the unwanted side effects of the conventional antipsychotic drugs. Side effects of the newer medications tend to be milder than those of the older antipsychotics. For that reason, the atypical antipsychotics are now usually the front-line treatments for schizophrenia (Marangell et al., 2003).

Antianxiety Medications

Antianxiety medications are *drugs that help reduce a person's experience of fear or anxiety.* The most commonly used antianxiety medications are the *benzodiazepines,* a type of tranquilizer that works by facilitating the action of the neurotransmitter gamma-aminobutyric acid (GABA; see Chapter 3). GABA inhibits certain neurons in the brain, producing a calming effect for the person. Recall from Chapter 8 that alcohol enhances GABA's actions and can also lead to a temporary reduction in anxiety. Because of this, mixing alcohol and tranquilizers can produce combined effects that are dangerous and potentially lethal. Commonly prescribed benzodiazepines include diazepam (Valium), lorazepam (Ativan), and alprazolam (Xanax). The benzodiazepines typically take effect in a matter of minutes and are effective for reducing symptoms of anxiety disorders (Roy-Byrne & Cowley, 2002).

Nonetheless, these days doctors are relatively cautious when prescribing benzodiazepines: They tend to prescribe them at lower dosages and for shorter periods than in the past. One concern is that these drugs have the potential for abuse. They are often associated with the development of tolerance, which is the need for higher dosages over time to achieve the same effects following long-term use (see Chapter 8). Furthermore, after people become tolerant of the drug, they risk significant withdrawal symptoms following discontinuation. Some withdrawal symptoms include increased heart rate, shakiness, insomnia, agitation, and anxiety—the very symptoms the drug was taken to eliminate! Therefore, patients who take benzodiazepines for extended periods may have difficulty coming off these drugs and should discontinue their medications gradually to minimize withdrawal symptoms (Schatzberg, Cole, & DeBattista, 2003). Another consideration when prescribing benzodiazepines is their side effects. The most common side effect is drowsiness, although benzodiazepines can also have negative effects on coordination and memory.

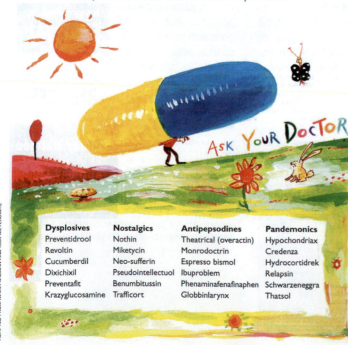

WHAT'S NEW IN PHARMACOLOGY
by Maira Kalman and Rick Meyerowitz

ASK YOUR DOCTOR

ADAPTED FROM MAIRA KALMAN AND RICK MEYEROWITZ

Dysplosives	Nostalgics	Antipepsodines	Pandemonics
Preventidrool	Nothin	Theatrical (overactin)	Hypochondriax
Revoltin	Miketycin	Monrodoctrin	Credenza
Cucumberdil	Neo-sufferin	Espresso bismol	Hydrocortidrek
Dixichixil	Pseudointellectuol	Ibuproblem	Relapsin
Preventafit	Benumbitussin	Phenaminafenafinaphen	Schwarzeneggra
Krazyglucosamine	Trafficort	Globbinlarynx	Thatsol

A newer drug, buspirone (Buspar), has been shown to reduce anxiety among individuals who suffer from generalized anxiety disorder (GAD). Buspirone is not as effective as the benzodiazepines for anxiety disorders other than generalized anxiety disorder, but it doesn't produce the drowsiness and withdrawal symptoms associated with benzodiazepines (Roy-Byrne & Cowley, 2002). Gabapentin (Neurontin), an antiseizure medication, has also been recently studied as a remedy for anxiety. Preliminary results suggest that this drug may be useful for treating social anxiety and panic disorder (Pande et al., 1999, 2000).

Antidepressants and Mood Stabilizers

Antidepressants are *a class of drugs that help lift people's mood.* Over the past few decades, the three most commonly prescribed antidepressants were the monoamine oxidase inhibitors (MAOIs), tricyclic antidepressants, and selective serotonin reuptake inhibitors (SSRIs). Antidepressants were first introduced in the 1950s, when iproniazid, a drug that was used to treat tuberculosis, was found to elevate mood (Selikoff, Robitzek, & Ornstein, 1952). Iproniazid is a *monoamine oxidase inhibitor (MAOI),* a medication that prevents the enzyme monoamine oxidase from breaking down neurotransmitters such as norepinephrine, serotonin, and dopamine. However, despite their effectiveness, MAOIs are rarely prescribed anymore. MAOI side effects such as dizziness and loss of sexual interest are often difficult to tolerate, and these drugs interact with many different medications, including over-the-counter cold medicines. They also can cause dangerous increases in blood pressure when taken with foods that contain tyramine, a natural substance formed from the breakdown of protein in certain cheeses, beans, aged meats, soy products, and draft beer.

A second category of antidepressants is the *tricyclic antidepressants,* which were also introduced in the 1950s. These include drugs such as imipramine (Tofranil) and amitriptyline (Elavil). These medications block the reuptake of norepinephrine and serotonin, thereby increasing the amount of neurotransmitter in the synaptic space between neurons. The most common side effects of tricyclic antidepressants include dry mouth, constipation, difficulty urinating, blurred vision, and racing heart (Marangell et al., 2003). Although these drugs are still prescribed, they are used much less frequently than they were in the past because of these side effects.

Among the most commonly used antidepressants today are the *selective serotonin reuptake inhibitors,* or SSRIs, which include drugs such as fluoxetine (Prozac), citalopram (Celexa), and paroxetine (Paxil). The SSRIs work by blocking the reuptake of serotonin in the brain, which makes more serotonin available in the synaptic space between neurons. The greater availability of serotonin in the synapse gives the neuron a better chance of "recognizing" and using this neurotransmitter in sending the desired signal. The SSRIs were developed based on hypotheses that low levels of serotonin are a causal factor in depression (see Chapter 13). Supporting this hypothesis, SSRIs are effective for depression, as well as for a wide range of other problems. SSRIs are called "selective" because, unlike the tricyclic antidepressants, which work on the serotonin and norepinephrine systems, SSRIs work more specifically on the serotonin system (see **FIGURE 14.3**).

Finally, in the past several years, a number of new antidepressants such as Effexor and Wellbutrin have been introduced. These antidepressants have characteristics that make them unique from the three classes of

ANTIDEPRESSANTS A class of drugs that help lift people's mood.

Figure 14.3 Antidepressant Drug Actions Antidepressant drugs, such as MAOIs, SSRIs and tricyclic antidepressants, act on neurotransmitters such as serotonin, dopamine, and norepinephrine by inhibiting their breakdown and blocking reuptake. These actions make more of the neurotransmitter available for release and leave more of the neurotransmitter in the synaptic gap to activate the receptor sites on the postsynaptic neuron. These drugs relieve depression and often alleviate anxiety and other disorders.

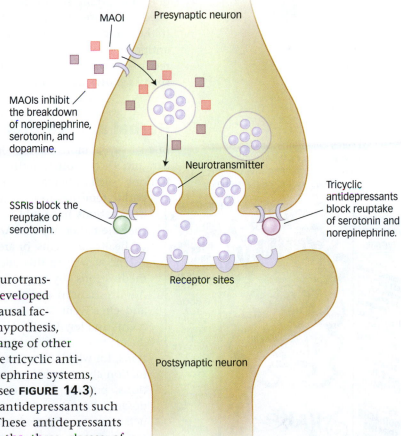

MAOI

Presynaptic neuron

MAOIs inhibit the breakdown of norepinephrine, serotonin, and dopamine.

Neurotransmitter

SSRIs block the reuptake of serotonin.

Tricyclic antidepressants block reuptake of serotonin and norepinephrine.

Receptor sites

Postsynaptic neuron

"More lithium."

antidepressants discussed so far and appear to have fewer side effects than the tricyclic antidepressants and MAOIs.

The antidepressants take from a few weeks to more than a month before they start to have an effect. Besides relieving symptoms of depression, almost all of the antidepressants effectively treat anxiety disorders, and many of them can resolve other problems, such as eating disorders. In fact, several companies that manufacture SSRIs have recently marketed their drugs as treatments for anxiety disorders rather than for their antidepressant effects. The general improvement in mood and outlook produced by antidepressants is attractive not only to people who are clinically depressed or anxious but also to many others seeking to level out the emotional hills and valleys of everyday life. Prozac is widely prescribed for people who are not suffering from specific disorders, and there is considerable debate about whether antidepressants should be used in this way to contribute to the well-being of people who are not sick (Kramer, 1997).

Although antidepressants are effective in treating unipolar depression, they are not recommended for treating bipolar disorder, which is characterized by manic or hypomanic episodes (see Chapter 13). Antidepressants are not prescribed because they might actually trigger a manic episode in a person with bipolar disorder. Instead, bipolar disorder is treated with *mood stabilizers,* which are medications used to suppress swings between mania and depression. Commonly used mood stabilizers include lithium and valproate. Even in unipolar depression, lithium is sometimes effective when combined with traditional antidepressants in people who do not respond to antidepressants alone.

Lithium has been associated with possible long-term kidney and thyroid problems, so people taking lithium must monitor their blood levels of lithium on a regular basis. Further, lithium has a precise range in which it is useful for each person, another reason it should be closely monitored with blood tests. Valproate, on the other hand, does not require such careful blood monitoring. Although valproate may have side effects of nausea and weight gain, it is currently the most commonly prescribed drug in the United States for bipolar disorder (Schatzberg et al., 2003). In sum, although the antidepressants are effective for a wide variety of problems, mood stabilizers may be required when a person's symptoms include extreme swings between highs and lows, such as experienced with bipolar disorder.

Herbal and Natural Products

In a survey of more than 2,000 Americans, 7% of those suffering from anxiety disorders and 9% of those suffering from severe depression reported using alternative "medications" such as herbal medicines, megavitamins, homeopathic remedies, or naturopathic remedies to treat these problems (Kessler et al., 2001). Even though these preparations have odd names such as St. John's wort (what's a wort, anyway?), they are rather popular. Are herbal and natural products effective in treating mental health problems, or are they just so much "snake oil"?

The answer to this question isn't simple. Herbal products are not considered medications by regulatory agencies (such as the U.S. Food and Drug Administration) and are exempt from rigorous research to establish their safety and effectiveness. Instead, herbal products are classified as nutritional supplements and regulated in the same way as foods. This means that it is easier for producers to market them and for people to buy them, unlike conventional medications, for which the rules are much more stringent. There is little scientific information about herbal products, including possible interactions with other medications, possible tolerance and withdrawal symptoms, side effects, appropriate dosages, how they work, or even *whether* they work—and the purity of these products often varies from brand to brand (Kressmann, Muller, & Blume, 2002). Major reasons people use them are that they are easily available over the counter, are less expensive, and are perceived as "natural" alternatives to "drugs."

"Snake oil cures" were often sold as miracle remedies for a variety of physical and mental ailments. Today the term has come to signify a treatment of dubious quality.

Many of the "natural" remedies and treatments available at health food and supplement stores come with little or no evidence of effectiveness and no claims for any specific benefit on the label—but the price tag is usually quite clear.

There is some research support for the effectiveness of herbal and natural products, but the evidence is not overwhelming. Products such as inositol (a bran derivative), kava (an herb related to black pepper), omega-3 fish oil (a fish oil), and SAM-e (. . . must be some kind of chemical) are sold as health foods and are described as having positive psychological effects of various kinds, but the evidence is mixed. For example, in the case of St. John's wort (a wort, it turns out, is an herb), some studies have shown it has an advantage over a placebo condition (e.g., Lecrubier et al., 2002), whereas others show no advantage (e.g., Hypericum Depression Trial Study Group, 2002). Although herbal medications and treatments are worthy of continued research, these products should be closely monitored and used judiciously until more is known about their safety and effectiveness.

Medications in Perspective

Psychologists looking for effective ways to treat psychological disorders get pretty excited about the progress of drug therapy. New drugs appear with some regularity, improving on prior medications and suggesting even greater improvements to come. At the same time, as we have seen, drugs can be blunt instruments as treatment devices, producing general changes in mood or relieving unpleasant symptoms—but leaving specific problems untreated. How can we bring medication and psychotherapy together to produce comprehensive treatments? One concern is how and when to combine treatments, and another concern is coordinating the treatments.

Combining Medication and Psychotherapy

Many studies have compared psychological treatments, medication, and combinations of these approaches for addressing psychological disorders. The results of these studies often depend on the particular problem being considered. For example, in the cases of schizophrenia and bipolar disorder, researchers have found that medication is a necessary part of treatment, and studies have tended to examine whether adding psychotherapeutic treatments such as social skills training or cognitive behavioral treatment can be helpful. For severe disorders, then, medication is usually a critical first step.

In the cases of anxiety disorders and depression, however, questions about treatment often involve deciding whether medication *or* psychotherapy should be used. CBT, medications, and their combinations have been found to be about equally effective. One study compared CBT, imipramine (the antidepressant also known as Tofranil), and the combination of these treatments (CBT plus imipramine) with a placebo (administration of an inert medication) for the treatment of panic disorder (Barlow et al., 2000). After 12 weeks of treatment, both CBT alone and imipramine

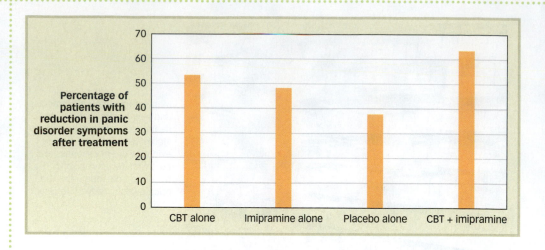

Figure 14.4 **The Effectiveness of Medication and Psychotherapy for Panic Disorder** One study of CBT and medication (imipramine) for panic disorder found that the effects of CBT, medication, and treatment that combined CBT and medication were not significantly different over the short term, though all three were superior to the placebo condition (Barlow et al., 2000).

alone were found to be superior to a placebo (see **FIGURE 14.4**). For the CBT-plus-imipramine condition, the response rate also exceeded the placebo one but was not significantly better than that for either CBT or imipramine alone. In other words, either treatment was better than nothing, but the combination of treatments was not significantly more effective than one or the other.

We do know that both therapy and medications are effective, so one question is whether they work through similar mechanisms. A recent study of people with social phobia examined patterns of cerebral blood flow following treatment using either citalopram (an SSRI) or CBT (Furmark et al., 2002). Patients in both groups were alerted to the possibility that they would soon have to speak in public. In both groups, those who responded to treatment showed similar reductions in activation in the amygdala, hippocampus, and neighboring cortical areas during this challenge. As you'll recall from Chapter 5, the amygdala and hippocampus play significant roles in memory for emotional information. These findings suggest that both therapy and medication affect the brain in regions associated with a reaction to threat. Although it might seem that events that influence the brain should be physical—after all, the brain is a physical object—both the physical administration of a drug and the psychological application of psychotherapy produce similar influences on the brain.

Findings such as these suggest that it is not always necessary to combine medication with psychotherapy; often, one type of treatment or the other will do just fine. There are other cases, however, in which both are helpful—such as when drugs help a person to become calm enough to interact successfully with a therapist or when therapy is used to help the person make cognitive or behavioral changes that will later allow medication to be reduced or eliminated (see **FIGURE 14.5**). Whatever magic medications can provide must be coordinated with the magic of psychotherapy.

Figure 14.5 **The Effects of Medication and Therapy in the Brain** PET scans of patients with social phobia showed similar reductions in activation of the amygdala/hippocampus region after they had received treatment with CBT (shown on the left) and citalopram, an SSRI (shown on the right) (from Furmark et al., 2002).

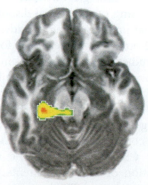

CBT

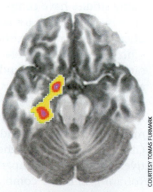

Medication

Coordinating Medication and Psychotherapy

Treatment can involve medication, psychotherapy, or both, but these treatments are often provided by different people. Psychiatrists are trained in the administration of medication in medical school (and they may also provide psychotherapy), whereas psychologists provide psychotherapy but not medication. This means that the coordination of treatment often involves cooperation between psychologists and psychiatrists. However, in 2002, New Mexico became the first state to allow appropriately trained psychologists to prescribe medications for mental health problems, and since then Louisiana has also granted this privilege. When New Mexico passed its legislation, there were only 18 psychiatrists serving the 72% of New Mexicans who lived outside Albuquerque and Santa Fe, and the wait for services was unacceptably long (Perina, 2002). Extending prescription privileges to psychologists was a way of serving people who might not otherwise have access to adequate care. The legislation in New Mexico requires that prescribing psychologists complete additional coursework and practical training under the supervision of a physician and also pass a national certification exam.

The question of whether psychologists should be licensed to prescribe medications has been a source of debate among physicians as well as among psychologists (Heiby, 2002; Lavoie & Fleet, 2002; Sammons, Paige, & Levant, 2003). Opponents argue that psychologists do not have the medical training to understand how medications interact with other drugs. The ability to prescribe medications also might make psychologists abandon their focus on psychotherapy and leave this important task understaffed. On the other hand, proponents of prescription privileges argue that patient safety would not be compromised due to rigorous training procedures and that underserved populations would benefit from more professionals being able to prescribe potentially helpful medications. This issue remains a focus of debate, so at present, the coordination of medication and psychotherapy usually involves a team effort of psychiatry and psychology.

Biological Treatments beyond Medication

Although medication can be an effective biological treatment, for some people medications do not work or side effects are intolerable. If this group of people doesn't respond to psychotherapy either, what other options do they have to achieve symptom relief? There are some additional avenues of help, but some are risky or poorly understood. In this section, we review biological treatments that go beyond medication and also look at the controversy that surrounds them. These biological treatments include electroconvulsive therapy, transcranial magnetic stimulation, phototherapy, and psychosurgery.

Electroconvulsive Therapy

More commonly known as "shock therapy," **electroconvulsive therapy (ECT)** is *a treatment that involves inducing a mild seizure by delivering an electrical shock to the brain.* The shock is applied to the person's scalp for less than a second. ECT is primarily used to treat severe depression, although it may also be useful for treating mania (Mukherjee, Sackeim, & Schnur, 1994). When first introduced, ECT was administered without any muscle relaxants or anesthetic, so participants often experienced muscle contractions and spasms during the seizure, some of which led to injuries. The procedure was frightening and painful for the recipient. The 1975 film *One Flew over the Cuckoo's Nest,* starring Jack Nicholson, raised public awareness that ECT might be used more as a punishment than a treatment by unscrupulous asylum attendants, and the technique became controversial and fell out of favor. Today, ECT is being used once again—but it is administered when the patient has been pretreated with muscle relaxants and is under general anesthetic, so the patient does not have convulsions and is not conscious of the procedure.

ELECTROCONVULSIVE THERAPY (ECT) A treatment that involves inducing a mild seizure by delivering an electrical shock to the brain.

TRANSCRANIAL MAGNETIC STIMULATION (TMS) A treatment that involves placing a powerful pulsed magnet over a person's scalp, which alters neuronal activity in the brain.

PHOTOTHERAPY A treatment for seasonal depression that involves repeated exposure to bright light.

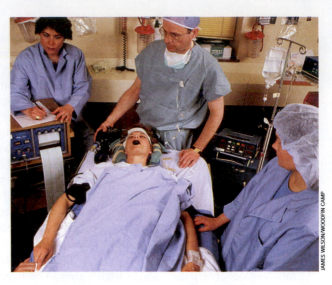

Electroconvulsive therapy (ECT) can be an effective treatment for severe depression. To reduce the side effects, it is administered under general anesthesia.

Controversy continues to mar the reputation of ECT, but some argue that it deserves higher status than a "last resort" treatment (Fink, 2001). The main side effect of ECT is impaired short-term memory, which usually improves over the first month or two after the end of treatment. In addition, patients undergoing this procedure sometimes report headaches and muscle aches afterward (Marangell et al., 2003). Despite these side effects, the treatment can be effective: About half the individuals who do not respond to medication alone may find ECT helpful in treating their depression (Prudic et al., 1996).

Transcranial Magnetic Stimulation

Transcranial magnetic stimulation (TMS) is *a treatment that involves placing a powerful pulsed magnet over a person's scalp, which alters neuronal activity in the brain* (George, Lisanby, & Sackeim, 1999). As a treatment for depression, the magnet is placed just above the right or left eyebrow in an effort to stimulate the right or left prefrontal cortex—areas of the brain implicated in depression. TMS is an exciting development because it is noninvasive and has fewer side effects than ECT (see Chapter 2). In fact, people do not require anesthetic for this procedure. Side effects are minimal; they may include mild headache and small risk of seizure, but TMS has no impact on memory or concentration. Enough studies have shown a positive effect on depression to suggest that TMS is useful (McNamara et al., 2001), even in treating depression that is unresponsive to medication (Fitzgerald et al., 2003; Kauffmann, Cheema, & Miller, 2004).

In fact, a recent study comparing TMS to ECT found that both procedures were effective, with no significant differences between them (Janicak et al., 2002). Other studies have investigated the utility of TMS for problems such as hallucinations, and early results are promising (Hoffman et al., 2003).

Phototherapy

Repeated exposure to bright light has been proven to be useful for treating seasonal affective disorder, a form of depression that occurs only in the winter months, probably in reaction to reduced sunlight.

Phototherapy, *a therapy that involves repeated exposure to bright light,* may be helpful to people who have a seasonal pattern to their depression. This could include people suffering with seasonal affective disorder (SAD; see Chapter 13) or those who experience depression only in the winter months due to the lack of light. Typically, the patient is exposed to bright light in the mornings, using a lamp designed for this purpose. Treatments lasting 2 hours each day for a week seem to be effective, at least in the short term (Terman et al., 1989).

Psychosurgery

In very rare cases, **psychosurgery,** *the surgical destruction of specific brain areas,* is used to treat certain psychological disorders, such as obsessive-compulsive disorder (OCD). Psychosurgery has a controversial history, beginning in the 1930s with the invention of the lobotomy by Portuguese physician Egas Moniz (1874–1955). After discovering that certain surgical procedures on animal brains calmed behavior, Moniz began to use similar techniques on violent or agitated human patients. Lobotomies involved inserting an instrument into the brain through the patient's eye socket or through holes drilled in the side of the head. The objective was to sever connections between the frontal lobes and inner brain structures such as the thalamus, known to be involved in emotion. Although some lobotomies produced highly successful results and Moniz received the 1949 Nobel Prize for his work, significant side effects such as extreme lethargy or childlike impulsivity detracted from these benefits. Lobotomy was used too widely for years, leaving many people devastated by these permanent side effects, and there is an ongoing movement challenging the award of the Nobel to Moniz. The development of antipsychotic drugs in the 1950s provided a safer way to treat violent patients and brought the practice of lobotomy to an end (Swayze II, 1995).

Today, psychosurgeries are far more precise than lobotomies of the 1930s and 1940s in targeting particular brain areas to lesion. This increased precision has produced better results. For example, patients suffering from obsessive-compulsive disorder who fail to respond to treatment (including several trials of medications and cognitive behavioral treatment) may benefit from specific surgical procedures called *cingulotomy* and *anterior capsulotomy.* Cingulotomy involves destroying part of the cingulate gyrus and corpus callosum (see Chapter 3). Anterior capsulotomy involves creating small lesions to disrupt the pathway between the caudate nucleus and putamen. Long-term follow-up studies suggest that more than a quarter of patients with OCD who do not respond to standard treatments report significant benefit following psychosurgery, with relatively few side effects (Baer et al., 1995; Cumming et al., 1995; Hay et al., 1993). A few case studies suggest that psychosurgery may be useful for some individuals with severe depression or bipolar disorder who don't respond to standard treatments (Bridges et al., 1994). However, due to the intrusive nature of psychosurgery and a lack of controlled studies, these procedures are currently reserved for the most severe cases.

In summary, the past 50 years have seen a revolution in the development of biomedical treatments for a wide range of mental illnesses. Medications have been developed to treat schizophrenia and psychotic disorders, depression, bipolar illness, and anxiety disorders. Medications are sometimes useful alone but are often combined with psychotherapy. In the case of depression, other biomedical treatments such as electroconvulsive therapy, transcranial magnetic stimulation, and phototherapy may provide relief. Psychosurgery in the form of lobotomy is no longer performed, but some psychosurgical treatments are effective when other forms of treatment have been exhausted. ■ ■

Treatment Effectiveness: For Better or for Worse

Think back to our fearful flyer Lisa at the beginning of the chapter. What if, instead of virtual reality therapy, Lisa had been assigned by her therapist to a drug treatment or to psychosurgery? For that matter, what if her therapy was to walk around for a week wearing a large false nose? Could these alternatives have been just as effective for treating her phobia? Through this chapter, we have explored various psychological and biomedical treatments that may help people with psychological disorders. But do these treatments actually work, and which ones work better than the others? To answer these questions, we'll first consider how we can evaluate the effectiveness of treatments. Then we'll turn to the evidence from these evaluations to see when therapy works. With any luck, false noses will not be necessary for anyone.

Rosemary Kennedy, sister of President John F. Kennedy, was intellectually challenged from childhood and had violent tantrums and rages that began in her early 20s. Her family agreed to her treatment with a lobotomy at St. Elizabeth's Hospital in Washington, DC, in 1942, but it went very wrong. She became permanently disabled—paralyzed on one side, incontinent, and unable to speak coherently—and spent the rest of her life in institutions.

PSYCHOSURGERY Surgical destruction of specific brain areas.

PLACEBO An inert substance or procedure that has been applied with the expectation that a healing response will be produced.

Evaluating Treatments

Treatment can have three possible outcomes: A client's symptoms can improve, stay the same, or worsen. How can we determine which of these has happened as a result of a particular treatment? The main problem in answering this question is the problem faced by researchers generally: figuring out whether one event has caused another. Did the treatment cause a cure?

As you learned in Chapter 2, this can be a difficult detective exercise. The detection is made even more difficult because people may approach treatment evaluation very unscientifically, often by simply noticing an improvement (or no improvement or that dreaded decline) and reaching a conclusion based on that sole observation. Treatment evaluation can be susceptible to illusions—mindbugs in how people process information about treatment effects—and these illusions can only be overcome by scientific evaluation.

Treatment Illusions

Imagine you're sick and the doctor says, "Take a pill." You follow the doctor's orders, and you get better. To what do you attribute your improvement? If you're like most people, you reach the conclusion that the pill cured you. How could this be an illusion? There are at least three ways: Maybe you would have gotten better anyway; maybe the pill wasn't the active ingredient in your cure; or maybe after you're better, you mistakenly remember having been more ill than you really were. These possibilities point to three potential illusions of treatment—illusions produced by natural improvement, by nonspecific treatment effects, and by reconstructive memory.

Natural improvement is the tendency of symptoms to return to their mean or average level, a process sometimes called *regression to the mean*. The illusion in this case happens when you conclude mistakenly that a treatment has made you better when you would have gotten better anyway. People typically turn to therapy or medication when their symptoms are at their worst, so they start their personal "experiment" to see if treatment makes them improve at a time when things couldn't get much worse. When this is the case, the client's symptoms will often improve regardless of whether there was any treatment at all; when you're at rock bottom, there's nowhere to move but up. In most cases, for example, depression that becomes severe enough to make a person a candidate for treatment will tend to lift in several months. A person who enters therapy for depression may develop an illusion that the therapy works because the therapy coincides with the typical course of the illness and the person's natural return to health.

Another treatment illusion occurs when a client or therapist attributes the client's improvement to a feature of treatment, although that feature wasn't really the active element that caused improvement. Recovery could be produced by *nonspecific treatment effects* that are not related to the specific mechanisms by which treatment is supposed to be working. For example, antidepressant medications are thought to work by changing brain chemistry to increase levels of serotonin, norepinephrine, and/or dopamine. However, the doctor prescribing the medication might simply be a pleasant and hopeful individual who gives the client a sense that things will improve. Client and doctor alike might attribute the client's improvement to brain changes—whereas the true active ingredient was the warm relationship with the good doctor.

Nonspecific treatment effects include many factors that might accompany a treatment: The client's decision to seek help, for example, might create a personal commitment, a kind of "turning over a new leaf," and the resulting behavior changes could be helpful. Another example: Staying away from alcohol because of its possible interaction with depression medication might be more useful as a treatment than the medication itself.

Simply knowing that you are getting a treatment can be a nonspecific treatment effect. These instances include the positive influences that can be

HIRAM S. DUDSON
1930 - 1993

Member,
Placebo Group

produced by a **placebo**, *an inert substance or procedure that has been applied with the expectation that a healing response will be produced*. For example, if you take a sugar pill that does not contain any painkiller for a headache thinking it is Tylenol or aspirin, this pill is a placebo. Placebos can have profound effects in the case of psychological treatments. Research shows that a large percentage of individuals with anxiety, depression, and other emotional problems experience significant improvement after a placebo treatment. Chapter 15 further discusses how placebo effects may occur as well as their influence on the brain.

One study compared the decrease in symptoms of obsessive-compulsive disorder between adolescents taking Prozac (fluoxetine) and those taking a placebo over the course of 13 weeks (Geller et al., 2001). Participants receiving medication showed a dramatic decrease in symptoms over time. Those taking a placebo also showed a reduction in symptoms over time, and the difference between the Prozac and placebo groups only became significant in the seventh week of treatment (see **FIGURE 14.6**). In fact, some psychologists estimate that up to 75% of the effects shown by antidepressant medications are due to the placebo effect (Kirsch & Sapirstein, 1998). Simply knowing that you're taking something for a problem can provide a measure of relief, even though what you're taking has no pharmacologically active ingredient.

A third treatment illusion can come about when the client's motivation to get well causes errors in *reconstructive memory* for the original symptoms. You might think that you've improved because of a treatment when in fact you're simply misremembering that your symptoms before treatment were worse than they actually were. This tendency was first observed in research examining the effectiveness of a study skills class (Conway & Ross, 1984). Some students who wanted to take the class indeed signed up and completed it, whereas others were randomly assigned to a waiting list until the class could be offered again. When their study abilities were measured afterward, those who took the class were no better at studying than their wait-listed counterparts. However, those who took the class *said* that they had improved. How could this be? Those participants recalled their study skills before the class as being worse than they actually had been. This motivated reconstruction of the past was dubbed by the researchers "getting what you want by revising what you had" (Conway & Ross, 1984). A client who forms a strong expectation of success in therapy might conclude later that even a useless treatment had worked wonders—by recalling past symptoms and troubles as worse than they were and thereby making the treatment seem effective.

A person who enters treatment is often anxious to get well and so may be especially likely to succumb to errors and illusions in assessing the effectiveness of the treatment. Treatments can look as if they worked when mindbugs lead us to ignore natural improvement, to overlook nonspecific treatment effects (such as the placebo effect), and to reconstruct our pretreatment history as worse than it was. Such treatment illusions can be overcome by using scientific methods to evaluate treatments—rather than trusting only our potentially faulty personal skills of observation.

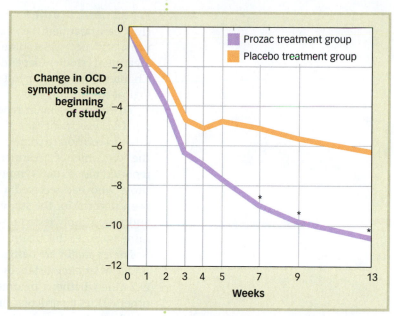

Figure 14.6 The Placebo Effect Two groups of patients were given pills to treat OCD. The first group was given Prozac, an antidepressant, and the second group was given an inert sugar pill, a placebo. Interestingly, both groups showed significant improvement in their depression symptoms until week 7, when the benefits of taking the placebo leveled off. As shown by the asterisks (*), Prozac reduced symptoms significantly more than did placebo pills by weeks 7, 9, and 13 (Geller et al., 2001).

INSADCO PHOTOGRAPHY/ALAMY

When you feel you've come a long way, you may remember where you started as farther down than it was. People who feel they have improved from a treatment program may reconstruct memories of the past that exaggerate their pretreatment problems.

Treatment Studies

How can treatment be evaluated in a way that allows us to choose treatments that work and not waste time with procedures that may be useless or even harmful? Treatment studies depend generally on the research design concepts covered in Chapter 2 but also depend on some ideas that are unique to the evaluation of psychological treatments.

There are two main types of treatment studies—outcome studies and process studies. *Outcome studies* are designed to evaluate *whether* a particular treatment works, often in relation to some other treatment or a control condition. For example, to study the outcome of treatment for depression, researchers might compare the self-reported moods and symptoms of two groups of people who were initially depressed—those who had received a treatment for 6 weeks and a control group who had also been selected for the study but had been assigned to a waiting list for later treatment and were simply tested 6 weeks after their selection. The outcome study could determine whether this treatment had any benefit.

Process studies are designed to answer questions regarding *why* a treatment works or under what circumstances a treatment works. For example, process researchers might examine whether a treatment for depression is more effective for certain clients than others: Does a particular drug have better effects for women than men? Process studies also can examine whether some parts of the treatment are particularly helpful, whereas others are irrelevant to the treatment's success: For example, in CBT for depression, is there more improvement if the therapy includes an assignment for the patient to write down a plan of activities each morning for the day? Process studies can refine therapies and target their influence to make them more effective.

Both outcome and process studies can be plagued by treatment illusions, so scientists usually design their research to overcome them. Ideally, for example, a treatment should be assessed in a *double-blind experiment*—a study in which both the patient and the researcher/therapist are uninformed about which treatment the patient is receiving (see Chapter 2). In the case of drug studies, this isn't hard to arrange because active drugs and placebos can be made to look alike to both the patients and the researchers during the study. Keeping both patients and researchers "in the dark" is much harder in the study of psychotherapy; in fact, it may even be impossible. Both the patient and the therapist can easily notice the differences in treatments such as psychoanalysis and behavior therapy, for example, so there's no way to keep the beliefs and expectations of both patient and therapist out of the picture in evaluating psychotherapy effectiveness.

The treatment illusions caused by natural improvement and reconstructive memory happen when people compare their symptoms before treatment to their symptoms after treatment—so treatment researchers typically try to avoid before/after comparisons within a single treatment group. A treatment (or experimental) group and a control group need to be randomly selected from the same population of patients before the study and then compared at the end of treatment. That way, natural improvement or motivated reconstructive memory can't cause illusions of effective treatment.

But what should happen to the control group during the treatment? If they simply stay home waiting until they can get treatment later (a wait-list control group), they won't receive the nonspecific effects of the treatment that the treatment group enjoys (such as visiting the comforting therapist or taking a medication). The researchers comparing *treatment* to *no treatment* might conclude erroneously that the treatment worked when in reality *any* treatment would have worked. For this reason, treatment studies commonly include a placebo treatment condition. In drug studies, the placebos are inactive medications given in the same way as the active medication; in psychotherapy studies, more elaborate activities that are like psychotherapy (e.g., yoga classes, meditation) are sometimes used to control for the nonspecific effects of psychotherapy. The scientific evaluation of treatment is designed to overcome the mindbugs that might make us jump to the conclusion that a treatment works when in fact it does not.

Which Treatments Work?

There are hundreds of published papers comparing various forms of psychotherapy to one another and to medication treatments. Every once in a while, someone takes a broad look at all this research and expresses the worry that treatment in general is not very effective and that psychotherapy in particular is a waste of everyone's time.

The distinguished psychologist Hans Eysenck (1916–97) reviewed the relatively few studies of psychotherapy effectiveness available in 1957 and raised a furor among therapists by concluding that psychotherapy—particularly psychoanalysis—was not only ineffective but seemed to *impede* recovery (Eysenck, 1957). Much larger numbers of studies have been examined statistically since then, and they support a more optimistic conclusion: The typical psychotherapy client is better off than three quarters of untreated individuals (Seligman, 1995; Smith, Glass, & Miller, 1980). Although critiques of psychotherapy continue to point out weaknesses in how patients are tested, diagnosed, and treated (Dawes, 1994), there is strong evidence generally supporting the effectiveness of many treatments. The key question then becomes: Which treatments are effective for which problems (Hunsley & Di Giulio, 2002)?

"Well, I do have this recurring dream that one day I might see some results."

Comparing Treatments

One of the most enduring debates in clinical psychology concerns how the various psychotherapies compare to one another. Some psychologists have argued for years that evidence supports the conclusion that most psychotherapies work about equally well. In this view, it is the nonspecific factors shared by all forms of psychotherapy, such as contact with and empathy from a professional, that contribute to change (Luborsky et al., 2002; Luborsky & Singer, 1975). In contrast, others have argued that there are important differences between therapies and that certain treatments are more effective than others, especially for treating particular types of problems (Beutler, 2002; Hunsley & Di Giulio, 2002). After all, you don't go to a foot doctor for a toothache: Different therapies ought to be differentially helpful for different problems. Some of these differences have been articulated in an attempt to compile a list of effective and helpful psychological treatments for particular problems.

St. Panacea was a shepherdess born in Italy in 1378. The name Panacea means "all healing," and a remedy for all that ails us is something we all would love. But a treatment that heals everything could be too much of a wish come true. Psychotherapy researchers worry that if any version of psychotherapy is effective for any mental disorder, the "active ingredient" of psychotherapy may be so general that the treatment could be meaningless.

Table 14.3	Some Well-Established Psychological Treatments
Type of Treatment	**Patient's Problem**
Cognitive behavior therapy	Panic disorder with and without agoraphobia
Cognitive therapy	Depression
Cognitive therapy	Bulimia
Interpersonal therapy	Depression
Behavior therapy (exposure and response prevention)	Obsessive-compulsive disorder
Behavior therapy	Childhood enuresis (bed wetting)
Behavior therapy	Marital difficulties

In 1995, the American Psychological Association (APA) published one of the first attempts to define criteria for determining whether a particular type of psychotherapy is effective for a particular problem (Task Force on Promotion and Dissemination of Psychological Procedures, 1995). The official criteria for empirically validated treatments defined two levels of empirical support: *well-established treatments,* those with a high level of support, and *probably efficacious treatments,* those with preliminary support. After these criteria were established, a list of empirically supported treatments was published by the APA (Chambless et al., 1998; Woody & Sanderson, 1998). **TABLES 14.3** and **14.4** show examples of each kind of treatment.

There is little doubt that clients should have the opportunity to receive treatments that work, but there is still much disagreement about what the best approaches to treatment are (see the Real World box on the facing page). Some well-known therapies are conspicuously absent in the list of well-established treatments—psychoanalysis, for example—and criticisms of the effectiveness of types of therapy have led their defenders to fault the list of well-established treatments as flawed or incomplete. For example, critics have argued that treatments such as long-term psychodynamic therapy are not easily studied and therefore may never make the list simply for this reason. Although the list is not perfect, the new emphasis on identifying which treatments are effective for which problems provides valuable information to psychotherapy consumers.

Table 14.4	Some Probably Efficacious Psychological Treatments
Type of Treatment	**Patient's Problem**
Behavior therapy	Cocaine abuse
Brief psychodynamic therapy	Opiate dependence
Cognitive behavior therapy	Opiate dependence
Brief psychodynamic therapy	Depression
Interpersonal therapy	Bulimia
Behavior therapy	Offensive sexual behavior

Dilbert

{ THE REAL WORLD } Controversial Treatment: Eye Movement Desensitization and Reprocessing

MANY EFFECTIVE TREATMENTS ARE founded on well-developed psychological research, so we have a pretty good idea of how and why they work. Some forms of psychotherapy, however, develop largely from one therapist's experience with clients and may offer unfounded and biased forms of treatment. There may be no scientific evidence for a therapy's effectiveness, or the evidence that exists may be based on tiny samples or faulty studies. But, of course, people still pay for the treatment, so someone is getting cheated.

One controversial treatment is *eye movement desensitization and reprocessing (EMDR)*, a treatment developed by psychologist Francine Shapiro in the 1980s to treat people who have experienced a trauma. While walking in a park, Dr. Shapiro noticed that her eye movements seemed to reduce the negative emotion associated with troubling memories. In her therapy sessions, Shapiro began to guide her clients to move their eyes back and forth as they recalled traumatic experiences and found that some reported improvement in dealing with troubling memories.

Essentially, EMDR involves bringing to mind and maintaining an image of a traumatic event while visually tracking the therapist's finger as it is moved back and forth in front of the client's face. EMDR also incorporates elements of other forms of psychotherapy, including CBT and psychodynamic therapy, but the eye movements are the unique component of the treatment.

This approach has generated controversy from its beginning, in part because of the extraordinary claims made by Shapiro and her colleagues. Described as a break-

Eye movement desensitization and reprocessing (EMDR) may be no more than exposure therapy with a fancy name.

through therapy for overcoming anxiety, stress, and trauma (Shapiro & Forrest, 2001), EMDR has been touted in a self-help book claiming that even self-administered EMDR could treat a wide range of problems, including anxiety and phobias, depression, anger, guilt, relationship problems, job dissatisfaction, and chronic pain (Friedberg, 2001). A website maintained by the EMDR Institute lists breathless quotes about the benefits of the treatment from the *Washington Post* and the *New York Times* (http://www.emdr.com). Therapists are trained in EMDR by taking pricey courses and workshops sanctioned exclusively by Shapiro's organization, and the costs are passed along to the client.

Does EMDR deserve this reputation as a breakthrough therapy? Comprehensive reviews of the research have concluded that people who have experienced a trauma do tend to report a reduction in symptoms following EMDR treatment (Antony & Swinson, 2000; Davidson & Parker, 2001; Feske, 1998; Herbert et al., 2000; Lohr, Tolin, & Lilienfeld, 1998; Spector & Read, 1999)—although it is not particularly effective for other problems. The odd finding, however, is that there is *no evidence that the eye movements are a necessary or even helpful part of the treatment.* At least 13 studies show that there is no significant effect of adding eye movements to the treatment (Davidson & Parker, 2001). This makes good sense since there really isn't any psychological theory that would explain why eye movements might be especially helpful in reducing the impact of troubling memories.

If the effects of EMDR have little to do with the eye movements, then why does EMDR work? In all likelihood, the active ingredient of EMDR is exposure. Recall that while the client engages in the eye-tracking exercises, he or she is instructed to bring the image of the feared trauma to mind. As you saw earlier in this chapter, exposure therapy relies on the finding that exposure to a feared stimulus, even in imagination, is effective in reducing fear. In the case of posttraumatic stress disorder, exposure can be an effective behavioral treatment (Rothbaum et al., 2000), and the eye-tracking elements of EMDR are peripheral. The therapist and the client share a peculiar superstitious rite of finger waving and eye movements while the real work of exposure therapy is going on.

Dangers of Treatment

Can psychotherapy or medication do damage? Psychologists who treat mental health problems adhere to the same Hippocratic ideal held by medical workers: "First, do no harm." But even the best intentions cannot keep some treatments from causing unintended harm. The psychiatrist Thomas Szasz (b. 1920) initiated a movement in the 1960s to hold psychiatry and psychology accountable for such effects by making the extreme argument that mental illness is a myth created by those who hope to make money treating it (Szasz, 1960). From this perspective, all treatments are worthless and any harm is too much harm. This cynical view certainly doesn't describe the thousands of mental health workers who devote themselves to improving the lives of

"First, I'd like to thank everyone who believed in me."

people with psychological disorders on a daily basis, but it does make you wonder about the harm psychological treatment might cause.

The dangers of drug treatment should be clear to anyone who has read a magazine ad for a drug—and studied the fine print with its list of side effects, potential drug interactions, and complications. Many drugs used for psychological treatment present the same types of problems as those associated with the recreational use of drugs or alcohol (see Chapter 8). For example, psychological medications may be addictive, creating long-term dependency with serious withdrawal symptoms. This is the case for Ritalin, often prescribed for attention deficit and hyperactivity disorder (ADHD) in children. Because it is chemically related to amphetamine, it can cause some of the same negative side effects to patients that have led lawmakers to ban amphetamines for the general public. The strongest critics of drug treatment claim that drugs do no more than trade one unwanted symptom for another—trading depression for sexual disinterest, anxiety for intoxication, or agitation for lethargy and dulled emotion (e.g., Breggin, 2000). The "magic bullet" of drug treatments may sometimes amount to shooting ourselves in the foot. Prescribing medication for psychological disorders is a serious step that mental health care workers must always take with caution.

Could there be dangers in psychotherapy as well? What could be harmful about sitting in a room talking with a sympathetic psychologist? Any chance the psychologist will bite? The dangers of psychotherapy are more subtle, but one is clear enough in some cases that there is actually a name for it: **Iatrogenic illness** is *a disorder or symptom that occurs as a result of a medical or psychotherapeutic treatment itself* (e.g., Boisvert & Faust, 2002). Such an illness might arise, for example, when a psychotherapist becomes convinced that a client has a disorder that in fact the client does not have. As a result, the therapist works to help the client accept that diagnosis and participate in psychotherapy to treat that disorder. Being treated for a disorder can, under certain conditions, make a person show signs of that very disorder—and so an iatrogenic illness is born.

There are cases of patients who have been influenced through hypnosis and repeated suggestions in therapy to believe that they have dissociative identity disorder (even coming to express multiple personalities) or to believe that they were subjected to traumatic events as a child and "recover" memories of such events when investigation reveals no evidence for these problems prior to therapy (Acocella, 1999; McNally, 2003; Ofshe & Watters, 1994). There are people who have entered therapy with a vague sense that something odd has happened to them and who emerge after hypnosis or other imagination-enhancing techniques with the conviction that their therapist's theory was right: They were abducted by space aliens (Clancy, 2005). Needless to say, a therapy that leads patients to develop such bizarre beliefs is doing more harm than good.

A client who enters therapy is often vulnerable, feeling defeated as a result of life problems that have led to the psychotherapist's office. People in this position may be open to a therapist's influence—and this is usually a good thing, if it's the beginning of an interaction that can bring the person back to health. But just as the therapeutic relationship has great power to heal, its abuse can produce problems that would not have existed otherwise. Psychotherapists must be aware of this power and take care to avoid harming those they would help.

To regulate the potentially powerful influence of therapies, psychologists hold themselves to a set of ethical standards for the treatment of people with mental disorders (American Psychological Association, 2002). Adherence to these standards is required for membership in the American Psychological Association, and there are also state licensing boards that monitor adherence to ethical principles in therapy. These ethical standards include (1) striving to benefit clients and taking care to do no harm; (2) establishing relationships of trust with clients; (3) promoting accuracy,

ONLY HUMAN

AT LEAST THE DUCK GOT REIMBURSED BY THE SPCA 1997—Ms. Nadean Cool won a settlement of $2.4 million in her lawsuit in Appleton, Wisconsin, against her former psychotherapist, Dr. Kenneth Olson. She claimed that he had first persuaded her that she had a multiple-personality disorder (120 personalities, including Satan and a duck) and then billed her insurance company for "group" therapy because he said he had to counsel so many people. (Olson, seeking greener pastures for his psychotherapy business, has since moved to Montana.)

honesty, and truthfulness; (4) seeking fairness in treatment and taking precautions to avoid biases; and (5) respecting the dignity and worth of all people. When people suffering from mental disorders come to psychologists for help, adhering to these guidelines is the least that psychologists can do. Ideally, in the hope of relieving this suffering, they can do much more.

IATROGENIC ILLNESS A disorder or symptom that occurs as a result of a medical or psychotherapeutic treatment.

In summary, observing improvement during treatment does not necessarily mean that the treatment is effective. The scientific evaluation of treatments is necessary because otherwise people may overlook natural improvement, nonspecific treatment effects such as the placebo effect, and reconstructive memory processes—illusions that can leave them thinking that treatment was effective when it was not. Treatment studies focus on both treatment outcomes and processes, using research methods such as double-blind techniques and placebo control groups that yield clear inferences about treatment effectiveness. Treatments for psychological disorders are generally more effective than no treatment at all, but certain treatments are more effective for certain disorders. Lists of treatments shown by research to be well established, or to be probably efficacious, are being recommended by psychology organizations to guide consumers. The evaluation of treatments also shows that they are not without drawbacks, and both medication and psychotherapy have dangers that ethical practitioners must consider carefully in designing treatments. ■ ■

Where Do You Stand?

Should Drugs Be Used to Prevent Traumatic Memories?

Medication can be an effective means of treating the symptoms of psychological disorders. Is medication also an effective way of *preventing* psychological disorders? Psychiatrist Roger Pitman's controversial studies of posttraumatic stress disorder (PTSD; see Chapter 15) focus on the use of the drug propranolol to prevent the consolidation of distressing memories after traumatic events. One of the key symptoms of PTSD is the presence of vivid and intrusive memories of a traumatic event such as a car accident or being the victim of a physical or sexual assault. If these memories are such prominent symptoms of PTSD, can we avoid the disorder if we prevent these memories from being associated with unpleasant emotions?

The idea that the emotional consequences of traumatic memories might be blocked is based on the role of brain structures and chemicals in the consolidation of emotional memories. Researchers have confirmed that the amygdala and the hippocampus are

involved in emotional memory (McNally, 2003). Propranolol is a drug that dampens emotional arousal by blocking beta-adrenergic receptors in the peripheral and central nervous system; this weakens the effects of chemicals such as adrenaline on receptors in these brain areas. If arousal cues were dampened by the administration of propranolol immediately after the trauma, perhaps the memories of the event would not be linked so strongly with the emotional response to the trauma.

To test this hypothesis, Pitman and his colleagues gave people who had experienced a traumatic event either propranolol or a placebo (sugar pill) when they arrived in an emergency room right after the trauma. On follow-up, the researchers found that the group given propranolol was significantly less physiologically reactive later when listening to a tape about their accident than those given the placebo (Pitman et al., 2002). This medication may not prevent traumatic memories from forming, but it seems to prevent them

from becoming associated with upsetting emotions.

Some people question whether researchers should be tampering with memory at all. A *New York Times Magazine* article argued that our painful memories are essential in shaping us into caring human beings with empathy toward others (Henig, 2004). Opponents of such research also point out that our memories, good and bad, make us who we are. On the practical side, because many people who experience traumas do not develop symptoms of PTSD, this approach could mean medicating a large number of people who do not need any intervention at all. People who suffer from the painful memories of a trauma, however, may be willing to take this chance. Where do you stand? Should people be given drugs to reduce the influence of traumatic events on their memories? Would you want to take such a drug if you suffered a trauma? By taking such a drug, do you feel you might be losing an experience that makes you you?

Chapter Review

Treatment: Getting Help to Those Who Need It

- Psychological disorders and mental illness are common problems with enormous social, financial, and personal costs. Psychological and biomedical treatments can help ameliorate these costs and provide a greater quality of life to people suffering with psychological disorders.

- There are several barriers to receiving effective treatments, including personal, familial, financial, and system barriers. People may not realize they need treatment, may not be able to afford it, or may not know how to get it. The delivery of treatment may be hampered by poor professional training, lack of funding, or resistance from family members.

Psychological Therapies: Healing the Mind through Interaction

- There are hundreds of different types of psychological therapies, with the most commonly used being psychodynamic, behavioral, cognitive, and humanistic/existential.

- Psychodynamic therapy is based on Freudian psychoanalysis and focuses on helping a client develop insight into his or her psychological problems. Techniques such as free association, dream analysis, interpretation of a client's statements and behaviors, and the analysis of resistance during treatment provide avenues toward insight.

- There are many varieties of psychodynamic therapies; most were originated by psychologists who studied with Freud but later broke away from his singular viewpoint.

- Behavior therapy helps clients change maladaptive behaviors to more adaptive ones. Aversion therapy, establishing a token economy, exposure therapy, and systematic desensitization are techniques based on traditional principles of learning theory.

- Cognitive therapy teaches clients to challenge maladaptive beliefs. Rational-emotive behavior therapy, cognitive restructuring, and mindfulness meditation are specific examples of this approach.

- Cognitive behavior therapy (CBT) combines the individual strategies of behavior therapy and cognitive therapy. CBT is problem focused and action oriented, structured, transparent, and flexible.

- Humanistic and existential therapies seek to help clients become more aware of their feelings and concerns in an effort to allow clients to continue on a natural path of growth. Humanistic therapies emphasize congruence, empathy, and unconditional positive regard in the therapist's treatment of a client. Gestalt therapy, an existentialist approach, uses methods such as focusing and the empty chair technique.

- Treatment delivered to people in groups includes couples and family therapy as well as group therapy. Group therapy allows multiple clients to work with a therapist and with each other toward overcoming psychological disorders. Self-help groups bring together individuals who can benefit from one another's experiences to deal with their problems.

Medical and Biological Treatments: Healing the Mind through the Brain

- Biomedical treatments include medications, herbal products, and other biologically based treatments, such as direct intervention in the brain.

- Medications have undergone significant improvement over the past several decades and can be effective for psychotic symptoms, anxiety, depression, and other disorders. However, side effects of these medications may be unpleasant or annoying for a patient.

- There is some preliminary evidence that some herbal products can be helpful for depression and anxiety, but little is done to regulate these products. Consumers need to be careful when using them.

- Treatments such as electroconvulsive therapy, transcranial magnetic stimulation, and psychosurgery can be of benefit for serious and intractable disorders, and phototherapy may be helpful for seasonal affective disorder. Radical techniques, such as the lobotomy, have been largely abandoned in favor of more focused, better-defined, and better-understood procedures.

Treatment Effectiveness: For Better or for Worse

- There is considerable interest in scientifically determining if a therapy is better than nothing, better than a placebo, or better than an alternative treatment. From this research, a number of treatments for particular problems have been shown to be effective.

- There are significant dangers of treatment, including the side effects of drugs and the potential for psychotherapy to create iatrogenic psychological disorders that were not present when the therapy was initiated.

Key Terms

psychotherapy (p. 541)

eclectic psychotherapy (p. 543)

psychodynamic
  psychotherapies (p. 543)

resistance (p. 544)

transference (p. 546)

interpersonal psychotherapy
  (IPT) (p. 547)

behavior therapy (p. 548)

aversion therapy (p. 548)

token economy (p. 549)

exposure therapy (p. 549)

systematic desensitization
  (p. 549)

cognitive therapy (p. 550)

cognitive restructuring (p. 551)

mindfulness meditation
  (p. 551)

cognitive behavioral therapy
  (CBT) (p. 552)

person-centered therapy
  (p. 553)

Gestalt therapy (p. 555)

group therapy (p. 557)

antipsychotic drugs (p. 560)

psychopharmacology (p. 560)

antianxiety medications (p. 562)

antidepressants (p. 563)

electroconvulsive therapy
  (ECT) (p. 567)

transcranial magnetic
  stimulation (TMS) (p. 568)

phototherapy (p. 568)

psychosurgery (p. 569)

placebo (p. 571)

iatrogenic illness (p. 576)

Recommended Readings

Drummond, E. (2000). *The complete guide to psychiatric drugs: Straight talk for best results.* New York: Wiley. This book is aimed at the consumer who is taking medication to deal with a psychological problem. It provides information to help make the decision, reviews which medications work for which problems, and offers practical advice about medication use.

El-Hai, J. (2005). *The lobotomist: A maverick medical genius and his tragic quest to rid the world of mental illness.* New York: Wiley. This biography of Dr. Walter Freeman, an American physician who promoted the use of lobotomies as a treatment for all kinds of mental illness, sheds light on the dark-

er history of psychiatry and medical approaches to treating psychological disorders.

Gurman, A. S., & Messer, S. B. (Eds.) (2003). *Essential psychotherapies,* 2nd ed. New York: Guilford Press. This is a great book for those interested in learning more about different types of psychotherapy.

Lilienfeld, S. O., Lynn, S. J., & Lohr, J. M. (Eds.) (2003). *Science and pseudoscience in clinical psychology.* New York: Guilford Press. A rigorous examination of techniques used in psychological assessment and therapy that are popular and influential but are also somewhat controversial, often lacking strong research to back them up.

15

Stress and Health

Sources of Stress: What Gets to You
Stressful Events
Chronic Stressors
Perceived Control over Stressful Events

Stress Reactions: All Shook Up
Physical Reactions
HOT SCIENCE Why Sickness Feels Bad: Psychological Effects of Immune Response
Psychological Reactions

Stress Management: Dealing with It
Mind Management
Body Management
THE REAL WORLD Rubbing the Right and Wrong Way: Massage and Therapeutic Touch
Situation Management

The Psychology of Illness: When It's in Your Head
Sensitivity to Illness
HOT SCIENCE This Is Your Brain on Placebos
On Being a Patient

The Psychology of Health: Feeling Good
Personality and Health
Health-Promoting Behaviors and Self-regulation
WHERE DO YOU STAND? Consider Yourself Warned

THE 53-YEAR-OLD PATIENT WAS SEMI- comatose with severe bronchial asthma when admitted to a hospital on July 13, 1960. Mr. X (fortunately, not his real name) was treated and discharged symptom free after a few days and went directly to his mother's home—where, in a matter of hours, he was wheezing so badly that he arrived back at the hospital in near-terminal condition. After two more severe attacks at his mother's house, a psychotherapist treating him for depression recommended that he not visit her again. A month later, just after completing some dental work, Mr. X phoned his mother. He was found an hour later blue and gasping for breath and was pronounced dead shortly thereafter.

How did Mr. X die? The autopsy report cited heart damage from lack of oxygen as the cause of death, but interviews with his family and doctors revealed a more complicated story (Mathis, 1964). A young teen when his father died, he became the "man of the house"—a responsibility he took literally. He lived with his mother until he was 31 years old. Two brief marriages failed; his mother was scornful of the marriages and had predicted their demise. His mother approved of his third wife, but even this wife resented the mother's demands.

Mr. X went into the nightclub business with his mother. She financed its purchase, and he worked as manager. His first asthma attack occurred shortly after he received a profitable offer for the business and told his mother he wanted to sell. His mother was upset but, urged on by his wife, he decided to take the offer. In an angry confrontation, his mother said, "Do this and something dire will happen to you." Two days later he had his first incident of mild wheezing.

His asthma became much worse after the partnership broke up. Although he had no previous history of respiratory difficulty, not even a common cold in 10 years, he rapidly developed bronchial asthma. At the sale, his mother was extremely agitated and reminded him of her prediction: "Something will strike you." During his many hospitalizations, Mr. X came to recognize that his troubles might be due to fear of his mother's curse, but this insight didn't do much to relieve his symptoms. On the day of his death, he expressed the belief that he was "allergic" to his mother and worried that her past predictions had been infallible. In the telephone conversation that preceded his death, he told his mother that he thought he was getting better. She replied by repeating her warning of "dire results."

Imagine that someone ordered an authentic voodoo doll from New Orleans, named it after you, and started sticking it with pins in your presence. Even if you didn't believe in curses at all, might this be stressful?

Scientists attempt to safely release the trapped gas in Lake Nyos, Cameroon, but it is unclear whether they will remove the threat of another mass asphyxiation.

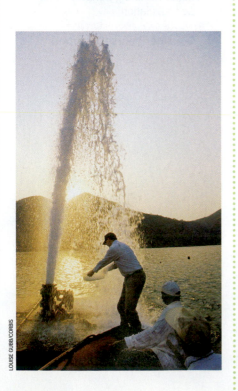

Can a person literally be frightened to death? Perhaps. The case of Mr. X resembles the phenomenon of "voodoo death" examined by physiologist Walter B. Cannon (1942). Cannon reviewed reports from around the world—often from traditional cultures in which death curses are taken very seriously—and found evidence for a profound connection between mind and body. Psychological and bodily injuries are similar, he reasoned. Just as physical trauma can cause a classic shock reaction—reduced blood pressure, rapid shallow pulse, and the deprivation of oxygen to the body's vital organs—so great fear can evoke physiological reactions that eventually result in death. Although such deaths are rare and their causes are always open to interpretation, the case of Mr. X shows how harm to the mind may provoke illness of the body. And asthma isn't the only condition that can be precipitated by anxiety and other psychological factors (Sandberg et al., 2000): A wide array of physical illnesses—from rashes to heart disease—can be traced to psychological causes.

Now, on an average day, you probably don't get a death curse from your mom. But modern life can present a welter of frights, bothers, and looming disasters that might make a nasty call from a loved one almost a relief. A wild driver may challenge your rights as a pedestrian, a band of evil professors may impose impossible project deadlines, or a fire may leave you out on the street. Perhaps it's just the really, really awful weather. Life has its **stressors**, *specific events or chronic pressures that place demands on a person or threaten the person's well-being.* Although such stressors rarely result in sudden death, they do have both immediate and cumulative effects that can influence health.

Cannon drew attention to the connection between mind and body, but his work was just the starting point for a long-term, interdisciplinary exploration of the influence of emotions and personality on health and illness. In this chapter, we'll look at what psychologists and physicians have learned about the kinds of life events that produce **stress**, *the physical and psychological response to internal or external stressors;* typical responses to such stressors; and ways to manage stress. Because sickness and health are not merely features of the physical body, we then consider the more general topic of **health psychology**, *the subfield of psychology concerned with ways psychological factors influence the causes and treatment of physical illness and the maintenance of health.* You will see how perceptions of illness can affect its course and how health-promoting behaviors can improve the quality of people's lives.

Sources of Stress: What Gets to You

Some 1,700 people living in the valley below Lake Nyos in northwestern Cameroon mysteriously died on the evening of August 26, 1986. Scientists discovered that a natural process in the lake, triggered by volcanic activity, had released a massive cloud of carbon dioxide gas that asphyxiated everyone nearby. Many people have resettled near the lake; it is beautiful, fertile land, and more importantly, there is nowhere else for them to go. Scientists have been working on a scheme to release the gas harmlessly, but no one knows whether this will work. So people stay, despite knowledge that another disaster could bubble up at any moment.

Catastrophes are obvious sources of stressors, but for most of us stressors are personal events that affect the comfortable pattern of our lives and little annoyances that bug us day after day. Let's look at the life events that can cause stress, chronic sources of stress, and the relationship between lack of perceived control and the impact of stressors.

Stressful Events

People often seem to get sick after major life events. In pioneering work, Thomas Holmes and Richard Rahe (1967) followed up on this observation, proposing that major life changes cause stress and that increased stress causes illness. To test their idea, they asked people to rate the magnitude of readjustment required by each of many events found to be associated with the onset of illness (Rahe et al., 1964). The resulting list of life events is remarkably predictive: Simply adding up the degree of life change for a person is a significant indicator of the person's future illness (Miller, 1996). A person who is divorced and loses a job and has a friend die all in a year, for example, is more likely to get sick than one who escapes the year with only a divorce.

A version of this list adapted for the life events of college students (and sporting the snappy acronym CUSS, for College Undergraduate Stress Scale) is shown in **TABLE 15.1**. To assess your stressful events, check off any events that have happened to you in the past year and sum your point total. In a sample of 257 students in an introductory psychology class at a state university in the eastern United States, the average was 1,247 points, varying on average by 441 points. The total scores in the class ranged from 182 to 2,571 (Renner & Mackin, 1998).

Looking at the list, you may wonder why positive events are included. Stressful life events are unpleasant, right? Why would getting married be stressful? Isn't a wedding supposed to be fun? Research has shown that compared with negative events, positive events produce less psychological distress and fewer physical symptoms (McFarlane et al., 1980), and the happiness can sometimes even counteract the effects of negative events (Fredrickson, 2000). However, positive events often require readjustment and preparedness that many people find extremely stressful (e.g., Brown & McGill, 1989), so these events are included in computing life-change scores.

STRESSORS Specific events or chronic pressures that place demands on a person or threaten the person's well-being.

STRESS The physical and psychological response to internal or external stressors.

HEALTH PSYCHOLOGY The subfield of psychology concerned with ways psychological factors influence the causes and treatment of physical illness and the maintenance of health.

Table 15.1	College Undergraduate Stress Scale		
Event	**Stress Rating**	**Event**	**Stress Rating**
Being raped	100	Talking in front of class	72
Finding out that you are HIV positive	100	Lack of sleep	69
Being accused of rape	98	Change in housing situation (hassles, moves)	69
Death of a close friend	97	Competing or performing in public	69
Death of a close family member	96	Getting in a physical fight	66
Contracting a sexually transmitted disease (other than AIDS)	94	Difficulties with a roommate	66
Concerns about being pregnant	91	Job changes (applying, new job, work hassles)	65
Finals week	90	Declaring a major or concerns about future plans	65
Concerns about your partner being pregnant	90	A class you hate	62
Oversleeping for an exam	89	Drinking or use of drugs	61
Flunking a class	89	Confrontations with professors	60
Having a boyfriend or girlfriend cheat on you	85	Starting a new semester	58
Ending a steady dating relationship	85	Going on a first date	57
Serious illness in a close friend or family member	85	Registration	55
Financial difficulties	84	Maintaining a steady dating relationship	55
Writing a major term paper	83	Commuting to campus or work or both	54
Being caught cheating on a test	83	Peer pressures	53
Drunk driving	82	Being away from home for the first time	53
Sense of overload in school or work	82	Getting sick	52
Two exams in one day	80	Concerns about your appearance	52
Cheating on your boyfriend or girlfriend	77	Getting straight A's	51
Getting married	76	A difficult class that you love	48
Negative consequences of drinking or drug use	75	Making new friends; getting along with friends	47
Depression or crisis in your best friend	73	Fraternity or sorority rush	47
Difficulties with parents	73	Falling asleep in class	40
		Attending an athletic event	20

Source: Renner and Mackin (1998). *Note:* To compute your personal life change score, sum the stress ratings for all events that have happened to you in the last year.

Crazybusy? The daily hassle of more work than time can become a significant stressor. Also a fire hazard.

Chronic Stressors

Life would be simpler if an occasional stressful event such as a wedding or a lost job were the only pressure we faced. At least each event would be limited in scope, with a beginning, a middle, and, ideally, an end. But unfortunately, life brings with it continued exposure to **chronic stressors,** *sources of stress that occur continuously or repeatedly.* Strained relationships, long lines at the supermarket, nagging relatives, overwork, money troubles—small stressors that may be easy to ignore if they happen only occasionally can accumulate to produce distress and illness. People who report having a lot of daily hassles also report more psychological symptoms (Kanner et al., 1981) and physical symptoms (Delongis et al., 1982), and these effects often have a greater and longer-lasting impact than major life events.

Of course, some people may simply be complainers—people who have so much to say about their daily hassles and health that they make it *look* as if hassles cause health problems. These same people may also complain about their heating bills and how the government is out to get them. And in fact, proneness toward complaints (also called *negative affectivity*) underlies part of the relationship between hassles and health (Dohrenwend et al., 1984). People who express negative emotions in one area of life tend to do so in other areas, creating an apparent relationship between hassles and health that may not reflect cause and effect. However, the bulk of research shows that even when this tendency is taken into account, life hassles still lead to psychological and physical problems (Critelli & Ee, 1996).

Many chronic stressors are linked to particular environments. For example, features of city life—noise, traffic, crowding, pollution, and even the threat of violence—provide particularly insistent sources of chronic stress. Rural areas have their own chronic stressors, of course, especially isolation and lack of access to amenities such as health care. The realization that chronic stressors are linked to environments has spawned the subfield *environmental psychology,* the scientific study of environmental effects on behavior and health.

In one study of the influence of noise on children, environmental psychologists looked at the impact of attending schools under the flight path to Los Angeles International Airport. Did the noise of more than 300 jets flying overhead each day have an influence beyond making kids yell to be heard? Compared with children matched for race, economic background, and ethnicity who attended nearby schools away from the noise, children going to school in the flight path had higher blood pressure and gave up more easily when working on difficult problems and puzzles (Cohen et al., 1980). Next time you fly into L.A., please try to do so more quietly for the children.

When the "Theme Building" was designed for Los Angeles International Airport in the early '60s to celebrate the modern age, few probably anticipated that it would someday be shown in a textbook as a reminder of the stress of airplane noise on children living nearby.

Perceived Control over Stressful Events

What do death curses, catastrophes, stressful life changes, and daily hassles have in common? What could possibly link vicious mothers, carbon dioxide bubbling up in a lake, weddings, and noisy jets? Right off the bat, of course, their threat to the person or the status quo is easy to see. Stressors challenge you to *do something*—to take some action to eliminate or overcome the stressor.

Paradoxically, events are most stressful when there is *nothing to do*—no way to deal with the challenge. Expecting that you will have control over what happens to you is associated with effectiveness in dealing with stress. Researchers David Glass and Jerome Singer (1972), in classic studies of *perceived control,* looked at the aftereffects of loud noise on people who could or could not control it. Participants were asked to solve puzzles and proofread in a quiet room or in a room filled with noise as loud as that in classrooms under the L.A. flight path. Glass and Singer found that bursts of such noise hurt people's performance on the tasks after the noise was over. However, this dramatic decline in performance was prevented among participants who were told during the noise period that they could stop the noise just by pushing a button. They didn't actually take this option, but access to the "panic button" shielded them from the detrimental effects of the noise.

Subsequent studies have found that a lack of perceived control underlies other stressors too. The stressful effects of crowding, for example, appear to stem from the feeling that you can't control getting away from the crowded conditions (Sherrod, 1974). Being jammed into a crowded dormitory room may be easier to handle, after all, the moment you learn of the button that drops open the trapdoor under your roommate's chair.

When the cabin attendant announces that "we have a full cabin on this flight," conditions can be stressful—not so much because of the crowding but because there is no obvious control over the crowding. Taking control—for example, by keeping busy or wearing headphones to decrease contact with others or even by talking with people and getting to know them—may help decrease the stress.

In summary, stressors include both major life events and minor hassles and can sometimes be traced to particular stressful environments. Stressors seem to add up over time: The more chronic the stressor, the more harmful the effects. Life events, hassles, and environmental stressors have in common the production of a threat to the person's well-being that is perceived as difficult or impossible to control. ■ ■

Stress Reactions: All Shook Up

An accident at the Three Mile Island nuclear plant near Harrisburg, Pennsylvania, on March 28, 1979, created a near meltdown in the reactor and released radioactivity into the air and into the Susquehanna River. The situation was out of control for 2 days, on the brink of a major disaster that was only averted when plant operators luckily made the right decision to repressurize the coolant system. Local residents learned that their lives were in grave danger, and 140,000 people packed up and fled the area. Most eventually returned when the danger had subsided, but they suffered lasting effects of the stress associated with this potentially deadly event.

A study conducted a year and a half later compared area residents with people from unaffected areas (Fleming et al., 1985). The local group showed physical signs of stress: They had relatively high levels of *catecholamines* (biochemicals indicating the activation of emotional systems), and they had fewer white blood cells available to fight infection (Schaeffer et al., 1985). The residents also suffered psychological effects, including higher levels of anxiety, depression, and alienation compared with people from elsewhere. Even on a simple proofreading task, residents performed more poorly than did people from unaffected areas. Because the radiation released

CHRONIC STRESSOR A source of stress that occurs continuously or repeatedly.

JOHN S. ZEEDICK/GETTY IMAGES

A near meltdown occurred at the Three Mile Island nuclear plant near Harrisburg, Pennsylvania, on March 28, 1979.

was not sufficient to account for any of these effects, they were attributed to the aftermath of stress. In short, stress can produce changes in every system of the body, influencing how people feel and how they act. Let's look at how the process works.

Physical Reactions

Before he became interested in voodoo death, Walter Cannon (1929) coined a phrase to describe the body's response to any threatening stimulus: the **fight-or-flight response**, *an emotional and physiological reaction to an emergency that increases readiness for action.* When the sirens began wailing at Three Mile Island, the area residents no doubt felt rattled in exactly this way. The mind asks, "Should I stay and battle this somehow, or should I run like mad?" And the body prepares to react. If you're a cat at this time, your hair stands on end. If you're a human, your hair stands on end too, but not as visibly. Cannon recognized this common response across species and suspected that it might be the body's first mobilization to any threat. Research conducted since Cannon's discovery has revealed what is happening in the brain and body during this reaction.

Brain activation in response to threat occurs in the hypothalamus, stimulating the nearby pituitary gland, which in turn releases adrenocorticotropic hormone (ACTH). The ACTH then travels through the bloodstream and stimulates the adrenal glands atop the kidneys (see **FIGURE 15.1**). In this cascading response of the *HPA axis* (for *h*ypothalamus, *p*ituitary, *a*drenal), the adrenal glands are then stimulated to release hormones, including the *catecholamines* mentioned earlier (epinephrine and norepinephrine), which increase sympathetic nervous system activation (and therefore increase heart rate, blood pressure, and respiration rate) and decrease parasympathetic activation (see Chapter 3). The increased respiration and blood pressure make more oxygen available to the muscles to energize attack or to initiate escape. The adrenal glands also release *cortisol*, a hormone that increases the concentration of glucose in the blood to make fuel available to the muscles. Everything is prepared for a full-tilt response to the threat.

Figure 15.1 HPA Axis Just a few seconds after a fearful stimulus is perceived, the hypothalamus activates the pituitary gland to release adrenocorticotropic hormone (ACTH). The ACTH then travels through the bloodstream to activate the adrenal glands to release catecholamines and cortisol, which energize the fight-or-flight response.

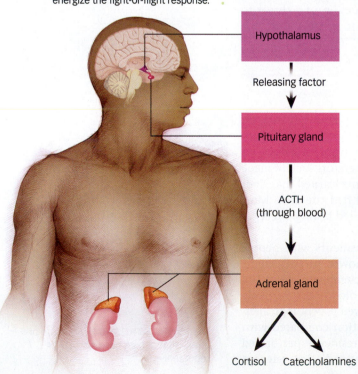

Hypothalamus

Releasing factor

Pituitary gland

ACTH (through blood)

Adrenal gland

Cortisol   Catecholamines

General Adaptation Syndrome

What might have happened to Three Mile Island's neighbors if the sirens had wailed again and again for days or weeks at a time? Starting in the 1930s, Hans Selye, a Canadian physician, undertook a variety of experiments that looked at the physiological consequences of severe threats to well-being, and the Three Mile Island investigation was part of a line of research on mind-body relationships that began with his work (1936, 1956).

Hans Selye with rat. Given all the stress Selye put rats under, this one looks surprisingly calm.

Selye studied rats. He subjected them to heat, cold, infection, trauma, hemorrhage, and other prolonged stressors, making few friends among the rats or their sympathizers but learning a lot about stress. His stressed-out rats developed physiological responses that included an enlarged adrenal cortex, shrinking of the thymus and lymph glands, and ulceration of the stomach and duodenum. Noting that so many different kinds of stressors caused similar patterns of physiological change, he called the reaction **general adaptation syndrome (GAS)**, which he defined as *a three-stage physiological stress response that appears regardless of the stressor that is encountered.* The GAS is *nonspecific*—that is, the "syndrome of just being sick" doesn't vary, no matter what the source of the repeated stress.

None of this is very good news. Although Friedrich Nietzsche once said, "What does not kill me makes me stronger," Selye found that he was wrong—that severe stress takes a toll on the body. He saw the GAS as occurring in three phases—alarm, resistance, and exhaustion (see **FIGURE 15.2**).

- *Alarm phase.* In this initial reaction, the body rapidly mobilizes its resources to respond to the threat. Energy is required, and the body calls on its stored fat and muscle. The alarm phase is equivalent to Cannon's fight-or-flight response. Resistance to stress is low.

- *Resistance phase.* The body adapts to its high state of arousal as it tries to cope with the stressor. Continuing to draw on resources of fat and muscle, it shuts down unnecessary processes: digestion, growth, and sex drive stall. Menstruation stops; production of testosterone and sperm decrease. The body is being taxed to generate resistance, not rebuilt, and all the fun stuff is put on hold.

- *Exhaustion phase.* The body's resistance collapses. Many of the resistance-phase defenses create gradual damage as they operate, leading to costs for the body. In the exhaustion phase, then, the costs of stress are finally calculated—aging, irreversible organ damage, or death.

FIGHT-OR-FLIGHT RESPONSE An emotional and physiological reaction to an emergency that increases readiness for action.

GENERAL ADAPTATION SYNDROME (GAS) A three-stage physiological response that appears regardless of the stressor that is encountered.

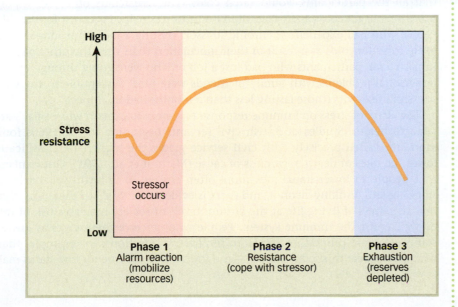

Figure 15.2 Selye's Three Phases of Stress Response In Selye's theory, resistance to stress builds over time but then can only last so long before exhaustion sets in.

Research inspired by Selye's theory has shown that exhaustion occurs when the prolonged production of *glucocorticoids* (hormones such as cortisol) that help in the metabolism of glucose and production of energy during resistance ends up damaging the body and brain. Glucocorticoids hinder the formation of some kinds of white blood cells, for example, compromising the immune system and increasing susceptibility to infection and tumor growth. Exposure to glucocorticoids in rats has even been connected to the degeneration of neurons in the hippocampus and so to memory loss (Sapolsky, 1992).

Stress Effects on the Immune Response

Stress can cause illness by increasing susceptibility to infections. For example, it raises the likelihood of herpes simplex flare-ups (Vanderplate, Aral, & Magder, 1988) and worsening of the bacterial infection called periodontal disease (Green et al., 1986). How does stress interfere with the bodily system that fights infection—the immune system?

The **immune system** is *a complex response system that protects the body from bacteria, viruses, and other foreign substances.* The system includes white blood cells such as **lymphocytes** (including T cells and B cells), *cells that produce antibodies that fight infection.* The immune system is remarkably responsive to psychological influences. *Psychoneuroimmunology* is the study of how the immune system responds to psychological variables, such as the presence of stressors. Stressors can cause hormones (those pesky glucocorticoids) to flood the brain, wearing down the immune system and making it less able to fight invaders. In one study of this, stress was found to interfere with the immune response that vaccinations ordinarily produce. People under stress (caregivers of patients with Alzheimer's disease) were given flu shots, and their immune responses were compared with those of noncaregivers similar in age, general health, and other characteristics. The expected immune response was muted in the caregivers compared with those in the control group. Apparently, the daily stress of caring for patients with a debilitating illness was enough to hamper antibody and T-cell response, leaving the caregivers vulnerable to flu (see the Hot Science box).

Stressful events can also compromise immune responses that heal wounds and ward off colds. In one study, medical student volunteers agreed to receive small wounds to the roof of the mouth. Researchers observed that these wounds healed more slowly during exam periods than during summer vacation (Marucha, Kiecolt-Glaser, & Favagehi, 1998). In another study, a set of selfless, healthy volunteers permitted researchers to swab common cold virus in their noses (Cohen et al., 1998). You might think that a direct application of the virus would be like exposure to a massive full-facial sneeze and that all the participants would catch colds. The researchers observed, though, that some people got colds and others didn't—and stress helped account for the difference. People who had experienced chronic stressors (lasting a month or longer) were more likely to suffer colds as a result of their inoculation than were the other people tested. In particular, participants who had lost a job or who were going through extended interpersonal problems with family or friends were most susceptible to the virus. Brief stressful life events (those lasting less than a month) had no impact.

The effect of stress on immune response may help to explain why social status is related to health. Studies of British civil servants beginning in the 1960s found that mortality varied precisely with civil service grade: the higher the classification, the lower the rates of death, regardless of cause (Marmot et al., 1991). One explanation is that people in lower-status jobs more often engage in unhealthy behavior such as smoking and drinking alcohol, and there is evidence of this. But there is also evidence that the stress of living life at the bottom levels of society increases risk of infections by weakening the immune system. People who perceive themselves as low in social status are more prone to suffer from respiratory infections, for example, than those who do not bear this social burden—and the same holds true for low-status male monkeys (Cohen, 1999).

IMMUNE SYSTEM A complex response system that protects the body from bacteria, viruses, and other foreign substances.

LYMPHOCYTES White blood cells that produce antibodies that fight infection.

{ HOT SCIENCE } Why Sickness Feels Bad: Psychological Effects of Immune Response

WHY DOES IT FEEL SO BAD TO BE SICK? YOU notice scratchiness in your throat or the start of sniffles, and you think you might be coming down with something. And in just a few short hours, you're achy all over, energy gone, no appetite, feverish, feeling so dull and listless that you can't even take advantage of that fabulous onetime offer on TV. You're sick. The question is: Why does it have to be like this? Why couldn't it feel good? As long as you're going to have to stay at home and miss out on things anyway, couldn't sickness be less of a pain?

Sickness makes you miserable for good reason. Misery is part of the *sickness response,* a coordinated, adaptive set of reactions to illness organized by the brain (Hart, 1988; Maier & Watkins, 1998; Watkins & Maier, 2005). Feeling sick keeps you home, where you'll spread germs to fewer people. More importantly, the sickness response makes you withdraw from activity and lie still, conserving the energy for fighting illness that you'd normally expend on other behavior. Appetite loss is similarly helpful: The energy spent on digestion is conserved. Thus, the behavioral changes that accompany illness are not random side effects; they help the body fight disease.

How does the brain know it should do this? The immune response to an infection conveys this information to the brain through a series of steps so that the sickness response can get under way. It begins with one of the components of the immune response, the activation of white blood cells

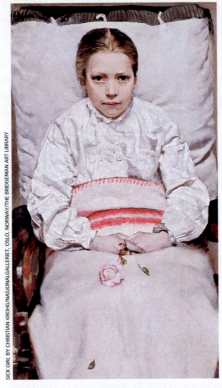

SICK GIRL BY CHRISTIAN KROHG/NASJONALGALLERIET, OSLO, NORWAY/THE BRIDGEMAN ART LIBRARY

Sickness not only feels bad but it also shows. The pain of being ill has an emotional wallop like mild depression.

called *macrophages* that "eat" microbes. These cells release *cytokines,* proteins that circulate through the body and communicate among the other white blood cells. *Cytokines* orchestrate the immune response at the cellular level, but they also communicate the sickness response to the brain (Maier & Watkins, 1998). Administration of cytokines to an animal can artificially create the sickness response, and administration of drugs that oppose the action of cytokines can block the sickness response even during an ongoing infection. Cytokines do not enter the brain, but they activate the vagus nerve that runs from the intestines, stomach, and chest to the brain and induce the "I am infected" message (Goehler et al., 2000). Perhaps this is why we often feel sickness in the "gut," a gnawing discomfort in the very center of the body.

Interestingly, the sickness response can be prompted without any infection at all—merely by the introduction of stress. The stressful presence of a predator's odor, for instance, can produce the sickness response of lethargy in an animal—oddly, along with symptoms of infection such as fever and increased white blood cell count (Maier & Watkins, 2000). In humans, the connection between sickness response, immune reaction, and stress is illustrated in depression, a condition in which all the sickness machinery runs at full speed. So in addition to fatigue and malaise, depressed people show signs characteristic of infection, including high levels of cytokines circulating in the blood (Maes, 1995). Just as illness can make you feel a bit depressed, severe depression seems to recruit the brain's sickness response and makes you feel ill (Watkins & Maier, 2005).

Stress and Cardiovascular Health

The heart and circulatory system are also sensitive to stress. For example, for several days after Iraq's 1991 missile attack on Israel, heart attack rates went up markedly among citizens in Tel Aviv (Meisel et al., 1991). The full story of how stress affects the cardiovascular system starts earlier than the occurrence of a heart attack, however: Chronic stress creates changes in the body that increase later vulnerability to this condition.

The main cause of coronary heart disease is *atherosclerosis,* a gradual narrowing of the arteries that occurs as fatty deposits, or plaque, build up on the inner walls of the arteries. Narrowed arteries result in a reduced blood supply and, eventually, when an artery is blocked by a blood clot or by detached plaque, in a heart attack. Although smoking, a sedentary lifestyle, and a diet high in fat and cholesterol can cause coronary heart disease, chronic stress is a major contributor (Krantz & McCeney, 2002). As a result of stress-activated arousal of the sympathetic nervous system, blood pressure goes up and stays up, and this gradually damages the blood vessels. The damaged vessels accumulate plaque, and the more plaque, the greater the likelihood of coronary heart disease.

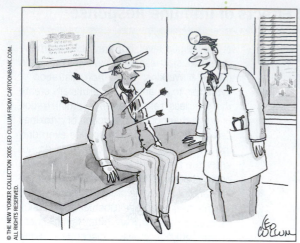

"I'd like to get your arrow count down."

Evidence for this process comes from a large, longitudinal study of Finnish men age 42 to 60 (Everson et al., 1997). Over a period of 4 years, men who exhibited elevated blood pressure in response to stress and who reported that their work environment was especially demanding showed progressive atherosclerosis of a major artery in the neck. Of course, stress alone did not hasten the progression of their disease: It was accelerated in men who were especially susceptible because they responded to stress with increased blood pressure.

In the 1950s, cardiologists Meyer Friedman and Ray Rosenman (1974) studied the relationship between behavior and coronary heart disease and noticed a curious effect: Even if husbands and wives shared unhealthy diets and lifestyles, the husbands were much more likely than their wives to suffer from coronary heart disease. Many American women were not in the workforce at that time, which suggested to the researchers that work-related stress might contribute to coronary heart disease. To find out, they interviewed and tested 3,000 healthy middle-age men and then tracked their subsequent cardiovascular health.

Based on their research, Friedman and Rosenman developed the concept of the **Type A behavior pattern**, which is characterized by *a tendency toward easily aroused hostility, impatience, a sense of time urgency, and competitive achievement strivings,* and they compared Type A individuals to those with a less driven behavior pattern (sometimes called Type B). The Type A men were identified not only by their answers to questions in the interview (agreeing that they walk and talk fast, work late, set goals for themselves, work hard to win, and easily get frustrated and angry at others) but also by their hard-driving manner. When the interviewer asked questions too slowly, for example, Type A people watched the clock, barked back answers, and interrupted the interviewer, at some points even slapping him with a fish. Okay, the part about the fish is wrong, but you get the idea: These people were pushy and intense. The researchers found that of the 258 men who had heart attacks in the 9 years following the interview, over two thirds had been classified as Type A and only one third had been classified as Type B.

Their findings were revolutionary—suggesting for the first time a link between mind and body in heart disease—and a flood of scientific research followed. Among the questions asked: Is Type A behavior truly lethal? Are there ways to explain this effect? Does the fact that Type A people are more likely to smoke and eat unhealthy diets contribute to the problem? After more than 30 years of follow-up work, the answer seems to be within reach: Apparently, two of the key forms of Type A behavior—time-consciousness and competitiveness—do *not* by themselves contribute to heart disease. Rather, it is the hostility and anger component of Type A behavior that contributes to heart disease. Research indicates that the complete Type A behavior pattern

TYPE A BEHAVIOR PATTERN The tendency toward easily aroused hostility, impatience, a sense of time urgency, and competitive achievement strivings.

Road rage starts to make sense when you believe that all the other drivers on the road are trying to kill you.

is *not* a significant cause of heart disease (Hemingway & Marmot, 1999). Instead, the tendency to react to stress and adversity with anger is the real problem (Rozanski, Blumenthal, & Kaplan, 1999).

One study of stress and anger tracked medical students for up to 48 years to see how their behavior while they were young related to their later susceptibility to coronary problems (Chang et al., 2002). Those who responded to stress with anger and hostility were found to be three times more likely later to develop premature heart disease and six times more likely to have an early heart attack than were students who did not respond with anger. Hostility, particularly in men, predicts heart disease better than any other major causal factor, such as smoking, high caloric intake, or even high levels of LDL cholesterol (Niaura et al., 2002) (see **FIGURE 15.3**). Stress affects the cardiovascular system to some degree in everyone but is particularly harmful in those people who respond to stressful events with hostility.

Psychological Reactions

The body's response to stress is intertwined with responses of the mind. Perhaps the first thing the mind does is try to sort things out—to interpret whether an event is threatening or not and, if it is, whether something can be done about it. When faced with stressful events that are perceived as uncontrollable, the mind, like the body, responds in ways that can lead to health problems. Psychological reactions to stress can eventually result in stress disorders such as posttraumatic stress disorder (PTSD) or the mental breakdown known as "burnout."

Stress Interpretation

The interpretation of a stimulus as stressful or not is called *primary appraisal* (Lazarus & Folkman, 1984). Primary appraisal allows you to realize that a small dark spot on your shirt is a stressor ("Spider!") or that a 70-mile-per-hour drop from a great height in a small car full of screaming people is not a stressor ("Roller coaster!").

In a demonstration of the importance of interpretation, researchers used a gruesome film of a subincision—a kind of genital surgery that is part of some tribal initiation rites—to severely stress volunteer participants (Speisman et al., 1964). Self-reports and participants' autonomic arousal (heart rate and skin conductance level) were the measures of stress. Before viewing the film, one group listened to an "intellectual" introduction that discussed the rite from an anthropologist's point of view, while another heard an introduction that downplayed the pain and emphasized the coming-of-age aspect of the initiation. Both interpretations markedly reduced the film viewers' stress compared with another group, whose viewing was preceded by a lecture accentuating the pain and trauma.

The next step in interpretation is *secondary appraisal*—determining whether the stressor is something you can handle or not—that is, whether you have control over the event (Lazarus & Folkman, 1984). Interestingly, the body responds differently depending on whether the stressor is perceived as a *threat* (a stressor you believe you might *not* be able to overcome) or a *challenge* (a stressor you feel fairly confident you can control) (Blascovich & Tomaka, 1996). The same midterm exam could be a challenge if you were well prepared and a threat if you neglected to study.

Although both threats and challenges raise heart rate, threats increase vascular reactivity (such as constriction of the blood vessels, which can lead to high blood pressure). In one study, researchers found that an interaction as innocuous as a conversation can produce threat or challenge responses depending on the race of the

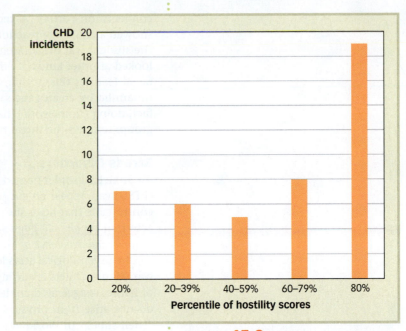

Figure 15.3 **Hostility and Coronary Heart Disease** Of 2,280 men studied over the course of 3 years, 45 suffered coronary heart disease (CHD) incidents (such as heart attack). Many more of these incidents occurred in the group who had initially scored above the 80th percentile in hostility (Niaura et al., 2002).

conversation partner. Asked to talk with another, unfamiliar student, white students showed a challenge reaction when the student was white and a threat reaction when the student was black (Mendes et al., 2002). Similar results were found in studies that looked at other kinds of differences, such as lower socioeconomic status or disfigured facial features (Blascovich, Mendes, Hunter, Lickel, Kowai-Bell, 2001). It's as if social unfamiliarity creates the same kind of stress as lack of preparedness for an exam. In fact, doing "homework" (having previously interacted with members of an unfamiliar group) tempers the threat reaction (Blascovich et al., 2001).

Stress Disorders

An anxiety disorder named for its relationship to stress, **posttraumatic stress disorder (PTSD)** can appear after a person lives through an experience so threatening and uncontrollable that he or she is left with feelings of terror and helplessness. PTSD is characterized by *chronic physiological arousal, recurrent unwanted thoughts or images of the trauma, and avoidance of things that call the traumatic event to mind.*

The psychological scars left by traumatic events are nowhere more apparent than in war. Many soldiers returning from combat have PTSD symptoms, including flashbacks of battle, exaggerated anxiety and startle reactions, and even medical conditions that do not arise from physical damage (such as paralysis or chronic fatigue). Known as "shell shock" in World War I and "combat fatigue" in World War II, the disorder was reported by veterans of the Vietnam War and the Gulf War.

PTSD symptoms do not quickly subside when service members come home. For example, the Centers for Disease Control (1988) found that even 20 years after the Vietnam War, 15% of veterans who had seen combat continued to report lingering symptoms. Florence Nightingale, the founder of modern nursing, is said to have returned to England from the Crimean War (1853–56) with chronic fatigue that continued for the rest of her life. This long-term psychological response is now recognized not only among the victims, witnesses, and perpetrators of war but also among ordinary people who are traumatized by any of life's terrible events. At some time over the course of their lives, about 8% of Americans are estimated to suffer from PTSD (Kessler, Sonnega, Bromet, Hughes, & Nelson, 1995).

One study tracked PTSD symptoms in 988 New York City residents after September 11, 2001 (Galea et al., 2002) (see **FIGURE 15.4**). One to 2 months after the 9/11 attacks, 7.5% of those interviewed reported multiple PTSD symptoms, such as recurrent intrusive memories or distressing dreams of the event, efforts to suppress thoughts of the event, and unusual nervousness or difficulty falling asleep. Among people in the study who lived in the immediate vicinity of the towers, 20% were diagnosed with PTSD.

On August 2, 1990, Iraqi leader Saddam Hussein commanded his troops to invade Kuwait and triggered a U.S. coalition response known as Operation Desert Storm. Many veterans returning from the Gulf War suffered symptoms of PTSD.

AP PHOTO/JOHN GAPS III

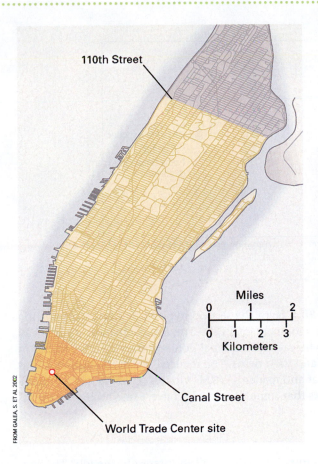

FROM GALEA, S. ET AL 2002

110th Street

Miles
0   1   2
0   1   2   3
Kilometers

Canal Street

World Trade Center site

Figure 15.4 **Manhattan** PTSD symptoms were more pronounced in New York City respondents who were near the World Trade Center towers at the time of the September 11 attacks. Participants were sampled from the area between 110th Street and Canal Street (yellow) and from south of Canal Street (orange)—the area nearest the towers.

Did people watching on television report PTSD symptoms following the attacks? The images of the flames and people jumping from the towers were hard to forget, and in fact, one study found that people who had watched the televised reports had higher rates of PTSD than those who did not watch (Ahern et al., 2003). But people who were prone to PTSD might have been more inclined to watch the news, so it is not clear in this case that viewing the images *caused* the disorder. Although news coverage of terrorism can increase anxiety (Slone, 2000), whether it typically increases the incidence of PTSD is not known.

Not everyone who is exposed to a traumatic event develops PTSD, suggesting that people differ in their degree of sensitivity to trauma. Research using magnetic resonance imaging (MRI) to examine brain structures has found one possible indication of such sensitivity. In some studies comparing people without and with PTSD, the hippocampus was found to be smaller in volume among individuals with PTSD (Stein et al., 1997). However, this finding was not supported in other studies (Yamasue et al., 2003), raising an important question: Does the reduced hippocampal volume reflect a pre-existing condition that makes the brain sensitive to stress, or does the traumatic stress itself somehow kill nerve cells?

To answer this question, Mark Gilbertson and colleagues (2002) collected MRI scans from four groups of men—Vietnam combat veterans who had developed PTSD, Vietnam combat veterans who had not developed PTSD, and the identical (monozygotic) twins of the men in each of these groups, none of whom themselves had had any combat exposure or developed PTSD. If reduced hippocampal volume is a result of traumatic experience, you would expect that combatants would show smaller hippocampal volume than their twin brothers. If reduced hippocampal volume reflects a preexisting source of sensitivity to stress that contributes to PTSD, however, you would expect instead that combatants who developed PTSD and their twin brothers would both show smaller hippocampal volumes than the combatants who did not develop PTSD or their twin brothers.

POSTTRAUMATIC STRESS DISORDER (PTSD) A psychological disorder characterized by chronic physiological arousal, recurrent unwanted thoughts or images of the trauma, and avoidance of things that call the trauma to mind.

Figure 15.5 **Hippocampal Volumes of Vietnam Veterans and Their Identical Twins** Average hippocampal volumes for four groups of participants: (1) combat-exposed veterans who developed PTSD; (2) their combat-unexposed twins with no PTSD themselves; (3) combat-exposed veterans who never developed PTSD; and (4) their un-exposed twins, also with no PTSD. Smaller hippocampal volumes were found both for the combat-exposed veterans with PTSD (group 1) and their twins who had not been exposed to combat (group 2) in comparison to veterans without PTSD (group 3) and their twins (group 4). This pattern of findings suggests that an inherited smaller hippocampus may make some people sensitive to conditions that cause PTSD.

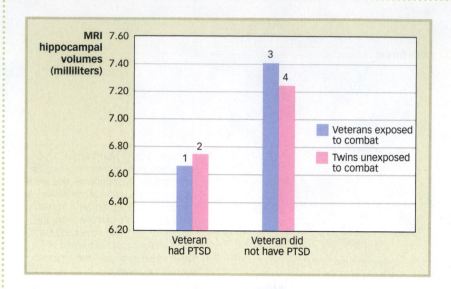

The results shown in **FIGURE 15.5** favor the second hypothesis—that a preexisting sensitivity contributes to the development of PTSD. The noncombatant groups had similar hippocampal volumes, whereas hippocampal volumes were clearly smaller in both the combatants with PTSD and their twins. The reduced size of the hippocampus apparently existed *prior* to combat and made the PTSD victims sensitive to the trauma of combat exposure. This suggests that some people who have a smaller hippocampus may be more susceptible to PTSD.

Burnout

Did you ever take a class from an instructor who had lost interest in the job? The syndrome is easy to spot: The teacher looks distant and blank, almost robotic, giving predictable and humdrum lessons each day—as if it doesn't matter whether anyone is listening. Now imagine *being* this instructor. You decided to teach because you wanted to shape young minds. You worked hard, and for a while things were great. But one day, you look up to see a roomful of miserable students who are bored and don't care about anything you have to say. They text-message while you talk and start shuffling papers and putting things away long before the end of class. You're happy at work only when you're not in class. When people feel this way, especially about their jobs or careers, they are suffering from **burnout**, *a state of physical, emotional, and mental exhaustion created by long-term involvement in an emotionally demanding situation and accompanied by lowered performance and motivation.*

Burnout is a particular problem in the helping professions (Freudenberger, 1974; Pines & Aronson, 1988). Teachers, nurses, clergy, doctors, dentists, psychologists, social workers, police officers, and others who repeatedly encounter emotional turmoil on the job may only be able to work productively for a limited time. Eventually, many succumb to symptoms of burnout: overwhelming exhaustion, a deep cynicism and detachment from the job, and a sense of ineffectiveness and lack of accomplishment (Maslach, 2003). Their unhappiness can even spread to others—people with burnout tend to become disgruntled employees who revel in their coworkers' failures and ignore their coworkers' successes (Brenninkmeijer, Vanyperen, & Buunk, 2001).

What causes burnout? One theory suggests that the culprit is using your job to give meaning to your life (Pines, 1993). If you define yourself only by your career and gauge your self-worth by success at work, you risk having nothing left when work fails. For example, a teacher in danger of burnout might do well to invest time in family, hobbies, or other self-expressions. Others argue that some emotionally stressful jobs lead to burnout no matter

An automatic nurse might be one solution to the problem of burnout among members of health professions. This "nursing table" patented in 1869 was to take care of the sick with minimal human intervention.

how they are approached and active efforts to overcome the stress before burnout occurs are important. The stress management techniques discussed in the next section may be lifesavers for such people.

In summary, the body and the mind both react to stress. The body responds with an initial fight-or-flight reaction that activates the hypothalamus-pituitary-adrenal (HPA) axis. Chronic repetition of this response generates the general adaptation syndrome (GAS), in which the body progresses through stages of alarm, resistance, and exhaustion in response to the prolonged stress. GAS affects the immune system and cardiovascular health, which in turn creates risks for overall health. While these body reactions are developing, primary appraisal and secondary appraisal are used to interpret the stress. The psychological costs of stress can be serious, in some cases eventually leading to anxiety disorders or depression. Some people exposed to traumatic stressors develop posttraumatic stress disorder, in which thoughts and images of the stressor plague the mind. Those who experience chronic stress in jobs that involve emotional turmoil can suffer from burnout. ■ ■

Stress Management: Dealing with It

Most college students (92%) say they occasionally feel overwhelmed by the tasks they face, and over a third say they have dropped courses or received low grades in response to severe stress (Deuenwald, 2003). No doubt you are among the lucky 8% who are entirely cool and report no stress. But just in case you're not, you may appreciate our exploration of stress management techniques—ways to counteract psychological and physical stress reactions directly by managing your mind and body and ways to sidestep stress by managing your situation. These techniques resemble some of the forms of cognitive behavior therapy we explored in Chapter 14, but they are strategies people often exercise on their own, without the help of a therapist.

Mind Management

"Cowards die many times before their deaths. The valiant never taste of death but once." Shakespeare's observation reminds us that stressful events are magnified in the mind. If you fear public speaking, for example, just the thought of an upcoming presentation to a group can create anxiety. And if you do break down during a presentation—going blank, for example, or blurting out something embarrassing—intrusive memories of this stressful event could echo in your mind afterward. A significant part of stress management, then, is control of the mind. A number of basic strategies are available, including ignoring the stressor, thinking about the stressor, and trying to think about the stressor in a new way. In the language of psychology, these techniques are known as *repressive coping, rational coping,* and *reframing.*

Repressive Coping

Controlling your thoughts isn't easy, but some people do seem to be able to banish unpleasant thoughts from mind. This style of dealing with stress, called **repressive coping,** is *characterized by avoiding situations or thoughts that are reminders of a stressor and maintaining an artificially positive viewpoint.* On self-report measures of coping style, *repressors* seldom report physical symptoms of anxiety such as sweaty palms, shakiness, a racing heart, or a nervous stomach (Weinberger, Schwartz, & Davidson, 1979). They paint an impossibly rosy picture of their lives, reporting, for example, that they are always polite and never lie, and they can't remember many events that made them sad or afraid. Everyone has *some* problems, of course, but repressors are good at deliberately ignoring them (Barnier, Levin, & Maher, 2004). So, for example, when repressors suffer a heart attack, they are less likely than other people to report intrusive thoughts of their heart problems in the days and weeks that follow (Ginzburg, Solomon, & Bleich, 2002).

BURNOUT A state of physical, emotional, and mental exhaustion created by long-term involvement in an emotionally demanding situation and accompanied by lowered performance and motivation.

REPRESSIVE COPING Avoiding situations or thoughts that are reminders of a stressor and maintaining an artificially positive viewpoint.

RATIONAL COPING Facing a stressor and working to overcome it.

REFRAMING Finding a new or creative way to think about a stressor that reduces its threat.

STRESS INOCULATION TRAINING (SIT) A therapy that helps people to cope with stressful situations by developing positive ways to think about the situation.

If you were an expert repressor, you might easily and quickly forget about *Boeuf à la Mode,* an anonymous French caricature from the early 19th century. If you were not an expert, you might wake up in the middle of the night and have this image come to mind.

Like Mr. X, who was persuaded to avoid his mother's home as a way of keeping her frightening threats out of mind, people often rearrange their lives in order to avoid stressful situations. Many victims of rape, for example, move away from home, and they typically avoid the place where the rape occurred (Ellis, 1983). Anticipating and attempting to avoid reminders of the traumatic experience, they become wary of strangers, especially men who resemble the assailant, and they check doors, locks, and windows more frequently than before. These kinds of *avoidance responses* may continue for years, and some victims only start to return to a normal life after psychotherapy (Foa & Rothbaum, 1998).

Clearly, repressive coping comes with costs. Although it may make sense to try to avoid stressful thoughts and situations when stress is at its peak, research indicates that longer-term use of such strategies can be harmful (Suls & Fletcher, 1985; Wegner & Pennebaker, 1993). The avoidance of thoughts and situations makes your world a bit smaller each day; a better approach is to come to grips with fears or problems. This is the basic idea of rational coping.

Rational Coping

Elvis Presley's motto was "Taking Care of Business," a saying that was embossed with the acronym TCB on the tail of his private jet, the *Lisa Marie.* TCB was his way of saying, "The show must go on," a reminder to overcome the impulse to shrink from challenges. His motto also suggests that toughing it out is always possible, that marching forcefully into the fray is the way to cope with fear. This approach may sound dangerous and probably is unwise in the face of serious threats. After all, Elvis wasn't exactly a model of successful coping with life stress, abusing prescription drugs and dying at an early age. Sometimes the show has to stop. However, there is a kernel of truth in Elvis's motto that is the basis of an effective stress-reduction method—the strategy of rational coping.

Rational coping involves *facing the stressor and working to overcome it.* This strategy is the opposite of repressive coping and so may seem to be the most unpleasant and unnerving thing you could do when faced with stress. It requires approaching rather than avoiding a stressor in order to lessen its longer-term negative impact (Hayes, Strosahl, & Wilson, 1999). Rational coping is a three-step process: *acceptance,* coming to realize that the stressor exists and cannot be wished away; *exposure,* attending to the stressor, thinking about it, and even seeking it out; and *understanding,* working to find the meaning of the stressor in your life.

When the trauma is particularly intense, rational coping may be difficult to undertake. In rape trauma, for example, even accepting that it happened takes time and effort; the initial impulse is to deny the event and try to live as though it had never occurred. Research on how psychotherapy helps people cope with rape trauma has focused on the exposure step by helping victims to confront and think about what happened. Using a technique called "prolonged exposure," rape survivors relive the traumatic event in

Elvis Presley's personal motto was "Taking Care of Business," so his backup group was the TCB Band; his fans joined TCB clubs; and his airplane, now parked at Graceland in Memphis, Tennessee, features the symbol with a lightning bolt on the tail.

COREY ROBINSON/AIRLINERS.NET

their imagination by recording a verbal account of the event and then listening to the recording daily. In one study, rape survivors were instructed to seek out objectively safe situations that caused them anxiety or that they had avoided. This sounds like bitter medicine indeed, but it is remarkably effective, producing significant reductions in anxiety and PTSD symptoms compared to no therapy and compared to other therapies that promote more gradual and subtle forms of exposure (Foa et al., 1999).

The third element of rational coping involves coming to an understanding of the meaning of the stressful events. A trauma victim may wonder again and again, "Why me?" or, "How did it happen?" or, "Why?" Survivors of incest frequently voice the desire to make sense of their trauma (Silver, Boon, & Stones, 1983)—a process that is difficult, even impossible, during bouts of suppression and avoidance.

How do you cope with a tidal wave? This tsunami survivor in Khao Lak, Thailand, December 2004, surveys the devastation of his life. The stress is massive, so the first steps in rational coping are very basic—find your loved ones and attend to the elements of survival.

Reframing

Changing the way you think is another way to cope with stressful thoughts. Rather than suppressing the thoughts or coping rationally, people sometimes engage in a strategy of **reframing**, which involves *finding a new or creative way to think about a stressor that reduces its threat*. If you experience anxiety at the thought of public speaking, for example, you might reframe by shifting from thinking of an audience as evaluating you to thinking of yourself as evaluating them, and this might make speech giving easier. Or you could focus on the people in the audience most responsive to your message and even seek them out afterward to ask what interested them about your speech. This way of reframing the stressor might not work for everyone. To be effective, reframing involves discovering a creative solution that will work for you.

Reframing can be an effective way to prepare for a moderately stressful situation, but if something like public speaking is so stressful that you can't bear to think about until you absolutely must, the technique may be not be usable. Psychotherapist Donald Meichenbaum introduced a reframing technique, **stress inoculation training (SIT)**, which *helps people to cope with stressful situations by developing positive ways to think about the situation*. This approach acknowledges that it is extremely difficult to change negative interpretations of a stressor *during* the emotional turmoil of the stressful event but suggests that proper preparation *beforehand* can arm the person with effectively reframed thoughts.

One study examined how SIT can help people who have difficulty controlling their anger (Novaco, 1977). Normally, the heat of anger powers up thoughts of being upset and lashing out. The training involved rehearsing thoughts such as, "Just roll with the punches; don't get bent out of shape," "You don't need to prove yourself," "I'm not going to let him get to me," "It's really a shame he has to act like this," and "I'll just let him make a fool of himself." Anger-prone people who practiced these thoughts were less likely to become physiologically aroused in response to laboratory-based provocations, both imaginary and real. Subsequent research on SIT has revealed that it can be useful, too, for helping people who have suffered prior traumatic events to become more comfortable living with those events (Foa & Meadows, 1997).

Reframing apparently can take place spontaneously if people are given the opportunity to spend time thinking and writing about stressful events. In an important series of studies, Jamie Pennebaker (1989) found that the physical health of a group of college students improved after they spent a few hours writing about their deepest thoughts and feelings. Compared with students who had written about something else, members of the self-disclosure group were less likely in subsequent months to visit the student health center; they also used less aspirin and achieved better grades (Pennebaker & Beall, 1986; Pennebaker, Colder, & Sharp, 1990). In fact, engaging in such expressive writing was found to improve immune function (Pennebaker, Kiecolt-Glaser, & Glaser, 1988), while suppressing emotional topics weakened it (Petrie, Booth, & Pennebaker, 1998). The positive effect of self-disclosing writing may reflect its usefulness in reframing trauma and reducing stress.

 **ONLY HUMAN**

REFRAMING NEEDED HERE 1992—In Asheville, North Carolina, in September, Shannon Marie Fogle, 22, a former Clemson University baton-twirling star and the current Miss Asheville, was arrested for DUI with a blood alcohol level of .21. Fogle's mother told reporters that her daughter had just that afternoon seen her replacement perform at Clemson and that when she was drinking later that evening, "the realization hit her" that she was no longer a star twirler. "It was overwhelming," the mother said.

Perhaps Ganesh, the Hindu god of wisdom, finds it therapeutic to write about his thoughts and feelings from time to time.

Body Management

Stress can express itself as tension in your neck muscles, back pain, a knot in your stomach, sweaty hands, or the harried face you glimpse in the mirror. Because stress so often manifests itself through bodily symptoms, bodily techniques such as relaxation, biofeedback, and aerobic exercise are useful in its management.

Relaxation

Imagine for a moment that you are scratching your chin. Don't actually do it; just think about it and notice that your body participates by moving ever so slightly, tensing and relaxing in the sequence of the imagined action. Physiologist and psychologist Edmund Jacobson (1932) discovered these effects with *electromyography* (EMG), a technique used to measure the subtle activity of muscles. He asked a subject to imagine scratching his chin, rowing a boat, or plucking a flower from a bush and observed that each of these thoughts can produce slight levels of tension in the muscles involved in performing the act. (This may be why, when you're balanced up high, thoughts of falling seem to make you teeter.) Jacobson also found that thoughts of relaxing the muscles sometimes reduced EMG readings when the people didn't even report feeling tense. Our bodies respond unconsciously to all the things we think about doing every day. These thoughts create muscle tension even when we think we're doing nothing at all.

These observations led Jacobson to develop **relaxation therapy**—*a technique for reducing tension by consciously relaxing muscles of the body.* A person in relaxation therapy may be asked to relax specific muscle groups one at a time or to imagine warmth flowing through the body or to think about a relaxing situation. Meditation, hypnosis, yoga, and prayer have some elements in common with relaxation therapy (see Chapter 8). These activities all draw on a **relaxation response**, *a condition of reduced muscle tension, cortical activity, heart rate, breathing rate, and blood pressure* (Benson, 1990). Basically, as soon as you get in a comfortable position, quiet down, and focus on something repetitive or soothing that holds your attention, you relax. Relaxation is not only healthy for overstimulated kindergarten children at nap time but it also benefits adults as well.

Relaxing on a regular basis can reduce symptoms of stress (Carlson & Hoyle, 1993). A few months of biweekly relaxation improves mood and even reduces blood levels of cortisol, the biochemical marker of the stress response (McKinney et al., 1997). Relaxation can improve health by reducing symptoms directly, improving coping, and preventing the development of stress-related illness. For example, in patients who are suffering from tension headache, relaxation reduces the tension that causes the headache; in people with cancer, relaxation makes it easier to cope with stressful treatments; in people with stress-related cardiovascular problems, relaxation can reduce the high blood pressure that puts the heart at risk (Mandle, Jacobs, Arcari, & Domar, 1996; see The Real World box).

Biofeedback

Wouldn't it be nice if, instead of having to learn to relax, you could just flip a switch and relax as fast as possible? **Biofeedback**, *the use of an external monitoring device to obtain information about a bodily function and possibly gain control over that function,* was developed with this goal of high-tech relaxation in mind.

Biofeedback can help people control physiological functions they are not likely to become aware of in other ways. For example, you probably have no idea right now what brain-wave patterns you are producing. In the late 1950s, Joe Kamiya (1969), a psychologist using the electroencephalograph (also called the EEG and discussed in Chapter 3), initiated a brain-wave biofeedback revolution when he found that people could change their brain waves from alert beta patterns to relaxed alpha patterns and back again when they were permitted to monitor their own EEG readings.

RELAXATION THERAPY A technique for reducing tension by consciously relaxing muscles of the body.

RELAXATION RESPONSE A condition of reduced muscle tension, cortical activity, heart rate, breathing rate, and blood pressure.

BIOFEEDBACK The use of an external monitoring device to obtain information about a bodily function and possibly gain control over that function.

{ THE REAL WORLD } Rubbing the Right and Wrong Way: Massage and Therapeutic Touch

THE GREEK PHYSICIAN HIPPOCRATES (CA. 460–ca. 377 BCE) advocated rubbing as a therapy for muscle stiffness, but many people think it can do more. Per Henrik Ling (1776–1839), who developed Swedish massage (the modern technique most of us think of as *massage*), saw it as a complement to medical treatments for arthritis, headache, fatigue, depression, multiple sclerosis, postoperative pain, asthma, and even cancer. Contemporary massage enthusiasts recommend it as a treatment for just about everything, but their claims have seldom been evaluated scientifically. Recent government interest in "alternative medicine," however, has shone a spotlight on its possible use.

A review of the conclusions of several hundred studies of massage effectiveness suggests that massage has some specific uses beyond that ancient cure for stiffness (Moyer, Rounds, & Hannum, 2004). Even a single massage can be more effective than comparison treatments such as relaxation or biofeedback in reducing blood pressure and decreasing heart rate, suggesting that massage may increase the activation of the parasympathetic nervous system and so counteract the sympathetic activation that usually accompanies stress and nervousness. However, a single massage does not decrease blood cortisol levels—a finding that argues against parasympathetic activation as the "active ingredient." A single massage also does not immediately decrease pain. So, one massage is basically a good way to relax for the moment but by itself probably won't work any miracles.

A regimen of massage treatments over the course of several weeks, however, can reduce chronic pain for days or weeks after treatment, as well as reduce chronic anxiety and depression. In fact, massage treatments were almost as effective as psychotherapy in reducing patient reports of anxiety and depression, suggesting the possibility of important parallels between the two types of treatment. Perhaps the therapeutic agent is the repeated, private contact between two people—whether the contact involves an hour-long conversation or massage. In both techniques, the client has positive expectations, the therapist is warm and positive, and the client and therapist work together to help the client feel better.

Massage therapy should not be confused with a more controversial technique known as therapeutic touch (TT). The therapeutic touch practitioner repeatedly passes his or her hands over the client a few inches away without directly touching the client. The client may not even be observing what is going on, so it is unclear how this therapy might work. Proponents of TT believe that the practitioner can sense "energy blockages" in the client's "energy field" and dissipate the blockages through these hand movements. The technique is widely used in nursing and has been defended by alternative healing supporters such as Andrew Weil. The small amount of research on this method supports skeptics' questions and suggests that TT involves nothing more than hand waving.

Nine-year-old Emily Rosa decided to study TT for a science fair project. Emily set up a cardboard screen with holes through which trained TT practitioners extended their hands. With their view blocked, she asked the practitioners to identify which of their hands she was placing her own hand near. She conducted a series of trials, tossing a coin each time to make sure her selection of hands was random. On average, the 21 practitioners chose the correct hand 44% of the time—which is less than the 50% chance they would have had by simply guessing. Emily's study doesn't examine whether TT helps people, but it does suggest that practitioners don't have a scientific explanation for how it might work. In fact, Emily's study made such an impact in the medical community that it was published in the *Journal of the American Medical Association* (Rosa et al., 1998).

Of course, TT might help people in ways that have nothing to do with energy fields, perhaps because it—like massage—is based on a positive therapeutic relationship between practitioner and client. For clients who are put off by magical notions of "energies," however, TT could undermine a positive therapeutic relationship. Like massage, TT is a technique for which an active ingredient is unknown. Unlike massage, however, it is not yet known whether TT has any ingredients at all.

Per Henrik Ling, father of massage therapy, is shown here on a Swedish postage stamp commemorating his life.

Emily Rosa, author of a science fair project on therapeutic touch, questioned the ability of therapists to sense the presence of patients—let alone their energy fields.

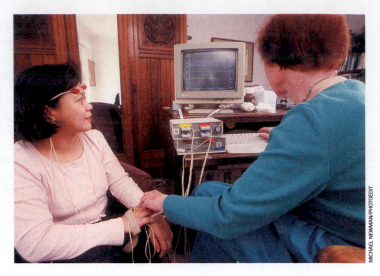

Biofeedback gives people access to visual or audio feedback showing levels of psychophysiological functions such as heart rate, breathing, or skin temperature that they would otherwise be unable to sense directly.

Recent studies suggest that EEG biofeedback (or neurofeedback) is moderately successful in treating brain-wave abnormalities in disorders such as epilepsy (Yucha & Gilbert, 2004). Often, however, the use of biofeedback to produce relaxation in the brain turns out to be a bit of technological overkill and may not be much more effective than simply having the person stretch out in a hammock and hum a happy tune. Unfortunately, biofeedback is not a magic bullet that gives people control over stress-induced health troubles, but it has proven useful as a technique for pursuing the benefits of relaxation (Moss, McGrady, Davies, & Wickramasekera, 2002).

Early experiments by Neal Miller (1978) had revealed that rats could be trained to reduce their heart rate when rewarded with pleasurable electric brain stimulation, and later studies found that humans could gain control of their heart rate, skin temperature, blood pressure, and so on when provided with indicators that enabled them to become conscious of these physiological processes. It seems impossible to control your skin temperature, for example, when you don't know from one minute to the next whether it's changing (even though you might very well notice you have cold hands). But with temperature sensors attached to their fingers, many people can learn to warm cold hands merely by watching a meter or listening to a tone that signals "warmer" or "colder" (e.g., Roberts & McGrady, 1996). This in turn may trigger a more general reduction in anxiousness because warming the hands is only achieved by relaxing some functions of the sympathetic nervous system. Thus, people who find that they cannot relax successfully through relaxation therapy may find that biofeedback provides a useful alternative.

Aerobic Exercise

A jogger nicely decked out in a neon running suit bounces back and forth in place at the crosswalk and then springs away when the signal changes. It is tempting to assume this jogger is the picture of psychological health—happy, unstressed, and even downright exuberant. It is also a bit tempting, if you're driving a car, to run up on the curb and mow the jogger down. As it turns out, the stereotype is true: Studies indicate that *aerobic exercise* (exercise that increases heart rate and oxygen intake for a sustained period) is associated with psychological well-being. One Finnish study surveyed around 3,400 people and found that those who exercised at least two to three times a week experienced less depression, anger, cynical distrust, and stress than those who exercised less frequently or who didn't exercise at all (Hassmen, Koivula, & Uutela, 2000).

But does exercise *cause* psychological well-being or does psychological well-being cause people to exercise? Perhaps general happiness is what inspires the jogger's bounce. Or could some unknown third factor (neon pants?) cause both the need to exercise and the sense of well-being? As we've mentioned many times, correlation does not always imply causation.

SOCIAL SUPPORT The aid gained through interacting with others.

To try to tease apart causal factors, researchers have randomly assigned people to aerobic exercise activities and no-exercise comparison groups and have found that exercise actually does promote stress relief and happiness. In one experiment, mildly depressed college women were randomly placed in either a 10-week program of aerobic exercise (1 hour, twice each week), a program of relaxation, or no treatment. The exercise group became less depressed over the course of the program, improving more than the relaxation group and the control group (McCann & Holmes, 1984). Subsequent studies have found that as little as 10 minutes of exercise at a time can yield a positive mood boost (Hanson, Stevens, & Coast, 2001).

So, exercise seems to improve well-being, but the reasons for this positive effect are unclear. Researchers have suggested that the effect results from increases in the body's production of neurotransmitters such as serotonin, which can have a positive effect on mood (as discussed in Chapter 3) or to increases in the production of endorphins—the endogenous opiates discussed in Chapters 3 and 8 (Jacobs, 1994).

Beyond boosting positive mood, exercise also stands to keep you healthy into the future. Current U.S. government recommendations suggest that 30 minutes of moderately vigorous exercise per day will reduce the risk of chronic illness (Dietary Guidelines Advisory Committee, 2005). Perhaps the simplest thing you can do to improve your happiness and health, then, is to regularly participate in an aerobic activity. Pick something you find fun; that will keep you coming back. Sign up for a dance class, get into a regular basketball game, or start paddling a canoe. If all else fails, park the car, get out a big foam rubber bat, and chase down the next bouncy jogger you see.

Exercise is helpful for the reduction of stress and even better if you get to carry the Olympic torch.

Situation Management

After you have tried to manage stress by managing your mind and managing your body, what's left to manage? Look around and you'll notice a whole world out there. Perhaps that could be managed as well. Situation management involves changing your life situation as a way of reducing the impact of stress on your mind and body. Ways to manage your situation can include seeking out social support and finding a place for humor in your life.

Social Support

The wisdom of the National Safety Council's first rule—"Always swim with a buddy"— is obvious when you're in water over your head, but people often don't realize that the same principle applies whenever danger threatens. Other people can offer help in times of stress. **Social support** is *aid gained through interacting with others*. One of the more self-defeating things you can do in life is to fail to connect to people in this way. Just failing to get married, for example, is bad for your health. Unmarried individuals have an elevated risk of mortality from cardiovascular disease, cancer, pneumonia and influenza, chronic obstructive pulmonary disease, and liver disease and cirrhosis (Johnson et al., 2000). More generally, good ongoing relationships with friends and family and participation in social activities and religious groups can be as healthy for you as exercising and avoiding smoking (House, Landis, & Umberson, 1988).

Social support is helpful on many levels:

- An intimate partner can help you remember to get your exercise and follow your doctor's orders, and together you'll probably follow a more healthy diet than you would all alone with your snacks.
- Talking about problems with friends and family can offer many of the benefits of professional psychotherapy, usually without the hourly fees.
- Sharing tasks and helping each other when times get tough can reduce the amount of work and worry in each other's lives.

The helpfulness of strong social bonds, though, transcends mere convenience. Lonely people are more likely than others to be stressed and depressed (Baumeister & Leary, 1995), and they can be more susceptible to illness because of lower-than-normal levels of immune functioning (Kiecolt-Glaser et al., 1984).

 ONLY HUMAN

TOO MUCH SOCIAL SUPPORT? 2003—In March, after someone reported a brick thrown through his window, authorities went to the neighboring home of Phillip and Jerry Logan in Wyandotte, Oklahoma, to question them. The Logans put out the word for other family members to come by and help them, and there soon broke out a series of fights that eventually involved 30 law enforcement officers from eight agencies. Six Logans (including the 61-year-old patriarch and the 55-year-old mother) were taken into custody. According to the Ottawa County sheriff, the immediate members of the Logan family have been charged with 250 crimes in the last 5 years.

Long-tailed macaques (*Macaca fascicularis*) living in mangroves in Thailand make friends. Like all good friends do, they clean each other for ticks and lice.

Even nonhuman primates suffer immune suppression when deprived of social support (Coe, 1993). In one study, 43 healthy, adult, male long-tailed macaque monkeys were randomly placed in stable or unstable social groups (Cohen et al., 1992). The four-to-five-member stable groups lived together for 26 months. The unstable groups were reorganized every month so that each monkey was forced to deal with three or four monkeys who were not in his previous group. Fights and disruption were common among the members of the unstable groups—just as they might have been if the monkeys encountered social strangers in the wild. Monkeys subjected to the unfriendly social environments showed reduced T-cell immune responses at the end of the experiment. Immune suppression was particularly severe among members of the unstable groups who didn't make friends with their new roommates—that is, who showed little affiliative behavior such as grooming or close contact.

Many first-year college students experience something of a crisis of social support. No matter how outgoing and popular they were in high school, newcomers typically find the task of developing satisfying new social relationships quite daunting. New friendships can seem shallow, connections with teachers may be perfunctory and even threatening, and social groups that are encountered can seem like islands of lost souls ("Hey, we're forming a club to investigate the lack of clubs on campus—want to join?"). Not surprisingly, research shows that students reporting the greatest feelings of isolation also show reduced immune responses to flu vaccinations (Pressman et al., 2005). Time spent getting to know people in new social situations can be an investment in your own health.

The value of social support in protecting against stress may be very different for women and men: Whereas women seek support under stress, men do not. The fight-or-flight response to stress may be largely a male reaction, according to research on sex differences by Shelley Taylor (2002). Taylor suggests that the female response to stress is to *tend-and-befriend* by taking care of people and bringing them together. Like males, human females respond to stressors with sympathetic nervous system arousal and the release of epinephrine and norepinephrine, but unlike males, they also release the hormone *oxytocin,* a hormone secreted by the pituitary gland in pregnant and nursing mothers. In the presence of estrogen, oxytocin triggers social responses—a tendency to seek out social contacts, nurture others, and create and maintain cooperative groups. After a hard day at work, a man may come home frustrated and worried about his job and end up drinking a beer and fuming alone. A woman under the same type of stress may instead play with her kids or talk to friends on the phone. The tend-and-befriend response to stress may help to explain why women are healthier and have a longer life span than do men. The typical male response amplifies the unhealthy effects of stress, whereas the female response takes a lesser toll on her mind and body—and provides social support for the people around her as well.

Humor

Wouldn't it be nice to laugh at your troubles and move on? Most of us recognize that humor can diffuse unpleasant situations and bad feelings, and it makes sense that bringing some fun into your life could help to reduce stress. The extreme point of view on this topic is staked out in self-help books with titles such as *Health, Healing, and the Amuse System* and *How Serious Is This? Seeing Humor in Daily Stress.* Is laughter truly the best medicine? Should we close down the hospitals and send in the clowns?

There is a kernel of truth to the theory that humor can help us cope with stress. For example, humor can reduce sensitivity to pain and distress, as researchers found when they subjected volunteers to an overinflated blood pressure cuff. Participants were more tolerant of the pain during a laughter-inducing comedy audiotape than during a neutral tape or instructed relaxation (Cogan, Cogan, Waltz, & McCue, 1987).

Humor can also reduce the time needed to calm down after a stressful event. For example, men viewing a highly stressful film about three industrial accidents were asked to either narrate the film aloud by describing the events seriously or by making their commentary as funny as possible. Although men in both groups reported feeling tense while watching the film and showed increased levels of sympathetic nervous arousal (increased heart rate and skin conductance, decreased skin temperature), those looking for humor in the experience bounced back to normal arousal levels more quickly than did those in the serious-story group. This fast recovery was true both for people who described themselves as having a good sense of humor and for those who characterized themselves as more serious (Newman & Stone, 1996).

If laughter and fun can alleviate stress quickly in the short term, do the effects accumulate to improve health and longevity? Sadly, the evidence suggests not (Provine, 2000). A study titled "Do Comics Have the Last Laugh?" tracked the longevity of comedians in comparison to other entertainers and nonentertainers (Rotton, 1992). It was found that the comedians died younger—perhaps after too many nights on stage thinking, *I'm dying out here.*

The same fate may befall comedians who don't go on the stage. A study of the long-term effects of having a cheerful personality found that such individuals have relatively brief (but no doubt happy) lives. Among 1,215 people whose childhood levels of cheerfulness and sense of humor had been rated by their parents and teachers, the more cheerful children tended to die younger, in part because such individuals grow up to be relatively careless about their health. These findings may be limited, however, because participants were selected on the basis of high IQ, and so they were not a random sample of the population (Martin et al., 2002).

Thus, current evidence suggests that in the short term, humor may help you get over the rough spots, but in the longer term, it may not be as helpful as a remedy for stress. The hypothesis that humor leads to health may be one of those overly simple remedies that come from thinking that all positive psychological qualities are linked. Self-help gurus who tout their own plans to make you happy, healthy, sexy, and rich do this by appealing to a pervasive mindbug—the tendency to group ideas together in terms of their goodness. You may love to laugh and love to be well, but you may not need to laugh *in order* to be well. Each of these positive qualities can coexist in a person without necessarily affecting the others.

"I don't think it's anything serious."

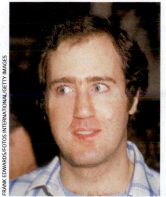

Is it dangerous to be funny or funny to be dangerous? The early deaths of comedians such as John Belushi (drug overdose), Andy Kaufman (lung cancer), John Candy (heart attack), Chris Farley (drug overdose), and Mitch Hedberg (drug overdose) make you wonder whether it's healthy to joke around for a living.

In summary, the management of stress involves strategies for influencing the mind, the body, and the situation. People often try to manage their minds by trying to suppress stressful thoughts or avoid situations that produce them. Such repressive coping is not particularly effective for most people, and better alternatives include rationally coping with the stressor and engaging in reframing to see it differently. Body management strategies revolve around the reduction of stress symptoms through relaxation, biofeedback, and aerobic exercise, and these can be very effective. Overcoming stress by managing your situation is also effective in the case of seeking out social support, and finding humor in stressful events can also be useful for helping you to cope with the events as they occur. ■ ■

NATIONAL LIBRARY OF MEDICINE, NATIONAL INSTITUTE OF HEALTH

Headache, as envisioned by caricaturist George Cruikshank (1792–1878).

The Psychology of Illness: When It's in Your Head

It's an insult to a patient seeking medical treatment if the physician says, "It's all in your head." Illness is in the body, isn't it? Suggesting that illness is all in your mind somehow says that it isn't "real" or, worse, that instead of the physical symptoms you feel, you have a mental illness. Yet in some sense, *everything* is in the head. The mind is indispensable when it comes to experiencing symptoms, recognizing illness, deciding to seek treatment, and working to recover. Certain psychological disorders can influence physical illness as well, making people hypersensitive or insensitive to symptoms and even creating physical symptoms that reflect underlying psychological problems. For psychologists, it is an insult to say, "It's all in your body."

Sensitivity to Illness

One of the mind's main influences on the body's health and illness is the mind's sensitivity to bodily symptoms. No doubt Mr. X, the poor victim of "voodoo death" discussed at the beginning of this chapter, had his attention radically reoriented toward his body by his mother's repeated warning that something bad would happen. This sensitivity may have then amplified his fear of dying and so aggravated his asthma. Noticing what is wrong with the body can be helpful when it motivates a search for treatment, but sensitivity can also lead to further problems when it snowballs into a preoccupation with illness that itself can cause harm.

Recognizing Illness and Seeking Treatment

You probably weren't thinking about your breathing a minute ago, but now that you're reading this sentence, you notice it. Breathe in, breathe out . . . breathe in, breathe out. Sometimes we are very attentive to our bodies. At other times, the body seems to be on "automatic," running along unnoticed until specific symptoms announce themselves or are pointed out by an annoying textbook writer. Psychologist Jamie Pennebaker has long been interested in the cognitive and emotional aspects of physical symptoms. In an early study, he looked at the impact of directing attention toward the body (Pennebaker & Lightner, 1980). Volunteers listened to audio feedback of their own breathing or street sounds as they jogged on a treadmill. When asked how they felt after running, the breath-focused group reported more physical symptoms such as headache, racing heart, and sweating than did the control group. Clearly, focusing inward on physical sensations can magnify symptoms that might otherwise go unnoticed.

Directing attention toward the body or away from it can influence the symptoms we perceive. When people are bored, for example, they have more attention available to direct toward their bodies and so focus more on physical symptoms. Pennebaker (1980) audiotaped classrooms and found that people are more likely to cough when someone else has just coughed—but that such psychological contagion is much more likely at boring points in a lecture. In fact, the overall amount of coughing is greater in classes taught by instructors who receive poor course evaluations. Interestingly, coughing is not something people do on purpose (as Pennebaker found when he recorded clusters of coughs among sleeping firefighters). Thus, awareness and occurrence of physical symptoms can be influenced by psychological factors beyond our control.

People differ substantially in the degree to which they attend to and report bodily symptoms. People who report many physical symptoms tend to be negative in other ways as well—describing themselves as anxious, depressed, and under stress (Watson & Pennebaker, 1989). In a study of college students, physical symptom reporting was found to be correlated with aspirin use, health center visits, and perceiving oneself as overweight—but was also related to having experienced stressful events such as rape, molestation, or parents' divorce (Pennebaker, 1982).

Do people with many symptom complaints truly have a lot of problems or are they just high-volume complainers? To answer this question, researchers used fMRI brain scans to compare severity of reported symptoms with degree of activation in brain areas usually associated with pain experience. Volunteers underwent several applications of a thermal stimulus (of 110 to 120°F) to the leg, and, as you might expect, some of the participants found it more painful than did others. Scans during the painful events revealed that the anterior cingulate cortex, somatosensory cortex, and prefrontal cortex (areas known to respond to painful body stimulation) were particularly active in those participants who reported higher levels of pain experience. Because other brain areas sensitive to pain such as the thalamus were not particularly active (see **FIGURE 15.6**), the researchers concluded that more reporting of pain is suggestive of greater activation but only of some of the brain areas linked with pain (Coghill, McHaffie, & Yen, 2003; see the Hot Science box on the next page).

In contrast to complainers are those who underreport symptoms and pain or ignore or deny the possibility that they are sick. Insensitivity to symptoms comes with costs: It can delay the search for treatment, sometimes with serious repercussions. Of 2,404 patients in one study who had been treated for a heart attack, 40% had delayed going to the hospital for over 6 hours from the time they first noticed suspicious symptoms (Gurwitz et al., 1997). Severe chest pain or a history of prior heart surgery did send people to the hospital in a hurry. Those with more subtle symptoms often waited around for hours, however, not calling an ambulance or their doctor, just hoping the problem would go away—which was not a good idea because many of the treatments that can reduce the damage of a heart attack are most useful when provided early.

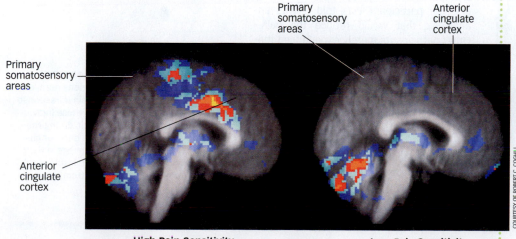

High Pain Sensitivity **Low Pain Sensitivity**

Figure 15.6 **The Brain in Pain** fMRI scans of brain activation in high- (left) and low-pain-sensitive (right) individuals during painful stimulation. The anterior cingulate cortex and primary somatosensory areas show greater activation in high-pain-sensitive individuals. Levels of activation are highest in yellow and red, then light blue and dark blue.
(Coghill, McHaffie, & Yen, 2003)

{ HOT SCIENCE } This Is Your Brain on Placebos

THERE IS SOMETHING MIRACULOUS ABOUT Band-Aids. Your standard household toddler typically *requires* one for any injury at all, expecting and often achieving immediate relief. It is not unusual to find the child who reports a stomachache "cured" if a Band-Aid has been applied to the tummy by a helpful adult. Of course, the Band-Aid is not *really* helping the pain—or is it?

Physicians and psychologists have long puzzled over the **placebo effect,** *a clinically significant psychological or physiological response to a therapeutically inert substance or procedure.* The classic placebo is the sugar pill, but Band-Aids, injections, heating pads, neck rubs, homeopathic remedies, and even kind words can have placebo effects. For the effect to occur, however, the recipient must know that a treatment is taking place (Stewart-Williams, 2004), and this is also true of active treatments such as morphine injections (Benedetti, Maggi, & Lopiano, 2003). Knowledge effects can be remarkably specific, mirroring in detail what patients believe about the nature of medicine—for example, that two pills work better than one and an injection works better than just a pill (de Craen et al., 1999).

How do placebos operate? Do people really feel pain but distort their report of the experience to make it consistent with their beliefs about treatment? Or does the placebo actually reduce the pain a patient experiences? Howard Fields and Jon Levine

"Find out who set up this experiment. It seems that half the patients were given a placebo, and the other half were given a different placebo."

(1984) discovered that placebos trigger the release of endorphins (or *endogenous opiates*), painkilling chemicals similar to morphine that are produced by the brain (see Chapter 8). In their experiments, they found that an injection of naloxone, an opiate-blocking drug, typically reduces the benefit both of an opiate such as morphine and a placebo injection, suggesting that the placebo has its painkilling effects because it triggers the release of endorphins.

In another advance in the study of these effects, placebos were found to lower the activation of specific brain areas associated with pain. One set of fMRI studies examined brain activation as volunteers were exposed to electric shock or heat (Wager et al., 2004). In preparation for some exposures to these painful stimuli, a placebo cream was applied to the skin, and the participant was told it was an analgesic that would reduce the pain. Other participants merely experienced the pain. As you can see in the accompanying figure, the fMRI scans showed decreased activation during placebo analgesia in the *thalamus, anterior cingulate cortex,* and *insula,* pain-sensitive brain regions that were activated during untreated pain. These findings suggest that placebos are not leading people to misreport their pain experience, but rather are reducing brain activity in areas that normally are active during pain experience.

Such findings don't mean that next time your stomach aches, you can break out the Band-Aids and heal yourself. What makes placebos effective is the *belief* that they will have an effect. Thus, placebo effects for a *known placebo* aren't possible. The fact that people need to be deceived to experience placebo effects and don't seem to be able to deceive themselves to create these effects shrouds the placebo effect in mystery—and even makes some researchers worry that the placebo effect is a myth. Some have even suggested that the effect doesn't exist at all (Hróbjartsson & Gøtzsche, 2001). The biochemical and physiological evidence makes placebo effects more concrete and therefore more believable. Still, it remains something of a puzzle how *believing* in a cure can make a person well, whereas just *wanting* a cure may not do much good at all.

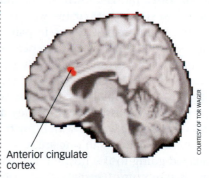

Anterior cingulate cortex

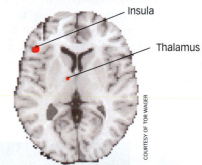

Insula

Thalamus

The Brain's Response to Placebo fMRI scans reveal that some brain regions normally activated when people report pain in response to shocks are deactivated when these individuals are given a placebo analgesic during the shock. These regions include the anterior cingulate cortex (shown in the top image, a right medial view of the brain) and the insula and thalamus (both shown in the bottom image, a ventral view of the brain).

(Wager et al., 2004)

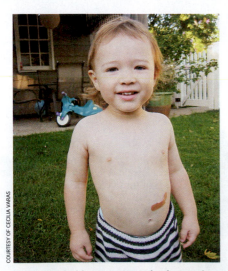

Can a Band-Aid cure a stomachache? Looks like someone here is feeling no pain.

Hoping that something bad isn't happening and worrying about the embarrassment if nothing is wrong can be dangerous—especially if it morphs into self-deception (Hackett & Cassem, 1975). For example, women with a family history of breast cancer may deny the importance of breast exams, or smokers may skip chest x-rays for fear that something will be discovered—even after they have noticed symptoms that should signal alarm. When it comes to your own health, such caution in protecting your mind from distress through the denial of illness is a mindbug that can result in exposing your body to great danger.

"Instead of an expensive, invasive procedure, we've decided to beat it out of you."

Somatoform Disorders

The flip side of denial is excessive sensitivity to illness, and it turns out that sensitivity also has its perils. Indeed, hypersensitivity to symptoms or to the possibility of illness is a mindbug that underlies a variety of psychological problems and can also undermine physical health. Psychologists studying **psychosomatic illness**, *an interaction between mind and body that can produce illness,* explore ways in which mind (psyche) can influence body (soma) and vice versa. The study of mind-body interactions focuses on psychological disorders called **somatoform disorders**, in which *the patient displays physical symptoms not fully explained by a general medical condition.* Hypochondriasis is the best known of these disorders, but other somatoform disorders include somatization disorder and conversion disorder.

Hypochondriasis is *a psychological disorder in which a person is preoccupied with minor symptoms and develops an exaggerated belief that the symptoms signify a life-threatening illness.* You may know people who constantly worry about their health, and these poor souls can mentally turn every cough into tuberculosis and every headache into a brain tumor. It is said that fairy-tale author Hans Christian Andersen (1805–75) was a hypochondriac, talking about his ailments and their possible meaning with anyone who would listen. It is also said that he had a morbid fear of being buried alive and placed a note by his bed each night as he slept explaining, "I only *appear* to be dead." For a hypochondriac, the tendency to catastrophize symptoms by imagining their worst-possible interpretation can become a chronic source of anxiety.

Somatization disorder involves *combinations of multiple physical complaints that have no medical explanation.* Chronic symptoms often lead the person to seek medical attention, sometimes from more than one physician at the same time. Unlike hypochondriasis, with its anxiety about an underlying disease, somatization disorder involves a greater focus on symptoms. The patient will usually complain of many symptoms—multiple pains in different parts of the body, gastrointestinal symptoms such as nausea or food intolerance, sexual symptoms such as irregular menstrual periods, and physical problems such as weakness or difficulty swallowing. Such patients seem to be searching for someone to sympathize with their many physical problems, but often they only succeed in alienating their loved ones and doctors with their persistent complaints.

Another somatoform disorder is **conversion disorder**, *a disorder characterized by apparently debilitating physical symptoms that appear to be voluntary—but that the person experiences as involuntary.* The patient might experience seizures, blindness, deafness, paralysis, or insensitivity to touch or pain in some body part, symptoms usually traced to neurological causes. On examination, however, the conversion disorder patient shows no neural basis for the symptom. The symptom may come or go over time and

PLACEBO EFFECT A clinically significant psychological or physiological response to a therapeutically inert substance or procedure.

PSYCHOSOMATIC ILLNESS An interaction between mind and body that can produce illness.

SOMATOFORM DISORDERS The set of psychological disorders in which the person displays physical symptoms not fully explained by a general medical condition.

HYPOCHONDRIASIS A psychological disorder in which a person is preoccupied with minor symptoms and develops an exaggerated belief that the symptoms signify a life-threatening illness.

SOMATIZATION DISORDER A psychological disorder involving combinations of multiple physical complaints with no medical explanation.

CONVERSION DISORDER A disorder characterized by apparently debilitating physical symptoms that appear to be voluntary—but that the person experiences as involuntary.

Augustine, a patient of Jean-Martin Charcot of the Sâlpetrière Hospital in France in 1876, photographed showing a conversion symptom of paralytic contraction of the right arm and leg. "All the joints are rigid; the fore-arm is in exaggerated pronation, the fingers are energetically flexed on the palm of the hand, the thumb is placed between ring finger and middle finger. . . . The pain in the right leg remains intense and the contracture of the limbs on the right is as total as possible" (Didi-Huberman, 2003, p. 246).

can sometimes be overcome when the patient's attention is diverted from it. A patient lying in bed with a "paralysis" of the leg, for example, might inadvertently move it to retain balance when the other leg is lifted by the physician. Yet such patients are not consciously feigning the symptoms and may be incapacitated for years with their "pseudoneurological" problems. Conversion symptoms may spontaneously resolve, but in some patients the absent symptoms are later replaced by others.

Such cases fascinated Sigmund Freud and other physicians early in the history of psychology because they demonstrated that the mind could produce physical illnesses without any physiological cause. More women than men develop conversion and somatization disorders, and early investigators called these disorders "hysteria" in the mistaken belief that these strange symptoms originated from the womb. Current theories focus on the idea that such symptoms occur as a result of breakdowns in the psychological processes underlying voluntary movement and attention (Hallett, Cloninger, Fahn, & Jankovic, 2005).

On Being a Patient

Getting sick is more than a change in physical state; it can involve a transformation of identity. This change can be particularly profound with a serious illness: A kind of cloud settles over you, a feeling that you are now different, and this transformation can influence everything you feel and do in this new world of illness. You take on a new role in life—that of the sick person—and you find yourself involved in a new set of social interactions in the world of health care providers whose job it is to help you get out of that role and back on your feet.

The Sick Role

Sociologist Talcott Parsons (1951) described the changes in self-perception and social relations that occur as the result of the adoption of a **sick role**—*a socially recognized set of rights and obligations linked with illness.* The sick person is absolved of responsibility for many everyday obligations and enjoys exemption from normal activities. For example, in addition to skipping school and homework and staying on the couch all day, a sick child can watch TV and avoid eating anything unpleasant at dinner. At the extreme, the sick person can get away with being rude, lazy, demanding, and picky. In return for these exemptions, the sick role also incurs obligations. The properly "sick" individual cannot appear to enjoy the illness or reveal signs of wanting to be sick and must also take care to pursue treatment to end this "undesirable" condition. The sick role accrues advantages to the person who takes it, but only as long as this individual appears not to want these advantages. Parsons observed that illness has psychological, social, and even moral components. You may recall times when you have felt the conflict between sickness and health as though it were a moral decision: Should you drag yourself out of bed and try to make it to the chemistry exam or just slump back under the covers and wallow in your "pain"?

Some people feign medical or psychological symptoms to achieve something they want, a type of behavior called *malingering.* Because many symptoms of illness cannot be faked—even facial expressions of pain are difficult to simulate (Williams, 2002)—

Is sickness a role we play? Michael Jackson arrived in court more than an hour late for his child molestation trial on March 10, 2005. He complained of severe back pain, and though he was acquitted of molestation, he was fined for his tardiness. Whether he was genuinely ill or using illness as an excuse to avoid the situation is something only Jacko knows.

malingering is possible only with a restricted number of illnesses. Faking illness is suspected when the secondary gains of illness—such as the ability to rest, to be freed from performing unpleasant tasks, or to be helped by others—outweigh the costs. Such gains can be very subtle, as when a child stays in bed because of the comfort provided by an otherwise distant parent, or they can be obvious, as when insurance benefits turn out to be a cash award for Best Actor. Some behaviors that may lead to illness may not be under the patient's control; for example, self-starvation may be part of an uncontrollable eating disorder. For this reason, malingering can be difficult to diagnose and treat (Feldman, 2004).

Patient-Practitioner Interaction

Medical care usually occurs through a strange interaction. On one side is a patient, often miserable, who expects to be questioned and examined and possibly prodded, pained, or given bad news. On the other side is a health care provider, who hopes to obtain useful information from the patient, help in some way, cope with the emotional part of the interaction, and achieve all of this as efficiently as possible because more patients are waiting. Seems less like a time for healing than an occasion for major awkwardness.

One of the keys to an effective medical care interaction is physician empathy (Spiro et al., 1994). The practitioner understands the patient as a physical body that needs care and must think carefully about how best to treat this body in light of a rapidly expanding base of medical information. In this sense, the practitioner is like an auto mechanic trying to work with the highest-tech car around. The patient, however, is not a machine but a person and comes to this interaction packed with emotions. After all, this is the patient's *life*.

To offer successful treatment, the physician must simultaneously understand the patient's physical state and psychological state. Physicians often err on the side of failing to acknowledge patients' emotions, focusing instead on technical issues of the case (Suchman et al., 1997). This is particularly unfortunate because a substantial percentage of patients who seek medical care do so for treatment of psychological and emotional problems (Taylor, 1986). As the Greek physician Hippocrates wrote in the fourth century BCE, "Some patients, though conscious that their condition is perilous, recover their health simply through their contentment with the goodness of the physician." The best physician treats the patient's mind as well as the patient's body.

"Next, an example of the very same procedure when done correctly."

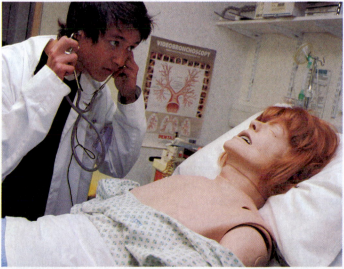

Doctor and patient have two modes of interaction, the technical and the interpersonal. Medical training with robot patients may help doctors learn the technical side of health care, but it is likely to do little to improve the interpersonal side.

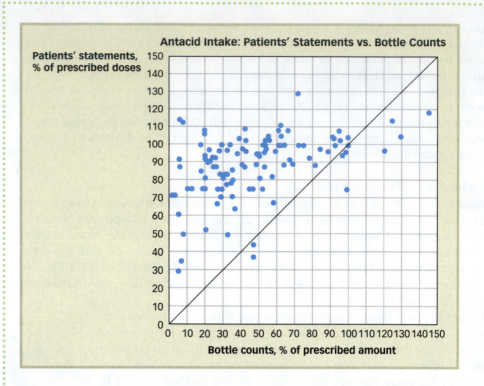

Figure 15.7 **Antacid Intake** A scatter plot of antacid intake measured by bottle count plotted against patient's stated intake for 116 patients. When the actual and stated intakes are the same, the point lies on the diagonal line; when stated intake is greater than actual, the point lies above the line. Most patients exaggerated their intake (Roth & Caron, 1978).

Another important part of the medical care interaction is motivating the patient to follow the prescribed regimen of care (Cohen, 1979). When researchers check compliance by counting the pills remaining in a patient's bottle after a prescription has been under way, they find that patients often do an astonishingly poor job of following doctors' orders (see **FIGURE 15.7**). Compliance deteriorates when the treatment must be *frequent,* as when eyedrops for glaucoma are required every few hours. Compliance is also poor when treatments are *inconvenient* or *painful,* such as drawing blood or performing injections in managing diabetes. Finally, compliance is a challenge *as the number of treatments increases.* This is a worrisome problem especially for older patients, who may have difficulty remembering when to take which pill. Failures in medical care may stem from the failure of health care providers to recognize mindbugs in the psychological processes that are involved in self-care. Helping people to follow doctors' orders involves psychology, not medicine, and is an essential part of promoting health.

In summary, the psychology of illness concerns how sensitivity to the body leads people to recognize illness and seek treatment and how somatoform disorders or psychosomatic illnesses can stem from too much or too little sensitivity. The psychology of illness also focuses on how people come to adopt the sick role, sometimes even faking illness, and how patients and their health care providers interact in ways that ensure the success of the medical treatment. ■ ■

The Psychology of Health: Feeling Good

Two types of psychological factors influence personal health: health-relevant personality traits and health behavior. Personality can influence health through relatively enduring traits that make some people particularly susceptible to health problems or stress while sparing or protecting others. The Type A behavior pattern is an example. Because personality is not typically something we choose ("I'd like a bit of that sense of humor and extroversion over there, please, but hold the whininess"), this source of health can be outside personal control. In contrast, engaging in positive health behaviors is something anyone can do. At least in principle, each of us has the capacity to take care of ourselves by choosing appropriate amounts of healthy food; engaging in safe sex; exercising; avoiding smoking, alcohol, and drugs; and engaging in other health-preserving behavior.

Personality and Health

Different health problems seem to plague different social groups. For example, men are more susceptible to heart disease than are women, and African Americans are more susceptible to asthma than are Asian or European Americans. Beyond these general social categories, are there other predictors of health? Personality turns out to be a factor in wellness, with individual differences in optimism and hardiness important influences.

Optimism

Pollyanna is one of literature's most famous optimists. Eleanor H. Porter's 1913 novel portrayed Pollyanna as a girl who greeted life with boundless good cheer even when she was orphaned and sent to live with her cruel aunt. Her response to a sunny day was to remark on the good weather, of course—but her response to a gloomy day was to point out how lucky it is that not every day is gloomy! Her crotchety Aunt Polly had exactly the opposite attitude, somehow managing to turn every happy moment into an opportunity for strict correction. A person's level of optimism or pessimism tends to be fairly stable over time, and research comparing the personalities of twins reared together versus those reared apart suggests that this stability arises because these traits are moderately heritable (Plomin et al., 1992). Perhaps Pollyanna and Aunt Polly were each "born that way."

Optimism has health benefits (Carver & Scheier, 2001). An optimist who believes that "in uncertain times, I usually expect the best" is likely to be healthier than a pessimist who believes that "if something can go wrong for me, it will." In a study of 309 patients who had undergone coronary artery bypass surgery, for example, researchers found that initial levels of optimism were related to patients' postoperative health (Scheier et al., 1999). Patients with higher levels of overall optimism (not merely optimism about the particular surgery) were less likely than other patients after their surgery to need rehospitalization for complications such as infection, heart attacks, or further surgery. Such findings are certainly encouraging for optimists (what wouldn't be?), but studies like this one showing that optimism directly improves physical health are relatively rare (Segerstrom, 2005). What *are* the benefits of optimism?

Optimism seems to aid in the maintenance of psychological health in the face of physical health problems. When sick, optimists are more likely than pessimists to maintain positive emotions, avoid negative emotions such as anxiety and depression, stick to medical regimens their caregivers have prescribed, and keep up their relationships with others. Among women who have surgery for breast cancer, for example, optimism reduces psychological harm. Optimists are less likely to experience distress and fatigue after treatment than are pessimists, largely because they keep up social contacts and recreational activities during their treatment (Carver, Lehman, & Antoni, 2003).

The benefits of optimism raise an important question: If the traits of optimism and pessimism are stable over time—even resistant to change—can pessimists ever hope to gain any of the advantages of optimism (Heatherton & Weinberger, 1994)? Research has shown that even die-hard pessimists can be trained to become significantly more optimistic and that this training can improve their psychosocial health outcomes. For example, pessimistic breast cancer patients who received 10 weeks of training in stress management techniques became more optimistic and were less likely than those who received only relaxation exercises to suffer distress and fatigue during their cancer treatments (Antoni et al., 2001).

A club badge distributed to members of the Pollyanna club in the United Kingdom, circa 1913.

The hope that optimism can help people, both psychologically and physically, is at the center of the positive psychology movement (discussed in Chapter 13), which has turned some researchers away from a focus on disorders, failures, and suffering (Gillham, 2000) and toward questions of how research can help people live meaningful and fulfilling lives, cultivate their personal strengths, and enhance their experiences. Positive psychology offers a kind of overarching optimism that recognizes that human errors and illusions are not the whole story. Still, the study of errors, illusions, and disorders—the mindbugs featured in this book—is essential if we are to understand and solve psychological problems. Perhaps the best approach is to take both the positive and the negative into account. After all, the half-full and the half-empty glasses are actually the same.

Hardiness

Some people seem to be thick-skinned, somehow able to take stress or abuse that could be devastating to others. Are there personality traits that contribute to such resilience and offer protection from stress-induced illness? To identify such traits, Suzanne Kobasa (1979) studied a group of stress-resistant business executives. These individuals reported high scores on the Holmes and Rahe (1967) index of stressful life events but had histories of relatively few illnesses compared with a similar group who succumbed to stress by getting sick. The stress-resistant group (Kobasa called them *hardy*) shared several traits, all conveniently beginning with the letter *C*. They showed a sense of *commitment,* an ability to become involved in life's tasks and encounters rather than just dabbling. They exhibited a belief in *control,* the expectation that their actions and words have a causal influence over their lives and environment. And they were willing to accept *challenge,* undertaking change and accepting opportunities for growth.

In addition to their exceptional coping skills (Maddi & Kobasa, 1984), hardy people seem to experience less stress when faced with events that others may feel are insurmountable. In one study, Israeli army recruits who took part in a grueling 4-month combat training program were tested for hardiness at the outset (Florian, Mikulciner, & Taubman, 1995). The recruits who were most hardy showed the best mental health after training, largely because they perceived the whole ordeal as less stressful than their less hardy counterparts.

Can just anyone develop hardiness, or is this a trait that is hard to change? As with other personality traits, hardiness is difficult to acquire. Researchers have attempted to teach hardiness with some success. In one such attempt, participants attended 10 weekly "hardiness training" sessions, in which they were encouraged to examine their stresses, develop action plans for dealing with them, explore their bodily reactions to stress, and find ways to compensate for unchangeable situations without falling into self-pity. Compared with control groups (who engaged in relaxation and meditation training or in group discussions about stress), the hardiness-training group reported greater reductions in their perceived personal stress as well as fewer symptoms of illness (Maddi, Kahn, & Maddi, 1998). The long-term effect of such training is not clear, but the possibility that some of the traits may be within anyone's reach is encouraging.

Health-Promoting Behaviors and Self-regulation

Even without changing our personalities at all, there are certain things we can do to be healthy. The importance of healthy eating, safe sex, and giving up smoking are common knowledge. But we don't seem to be acting on the basis of this knowledge. At the turn of the 21st century, 21% of Americans are obese (Mokdad et al., 2003). The prevalence of unsafe sex is difficult to estimate, but 65 million Americans currently suffer from an incurable sexually transmitted disease (STD), while 15 million contract one or more new STDs each year (Centers for Disease Control, 2000)—and another million live with human immunodeficiency virus/acquired immune deficiency syndrome

Table 15.2	STDs in the USA: Estimates of Numbers of New Cases and Existing Infections	
STDs	**U.S. Incidence (Estimated New Cases per Year)**	**U.S. Prevalence* (Estimated Number of People Currently Infected)**
Chlamydia	3 million	2 million
Gonorrhea	650,000	Not available
Syphilis	70,000	Not available
Herpes	1 million	45 million
Human papillomavirus (cause of genital warts)	5.5 million	20 million
Hepatitis B	120,000	417,000
Trichomoniasis	5 million	Not available
HIV/AIDS (both sexually transmitted and nonsexually transmitted)	40,000	1 million

*No recent surveys on national prevalence for gonorrhea, syphilis, or trichomoniasis have been conducted.
Sources: Cates (1999), Centers for Disease Control (2006).

(HIV/AIDS) (Centers for Disease Control, 2006) (see **TABLE 15.2**). And despite endless warnings, 29.5% of Americans use tobacco on a regular basis (National Household Survey on Drug National Household Survey on Drug Abuse, 2001). What's going on?

Self-regulation

Doing what is good for you is not necessarily easy. Mark Twain once remarked, "The only way to keep your health is to eat what you don't want, drink what you don't like, and do what you'd druther not." Engaging in health-promoting behaviors involves **self-regulation**, *the exercise of voluntary control over the self to bring the self into line with preferred standards.* When you decide on a salad rather than a cheeseburger, for instance, you control your impulse and behave in a way that will help to make you the kind of person you would prefer to be—a healthy one. Self-regulation often involves putting off immediate gratification for longer-term gains, one of those life tasks that is so difficult it qualifies as a mindbug (see Chapter 8).

Self-regulation requires a kind of inner strength or willpower. One theory suggests that self-control is a kind of strength that can be fatigued (Schmeichel & Baumeister, 2004). In other words, trying to exercise control in one area may exhaust self-control, leaving behavior in other areas unregulated. To test this theory, researchers seated hungry volunteers near a batch of fresh, hot, chocolate chip cookies. They asked some participants to leave the cookies alone but help themselves to a healthy snack of radishes, whereas others were allowed to indulge. When later challenged with an impossibly difficult figure-tracing task, the self-control group was more likely than the self-indulgent group to abandon the difficult task—behavior interpreted as evidence that they had depleted their pool of self-control (Baumeister et al., 1998). The take-home message from this experiment is that to control behavior successfully, we need to choose our battles, exercising self-control mainly on the personal weaknesses that are most harmful to health.

Sometimes, though, self-regulation is less a matter of brute force than of strategy. Martial artists claim that anyone can easily overcome a large attacker with the use of the right moves, and overcoming our own unhealthy impulses may also be a matter of finesse. Let's look carefully at healthy approaches to some key challenges for self-regulation—eating, safe sex, and smoking—to learn what "smart moves" can aid us in our struggles.

SELF-REGULATION The exercise of voluntary control over the self to bring the self into line with preferred standards.

Eating Wisely

In many Western cultures, the weight of the average citizen is increasing alarmingly. One explanation is based on our evolutionary history: In order to ensure their survival, our ancestors found it useful to eat well in times of plenty to store calories for leaner times. In postindustrial societies in the 21st century, however, there are no leaner times, and people can't burn all of the calories they consume (Pinel, Assanand, & Lehman, 2000). But why, then, isn't obesity endemic throughout the Western world? Why are people in France leaner on average than Americans even though their foods are high in fat? One reason has to do with average portion, which is far smaller in France than in the United States. Activity level in France is also greater. Research by Paul Rozin and his colleagues finds that the time people spend eating differs between cultures as well. At a McDonald's in France, meals take an average of 22 minutes, whereas in the United States, they take under 15 minutes (Rozin, Kabnick, Pete, Fischler, & Shields, 2003). Right now Americans seem to be involved in some kind of national eating contest.

Short of moving to France, what can you do? Studies indicate that dieting doesn't always work because the process of conscious self-regulation can be easily undermined by stress, leading people who are trying to control themselves to lose control by overindulging in the very behavior they had been trying to overcome. Evidence for this process comes from studies comparing dieters (who are currently dieting or who had dieted in the past) with people who had never dieted. In one such study, researchers divided dieters and nondieters into groups that either were or were not subjected to various stressors (a "fairly painful" electric shock, a task that looked easy but was rigged to make them fail, a warning that they'd be giving a 2-minute speech to five critical classmates) and then offered everyone ice cream in a "taste test."

Participants in the no-stress condition behaved as you might expect—the dieters sampled less ice cream than the nondieters. Balanced on their diet tightrope, these folks didn't fall off (see **FIGURE 15.8**). In comparison, the dieting participants in all of the stressful situations took a hard fall, no matter what kind of stress they encountered: They lost any pretense of dieting and instead ate more ice cream than the nondieters (Heatherton, Herman, & Polivy, 1991). This outcome may remind you of a general principle discussed in Chapter 8: Trying hard not to do something can often directly produce the unwanted behavior (Wegner, 1994).

Researchers Janet Polivy and Peter Herman (1992) suggest that the restraint problem is inherent in the very act of self-control; they even suggest that people who don't diet shouldn't start. Rather than dieting, heading toward normal weight once you

Is eating a contest? North American culture makes excessive eating almost a competition, but it's hard to find winners.

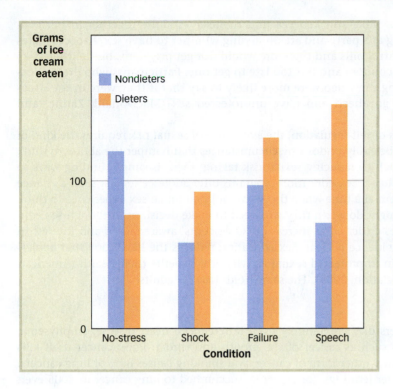

Grams of ice cream eaten

■ Nondieters
■ Dieters

100

0

No-stress Shock Failure Speech

Condition

Figure 15.8 Ice Cream "Sampling" in Response to Stress People who diet took less ice cream than nondieters in a non-stressful control condition but increased their sampling of ice cream in response to the stresses of shock, failure, or the threat of having to give a speech.

have lost your way should involve a new emphasis on exercise and nutrition (Pro-chaska & Sallis, 2004). Reframing eating in terms of getting nutrition can move people toward a better diet without "dieting." In emphasizing what is good to eat, the person can freely think about food rather than trying to suppress thoughts about it. A focus on increasing activity rather than reducing food intake, in turn, gives people another positive and active goal to pursue. Self-regulation is more effective when it focuses on what to do rather than on what not to do (Wegner & Wenzlaff, 1996).

Avoiding Sexual Risks

People put themselves at risk when they have unprotected vaginal, oral, or anal inter-course with many sexual partners or with partners who themselves have many sexual partners, exhibit symptoms of sexually transmitted diseases (STDs), are HIV positive, or are intravenous drug users. Sexually active adolescents and adults are usually aware of such risks, not to mention the risk of unwanted pregnancy, and yet many behave in risky ways nonetheless.

Why doesn't awareness translate into avoidance? People may believe—as they do with any health problem—"If you don't have it now, you don't worry about it." Risk takers harbor an *illusion of unique invulnerability,* a systematic bias toward be-lieving that they are less likely to fall victim to the problem than are others (Perloff & Fetzer, 1986). For example, a study of sexually active female college students found that respondents judged their own likelihood of getting pregnant in the next year as under 10% but estimated the average for other females at the university to be 27% (Burger & Burns, 1988). Paradoxically, this illusion was *even stronger* among women in the sample who reported using inadequate or no contraceptive tech-niques. The tendency to think, *It won't happen to me,* may be most pronounced when it probably will.

Risky sex is often the impulsive result of last-minute emotions. When thought is further blurred by alcohol or recreational drugs, people often fail to use the latex condoms that can reduce their exposure to the risks of pregnancy, HIV, and many other STDs. In a study of the relationship of alcohol to these lapses in sexual judg-ment, researchers asked male students to imagine themselves in a sexual scenario shown on a video: Mike and Rebecca find themselves alone together in her bedroom after meeting at a party and are discussing whether to have sex. Rebecca states she takes birth control pills and therefore would not get pregnant, but neither Mike nor Rebecca has a condom and it is too late to get one. Participants who drank alcohol before watching the video were more likely to say that if they were in the situation, they would go ahead and have unprotected sex (MacDonald, Zanna, and Fong, 1996).

Like other forms of self-regulation, the avoidance of sexual risk requires the kind of planning that can be easily undone by circumstances that hamper the ability to think ahead. One approach to reducing sexual risk taking, then, is simply finding ways to help people plan ahead. Sex education programs offer adolescents just such a chance by encouraging them at a time when they have not had much sex experience to think about what they might do when they will need to make decisions. Although sex education is sometimes criticized as increasing adolescents' awareness of and interest in sex, the research evidence is clear: Sex education reduces the likelihood that adolescents will engage in unprotected sexual activity and benefits their health (American Psychological Association, 2005). The same holds true for adults.

Not Smoking

One in two smokers dies prematurely from lung cancer, heart disease, emphysema, and other diseases such as cancer of the mouth and throat. Lung cancer itself kills more people than any other form of cancer, and smoking causes 80% of lung cancers. ABC newscaster Peter Jennings, for example, succumbed to lung cancer in 2005 even though he had quit smoking 20 years earlier. And if these effects aren't bad enough, they don't even include the burden of secondhand smoke, which increases risk of disease in everyone who lives with a smoker, especially children. Although the overall rate of smoking in the United States is declining, new smokers abound, and many can't seem to stop. College students are puffing away along with everyone else, with 28.5% of students currently smoking (Wechsler et al., 1998). In the face of all the devastating health consequences, why don't people quit?

Nicotine, the active ingredient in cigarettes, is addictive, and so smoking is difficult to stop once the habit is established (discussed in Chapter 8). And as in other forms of self-regulation, the resolve to quit smoking is fragile and seems to break down under

Newscaster Peter Jennings died in 2005 of lung cancer, attributed to decades of smoking.

Some people like to smoke because it enhances their overall "look."

IMAGESHOP/ALAMY

stress. In the months following 9/11, for example, cigarette sales jumped 13% in the state of Massachusetts (Phillips, 2002). In fact, Peter Jennings reported that he started smoking again occasionally during that stressful time. And for some time after quitting, ex-smokers remain sensitive to cues in the environment: Eating or drinking, a bad mood, anxiety, or just seeing someone else smoking is enough to make them want a cigarette (Shiffman et al., 1996). For people who have just quit, the urge even crops up in the form of dreams about smoking (Hajek & Belcher, 1991). The good news is that the urge decreases and people become less likely to relapse the longer they've been away from nicotine.

Psychological programs and techniques to help people kick the habit include nicotine replacement systems such as gum and skin patches, counseling programs, and hypnosis—but these programs are not always successful. Trying again and again in different ways is apparently the best approach (Schachter, 1982). After all, to quit smoking forever, you only need to quit one more time than you start up. But like the self-regulation of eating and sexuality, the self-regulation of smoking can require effort and thought. The ancient Greeks blamed self-control problems on *akrasia*, or "weakness of will." Modern psychology focuses less on blaming a person's character for poor self-regulation and points instead toward the difficulty of the task. Keeping healthy by behaving in healthy ways is one of the great challenges of life.

In summary, health psychology reveals the connection between mind and body both through the influence of personality on health and through the influence of the self-regulation of behavior on health. Research on personality traits reveals benefits of optimism for psychological health among people who have physical health problems. Research on traits such as hardiness, in turn, reveals that some people have resiliency that can help them fend off stress-related illness. The self-regulation of behaviors such as eating, sexuality, and smoking is difficult for many people because self-regulation is easily disrupted by stress. Time and thought devoted to strategies for maintaining self-control can pay off, though, with significant improvements in health and quality of life. ■ ■

Where Do You Stand?

Consider Yourself Warned

Just 6 months after the terrorist attack of September 11, 2001, President George W. Bush created the Homeland Security Advisory System. This official gauge of the danger of a new attack provides color codes for "threat conditions" from low (green) through guarded (blue), elevated (yellow), high (orange), and severe (red). The Presidential Directive creating the system described it as a "comprehensive and effective means to disseminate information regarding the risk of terrorist acts to Federal, State, and local authorities and to the American people" (Office of the Press Secretary, 2002).

In fact, the warning level has never been below yellow. Although it has been raised to red only once (and just for flights from the United Kingdom to the United States), it has been orange eight times. The specific government actions triggered by the different levels have not been revealed to the public, but higher threat conditions prompt warnings for citizens "to be vigilant, take notice of their surroundings, and report suspicious items or activities to local authorities immediately." These are probably good ideas no matter what the threat conditions, so it is unclear

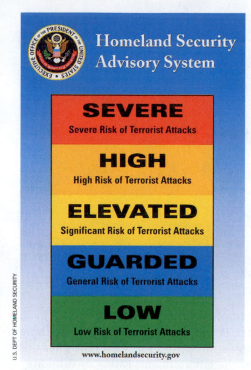

U.S. DEPT OF HOMELAND SECURITY

The Homeland Security Advisory System communicates U.S. government estimates of terrorist "threat conditions" on a color-coded scale.

whether this warning system is a useful response to terrorist threat. Certainly, if the level is raised to red, people could respond by avoiding travel or through other emergency actions that could protect them. But as long as the warning gauge merely wavers between yellow and orange, it's hard not to agree with psychologist Philip Zimbardo that the government's creation does nothing more than promote a "pre–traumatic stress syndrome" (Zhang, 2004). Perhaps all these warnings are simply doing the terrorists' work for them and putting citizens under constant stress.

We are surrounded every day with silly warnings—the steam iron label that warns "Do not use while wearing clothing" or the matchbook that says "Warning: Contents may catch fire." Are there times when we warn ourselves needlessly? Should we limit warnings such as the Homeland Security Advisory System to a more specific function, only telling us when there is a known threat rather than triggering stress about vague possibilities? Or is ongoing warning about terrorism a good idea, something that keeps all of us on our toes? Should we always know how worried we should be? Where do you stand?

Chapter Review

Sources of Stress: What Gets to You

- Stressors include both major life changes and minor hassles and can sometimes be traced to particular stressful environments.
- Stressors add up over time, with more chronic stressors producing more harmful effects. Stressors have in common the production of a threat to the person's well-being that is perceived as difficult or impossible to control.

Stress Reactions: All Shook Up

- The body responds to stress with an initial "fight-or-flight" reaction and the activation of the hypothalamus-pituitary-adrenal (HPA) axis.
- Repetition of this response generates the general adaptation syndrome, progressing in stages of alarm, resistance, and exhaustion.

- Both the immune response and the cardiovascular system can be affected by stress, and people with the Type A behavior pattern who respond to stress with hostility are particularly likely to suffer cardiovascular health problems.
- The mind's reaction to stress begins with primary and secondary appraisal and can yield disorders such as depression, burnout, or posttraumatic stress disorder (PTSD) in which thoughts of the stressor plague the mind.

Stress Management: Dealing with It

- People manage their stress by controlling their minds, their bodies, and their situations.
- Repressive coping is not effective for most people, and better alternatives include rationally coping with the stressor and engaging in reframing to see things differently.

- Body-oriented stress management strategies focus on reducing symptoms through relaxation, biofeedback, and aerobic exercise, and these can be effective.
- Overcoming stress by managing your situation is also effective in the case of seeking out social support and finding humor in stressful events.

The Psychology of Illness: When It's in Your Head

- Sensitivity to the body leads people to recognize illness and seek treatment, but somatoform disorders or psychosomatic illnesses can stem from sensitivity that is too great or too little.
- People come to adopt the sick role, sometimes even faking illness, and patients and their health care providers interact in ways that influence the success of the medical treatment.

The Psychology of Health: Feeling Good

- Personality traits such as optimism can make some people respond well psychologically when they experience physical health problems, whereas traits promoting hardiness give others special resilience to stress-related illness.
- Controlling health-relevant behaviors such as eating, sexuality, and smoking is difficult because self-regulation is easily disrupted by stress but can be managed through the devotion of time and thought to effective self-regulation strategies.

Key Terms

stressors (p. 582)

stress (p. 582)

health psychology (p. 582)

chronic stressor (p. 584)

fight-or-flight response (p. 586)

general adaptation syndrome (GAS) (p. 587)

immune system (p. 588)

lymphocytes (p. 588)

Type A behavior pattern (p. 590)

posttraumatic stress disorder (PTSD) (p. 592)

burnout (p. 594)

repressive coping (p. 595)

rational coping (p. 596)

reframing (p. 597)

stress inoculation training (SIT) (p. 597)

relaxation therapy (p. 598)

relaxation response (p. 598)

biofeedback (p. 598)

social support (p. 601)

placebo effect (p. 607)

psychosomatic illness (p. 607)

somatoform disorders (p. 607)

hypochondriasis (p. 607)

somatization disorder (p. 607)

conversion disorder (p. 607)

sick role (p. 608)

self-regulation (p. 613)

Recommended Readings

Pennebaker, J. W. (1990). *Opening up: The healing power of confiding in others*. New York: Morrow. This engaging book explains why self-disclosure is useful, recounting Pennebaker's experiments, which found that people who are encouraged to express their thoughts and feelings about their stresses and traumas showed health improvements.

Sapolsky, R. M. (1998). *Why zebras don't get ulcers: An updated guide to stress, stress-related diseases, and coping*. San Francisco: Freeman. This book covers the technical side of stress in a way that is accessible to the layperson. Sapolsky masterfully presents a wide range of facts, discoveries, and anecdotes on the biology and psychology of stress in humans and other species.

Taylor, S. E. (2003). *The tending instinct: Women, men, and the biology of relationships*. New York: Owl Books. Women and men react to stress differently, a point beautifully made in a book that fosters in the reader a new appreciation of the importance of nurturance and communication in health and relationships.

Wall, P. (2000). *Pain: The science of suffering*. New York: Columbia University Press. We are all frightened of pain, but we also need to have it to keep us alert to our bodies. This book explores fascinating cases and experiments to illustrate how pain happens and what can be done when it becomes a burden.

16

Social Psychology

Social Behavior: Interacting with People
 Survival: The Struggle for Resources
 Reproduction: The Quest for Immortality
 THE REAL WORLD An Affair to Remember
 HOT SCIENCE Beautifully Average

Social Influence: Controlling People
 The Hedonic Motive: The Power of Pleasure
 The Approval Motive: The Power of Social Acceptance
 The Accuracy Motive: The Power of Being Right
 THE REAL WORLD This Just In

Social Cognition: Understanding People
 Stereotyping: Drawing Inferences from Categories
 Attribution: Drawing Inferences from Actions
 WHERE DO YOU STAND? Are You Prejudiced?

IN 1999, 16 MEN AND WOMEN VOLUNTEERED for one of the most unusual psychology experiments ever conducted. They agreed to leave their homes, their jobs, their families and friends and to be flown to an uninhabited island off the coast of Borneo, where they would be left to survive on their own. The rules of the experiment were simple: The volunteers would meet every few days and vote to evict one of them, and the last volunteer to remain would receive $1 million. One of the things that made this psychology experiment so unusual was that it was captured on film and broadcast as a national television show called *Survivor*.

Surviving on the island of Pulau Tiga wasn't easy: The jungle was infested with rats and the ocean was infested with snakes. The volunteers faced many challenges but none more daunting than each other. "I thought this was going to be tough," one of them said early on, "but the hardest part, though, is the people" (CBS, 2000). Indeed, for 13 weeks, television viewers watched a remarkable interpersonal drama unfold as each volunteer tried to avoid being eliminated by the others. Some volunteers tried to make themselves essential by becoming expert at construction or fishing, some tried to make themselves liked by telling jokes and helping others, some tried to make themselves respected by voting to eliminate others in alphabetical order, and some just tried to make themselves scarce. In the very first week, coalitions began to form: The two Black volunteers agreed never to vote against each other, and the women agreed to begin by voting against the men. But within a short time, the nature of these alliances began to shift as the volunteers formed new bonds based on personalities, abilities, and romantic attractions rather than ethnicity or gender. The group initially voted to eliminate its weakest members—those who couldn't hunt, swim, or tolerate the heat—but as the weeks wore on, fear of competition led the group to start eliminating its strongest members instead. Finally, after 3 months of backstabbing, treachery, and mosquito bites, 51 million viewers watched as a 39-year-old corporate trainer named Richard Hatch won the prize by a single vote.

Study this chapter carefully. Richard Hatch earned a million dollars by knowing more about social psychology than anyone else on his island.

AP PHOTO/DAMIAN DOVARGANES

How did Mr. Hatch manage to be the last survivor? "The first hour on the island I stepped into my strategy and thought, 'I'm going to focus on how to establish an alliance with four people early on.' I spend a lot of time thinking about who people are and why they interact the way they do" (CBS, 2000).

Although you won't be receiving any money for your efforts, in this chapter you too will spend time thinking about who people are and why they interact the way they do, because when stripped to its bare essentials, the game of life is not unlike the game of *Survivor*. People have many needs—for food and shelter, for love and meaning—and they satisfy those needs by harming each other and helping each other (*social behavior*); by influencing others to think, feel, and act in a particular way (*social influence*); and by figuring out what others are like and why they behave as they do (*social cognition*). As you will see, *social psychology*—the study of the causes and consequences of interpersonal behavior—is critical for understanding how our species has managed to become the ultimate survivor on this island we call earth.

Social Behavior: Interacting with People

On any given day, most of us interact with a wide variety of people—such as friends, coworkers, family members, and strangers—in a variety of contexts—such as work, school, commerce, and recreation. We confide, conflict, cajole, carouse, criticize, and collaborate. We make dates, we make friends, we make lunch, we make love. We marry each other, we murder each other, and we do just about everything in between. Indeed, social behavior is so diverse and multifaceted that one of the challenges facing the psychologists who wish to understand it is to find a single framework within which all of the many forms of social behavior can be organized and understood.

The theory of evolution by natural selection provides one such framework (Dawkins, 1976). As you learned in Chapter 3, parents pass along some of their genes to their children, who in turn pass along some of *their* genetic material to their children, and so on. Individual humans disappear after 80 years or so, but their genetic material may be transmitted across generations indefinitely. It's convenient to think of ourselves as people who happen to have genes inside them, but the evolutionary perspective suggests that we are really genes that happen to have people around them.

"Selective breeding has given me an aptitude for the law, but I still love fetching a dead duck out of freezing water."

LEO CULLUM/CARTOONBANK.COM

We are *vehicles* for our genes, and our genes are the *designers* of and *passengers* in these vehicles. Genes are designers because they determine how the vehicles are constructed and thereby influence how the vehicles operate. Your genes help determine your size and shape, traits and tastes, and capabilities and limitations, rendering some of us finely tuned Ferraris and some of us serviceable sedans. And genes are passengers because they can potentially ride around forever if they can just get their old vehicles to build new vehicles before the old vehicles wear out. After three and a half billion years of practice, genes have gotten pretty good at designing vehicles of this kind, and the latest model on the showroom floor is you.

So how do these facts help us understand social behavior? The evolutionary perspective suggests that because we are short-lived vehicles for our genes, much of our social behavior revolves around the two fundamental tasks of *survival* and *reproduction*.

Survival: The Struggle for Resources

For most animals, survival is a struggle because the resources that life requires—food, water, and shelter—are scarce. Human beings engage in social behaviors that range from hurting each other to helping each other. *Hurting* and *helping* are antonyms, so you might expect them to have little in common. But as you will see, these opposite forms of social behavior are often different solutions to the same problem of scarce resources.

Aggression

The simplest way to solve the problem of scarce resources is to take what you want and smack the stripes off of anyone who tries to stop you. **Aggression** is *behavior whose purpose is to harm another,* and a quick glance at the front page of the newspaper reveals that human beings are as capable of aggression as any other animal and better at it than most (Anderson & Bushman, 2002; Geen, 1998). Sometimes people engage in *premeditated aggression,* which occurs when people consciously decide to use aggression to achieve their goals. The bank robber who threatens a teller wants to be wealthier, the zealot who assassinates a politician wants the government to change its policies, and the fighter pilot who bombs an enemy wants his or her nation to win a war. Each of these individuals has a goal, and each inflicts harm in order to achieve it. However, this harm does not necessarily entail violence: Check forgers and computer hackers can aggress with the stroke of a pen or the stroke of a key. The idea that aggression can be a means to an end is captured by the **frustration-aggression principle**, which suggests that *people aggress when their goals are thwarted* (Berkowitz, 1989; Dollard et al., 1939). The robber's goal of having money is thwarted by the clerk who is standing in front of the cash register, and so the robber aggresses in order to eliminate that obstacle.

But the newspaper stories that make us shake our heads in disbelief are those that describe *impulsive aggression,* which occurs when people aggress spontaneously and without premeditation. Impulsive aggression is rarely about scarce resources. Studies of violent crime suggest that about a third of all murders begin with a quarrel over a trivial matter (Daly & Wilson, 1988), and the stabbings, beatings, lootings, and shootings that make headlines are not calculated attempts to achieve a goal. Rather, impulsive aggression is a response to an unpleasant internal state, such as frustration, anger, or pain (Berkowitz, 1990). When a laboratory rat is given a painful electric shock, it will attack anything in its cage, including other animals, stuffed dolls, or even tennis balls (Berkowitz, 1993). Injecting a rat with stress hormones can lead it to attack as well (Kruk et al., 2004). In the natural environment, the source of an animal's pain is often nearby, such as a predator or a bush full of prickly thorns, and thus impulsive aggression may have evolved as a way to eliminate sources of pain.

Some human aggression is also a response to an unpleasant internal state. For instance, when people feel hot and bothered, they tend to behave aggressively (Anderson, 1989; Anderson, Bushman, & Groom, 1997). The correlation between a city's average daytime temperature and its rate of violent crime is so strong that we can predict with confidence that if the average temperature in the United States were to increase by just 2 degrees Fahrenheit (which is what you should expect from global warming in your lifetime), we would observe about 50,000 more violent crimes per year (**FIGURE 16.1**). Unpleasant odors, immersing your hand in painfully cold water,

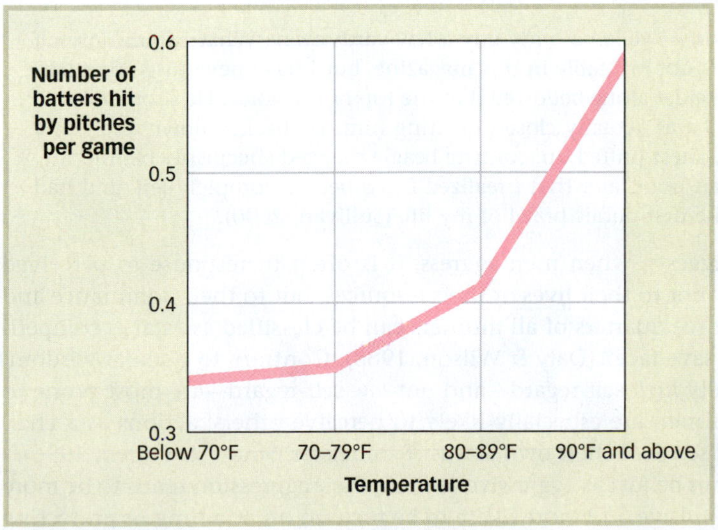

AGGRESSION Behavior whose purpose is to harm another.

FRUSTRATION-AGGRESSION PRINCIPLE A principle stating that people aggress when their goals are thwarted.

Figure 16.1
Temper and Temperature Professional pitchers have awfully good aim, so when they hit batters with the baseball, it's safe to assume that it wasn't an accident. This figure shows the average number of batters who were hit by pitches per game during the 1986–88 major-league baseball seasons. As you can see, the temperature on the field was highly correlated with the likelihood of being beaned.

AP PHOTO/UNSOLVED MYSTERIES

AP PHOTO/LOUIS LANZANO

Aggression is a way of attaining a goal by harming others. The unknown robber on the left engaged in violence, which is just one of many ways to aggress. When Tyco CEO Dennis Kozlowski (right) defrauded shareholders and stole hundreds of millions of dollars, he aggressed without engaging in violence.

 **ONLY HUMAN**

AH, NOW I FEEL BETTER In 1996, Domenico Germano was sentenced to 4 years of probation and ordered to reimburse a bank more than $5,000 for repairs. Six months earlier he had become frustrated because the bank's ATM wouldn't give him any money, so he pulled out a gun and shot it four times.

and even seeing a disgusting scene can lead to unpleasant internal states and hence trigger aggressive behavior (Berkowitz, 1990). What's notable about these instances of impulsive aggression is that they are often directed toward people who are not responsible for the unpleasant state, and as such, they have little chance of alleviating it. Like a shocked rat that attacks the tennis ball in its cage, people who feel frustrated, hurt, or angry often aggress against others simply because they are nearby.

Not everyone aggresses when they are hot and bothered. So who does, and when and why? The single best predictor of impulsive aggression is gender (Wrangham & Peterson, 1997). Crimes such as assault, battery, and murder are almost exclusively perpetrated by men—and especially by young men—who were responsible for 97% of the same-sex murders in the United States, Britain, and Canada (Archer, 1994). Although most societies encourage males to be more aggressive than females, male aggressiveness is not merely the product of socialization. Many studies show that impulsive aggression is strongly correlated with the presence of testosterone, which is typically higher in men than in women (see Chapter 11), in young men than in older men, and in violent criminals than in nonviolent criminals (Dabbs et al., 1995).

Testosterone doesn't cause aggression directly, but it does seem to prepare men for aggressing by making them feel extremely powerful and overconfident in their ability to prevail in a fight. Male chimpanzees with high testosterone tend to stand tall and hold their chins high (Muller & Wrangham, 2004), and human beings with high testosterone walk more purposefully, focus more directly on the people they are talking to, and speak in a more forward and independent manner (Dabbs, Bernieri, Strong, Campo, & Milun, 2001). Not only does testosterone cause men to feel confident and powerful but it also leaves them feeling easily irritated and frustrated (Dabbs, Strong, & Milun, 1997). A journalist who took a testosterone injection described an incident that began when he gave his wayward dog a swat on the hindquarters:

> "Don't smack your dog!" yelled a burly guy a few yards away. What I found myself yelling back at him is not printable in this magazine, but I have never used that language in public before, let alone bellowed it at the top of my voice. He shouted back, and within seconds I was actually close to hitting him. He backed down and slunk off. I strutted home, chest puffed up, contrite beagle dragged sheepishly behind me. It wasn't until half an hour later that I realized I had been a complete jerk and had nearly gotten into the first public brawl of my life (Sullivan, 2000).

As this incident suggests, when men aggress, it is often in response to perceived challenges or threats—not to their lives or their resources, but to their dominance and their status. Indeed, three quarters of all murders can be classified as "status competitions" or "contests to save face" (Daly & Wilson, 1988). Contrary to popular wisdom, men with unrealistically *high* self-regard—and not *low* self-regard—are most prone to violence because such men are especially likely to perceive others' actions as a challenge to their inflated sense of their own status (Baumeister, Smart, & Loden, 1996).

Although women can be just as aggressive as men, their aggression tends to be more premeditated than impulsive and more likely to be focused on attaining or protecting a resource than on attaining or protecting their status. Women are *much* less likely than men to aggress without provocation or to aggress in ways that cause physical injury, but they are only *slightly* less likely than men to aggress when provoked or to aggress in ways that cause psychological injury (Bettencourt & Miller, 1996; Eagly & Steffen, 1986). Indeed, women may even be *more* likely than men to aggress by causing social harm—for example, by ostracizing others or by spreading malicious rumors about them (Crick & Grotpeter, 1995).

Perhaps William James (1911, p. 272) was right when he wrote that "our ancestors have bred pugnacity into our bone and marrow and thousands of years of peace won't breed it out of us." But just because aggression is part of our evolutionary past doesn't mean that it has to be part of our future. Cultures can effectively encourage or discourage aggression, which is why violent crime rates vary so much between otherwise similar countries, such as the United States and Canada. Even within a country, aggression has a distinct cultural geography. For example, violent crime in the United States is much more prevalent in the South, where men are taught to react aggressively when they feel their status has been challenged (Nisbett & Cohen, 1996). In one set of experiments, researchers Dov Cohen, Richard Nisbett, and their colleagues insulted volunteers from northern and southern states and found that the southerners were more likely to feel that their status had been diminished by the insult (Cohen et al., 1996). The southerners also experienced a greater increase in testosterone than did the northerners, and they were physically more assertive when a 6-foot 3-inch, 250-pound man got in their way as they left the experimental room. People learn by example, and when cultures exemplify violence, violence increases measurably. Despite what the film and game industries may claim, studies clearly show that watching violent television shows and playing violent video games makes people more aggressive (Anderson & Bushman, 2001) and less cooperative (Sheese & Graziano, 2005).

On the other hand, when cultures exemplify peaceful behavior, aggression decreases. For example, in the mid-1980s, an unusual disease killed the aggressive males in a particular troop of wild baboons in Kenya, leaving only the less aggressive males to reproduce. A decade later, researchers discovered that a new "culture" had emerged among the descendants of the peaceful males. This new generation of male baboons were less aggressive, they groomed and affiliated with females, they were more tolerant of low-ranking males, and they showed fewer signs of physiological stress (Sapolsky & Share, 2004). If baboons can learn to get along, then surely people can too.

Cooperation

Physical prowess may enable individuals to win conflicts over resources, but when individuals work together, they can often attain more resources for themselves than either could have attained alone. **Cooperation** is *behavior by two or more individuals that leads to mutual benefit* (Deutsch, 1949; Pruitt, 1998), and it is one of our species' greatest achievements—right up there with language, fire, and opposable thumbs (Axelrod, 1984; Axelrod & Hamilton, 1981). Every roadway and supermarket, every television and compact disc, every ballet and surgery is the result of cooperation, and it is difficult to think of an important human achievement that could have occurred without it.

If the benefits of cooperation are plentiful and clear, then why don't people cooperate all the time? The answer is that cooperation is *risky,* as a simple game called *the prisoner's dilemma* illustrates. Imagine that you and your friend have been arrested for bank robbery and are being interrogated separately. The detectives tell you that if you and your friend both confess, you'll each get 10 years in prison, and if you both refuse to confess, you'll each get 1 year in prison. However, if one of you confesses and the other doesn't, then the one who confesses will go free and the one who doesn't confess will be put away for 30 years. What should you do? If you study **FIGURE 16.2** on the next page, you'll see that you and your friend would be wise to cooperate. If you trust your friend and refuse to confess and if your friend trusts you and does the same, then you will both get a light sentence. But if you refuse to confess and your friend betrays you by confessing, then your friend gets to go home and wash his car while you spend the next few decades making license plates.

"What's amazing to me is that this late in the game we _still_ have to settle our differences with rocks."

COOPERATION Behavior by two or more individuals that leads to mutual benefit.

Figure 16.2 The Prisoner's Dilemma Game The prisoner's dilemma game illustrates the benefits and costs of cooperation. Players A and B receive benefits whose size depends on whether they independently decide to cooperate. Mutual cooperation leads to a relatively moderate benefit to both players, but if only one player cooperates, then the cooperator gets no benefit and the noncooperator gets a large benefit.

	COOPERATION (B does not confess)	NONCOOPERATION (B confesses)
COOPERATION (A does not confess)	A gets 1 year B gets 1 year	A gets 30 years B gets 0 years
NONCOOPERATION (A confesses)	A gets 0 years B gets 30 years	A gets 10 years B gets 10 years

The prisoner's dilemma is interesting because it mirrors the risks and benefits of cooperation in everyday life. For example, if everyone pays his or her taxes, then the tax rate stays low and everyone enjoys the benefits of sturdy bridges and first-rate museums. If no one pays taxes, then the bridges fall down and the museums shut their doors. There is clearly a *moderate* benefit to everyone if everyone pays taxes, but there is a *huge* benefit to the few noncooperators who don't pay taxes while everyone else does because they get to use the bridges and enjoy the museums while keeping their entire incomes. This dilemma makes it difficult for people to decide whether to pay taxes and risk being chumps or to cheat and risk having the bridges collapse and the museums shut down. If you are like most people, you would be perfectly willing to cooperate in this sort of dilemma but you worry that others won't do the same. So what can you do to minimize your risks?

First, you can learn to tell when someone is cheating, and some studies suggest that people have a finely honed ability to do just that. In the Wason card-selection task (shown in **FIGURE 16.3**), participants are asked to turn over two cards to test for violations of an abstract rule of the form "If P, then Q." Logic dictates that best way to test for violations in this case is to turn over the cards marked P and Not Q. But because people have a mindbug called the *hypothesis-confirming bias,* only about 25% of the participants turn over the correct cards, and most turn over the cards marked P and Q. People find this abstract logical exercise quite difficult. But when participants are asked to determine whether a *cheater* is violating a social rule that has precisely the same form—for example, "If the man is drinking beer (P), then he is over 21 (Q)"—the number of participants who turn over the correct cards nearly triples (Cosmides, 1989). There is some controversy about why this happens (Cheng & Holyoak, 1989; Fodor, 2000; Gigerenzer & Hug, 1992), but one explanation is that human beings have a uniquely powerful capacity to detect cheaters that surpasses their capacity for logical reasoning in general. People not only detect cheaters but they also have a powerful reaction to them. The *ultimatum game* requires one player (the divider) to divide a monetary prize into two parts and offer one of the parts to a second player (the decider), who can either accept or reject the offer. If the decider rejects the offer, then both players get nothing and the game is over. Studies show that deciders typically reject offers

Figure 16.3 The Wason Card-Selection Task In the Wason card-selection task, participants are asked to turn over two cards to test a rule of the form "If P, then Q." Logic dictates that they should turn over the card that says P and the card that says Not Q (top row). Studies show that very few people pick the correct cards. For example, when asked to determine whether a card with a vowel on one side has an even number on the other side (middle row), most people turn over E and 4 rather than E and 7. However, when the rule is a social rule (bottom row), people do much better. For instance, when people are shown the set of cards in the bottom row and are asked to turn over two cards to determine whether it is true that "anyone at the bar who is drinking beer is over 21," people usually pick the correct cards—Beer and 16—because they realize that turning over Coke and 25 will provide no information about whether a minor is drinking. The problems are logically identical, so why does it seem so easy in one case and so hard in another?

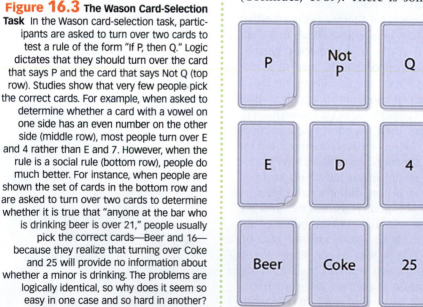

that they consider unfair because they'd rather get nothing than get cheated (Fehr & Gaechter, 2002; Thaler, 1988). Indeed, even nonhuman primates object to being cheated by an experimenter. In one study, monkeys were willing to work for a slice of cucumber before—but not after—they saw the experimenter give another monkey a more delicious food for doing less work (Brosnan & DeWaal, 2003).

Kevin Hart owns the Gator Motel in Fargo, Georgia, which he runs on an honor system: Guests arrive, stay as long as they like, and leave their payment on the dresser. If just a few people cheated, it would not affect the room rates, but if too many cheated, then prices would have to rise. How would you decide whether to pay or to cheat? Before answering this question, please notice the large dog.

Altruism

When people cooperate, they can realize great benefits. But is cooperation always driven by self-interest? Although human beings and other animals appear to engage in **altruism**, which is *behavior that benefits another without benefiting oneself,* such behavior often benefits the apparent altruist in subtle ways. For example, birds and squirrels give "alarm calls" when they see a predator, which puts them at increased risk of being eaten but allows their fellow birds and squirrels to escape. Ants and bees spend their lives caring for the offspring of the queen rather than bearing offspring of their own. Although such behaviors may appear to be altruistic, they are actually self-interested because individuals who promote the survival of their relatives are promoting the survival of their own genes (Hamilton, 1964). **Kin selection** is *the process by which evolution selects for genes that cause individuals to provide benefits to their relatives,* and research shows that animals are much more "altruistic" toward their own kin. The squirrels that give alarm calls are those that are most closely related to the other squirrels with which they live (Maynard-Smith, 1965). Honeybees may raise the queen's offspring, but as it turns out, an odd genetic quirk makes honeybees more closely related to the queen's offspring than they would be to their own. In short, nonhuman animals cooperate with relatives, but cooperating with relatives is not necessarily altruistic.

Not all cooperation takes place between closely related individuals. For example, male baboons will risk injury to help an unrelated baboon win a fight, and monkeys will spend time grooming unrelated monkeys when they could be looking out for themselves. Such behaviors may appear to be instances of noble generosity, but careful studies of primates have revealed that the individuals who perform such favors tend to receive favors in return. **Reciprocal altruism** is *behavior that benefits another with the expectation that those benefits will be returned in the future,* and despite the second word in its name, it isn't very altruistic at all (Trivers, 1972b). Indeed, reciprocal altruism is merely cooperation extended over long periods of time.

So what about people? Like other animals, people are generally willing to contribute to the benefit of others in direct proportion to their degree of relatedness (Burnstein, Crandall, & Kitayama, 1994). Unlike other animals, however, human beings are also willing to provide benefits to complete strangers who will never be able to return the favor (Batson, 2002). As the World Trade Center burned on the morning of September 11, 2001, civilians in sailboats headed *toward* the destruction rather than away from it, initiating the largest waterborne evacuation in the history of the United States. As one observer remarked, "If you're out on the water in a pleasure craft and you see those buildings on fire, in a strictly rational sense you should head to New Jersey. Instead, people

ALTRUISM Behavior that benefits another without benefiting oneself.

KIN SELECTION The process by which evolution selects for genes that cause individuals to provide benefits to their relatives.

RECIPROCAL ALTRUISM Behavior that benefits another with the expectation that those benefits will be returned in the future.

Ground squirrels put themselves in danger when they warn others about predators, but those they warn share their genes, so the behavior is not truly altruistic. In contrast, Christine Karg-Palreiro anonymously donated her kidney to an unrelated individual in 2003 and later remarked, "If I had a spare, I'd do it again." The United Network for Organ Sharing reports that in the past 20 years, more than 100 people have made anonymous organ donations to strangers.

GROUP A collection of two or more people who believe they have something in common.

PREJUDICE A positive or negative evaluation of another person based on their group membership.

DISCRIMINATION Positive or negative behavior toward another person based on their group membership.

IN-GROUP A human category of which a person is a member.

OUT-GROUP A human category of which a person is not a member.

DEINDIVIDUATION A phenomenon that occurs when immersion in a group causes people to become less aware of their individual values.

SOCIAL LOAFING The tendency for people to expend less effort when in a group than alone.

BYSTANDER INTERVENTION The act of helping strangers in an emergency situation.

DIFFUSION OF RESPONSIBILITY The tendency for individuals to feel diminished responsibility for their actions when they are surrounded by others who are acting the same way.

GROUP POLARIZATION The tendency for a group's initial leaning to get stronger over time.

went into potential danger and rescued strangers. That's social" (Dreifus, 2003). Indeed, heroism may be uncommon but it is not unheard of, which is to say that human beings are clearly capable of genuine altruism. Some studies even suggest that we tend to underestimate just how altruistic most people really are (Miller & Ratner, 1998).

Groups

People benefit from cooperation, but how does cooperation ever get started in the first place? After all, cooperation requires that someone take an initial risk by benefiting an individual who has not yet benefited them and then *trust* that that individual will someday repay the favor. Human beings have developed a remarkably inventive way to minimize the risk of initial cooperation, and it is called the **group**, which is *a collection of two or more people who believe they have something in common*. Every one of us is a member of many such groups. We refer to the smaller ones as families and teams, and we refer to the larger ones as religions and nations.

Although there are profound differences between such groups, they all seem to have one thing in common: The people in them tend to display **prejudice**, which is *a positive or negative evaluation of another person based on their group membership,* and **discrimination**, which is *positive or negative behavior toward another person based on their group membership*. Specifically, people tend to be positively prejudiced toward members of their own groups, they tend to discriminate in favor of their own groups, and they tend to expect that their fellow group members will do the same for them in the future (see the Where Do You Stand? box on page 660). Because people favor members of their own groups, group membership allows people to know in advance who is most and least likely to repay their efforts to cooperate, and this knowledge reduces the risks of cooperation.

Research shows that people do indeed favor members of the **in-group**, *a human category of which a person is a member,* more than they favor members of the **out-group**, *a human category of which a person is not a member* (Sumner, 1906), and that it doesn't take much to create this kind of favoritism. In one set of studies, participants were shown abstract paintings by two artists and were then divided into two groups based on their preference for one artist or the other (Tajfel, 1970; Tajfel et al., 1971). When participants were subsequently asked to allocate money to other participants, they consistently allocated more money to those in their group (Brewer, 1979). Indeed, participants show positive prejudice and discrimination even when they are randomly assigned to completely meaningless groups such as "Group X" and "Group Y" (Hodson & Sorrentino, 2001; Locksley, Ortiz, & Hepburn, 1980). In other words, just knowing that "I'm one of *us* and not one of *them*" seems sufficient to produce this kind of favoritism. Just as people feel positively about and act positively toward members of their own groups, they think negatively about and act negatively toward members of other groups (Hewstone, Rubin, & Willis, 2002), and this happens even when group membership is determined by nothing more meaningful than a coin flip (Locksley et al., 1980).

Why do people have negative prejudice toward members of out-groups? First, derogating the out-group can raise our self-esteem. If we see the out-group as lazy, immoral, and stupid, it makes it all that much easier to see the in-group (and that includes us!) as industrious, virtuous, and wise (Crocker & Luhtanen, 1990; Fein & Spencer, 1997; Lemyre & Smith, 1985). Second, groups often compete for scarce resources, and if we see the out-group as lazy, immoral, and stupid, it makes it all that much easier to justify treating them badly. In fact, research has shown that putting groups into competition for scarce resources is one of the very best ways to ensure that they will be prejudiced and discriminate against each other (Campbell, 1965; Sherif et al., 1961).

In 1935, Rubin Stacy was lynched by a mob of masked men after allegedly assaulting a White woman. What effect might wearing masks have on members of a mob?

Prejudice and discrimination may sound bad, but groups are capable of much worse things, such as riots, lynchings, gang rapes, and stampedes (Milgram & Toch, 1968). If we take death and destruction as our measure, then a group of humans is clearly among the most dangerous of all natural phenomena. Why do people in groups do dreadful things that few (if any) of their individual members would ever do alone? This is a particularly compelling mindbug: Law-abiding, rational individuals often behave differently when they start hanging around together in a group. There are at least three reasons for this:

- Everyone has urges and impulses that they hold in check. We may want to slap the guy who blasts his music on the bus, grab the Rolex from the jeweler's window, or plant a kiss on the attractive stranger in the library, but we don't do these things because we have self-control and scruples. Research has shown that people are most likely to exert self-control and adhere to their scruples when their attention is focused on themselves (Wicklund, 1975), which is why people are less likely to cheat when they can see themselves in a mirror (Diener & Wallbom, 1976; Vallacher & Solodky, 1979). When people assemble in groups, their attention is naturally drawn to others and *away* from themselves, and thus they are less likely to abide by their own moral values (Mullen, 1986; Mullen, Chapman, & Peaugh, 1989; Wegner & Schaefer, 1978). There's a name for this kind of shift in focus: **Deindividuation** occurs *when immersion in a group causes people to become less aware of their individual values.*

- Groups can diminish our sense of personal responsibility for our own actions. For example, **social loafing** occurs when *people expend less effort when in a group than alone*. People applaud less loudly when they are in a large audience than a small one (Latane, Williams, & Harkins, 1979), and athletes exert less effort in team events than in solo events (Williams et al., 1989). People in groups leave worse tips at restaurants (Freeman et al., 1975), donate less money to charitable causes (Wiesenthal, Austrom, & Silverman, 1983), and are less likely to respond when someone says hello (Jones & Foshay, 1984). Studies of **bystander intervention**— which is *the act of helping strangers in an emergency situation*—reveal that bystanders are less likely to step forward and help an innocent person in distress when there are many other bystanders present (Darley & Latané, 1968; Latane & Nida, 1981). When a young woman named Kitty Genovese was stabbed to death in view of 38 witnesses who did nothing to help her, the newspapers blamed urban apathy. But research revealed that the witnesses were not apathetic—they'd simply assumed that one of the *other* bystanders was more responsible for calling the police than they were. **Diffusion of responsibility** occurs when *individuals feel diminished responsibility for their actions because they are surrounded by others who are acting the same way.*

- It is said that two heads are better than one, but studies suggest that groups tend to make decisions that are about as good as the decision made by the average member—or *worse* (Gigone & Hastie, 1997; Hill, 1982; Levine & Moreland, 1998). One reason for this is that groups tend to spend most of their time talking about the *common information* that all members share rather than the *unique information* that only a few members possess (Larson, Foster-Fishman, & Keys, 1994; Stasser & Titus, 1985). One member of a student entertainment committee may know a lot about a restaurant's cuisine ("Superb!"), and another may know a lot about its loudspeaker system ("Amazing!"), but if every member of the committee knows about the restaurant's location ("A bit far away"), then location may be weighted too heavily in the group's decision—despite the fact that it may be the least relevant piece of information (Gigone & Hastie, 1996).

Groups may also make poor decisions because their leaders can be extraordinarily influential despite the fact that they are not necessarily well informed (Hollander, 1964). You might expect that mixing a lot of people who have one opinion with a few people who have the opposite opinion would lead a group to moderate its views, but, in fact, the result is often **group polarization**, which is *the tendency for a group's*

Groups can lead people to feel deindividuated and hence less responsible for their actions. What are the chances that any of these individuals would stroll through the mall naked if they were alone?

In the 1957 film *Twelve Angry Men*, a jury is prepared to convict an innocent teenager of murder until one lone juror bravely voices his disagreement and ultimately changes the other jurors' minds. Alas, it is all too rare for group members who hold minority opinions to change—or even to try to change—the decision of a group.

initial leaning to get stronger over time (Lamm & Myers, 1978). After a bit of group discussion, an initial opinion of, "That's a pretty good idea," becomes, "This is the greatest idea we've ever had!" Some psychologists have suggested that groups make poor decisions because group members are so concerned with preserving group cohesiveness that they fail to challenge each other's ideas and suggestions (Janis, 1982), but not much evidence supports this *groupthink hypothesis* (Esser, 1998; Kramer, 1998).

The misbehavior of groups is so well documented that one psychologist was moved to write an article titled "Humans Would Be Better without Groups" (Buys, 1978). A provocative claim, to be sure, but ultimately a false one. Psychologists are more intrigued by the mindbugs of group failures than the seamless synchrony of group successes precisely because the latter are so much more common. For every street gang that murders an innocent victim, there are many civic groups that clean trash from a neighborhood park; for every bloody riot, there are many peaceful protests; and for every stampede, there are more than a few parades. Groups provide more benefits than costs, so it is not surprising that our species has developed a need for belonging to groups that is every bit as fundamental as our need for eating, drinking, and sleeping (Baumeister & Leary, 1995).

In fact, one of the very best predictors of a person's general happiness and life satisfaction is the quality and extent of their social relationships and group memberships (Myers & Diener, 1995), and people who are excluded from groups are invariably anxious, lonely, depressed, and at increased risk for illness and premature death (Cacioppo, Hawkley, & Berntson, 2003; Cohen, 1988; Leary, 1990). Indeed, recent studies reveal that being excluded from a group activates areas of the brain that are normally activated by physical pain (Eisenberger, Lieberman, & Williams, 2003). Belonging is not just a source of psychological and physical well-being but also a source of identity (Tajfel & Turner, 1986), which is why people typically describe themselves by listing the groups of which they are members ("I'm a Canadian, an architect, and a mother of two"). Groups are a way to lower the risks of cooperation and increase the odds of survival, but they are more than that. We are not merely *in* our groups: We *are* our groups.

A recent study revealed that when people are excluded from a social group, (a) the anterior cingulate cortex (ACC) and (b) the right ventral prefrontal cortex (RVPC) become active. Interestingly, the ACC is commonly associated with the experience of physical pain and the RVPC is commonly associated with pain relief. Apparently, social exclusion causes people to feel pain and to make an effort to diminish it.

Eisenberger, N. I., Lieberman, M. D., & Williams, K. D. (2003). *Science, 302,* 290–292.

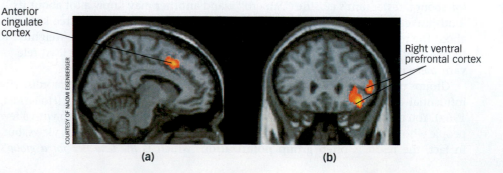

Anterior cingulate cortex

Right ventral prefrontal cortex

(a)   (b)

Reproduction: The Quest for Immortality

Survival matters. But from an evolutionary point of view, survival only matters because it is a prerequisite for reproduction. A vehicle for genes must stay alive in order to build the next vehicle, so it is not surprising that our urge to reproduce—which involves everything from having sex to raising children—is every bit as strong as our urge to stay alive. Indeed, a great deal of our social behavior can be understood in terms of our basic reproductive drive (Buss & Kenrick, 1998).

Selectivity

Survival is the first step on the road to reproduction, but the second step involves finding someone of the opposite sex who has taken the first step too. You need only look around whatever room you are in to know that not just anyone will do. People *select* their reproductive and sexual partners, and perhaps the most striking fact about this selection is that women are more selective than men (Feingold, 1992a). In one study, an attractive person (who was working for the experimenters) approached an opposite-sex stranger on a college campus and asked one of two questions: "Would you go out tonight?" or, "Would you go to bed with me?" About half of the men and women who were approached agreed to go out with the attractive person. Although *none* of the women agreed to go to bed with the person, *three quarters* of the men did (Clark & Hatfield, 1989).

What makes women the choosier sex? One explanation focuses on differences in male and female reproductive biology (Buss & Schmitt, 1993; Trivers, 1972a). Men produce billions of sperm in their lifetimes, their ability to conceive a child tomorrow is not inhibited by having conceived one today, and conception has no significant physical costs. On the other hand, women produce a small number of eggs in their lifetimes, conception eliminates their ability to conceive for at least 9 more months, and pregnancy produces physical changes that increase their nutritional requirements and put them at risk of illness and death. Therefore, if a man makes an "evolutionary mistake" by mating with a woman whose genes do not produce healthy offspring or who won't do her part to raise them, he has lost nothing except a few sperm. But if a woman makes the same mistake by mating with a man whose genes do not produce healthy offspring or who won't do his part to raise them, she has lost a precious egg, borne the costs of pregnancy, risked her life in childbirth, and missed at least 9 months of other reproductive opportunities. Women are naturally more selective because reproduction is much more costly for women than for men.

Although reproductive biology makes sex a more expensive proposition for women than for men, it is important to note two things. First, women are more selective than men *on average,* but there is still tremendous variability *among* men and *among* women (Gangestad & Simpson, 2000). We've described the typical reproductive strategies of *most* women and men but certainly not the strategy of any particular woman or man. Second, like biology, social norms can also make sex differentially expensive for women and men and can thereby increase or decrease gender differences in selectivity (Eagly & Wood, 1999). For example, in cultures that glorify promiscuous men as *playboys* and disparage promiscuous women as *sluts,* women are likely to be much more selective than men because the reputational costs of sex are much higher. When cultures lower the costs of sex for women by providing access to effective birth control, by promoting the financial independence of women, or by adopting communal styles of child-rearing, women do indeed become less selective (Kasser & Sharma, 1999). Similarly, when sex is expensive for men—for example, when they are choosing a long-term mate for a monogamous relationship rather than a short-term mate for a weekend in Vermont—they can be every bit as selective as women (Kenrick, Sadalla, Groth, & Troste, 1990). Our basic biology generally makes sex a more expensive proposition for women than for men, but social forces can exaggerate, equalize, or reverse those costs. The higher the costs, the greater the selectivity.

If men could become pregnant, how might their behavior change? Among seahorses, it is the male that carries the young, and not coincidentally, males are more selective than are females.

DR. PAUL ZAHL/PHOTO RESEARCHERS

CREATAS IMAGES/PICTUREQUEST

MERE EXPOSURE EFFECT The tendency for liking to increase with the frequency of exposure.

Attraction

For most of us, there are a very small number of people with whom we are willing to have sex, an even smaller number of people with whom we are willing to have children, and a staggeringly large number of people with whom we are unwilling to have either. So when we meet someone new, how do we decide which of these categories they belong in? Many things go into choosing a date, a lover, or a partner for life, but perhaps none is more important than the simple feeling we call *attraction* (Berscheid & Reiss, 1998). Sonnets and symphonies have been written about this feeling, wars have been waged and kingdoms have been lost over it. It may be difficult to describe the feeling with precision, but one thing about it is perfectly clear: Some people cause us to experience it and others do not. Research suggests that attraction is caused by a wide range of factors that can be roughly divided into the situational, the physical, and the psychological.

Situational factors. One of the best predictors of any kind of interpersonal relationship is the physical proximity of the people involved (Nahemow & Lawton, 1975). For example, in one study, students who had been randomly assigned to university housing were asked to name their three closest friends, and nearly half named their next-door neighbor (Festinger, Schachter, & Back, 1950). We tend to think that we select our friends and romantic partners on the basis of their personalities, appearances, and so on—and we do—but we only get to select from the pool of people whom we have met, and the likelihood of meeting a potential partner naturally increases with proximity. Before you ever start auditioning and ruling out potential mates, geography has already ruled out 99.999% of the world's population for you. Proximity not only provides the opportunity for attraction but it also provides the motivation. People naturally work hard to like those with whom they expect to have social interactions (Darley & Berscheid, 1967). When new neighbors move into the apartment next door, you know your day-to-day existence will be better if you like them than if you detest them, and so you make every effort to like them. In fact, the closer they live, the more effort you make.

Proximity provides something else as well. Every time we encounter a person, that person becomes a bit more familiar to us, and people—like other animals—generally prefer familiar to novel stimuli. *The tendency for liking to increase with the frequency of exposure* is called the **mere exposure effect** (Bornstein, 1989; Zajonc, 1968), and it is so powerful that it even occurs when we don't know we've been exposed to it. For instance, in some experiments, geometric shapes, faces, or alphabetical characters were flashed on a computer screen so quickly that participants were unaware of having seen them. These participants were then shown some of the "old" stimuli that had been flashed across the screen as well as some "new" stimuli that had not. Although they could not reliably tell which stimuli were old and which were new, participants tended to *like* the old stimuli better than the new ones (Monahan, Murphy, & Zajonc, 2000). In other words, the mere act of being exposed to some things (rather than others) in the environment led to increased liking for those things.

Proximity exposes us to certain people on a regular basis, and being exposed causes those people to feel familiar to us and hence increases our liking of them (Brockner & Swap, 1976). This effect can have some unusual consequences. In one study, police trainees who lined up alphabetically at the start of each class ended up being most attracted to other trainees whose surnames began with letters that were the same as (or close to) the first letters of their own surnames (Segal, 1974). We might like to think that attraction is determined solely by the qualities of the people involved, but research demonstrates that it is often the result of geographical accidents that put people in the same place at the same time.

Of course, some places and times are better than others. What kinds of situations promote attraction? You may recall from Chapter 10 that people can misinterpret physiological arousal as a sign of attraction (Byrne et al., 1975; Schachter & Singer, 1962). In one study, experimenters observed men as they crossed a swaying suspension bridge. A young woman who was actually working for the experimenters approached the men either when they were in the middle of the bridge or after they

In 2003, actress Carol Channing (then 82) married the boy next door—her childhood sweetheart, Harry Kullijian (then 83). Research on proximity and attraction suggests that Carol and Harry had a good chance of ending up together, though in this case it seems to have taken a while.

AP PHOTO/SAN FRANCISCO CHRONICLE, DEANNE FITZMAURICE

The woman pictured here prefers the photograph on the right, but her husband prefers the one on the left. Why? The photograph on the left is printed normally and the one on the right is printed in reverse. Because we tend to see ourselves mostly in the mirror, reverse-printed photographs look to us more like the image we are used to seeing (Mita, Dermer, & Knight, 1977). Because of the mere exposure effect, people tend to favor reverse-printed photographs of themselves.

had finished crossing it. The woman asked the men to complete a survey, and after they did so, she gave each man her telephone number and offered to explain her project in greater detail if he called. The men who had met the woman in the middle of the swaying bridge were much more likely to call than were the men who had met the woman only after they had crossed the bridge (Dutton & Aron, 1974). Why? The men experienced more physiological arousal when they completed the questionnaire on the suspension bridge, and some of those men mistook that arousal for attraction. Apparently, a sheer blouse and a sheer drop have similar effects on men, who easily confuse the two (see the Real World box on the next page).

Physical factors. Once people are in the same place at the same time, they can begin to learn about each other's personal qualities, and in most cases, the first quality they learn about is the other person's appearance. You know from experience that a person's appearance influences your attraction toward that person, but research suggests that this influence is stronger than most of us might suspect. In one study, Elaine Walster and her colleagues arranged a dance for first-year university students and randomly assigned each student to an opposite-sex partner. Midway through the dance, the students confidentially reported how much they liked their partner, how attractive they thought their partner was, and how much they would like to see their partner again. The researchers measured many of the students' attributes—from their attitudes to their personalities—and they found that the partner's physical appearance was the *only* attribute that influenced the students' feelings of attraction (Walster et al., 1966). Field studies have revealed the same thing. For instance, one study found that a man's height and a woman's weight were among the best predictors of how many responses a personal ad received (Lynn & Shurgot, 1984), and another study found that physical attractiveness was the *only* factor that predicted the online dating choices of both women and men (Green, Buchanan, & Heuer, 1984).

Physical beauty is important in just about every interpersonal context (Etcoff, 1999; Langlois et al., 2000). Beautiful people have more friends, more dates, more sex, and more fun than the rest of us do (Curran & Lippold, 1975), and they can even expect to earn 10% more money over the courses of their lives (Hamermesh & Biddle, 1994). People tend to believe that beautiful people have superior personal qualities (Dion, Berscheid, & Walster, 1972; Eagly et al., 1991), and in some cases they actually do. For instance, because beautiful people have more friends and more opportunities for social interaction, they tend to have better social skills than do less beautiful people (Feingold, 1992b). Beauty is so powerful that it even influences how mothers treat their own children: Mothers of attractive children are more affectionate and playful with their children compared to mothers of less attractive children (Langlois et al., 1995). It is interesting to note that although men and women are equally influenced by the beauty of their potential partners, men are more likely than women to acknowledge this fact (Feingold, 1990).

Research on how people misinterpret their arousal may help explain why Brandon Harding proposed marriage (and why Melani Dino said yes) right after they finished skydiving in Snohomish, Washington.

In a commercial for Pantene hair products, model Kelly LeBrock pleaded with viewers, "Don't hate me because I'm beautiful." Research on the power of physical attractiveness suggests that there was not much danger of that happening.

{ THE REAL WORLD } An Affair to Remember

ROMANCE TURNS US ALL INTO PUBLICITY hounds. First we show our friends photographs of the new person we've been dating, then we let everyone have a good look at the engagement ring, then we make a public spectacle of getting married, and finally we end up wearing matching T-shirts and golf caps. Couples usually take great delight in broadcasting their togetherness, but not *all* relationships are so eager to be advertised. If you happen to be dating your best friend's ex, your best friend's spouse, or either of your best friend's parents, then the two of you have probably decided that the rest of the world really doesn't need to know about it. Research suggests that such secret relationships are psychologically special. Whether they end up being milestones or millstones, delightful or destructive, these are the relationships that people look back on most often (Wegner, Lane, & Dimitri, 1994). But are secret relationships special because we tend to have such relationships with special people, or does their secrecy itself make them seem more special than they actually are?

In a study designed to investigate this question, Daniel Wegner and his colleagues invited two men and two women to play a card game in the laboratory. Each woman was paired with one of the men, and the two teams sat down to play against each other. The experimenter claimed to be studying nonverbal communication, and so before the game began, he asked one of the couples to touch their feet together. The experimenter told the couple that throughout the game, they should keep their feet in constant contact to exchange signals about which cards to play. In the *nonsecret* condition, both couples were aware that one of the couples was doing this, but in the *secret* condition, the couple playing footsie was

AP PHOTO

White House intern Monica Lewinsky and President Bill Clinton had a secret romantic relationship. If they hadn't been forced to hide their relationship from the public, would they have found each other so attractive?

instructed in private not to let the other couple find out what they were up to. After the game was over, the participants rated each other in private. The results showed that the couple who had played footsie found each other much more attractive when they'd been forced to keep their under-the-table shenanigans a secret (Wegner et al., 1994).

But *why* does secrecy make relationships so darn spicy?

- *Forbidden fruit:* Sometimes things seem most appealing when they're least available. Secret relationships are often secret because they involve people with whom romance is forbidden. Research shows that when potential partners are made unavailable, our attraction to them often grows (Pennebaker et al., 1979; Walster et al., 1973). Indeed, when parents try to keep young people

apart, they usually become more—and not less—attracted to each other (Driscoll, Davis, & Lipetz, 1972).

- *Risky business:* A key feature of secret relationships is that they always run the risk of discovery, and this fact can have several consequences. For example, when we risk losing our friendships and reputations by having a secret romance, we may be compelled to justify our behavior by overvaluing the relationship (Aronson & Mills, 1958). In addition, the prospect of "getting caught" can itself be quite arousing, and it is all too easy to misattribute that arousal to the attractiveness of a secret partner (Dienstbier, 1979).

- *Mental boomerang:* Our thoughts have a way of doing precisely the opposite of what we want them to do. Just as we often cannot recall the things we most want to remember, we often find ourselves remembering the things we want least to recall (see Chapter 8). One of the best ways to keep a secret is not to think about it in the presence of others, but attempts to suppress thoughts often backfire and lead us to become obsessed with the very things we are trying not to think about (Wegner, 1994). Indeed, when people are instructed to suppress thoughts of a romantic relationship, they tend to find those relationships more exciting (Wegner & Gold, 1995).

In short, research suggests that secret relationships derive some of their allure from the very fact of their secrecy. So the next time someone you like asks if you'll go out with them, you might just smile and say, "Only if you promise not to tell."

So it pays to be beautiful. But what exactly constitutes beauty? Those of us who are less than perfect like to think that beauty is in the eye of the beholder. Although standards of beauty do indeed vary from person to person and culture to culture, many aspects of physical appearance seem to be universally appreciated or disdained (Cunningham et al., 1995). For example:

- Male bodies are considered most attractive when they approximate an inverted triangle (i.e., broad shoulders with a narrow waist and hips), and female bodies are considered most attractive when they approximate an hourglass (i.e., broad shoulders and hips with a narrow waist). In fact, the most attractive female body across many cultures seems to be the "perfect hourglass" in which the waist is precisely 70% the size of the hips (Singh, 1993).

- Human faces and human bodies are generally considered more attractive when they are *bilaterally symmetrical*—that is, when the left half is a mirror image of the right (Perrett et al., 1999).

- Characteristics such as large eyes, high eyebrows, and a small chin make people look immature or "baby-faced" (Berry & McArthur, 1985). As a general rule, female faces are considered more attractive when they have immature features, but male faces are considered more attractive when they have mature features (Cunningham, Barbee, & Pike, 1990; Zebrowitz & Montepare, 1992).

Is there any rhyme or reason to this list of scenic attractions? The evolutionary perspective suggests that we should be attracted to people who have the *genes* and the propensity for *parental behavior* that will enable our children to grow, prosper, and become parents themselves. In other words, the things we find attractive in others should be reasonably reliable indicators of their genetic qualities and parental tendencies. Are they?

- Testosterone causes male bodies to become "inverted triangles" just as estrogen causes female bodies to become "hourglasses." Men who are high in testosterone tend to be socially dominant and therefore have more resources to devote to their offspring, whereas women who are high in estrogen tend to be especially fertile and potentially have more offspring to make use of those resources. In other words, body shape is an indicator of male dominance and female fertility. In fact, women who have the "perfect hourglass" figure tend to bear healthier children than do women with other waist-to-hip ratios (Singh, 1993).

- Asymmetrical features can be signs of genetic mutation, prenatal exposure to pathogens, or susceptibility to disease (Jones et al., 2001; Thornhill & Gangestad, 1993), so physical symmetry is an indicator of overall health. People not only *prefer* symmetrical features, but they are expert at detecting it. For instance, women can discriminate symmetrical and asymmetrical men *by smell,* and their preference for symmetrical men is more pronounced when they are ovulating (Thornhill & Gangestad, 1999).

- Younger women are generally more fertile than older women, whereas older men generally have more resources than younger men. Thus, a youthful appearance is a signal of a woman's ability to bear children, just as a mature appearance is a signal of a man's ability to raise them. Studies have shown that women prefer older men and men prefer younger women across a wide variety of human cultures (Buss, 1989).

The evolutionary perspective suggests that the feeling we call *attraction* is simply our genes' way of telling us that we are in the presence of a person who has both the genes and the propensity toward parental behavior to make those genes immortal. It is no coincidence that people in different epochs and people in different cultures appreciate many of the same features in the opposite sex.

Artists have been sculpting and painting the Three Graces for thousands of years, and the body types they depict show how standards of beauty change across time. Nonetheless, research suggests that even as the size of the ideal female changes across time, the ideal hip-to-waist ratio remains constant (Singh, 1993).

RÉUNION DES MUSÉES NATIONAUX/ART RESOURCE, NY

ERICH LESSING/ART RESOURCE, NY

ERICH LESSING/ART RESOURCE, NY

CARLISLE MUSEUM & ART GALLERY/BRIDGEMAN ART LIBRARY

After the 1992 presidential election, Bill Clinton's chief strategist, James Carville, married George H. W. Bush's chief strategist, Mary Matalin. Despite the occasional odd couple, most people are attracted to those with similar attitudes and beliefs. Perhaps this couple's shared passion for politics outweighed their party affiliations.

Psychological factors. If attraction is all about big biceps and high cheekbones, then why don't we just skip the small talk and pick our mates from photographs? Because attraction is about much more than physical signals of fertility and resources. Physical attributes may determine who draws our attention and quickens our pulse, but after people begin interacting, they quickly go beyond appearances (Cramer, Schaefer, & Reid, 1996; Regan, 1998). People's *inner* qualities—personalities, points of view, attitudes, beliefs, values, ambitions, and abilities—play an important role in determining their sustained interest in each other, and there isn't much mystery about the kinds of inner qualities that people find most attractive. For example, intelligence, sense of humor, sensitivity, and ambition are high on just about everybody's list (Daniel et al., 1985).

Although we may be attracted to the person with the quickest wit and the highest IQ, research suggests that we typically interact with people whose standing on these dimensions is roughly *similar* to our own (Byrne, Ervin, & Lamberth, 1970; Byrne & Nelson, 1965; Hatfield & Rapson, 1992; Neimeyer & Mitchell, 1988). We marry people with similar levels of education, religious backgrounds, ethnicities, socioeconomic statuses, and personalities (Botwin, Buss, & Shackelford, 1997; Buss, 1985; Caspi & Herbener, 1990), and some research even suggests that we are unusually likely to marry someone whose surname starts with the same letter of the alphabet that ours does (Jones et al., 2004). Indeed, of all the variables psychologists have ever studied, *gender* appears to be the only one for which the majority of people have a consistent preference for dissimilarity.

Why is similarity so attractive? First, it's easy to interact with people who are similar to us because we can instantly agree on a wide range of issues, such as what to eat, where to live, how to raise children, and how to spend our money. Second, when someone shares our attitudes and beliefs, we feel a bit more confident that those attitudes and beliefs are correct (Byrne & Clore, 1970). Indeed, research shows that when the accuracy of a person's attitudes and beliefs is challenged, similarity becomes an even more important determinant of their attraction to others (Greenberg et al., 1990; Hirschberger, Florian, & Mikulincer, 2002). Third, if we like people who share our attitudes and beliefs, then we can reasonably expect them to like us for the same reason—and *being* liked is a powerful source of attraction (Aronson & Worchel, 1966; Backman & Secord, 1959; Condon & Crano, 1988).

It is worth noting that our desire for similarity goes beyond attitudes and beliefs. For example, we may admire extraordinary skill in athletes and actors, but when it comes to friends and lovers, extraordinary people can threaten our self-esteem and make us feel a bit nervous about our own competence (Tesser, 1991). As such, we are generally attracted to competent people who, just like us, have small pockets of incompetence. Why? It seems that people who are annoyingly perfect are perfectly annoying. Having a flaw or two "humanizes" people and makes them seem more accessible—and similar—to us (see the Hot Science box) (Aronson, Willerman, & Floyd, 1966).

Relationships

Selecting an attractive mate is the beginning of the reproductive process, but the real work consists of bearing and raising children. For human beings, that work is ordinarily done in the context of committed, long-term, romantic relationships such as a marriage. Only a few animals have relationships of this kind, so why are we among them? The answer is that we're born too soon. Human beings have large heads to house their large brains, and thus a fully developed human infant could not pass through its mother's birth canal. As such, human infants are *born before they are fully developed* and thus need a great deal of care—often more than one parent can provide. If human infants were more like tadpoles—ready at birth to swim, find food, and escape predators—then their parents might not need to form and maintain relationships. But human infants are remarkably helpless creatures that require years of intense care before they can fend for themselves, and so human adults do almost all of their reproducing in the context of committed, long-term relationships. (By the way, some baby birds also require more food than one adult caretaker can provide, and the adults of those species also tend to form long-term relationships.)

{ HOT SCIENCE }   Beautifully Average

IF SOMEONE DESCRIBED YOU AS "average-looking," you might not be insulted, but odds are that your mother would be furious. Tell Mom to relax. Psychologists have recently learned that when it comes to faces, average-looking is awfully hard to beat.

A face can be beautiful for many reasons, but research shows that faces are considered especially beautiful when their features approximate the average of the human population. In a clever series of studies, researchers digitized the photographs of many college students and then used a computer program to "morph" those faces together (Langlois & Roggman, 1990; Langlois, Roggman, & Musselman, 1994). Specifically, the program averaged the value of each pixel in the digitized photographs, producing a "composite face" that was the average of its components. The composite face and the component faces were then shown to participants, who rated the attractiveness of each. The participants tended to rate the composite as more attractive than the component faces. Interestingly, the more components that went into making a composite, the more attractive that composite was judged to be:

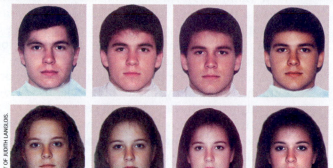

COURTESY OF JUDITH LANGLOIS.

Most people find the composite faces more attractive when more faces are used to make the composite. From left to right, the faces above are composites of 4 faces, 8 faces, 16 faces, and 32 faces.

Langlois, J. H., & Roggman, L. A. (1990). *Psychological Science, 1,* 115–121.

The average of 100 faces is more attractive than the average of 10.

Why do people find averageness so attractive? Nature experiments with organisms by generating mutations and seeing which ones work. Some mutations prove so valuable that those who have them out-reproduce those who don't, and soon the entire species has the mutation too. But *most* of nature's experiments are failures, and most mutations are unimportant at best and harmful at worst. The mutations that make some people vulnerable to certain diseases are good examples. One reason why we are attracted to averageness might be that people who look like everyone else are unlikely to carry a mutant gene. If this speculation is true, then our preference for averageness shouldn't be something we have to learn. In fact, research shows that people in a variety of cultures prefer composites to components (Rhodes et al., 2001). Perhaps even more startling is the fact that newborn babies seem to have the same preference (Langlois, Roggman, & Rieser-Danner, 1990; Rubenstein, Kalakanis, & Langlois, 1999).

Remember that averageness is just one of the many things we find attractive in a face, and it's not always the most important one. There are many movie stars with unusual facial features whom we would all consider extremely attractive. Nonetheless, research shows that even if an average face isn't more attractive than every face, it's more attractive than most faces picked at random. In other words, tell Mom not to beat anyone up just yet.

If a committed, long-term relationship hasn't happened to you yet, you can be almost certain that it will. About 90% of Americans marry, and about 80% of those who divorce marry a second time (Norton, 1987). How do we decide whom to marry? The evolutionary perspective suggests that marriage is all about making and raising babies, but if you're like most people, *you* think that marriage is all about love. Indeed, about 85% of Americans say that they would not marry without love (Kephart, 1967; Simpson, Campbell, & Berscheid, 1986), the vast majority say they would sacrifice their other life goals to attain it (Hammersla & Frease-McMahan, 1990), and most list love as one of the two most important sources of happiness in life (Freedman, 1978).

Are people more like cattle or robins? In most ways, we are more like any mammal than we are like any bird, but songbirds and people do share one thing that cattle don't: Their young are helpless at birth and thus require significant parental care. Interestingly, adult robins and adult human beings (but not adult cattle) have enduring relationships. And sing.

PAUL A. SOUDERS/CORBIS

CRAIG LOVELL/CORBIS

LIGHTSCAPES PHOTOGRAPHY, INC./CORBIS

PASSIONATE LOVE An experience involving feelings of euphoria, intimacy, and intense sexual attraction.

COMPANIONATE LOVE An experience involving affection, trust, and concern for a partner's well-being.

SOCIAL EXCHANGE The hypothesis that people remain in relationships only as long as they perceive a favorable ratio of costs to benefits.

COMPARISON LEVEL The cost-benefit ratio that people believe they deserve or could attain in another relationship.

EQUITY A state of affairs in which the cost-benefit ratios of two partners are roughly equal.

The fact that marriage is all about love seems so obvious that people are often surprised to learn that this so-called fact is a rather recent invention (Brehm, 1992; Fisher, 1993; Hunt, 1959). Throughout history and across cultures, marriage has traditionally served a variety of economic (and decidedly unromantic) functions, ranging from cementing agreements between clans to paying back debts. Ancient Greeks and Romans married, but they considered love a form of madness. Twelfth-century Europeans married but thought of love as a game to be played by knights and ladies of the court (who happened to be married, but not to the knights). Indeed, it wasn't until the 17th century that westerners began seriously considering the possibility that love might actually be a *reason* to get married.

But is it? Most people who get married expect to stay married, and in this respect, most people are wrong. About 65% of marriages in the United States end in permanent separation or divorce (Castro-Martin & Bumpass, 1989). Although there are many reasons for this (Gottman, 1994; Karney & Bradbury, 1995), one is that couples don't always have a clear understanding of what love is. Indeed, a language that uses the same word to describe the deepest forms of intimacy ("I love Emily") and the most shallow forms of satisfaction ("I love ketchup") is bound to confuse the people who speak it—which is why people debate endlessly the question of whether they are really "in love." Psychologists try to sidestep this confusion by distinguishing between two basic kinds of love—**passionate love**, which is *an experience involving feelings of euphoria, intimacy, and intense sexual attraction,* and **companionate love**, which is *an experience involving affection, trust, and concern for a partner's well-being* (Hatfield, 1988; Rubin, 1973; Sternberg, 1986). The ideal romantic relationship gives rise to both types of love, but the speeds, trajectories, and durations of the two experiences are markedly different (**FIGURE 16.4**).

Passionate love has a rapid onset, reaches its peak quickly, and begins to diminish within just a few months. Companionate love, on the other hand, takes some time to get started, grows slowly, and need never stop. As such, the love we feel early in a relationship is not the same love we feel later. When people marry for passionate love, they may not choose a partner with whom they can easily develop companionate love, and if they don't understand how quickly passionate love cools, they may blame their partners when it does. In many cultures, parents try to keep children from making these mistakes by choosing their marriage partners for them. Some studies suggest that arranged marriages yield greater satisfaction over the long term than do "love matches" (Yelsma & Athappilly, 1988), but other studies suggest just the opposite (Xiaohe & Whyte, 1990). If there *are* any benefits to arranged marriage, they may derive from the fact that parents are less likely to pick partners on the basis of passionate love and more likely to pick partners who have a high potential for companionate love (Haidt, 2006).

We've examined some of the factors that draw people into intimate relationships, but what determines when people will be drawn out? Although feelings of love, happiness, and satisfaction may lead us to marriage, the lack of those feelings doesn't seem to lead us to divorce. Marital satisfaction is only weakly correlated with marital

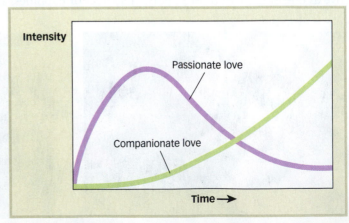

Figure 16.4
Passionate and Companionate Love Companionate and passionate love have different time courses and trajectories. Passionate love begins to cool within just a few months, but companionate love can grow slowly but steadily over years.

As relationships endure, passionate love fades and companionate love endures. Ronald Reagan and Nancy Davis were "crazy" about each other when they met in 1951, but after many decades, what they valued most about their marriage was the fact that they were "best friends."

stability (Karney & Bradbury, 1995), suggesting that relationships break up or remain intact for reasons other than the satisfaction of those involved (Drigotas & Rusbult, 1992; Rusbult & Van Lange, 2003). Relationships offer benefits, such as love, sex, and financial security, but they exact costs, such as increased responsibility, increased conflict, and loss of freedom. **Social exchange** is *the hypothesis that people remain in relationships only as long as they perceive a favorable ratio of costs to benefits* (Homans, 1961; Thibaut & Kelley, 1959). For example, a relationship that provides an acceptable level of benefits at a reasonable cost would probably be maintained. Research suggests that this hypothesis is generally true with three important additions:

- People calculate their cost-benefit ratios by comparing them to alternatives. A person's **comparison level** refers to *the cost-benefit ratio that people believe they deserve or could attain in another relationship* (Rusbult et al., 1991; Thibaut & Kelley, 1959). A cost-benefit ratio that is acceptable to two people who are stranded on a desert island might not be acceptable to the same two people if they were living in a large city where each had access to other potential partners. A cost-benefit ratio seems favorable when we feel that it is the best we can or should do.

- People may hope to maximize their cost-benefit ratios, but they do not want them to be markedly different from their partner's. Most people seek **equity**, which is *a state of affairs in which the cost-benefit ratios of two partners are roughly equal* (Messick & Cook, 1983; Walster, Walster, & Berscheid, 1978). For example, spouses are more distressed when their respective cost-benefit ratios are *different* than when their cost-benefit ratios are *unfavorable*—and this is true even when their cost-benefit ratio is *more* favorable than their partner's (Schafer & Keith, 1980).

- Relationships can be thought of as investments into which people pour resources such as time, money, and affection, and research suggests that after people have poured significant resources into their relationships, they are more willing to settle for less favorable cost-benefit ratios (Kelley, 1983; Rusbult, 1983). This is one of the reasons why people are much more likely to end new marriages than old ones (Bramlett & Mosher, 2002; Cherlin, 1992).

"This next one goes out to all those who have ever been in love, then become engaged, gotten married, participated in the tragic deterioration of a relationship, suffered the pains and agonies of a bitter divorce, subjected themselves to the fruitless search for a new partner, and ultimately resigned themselves to remaining single in a world full of irresponsible jerks, noncommittal weirdos, and neurotic misfits."

In summary, evolutionary pressures have made survival and reproduction two fundamental challenges for humans and other animals. Survival requires scarce resources, and two ways to get them are aggression and cooperation. Impulsive aggression is a reaction to a negative internal state, and males are particularly prone to use aggression to ensure their status. Cooperation comes with risks; one strategy to reduce those risks is to form groups whose members are biased in favor of each other. Unfortunately, groups often show prejudice and discrimination toward those who are not members, they sometimes make poor decisions, and they may even take extreme actions that no individual member would take alone. Deindividuation, social loafing, and diffusion of responsibility are some of the causes of this behavior.

Organisms survive to reproduce, and reproduction requires choosing the right mate. Biology and culture tend to make the costs of reproduction higher for women than for men, so women tend to be choosier when selecting potential mates. Attraction is a feeling that draws us closer to a potential mate, and it has both situational and personal determinants. Physical appearance plays an unusually important role, but psychological determinants are also important, and people seem to be most attracted to those who are similar to them on a wide variety of dimensions. Reproduction is usually accomplished within the context of a long-term, committed relationship. People weigh the costs and benefits of their relationships and tend to dissolve them when they think they can or should do better, when they and their partners have very different cost-benefit ratios, or when they have little invested in the relationship. ■ ■ ■

Social Influence: Controlling People

Those of us who grew up watching Wonder Woman and Superman cartoons on Saturday mornings have usually thought a bit about which of the standard superpowers we'd most like to have. Super-strength and super-speed have obvious benefits, invisibility and x-ray vision could be interesting as well as lucrative, and there's a lot to be said for flying. But when it comes right down to it, the ability to control other people would probably be more useful. After all, who needs to leap tall buildings, change the course of mighty rivers, or bend steel in their bare hands if they can get someone else to do it for them? The things we want from life—gourmet food, interesting jobs, big houses, fancy cars—can be given to us by others, and the things we want most—loving families, loyal friends, admiring children, appreciative employers—cannot be had in any other way.

Social influence is *the control of one person's behavior by another,* and those who know how to exert such influence can have and be just about anything they please (Cialdini & Trost, 1998). Human beings are not unique in their exercise of—or susceptibility to—social influence. Indeed, influence is the fundamental force that binds the individual members of any social species together, and without it there could be no groups, no cooperation, and no altruism. All social animals exert and yield to social influence, but human beings have raised influence to the status of an art, developing subtle and complex techniques not observed anywhere else in the natural world.

How does social influence work? If you wanted someone to give you their time, money, allegiance, or affection, you'd be wise to consider first what it is *they* want. People have three basic wants that make them susceptible to social influence. First, people have a *hedonic motive,* or a desire to experience pleasure and avoid pain. Second, people have an *approval motive,* or a desire to be accepted and to avoid being rejected. Third, people have an *accuracy motive,* or a desire to believe what is true and to avoid believing what is false. As we shall see, most forms of social influence appeal to one or more of these motives.

The Hedonic Motive: The Power of Pleasure

Pleasure-seeking is probably the most fundamental of all motives, and social influence often involves creating situations in which others can achieve more pleasure by doing what we want them to do than by doing something else. Parents, teachers, governments, and businesses constantly try to influence our behavior by offering rewards and threatening punishments. There's nothing mysterious about these influence attempts, and they are often quite effective. When the Republic of Singapore warned its citizens

SOCIAL INFLUENCE The control of one person's behavior by another.

OBSERVATIONAL LEARNING Learning that occurs when one person observes another person being rewarded or punished.

in 1992 that anyone caught chewing gum in public would face a year in prison and a $5,500 fine, the rest of the world seemed either outraged or amused. When all the criticism and chuckling subsided, though, it was hard to ignore the fact that the incidence of felonious gum-chewing in Singapore had fallen to an all-time low.

You'll recall from Chapter 5 that even a sea slug will repeat behaviors that are followed by rewards and avoid behaviors that are followed by punishments. Although the same is generally true of human beings, there are at least two notable exceptions:

■ Reward and punishment are sometimes *more effective* influences on human than nonhuman behavior because people are especially good at **observational learning**, which is *the process of learning by observing others being rewarded and punished*. In a classic study by Albert Bandura, children who saw an adult behave aggressively were more likely to behave aggressively themselves if they observed the adult being rewarded rather than punished (Bandura, 1965). This method of social influence can be effective even when rewards and punishments are quite subtle. For instance, toddlers in one study watched their mothers being exposed to a rubber snake (Gerull & Rapee, 2002). Those who saw their mothers frown were more likely to avoid the snake than were those who saw their mothers smile. The mothers' facial expressions indicated whether they found the experience rewarding, and those expressions were sufficient to influence the child's subsequent behavior. Indeed, 1-year-old children will avoid a toy if an unfamiliar woman on television appears to be unhappy when she looks at it (Mumme & Fernald, 2003).

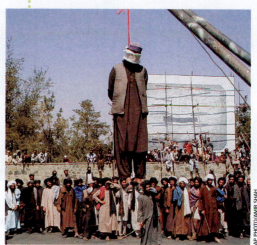

Spectators watch as convicted criminal Meya Gul is hanged in front of a hotel in Kabul, Afghanistan, on September 23, 2000. Whether or not public punishment is ethical, research on observational learning suggests that it can be effective.

■ Sometimes reward and punishment are *less effective* influences on human behavior. This unusual mindbug can occur because, unlike other animals, people tend to think about the *causes* of their rewards and punishments (Deci, Koestner, & Ryan, 1999). For example, children in one study were allowed to play with some colored markers. After drawing for a while, some of the children were given a "Good Player Award" and others were not (see Chapter 6). All the children were given markers the next day. You might think that receiving an award on the first day would make children more interested in playing with the markers on the next day, but in fact, the reward had precisely the *opposite* effect (Lepper, Greene, & Nisbett, 1973). Why? Because children who had received an award the first day assumed that drawing was something one did to receive rewards, and if no one was going to reward them for it the next day, then why should they do it?

Social influence attempts that are based on reward and punishment can also backfire because people don't always take kindly to being manipulated. Researcher James Pennebaker placed signs in two restrooms on a college campus. One sign read, "Please don't write on these walls," and the other read, "Do not write on these walls under any circumstances." Two weeks later, the walls in the second restroom had more graffiti than the walls in the first restroom did, presumably because students didn't appreciate the threatening tone of the second sign and thus wrote on the walls just to prove that they could (Pennebaker & Sanders, 1976).

The Approval Motive: The Power of Social Acceptance

Other people stand between us and starvation, predation, loneliness, and all the other things that make getting shipwrecked such a bad idea. We depend on others for safety, sustenance, and solidarity, all of which become conspicuous by their absence. Social rejection is not just a blow to our self-esteem but also a hazard to our health. Indeed, being isolated and lonely makes people susceptible to a wide variety of physical illnesses (Pressman et al., 2005). Having others like us, accept us, and approve of us is a powerful human motive (Baumeister & Leary, 1995; Leary, Tambor, Terdal & Downs, 1995), and like any motive, it leaves us vulnerable to social influence. This influence comes in several different forms.

People (and other social animals) are motivated by a need for approval, which leads them to obey norms.

Normative Influence

You probably know that you are supposed to face forward in an elevator and that you shouldn't talk to the person next to you even if you were talking to that person before you got on the elevator unless you are the only two people on the elevator, in which case, it's okay to talk and face sideways but still not backward. What's so interesting about rules such as these is that they are both elaborate and unwritten. No one ever taught you this complicated elevator etiquette, but you nonetheless managed to pick it up along the way. The unwritten rules that govern social behavior are called **norms**, which are *customary standards for behavior that are widely shared by members of a culture* (Miller & Prentice, 1996). We learn norms with exceptional ease and we obey them with exceptional fidelity because we know that if we don't, others won't approve of us.

Our slavish devotion to norms provides a powerful lever for influence. **Normative influence** occurs when *one person's behavior is influenced by another person's behavior because the latter provides information about what is appropriate*. For example, every human culture has a **norm of reciprocity**, which is *the unwritten rule that people should benefit those who have benefited them* (Gouldner, 1960). If a stranger helped you jumpstart your car in a parking lot, you would find it difficult to refuse his request to use your cell phone because you know that those who accept kindness without returning it do not meet with social approval. Similarly, when a friend pays for lunch, you probably feel an immediate urge to repay the favor, perhaps even offering, "My treat next time," or words to that effect. Indeed, the norm of reciprocity is so strong that when

Have you ever wondered which big spender left the bill as a tip? In fact, the bills are often put there by the very people you are tipping because they know that the presence of paper money will suggest to you that others are leaving big tips and that it would be socially appropriate for you to do the same. By the way, the customary gratuity for someone who writes a textbook for you is 15%. But most students send more.

researchers randomly pulled the names of strangers from a telephone directory and sent them all Christmas cards, they received Christmas cards back from most (Kunz & Woolcott, 1976). Some social influence techniques trade on this norm of reciprocity. For example, waiters and waitresses get bigger tips when they give customers a piece of candy along with the bill because customers feel obligated to do "a little extra" for those who have done "a little extra" for them (Strohmetz et al., 2002). For the same reason, panhandlers may hand you a newspaper or a flower that you didn't really want because they know it will increase the odds that you'll acquiesce to their subsequent request for money.

The norm of reciprocity always involves swapping, but the swapping doesn't always involve favors. The **door-in-the-face technique** is *a strategy that uses reciprocating concessions to influence behavior*. Here's how it works: You ask someone for something more valuable than you really want, you wait for that person to refuse (to "slam the door in your face"), and then you ask the person for what you really want. This technique works like a charm. In one study, researchers asked college students to volunteer to supervise adolescents who were going on a field trip, and only 17% of the students agreed. But when the researchers first asked students to commit to spending 2 hours per week for 2 years working at a youth detention center (to which every one of the students said no)

Blondie

and *then* asked them if they'd be willing to supervise the field trip, 50% of the students agreed (Cialdini et al., 1975). There's a mindbug at work: People were more likely to endorse the second request *because* they refused the first request, although most people would balk at the second request if they heard it all by itself. How does this technique involve the norm of reciprocity? The researchers began by asking for a large favor, which the student firmly refused. They then made a concession by asking for a smaller favor. Because the researchers made a concession, the norm of reciprocity demanded that the student make one too.

Conformity

People can influence us by invoking familiar norms. But if you've ever found yourself sneaking a peek at the diner next to you, hoping to discover whether the little fork is supposed to be used for the shrimp or the salad, then you know that other people can also influence us by defining *new* norms in ambiguous, confusing, or novel situations. **Conformity** is *the tendency to do what others do simply because others are doing it,* and it results in part from normative influence.

In a classic study, Solomon Asch had participants sit in a room with seven other people who appeared to be ordinary participants but who were actually trained actors (Asch, 1951; Asch, 1956). An experimenter explained that the participants would be shown cards with three lines printed on them and that their job was to state which of the three lines matched a "standard line" that was printed on another card (**FIGURE 16.5**). The experimenter held up a card and then went around the room, asking each person to answer aloud in turn. The real participant was among the last to be called on. Everything was normal on the first two trials, but on the third trial, something odd happened: The actors all began giving the same wrong answer! What did the real participant do? Results showed that 75% of them conformed and announced the wrong answer on at least one trial. Subsequent research has shown that these participants were indeed succumbing to normative influence. For example, when the number of actors was increased, participants in this situation were even more likely to conform; but if even one actor did not conform, then the participants were much less likely to do so (Asch, 1955; Nemeth & Chiles, 1988). Participants didn't actually misperceive the length of the lines; that'd be pretty difficult for someone with normal vision to do. Rather, they merely said something they didn't believe in order to gain social approval.

The perplexed research participant (center), flanked by confederates (who are "in" on the experiment), is on the verge of conformity in one of Solomon Asch's line-judging experiments.

WILLIAM VANDIVERT/SCIENTIFIC AMERICAN

NORM A customary standard for behavior that is widely shared by members of a culture.

NORMATIVE INFLUENCE A phenomenon whereby one person's behavior is influenced by another person's behavior because the latter provides information about what is appropriate.

NORM OF RECIPROCITY The norm that people should benefit those who have benefited them.

DOOR-IN-THE-FACE TECHNIQUE A strategy that uses reciprocating concessions to influence behavior.

CONFORMITY The tendency to do what others do simply because others are doing it.

Standard	A B C

Figure 16.5 Asch's **Conformity Study** If you were asked which of the lines on the right—A, B, or C—matches the standard line on the left, what would you say? Research on conformity suggests that your answer would depend, in part, on how other people in the room answered the same question.

Private Lynndie England faced a court martial for her role in the abuse of Iraqi prisoners at the Abu Ghraib prison. When the judge asked her why she had abused the prisoners, she implicated her fellow soldiers. "I refused at first . . . [but] they were being very persistent, bugging me, so I said, 'Okay, whatever.'" Then she added, "I was yielding to peer pressure."

The behavior of others can tell us what is proper, appropriate, expected, and accepted—in other words, it can define a norm—and once a norm is defined, anyone who cares about social approval will experience tremendous pressure to honor it. When a Holiday Inn in Tempe, Arizona, left a variety of different "message cards" in their guests' bathrooms in the hopes of convincing those guests to reuse their towels rather than laundering them every day, they discovered that the single most effective message was the one that simply read: "Seventy five percent of our guests use their towels more than once" (Cialdini, 2005).

Obedience

Other people's behavior can provide information about norms, but in most situations there are a few people whom we all recognize as having special authority both to define and enforce the norms. The usher at a movie theater may be an underpaid high school student who isn't allowed to drink, drive, vote, or stay up past 10 on a school night, but in the context of the theater, the usher is the authority. So when the usher asks you to take your feet off the seat in front of you, you obey. **Obedience** is *the tendency to do what authorities tell us to do simply because they tell us to do it.*

Why do we obey authorities? Well, okay, sometimes they have guns. Authorities can influence us by threatening punishment and promising reward, but research suggests that much of their influence is *normative* (Tyler, 1990). Stanley Milgram demonstrated this in one of psychology's most infamous experiments (Milgram, 1963). The participants in this experiment were people of all ages who answered an ad in the local newspaper asking them to take part in a study of learning and memory. When they arrived at the laboratory, they met a middle-aged man who was introduced as another participant but who was actually a trained actor. An experimenter in a lab coat explained that the participant would play the role of *teacher* and the actor would play the role of *learner*. The teacher and learner would sit in different rooms, the teacher would read words to the learner over a microphone, and the learner would then repeat the words back to the teacher. If the learner made a mistake, the teacher would press a button that delivered an electric shock to the learner. Each time the learner made an error, the teacher would increase the level of shock (**FIGURE 16.6**). The shock-generating machine (which wasn't actually hooked up, of course) offered 30 levels of shock, ranging from 15 volts (labeled "slight shock") to 450 volts (labeled "Danger: Severe shock").

After the learner was strapped into his chair, the experiment began. When the learner made his first mistake, the participant dutifully delivered a 15-volt shock. As the learner

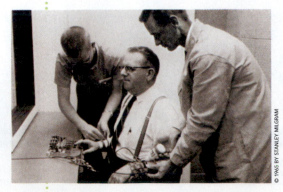

Figure 16.6 Milgram's Obedience Studies The learner (left) being hooked up to the shock generator (right) that was used in Stanley Milgram's obedience studies.

made more mistakes, he received more shocks. When the participant delivered the 75-volt shock, the learner cried out in pain. At 150 volts, the learner screamed, *"Get me out of here. I told you I have heart trouble . . . I refuse to go on. Let me out!"* With every shock, the learner's screams became more agonized as he pleaded pitifully for his freedom. Then, after receiving the 330-volt shock, the learner stopped responding altogether. Participants were naturally upset by all of this, and they typically asked the experimenter to stop the experiment. But the experimenter simply replied, *"You have no choice; you must go on."* The experimenter never threatened the participant with punishment of any kind. Rather, he just stood there with his clipboard in hand and calmly instructed the participant to continue. What did the participants do? Eighty percent of the participants continued to shock the learner even after he screamed, complained, pleaded, and then fell silent. And 62% went all the way, delivering the highest possible voltage.

Is this the face of a monster? In this photo, Nazi war criminal Adolph Eichmann sits before the District Court of Jerusalem. Eichmann acknowledged that he sent millions of Jews to their deaths but argued that he was merely obeying authority. He was sentenced to death and hanged in 1962.

Were these people psychopathic sadists? Would a normal person electrocute a stranger just because some guy in a lab coat told them to? The answer, it seems, is yes, because being *normal* means being sensitive to and respectful of social norms. The participants in this experiment knew that hurting others is *often* wrong but not *always* wrong. Doctors give painful injections, and teachers give painful exams. There are many situations in which it is permissible—and even desirable—to cause someone to suffer in the service of a higher goal. The experimenter's calm demeanor and persistent instruction suggested that he, and not

"Sure, I follow the herd—not out of brainless obedience, mind you, but out of a deep and abiding respect for the concept of community."

the participant, knew what was appropriate in this particular situation. Indeed, subsequent research confirmed that participants' obedience was due to normative pressure. When the experimenter's authority to define the norm was undermined—for example, when a second experimenter appeared to disagree with the first or when the instructions were given by a person who wasn't wearing a lab coat—participants rarely obeyed the instructions (Milgram, 1974; Miller, 1986).

The Accuracy Motive: The Power of Being Right

Just about every action relies on an **attitude**, which is *an enduring positive or negative evaluation of an object or event,* and a **belief**, which is *an enduring piece of knowledge about an object or event.* Even the simplest actions are based on attitudes and beliefs. When we are hungry, we open the refrigerator and grab an apple because our attitudes tell us that apples taste good and our beliefs tell us that those good-tasting apples are to be found in the refrigerator. In a sense, attitudes tell us what we should do ("Eat an apple") and beliefs tell us how we should do it ("Start by opening the fridge"). If attitudes or beliefs are inaccurate—that is, if we don't know what is good and we don't know what is true—then our actions are fruitless. Because we rely so heavily on our attitudes and beliefs to guide our actions, it isn't surprising that we want to have the right ones. We are motivated to be accurate, and like any motive, this one leaves us vulnerable to social influence.

Informational Influence

Other human beings have pretty much the same sensory apparatus that we do, and thus we rely on their reactions to the world to tell us *about* the world. If everyone in a movie theater suddenly jumped up and ran screaming for the exit, you'd probably join them—

OBEDIENCE The tendency to do what authorities tell us to do simply because they tell us to do it.

ATTITUDE An enduring positive or negative evaluation of an object or event.

BELIEF An enduring piece of knowledge about an object or event.

The behavior of others provides information about the world to which they are reacting. When a social animal flees, others tend to follow.

COURTESY OF J.J. PASCOE

AP PHOTO/SUZANNE PLUNKETT

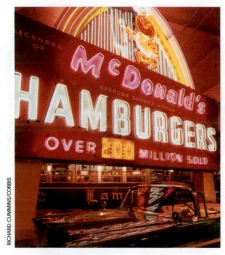

RICHARD CUMMINS/CORBIS

Is McDonald's trying to keep track of sales from the parking lot? Probably not. Rather, they want you to know that other people are buying their hamburgers, which suggests that they are worth buying, which, in turn, suggests that you just might want to stop and have one yourself right about now.

not because you were afraid that they'd think less of you if you didn't, but because their behavior would suggest that there was something worth running from. **Informational influence** occurs when *a person's behavior is influenced by another person's behavior because the latter provides information about what is good or true.* You can demonstrate the power of informational influence by standing in the middle of the sidewalk, tilting back your head, and staring at the top of a tall building. Research shows that within just a few minutes, other people will begin stopping and staring too, believing that you must know something they don't (Milgram, Bickman, & Berkowitz, 1969).

You are the constant target of informational influence. When a salesperson tells you that "most people buy the deluxe model," she is artfully suggesting that you should consider how others behave and then take that behavior as information about the quality of the product. Advertisements that refer to soft drinks as "popular" or books as "best sellers" are reminding you that other people are buying these particular sodas and novels, which suggests that they know something you don't and that you'd be wise to follow their example. Situation comedies provide "laugh tracks" because the producers know that when you hear other people laughing, you will mindlessly assume that something must be funny (Nosanchuk & Lightstone, 1974). Bars and nightclubs may waive the cover charge for the first group of patrons because they know that when a club looks full, passersby will assume that others spent money to get into the club and that the club must be worth the expense. In short, the world is full of objects and events that we know little about, and we can often cure our ignorance by paying attention to the way in which others are acting toward them. Observing the reactions of other people is a bit like having an extra pair of eyes. Alas, the very thing that makes us open to information leaves us open to manipulation as well.

In 1953, Charlie Douglass (1910–2003) invented the Laff Box because he suspected that television viewers would think a show was funny if they heard other people laughing. Research has since shown that Douglass's intuition was right.

STEVE KELLEY, COURTESY OF BOB DOUGLASS

Persuasion

When the next presidential election rolls around, two things will happen. First, the candidates will say that they intend to win your vote by making arguments that focus on the issues. Second, the candidates will then avoid arguments, ignore issues, and attempt to win your vote with a variety of cheap tricks. What the candidates promise to do and what they actually do reflect two basic forms of **persuasion**, which occurs when *a person's attitudes or beliefs are influenced by a communication from another person* (Petty & Wegener, 1998). The candidates will promise to persuade you by demonstrating that their positions on the issues are the most practical, intelligent, fair, and beneficial. Having made that promise, they will then devote most of their financial resources to persuading you by other means—for example, by dressing nicely and smiling a lot, by surrounding themselves with famous athletes and movie stars, by repeatedly pairing their opponent's name with words and images that nobody much cares for, and so on. In other words, the candidates will promise to engage in **systematic persuasion**, which refers to *a change in attitudes or beliefs that is brought about by appeals to reason,* but they will spend most of their time and money engaged in **heuristic persuasion,** which refers to *a change in attitudes or beliefs that is brought about by appeals to habit or emotion* (Chaiken, 1980; Petty & Cacioppo, 1986).

How do these two forms of persuasion work? *Systematic persuasion* appeals to logic and reason. People should be more persuaded when evidence and arguments are strong rather than weak. Although this is often true, there are many rhetorical devices that can make arguments and evidence seem stronger than they actually are. For example, it is often tempting to ignore one's opponents—as presidential candidate John Kerry did when his military record was challenged in 2004—but research suggests that people are generally more persuaded by communications that refute opposing positions than by communications that ignore them (Hovland & Weiss, 1951). Similarly, research shows that people generally pay more attention to the argument they hear first but remember best the argument they hear last. As such, a candidate may prefer to speak first if the debate is being held 1 day before the election but may prefer to speak last if the debate is being held 1 month before the election (Miller & Campbell, 1959).

Heuristic persuasion appeals to habit and emotion. Rather than weighing evidence and analyzing arguments, people often use *heuristics*—which are simple shortcuts or "rules of thumb"—to help them decide whether to believe a communication (see Chapter 7). For instance, participants in one study read the statement, "When a government becomes oppressive, it is the right of the people to abolish it." Those who were told that the remark had been made by Abraham Lincoln were more persuaded by it than were those who were told that the remark had been made by Communist leader Vladimir Lenin (Lorge, 1936). (In case you're wondering, the sentence paraphrases a statement in the U.S. Declaration of Independence.) Rather than analyzing the content of the remark, participants used a simple heuristic ("Always trust Honest Abe," or, "Never trust a Commie") to help them decide whether to accept the communication. Emotions can also function as heuristics. In one study, participants who drank a sweet cola were more persuaded by a speech about comprehensive exams than were participants who drank a bitter tonic (Albarracin & Kumkale, 2003). Rather than evaluating the arguments and evidence, participants seemed to rely

INFORMATIONAL INFLUENCE A phenomenon whereby a person's behavior is influenced by another person's behavior because the latter provides information about what is good or true.

PERSUASION A phenomenon that occurs when a person's attitudes or beliefs are influenced by a communication from another person.

SYSTEMATIC PERSUASION A change in attitudes or beliefs that is brought about by appeals to reason.

HEURISTIC PERSUASION A change in attitudes or beliefs that is brought about by appeals to habit or emotion.

The order in which information is presented can have an influence on the persuasiveness of a communication.

Systematic and heuristic persuasion have long been the staples of advertising. The automobile advertisement on the left presents facts about the car and invites you to "see for yourself," whereas the advertisement on the right tells you only that most people choose this ketchup. Can you guess why advertisers include more facts when selling cars than ketchup?

Answer: Cars are more expensive (and thus people are strongly motivated to consider evidence for or against buying them), but ketchup is cheap.

on a simple heuristic: "If I feel good when I hear an argument, it's probably right." These are only two of the many heuristics people use to decide whether to accept or reject a communication. Other examples, such as, "If everyone else says it, then it must be true," or, "Experts know more than I do," are familiar to all of us.

Which of these forms of persuasion is more effective? It depends on how closely the audience is listening. Weighing evidence and analyzing arguments is more effortful and time consuming than using a simple heuristic, and thus people tend to weigh and analyze only when the communication is about something they consider important. For example, in one study, university students heard a speech that contained either strong or weak arguments in favor of instituting comprehensive exams at their school (Petty, Cacioppo, & Goldman, 1981). Some students were told that the speaker was a Princeton University professor, and others were told that the speaker was a high school student. Some students were told that their university was considering implementing these exams right away, whereas others were told that their university was considering implementing these exams in 10 years. As **FIGURE 16.7** shows, when students thought the new exams might affect them personally, they were motivated to consider the evidence, and they were systematically persuaded. That is, their attitudes and beliefs were influenced by the strength of the arguments and not by the status of the speaker. But when students thought the new exams would not affect them personally, they were not motivated to consider the evidence, and thus they were heuristically persuaded. That is, their attitudes and beliefs were influenced by the status of the speaker but not by the strength of the arguments (see the Real World box).

Figure 16.7 **Systematic and Heuristic Persuasion** (a) *Systematic persuasion.* When students were motivated to analyze arguments because they would be personally affected by them, their attitudes were influenced by the strength of the arguments (strong arguments were more persuasive than weak arguments) but not by the status of the communicator (the Princeton professor was not more persuasive than the high school student). (b) *Heuristic persuasion.* When students were not motivated to analyze arguments because they would not be personally affected by them, their attitudes were influenced by the status of the communicator (the Princeton professor was more persuasive than the high school students) but not by the strength of the arguments (strong arguments were no more persuasive than weak arguments) (Petty, Cacioppo, & Goldman, 1981).

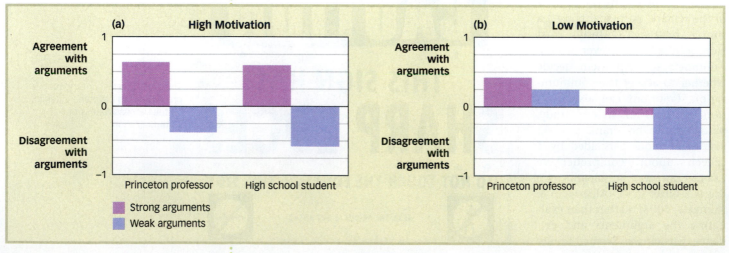

{ THE REAL WORLD } **This Just In**

DOES A COLLEGE STUDENT'S CHOICE OF majors reveal anything about him or her? Research suggests that it does. In a recent study of 18,521 students at 129 public and private universities, researchers found that psychology majors have better social skills and more active social lives than do students who major in other subjects. Indeed, among seniors, psychology majors were the most likely to be involved in a long-term romantic relationship, to have a "warm and trusting" relationship with their parents, and to have remained in contact with their high school friends. Perhaps the most amazing thing about the results of this survey is that we made them up. That's right. Everything you just read is a lie.

Now, if you had to guess which majors really *do* have the best social skills, what would your answer be? If you're like most people who read the preceding paragraph, you would be especially willing to entertain the possibility that the correct answer is *psychology majors.* Even though you were explicitly told that the sentences you read were fiction, research provides three reasons to suspect that you nonetheless will tend to believe them—at least at first, at least a little, and maybe even a lot later on.

- *The perseverance effect:* Judges often tell juries to ignore what they've just heard, but this is easier to say than do. For example, participants in one study performed a task and were then told that they had performed very well or very poorly (Ross, Lepper, & Hubbard, 1975). After a few minutes, the experimenter confessed that the participant had actually been given success or failure feedback that had nothing whatsoever to do with his or her actual performance. When participants were then asked to predict how they thought they would *really* perform on the task, those who had received success feedback predicted that they would perform better than did those who received failure feedback—despite the fact that they now knew the feedback was false. Subsequent studies have shown that this happened because the participants invented explanations for their success or their failure, and when the performance feedback was later discredited,

SUSAN VAN ETTEN/PHOTOEDIT

these explanations remained (Anderson, Lepper, & Ross, 1980). Because people explain things to themselves, they cannot easily "undo" the effects of information after they find out it is false.

- *The unbelieving effect:* When someone tells you something, it *feels* as though you first consider it and then decide whether to believe it or not. But research suggests that this feeling is an illusion and that the human mind actually believes *everything* it hears and then quickly "unbelieves" some of it. For example, participants in one study were told about a robbery and given false information that made the robber seem unusually cruel ("Kevin threatened to sexually assault the clerk") or unusually kind ("Kevin apologized to the clerk for having to rob the store") (Gilbert, Tafarodi, & Malone, 1993). All participants knew that this information was completely false, but while they were reading the information, some were interrupted with another task. The results showed that interruption prevented these participants from unbelieving the false information that they initially believed despite the fact that they knew it was false. As such, these participants recommended a longer prison term for the "cruel robber" than the "kind robber." It seems that people

believe first and ask questions later, which tends to make them a bit more gullible than they should be (Arkes, Boehm, & Xu, 1991; Gilbert, Krull, & Malone, 1990).

- *The sleeper effect:* You probably know that eccentric pop star Michael Jackson sleeps in a hyperbaric chamber. But where did you hear about it? Chances are that you read about this while standing in line at the supermarket because the story (which is completely false) appeared in the *National Enquirer.* You already know that information in the *National Enquirer* deserves to be treated with maximal skepticism, and you probably didn't believe the story when you read it. So why do you believe it now? Research suggests that communications from unreliable sources can have a delayed impact because people tend to forget the source of information before they forget the information itself (Hovland, Lumsdaine, & Sheffield, 1949). In one study, participants heard an essay touting a new consumer product and then learned that the essay had been written either by the manufacturer or by *Consumer Reports* (Pratkanis et al., 1988). Although participants were not initially persuaded by the manufacturer's essay, they *were* persuaded later on—in fact, they were ultimately *just as persuaded* by the essay when it was written by the manufacturer as when it was written by *Consumer Reports.* Information that makes us initially skeptical can remain in memory long after our skepticism has evaporated.

The sad part of this story is that there really are no data to suggest that psychology majors have better social skills or more active social lives than other students. However, the happy part of this story is that psychology majors are much more likely than other students to have a sophisticated understanding of the perseverance effect, the unbelieving effect, and the sleeper effect. Of course, knowing about these phenomena doesn't necessarily prevent them from occurring, so the next time you are in line at the grocery store, you might consider reading the candy bar labels instead of the tabloids.

FOOT-IN-THE-DOOR TECHNIQUE A strategy that uses a person's desire for consistency to influence that person's behavior.

COGNITIVE DISSONANCE An unpleasant state that arises when a person recognizes the inconsistency of his or her actions, attitudes, or beliefs.

Consistency

If a friend told you that rabbits had just staged a coup in Antarctica and were halting all carrot exports, you probably wouldn't turn on CNN to see if it was true. You'd know right away that your friend was joking because the statement is logically inconsistent with other things that you know are true—for example, that rabbits rarely foment revolution and that Antarctica does not export carrots. People evaluate the accuracy of new beliefs by assessing their *consistency* with old beliefs, and although this is not a foolproof method for determining whether something is true, it provides a pretty good approximation. Most people have a desire for accuracy, and because consistency is a rough measure of accuracy, most of us have a desire for consistency as well (Cialdini, Trost, & Newsom, 1995).

Our desire for consistency can leave us vulnerable to social influence. For example, the **foot-in-the-door technique** is *a strategy that uses a person's desire for consistency to influence that person's behavior* (Burger, 1999). In one study, experimenters went to a neighborhood, knocked on doors, and asked homeowners if they would install in their front yards a large, unsightly sign that said, "Drive Carefully." Only 17% of the homeowners agreed to install the sign. The experimenters asked some other homeowners to sign a petition urging the state legislature to promote safe driving, which almost all agreed to do, and *then* asked those homeowners if they would install the unsightly sign. Fifty-five percent of *these* homeowners agreed to install the sign (Freedman & Fraser, 1966)! Why would a homeowner be more likely to grant two requests than one?

Just imagine how the homeowners probably felt. They had just signed a petition stating that safe driving was important to them, and they knew that refusing to install the sign would be inconsistent with that action. As they wrestled with these facts, they probably began to experience a feeling that you might call "squirming" but that Leon Festinger called **cognitive dissonance**, which is *an unpleasant state that arises when a person recognizes the inconsistency of his or her actions, attitudes, or beliefs* (Festinger, 1957). Festinger made many major contributions to the field of social psychology, one of which started with this simple observation: When people experience the unpleasant state of cognitive dissonance, they naturally try to alleviate it, and one way to alleviate cognitive dissonance is to change one's actions, attitudes, or beliefs in order to restore consistency among them (Aronson, 1969; Cooper & Fazio, 1984). In other words, if you want to stop squirming, then just move the lawn furniture and make way for the yard sign.

The fact that we often alleviate cognitive dissonance by changing our actions, attitudes, or beliefs can leave us vulnerable to other people's efforts to change them for us. In one study, female college students applied to join a weekly discussion on "the psychology of sex." Women in the control group were allowed to join the discussion, but women in the experimental group were allowed to join the discussion only after first passing an embarrassing test that involved reading pornographic fiction to a strange man. Although the carefully staged discussion was as dull as possible, the researchers found that women in the experimental group found it more interesting than did women in the control group (Aronson & Mills, 1958). As **FIGURE 16.8** shows, women in the experimental group knew that they had paid a steep price to join the group ("I read all that lurid pornography out loud!"), but that belief was inconsistent with the belief that the discussion was worthless ("This discussion isn't interesting at all . . ."). As such, the women experienced cognitive dissonance, which they alleviated by changing their beliefs about the value of the discussion ("You know, this discussion is much more interesting than I first thought"). We normally think that people pay for things because they value them, but as this study shows, people sometimes value things because they've paid for them. It is little wonder that some fraternities use hazing to breed loyalty, that some religions require their adherents to make large personal or monetary sacrifices, that some gourmet restaurants charge outrageous amounts to keep their patrons coming back, or that some men and women play hard to get to maintain their suitors' interest.

Figure 16.8 Effort Justification and Cognitive Dissonance Suffering for something of little value can cause cognitive dissonance. One way to eliminate that dissonance is to change your belief about the value of the thing you suffered for.

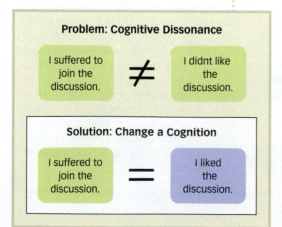

Members of the Virginia Military Institute freshman class scramble up a muddy hill while upperclassmen hold their feet (far left), and members of Michigan Tech University's Sigma Tau Gamma fraternity brave subzero wind-chill to participate in the group's annual "Grundy Run" through the campus (immediate left). Why do social groups "haze" their initiates so often?

We desire consistency, but there are inevitably occasions when we just can't help but be inconsistent—for example, when we tell a friend that her new hair-style is "unusually trendy" when it actually resembles a wet skunk after an unfortunate encounter with a blender. Why don't we experience cognitive dissonance under such circumstances and come to believe our own lies? Because telling a friend that her hairstyle is trendy is inconsistent with the belief that her hairstyle is hideous, but it is perfectly consistent with the belief that one should be nice to one's friends. When small inconsistencies are *justified* by large consistencies, cognitive dissonance does not occur.

For example, participants in one study were asked to perform a dull task that involved turning knobs one way, then the other, and then back again. After the participants were sufficiently bored, the experimenter explained that he desperately needed a few more people to volunteer for the study, and he asked the participants to go into the hallway, find another person, and tell that person that the knob-turning task was great fun. The experimenter offered some participants $1 to tell this lie, and he offered other participants $20. All participants agreed to tell the lie, and after they did so, they were asked to report their true enjoyment of the knob-turning task. The results showed that participants liked the task *more* when they were paid $1 than $20 to lie about it (Festinger & Carlsmith, 1959). Why? Because the belief that *the knob-turning task was dull* was inconsistent with the belief that *I recommended the task to that person in the hallway,* but the latter belief was perfectly consistent with the belief that *$20 is a lot of money.* For some participants, the large payment justified the lie, so only those people who received the small payment experienced cognitive dissonance. As such, only the participants who received $1 felt the need to restore consistency by changing their beliefs about the enjoyableness of the task (**FIGURE 16.9**).

In summary, social influence requires understanding basic motives, one of which is to experience pleasure and avoid pain. People can be influenced by rewards and punishments, but they also can be influenced by observing *others* being rewarded or punished and can think about the *causes* of the rewards and punishments they receive, which can cause influence attempts to backfire. People want to be accepted by others, so they try not to violate social norms. One particularly strong norm is that people should benefit those who have benefited them, and several influence techniques put people in a position where they must either comply with a request or risk violating that norm. When people look to the behavior of others as a guide for their own actions, they often end up conforming or obeying, sometimes with disastrous results. Finally, people are motivated to have accurate attitudes and beliefs, and they achieve these in three ways. First, people use the behavior of others to help them decide what is true. Second, people use communications from others to help them decide what is true, although some of those communications appeal to reason and some appeal to habit or emotion. Third, people decide what is true by comparing new information to old information. When they recognize inconsistencies among their attitudes, beliefs, and actions, they may experience cognitive dissonance. ■ ■

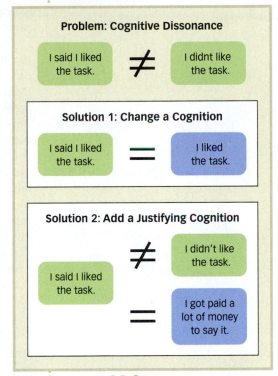

Figure 16.9 Reducing Cognitive Dissonance Behaving in ways that are inconsistent with our attitudes and beliefs can cause cognitive dissonance. One way to eliminate that dissonance is to change your attitude or belief. Another way is to add a justification.

SOCIAL COGNITION The processes by which people come to understand others.

CATEGORIZATION The process by which people identify a stimulus as a member of a class of related stimuli.

STEREOTYPING The process by which people draw inferences about others based on their knowledge of the categories to which others belong.

Social Cognition: Understanding People

Now, what's with Big Tom? Can he really be as clueless as he appears? He seems to still just be trying to float and hope for the best. . . . I can't quite make out what Jenna's trying to do either. She knows from experience that she yaps far too much and I would have thought she would have tempered that trait by now. Rob's . . . personality is humorous, but he's created animosity in several of the others . . . so he could be in serious trouble.

These words aren't great poetry. They're not even grammatical prose. But they are worth a million bucks because they represent the musings of Richard Hatch, who won the game of *Survivor* by thinking long and hard about the other people on his island—about who they were, what they did, and why (Hatch, 2005). Richard Hatch was an informal specialist in **social cognition**, which refers to *the processes by which people come to understand others,* and most of us specialize in precisely the same subject.

Indeed, the human brain itself seems specialized for social cognition. For example, the medial prefrontal cortex is activated when people think about the attributes of other people but not about the attributes of inanimate objects such as houses or tools (Mitchell, Heatherton, & Macrae, 2002). Although most brain areas show diminished activity when a person is at rest, the medial prefrontal cortex remains active all the time (Gusnard & Raichle, 2001). Why should the brain have specific areas that are dedicated to processing information about just *one* of the millions of objects it might encounter, and why should those areas remain active day and night? Because of the millions of objects a person might encounter, another person is the single most important one. We all specialize in drawing inferences about other people—about their thoughts and feelings, their beliefs and desires, their abilities and aspirations, their intentions, needs, and characters—because other people can provide us with the greatest benefits and exact from us the greatest costs.

As it turns out, the inferences we draw about other people are based on the categories to which they belong and on the things they say and do. Let's examine these two kinds of inferences in turn.

Stereotyping: Drawing Inferences from Categories

You'll recall from Chapter 7 that **categorization** is *the process by which people identify a stimulus as a member of a class of related stimuli.* Once we have identified a novel stimulus as a member of a category ("That's a textbook"), we can then use our knowledge of the category to make educated guesses about the properties of the novel stimulus ("It's probably expensive") and act accordingly ("I think I'll borrow it from the library"). The same is true of people. **Stereotyping** is *the process by which people draw inferences about others based on their knowledge of the categories to which others belong.* The moment we categorize a person as an adult, a male, a baseball player, and a Russian, we can use our knowledge of those categories to make some educated guesses about him—for example, that he shaves his face but not his legs, that he understands the infield fly rule, and that he knows more about Chekhov than we do. When we offer children candy instead of liquor or ask gas station attendants for directions instead of dating advice, we are making inferences about people whom we have never met before based solely on their category membership. As these examples suggest, stereotyping is a very useful process (Allport, 1954). And yet, ever since the word was coined in 1936, it has had a distasteful connotation. Why? Because stereotyping is a useful process that can often produce harmful results, and it does so because stereotypes can be inaccurate, overused, self-perpetuating, and automatic.

These photos show a former basketball player who was recently elected to the city council in Athens, Greece, and a Brazilian poet who wrote, "To not contemplating, I prefer eternal blindness." Despite what your stereotypes might suggest, Thiago de Mello (left) is the Brazilian poet and Yvette Jarvis (right) is the former basketball player and Greek politician.

Stereotypes Can Be Inaccurate

The inferences we draw about individuals are only as accurate as our stereotypes about the categories to which they belong. There is no evidence to indicate that Jews are especially materialistic or that Blacks are especially lazy, and yet surveys show that most American college students have held such beliefs for most of the past century (G. M. Gilbert, 1951; Karlins, Coffman, & Walters, 1969; Katz & Braly, 1933). We aren't born holding these beliefs, so how do we acquire them? There are only two ways to acquire a belief about anything: to see for yourself or to take somebody else's word for it. In fact, most of what we know about the members of human categories is hearsay—stuff we picked up from friends and uncles, from novels and newspapers, from jokes and movies and late-night television. Many of the people who believe that Jews are materialistic and Blacks are lazy have never actually met someone who is Jewish or Black, and their beliefs are a result of listening too closely to what others told them. In the process of inheriting the wisdom of our culture, it is inevitable that we also will inherit its ignorance.

But even direct observation can produce inaccurate stereotypes. For example, research participants in one study were shown a long series of positive and negative behaviors and were told that each behavior had been performed by a member of one of two groups: Group A or Group B (**FIGURE 16.10**). There were more positive than negative behaviors in the series, and there were more members of Group A than of Group B. In other words, negative behaviors were rarer than positive behaviors, and Group B members were rarer than Group A members. The series of behaviors was carefully arranged so that each group behaved negatively exactly one third of the time. After seeing the series, participants correctly remembered that Group A had behaved negatively one third of the time. However, they incorrectly remembered that Group B had behaved negatively more than *half* the time (Hamilton & Gifford, 1976).

Why did this happen? Bad behavior was rare and being a member of Group B was rare; thus participants were especially likely to notice when the two co-occurred ("Aha! There's one of those unusual Group B people doing an unusually awful thing again"). This is an example of an *illusory correlation,* or seeing a strong pattern of relationship between two things when actually little or no relationship exists. These findings help explain why members of majority groups tend to overestimate the number of crimes (which are relatively rare events) committed by members of minority groups (who are relatively rare people; that's why they're in the minority). Even when we directly observe people, we can end up with inaccurate beliefs about the groups to which they belong. This mindbug has the potential to create disastrous consequences for societies and for social relationships.

Stereotypes Can Be Overused

Because all thumbtacks are pretty much alike, our beliefs about thumbtacks ("small, cheap, painful when chewed") are quite useful, and we will rarely be mistaken if we generalize from one thumbtack to another. Human categories, however, are so variable that our stereotypes may offer only the vaguest of clues about the individuals who populate those categories. You probably believe that men have greater upper body strength than women do, and this belief is right *on average*. But the upper body strength of individuals *within* each of these categories is so varied that you cannot easily predict how much weight a particular person can lift simply by knowing that person's gender (**FIGURE 16.11**). The inherent variability of human categories makes stereotypes much less useful than they might otherwise be. In our quest to define the forest, we often miss the uniqueness of each tree.

Alas, we don't always recognize this because the mere act of categorizing a stimulus tends to warp our perceptions of that category's variability. For instance, participants in some studies were shown a series of lines of different lengths (**FIGURE 16.12** on the next page) (McGarty & Turner, 1992; Tajfel & Wilkes, 1963). For one group of participants, the

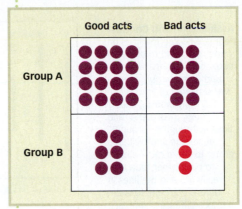

Figure 16.10 **Illusory Correlation** Both Group A and Group B each perform two-thirds good acts and one-third bad acts. However, "Group B" and "bad acts" are both rare, leading people to notice and remember their co-occurrence, which leads them to perceive a correlation between group membership and behavior that isn't really there.

Figure 16.11 **Intracategory and Intercategory Variability** As these hypothetical data show, when people are asked to lift a stool, a chair, or a desk above their heads, a larger percentage of men than women succeed at each task. But notice that although men seem to have greater upper body strength on average, there are still plenty of women who can lift a desk and plenty of men who can't lift a stool. In other words, because individuals *within* each of these gender categories differ so much, it is difficult to predict how much weight a person can lift simply by knowing his or her gender.

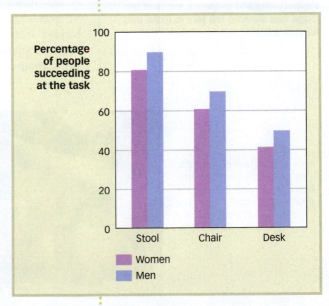

Figure 16.12
Assimilation and Contrast
People who see the lines on the right tend to *overestimate the similarity* of lines 1 and 3 and *underestimate the similarity* of lines 3 and 4. Simply labeling lines 1 through 3 "Group A" and lines 4 through 6 "Group B" causes the lines within a group to seem more similar to each other than they really are and the lines in different groups to seem more different from each other than they really are.

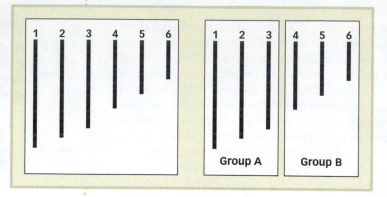

longest lines were labeled *A* and the shortest lines were labeled *B*, as they are on the right side of Figure 16.12. For the second group of participants, the lines were shown without these category labels, as they are on the left side of Figure 16.12. Interestingly, those participants who saw the category labels *overestimated* the similarity of the lines that shared a label and *underestimated* the similarity of lines that did not.

You've probably experienced this phenomenon yourself. For instance, we all identify colors as members of categories such as *blue* or *green,* and this leads us to overestimate the similarity of colors that share a category label and to underestimate the similarity of colors that do not. This is why we see discrete *bands* of color when we look at rainbows, which are actually a smooth continuum of colors. This is also why we tend to underestimate the distance between cities that are in the same country, such as Memphis, Tennessee, and Pierre, South Dakota, and overestimate the distance between cities that are in different countries, such as Memphis, Tennessee, and Toronto, Canada (Burris & Branscombe, 2005). What's true of colors and distances is true of people as well. The mere act of categorizing people as Blacks or Whites, Jews or Gentiles, artists or accountants can cause us to underestimate the variability within those categories ("All artists are wacky") and to overestimate the variability between them ("They're much wackier than accountants"). When we underestimate the variability of a human category, we feel justified in using our stereotypes.

The tendency to underestimate variability is especially likely when the person we are judging is a member of an out-group rather than a member of our in-group. In one study, Princeton students were shown a videotape of a person choosing to listen to a particular kind of music, such as jazz rather than classical (Quattrone & Jones, 1980). When the participants were told that the person shown in the videotape was a fellow Princeton student, they were reluctant to conclude that "the average Princeton student" preferred jazz to classical because *these* Princeton students in the study recognized how distinctive and unique each Princeton student is. But when these Princeton students were told that the person in the videotape was a Rutgers student, they readily concluded that the average Rutgers student preferred jazz to classical. After all, Rutgers students are all pretty much alike! And yet when the same study was performed with Rutgers students as participants, the Rutgers students were reluctant to draw conclusions about the average Rutgers student but were quick to draw conclusions about the average Princeton student.

ONLY HUMAN

SHOULD STEREOTYPING BE ILLEGAL?
In 1993, Richard Jacobs was convicted of stealing court documents. On appeal, he claimed that he was the victim of stereotyping and prejudice because the judge had allowed the jury to learn that he was a lawyer.

They may all look alike to you, but if you confuse the harmless snake on the left with the deadly snake on the right, you won't be around to do it a second time.

Stereotypes Can Be Self-Perpetuating

When we meet a man who likes ballet more than football or a senior citizen who likes hip-hop more than easy-listening, why don't we recognize that our stereotypes are inaccurate? Stereotypes are a bit like viruses, and once they take up residence inside us, they perpetuate themselves and resist even our most concerted efforts to eradicate them. Stereotypes are self-perpetuating because we see what we expect to see, we cause others to behave as we expect them to behave, and we tend to modify our stereotypes rather than abandon them. Each of these mindbugs contributes to the maintenance of stereotypic thinking. Let's look at them in turn:

- **Perceptual confirmation** is *the tendency for observers to perceive what they expect to perceive*. You may recall the study described in Chapter 2 in which students who were falsely told that a particular rat was bred to be stupid tended to underestimate that rat's performance in a maze. The same thing can happen with people. In one study, participants listened to a college basketball game and were asked to evaluate the performance of one of the players. Although all participants heard the same pre-recorded game, some were led to believe that the player was Black and others were led to believe that the player was White. Participants' stereotypes led them to expect different performances from athletes of different ethnic origins. In fact, the participants perceived just what they expected. Those who believed the player was Black thought he had exhibited greater athletic ability but less intelligence than did those who thought he was White (Stone, Perry, & Darley, 1997). Although people are especially inclined to notice and remember behaviors that are clearly at odds with their stereotypes (e.g., a skinhead reciting Shakespearean sonnets or a senator robbing a convenience store), most ordinary behaviors are ambiguous, and thus we tend to see them as confirming rather than disconfirming our stereotypes (Stangor & McMillan, 1992). Stereotypes perpetuate themselves in part by biasing our perception of individuals, leading us to believe that those individuals have confirmed our stereotypes when, in fact, they have not (Fiske, 1998).

- Stereotypes influence perception, but they also influence reality. **Self-fulfilling prophecy** is *a phenomenon whereby observers bring about what they expect to perceive*. When people know that observers have a negative stereotype about them, they may experience *stereotype threat*, or fear of confirming an observer's stereotype. Ironically, this fear can cause people to behave in precisely the way that the stereotype predicts. In one study, American students of African or European ancestry were given a test, and half of the students in each group were asked to list their race at the top of the exam. Students who were not asked to list their race performed as well as their SAT scores suggested they should (Steele & Aronson, 1995). But when students were asked to list their races, African American students performed more poorly than their SAT scores suggested they should (**FIGURE 16.13**). Other measures confirmed that the African American students who had been asked to list their race were worried about confirming a stereotype about their group, and this worry impaired their performance.

  Stereotype threat is just one of many ways in which observers may cause others to confirm a stereotype. For example, observers tend to behave unpleasantly toward people about whom they hold negative stereotypes, which leads those people to behave unpleasantly in turn, thus confirming the observer's initial belief that "those kinds of people" just aren't very nice (Harris & Rosenthal, 1985). Similarly, observers tend to seek information that confirms rather than disconfirms their stereotypes (Snyder & Swann, 1978). When a man asks a woman, "Do you like cooking more than sewing?" he is giving her very little opportunity to explain that she actually prefers sumo wrestling to both. Stereotypes perpetuate themselves in part by causing the stereotyped individual to behave in ways that confirm the stereotype.

PERCEPTUAL CONFIRMATION A phenomenon that occurs when observers perceive what they expect to perceive.

SELF-FULFILLING PROPHECY A phenomenon whereby observers bring about what they expect to perceive.

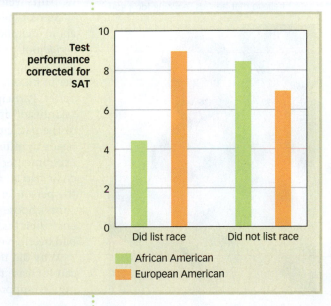

Figure 16.13 Stereotype Threat and Exam Performance When asked to indicate their race before starting a test, African American students perform more poorly than their SAT scores suggest they should.

Many of us think that nuns are traditional and proper. Does this photo of Sister Rosa Elena nailing Sister Amanda de Jesús with a snowball change your stereotype, or are you tempted to subtype them instead?

Ahmed Amadou Diallo was gunned down at his home in the Bronx on February 4, 1999. Four White police officers fired 41 shots at Diallo, who had no police record and was unarmed. Diallo was hit 19 times and died instantly. The officers testified that Diallo had gestured with his hands, leading them to believe that he was reaching for a gun.

- When a person clearly disconfirms an observer's stereotype, the observer may find ways to modify—and therefore retain—the stereotype (Weber & Crocker, 1983). For example, people tend to believe that public relations agents are sociable. In one study, participants learned about a PR agent who was *slightly* unsociable, and the results showed that their stereotypes about PR agents shifted a bit to accommodate this new information. But when participants learned about a PR agent who was *extremely* unsociable, their stereotypes did not change at all (Kunda & Oleson, 1997). Why? Because when participants encountered an *extremely* unsociable PR agent ("Rick—a PR agent from Des Moines who works primarily with divorce attorneys—just can't stand the company of other people"), they engaged in *subtyping*. Rather than changing their stereotypes of PR agents ("I guess they aren't such a sociable bunch"), they created a new, highly specialized subcategory of PR agents ("PR agents from Iowa who work for small law firms are very unsociable"), which allowed them to think of the extremely unsociable PR agent as "an exception to the rule" and thereby preserve their stereotypes about PR agents in general. Subtyping is a powerful method for preserving our stereotypes in the face of contradictory evidence.

Stereotyping Can Be Automatic

If stereotypes are inaccurate and self-perpetuating, then why don't we just stop using them? Because stereotyping can happen *unconsciously* (which means that we don't always know we are using them) and *automatically* (which means that we often cannot avoid using them even when we try). For example, in one study, photos of Black or White men holding guns or cameras were flashed on a computer screen for less than 1 second each. Participants earned money by pressing a button labeled "shoot" whenever the man on the screen was holding a gun but lost money if they shot a man holding a camera. The participants made some mistakes, of course, but the kinds of mistakes they made were quite disturbing: Participants were more likely to shoot a man holding a gun when that man was Black and less likely to shoot a man holding a camera when that man was White (Correll et al., 2002). Although the photos appeared on the screen so quickly that participants did not have enough time to consciously consult their stereotypes, those stereotypes worked unconsciously, causing them to mistake a camera for a gun when it was in the hands of a Black man and a gun for a camera when it was in the hands of a White man. Interestingly, Black participants were just as likely to make this pattern of errors as were White participants.

Stereotypes comprise all the information that we have absorbed over the years about members of different human categories, for better or for worse, and we can't *decide* not to use that information any more than we can *decide* not to see the color green, not to remember our high school graduation, or not to enjoy the smell of lavender in bloom. In fact, trying not to use stereotypes can make matters worse instead of better. Participants in one study were shown a photograph of a tough-looking male "skinhead" and were asked to write an essay describing a typical day in his life. Some of the participants were told that they should not allow their stereotypes about skinheads to influence their essays, and others were given no such instructions. Next, the experimenter brought each participant to a room with eight empty chairs. The first chair had a jacket draped over it, and the experimenter explained that it belonged to the person in the photograph, who had gone to use the restroom. Where did participants choose to sit? Participants who had been told not to let their stereotypes influence their essays sat farther away from the skinhead's jacket than did participants who had been given no instructions (Macrae et al., 1994).

Why did this happen? As you learned in Chapter 8, attempts to suppress a thought can increase the likelihood that people will experience the very thought they are trying to suppress (Wegner et al., 1987). Stereotypical thoughts are no exception.

BRIAN PLONKA/THE SPOKESMAN REVIEW

AP PHOTO/HO

Although stereotyping is often unconscious and automatic, it is not inevitable (Blair, 2002). We cannot stop using stereotypes with the flick of a mental switch, but research shows that stereotyping effects can be reduced (and sometimes eliminated) by a variety of factors ranging from educational programs (Kawakami et al., 2000; Rudman, Ashmore, & Gary, 2001) to damage to the prefrontal cortex (Milne & Grafman, 2001). Education is probably the better social policy.

Attribution: Drawing Inferences from Actions

In 1963, Dr. Martin Luther King Jr. gave a speech in which he described his vision for America. "I have a dream that my four children will one day live in a nation where they will not be judged by the color of their skin but by the content of their character." Research on stereotyping demonstrates that Dr. King's concerns were well justified. We do indeed judge others by the color of their skin—as well as by their gender, nationality, religion, age, and occupation—and in so doing, we sometimes make tragic errors. But are we any better at judging people by the content of their character? If we could "turn off" our stereotypes and treat each person as an individual, would we judge these individuals accurately?

Not necessarily. Treating a person as an individual means judging them by their own words and deeds. This is more difficult than it sounds because the relationship between what a person *is* and what a person *says or does* is not always straightforward. An honest person may lie to save a friend from embarrassment, and a dishonest person may tell the truth to bolster her credibility. Happy people have some rotten days, polite people can be rude in traffic, and people who despise us can be flattering when they need a favor. In short, a person's behavior *sometimes* tells us about the kind of person they are, but sometimes it simply tells us about the kind of situation they happen to be in.

To judge a person accurately we need to know not only *what* they did but also *why* they did it. Is the batter who hit the home run a talented slugger, or was the wind blowing in just the right direction? Is the politician who gave the pro-life speech really opposed to abortion, or was she just trying to win the conservative vote? When we answer questions such as these, we are making **attributions**, which are *inferences about the causes of people's behaviors* (Gilbert, 1998; Heider, 1958; Jones & Davis, 1965; Kelley, 1967). We make *situational attributions* when we decide that a person's behavior was caused by some temporary aspect of the situation in which it happened ("He was lucky that the wind carried the ball into the stands"), and we make *dispositional attributions* when we decide that a person's behavior was caused by his or her relatively enduring tendency to think, feel, or act in a particular way ("He's got a great eye and a powerful swing").

How do we know whether to make a dispositional or a situational attribution? According to Harold Kelley's *covariation model* (Kelley, 1967), we use three kinds of information: consistency, distinctiveness, and consensus. For example, imagine that you wanted to know why your neighbor didn't mow his lawn last weekend. Is he lazy, or did bad weather keep him indoors? According to the covariation model, we should consider information about the *regularity* of his action (consistency information), information about the *generality* of his action (distinctiveness information), and information about the *typicality* of his action (consensus information). If your neighbor rarely mows his lawn ("not mowing" is consistent over time), if he avoided every other form of work last weekend (lawn mowing is not distinctive), and if everyone else on the block mowed their lawns last weekend (his action is not consensual with the actions of others), then you should probably make a dispositional attribution, such as, "My neighbor is lazy." On the other hand, if your neighbor usually mows his lawn on the weekend (his current action of "not mowing" is inconsistent over time), if he fixed the screen door and painted the kitchen last weekend (his action is distinctive), and if no one else on the block mowed their lawns last weekend (his action is consensual with the actions of others), then

ATTRIBUTION An inference about the cause of a person's behavior.

"For God's sake, think! Why is he being so nice to you?"

Figure 16.14 The Covariation Model of Attribution Harold Kelley's covariation model tells us how to use information to make an attribution for another person's action, such as his failure to mow the lawn last week. If the person's action is consistent (he often fails to mow the lawn) but not distinctive (he avoids other kinds of work) and not consensual (other people did mow their lawns last week), then the model tells us to make a dispositional attribution. If the person's action is not consistent (he usually mows his lawn) but is distinctive (he doesn't avoid other kinds of work) and consensual (other people didn't mow their lawns last week), the model tells us to make a situational attribution.

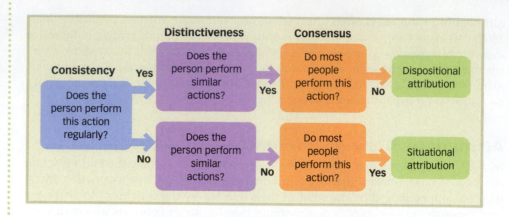

you should probably make a situational attribution, such as, "It must have been raining." As **FIGURE 16.14** shows, patterns of consistency, distinctiveness, and consensus provide useful information about the cause of a person's behavior.

Research suggests that people don't always use this information as they should. The psychologist Edward E. Jones discovered the **correspondence bias**, which is *the tendency to make a dispositional attribution even when a person's behavior was caused by the situation* (Gilbert & Malone, 1995; Jones & Harris, 1967; Ross, 1977). This bias is one of the most commonly observed mindbugs, which is why the psychologist Lee Ross has called it the *fundamental attribution error*. For example, volunteers in one experiment played a trivia game in which one participant acted as the "quizmaster" and made up a list of unusual questions, another participant acted as the "contestant" and tried to answer those questions, and a third participant acted as the "observer" and simply watched the game. The quizmasters tended to ask tricky questions based on their own idiosyncratic knowledge, and contestants were generally unable to answer them. After watching the game, the observers were asked to decide how knowledgeable the quizmaster and the contestant were. Although the quizmasters had asked good questions and the contestants had given bad answers, it should have been clear to the observers that all this asking and answering was a product of the roles they had been assigned to play and that the contestant would have asked equally good questions and the quizmaster would have given equally bad answers had their roles been reversed. And yet observers tended to rate the quizmaster as more knowledgeable than the contestant (Ross, Amabile, & Steinmetz, 1977) and were

Do abusive people seek power or does power lead people to be abusive? In Philip Zimbardo's infamous "Stanford Prison Experiment," researchers built a simulated prison in the basement of the psychology department and randomly assigned volunteers to play the role of prisoner or guard. The study had to be abandoned when many of the "guards" began abusing the "prisoners." In a situation where ordinary people were given the power to harm, they used it. The researchers wrote, "If these reactions had been observed within the confines of an existing penal institution, it is probable that a dispositional hypothesis [or, attribution] would be invoked as an explanation" (Haney, Banks, & Zimbardo, 1973). Indeed, more than 30 years later, the prisoner abuse and torture at Abu Ghraib in Iraq was officially denounced as the work of "a few bad apples."

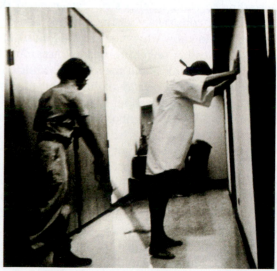

more likely to choose the quizmaster as their own partner in an upcoming game (Quattrone, 1982). Even when we know that a successful athlete had a home field advantage or that a successful entrepreneur had family connections, we tend to attribute their success to talent and tenacity.

The tendency toward correspondence bias varies from person to person (D'Agostino & Fincher-Kiefer, 1992), situation to situation (Fein, Hilton, & Miller, 1990), and culture to culture (Choi, Nisbett, & Norenzayan, 1999), but research suggests that, as a general rule, people tend to make dispositional attributions even when other people's actions were clearly caused by the situations in which they happened. Indeed, people often make dispositional attributions even when *they themselves* have caused the other person's actions (which is why "Tell me you love me" remains such a popular request) (Gilbert & Jones, 1986). Why do we make dispositional attributions even when we shouldn't?

First, the situational causes of behavior are often invisible (Ichheiser, 1949). For example, professors tend to assume that fawning students really do admire them in spite of the strong incentive for students to suck up to those who control their grades. The problem is that professors can literally *see* the student laughing at witless jokes and applauding after boring lectures, but they cannot *see* "control over grades." Situations are not as tangible or visible as behaviors, so it is all too easy to ignore them (Taylor & Fiske, 1978). Second, even when situations are too obvious to ignore, we find it difficult to *use* the information we have about them. For example, when participants in one study were asked to perform a mentally taxing task (such as keeping a seven-digit number in mind) while making attributions, they had no difficulty making dispositional attributions, but they found it quite difficult to make situational attributions (Gilbert, Pelham, & Krull, 1988; Winter & Uleman, 1984). Situational attributions tend to be more complex and require more time and attention, which means that they are less likely to be made in the busy world of everyday life. Information about situations is hard to get and hard to use, and thus we are prone to believe that others' actions are caused by their dispositions.

We are more prone to correspondence bias when judging others than when judging ourselves. The **actor-observer effect** is *the tendency to make situational attributions for our own behaviors while making dispositional attributions for the identical behavior of others* (Jones & Nisbett, 1972). When college students were asked to explain why they and their friends had chosen their majors, they tended to explain their own choices in terms of situations ("I chose economics because my parents told me I have to support myself as soon as I'm done with college") but tended to explain their friends' choices in terms of dispositions ("Norma chose economics because she's materialistic") (Nisbett et al., 1973). The actor-observer effect occurs because people typically have *more information* about the situations that caused their own behavior than about the situations

CORRESPONDENCE BIAS The tendency to make a dispositional attribution even when a person's behavior was caused by the situation.

ACTOR-OBSERVER EFFECT The tendency to make situational attributions for our own behaviors while making dispositional attributions for the identical behavior of others.

The Kennedy brothers (Senator Robert, Senator Ted, and President John) and the Bush brothers (Governor Jeb and President George) were all very successful men with very successful fathers. Was their success due to the content of their characters or to the money and fame that came with their family names?

that caused other people's behavior. We can remember getting the please-major-in-something-practical lecture from our parents, but we weren't at Norma's house to see her get the same lecture. As observers, we are focused on another person's behavior, but as actors, we are focused—quite literally—on the situations in which our behavior occurs. In fact, when conversationalists are shown a videotape of their conversation that allows them to see it from their partner's point of view, they tend to make dispositional attributions for their own behavior and situational attributions for their partner's (Storms, 1973; Taylor & Fiske, 1975).

In summary, we make inferences about people based on the categories to which they belong, which is the basis of stereotyping. This method can lead us to misjudge others for four reasons: Stereotypes can be inaccurate; stereotypes can be overused; stereotypes can perpetuate themselves; and stereotypes can operate unconsciously and automatically, which makes it difficult to avoid using them. We also make inferences about people based on their behaviors, assuming that others act as they do because of the situations in which they find themselves or because of their own dispositions. However, we tend to attribute actions to dispositions even when we should not. We are less prone to this error when making attributions for our own behavior. ■ ■

Where Do You Stand?

Are You Prejudiced?

The satirist Ambrose Bierce (1911) defined a *bigot* as "one who is obstinately and zealously attached to an opinion that you do not entertain." Indeed, most of us think of prejudice as a bad habit whose defining feature is that other people do it and we don't. Not so fast. Just because you don't sit around thinking evil thoughts about people who don't share your religious or ethnic background doesn't mean that you are free of prejudice. Recent research by psychologists Anthony Greenwald, Mahzarin Banaji, and their colleagues using the *implicit association test* (IAT) suggests that even people who think of themselves as egalitarian can harbor unconscious prejudices against members of out-groups.

In one study, White participants were asked to classify a series of words (Greenwald, McGhee, & Schwartz, 1998). Some of the words were common nouns such as *tulip* or *aunt*, and some of the words were proper names such as *Greg* or *Jamal*. The common nouns were related to a dislikable category such as *insects* or to a likable category such as *flowers*. The proper names were related to the participant's in-group (Whites) or to his or her out-group (Blacks). When one of these words appeared on the computer screen, the

participant's job was to press a button as quickly as possible to indicate whether it was a flower, an insect, a predominantly White name, or a predominantly Black name.

Now comes the interesting part. Although the participants were asked to classify the words as belonging to one of four categories, the experimental apparatus only had two buttons! On the *consistent* trials, participants were told to press the right-hand button if the word was either an insect or a Black name and to press the left-hand button if the word was a flower or a White name. On the *inconsistent* trials, participants were told to press the left-hand button if the word was a flower or a Black name and to press the right-hand button if the word was an insect or a White name (see the figure below). Why did the experimenters arrange and rearrange the apparatus this way? Because previous

a) Consistent Trials

b) Inconsistent Trials

research has shown that a classification task of this sort is much easier if the dislikable words (or the likable words) share a single button. Thus, if White participants disliked Black names, they should have found the classification task easier when Black names and insects shared one button and White names and flowers shared the other. Consistent trials should have been easier than inconsistent trials *only* if participants disliked Black names and liked White names. As the results in the figure to the right show, White participants were much faster on the consistent than the inconsistent trials.

Do these results mean that these White participants were a bunch of hate-mongers? Probably not. Psychologists since Freud have recognized that people can consciously think one thing while unconsciously feeling another. Whites who honestly believe in tolerance, diversity, and racial equality and who harbor no conscious prejudice toward Blacks may still show evidence of unconscious prejudice on the IAT (Greenwald & Nosek, 2001). In fact, Black participants also show unconscious prejudice against Blacks (Lieberman et al., 2005).

How can our conscious and unconscious attitudes be so different? You know from Chapter 6 that if an experimenter repeatedly exposed you to the word *democracy* while administering an electric shock, you would eventually develop a negative association with that word. Yet if the experimenter

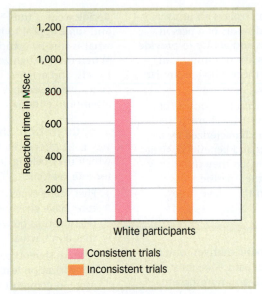

Results of an IAT Experiment In this IAT experiment, White participants respond faster on consistent trials when a likable object is paired with a White name. The reaction time on inconsistent trials is considerably slower. (Greenwald, McGhee, & Schwartz, 1998)

explicitly asked you how you felt about democracy, you would probably say you liked it. In other words, you would have *both* a negative unconscious attitude toward democracy that was based on nothing more than the pairing of the word with electric shock and a positive conscious attitude

toward democracy that was based on your knowledge of world politics (Wilson, Lindsey, & Schooler, 2000). Similarly, Whites who have positive conscious attitudes toward Blacks may nonetheless develop negative unconscious attitudes simply by watching movies and reading newspapers that pair Black names and faces with negative concepts, such as *poverty* and *crime*. Because all Americans are exposed to the same media, Blacks have the same unconscious attitudes toward their own group that Whites do (Greenwald et al., 2002). Both conscious and unconscious attitudes are real, and each influences behavior under different circumstances (Eberhardt, 2005; Phelps et al., 2000).

This research has potentially profound social, moral, legal, and ethical implications. For instance, in the United States, employers are not allowed to discriminate against applicants on the basis of gender or race (among other things), and they face severe legal repercussions if they are found to have done so. Yet, if people have prejudices that they don't know about and can't control—if they consciously believe all the right things but unconsciously believe some of the wrong ones—then how can they be held accountable for any ill actions that their prejudices may produce? Before you decide where you stand on this issue, you might want to take the IAT yourself at https://implicit.harvard.edu/implicit/demo/.

Chapter Review

Social Behavior: Interacting with People

- Human beings are social animals, and social psychology is the study of the causes and consequences of their social interaction. Like all animals, human beings are designed to survive and reproduce.
- Survival requires scarce resources, and two primary ways to get them are aggression and cooperation. Impulsive aggression is a reaction to a negative internal state, and males are particularly prone to use aggression to ensure their status. The primary risk of cooperation is that others may take benefits without bearing costs.

- Belonging to a group tends to reduce the risks associated with cooperation. Unfortunately, groups often disparage those who are not members, they sometimes make poor decisions, and they may even take reprehensible actions that no individual member would take alone.
- Reproduction requires choosing the right mate. Because both biology and culture make the costs of reproduction so much higher for women than for men, women tend to be choosier.
- Attraction is a feeling that draws us closer to a potential mate, and it has both situational and personal determinants. Of the

personal determinants, physical appearance plays an unusually important role because it can provide indicators of a person's genetic endowment and their willingness and ability to provide for offspring. Psychological determinants are also important, and people seem to be most attracted to those who are similar to them on a wide variety of dimensions.

■ Reproduction is usually accomplished within the context of a long-term romantic relationship that is initially characterized by feelings of intense attraction and later characterized by feelings of friendship. People weigh the costs and benefits of their relationships and tend to dissolve them when they think they can or should do better, when they and their partners have very different cost-benefit ratios, or when they have little invested in the relationship.

Social Influence: Controlling People

■ Social influence requires understanding basic motives, one of which is to experience pleasure and avoid pain. Like most animals, people can be influenced by rewards and punishments. But unlike most animals, people can be influenced by observing others being rewarded or punished and think about the causes of the rewards and punishments they receive, which can cause influence attempts to backfire.

■ People want to be accepted by others, and thus they try not to violate norms. One particularly strong norm is that people should benefit those who have benefited them, and several influence techniques put people in a position where they must either comply with a request or risk violating that norm.

■ When people do not know the norms in a particular situation, they look to the behavior of others. As such, they often end up doing what others are doing or doing what they are told to do. This kind of conformity and obedience can sometimes lead to shocking outcomes.

■ Finally, people are motivated to have accurate attitudes and beliefs, and they achieve these in three ways. First, people use the behavior of others to help them decide what is true. Second, people use communications from others to help them decide what is true. Some communications appeal to reason and some appeal to habit or emotion. Third, people decide what is true by comparing new information to old information. When they recognize inconsistencies among their attitudes, beliefs, and actions, they may experience an unpleasant state of cognitive dissonance. To alleviate this state, people may attempt to eliminate the inconsistency or to justify it.

Social Cognition: Understanding People

■ We make inferences about people based on the categories to which they belong. This method can lead us to misjudge others for four reasons.

1. First, stereotypes can be inaccurate, either because our cultures have given us misinformation or because we have seen relationships between category membership and behavior that don't actually exist.

2. Second, stereotypes can be overused because the mere act of categorization leads us to see category members as having more in common than they actually do. This is especially likely to happen when we are judging members of categories to which we do not belong.

3. Third, stereotypes can perpetuate themselves by causing us to see what we expect to see, to treat others in ways that lead them to behave as we expected, and to "explain away" disconfirming evidence.

4. Fourth, stereotypes can operate unconsciously and automatically, which makes it difficult to avoid using them.

■ We also make inferences about people based on their actions. We assume that other people act as they do because of the situations in which they find themselves or because of their own dispositions.

■ When a person's action is low in consistency, high in distinctiveness, and high in consensus, we should attribute the action to the situation. But research shows that we tend to attribute actions to dispositions even when we should not. This happens because situations are difficult to see and because information about situations is difficult to use.

Key Terms

aggression (p. 623)

frustration-aggression principle (p. 623)

cooperation (p. 625)

altruism (p. 627)

kin selection (p. 627)

reciprocal altruism (p. 627)

group (p. 628)

prejudice (p. 628)

discrimination (p. 628)

in-group (p. 628)

out-group (p. 628)

deindividuation (p. 629)

social loafing (p. 629)

bystander intervention (p. 629)

diffusion of responsibility (p. 629)

group polarization (p. 629)

mere exposure effect (p. 632)

passionate love (p. 638)

companionate love (p. 638)

social exchange (p. 639)

comparison level (p. 639)

equity (p. 639)

social influence (p. 640)

observational learning (p. 641)

norms (p. 642)

normative influence (p. 642)

norm of reciprocity (p. 642)

door-in-the-face technique (p. 642)

conformity (p. 643)

obedience (p. 644)

attitude (p. 645)

belief (p. 645)

informational influence (p. 646)

persuasion (p. 647)

systematic persuasion (p. 647)

heuristic persuasion (p. 647)

foot-in-the-door technique (p. 650)

cognitive dissonance (p. 650)

social cognition (p. 652)

categorization (p. 652)

stereotyping (p. 652)

perceptual confirmation (p. 655)

self-fulfilling prophecy (p. 655)

attributions (p. 657)

correspondence bias (p. 658)

actor-observer effect (p. 659)

Recommended Readings

Baumeister, R. F. (1999). *Evil: Inside human violence and cruelty.* New York: Freeman. A leading social psychologist presents a discussion of the psychological roots of human aggression and violence. Roy Baumeister challenges much of the conventional wisdom regarding where violence comes from.

Buss, D. M. (1995). *The evolution of desire: Strategies of human mating.* New York: Basic Books. David Buss surveys research on intimate relationships from the evolutionary perspective. The adaptive significance of behaviors related to love and relationships receives special attention.

Cialdini, R. B. (2000). *Influence: Science and practice* (4th ed.). New York: Morrow. This classic volume presents an engaging, witty, and scientific discussion of techniques for wielding and escaping social influence. Robert Cialdini himself has conducted a wealth of studies in this area.

Etcoff, N. (1999). *Survival of the prettiest: The science of beauty.* New York: Doubleday. Nancy Etcoff reviews research on physical attractiveness from a variety of perspectives: social, biological, archaeological, and cross-cultural.

Gilovich, T. (1991). *How we know what isn't so: The fallibility of human reason in everyday life.* New York: Free Press. Tom Gilovich discusses the mistakes people make when judging others. This book has several illuminating examples drawn from real-life situations.

Glossary

absentmindedness A lapse in attention that results in memory failure. (p. 189)

absolute threshold The minimal intensity needed to just barely detect a stimulus. (p. 124)

accommodation The process by which infants revise their schemas in light of new information. (p. 413)

accommodation The process by which the eye maintains a clear image on the retina. (p. 132)

acetylcholine (ACh) A neurotransmitter involved in a number of functions, including voluntary motor control. (p. 83)

acquisition The phase of classical conditioning when the CS and the US are presented together. (p. 214)

action potential An electric signal that is conducted along an axon to a synapse. (p. 80)

activation-synthesis model The theory that dreams are produced when the brain attempts to make sense of activations that occur randomly during sleep. (p. 317)

actor-observer effect The tendency to make situational inferences for our own behaviors while making dispositional inferences for the identical behavior of others. (p. 659)

adolescence The period of development that begins with the onset of sexual maturity (about 11 to 14 years of age) and lasts until the beginning of adulthood (about 18 to 21 years of age). (p. 430)

adulthood The period of development that begins around 18 to 21 years and ends at death. (p. 438)

affective forecasting The process by which people predict their emotional reactions to future events. (p. 378)

aggression Behavior whose purpose is to harm another. (p. 623)

agonists Drugs that increase the action of a neurotransmitter. (p. 85)

agoraphobia An extreme fear of venturing out into public places. (p. 505)

alcohol myopia A condition that results when alcohol hampers attention, leading people to respond in simple ways to complex situations. (p. 322)

algorithm A well-defined sequence of procedures or rules that guarantees a solution to a problem. (p. 275)

altered states of consciousness Forms of experience that depart from the normal subjective experience of the world and the mind. (p. 309)

altruism Behavior that benefits another without benefiting oneself. (p. 627)

amygdala A part of the limbic system that plays a central role in many emotional processes, particularly the formation of emotional memories. (p. 96)

anal stage The second psychosexual stage, which is dominated by the pleasures and frustrations associated with the anus, retention and expulsion of feces and urine, and toilet training. (p. 468)

analogical problem solving Solving a problem by finding a similar problem with a known solution and applying that solution to the current problem. (p. 281)

anorexia nervosa An eating disorder characterized by an intense fear of being fat and severe restriction of food intake. (p. 392)

antagonists Drugs that block the function of a neurotransmitter. (p. 85)

anterograde amnesia The inability to transfer new information from the short-term store into the long-term store. (p. 177)

antianxiety medications Drugs that help reduce a person's experience of fear or anxiety. (p. 562)

antidepressants A class of drugs that help lift people's mood. (p. 563)

antipsychotic drugs Medications that are used to treat schizophrenia and related psychotic disorders. (p. 560)

antisocial personality disorder (APD) A pervasive pattern of disregard for and violation of the rights of others that begins in childhood or early adolescence and continues into adulthood. (p. 529)

anxiety disorder The class of mental disorder in which anxiety is the predominant feature. (p. 501)

aphasia Difficulty in producing or comprehending language. (p. 262)

apparent motion The perception of movement as a result of alternating signals appearing in rapid succession in different locations. (p. 149)

appraisal An evaluation of the emotion-relevant aspects of a stimulus that is performed by the amygdala. (p. 374)

approach motivation A motivation to experience positive outcomes. (p. 400)

area A1 A portion of the temporal lobe that contains the primary auditory cortex. (p. 152)

area V1 The part of the occipital lobe that contains the primary visual cortex. (p. 138)

assimilation The process by which infants apply their schemas in novel situations. (p. 413)

association areas Areas of the cerebral cortex that are composed of neurons that help provide sense and meaning to information registered in the cortex. (p. 99)

attachment The emotional bond that forms between newborns and their primary caregivers. (p. 422)

attitude An enduring positive or negative evaluation of an object or event. (p. 645)

attribution An inference about the cause of a person's behavior. (p. 657)

autonomic nervous system (ANS) A set of nerves that carries involuntary and automatic commands that control blood vessels, body organs, and glands. (p. 88)

availability bias Items that are more readily available in memory are judged as having occurred more frequently. (p. 275)

aversion therapy A form of behavior therapy that uses positive punishment to reduce the frequency of an undesirable behavior. (p. 548)

avoidance motivation A motivation not to experience negative outcomes. (p. 400)

axon The part of a neuron that transmits information to other neurons, muscles, or glands. (p. 75)

balanced placebo design A study design in which behavior is observed following the presence or absence of an actual stimulus and also following the presence or absence of a placebo stimulus. (p. 322)

basal ganglia A set of subcortical structures that directs intentional movements. (p. 97)

basilar membrane A structure in the inner ear that undulates when vibrations from the ossicles reach the cochlear fluid. (p. 152)

behavior Observable actions of human beings and nonhuman animals. (p. 2)

behavior therapy A type of therapy that assumes that disordered behavior is learned, and symptom relief is achieved through changing overt maladaptive behaviors to more constructive behaviors. (p. 548)

behavioral neuroscience An approach to psychology that links psychological processes to activities in the nervous system and other bodily processes. (p. 24)

behaviorism An approach that advocates that psychologists restrict themselves to the scientific study of objectively observable behavior. (p. 17)

belief An enduring piece of knowledge about an object or event. (p. 645)

belief bias People's judgments about whether to accept conclusions depend more on how believable the conclusions are than on whether the arguments are logically valid. (p. 287)

bias The distorting influences of present knowledge, beliefs, and feelings on recollection of previous experiences. (p. 200)

Big Five The traits of the five-factor model: conscientiousness, agreeableness, neuroticism, openness to experience, and extraversion. (p. 457)

binocular disparity The difference in the retinal images of the two eyes that provides information about depth. (p. 146)

biofeedback The use of an external monitoring device to obtain information about a bodily function and possibly gain control over that function. (p. 598)

biological preparedness A propensity for learning particular kinds of associations over others. (p. 223)

bipolar disorder An unstable emotional condition characterized by cycles of abnormal, persistent high mood (mania) and low mood (depression). (p. 515)

blind spot An area of the retina that contains neither rods nor cones and therefore has no mechanism to sense light. (p. 134)

blocking A failure to retrieve information that is available in memory even though you are trying to produce it. (p. 192)

bulimia nervosa An eating disorder characterized by binge eating followed by purging. (p. 392)

burnout A state of physical, emotional, and mental exhaustion created by long-term involvement in an emotionally demanding situation and accompanied by lowered performance and motivation. (p. 594)

bystander intervention The act of helping strangers in an emergency situation. (p. 629)

Cannon-Bard theory A theory about the relationship between emotional experience and physiological activity suggesting that a stimulus simultaneously triggers activity in the autonomic nervous system and emotional experience in the brain. (p. 370)

Cartesian Theater (after philosopher René Descartes) A mental screen or stage on which things appear to be presented for viewing by the mind's eye. (p. 294)

case method A method of gathering scientific knowledge by studying a single individual. (p. 44)

catatonic behavior A marked decrease in all movement or an increase in muscular rigidity and overactivity. (p. 521)

categorization The process by which people identify a stimulus as a member of a class of related stimuli. (p. 652)

category-specific deficit A neurological syndrome that is characterized by an inability to recognize objects that belong to a particular category while leaving the ability to recognize objects outside the category undisturbed. (p. 268)

cell body The part of a neuron that coordinates information-processing tasks and keeps the cell alive. (p. 75)

central nervous system (CNS) The part of the nervous system that is composed of the brain and spinal cord. (p. 87)

cephalocaudal rule The "top-to-bottom" rule that describes the tendency for motor skills to emerge in sequence from the head to the feet. (p. 411)

cerebellum A large structure of the hindbrain that controls fine motor skills. (p. 93)

cerebral cortex The outermost layer of the brain, visible to the naked eye and divided into two hemispheres. (p. 95)

childhood The stage of development that begins at about 18 to 24 months and lasts until adolescence. (p. 415)

chromosomes Strands of DNA wound around each other in a double-helix configuration. (p. 104)

chronic stressor A source of stress that occurs continuously or repeatedly. (p. 584)

chunking Combining small pieces of information into larger clusters or chunks that are more easily held in short-term memory. (p. 175)

circadian rhythm A naturally occurring 24-hour cycle. (p. 309)

classical conditioning When a neutral stimulus evokes a response after being paired with a stimulus that naturally evokes a response. (p. 212)

cochlea A fluid-filled tube that is the organ of auditory transduction. (p. 152)

cocktail party phenomenon A phenomenon in which people tune in one message even while they filter out others nearby. (p. 299)

cognitive behavioral therapy (CBT) A blend of cognitive and behavioral therapeutic strategies. (p. 552)

cognitive development The emergence of the ability to understand the world. (p. 412)

cognitive dissonance An unpleasant state that arises when a person recognizes the inconsistency of his or her actions, attitudes, or beliefs. (p. 650)

cognitive map A mental representation of the physical features of the environment. (p. 238)

cognitive neuroscience A field that attempts to understand the links between cognitive processes and brain activity. (p. 25)

cognitive psychology The scientific study of mental processes, including perception, thought, memory, and reasoning. (p. 21)

cognitive restructuring A therapeutic approach that teaches clients to question the automatic beliefs, assumptions, and predictions that often lead to negative emotions and to replace negative thinking with more realistic beliefs. (p. 551)

cognitive therapy A form of psychotherapy that involves helping a client identify and correct any distorted thinking about self, others, or the world. (p. 550)

cognitive unconscious The mental processes that give rise to the person's thoughts, choices, emotions, and behavior even though they are not experienced by the person. (p. 306)

color-opponent system Pairs of visual neurons that work in opposition. (p. 137)

comorbidity The co-occurrence of two or more disorders in a single individual. (p. 496)

companionate love An experience involving affection, trust, and concern for a partner's well-being. (p. 638)

comparison level The cost-benefit ratio that people believe they deserve or could attain in another relationship. (p. 638)

concept A mental representation that groups or categorizes shared features of related objects, events, or other stimuli. (p. 267)

concrete operational stage The stage of development that begins at about 6 years and ends at about 11 years, in which children acquire a basic understanding of the physical world and a preliminary understanding of their own and others' minds. (p. 415)

conditioned response (CR) A reaction that resembles an unconditioned response but is produced by a conditioned stimulus. (p. 213)

conditioned stimulus (CS) A stimulus that is initially neutral and produces no reliable response in an organism. (p. 213)

cones Photoreceptors that detect color, operate under normal daylight conditions, and allow us to focus on fine detail. (p. 132)

conformity The tendency to do what others do simply because others are doing it. (p. 643)

conjunction fallacy When people think that two events are more likely to occur together than either individual event. (p. 276)

conscious motivation A motivation of which one is aware. (p. 399)

consciousness A person's subjective experience of the world and the mind. (pp. 8, 294)

conservation The notion that the properties of an object are invariant despite changes in the object's appearance. (p. 415)

construct validity The tendency for an operational definition and a property to have a clear conceptual relation. (p. 43)

control group One of the two groups of participants created by the manipulation of an independent variable in an experiment that is not exposed to the stimulus being studied. (p. 60)

conventional stage A stage of moral development in which the morality of an action is primarily determined by the extent to which it conforms to social rules. (p. 427)

conversion disorder A disorder characterized by apparently debilitating physical symptoms that appear to be voluntary—but that the person experiences as involuntary. (p. 607)

cooperation Behavior by two or more individuals that leads to mutual benefit. (p. 625)

corpus callosum A thick band of nerve fibers that connects large areas of the cerebral cortex on each side of the brain and supports communication of information across the hemispheres. (p. 98)

correlation The "co-relationship" or pattern of covariation between two variables, each of which has been measured several times. (p. 53)

correlation coefficient A statistical measure of the direction and strength of a correlation, which is signified by the letter *r*. (p. 54)

correspondence bias The tendency to make a dispositional attribution even when a person's behavior was caused by the situation. Also known as the fundamental attribution error. (p. 658)

crystallized intelligence The accuracy and amount of information available for processing (see *fluid intelligence*). (p. 348)

cultural psychology The study of how cultures reflect and shape the psychological processes of their members. (p. 29)

debriefing A verbal description of the true nature and purpose of a study that psychologists provide to people after they have participated in the study. (p. 68)

deep structure The meaning of a sentence. (p. 256)

defense mechanisms Unconscious coping mechanisms that reduce anxiety generated by threats from unacceptable impulses. (p. 466)

deindividuation A phenomenon that occurs when immersion in a group causes people to become less aware of their individual values. (p. 629)

delusion A patently false belief system, often bizarre and grandiose, that is maintained in spite of its irrationality. (p. 520)

demand characteristics Those aspects of an observational setting that cause people to behave as they think an observer wants or expects them to behave. (p. 49)

dendrites The part of a neuron that receives information from other neurons and relays it to the cell body. (p. 75)

dependent variable The variable that is measured in a study. (p. 60)

depressants Substances that reduce the activity of the central nervous system. (p. 321)

developmental psychology The study of continuity and change across the life span. (p. 406)

deviation IQ A statistic obtained by dividing a person's test score by the average test score of people in the same age group and then multiplying the quotient by 100 (see *ratio IQ*). (p. 340)

diathesis-stress model Suggests that a person may be predisposed for a mental disorder that remains unexpressed until triggered by stress. (p. 498)

dichotic listening A task in which people wearing headphones hear different messages presented to each ear. (p. 298)

diffusion of responsibility The tendency for individuals to feel diminished responsibility for their actions when they are surrounded by others who are acting the same way. (p. 629)

discrimination Positive or negative behavior toward another person based on their group membership. (p. 628)

discrimination The capacity to distinguish between similar but distinct stimuli. (p. 217)

disorganized speech Severe disruption of verbal communication in which ideas shift rapidly and incoherently from one to another unrelated topic. (p. 521)

displacement A defense mechanism that involves shifting unacceptable wishes or drives to a neutral or less-threatening alternative. (p. 467)

display rules Norms for the control of emotional expression. (p. 383)

dissociative amnesia The sudden loss of memory for significant personal information. (p. 510)

dissociative disorder A disorder in which normal cognitive processes are severely disjointed and fragmented, creating significant disruptions in memory, awareness, or personality that can vary in length from a matter of minutes to many years. (p. 508)

dissociative fugue The sudden loss of memory for one's personal history, accompanied by an abrupt departure from home and the assumption of a new identity. (p. 510)

dissociative identity disorder (DID) The presence within an individual of two or more distinct identities that at different times take control of the individual's behavior. (p. 508)

dissociative identity disorder A condition that involves the occurrence of two or more distinct identities within the same individual. (p. 14)

DMS-IV-TR Diagnostic and Statistical Manual of Mental Disorders (Fourth Edition, Text Revision). (p. 491)

door-in-the-face technique A strategy that uses reciprocating concessions to influence behavior. (p. 642)

dopamine A neurotransmitter that regulates motor behavior, motivation, pleasure, and emotional arousal. (p. 84)

dopamine hypothesis The idea that schizophrenia involves an excess of dopamine activity. (p. 524)

double depression A moderately depressed mood that persists for at least 2 years and is punctuated by periods of major depression. (p. 512)

double-blind An observation whose true purpose is hidden from the researcher as well as from the participant. (p. 51)

drive An internal state generated by departures from physiological optimality. (p. 390)

drug tolerance The tendency for larger doses of a drug to be required over time to achieve the same effect. (p. 319)

dynamic unconscious An active system encompassing a lifetime of hidden memories, the person's deepest instincts and desires, and the person's inner struggle to control these forces. (pp. 305, 463)

dysthymia A disorder that involves the same symptoms as in depression only less severe, but the symptoms last longer, persisting for at least 2 years. (p. 512)

echoic memory A fast-decaying store of auditory information. (p. 174)

eclectic psychotherapy Treatment that draws on techniques from different forms of therapy, depending on the client and the problem. (p. 543)

ego The component of personality, developed through contact with the external world, that enables us to deal with life's practical demands. (p. 464)

egocentrism The failure to understand that the world appears differently to different observers. (p. 416)

elaborative encoding The process of actively relating new information to knowledge that is already in memory. (p. 170)

electroconvulsive therapy (ECT) A treatment that involves inducing a mild seizure by delivering an electric shock to the brain. (p. 567)

electroencephalogram (EEG) A device used to record electrical activity in the brain. (p. 110)

electromyograph (EMG) A device that measures muscle contractions under the surface of a person's skin. (p. 42)

electrooculograph (EOG) An instrument that measures eye movements. (p. 311)

embryonic stage The period of prenatal development that lasts from the second week until about the eighth week. (p. 407)

emotion A positive or negative experience that is associated with a particular pattern of physiological activity. (p. 307)

emotion regulation The use of cognitive and behavioral strategies to influence one's emotional experience. (p. 376)

emotional expression Any observable sign of an emotional state. (p. 377)

empiricism Originally a Greek school of medicine that stressed the importance of observation, and now generally used to describe any attempt to acquire knowledge by observing objects or events. (p. 40)

encoding The process by which we transform what we perceive, think, or feel into an enduring memory. (p. 169)

encoding specificity principle The idea that a retrieval cue can serve as an effective reminder when it helps re-create the specific way in which information was initially encoded. (p. 180)

endorphins or **endogenous opiates** Neurotransmitters that have a similar structure to opiates and that appear to play a role in how the brain copes internally with pain and emotion. (pp. 84, 325)

episodic memory The collection of past personal experiences that occurred at a particular time and place. (p. 185)

equity A state of affairs in which the cost-benefit ratios of two partners are roughly equal. (p. 638)

evolutionary psychology A psychological approach that explains mind and behavior in terms of the adaptive value of abilities that are preserved over time by natural selection. (p. 26)

exemplar theory A theory of categorization that argues that we make category judgments by comparing a new instance with stored memories for other instances of the category. (p. 272)

existential approach A school of thought that regards personality as governed by an individual's ongoing choices and decisions in the context of the realities of life and death. (p. 472)

expectancy theory The idea that alcohol effects can be produced by people's expectations of how alcohol will influence them in particular situations. (p. 321)

experiment A technique for establishing the causal relationship between variables. (p. 58)

experimental group One of the two groups of participants created by the manipulation of an independent variable in an experiment; the experimental group is exposed to the stimulus being studied and the *control group* is not. (p. 60)

explicit memory The act of consciously or intentionally retrieving past experiences. (p. 183)

exposure therapy An approach to treatment that involves confronting an emotion-arousing stimulus directly and repeatedly, ultimately leading to a decrease in the emotional response. (p. 549)

expressed emotion Emotional overinvolvement (intrusiveness) and excessive criticism directed toward the former patient by his or her family. (p. 525)

external validity A characteristic of an experiment in which the independent and dependent variables are operationally defined in a normal, typical, or realistic way. (p. 65)

extinction The gradual elimination of a learned response that occurs when the US is no longer presented. (p. 216)

extrinsic motivation A motivation to take actions that are not themselves rewarding but that lead to reward. (p. 397)

facial feedback hypothesis The hypothesis that emotional expressions can cause the emotional experiences they signify. (p. 381)

factor analysis A statistical technique that explains a large number of correlations in terms of a small number of underlying factors. (p. 345)

false recognition A feeling of familiarity about something that hasn't been encountered before. (p. 194)

family resemblance theory Members of a category have features that appear to be characteristic of category members but may not be possessed by every member. (p. 269)

fast mapping The fact that children can map a word onto an underlying concept after only a single exposure. (p. 258)

fetal alcohol syndrome A developmental disorder that stems from heavy alcohol use by the mother during pregnancy. (p. 408)

fetal stage The period of prenatal development that lasts from the ninth week until birth. (p. 408)

fight-or-flight response An emotional and physiological reaction to an emergency that increases readiness for action. (p. 586)

fixation A phenomenon in which a person's pleasure-seeking drives become psychologically stuck, or arrested, at a particular psychosexual stage. (p. 468)

fixed interval schedule (FI) An operant conditioning principle in which reinforcements are presented at fixed time periods, provided that the appropriate response is made. (p. 231)

fixed ratio schedule (FR) An operant conditioning principle in which reinforcement is delivered after a specific number of responses have been made. (p. 232)

flashbulb memories Detailed recollections of when and where we heard about shocking events. (p. 201)

fluid intelligence The ability to process information (see *crystallized intelligence*). (p. 348)

foot-in-the-door technique A strategy that uses a person's desire for consistency to influence that person's behavior. (p. 650)

formal operations stage The stage of development that begins around the age of 11 and lasts through adulthood, in which children gain a deeper understanding of their own and others' minds and learn to reason abstractly. (p. 416)

fovea An area of the retina where vision is the clearest and there are no rods at all. (p. 133)

framing effects When people give different answers to the same problem depending on how the problem is phrased (or framed). (p. 277)

fraternal twins (also called **dizygotic twins**) Twins who develop from two different eggs that were fertilized by two different sperm (see *identical twins*). (p. 352)

frequency distribution A graphical representation of the measurements of a sample that are arranged by the number of times each measurement was observed. (p. 46)

frequency format hypothesis The proposal that our minds evolved to notice how frequently things occur, not how likely they are to occur. (p. 280)

frontal lobe A region of the cerebral cortex that has specialized areas for movement, abstract thinking, planning, memory, and judgment. (p. 99)

frustration-aggression principle A principle stating that people aggress when their goals are thwarted. (p. 623)

full consciousness Consciousness in which you know and are able to report your mental state. (p. 300)

functional fixedness The tendency to perceive the functions of objects as fixed. (p. 284)

functionalism The study of the purpose mental processes serve in enabling people to adapt to their environment. (p. 10)

fundamental attribution error See *correspondence bias*.

GABA (gamma-aminobutyric acid) The primary inhibitory neurotransmitter in the brain. (p. 84)

gate-control theory A theory of pain perception based on the idea that signals arriving from pain receptors in the body can be stopped, or *gated*, by interneurons in the spinal cord via feedback from two directions. (p. 157)

gene The unit of hereditary transmission. (p. 104)

general adaptation syndrome (GAS) A three-stage physiological response that appears regardless of the stressor that is encountered. (p. 587)

generalization A process in which the CR is observed even though the CS is slightly different from the original one used during acquisition. (p. 217)

generalized anxiety disorder (GAD) A disorder characterized by chronic excessive worry accompanied by three or more of the following symptoms: restlessness, fatigue, concentration problems, irritability, muscle tension, and sleep disturbance. (p. 502)

genetic dysphasia A syndrome characterized by an inability to learn the grammatical structure of language despite having otherwise normal intelligence. (p. 260)

genital stage The final psychosexual stage, a time for the coming together of the mature adult personality with a capacity to love, work, and relate to others in a mutually satisfying and reciprocal manner. (p. 470)

germinal stage The 2-week period of prenatal development that begins at conception. (p. 407)

Gestalt psychology A psychological approach that emphasizes that we often perceive the whole rather than the sum of the parts. (p. 13)

Gestalt therapy An existentialist approach to treatment with the goal of helping the client become aware of his or her thoughts, behaviors, experiences, and feelings and to "own" or take responsibility for them. (p. 555)

glial cells Support cells found in the nervous system. (p. 76)

glutamate A major excitatory neurotransmitter involved in information transmission throughout the brain. (p. 84)

grammar A set of rules that specify how the units of language can be combined to produce meaningful messages. (p. 255)

grossly disorganized behavior Behavior that is inappropriate for the situation or ineffective in attaining goals, often with specific motor disturbances. (p. 521)

group A collection of two or more people who believe they have something in common. (p. 628)

group polarization The tendency for a group's initial leaning to get stronger over time. (p. 629)

group therapy Therapy in which multiple participants (who often do not know one another at the outset) work on their individual problems in a group atmosphere. (p. 557)

habituation A general process in which repeated or prolonged exposure to a stimulus results in a gradual reduction in responding. (p. 211)

hair cells Specialized auditory receptor neurons embedded in the basilar membrane. (p. 152)

hallucination A false perceptual experience that has a compelling sense of being real despite the absence of external stimulation. (p. 520)

hallucinogens Drugs that alter sensation and perception and often cause visual and auditory hallucinations. (p. 326)

haptic perception The active exploration of the environment by touching and grasping objects with our hands. (p. 155)

harm reduction approach A response to high-risk behaviors that focuses on reducing the harm such behaviors have on people's lives. (p. 325)

health psychology The subfield of psychology concerned with ways psychological factors influence the causes and treatment of physical illness and the maintenance of health. (p. 582)

hedonic principle The notion that all people are motivated to experience pleasure and avoid pain. (p. 388)

helplessness theory The idea that individuals prone to depression automatically attribute negative experiences to causes that are internal (i.e., their own fault), stable (i.e., unlikely to change), and global (i.e., widespread). (p. 514)

heritability A measure of the variability of behavioral traits among individuals that can be accounted for by genetic factors. (p. 106)

heritability coefficient A statistic (commonly denoted as $h2$) that describes the proportion of the difference between people's scores that can be explained by differences in their genetic makeup. (p. 353)

heuristic A fast and efficient strategy that may facilitate decision making but does not guarantee that a solution will be reached. (p. 275)

heuristic persuasion A change in attitudes or beliefs that is brought about by appeals to habit or emotion. (p. 647)

hindbrain An area of the brain that coordinates information coming into and out of the spinal cord. (p. 93)

hippocampus A structure critical for creating new memories and integrating them into a network of knowledge so that they can be stored indefinitely in other parts of the cerebral cortex. (p. 96)

homeostasis The tendency for a system to take action to keep itself in a particular state. (p. 390)

human sexual response cycle The stages of physiological arousal during sexual activity. (p. 396)

humanistic psychology An approach to understanding human nature that emphasizes the positive potential of human beings. (p. 16)

hypnosis An altered state of consciousness characterized by suggestibility and the feeling that one's actions are occurring involuntarily. (p. 327)

hypnotic analgesia The reduction of pain through hypnosis in people who are susceptible to hypnosis. (p. 330)

hypochondriasis A psychological disorder in which a person is preoccupied with minor symptoms and develops an exaggerated belief that the symptoms signify a life-threatening illness. (p. 607)

hypothalamus A subcortical structure that regulates body temperature, hunger, thirst, and sexual behavior. (p. 95)

hypothesis A specific and testable prediction that is usually derived from a *theory*. (p. 65)

hysteria A temporary loss of cognitive or motor functions, usually as a result of emotionally upsetting experiences. (p. 14)

iatrogenic illness A disorder or symptom that occurs as a result of a medical or psychotherapeutic treatment. (p. 576)

iconic memory A fast-decaying store of visual information. (p. 174)

id The part of the mind containing the drives present at birth; it is the source of our bodily needs, wants, desires, and impulses, particularly our sexual and aggressive drives. (p. 464)

identical twins (also called **monozygotic twins**) Twins who develop from the splitting of a single egg that was fertilized by a single sperm (see *fraternal twins*). (p. 352)

identification A defense mechanism that helps deal with feelings of threat and anxiety by enabling us unconsciously to take on the characteristics of another person who seems more powerful or better able to cope. (p. 467)

illusions Errors of perception, memory, or judgment in which subjective experience differs from objective reality. (p. 12)

immune system A complex response system that protects the body from bacteria, viruses, and other foreign substances. (p. 588)

implicit learning Learning that takes place largely independent of awareness of both the process and the products of information acquisition. (p. 246)

implicit memory The influence of past experiences on later behavior and performance, even though people are not trying to recollect them and are not aware that they are remembering them. (p. 183)

in-group A human category of which a person is a member. (p. 628)

independent variable The variable that is manipulated in an experiment. (p. 60)

infancy The stage of development that begins at birth and lasts between 18 and 24 months. (p. 410)

informational influence A phenomenon whereby a person's behavior is influenced by another person's behavior because the latter provides information about what is good or true. (p. 646)

informed consent A written agreement to participate in a study made by a person who has been informed of all the risks that participation may entail. (p. 68)

insomnia Difficulty in falling asleep or staying asleep. (p. 313)

intelligence A hypothetical mental ability that enables people to direct their thinking, adapt to their circumstances, and learn from their experiences. (p. 351)

intermittent reinforcement An operant conditioning principle in which only some of the responses made are followed by reinforcement. (p. 233)

intermittent-reinforcement effect The fact that operant behaviors that are maintained under intermittent reinforcement schedules resist extinction better than those maintained under continuous reinforcement. (p. 233)

internal validity The characteristic of an experiment that allows one to draw accurate inferences about the causal relationship between an independent and dependent variable. (p. 64)

internal working model of attachment A set of expectations about how the primary caregiver will respond when the child feels insecure. (p. 424)

interneurons Neurons that connect sensory neurons, motor neurons, or other interneurons. (p. 77)

interpersonal psychotherapy (IPT) A form of psychotherapy that focuses on helping clients improve their social relationships. (p. 547)

intrinsic motivation A motivation to take actions that are themselves rewarding. (p. 397)

introspection The subjective observation of one's own experience. (p. 8)

ironic processes of mental control Mental processes that can produce ironic errors because monitoring for errors can itself produce them. (p. 304)

James-Lange theory A theory about the relationship between emotional experience and physiological activity suggesting that stimuli trigger activity in the autonomic nervous system, which in turn produces an emotional experience in the brain. (p. 370)

just noticeable difference (JND) The minimal change in a stimulus that can just barely be detected. (p. 126)

kin selection The process by which evolution selects for genes that cause individuals to provide benefits to their relatives. (p. 627)

language A system for communicating with others using signals that convey meaning and are combined according to rules of grammar. (p. 254)

language acquisition device (LAD) A collection of processes that facilitate language learning. (p. 260)

latency stage The fourth psychosexual stage, in which the primary focus is on the further development of intellectual, creative, interpersonal, and athletic skills. (p. 469)

latent content A dream's true underlying meaning. (p. 317)

latent learning A condition in which something is learned but it is not manifested as a behavioral change until sometime in the future. (p. 238)

law of effect The principle that behaviors that are followed by a "satisfying state of affairs" tend to be repeated and those that produce an "unpleasant state of affairs" are less likely to be repeated. (p. 225)

law of large numbers A statistical law stating that as sample size increases, the attributes of a sample will more closely reflect the attributes of the population from which it was drawn. (p. 45)

learning Some experience that results in a relatively permanent change in the state of the learner. (p. 210)

limbic system A group of forebrain structures including the hypothalamus, the amygdala, and the hippocampus, which are involved in motivation, emotion, learning, and memory. (p. 96)

linguistic relativity hypothesis The proposal that language shapes the nature of thought. (p. 266)

locus of control A person's tendency to perceive the control of rewards as internal to the self or external in the environment. (p. 476)

long-term memory store A place where information can be kept for hours, days, weeks, or years. (p. 177)

long-term potentiation (LTP) Enhanced neural processing that results from the strengthening of synaptic connections. (p. 178)

loudness A sound's intensity. (p. 150)

lymphocytes White blood cells that produce antibodies that fight infection. (p. 588)

major depressive disorder A disorder characterized by a severely depressed mood that lasts 2 weeks or more and is accompanied by feelings of worthlessness and lack of pleasure, lethargy, and sleep and appetite disturbances. (p. 512)

manifest content A dream's apparent topic or superficial meaning. (p. 317)

manipulation A characteristic of experimentation in which the researcher artificially creates a pattern of variation in an independent variable in order to determine its causal powers. Manipulation usually results in the creation of an *experimental group* and a *control group*. (p. 59)

marijuana The leaves and buds of the hemp plant. (p. 326)

matched pairs An observational technique that involves matching each participant in the experimental group with a specific participant in the control group in order to eliminate the possibility that a third variable (and not the independent variable) caused changes in the dependent variable. (p. 57)

matched samples An observational technique that involves matching the average of the participants in the experimental and control groups in order to eliminate the possibility that a third variable (and not the independent variable) caused changes in the dependent variable. (p. 57)

mean The average of the measurements in a frequency distribution. (p. 47)

means-ends analysis A process of searching for the means or steps to reduce differences between the current situation and the desired goal. (p. 281)

measure A device that can detect the measurable events to which an operational definition refers. (p. 42)

median The "middle" measurement in a frequency distribution. Half the measurements in a frequency distribution are greater than or equal to the median and half are less than or equal to the median. (p. 47)

medical model The conceptualization of psychological abnormalities as diseases that, like biological diseases, have symptoms and causes and possible cures. (p. 491)

meditation The practice of intentional contemplation. (p. 332)

medulla An extension of the spinal cord into the skull that coordinates heart rate, circulation, and respiration. (p. 93)

memory The ability to store and retrieve information over time. (p. 168)

memory misattribution Assigning a recollection or an idea to the wrong source. (p. 193)

memory storage The process of maintaining information in memory over time. (p. 173)

mental control The attempt to change conscious states of mind. (p. 303)

mere exposure effect The tendency for liking to increase with the frequency of exposure. (p. 632)

metabolism The rate at which energy is used by the body. (p. 394)

method A set of rules and techniques for observation that allow researchers to avoid the illusions, mistakes, and erroneous conclusions that simple observation can produce. (p. 40)

mind Our private inner experience of perceptions, thoughts, memories, and feelings. (p. 2)

mind/body problem The issue of how the mind is related to the brain and body. (p. 297)

mindfulness meditation A form of cognitive therapy that teaches an individual to be fully present in each moment; to be aware of his or her thoughts, feelings and sensations; and to detect symptoms before they become a problem. (p. 551)

minimal consciousness A low-level kind of sensory awareness and responsiveness that occurs when the mind inputs sensations and may output behavior. (p. 300)

Minnesota Multiphasic Personality Inventory (MMPI) A well-researched, clinical questionnaire used to assess personality and psychological problems. (p. 452)

mode The "most frequent" measurement in a frequency distribution. (p. 47)

monocular depth cues Aspects of a scene that yield information about depth when viewed with only one eye. (p. 145)

mood disorders Mental disorders that have a disturbance in mood as their predominant feature. (p. 511)

morphemes The smallest meaningful units of language. (p. 255)

morphological rules A set of rules that indicate how morphemes can be combined to form words. (p. 255)

motion parallax A depth cue based on the movement of the head over time. (p. 147)

motivation The purpose for or cause of an action. (p. 386)

motor development The emergence of the ability to execute physical action. (p. 411)

motor neurons Neurons that carry signals from the spinal cord to the muscles to produce movement. (p. 77)

myelin sheath An insulating layer of fatty material. (p. 76)

myelination The formation of a fatty sheath around the axons of a brain cell. (p. 408)

narcissism A trait that reflects a grandiose view of the self combined with a tendency to seek admiration from and exploit others. (p. 484)

narcolepsy A disorder in which sudden sleep attacks occur in the middle of waking activities. (p. 314)

narcotics or **opiates** Highly addictive drugs derived from opium that relieve pain. (p. 324)

nativism The philosophical view that certain kinds of knowledge are innate or inborn. (p. 5)

nativist theory The view that language development is best explained as an innate, biological capacity. (p. 260)

natural correlation A correlation observed between naturally occurring variables. (p. 56)

natural selection Charles Darwin's theory that the features of an organism that help it survive and reproduce are more likely than other features to be passed on to subsequent generations. (p. 10)

naturalistic observation A method of gathering scientific knowledge by unobtrusively observing people in their natural environments. (p. 49)

need for achievement The motivation to solve worthwhile problems. (p. 399)

negative symptoms Emotional and social withdrawal, apathy, poverty of speech, and other indications of the absence or insufficiency of normal behavior, motivation, and emotion. (p. 521)

nervous system An interacting network of neurons that conveys electrochemical information throughout the body. (p. 87)

neurons Cells in the nervous system that communicate with one another to perform information-processing tasks. (p. 74)

neurotransmitters Chemicals that transmit information across the synapse to a receiving neuron's dendrites. (p. 81)

night terrors (or sleep terrors) Abrupt awakenings with panic and intense emotional arousal. (p. 314)

NMDA receptor A hippocampal receptor site that influences the flow of information from one neuron to another across the synapse by controlling the initiation of long-term potentiation. (p. 178)

nonshared environment Those environmental factors that are not experienced by all relevant members of a household (see *shared environment*). (p. 355)

norepinephrine A neurotransmitter that influences mood and arousal. (p. 84)

norm A customary standard for behavior that is widely shared by members of a culture. (p. 642)

norm of reciprocity The norm that people should benefit those who have benefited them. (p. 642)

normal distribution A frequency distribution in which most measurements are concentrated around the mean and fall off toward the tails, and the two sides of the distribution are symmetrical. (p. 47)

normative influence A phenomenon whereby one person's behavior is influenced by another person's behavior because the latter provides information about what is appropriate. (p. 642)

obedience The tendency to do what authorities tell us to do simply because they tell us to do it. (p. 644)

object permanence The idea that objects continue to exist even when they are not visible. (p. 413)

observational learning A condition in which learning takes place by watching the actions of others. (p. 243)

observational learning Learning that occurs when one person observes another person being rewarded or punished. (p. 641)

obsessive-compulsive disorder (OCD) A disorder in which repetitive, intrusive thoughts (obsessions) and ritualistic behaviors (compulsions) designed to fend off those thoughts interfere significantly with an individual's functioning. (p. 507)

occipital lobe A region of the cerebral cortex that processes visual information. (p. 98)

Oedipus conflict A developmental experience in which a child's conflicting feelings toward the opposite-sex parent is (usually) resolved by identifying with the same-sex parent. (p. 469)

olfactory bulb A brain structure located above the nasal cavity beneath the frontal lobes. (p. 159)

olfactory receptor neurons (ORNs) Receptor cells that initiate the sense of smell. (p. 158)

operant behavior Behavior that an organism produces that has some impact on the environment. (p. 225)

operant conditioning A type of learning in which the consequences of an organism's behavior determine whether it will be repeated in the future. (p. 224)

operational definition A description of an abstract property in terms of a concrete condition that can be measured. (p. 41)

oral stage The first psychosexual stage, in which experience centers on the pleasures and frustrations associated with the mouth, sucking, and being fed. (p. 468)

organizational encoding The act of categorizing information by noticing the relationships among a series of items. (p. 172)

out-group A human category of which a person is not a member. (p. 628)

outcome expectancies A person's assumptions about the likely consequences of a future behavior. (p. 476)

overjustification effect Circumstances when external rewards can undermine the intrinsic satisfaction of performing a behavior. (p. 229)

panic disorder A disorder characterized by the sudden occurrence of multiple psychological and physiological symptoms that contribute to a feeling of stark terror. (p. 505)

parasympathetic nervous system A set of nerves that helps the body return to a normal resting state. (p. 88)

parietal lobe A region of the cerebral cortex whose functions include processing information about touch. (p. 98)

passionate love An experience involving feelings of euphoria, intimacy, and intense sexual attraction. (p. 638)

perception The organization, identification, and interpretation of a sensation in order to form a mental representation. (p. 123)

perceptual confirmation A phenomenon that occurs when observers perceive what they expect to perceive. (p. 655)

perceptual constancy A perceptual principle stating that even as aspects of sensory signals change, perception remains consistent. (p. 142)

peripheral nervous system (PNS) The part of the nervous system that connects the central nervous system to the body's organs and muscles. (p. 87)

persistence The intrusive recollection of events that we wish we could forget. (p. 201)

person-centered therapy An approach to therapy that assumes all individuals have a tendency toward growth and that this growth can be facilitated by acceptance and genuine reactions from the therapist. (p. 553)

person-situation controversy The question of whether behavior is caused more by personality or by situational factors. (p. 474)

personal constructs Dimensions people use in making sense of their experiences. (p. 475)

personality An individual's characteristic style of behaving, thinking, and feeling. (p. 450)

personality disorder A disorder characterized by deeply ingrained, inflexible patterns of thinking, feeling, relating to others, or controlling impulses that causes distress or impaired functioning. (p. 526)

persuasion A phenomenon that occurs when a person's attitudes or beliefs are influenced by a communication from another person. (p. 647)

phallic stage The third psychosexual stage, during which experience is dominated by the pleasure, conflict, and frustration associated with the phallic-genital region as well as powerful incestuous feelings of love, hate, jealousy, and conflict. (p. 469)

phenomenology How things seem to the conscious person. (p. 295)

pheromones Biochemical odorants emitted by other members of their species that can affect an animal's behavior or physiology. (p. 160)

philosophical empiricism The philosophical view that all knowledge is acquired through experience. (p. 5)

phobic disorders Disorders characterized by marked, persistent, and excessive fear and avoidance of specific objects, activities, or situations. (p. 503)

phoneme The smallest unit of sound that is recognizable as speech rather than as random noise. (p. 254)

phonological rules A set of rules that indicate how phonemes can be combined to produce speech sounds. (p. 255)

phototherapy A treatment for seasonal depression that involves repeated exposure to bright light. (p. 568)

phrenology A now defunct theory that specific mental abilities and characteristics, ranging from memory to the capacity for happiness, are localized in specific regions of the brain. (p. 7)

physiology The study of biological processes, especially in the human body. (p. 7)

pitch How high or low a sound is. (p. 150)

pituitary gland The "master gland" of the body's hormone-producing system, which releases hormones that direct the functions of many other glands in the body. (p. 96)

place code The cochlea encodes different frequencies at different locations along the basilar membrane. (p. 153)

placebo An inert substance or procedure that has been applied with the expectation that a healing response will be produced. (p. 571)

placebo effect A clinically significant psychological or physiological response to a therapeutically inert substance or procedure. (p. 606)

pleasure principle The psychic force that motivates the tendency to seek immediate gratification of any impulse. (p. 464)

pons A brain structure that relays information from the cerebellum to the rest of the brain. (p. 94)

population The complete collection of participants who might possibly be measured. (p. 45)

postconventional stage A stage of moral development at which the morality of an action is determined by a set of general principles that reflect core values. (p. 427)

posthypnotic amnesia The failure to retrieve memories following hypnotic suggestions to forget. (p. 330)

posttraumatic stress disorder (PTSD) A psychological disorder characterized by chronic physiological arousal, recurrent unwanted thoughts or images of the trauma, and avoidance of things that call the trauma to mind. (p. 592)

power The tendency for a measure to produce different results when it is used to measure different things. (p. 44)

practical reasoning Figuring out what to do, or reasoning directed toward action. (p. 286)

preconventional stage A stage of moral development in which the morality of an action is primarily determined by its consequences for the actor. (p. 427)

predictive validity The tendency for an operational definition to be related to other operational definitions. (p. 43)

prejudice A positive or negative evaluation of another person based on their group membership. (p. 628)

preoperational stage The stage of development that begins at about 2 years and ends at about 6 years, in which children have a preliminary understanding of the physical world. (p. 415)

preparedness theory The idea that people are instinctively predisposed toward certain fears. (p. 504)

primary sex characteristics Bodily structures that are directly involved in reproduction. (p. 431)

priming An enhanced ability to think of a stimulus, such as a word or object, as a result of a recent exposure to the stimulus. (p. 184)

proactive interference Situations in which earlier learning impairs memory for information acquired later. (p. 189)

problem of other minds The fundamental difficulty we have in perceiving the consciousness of others. (p. 295)

procedural memory The gradual acquisition of skills as a result of practice, or "knowing how," to do things. (p. 183)

prodigy A person of normal intelligence who has an extraordinary ability. (p. 350)

projection A defense mechanism that involves attributing one's own threatening feelings, motives, or impulses to another person or group. (p. 466)

projective techniques A standard series of ambiguous stimuli designed to elicit unique responses that reveal inner aspects of an individual's personality. (p. 452)

prospect theory Proposes that people choose to take on risk when evaluating potential losses and avoid risks when evaluating potential gains. (p. 279)

prospective memory Remembering to do things in the future. (p. 191)

prototype The "best" or "most typical member" of a category. (p. 270)

proximodistal rule The "inside-to-outside" rule that describes the tendency for motor skills to emerge in sequence from the center to the periphery. (p. 411)

psychoactive drug A chemical that influences consciousness or behavior by altering the brain's chemical message system. (p. 318)

psychoanalysis A therapeutic approach that focuses on bringing unconscious material into conscious awareness to better understand psychological disorders. (p. 15)

psychoanalytic theory Sigmund Freud's approach to understanding human behavior that emphasizes the importance of unconscious mental processes in shaping feelings, thoughts, and behaviors. (p. 15)

psychodynamic approach An approach that regards personality as formed by needs, strivings, and desires, largely operating outside of awareness—motives that can also produce emotional disorders. (p. 463)

psychodynamic psychotherapies A general approach to treatment that explores childhood events and encourages individuals to develop insight into their psychological problems. (p. 543)

psychology The scientific study of mind and behavior. (p. 2)

psychopharmacology The study of drug effects on psychological states and symptoms. (p. 560)

psychophysics Methods that measure the strength of a stimulus and the observer's sensitivity to that stimulus. (p. 124)

psychosexual stages Distinct early life stages through which personality is formed as children experience sexual pleasures from specific body areas and caregivers redirect or interfere with those pleasures. (p. 468)

psychosomatic illness An interaction between mind and body that can produce illness. (p. 607)

psychosurgery Surgical destruction of specific brain areas. (p. 569)

psychotherapy An interaction between a therapist and someone suffering from a psychological problem with the goal of providing support or relief from the problem. (p. 541)

puberty The bodily changes associated with sexual maturity. (p. 431)

punisher Any stimulus or event that functions to decrease the likelihood of the behavior that led to it. (p. 226)

random sampling A technique for choosing participants that ensures that every member of a population has an equal chance of being included in the sample. (p. 66)

randomization A procedure to ensure that a participant's inclusion in the experimental or control group is not determined by a third variable. (p. 61)

range The numerical difference between the smallest and largest measurements in a frequency distribution. (p. 47)

ratio IQ A statistic obtained by dividing a person's mental age by the person's physical age and then multiplying the quotient by 100 (see *deviation IQ*). (p. 339)

rational choice theory The classical view that we make decisions by determining how likely something is to happen, judging the value of the outcome, and then multiplying the two. (p. 274)

rational coping Facing a stressor and working to overcome it. (p. 596)

rationalization A defense mechanism that involves supplying a reasonable-sounding explanation for unacceptable feelings and behavior to conceal (mostly from oneself) one's underlying motives or feelings. (p. 466)

reaction formation A defense mechanism that involves unconsciously replacing threatening inner wishes and fantasies with an exaggerated version of their opposite. (p. 466)

reaction time The amount of time taken to respond to a specific stimulus. (p. 7)

reality principle The regulating mechanism that enables the individual to delay gratifying immediate needs and function effectively in the real world. (p. 464)

reappraisal A strategy that involves changing one's emotional experience by changing the meaning of the emotion- eliciting stimulus. (p. 376)

reasoning A mental activity that consists of organizing information or beliefs into a series of steps to reach conclusions. (p. 285)

rebound effect of thought suppression The tendency of a thought to return to consciousness with greater frequency following suppression. (p. 303)

receptive field The region of the sensory surface that, when stimulated, causes a change in the firing rate of that neuron. (p. 134)

receptors Parts of the cell membrane that receive the neurotransmitter and initiate a new electric signal. (p. 81)

reciprocal altruism Behavior that benefits another with the expectation that those benefits will be returned in the future. (p. 627)

referred pain Feeling of pain when sensory information from internal and external areas converge on the same nerve cells in the spinal cord. (p. 156)

reflexes Specific patterns of motor response that are triggered by specific patterns of sensory stimulation. (p. 411)

refractory period The time following an action potential during which a new action potential cannot be initiated. (p. 81)

reframing Finding a new or creative way to think about a stressor that reduces its threat. (p. 597)

regression A defense mechanism in which the ego deals with internal conflict and perceived threat by reverting to an immature behavior or earlier stage of development. (p. 467)

rehearsal The process of keeping information in short-term memory by mentally repeating it. (p. 174)

reinforcement The consequences of a behavior that determine whether it will be more likely that the behavior will occur again. (p. 19)

reinforcer Any stimulus or event that functions to increase the likelihood of the behavior that led to it. (p. 226)

relaxation response A condition of reduced muscle tension, cortical activity, heart rate, breathing rate, and blood pressure. (p. 598)

relaxation therapy A technique for reducing tension by consciously relaxing muscles of the body. (p. 598)

reliability The tendency for a measure to produce the same result whenever it is used to measure the same thing. (p. 44)

REM sleep A stage of sleep characterized by rapid eye movements and a high level of brain activity. (p. 310)

representativeness heuristic A mental shortcut that involves making a probability judgment by comparing an object or event to a prototype of the object or event. (p. 277)

repression A mental process that removes unacceptable thoughts and memories from consciousness. (p. 305)

repressive coping Avoiding situations or thoughts that are reminders of a stressor and maintaining an artificially positive viewpoint. (p. 595)

resistance A reluctance to cooperate with treatment for fear of confronting unpleasant unconscious material. (p. 544)

response An action or physiological change elicited by a stimulus. (p. 19)

resting potential The difference in electric charge between the inside and outside of a neuron's cell membrane. (p. 79)

reticular formation A brain structure that regulates sleep, wakefulness, and levels of arousal. (p. 93)

retina Light-sensitive tissue lining the back of the eyeball. (p. 132)

retrieval The process of bringing to mind information that has been previously encoded and stored. (p. 169)

retrieval cue External information that is associated with stored information and helps bring it to mind. (p. 180)

retroactive interference Situations in which later learning impairs memory for information acquired earlier. (p. 189)

retrograde amnesia The inability to retrieve information that was acquired before a particular date, usually the date of an injury or operation. (p. 177)

rods Photoreceptors that become active only under low-light conditions for night vision. (p. 132)

Rorschach Inkblot Test A projective personality test in which individual interpretations of the meaning of a set of unstructured inkblots are analyzed to identify a respondent's inner feelings and interpret his or her personality structure. (p. 453)

sample The partial collection of people who actually were measured in a study. (p. 45)

savant A person of low intelligence who has an extraordinary ability. (p. 350)

schemas Theories or models of the way the world works. (p. 413)

schizophrenia A disorder characterized by the profound disruption of basic psychological processes, a distorted perception of reality, altered or blunted emotion, and disturbances in thought, motivation, and behavior. (p. 519)

seasonal affective disorder (SAD) Depression that involves recurrent depressive episodes in a seasonal pattern. (p. 512)

second-order conditioning Conditioning where the US is a stimulus that acquired its ability to produce learning from an earlier procedure in which it was used as a CS. (p. 215)

secondary sex characteristics Bodily structures that change dramatically with sexual maturity but that are not directly involved in reproduction. (p. 431)

self-actualizing tendency The human motive toward realizing our inner potential. (p. 471)

self-concept A person's explicit knowledge of his or her own behaviors, traits, and other personal characteristics. (p. 478)

self-consciousness A distinct level of consciousness in which the person's attention is drawn to the self as an object. (p. 301)

self-esteem The extent to which an individual likes, values, and accepts the self. (p. 480)

self-fulfilling prophecy A phenomenon whereby observers bring about what they expect to perceive. (p. 655)

self-regulation The exercise of voluntary control over the self to bring the self into line with preferred standards. (p. 613)

self-report A series of answers to a questionnaire that asks people to indicate the extent to which sets of statements or adjectives accurately describe their own behavior or mental state. (p. 452)

self-selection The case in which a participant's inclusion in the experimental or control group is determined by the participant. (p. 61)

self-serving bias People's tendency to take credit for their successes but downplay responsibility for their failures. (p. 484)

self-verification The tendency to seek evidence to confirm the self-concept. (p. 480)

semantic memory A network of associated facts and concepts that make up our general knowledge of the world. (p. 185)

sensation Simple awareness due to the stimulation of a sense organ. (p. 123)

sensorimotor stage A stage of development that begins at birth and lasts through infancy in which infants acquire information about the world by sensing it and moving around within it. (p. 413)

sensory adaptation Sensitivity to prolonged stimulation tends to decline over time as an organism adapts to current conditions. (p. 128)

sensory memory store The place in which sensory information is kept for a few seconds or less. (p. 173)

sensory neurons Neurons that receive information from the external world and convey this information to the brain via the spinal cord. (p. 77)

serotonin A neurotransmitter that is involved in the regulation of sleep and wakefulness, eating, and aggressive behavior. (p. 84)

shaping Learning that results from the reinforcement of successive approximations to a final desired behavior. (p. 233)

shared environment Those environmental factors that are experienced by all relevant members of a household (see *nonshared environment*). (p. 355)

short-term memory store A place where nonsensory information is kept for more than a few seconds but less than a minute. (p. 174)

sick role A socially recognized set of rights and obligations linked with illness. (p. 608)

signal detection theory An observation that the response to a stimulus depends both on a person's sensitivity to the stimulus in the presence of noise and on a person's response criterion. (p. 127)

sleep apnea A disorder in which the person stops breathing for brief periods while asleep. (p. 313)

sleep paralysis The experience of waking up unable to move. (p. 314)

social cognition The processes by which people come to understand others. (p. 650)

social cognitive approach An approach that views personality in terms of how the person thinks about the situations encountered in daily life and behaves in response to them. (p. 473)

social exchange The hypothesis that people remain in relationships only as long as they perceive a favorable ratio of costs to benefits. (p. 639)

social influence The control of one person's behavior by another. (p. 640)

social loafing The tendency for people to expend less effort when in a group than alone. (p. 629)

social phobia A disorder that involves an irrational fear of being publicly humiliated or embarrassed. (p. 504)

social psychology A subfield of psychology that studies the causes and consequences of interpersonal behavior. (p. 28)

social support The aid gained through interacting with others. (p. 601)

somatic nervous system A set of nerves that conveys information into and out of the central nervous system. (p. 87)

somatization disorder A psychological disorder involving combinations of multiple physical complaints with no medical explanation. (p. 607)

somatoform disorders The set of psychological disorders in which the person displays physical symptoms not fully explained by a general medical condition. (p. 607)

somnambulism (sleepwalking) Occurs when the person arises and walks around while asleep. (p. 313)

source memory Recall of when, where, and how information was acquired. (p. 194)

specific phobia A disorder that involves an irrational fear of a particular object or situation that markedly interferes with an individual's ability to function. (p. 503)

spinal reflexes Simple pathways in the nervous system that rapidly generate muscle contractions. (p. 90)

spontaneous recovery The tendency of a learned behavior to recover from extinction after a rest period. (p. 216)

state-dependent retrieval The tendency for information to be better recalled when the person is in the same state during encoding and retrieval. (p. 181)

stereotyping The process by which people draw inferences about others based on their knowledge of the categories to which others belong. (p. 650)

stimulants Substances that excite the central nervous system, heightening arousal and activity levels. (p. 323)

stimulus Sensory input from the environment. (p. 7)

storage The process of maintaining information in memory over time. (p. 169)

strange situation A behavioral test developed by Mary Ainsworth that is used to determine a child's attachment style. (p. 423)

stress inoculation training (SIT) A therapy that helps people to cope with stressful situations by developing positive ways to think about the situation. (p. 597)

stress The physical and psychological response to internal or external stressors. (p. 582)

stressors Specific events or chronic pressures that place demands on a person or threaten the person's well-being. (p. 582)

structuralism The analysis of the basic elements that constitute the mind. (p. 8)

subcortical structures Areas of the forebrain housed under the cerebral cortex near the very center of the brain. (p. 95)

sublimation A defense mechanism that involves channeling unacceptable sexual or aggressive drives into socially acceptable and culturally enhancing activities. (p. 467)

subliminal perception A thought or behavior that is influenced by stimuli that a person cannot consciously report perceiving. (p. 306)

suggestibility The tendency to incorporate misleading information from external sources into personal recollections. (p. 197)

sunk-cost fallacy A framing effect in which people make decisions about a current situation based on what they have previously invested in the situation. (p. 277)

superego The mental system that reflects the internalization of cultural rules, mainly learned as parents exercise their authority. (p. 464)

surface structure How a sentence is worded. (p. 256)

syllogistic reasoning Determining whether a conclusion follows from two statements that are assumed to be true. (p. 287)

sympathetic nervous system A set of nerves that prepares the body for action in threatening situations. (p. 88)

synapse The junction or region between the axon of one neuron and the dendrites or cell body of another. (p. 76)

synesthesia The perceptual experience of one sense that is evoked by another sense. (p. 122)

syntactical rules A set of rules that indicate how words can be combined to form phrases and sentences. (p. 255)

systematic desensitization A procedure in which a client relaxes all the muscles of his or her body while imagining being in increasingly frightening situations. (p. 549)

systematic persuasion A change in attitudes or beliefs that is brought about by appeals to reason. (p. 647)

taste buds The organ of taste transduction. (p. 161)

tectum A part of the midbrain that orients an organism in the environment. (p. 94)

tegmentum A part of the midbrain that is involved in movement and arousal. (p. 94)

telegraphic speech Speech that is devoid of function morphemes and consists mostly of content words. (p. 258)

temperaments Characteristic patterns of emotional reactivity. (p. 424)

template A mental representation that can be directly compared to a viewed shape in the retinal image. (p. 143)

temporal code The cochlea registers low frequencies via the firing rate of action potentials entering the auditory nerve. (p. 153)

temporal lobe A region of the cerebral cortex responsible for hearing and language. (p. 99)

teratogens Agents that damage the process of development, such as drugs and viruses. (p. 408)

terminal buttons Knoblike structures that branch out from an axon. (p. 81)

thalamus A subcortical structure that relays and filters information from the senses and transmits the information to the cerebral cortex. (p. 95)

Thematic Apperception Test (TAT) A projective personality test in which respondents reveal underlying motives, concerns, and the way they see the social world through the stories they make up about ambiguous pictures of people. (p. 453)

theoretical reasoning Reasoning directed toward arriving at a belief. (p. 286)

theory A hypothetical account of how and why a phenomenon occurs, usually in the form of a statement about the causal relationship between two or more properties. Theories lead to *hypotheses*. (p. 65)

theory of mind The idea that human behavior is guided by mental representation, which gives rise to the realization that the world is not always the way it looks and that different people see it differently. (p. 416)

third-variable correlation The fact that two variables may be correlated only because they are both caused by a third variable. (p. 57)

third-variable problem The fact that the causal relationship between two variables cannot be inferred from the correlation between them because of the ever-present possibility of third-variable correlation. (p. 58)

thought suppression The conscious avoidance of a thought. (p. 303)

timbre A listener's experience of sound quality or resonance. (p. 151)

tip-of-the-tongue experience The temporary inability to retrieve information that is stored in memory, accompanied by the feeling that you are on the verge of recovering the information. (p. 192)

token economy A form of behavior therapy in which clients are given "tokens" for desirable behavior, which they can later trade for rewards. (p. 549)

trait A relatively stable disposition to behave in a particular and consistent way. (p. 454)

transcranial magnetic stimulation (TMS) A treatment that involves placing a powerful pulsed magnet over a person's scalp, which alters neuronal activity in the brain. (p. 568)

transduction What takes place when many sensors in the body convert physical signals from the environment into neural signals sent to the central nervous system. (p. 123)

transfer-appropriate processing The idea that memory is likely to transfer from one situation to another when we process information in a way that is appropriate to the retrieval cues that will be available later. (p. 181)

transference An event that occurs in psychoanalysis when the therapist begins to assume a major significance in the client's life and the client reacts to the therapist based on unconscious childhood fantasies. (p. 546)

transience Forgetting what occurs with the passage of time. (p. 187)

trichromatic color representation The pattern of responding across the three types of cones that provides a unique code for each color. (p. 137)

two-factor theory A theory about the relationship between emotional experience and physiological activity suggesting that emotions are inferences about the causes of undifferentiated physiological arousal. (p. 371)

two-factor theory of intelligence Spearman's theory suggesting that every task requires a combination of a general ability (which he called *g*) and skills that are specific to the task (which he called *s*). (p. 346)

Type A behavior pattern The tendency toward easily aroused hostility, impatience, a sense of time urgency, and competitive achievement strivings. (p. 590)

unconditional positive regard An attitude of nonjudgmental acceptance toward another person. (p. 471)

unconditioned response (UR) A reflexive reaction that is reliably elicited by an unconditioned stimulus. (p. 212)

unconditioned stimulus (US) Something that reliably produces a naturally occurring reaction in an organism. (p. 212)

unconscious The part of the mind that operates outside of conscious awareness but influences conscious thoughts, feelings, and actions. (p. 15)

unconscious motivation A motivation of which one is not aware. (p. 399)

universality hypothesis The hypothesis that emotional expressions have the same meaning for everyone. (p. 379)

validity The characteristic of an observation that allows one to draw accurate inferences from it. (p. 43)

variable A property whose value can vary or change. (p. 53)

variable interval schedule (VI) An operant conditioning principle in which behavior is reinforced based on an average time that has expired since the last reinforcement. (p. 231)

variable ratio schedule (VR) An operant conditioning principle in which the delivery of reinforcement is based on a particular average number of responses. (p. 232)

vestibular system The three fluid-filled semicircular canals and adjacent organs located next to the cochlea in each inner ear. (p. 158)

visual acuity The ability to see fine detail. (p. 130)

visual-form agnosia The inability to recognize objects by sight. (p. 140)

visual imagery encoding The process of storing new information by converting it into mental pictures. (p. 171)

Weber's law The just noticeable difference of a stimulus is a constant proportion despite variations in intensity. (p. 126)

working memory Active maintenance of information in short-term storage. (p. 175)

zygote A single cell that contains chromosomes from both a sperm and an egg. (p. 407)

References

Abel, T., Alberini, C., Ghirardi, M., Huang, Y.-Y., Nguyen, P., & Kandel, E. R. (1995). Steps toward a molecular definition of memory consolidation. In D. L. Schacter (Ed.), *Memory distortion: How minds, brains and societies reconstruct the past* (pp. 298–328). Cambridge, MA: Harvard University Press.

Abrams, M., & Reber, A. S. (1988). Implicit learning: Robustness in the face of psychiatric disorders. *Journal of Psycholinguistic Research, 17,* 425–439.

Abramson, L. Y., Alloy, L. B., Hankin, B. L., Haeffel, G. J., MacCoon, D. G., & Gibb, B. E. (2002). Cognitive vulnerability-stress models of depression in a self-regulatory and psychobiological context. In I. H. Gotlib & C. L. Hammen (Eds.), *Handbook of depression* (pp. 268–294). New York: Guilford Press.

Abramson, L. Y., Seligman, M. E. P., & Teasdale, J. D. (1978). Learned helplessness in humans: Critique and reformulation. *Journal of Abnormal Psychology, 87,* 49–74.

Abromov, I., & Gordon, J. (1994). Color appearance: On seeing red—or yellow, or green, or blue. *Annual Review of Psychology, 45,* 451–485.

Acevedo-Garcia, D., McArdle, N., Osypuk, T. L., Lefkowitz, B., & Krimgold, B. K. (2007). *Children left behind: How metropolitan areas are failing America's children.* Boston: Harvard School of Public Health.

Achter, J. A., Lubinski, D., & Benbow, C. P. (1996). Multipotentiality among the intellectually gifted: "It was never there and already it's vanishing." *Journal of Counseling Psychology, 43,* 65–76.

Ackroff, K., Luxas, F., & Sclafani, A. (2005). Flavor preference conditioning as a function of fat source. *Physiology and Behavior, 85,* 448–460.

Acocella, J. (1999). *Creating hysteria: Women and multiple personality disorder.* San Francisco: Jossey-Bass.

Acton, G. S., & Schroeder, D. H. (2001). Sensory discrimination as related to general intelligence. *Intelligence, 29,* 263–271.

Adams, H. E., Wright, L. W., Jr., & Lohr, B. A. (1996). Is homophobia associated with homosexual arousal? *Journal of Abnormal Psychology, 105,* 440–445.

Addis, D. R., Wong, A. T., & Schacter, D. L. (2007). Remembering the past and imagining the future: Common and distinct neural substrates during event construction and elaboration. *Neuropsychologia, 45,* 1363–1377.

Adelmann, P. K., & Zajonc, R. B. (1989). Facial efference and the experience of emotion. *Annual Review of Psychology, 40,* 249–280.

Adler, A. (1927). *Understanding human nature.* Greenwich, CT: Fawcett.

Adolph, K. E., & Avoilio, A. M. (2000). Walking infants adapt locomotion to changing body dimensions. *Journal of Experimental Psychology: Human Perception and Performance, 26,* 1148–1166.

Adolphs, R., Cahil, L., Schul, R., & Babinsky, R. (1997). Impaired declarative memory for emotional material following bilateral amygdala damage in humans. *Learning and Memory, 4,* 291–300.

Adolphs, R., Russell, J. A., & Tranel, D. (1999). A role for the human amygdala in recognizing emotional arousal from unpleasant stimuli. *Psychological Science, 10,* 167–171.

Adolphs, R., Tranel, D., Damasio, H., & Damasio, A. R. (1995). Fear and the human amygdala. *Journal of Neuroscience 15,* 5879–5891.

Adorno, T. W., Frenkel-Brunswik, E., Levinson, D. J., & Sanford, R. N. (1950). *The authoritarian personality.* New York: Harper & Row.

Aggleton, J. (Ed.). (1992). *The amygdala: Neurobiological aspects of emotion, memory and mental dysfunction.* New York: Wiley-Liss.

Aharon, I., Etcoff, N., Ariely, D., Chabris, C. F., O'Conner, E., & Breiter, H. C. (2001). Beautiful faces have variable reward value: fMRI and behavioral evidence. *Neuron, 32,* 537–551.

Ahern, J., Galea, S., Resnick, H., Kilpatrick D., Bucuvalas, M., Gold, J., et al. (2003). Television images and psychological symptoms after the September 11 terrorist attacks. *Psychiatry, 65*(4), 289–300.

Ahlers, M. (2003, September 23). Bitter divorce blamed for sniper shootings. *CNN.com.* Retrieved September 15, 2007, from http://www.cnn.com/2003/LAW/09/23/sprj.dcsp.sniper.hearing/index.html

Ainslie, G. (2001). *Breakdown of will.* New York: Cambridge University Press.

Ainsworth, M. D. S., Blehar, M. C., Waters, E., & Wall, S. (1978). *Patterns of attachment: A psychological study of the strange situation.* Hillsdale, NJ: Erlbaum.

Albarracin, D., & Kumkale, G. T. (2003). Affect as information in persuasion: A model of affect identification and discounting. *Journal of Personality & Social Psychology, 84,* 453–469.

Albee, E. (1962). *Who's afraid of Virginia Woolf?* New York: Atheneum.

Alicke, M. D., Klotz, M. L., Breitenbecher, D. L., Yurak, T. J., & Vredenburg, D. S. (1995). Personal contact, individuation, and the better-than-average effect. *Journal of Personality and Social Psychology, 68,* 804–824.

Allison, D. B., Fontaine, K. R., Manson, J. E., Stevens, J., & VanItallie, T. B. (1999). Annual deaths attributable to obesity in the United States. *Journal of the American Medical Association, 282,* 1530–1538.

Alloy, L. B., Jacobson, N. H., & Acocella, J. (1999). *Casebook in abnormal psychology* (4th ed.). New York: McGraw-Hill.

Allport, G. W. (1937). *Personality: A psychological interpretation.* New York: Holt.

Allport, G. W. (1954). *The nature of prejudice.* Cambridge, MA: Addison-Wesley.

Allport, G. W., & Odbert, H. S. (1936). Trait-names: A psycholexical study. *Psychological Monographs, 47,* 592.

Alt, K. W., Jeunesse, C., Buitrago-Téllez, C. H., Wächter, R., Boës, E., & Pichler, S. L. (1997). Evidence for stone age cranial surgery. *Nature, 387,* 360.

Alvarez, L. W. (1965). A pseudo experience in parapsychology. *Science, 148,* 1541.

Amabile, T. M. (1996). *Creativity in context.* Boulder, CO: Westview Press.

American Psychiatric Association. (2000). *Diagnostic and statistical manual of mental disorders DSM-IV-TR* (4th ed.). Washington, DC: American Psychiatric Press.

American Psychological Association. (2002). *Ethical principles of psychologists and code of conduct.* Washington, DC: Author.

American Psychological Association. (2005). Resolution in favor of empirically supported sex education and HIV prevention programs for adolescents. Washington, DC.

Andersen, S. M., & Berk, J. S. (1998). Transference in everyday experience: Implications of experimental research for relevant clinical phenomena. *Review of General Psychology, 2,* 81–120.

Anderson, C. A. (1989). Temperature and aggression: Ubiquitous effects of heat on occurrence of human violence. *Psychological Bulletin, 106,* 74–96.

Anderson, C. A., Berkowitz, L., Donnerstein, E., Huesmann, L. R., Johnson, J. D., Linz, D., et al. (2003). The influence of media violence on youth. *Psychological Science in the Public Interest, 4,* 81–110.

Anderson, C. A., & Bushman, B. J. (2001). Effects of violent video games on aggressive behavior, aggressive cognition, aggressive affect, physiological arousal, and prosocial behavior: A meta-analytic review of the scientific literature. *Psychological Science, 12,* 353–359.

Anderson, C. A., & Bushman, B. J. (2002). Human aggression. *Annual Review of Psychology, 53,* 27–51.

Anderson, C. A., Bushman, B. J., & Groom, R. W. (1997). Hot years and serious and deadly assault: Empirical tests of the heat hypothesis. *Journal of Personality and Social Psychology, 73,* 1213–1223.

Anderson, C. A., Lepper, M. R., & Ross, L. (1980). Perseverance of social theories: The role of explanation in the persistence of discredited information. *Journal of Personality and Social Psychology, 39,* 1037–1049.

Anderson, J. R., & Fincham, J. M. (1994). Acquisition of procedural skills from examples. *Journal of Experimental Psychology: Learning, Memory, and Cognition, 20,* 1322–1340.

Anderson, J. R., & Schooler, L. J. (1991). Reflections of the environment in memory. *Psychological Science, 2,* 396–408.

Anderson, J. R., & Schooler, L. J. (2000). The adaptive nature of memory. In E. Tulving & F. I. M. Craik (Eds.), *The Oxford handbook of memory* (pp. 557–570). Oxford, England: Oxford University Press.

Anderson, M. C., Ochsner, K. N., Kuhl, B., Cooper, J., Robertson, E., Gabrieli, S. W., et al. (2004). Neural systems underlying the suppression of unwanted memories. *Science, 303,* 232–235.

Anderson, R. C., Pichert, J. W., Goetz, E. T., Schallert, D. L., Stevens, K. V., & Trollip, S. R. (1976). Instantiation of general terms. *Journal of Verbal Learning and Verbal Behavior, 15,* 667–679.

Andrewes, D. (2001). *Neuropsychology: From theory to practice.* Hove, England: Psychology Press.

Andrews, I. (1982). Bilinguals out of focus: A critical discussion. *IRAL: International Review of Applied Linguistics in Language Teaching, 20,* 297–305.

Angermeyer, M. C., & Matschinger, H. (1996a). Lay beliefs about the causes of mental disorders: A new methodological approach. *Social Psychiatry & Psychiatric Epidemiology, 21,* 309–315.

Angermeyer, M. C., & Matschinger, H. (1996b). The effect of violent attacks by schizophrenic persons on the attitude of the public towards the mentally ill. *Social Science and Medicine, 43,* 1721–1728.

Angier, N. (1997, December 23). Joined for life, and living life to the full. *New York Times,* p. F1.

Ansfield, M., Wegner, D. M., & Bowser, R. (1996). Ironic effects of sleep urgency. *Behavior Research and Therapy, 34,* 523–531.

Ansuini, C. G., Fiddler-Woite, J., & Woite, R. S. (1996). The source, accuracy, and impact of initial sexuality information on lifetime wellness. *Adolescence, 31,* 283–289.

Antoni, M. H., Lehman, J. M., Klibourn, K. M., Boyers, A. E., Culver, J. L., Alferi, S. M., et al. (2001). Cognitive-behavioral stress management intervention decreases the prevalence of depression and enhances benefit finding among women under treatment for early-stage breast cancer. *Health Psychology, 20,* 20–32.

Antony, M. M., Downie, F., & Swinson, R. (1998). Diagnostic issues and epidemiology in obsessive-compulsive disorder. In R. Swinson, M. Antony, S. Rachman, & M. Richter (Eds.), *Obsessive-compulsive disorder: Theory, research, and treatment* (pp. 3–32). New York: Guilford Press.

Antony, M. M., Roth, D., Swinson, R. P., Huta, V., & Devins, G. M. (1998). Illness intrusiveness in individuals with panic disorder, obsessive compulsive disorder, or social phobia. *Journal of Nervous and Mental Disease, 186,* 311–315.

Antony, M. M., & Swinson, R. P. (2000). *Phobic disorders and panic in adults: A guide to assessment and treatment.* Washington, DC: American Psychological Association.

Archer, J. E. (Ed.). (1994). *Male violence.* London: Routledge.

Archibold, R. C. (2006, July 17). Arizona ballot could become lottery ticket. *New York Times,* pp. A1/A15.

Aristotle. (1998). *The Nichomachean ethics* (D. W. Ross, Trans.). Oxford, England: Oxford University Press.

Ariyasu, H., Takaya, K., Tagami, T., Ogawa, Y., Hosoda, K., Akamizu, T., et al. (2001). Stomach is a major source of circulating ghrelin, and feeding state determines plasma ghrelin-like immunoreactivity levels in humans. *Journal of Clinical Endocrinology and Metabolism, 86,* 4753–4758.

Arkes, H. R., Boehm, L. E., & Xu, G. (1991). Determinants of judged validity. *Journal of Experimental Social Psychology, 27,* 576–605.

Arlitt, A. H. (1921). On the need for caution in establishing race norms. *Journal of Applied Psychology, 5,* 179–183.

Arlow, J. A. (2000). Psychoanalysis. In R. J. Corsini & D. Wedding (Eds.), *Current psychotherapies* (6th ed., pp. 16–53). Itasca, IL: F. E. Peacock, Publishers.

Armstrong, D. M. (1980). *The nature of mind.* Ithaca, NY: Cornell University Press.

Arnold, M. B. (Ed.). (1960). *Emotion and personality: Psychological aspects* (Vol. 1). New York: Columbia University Press.

Arnold, S. E., Trojanowski, J. Q., Gur, R. E., Blackwell, P., Han, L., & Choi, C. (1998). Absence of neurodegeneration and neural injury in the cerebral cortex in a sample of elderly patients with schizophrenia. *Archives of General Psychiatry, 55,* 225–232.

Aronson, E. (1963). Effect of the severity of threat on the devaluation of forbidden behavior. *Journal of Abnormal and Social Psychology, 66,* 584–588.

Aronson, E. (1969). The theory of cognitive dissonance: A current perspective. In L. Berkowitz (Ed.), *Advances in experimental social psychology* (Vol. 4, pp. 1–34): Academic Press.

Aronson, E., & Mills, J. (1958). The effect of severity of initiation on liking for a group. *Journal of Abnormal and Social Psychology, 59,* 177–181.

Aronson, E., Willerman, B., & Floyd, J. (1966). The effect of a pratfall on increasing interpersonal attractiveness. *Psychonomic Science, 4,* 227–228.

Aronson, E., & Worchel, P. (1966). Similarity versus liking as determinants of interpersonal attractiveness. *Psychonomic Science, 5,* 157–158.

Asch, S. E. (1946). Forming impressions of personality. *Journal of Abnormal and Social Psychology, 41,* 258–290.

Asch, S. E. (1951). Effects of group pressure on the modification and distortion of judgments. In H. Guetzkow (Ed.), *Groups, leadership, and men* (pp. 177–190). Pittsburgh: Carnegie Press.

Asch, S. E. (1955). Opinions and social pressure. *Scientific American, 193,* 31–35.

Asch, S. E. (1956). Studies of independence and conformity: 1 A minority of one against a unanimous majority. *Psychological Monographs: General and Applied, 70,* 1–70.

Aschoff, J. (1965). Circadian rhythms in man. *Science, 148,* 1427–1432.

Aserinsky, E., & Kleitman, N. (1953). Regularly occurring periods of eye motility, and concomitant phenomena, during sleep. *Science, 118,* 273–274.

Ashby, F. G., & Ell, S. W. (2001). The neurobiology of human category learning. *Trends in Cognitive Sciences, 5,* 204–210.

Ashcraft, M. H. (1998). *Fundamentals of cognition.* New York: Longman.

Associated Press. (2007). Former stripper guilty of posing as psychologist. Boston: BostonHerald.com.

Astington, J. W., & Baird, J. (2005). *Why language matters for theory of mind.* Oxford, England: Oxford University Press.

Atkinson, J. W., & Litwin, G. H. (1960). Achievement motive and test anxiety conceived as motive to approach success and motive to avoid failure. *Journal of Abnormal and Social Psychology, 60,* 52–63.

Avolio, B. J., & Waldman, D. A. (1994). Variations in cognitive, perceptual, and psychomotor abilities across the working life span: Examining the effects of race, sex, experience, education, and occupational type. *Psychology and Aging, 9,* 430–442.

Axelrod, R. (1984). *The evolution of cooperation.* New York: Basic Books.

Axelrod, R., & Hamilton, W. D. (1981). The evolution of cooperation. *Science, 211,* 1390–1396.

Ayres, C. E. (1921). Instinct and capacity. 1. The instinct of belief-in-instincts. *Journal of Philosophy, 18,* 561–565.

Azam, E. (1876). Dé doublement de la personnalité: Suite de l'histoié de Felida X. *Revue Scientifique, 6,* 265–269.

Azuma, H., & Kashiwagi, K. (1987). Descriptors for an intelligent person: A Japanese study. *Japanese Psychological Research, 29,* 17–26.

Baars, B. J. (1986). *The cognitive revolution in psychology.* New York: Guilford Press.

Backman, C. W., & Secord, P. F. (1959). The effect of perceived liking on interpersonal attraction. *Human Relations, 12,* 379–384.

Bäckman, L., & Dixon, R. A. (1992). Psychological compensation: A theoretical framework. *Psychological Bulletin, 112,* 259–283.

Baddeley, A. D., & Hitch, G. J. (1974). Working memory. In S. Dornic (Ed.), *Attention and performance.* Hillsdale, NJ: Erlbaum.

Baer, L., Rauch, S. L., Ballantine, H. T., Jr., Martuza, R., Cosgrove, R., Cassem, E., et al. (1995). Cingulotomy for intractable obsessive-compulsive disorder: Prospective long-term follow-up of 18 patients. *Archives of General Psychiatry, 52,* 384–392.

Bagby, R. M., Levitan, R. D., Kennedy, S. H., Levitt, A. J., & Joffe, R. T. (1999). Selective alteration of personality in response to noradrenergic and serotonergic antidepressant medication in depressed sample: Evidence of non-specificity. *Psychiatry Research, 86,* 211–216.

Bahrick, H. P. (1984). Semantic memory content in permastore: 50 years of memory for Spanish learned in school. *Journal of Experimental Psychology: General, 113,* 1–29.

Bahrick, H. P. (2000). Long-term maintenance of knowledge. In E. Tulving & F. I. M. Craik (Eds.), *The Oxford handbook of memory* (pp. 347–362). New York: Oxford University Press.

Bahrick, H. P., Hall, L. K., & Berger, S. A. (1996). Accuracy and distortion in memory for high school grades. *Psychological Science, 7,* 265–271.

Bailey, J. M., & Pillard, R. C. (1991). A genetic study of male sexual orientation. *Archives of General Psychiatry, 48,* 1089–1096.

Bailey, J. M., Pillard, R. C., Dawood, K., Miller, M. B., Farrer, L. A., Trivedi, S., et al. (1999). A family history study of make sexual orientation using three independent samples. *Behavior Genetics, 29,* 79–86.

Bailey, J. M., Pillard, R. C., Neale, M. C., & Agyes, Y. (1993). Heritable factors influence sexual orientation in women. *Archives of General Psychiatry, 50,* 217–223.

Bailey, R. (2002, March 6). Hooray for designer babies! *Reason.com.* Retrieved September 30, 2007, from http://www.reason.com/news/show/34776.html

Baillargeon, R., Spelke, E. S., & Wasserman, S. (1985). Object permanence in 5-month-old infants. *Cognition, 20,* 191–208.

Baldwin, M. W., Carrell, S. E., & Lopez, D. F. (1989). Priming relationship schemas: My advisor and the Pope are watching me from the back of my mind. *Journal of Experimental Social Psychology, 26,* 435–454.

Baler, R. D., & Volkow, N. D. (2006). Drug addiction: the neurobiology of disrupted self-control. *Trends in Molecular Medicine 12,* 559–566.

Baltes, P. B., & Reinert, G. (1969). Cohort effects in cognitive development of children as revealed by cross-sectional sequences. *Developmental Psychology, 1,* 169–177.

Bandura, A. (1965). Influence of models' reinforcement contingencies on the acquisition of imitative responses. *Journal of Social and Personality Psychology, 1,* 589–595.

Bandura, A. (1977). *Social learning theory.* Englewood Cliffs, NJ: Prentice Hall.

Bandura, A. (1986). *Social foundations of thought and action: A social cognitive theory.* Englewood Cliffs, NJ: Prentice Hall.

Bandura, A. (1994). Social cognitive theory of mass communication. In J. Bryant & D. Zillmann (Eds.), *Media effects: Advances in theory and research* (pp. 61–90). Hillsdale, NJ: Erlbaum.

Bandura, A., Ross, D., & Ross, S. (1961). Transmission of aggression through imitation of adult models. *Journal of Abnormal and Social Psychology, 63,* 575–582.

Bandura, A., Ross, D., & Ross, S. (1963). Vicarious reinforcement and imitative learning. *Journal of Abnormal and Social Psychology, 67,* 601–607.

Banks, M. S., & Salapatek, P. (1983). Infant visual perception. In M. Haith & J. Campos (Eds.), *Handbook of child psychology: Biology and infancy.* New York: Wiley.

Banse, R., & Scherer, K. R. (1996). Acoustic profiles in vocal emotion expression. *Journal of Personality and Social Psychology, 70,* 614–636.

Barchas, J. D., Berger, P. A., Ciranello, R. D., & Elliot, G. R. (1980). *Psychopharmacology: From theory to practice.* New York: Oxford University Press.

Bard, P. (1934). On emotional experience after decortication with some remarks on theoretical views. *Psychological Review, 41,* 309–329.

Bargh, J. A., & Chartrand, T. L. (1999). The unbearable automaticity of being. *American Psychologist, 54,* 462–479.

Bargh, J. A., Chen, M., & Burrows, L. (1996). The automaticity of social behavior: Direct effects of trait concept and stereotype activation on action. *Journal of Personality and Social Psychology, 71,* 230–244.

Bargh, J. A., Gollwitzer, P. M., Lee-Chai, A., Barndollar, K., & Trötschel, R. (2001). Bypassing the will: Automatic and controlled self-regulation. *Journal of Personality and Social Psychology, 81,* 1014–1027.

Barker, A. T., Jalinous, R., & Freeston, I. L. (1985). Noninvasive magnetic stimulation of the human motor cortex. *Lancet, 2,* 1106–1107.

Barkow, J. (1980). Prestige and self-esteem: A biosocial interpretation. In D. R. Omark, F. F. Stayer, & D. G. Freedman (Eds.), *Dominance relations* (pp. 319–322). New York: Garland.

Barlow, D. H., Gorman, J. M., Shear, M. K., & Woods, S. W. (2000). Cognitive-behavioral therapy, imipramine, or their combination for panic disorder: A randomized controlled trial. *Journal of the American Medical Association, 283*(19), 2529–2536.

Barlow, D. H., O'Brien, G. T., & Last, C. G. (1984). Couples treatment of agoraphobia. *Behavior Therapy, 15,* 41–58.

Barnier, A. J., Levin, K., & Maher, A. (2004). Suppressing thoughts of past events: Are repressive copers good suppressors? *Cognition and Emotion, 18,* 457–477.

Baron-Cohen, S. (1991). Do people with autism understand what causes emotion? *Child Development, 62,* 385–395.

Baron-Cohen, S., Leslie, A., & Frith, U. (1985). Does the autistic child have a "theory of mind"? *Cognition, 21,* 37–46.

Barondes, S. (2003). *Better than Prozac.* New York: Oxford University Press.

Barrett, T. R., & Etheridge, J. B. (1992). Verbal hallucinations in normals: I: People who hear voices. *Applied Cognitive Psychology, 6,* 379–387.

Barsalou, L. W., & Ross, B. H. (1986). The roles of automatic and strategic processing in sensitivity to superordinate and property frequency. *Journal of Experimental Psychology: Learning, Memory, & Cognition, 12,* 116–134.

Bartlett, F. C. (1932). *Remembering.* Cambridge, England: Cambridge University Press.

Bartol, C. R., & Costello, N. (1976). Extraversion as a function of temporal duration of electric shock: An exploratory study. *Perceptual and Motor Skills, 42,* 1174.

Bartoshuk, L. M. (2000). Comparing sensory experiences across individuals: Recent psychophysical advances illuminate genetic variation in taste perception. *Chemical Senses, 25,* 447–460.

Bartoshuk, L. M., & Beauchamp, G. K. (1994). Chemical senses. *Annual Review of Psychology, 45,* 419–445.

Bartoshuk, L. M., Duffy, V. B., & Miller, I. J. (1994). PTC/PROP tasting: Anatomy, psychophysics, and sex effects. *Physiology and Behavior, 56,* 1165–1171.

Batson, C. D. (2002). Addressing the altruism question experimentally. In S. G. Post & L. G. Underwood (Eds.), *Altruism & altruistic love: Science, philosophy, & religion in dialogue* (pp. 89–105). London: Oxford University Press.

Baumeister, R. F. (1999). *Evil: Inside human violence and cruelty.* New York: Freeman.

Baumeister, R. F. (2004). Gender and erotic plasticity: Sociocultural influences on the sex drive. *Sexual & Relationship Therapy, 19,* 133–139.

Baumeister, R. F., Bratslavsky, E., Muraven, M., & Tice, D. M. (1998). Ego depletion: Is the active self a limited resource? *Journal of Personality and Social Psychology, 74,* 1252–1265.

Baumeister, R. F., Campbell, J. D., Krueger, J. I., & Vohs, K. D. (2003). Does high self-esteem cause better performance, interpersonal success, happiness, or healthier lifestyles? *Psychological Science in the Public Interest, 4,* 1–44.

Baumeister, R. F., Cantanese, K. R., & Vohs, K. D. (2001). Is there a gender difference in strength of sex drive? Theoretical views, conceptual distinctions, and a review of relevant evidence. *Personality and Social Psychology Review, 5,* 242–273.

Baumeister, R. F., & Leary, M. R. (1995). The need to belong: Desire for interpersonal attachments as a fundamental human motivation. *Psychological Bulletin, 117,* 497–529.

Baumeister, R. F., Smart, L., & Boden, J. M. (1996). Relation of threatened egotism to violence and aggression: The dark side of high self-esteem. *Psychological Review, 103,* 5–33.

Baumeister, R. F., & Tice, D. M. (1990). Anxiety and social exclusion. *Journal of Social and Clinical Psychology, 9,* 165–195.

Baxter, L. R., Schwartz, J. M., Bergman, K. S., Szuba, M. P., Guze, B. H., Mazziotta, J. C., Alazraki, A., et al. (1992). Caudate glucose metabolic rate changes with both drug behavior therapy for obsessive-compulsive disorder. *Archives of General Psychiatry, 49,* 681–689.

Bayley, P. J., Gold, J. J., Hopkins, R. O., & Squire, L. R. (2005). The neuroanatomy of remote memory. *Neuron, 46,* 799–810.

Bechara, A., Damasio, A. R., Damasio, H., & Anderson, S. W. (1994). Insensitivity to future consequences following damage to human prefrontal cortex. *Cognition, 50,* 7–15.

Bechara, A., Damasio, H., Tranel, D., & Damasio, A. R. (1997). Deciding advantageously before knowing the advantageous strategy. *Science, 275,* 1293–1295.

Bechara, A., Dolan, S., Denburg, N., Hindes, A., & Anderson, S. W. (2001). Decision-making deficits, linked to a dysfunctional ventromedial prefrontal cortex, revealed in alcohol and stimulant abusers. *Neuropsychologia, 39,* 376–389.

Bechara, A., Tranel, D., & Damasio, H. (2000). Characterization of the decision-making deficit of patients with ventromedial prefrontal cortex lesions. *Brain, 123,* 2189–2202.

Beck, A. T. (1967). *Depression: Causes and treatment.* Philadelphia: University of Pennsylvania Press.

Beck, A. T., & Weishaar, M. (2000). Cognitive therapy. In R. J. Corsini & D. Wedding (Eds.), *Current psychotherapies* (6th ed., pp. 241–272). Itasca, IL: F. E. Peacock, Publishers.

Beckers, G., & Zeki, S. (1995). The consequences of inactivating areas V1 and V5 on visual motion perception. *Brain, 118,* 49–60.

Békésy, G. von. (1960). *Experiments in hearing.* New York: McGraw-Hill.

Bell, A. P., Weinberg, M. S., & Hammersmith, S. K. (1981). *Sexual preference: Its development in men and women.* Bloomington: Indiana University Press.

Belsky, G., & Gilovich, T. (2000). *Why smart people make big money mistakes—and how to correct them: Lessons from the new science of behavioral economics.* New York: Fireside.

Belsky, J., Spritz, B., & Crnic, K. (1996). Infant attachment security and affective-cognitive information processing at age 3. *Psychological Science, 7,* 111–114.

Bem, S. L. (1974). The measure of psychological androgyny. *Journal of Consulting & Clinical Psychology, 42,* 155–162.

Benedetti, F., Maggi, G., & Lopiano, L. (2003). Open versus hidden medical treatment: The patient's knowledge about a therapy affects the therapy outcome. *Prevention & Treatment, 6,* Article 1. Retrieved June 23, 2003, from http://content.apa.org/psycarticles/2003-07872-001

Benes, F. M. (1998). Model generation and testing to probe neural circuitry in the cingulated cortex of postmortem schizophrenia brain. *Schizophrenia Bulletin, 24,* 219–230.

Benjamin, L. T., Jr. (Ed.). (1988). *A history of psychology: Original sources and contemporary research.* New York: McGraw-Hill.

Bennett, D. J. (1998). *Randomness.* Cambridge, MA: Harvard University Press.

Benson, H. (Ed.). (1990). *The relaxation response.* New York: Harper Torch.

Bereczkei, T., Vorgos, S., Gal, A., & Bernath, L. (1997). Resources, attractiveness, family commitment; reproductive decisions in human mate choice. *Journal of Ethology, 103,* 681–699.

Berger, H. (1929). Über das Elektroenkephalogram des Menschen. *Archiv fuer Psychiatrie, 87,* 527–570.

Berglund, H., Lindstrom, P., & Savic, I. (2006). Brain response to putative pheromones in lesbian women. *Proceedings of the National Academy of Sciences, 103,* 8269–8274.

Berkerian, D. A., & Bowers, J. M. (1983). Eyewitness testimony: Were we misled? *Journal of Experimental Psychology: Learning, Memory, and Cognition, 9,* 139–145.

Berkowitz, L. (1989). Frustration-aggression hypothesis: Examination and reformulation. *Psychological Bulletin, 106,* 59–73.

Berkowitz, L. (1990). On the formation and regulation of anger and aggression: A cognitive-neoassociationistic analysis. *American Psychologist, 45,* 494–503.

Berkowitz, L. (1993). Pain and aggression: Some findings and implications. *Motivation and Emotion, 17,* 277–293.

Berman, D. (2005, January 10). *Berman's bits.* Retrieved March 3, 2007, from http://www.bermansbits.com/archive/2005/v10n_02.html

Bernard, L. L. (1924). *Instinct: A study in social psychology.* New York: Holt.

Berry, D. S., & McArthur, L. Z. (1985). Some components and consequences of a babyface. *Journal of Personality and Social Psychology, 48,* 312–323.

Berry, J. W., Poortinga, Y. H., Segall, M. H., & Dasen, P. R. (1992). *Cross-cultural psychology: Research and applications.* New York: Cambridge University Press.

Berscheid, E., & Reiss, H. T. (1998). Interpersonal attraction and close relationships. In D. T. Gilbert, S. T. Fiske, & G. Lindzey (Eds.), *The handbook of social psychology* (4th ed., Vol. 2, pp. 193–281). New York: McGraw-Hill.

Bertelsen, A. (1999). Reflections on the clinical utility of the ICD-10 and DSM-IV classifications and their diagnostic criteria. *Australian and New Zealand Journal of Psychiatry, 33,* 166–173.

Bertelsen, B., Harvald, B., & Hauge, M. (1977). A Danish twin study of manic-depressive disorders. *British Journal of Psychiatry, 130,* 330–351.

Bertenthal, B. I., Rose, J. L., & Bai, D. L. (1997). Perception-action coupling in the development of visual control of posture. *Journal of Experimental Psychology: Human Perception & Performance, 23,* 1631–1643.

Best, J. B. (1992). *Cognitive psychology* (3rd ed.). New York: West Publishing.

Bettencourt, B. A., & Miller, N. (1996). Gender differences in aggression as a function of provocation: A meta-analysis. *Psychological Bulletin, 119,* 422–447.

Beutler, L. E. (2002). The dodo bird is extinct. *Clinical Psychology: Science and Practice, 9,* 30–34.

Bialystok, E. (1999). Cognitive complexity and attentional control in the bilingual mind. *Child Development, 70,* 636–644.

Bialystok, E., & Hakuta, K. (1994). *In other words: The science and psychology of second-language acquisition.* New York: Basic Books.

Bickerton, D. (1990). *Language and species.* Chicago: Chicago University Press.

Biederman, I. (1987). Recognition-by-components: A theory of human image understanding. *Psychological Review, 94,* 115–147.

Bierce, A. (1911). *The devil's dictionary.* New York: A. & C. Boni.

Billet, E., Richter, J., & Kennedy, J. (1998). Genetics of obsessive-compulsive disorder. In R. Swinson, M. Anthony, S. Rachman & M. Richter (Eds.), *Obsessive-compulsive disorder: Theory, research, and treatment* (pp. 181–206). New York: Guilford Press.

Binet, A. (1905). New methods for the diagnosis of the intellectual level of subnormals. *L'Année Psychologique, 12,* 191–244.

Binet, A. (1909). *Les idées modernes sur les enfants.* Paris: Flammarion.

Binswanger, L. (1958). The existential analysis school of thought. In R. May (Ed.), *Existence: A new dimension in psychiatry and psychology.* New York: Basic Books.

Bjork, D. W. (1983). *The compromised scientist: William James in the development of American psychology.* New York: Columbia University Press.

Bjork, D. W. (1993). *B. F. Skinner: A life.* New York: Basic Books.

Bjork, R. A., & Bjork, E. L. (1988). On the adaptive aspects of retrieval failure in autobiographical memory. In M. M. Gruneberg, P. E. Morris, R. N. Sykes (Eds.), *Practical aspects of memory: Current research and issues* (pp. 283–288). Chichester, England: Wiley.

Blackmore, S. (2004). *Consciousness: An introduction.* New York: Oxford University Press.

Blair, I. V. (2002). The malleability of automatic stereotypes and prejudice. *Personality and Social Psychology Review, 6,* 242–261.

Blair, J., Peschardt, K., & Mitchell, D. R. (2005). *Psychopath: Emotion and the brain.* Oxford, England: Blackwell.

Blascovich, J., Mendes, W. B., Hunter, S. B., Lickel, B., & Kowai-Bell, N. (2001). Perceiver threat in social interactions with stigmatized others. *Journal of Personality and Social Psychology, 80,* 253–267.

Blascovich, J., & Tomaka, J. (1996). The biopsychosocial model of arousal regulation. In M. P. Zanna (Ed.), *Advances in experimental social psychology* (Vol. 28, pp. 1–51). San Diego, CA: Academic Press.

Blasi, A. (1980). Bridging moral cognition and moral action: A critical review of the literature. *Psychological Bulletin, 88,* 1–45.

Blatt, S. J., & Homann, E. (1992). Parent-child interaction in the etiology of dependent and self-critical depression. *Clinical Psychology Review, 12,* 47–91.

Blatt, S. J., & Zuroff, D. C. (1992). Interpersonal relatedness and self-definition: Two prototypes for depression. *Clinical Psychology Review, 12,* 527–562.

Blazer, D. G., Hughes, D., & George, L. D. (1987). Stressful life events and the onset of a generalized anxiety syndrome. *American Journal of Psychiatry, 144,* 1178–1183.

Blazer, D. G., Hughes, D. J., George, L. K., Swartz, M., & Boyer, R. (1991). Generalized anxiety disorder. In L. N. Robins & D. A. Regier (Eds.), *Psychiatric disorders in America* (Vol. 180–203). New York: Free Press.

Bliss, T. V. P. (1999). Young receptors make smart mice. *Nature, 401,* 25–27.

Bliss, T. V. P., & Lømo, W. T. (1973). Long-lasting potentiation of synaptic transmission in the dentate area of the anesthetized rabbit following stimulation of the perforant path. *Journal of Physiology, 232,* 331–356.

Bloom, P. (2004). *Descartes' baby: How the science of child development explains what makes us human.* New York: Basic Books.

Bohan, J. S. (1996). *Psychology and sexual orientation: Coming to terms.* New York: Routledge.

Boisvert, C. M., & Faust, D. (2002). Iatrogenic symptoms in psychotherapy: A theoretical exploration of the potential impact of labels, language, and belief systems. *American Journal of Psychotherapy, 56,* 244–259.

Boomsma, D., Busjahn, A., & Peltonen, L. (2002). Classical twin studies and beyond. *Nature Reviews Genetics, 3,* 872–882.

Bootzin, R. R., Manber, R., Perlis, M. L., Salvio, M. A., & Wyatt, J. K. (1993). Sleep disorders. In P. B. Sutker & H. E. Adams (Eds.), *Comprehensive handbook of psychopathology* (2nd ed.). New York: Plenum Press.

Borkenau, P., & Liebler, A. (1995). Observable attributes as manifestations and cues of personality and intelligence. *Journal of Personality, 63,* 1–25.

Borkevec, T. D. (1982). Insomnia. *Journal of Consulting and Clinical Psychology, 50,* 880–895.

Born, R. T., & Bradley, D. C. (2005). Structure and function of visual area MT. *Annual Review of Neuroscience, 28,* 157–189.

Bornstein, R. F. (1989). Exposure and affect: Overview and meta-analysis of research, 1968–1987. *Psychological Bulletin, 106,* 265–289.

Boroditsky, L. (2001). Does language shape thought? Mandarin and English speakers' conceptions of time. *Cognitive Psychology, 43,* 1–22.

Bostwick, J. M., & Pankratz, S. (2000). Affective disorders and suicide risk: A reexamination. *American Journal of Psychiatry, 157,* 1925–1932.

Botwin, M. D., Buss, D. M., & Shackelford, T. K. (1997). Personality and mate preferences: Five factors in mate selection and marital satisfaction. *Journal of Personality, 65,* 107–136.

Bouchard, T. J., & Loehlin, J. C. (2001). Genes, evolution, and personality. *Behavioral Genetics, 31,* 243–273.

Bouchard, T. J., & McGue, M. (1981). Familial studies of intelligence: A review. *Science, 212,* 1055–1059.

Boucher, J. D., & Carlson, G. E. (1980). Recognition of facial expressions in three cultures. *Journal of Cross-Cultural Psychology, 11,* 263–280.

Bourguignon, E. (1968). World distribution and patterns of possession states. In R. Prince (Ed.), *Trance and possession states* (pp. 3–34). Montreal, Canada: R. M. Burke Memorial Society.

Bower, B. (1999, Oct. 30). The mental butler did it—research suggests that subconscious affects behavior more than thought. *Science News.*

Bower, G. H. (1981). Mood and memory. *American Psychologist, 36,* 129–148.

Bower, G. H., Clark, M. C., Lesgold, A. M., & Winzenz, D. (1969). Hierarchical retrieval schemes in recall of categorical word lists. *Journal of Verbal Learning and Verbal Behavior, 8,* 323–343.

Bowers, K. S., Regehr, G., Balthazard, C., & Parker, D. (1990). Intuition in the context of discovery. *Cognitive Psychology, 22,* 72–110.

Bowlby, J. (1969). *Attachment and loss: Vol. 1. Attachment.* New York: Basic Books.

Bowlby, J. (1973). *Attachment and loss: Vol. 2. Separation.* New York: Basic Books.

Bowlby, J. (1980). *Attachment and loss: Vol. 3. Loss: Sadness and depression.* New York: Basic Books.

Bozarth, M. A. (Ed.). (1987). *Methods of assessing the reinforcing properties of abused drugs.* New York: Springer-Verlag.

Bozarth, M. A., & Wise, R. A. (1985). Toxicity associated with long-term intravenous heroin and cocaine self-administration in the rat. *Journal of the American Medical Association, 254,* 81–83.

Bradford, D., Stroup, S., & Lieberman, J. (2002). Pharmacological treatments for schizophrenia. In P. E. Nathan & J. M. Gorman (Eds.), *A guide to treatments that work* (2nd ed., pp. 169–199). New York: Oxford University Press.

Bradmetz, J., & Schneider, R. (2004). The role of the counterfactually satisfied desire in the lag between false-belief and false-emotion attributions in children aged 4–7. *British Journal of Developmental Psychology, 22,* 185–196.

Brainerd, C. J., & Reyna, V. E. (2005). *The science of false memory.* New York: Oxford University Press.

Bramlett, M. D., & Mosher, W. D. (2001). *First marriage dissolution, divorce, and remarriage: United States.* (Advance data from vital and health statistics, 323.) Hyattsville, MD: National Center for Health Statistics.

Bramlett, M. D., & Mosher, W. D. (2002). *Cohabitation, marriage, divorce, and remarriage in the United States* (Vital and Health Statistics Series 23, No. 22). Hyattsville, MD: National Center for Health Statistics.

Braun, A. R., Balkin, T. J., Wesensten, N. J., Gwadry, F., Carson, R. E., Varga, M., et al. (1998). Dissociated pattern of activity in visual cortices and their projections during rapid eye movement sleep. *Science, 279,* 91–95.

Breckler, S. J. (1994). Memory for the experiment of donating blood: Just how bad was it? *Basic and Applied Social Psychology, 15,* 467–488.

Brédart, S., & Valentine, T. (1998). Descriptiveness and proper name retrieval. *Memory, 6,* 199–206.

Breggin, P. R. (1990). Brain damage, dementia, and persistent cognitive dysfunction associated with neuroleptic drugs: Evidence, etiology, implications. *Journal of Mind and Behavior, 11,* 425–463.

Breggin, P. R. (2000). *Reclaiming our children.* Cambridge, MA: Perseus Books.

Brehm, J. W. (1956). Post-decision changes in the desirability of alternatives. *Journal of Abnormal and Social Psychology, 52,* 384–389.

Brehm, S. S. (1992). *Intimate relationships* (2nd ed.). New York: McGraw-Hill.

Breland, K., & Breland, M. (1961). The misbehavior of organisms. *American Psychologist, 16,* 681–684.

Brennan, P. A., & Zufall, F. (2006). Pheromonal communication in vertebrates. *Nature, 444,* 308–315.

Brenneis, C. B. (2000). Evaluating the evidence: Can we find authenticated recovered memory? *Journal of the American Psychoanalytic Association, 17,* 61–77.

Brenninkmeijer, V., Vanyperen, N. W., & Buunk, B. P. (2001). I am not a better teacher, but others are doing worse: Burnout and perceptions of superiority among teachers. *Social Psychology of Education, 4*(3–4), 259–274.

Brewer, M. B. (1979). In-group bias in the minimal intergroup situation: A cognitive-motivational analysis. *Psychological Bulletin, 86,* 307–324.

Brewer, W. F. (1996). What is recollective memory? In D. C. Rubin (Ed.), *Remembering our past: Studies in autobiographical memory* (pp. 19–66). New York: Cambridge University Press.

Brickman, P., Coates, D., & Janoff-Bulman, R. J. (1978). Lottery winners and accident victims: Is happiness relative? *Journal of Personality and Social Psychology, 36,* 917–927.

Bridges, P. K., Bartlett, J. R., Hale, A. S., Poynton, A. M., Malizia, A. L., & Hodgkiss, A. D. (1994). Psychosurgery: stereotactic subcaudate tractomy: An indispensable treatment. *British Journal of Psychiatry, 165,* 599–611.

Broadbent, D. E. (1958). *Perception and communication.* London: Pergamon Press.

Broberg, D. J., & Bernstein, I. L. (1987). Candy as a scapegoat in the prevention of food aversions in children receiving chemotherapy. *Cancer, 60,* 2344–2347.

Broca, P. (1861). Remarques sur le siège de la faculté du langage articulé; suivies d'une observation d'aphemie (perte de la parole). *Bulletin de la société anatomique de Paris, 36,* 330–357.

Broca, P. (1863). Localisation des fonction cerebrales: Siège du langage articulé. *Bulletin de la société d'anthropologie de Paris, 4,* 200–202.

Brock, A. (1993). Something old, something new: The "reappraisal" of Wilhelm Wundt in textbooks. *Theory & Psychology, 3*(2), 235–242.

Brockner, J., & Swap, W. C. (1976). Effects of repeated exposure and attitudinal similarity on self-disclosure and interpersonal attraction. *Journal of Personality and Social Psychology, 33,* 531–540.

Broderick, C. B., & Schrader, S. S. (1991). The history of professional marriage and family therapy. In A. S. Gurman & D. P. Kniskern (Eds.), *Handbook of family therapy* (pp. 3–40). New York: Brunner/Mazel.

Brody, N. (2003). Construct validation of the Sternberg Triarchic Abilities Test: Comment and reanalysis. *Intelligence, 31*(4), 319–329.

Brooks-Gunn, J., Graber, J. A., & Paikoff, R. L. (1994). Studying links between hormones and negative affect: Models and measures. *Journal of Research on Adolescence, 4,* 469–486.

Brosnan, S. F., & DeWaal, F. B. M. (2003). Monkeys reject unequal pay. *Nature, 425,* 297–299.

Brown, B. B., Mory, M., & Kinney, D. (1994). Casting crowds in a relational perspective: Caricature, channel, and context. In G. A. R.

Montemayor & T. Gullotta (Eds.), *Advances in adolescent development: Personal relationships during adolescence* (Vol. 5, pp. 123–167). Newbury Park, CA: Sage.

Brown, J. D. (1993). Self-esteem and self-evaluation: Feeling is believing. In J. M. Suls (Ed.), *The self in social perspective: Psychological perspectives on the self* (Vol. 4, pp. 27–58). Hillsdale, NJ: Erlbaum.

Brown, J. D., & McGill, K. L. (1989). The cost of good fortune: When positive life events produce negative health consequences. *Journal of Personality & Social Psychology, 57*, 1103–1110.

Brown, R. (1958). *Words and things.* New York: Free Press.

Brown, R., & Hanlon, C. (1970). Derivational complexity and order of acquisition in child speech. In J. R. Hayes (Ed.), *Cognition and the development of language* (pp. 11–53). New York: Wiley.

Brown, R., & Kulik, J. (1977). Flashbulb memories. *Cognition, 5,* 73–99.

Brown, R., & McNeill, D. (1966). The "tip-of-the-tongue" phenomenon. *Journal of Verbal Learning and Verbal Behavior, 5,* 325–337.

Brown, S. C., & Craik, F. I. M. (2000). Encoding and retrieval of information. In E. Tulving & F. I. M. Craik (Eds.), *The Oxford handbook of memory* (pp. 93–107). New York: Oxford University Press.

Brown, T. A., & Barlow, D. H. (2002). Classification of anxiety and mood disorders. In D. H. Barlow (Ed.), *Anxiety and its disorders: The nature and treatment of anxiety and panic* (2nd ed.). New York: Guilford Press.

Brown, T. A., Campbell, L. A., Lehman, C. L., Grisham, J. R., & Mancill, R. B. (2001). Current and lifetime comorbidity of the *DSM-IV* anxiety and mood disorders in a large clinical sample. *Journal of Abnormal Psychology, 110,* 585–599.

Brownell, K. D., Greenwood, M. R. C., Stellar, E., & Shrager, E. E. (1986). The effects of repeated cycles of weight loss and regain in rats. *Physiology and Behavior, 38,* 459–464.

Brownlee, S. (2002, March). Designer babies. *The Washington Monthly.*

Bruner, J. S. (1983). Education as social invention. *Journal of Social Issues, 39,* 129–141.

Brunner, D. P., Dijk, D. J., Tobler, I., & Borbely, A. A. (1990). Effect of partial sleep deprivation on sleep stages and EEG power spectra. *Electroencephalography and Clinical Neurophysiology, 75,* 492–499.

Buchanan, C. M., Eccles, J. S., & Becker, J. B. (1992). Are adolescents the victims of raging hormones? Evidence for activational effects of hormones on moods and behavior at adolescence. *Psychological Bulletin, 111,* 62–107.

Buchanan, P. J. (2002, October 30). The Beltway sniper and the media. Retrieved September 15, 2006, from http://www.townhall.com/columnists/PatrickJBuchanan/2002/10/30/the_beltway_sniper_and_the_media

Buck, L., & Axel, R. (1991). A novel multigene family may encode odorant receptors: A molecular basis for odor recognition. *Cell, 65,* 175–187.

Buckley, K. W. (1989). *Mechanical man: John Broadus Watson and the beginnings of behaviorism.* New York: Guilford Press.

Buckner, R. L., Petersen, S. E., Ojemann, J. G., Miezin, F. M., Squire, L. R., & Raichle, M. E. (1995). Functional anatomical studies of explicit and implicit memory retrieval tasks. *Journal of Neuroscience, 15,* 12–29.

Buckner, R. L., Snyder, A. Z., Shannon, B. J., LaRossa, G., Sachs, R., Fotenos, A. F., et al. (2005). Molecular, structural, and functional characterization of Alzheimer's disease: Evidence for a relationship between default activity, amyloid, and memory. *Journal of Neuroscience, 25,* 7709–7717.

Bureau of Justice Statistics. (2001). *Prisoners in 2000* (No. NCJ 188207). Washington, DC: U.S. Department of Justice.

Burger, J. M. (1999). The foot-in-the-door compliance procedure: A multiple-process analysis and review. *Personality and Social Psychology Review, 3,* 303–325.

Burger, J. M., & Burns, L. (1988). The illusion of unique invulnerability and the use of effective contraception. *Personality and Social Psychology Bulletin, 14,* 264–270.

Burke, D., MacKay, D. G., Worthley, J. S., & Wade, E. (1991). On the tip of the tongue: What causes word failure in young and older adults? *Journal of Memory and Language, 30,* 237–246.

Burnstein, E., Crandall, C., & Kitayama, S. (1994). Some neo-Darwinian decision rules for altruism: Weighing cues for inclusive fitness as a function of the biological importance of the decision. *Journal of Personality & Social Psychology, 67,* 773–789.

Burris, C. T., & Branscombe, N. R. (2005). Distorted distance estimation induced by a self-relevant national boundary. *Journal of Experimental Social Psychology, 41,* 305–312.

Bushman, B. J., & Baumeister, R. F. (1998). Threatened egotism, narcissism, self-esteem, and direct and displaced aggression: Does self-love or self-hate lead to violence? *Journal of Personality and Social Psychology, 75,* 219–229.

Buss, D. M. (1985). Human mate selection. *American Scientist, 73,* 47–51.

Buss, D. M. (1989). Sex differences in human mate preferences: Evolutionary hypotheses tested in 37 cultures. *Behavioral and Brain Sciences, 12,* 1–49.

Buss, D. M. (1994). *The evolution of desire: Strategies of human mating.* New York: Basic Books.

Buss, D. M. (1996). Social adaptation and five major factors of personality. In J. S. Wiggins (Ed.), *The five-factor model of personality: Theoretical perspectives* (pp. 180–208). New York: Guilford Press.

Buss, D. M. (1999). *Evolutionary psychology: The new science of the mind.* Boston: Allyn and Bacon.

Buss, D. M. (2000). *The dangerous passion: Why jealousy is as necessary as love and sex.* New York: Free Press.

Buss, D. M., Abbott, M., Angleitner, A., Asherian, A., Biaggio, A., Blanco-Villasenor, A., et al. (1990). International preferences in selecting mates: A study of 37 cultures. *Journal of Cross-Cultural Psychology, 21,* 5–47.

Buss, D. M., Haselton, M. G., Shackelford, T. K., Bleske, A. L., & Wakefield, J. C. (1998). Adaptations, exaptations, and spandrels. *American Psychologist, 53,* 533–548.

Buss, D. M., & Kenrick, D. T. (1998). Evolutionary social psychology. In D. T. Gilbert, S. T. Fiske, & G. Lindzey (Eds.), *The handbook of social psychology* (4th ed., pp. 982–1026). New York: McGraw-Hill.

Buss, D. M., & Schmitt, D. P. (1993). Sexual strategies theory: An evolutionary perspective on human mating. *Psychological Review, 100,* 204–232.

Butzlaff, R. L., & Hooley, J. M. (1998). Expressed emotion and psychiatric relapse: A meta-analysis. *Archives of General Psychiatry, 55,* 547–552.

Buys, C. J. (1978). Humans would do better without groups. *Personality and Social Psychology Bulletin, 4,* 123–125.

Byrne, D., Allgeier, A. R., Winslow, L., & Buckman, J. (1975). The situational facilitation of interpersonal attraction: A three-factor hypothesis. *Journal of Applied Social Psychology, 5,* 1–15.

Byrne, D., & Clore, G. L. (1970). A reinforcement model of evaluative responses. *Personality: An International Journal, 1,* 103–128.

Byrne, D., Ervin, C. R., & Lamberth, J. (1970). Continuity between the experimental study of attraction and real-life computer dating. *Journal of Personality and Social Psychology, 16,* 157–165.

Byrne, D., & Nelson, D. (1965). Attraction as a linear function of proportion of positive reinforcements. *Journal of Personality and Social Psychology, 1,* 659–663.

Cabeza, R. (2002). Hemispheric asymmetry reduction in older adults: The HAROLD model. *Psychology and Aging, 17,* 85–100.

Cabeza, R., Rao, S., Wagner, A. D., Mayer, A., & Schacter, D. L. (2001). Can medial temporal lobe regions distinguish true from false? An event-related fMRI study of veridical and illusory recognition memory. *Proceedings of the National Academy of Sciences (USA), 98,* 4805–4810.

Cacioppo, J. T., Hawkley, L. C., & Berntson, G. G. (2003). The anatomy of loneliness. *Current Directions in Psychological Science, 12,* 71–74.

Cahill, L., Haier, R. J., Fallon, J., Alkire, M. T., Tang, C., Keator, D., et al. (1996). Amygdala activity at encoding correlated with long-term, free recall of emotional information. *Proceedings of the National Academy of Sciences (USA), 93,* 8016–8021.

Cahill, L., & McGaugh, J. L. (1998). Mechanisms of emotional arousal and lasting declarative memory. *Trends in Neurosciences, 21,* 294–299.

Calder, A. J., Young, A. W., Rowland, D., Perrett, D. I., Hodges, J. R., & Etcoff, N. L. (1996). Facial emotion recognition after bilateral amygdala damage: Differentially severe impairment of fear. *Cognitive Neuropsychology, 13,* 699–745.

Calkins, M. W. (Ed.). (1930). *Mary Whiton Calkins* (Vol. 1). Worcester, MA: Clark University Press.

Callaghan, T., Rochat, P., Lillard, A., Claux, M. L., Odden, H., Itakura, S., et al. (2005). Synchrony in the onset of mental-state reasoning: Evidence from five cultures. *Psychological Science, 16,* 378–384.

Campbell, A. (1999). Staying alive: Evolution, culture, and women's intra-sexual aggression. *Behavioral & Brain Sciences, 22,* 203–252.

Campbell, C. M., Edward, R. R., & Fillingim, R. B. (2005). Ethnic differences in responses to multiple experimental pain stimuli. *Pain, 113,* 20–26.

Campbell, D. T. (1965). Ethnocentric and other altruistic motives. In D. Levine (Ed.), *Nebraska symposium on motivation* (pp. 283–311). Lincoln: University of Nebraska Press.

Campbell, R., & Sais, E. (1995). Accelerated metalinguistic (phonological) awareness in bilingual children. *British Journal of Developmental Psychology, 13,* 61–68.

Canetto, S., & Lester, D. (1995). Gender and the primary prevention of suicide mortality. *Suicide and Life Threatening Behavior, 25,* 85–89.

Cannon, W. B. (1927). The James-Lange theory of emotion: A critical examination and alternate theory. *American Journal of Psychology, 39,* 106–124.

Cannon, W. B. (1929). *Bodily changes in pain, hunger, fear, and rage: An account of recent research into the function of emotional excitement* (2nd ed.). New York: Appleton-Century-Crofts.

Cannon, W. B. (1942). "Voodoo" death. *American Anthropologist, 44,* 182–190.

Cantor, N. (1990). From thought to behavior: "Having" and "doing" in the study of personality and cognition. *American Psychologist, 45,* 735–750.

Caplan, A. L. (Ed.). (1992). *When medicine went mad: Bioethics and the Holocaust.* Totowa, NJ: Humana Press.

Carlson, C., & Hoyle, R. (1993). Efficacy of abbreviated progressive muscle relaxation training: A quantitative review of behavioral medicine research. *Journal of Consulting & Clinical Psychology, 61,* 1059–1067.

Carmena, J. M., Lebedev, M. A., Crist, R. E., O'Doherty, J. E., Santucci, D. M., Dimitrov, D. F., et al. (2003). Learning to control a brain-machine interface for reaching and grasping by primates. *Public Library of Science Biology, 1,* 193–208.

Carmichael Olson, H., Streissguth, A. P., Sampson, P. D., Barr, H. M., Bookstein, F. L., & Thiede, K. (1997). Association of prenatal alcohol exposure with behavioral and learning problems in early adolescence. *Journal of the American Academy of Child and Adolescent Psychiatry, 36,* 1187–1194.

Carolson, E. A. (1998). A prospective longitudinal study of attachment disorganization/disorientation. *Child Development, 69,* 1107–1128.

Carr, L., Iacoboni, M., Dubeau, M., Mazziotta, J. C., & Lenzi, G. L. (2003). Neural mechanisms of empathy in humans: A relay from neural systems for imitation to limbic areas. *Proceedings of the National Academy of Sciences, 100,* 5497–5502.

Carroll, J. B. (1993). *Human cognitive abilities.* Cambridge, England: Cambridge University Press.

Carson, R. C., Butcher, J. N., & Mineka, S. (2000). *Abnormal psychology and modern life* (11th ed.). Boston: Allyn and Bacon.

Carstensen, L. L. (1992). Social and emotional patterns in adulthood: Support for socioemotional selectivity theory. *Psychology and Aging, 7,* 331–338.

Carstensen, L. L., & Fredrickson, B. L. (1998). Influence of HIV status and age on cognitive representations of others. *Health Psychology, 17,* 1–10.

Carstensen, L. L., Isaacowitz, D. M., & Charles, S. T. (1999). Taking time seriously: A theory of socioemotional selectivity. *American Psychologist, 54,* 165–181.

Carstensen, L. L., Pasupathi, M., Mayr, U., & Nesselroade, J. R. (2000). Emotional experience in everyday life across the adult life span. *Journal of Personality & Social Psychology, 79,* 644–655.

Carstensen, L. L., & Turk-Charles, S. (1994). The salience of emotion across the adult life span. *Psychology and Aging, 9,* 259–264.

Carver, C. S., Lehman, J. M., & Antoni, M. H. (2003). Dispositional pessimism predicts illness-related disruption of social and recreational activities among breast cancer patients. *Journal of Personality & Social Psychology, 84,* 813–821.

Carver, C. S., & Scheier, M. F. (2001). Optimism, pessimism, and self-regulation. In E. C. Chang (Ed.), *Optimism and pessimism: Implications for theory, research, and practice.* Washington, DC: American Psychological Association.

Caspi, A., Henry, B., McGee, R. O., Moffitt, T. E., & Silva, P. A. (1995). Temperamental origins of child and adolescent behavior problems: From age three to age fifteen. *Child Development, 66,* 55–68.

Caspi, A., & Herbener, E. S. (1990). Continuity and change: Assortative marriage and the consistency of personality in adulthood. *Journal of Personality and Social Psychology, 58,* 250–258.

Caspi, A., Lynam, D., Moffitt, T. E., & Silva, P. A. (1993). Unraveling girls' delinquency: Biological, dispositional, and contextual contributions to adolescent misbehavior. *Developmental Psychology, 29,* 19–30.

Caspi, A., & Moffitt, T. E. (1991). Individual differences are accentuated during periods of social change: The sample case of girls at puberty. *Journal of Personality and Social Psychology, 61,* 157–168.

Caspi, A., Roberts, B. W., & Shiner, R. L. (2005). Personality development: Stability and change. *Annual Review of Psychology, 56,* 453–484.

Cassidy, K. W., Fineberg, D. S., Brown, K., & Perkins, A. (2005). Theory of mind may be contagious, but you don't catch it from your twin. *Child Development, 76,* 97–106.

Castro-Martin, T., & Bumpass, L. (1989). Recent trends in marital disruption. *Demography, 26,* 37–51.

Cates, W. (1999). Estimates of the incidence and prevalence of sexually transmitted diseases in the United States. *Sexually Transmitted Disease, 26*(Suppl.), S2–S7.

Catrambone, R. (2002). The effects of surface and structural feature matches on the access of story analogs. *Journal of Experimental Psychology: Learning, Memory, & Cognition, 28,* 318–334.

Cattell, R. B. (1950). *Personality: A systematic, theoretical, and factual study.* New York: McGraw-Hill.

CBS. (2000). *Survivor.* Retrieved July 2, 2003, from http://www.cbs.com/primetime/survivor

Ceci, S. J. (1991). How much does schooling influence general intelligence and its cognitive components? A reassessment of the evidence. *Developmental Psychology, 27,* 703–722.

Ceci, S. J., DeSimone, M., & Johnson, S. (1992). Memory in context: A case study of "Bubbles P.," a gifted but uneven memorizer. In D. J. Herrmann, H. Weingartner, A. Searleman, & C. McEvoy (Eds.), *Memory improvement: Implications for memory theory* (pp. 169–186). New York: Springer-Verlag.

Ceci, S. J., & Williams, W. M. (1997). Schooling, intelligence, and income. *American Psychologist, 52,* 1051–1058.

Centers for Disease Control (CDC). (1988). Health status of Vietnam veterans: I. Psychosocial characteristics. *Journal of the American Medical Association, 259,* 2701–2708.

Centers for Disease Control (CDC). (2000). *Tracking the hidden epidemics.* Washington, DC: author.

Centers for Disease Control (CDC). (August 18, 2000). Surveillance summary. *49* (No. SS-8). Washington, DC: author.

Centers for Disease Control (CDC). (June 28, 2002). Surveillance summary. *51* (No. SS-54). Washington, DC: author.

Centers for Disease Control (CDC). (2006). Epidemiology of HIV/AIDS—United States, 1981–2005. *Morbidity and Mortality Weekly Report, 55,* 589–592.

Chaiken, S. (1980). Heuristic versus systematic information processing and the use of source versus message cues in persuasion. *Journal of Personality and Social Psychology, 39,* 752–766.

Chalmers, D. (1996). *The conscious mind: In search of a fundamental theory.* New York: Oxford University Press.

Chambless, D. L., Baker, M. J., Baucom, D. H., Beutler, L. E., Calhoun, K. S., Crits-Christoph, P., et al. (1998). Update on empirically validated therapies, II. *Clinical Psychologist, 51*(1), 3–14.

Chandrashekar, J., Hoon, M. A., Ryba, N. J., & Zuker, C. S. (2006). The receptors and cells for human tastes. *Nature, 444,* 288–294.

Chang, P. P., Ford, D. E., Meoni, L. A., Wang, N., & Klag, M. J. (2002). Anger in young men and subsequent premature cardiovascular disease. *Archives of Internal Medicine, 162,* 901–906.

Charles, S. T., Reynolds, C. A., & Gatz, M. (2001). Age-related differences and change in positive and negative affect over 23 years. *Journal of Personality and Social Psychology, 80,* 136–151.

Charness, N. (1981). Aging and skilled problem solving. *Journal of Experimental Psychology: General, 110,* 21–38.

Chartrand, T. L., & Bargh, J. A. (1999). The chameleon effect: The perception-behavior link and social interaction. *Journal of Personality and Social Psychology, 76,* 893–910.

Chartrand, T. L., & Kay, A. (in press). Mystery moods and perplexing performance: Consequences of succeeding and failing at a nonconscious goal.

Chebium, R. (2000). Kirk Bloodsworth, twice convicted of rape and murder, exonerated by DNA evidence. *CNN.com.* Retrieved June 20, 2000, from http://www.cnn.com/2000/LAW/06/20/bloodsworth.profile

Cheney, D. L., & Seyfarth, R. M. (1990). *How monkeys see the world.* Chicago: University of Chicago Press.

Cheng, P. W., & Holyoak, K. J. (1989). On the natural selection of reasoning theories. *Cognition, 33,* 285–313.

Cherlin, A. J. (Ed.). (1992). *Marriage, divorce, remarriage* (2nd ed.). Cambridge, MA: Harvard University Press.

Cherry, A., Dillon, M. E., & Rugh, D. (Eds.). (2002). *Substance abuse: A global view.* Westport, CT: Greenwood.

Cherry, C. (1953). Some experiments on the recognition of speech with one and two ears. *Journal of the Acoustical Society of America, 25,* 275–279.

Choi, I., Nisbett, R. E., & Norenzayan, A. (1999). Causal attribution across cultures: Variation and universality. *Psychological Bulletin, 125,* 47–63.

Chomsky, N. (1957). *Syntactic structures.* The Hague: Mouton.

Chomsky, N. (1959). A review of *Verbal Behavior* by B. F. Skinner. *Language, 35,* 26–58.

Chomsky, N. (1986). *Knowledge of language: Its nature, origin, and use.* New York: Praeger.

Chorover, S. L. (1980). *From Genesis to genocide: The meaning of human nature and the power of behavior control.* Cambridge, MA: MIT Press.

Christianson, S.-Å., & Loftus, E. F. (1987). Memory for traumatic events. *Applied Cognitive Psychology, 1,* 225–239.

Cialdini, R. B. (2000). *Influence: Science and practice* (4th ed.). New York: Morrow.

Cialdini, R. B. (2005). Don't throw in the towel: Use social influence research. *American Psychological Society, 18,* 33–34.

Cialdini, R. B., & Trost, M. R. (1998). Social influence: Social norms, conformity, and compliance. In D. T. Gilbert, S. T. Fiske, & G. Lindzey (Eds.), *The handbook of social psychology* (4th ed., Vol. 2, pp. 151–192). New York: McGraw-Hill.

Cialdini, R. B., Trost, M. R., & Newsom, J. T. (1995). Preference for consistency: The development of a valid measure and the discovery of surprising behavioral implications. *Journal of Personality and Social Psychology, 69,* 318–328.

Cialdini, R. B., Vincent, J. E., Lewis, S. K., Catalan, J., Wheeler, D., & Darby, B. L. (1975). Reciprocal concessions procedure for inducing compliance: The door-in-the-face technique. *Journal of Personality and Social Psychology, 31,* 206–215.

Cicchetti, D., & Toth, S. L. (1998). Perspectives on research and practice in developmental psychopathology. In I. E. Sigel & K. A. Renninger (Eds.), *Handbook of child psychology: Vol. 4. Child psychology in practice* (5th ed., pp. 479–583). New York: Wiley.

Clancy, S. A. (2005). *Abducted: How people come to believe they were kidnapped by aliens.* Cambridge. MA: Harvard University Press.

Clark, L. A. (2007). Assessment and diagnosis of personality disorder: Perennial issues and emerging conceptualization. *Annual Review of Psychology, 58,* 227–257.

Clark, R. D., & Hatfield, E. (1989). Gender differences in receptivity to sexual offers. *Journal of Psychology and Human Sexuality, 2,* 39–55.

Clayton, N. S., & Dickinson, A. (1998). Episodic-like memory during cache recovery by scrub jays. *Nature, 395,* 272–274.

Cleckley, H. M. (1976). *The mask of sanity* (5th ed.). St. Louis: Mosby.

Coe, C. (1993). Psychosocial factors and immunity in nonhuman primates: A review. *Psychosomatic Medicine, 55,* 298–308.

Cogan, R., Cogan, D., Waltz, W., & McCue, M. (1987). Effects of laughter and relaxation on discomfort thresholds. *Journal of Behavioral Medicine, 10,* 139–144.

Coghill, R. C., McHaffie, J. G., & Yen, Y. (2003). Neural correlates of individual differences in the subjective experience of pain. *Proceedings of the National Academy of Sciences, (USA), 100,* 8538–8542.

Cohen, D. (1997). A critique of the use of neuroleptic drugs in psychiatry. In S. Fisher & R. P. Greenberg (Eds.), *From placebo to panacea: Putting psychiatric drugs to test* (pp. 173–228). New York: Wiley.

Cohen, D., Nisbett, R. E., Bowdle, B. F., & Schwarz, N. (1996). Insult, aggression, and the southern culture of honor: An "experimental ethnography." *Journal of Personality and Social Psychology, 70,* 945–960.

Cohen, G. (1990). Why is it difficult to put names to faces? *British Journal of Psychology, 81,* 287–297.

Cohen, N. J., & Squire, L. R. (1980). Preserved learning and retention of pattern analyzing skill in amnesics: Dissociation of knowing how and knowing that. *Science, 210,* 207–210.

Cohen, S. (1988). Psychosocial models of the role of social support in the etiology of physical disease. *Health Psychology, 7,* 269–297.

Cohen, S. (1999). Social status and susceptibility to respiratory infections. *New York Academy of Sciences, 896,* 246–253.

Cohen, S., Evans, G. W., Krantz, D. S., & Stokols, D. (1980). Physiological, motivational, and cognitive effects of aircraft noise on children. *American Psychologist, 35,* 231–243.

Cohen, S., Frank, E., Doyle, W. J., Skoner, D. P., Rabin, B. S., & Gwaltney, J. M., Jr. (1998). Types of stressors that increase susceptibility to the common cold in healthy adults. *Health Psychology, 17,* 214–223.

Cohen, S., Kaplan, J. R., Cunnick, J. E., Manuck, S. B., & Rabin, B. S. (1992). Chronic social stress, affiliation, and cellular immune response in nonhuman primates. *Psychological Science, 3,* 301–304.

Cohen, S. J. (Ed.). (1979). *New directions in patient compliance.* Lexington, MA: Heath.

Cole, M. (1996). *Cultural psychology: A once and future discipline.* Cambridge, MA: Belknap Press of Harvard University Press.

Coley, R. L., & Chase-Landale, P. L. (1998). Adolescent pregnancy and parenthood: Recent evidence and future directions. *American Psychologist, 53,* 152–166.

Condon, J. W., & Crano, W. D. (1988). Inferred evaluation and the relation between attitude similarity and interpersonal attraction. *Journal of Personality and Social Psychology, 54,* 789–797.

Connors, E., Lundregan, T., Miller, N., & McEwen, T. (1997). *Convicted by juries, exonerated by science: Case studies in the use of DNA evidence to establish innocence after trial.* Collingdale, PA: Diane Publishing.

Conway, M., & Ross, M. (1984). Getting what you want by revising what you had. *Journal of Personality and Social Psychology, 47,* 738–748.

Conwell, Y., Duberstein, P. R., Cox, C., Hermmann, J. H., Forbes, N. T., & Caine, E. D. (1996). Relationships of age and axis I diagnoses in victims of completed suicide: A psychological autopsy study. *American Journal of Psychiatry, 153,* 1001–1008.

Cook, E. P. (1985). *Psychological androgyny.* New York: Pergamon Press.

Cook, M., & Mineka, S. (1989). Observational conditioning of fear to fear-relevant versus fear-irrelevant stimuli in rhesus monkeys. *Journal of Abnormal Psychology, 98,* 448–459.

Cook, M., & Mineka, S. (1990). Selective associations in the observational conditioning of fear in rhesus monkeys. *Journal of Experimental Psychology: Animal Behavior Process, 16,* 372–389.

Coombs, R. H. (1991). Marital status and personal well-being: A literature review. *Family Relations, 40,* 97–102.

Coons, P. M. (1994). Confirmation of childhood abuse in child and adolescent cases of multiple personality disorder and dissociative disorder not otherwise specified. *Journal of Nervous and Mental Disease, 182,* 461–464.

Cooper, J., & Fazio, R. H. (1984). A new look at dissonance theory. In L. Berkowitz (Ed.), *Advances in experimental social psychology* (Vol. 17, pp. 229–266). New York: Academic Press.

Cooper, J. R., Bloom, F. E., & Roth, R. H. (2003). *Biochemical basis of neuropharmacology.* New York: Oxford University Press.

Cooper, M. L., Shapiro, C. M., & Powers, A. M. (1998). Motivations for sex and risky sexual behavior among adolescents and young adults: A functional perspective. *Journal of Personality and Social Psychology, 75,* 1528–1558.

Coren, S. (1997). *Sleep thieves.* New York: Free Press.

Corkin, S. (1984). Lasting consequences of bilateral medial temporal lobectomy: Clinical course and experimental findings in H. M. *Seminars in Neurology, 4,* 249–259.

Corkin, S. (2002). What's new with the amnesic patient HM? *Nature Reviews Neuroscience, 3,* 153–160.

Correll, J., Park, B., Judd, C. M., & Wittenbrink, B. (2002). The police officer's dilemma: Using ethnicity to disambiguate potentially threatening individuals. *Journal of Personality and Social Psychology, 83,* 1314–1329.

Corsi, P. (1991). *The enchanted loom: Chapters in the history of neuroscience.* New York: Oxford University Press.

Corsini, R. J. (2000). Introduction. In R. J. Corsini & D. Wedding (Eds.), *Current psychotherapies* (6th ed., pp. 1–15). Itasca, IL: F. E. Peacock, Publishers.

Corti, E. (1931). *A history of smoking* (P. England, Trans.). London: Harrap.

Coryell, W., Endicott, J., Maser, J. D., Mueller, T., Lavori, P., & Keller, M. (1995). The likelihood of recurrence in bipolar affective disorder: The importance of episode recency. *Journal of Affective Disorders, 33,* 201–206.

Cosmides, L. (1989). The logic of social exchange: Has natural selection shaped how humans reason? Studies with the Wason selection task. *Cognition, 31,* 187–276.

Cox, D., & Cowling, P. (1989). *Are you normal?* London: Tower Press.

Coyne, J. A. (2000, April 3). Of vice and men: Review of R. Tornhill and C. Palmer, *A natural history of rape. The New Republic,* 27–34.

Coyne, J. C., & Whiffen, V. E. (1995). Issues in personality as diathesis for depression: The case of sociotropy-dependency and autonomy self-criticism. *Psychological Bulletin, 118,* 358–378.

Craik, F. I. M., Govoni, R., Naveh-Benjamin, M., & Anderson, N. D. (1996). The effects of divided attention on encoding and retrieval processes in human memory. *Journal of Experimental Psychology: General, 125,* 159–180.

Craik, F. I. M., & Tulving, E. (1975). Depth of processing and the retention of words in episodic memory. *Journal of Experimental Psychology: General, 104,* 268–294.

Cramer, R. E., Schaefer, J. T., & Reid, S. (1996). Identifying the ideal mate: More evidence for male-female convergence. *Current Psychology: Developmental, Learning, Personality, Social, 15,* 157–166.

Craske, M. G. (1999). *Anxiety disorders: Psychological approaches to theory and treatment.* Boulder, CO: Westview.

Crespi, L. P. (1942). Quantitative variation in incentive and performance in the white rat. *American Journal of Psychology, 55,* 467–517.

Crick, N. R., & Grotpeter, J. K. (1995). Relational aggression, gender, and social-psychological adjustment. *Child Development, 66,* 710–722.

Critelli, J. W., & Ee, J. S. (1996). Stress and physical illness: Development of an integrative model. In T. W. Miller (Ed.), *Theory and assessment of stressful life events* (pp. 139–159). Madison, CT: International Universities Press.

Crocker, J., & Luhtanen, R. (1990). Collective self-esteem and in-group bias. *Journal of Personality and Social Psychology, 58,* 60–67.

Crocker, J., & Wolfe, C. T. (2001). Contingencies of self-worth. *Psychological Review, 108*(3), 593–623.

Crombag, H. F. M., Wagenaar, W. A., & Van Koppen, P. J. (1996). Crashing memories and the problem of "source monitoring." *Applied Cognitive Psychology, 10,* 95–104.

Cross, P. (1977). Not can but will college teachers be improved? *New Directions for Higher Education, 17,* 1–15.

Cross-National Collaborative Research Group. (1992). The changing rate of major depression: Cross-national comparison. *Journal of the American Medical Association, 268,* 3098–3105.

Crowe, R. (1990). Panic disorder: Genetic considerations. *Journal of Psychiatric Researchers, 24,* 129–134.

Csermansky, J. G., & Grace, A. A. (1998). New models of the pathophysiology of schizophrenia: Editor's introduction. *Schizophrenia Bulletin, 24,* 185–187.

Csikszentmihalyi, M. (1990). *Flow: The psychology of optimal experience.* New York: Harper & Row.

Csikszentmihalyi, M., & Larson, R. (1987). Validity and reliability of the experience-sampling method. *Journal of Nervous & Mental Disease, 175,* 526–536.

Cumming, S., Hay, P., Lee, T., & Sachdev, P. (1995). Neuropsychological outcome from psychosurgery for obsessive-compulsive disorder. *Australian and New Zealand Journal of Psychiatry, 29,* 293–298.

Cummings, D. E., Purnell, J. Q., Frayo, R. S., Schmidova, K., Wisse, B. E., & Weigle, D. S. (2001). A preprandial rise in plasma ghrelin levels suggests a role in meal initiation in humans. *Diabetes, 50,* 1714–1719.

Cummins, D. D., & Allen, C. A. (2000). *The evolution of mind.* New York: Oxford University Press.

Cunningham, M. R., Barbee, A. P., & Pike, C. L. (1990). What do women want? Facialmetric assessment of multiple motives in the perception of male facial physical attractiveness. *Journal of Personality & Social Psychology, 59,* 61–72.

Cunningham, M. R., Roberts, A. R., Barbee, A. P., Druen, P. B., & Wu, C.-H. (1995). "Their ideas of beauty are, on the whole, the same as ours": Consistency and variability in the cross-cultural perception of female physical attractiveness. *Journal of Personality and Social Psychology, 68,* 261–279.

Curran, J. P., & Lippold, S. (1975). The effects of physical attraction and attitude similarity on attraction in dating dyads. *Journal of Personality, 43,* 528–539.

Curtiss, S. (1977). Genie: A psycholinguistic study of a modern-day "wild-child." New York: Academic Press.

Cutler, D. L., Bevilacqua, J., & McFarland, B. H. (2003). Four decades of community mental health: A symphony in four movements. *Community Mental Health Journal, 39,* 381–398.

Cutler, S., & Nolen-Hoeksema, S. (1991). Accounting for sex differences in depression through female victimization: Childhood sexual abuse. *Sex Roles, 24,* 425–438.

Cytowic, R. (2003). *The man who tasted shapes.* Cambridge, MA: MIT Press.

Dabbs, J. M., Bernieri, F. J., Strong, R. K., Campo, R., & Milun, R. (2001). Going on stage: Testosterone in greetings and meetings. *Journal of Research in Personality, 35,* 27–40.

Dabbs, J. M., Carr, T. S., Frady, R. L., & Riad, J. K. (1995). Testosterone, crime, and misbehavior among 692 male prison inmates. *Personality and Individual Differences, 18,* 627–633.

Dabbs, J. M., Strong, R., & Milun, R. (1997). Exploring the mind of testosterone: A beeper study. *Journal of Research in Personality, 31,* 577–587.

D'Agostino, P. R., & Fincher-Kiefer, R. (1992). Need for cognition and correspondence bias. *Social Cognition, 10,* 151–163.

Dally, P. (1999). *The marriage of heaven and hell: Manic depression and the life of Virginia Woolf.* New York: St. Martin's Griffin.

Dalton, P. (2003). Olfaction. In H. Pashler & S. Yantis (Eds.), *Stevens' handbook of experimental psychology: Vol. 1. Sensation and perception* (3rd ed., pp. 691–746). New York: Wiley.

Daly, M., & Wilson, M. (1988). Evolutionary social psychology and family homicide. *Science, 242,* 519–524.

Damasio, A. R. (1989). Time-locked multiregional retroactivation: A systems-level proposal for the neural substrates of recall and recognition. *Cognition, 33,* 25–62.

Damasio, A. R. (1994). *Descartes' error: Emotion, reason, and the human brain.* New York: Putnam.

Damasio, A. R. (2005). *Descartes' error: Emotion, reason, and the human brain.* (ppbk. ed). New York: Penguin.

Damasio, A. R., Grabowski, T. J., Bechara, A., Damasio, H., Ponto, L. L. B., Parvisi, J., et al. (2000). Subcortical and cortical brain activity during the feeling of self-generated emotions. *Nature Neuroscience, 3,* 1049–1056.

Damasio, H., Grabowski, T. J., Tranel, D., Hichwa, R. D., & Damasio, A . R. (1996). A neural basis for lexical retrieval. *Nature, 380,* 499–505.

Damsma, G., Pfaus, J. G., Wenkstern, D., Phillips, A. G., & Fibiger, H. C. (1992). Sexual behavior increases dopamine transmission in the nucleus accumbens and striatum of male rats: Comparison with novelty and locomotion. *Behavioral Neurosciences, 106,* 181–191.

Daniel, H. J., O'Brien, K. F., McCabe, R. B., & Quinter, V. E. (1985). Values in mate selection: A 1984 campus survey. *College Student Journal, 19,* 44–50.

Darley, J. M., & Berscheid, E. (1967). Increased liking caused by the anticipation of interpersonal contact. *Human Relations, 10,* 29–40.

Darley, J. M., & Latané, B. (1968). Bystander intervention in emergencies: Diffusion of responsibility. *Journal of Personality and Social Psychology, 8,* 377–383.

Dar-Nimrod, I., & Heine, S. J. (2006). Exposure to scientific theories affects women's math performance. *Science, 314,* 435.

Darroch, J. E., Singh, S., Frost, J. J., & Study Team. (2001). Differences in teenage pregnancy rates among five developed countries: The roles of sexuality and contraceptive use. *Family Planning Perspectives, 33,* 244–250.

Darwin, C. (1859). *On the origin of species by means of natural selection.* London: J. Murray.

Darwin, C. (1998). *The expression of the emotions in man and animals.* (P. Ekman, Ed.) New York: Oxford University Press. (Originally published 1872)

Darwin, C. J., Turvey, M. T., & Crowder, R. G. (1972). An auditory analogue of the Sperling partial report procedure: Evidence for brief auditory storage. *Cognitive Psychology, 3,* 255–267.

Dauer, W., & Przedborski, S. (2003). Parkinson's disease: Mechanisms and models. *Neuron, 39,* 889–909.

Davidson, P. R., & Parker, K. C. H. (2001). Eye movement desensitization and reprocessing (EMDR): A meta-analysis. *Journal of Consulting and Clinical Psychology, 69,* 305–316.

Davidson, R. J. (2004). What does the prefrontal cortex "do" in affect: Perspectives on frontal EEG asymmetry research. *Biological Psychology, 67,* 219–233.

Davidson, R. J., Ekman, P., Saron, C., Senulis, J., & Friesen, W. V. (1990). Emotional expression and brain physiology I: Approach/withdrawal and cerebral asymmetry. *Journal of Personality and Social Psychology, 58,* 330–341.

Davidson, R. J., Pizzagalli, D., Nitschke, J. B., & Putnam, K. (2002). Depression: Perspectives from affective neuroscience. *Annual Review of Psychology, 53,* 545–574.

Davidson, R. J., Putnam, K. M., & Larson, C. L. (2000). Dysfunction in the neural circuitry of emotion regulation—a possible prelude to violence. *Science, 289,* 591–594.

Davies, G. (1988). Faces and places: Laboratory research on context and face recognition. In G. M. Davies & D. M. Thomson (Eds.), *Memory in context: Context in memory* (pp. 35–53). New York: Wiley.

Davis, K. (1947). Final note on a case of extreme social isolation. *American Journal of Sociology, 52,* 432–437.

Dawes, R. M. (1986). Representative thinking in clinical judgment. *Clinical Psychology Review, 6,* 425–441.

Dawes, R. M. (1994). *House of cards: Psychology and psychotherapy built on myth.* New York: Free Press.

Dawes, R. M. (2001). *Everyday irrationality: How pseudo scientists, lunatics, and the rest of us systematically fail to think rationally.* Boulder, CO: Westview Press.

Dawkins, R. J. (1976). *The selfish gene.* Oxford, England: Oxford University Press.

Dawood, K., Kirk, K. M., Bailey, J. M., Andrews, P. W., & Martin, N. G. (2005). Genetic and environmental influences on the frequency of orgasm in women. *Twin Research, 8,* 27–33.

de Craen, A. J. M., Moerman, D. E., Heisterkamp, S. H., Tytgat, G. N. J., Tijssen, J. G. P., & Kleijnen, J. (1999). Placebo effect in the treatment of duodenal ulcer. *British Journal of Clinical Pharmacology, 48,* 853–860.

De Valois, R. L., Abramov, I., & Jacobs, G. (1966). Analysis of response patterns of LGN cells. *Journal of the Optical Society of America [A], 56,* 966–977.

De Witte, P. (1996). The role of neurotransmitters in alcohol dependency. *Alcohol & Alcoholism, 31*(Suppl. 1), 13–16.

De Wolff, M., & van IJzendoorn, M. H. (1997). Sensitivity and attachment: A meta-analysis on parental antecedents of infant attachment. *Child Development, 68,* 571–591.

Deary, I. J. (2000). *Looking down on human intelligence: From psychometrics to the brain.* New York: Oxford University Press.

Deary, I. J. (2001). *Intelligence: A very short introduction.* Oxford, England: Oxford University Press.

Deary, I. J., Der, G., & Ford, G. (2001). Reaction time and intelligence differences: A population based cohort study. *Intelligence, 29,* 389–399.

Deary, I. J., & Stough, C. (1996). Intelligence and inspection time: Achievements, prospects, and problems. *American Psychologist, 51,* 599–608.

Deary, I. J., Whalley, L. J., Lemmon, H., Crawford, J. R., & Starr, J. M. (2000). The stability of individual differences in mental ability from childhood to old age: Follow-up of the 1932 Scottish Mental Survey. *Intelligence, 28,* 49–55.

Deary, I. J., Whiteman, M. C., Starr, J. M., Whalley, L. J., & Fox, H. C. (2004). The impact of childhood intelligence on later life: Following up the Scottish mental surveys of 1932 and 1947. *Journal of Personality and Social Psychology, 86,* 130–147.

DeCasper, A. J., & Spence, M. J. (1986). Prenatal maternal speech influences newborns' perception of speech sounds. *Infant Behavior and Development, 9,* 133–150.

Deci, E. L. (1971). Effects of externally mediated rewards on intrinsic motivation. *Journal of Personality and Social Psychology, 18,* 105–115.

Deci, E. L., Koestner, R., & Ryan, R. M. (1999). A meta-analytic review of experiments examining the effects of extrinsic rewards on intrinsic motivation. *Psychological Bulletin, 125,* 627–668.

Deese, J. (1959). On the prediction of occurrence of particular verbal intrusions in immediate recall. *Journal of Experimental Psychology, 58,* 17–22.

DeFelipe, J., & Jones, E. G. (1988). *Cajal on the cerebral cortex: An annotated translation of the complete writings.* New York: Oxford University Press.

DeLisi, L. E., Crow, T. J., & Hirsch, S. R. (1986). The third biannual workshops on schizophrenia. *Archives of General Psychiatry, 43,* 706–711.

DeLoache, J. S., & Gottlieb, A. (2000). *A world of babies: Imagined childcare guides for seven societies.* Cambridge, England: Cambridge University Press.

Delongis, A., Coyne, J. C., Dakof, G., Folkman, S., & Lazarus, R. S. (1982). Relationship of daily hassles, uplifts, and major life events to health status. *Health Psychology, 1,* 119–136.

Demb, J. B., Desmond, J. E., Wagner, A. D., Vaidya, C. J., Glover, G. H., & Gabrieli, J. D. E. (1995). Semantic encoding and retrieval in the left inferior prefrontal cortex: A functional MRI study of task difficulty and process specificity. *Journal of Neuroscience, 15,* 5870–5878.

Dement, W. C. (1959, Nov. 30). Dreams. *Time.*

Dement, W. C. (1978). *Some must watch while some must sleep.* New York: Norton.

Dement, W. C. (1999). *The promise of sleep.* New York: Delacorte Press.

Dement, W. C., & Kleitman, N. (1957). The relation of eye movements during sleep to dream activity: An objective method for the study of dreaming. *Journal of Experimental Psychology, 53,* 339–346.

Dement, W. C., & Wolpert, E. (1958). Relation of eye movements, body motility, and external stimuli to dream content. *Journal of Experimental Psychology, 55,* 543–553.

Dennett, D. (1991). *Consciousness explained.* New York: Basic Books.

DePaulo, B. M., Charlton, K., Cooper, H., Lindsay, J. J., & Muhlenbruck, L. (1997). The accuracy-confidence correlation in the detection of deception. *Personality and Social Psychology Review, 1,* 346–357.

DePaulo, B. M., Lindsay, J. J., Malone, B. E., Muhlenbruck, L., Charlton, K., & Cooper, H. (2003). Cues to deception. *Psychological Bulletin, 129,* 74–118.

DePaulo, B. M., Stone, J. I., & Lassiter, G. D. (1985). Deceiving and detecting deceit. In B. R. Schlenker (Ed.), *The self and social life* (pp. 323–370). New York: McGraw-Hill.

DeRosnay, M., Pons, F., Harris, P. L., & Morrell, J. M. B. (2004). A lag between understanding false belief and emotion attribution in young children: Relationships with linguistic ability and mothers' mental-state language. *British Journal of Developmental Psychology, 197–218.*

DesJardin, J. L., Eisenberg, L. S., & Hodapp, R. M. (2006). Sound beginnings: Supporting families of young deaf children with cochlear implants. *Infants and Young Children, 19,* 179–189.

Deuenwald, M. (2003, June 12). Students find another staple of campus life: Stress. *New York Times.*

Deutsch, M. (1949). A theory of cooperation and competition. *Human Relations, 2,* 129–152.

DeVilliers, P. (2005). The role of language in theory-of-mind development: What deaf children tell us. In J. W. Astington & J. A. Baird (Eds.), *Why language matters for theory of mind* (pp. 266–297). Oxford, England: Oxford University Press.

Diaconis, P., & Mosteller, F. (1989). Methods for studying coincidences. *Journal of the American Statistical Association, 84,* 853–861.

Diamond, M., & Schiebel, A. B. (1986). *The human brain coloring book.* New York: Collins.

Dickens, W. T., & Flynn, J. R. (2001). Heritability estimates versus large environmental effects: The IQ paradox resolved. *Psychological Review, 108,* 346–369.

Didi-Huberman, G. (2003). *Invention of hysteria: Charcot and the photographic iconography of the Sâlpetrière* (A. Hartz, Trans.). Cambridge, MA: MIT Press.

Diener, E., & Biswas-Diener, R. (2002). Will money increase subjective well-being? *Social Indicators Research, 57,* 119–169.

Diener, E., Horwitz, J., & Emmons, R. A. (1985). Happiness of the very wealthy. *Social Indicators Research, 16,* 263–274.

Diener, E., & Wallbom, M. (1976). Effects of self-awareness on anti-normative behavior. *Journal of Research in Personality, 10,* 107–111.

Dienstbier, R. A. (1979). Attraction increases and decreases as a function of emotion-attribution and appropriate social cues. *Motivation and Emotion, 3,* 201–218.

Dietary Guidelines Advisory Committee. (2005). Dietary guidelines for Americans 2005. Retrieved October 15, 2007, from http://www.health.gov/dietaryguidelines

Dijksterhuis, A. (2004). Think different: The merits of unconscious thought in preference development and decision making. *Journal of Personality and Social Psychology, 87,* 586–598.

Dijksterhuis, A., Aarts, H., & Smith, P. K. (2005). The power of the subliminal: On subliminal persuasion and other potential applications. In J. S. U. R. Hassin & J. A. Bargh (Eds.), *The new unconscious* (pp. 77–106). New York: Oxford University Press.

Dillbeck, M. C., & Orme-Johnson, D. W. (1987). Physiological differences between Transcendental Meditation and rest. *American Psychologist, 42,* 879–881.

Dimberg, U. (1982). Facial reactions to facial expressions. *Psychophysiology, 19,* 643–647.

Dion, K., Berscheid, E., & Walster, E. (1972). What is beautiful is good. *Journal of Personality and Social Psychology, 24,* 285–290.

DiTella, R., MacCulloch, R. J., & Oswald, A. J. (2003). The macroeconomics of happiness. *Review of Economics and Statistics, 85,* 809–827.

Dittrich, W. H., Troscianko, T., Lea, S., & Morgan, D. (1996). Perception of emotion from dynamic point-light displays represented in dance. *Perception, 25,* 727–738.

Dohrenwend, B. S., Dohrenwend, B. P., Dodson, M., & Shrout, P. E. (1984). Symptoms, hassles, social supports, and life events: Problem of confounded measures. *Journal of Abnormal Psychology, 93,* 222–230.

Dollard, J., Doob, L. W., Miller, N. E., Mowrer, O. H., & Sears, R. R. (1939). *Frustration and aggression.* Oxford, England: Yale University Press.

Domjan, M. (2005). Pavlovian conditioning: A functional perspective. *Annual Review of Psychology, 56,* 179–206.

Dorahy, M. J. (2001). Dissociative identity disorder and memory dysfunction: The current state of experimental research and its future directions. *Clinical Psychology Review, 21,* 771–795.

Dornbusch, S. M., Hastorf, A. H., Richardson, S. A., Muzzy, R. E., & Vreeland, R. S. (1965). The perceiver and perceived: Their relative influence on categories of interpersonal perception. *Journal of Personality and Social Psychology, 1,* 434–440.

Dorus, S., Vallender, E. J., Evans, P. D., Anderson, J. R., Gilbert, S. L., Mahowald, M., et al. (2004). Accelerated evolution of nervous system genes in the origin of *Homo sapiens. Cell, 119,* 1027–1040.

Dostoevsky, F. (1955). *Winter notes on summer impressions* (R. L. Reinfield, Trans.). New York: Criterion Books. (Original work published 1863)

Dowling, J. E. (1992). *Neurons and networks: An introduction to neuroscience.* Cambridge, MA: Harvard University Press.

Downer, J. D. C. (1961). Changes in visual gnostic function and emotional behavior following unilateral temporal damage in the "split-brain" monkey. *Nature, 191,* 50–51.

Downing, P. E., Chan, A. W. Y., Peelen, M. V., Dodds, C. M., & Kanwisher, N. (2006). Domain specificity in visual cortex. *Cerebral Cortex, 16,* 1453–1461.

Draguns, J. G. (1980). Psychological disorders of clinical severity. In H. C. Triandis & J. G. Draguns (Eds.), *Handbook of cross-cultural psychology* (Vol. 6, pp. 99–174). Boston: Allyn and Bacon.

Dreger, A. D. (1998). The limits of individuality: Ritual and sacrifice in the lives and medical treatment of conjoined twins. *Studies in History and Philosophy of Biological and Biomedical Sciences, 29,* 1–29.

Dreifus, C. (2003, May 20). Living one disaster after another, and then sharing the experience. *New York Times,* p. D2.

Drigotas, S. M., & Rusbult, C. E. (1992). Should I stay or should I go? A dependence model of breakups. *Journal of Personality and Social Psychology, 62,* 62–87.

Driscoll, R., Davis, K. E., & Lipetz, M. E. (1972). Parental interference and romantic love: The Romeo and Juliet effect. *Journal of Personality and Social Psychology, 24,* 1–10.

Druckman, D., & Bjork, R. A. (1994). *Learning, remembering, believing: Enhancing human performance.* Washington, DC: National Academy Press.

Drummond, E. (2000). *The complete guide to psychiatric drugs: Straight talk for best results.* New York: Wiley.

Duchaine, B. C., Yovel, G., Butterworth, E. J., & Nakayama, K. (2006). Prosopagnosia as an impairment to face-specific mechanisms: Elimination of the alternative hypotheses in a developmental case. *Cognitive Neuropsychology, 23,* 714–747.

Duckworth, A. L., & Seligman, M. E. P. (2005). Self-discipline outdoes IQ in predicting academic performance of adolescents. *Psychological Science, 16,* 939–944.

Dudycha, G. J., & Dudycha, M. M. (1933). Some factors and characteristics of childhood memories. *Child Development, 4,* 265–278.

Duncker, K. (1945). On problem-solving. *Psychological Monographs, 58,* No. 5.

Dunlap, K. (1919). Are there any instincts? *Journal of Abnormal Psychology, 14,* 307–311.

Dunphy, D. C. (1963). The social structure of urban adolescent peer groups. *Sociometry, 26,* 230–246.

Durkheim, E. (1951). *Suicide: A study in sociology* (G. Simpson, Trans.). New York: Free Press.

Dutton, D. G., & Aron, A. P. (1974). Some evidence for heightened sexual attraction under conditions of high anxiety. *Journal of Personality and Social Psychology, 30,* 510–517.

Duval, S., & Wicklund, R. A. (1972). *A theory of objective self awareness.* New York: Academic Press.

Eacott, M. J., & Crawley, R. A. (1998). The offset of childhood amnesia: Memory for events that occurred before age 3. *Journal of Experimental Psychology: General, 127,* 22–33.

Eagly, A. H., Ashmore, R. D., Makhijani, M. G., & Longo, L. C. (1991). What is beautiful is good, but . . . : A meta-analytic review of research on the physical attractiveness stereotype. *Psychological Bulletin, 110,* 109–128.

Eagly, A. H., & Steffen, V. J. (1986). Gender and aggressive behavior: A meta-analytic review of the social psychological literature. *Psychological Bulletin, 100,* 309–330.

Eagly, A. H., & Wood, W. (1999). The origins of sex differences in human behavior: Evolved dispositions versus social roles. *American Psychologist, 54,* 408–423.

Eaton, W. W., Kessler, R. C., Wittchen, H. U., & McGee, W. J. (1994). Panic and panic disorder in the United States. *American Journal of Psychiatry, 151,* 413–420.

Eaton, W. W., Romanoski, A., Anthony, J. C., & Nestadt, G. (1991). Screening for psychosis in the general population with a self-report interview. *Journal of Nervous and Mental Disease, 179,* 689–693.

Ebbinghaus, H. (1964). *Memory: A contribution to experimental psychology.* New York: Dover. (Originally published 1885)

Eberhardt, J. L. (2005). Imaging race. *American Psychologist, 60,* 181–190.

Eddy, D. M. (1982). Probabilistic reasoning in clinical medicine: Problems and opportunities. In D. Kahneman, P. Slovic, & A. Tversky (Eds.), *Judgments under uncertainty: Heuristics and biases* (pp. 249–267). Cambridge, MA: Cambridge University Press.

Edgerton, V. R., Tillakaratne, J. K. T., Bigbee, A. J., deLeon, R. D., & Roy, R. R. (2004). Plasticity of the spinal neural circuitry after injury. *Annual Review of Neuroscience, 27,* 145–167.

Edwards, W. (1955). The theory of decision making. *Psychological Bulletin, 51,* 201–214.

Eich, J. E. (1980). The cue-dependent nature of state-dependent retention. *Memory & Cognition, 8,* 157–173.

Eich, J. E. (1995). Searching for mood dependent memory. *Psychological Science, 6,* 67–75.

Eichenbaum, H., & Cohen, N. J. (2001). *From conditioning to conscious recollection: Memory systems of the brain.* New York: Oxford University Press.

Eimas, P. D., Siqueland, E. R., Jusczyk, P., & Vigorito, J. (1971). Speech perception in infants. *Science, 171,* 303–306.

Einstein, G. O., & McDaniel, M. A. (1990). Normal aging and prospective memory. *Journal of Experimental Psychology: Learning, Memory, and Cognition, 16,* 717–726.

Eisenberger, N. I., Lieberman, M. D., & Williams, K. D. (2003). Does rejection hurt? An fMRI study of social exclusion. *Science, 302,* 290–292.

Ekman, P. (1965). Differential communication of affect by head and body cues. *Journal of Personality and Social Psychology, 2,* 726–735.

Ekman, P. (1972). Universals and cultural differences in facial expressions of emotion. In J. K. Cole (Ed.), *Nebraska Symposium on Motivation, 1971* (pp. 207–283). Lincoln: University of Nebraska Press.

Ekman, P. (1992). *Telling lies.* New York: Norton.

Ekman, P. (2003a). Darwin, deception, and facial expression. *Annals of the New York Academy of Science, 1000,* 205–221.

Ekman, P. (2003b). *Emotions revealed: Recognizing faces and feelings to improve communication and emotional life.* New York: Times Books.

Ekman, P., & Friesen, W. V. (1968). Nonverbal behavior in psychotherapy research. In J. M. Shlien (Ed.), *Research in psychotherapy* (Vol. 3, pp. 179–216). Washington, DC: American Psychological Association.

Ekman, P., & Friesen, W. V. (1971). Constants across cultures in the face and emotion. *Journal of Personality and Social Psychology, 17,* 124–129.

Ekman, P., & Friesen, W. V. (1978). *The Facial Action Coding System.* Palo Alto, CA: Consulting Psychologists Press.

Ekman, P., & Friesen, W. V. (1982). Felt, false, and miserable smiles. *Journal of Nonverbal Behavior, 6,* 238–252.

Ekman, P., Friesen, W. V., O'Sullivan, M., Chan, A., Diacoyanni-Tarlatzis, I., Heider, K., et al. (1987). Universals and cultural differences in the judgments of facial expressions of emotion. *Journal of Personality and Social Psychology, 53,* 712–717.

Ekman, P., Levenson, R. W., & Friesen, W. V. (1983). Autonomic nervous system activity distinguishes among emotions. *Science, 221,* 1208–1210.

Ekman, P., & O'Sullivan, M. (1991). Who can catch a liar? *American Psychologist, 46*(9), 913–920.

Ekman, P., O'Sullivan, M., & Frank, M. G. (1999). A few can catch a liar. *Psychological Science, 10,* 263–266.

Elder, G. H., & Conger, R. D. (2000). *Children of the land: Adversity and success in rural America.* Chicago: University of Chicago Press.

Eldridge, L. L., Knowlton, B. J., Furmanski, C. S., Bookheimer, S. Y., & Engel, S. A. (2000). Remembering episodes: A selective role for the hippocampus during retrieval. *Nature Neuroscience, 3,* 1149–1152.

Eldridge, M. A., Barnard, P. J., & Bekerian, D. A. (1994). Autobiographical memory and daily schemas at work. *Memory, 2,* 51–74.

Elfenbein, H. A., & Ambady, N. (2002). On the universality and cultural specificity of emotion recognition: A meta-analysis. *Psychological Bulletin, 128,* 203–235.

El-Hai, J. (2005). *The lobotomist: A maverick medical genius and his tragic quest to rid the world of mental illness.* New York: Wiley.

Ellenberger, H. F. (1954). The life and work of Hermann Rorschach (1884–1922). *Bulletin of the Menninger Clinic, 18,* 173–213.

Ellicot, A., Hammen, C., Gitlin, M., Brown, G., & Jaminson, K. (1990). Life events and course of bipolar disorder. *American Journal of Psychiatry, 147,* 1194–1198.

Elliott, R., Sahakian, B. J., Matthews, K., Bannerjea, A., Rimmer, J., & Robbins, T. W. (1997). Effects of methylphenidate on spatial working memory and planning in healthy young adults. *Psychopharmacology, 131,* 196–206.

Ellis, A. (2000). Rational emotive behavior therapy. In R. J. Corsini & D. Wedding (Eds.), *Current psychotherapies* (6th ed., pp. 168–204). Itasca, IL: F. E. Peacock, Publishers.

Ellis, B. J., & Garber, J. (2000). Psychosocial antecedents of variation in girls' pubertal timing: Maternal depression, stepfather presence, and marital and family stress. *Child Development, 71,* 485–501.

Ellis, E. M. (1983). A review of empirical rape research: Victim reactions and response to treatment. *Clinical Psychology Review, 3,* 473–490.

Ellis, L., & Ames, M. A. (1987). Neurohormonal functioning in sexual orientation: A theory of homosexuality-heterosexuality. *Psychological Bulletin, 101,* 233–258.

Ellman, S. J., Spielman, A. J., Luck, D., Steiner, S. S., & Halperin, R. (1991). REM deprivation: A review. In S. J. Ellman & J. S. Antrobus (Eds.), *The mind in sleep: Psychology and psychophysiology* (2nd ed., pp. 329–376). New York: Wiley.

Emerson, R. C., Bergen, J. R., & Adelson, E. H. (1992). Directionally selective complex cells and the computation of motion energy in cat visual cortex. *Vision Research, 32,* 203–218.

Emmelkamp, P. M. G., Krijn, M., Hulsbosch, A. M., de Vries, S., Schuemie, M. J., & van der Mast, C. A. (2002). Virtual reality treatment versus exposure in vivo: A comparative evaluation in acrophobia. *Behaviour Research and Therapy, 40*(5), 509–516.

Emmelkamp, P. M. G., & Wessels, H. (1975). Flooding in imagination vs. flooding in vivo: A comparison with agoraphobics. *Behaviour Research and Therapy, 13,* 7–15.

Empson, J. A. (1984). Sleep and its disorders. In R. Stevens (Ed.), *Aspects of consciousness.* New York: Academic Press.

Enns, J. T. (2004). *The thinking eye, the seeing brain.* New York: Norton.

Epley, N., Savitsky, K., & Kachelski, R. A. (1999). What every skeptic should know about subliminal persuasion. *Skeptical Inquirer, 23,* 40–45, 58.

Erber, R., Wegner, D. M., & Therriault, N. (1996). On being cool and collected: Mood regulation in anticipation of social interaction. *Journal of Personality and Social Psychology, 70,* 757–766.

Erffmeyer, E. S. (1984). Rule-violating behavior on the golf course. *Perceptual and Motor Skills, 59,* 591–596.

Erickson, E. (1959). *Identity and the life cycle: Selected papers.* New York: International Universities Press.

Ericsson, K. A., & Charness, N. (1999). Expert performance: Its structure and acquisition. In S. J. Ceci & W. M. Williams (Eds.), *The nature-nurture debate: The essential readings* (pp. 200–256). Oxford, England: Blackwell.

Eronen, M., Angermeyer, M. C., & Schulze, B. (1998). The psychiatric epidemiology of violent behavior. In *Social Psychiatry & Psychiatric Epidemiology* (Vol. 33). Leipzig, Germany: Springer.

Esser, J. K. (1998). Alive and well after 25 years: A review of groupthink research. *Organizational Behavior and Human Decision Processes, 73,* 116–141.

Etcoff, N. (1999). *Survival of the prettiest: The science of beauty.* New York: Doubleday.

Evans, J. St. B., Barston, J. L., & Pollard, P. (1983). On the conflict between logic and belief in syllogistic reasoning. *Memory & Cognition, 11,* 295–306.

Evans, P. D., Gilbert, S. L, Mekel-Bobrov, N., Vallender, E. J., Anderson, J. R., Vaez-Azizi, L. M., et al. (2005). Microcephalin, a gene regulating brain size, continues to evolve adaptively in humans. *Science, 309,* 1717–1720.

Everson, S. A., Lynch, J. W., Chesney, M. A., Kaplan, G. A., Goldberg, D. E., Shade, S. B., et al. (1997). Interaction of workplace demands and cardiovascular reactivity in progression of carotid atherosclerosis: Population based study. *British Medical Journal, 314,* 553–558.

Exner, J. E. (1993). *The Rorschach: A comprehensive system: Vol. 1. Basic foundations.* New York: Wiley.

Eysenck, H. J. (1957). The effects of psychotherapy: An evaluation. *Journal of Consulting Psychology, 16,* 319–324.

Eysenck, H. J. (1960). *Behavior therapy and the neuroses.* Oxford, England: Pergamon Press.

Eysenck, H. J. (1967). *The biological basis of personality.* Springfield, IL: Charles C. Thomas.

Eysenck, H. J. (1990). Biological dimensions of personality. In L. A. Pervin (Ed.), *Handbook of personality: Theory and research* (pp. 244–276). New York: Guilford Press.

Eysenck, S. B. G., & Eysenck, H. J. (1963). The validity of questionnaire and rating assessments of extraversion and neuroticism, and their factorial stability. *British Journal of Psychology, 54,* 51–62.

Eysenck, S. B. G., & Eysenck, H. J. (1985). *Personality and individual differences: A natural science approach.* New York: Plenum Press.

Falk, R., & McGregor, D. (1983). The surprisingness of coincidences. In P. Humphreys, O. Svenson, & A. Vari (Eds.), *Analysing and aiding decision processes* (pp. 489–502). New York: North Holland.

Fancher, R. E. (1979). *Pioneers of psychology.* New York: Norton.

Fantz, R. L. (1964). Visual experience in infants: Decreased attention to familiar patterns relative to novel ones. *Science, 164,* 668–670.

Farah, M. J., Illes, J. Cook-Deegan, R., Gardner, H., Kandel, E., King, P., et al. (2004). Neurocognitive enhancement: What can we do and what should we do? *Nature Reviews Neuroscience, 5,* 421–426.

Farah, M. J., & Rabinowitz, C. (2003). Genetic and environmental influences on the organization of semantic memory in the brain: Is "living things" an innate category? *Cognitive Neuropsychology, 20,* 401–408.

Farrar, M. J. (1990). Discourse and the acquisition of grammatical morphemes. *Journal of Child Language, 17,* 607–624.

Farries, M. A. (2004). The avian song system in comparative perspective. *Annals of the New York Academy of Sciences, 1016,* 61–76.

Fazel, S., & Danesh, J. (2002). Serious mental disorder in 23,000 prisoners: A review of 62 surveys. *Lancet, 359,* 545–550.

Fechner, G. T. (1966). *Elements of psychophysics.* (H. E. Alder, Trans.). New York: Holt, Reinhart and Wilson. (Original work published 1860)

Fehr, E., & Gaechter, S. (2002). Altruistic punishment in humans. *Nature, 415,* 137–140.

Fein, S., Hilton, J. L., & Miller, D. T. (1990). Suspicion of ulterior motivation and the correspondence bias. *Journal of Personality and Social Psychology, 58,* 753–764.

Fein, S., & Spencer, S. J. (1997). Prejudice as self-image maintenance: Affirming the self through derogating others. *Journal of Personality and Social Psychology, 73,* 31–44.

Feinberg, T. E. (2001). *Altered egos: How the brain creates the self.* New York: Oxford University Press.

Feingold, A. (1990). Gender differences in effects of physical attractiveness on romantic attraction: A comparison across five research paradigms. *Journal of Personality and Social Psychology, 59,* 981–993.

Feingold, A. (1992a). Gender differences in mate selection preferences: A test of the parental investment model. *Psychological Bulletin, 112,* 125–139.

Feingold, A. (1992b). Good-looking people are not what we think. *Psychological Bulletin, 111,* 304–341.

Feingold, A. (1994). Gender differences in personality: A meta-analysis. *Psychological Bulletin, 116,* 429–456.

Feldman, M. D. (2004). *Playing sick.* New York: Brunner-Routledge.

Ferster, C. B., & Skinner, B. F. (1957). *Schedules of reinforcement.* New York: Appleton-Century-Crofts.

Feske, U. (1998). Eye movement desensitization and reprocessing treatment for posttraumatic stress disorder. *Clinical Psychology: Science and Practice, 5,* 171–181.

Festinger, L. (1957). *A theory of cognitive dissonance.* Stanford, CA: Stanford University Press.

Festinger, L., & Carlsmith, J. M. (1959). Cognitive consequences of forced compliance. *Journal of Abnormal and Social Psychology, 58,* 203–210.

Festinger, L., Schachter, S., & Back, K. (1950). *Social pressures in informal groups: A study of human factors in housing.* Oxford, England: Harper & Row.

Fiedler, E. R., Oltmanns, T. F., & Turkheimer, E. (2004). Traits associated with personality disorders and adjustment to military life: Predictive validity of self and peer reports. *Military Medicine, 169,* 32–40.

Field, G. C. (1921). Faculty psychology and instinct psychology. *Mind, 30,* 257–270.

Fields, H. L., & Levine, J. D. (1984). Placebo analgesia: A role for endorphins? *Trends in Neurosciences, 7,* 271–273.

Fiering, C., & Taft, L. (1985). The gifted learning disabled: Not a paradox. *Pediatric Annals, 14,* 729–732.

Fink, M. (2001) Convulsive therapy: A review of the first 55 years. *Journal of Affective Disorders, 63,* 1–15.

Finkelstein, K. E. (1999, October 17). Yo-Yo Ma's lost Stradivarius is found after wild search. *New York Times,* p. 34.

Finn, R. (1991). Different minds. *Discover, 12,* 54–59.

Fiorentine, R. (1999). After drug treatment: Are 12-step programs effective in maintaining abstinence? *American Journal of Drug and Alcohol Abuse, 25,* 93–116.

Fisher, H. E. (1993). *Anatomy of love: The mysteries of mating, marriage, and why we stray.* New York: Fawcett.

Fisher, R. P., & Craik, F. I. M. (1977). The interaction between encoding and retrieval operations in cued recall. *Journal of Experimental Psychology: Human Learning and Perception, 3,* 153–171.

Fiske, S. T. (1998). Stereotyping, prejudice, and discrimination. In D. T. Gilbert, S. T. Fiske, & G. Lindzey (Eds.), *The handbook of social psychology* (4th ed., Vol. 2, pp. 357–411). New York: McGraw-Hill.

Fitzgerald, P. B., Brown, T. L., Marston, N. A. U., Daskalakis, Z. J., de Castella, A., Kulkarni, J., et al. (2003). Transcranial magnetic stimulation in the treatment of depression: A double-blind, placebo-controlled trial. *Archives of General Psychiatry, 60,* 1002–1008.

Fleming, R., Baum, A., Gisriel, M. M., & Gatchel, R. J. (1985). Mediating influences of social support on stress at Three Mile Island. In A. Monat & R. S. Lazarus (Eds.), *Stress and coping: An anthology* (2nd ed.) (pp. 95–106). New York: Columbia University Press.

Fletcher, P. C., Shallice, T., & Dolan, R. J. (1998). The functional roles of prefrontal cortex in episodic memory. I. Encoding. *Brain, 121,* 1239–1248.

Flor, H., Nikolajsen, L., & Jensen, T. S. (2006). Phantom limb pain: A case of maladaptive CNS plasticity? *Nature Reviews Neuroscience, 7,* 873–881.

Florian, V., Mikulciner, M., & Taubman, O. (1995). Does hardiness contribute to mental health during a stressful real-life situation? The roles of appraisal and coping. *Journal of Personality and Social Psychology, 68,* 687–695.

Flynn, J. R. (1984). The mean IQ of Americans: Massive gains 1932 to 1978. *Psychological Bulletin, 95,* 29–51.

Foa, E. B., Dancu, C. V., Hembree, E. A., Jaycox, L. H., Meadows, E. A., & Street, G. P. (1999). A comparison of exposure therapy, stress inoculation training, and their combination for reducing posttraumatic stress disorder in female assault victims. *Journal of Consulting & Clinical Psychology, 67,* 194–200.

Foa, E. B, & Meadows, E. A. (1997). Psychosocial treatments for posttraumatic stress disorder: A critical review. *Annual Review of Psychology, 48,* 449–480.

Foa, E. B., & Rothbaum, B. O. (1998). *Treating the trauma of rape: Cognitive-behavioral therapy for PTSD.* New York: Guilford Press.

Fodor, J. (2000). Why we are so good at catching cheaters. *Cognition, 75,* 2932.

Fogassi, L., Ferrari, P. F., Gesierich, B., Rozzi, S., Chersi, F., & Rizzolatti, G. (2005). Parietal lobe: From action organization to intention understanding. *Science, 308,* 662–667.

Fornazzari, L., Wilkinson, D. A., Kapur, B. M., & Carlen, P. L. (1983). Cerebellar, cortical and functional impairment in toluene abusers. *Acta Neurologica Scandinavica, 67,* 319–329.

Fouts, R. S., & Bodamer, M. (1987). Preliminary report to the National Geographic Society on "Chimpanzee intrapersonal signing." *Friends of Washoe, 7,* 4–12.

Fowler, D. (1985). Landmarks in computer-assisted psychological assessment. *Journal of Consulting and Clinical Psychology, 53,* 748–759.

Fox, P. T., Mintun, M. A., Raichle, M. E., Miezin, F. M., Allman, J. M., & Van Essen, D. C., et al. (1986). Mapping human visual cortex with positron emission tomography. *Nature, 323,* 806–809.

Frank, M. G., Ekman, P., & Friesen, W. V. (1993). Behavioral markers and recognizability of the smile of enjoyment. *Journal of Personality and Social Psychology, 64,* 83–93.

Frank, M. G., & Stennet, J. (2001). The forced-choice paradigm and the perception of facial expressions of emotion. *Journal of Personality and Social Psychology, 80,* 75–85.

Frankl, V. (2000). *Man's search for meaning.* New York: Beacon Press.

Fredrickson, B. L. (2000). Cultivating positive emotions to optimize health and well-being. *Prevention and Treatment, 3.*

Fredrickson, B. L. (2001). The role of positive emotions in positive psychology: The broaden-and-build theory of positive emotions. *American Psychologist, 56,* 218–226.

Freedman, J. (1978). *Happy people: What happiness is, who has it, and why.* New York: Harcourt Brace Jovanovich.

Freedman, J. L., & Fraser, S. C. (1966). Compliance without pressure: The foot-in-the-door technique. *Journal of Personality and Social Psychology, 4,* 195–202.

Freeman, S., Walker, M. R., Borden, R., & Latané, B. (1975). Diffusion of responsibility and restaurant tipping: Cheaper by the bunch. *Personality and Social Psychology Bulletin, 1,* 584–587.

Freud, A. (1936). *The ego and the mechanisms of defense.* New York: International Universities Press.

Freud, S. (1938). The psychopathology of everyday life. In A. A. Brill (Ed.), *The basic writings of Sigmund Freud.* New York: Basic Books. (Originally published 1901)

Freud, S. (1952). *A general introduction to psychoanalysis.* New York: Pocket Books. (Originally published 1920)

Freud, S. (1953). Three essays on the theory of sexuality. In J. Strachey (Ed.), *The standard edition of the complete psychological works of Sigmund Freud* (Vol. 7, pp. 135–243). London: Hogarth Press. (Originally published 1905)

Freud, S. (1965). *The interpretation of dreams* (J. Strachey, Trans.). New York: Avon. (Originally published 1900)

Freudenberger, H. J. (1974). Staff burnout. *Journal of Social Issues, 30,* 159–165.

Freyd, J. J. (1996). *Betrayal trauma: The logic of forgetting childhood abuse.* Cambridge, MA: Harvard University Press.

Frick, R. W. (1985). Communicating emotion: The role of prosodic features. *Psychological Bulletin, 97,* 412–429.

Fried, P. A., & Watkinson, B. (2000). Visuoperceptual functioning differs in 9- to 12-year-olds prenatally exposed to cigarettes and marijuana. *Neurotoxicology and Teratology, 22,* 11–20.

Friedberg, F. (2001). *Do-it-yourself eye movement technique for emotional healing.* Oakland, CA: New Harbinger Publications.

Friedman, M., & Rosenman, R. H. (1974). *Type A behavior and your heart.* New York: Knopf.

Friedman, W. J. (1993). Memory for the time of past events. *Psychological Bulletin, 113,* 44–66.

Friesen, W. V. (1972). Cultural differences in facial expressions in a social situation: An experimental test of the concept of display rules. Unpublished doctoral dissertation, University of California, San Francisco.

Frith, C. D., & Fletcher, P. (1995). Voices from nowhere. *Critical Quarterly, 37,* 71–83.

Frith, U. (2001). Mind blindness and the brain in autism. *Neuron, 32,* 969–979.

Frith, U. (2003). *Autism: Explaining the enigma.* Oxford, England: Blackwell.

Fryer, A. J., Mannuzza, S., Gallops, M. S., Martin, L. Y., Aaronson, C., Gorman, J. M., et al. (1990). Familial transmission of simple phobias and fears: A preliminary report. *Archives of General Psychiatry, 47,* 252–256.

Furmark, T., Tillfors, M., Marteinsdottir, I., Fischer, H., Pissiota, A., Långström, B., et al. (2002). Common changes in cerebral blood flow in patients with social phobia treated with citalopram or cognitive-behavioral therapy. *Archives of General Psychiatry, 59*(5), 425–433.

Fuster, J. M. (2003). *Cortex and mind.* New York: Oxford University Press.

Gable, S. L., & Haidt, J. (2005). What (and why) is positive psychology? *Review of General Psychology, 9,* 102–110.

Gais, S., & Born, J. (2004). Low acetylcholine during slow-wave sleep is critical for declarative memory consolidation. *Proceedings of the National Academy of Sciences (USA), 101,* 2140–2144.

Galanter, E. (1962). Contemporary psychophysics. In R. Brown, E. Galanter, E. H. Hess, & G. Mandler (Eds.), *New directions in psychology* (pp. 87–156). New York: Holt, Rinehart, & Winston.

Galati, D., Scherer, K. R., & Ricci-Bitt, P. E. (1997). Voluntary facial expression of emotion: Comparing congenitally blind with normally sighted encoders. *Journal of Personality and Social Psychology, 73,* 1363–1379.

Galea, S., Ahern, J., Resnick, H., Kilpatrick, D., Bucuvalas, M., Gold, J., et al. (2002). Psychological sequelae of the September 11 terrorist attacks in New York City. *New England Journal of Medicine, 346*(13), 982–987.

Galef, B. (1998). Edward Thorndike: Revolutionary psychologist, ambiguous biologist. *American Psychologist, 53,* 1128–1134.

Gallistel, C. R. (2000). The replacement of general-purpose learning models with adaptively specialized learning modules. In M. S. Gazzaniga (Ed.), *The new cognitive neurosciences* (pp. 1179–1191). Cambridge, MA: MIT Press.

Gallistel, C. R., & Gelman, R. (1992). Preverbal and verbal counting and computation. *Cognition,* Special issue: *Numerical Cognition, 44,* 43–74.

Gallup, G. G. (1977). Self-recognition in primates: A comparative approach to the bidirectional properties of consciousness. *American Psychologist, 32,* 329–338.

Gallup, G. G. (1997). On the rise and fall of self-conception in primates. *Annals of the New York Academy of Sciences, 818,* 73–84.

Galton, F. (1869). *Hereditary genius: An inquiry into its laws and consequences.* London: Macmillan/Fontana.

Gangestad, S. W., & Simpson, J. A. (2000). On the evolutionary psychology of human mating: Trade-offs and strategic pluralism. *Behavioral and Brain Sciences, 23,* 573–587.

Garb, H. N. (1998). *Studying the clinician: Judgment research and psychological assessment.* Washington, DC: American Psychological Association.

Garb, H. N. (1999). Call for a moratorium on the use of the Rorschach inkblot test in clinical and forensic settings. *Assessment, 6,* 313–315.

Garcia, J. (1981). Tilting at the windmills of academe. *American Psychologist, 36,* 149–158.

Garcia, J., & Koelling, R. A. (1966). Relation of cue to consequence in avoidance learning. *Psychonomic Science, 4,* 123–124.

Gardner, R. A., & Gardner, B. T. (1969). Teaching sign language to a chimpanzee. *Science, 165,* 664–672.

Garofalo, R., Cameon, W., Wissow, L. S., Woods, E. R., & Goodman, E. (1999). Sexual orientation and risk of suicide. *Archives of Pediatrics and Adolescent Medicine, 513,* 487.

Garry, M., Manning, C., Loftus, E. F., & Sherman, S. J. (1996). Imagination inflation: Imagining a childhood event inflates confidence that it occurred. *Psychonomic Bulletin and Review, 3,* 208–214.

Gauld, A. (1992). *The history of hypnotism.* Cambridge, England: Cambridge University Press.

Gazzaniga, M. S. (Ed.). (2000). *The new cognitive neurosciences.* Cambridge, MA: MIT Press.

Gazzaniga, M. S. (2006). Forty-five years of split brain research and still going strong. *Nature Reviews Neuroscience, 6,* 653–659.

Ge, X. J., Conger, R. D., & Elder, G. H. (1996). Coming of age too early: Pubertal influences on girls' vulnerability to psychological distress. *Child Development, 67,* 3386–3400.

Geen, R. G. (1984). Preferred stimulation levels in introverts and extraverts: Effects on arousal and performance. *Journal of Personality and Social Psychology, 46,* 1303–1312.

Geen, R. G. (1998). Aggression and antisocial behavior., *The handbook of social psychology,* (4th ed., Vol. 2, pp. 317–356). New York: McGraw-Hill.

Gegenfurtner, K. R., & Kiper, D. C. (2003). Color vision. *Annual Review of Neuroscience, 26,* 181–206.

Geller, D. A., Hoog, S. L., Heiligenstein, J. H., Ricardi, R. K., Tamura, R., Kluszynski, S., Jacobson, J. G., et al. (2001). Fluoxetine treatment for obsessive-compulsive disorder in children and adolescents: A placebo-controlled clinical trial. *Journal of the American Academy of Child and Adolescent Psychiatry, 40,* 773–779.

George, D. (1981). *Sweet man: The real Duke Ellington.* New York: Putnam.

George, M. S., Lisanby, S. H., Sackeim, H. A. (1999). Transcranial magnetic stimulation: Applications in neuropsychiatry. *Archives of General Psychiatry, 56,* 300–311.

Gerard, H. B., & White, G. L. (1983). Post-decisional reevaluation of choice alternatives. *Personality and Social Psychology Bulletin, 9,* 365–369.

Gershoff, E. T. (2002). Corporal punishment by parents and associated child behaviors and experiences: A meta-analytic and theoretical review. *Psychological Bulletin, 128,* 539–579.

Gerull, F. C., & Rapee, R. M. (2002). Mother knows best: The effects of maternal modelling on the acquisition of fear and avoidance behaviour in toddlers. *Behaviour Research and Therapy, 40,* 279–287.

Gibb, B. E., Alloy, L. B., & Tierney, S. (2001). History of childhood maltreatment, negative cognitive styles, and episodes of depression in adulthood. *Cognitive Therapy and Research, 25,* 425–446.

Gibbons, F. X. (1990). Self-attention and behavior: A review and theoretical update. In M. P. Zanna (Ed.), *Advances in experimental social psychology* (Vol. 23, pp. 249–303). San Diego, CA: Academic Press.

Gibbs, N. A. (1996). Nonclinical populations in research on obsessive-compulsive disorder: A critical review. *Clinical Psychology Review, 16,* 729–773.

Gick, M. L., & Holyoak, K. J. (1980). Analogical problem solving. *Cognitive Psychology, 12,* 306–355.

Giedd, J. N., Blumenthal, J., Jeffries, N. O., Castellanos, F. X., Liu, H., Zijdenbos, A., et al. (1999). Brain development during childhood and adolescence: A longitudinal MRI study. *Nature Neuroscience, 2,* 861–863.

Giesler, R. B., Josephs, R. A., & Swann, W. B., Jr. (1996). Self-verification in clinical depression: The desire for negative evaluation. *Journal of Abnormal Psychology, 105,* 358–368.

Gigerenzer, G. (1996). The psychology of good judgment: Frequency formats and simple algorithms. *Journal of Medical Decision Making, 16,* 273–280.

Gigerenzer, G. (2002). *Calculated risks: How to know when numbers deceive you.* New York: Simon & Schuster.

Gigerenzer, G., & Hoffrage, U. (1995). How to improve Bayesian reasoning without instruction: Frequency formats. *Psychological Review, 102,* 684–704.

Gigerenzer, G., & Hug, K. (1992). Domain-specific reasoning: Social contracts, cheating, and perspective change. *Cognition, 43,* 127–171.

Gigone, D., & Hastie, R. (1996). The impact of information on group judgment: A model and computer simulation. In E. H. Witte & J. H. Davis (Eds.), *Understanding group behavior: Consensual action by small groups* (Vol. 1, pp. 221–251). Mahwah, NJ: Erlbaum.

Gigone, D., & Hastie, R. (1997). Proper analysis of the accuracy of group judgments. *Psychological Bulletin, 121,* 149–167.

Gilbert, D. T. (1991). How mental systems believe. *American Psychologist, 46,* 107–119.

Gilbert, D. T. (1998). Ordinary personology. In D. T. Gilbert, S. T. Fiske, & G. Lindzey (Eds.), *The handbook of social psychology* (4th ed., Vol. 2, pp. 89–150). New York: McGraw-Hill.

Gilbert, D. T. (2006). *Stumbling on happiness.* New York: Knopf.

Gilbert, D. T., Brown, R. P., Pinel, E. C., & Wilson, T. D. (2000). The illusion of external agency. *Journal of Personality and Social Psychology, 79,* 690–700.

Gilbert, D. T., Driver-Linn, E., & Wilson, T. D. (2002). The trouble with Vronsky: Impact bias in the forecasting of future affective states. In L. F. Barrett & P. Salovey (Eds.), *The wisdom in feeling: Psychological processes in emotional intelligence* (pp. 114–143). New York: Guilford Press.

Gilbert, D. T., Gill, M. J., & Wilson, T. D. (2002). The future is now: Temporal correction in affective forecasting. *Organizational Behavior and Human Decision Processes, 88,* 430–444.

Gilbert, D. T., & Jones, E. E. (1986). Perceiver-induced constraint: Interpretations of self-generated reality. *Journal of Personality and Social Psychology, 50,* 269–280.

Gilbert, D. T., Krull, D. S., & Malone, P. S. (1990). Unbelieving the unbelievable: Some problems in the rejection of false information. *Journal of Personality and Social Psychology, 59,* 601–613.

Gilbert, D. T., & Malone, P. S. (1995). The correspondence bias. *Psychological Bulletin, 117,* 21–38.

Gilbert, D. T., Pelham, B. W., & Krull, D. S. (1988). On cognitive busyness: When persons perceive meet persons perceived. *Journal of Personality and Social Psychology, 54,* 733–740.

Gilbert, D. T., Pinel, E. C., Wilson, T. D., Blumberg, S. J., & Wheatley, T. P. (1998). Immune neglect: A source of durability bias in affective forecasting. *Journal of Personality and Social Psychology, 75,* 617–638.

Gilbert, D. T., Tafarodi, R. W., & Malone, P. S. (1993). You can't not believe everything you read. *Journal of Personality and Social Psychology, 65,* 221–233.

Gilbert, G. M. (1951). Stereotype persistence and change among college students. *Journal of Abnormal and Social Psychology, 46,* 245–254.

Gilbertson, M. W., Shenton, M. E., Ciszewski, A., Kasai, K., Lasko, N. B., Orr, S. P., et al. (2002). Smaller hippocampal volume predicts pathological vulnerability to psychological trauma. *Nature Neuroscience, 5,* 1242–1247.

Gillham, J. E. (Ed.). (2000). *The science of optimism and hope: Research essays in honor of Martin E. P. Seligman.* West Conshohoken, PA: Templeton Foundation Press.

Gilligan, C. (1982). *In a different voice: Psychological theory and women's development.* Cambridge, MA: Harvard University Press.

Gilovich, T. (1991). *How we know what isn't so: The fallibility of human reason in everyday life.* New York: Free Press.

Gilovich, T., Kruger, J., & Savitsky, K. (1999). Everyday egocentrism and everyday interpersonal problems. In R. M. Kowalski & M. R. Leary (Eds.), *The social psychology of emotional and behavioral problems: Interfaces of social and clinical psychology* (pp. 69–95). Washington, DC: American Psychological Association.

Ginzburg, K., Solomon, Z., & Bleich, A. (2002). Repressive coping style, acute stress disorder, and posttraumatic stress disorder after myocardial infarction. *Psychosomatic Medicine, 64,* 748–757.

Gladue, B. A. (1994). The biopsychology of sexual orientation. *Current Directions in Psychological Science, 3,* 150–154.

Glass, D. C., & Singer, J. E. (1972). *Urban stress.* New York: Academic Press.

Gleaves, D. H., Smith, S. M., Butler, L. D., & Spiegel, D. (2004). False and recovered memories in the laboratory and clinic: A review of experimental and clinical evidence. *Clinical Psychology: Science and Practice, 11,* 3–28.

Glenwick, D. S., Jason, L. A., & Elman, D. (1978). Physical attractiveness and social contact in the singles bar. *Journal of Social Psychology, 105,* 311–312.

Glick, P., Gottesman, D., & Jolton, J. (1989). The fault is not in the stars: Susceptibility of skeptics and believers in astrology to the Barnum effect. *Personality & Social Psychology Bulletin, 15,* 572–583.

Glisky, E. L., Schacter, D. L., & Tulving, E. (1986). Computer learning by memory-impaired patients: Acquisition and retention of complex knowledge. *Neuropsychologia, 24,* 313–328.

Glynn, S. M. (1990). Token economy approaches for psychiatric patients: Progress and pitfalls over 25 years. *Behavior Modification, 14,* 383–407.

Gneezy, U., & Rustichini, A. (2000). A fine is a price. *Journal of Legal Studies, 29,* 1–17.

Gobert, A., Rivet, J. M., Cistarelli, L., Melon, C., & Millan, M. J. (1999). Buspirone modulates basal and fluoxetine-stimulated dialysate levels of dopamine, noradrenaline, and serotonin in the frontal cortex of freely moving rats: Activation of serotonin 1A receptors and blockade of alpha2-adrenergic receptors underlie its actions. *Neuroscience, 93,* 1251–1262.

Goddard, H. H. (1913). *The Kallikak family: A study in the heredity of feeble-mindedness.* New York: Macmillan.

Godden, D. R., & Baddeley, A. D. (1975). Context-dependent memory in two natural environments: On land and underwater. *British Journal of Psychology, 66,* 325–331.

Goehler, L. E., Gaykema, R. P. A., Hansen, M. K., Anderson, K., Maier, S. F., & Watkins, L. R. (2000). Vagal immune-to-brain communication: A visceral chemosensory pathway. *Autonomic Neuroscience: Basic and Clinical, 85,* 49–59.

Goel, V., & Dolan, R. J. (2003). Explaining modulation of reasoning by belief. *Cognition, 87,* 11–22.

Goetzman, E. S., Hughes, T., & Klinger, E. (1994). *Current concerns of college students in a midwestern sample.* Unpublished report, University of Minnesota, Morris.

Goff, L. M., & Roediger, H. L., III. (1998). Imagination inflation for action events—Repeated imaginings lead to illusory recollections. *Memory & Cognition, 26,* 20–33.

Gold, R. B., & Nash, E. (2001). State-level policies on sexuality, STD education. *The Guttmacher Report on Public Policy, 4,* 4–7.

Goldman, M. S., Brown, S. A., & Christiansen, B. A. (1987). Expectancy theory: Thinking about drinking. In H. T. Blane & K. E. Leonard (Eds.), *Psychological theories of drinking and alcoholism* (pp. 181–266). New York: Guilford Press.

Gollaher, D. (1995). *Voice for the mad: The life of Dorothea Dix.* New York: Free Press.

Gomez, C., Argandota, E. D., Solier, R. G., Angulo, J. C., & Vazquez, M. (1995). Timing and competition in networks representing ambiguous figures. *Brain and Cognition, 29,* 103–114.

Goodale, M. A., & Milner, A. D. (1992). Separate visual pathways for perception and action. *Trends in Neurosciences, 15,* 20–25.

Goodale, M. A., Milner, A. D., Jakobson, L. S., & Carey, D. P. (1991). A neurological dissociation between perceiving objects and grasping them. *Nature, 349,* 154–156.

Goodale, M. A., & Milner, D. (2004). *Sight unseen.* Oxford, England: Oxford University Press.

Goodwin, F. K., & Ghaemi, S. N. (1998). Understanding manic-depressive illness. *Archives of General Psychiatry, 55,* 23–25.

Goodwin, F. K., & Jamison, K. R. (1990). *Manic depressive illness.* New York: Oxford University Press.

Gopnik, A., & Astington, J. W. (1988). Children's understanding of representational change and its relation to the understanding of false belief and the appearance reality distinction. *Child Development, 59,* 26–37.

Gopnik, A., Meltzoff, A., & Kuhl, P. (1999). *The scientist in the crib: What early learning tells us about the mind.* New York: HarperCollins.

Gopnik, M. (1990a). Feature-blind grammar and dysphasia. *Nature, 344,* 715.

Gopnik, M. (1990b). Feature blindness: A case study. *Language Acquisition: A Journal of Developmental Linguistics, 1,* 139–164.

Gordon, P. (2004). Numerical cognition without words: Evidence from Amazonia. *Science, 306,* 496–499.

Gosling, S. D. (1998). Personality dimensions in spotted hyenas (*Crocuta crocuta*). *Journal of Comparative Psychology, 112,* 107–118.

Gosling, S. D., & John, O. P. (1999). Personality dimensions in nonhuman animals: A cross-species review. *Current Directions in Psychological Science, 8,* 69–75.

Gottesman, I. I. (1991). *Schizophrenia genesis: The origins of madness.* New York: Freeman.

Gottesman, I. I., & Hanson, D. R. (2005). Human development: Biological and genetic processes. *Annual Review of Psychology, 56,* 263–286.

Gottfredson, L. S. (1997). Mainstream science on intelligence: An editorial with 52 signatories, history, and bibliography. *Intelligence, 24,* 13–23.

Gottfredson, L. S. (1998). The general intelligence factor. *Scientific American Presents, 9,* 24–29.

Gottfredson, L. S. (2003). Dissecting practical intelligence theory: Its claims and evidence. *Intelligence, 31*(4), 343–397.

Gottfredson, L. S., & Deary, I. J. (2004). Intelligence predicts health and longevity, but why? *Current Directions in Psychological Science, 13,* 1–4.

Gottman, J. M. (1994). *What predicts divorce? The relationship between marital processes and marital outcomes.* Hillsdale, NJ: Erlbaum.

Gould, M. S. (1990). Suicide clusters and media exposure. In S. J. Blumenthal & D. J. Kupfer (Eds.), *Suicide over the life cycle: Risk factors, assessment, and treatment of suicidal patients* (pp. 517–532). Washington, DC: American Psychiatric Press.

Gouldner, A. W. (1960). The norm of reciprocity. *American Sociological Review, 25,* 161–178.

Grace, A. A., & Moore, H. (1998). Regulation of information flow in the nucleus accumbens: A model for the pathophysiology of schizophrenia. In M. F. Lanzenweger & R. H. Dworkin (Eds.), *Origins and development of schizophrenia* (pp. 123–160). Washington, DC: American Psychological Association.

Graf, P., & Schacter, D. L. (1985). Implicit and explicit memory for new associations in normal subjects and amnesic patients. *Journal of Experimental Psychology: Learning, Memory, and Cognition, 11,* 501–518.

Graf, P., Squire, L. R., & Mandler, G. (1984). The information that amnesic patients do not forget. *Journal of Experimental Psychology: Learning, Memory, and Cognition, 10,* 164–178.

Grant, B. F., Hasin, D. S., Stinson, F. S., Dawson, D. A., Chou, S. P., & Ruan, W. J. (2004). Prevalence, correlates, and disability of personality disorders in the U.S.: Results from the National Epidemiologic Survey on Alcohol and Related Conditions. *Journal of Clinical Psychiatry, 65,* 948–958.

Gray, H. M., Gray, K., & Wegner, D. M. (2007). Dimensions of mind perception. *Science, 315,* 619.

Gray, J. A. (1970). The psychophysiological basis of introversion-extraversion. *Behavior Research and Therapy, 8,* 249–266.

Greeley, A. M. (1975). *The sociology of the paranormal: A reconnaissance.* Beverly Hills, CA: Sage.

Green, D. A., & Swets, J. A. (1966). *Signal detection theory and psychophysics.* New York: Wiley.

Green, L. W., Tryon, W. W., Marks, B., & Huryn, J. (1986). Periodontal disease as a function of life events. *Journal of Human Stress, 12,* 32–36.

Green, S. K., Buchanan, D. R., & Heuer, S. K. (1984). Winners, losers, and choosers: A field investigation of dating initiation. *Personality & Social Psychology Bulletin, 10,* 502–511.

Greenberg, J., Pyszczynski, T., Solomon, S., Rosenblatt, A., Veeder, M., Kirkland, S., et al. (1990). Evidence for terror management theory II: The effects of mortality salience on reactions to those who threaten or bolster the cultural worldview. *Journal of Personality and Social Psychology, 58,* 308–318.

Greenberg, P. E., Sisitsky, T., Kessler, R. C., Finkelstein, S. N., Berndt, E. R., Davidson, J. R. T., et al. (1999). The economic burden of anxiety disorders in the 1990s. *Journal of Clinical Psychiatry, 60,* 427–435.

Greene, J. D., Sommerville, R. B., Nystrom, L. E., Darley, J. M., & Cohen, J. D. (2001). An fMRI investigation of emotional engagement in moral judgment. *Science, 293,* 2105–2108.

Greenfield, P. M., Keller, H., Fuligni, A., & Maynard, A. (2003). Cultural pathways through universal development. *Annual Review of Psychology, 54,* 461–490.

Greenwald, A. G. (1992). New Look 3: Unconscious cognition reclaimed. *American Psychologist, 47,* 766–779.

Greenwald, A. G., Banaji, M. R., Rudman, L. A., Farnham, S. D., Nosek, B. A., & Mellott, D. S. (2002). A unified theory of implicit attitudes, stereotypes, self-esteem, and self-concept. *Psychological Review, 109,* 3–25.

Greenwald, A. G., McGhee, D. E., & Schwartz, J. L. K. (1998). Measuring individual differences in implicit cognition: The implicit association test. *Journal of Personality & Social Psychology, 74,* 1464–1480.

Greenwald, A. G., & Nosek, B. A. (2001). Health of the Implicit Association Test at age 3. *Zeitschrift für Experimentelle Psychologie, 48,* 85–93.

Gropp, E., Shanabrough, M., Borok, E., Xu, A. W., Janoschek, R., Buch, T., et al. (2005). Agouti-related peptide-expressing neurons are mandatory for feeding. *Nature Neuroscience, 8,* 1289–1291.

Gross, J. J. (1998). Antecedent- and response-focused emotion regulation: Divergent consequences for experience, expression, and physiology. *Journal of Personality and Social Psychology, 74,* 224–237.

Gross, J. J., & Munoz, R. F. (1995). Emotion regulation and mental health. *Clinical Psychology: Science and Practice, 2,* 151–164.

Groves, B. (2004, August 2). Unwelcome awareness. *The San Diego Union-Tribune,* p. 24.

Grudnick, J. L., & Kranzler, J. H. (2001). Meta-analysis of the relationship between intelligence and inspection time. *Intelligence, 29,* 523–535.

Guillery, R. W., & Sherman, S. M. (2002). Thalamic relay functions and their role in corticocortical communication: Generalizations from the visual system. *Neuron, 33,* 163–175.

Gur, R. E., Cowell, P., Turetsky, B. I., Gallacher, F., Cannon, T., Bilker, W., et al. (1998). A follow-up magnetic resonance imaging study of schizophrenia: Relationship of neuranatomical changes to clinical and neurobehavioral measures. *Archives of General Psychiatry, 55,* 145–152.

Gurman, A. S., & Messer, S. B. (Eds.). (2003). *Essential psychotherapies,* (2nd ed). New York: Guilford Press.

Gurwitz, J. H., McLaughlin, T. J., Willison, D. J., Guadagnoli, E., Hauptman, P. J., Gao, X., et al. (1997). Delayed hospital presentation in patients who have had acute myocardial infarction. *Annals of Internal Medicine, 126,* 593–599.

Gusnard, D. A., & Raichle, M. E. (2001). Searching for a baseline: Functional imaging and the resting human brain. *Nature Reviews: Neuroscience, 2,* 685–694.

Gustafsson, J.-E. (1984). A unifying model for the structure of intellectual abilities. *Intelligence, 8,* 179–203.

Guthrie, R. V. (2000). Kenneth Bancroft Clark (1914–). In A. E. Kazdin (Ed.), *Encyclopedia of Psychology* (Vol. 2, p. 91). Washington, DC: American Psychological Association.

Hackett, T. P., & Cassem, N. H. (1975). Psychological management of the myocardial infarction patient. *Journal of Human Stress, 1,* 25–38.

Hacking, I. (1975). *The emergence of probability.* Cambridge, MA: Cambridge University Press.

Haidt, J. (2001). The emotional dog and its rational tail: A social intuitionist approach to moral judgment. *Psychological Review, 108,* 814–834.

Haidt, J. (2006). *The happiness hypothesis: Finding modern truth in ancient wisdom.* New York: Basic Books.

Haidt, J., & Keltner, D. (1999). Culture and facial expression: Open-ended methods find more expressions and a gradient of recognition. *Cognition and Emotion, 13,* 225–266.

Hajek, P., & Belcher, M. (1991). Dream of absent-minded transgression: An empirical study of a cognitive withdrawal symptom. *Journal of Abnormal Psychology, 100,* 487–491.

Hakuta, K. (1986). *Cognitive development of bilingual children.* Center for Language Education and Research, University of California, Los Angeles.

Hakuta, K. (1999). The debate on bilingual education. *Journal of Developmental and Behavioral Pediatrics, 20,* 36–37.

Hallett, M. (2000). Transcranial magnetic stimulation and the human brain. *Nature, 406,* 147–150.

Hallett, M., Cloninger, C. R., Fahn, S., & Jankovic, J. J. (Eds.). (2005). *The psychogenic movement disorders: Neurology and neuropsychiatry.* Philadelphia: Lippincott, Williams & Wilkins.

Halliday, R., Naylor, H., Brandeis, D., Callaway, E., Yano, L., & Herzig, K. (1994). The effect of D-amphetamine, clonidine, and yohimbine on human information processing. *Psychophysiology, 31,* 331–337.

Halpern, B. (2002). Taste. In H. Pashler & S. Yantis (Eds.), *Stevens' handbook of experimental psychology: Vol 1. Sensation and perception* (3rd ed., pp. 653–690). New York: Wiley.

Halpern, D. F. (1997). Sex differences in intelligence: Implications for education. *American Psychologist, 52,* 1091–1102.

Hamermesh, D. S., & Biddle, J. E. (1994). Beauty and the labor market. *American Economic Review, 84,* 1174–1195.

Hamilton, D. L., & Gifford, R. K. (1976). Illusory correlation in interpersonal perception: A cognitive basis of stereotypic judgements. *Journal of Experimental Social Psychology, 12,* 392–407.

Hamilton, W. D. (1964). The genetical evolution of social behaviour. *Journal of Theoretical Biology, 7,* 1–16.

Hammen, C. L. (1995). Stress and the course of unipolar disorders. In C. M. Mazure (Ed.), *Does stress cause psychiatric illness?* Washington, DC: American Psychiatric Press.

Hammersla, J. F., & Frease-McMahan, L. (1990). University students' priorities: Life goals vs. relationships. *Sex Roles, 23,* 1–14.

Haney, C., Banks, C., & Zimbardo, P. G. (1973). Interpersonal dynamics in a simulated prison. *International Journal of Criminology and Penology, 1,* 69–97.

Hansen, E. S., Hasselbalch, S., Law, I., & Bolwig, T. G. (2002). The caudate nucleus in obsessive-compulsive disorder. Reduced metabolism following treatment with paroxetine: A PET study. *International Journal of Neuropsychopharmacology, 5,* 1–10.

Hanson, C. J., Stevens, L. C., & Coast, J. R. (2001). Exercise duration and mood state: How much is enough to feel better? *Health Psychology, 20,* 267–275.

Happe, F. G. E. (1995). The role of age and verbal ability in the theory-of-mind performance of subjects with autism. *Child Development, 66,* 843–855.

Hare, R. D. (1998). *Without conscience: The disturbing world of the psychopaths among us.* New York: Guilford Press.

Harkness, S., Edwards, C. P., & Super, C. M. (1981). Social roles and moral reasoning: A case study in a rural African community. *Developmental Psychology, 17,* 595–603.

Harlow, H. F. (1958). The nature of love. *American Psychologist, 13,* 573–685.

Harlow, H. F., & Harlow, M. L. (1965). The affectional systems. In A. M. Schrier, H. F. Harlow, & F. Stollnitz (Eds.), *Behavior of nonhuman primates* (Vol. 2). New York: Academic Press.

Harlow, J. M. (1848). Passage of an iron rod through the head. *Boston Medical and Surgical Journal, 39,* 389–393.

Harris, B. (1979). Whatever happened to Little Albert? *American Psychologist, 34,* 151–160.

Harris, M. J., & Rosenthal, R. (1985). Mediation of interpersonal expectancy effects: 31 meta-analyses. *Psychological Bulletin, 97,* 363–386.

Harris, P. L., de Rosnay, M., & Pons, F. (2005). Language and children's understanding of mental states. *Current Directions in Psychological Science, 14,* 69–73.

Harris, P. L., Johnson, C. N., Hutton, D., Andrews, G., & Cooke, T. (1989). Young children's theory of mind and emotion. *Cognition and Emotion, 3,* 379–400.

Hart, B. L. (1988). Biological basis of the behavior of sick animals. *Neuroscience and Biobehavioral Reviews, 12,* 123–137.

Hartley, M., & Commire, A. (1990). *Breaking the silence.* New York: Putnam Group.

Hartshorne, H., & May, M. (1928). *Studies in deceit.* New York: Macmillan.

Hasher, L., & Zacks, R. T. (1984). Automatic processing of fundamental information: The case of frequency of occurrence. *American Psychologist, 39,* 1372–1388.

Hasselmo, M. E. (2006). The role of acetylcholine in learning and memory. *Current Opinion in Neurobiology, 16,* 710–715.

Hassmen, P., Koivula, N., & Uutela, A. (2000). Physical exercise and psychological well-being: A population study in Finland. *Preventive Medicine, 30,* 17–25.

Hasson, U., Hendler, T., Bashat, D. B., & Malach, R. (2001). Vase or face? A neural correlate of shape-selective grouping processes in the human brain. *Journal of Cognitive Neuroscience, 13,* 744–753.

Hatch, R. (2005). *Richard Hatch homepage.* Retrieved August 24, 2005, from http://www.richardhatch.com

Hatfield, E. (1988). Passionate and companionate love. In R. J. Sternberg & M. L. Barnes (Eds.), *The psychology of love* (pp. 191–217). New Haven, CT: Yale University Press.

Hatfield, E., & Rapson, R. L. (1992). Similarity and attraction in close relationships. *Communication Monographs, 59,* 209–212.

Hathaway, S. R., & McKinley, J. C. (1951). *Minnesota Multiphasic Personality Inventory manual.* New York: Psychological Corporation.

Hausser, M. (2000). The Hodgkin-Huxley theory of the action potential. *Nature Neuroscience, 3,* 1165.

Haxby, J. V., Gobbini, M. I., Furey, M. L. Ishai, A., Schouten, J. L., & Pietrini, P. (2001). Distributed and overlapping representations of faces and objects in ventral temporal cortex. *Science, 293,* 2425–2430.

Hay, P., Sachdev, P., Cumming, S., Smith, J. S., Lee, T., Kitchener, P., et al. (1993). Treatment of obsessive-compulsive disorder by psychosurgery. *Acta Psychiatrica Scandinavica, 87,* 197–207.

Hayes, D. P., & Grether, J. (1983). The school year and vacations: When do students learn? *Cornell Journal of Social Relations, 17,* 56–71.

Hayes, K., & Hayes, C. (1951). The intellectual development of a home-raised chimpanzee. *Proceedings of the American Philosophical Society, 95,* 105–109.

Hayes, S. C., Strosahl, K., & Wilson, K. G. (1999). *Acceptance and commitment therapy: An experiential approach to behavior change.* New York: Guilford Press.

Health, United States. (2001). Hyattsville, MD: National Center for Health Statistics.

Heatherton, T. F., Herman, C. P., & Polivy, J. (1991). Effects of physical threat and ego threat on eating behavior. *Journal of Personality and Social Psychology, 60,* 138–143.

Heatherton, T. F., & Weinberger, J. L. (Eds.). (1994). *Can personality change?* Washington, DC: American Psychological Association.

Heaton, R., Paulsen, J. S., McAdams, L. A., Kuck, J., Zisook, S., Bra, D., et al. (1994). Neuropsychological deficits in schizophrenia: Relationship to age, chronicity, and dementia. *Archives of General Psychiatry, 51,* 469–476.

Hebb, D. O. (1949). *The organization of behavior.* New York: Wiley.

Hebl, M. R., & Heatherton, T. F. (1997). The stigma of obesity in women: The difference is Black and White. *Personality and Social Psychology Bulletin, 24,* 417–426.

Hebl, M. R., & Mannix, L. M. (2003). The weight of obesity in evaluating others: A mere proximity effect. *Personality and Social Psychology Bulletin, 29,* 28–38.

Hecht, S., & Mandelbaum, M. (1938). Rod-cone dark adaptation and vitamin A. *Science, 88,* 219–221.

Heerey, E. A., Keltner, D., & Capps, L. M. (2003). Making sense of self-conscious emotion: Linking theory of mind and emotion in children with autism. *Emotion, 3,* 394–400.

Heiby, E. M. (2002). Prescription privileges for psychologists: Can differing views be reconciled? *Journal of Clinical Psychology, 58,* 589–597.

Heider, F. (1958). *The psychology of interpersonal relations.* New York: Wiley.

Heider, F., & Simmel, M. (1944). An experimental study of apparent behavior. *American Journal of Psychology, 57,* 243–259.

Hemingway, H., & Marmot, M. (1999). Evidence-based cardiology: Psychosocial factors in the aetiology and prognosis of coronary heart disease: Systematic review of prospective cohort studies. *British Medical Journal, 318,* 1460–1467.

Henderlong, J., & Lepper, M. R. (2002). The effects of praise on children's intrinsic motivation: A review and synthesis. *Psychological Bulletin, 128,* 774–795.

Henig, R. M. (2004, April 4). The quest to forget. *New York Times Magazine,* 32–37.

Henriques, J. B., & Davidson, R. J. (1990). Regional brain electrical asymmetries discriminate between previously depressed and healthy control subjects. *Journal of Abnormal Psychology, 99,* 22–31.

Henry, W. P., Strupp, H. H., Schacht, T. E., & Gaston, L. (1994). Psychodynamic approaches. In A. E. Bergin & S. L. Garfield (Eds.), *Handbook of psychotherapy and behavior change* (pp. 467–508). New York: Wiley.

Herbert, J. D., Lilienfeld, S. O., Lohr, J. M., Montgomery, R. W., O'Donohue, W. T., Rosen, G. M., et al. (2000). Science and pseudoscience in the development of eye movement desensitization and reprocessing: Implications for clinical psychology. *Clinical Psychology Review, 20,* 945–971.

Herek, G. M. (2002). Gender gaps in public opinion about lesbians and gay men. *Public Opinion Quarterly, 66,* 40–67.

Herman, J. L. (1992). *Trauma and recovery.* New York: Basic Books.

Herman-Giddens, M. E., Slora, E. J., Wasserman, R. C., Bourdony, C. J., Bhapkar, M. V., Koch, G. G., et al. (1997). Secondary sexual characteristics and menses in young girls seen in office practice: A study from the pediatric research in office settings network. *Pediatrics and Perinatal Epidemiology, 99,* 505–512.

Herrmann, D. J., Raybeck, D., & Gruneberg, M. (2002). *Improving memory and study skills: Advances in theory and practice.* Seattle: Hogrefe and Huber.

Herrnstein, R. J. (1972). Nature as nurture: Behaviorism and the instinct doctrine. *Behaviorism, 1,* 23–52.

Herrnstein, R. J. (1977). The evolution of behaviorism. *American Psychologist, 32,* 593–603.

Herrnstein, R. J., & Murray, C. (1994). *The bell curve.* New York: Free Press.

Hershenson, M. (Ed.). (1989). *The moon illusion.* Hillsdale, NJ: Erlbaum.

Hertwig, R., & Gigerenzer, G. (1999). The "conjunction fallacy" revisited: How intelligent inferences look like reasoning errors. *Journal of Behavioral Decision Making, 12,* 275–305.

Hess, T. M. (2005). Memory and aging in context. *Psychological Bulletin, 131,* 383–406.

Hettema, J. M., Neale, M. C., & Kendler, K. S. (2001). A review and meta-analysis of the genetic epidemiology of anxiety disorders. *American Journal of Psychiatry, 158,* 1568–1578.

Hewstone, M., Rubin, M., & Willis, H. (2002). Intergroup bias. *Annual Review of Psychology, 53,* 575–604.

Heyns, B. (1978). *Summer learning and the effects of schooling.* New York: Academic Press.

Higgins, E. T. (1987). Self-discrepancy theory: A theory relating self and affect. *Psychological Review, 94,* 319–340.

Hilgard, E. R. (1965). *Hypnotic susceptibility.* New York: Harcourt, Brace and World.

Hilgard, E. R. (1986). *Divided consciousness: Multiple controls in human thought and action.* New York: Wiley-Interscience.

Hill, G. W. (1982). Group versus individual performance: Are N + 1 heads better than one? *Psychological Bulletin, 91,* 517–539.

Hilts, P. (1995). *Memory's ghost: The strange tale of Mr. M and the nature of memory.* New York: Simon & Schuster.

Hintzman, D. L., Asher, S. J., & Stern, L. D. (1978). Incidental retrieval and memory for coincidences. In M. M. Gruneberg, P. E. Morris, & R. N. Sykes (Eds.), *Practical aspects of memory* (pp. 61–68). New York: Academic Press.

Hirschberger, G., Florian, V., & Mikulincer, M. (2002). The anxiety buffering function of close relationships: Mortality salience effects on the readiness to compromise mate selection standards. *European Journal of Social Psychology, 32,* 609–625.

Hirschfeld, D. R., Rosenbaum, J. F., Biederman, J., Bolduc, E. A., Faraone, S. V., Snidman, N., et al. (1992). Stable behavioral inhibition and its association with anxiety disorder. *Journal of the American Academy of Child and Adolescent Psychiatry, 31,* 103–111.

Hirschfeld, R. M. A. (1996). Panic disorder: Diagnosis, epidemiology, and clinical course. *Journal of Clinical Psychiatry, 57,* 3–8.

Hirstein, W., & Ramachandran, V. S. (1997). Capgras syndrome: A novel probe for understanding the neural representation of the identity and familiarity of persons. *Proceedings: Biological Sciences, 264,* 437–444.

Hishakawa, Y. (1976). Sleep paralysis. In C. Guilleminault, W. C. Dement, & P. Passouant (Eds.), *Narcolepsy: Advances in sleep research* (Vol. 3, pp. 97–124). New York: Spectrum.

Hitchcock, S. T. (2005). *Mad Mary Lamb: Lunacy and murder in literary London.* New York: Norton.

Hobson, J. A. (1988). *The dreaming brain.* New York: Basic Books.

Hobson, J. A., & McCarley, R. W. (1977). The brain as a dream-state generator: An activation-synthesis hypothesis of the dream process. *American Journal of Psychiatry, 134,* 1335–1368.

Hodgkin, A. L., & Huxley, A. F. (1939). Action potential recorded from inside a nerve fibre. *Nature, 144,* 710–712.

Hodson, G., & Sorrentino, R. M. (2001). Just who favors in in-group? Personality differences in reactions to uncertainty in the minimal group paradigm. *Group Dynamics, 5,* 92–101.

Hoek, H. W., & van Hoeken, D. (2003). Review of the prevalence and incidence of eating disorders. *International Journal of Eating Disorders, 34,* 383–396.

Hoffman, R. E., Hawkins, K. A., Gueorguieva, R., Boutros, N. N., Rachid, F., Carroll, K., et al. (2003). Transcranial magnetic stimulation of left temporoparietal cortex and medication-resistant auditory hallucinations. *Archives of General Psychiatry, 60,* 49–56.

Hoffrage, U., & Gigerenzer, G. (1996). The impact of information representation on Bayesian reasoning. In G. Cottrell (Ed.), *Proceedings of the Eighteenth Annual Conference of the Cognitive Science Society* (pp. 126–130). Mahwah, NJ: Erlbaum.

Hoffrage, U., & Gigerenzer, G. (1998). Using natural frequencies to improve diagnostic inferences. *Academic Medicine, 73*, 538–540.

Hogan, D. P., Sun, R., & Cornwell, G. T. (2000). Sexual and fertility behaviors of American females age 15–19 years: 1985, 1990 and 1995. *American Journal of Public Health, 90*, 1421–1425.

Hollander, E. P. (1964). *Leaders, groups, and influence.* Oxford, England: Oxford University Press.

Holloway, G. (2001). *The complete dream book: What your dreams tell about you and your life.* Naperville, IL: Sourcebooks.

Holloway, M. (1999). Flynn's effect. *Scientific American, 280*(1), 37–38.

Holmbeck, G. N., & O'Donnell, K. (1991). Discrepancies between perceptions of decision making and behavioral autonomy. In R. L. Paikoff (Ed.), *New directions for child development: No. 51. Shared views in the family during adolescence.* San Francisco: Jossey-Bass.

Holmes, T. H., & Rahe, R. H. (1967). The social readjustment rating scale. *Journal of Psychosomatic Research, 11*, 213–318.

Homans, G. C. (1961). *Social behavior.* New York: Harcourt, Brace and World.

Hooley, J. M., & Hiller, J. B. (1998). Expressed emotion and the pathogenesis of relapse in schizophrenia. In M. F. Lenzenweger & R. H. Dworkin (Eds.), *Origins and development of schizophrenia* (pp. 447–468). Washington, DC: American Psychological Association.

Horn, J. L., & Cattell, R. B. (1966). Refinement and test of the theory of fluid and crystallized general intelligences. *Journal of Educational Psychology, 5*, 253–270.

Horney, K. (1937). *The neurotic personality of our time.* New York: Norton.

Horta, B. L., Victoria, C. G., Menezes, A. M., Halpern, R., & Barros, F. C. (1997). Low birthweight, preterm births and intrauterine growth retardation in relation to maternal smoking. *Pediatrics and Perinatal Epidemiology, 11*, 140–151.

Horwitz, S., & Ruane, M. (2003). *Sniper: Inside the hunt for the killers who terrorized the nation.* New York: Ballantine Books.

House, J., Landis, K., & Umberson, D. (1988). Social relationships and health. *Science, 241*, 540–545.

Hovland, C. I., Lumsdaine, A. A., & Sheffield, F. D. (1949). *Experiments on mass communications.* Princeton, NJ: Princeton University Press.

Hovland, C. I., & Weiss, W. (1951). The influence of source credibility on communication effectiveness. *Public Opinion Quarterly, 15*, 635–650.

Howard, I. P. (2002). Depth perception. In S. Yantis & H. Pashler (Eds.), *Stevens' handbook of experimental psychology: Vol 1. Sensation and perception* (3rd ed., pp. 77–120). New York: Wiley.

Howard, J. H., Jr., & Howard, D. V. (1997). Age differences in implicit learning of higher order dependencies in serial patterns. *Psychology and Aging, 12*, 634–656.

Howes, M., Siegel, M., & Brown, F. (1993). Early childhood memories—accuracy and affect. *Cognition, 47*, 95–119.

Hróbjartsson, A., & Gøtzsche, P. C. (2001). Is the placebo powerless? An analysis of clinical trials comparing placebo with no treatment. *New England Journal of Medicine, 344*, 1594–1602.

Hsu, L. K. G. (1990). *Eating disorders.* New York: Guilford Press.

Hubbard, E. M., & Ramachandran, V. S. (2003). Refining the experimental lever. *Journal of Consciousness Studies, 10*, 77–84.

Hubbard, E. M., & Ramachandran, V. S. (2005). Neurocognitive mechanisms of synesthesia. *Neuron, 48*, 509–520.

Hubel, D. H. (1988). *Eye, brain, and vision.* New York: Freeman.

Hubel, D. H., & Wiesel, T. N. (1962). Receptive fields, binocular interaction and functional architecture in the cat's visual cortex. *Journal of Physiology, 160*, 106–154.

Hubel, D. H., & Wiesel, T. N. (1998). Early exploration of the visual cortex. *Neuron, 20*, 401–412.

Huesmann, L. R., Moise-Titus, J., Podolski, C.-L., & Eron, L. D. (2003). Longitudinal relations between children's exposure to TV violence and their aggressive and violent behavior in young adulthood: 1977–1992. *Developmental Psychology, 39*, 201–221.

Hughs, S., Power, T., & Francis, D. (1992). Defining patterns of drinking in adolescence: A cluster analytic approach. *Journal of Studies on Alcohol, 53*, 40–47.

Humphreys, N., & Dennett, D. C. (1989). Speaking for our selves. *Raritan: A Quarterly Review, 9*, 68–98.

Hunsley, J., & Di Giulio, G. (2002). Dodo bird, phoenix, or urban legend? The question of psychotherapy equivalence. *Scientific Review of Mental Health Practice, 1*, 13–24.

Hunt, M. (1959). *The natural history of love.* New York: Knopf.

Hunt, R. R., & McDaniel, M. A. (1993). The enigma of organization and distinctiveness. *Journal of Memory and Language, 32*, 421–445.

Hunter, J. E., & Hunter, R. F. (1984). Validity and utility of alternative predictors of job performance. *Psychological Bulletin, 96*, 72–98.

Hurvich, L. M., & Jameson, D. (1957). An opponent process theory of color vision. *Psychological Review, 64*, 384–404.

Huttenlocher, P. R. (1979). Synaptic density in human frontal cortex—developmental changes and effects of aging. *Brain Research, 163*, 195–205.

Huxley, A. (1954). *The doors of perception.* New York: Harper & Row.

Hyman, I. E., Jr., & Billings, F. J. (1998). Individual differences and the creation of false childhood memories. *Memory, 6*, 1–20.

Hyman, I. E., Jr., & Pentland, J. (1996). The role of mental imagery in the creation of false childhood memories. *Journal of Memory and Language, 35*, 101–117.

Hypericum Depression Trial Study Group. (2002). Effect of *Hypericum perforatum* (St. John's wort) in major depressive disorder: A randomized controlled trial. *Journal of the American Medical Association, 287*, 1807–1814.

Iacoboni, M., & Dapretto, M. (2006). The mirror neuron system and the consequences of its dysfunction. *Nature Reviews Neuroscience, 7*, 942–951.

Iacoboni, M., Molnar-Szakacs, I., Gallese, V., Buccino, G., Mazziotta, J. C., & Rizzolatti, G. (2005). Grasping the intentions of others with one's own mirror neuron system. *PLoS Biology, 3*, 529–535.

Iacono, W. G., & Beiser, M. (1992). Where are women in first-episode studies of schizophrenia? *Schizophrenia Bulletin, 18*, 471–480.

Ichheiser, G. (1949). Misunderstandings in human relations: A study in false social perceptions. *American Journal of Sociology, 55* (Part 2):1–70.

Inciardi, J. A. (2001). *The war on drugs III.* New York: Allyn and Bacon.

Ingram, R. E., Miranda, J., & Segal, Z. V. (1998). *Cognitive vulnerability to depression.* New York: Guilford Press.

Ingvar, M., Ambros-Ingerson, J., Davis, M., Granger, R., Kessler, M., Rogers, G. A., et al. (1997). Enhancement by an ampakine of memory encoding in humans. *Experimental Neurology, 146*, 553–559.

Inoff-Germain, G., Arnold, G. S., Nottelmann, E. D., & Susman, E. J. (1988). Relations between hormone levels and observational measures of aggressive behavior of young adolescents in family interactions. *Developmental Psychology, 24*, 129–139.

Inui, A. (2001). Ghrelin: An orexigenic and somatotrophic signal from the stomach. *Nature Reviews Neuroscience, 2*, 551–560.

Irvine, J. T. (1978). Wolof magical thinking: Culture and conservation revisited. *Journal of Cross Cultural Psychology, 9*, 300–310.

Isabelle, R. A. (1993). Origins of attachment: Maternal interactive behavior across the first year. *Child Development, 64,* 605–621.

Isacsson, G., & Rich, C. L. (1997). Depression and antidepressants, and suicide: Pharmacoepidemiological evidence for suicide prevention. In R. W. Maris, M. M. Silverman, & S. S. Canetton (Eds.), *Review of suicidology* (pp. 168–201). New York: Guilford Press.

Isen, A. M., & Patrick, R. (1983). The effect of positive feelings on risk-taking: When the chips are down. *Organizational Behavior and Human Performance, 31,* 194–202.

Ittelson, W. H. (1952). *The Ames demonstrations in perception.* Princeton, NJ: Princeton University Press.

Izard, C. E. (1971). *The face of emotion.* New York: Appleton-Century-Crofts.

Jablensky, A. (1997). The 100-year epidemiology of schizophrenia. *Schizophrenia Research, 28,* 111–125.

Jaccard, J., Dittus, P. J., & Gordon, V. V. (1998). Parent-adolescent congruency in reports of adolescent sexual behavior and in communications about sexual behavior. *Child Development, 69,* 247–261.

Jacobs, B. L. (1994). Serotonin, motor activity, and depression-related disorders. *American Scientist, 82,* 456–463.

Jacobson, E. (1932). The electrophysiology of mental activities. *American Journal of Psychology, 44,* 677–694.

Jacobson, T., & Hoffman, V. (1997). Children's attachment representations: Longitudinal relations to school behavior and academic competency in middle childhood and adolescence. *Developmental Psychology, 33,* 703–710.

Jaffee, S., & Hyde, J. S. (2000). Gender differences in moral orientation: A meta-analysis. *Psychological Bulletin, 126,* 703–726.

Jahoda, G. (1993). *Crossroads between culture and mind.* Cambridge, MA: Harvard University Press.

James, T. W., Culham, J., Humphrey, G. K., Milner, A. D., & Goodale, M. A. (2003). Ventral occipital lesions impair object recognition but not object-directed grasping: An fMRI study. *Brain, 126,* 2463–2475.

James, W. (1884). What is an emotion? *Mind, 9,* 188–205.

James, W. (1890). *The principles of psychology.* Cambridge, MA: Harvard University Press.

James, W. (1902). *The varieties of religious experience: A study in human nature.* New York: Longman.

James, W. (1911). *Memories and studies.* New York: Longman.

Jamison, K. R. (1999). *Night falls fast: Understanding suicide.* New York: Random House.

Janicak, P. G., Dowd, S. M., Martis, B., Alam, D., Beedle, D., Krasuski, J., et al. (2002). Repetitive transcranial magnetic stimulation versus electroconvulsive therapy for major depression: Preliminary results of a randomized trial. *Biological Psychiatry, 51,* 659–667.

Janis, I. L. (1982). *Groupthink: Scientific studies of policy decisions and fiascoes* (2nd ed.). Boston: Houghton Mifflin.

Jarvella, R. J. (1970). Effects of syntax on running memory span for connected discourse. *Psychonomic Science, 19,* 235–236.

Jarvella, R. J. (1971). Syntactic processing of connected speech. *Journal of Verbal Learning & Verbal Behavior, 10,* 409–416.

Jaynes, J. (1976). *The origin of consciousness in the breakdown of the bicameral mind.* London: Allen Lane.

Jencks, C. (1979). *Who gets ahead? The determinants of economic success in America.* New York: Wiley.

Jenike, M. A., Baer, L., & Minichiello, W. E. (1986). *Obsessive-compulsive disorders: Theory and management.* Littleton, MA: PSG Publishing.

Jenkins, H. M., Barrera, F. J., Ireland, C., & Woodside, B. (1978). Signal-centered action patterns of dogs in appetitive classical conditioning. *Learning and Motivation, 9,* 272–296.

Jobes, D. A., Berman, A. L., O'Carroll, P. W., Eastgard, S., & Knickmeyer, S. (1996). The Kurt Cobain suicide crisis: Perspectives from research, public health, and the news media. *Suicide and Life-Threatening Behavior, 26,* 269–271.

John, O. P., & Srivastava, S. (1999). The Big Five trait taxonomy: History, measurement, and theoretical perspectives. In L. A. Pervin & O. P. John (Eds.), *Handbook of personality: Theory and research* (2nd ed., pp. 102–138). New York: Guilford Press.

Johnson, D. H. (1980). The relationship between spike rate and synchrony in responses of auditory-nerve fibers to single tones. *Journal of the Acoustical Society of America, 68,* 1115–1122.

Johnson, D. R., & Wu, J. (2002). An empirical test of crisis, social selection, and role explanations of the relationship between marital disruption and psychological distress: A pooled time-series analysis of four-wave panel data. *Journal of Marriage and the Family, 64,* 211–224.

Johnson, J. D., Noel, N. E., & Sutter-Hernandez, J. (2000). Alcohol and male sexual aggression: A cognitive disruption analysis. *Journal of Applied Social Psychology, 30,* 1186–1200.

Johnson, J. S., & Newport, E. L. (1989). Critical period effects in second language learning: The influence of maturational state on the acquisition of English as a second language. *Cognitive Psychology, 21,* 60–99.

Johnson, K. (2002). Neural basis of haptic perception. In H. Pashler & S. Yantis (Eds.), *Stevens' handbook of experimental psychology: Vol. 1. Sensation and perception* (3rd ed., pp. 537–583). New York: Wiley.

Johnson, M. H., Dziurawiec, S., Ellis, H. D., & Morton, J. (1991). Newborns' preferential tracking of face-like stimuli and its subsequent decline. *Cognition, 40,* 1–19.

Johnson, M. K., Hashtroudi, S., & Lindsay, D. S. (1993). Source monitoring. *Psychological Bulletin, 114,* 3–28.

Johnson, N. J., Backlund, E., Sorlie, P. D., & Loveless, C. A. (2000). Marital status and mortality: The National Longitudinal Mortality Study. *Annual Review of Epidemiology, 10,* 224–238.

Johnson, R. (2005, February 12). A genius explains. *The Guardian.*

Johnson, S. (2004). *Mind wide open: Your brain and the neuroscience of everyday life.* New York: Scribner.

Johnson, S. L., & Miller, I. (1997). Negative life events and time to recover from episodes of bipolar disorder. *Journal of Abnormal Psychology, 106,* 449–457.

Johnston, L., Bachman, J., & O'Malley, P. (1997). *Monitoring the future.* Ann Arbor, MI: Institute for Social Research.

Johnstone, E. C., Crow, T. J., Frith, C., Husband, J., & Kreel, L. (1976). Cerebral ventricular size and cognitive impairment in chronic schizophrenia. *Lancet, 2,* 924–926.

Joiner, T. E., Jr. (2002). Depression in its interpersonal context. In I. H. Gotlib & C. Hammen (Eds.), *Handbook of depression* (pp. 295–313). New York: Guilford Press.

Joiner, T. E., Jr. (2006). *Why people die by suicide.* Cambridge, MA: Harvard University Press.

Joiner, T. E., Jr., Katz, J., & Lew, A. S. (1997). Self-verification and depression among youth psychiatric inpatients. *Journal of Abnormal Psychology, 106,* 608–618.

Joiner, T. E., Jr., & Metalsky, G. I. (1995). A prospective test of an integrative interpersonal theory of depression: A naturalistic study of college roommates. *Journal of Personality and Social Psychology, 69,* 778–788.

Joiner, T. E., Jr., Metalsky, G. I., Katz, J., & Beach, S. R. H. (1999). Be (re)assured: Excessive reassurance-seeking has (at least) some explanatory power regarding depression. *Psychological Inquiry, 10,* 305–308.

Jones, B. C., Little, A. C., Penton-Voak, I. S., Tiddeman, B. P., Burt, D. M., & Perrett, D. I. (2001). Facial symmetry and judgements of apparent health: Support for a "good genes" explanation of the attractiveness-symmetry relationship. *Evolution and Human Behavior, 22,* 417–429.

Jones, E. E., & Davis, K. E. (1965). From acts to dispositions: The attribution process in person perception. In L. Berkowitz (Ed.), *Advances in experimental social psychology* (Vol. 2, pp. 219–266). New York: Academic Press.

Jones, E. E., & Harris, V. A. (1967). The attribution of attitudes. *Journal of Experimental Social Psychology, 3,* 1–24.

Jones, E. E., & Nisbett, R. E. (1972). The actor and the observer: Divergent perceptions of the causes of behavior. In E. E. Jones, D. E. Kanouse, H. H. Kelley, R. E. Nisbett, S. Valins, & B. Weiner (Eds.), *Attribution: Perceiving the causes of behavior* (pp. 79–94). Morristown, NJ: General Learning Press.

Jones, J. T., Pelham, B. W., Carvallo, M., & Mirenberg, M. C. (2004). How do I love thee? Let me count the Js: Implicit egotism and interpersonal attraction. *Journal of Personality and Social Psychology, 87,* 665–683.

Jones, K. (1972). *A history of mental health services.* London: Routledge and Kegan Paul.

Jones, L. M., & Foshay, N. N. (1984). Diffusion of responsibility in a nonemergency situation: Response to a greeting from a stranger. *Journal of Social Psychology, 123,* 155–158.

Jost, J. T., Glaser, J., Kruglanski, A. W., & Sullaway, F. J. (2003). Political conservatism as motivated social cognition. *Psychological Bulletin, 129,* 339–375.

Jouvet, M., & Mounier, D. (1961). Identification of the neural structures responsible for rapid cortical activity during normal sleep. *Journal de Physiologie, 53,* 379–380.

Joyce, J. (1994). *Ulysses: The 1922 Text.* Introduction and notes by Jeri Johnson. New York: Oxford University Press.

Judd, L. L. (1997). The clinical course of unipolar major depressive disorders. *Archives of General Psychiatry, 54,* 989–991.

Jurewicz, I., Owen, R. J., & O'Donovan, M. C. (2001). Searching for susceptibility genes in schizophrenia. *European Neuropsychopharmacology, 11,* 395–398.

Kaas, J. H. (1991). Plasticity of sensory and motor maps in adult mammals. *Annual Review of Neuroscience, 14,* 137–167.

Kagan, J. (1997). Temperament and the reactions to unfamiliarity. *Child Development, 68,* 139–143.

Kahneman, D., Krueger, A. B., Schkade, D. A., Schwarz, N., & Stone, A. A. (2004). A survey method for characterizing daily life experience: The day reconstruction method. *Science, 306,* 1776–1780.

Kahneman, D., & Tversky, A. (1973). On the psychology of prediction. *Psychological Review, 80,* 237–251.

Kahneman, D., & Tversky, A. (1979). Prospect theory: An analysis of decision under risk. *Econometrica, 47,* 263–291.

Kalman, M., & Meyerowitz, R. (2003, September 8). What's new in pharmacology. *New Yorker,* back cover.

Kamil, A. C., & Jones, J. E. (1997). The seed-storing corvid Clark's nutcracker learns geometric relationships among landmarks. *Nature, 390,* 276–279.

Kaminski, J., Call, J., & Fischer, J. (2004). Word learning in a domestic dog: Evidence for "fast mapping." *Science, 304,* 1682–1683.

Kamiya, J. (1969). Operant control of the EEG alpha rhythm and some of its reported effects on consciousness. In C. S. Tart (Ed.), *Altered states of consciousness* (pp. 519–529). Garden City, NY: Anchor Books.

Kandel, E. R. (2000). Nerve cells and behavior. In E. R. Kandel, G. H. Schwartz, & T. M. Jessell (Eds.), *Principles of neural science* (pp. 19–35). New York. McGraw-Hill.

Kanner, A. D., Coyne, J. C., Schaefer, C., & Lazarus, R. S. (1981). Comparison of two modes of stress management: Daily hassles and uplifts versus major life events. *Journal of Behavioral Medicine, 4,* 1–39.

Kant, I. (1965). *Critique of pure reason* (N. K. Smith, Trans.). New York: St. Martin's Press. (Originally published 1781)

Kanwisher, N. (2000). Domain specificity in face perception. *Nature Neuroscience, 3,* 759–763.

Kanwisher, N., McDermott, J., & Chun, M. M. (1997). The fusiform face area: A module in human extrastriate cortex specialized for face perception. *Journal of Neuroscience, 17,* 4302–4311.

Kanwisher, N., & Yovel, G. (2006). The fusiform face area: A cortical region specialized for the perception of faces. *Philosophical Transactions of the Royal Society (B), 361,* 2109–2128.

Kapur, S., Craik, F. I. M., Tulving, E., Wilson, A. A., Houle, S., & Brown, G. M. (1994). Neuroanatomical correlates of encoding in episodic memory: Levels of processing effects. *Proceedings of the National Academy of Sciences (USA), 91,* 2008–2011.

Karlins, M., Coffman, T. L., & Walters, G. (1969). On the fading of social stereotypes: Studies in three generations of college students. *Journal of Personality and Social Psychology, 13,* 1–16.

Karney, B. R., & Bradbury, T. N. (1995). The longitudinal course of marital quality and stability: A review of theory, methods, and research. *Psychological Bulletin, 118,* 3–34.

Karno, M., & Golding, J. M. (1991). Obsessive-compulsive disorder. In L. N. Robins & D. A. Regier (Eds.), *Psychiatric disorders in America: The epidemiologic catchment area study.* New York: Free Press.

Kaslow, N. J., & Celano, M. P. (1995). The family therapies. In A. S. Gurman, & A. S. Messer (Eds.), *Essential psychotherapies* (6th ed., pp. 343–402). New York: Guilford Press.

Kasser, T., & Sharma, Y. S. (1999). Reproductive freedom, educational equality, and females' preference for resource-acquisition characteristics in mates. *Psychological Science, 10,* 374–377.

Katon, W. (1994). Primary care–psychiatry panic disorder management. In B. E. Wolfe & J. D. Maser (Eds.), *Treatment of panic disorder: A consensus development conference* (pp. 41–56). Washington, DC: American Psychiatric Press.

Katz, D., & Braly, K. (1933). Racial stereotypes of one hundred college students. *Journal of Abnormal and Social Psychology, 28,* 280–290.

Katz, R., & McGuffin, P. (1993). The genetics of affective disorders. In J. P. Chapman & D. C. Fowles (Eds.), *Progress in experimental personality and psychopathology research* (Vol. 16). New York: Springer.

Kauffmann, C. D., Cheema, M. A., & Miller, B. E. (2004). Slow right prefrontal transcranial magnetic stimulation as a treatment for medication-resistant depression: A double-blind, placebo-controlled study. *Depression and Anxiety, 19,* 59–62.

Kawakami, K., Dovidio, J. F., Moll, J., Hermsen, S., & Russin, A. (2000). Just say no (to stereotyping): Effects of training in the negation of stereotypic associations on stereotype activation. *Journal of Personality and Social Psychology, 78,* 871–888.

Keefe, F. J., Abernathy, A. P., & Campbell, L. C. (2005). Psychological approaches to understanding and treating disease-related pain. *Annual Review of Psychology, 56,* 601–630.

Keefe, F. J., Lumley, M., Anderson, T., Lynch, T., & Carson, K. L. (2001). Pain and emotion: New research directions. *Journal of Clinical Psychology, 57,* 587–607.

Keisler, D. J. (1999). *Beyond the disease model of mental disorders.* New York: Praeger.

Keller, M. B., Klein, D. N., Hirschfeld, R. M., Kocsis, J. H., McCullough, J. P., Miller, I., et al. (1995). Results of the *DSM-IV* mood disorders field trial. *American Journal of Psychiatry, 152,* 843–849.

Kelley, H. H. (1967). Attribution theory in social psychology. In D. Levine (Ed.), *Nebraska Symposium on Motivation.* (Vol. 15, pp. 192–238). Lincoln: University of Nebraska Press.

Kelley, H. H. (1983). Love and commitment. In H. H. Kelley, E. Berscheid, A. Christensen, & J. H. Harvey (Eds.), *Close relationships* (pp. 265–314). New York: Freeman.

Kelley, W. M., Macrae, C. N., Wyland, C. L., Caglar, S., Inati, S., & Heatherton, T. F. (2002). Finding the self? An event-related fMRI study. *Journal of Cognitive Neuroscience, 14,* 785–794.

Kellman, P. J., & Spelke, E. S. (1983). Perception of partly occluded objects in infancy. *Cognitive Psychology, 15,* 483–524.

Kelly, C., & McCreadie, R. (2000). Cigarette smoking and schizophrenia. *Advances in Psychiatric Treatment, 6,* 327–331.

Kelly, G. (1955). *The psychology of personal constructs.* New York: Norton.

Keltner, D. (1995). Signs of appeasement: Evidence for the distinct displays of embarrassment, amusement, and shame. *Journal of Personality and Social Psychology, 68,* 441–454.

Keltner, D., & Buswell, B. N. (1996). Evidence for the distinctness of embarrassment, shame, and guilt: A study of recalled antecedents and facial expressions of emotion. *Cognition and Emotion, 10,* 155–171.

Keltner, D., & Haidt, J. (1999). Social functions of emotions at four levels of analysis. *Cognition and Emotion, 13,* 505–521.

Keltner, D., & Harker, L. A. (1998). The forms and functions of the nonverbal signal of shame. In P. Gilbert & B. Andrews (Eds.), *Shame: Interpersonal behavior, psychopathology, and culture* (pp. 78–98). New York: Oxford University Press.

Keltner, D., & Shiota, M. N. (2003). New displays and new emotions: A commentary on Rozin and Cohen (2003). *Emotion, 3,* 86–91.

Kendler, K. S., Myers, J., & Prescott, C. A. (2002). The etiology of phobias: An evaluation of the stress-diathesis model. *Archives of General Psychiatry, 59,* 242–248.

Kendler, K. S., Neale, M., Kessler, R. C., & Heath, A. (1992). Generalized anxiety disorder in women: A population-based twin study. *Archives of General Psychiatry, 49,* 267–272.

Kendler, K. S., Walters, E. E., Neale, M. C., Kessler, R. C., Heath, A. C., & Eaves, L. J. (1995). The structure of the genetic and environmental risk factors for six major psychiatric disorders in women: Phobia, generalized anxiety disorder, panic disorder, bulimia, major depression, and alcoholism. *Archives of General Psychiatry, 52,* 374–383.

Kennedy, Q., Mather, M., & Carstensen, L. L. (2004). The role of motivation in the age-related positivity effect in autobiographical memory. *Psychological Science, 15,* 208–214.

Kenrick, D. T., Sadalla, E. K., Groth, G., & Trost, M. R. (1990). Evolution, traits, and the stages of human courtship: Qualifying the parental investment model. *Journal of Personality, 58,* 97–116.

Kensinger, E. A., & Schacter, D. L. (2005). Emotional content and reality monitoring ability: fMRI evidence for the influence of encoding processes. *Neuropsychologia, 43,* 1429–1443.

Kephart, W. M. (1967). Some correlates of romantic love. *Journal of Marriage and the Family, 29,* 470–474.

Kernis, M. H. (2003). Toward a conceptualization of optimal self-esteem. *Psychological Inquiry, 14,* 1–26.

Kessler, R. C. (1997). The effects of stressful life events on depression. *Annual Review of Psychology, 48,* 191–214.

Kessler, R. C., McGonagle, K. A., Zhao, S., Nelson, C. B., Hughes, M., Eshleman, S., et al. (1994). Lifetime and 12-month prevalence of *DSM-III-R* psychiatric disorders in the United States: Results from the National Comorbidity Study. *Archives of General Psychiatry, 51,* 8–19.

Kessler, R. C., Nelson, C. B., McGonagle, K. A., Liu, J., Swartz, M., & Blazer, D. (1996). Comorbidity of *DSM-III-R* major depressive disorder in the general population: Results from the U.S. national comorbidity survey. *British Journal of Psychiatry, 168,* 17–30.

Kessler, R. C., Sonnega, A., Bromet, E., Hughes, M., & Nelson, C. B. (1995). Posttraumatic stress disorder in the National Comorbidity Survey. *Archives of General Psychiatry, 52,* 1048–1060.

Kessler, R. C., Soukup, J., Davis, R. B., Foster, D. F., Wilkey, S. A., Van Rompay, M. I., et al. (2001). The use of complementary and alternative therapies to treat anxiety and depression in the United States. *American Journal of Psychiatry, 158,* 289–294.

Kety, S. S. (1990). Genetic factors in suicide: Family, twin, and adoption studies. In S. J. Blumenthal & D. J. Kupfer (Eds.), *Suicide over the life cycle: Risk factors, assessment, and treatment of suicidal patients* (pp. 127–133). Washington, DC: American Psychiatric Press.

Keuler, D. J., & Safer, M. A. (1998). Memory bias in the assessment and recall of pre-exam anxiety: How anxious was I? *Applied Cognitive Psychology, 12,* S127–S137.

Khalid, R. (1991). Personality and academic achievement: A thematic apperception perspective. *British Journal of Projective Psychology, 36,* 25–34.

Kiecolt-Glaser, J. K., Garner, W., Speicher, C., Penn, G., & Glaser, R. (1984). Psychosocial modifiers of immunocompetence in medical students. *Psychosomatic Medicine, 46,* 7–14.

Kiehl, K. A., Smith, A. M., Hare, R. D., Mendrek, A., Forster, B. B., Brink, J., et al. (2001). Limbic abnormalities in affective processing by criminal psychopaths as revealed by functional magnetic resonance imaging. *Biological Psychiatry, 50,* 677–684.

Kihlstrom, J. F. (1985). Hypnosis. *Annual Review of Psychology, 36,* 385–418.

Kihlstrom, J. F. (1987). The cognitive unconscious. *Science, 237,* 1445–1452.

Kihlstrom, J. F. (2005). Dissociative disorders. *Annual Review of Clinical Psychology, 1,* 227–253.

Kihlstrom, J. F., & Klein, S. B. (1994). The self as a knowledge structure. In R. S. Wyer & T. K. Srull (Eds.), *Handbook of social cognition* (2nd ed., Vol. 1, pp. 153–208). Hillsdale, NJ: Erlbaum.

Kim, K., & Smith, P. K. (1998). Childhood stress, behavioural symptoms and mother-daughter pubertal development. *Journal of Adolescence, 21,* 231–240.

King, C. A. (1997). Suicidal behavior in adolescence. In R. W. Maris, M. M. Silverman, & S. S. Canetton (Eds.), *Review of suicidology, 1997* (pp. 61–95). New York: Guilford Press.

King, F. (1990). *Lump it or leave it.* New York: St. Martin's Press.

Kinney, D. A. (1993). From nerds to normals—The recovery of identity among adolescents from middle school to high school. *Sociology of Education, 66,* 21–40.

Kirchner, W. H., & Towne, W. F. (1994). The sensory basis of the honeybee's dance language. *Scientific American, 270*(6), 74–80.

Kirsch, I., & Sapirstein, G. (1998). Listening to Prozac but hearing placebo: A meta-analysis of antidepressant medication. *Prevention and Treatment, 1,* Article 0002. Retrieved May 18, 2007, from www.journals.apa.org/pt/prevention/volume1/pre0010002a.html

Klein, S. B. (2004). The cognitive neuroscience of knowing one's self. In M. Gazzaniga (Ed.), *The cognitive neurosciences* (3rd ed.). Cambridge, MA: MIT Press.

Kleinman, A. M. (1986). *Social origins of distress and disease: Depression, neurasthenia and pain in modern China.* New Haven: Yale University Press.

Kleinman, A. M. (1988). *Rethinking psychiatry: From cultural category to personal experience.* New York: Free Press.

Kleinschmidt, A., & Cohen, L. (2006). The neural bases of prosopagnosia and pure alexia: Recent insights from functional neuroimaging. *Current Opinion in Neurology, 19,* 386–391.

Klinger, E. (1975). Consequences of commitment to and disengagement from incentives. *Psychological Review, 82,* 1–25.

Klinger, E. (1977). *Meaning and void.* Minneapolis: University of Minnesota Press.

Klopfer, B., & Kelley, D. (1942). *The Rorschach technique.* Yonkers, NY: World Book.

Kluft, R. P. (1984). Treatment of multiple personality. *Psychiatric Clinics of North America, 7,* 9–29.

Kluft, R. P. (1991). Multiple personality disorder. In A. Tasman & S. M. Goldfinger (Eds.), *American Psychiatric Press Review of Psychiatry* (Vol. 10, pp. 161–188). Washington, DC: American Psychiatric Press.

Klüver, H. (1951). Functional differences between the occipital and temporal lobes with special reference to the interrelations of behavior and extracerebral mechanisms. In L. A. Jeffress (Ed.), *Cerebral mechanisms in behavior* (pp. 147–199). New York: Wiley.

Klüver, H., & Bucy, P. C. (1937). "Psychic blindness" and other symptoms following bilateral temporary lobectomy in rhesus monkeys. *American Journal of Physiology, 119,* 352–353.

Klüver, H., & Bucy, P. C. (1939). Preliminary analysis of functions of the temporal lobes in monkeys. *Archives of Neurology and Psychiatry, 42,* 979–1000.

Knowlton, B. J., Ramus, S. J., & Squire, L. R. (1992). Intact artificial grammar learning in amnesia: Dissociation of classification learning and explicit memory for specific instances. *Psychological Science, 3,* 173–179.

Knutson, B., Adams, C. M., Fong, G. W., & Hommer, D. (2001). Anticipation of increasing monetary reward selectively recruits nucleus accumbens. *Journal of Neurosciences, 21,* 1–5.

Knutson, B., Wolkowitz, O. M., Cole, S. W., Chan, T., Moore, E. A., Johnson, R. C., et al. (1998). Selective alteration of personality and social behavior by serotonergic intervention. *American Journal of Psychiatry, 155,* 373–379.

Kobasa, S. (1979). Stressful life events, personality, and health: An inquiry into hardiness. *Journal of Personality and Social Psychology, 37,* 1–11.

Koch, C. (2004). *The quest for consciousness: A neurobiological approach.* Englewood, CO: Roberts & Co.

Koffka, K. (1935). *Principles of Gestalt psychology.* New York: Harcourt, Brace and World.

Kohlberg, L. (1963). Development of children's orientation towards a moral order (Part I). Sequencing in the development of moral thought. *Vita Humana, 6,* 11–36.

Kohlberg, L. (1986). A current statement on some theoretical issues. In S. Modgil & C. Modgil (Eds.), *Lawrence Kohlberg.* Philadelphia: Falmer.

Kolb, B., & Whishaw, I. Q. (2003). *Fundamentals of human neuropsychology* (5th ed.). New York: Worth.

Kolotkin, R. L., Meter, K., & Williams, G. R. (2001). Quality of life and obesity. *Obesity Reviews,* 219–229.

Komiya, N., Good, G. E., & Sherrod, N. B. (2000). Emotional openness as a predictor of college students' attitudes toward seeking psychological help. *Journal of Counseling Psychology, 47,* 138–143.

Koole, S. L., Dijksterhuis, A., & van Knippenberg, A. (2001). What's in a name: Implicit self-esteem and the automatic self. *Journal of Personality and Social Psychology, 80,* 669–685.

Koss, M. P. (1990). The women's mental health research agenda: Violence against women. *American Psychologist, 45,* 374–380.

Kosslyn, S. M., Alpert, N. M., Thompson, W. L., Chabris, C. F., Rauch, S. L., & Anderson, A. K. (1993). Visual mental imagery activates topographically organized visual cortex: PET investigations. *Journal of Cognitive Neuroscience, 5,* 263–287.

Kosslyn, S. M., Pascual-Leone, A., Felician, O., Camposano, S., Keenan, J. P., Thompson, W. L., et al. (1999). The role of area 17 in visual imagery: Convergent evidence from PET and rTMS. *Science, 284,* 167–170.

Kraepelin, E. (1899). *Psychiatrie.* Leipzig, Germany: Barth.

Kramer, P. D. (1997). *Listening to Prozac* (Rev. ed.). New York: Penguin.

Kramer, R. M. (1998). Revisiting the Bay of Pigs and Vietnam decisions 25 years later: How well has the groupthink hypothesis stood the test of time? *Organizational Behavior and Human Decision Processes, 73,* 236–271.

Krantz, D. S., & McCeney, M. K. (2002). Effects of psychological and social factors on organic disease: A critical assessment of research on coronary heart disease. *Annual Review of Psychology, 53,* 341–369.

Krebs, J. R., & Davies, N. B. (1991). *Behavioural ecology: An evolutionary approach* (3rd ed.). Sutherland, MA: Sinauer Associates.

Kreider, R. M., & Fields, J. M. (2002). *Number, timing, and duration of marriages and divorces: 1996.* Washington, DC: U.S. Census Bureau, Current Population Reports.

Kressmann, S., Muller, W. E., & Blume, H. H. (2002). Pharmaceutical quality of different Ginkgo biloba brands. *Journal of Pharmacy and Pharmacology, 54,* 661–669.

Krings, T., Topper, R., Foltys, H., Erberich, S., Sparing, R., Willmes, K., et al. (2000). Cortical activation patterns during complex motor tasks in piano players and control subjects. A functional magnetic resonance imaging study. *Neuroscience Letters, 278,* 189–193.

Kroeze, W. K., & Roth, B. L. (1998). The molecular biology of serotonin receptors: Therapeutic implications for the interface of mood and psychosis. *Biological Psychiatry, 44,* 1128–1142.

Kronig, M. H., Apter, J., Asnis, G., Bystritsky, A., Curtis, G., Ferguson, J., et al. (1999). Placebo-controlled multicenter study of sertraline treatment for obsessive-compulsive disorder. *Journal of Clinical Psychopharmacology, 19,* 172–176.

Kruk, M. R., Halasz, J., Meelis, W., & Haller, J. (2004). Fast positive feedback between the adrenocortical stress response and a brain mechanism involved in aggressive behavior. *Behavioral Neuroscience, 118,* 1062–1070.

Kubovy, M. (1981). Concurrent-Pitch segregation and the theory of indispensable attributes. In M. Kubovy & J. R. Pomerantz (Eds.), *Perceptual organization* (pp. 55–96). Hillsdale, NJ: Erlbaum.

Kuffler, S. W. (1953). Discharge patterns and function organization of mammalian retina. *Journal of Neurophysiology, 16,* 37–68.

Kunda, Z., & Oleson, K. C. (1997). When exceptions prove the rule: How extremity of deviance determines the impact of deviant examples on stereotypes. *Journal of Personality and Social Psychology, 72,* 965–979.

Kunugi, H., Urushibara, T., Murray, R. M., Nanko, S., & Hirose, T. (2003). Prenatal underdevelopment and schizophrenia: A case report of monozygotic twins. *Psychiatry and Clinical Neurosciences, 57,* 271–274.

Kunz, P. R., & Woolcott, M. (1976). Season's greetings: From my status to yours. *Social Science Research, 5,* 269–278.

Kutchins, H., & Kirk, S. A. (1997). *Making us crazy: DSM: The psychiatric bible and the creation of mental disorders.* New York: Free Press.

LaBar, K. S., & Phelps, E. A. (1998). Arousal-mediated memory consolidation: Role of the medial temporal lobe in humans. *Psychological Science, 9,* 490–493.

LaBerge, S., & Rheingold, H. (1990). *Exploring the world of lucid dreaming.* New York: Ballantine.

Lachman, R., Lachman, J. L., & Butterfield, E. C. (1979). *Cognitive psychology and information processing: An introduction.* Hillsdale, NJ: Erlbaum.

Lackner, J. R., & DiZio, P. (2005). Vestibular, proprioceptive, and haptic contributions to spatial orientation. *Annual Review of Psychology, 56,* 115–147.

Lai, Y., & Siegal, J. (1999). Muscle atonia in REM sleep. In B. Mallick & S. Inoue (Eds.), *Rapid eye movement sleep* (pp. 69–90). New Delhi, India: Narosa Publishing House.

Lalonde, J. K., Hudson, J. I., Gigante, R. A., & Pope, H. G., Jr. (2001). Canadian and American psychiatrists' attitudes toward dissociative disorders diagnoses. *Canadian Journal of Psychiatry, 46,* 407–412.

Lamb, M. E., Sternberg, K. J., & Prodromidis, M. (1992). Nonmaternal care and the security of infant/mother attachment: A reanalysis of the data. *Infant Behavior & Development, 15,* 71–83.

Lamb, M. E., Thompson, R. A., Gardner, W., & Charnov, E. L. (1985). *Infant-mother attachment: The origins and developmental significance of individual differences in strange situation behavior.* Hillsdale, NJ: Erlbaum.

Lamm, H., & Myers, D. G. (1978). Group-induced polarization of attitudes and behavior. *Advances in Experimental Social Psychology, 11,* 145–195.

Landauer, T. K., & Bjork, R. A. (1978). Optimum rehearsal patterns and name learning. In M. M. Gruneberg, P. E. Morris, & R. N. Sykes (Eds.), *Practical aspects of memory.* (pp. 625–632). New York: Academic Press.

Lang, F. R., & Carstensen, L. L. (1994). Close emotional relationships in late life: Further support for proactive aging in the social domain. *Psychology and Aging, 9,* 315–324.

Lange, C. G., & James, W. (1922). *The emotions.* Baltimore: Williams and Wilkins.

Langer, E. J., & Abelson, R. P. (1974). A patient by any other name . . . Clinician group difference in labeling bias. *Journal of Consulting & Clinical Psychology, 42,* 4–9.

Langleben, D. D., Loughead, J. W., Bilker, W. B., Ruparel, K., Childress, A. R., Busch, S. I., et al. (2005). Telling truth from lie in individual subjects with fast event-related fMRI. *Human Brain Mapping 26,* 262–272.

Langlois, J. H., Kalakanis, L., Rubenstein, A. J., Larson, A., Hallam, M., & Smoot, M. (2000). Maxims or myths of beauty? A meta-analytic and theoretical review. *Psychological Bulletin, 126,* 390–423.

Langlois, J. H., Ritter, J. M., Casey, R. J., & Sawin, D. B. (1995). Infant attractiveness predicts maternal behaviors and attitudes. *Developmental Psychology, 31,* 464–472.

Langlois, J. H., & Roggman, L. A. (1990). Attractive faces are only average. *Psychological Science, 1,* 115–121.

Langlois, J. H., Roggman, L. A., & Musselman, L. (1994). What is average and what is not average about attractive faces? *Psychological Science, 5,* 214–220.

Langlois, J. H., Roggman, L. A., & Rieser-Danner, L. A. (1990). Infants' differential social responses to attractive and unattractive faces. *Developmental Psychology, 26,* 153–159.

Langston, J. W. (1995). *The case of the frozen addicts.* New York: Pantheon.

Larsen, S. F. (1992). Potential flashbulbs: Memories of ordinary news as baseline. In E. Winograd & U. Neisser (Eds.), *Affect and accuracy in recall: Studies of "flashbulb memories"* (pp. 32–64). New York: Cambridge University Press.

Larson, J. R., Foster-Fishman, P. G., & Keys, C. B. (1994). Discussion of shared and unshared information in decision-making groups. *Journal of Personality & Social Psychology, 67,* 446–461.

Larson, R., & Richards, M. H. (1991). Daily companionship in late childhood and early adolescence—changing developmental contexts. *Child Development, 62,* 284–300.

Lashley, K. S. (1960). In search of the engram. In F. A. Beach, D. O. Hebb, C. T. Morgan, & H. W. Nissen (Eds.), *The neuropsychology of Lashley.* New York: McGraw-Hill.

Latané, B., & Nida, S. (1981). Ten years of research on group size and helping. *Psychological Bulletin, 89,* 308–324.

Latané, B., Williams, K., & Harkins, S. (1979). Many hands make light the work: The causes and consequences of social loafing. *Journal of Personality and Social Psychology, 37,* 822–832.

Laupa, M., & Turiel, E. (1986). Children's conceptions of adult and peer authority. *Child Development, 57,* 405–412.

Laurence, J., & Perry, C. (1983). Hypnotically created memory among high hypnotizable subjects. *Science, 222,* 523–524.

Laureys, S., Giacino, J. T., Schiff, N. D., Schabus, M., & Owen, A. M. (2006). How should functional imaging of patients with disorders of consciousness contribute to their clinical rehabilitation needs? *Current Opinion in Neurology, 19,* 520–527.

Lavie, P. (2001). Sleep-wake as a biological rhythm. *Annual Review of Psychology, 52,* 277–303.

Lavoie, K. L., & Fleet, R. P. (2002). Should psychologists be granted prescription privileges? A review of the prescription privilege debate for psychiatrists. *Canadian Journal of Psychiatry, 47*(5), 443–449.

Lavori, P. W., Klerman, G. L., Keller, M. B., Reich, T., Rice, J., & Endicott, J. (1987). Age-period-cohort analysis of secular trends in onset of major depression: Findings in siblings of patients with major affective disorder. *Journal of Psychiatric Researchers, 21,* 23–25.

Lawton, M. P., Kleban, M. H., Rajagopal, D., & Dean, J. (1992). The dimensions of affective experience in three age groups. *Psychology and Aging, 7,* 171–184.

Lazarus, R. S. (1984). On the primacy of cognition. *American Psychologist, 39,* 124–129.

Lazarus, R. S., & Alfert, E. (1964). Short-circuiting of threat by experimentally altering cognitive appraisal. *Journal of Abnormal and Social Psychology, 69,* 195–205.

Lazarus, R. S., & Folkman, S. (1984). *Stress, appraisal, and coping.* New York: Springer.

Leary, M. R. (1990). Responses to social exclusion: Social anxiety, jealousy, loneliness, depression, and low self-esteem. *Journal of Social and Clinical Psychology, 9,* 221–229.

Leary, M. R., & Baumeister, R. F. (2000). The nature and function of self-esteem: Sociometer theory. In M. P. Zanna (Ed.), *Advances in experimental social psychology* (Vol. 32, pp. 1–62). San Diego: Academic Press.

Leary, M. R., Britt, T. W., Cutlip, W. D., & Templeton, J. L. (1992). Social blushing. *Psychological Bulletin, 112,* 446–460.

Leary, M. R., Tambor, E. S., Terdal, S. K., & Downs, D. L. (1995). Self-esteem as an interpersonal monitor: The sociometer hypothesis. *Journal of Personality and Social Psychology, 68,* 518–530.

Leaton, R. N. (1976). Long-term retention of the habituation of lick suppression and startle response produced by a single auditory stimulus. *Journal of Experimental Psychology: Animal Behavior Processes, 2,* 248–259.

Lecky, P. (1945). *Self-consistency: A theory of personality.* New York: Island Press.

Lecrubier, Y., Clerc, G., Didi, R., & Kieser, M. (2002). Efficacy of St. John's Wort Extract WS 5570 in major depression: A double-blind, placebo-controlled trial. *American Journal of Psychiatry, 159,* 1361–1366.

LeDoux, J. E. (1992). Brain mechanisms of emotion and emotional learning. *Current Opinion in Neurobiology, 2,* 191–197.

LeDoux, J. E. (1996). *The emotional brain: The mysterious underpinnings of emotional life.* New York: Simon & Schuster.

LeDoux, J. E. (1998). Fear and the brain: Where have we been, and where are we going? *Biological Psychiatry, 153,* 1229–1238.

LeDoux, J. E. (2000). Emotion circuits in the brain. *Annual Review of Neuroscience, 23*, 155–184.

LeDoux, J. E. (2002). *The synaptic self: How our brains become who we are.* New York: Viking.

LeDoux, J. E., Iwata, J., Cicchetti, P., & Reis, D. J. (1988). Different projections of the central amygdaloid nucleus mediate autonomic and behavioral correlates of conditioned fear. *Journal of Neuroscience, 8*, 2517–2529.

Lee, D. N., & Aronson, E. (1974). Visual proprioceptive control of standing in human infants. *Perception & Psychophysics, 15*, 529–532.

Lefcourt, H. M. (1982). *Locus of control: Current trends in theory and research* (2nd ed.). Hillsdale, NJ: Erlbaum.

Leighton, J. P., & Sternberg, R. J. (Eds.). (2003). *The nature of reasoning.* Cambridge, England: Cambridge University Press.

Lemyre, L., & Smith, P. M. (1985). Intergroup discrimination and self-esteem in the minimal group paradigm. *Journal of Personality and Social Psychology, 49*, 660–670.

Lentz, M. J., Landis, C. A., Rothermel, J., & Shaver, J. L. (1999). Effects of selective slow wave sleep disruption on musculoskeletal pain and fatigue in middle aged women. *Journal of Rheumatology, 26*, 1586–1592.

Leonard, M. (2002, October 27). Arrest in sniper case; sniper suspect defies profile. *Boston Globe*, p. A1.

Lepage, M., Ghaffar, O., Nyberg, L., & Tulving, E. (2000). Prefrontal cortex and episodic memory retrieval mode. *Proceedings of the National Academy of Sciences (USA), 97*, 506–511.

Lepper, M. R., & Greene, D. (1976). *The hidden costs of reward.* Hillsdale, NJ: Erlbaum.

Lepper, M. R., & Greene, D. (1978). Overjustification research and beyond: Toward a means-end analysis of intrinsic and extrinsic motivation. In M. R. Lepper & D. Greene (Eds.), *The hidden costs of reward: New perspectives on the psychology of human motivation.* New York: Wiley.

Lepper, M. R., Greene, D., & Nisbett, R. E. (1973). Undermining children's intrinsic interest with extrinsic rewards: A test of the "overjustification" hypothesis. *Journal of Personality and Social Psychology, 28*, 129–137.

Levenson, R. W., Cartensen, L. L., Friesen, W. V., & Ekman, P. (1991). Emotion physiology, and expression in old age. *Psychology and Aging, 6*, 28–35.

Levenson, R. W., Ekman, P., & Friesen, W. V. (1990). Voluntary facial action generates emotion-specific autonomic nervous system activity. *Psychophysiology, 27*, 363–384.

Levenson, R. W., Ekman, P., Heider, K., & Friesen, W. V. (1992). Emotion and automatic nervous system activity in the Minangkabau of West Sumatra. *Journal of Personality and Social Psychology, 62*, 972–988.

Levine, J. M., & Moreland, R. L. (1998). Small groups. In D. T. Gilbert, S. T. Fiske, & G. Lindzey (Eds.), *The handbook of social psychology* (4th ed., Vol. 2, pp. 415–469). New York: McGraw-Hill.

Levine, M. (1981). *History and politics of community mental health.* New York: Oxford University Press.

Levy, J., Trevarthen, C., & Sperry, R. W. (1972). Perception of bilateral chimeric figures following hemispheric disconnection. *Brain, 95*, 61–78.

Lewin, K. (1936). *Principles of topological psychology.* New York: McGraw-Hill.

Lewin, K. (1951). Behavior and development as a function of the total situation. In K. Lewin, *Field theory in social science: Selected theoretical papers* (pp. 791–843). New York: Harper & Row.

Lewis, M., & Brooks-Gunn, J. (1979). *Social cognition and the acquisition of self.* New York: Plenum Press.

Lewis, R., Kapur, S., Jones, C., DaSilva, J., M. Brown, G. M., Wilson, A. A., et al. (1999). Serotonin 5-HT-sub-2 receptors in schizophrenia: A PET study using [-sup-1-sup-8F] setoperone in neuroleptic-naive patients and normal subjects. *American Journal of Psychiatry, 156*, 72–78.

Lewontin, R., Rose, S., & Kamin, L. J. (1984). *Not in our genes.* New York: Pantheon.

Li, H. Z., & Browne, A. J. (2000). Defining mental illness and accessing mental health services: Perspectives of Asian Canadians. *Canadian Journal of Community Mental Health, 19*, 143–159.

Li, W., Lexenberg, E., Parrish, T., & Gottfried, J. A. (2006). Learning to smell the roses: Experience-dependent neural plasticity in human piriform and orbitofrontal cortices. *Neuron, 52*, 1097–1108.

Libet, B. (1985). Unconscious cerebral initiative and the role of conscious will in voluntary action. *Behavioral and Brain Sciences, 8*, 529–566.

Liebenluft, E. (1996). Women with bipolar illness: Clinical and research issues. *American Journal of Psychiatry, 153*, 163–173.

Lieberman, M. D., Hariri, A., Jarcho, J. M., Eisenberger, N. I., & Bookheimer, S. Y. (2005). An fMRI investigation of race-related amygdala activity in African American and Caucasian-American individuals. *Nature Neuroscience, 8*, 720–722.

Lieberman, M. D., Ochsner, K. N., Gilbert, D. T., & Schacter, D. L. (2001). Do amnesics exhibit cognitive dissonance reduction? The role of explicit memory and attention in attitude change. *Psychological Science, 12*, 135–140.

Lieberman, M. D., & Rosenthal, R. (2001). Why introverts can't always tell who likes them: Multitasking and nonverbal decoding. *Journal of Personality and Social Psychology, 80*, 294–310.

Liebowitz, M. R., Fyer, A. J., Gorman, J. M., Dillon, D., Davies, S., Stein, J. M., et al. (1985a). Specificity of lactate infusions in social phobia versus panic disorders. *American Journal of Psychiatry, 142*, 947–950.

Liebowitz, M. R., Gorman, J. M., Fyer, A. J., Levitt, M., Dillon, D., Levy, G., et al. (1985b). Lactate provocation of panic attacks: II. Biochemical and physiological findings. *Archives of General Psychiatry, 42*, 709–719.

Lilienfeld, S. O., Lynn, S. J., & Lohr, J. M. (Eds.). (2003). *Science and pseudoscience in clinical psychology.* New York: Guilford Press.

Lilienfeld, S. O., Wood, J. M., & Garb, H. N. (2000). The scientific status of projective techniques. *Psychological Science in the Public Interest, 1*, 27–66.

Lillard, L. A., & Waite, L. J. (1995). 'Til death do us part: Marital disruption and mortality. *American Journal of Sociology, 100*, 1131–1156.

Lindenberger, U., & Baltes, P. B. (1997). Intellectual functioning in old and very old age: Cross-sectional results from the Berling aging study. *Psychology and Aging, 12*, 410–432.

Lindsay, D. S., & Read, J. D. (1994). Psychotherapy and memories of childhood sexual abuse: A cognitive perspective. *Applied Cognitive Psychology, 8*, 281–338.

Lindsley, O. R., Skinner, B. F., & Solomon, H. C. (1953). *Studies in behavior therapy (status report 1).* Waltham, MA: Metropolitan State Hospital.

Lindstrom, M. (2005). *Brand sense: How to build powerful brands through touch, taste, smell, sight and sound.* London: Kogan Page.

Link, B. G., Phelan, J. C., Bresnahan, M., Stueve, A., & Pescosolido, B. A. (1999). Public conceptions of mental illness: Labels, causes, dangerousness, and social distance. *American Journal of Public Health, 89*, 1328–1333.

Link, S. W. (1994). Rediscovering the past: Gustav Fechner and signal detection theory. *Psychological Science, 5*, 335–340.

Linszen, D. H., Dingemans, P. M., Nugter, M. A., Van der Does, A. J., Scholte, W. F., & Lenoir, M. A. (1997). Patient attributes and expressed emotion as risk factors for psychotic relapse. *Schizophrenia Bulletin, 23,* 119–130.

Lipps, T. (1907). Das Wissen von fremden Ichen. In T. Lipps (Ed.), *Psychologische Untersuchungen* (Vol. 1, pp. 694–722). Leipzig: Engelmann.

Little, B. R. (1983). Personal projects: A rationale and method for investigation. *Environment and Behavior, 15,* 273–309.

Little, B. R. (1993). Personal projects and the distributed self: Aspects of a conative psychology. In J. R. Suls (Ed.), *Psychological perspectives on the self* (Vol. 4, pp. 157–185). Hillsdale, NJ: Erlbaum.

Livingstone, M., & Hubel, D. (1988). Segregation of form, color, movement, and depth: Anatomy, physiology, and perception. *Science, 240,* 740–749.

Locksley, A., Ortiz, V., & Hepburn, C. (1980). Social categorization and discriminatory behavior: Extinguishing the minimal intergroup discrimination effect. *Journal of Personality and Social Psychology, 39,* 773–783.

Loehlin, J. C. (1992). *Genes and environment in personality development.* Newbury Park, CA: Sage.

Loftus, E. F. (1975). Leading questions and eyewitness report. *Cognitive Psychology, 7,* 560–572.

Loftus, E. F. (1993). The reality of repressed memories. *American Psychologist, 48,* 518–537.

Loftus, E. F. (2003). Make-believe memories. *American Psychologist, 58,* 867–873.

Loftus, E., & Ketchum, K. (1994). *The myth of repressed memory.* New York: St. Martin's Press.

Loftus, E. F., & Klinger, M. R. (1992). Is the unconscious smart or dumb? *American Psychologist, 47,* 761–765.

Loftus, E. F., Miller, D. G., & Burns, H. J. (1978). Semantic integration of verbal information into a visual memory. *Journal of Experimental Psychology: Human Learning and Memory, 4,* 19–31.

Loftus, E. F., & Pickrell, J. E. (1995). The formation of false memories. *Psychiatric Annals, 25,* 720–725.

Logan, G. D. (1988). Toward an instance theory of automatization. *Psychological Review, 95,* 492–527.

Lohr, J. M., Tolin, D. F., & Lilienfeld, S. O. (1998). Efficacy of eye movement desensitization and reprocessing: Implications for behavior therapy. *Behavior Therapy, 29,* 123–156.

Lorenz, K. (1952). *King Solomon's ring.* New York: Crowell.

Lorge, I. (1936). Prestige, suggestion, and attitudes. *Journal of Social Psychology, 7,* 386–402.

Lozano, B. E., & Johnson, S. L. (2001). Can personality traits predict increases in manic and depressive symptoms? *Journal of Affective Disorders, 63,* 103–111.

Lubinski, D., Webb, R. M., Morelock, M. J., & Benbow, C. P. (2001). Top 1 in 10,000: A 10-year follow-up of the profoundly gifted. *Journal of Applied Psychology, 86,* 718–729.

Luborsky, L., Rosenthal, R., Diguer, L., Andrusyna, T. P., Berman, J. S., Levitt, J. T., et al. (2002). The dodo bird verdict is alive and well—mostly. *Clinical Psychology: Science and Practice, 9,* 2–12.

Luborsky, L., & Singer, B. (1975). Comparative studies of psychotherapies: Is it true that "everywon has one and all must have prizes"? *Archives of General Psychiatry, 32*(8), 995–1008.

Lucas, R. E., Clark, A. E., Georgellis, Y., & Diener, E. (2003). Reexamining adaptation and the set point model of happiness: Reactions to changes in marital status. *Journal of Personality and Social Psychology, 84,* 527–539.

Ludwig, A. M. (1966). Altered states of consciousness. *Archives of General Psychiatry, 15,* 225–234.

Luria, A. R. (1968). *The mind of a mnemonist: A little book about a vast memory* (L. Solotaroff, Trans.). New York: Basic Books.

Lustman, P. J., Caudle, M. L., & Clouse, R. E. (2002). Case study: Nondysphoric depression in a man with type 2 diabetes. *Clinical Diabetes, 20,* 122–123.

Lykken, D. T. (1995). *The antisocial personalities.* Hillsdale, NJ: Erlbaum.

Lykken, D. T., & Tellegen, A. (1996). Happiness is a stochastic phenomenon. *Psychological Science, 7,* 186–189.

Lynn, M., & Shurgot, B. A. (1984). Responses to lonely hearts advertisements: Effects of reported physical attractiveness, physique, and coloration. *Personality and Social Psychology Bulletin, 10,* 349–357.

Lynn, R., & Vanhanen, T. (2002). *IQ and the wealth of nations.* Westport, CT: Praeger/Greenwood.

Lynn, S. J., Rhue, J. W., & Weekes, J. R. (1990). Hypnotic involuntariness: A social cognitive analysis. *Psychological Review, 97,* 169–184.

MacDonald, S., Uesiliana, K., & Hayne, H. (2000). Cross-cultural and gender differences in childhood amnesia. *Memory, 8,* 365–376.

MacDonald, T. K., Zanna, M. P., & Fong, G. T. (1996). Why common sense goes out the window: Effects of alcohol on intentions to use condoms. *Personality and Social Psychology Bulletin, 22,* 763–775.

MacGregor, J. N., Ormerod, T. C., & Chronicle, E. P. (2001). Information processing and insight: A process model of performance on the nine-dot and related problems. *Journal of Experimental Psychology: Learning, Memory, & Cognition, 27,* 176–201.

Mack, A. H., Franklin, J. E., Jr., & Frances, R. J. (2003). Substance use disorders. In R. E. Hales & S. C. Yudofsky (Eds.), *The American Psychiatric Publishing textbook of clinical psychiatry* (4th ed., pp. 309–377). Washington, DC: American Psychiatric Publishing.

Mackinnon, A., & Foley, D. (1996). The genetics of anxiety disorders. In H. G. Westenberg, J. A. Den Boer & D. L. Murphy (Eds.), *Advances in the neurobiology of anxiety disorders* (pp. 39–59). Chichester, England: Wiley.

Maclean, P. D. (1970). The triune brain, emotion, and scientific bias. In F. O. Schmitt (Ed.), *The neurosciences: A second study program* (pp. 336–349). New York: Rockefeller University Press.

Macmillan, M. (2000). *An odd kind of fame: Stories of Phineas Gage.* Cambridge, MA: MIT Press.

Macmillan, N. A., & Creelman, C. D. (2005). *Detection theory.* Mahwah, NJ: Erlbaum.

Macrae, C. N., Bodenhausen, G. V., Milne, A. B., & Jetten, J. (1994). Out of mind but back in sight: Stereotypes on the rebound. *Journal of Personality and Social Psychology, 67,* 808–817.

Macrae, C. N., Moran, J. M., Heatherton, T. F., Banfield, J. F., & Kelley, W. M. (2004). Medial prefrontal activity predicts memory for self. *Cerebral Cortex, 14,* 647–654.

Maddi, S. R., Kahn, S., & Maddi, K. L. (1998). The effectiveness of hardiness training. *Consulting Psychology Journal: Practice and Research, 50,* 78–86.

Maddi, S. R., & Kobasa, S. (1984). *The hardy executive: Health under stress.* Homewood, IL: Dow Jones–Irwin.

Maes, M. (1995). Evidence for an immune response in major depression: A review and hypothesis. *Progress in Neuro-Psychopharmacology and Biological Psychiatry, 19,* 11–38.

Magee, W. J., Eaton, W. W., Wittchen, H.-U., McGonagle, K. A., & Kessler, R. C. (1996). Agoraphobia, simple phobia, and social phobia in the National Comorbidity Survey. *Archives of General Psychiatry, 53,* 159–168.

Maguire, E. A., Woollett, K., & Spiers, H. J. (2006). London taxi drivers and bus drivers: A structural MRI and neuropsychological analysis. *Hippocampus, 16,* 1091–1101.

Mah, K., & Binik, Y. M. (2002). Do all orgasms feel alike? Evaluating a two-dimensional model of the orgasm experience across gender and sexual context. *Journal of Sex Research, 39,* 104–113.

Maier, S. F., & Watkins, L. R. (1998). Cytokines for psychologists: Implications of bidirectional immune-to-brain communication for understanding behavior, mood, and cognition. *Psychological Review, 105,* 83–107.

Maier, S. F., & Watkins, L. R. (2000). The immune system as a sensory system: Implications for psychology. *Current Directions in Psychological Science, 9,* 98–102.

Makin, J. E., Fried, P. A., & Watkinson, B. (1991). A comparison of active and passive smoking during pregnancy: Long-term effects. *Neurotoxicology and Teratology, 16,* 5–12.

Maldonado, J. R., & Butler, L. D. (1998). *Treatments for dissociative disorders.* New York: Oxford University Press.

Malina, R. M., Bouchard, C., & Beunen, G. (1988). Human growth: Selected aspects of current research on well-nourished children. *Annual Review of Anthropology, 17,* 187–219.

Malinoski, P. T., & Lynn, S. J. (1999). The plasticity of early memory reports: Social pressure, hypnotizability, compliance, and interrogative suggestibility. *The International Journal of Clinical and Experimental Hypnosis, 47,* 320–345.

Mandel, D. R., & Lehman, D. R. (1998). Integration of contingency information in judgments of cause, covariation, and probability. *Journal of Experimental Psychology: General, 127,* 269–285.

Mandle, C. L., Jacobs, S. C., Arcari, P. M., & Domar, A. D. (1996). The efficacy of relaxation response interventions with adult patients: A review of the literature. *Journal of Cardiovascular Nursing, 10,* 4–26.

Mandler, G. (1967). Organization and memory. In K. W. Spence & J. T. Spence (Eds.), *The psychology of learning and motivation* (Vol. 1, pp. 327–372). New York: Academic Press.

Mann, J. J., Waternaux, C., Haas, G. L, & Malone, K. M. (1999). Toward a clinical model of suicidal behavior in psychiatric patients. *American Journal of Psychiatry, 156,* 181–189.

Marangell, L. B., Silver, J. M., Goff, D. M., & Yudofsky, S. C. (2003). Psychopharmacology and electroconvulsive therapy. In R. E. Hales & S. C. Yudofsky (Eds.), *The American Psychiatric Publishing textbook of clinical psychiatry* (4th ed., pp. 1047–1149). Washington, DC: American Psychiatric Publishing.

Marcus, G. B. (1986). Stability and change in political attitudes: Observe, recall, and "explain." *Political Behavior, 8,* 21–44.

Marcus, J., Hans, S. L., Auerbach, J. G., & Auerbach, A. G. (1993). Children at risk for schizophrenia: The Jerusalem infant development study: II. Neurological deficits at school age. *Archives of General Psychiatry, 50,* 797–809.

Marks, I. M., & Nesse, R. M. (1994). Fear and fitness: An evolutionary analysis of anxiety disorders. *Ethology and Sociobiology, 15,* 247–261.

Markus, H. (1977). Self-schemata and processing information about the self. *Journal of Personality and Social Psychology, 35,* 63–78.

Marlatt, G. A. (Ed.). (1998). *Harm reduction: Pragmatic strategies for managing high-risk behaviors.* New York: Guilford Press.

Marlatt, G. A., Larimer, M. E., Baer, J. S., & Quigley, L. A. (1993). Harm reduction for alcohol problems: Moving beyond the controlled drinking controversy. *Behavior Therapy, 24,* 461–504.

Marlatt, G. A., & Rohsenow, D. (1980). Cognitive processes in alcohol use: Expectancy and the balanced placebo design. In N. K. Mello (Ed.), *Advances in substance abuse: Behavioral and biological research* (pp. 159–199). Greenwich, CT: JAI Press.

Marmot, M. G., Stansfeld, S., Patel, C., North, F., Head, J., White, L., et al. (1991). Health inequalities among British civil servants: The Whitehall II study. *Lancet, 337,* 1387–1393.

Marr, D., & Nishihara, H. K. (1978). Representation and recognition of the spatial organization of three-dimensional shapes. *Proceedings of the Royal Society of London B, 200,* 269–294.

Marsolek, C. J. (1995). Abstract visual-form representations in the left cerebral hemispheres. *Journal of Experimental Psychology: Human Perception and Performance, 21,* 375–386.

Martin, A. (2007). The representation of object concepts in the brain. *Annual Review of Psychology, 58,* 25–45.

Martin, A., & Caramazza, A. (2003). Neuropsychological and neuroimaging perspectives on conceptual knowledge: An introduction. *Cognitive Neuropsychology, 20,* 195–212.

Martin, A., & Chao, L. L. (2001). Semantic memory and the brain: Structure and processes. *Current Opinion in Neurobiology, 11,* 194–201.

Martin, G., & Koo, L. (1997). Celebrity suicide: Did the death of Kurt Cobain influence young suicides in Australia? *Archives of Suicide Research, 3,* 187–198.

Martin, L. R., Friedman, H. S., Tucker, J. S., Tomlinson-Keasey, C., Criqui, M. H., & Schwartz, J. E. (2002). A life course perspective on childhood cheerfulness and its relation to mortality risk. *Personality and Social Psychology Bulletin, 28,* 1155–1165.

Martin, N. G., Eaves, L. J., Geath, A. R., Jarding, R., Feingold, L. M., & Eysenck, H. J. (1986). Transmission of social attitudes. *Proceedings of the National Academy of Sciences (USA), 83,* 4364–4368.

Marucha, P. T., Kiecolt-Glaser, J. K., & Favagehi, M. (1998). Mucosal wound healing is impaired by examination stress. *Psychosomatic Medicine, 60,* 362–365.

Maslach, C. (2003). Job burnout: New directions in research and intervention. *Current Directions in Psychological Science, 12,* 189–192.

Maslow, A. H. (1937). Dominance-feeling, behavior, and status. In R. J. Lowry (Ed.), *Dominance, self-esteem, self-actualization: Germinal papers by A. H. Maslow.* Monterey, CA: Brooks-Cole.

Maslow, A. H. (1954). *Motivation and personality.* New York: Harper & Row.

Maslow, A. H. (1962). *Toward a psychology of being.* New York: Van Nostrand Reinhold.

Maslow, A. H. (1970). *Motivation and personality* (2nd ed.). New York: Harper & Row.

Masserman, J. H. (1961). *Principles of dynamic psychiatry* (2nd ed.). Philadelphia: W. B. Saunders.

Masters, W. H., & Johnson, V. E. (1966). *Human sexual response.* Boston: Little, Brown.

Mather, M., Canli, T., English, T., Whitfield, S., Wais, P., Ochsner, K., et al. (2004). Amygdala responses to emotionally valenced stimuli in older and younger adults. *Psychological Science, 15,* 259–263.

Mather, M., & Carstensen, L. L. (2003). Aging and attentional biases for emotional faces. *Psychological Science, 14,* 409–415.

Mathis, J. L. (1964). A sophisticated version of voodoo death. *Psychosomatic Medicine, 26,* 104–107.

Matthews, G., & Gilliland, K. (1999). The personality theories of H. J. Eysenck and J. A. Gray: A comparative review. *Personality and Individual Differences, 26,* 583–626.

Maudsley, H. (1886). *Natural causes and supernatural seemings.* London: Kegan Paul, Trench.

May, R. (1983). *The discovery of being: Writings in existential psychology.* New York: Norton.

Maynard-Smith, J. (1965). The evolution of alarm calls. *American Naturalist, 100,* 637–650.

Maynard-Smith, J., & Szathmary, E. (1995). *The major transitions in evolution.* Oxford, England: Oxford University Press.

McAdams, D. (1993). *The stories we live by: Personal myths and the making of the self.* New York: Morrow.

McAndrew, F. T. (1986). A cross-cultural study of recognition thresholds for facial expression of emotion. *Journal of Cross-Cultural Psychology, 17,* 211–224.

McCann, I. L., & Holmes, D. S. (1984). Influence of aerobic exercise on depression. *Journal of Personality and Social Psychology, 46,* 1142–1147.

McClelland, D. C., Atkinson, J. W., Clark, R. A., & Lowell, E. L. (1953). *The achievement motive.* New York: Appleton-Century-Crofts.

McClintock, M. K. (1971). Menstrual synchrony and suppression. *Nature, 299,* 244–245.

McClintock, M. K., & Herdt, G. (1996). Rethinking puberty: The development of sexual attraction. *Current Directions in Psychological Science, 5,* 178–183.

McCloskey, M., & Zaragoza, M. (1985). Misleading postevent information and memory for events: Arguments and evidence against memory impairment hypotheses. *Journal of Experimental Psychology: General, 114,* 1–16.

McConkey, K. M., Barnier, A. J., & Sheehan, P. W. (1998). Hypnosis and pseudomemory: Understanding the findings and their implications. In S. J. Lynn & K. M. McConkey (Eds.), *Truth in memory* (pp. 227–259). New York: Guilford Press.

McCrae, R. R., & Costa, P. T. (1990). *Personality in adulthood.* New York: Guilford Press.

McCrae, R. R., & Costa, P. T. (1999). A five-factor theory of personality. In L. A. Pervin & O. P. John (Eds.), *Handbook of personality: Theory and research.* New York: Guilford Press.

McDaniel, M. A. (2005). Big-brained people are smarter: A meta-analysis of the relationship between in vivo brain volume and intelligence. *Intelligence, 33,* 337–346.

McDougall, W. (1930). The hormic psychology. In C. Murchison (Ed.), *Psychologies of 1930* (pp. 3–36). Worcester, MA: Clark University Press.

McDougall, W. (2003). *Introduction to social psychology.* Mineola, NY: Dover Publications. (Originally published 1908)

McEvoy, S. P., Stevenson, M. R., McCartt, A. T., Woodward, M., Haworth, C., Palamara, P., et al. (2005). Role of mobile phones in motor vehicle crashes resulting in hospital attendance: A case-crossover study. *British Medical Journal, 331,* 428–430.

McFall, R. M., & Treat, T. A. (1999). Quantifying the information value of clinical assessments with signal detection theory. *Annual Review of Psychology, 50,* 215–241.

McFarland, C., & Ross, M. (1987). The relation between current impressions and memories of self and dating partners. *Personality and Social Psychology Bulletin, 13,* 228–238.

McFarlane, A. H., Norman, G. R., Streiner, D. L., Roy, R., & Scott, D. J. (1980). A longitudinal study of the influence of the psychosocial environment on health status: A preliminary report. *Journal of Health and Social Behavior, 21,* 124–133.

McGarty, C., & Turner, J. C. (1992). The effects of categorization on social judgement. *British Journal of Social Psychology, 31,* 253–268.

McGue, M., & Bouchard, T. J. (1998). Genetic and environmental influences on human behavioral differences. *Annual Review of Neuroscience, 21,* 1–24.

McGuire, P. K., Shah, G. M., & Murray, R. M. (1993). Increased blood flow in Broca's area during auditory hallucinations in schizophrenia. *Lancet, 342,* 703–706.

McHugh, P. R., Lief, H. I., Freyd, P. P., & Fetkewicz, J. M. (2004). From refusal to recollection: Family relationships after an accusation based on recovered memories. *Journal of Nervous and Mental Disease, 192,* 525–532.

McKetin, R., McLaren, J., Lubman, D. I., & Hides, L. (2006). The prevalence of psychotic symptoms among methamphetamine users. *Addiction, 101,* 1473–1478.

McKetin, R., Ward, P. B., Catts, S. V., Mattick, R. P., & Bell, J. R. (1999). Changes in auditory selective attention and event-related potentials following oral administration of D-amphetamine in humans. *Neuropsychopharmacology,* 380–390.

McKinney, C. H., Antoni, M. H., Kumar, M., Tims, F. C., & McCabe, P. M. (1997). Effects of guided imagery and music (GIM) therapy on mood and cortisol in healthy adults. *Health Psychology, 16,* 390–400.

McNally, R. J. (2003). *Remembering trauma.* Cambridge, MA: Belknap Press/Harvard University Press.

McNally, R. J., & Steketee, G. S. (1985). Etiology and maintenance of severe animal phobias. *Behavioral Research and Therapy, 23,* 431–435.

McNamara, B., Ray, J. L., Arthurs, O. J., & Boniface, S. (2001). Transcranial magnetic stimulation for depression and other psychiatric disorders. *Psychological Medicine, 31,* 1141–1146.

McNeilly, A. S., Robinson, I. C., Houston, M. J., & Howie, P. W. (1983). Release of oxytocin and prolactin in response to suckling. *British Medical Journal, 286,* 257–259.

McWilliams, N. (1994). *Psychoanalytic diagnosis: Understanding personality structure in the clinical process.* New York: Guilford Press.

McWilliams, P. (1993). *Ain't nobody's business if you do: The absurdity of consensual crimes in a free society.* Los Angeles: Prelude Press.

Mead, G. H. (1934). *Mind, self, and society.* Chicago: University of Chicago Press.

Mead, M. (1968). *Sex and temperament in three primitive societies.* New York: Dell. (Originally published 1935)

Mechelli, A., Crinion, J. T., Noppeney, U., O'Doherty, J., Ashburner, J., Frackowiak, R. S., et al. (2004). Neurolinguistics: Structural plasticity in the human brain. *Nature, 431,* 757.

Medin, D. L., & Schaffer, M. M. (1978). Context theory of classification learning. *Psychological Review, 85,* 207–238.

Medvec, V. H., Madey, S. F., & Gilovich, T. (1995). When less is more: Counterfactual thinking and satisfaction among Olympic medalists. *Journal of Personality and Social Psychology, 69,* 603–610.

Meins, E. (2003). Emotional development and attachment relationships. In A. Slater & G. Bremner (Eds.), *An introduction to developmental psychology* (pp. 141–164). Malden, MA: Blackwell.

Meins, E., Fernyhough, C., Fradley, E., & Tuckey, M. (2001). Rethinking maternal sensitivity: Mothers' comments on infants' mental processes predict security of attachment at 12 months. *Journal of Child Psychology & Psychiatry & Allied Disciplines, 42,* 637–648.

Meisel, S. R., Dayan, K. I., Pauzner, H., Chetboun, I., Arbel, Y., David, D., et al. (1991). Effect of Iraqi missile war on incidence of acute myocardial infarction and sudden death in Israeli citizens. *Lancet, 338,* 660–661.

Mekel-Bobrov, N., Gilbert, S. L., Evans, P. D., Vallender, E. J., Anderson, J. R., Hudson, R. R., et al. (2005). Ongoing adaptive evolution of ASPM, a brain size determinant in *Homo sapiens. Science, 309,* 1720–1722.

Meltzoff, A. N., & Moore, M. K. (1977). Imitation of facial and manual gestures by human neonates. *Science, 198,* 75–78.

Melzack, R., & Wall, P. D. (1965). Pain mechanisms: A new theory. *Science, 150,* 971–979.

Mendes, W. B., Blascovich, J., Lickel, B., & Hunter, S. (2002). Challenge and threat during social interaction with white and black men. *Personality & Social Psychology Bulletin, 28,* 939–952.

Merikangas, K. R., Wicki, W., & Angst, J. (1994). Heterogeneity of depression: Classification of depressive subtype by longitudinal course. *British Journal of Psychiatry, 164,* 342–348.

Mervis, C. B., & Bertrand, J. (1994). Acquisition of the "Novel Name" Nameless Category (N3C) principle. *Child Development, 65,* 1646–1662.

Merzenich, M. M., Recanzone, G. H., Jenkins, W. M., & Grajski, K. A. (1990). Adaptive mechanisms in cortical networks underlying cortical contributions to learning and nondeclarative memory. *Cold Spring Harbor Symposia on Quantitative Biology, 55,* 873–887.

Messick, D. M., & Cook, K. S. (1983). *Equity theory: Psychological and sociological perspectives.* New York: Praeger.

Metcalfe, J., & Wiebe, D. (1987). Intuition in insight and noninsight problem solving. *Memory & Cognition, 15,* 238–246.

Meyer-Bahlberg, H. F. L., Ehrhardt, A. A., Rosen, L. R., & Gruen, R. S. (1995). Prenatal estrogens and the development of homosexual orientation. *Developmental Psychology, 31,* 12–21.

Michael, R. T. (1994). *Sex in America: A definitive survey.* Boston: Little, Brown.

Michelson, D., Pollack, M., Lydiard, R. D., Tamura, R., Tepner, R., & Tollefson, G. (1999). Continuing treatment of panic disorder after acute responses: Randomized, placebo-controlled trail with fluoxetine. The Fluoxitine Panic Disorder Study Group. *British Journal of Psychiatry, 174,* 213–218.

Michotte, A. (1963). *The perception of causality.* New York: Basic Books.

Miklowitz, D. J., Goldstein, M. J., Nuechterlein, K. H., Snyder, K. S., & Mintz, J. (1988). Family factors and the course of bipolar affective disorder. *Archives of General Psychiatry, 45,* 225–231.

Milgram, S. (1963). Behavioral study of obedience. *Journal of Abnormal and Social Psychology, 67,* 371–378.

Milgram, S. (1974). *Obedience to authority.* New York: Harper & Row.

Milgram, S., Bickman, L., & Berkowitz, O. (1969). Note on the drawing power of crowds of different size. *Journal of Personality and Social Psychology, 13,* 79–82.

Milgram, S., & Toch, H. (1968). Collective behavior: Crowds and social movements. In G. Lindzey & E. Aronson (Eds.), *The handbook of social psychology* (2nd ed., Vol. 4, pp. 507–610). Reading, MA: Addison-Wesley.

Miller, A. J. (1986). *The obedience experiments: A case study of controversy in social science.* New York: Praeger.

Miller, D. T., & Prentice, D. A. (1996). The construction of social norms and standards. In E. T. Higgins, & A. W. Kruglanski (Ed.), *Social psychology: Handbook of basic principles* (pp. 799–829). New York: Guilford Press.

Miller, D. T., & Ratner, R. K. (1998). The disparity between the actual and assumed power of self-interest. *Journal of Personality and Social Psychology, 74,* 53–62.

Miller, G. A. (1956). The magical number seven, plus or minus two: Some limits on our capacity for processing information. *Psychological Review, 63,* 81–96.

Miller, J. (1994). On the internal structure of phonetic categories: A progress report. *Cognition, 50,* 271–285.

Miller, K. F., Smith, C. M., & Zhu, J. (1995). Preschool origins of cross-national differences in mathematical competence: The role of number-naming systems. *Psychological Science, 6,* 56–60.

Miller, N. E. (1960). Motivational effects of brain stimulation and drugs. *Federation Proceedings, 19,* 846–854.

Miller, N. E. (1978). Biofeedback and visceral learning. *Annual Review of Psychology, 29,* 373–404.

Miller, N. E., & Campbell, D. T. (1959). Recency and primacy in persuasion as a function of the timing of speeches and measurements. *Journal of Abnormal & Social Psychology, 59,* 1–9.

Miller, T. W. (Ed.). (1996). *Theory and assessment of stressful life events.* Madison, CT: International Universities Press.

Miller, W. R. (1978). Behavioral treatment of problem drinkers: A comparative outcome study of three controlled drinking therapies. *Journal of Consulting and Clinical Psychology, 46,* 74–86.

Mills, P. J., & Dimsdale, J. E. (1991). Cardiovascular reactivity to psychosocial stressors. A review of the effects of beta-blockade. *Psychosomatics, 32,* 209–220.

Milne, E., & Grafman, J. (2001). Ventromedial prefrontal cortex lesions in humans eliminate implicit gender stereotyping. *Journal of Neuroscience, 21,* 1–6.

Milner, A. D., & Goodale, M. A. (1995). *The visual brain in action.* Oxford, England: Oxford University Press.

Milner, B. (1962). Laterality effects in audition. In V. B. Mountcastle (Ed.), *Interhemispheric relations and cerebral dominance* (pp. 177–195). Baltimore: Johns Hopkins University Press.

Mineka, S., & Cook, M. (1988). Social learning and the acquisition of snake fear in monkeys. In T. Zentall & B. G. Galef, Jr. (Eds.), *Social learning* (pp. 51–73). Hillsdale, NJ: Erlbaum.

Mineka, S., & Ohman, A. (2002). Born to fear: Non-associative vs. associative factors in the etiology of phobia. *Behaviour Research and Therapy, 40,* 173–184.

Minsky, M. (1986). *The society of mind.* New York: Simon & Schuster.

Mischel, W. (1968). *Personality and assessment.* New York: Wiley.

Mischel, W., & Shoda, Y. (1999). Integrating dispositions and processing dynamics within a unified theory of personality: The Cognitive-Affective Personality System. In L. A. Pervin & O. P. John (Eds.), *Handbook of personality: Theory and research.* New York: Guilford Press.

Mischel, W., Shoda, Y., & Rodriguez, M. L. (1989). Delay of gratification in children. *Science, 244,* 933–938.

Mita, T. H., Dermer, M., & Knight, J. (1977). Reversed facial images and the mere-exposure hypothesis. *Journal of Personality and Social Psychology, 35,* 597–601.

Mitchell, J. P., Heatherton, T. F., & Macrae, C. N. (2002). Distinct neural systems subserve person and object knowledge. *Proceedings of the National Academy of Sciences (USA), 99,* 15238–15243.

Miura, I. T., Okamoto, Y., Kim, C. C., & Chang, C. M. (1994). Comparisons of children's cognitive representation of number: China, France, Japan, Korea, Sweden and the United States. *International Journal of Behavioral Development, 17,* 401–411.

Moffitt, T. E. (1993). Adolescence-limited and life-course-persistent antisocial behavior: A developmental taxonomy. *Psychological Review, 100,* 674–701.

Moghaddam, B., & Bunney, B. S. (1989). Differential effect of cocaine on extracellular dopamine levels in rat medial prefrontal cortex and nucleus accumbens: Comparison to amphetamine. *Synapse, 4,* 156–161.

Mokdad, A. H. P., Ford, E. S., Bowman, B. A., Dietz, W. H., Vinicor, F., Bales, V. S., et al. (2003). Prevalence of obesity, diabetes, and obesity-related health risk factors, 2001. *Journal of the American Medical Association, 289*(1), 76–79.

Monahan, J. L., Murphy, S. T., & Zajonc, R. B. (2000). Subliminal mere exposure: Specific, general, and diffuse effects. *Psychological Science, 11,* 462–466.

Mook, D. G. (1983). In defense of external invalidity. *American Psychologist, 38,* 379–387.

Mook, D. G. (1996). *Motivation.* New York: Norton.

Moore, K. L. (1977). *The developing human* (2nd ed.). Philadelphia: Saunders.

Moray, N. (1959). Attention in dichotic listening: Affective cues and the influence of instructions. *Quarterly Journal of Experimental Psychology, 11,* 56–60.

Morgan, H. (1990). Dostoevsky's epilepsy: A case report and comparison. *Surgical Neurology, 33,* 413–416.

Morgenstern, J., Labouvie, E., McCrady, B. S., Kahler, C. W., & Frey, R. M. (1997). Affiliation with Alcoholics Anonymous after treatment: A study of its therapeutic effects and mechanisms of action. *Journal of Consulting and Clinical Psychology, 65,* 768–777.

Morin, A. (2002). Right hemisphere self-awareness: A critical assessment. *Consciousness & Cognition, 11,* 396–401.

Morris, C. D., Bransford, J. D., & Franks, J. J. (1977). Levels of processing versus transfer-appropriate processing. *Journal of Verbal Learning and Verbal Behavior, 16,* 519–533.

Morris, R. G., Anderson, E., Lynch, G. S., & Baudry, M. (1986). Selective impairment of learning and blockade of long-term potentiation by an N-methyl-D-aspartate receptor antagonist, AP5. *Nature, 319,* 774–776.

Morris, T. L. (2001). Social phobia. In M. W. Vasey & M. R. Dadds (Eds.), *The developmental psychopathology of anxiety* (pp. 435–458). New York: Oxford University Press.

Morrow, D., Leirer, V., Altiteri, P., & Fitzsimmons, C. (1994). When expertise reduces age differences in performance. *Psychology and Aging, 9,* 134–148.

Moruzzi, G., & Magoun, H. W. (1949). Brain stem reticular formation and activation of the EEG. *Electroencephalography and Clinical Neurophysiology, 1,* 455–473.

Moscovitch, M. (1994). Memory and working-with-memory: Evaluation of a component process model and comparisons with other models. In D. L. Schacter & E. Tulving (Eds.), *Memory systems 1994* (pp. 269–310). Cambridge, MA: MIT Press.

Moscovitch, M., Nadel, L., Winocur, G., Gilboa, A., & Rosenbaum, R. S. (2006). The cognitive neuroscience of remote episodic, semantic and spatial memory. *Current Opinion in Neurobiology, 16,* 179–190.

Moss, D., McGrady, A., Davies, T., & Wickramasekera, I. (2002). *Handbook of mind-body medicine for primary care.* Newbury Park, CA: Sage.

Motley, M. T., & Baars, B. J. (1979). Effects of cognitive set upon laboratory induced verbal (Freudian) slips. *Journal of Speech & Hearing Research, 22,* 421–432.

Moyer, C. A., Rounds, J., & Hannum, J. W. (2004). A meta-analysis of massage therapy research. *Psychological Bulletin, 130,* 3–18.

Mroczek, D. K., & Spiro, A. (2005). Change in life satisfaction during adulthood: Findings from the Veterans Affairs Normative Aging Study. *Journal of Personality and Social Psychology, 88,* 189.

Mueller, E. T. (1990). *Daydreaming in humans and machines : A computer model of the stream of thought.* New York: Ablex.

Mueller, T. I., Leon, A. C., Keller, M. B., Solomon, D. A., Endicott, J., Coryell, W., et al. (1999). Recurrence after recovery from major depressive disorder during 15 years of observational follow-up. *American Journal of Psychiatry, 156,* 1000–1006.

Muenter, M. D., & Tyce, G. M. (1971). L-dopa therapy of Parkinson's disease: Plasma L-dopa concentration, therapeutic response, and side effects. *Mayo Clinic Proceedings, 46,* 231–239.

Mukherjee, S., Sackeim, H. A., & Schnur, D. B. (1994). Electroconvulsive therapy of acute manic episodes: a review of 50 years' experience. *American Journal of Psychiatry, 151,* 169–176.

Mullen, B. (1986). Atrocity as a function of lynch mob composition: A self-attention perspective. *Personality and Social Psychology Bulletin, 12,* 187–197.

Mullen, B., Chapman, J. G., & Peaugh, S. (1989). Focus of attention in groups: A self-attention perspective. *Journal of Social Psychology, 129,* 807–817.

Mullen, M. K. (1994). Earliest recollections of childhood: A demographic analysis. *Cognition, 52,* 55–79.

Muller, M. N., & Wrangham, R. W. (2004). Dominance, aggression and testosterone in wild chimpanzees: A test of the "challenge hypothesis." *Animal Behaviour, 67,* 113–123.

Multhaup, K. S., Johnson, M. D., & Tetirick, J. C. (2005). The wane of childhood amnesia for autobiographical and public event memories. *Memory, 13,* 161–173.

Mumford, D. B., Whitehouse, A. M., & Platts, M. (1991). Sociocultural correlates of eating disorders among Asian schoolgirls in Bradford. *British Journal of Psychiatry, 158,* 222–228.

Mumme, D. L., & Fernald, A. (2003). The infant as onlooker: Learning from emotional reactions observed in a television scenario. *Child Development, 74,* 221–237.

Murphy, N. A., Hall, J. A., & Colvin, C. R. (2003). Accurate intelligence assessments in social interactions: Mediators and gender effects. *Journal of Personality, 71,* 465–493.

Murray, C. J. L., & Lopez, A. D. (1996). *The global burden of disease: A comprehensive assessment of mortality and disability from diseases, injuries, and risk factors in 1990 and projected to 2020.* Cambridge, MA: Harvard School of Public Health.

Murray, H. A. (1938). *Explorations in personality.* New York: Oxford University Press.

Murray, H. A. (1943). *Thematic Apperception Test Manual.* Cambridge, MA: Harvard University Press.

Murray, H. A., & Kluckhohn, C. (1953). Outline of a conception of personality. In C. Kluckhohn, Murray, H. A., & Schneider, D. M. (Eds.), *Personality in nature, society, and culture* (2nd ed., pp. 3–52). New York: Knopf.

Myers, D. G., & Diener, E. (1995). Who is happy? *Psychological Science, 6,* 10–19.

Nadasdy, A. (1995). Phonetics, phonology, and applied linguistics. *Annual Review of Applied Linguistics, 15,* 68–77.

Nadel, L., & Zola-Morgan, S. (1984). Infantile amnesia: A neurobiological perspective. In M. Moscovitch (Ed.), *Infant memory* (pp. 145–172). New York: Plenum Press.

Nagasako, E. M., Oaklander, A. L., & Dworkin, R. H. (2003). Congenital insensitivity to pain: An update. *Pain, 101,* 213–219.

Nagel, T. (1974). What is it like to be a bat? *Philosophical Review, 83,* 433–450.

Nahemow, L., & Lawton, M. P. (1975). Similarity and propinquity in friendship formation. *Journal of Personality and Social Psychology, 32,* 205–213.

Nakazato, M., Murakami, N., Date, Y., Kojima, M., Matsuo, H., Kangawa, K., et al. (2001). A role for ghrelin in the central regulation of feeding. *Nature, 409,* 194–198.

Narrow, W. E., Rae, D. S., Robins, L. N., & Regier, D. A. (2002). Revised prevalence estimates of mental disorders in the United States: Using a clinical significance criterion to reconcile 2 surveys' estimates. *Archives of General Psychiatry, 59,* 115–123.

Nasar, S. (1998). *A beautiful mind.* New York: Simon & Schuster.

Nash, M. (1987). What, if anything, is regressed about hypnotic age regression? A review of the empirical literature. *Psychological Bulletin, 102,* 42–52.

Nasser, M. (1986). Comparative study of the prevalence of abnormal eating attitudes among Arab female students of both London and Cairo universities. *Psychological Medicine, 16,* 621–625.

Nathan, P. E., & Lagenbucher, J. W. (1999). Psychopathology: Description and classification. *Annual Review of Psychology, 50,* 79–107.

National Center for Health Statistics. (2001). *Health, United States.* Hyattsville, MD: National Center for Health Statistics.

National Center for Health Statistics. (2004). *Health, United States, 2004, with chartbook on trends in the health of Americans.* Hyattsville, MD: Author.

National Center for Injury Prevention and Control. (2001–2002). *Injury Fact Book.* Atlanta, GA: Centers for Disease Control and Prevention.

National Household Survey on Drug Abuse. (2001). Washington, DC: Substance Abuse and Mental Health Services Administration.

National Institute of Mental Health. (2003). In harm's way (NIH Publication No. 03-4594). Washington, DC: National Institutes of Health, U.S. Department of Health and Human Services.

National Research Council. (2003). *The polygraph and lie detection.* Washington, DC: National Academies Press.

Neilson, T. A., Deslauriers, D., & Baylor, G. W. (1991). Emotions in dream and waking event reports. *Dreaming, 1,* 287–300.

Neimeyer, R. A., & Mitchell, K. A. (1988). Similarity and attraction: A longitudinal study. *Journal of Social and Personal Relationships, 5,* 131–148.

Neisser, U. (1967). *Cognitive psychology.* New York: Appleton-Century-Crofts.

Neisser, U. (Ed.). (1998). *The rising curve: Long-term gains in IQ and related measures.* Washington, DC: American Psychological Association.

Neisser, U., & Becklen, R. (1975). Selective looking: Attending to visually significant events. *Cognitive Psychology, 7,* 480–494.

Neisser, U., Boodoo, G., Bouchard, T. J., Jr., Boykin, A. W., Brody, N., Ceci, S. J., et al. (1996). Intelligence: Knowns and unknowns. *American Psychologist, 51,* 77–101.

Neisser, U., & Harsch, N. (1992). Phantom flashbulbs: False recollections of hearing the news about Challenger. In E. Winograd & U. Neisser (Eds.), *Affect and accuracy in recall: Studies of "flashbulb memories"* (pp. 9–31). Cambridge, England: Cambridge University Press.

Neisser, U., & Hyman, I. E. (Eds.). (2000). *Memory observed: Remembering in natural contexts.* New York: Worth.

Nemeth, C., & Chiles, C. (1988). Modelling courage: The role of dissent in fostering independence. *European Journal of Social Psychology, 18,* 275–280.

Netherlands Ministry of Justice. (1999). *Fact Sheet: Dutch Drugs Policy.* Utrecht, Netherlands: Trimbos Institute, Netherlands Institute of Mental Health and Addiction.

Nettleback, T., & Lally, M. (1976). Inspection time and measured intelligence. *British Journal of Psychology, 67,* 17–22.

Neugebauer, R., Hoek, H. W., & Susser, E. (1999). Prenatal exposure to wartime famine and development of antisocial personality in early adulthood. *Journal of the American Medical Association, 282,* 455–462.

Newberg, A., Alavi, A., Baime, M., Pourdehnad, M., Santanna, J., & d'Aquili, E. (2001). The measurement of regional cerebral blood flow during the complex cognitive task of meditation: A preliminary SPECT study. *Psychiatry Research: Neuroimaging, 106,* 113–122.

Newell, A., Shaw, J. C., & Simon, H. A. (1958). Elements of a theory of human problem solving. *Psychological Review, 65,* 151–166.

Newman, A. J., Bavelier, D., Corina, D., Jezzard, P., & Neville, H. J. (2002). A critical period for right hemisphere recruitment in American Sign Language processing. *Nature Neuroscience, 5,* 76–80.

Newman, L. S., Baumeister, R. F., & Duff, K. J. (1995). A new look at defensive projection: Thought suppression, accessibility, and biased person perception, *Journal of Personality and Social Psychology, 72,* 980–1001.

Newman, M. G., & Stone, A. A. (1996). Does humor moderate the effects of experimentally induced stress? *Annals of Behavioral Medicine, 18,* 101–109.

Newsome, W. T., & Paré, E. B. (1988). A selective impairment of motion perception following lesions of the middle temporal visual area (MT). *Journal of Neuroscience, 8,* 2201–2211.

Neylan, T. C., Metzler, T. J., Best, S. R., Weiss, D. S., Fagan, J. A., Libermans, A., et al. (2002). Critical incident exposure and sleep quality in police officers. *Psychosomatic Medicine, 64,* 345–352.

Niaura, R., Todaro, J. F., Stroud, L., Spiro III, A., Ward, K. D., Weiss, S., et al. (2002). Hostility, the metabolic syndrome, and incident coronary heart disease. *Health Psychology, 21,* 588–593.

NICHD Early Child Care Research Network. (1997). The effects of infant child care on infant-mother attachment security: Results of the NICHD study of early child care. *Child Development, 68,* 860–879.

NICHD Early Child Care Research Network. (1999). Child care and mother-infant interaction in the first three years of life. *Developmental Psychology, 35,* 1399–1413.

NICHD Early Child Care Research Network. (2002). Child-care structure to process to outcome: Direct and indirect effects of child-care quality on young children's development. *Psychological Science, 13,* 199–206.

Nicoladis, E., & Genesee, F. (1997). Language development in preschool bilingual children. *Journal of Speech-Language Pathology & Audiology, 21,* 258–270.

Nicolelis, M. A. L. (2001). Actions from thoughts. *Nature, 409,* 403–407.

Nikles, C. D., II, Brecht, D. L., Klinger, E., & Bursell, A. L. (1998). The effects of current concern- and nonconcern-related waking suggestions on nocturnal dream content. *Journal of Personality and Social Psychology, 75,* 242–255.

Nikula, R., Klinger, E., & Larson-Gutman, M. K. (1993). Current concerns and electrodermal reactivity: Responses to words and thoughts. *Journal of Personality, 61,* 63–84.

Ninan, P. T. (1999). The functional anatomy, neurochemistry, and pharmacology of anxiety. *Journal of Clinical Psychiatry, 60,* 12–17.

Nisbett, R. E., Caputo, C., Legant, P., & Maracek, J. (1973). Behavior as seen by the actor and as seen by the observer. *Journal of Personality and Social Psychology, 27,* 154–164.

Nisbett, R. E., & Cohen, D. (1996). *Culture of honor: The psychology of violence in the south.* Boulder, CO: Westview Press.

Nisbett, R. E., & Wilson, T. D. (1977). Telling more than we can know: Verbal reports on mental processes. *Psychological Review, 84,* 231–259.

Nishino, S., Mignot, E., & Dement, W. C. (1995). Sedative-hypnotics. In A. F. Schatzberg & C. B. Nemeroff (Eds.), *American Psychiatric Press textbook of psychopharmacology.* (pp. 405–416). Washington, DC: American Psychiatric Press.

Nissen, M. J., & Bullemer, P. (1987). Attentional requirements of learning: Evidence from performance measures. *Cognitive Psychology, 19,* 1–32.

Nolen-Hoeksema, S. (1987). Sex differences in unipolar depression: Evidence and theory. *Psychological Bulletin, 101,* 259–282.

Nolen-Hoeksema, S. (1990). *Sex differences in depression.* Stanford: Stanford University Press.

Norcross, J. C., Hedges, M., & Castle, P. H. (2002). Psychologists conducting psychotherapy in 2001: A study of the Division 29 membership. *Psychotherapy: Theory/Research/Practice/Training, 39,* 97–102.

Norton, A. J. (1987). Families and children in the year 2000. *Children Today,* July–August, 6–9.

Norton, G. R., Harrison, B., Hauch, J., & Rhodes, L. (1985). Characteristics of people with infrequent panic attacks. *Journal of Abnormal Psychology, 94,* 216–221.

Nosanchuk, T. A., & Lightstone, J. (1974). Canned laughter and public and private conformity. *Journal of Personality & Social Psychology, 29,* 153–156.

Novaco, R. W. (1977). Stress inoculation: A cognitive therapy for anger. *Journal of Consulting & Clinical Psychology, 45,* 600–608.

Nunn, J. A., Gregory, L. J., & Brammer, M. (2002). Functional magnetic resonance imaging of synesthesia: Activation of V4/V8 by spoken words. *Nature Neuroscience, 5,* 371–375.

Nuttin, J. M. (1985). Narcissism beyond Gestalt and awareness: The name letter effect. *European Journal of Social Psychology, 15,* 353–361.

Nyberg, L., McIntosh, A. R., Houle, S., Nilsson, L.-G., & Tulving, E. (1996). Activation of medial temporal structures during episodic memory retrieval. *Nature, 380,* 715–717.

O'Connor, T. G., & Ruter, M. (2000). Attachment disorder following early severe deprivation: Extension and longitudinal follow-up. *Journal of the American Academy of Child and Adolescent Psychiatry, 39,* 703–712.

O'Laughlin, M. J., & Malle, B. F. (2002). How people explain actions performed by groups and individuals. *Journal of Personality and Social Psychology, 82,* 33–48.

O'Sullivan, L. F., & Allegeier, E. R. (1998). Feigning sexual desire: Consenting to unwanted sexual activity in heterosexual dating relationships. *Journal of Sex Research, 35,* 234–243.

Oakes, L. M., & Cohen, L. B. (1990). Infant perception of a causal event. *Cognitive Development, 5,* 193–207.

Oately, K., Keltner, D., & Jenkins, J. M. (2006). *Understanding emotions* (2nd ed.). Malden, MA: Blackwell.

Ochsner, K. N. (2000). Are affective events richly recollected or simply familiar? The experience and process of recognizing feelings past. *Journal of Experimental Psychology: General, 129,* 242–261.

Ochsner, K. N., Bunge, S. A., Gross, J. J., & Gabrieli, J. D. E. (2002). Rethinking feelings: An fMRI study of the cognitive regulation of emotion. *Journal of Cognitive Neuroscience, 14,* 1215–1229.

Office of the Press Secretary. (2002, July 21). Homeland Security presidential directive 3. Retrieved August 2007 from http://www.whitehouse.gov/news/releases/2002/03/20020312-5.html

Ofshe, R. J. (1992). Inadvertent hypnosis during interrogation: False confession due to dissociative state, misidentified multiple personality, and the satanic cult hypothesis. *International Journal of Clinical and Experimental Hypnosis, 40,* 125–126.

Ofshe, R., & Watters, E. (1994). *Making monsters: False memories, psychotherapy, and sexual hysteria.* New York: Scribner/Macmillan.

Öhman, A., & Dimberg, U. (1978). Facial expressions as conditioned stimuli for electrodermal responses: A case of preparedness? *Journal of Personality and Social Psychology, 36,* 1251–1258.

Öhman, A., Dimberg, U., & Öst, L. G. (1985). Animal and social phobias: Biological constraints on learned fear responses. In S. Reiss & R. Bootzin (Eds.), *Theoretical issues in behavior therapy* (pp. 123–175). New York: Academic Press.

Öhman, A., & Mineka, S. (2001). Fears, phobias, and preparedness: Toward an evolved model of fear and fear learning. *Psychological Review, 108,* 483–522.

Okagaki, L., & Sternberg, R. J. (1993). Parental beliefs and children's school performance. *Child Development, 64,* 36–56.

Olausson, P. O., Haglund, B., Weitoft, G. R., & Cnattingius, S. (2001). Teenage child-bearing and long-term socioeconomic consequences: A case study in Sweden. *Family Planning Perspectives, 33,* 70–74.

Oldham, J. M., Skodol, A. E., & Bender, D. S. (2005). *The American Psychiatric Publishing textbook of personality disorders.* Washington, DC: American Psychiatric Publishing.

Olds, J. (1956, October). Pleasure center in the brain. *Scientific American, 195,* 105–116.

Olds, J., & Fobes, J. I. (1981). The central basis of motivation: Intracranial self-stimulation studies. *Annual Review of Psychology, 32,* 523–574.

Olds, J., & Milner, P. (1954). Positive reinforcement produced by electrical stimulation of septal areas and other regions of rat brains. *Journal of Comparative and Physiological Psychology, 47,* 419–427.

Ollers, D. K., & Eilers, R. E. (1988). The role of audition in infant babbling. *Child Development, 59,* 441–449.

Oltmanns, T. F., Neale, J. M., & Davison, G. C. (1991). *Case studies in abnormal psychology* (3rd ed.). New York: Wiley.

Oltmanns, T. F., & Turkheimer, E. (2006). Perceptions of self and others regarding pathological personality traits. In R. Kreuger & J. Tackett (Eds.), *Personality and psychopathology* (pp. 71–111). New York: Guilford Press.

Olton, D. S., & Samuelson, R. J. (1976). Remembrance of places passed: Spatial memory in rats. *Journal of Experimental Psychology: Animal Behavior Processes, 2,* 97–116.

Orban, G. A., Van Essen, D., & Vanduffel, W. (2004). Comparative mapping of higher visual areas in monkeys and humans. *Trends in Cognitive Sciences, 8,* 315–324.

Orne, M. T., & Evans, F. J. (1965). Social control in the psychological experiment: Antisocial behavior and hypnosis. *Journal of Personality and Social Psychology, 1,* 189–200.

Öst, L.-G., Lindahl, I.-L., Sterner, U., & Jerremalm, A. (1984). Exposure in vivo vs. applied relaxation in the treatment of blood phobia. *Behaviour Research and Therapy, 22,* 205–216.

Oswald, L., Taylor, A. M., & Triesman, M. (1960). Discriminative responses to stimulation during human sleep. *Brain, 83,* 440–453.

Owen, A. M., Coleman, M. R., Boly, M., Davis, M. H., Laureys, S., & Pickard, J. D. (2006). Detecting awareness in the vegetative state. *Science, 313,* 1402.

Owens, W. A. (1966). Age and mental abilities: A second adult follow-up. *Journal of Educational Psychology, 57,* 311–325.

Paivio, A. (1969). Mental imagery in associative learning and memory. *Psychological Review, 76,* 241–263.

Paivio, A. (1971). *Imagery and verbal processes.* New York: Holt, Reinhart and Winston.

Paivio, A. (1986). *Mental representations: A dual coding approach.* New York: Oxford University Press.

Palmieri, R. M., Ingersoll, C. D., & Stone, M. B. (2002). Center-of-pressure parameters used in the assessment of postural control. *Journal of Sport Rehabilitation, 11,* 51–66.

Pande, A. C., Davidson, J. R. T., Jefferson, J. W., Janney, C. A., Katzelnick, D. J., Weisler, R. H., et al. (1999). Treatment of social phobia with gabapentin: A placebo-controlled study. *Journal of Clinical Psychopharmacology, 19,* 341–348.

Pande, A. C., Pollack, M. H., Crockatt, J., Greiner, M., Chouinard, G., R. Bruce Lydiard, R., et al. (2000). Placebo-controlled study of gabapentin treatment of panic disorder. *Journal of Clinical Psychopharmacology, 20,* 467–471.

Papez, J. W. (1937). A proposed mechanism of emotion. *Archives of Neurology and Pathology, 38,* 725–743.

Parkinson, B., & Totterdell, P. (1999). Classifying affect-regulation strategies. *Cognition and Emotion, 13,* 277–303.

Parrott, A. C. (2001). Human psychopharmacology of Ecstasy (MDMA): A review of 15 years of empirical research. *Human Psychopharmacology, 16,* 557–577.

Parrott, A. C., Morinan, A., Moss, M., & Scholey, A. (2004). *Understanding drugs and behavior.* Chichester, England: Wiley.

Parrott, W. G. (1993). Beyond hedonism: Motives for inhibiting good moods and for maintaining bad moods. In D. M. Wegner & J. W. Pennebaker (Eds.), *Handbook of mental control* (pp. 278–308). Englewood Cliffs, NJ: Prentice Hall.

Parsons, T. (1951). *The social system.* Glencoe, IL: Free Press.

Partinen, M. (1994). Epidemiology of sleep disorders. In M. H. Kryger, T. Roth, & W. C. Dement (Eds.), *Principles and practice of sleep medicine* (2nd ed.). Philadelphia: Saunders.

Pasqual-Leone, A., Amedi, A., Fregni, F., & Merabet, L. B. (2005). The plastic human brain cortex. *Annual Review of Neuroscience, 28,* 377–401.

Pascual-Leone, A., Houser, C. M., Reese, K., Shotland, L. I., Grafman, J., Sato, S., et al. (1993). Safety of rapid-rate transcranial magnetic stimulation in normal volunteers. *Electroencephalography and Clinical Neurophysiology, 89,* 120–130.

Passini, F. T., & Norman, W. T. (1966). A universal conception of personality structure? *Journal of Personality and Social Psychology, 4,* 44–49.

Patrick, C. J., Cuthbert, B. N., & Lang, P. J. (1994). Emotion in the criminal psychopath: Fear image processing. *Journal of Abnormal Psychology, 103,* 523–534.

Patterson, C. J. (1995). Lesbian mothers, gay fathers, and their children. In A. R. D'Augelli & C. J. Patterson (Eds.), *Lesbian, gay and bisexual identities across the lifespan: Psychological perspectives* (pp. 262–290). New York: Oxford University Press.

Paul, A. M. (2004). *The cult of personality testing.* New York: Free Press.

Pavlidis, I., Eberhardt, N. L., & Levine, J. A. (2002). Human behaviour: Seeing through the face of deception. *Nature, 415,* 35.

Pavlov, I. P. (1923a). New researches on conditioned reflexes. *Science, 58,* 359–361.

Pavlov, I. P. (1923b, July 23). Pavloff. *Time, 1*(21), 20–21.

Pavlov, I. P. (1927). *Conditioned reflexes.* Oxford, England: Oxford University Press.

Pawlowski, B., Dunbar, R. I. M., & Lipowicz, A. (2000). Tall men have more reproductive success. *Nature, 362,* 156.

Pearce, J. M. (1987). A model of stimulus generalization for Pavlovian conditioning. *Psychological Review, 84,* 61–73.

Peissig, J. J., & Tarr, M. J. (2007). Visual object recognition: Do we know more now than we did 20 years ago? *Annual Review of Psychology, 58,* 75–96.

Pelham, B. W. (1985). Self-investment and self-esteem: Evidence for a Jamesian model of self-worth. *Journal of Personality and Social Psychology, 69,* 1141–1150.

Pelham, B. W., & Blanton, H. (2003). *Conducting research in psychology: Measuring the weight of smoke* (2nd ed.). Pacific Grove, CA: Thomson Wadsworth.

Pelham, B. W., Carvallo, M., & Jones, J. T. (2005). Implicit egotism. *Current Directions in Psychological Science, 14,* 106–110.

Pelham, B. W., Mirenberg, M. C., & Jones, J. T. (2002). Why Susie sells seashells by the seashore: Implicit egotism and major life decisions. *Journal of Personality and Social Psychology, 82,* 469–487.

Pendergrast, M. (1995). *Victims of memory: Incest accusations and shattered lives.* Hinesburg, VT: Upper Access.

Penfield, W., & Rasmussen, T. (1950). *The cerebral cortex of man: A clinical study of localization of function.* New York: Macmillan.

Pennebaker, J. W. (1980). Perceptual and environmental determinants of coughing. *Basic and Applied Social Psychology, 1,* 83–91.

Pennebaker, J. W. (1982). *The psychology of physical symptoms.* New York: Springer.

Pennebaker, J. W. (1989). Confession, inhibition, and disease. *Advances in Experimental Social Psychology, 22,* 211–244.

Pennebaker, J. W. (1990). *Opening up: The healing power of confiding in others.* New York: Morrow.

Pennebaker, J. W., & Beall, S. K. (1986). Confronting a traumatic event: Toward an understanding of inhibition and disease. *Journal of Abnormal Psychology, 95,* 274–281.

Pennebaker, J. W., Colder, M., & Sharp, L. K. (1990). Accelerating the coping process. *Journal of Personality and Social Psychology, 58,* 528–537.

Pennebaker, J. W., Dyer, M. A., Caulkins, R. S., Litowitz, D. L., Ackreman, P. L., Anderson, D. B., et al. (1979). Don't the girls get prettier at closing time: A country and western application to psychology. *Personality and Social Psychology Bulletin, 5,* 122–125.

Pennebaker, J. W., Kiecolt-Glaser, J. K., & Glaser, R. (1988). Disclosure of traumas and immune function: Health implications for psychotherapy. *Journal of Consulting and Clinical Psychology, 56,* 239–245.

Pennebaker, J. W., & Lightner, J. M. (1980). Competition of internal and external information in an exercise setting. *Journal of Personality and Social Psychology, 39,* 165–174.

Pennebaker, J. W., & Sanders, D. Y. (1976). American graffiti: Effects of authority and reactance arousal. *Personality and Social Psychology Bulletin, 2,* 264–267.

Perenin, M.-T., & Vighetto, A. (1988). Optic ataxia: A specific disruption in visuomotor mechanisms. I. Different aspects of the deficit in reaching for objects. *Brain, 111,* 643–674.

Perina, K. (2002, May–June). Rx without the M.D. *Psychology Today, 46.*

Perkins, D. N., & Grotzer, T. A. (1997). Teaching intelligence. *American Psychologist, 52,* 1125–1133.

Perloff, L. S., & Fetzer, B. K. (1986). Self-other judgments and perceived vulnerability to victimization. *Journal of Personality and Social Psychology, 50,* 502–510.

Perls, F. S., Hefferkine, R., & Goodman, P. (1951). *Gestalt therapy: Excitement and growth in the human personality.* New York: Julian Press.

Perrett, D. I., Burt, D. M., Penton-Voak, I. S., Lee, K. J., Rowland, D. A., & Edwards, R. (1999). Symmetry and human facial attractiveness. *Evolution and Human Behavior, 20,* 295–307.

Perrett, D. I., Rolls, E. T., & Caan, W. (1982). Visual neurons responsive to faces in the monkey temporal cortex. *Experimental Brain Research, 47,* 329–342.

Perris, C. (1992). *Bipolar-unipolar distinction* (2nd ed.). New York: Guilford Press.

Persons, J. B. (1986). The advantages of studying psychological phenomena rather than psychiatric diagnoses. *American Psychologist, 41,* 1252–1260.

Peskin, H. (1973). Influence of the developmental schedule of puberty on learning and ego functioning. *Journal of Youth and Adolescence, 2,* 273–290.

Peters, E. R., Joseph, S. A., & Garety, P. A. (1999). Measurement of delusional ideation in the normal population: Introducing the PDI (Peters et al. Delusions Inventory). *Schizophrenia Bulletin, 25,* 553–576.

Petersen, A. C. (1985). Pubertal development as a cause of disturbance—Myths, realities, and unanswered questions. *Genetic Social and General Psychology Monographs, 111,* 205–232.

Petersen, A. C., & Grockett, L. (1985). Pubertal timing and grade effects on adjustment. *Journal of Youth and Adolescence, 14,* 191–206.

Peterson, C., & Seligman, M. E. P. (2004). *Character strengths and virtues: A handbook and classification.* Washington, DC: American Psychological Association.

Peterson, C., & Siegal, M. (1999). Representing inner worlds: Theory of mind in autistic, deaf and normal hearing children. *Psychological Science, 10,* 126–129.

Peterson, L. R., & Peterson, M. J. (1959). Short-term retention of individual verbal items. *Journal of Experimental Psychology, 58,* 193–198.

Peterson, S. E., Fox, P. T., Posner, M. I., Mintun, M. A., & Raichle, M. E. (1989). Positron emission tomographic studies of the processing of single words. *Journal of Cognitive Neuroscience, 1,* 154–170.

Petitto, L. A., & Marentette, P. F. (1991). Babbling in the manual mode: Evidence for the ontogeny of language. *Science, 251,* 1493–1496.

Petrie, K. P., Booth, R. J., & Pennebaker, J. W. (1998). The immunological effects of thought suppression. *Journal of Personality and Social Psychology, 75,* 1264–1272.

Petty, R. E., & Cacioppo, J. T. (1986). The elaboration likelihood model of persuasion. In L. Berkowitz (Ed.), *Advances in experimental social psychology* (Vol. 19, pp. 123–205). New York: Academic Press.

Petty, R. E., Cacioppo, J. T., & Goldman, R. (1981). Personal involvement as a determinant of argument-based persuasion. *Journal of Personality & Social Psychology, 41,* 847–855.

Petty, R. E., & Wegener, D. T. (1998). Attitude change: Multiple roles for persuasion variables. In D. T. Gilbert, S. T. Fiske, & G. Lindzey (Eds.), *The handbook of social psychology* (4th ed., Vol. 1, pp. 323–390). Boston: McGraw-Hill.

Pew Research Center for the People & the Press. (1997). *Motherhood today: A tougher job, less ably done.* Pew Research Center: Author.

Pew Research Center for the People & the Press. (2006). *Attitudes toward homosexuality in African countries.* Pew Research Center: Author.

Phelan, J., Link, B., Stueve, A., & Pescosolido, B. (1997). *Public conceptions of mental illness in 1950 in 1996: Has sophistication increased? Has stigma declined?* Paper presented at the American Sociological Association, Toronto, Ontario.

Phelan, J., Link, B., Stueve, A., & Pescosolido, B. (2000). Public conceptions of mental illness in 1950 and 1996: What is mental illness and is it to be feared? *Journal of Health and Social Behavior, 41,* 188–207.

Phelps, E. A. (2006). Emotion and cognition: Insights from studies of the human amygdala. *Annual Review of Psychology, 24,* 27–53.

Phelps, E. A., & LeDoux, J. L. (2005). Contributions of the amygdala to emotion processing: From animal models to human behavior. *Neuron, 48,* 175–187.

Phelps, E. A., O'Connor, K. J., Cunningham, W. A., Funayama, E. S., Gatenby, J. C., Gore, J. C., et al. (2000). Performance on indirect measures of race evaluation predicts amygdala activation. *Journal of Cognitive Neuroscience, 12,* 729–738.

Phillips, D. P., & Carstensen, L. L. (1986). Clustering of teenage suicides after television news stories about suicide. *New England Journal of Medicine, 315,* 685–689.

Phillips, F. (2002, January 24). Jump in cigarette sales tied to Sept. 11 attacks. *Boston Globe,* p. B1.

Piaf, E. (1990). *My life.* London: Peter Owen.

Piaget, J. (1954a). *The construction of reality in the child.* New York: Basic Books.

Piaget, J. (1954b). *The child's concept of number.* New York: Norton.

Piaget, J. (1965). *The moral judgment of the child.* New York: Free Press. (Originally published 1932)

Piaget, J. (1977). The first year of life of the child. In H. E. Gruber & J. J. Voneche (Eds.), *The essential Piaget: An interpretative reference and guide* (pp. 198–214). New York: Basic Books. (Originally published 1927)

Piaget, J., & Inhelder, B. (1969). *The psychology of the child* (H. Weaver, Trans.). New York: Basic Books.

Pinel, J. P. J., Assanand, S., & Lehman, D. R. (2000). Hunger, eating, and ill health. *American Psychologist, 55,* 1105–1116.

Pines, A. M. (1993). Burnout: An existential perspective. In W. B. Schaufeli, C. Maslach & T. Marek (Eds.), *Professional burnout: Recent developments in theory and research* (pp. 33–51). Washington, DC: Taylor & Francis.

Pines, A., M., & Aronson, E. (1988). *Career burnout: Causes and cures* (2nd ed.). New York: Free Press.

Pinker, S. (1994). *The language instinct.* New York: Morrow.

Pinker, S. (1997a). *How the mind works.* New York: Norton.

Pinker, S. (1997b). Evolutionary psychology: An exchange. *New York Review of Books, 44,* 55–58.

Pinker, S., & Bloom, P. (1990). Natural language and natural selection. *Behavioral & Brain Sciences, 13,* 707–784.

Pipes, D. (2002, October 29). The snipers: Crazy or jihadis? *New York Post.* Retrieved September 15, 2007, from http://www.danielpipes.org/article/493

Pitman, R. K., Sanders, K. M., Zusman, R. M., Healy, A. R., Cheema, F., Lasko, N. B., Cahill, L., et al. (2002). Pilot study of secondary prevention of posttraumatic stress disorder with propranolol. *Biological Psychiatry, 51,* 189–192.

Plato. (1956). *Protagoras* (O. Jowett, Trans.). New York: Prentice Hall.

Plomin, R., & Caspi, A. (1999). Behavioral genetics and personality. In L. A. Pervin & O. P. John (Eds.), *Handbook of personality: Theory and research* (Vol. 2, pp. 251–276). New York: Guilford Press.

Plomin, R., De Fries, J. C., McClearn, G. E., & Rutter, M. (1997). *Behavior genetics* (3rd ed.). New York: Freeman.

Plomin, R., DeFries, J. C., McClearn, G. E., & McGuffin, P. (2001a). *Behavioral genetics.* (4th ed.). New York: Freeman.

Plomin, R., Hill, L., Craig, I. W., McGuffin, P., Purcell, S., Sham, P., et al. (2001b). A genome-wide scan of 1842 DNA markers for allelic associations with general cognitive ability: A five-stage design using DNA pooling and extreme selected groups. *Behavior Genetics, 31,* 497–509.

Plomin, R., Scheier, M. F., Bergeman, C. S., Pedersen, N. L., Nesselroade, J. R., & McClearn, G. E. (1992). Optimism, pessimism, and mental health: A twin/adoption analysis. *Personality and Individual Differences, 13,* 921–930.

Plomin, R., & Spinath, F. M. (2004). Intelligence: Genetics, genes, and genomics. *Journal of Personality and Social Psychology, 86,* 112–129.

Plotnik, J. M., de Waal, F. B. M., & Reiss, D. (2006). Self-recognition in an Asian elephant. *Proceedings of the National Academy of Science, 103,* 17053–17057.

Polivy, J., & Herman, C. P. (1992). Undieting: A program to help people stop dieting. *International Journal of Eating Disorders, 11,* 261–268.

Poole, D. A., Lindsay, S. D., Memon, A., & Bull, R. (1995). Psychotherapy and the recovery of memories of childhood sexual abuse: U.S. and British practitioners' opinions, practices, and experiences. *Journal of Consulting and Clinical Psychology, 63,* 426–487.

Pope, A. W., & Bierman, K. L. (1999). Predicting adolescent peer problems and antisocial activities: The relative roles of aggression and dysregulation. *Developmental Psychology, 35,* 335–346.

Posey, T. B., & Losch, M. E. (1983). Auditory hallucinations of hearing voices in 375 normal subjects. *Imagination, Cognition and Personality, 3,* 99–113.

Posner, M. I., & Raichle, M. E. (1994). *Images of mind.* New York: Freeman.

Post, R. M. (2004). Differing psychotropic profiles of the anticonvulsants in bipolar and other psychiatric disorders. *Clinical Neuroscience Research, 4,* 9–30.

Posthuma, D., & de Geus, E. J. C. (2006). Progress in the molecular-genetic study of intelligence. *Current Directions in Psychological Science, 15,* 151–155.

Postman, L., & Underwood, B. J. (1973). Critical issues in interference theory. *Memory & Cognition, 1,* 19–40.

Prasada, S., & Pinker, S. (1993). Generalizations of regular and irregular morphology. *Language and Cognitive Processes, 8,* 1–56.

Pratkanis, A. R. (1992). The cargo-cult science of subliminal persuasion. *Skeptical Inquirer, 16,* 260–272.

Pratkanis, A. R., Greenwald, A. G., Leippe, M. R., & Baumgardner, M. H. (1988). In search of reliable persuasion effects: III. The sleeper effect is dead: Long live the sleeper effect. *Journal of Personality and Social Psychology, 54,* 203–218.

Premack, D. (1962). Reversibility of the reinforcement relation. *Science, 136,* 255–257.

Pressman, S. D., Cohen, S., Miller, G. E., Barkin, A., Rabin, B. S., & Treanor, J. J. (2005). Loneliness, social network size, and immune response to influenza vaccination in college freshmen. *Health Psychology, 24,* 297–306.

Prochaska, J. J., & Sallis, J. F. (2004). A randomized controlled trial of single versus multiple health behavior change: Promoting physical activity and nutrition among adolescents. *Health Psychology, 23,* 314–318.

Provine, R. R. (2000). *Laughter: A scientific investigation.* New York: Viking.

Prudic, J., Haskett, R. F., Mulsant, B., Malone, K. M., Pettinati, H. M., Stephens, S., et al. (1996). Resistance to antidepressant medications and short-term clinical response to ECT. *American Journal of Psychiatry, 153,* 985–992.

Pruitt, D. G. (1998). Social conflict. In D. T. Gilbert, S. T. Fiske, & G. Lindzey (Eds.), *The handbook of social psychology* (4th ed., Vol. 2, pp. 470–503). New York: McGraw-Hill.

Putnam, F. W., Guroff, J. J., Silberman, E. K., Barban, L., & Post, R. M. (1986). The clinical phenomenology of multiple personality disorder: Review of 100 recent cases. *Journal of Clinical Psychiatry, 47,* 285–293.

Pyszczynski, T., Holt, J., & Greenberg, J. (1987). Depression, self-focused attention, and expectancy for positive and negative future life events for self and others. *Journal of Personality and Social Psychology, 52,* 994–1001.

Pyszczynski, T., Solomon, S., & Greenberg, J. (2003). *In the wake of 9/11: The psychology of terror.* Washington, DC: American Psychological Association.

Quattrone, G. A. (1982). Behavioral consequences of attributional bias. *Social Cognition, 1,* 358–378.

Quattrone, G. A., & Jones, E. E. (1980). The perception of variability within in-groups and out-groups: Implications for the law of small numbers. *Journal of Personality and Social Psychology, 38,* 141–152.

Querleu, D., Lefebvre, C., Titran, M., Renard, X., Morillon, M., & Crepin, G. (1984). Reactivite de bouveau-ne de moins de deux heures de vie a la voix maternelle. *Journal de Gynecologie Obstetrique et de Biologie de la Reproduction, 13,* 125–134.

Quiroga, R. Q., Reddy, L., Kreiman, G., Koch, C., & Fried, I. (2005). Invariant visual representation by single neurons in the human brain. *Nature, 435,* 1102–1107.

Rabin, B. M., & Rabin, J. S. (1984) Acquisition of radiation- and lithium chloride-induced conditioned taste aversions in anesthetized rats. *Animal Learning & Behavior, 12,* 439–441.

Rachman, S. J., & DeSilva, P. (1978). Abnormal and normal obsessions. *Behavioral Research and Therapy, 16,* 223–248.

Radford, E., & Radford, M. A. (1949). *Encyclopedia of superstitions.* New York: Philosophical Library.

Rahe, R. H., Meyer, M., Smith, M., Klaer, G., & Holmes, T. H. (1964). Social stress and illness onset. *Journal of Psychosomatic Research, 8,* 35–44.

Raichle, M. E., Fiez, J. A., Videen, T. O., MacLeod, A.-M. K., Pardo, J. V., Fox, P. T., et al. (1994). Practice-related changes in human brain functional anatomy during nonmotor learning. *Cerebral Cortex, 4,* 8–26.

Raichle, M. E., & Mintun, M. A. (2006). Brain work and brain imaging. *Annual Review of Neuroscience, 29,* 449–476.

Ramachandran, V. S., & Blakeslee, S. (1998). *Phantoms in the brain: Probing the mysteries of the human mind.* New York: Morrow.

Ramachandran, V. S., & Hubbard, E. M. (2003). Hearing colors, tasting shapes. *Scientific American, 288,* 52–59.

Ramachandran, V. S., Rodgers-Ramachandran, D., & Stewart, M. (1992). Perceptual correlates of massive cortical reorganization. *Science, 258,* 1159–1160.

Rapaport, D. (1946). *Diagnostic Psychological Testing: The theory, statistical evaluation, and diagnostic application of a battery of tests.* Chicago: Year Book Publishers.

Rapoport, J. (1989). *The boy who couldn't stop washing: The experience and treatment of obsessive-compulsive disorder.* New York: Penguin.

Rapport, R. (2005). *Nerve endings: The discovery of the synapse.* New York: Norton.

Raskin, N. J., & Rogers, C. R. (2000). Person-centered therapy. In R. J. Corsini & D. Wedding (Eds.), *Current psychotherapies* (6th ed., pp. 133–167). Itasca, IL: F. E. Peacock, Publishers.

Raz, N. (2000). Aging of the brain and its impact on cognitive performance: Integration of structural and functional findings. In F. I. M. Craik & T. A. Salthouse (Eds.), *The handbook of aging and cognition* (pp. 1–90). Mahwah, NJ: Erlbaum.

Read, K. E. (1965). *The high valley.* London: Allen and Unwin.

Reason, J., & Mycielska, K. (1982). *Absent-minded?: The psychology of mental lapses and everyday errors.* Englewood Cliffs: Prentice-Hall.

Reber, A. S. (1967). Implicit learning of artificial grammars. *Journal of Verbal Learning and Verbal Behavior, 6,* 855–863.

Reber, A. S. (1996). *Implicit learning and tacit knowledge: An essay on the cognitive unconscious.* New York: Oxford University Press.

Reber, A. S., & Allen, R. (2000). Individual differences in implicit learning. In R. G. Kunzendorf & B. Wallace (Eds.), *Individual differences in conscious experience.* Philadelphia: John Benjamins.

Reber, A. S., Walkenfeld, F. F., & Hernstadt, R. (1991). Implicit learning: Individual differences and IQ. *Journal of Experimental Psychology: Learning, Memory, and Cognition, 17,* 888–896.

Reber, P. J., Gitelman, D. R., Parrish, T. B., & Mesulam, M. M. (2003). Dissociating explicit and implicit category knowledge with fMRI. *Journal of Cognitive Neuroscience, 15,* 574–583.

Rechsthaffen, A., Gilliland, M. A., Bergmann, B. M., & Winter, J. B. (1983). Physiological correlates of prolonged sleep deprivation in rats. *Science, 221,* 182–184.

Reed, G. (1988). *The psychology of anomalous experience* (Rev. ed.). Buffalo, NY: Prometheus Books.

Regan, P. C. (1998). What if you can't get what you want? Willingness to compromise ideal mate selection standards as a function of sex, mate value, and relationship context. *Personality and Social Psychology Bulletin, 24,* 1294–1303.

Regier, D. A., Narrow, W. E., Rae, D. S., Manderscheid, R. W., Locke, B. Z., & Goodwin, F. K. (1993). The de facto US mental and addictive disorders service system: Epidemiologic Catchment Area prospective 1-year prevalence rates of disorders and services. *Archives of General Psychiatry, 41,* 934–941.

Reichhardt, T. (2003). Playing with fire? *Nature, 424,* 367–368.

Reinarman, C., Cohen, P. D. A., & Kaal, H. L. (2004). The limited relevance of drug policy: Cannabis in Amsterdam and San Francisco. *American Journal of Public Health, 94,* 836–842.

Reis, S. M., Neu, T. W., & McGuire, J. M. (1995). *Talents in two places: Case studies of high ability students with learning disabilities who have achieved.* Storrs, CT: University of Connecticut, National Research Center on the Gifted and Talented.

Reiss, D., & Marino, L. (2001). Mirror self-recognition in the bottlenose dolphin: A case of cognitive convergence. *Proceedings of the National Academy of Sciences, 98,* 5937–5942.

Reissland, N. (1988). Neonatal imitation in the first hour of life: Observations in rural Nepal. *Developmental Psychology, 24,* 464–469.

Reiter, E. O., & Lee, P. A. (2001). Have the onset and tempo of puberty changed? *Archives of Pediatrics and Adolescent Medicine, 155,* 988–989.

Renner, M. J., & Mackin, R. (1998). A life stress instrument for classroom use. *Teaching of Psychology, 25,* 46–48.

Repacholi, B. M., & Gopnik, A. (1997). Early reasoning about desires: Evidence from 14- and 18-month-olds. *Developmental Psychology, 33,* 12–21.

Rescorla, R. A. (1966). Predictability and number of pairings in Pavlovian fear conditioning. *Psychonomic Science, 4,* 383–384.

Rescorla, R. A. (1988). Classical conditioning: It's not what you think it is. *American Psychologist, 43,* 151–160.

Rescorla, R. A. (2006). Stimulus generalization of excitation and inhibition. *Quarterly Journal of Experimental Psychology, 59,* 53–67.

Rescorla, R. A., & Wagner, A. R. (1972). A theory of Pavlovian conditioning: Variations in effectiveness of reinforcement and nonreinforcement. In A. Black & W. F. Prokasky, Jr. (Eds.), *Classical conditioning II.* New York: Appleton-Century-Crofts.

Ressler, K. J., & Nemeroff, C. B. (1999) Role of norepinephrine in the pathophysiology and treatment of mood disorders. *Biological Psychiatry, 46,* 1219–1233.

Rhodes, G., Yoshikawa, S., Clark, A., Lee, K., McKay, R., & Akamatsu, S. (2001). Attractiveness of facial averageness and symmetry in non-Western cultures: In search of biologically based standards of beauty. *Perception, 30,* 611–625.

Richards, M. H., Crowe, P. A., Larson, R., & Swarr, A. (1998). Developmental patterns and gender differences in the experience of peer companionship during adolescence. *Child Development, 69,* 154–163.

Richert, E. S. (1997). Excellence with equity in identification and programming. In N. Colangelo & G. A. Davis (Eds.), *Handbook of gifted education* (2nd ed., pp. 75–88). Boston: Allyn & Bacon.

Richters, J., de Visser, R., Rissel, C., & Smith, A. (2006). Sexual practices at last heterosexual encounter and occurrence of orgasm in a national survey. *Journal of Sex Research, 43,* 217–226.

Rieber, R. W. (Ed.). (1980). *Wilhelm Wundt and the making of scientific psychology.* New York: Plenum Press.

Riefer, D. M., Kevari, M. K., & Kramer, D. L. F. (1995). Name that tune: Eliciting the tip-of-the-tongue experience using auditory stimuli. *Psychological Reports, 77,* 1379–1390.

Rizzolatti, G. (2004). The mirror-neuron system and imitation. In S. Hurley & N. Chater (Eds.), *Perspectives on imitation: From mirror neurons to memes* (pp. 55–76). Cambridge, MA: MIT Press.

Rizzolatti, G., & Craighero, L. (2004.) The mirror-neuron system. *Annual Review of Neuroscience, 27,* 169–192.

Roberson, D., Davidoff, J., Davies, I. R. L., & Shapiro, L. R. (2004). The development of color categories in two languages: A longitudinal study. *Journal of Experimental Psychology: General, 133,* 554–571.

Roberts, G. A. (1991). Delusional belief and meaning in life: A preferred reality? *British Journal of Psychiatry, 159,* 20–29.

Roberts, G. A., & McGrady, A. (1996). Racial and gender effects on the relaxation response: Implications for the development of hypertension. *Biofeedback and Self-Regulation, 21,* 51–62.

Robins, E., & Guze, S. B. (1972). Classification of affective disorders: The primary-secondary, the endogenous-reactive, and the neurotic-psychotic concepts. In T. A. Williams, M. M. Katz & J. A. Shields (Eds.), *Recent advances in the psychobiology of depressive illnesses* (pp. 283–293). Washington, DC: U.S. Government Printing Office.

Robins, L. N., Helzer, J. E., Hesselbrock, M., & Wish, E. (1980). Vietnam veterans three years after Vietnam. In L. Brill & C. Winick (Eds.), *The yearbook of substance use and abuse* (Vol. 11). New York: Human Sciences Press.

Robins, L. N., Helzer, J. E., Weissman, M. M., Orvaschel, H., Gruenberg, E., Burke, J. D., et al. (1984). Lifetime prevalence of specific psychiatric disorders in three sites. *Archives of General Psychiatry, 41,* 949–958.

Robins, L. N., & Regier, D. A. (1991). *Psychiatric disorders in America.* New York: Free Press.

Robinson, A., & Clinkenbeard, P. R. (1998). Giftedness: An exceptionality examined. *Annual Review of Psychology, 49,* 117–139.

Robinson, D. N. (1995). *An intellectual history of psychology.* Madison: University of Wisconsin Press.

Robinson, R. G., & Downhill, J. E. (1995). Lateralization of psychopathology in response to focal brain injury. In R. J. Davidson & K. Hugdahl (Eds.), *Brain asymmetry* (pp. 693–711). Cambridge, MA: MIT Press.

Robinson, W. A. (2006). *The last man who knew everything: Thomas Young.* London: Pi Press.

Rodieck, R. W. (1998). *The first steps in seeing.* Sunderland, MA: Sinauer.

Roediger III, H. L. (2000). Why retrieval is the key process to understanding human memory. In E. Tulving (Ed.), *Memory, consciousness, and the brain: The Tallinn conference* (pp. 52–75). Philadelphia: Psychology Press.

Roediger III, H. L., & McDermott, K. B. (1995). Creating false memories: Remembering words not presented in lists. *Journal of Experimental Psychology: Learning, Memory, and Cognition, 21,* 803–814.

Roediger III, H. L., & McDermott, K. B. (2000). Tricks of memory. *Current Directions in Psychological Science, 9,* 123–127.

Roediger III, H. L., Weldon, M. S., & Challis, B. H. (1989). Explaining dissociations between implicit and explicit measures of retention: A processing account. In H. L. I. Roediger & F. I. M. Craik (Eds.), *Varieties of memory and consciousness: Essays in honor of Endel Tulving* (pp. 3–41). Hillsdale, NJ: Erlbaum.

Rogers, C. R. (1951). *Client-centered therapy: Its current practice, implications, and theory.* Boston: Houghton Mifflin.

Rogers, C. R. (1957). The necessary and sufficient conditions for therapeutic personality change. *Journal of Consulting Psychology, 21,* 95–103.

Rogers, C. R. (1961). *On becoming a person.* Boston: Houghton Mifflin.

Rogers, T. B., Kuiper, N. A., & Kirker, W. S. (1977). Self-reference and the encoding of personal information. *Journal of Personality and Social Psychology, 35,* 677–688.

Rosa, L., Rosa, E., Sarner, L., & Barrett, S. (1998). A close look at therapeutic touch. *Journal of the American Medical Association, 279,* 1005–1010.

Rosch, E. H. (1973). Natural categories. *Cognitive Psychology, 4,* 328–350.

Rosch, E. H. (1975). Cognitive representations of semantic categories. *Journal of Experimental Psychology: General, 104,* 192–233.

Rosch, E. H., & Mervis, C. B. (1975). Family resemblances: Studies in the internal structure of categories. *Cognitive Psychology, 7,* 573–605.

Rose, S. P. R. (2002). Smart drugs: Do they work? Are they ethical? Will they be legal? *Nature Reviews Neuroscience 3,* 975–979.

Roseman, I. J. (1984). Cognitive determinants of emotion: A structural theory. *Review of Personality and Social Psychology, 5,* 11–36.

Roseman, I. J., & Smith, C. A. (2001). Appraisal theory: Overview, assumptions, varieties and controversies. In K. R. Scherer, A. Schorr, & T. Johnstone (Eds.), *Appraisal processes in emotion: Theory, methods, research* (pp. 3–19). New York: Oxford University Press.

Rosenberg, M. (1965). *Society and the adolescent self-image.* Princeton, NJ: Princeton University Press.

Rosenhan, D. (1973). On being sane in insane places. *Science, 179,* 250–258.

Rosenstein, M. J., Milazzo-Sayre, L. J., & Manderscheid, R. W. (1990). Characteristics of persons using specifically inpatient, outpatient, and partial care programs in 1986. In M. A. Sonnenschein (Ed.), *Mental health in the United States* (pp. 139–172). Washington, DC: U.S. Government Printing Office.

Rosenthal, R., & Fode, K. L. (1963). The effect of experimenter bias on the performance of the albino rat. *Behavioral Science, 8,* 183–189.

Ross, B. H. (1984). Reminders and their effects in learning a cognitive skill. *Cognitive Psychology, 16,* 371–416.

Ross, D. F., Ceci, S. J., Dunning, D., & Toglia, M. P. (1994). Unconscious transference and mistaken identity: When a witness misidentifies a familiar but innocent person. *Journal of Applied Psychology, 79,* 918–930.

Ross, L. (1977). The intuitive psychologist and his shortcomings: Distortions in the attribution process. *Advances in Experimental Social Psychology, 10,* 173–220.

Ross, L., Amabile, T. M., & Steinmetz, J. L. (1977). Social roles, social control, and biases in social-perception processes. *Journal of Personality and Social Psychology, 35,* 485–494.

Ross, L., Lepper, M. R., & Hubbard, M. (1975). Perseverance in self-perception and social perception: Biased attribution processes in the debriefing paradigm. *Journal of Personality and Social Psychology, 32,* 880–892.

Ross, L., & Nisbett, R. E. (1991). *The person and the situation.* New York: McGraw-Hill.

Roth, H. P., & Caron, H. S. (1978). Accuracy of doctors' estimates and patients' statements on adherence to a drug regimen. *Clinical Pharmacology and Therapeutics, 23,* 361–370.

Roth, M., & Mountjoy, C. Q. (1997). The need for the concept of neurotic depression. In G. B. C. H. S. Akiskal (Ed.), *Dysthymia and the spectrum of chronic depressions* (pp. 96–129). New York: Guilford Press.

Rothbart, M. K., & Bates, J. E. (1998). Temperament. In W. Damon (Series Ed.) & N. Eisenberg (Vol. Ed.), *Handbook of child psychology: Vol. 3. Social emotional and personality development* (5th ed., pp. 105–176). New York: Wiley.

Rothbaum, B. O., Hodges, L., Watson, B. A., Kessler, G. D., & Opdyke, D. (1996). Virtual reality exposure therapy in the treatment of fear of flying: A case report. *Behaviour Research & Therapy, 34,* 477–481.

Rothbaum, B. O., Meadows, E. A., Resick, P., & Foy, D. W. (2000). Cognitive-behavioral therapy. In E. B. Foa, T. M. Keane, & M. J. Friedman (Eds.), *Effective treatments for PTSD* (pp. 60–83). New York: Guilford Press.

Rothermundt, M., Arolt, V., & Bayer, T. A. (2001). Review of immunological and immunopathological findings in schizophrenia. *Brain, Behavior, and Immunity, 15,* 319–339.

Rotstein, A. H. (2006, November 11). Despite 2–1 defeat on Election Day, backer of $1 million voter lottery still likes the idea. *Associated Press.*

Rotter, J. B. (1966). Generalized expectancies for internal versus external locus of control of reinforcement. *Psychological Monographs: General and Applied, 80.* 1–28.

Rotton, L. (1992). Trait humor and longevity: Do comics have the last laugh? *Health Psychology, 11,* 262–266.

Rowa, K., Antony, M. M., Brar, S., Summerfeldt, L. J., & Swinson, R. P. (2000). Treatment histories of patients with three anxiety disorders. *Depression and Anxiety, 12,* 92–98.

Rowland, L. W. (1939). Will hypnotized persons try to harm themselves or others? *Journal of Abnormal and Social Psychology, 34,* 114–117.

Roy-Byrne, P. P., & Cowley, D. (1998). *Pharmacological treatment of panic, generalized anxiety, and phobic disorders.* New York: Oxford University Press.

Roy-Byrne, P. P., & Cowley, D. S. (2002). Pharmacological treatments for panic disorder, generalized anxiety disorder, specific phobia, and social anxiety disorder. In P. E. Nathan & J. M. Gorman (Eds.), *A guide to treatments that work* (2nd ed., pp. 337–365). New York: Oxford University Press.

Royzman, E. B., Cassidy, K. W., & Baron, J. (2003). "I know, you know": Epistemic egocentrism in children and adults. *Review of General Psychology, 7,* 38–65.

Rozanski, A., Blumenthal, J. A., & Kaplan, J. (1999). Impact of psychological factors on the pathogenesis of cardiovascular disease and implications for therapy. *Circulation, 99,* 2192–2217.

Rozin, P. (1968). Are carbohydrate and protein intakes separately regulated? *Journal of Comparative and Physiological Psychology, 65,* 23–29.

Rozin, P., Bauer, R., & Catanese, D. (2003). Food and life, pleasure and worry, among American college students: Gender differences and regional similarities. *Journal of Personality and Social Psychology, 85,* 132–141.

Rozin, P., Dow, S., Moscovitch, M., & Rajaram, S. (1998). What causes humans to begin and end a meal? A role for memory for what has been eaten, as evidenced by a study of multiple meal eating in amnesic patients. *Psychological Science, 9,* 392–396.

Rozin, P., & Fallon, A. E. (1987). A perspective on disgust. *Psychological Review, 94,* 23–41.

Rozin, P., Haidt, J., & McCauley, C. R. (1999). Disgust: The body and soul emotion. In T. Dalgleish & M. J. Power (Eds.), *Handbook of cognition and emotion* (pp. 429–445). New York: Wiley.

Rozin, P., Hammer, L., Oster, H., Horowitz, T., & Marmora, V. (1986a). The child's concept of food: Differentiation of categories of rejected substances in the 1.4 to 5 years range. *Appetite, 7,* 141–151.

Rozin, P., Kabnick, K., Pete, E., Fischler, C., & Schields, C. (2003). The ecology of eating: Smaller portion sizes in France than in the United States help explain the French paradox. *Psychological Science, 14,* 450–454.

Rozin, P., & Kalat, J. W. (1971). Specific hungers and poison avoidance as adaptive specializations of learning. *Psychological Review, 78,* 459–486.

Rozin, P., Millman, L., & Nemeroff, C. (1986b). Operation of the laws of sympathetic magic in disgust and other domains. *Journal of Personality and Social Psychology, 50,* 703–712.

Rozin, P., Trachtenberg, S., & Cohen, A. B. (2001). Stability of body image and body image dissatisfaction in American college students over about the last 15 years. *Appetite, 37,* 245–248.

Rubenstein, A. J., Kalakanis, L., & Langlois, J. H. (1999). Infant preferences for attractive faces: A cognitive explanation. *Developmental Psychology, 35,* 848–855.

Rubin, B. D., & Katz, L. C. (1999). Optical imaging of odorant representations in the mammalian olfactory bulb. *Neuron, 23,* 499–511.

Rubin, Z. (1973). *Liking and loving.* New York: Holt, Reinhart and Winston.

Rude, S. S., Wenzlaff, R. M., Gibbs, B., Vane, J., & Whitney, T. (2002). Negative processing biases predict subsequent depressive symptoms. *Cognition and Emotion, 16,* 423–440.

Rudman, L. A., Ashmore, R. D., & Gary, M. L. (2001). "Unlearning" automatic biases: The malleability of implicit prejudice and stereotypes. *Journal of Personality and Social Psychology, 81,* 856–868.

Rusbult, C. E. (1983). A longitudinal test of the investment model: The development (and deterioration) of satisfaction and commitment in heterosexual involvements. *Journal of Personality and Social Psychology, 45,* 101–117.

Rusbult, C. E., & Van Lange, P. A. M. (2003). Interdependence, interaction and relationships. *Annual Review of Psychology, 54,* 351–375.

Rusbult, C. E., Verette, J., Whitney, G. A., & Slovik, L. F. (1991). Accommodation processes in close relationships: Theory and preliminary empirical evidence. *Journal of Personality and Social Psychology, 60,* 53–78.

Rushton, J. P. (1995). Asian achievement, brain size, and evolution: Comment on A. H. Yee. *Educational Psychology Review, 7,* 373–380.

Russell, J. A. (1980). A circumplex model of affect. *Journal of Personality and Social Psychology, 39,* 1161–1178.

Rutter, M., O'Connor, T. G., & the English and Romanian Adoptees Study Team (2004). Are there biological programming effects for psychological development? Findings from a study of Romanian adoptees. *Developmental Psychology, 40,* 81–94.

Rutter, M., & Silberg, J. (2002). Gene-environment interplay in relation to emotional and behavioral disturbance. *Annual Review of Psychology, 53,* 463–490.

Ryan, R. M., & Deci, E. L. (2000). Self-determination theory and the facilitation of intrinsic motivation, social development, and well-being. *American Psychologist, 55,* 68–78.

Sachs, J. S. (1967). Recognition of semantic, syntactic, and lexical changes in sentences. *Psychonomic Bulletin, 1,* 17–18.

Sackeim, H. A., & Devanand, D. P. (1991). Dissociative disorders. In M. Hersen & S. M. Turner (Eds.), *Adult psychopathology and diagnosis* (2nd ed., pp. 279–322). New York: Wiley.

Sacks, O. (1995). *An anthropologist on Mars.* New York: Knopf.

Saffran, J. R., Aslin, R. N., & Newport, E. I. (1996). Statistical learning by 8-month-old infants. *Science, 274,* 1926–1928.

Salge, R. A., Beck, J. G., & Logan, A. (1988). A community survey of panic. *Journal of Anxiety Disorder, 2,* 157–167.

Salthouse, T. A. (1984). Effects of age and skill in typing. *Journal of Experimental Psychology: General, 113,* 345–371.

Salthouse, T. A. (1987). Age, experience, and compensation. In C. Schooler & K. W. Schaie (Eds.), *Cognitive functioning and social structure over the life course* (pp. 142–150). New York: Ablex.

Salthouse, T. A. (1996a). General and specific mediation of adult age differences in memory. *Journal of Gerontology: Series B: Psychological Sciences and Social Sciences, 51B,* P30–P42.

Salthouse, T. A. (1996b). The processing-speed theory of adult age differences in cognition. *Psychological Review, 103,* 403–428.

Salthouse, T. A. (2000). Pressing issues in cognitive aging. In D. Park & N. Schwartz (Eds.), *Cognitive aging: A primer.* Philadelphia: Psychology Press.

Salthouse, T. A. (2001). Structural models of the relations between age and measures of cognitive functioning. *Intelligence, 29,* 93–115.

Sammons, M. T., Paige, R. U., & Levant, R. F. (Eds.). (2003). *Prescriptive authority for psychologists: A history and guide.* Washington, DC: American Psychological Association.

Sampson, R. J., & Laub, J. H. (1995). Understanding variability in lives through time: Contributions of life-course criminology. *Studies of Crime Prevention, 4,* 143–158.

Sandberg, S., Paton, J. Y., Ahola, S., McCann, D. C., McGuinness, D., Hillary, C. R., et al. (2000). The role of acute and chronic stress in asthma attacks in children. *Lancet, 356,* 982–987.

Sandin, R. H., Enlund, G., Samuelsson, P., & Lenmarken, C. (2000). Awareness during anesthesia: A prospective case study. *The Lancet, 355,* 707–711.

Sapolsky, R. M. (1992). *Stress, the aging brain, and the mechanisms of neuron death.* Cambridge, MA: MIT Press.

Sapolsky, R. M. (1998). *Why zebras don't get ulcers: An updated guide to stress, stress-related diseases, and coping.* New York: Freeman.

Sapolsky, R. M., & Share, L. J. (2004). A pacific culture among wild baboons: Its emergence and transmission. *PLoS Biology, 2,* e106.

Sarris, V. (1989). Max Wertheimer on seen motion: Theory and evidence. *Psychological Research, 51,* 58–68.

Sarter, M. (2006). Preclinical research into cognition enhancers. *Trends in Pharmacological Sciences, 27,* 602–608.

Satcher, D. (2001). *The Surgeon General's call to action to promote sexual health and responsible sexual behavior.* Washington, DC: U.S. Government Printing Office.

Savage, C. R., Deckersbach, T., Heckers, S., Wagner, A. D., Schacter, D. L., Alpert, N. M., et al. (2001). Prefrontal regions supporting spontaneous and directed application of verbal learning strategies: Evidence from PET. *Brain, 124,* 219–231.

Savage-Rumbaugh, S., & Lewin, R. (1996). *Kanzi: The ape on the brink of the human mind.* New York: Wiley.

Savage-Rumbaugh, S., Shanker, S. G., & Taylor, T. J. (1998). *Apes, language, and the human mind.* Oxford, England: Oxford University Press.

Saver, J. L., & Rabin, J. (1997). The neural substrates of religious experience. *Journal of Neuropsychiatry and Clinical Neurosciences, 9,* 498–510.

Savic, I., Berglund, H., & Lindstrom, P. (2005). Brain response to putative pheromones in homosexual men. *Proceedings of the National Academy of Sciences, 102,* 7356–7361.

Savin-Williams, R. C. (1998). Disclosure to families of same-sex attraction by lesbian, gay and bisexual youth. *Journal of Research on Adolescence, 8,* 49–68.

Sawa, A., & Snyder, S. H. (2002). Schizophrenia: Diverse approaches to a complex disease. *Science, 295,* 692–695.

Sawyer, T. F. (2000). Francis Cecil Sumner: His views and influence on African American higher education. *History of Psychology, 3*(2), 122–141.

Scarborough, E., & Furumoto, L. (1987). *Untold lives: The first generation of American women psychologists.* New York: Columbia University Press.

Scarr, S., & McCartney, K. (1983). How people make their own environments: A theory of genotype-to-environment factors. *Child Development, 54,* 424–435.

Scazufca, M., & Kuipers, E. (1998). Stability of expressed emotion in relatives of those with schizophrenia and its relationship with burden of care and perception of patients' social functioning. *Psychological Medicine, 28,* 453–461.

Schachter, S. (1982). Recidivism and self-cure of smoking and obesity. *American Psychologist, 37,* 436–444.

Schachter, S., & Singer, J. E. (1962). Cognitive, social, and psychological determinants of emotional state. *Physiological Review, 69,* 379–399.

Schacter, D. L. (1987). Implicit memory: History and current status. *Journal of Experimental Psychology: Learning, Memory, and Cognition, 13,* 501–518.

Schacter, D. L. (1996). *Searching for memory: The brain, the mind, and the past.* New York: Basic Books.

Schacter, D. L. (1999). The seven sins of memory: Insights from psychology and cognitive neuroscience. *American Psychologist, 54*(3), 182–203.

Schacter, D. L. (2001a). *Forgotten ideas, neglected pioneers: Richard Semon and the story of memory.* Philadelphia: Psychology Press.

Schacter, D. L. (2001b). *The seven sins of memory: How the mind forgets and remembers.* Boston: Houghton Mifflin.

Schacter, D. L., Alpert, N. M., Savage, C. R., Rauch, S. L., & Albert, M. S. (1996a). Conscious recollection and the human hippocampal formation: Evidence from positron emission tomography. *Proceedings of the National Academy of Sciences (USA) 93,* 321–325.

Schacter, D. L., & Buckner, R. L. (1998). Priming and the brain. *Neuron, 20,* 185–195.

Schacter, D. L., & Curran, T. (2000). Memory without remembering and remembering without memory: Implicit and false memories. In M. S. Gazzaniga (Ed.), *The new cognitive neurosciences* (2nd ed.). Cambridge, MA: MIT Press.

Schacter, D. L., Dobbins, I. G., & Schnyer, D. M. (2004). Specificity of priming: A cognitive neuroscience perspective. *Nature Reviews Neuroscience, 5,* 853–862.

Schacter, D. L., Harbluk, J. L., & McLachlan, D. R. (1984). Retrieval without recollection: An experimental analysis of source amnesia. *Journal of Verbal Learning and Verbal Behavior, 23,* 593–611.

Schacter, D. L., Israel, L., & Racine, C. A. (1999). Suppressing false recognition in younger and older adults: The distinctiveness heuristic. *Journal of Memory and Language, 40,* 1–24.

Schacter, D. L., & Moscovitch, M. (1984). Infants, amnesics, and dissociable memory systems. In M. Moscovitch (Ed.), *Infant memory* (pp. 173–216). New York: Plenum Press.

Schacter, D. L., Reiman, E., Curran, T., Yun, L. S., Bandy, D., McDermott, K. B., et al. (1996b). Neuroanatomical correlates of veridical and illusory recognition memory: Evidence from positron emission tomography. *Neuron, 17,* 267–274.

Schacter, D. L., & Tulving, E. (1994). *Memory systems 1994.* Cambridge, MA: MIT Press.

Schacter, D. L., Wagner, A. D., & Buckner, R. L. (2000). Memory systems of 1999. In E. Tulving & F. I. M. Craik (Eds.), *The Oxford handbook of memory.* New York: Oxford University Press.

Schaeffer, M. A., McKinnon, W., Baum, A., Reynolds, C. P., Rikli, P., & Davidson, L. M. (1985). Immune status as a function of chronic stress at Three-Mile Island [Abstract]. *Psychosomatic Medicine, 47,* 85.

Schafer, R. B., & Keith, P. M. (1980). Equity and depression among married couples. *Social Psychology Quarterly, 43,* 430–435.

Schaie, K. W. (1996). *Intellectual development in adulthood: The Seattle longitudinal study.* New York: Cambridge University Press.

Schaie, K. W. (2005). *Developmental influences on adult intelligence: The Seattle longitudinal study.* New York: Oxford University Press.

Schatzberg, A. F., Cole, J. O., & DeBattista, C. (2003). *Manual of clinical psychopharmacology* (4th ed.). Washington, DC: American Psychiatric Publishing.

Scheff, T. J. (1984). *Being mentally ill: A sociological theory.* Chicago: Aldine.

Scheier, M. F., Matthews, K. A., Owens, J. F., Schulz, R., Bridges, M. W., Magovern, Sr., G. J., et al. (1999). Optimism and rehospitalization after coronary artery bypass graft surgery. *Archives of Internal Medicine, 159,* 829–835.

Scherer, K. R. (1999). Appraisal theory. In T. Dalgleish & M. Power (Eds.), *Handbook of cognition and emotion* (pp. 637–663). New York: Wiley.

Scherer, K. R. (2001). The nature and study of appraisal: A review of the issues. In K. R. Scherer, A. Schorr, & T. Johnstone (Eds.), *Appraisal processes in emotion: Theory, methods, research* (pp. 369–391). New York: Oxford University Press.

Schildkraut, J. J. (1965). The catecholamine hypothesis of affective disorders: A review of supporting evidence. *American Journal of Psychiatry, 122,* 509–522.

Schlafly, P. (2001, May 2). Daycare bombshell hits the "village." Retrieved October 7, 2007, from http://www.eagleforum.org/column/2001/may01/01-05-02.shtml

Schmeichel, B. J., & Baumeister, R. F. (2004). Self-regulatory strength. In R. F. Baumeister & K. D. Vohs (Eds.), *Handbook of self-regulation* (pp. 84–98). New York: Guilford Press.

Schmidt, F. L., & Hunter, J. E. (1998). The validity and utility of selection methods in personnel psychology: Practical and theoretical implications of 85 years of research findings. *Psychological Bulletin, 124,* 262–274.

Schmidt, N. B., Lerew, D. R., & Jackson R. J. (1997). The role of anxiety sensitivity in the pathogenesis of panic: Prospective evaluation of spontaneous panic attacks during acute stress. *Journal of Abnormal Psychology, 106,* 355–365.

Schmitt, W. B., Deacon, R. M. J., Reisel, D., Sprengel, R., Seeburg, P. H., Rawlins, J. N. P., et al. (2004). Spatial reference memory in GluR-A.-deficient mice using a novel hippocampal-dependent paddling pool escape task. *Hippocampus, 14,* 216–223.

Schnapf, J. L., Kraft, T. W., & Baylor, D. A. (1987). Spectral sensitivity of human cone photoreceptors. *Nature, 325,* 439–441.

Schneider, B. H., Atkinson, L., & Tardif, C. (2001). Child-parent attachment and children's peer relations: A quantitative review. *Developmental Psychology, 37,* 86–100.

Schneider, M. (2001). Toward a reconceptualization of the coming-out process for adolescent females. In A. R. D'Augelli & C. J. Patterson (Eds.), *Lesbian, gay and bisexual identities and youth: Psychological perspectives* (pp. 71–96). New York: Oxford University Press.

Schneier, F., Johnson, J., Hornig, C. D., Liebowitz, M. R., & Weissman, M. M. (1992). Social phobia: Comorbidity and morbidity in an epidemiologic sample. *Archives of General Psychiatry, 49,* 282–288.

Schnorr, J. A., & Atkinson, R. C. (1969). Repetition versus imagery instructions in the short- and long-term retention of paired associates. *Psychonomic Science, 15,* 183–184.

Schooler, J. W., Bendiksen, M., & Ambadar, Z. (1997). Taking the middle line: Can we accommodate both fabricated and recovered memories of sexual abuse? In M. A. Conway (Ed.), *Recovered memories and false memories* (pp. 251–292). Oxford, England: Oxford University Press.

Schooler, J. W., Reichle, E. D., & Halpern, D. V. (2001). *Zoning-out during reading: Evidence for dissociations between experience and meta-consciousness.* Paper presented at the Annual Meeting of the Psychonomic Society, Orlando, FL.

Schouwenburg, H. C. (1995). Academic procrastination: Theoretical notions, measurement, and research. In J. R. Ferrari, J. L. Johnson, & W. G. McCown (Eds.), *Procrastination and task avoidance: Theory, research, and treatment.* New York: Plenum Press.

Schreiner, C. E., Read, H. L., & Sutter, M. L. (2000). Modular organization of frequency integration in primary auditory cortex. *Annual Review of Neuroscience, 23,* 501–529.

Schultz, D. P., & Schultz, S. E. (1987). *A history of modern psychology* (4th ed.). San Diego: Harcourt Brace Jovanovich.

Schwartz, C. E., Wright, C. I., Shin, L. M., Kagan, J., & Rauch, S. L. (2003). Inhibited and uninhibited infants "grown up": Adult amygdalar response to novelty. *Science, 300,* 1952–1953.

Schwartz, J. H., & Westbrook, G. L. (2000). The cytology of neurons. In E. R. Kandel, G. H. Schwartz, & T. M. Jessell (Eds.), *Principles of neural science* (pp. 67–104). New York: McGraw-Hill.

Schwartz, S., & Maquet, P. (2002). Sleep imaging and the neuropsychological assessment of dreams. *Trends in Cognitive Sciences, 6,* 23–30.

Schwartzman, A. E., Gold, D., & Andres, D. (1987). Stability of intelligence: A 40-year follow-up. *Canadian Journal of Psychology, 41,* 244–256.

Schwarz, N., & Clore, G. L. (1983). Mood, misattribution, and judgments of well-being: Informative and directive functions of affective states. *Journal of Personality and Social Psychology, 45,* 513–523.

Schwarz, N., Mannheim, Z., & Clore, G. L. (1988). How do I feel about it? The informative function of affective states. In K. Fiedler & J. Forgas (Eds.), *Affect cognition and social behavior: New evidence and integrative attempts* (pp. 44–62). Toronto: C. J. Hogrefe.

Sclafani, A. (1995). How food preferences are learned—laboratory animal models. *Proceedings of the Nutrition Society, 54,* 419–427.

Scoville, W. B., & Milner, B. (1957). Loss of recent memory after bilateral hippocampal lesions. *Journal of Neurology, Neurosurgery, and Psychiatry, 20,* 11–21.

Scribner, S. (1975). Recall of classical syllogisms: A cross-cultural investigation of errors on logical problems. In R. J. Falmagne (Ed.), *Reasoning: Representation and process in children and adults.* Hillsdale, NJ: Erlbaum.

Scribner, S. (1984). Studying working intelligence. In B. Rogoff & J. Lave (Eds.), *Everyday cognition: Its development in social context* (pp. 9–40). Cambridge, MA: Harvard University Press.

Segal, M. W. (1974). Alphabet and attraction: An unobtrusive measure of the effect of propinquity in a field setting. *Journal of Personality and Social Psychology, 30,* 654–657.

Segall, M. H., Lonner, W. J., & Berry, J. W. (1998). Cross-cultural psychology as a scholarly discipline: On the flowering of culture in behavioral research. *American Psychologist, 53*(10), 1101–1110.

Segerstrom, S. C. (2005). Optimism and immunity: Do positive thoughts always lead to positive effects? *Brain, Behavior, and Immunity, 19,* 195–200.

Seligman, M. E. P. (1971). Phobias and preparedness. *Behavior Therapy, 2,* 307–320.

Seligman, M. E. P. (1995). The effectiveness of psychotherapy: The consumer reports study. *American Psychologist, 48,* 966–971.

Selikoff, I. J., Robitzek, E. H., & Ornstein, G. G. (1952). Toxicity of hydrazine derivatives of isonicotinic acid in the chemotherapy of human tuberculosis. *Quarterly Bulletin of SeaView Hospital, 13,* 17–26.

Selye, H. (1936). A syndrome produced by diverse nocuous agents. *Nature, 138,* 32.

Selye, H. (1956). *The stress of life.* New York: McGraw-Hill.

Selye, H., & Fortier, C. (1950). Adaptive reaction to stress. *Psychosomatic Medicine, 12,* 149–157.

Semenza, C., & Zettin, M. (1989). Evidence from aphasia from proper names as pure referring expressions. *Nature, 342,* 678–679.

Senghas, A., Kita, S., & Ozyurek, A. (2004). Children create core properties of language: Evidence from an emerging sign language in Nicaragua. *Science, 305,* 1782.

Serpell, R. (1974). Aspects of intelligence in a developing country. *African Social Research, 17,* 578–596.

Shackelford, T. K., & Larsen, R. J. (1999). Facial attractiveness and physical health. *Evolution and Human Behavior, 20,* 71–76.

Shah, J., Higgins, E. T., & Friedman, R. S. (1998). Performance incentives and means: How regulatory focus influences goal attainment. *Journal of Personality and Social Psychology, 74,* 285–293.

Shallice, T., Fletcher, P., Frith, C. D., Grasby, P., Frackowiak, R. S. J., & Dolan, R. J. (1994). Brain regions associated with acquisition and retrieval of verbal episodic memory. *Nature, 368,* 633–635.

Shapiro, F., & Forrest, M. S. (2001). *EMDR: The breakthrough therapy for overcoming anxiety, stress, and trauma.* New York: Basic Books.

Shapiro, N. (2005, October 5–11). The day care scare. *Seattle Weekly.*

Shaw, P., Greenstein, D., Lerch, J., Clasen, L., Lenroot, R., N. Gogtay, N., et al. (2006). Intellectual ability and cortical development in children and adolescents. *Nature, 440,* 676–679.

Shedler, J., & Block, J. (1990). Adolescent drug use and psychological health: A longitudinal inquiry. *American Psychologist, 45,* 612–630.

Sheehan, P. (1979). Hypnosis and the process of imagination. In E. Fromm & R. S. Shor (Eds.), *Hypnosis: Developments in research and new perspectives.* Chicago: Aldine.

Sheese, B. E., & Graziano, W. G. (2005). Deciding to defect: The effects of video-game violence on cooperative behavior. *Psychological Science, 16,* 354–357.

Sheingold, K., & Tenney, Y. J. (1982). Memory for a salient childhood event. In U. Neisser (Ed.), *Memory observed* (pp. 201–212). New York: Freeman.

Shenton, M. E., Dickey, C. C., Frumin, M., & McCarley, R. W. (2001). A review of MRI findings in schizophrenia. *Schizophrenia Research, 49,* 1–52.

Shepherd, G. M. (1988). *Neurobiology.* New York: Oxford University Press.

Sherif, M., Harvey, O. J., White, B. J., Hood, W. R., & Sherif, C. (1961). *Intergroup conflict and cooperation: The Robbers Cave experiment.* Norman, OK: University of Oklahoma Book Exchange.

Sherrod, D. (1974). Crowding, perceived control, and behavioral aftereffects. *Journal of Applied Social Psychology, 4,* 171–186.

Shettleworth, S. J. (1995). Memory in food-storing birds: From the field to the Skinner box. In E. Alleva, A. Fasolo, H. P. Lipp, L. Nadel, & L. Ricceri (Eds.), *Behavioural brain research in naturalistic and seminaturalistic settings* (pp. 159–192). Boston: Kluwer Academic Publishers.

Shiffman, S., Gnys, M., Richards, T. J., Paty, J. A., & Hickcox, M. (1996). Temptations to smoke after quitting: A comparison of lapsers and maintainers. *Health Psychology, 15,* 455–461.

Shih, M., Pittinsky, T. L., & Ambady, N. (1999). Stereotype susceptibility: Identity salience and shifts in quantitative performance. *Psychological Science, 10,* 80–83.

Shimamura, A. P., & Squire, L. R. (1987). A neuropsychological study of fact memory and source amnesia. *Journal of Experimental Psychology: Learning, Memory, and Cognition, 13,* 464–473.

Shimoda, K., Argyle, M., & Ricci-Bitt, P. E. (1978). The intercultural recognition of emotional expressions by three national racial groups: English, Italian, and Japanese. *European Journal of Social Psychology, 8,* 169–179.

Shiv, B., Loewenstein, G., Bechara, A., Damasio, H., & Damasio, A. R. (2005). Investment behavior and the negative side of emotion. *Psychological Science, 16,* 435–439.

Shomstein, S., & Yantis, S. (2004). Control of attention shifts between vision and audition in human cortex. *Journal of Neuroscience, 24,* 10702–10706.

Shweder, R. A. (1991). *Thinking through cultures: Expeditions in cultural psychology.* Cambridge, MA: Harvard University Press.

Shweder, R. A., & Sullivan, M. A. (1993). Cultural psychology: Who needs it? *Annual Review of Psychology, 44,* 497–523.

Siegel, A., Roeling, T. A. P., Gregg, T. R., & Kruk, M. R. (1999). Neuropharmacology of brain-stimulation-evoked aggression. *Neuroscience and Biobehavioral Reviews, 23,* 359–389.

Siegel, B. (1988, October 30). Can evil beget good? Nazi data: A dilemma for science. *Los Angeles Times.*

Siegel, S. (1976). Morphine analgesia tolerance: Its situational specificity supports a Pavlovian conditioning model. *Science, 193,* 323–325.

Siegel, S. (1984). Pavlovian conditioning and heroin overdose: Reports by overdose victims. *Bulletin of the Psychonomic Society, 22,* 428–430.

Sigl, J. C., & Chamoun, N. (1994). An introduction to bispectral analysis for the electroencephalogram. *Journal of Clinical Monitoring, 10,* 392–404.

Silver, R. L., Boon, C., & Stones, M. H. (1983). Searching for meaning in misfortune: Making sense of incest. *Journal of Social Issues, 39,* 81–102.

Simon, L. (1998). *Genuine reality: A life of William James.* New York: Harcourt Brace.

Simpson, E. L. (1974). Moral development research: A case study of scientific cultural bias. *Human Development, 17,* 81–106.

Simpson, J. A., Campbell, B., & Berscheid, E. (1986). The association between romantic love and marriage: Kephart (1967) twice revisited. *Personality and Social Psychology Bulletin, 12,* 363–372.

Singer, T., Seymour, B., O'Doherty, J., Kaube, H., Dolan, R. J., & Frith, C. D. (2004). Empathy for pain involves the affective but not sensory components of pain. *Science, 303,* 1157–1162.

Singh, D. (1993). Adaptive significance of female physical attractiveness: Role of waist-to-hip ratio. *Journal of Personality and Social Psychology, 65,* 293–307.

Sipe, K. (2006). Muhammad trial journal. Retrieved September 15, 2007, from http://home.hamptonroads.com/guestbook/journal.cfm?startrow=11&question=1&id=53

Skinner, B. F. (1932a). Drive and reflex strength. *Journal of General Psychology, 6,* 22–37.

Skinner, B. F. (1932b). Drive and reflex strength II. *Journal of General Psychology, 6,* 38–48.

Skinner, B. F. (1938). *The behavior of organisms: An experimental analysis.* New York: Appleton-Century-Crofts.

Skinner, B. F. (1947). "Superstition" in the pigeon. *Journal of Experimental Psychology, 38,* 168–172.

Skinner, B. F. (1948/1986). *Walden II.* Englewood Cliffs, NJ: Prentice Hall.

Skinner, B. F. (1950). Are theories of learning necessary? *Psychological Review, 57,* 193–216.

Skinner, B. F. (1953). *Science and human behavior.* New York: Macmillan.

Skinner, B. F. (1957). *Verbal behavior.* New York: Appleton-Century-Crofts.

Skinner, B. F. (1958). Teaching machines. *Science, 129,* 969–977.

Skinner, B. F. (1971). *Beyond freedom and dignity.* New York: Bantam Books.

Skinner, B. F. (1979). The shaping of a behaviorist: Part two of an autobiography. New York: Knopf.

Slater, A., Morison, V., & Somers, M. (1988). Orientation discrimination and cortical function in the human newborn. *Perception, 17,* 597–602.

Sleepwalker found dozing high atop crane. (2005, July 6). Retrieved March 3, 2007, from http://www.accessmylibrary.com

Slone, M. (2000). Responses to media coverage of terrorism. *Journal of Conflict Resolution, 44,* 508–522.

Slotnick, S. D., & Schacter, D. L. (2004). A sensory signature that distinguished true from false memories. *Nature Neuroscience, 7,* 664–672.

Smetacek, V. (2002). Balance: Mind-grasping gravity. *Nature, 415,* 481.

Smetana, J. G. (1981). Preschool children's conceptions of moral and social rules. *Child Development, 52,* 1333–1336.

Smetana, J. G., & Braeges, J. L. (1990). The development of toddler's moral and conventional judgments. *Merrill-Palmer Quarterly, 36,* 329–346.

Smith, E. E., & Jonides, J. (1997). Working memory: A view from neuroimaging. *Cognitive Psychology, 33,* 5–42.

Smith, M. L., Glass, G. V., & Miller, T. I. (1980). *The benefits of psychotherapy.* Baltimore: Johns Hopkins University Press.

Smith, N., & Tsimpli, I-M. (1995). *The mind of a savant.* Oxford, England: Oxford University Press.

Snyder, M., & Swann, W. B., Jr. (1978). Hypothesis testing processes in social interaction. *Journal of Personality and Social Psychology, 36,* 1202–1212.

Sobel, D. (1995). *Longitude: The true story of a lone genius who solved the greatest scientific problem of his time.* New York: Walker.

Sobell, M. B., & Sobell, L. C. (1995). Controlled drinking after 25 years: How important was the great debate? *Addiction, 90,* 1149–1153.

Solomon, J., & George, C. (1999). The measurement of attachment security in infancy and childhood. In J. Cassidy & P. R. Shaver (Eds.), *Handbook of attachment: Theory, research and clinical applications* (pp. 287–316). New York: Guilford Press.

Solomon, S., Greenberg, J., & Pyszczynski, T. (1991). A terror management theory of social behavior: The psychological functions of self-esteem and cultural worldviews. In M. P. Zanna (Ed.), *Advances in experimental social psychology* (Vol. 24, pp. 93–159). New York: Academic Press.

Sonnby-Borgstrom, M., Jonsson, P., & Svensson, O. (2003). Emotional empathy as related to mimicry reactions at different levels of information processing. *Journal of Nonverbal Behavior, 27,* 3–23.

Spanos, N. P. (1994). Multiple identity enactments and multiple personality disorder: A sociocognitive perspective. *Psychological Bulletin, 116,* 143–165.

Spearman, C. (1904). "General intelligence," objectively determined and measured. *American Journal of Psychology, 15,* 201–293.

Spector, J., & Read, J. (1999). The current status of eye movement desensitization and reprocessing (EMDR). *Clinical Psychology and Psychotherapy, 6,* 165–174.

Speisman, J. C., Lazarus, R. S., Moddkoff, A., & Davison, L. (1964). Experimental reduction of stress based on ego-defense theory. *Journal of Abnormal and Social Psychology, 68,* 367–380.

Spellman, B. A. (1996). Acting as intuitive scientists: Contingency judgments are made while controlling for alternative potential causes. *Psychological Science, 7,* 337–342.

Spencer, L. G. (1929). *Illustrated phenomenology: The science and art of teaching how to read character—A manual of mental science.* London: Fowler.

Sperling, G. (1960). The information available in brief visual presentations. *Psychological Monographs, 74* (Whole No. 48).

Sperry, R. W. (1964). The great cerebral commissure. *Scientific American, 210,* 42–52.

Spinoza, B. (1982). *The ethics and selected letters* (S. Feldman, Ed., & S. Shirley, Trans.). Indianapolis, IN: Hackett. (Original work published 1677)

Spiro, H. M., McCrea Curnan, M. G., Peschel, E., & St. James, D. (1994). *Empathy and the practice of medicine: Beyond pills and the scalpel.* New Haven, CT: Yale University Press.

Spitz, R. A. (1949). Motherless infants. *Child Development, 20,* 145–155.

Spitzer, R. L., Gibbon, M., Skodol, A. E., Williams, J. B. W., & First, M. B. (1994). DSM-IV Casebook: *A learning companion to the diagnostic & statistical manual of mental disorders* (4th ed.). Washington, DC: American Psychiatric Press.

Sprecher, S. (1999). "I love you more today than yesterday": Romantic partners' perceptions of changes in love and related affect over time. *Journal of Personality and Social Psychology, 76,* 46–53.

Squire, L. R. (1992). Memory and the hippocampus: A synthesis from findings with rats, monkeys, and humans. *Psychological Review, 99,* 195–231.

Squire, L. R., & Kandel, E. R. (1999). *Memory: From mind to molecules.* New York: Scientific American Library.

Squire, L. R., Knowlton, B., & Musen, G. (1993). The structure and organization of memory. *Annual Review of Psychology, 44,* 453–495.

Squire, L. R., Ojemann, J. G., Miezin, F. M., Petersen, S. E., Videen, T. O., & Raichle, M. E. (1992). Activation of the hippocampus in normal humans: A functional anatomical study of memory. *Proceedings of the National Academy of Sciences (USA), 89,* 1837–1841.

Sroufe, L. A., Egeland, B., & Kruetzer, T. (1990). The fate of early experience following developmental change: Longitudinal approaches to individual adaptation in childhood. *Child Development, 61,* 1363–1373.

Stadler, M. A., & Frensch, P. A. (Eds.). (1998). *Handbook of implicit learning.* Thousand Oaks, CA: Sage.

Stangor, C., & McMillan, D. (1992). Memory for expectancy-congruent and expectancy-incongruent information: A review of the social and social developmental literature. *Psychological Bulletin, 111,* 42–61.

Starkey, P., Spelke, E. S., & Gelman, R. (1983). Detection of intermodal numerical correspondences by human infants. *Science, 222,* 179–181.

Starkey, P., Spelke, E. S., & Gelman, R. (1990). Numerical abstraction by human infants. *Cognition, 36,* 97–127.

Stasser, G., & Titus, W. (1985). Pooling of unshared information in group decision making: Biased information sampling during discussion. *Journal of Personality and Social Psychology, 48,* 1467–1478.

Staw, B. M., & Hoang, H. (1995). Sunk costs in the NBA: Why draft order affects playing time and survival in professional basketball. *Administrative Science Quarterly 40,* 474–494.

Steadman, H. J., Mulvey, E. P., Monahan, J., Robbins, P. C., Appelbaum, P. S., Grisso, T., et al. (1998). Violence by people discharged from acute psychiatric inpatient facilities and by others in the same neighborhoods. *Archives of General Psychiatry, 55,* 393–401.

Steele, C. M., & Aronson, J. (1995). Stereotype threat and the intellectual test performance of African Americans. *Journal of Personality and Social Psychology, 69,* 797–811.

Steele, C. M., & Josephs, R. A. (1990). Alcohol myopia: Its prized and dangerous effects. *American Psychologist, 45,* 921–933.

Steele, H., Steele, M., Croft, C., & Fonagy, P. (1999). Infant-mother attachment at one year predicts children's understanding of mixed emotions at six years. *Social Development, 8,* 161–178.

Stein, M. B. (1998). Neurobiological perspectives on social phobia: From affiliation to zoology. *Biological Psychiatry, 44,* 1277–1285.

Stein, M. B., Chavira, D. A., & Jang, K. L. (2001). Bringing up bashful baby: Developmental pathways to social phobia. *Psychiatric Clinics of North America, 24,* 661–675.

Stein, M. B., Koverola, C., Hanna, C., Torchia, M. G., & McClarty, B. (1997). Hippocampal volume in women victimized by childhood sexual abuse. *Psychological Medicine, 27,* 951–959.

Stein, Z., Susser, M., Saenger, G., & Marolla, F. (1975). *Famine and development: The Dutch hunger winter of 1944–1945.* Oxford, England: Oxford University Press.

Steinbaum, E. A., & Miller, N. E. (1965). Obesity from eating elicited by daily stimulation of hypothalamus. *American Journal of Physiology, 208,* 1–5.

Steinberg, L. (1999). *Adolescence* (5th ed.). Boston: McGraw-Hill.

Steinberg, L., & Morris, A. S. (2001). Adolescent development. *Annual Review of Psychology, 52,* 83–110.

Steinem, G. (1970). Testimony on May 6, 1970, *Subcommittee on Constitutional Amendments of the Committee on the Judiciary* (2nd Session on S. J. Res. 61 5–7 ed., pp. 335–337). Washington, DC: U.S. Government Printing Office.

Steiner, F. (1986). Differentiating smiles. In E. Branniger-Huber & F. Steiner (Eds.), *FACS in psychotherapy research* (pp. 139–148). Zurich: Department of Clinical Psychology, Universität Zürich.

Steiner, J. E. (1973). The gustofacial response: Observation on normal and anencephalic newborn infants. In J. F. Bosma (Ed.), *Fourth symposium on oral sensation and perception: Development in the fetus and infant* (pp. 254–278). Bethesda, MD: U.S. Department of Heath, Education, and Welfare (DHEW 73-546).

Steiner, J. E. (1979). Human facial expressions in response to taste and smell stimulation. *Advances in Child Development and Behavior, 13,* 257–295.

Steinman, R. B., Pizlo, Z., & Pizlo, F. J. (2000). Phi is not beta, and why Wertheimer's discovery launched the Gestalt revolution. *Vision Research, 40,* 2257–2264.

Stellar, J. R., Kelley, A. E., & Corbett, D. (1983). Effects of peripheral and central dopamine blockade on lateral hypothalamic self-stimulation: Evidence for both reward and motor deficits. *Pharmacology, Biochemistry, and Behavior, 18,* 433–442.

Stellar, J. R., & Stellar, E. (1985). *The neurobiology of motivation and reward.* New York: Springer-Verlag.

Stelmack, R. M. (1990). Biological bases of extraversion: Psychophysiological evidence. *Journal of Personality, 58,* 293–311.

Stephens, R. S. (1999). Cannabis and hallucinogens. In B. S. McCrady & E. E. Epstein (Eds.), *Addictions: A comprehensive guidebook.* New York: Oxford University Press.

Sterelny, K., & Griffiths, P. E. (1999). *Sex and death: An introduction to philosophy of biology.* University of Chicago Press.

Stern, J. A., Brown, M., Ulett, A., & Sletten, I. (1977). A comparison of hypnosis, acupuncture, morphine, valium, aspirin, and placebo in the management of experimentally induced pain. In W. E. Edmonston (Ed.), *Conceptual and investigative approaches to hypnosis and hypnotic phenomena* (Vol. 296, pp. 175–193). New York: Annals of the New York Academy of Sciences.

Stern, R., & Marks, I. (1973). Brief and prolonged flooding: A comparison in agoraphobic patients. *Archives of General Psychiatry, 28,* 270–276.

Stern, W. (1914). *The psychological methods of testing intelligence* (G. M. Whipple, Trans.). Baltimore: Warwick & York.

Sternberg, R. J. (1986). A triangular theory of love. *Psychological Review, 93,* 119–135.

Stevens, G., & Gardner, S. (1982). *The women of psychology* (Vol. 1). Rochester: Schenkman Books.

Stevens, J. (1988). An activity approach to practical memory. In M. M. Gruneberg, P. E. Morris, & R. N. Sykes (Eds.), *Practical aspects of memory: Current research and issues* (Vol. 1, pp. 335–341). New York: Wiley.

Stevens, L. A. (1971). *Explorers of the brain.* New York: Knopf.

Stevenson, R. L. (1886). *Strange Case of Dr. Jekyll and Mr. Hyde.* London: Longmans, Green & Co.

Stewart-Williams, S. (2004). The placebo puzzle: Putting together the pieces. *Health Psychology, 23,* 198–206.

Stickgold, R., Hobson, J. A., Fosse, R., & Fosse, M. (2001). Sleep, learning, and dreams: Off-line memory reprocessing. *Science, 294,* 1052–1057.

Stickgold, R., James, L., & Hobson, J. A. (2000). Visual discrimination learning requires post-training sleep. *Nature Neuroscience, 3,* 1237–1238.

Stickgold, R., Malia, A., Maguire, D., Roddenberry, D., & O'Connor, M. (2000). Replaying the game: Hypnagogic images in normals and anmesics. *Science, 290,* 350–353.

Stigler, J. W., Shweder, R., & Herdt, G. (Eds.). (1990). *Cultural psychology: Essays on comparative human development.* Cambridge, England: Cambridge University Press.

Stone, J., Perry, Z. W., & Darley, J. M. (1997). "White men can't jump": Evidence for the perceptual confirmation of racial stereotypes following a basketball game. *Basic and Applied Social Psychology, 19,* 291–306.

Storms, M. D. (1973). Videotape and the attribution process: Reversing actors' and observers' points of view. *Journal of Personality and Social Psychology, 27,* 165–175.

Strack, F., Martin, L. L., & Stepper, S. (1988). Inhibiting and facilitating conditions of the human smile: A nonobtrusive test of the facial feedback hypothesis. *Journal of Personality and Social Psychology, 54,* 768–777.

Strahan, E. J., Spencer, S. J., & Zanna, M. P. (2002). Subliminal priming and persuasion: Striking while the iron is hot. *Journal of Experimental Social Psychology, 38,* 556–568.

Strayer, D. L., Drews, F. A., & Johnston, W. A. (2003). Cell phone induced failures of visual attention during simulated driving. *Journal of Experimental Psychology: Applied, 9,* 23–32.

Streissguth, A. P., Barr, H. M., Bookstein, F. L., Sampson, P. D., & Carmichael Olson, H. (1999). The long-term neurocognitive consequences of prenatal alcohol exposure: A 14-year study. *Psychological Science, 10,* 186–190.

Strickland, L. H. (1991). Russian and Soviet social psychology. *Canadian Psychology, 32,* 580–595.

Strohmetz, D. B., Rind, B., Fisher, R., & Lynn, M. (2002). Sweetening the till: The use of candy to increase restaurant tipping. *Journal of Applied Social Psychology, 32,* 300–309.

Stuss, D. T., & Benson, D. F. (1986). *The frontal lobes.* New York: Raven Press.

Substance Abuse and Mental Health Services Administration. (2005). *Suicide warning signs.* Washington, DC: U.S. Department of Health and Human Services.

Suchman, A. L., Markakis, K., Beckman, H. B., & Frankel, R. (1997). A model of empathic communication in the medical interview. *Journal of the American Medical Association, 277,* 678–682.

Sue, S., Fujino, D. C., Hu, L., Takeuchi, D. T., & Zane, N. W. S. (1991). Community mental health services for ethnic minority groups: A test of the cultural responsiveness hypothesis. *Journal of Counseling and Clinical Psychology, 59,* 533–540.

Sullivan, A. (2000, April 2). The he hormone. *New York Times Magazine,* pp. SM46.

Sullivan, H. S. (1953). *The interpersonal theory of psychiatry.* New York: Norton.

Sulloway, F. J. (1992). *Freud, biologist of the mind.* Cambridge, MA: Harvard University Press.

Suls, J., & Fletcher, B. (1985). The relative efficacy of avoidant and nonavoidant coping strategies: A meta-analysis. *Health Psychology, 4,* 249–288.

Sumner, W. (1906). *Folkways.* New York: Ginn.

Susman, S., Dent, C., McAdams, L., Stacy, A., Burton, D., & Flay, B. (1994). Group self-identification and adolescent cigarette smoking: a 1-year prospective study. *Journal of Abnormal Psychology, 103,* 576–580.

Susser, E. B., Brown, A., & Matte, T. D. (1999). Prenatal factors and adult mental and physical health. *Canadian Journal of Psychiatry, 44*(4) 326–334.

Sussman, L. K., Robins, L. N., & Earls, F. (1987). Treatment-seeking for depression by black and white Americans. *Social Science and Medicine, 24,* 187–196.

Suzuki, L. A., & Valencia, R. R. (1997). Race-ethnicity and measured intelligence: Educational implications. *American Psychologist, 52,* 1103–1114.

Swann, W. B. (1983). Self-verification: Bringing social reality into harmony with the self. In J. M. Suls & Greenwald, A. G. (Eds.), *Psychological perspectives on the self* (Vol. 2, pp. 33–66). Hillsdale, NJ: Erlbaum.

Swann, W. B., Wenzlaff, R. M., & Tafarodi, R. W. (1992). Depression and the search for negative evaluations: More evidence of the role of self-verification strivings. *Journal of Abnormal Psychology, 10,* 314–317.

Swanson, J. W. (1994). Mental disorder, substance abuse, and community violence: An epidemiological approach. In J. Monahan & H. J.

Steadman (Eds.), *Violence and mental disorder: Developments in risk assessment* (pp. 101–136). Chicago: University of Chicago Press.

Swayze II, V. W. (1995). Frontal leukotomy and related psychosurgical procedures before antipsychotics (1935–1954): A historical overview. *American Journal of Psychiatry, 152,* 505–515.

Swednsen, J., Hammen, C., Heller, T., & Gitlin, M. (1995). Correlates of stress reactivity in patients with bipolar disorder. *American Journal of Psychiatry, 152,* 795–797.

Swets, J. A., Dawes, R. M., & Monahan, J. (2000). Psychological science can improve diagnostic decisions. *Psychological Science in the Public Interest, 1,* 1–26.

Swinkels, A. (2003). An effective exercise for teaching cognitive heuristics. *Teaching of Psychology, 30,* 120–122.

Szasz, T. (1960). The myth of mental illness. *American Psychologist, 15,* 113–118.

Szechtman, H., Woody, E., Bowers, K. S., & Nahmias, C. (1998). Where the imaginal appears real: A positron emission tomography study of auditory hallucinations. *Proceedings of the National Academy of Sciences, 95,* 1956–1960.

Szpunar, K. K., Watson, J. M., & McDermott, K. B. (2007). Neural substrates of envisioning the future. *Proceedings of the National Academy of Sciences (USA), 104,* 642–647.

Tajfel, H. (1970). Experiments in intergroup discrimination. *Scientific American, 223,* 96–102.

Tajfel, H., Billig, M. G., Bundy, R. P., & Flament, C. (1971). Social categorization and intergroup behaviour. *European Journal of Social Psychology, 1,* 149–178.

Tajfel, H., & Turner, J. C. (1986). The social identity theory of intergroup behavior. In S. Worchel & W. G. Austin (Eds.), *Psychology of intergroup relations* (pp. 7–24). Chicago: Nelson.

Tajfel, H., & Wilkes, A. L. (1963). Classification and quantitative judgement. *British Journal of Psychology, 54,* 101–114.

Takahashi, K. (1986). Examining the strange-situation procedure with Japanese mothers and 12-month-old infants. *Developmental Psychlogy, 22,* 265–270.

Tam, E. M., Lam, R. W., & Levitt, A. J. (1995). Treatment of seasonal affective disorder: A review. *Canadian Journal of Psychiatry, 40,* 457–466.

Tamminga, C. A. (2006). The neurobiology of cognition in schizophrenia. *Journal of Clinical Psychiatry, 67*(Suppl. 9), 9–13.

Tamminga, C. A., Nemeroff, C. B., Blakely, R. D., Brady, L., Carter, C. S., Davis, K. L, Dingledine, R., et al. (2002). Developing novel treatments for mood disorders: Accelerating discovery. *Biological Psychiatry, 52,* 589–609.

Tanaka, K. (1996). Inferotemporal cortex and object vision. *Annual Review of Neuroscience, 19,* 109–139.

Tang, Y.-P., Shimizu, E., Dube, G. R., Rampon, C., Kerchner, G. A., Zhuo, M., et al. (1999). Genetic enhancement of learning and memory in mice. *Nature, 401,* 63–69.

Tanner, L. (February 7, 2002). Woman gives birth after pre-pregnancy test is used to screen for early Alzheimer's gene. Associated Press.

Tapert, S. F., Brown, G. G., Kindermann, S., Cheung, E. Frank, L. R., & Brown, S. A. (2001). fMRI measurement of brain dysfunction in alcohol-dependent young women. *Alcoholism: Clinical and Experimental Research, 25,* 236–245.

Tarr, M. J., & Vuong, Q. C. (2002). Visual object recognition. In S. Yantis & H. Pashler (Eds.), *Stevens' handbook of experimental psychology: Vol. 1. Sensation and perception* (3rd ed., pp. 287–314). New York: Wiley.

Tart, C. T. (Ed.). (1969). *Altered states of consciousness.* New York: Wiley.

Task Force on Promotion and Dissemination of Psychological Procedures. (1995). Training in and dissemination of empirically-validated psychological treatments: Report and recommendations. *Clinical Psychologist, 48*, 3–23.

Tavris, C. (1989). *Anger: The misunderstood emotion* (Rev. ed.). New York: Simon & Schuster.

Taylor, D., & Lambert, W. (1990). *Language and culture in the lives of immigrants and refugees.* Austin, TX: Hogg Foundation for Mental Health.

Taylor, E. (2001). *William James on consciousness beyond the margin.* Princeton, NJ: Princeton University Press.

Taylor, S. E. (1986). *Health psychology.* New York: Random House.

Taylor, S. E. (1989). *Positive illusions.* New York: Basic Books.

Taylor, S. E. (2002). *The tending instinct: How nurturing is essential to who we are and how we live.* New York: Times Books.

Taylor, S. E. (2003). *The tending instinct: Women, men, and the biology of relationships.* New York: Owl Books.

Taylor, S. E., & Brown, J. D. (1988). Illusion and well-being: A social psychological perspective on mental health. *Psychological Bulletin, 103*, 193–210.

Taylor, S. E., & Fiske, S. T. (1975). Point-of-view and perceptions of causality. *Journal of Personality and Social Psychology, 32*, 439–445.

Taylor, S. E., & Fiske, S. T. (1978). Salience, attention, and attribution: Top of the head phenomena. In L. Berkowitz (Ed.), *Advances in experimental social psychology* (Vol. 11, pp. 249–288). New York: Academic Press.

Teasdale, J. D., Segal, Z. V., & Williams, J. M. G. (2000). Prevention of relapse/recurrence in major depression by Mindfulness-Based Cognitive Therapy. *Journal of Consulting and Clinical Psychology, 68*, 615–623.

Telch, M. J., Lucas, J. A., & Nelson, P. (1989). Non-clinical panic in college students: An investigation of prevalence and symptomology. *Journal of Abnormal Psychology, 98*, 300–306.

Tellegen, A., & Atkinson, G. (1974). Openness to absorbing and self-altering experiences ("absorption"), a trait related to hypnotic susceptibility. *Journal of Abnormal Psychology, 83*, 268–277.

Tellegen, A., Lykken, D. T., Bouchard, T. J., Wilcox, K., Segal, N., & Rich, A. (1988). Personality similarity in twins reared together and apart. *Journal of Personality and Social Psychology, 54*, 1031–1039.

Temerlin, M. K., & Trousdale, W. W. (1969). The social psychology of clinical diagnosis. *Psychotherapy: Theory, Research & Practice, 6*, 24–29.

Tempini, M. L., Price, C. J., Josephs, O., Vandenberghe, R., Cappa, S. F., Kapur, N., et al. (1998). The neural systems sustaining face and proper-name processing. *Brain, 121*, 2103–2118.

Terman, L. M. (1916). *The measurement of intelligence.* Boston: Houghton Mifflin.

Terman, L. M., & Oden, M. H. (1959). *Genetic studies of genius: Vol. 5. The gifted group at mid-life.* Stanford, CA: Stanford University Press.

Terman, M., Terman, J. S., Quitkin, F. M., McGrath, P. J., Stewart, J. W., & Rafferty, B. (1989). Light therapy for seasonal affective disorder. A review of efficacy. *Neuropsychopharmacology, 2*, 1–22.

Tesser, A. (1991). Emotion in social comparison and reflection processes. In J. Suls, & T. A. Wills (Ed.), *Social comparison: Contemporary theory and research* (pp. 117–148). Hillsdale, NJ: Erlbaum.

Tesser, A. (1993). The importance of heritability in psychological research: The case of attitudes. *Psychological Review, 100*, 129–142.

Teyler, T. J., & DiScenna, P. (1986). The hippocampal memory indexing theory. *Behavioral Neuroscience, 100*, 147–154.

Thaker, G. K. (2002). Current progress in schizophrenia research. Search for genes of schizophrenia: Back to defining valid phenes. *Journal of Nervous and Mental Disease, 190*, 411–412.

Thaler, R. H. (1988). The ultimatum game. *Journal of Economic Perspectives, 2*, 195–206.

Tharp, R. G. (1991). Cultural diversity and treatment of children. *Journal of Counseling and Clinical Psychology, 59*, 799–812.

Thase, M. E., & Howland, R. H. (1995). Biological processes in depression: An updated review and integration. In E. E. Beckham & W. R. Leber (Eds.), *Handbook of depression* (2nd ed., pp. 213–279). New York: Guilford Press.

The UP Series: *Seven up, Seven plus seven, 21 up, 28 up, 35 up, 42 up, 49 up.* (1964–2005). Paul Almond, dir./Michael Apted, dir. Granada Television of England Productions.

Thelen, E., Corbetta, D., Kamm, K., Spencer, J. P., Schneider, K., & Zernicke, R. F. (1993). The transition to reaching: Mapping intention and intrinsic dynamics. *Child Development, 64*, 1058–1098.

Thibaut, J. W., & Kelley, H. H. (1959). *The social psychology of groups.* New Brunswick, NJ: Transaction Publishers.

Thoma, S. J., Narvaez, D., Rest, J., & Derryberry, P. (1999). Does moral judgment development reduce to political attitudes or verbal ability? Evidence using the defining issues test. *Educational Psychology Review*, 325–341.

Thomas, A., & Chess, S. (1977). *Temperament and development.* New York: Brunner/Mazel.

Thomas, G. V. (1981). Continuity, reinforcement rate and the law of effect. *Quarterly Journal of Experimental Psychology, 33B*, 33–43.

Thompson, C. P., Skowronski, J., Larsen, S. F., & Betz, A. (1996). *Autobiographical memory: Remembering what and remembering when.* Mahwah, NJ: Erlbaum.

Thompson, P. M., Giedd, J. N., Woods, R. P., MacDonald, D., Evans, A. C., & Toga, A. W. (2000). Growth patterns in the developing brain detected by using continuum mechanical tensor maps. *Nature, 404*, 190–193.

Thompson, P. M., Vidal, C., Giedd, J. N., Gochman, P., Blumenthal, J., Nicolson, R., et al. (2001). Accelerated gray matter loss in very early-onset schizophrenia. *Proceedings of the National Academy of Science (USA), 98*, 11650–11655.

Thomson, D. M. (1988). Context and false recognition. In G. M. Davies & D. M. Thomson (Eds.), *Memory in context: Context in memory* (pp. 285–304). Chichester, England: Wiley.

Thorndike, E. L. (1898). Animal intelligence: An experimental study of associative processes in animals. *Psychological Review Monograph Supplements, 2*, 4–160.

Thornhill, R., & Gangestad, S. W. (1993). Human facial beauty: Averageness, symmetry, and parasite resistance. *Human Nature, 4*, 237–269.

Thornhill, R., & Gangestad, S. W. (1999). The scent of symmetry: A human sex pheromone that signals fitness? *Evolution and Human Behavior, 20*, 175–201.

Thurber, J. (1956). *Further fables of our time.* New York: Simon & Schuster.

Thurstone, L. L. (1938). *Primary mental abilities.* Chicago: University of Chicago Press.

Tice, D. M., & Baumeister, R. F. (1997). Longitudinal study of procrastination, performance, stress, and health: The costs and benefits of dawdling. *Psychological Science, 8*(6), 454–458.

Tienari, P., Wynne, L. C., Sorri, A., Lahti, I., Läksy, K., Moring, J., et al. (2004). Genotype-environment interaction in schizophrenia-spectrum disorder: Long-term follow-up study of Finnish adoptees. *British Journal of Psychiatry, 184*, 216–222.

Time poll. (2005, January 17). Just how happy are we? *Time*, A4.

Titchener, E. B. (1896). *An outline of psychology.* New York: Macmillan.

Tittle, P. (Ed.). (2004). *Should parents be licensed?: Debating the issues.* New York: Prometheus Books.

Todd, J. T., & Morris, E. K. (1992). Case histories in the great power of steady misrepresentation. *American Psychologist, 47*(11), 1441–1453.

Todes, D. P. (2000). Pavlov: *Exploring the animal machine*. New York: Oxford University Press.

Tolman, E. C., & Honzik, C. H. (1930a). Introduction and removal of reward and maze performance in rats. *University of California Publications in Psychology, 4*, 257–275.

Tolman, E. C., & Honzik, C. H. (1930b). "Insight" in rats. *University of California Publications in Psychology, 4*, 215–232.

Tolman, E. C., Ritchie, B. F., & Kalish, D. (1946). Studies in spatial learning: I: Orientation and short cut. *Journal of Experimental Psychology, 36*, 13–24.

Tomarken, A. J., Simien, C., & Garber, J. (1994). Retesting frontal brain asymmetry discriminates adolescent children of depressed mothers from low-risk controls. *Psychophysiology, 31*, 97–98.

Tomkins, S. S. (1981). The role of facial response in the experience of emotion. *Journal of Personality and Social Psychology, 40*, 351–357.

Tooby, J., & Cosmides, L. (2000). Mapping the evolved functional organization of mind and brain. In M. S. Gazzaniga (Ed.), *The cognitive neurosciences* (pp. 1185–1198). Cambridge, MA: MIT Press.

Tootell, R. B. H., Reppas, J. B., Dale, A. M., Look, R. B., Sereno, M. I., Malach, R., et al. (1995). Visual-motion aftereffect in human cortical area MT revealed by functional magnetic resonance imaging. *Nature, 375*, 139–141.

Torgensen, S. (1983). Genetic factors in anxiety disorders. *Archives of General Psychiatry, 40*, 1085–1089.

Torgensen, S. (1986). Childhood and family characteristics in panic and generalized anxiety disorder. *American Journal of Psychiatry, 143*, 630–639.

Torrey, E. F. (1994). Violent behavior by individuals with serious mental illness. *Hospital & Community Psychiatry, 45*, 653–662.

Torrey, E. F., Bower, A. E., Taylor, E. H., & Gottesman, I. I. (1994). *Schizophrenia and manic-depressive disorder: The biological roots of mental illness as revealed by the landmark study of identical twins*. New York: Basic Books.

Trebach, A. S., & Zeese, K. B. (Eds.). (1992). *Friedman and Szasz on liberty and drugs: Essays on the free market and prohibition*. Washington, DC: Drug Policy Foundation Press.

Treede, R. D., Kenshalo, D. R., Gracely, R. H., & Jones, A. K. (1999). The cortical representation of pain. *Pain, 79*, 105–111.

Trevelyan, A. J., Sussillo, D., Watson, B. O., & Yuste, R. (2006). Modular propagation of epileptiform activity: Evidence for an inhibitory veto in neocortex. *Journal of Neuroscience, 26*, 12447–12455.

Trivers, R. L. (1972a). Parental investment and sexual selection. In B. Campbell (Ed.), *Sexual selection and the descent of man, 1871–1971* (pp. 139–179). Chicago: Aldine.

Trivers, R. L. (1972b). The evolution of reciprocal altruism. *The Quarterly Review of Biology, 46*, 35–57.

Trull, T. J., & Durrett, C. A. (2005). Categorical and dimensional models of personality disorder. *Annual Review of Clinical Psychology, 1*, 355–380.

Tucker, E. (2003, June 25). Move over, Fido! Chickens are becoming hip suburban pets. *USA Today*.

Tuerlinckx, F., De Boeck, P., & Lens, W. (2002). Measuring needs with the Thematic Apperception Test: A psychometric study. *Journal of Personality and Social Psychology, 82*, 448–461.

Tulving, E. (1972). Episodic and semantic memory. In E. Tulving & W. Donaldson (Eds.), *Organization of memory* (pp. 381–403). New York: Academic Press.

Tulving, E. (1983). *Elements of episodic memory*. Oxford, England: Clarendon Press.

Tulving, E. (1998). Neurocognitive processes of human memory. In C. von Euler & I. Lundberg & R. Llins (Eds.), *Basic mechanisms in cognition and language* (pp. 261–281). Amsterdam: Elsevier.

Tulving, E., Kapur, S., Craik, F. I. M., Moscovitch, M., & Houle, S. (1994). Hemispheric encoding/retrieval asymmetry in episodic memory: Positron emission tomography findings. *Proceedings of the National Academy of Sciences (USA), 91*, 2016–2020.

Tulving, E., & Pearlstone, Z. (1966). Availability versus accessibility of information in memory for words. *Journal of Verbal Learning & Verbal Behavior, 5*, 381–391.

Tulving, E., & Schacter, D. L. (1990). Priming and human memory systems. *Science, 247*, 301–306.

Tulving, E., Schacter, D. L., & Stark, H. (1982). Priming effects in word-fragment completion are independent of recognition memory. *Journal of Experimental Psychology: Learning, Memory, and Cognition, 8*, 336–342.

Tulving, E., & Thompson, D. M. (1973). Encoding specificity and retrieval processes in episodic memory. *Psychological Review, 80*, 352–373.

Turiel, E. (1998). The development of morality. In N. Eisenberg (Ed.), *Handbook of child psychology: Vol. 3. Social, emotional and personality development* (pp. 863–932). New York: Wiley.

Turkheimer, E. (2000). Three laws of behavior genetics and what they mean. *Current Directions in Psychological Science, 9*, 160–164.

Turkheimer, E., Haley, A., Waldron, M., D'Onofrio, B., & Gottesman, I. I. (2003). Socioeconomic status modifies heritability of IQ in young children. *Psychological Science, 14*, 623–628.

Turkheimer, E., & Waldron, M. (2000). Nonshared environment: A theoretical, methodological, and quantitative review. *Psychological Bulletin, 126*, 78–108.

Turner, D. C., Robbins, T. W., Clark, L., Aron, A. R., Dowson, J., & Sahakian, B. J. (2003). Cognitive enhancing effects of modafinil in healthy volunteers. *Psychopharmacology, 165*, 260–269.

Turner, D. C., & Sahakian, B. J. (2006). Neuroethics of cognitive enhancement. *BioSocieties, 1*, 113–123.

Tversky, A., & Kahneman, D. (1973). Availability: A heuristic for judging frequency and probability. *Cognitive Psychology, 5*, 207–232.

Tversky, A., & Kahneman, D. (1974). Judgment under uncertainty: Heuristics and biases. *Science, 185*, 1124–1131.

Tversky, A., & Kahneman, D. (1981). The framing of decisions and the psychology of choice. *Science, 211*, 453–458.

Tversky, A., & Kahneman, D. (1983). Extensional versus intuitive reasoning: The conjunction fallacy in probability judgment. *Psychological Review, 90*, 293–315.

Tversky, A., & Kahneman, D. (1992). Advances in prospect theory: Cumulative representation of uncertainty. *Journal of Risk and Uncertainty, 5*, 297–323.

Twenge, J. M., Campbell, W. K., & Foster, C. A. (2003). Parenthood and marital satisfaction: A meta-analytic review. *Journal of Marriage and Family, 65*, 574–583.

Tyler, T. R. (1990). *Why people obey the law*. New Haven, CT: Yale University Press.

Ungerleider, L. G., & Mishkin, M. (1982). Two cortical visual systems. In D. J. Ingle, M. A. Goodale, & R. J. W. Mansfield (Eds.), *Analysis of visual behavior* (pp. 549–586). Cambridge, MA: MIT Press.

Ursano, R. J., & Silberman, E. K. (2003). Psychoanalysis, psychoanalytic psychotherapy, and supportive psychotherapy. In R. E. Hales & S. C. Yudofsky (Eds.), *The American Psychiatric Publishing textbook of clinical psychiatry* (4th ed., pp. 1177–1203). Washington, DC: American Psychiatric Publishing.

Usher, J. A., & Neisser, U. (1993). Childhood amnesia and the beginnings of memory for four early life events. *Journal of Experimental Psychology: General, 122*, 155–165.

Valenstein, E. S. (1973). *Brain control: A critical examination of brain stimulation and psychosurgery.* New York: Wiley.

Valenstein, E. S. (1986). *Great and desperate cures: The rise and decline of psychosurgery and other radical treatments for mental illness.* New York: Basic Books.

Valentine, T., Brennen, T., & Brédart, S. (1996). *The cognitive psychology of proper names: On the importance of being Ernest.* London: Routledge.

Valins, S. (1966). Cognitive effects of false heart-rate feedback. *Journal of Personality and Social Psychology, 4,* 400–408.

Vallacher, R. R., & Solodky, M. (1979). Objective self-awareness, standards of evaluation, and moral behavior. *Journal of Experimental Social Psychology, 15,* 254–262.

Vallacher, R. R., & Wegner, D. M. (1985). *A theory of action identification.* Hillsdale, NJ: Erlbaum.

Vallacher, R. R., & Wegner, D. M. (1987). What do people think they're doing? Action identification and human behavior. *Psychological Review, 94,* 3–15.

van den Boon, D. C. (1994). The influence of temperament and mothering on attachment and exploration: An experimental manipulation of sensitive responsiveness among lower-class mothers with irritable infants. *Child Development, 65,* 1457–1477.

van den Boon, D. C. (1995). Do first year intervention effects endure? Follow-up during toddlerhood of a sample of Dutch irritable infants. *Child Development, 66,* 1798–1816.

Van Essen, D. C., Anderson, C. H., & Felleman, D. J. (1992). Information processing in the primate visual system: An integrated systems perspective. *Science, 255,* 419–423.

van IJzendoorn, M. H. (1995). Adult attachment representations, parental responsiveness, and infant attachment: A meta-analysis on the predictive validity of the Adult Attachment Interview. *Psychological Bulletin, 117,* 387–403.

van IJzendoorn, M. H., & Kroonenberg, P. M. (1988). Cross-cultural patterns of attachment: A meta-analysis of the strange situation. *Child Development, 59,* 147–156.

van IJzendoorn, M. H., & Sagi, A. (1999). Cross-cultural patterns of attachment: Universal and contextual dimensions. In J. Cassidy & P. R. Shaver (Eds.), *Handbook of attachment: Theory, research and clinical applications* (pp. 713–734). New York: Guilford Press.

van Stegeren, A. H., Everaerd, W., Cahill, L., McGaugh, J. L., & Gooren, L. J. G. (1998). Memory for emotional events: Differential effects of centrally versus peripherally acting blocking agents. *Psychopharmacology, 138,* 305–310.

Van Velzen, C. J. M., & Emmelkamp, P. M. G. (1996). The assessment of personality disorders: Implications for cognitive and behavior therapy. *Behaviour Research and Therapy, 34,* 655–668.

Vance, E. B., & Wagner, N. N. (1976). Written descriptions of orgasm: A study of sex differences. *Archives of Sexual Behavior, 5,* 87–98.

Vanderplate, C., Aral, S. O., & Magder, L. (1988). The relationship among genital herpes simplex virus, stress, and social support. *Health Psychology, 7,* 159–168.

Vargha-Khadem, F., Gadian, D. G., Watkins, K. E., Connelly, A., Van Paesschen, W., & Mishkin, M. (1997). Differential effects of early hippocampal pathology on episodic and semantic memory. *Science, 277,* 376–380.

Vitkus, J. (1996). *Casebook in abnormal psychology* (3rd ed.). New York: McGraw-Hill.

Vitkus, J. (1999). *Casebook in abnormal psychology* (4th ed.). New York: McGraw-Hill.

Von Frisch, K. (1974). Decoding the language of the bee. *Science, 185,* 663–668.

von Restorff, H. (1933). Analyse von Vörgangen in Spurenfeld. I. Über die Wirkung von Bereichsbildung im Spurenfeld. *Psychologische Forschung, 18,* 299–342.

Vondra, J. I., Shaw, D. S., Swearingen, L., Cohen, M., & Owens, E. B. (2001). Attachment stability and emotional and behavioral regulation from infancy to preschool age. *Development and Psychopathology, 13,* 13–33.

Vonnegut, M. (1976). *The Eden express.* New York: Bantam.

Vortac, O. U., Edwards, M. B., & Manning, C. A. (1995). Functions of external cues in prospective memory. *Memory, 3,* 201–219.

Wade, N. J. (2005). *Perception and illusion: Historical perspectives.* New York: Springer.

Wager, T. D., Rilling, J., K., Smith, E. E., Sokolik, A., Casey, K. L., Davidson, R. J., et al. (2004). Placebo-induced changes in fMRI in the anticipation and experience of pain. *Science, 303,* 1162–1167.

Wagner, A. D., Schacter, D. L., Rotte, M., Koustaal, W., Maril, A., Dale, A. M., et al. (1998). Remembering and forgetting of verbal experiences as predicted by brain activity. *Science, 281,* 1188–1190.

Wagner, U., Gais, S., Haider, H., Verleiger, R., & Born, J. (2004). Sleep inspires insight. *Nature, 427,* 352–355.

Wahba, M. A., & Bridwell, L. G. (1976). Maslow reconsidered: A review of research on the need hierarchy theory. *Organizational Behavior & Human Performance, 15,* 212–240.

Wahl, O. F. (1976). Monozygotic twins discordant for schizophrenia: A review. *Psychological Bulletin, 83,* 91–106.

Waite, L. J. (1995). Does marriage matter? *Demography, 32,* 483–507.

Waldfogel, S. (1948). The frequency and affective character of childhood memories. *Psychological Monographs, 62* (Whole No. 291).

Waldmann, M. R. (2000). Competition among causes but not effects in predictive and diagnostic learning. *Journal of Experimental Psychology: Learning, Memory, and Cognition, 26,* 53–76.

Walker, C. (1977). Some variations in marital satisfaction. In R. C. J. Peel (Ed.), *Equalities and inequalities in family life* (pp. 127–139). London: Academic Press.

Walker, L. J. (1988). The development of moral reasoning. *Annals of Child Development, 55,* 677–691.

Wall, P. (2000). *Pain: The science of suffering.* New York: Columbia University Press.

Wallace, J., Schnieder, T., & McGuffin, P. (2002). Genetics of depression. In I. H. Gottlieb & C. L. Hammen (Eds.), *Handbook of depression* (pp. 169–191). New York: Guilford Press.

Wallbott, H. G. (1998). Bodily expression of emotion. *European Journal of Social Psychology, 28,* 879–896.

Walster, E., Aronson, V., Abrahams, D., & Rottmann, L. (1966). Importance of physical attractiveness in dating behavior. *Journal of Personality and Social Psychology, 4,* 508–516.

Walster, E., Walster, G. W., & Berscheid, E. (1978). *Equity: Theory and research.* Boston: Allyn and Bacon.

Walster, E., Walster, G. W., Piliavin, J., & Schmidt, L. (1973). "Playing hard to get": Understanding an elusive phenomenon. *Journal of Personality and Social Psychology, 26,* 113–121.

Walton, D. N. (1990). What is reasoning? What is an argument? *Journal of Philosophy, 87,* 399–419.

Waltzman, S. B. (2006). Cochlear implants: Current status. *Expert Review of Medical Devices, 3,* 647–655.

Wang, L. H., McCarthy, G., Song, A. W., & LaBar, K. S. (2005). Amygdala activation to sad pictures during high-field (4 tesla) functional magnetic resonance imaging. *Emotion, 5,* 12–22.

Ward, J., Parkin, A. J., Powell, G., Squires, E. J., Townshend, J., & Bradley, V. (1999). False recognition of unfamiliar people: "Seeing film stars everywhere." *Cognitive Neuropsychology, 16,* 293–315.

Warnock, M. (2003). *Making babies: Is there a right to have children?* Oxford, England: Oxford University Press.

Warrington, E. K., & McCarthy, R. A. (1983). Category specific access dysphasia. *Brain, 106,* 859–878.

Warrington, E. K., & Shallice, T. (1984). Category specific semantic impairments. *Brain, 107,* 829–854.

Watanabe, S., Sakamoto, J., & Wakita, M. (1995). Pigeons' discrimination of painting by Monet and Picasso. *Journal of the Experimental Analysis of Behavior, 63,* 165–174.

Waters, E., & Cummings, E. M. (2000). A secure base from which to explore close relationships. *Child Development, 71,* 164–173.

Watkins, L. R., & Maier, S. F. (2005). Immune regulation of central nervous system functions: From sickness responses to pathological pain. *Journal of Internal Medicine, 257,* 139–155.

Watson, D., & Pennebaker, J. W. (1989). Health complaints, stress, and distress: Exploring the central role of negative affectivity. *Psychological Review, 96,* 234–254.

Watson, D., & Tellegen, A. (1985). Toward a consensual structure of mood. *Psychological Bulletin, 98,* 219–235.

Watson, J. B. (1913). Psychology as the behaviorist views it. *Psychological Review, 20,* 158–177.

Watson, J. B. (1924a). *Behaviorism.* New York: People's Institute.

Watson, J. B. (1924b). The unverbalized in human behavior. *Psychological Review, 31,* 339–347.

Watson, J. B. (1928). *Psychological care of infant and child.* New York: Norton.

Watson, J. B. (1930). *Behaviorism* (Rev. ed.). Chicago: University of Chicago Press.

Watson, J. B., & Rayner, R. (1920). Conditioned emotional reactions. *Journal of Experimental Psychology, 3,* 1–14.

Watson, R. I. (1978). *The great psychologists.* New York: Lippincott.

Watt, H. J. (1905). Experimentelle Beitraege zu einer Theorie des Denkens (Experimental contributions to a theory of thinking). *Archiv fuer die gesamte Psychologie, 4,* 289–436.

Watzlawick, P., Beavin, J., & Jackson, D. D. (1967). *Pragmatics of human communication: A study of interactional patterns, pathologies, and paradoxes.* New York: Norton.

Wearing, D. (2006). *Forever today.* London: Corgi Books.

Weber, R., & Crocker, J. (1983). Cognitive processes in the revision of stereotypic beliefs. *Journal of Personality and Social Psychology, 45,* 961–977.

Wechsler, H., Davenport, A., Dowdall, G., Moeykens, B., & Castillo, S. (1994). Health and behavioral consequences of binge drinking in college: A national survey of students at 140 campuses. *Journal of the American Medical Association, 272,* 1672–1677.

Wechsler, H., Rigotti, N. A., Gledhill-Hoyt, J., & Lee, H. (1998). Increased levels of cigarette use among college students: A cause for national concern. *Journal of the American Medical Association, 280,* 1673–1678.

Wegner, D. M. (1994a). Ironic processes of mental control. *Psychological Review, 101,* 34–52.

Wegner, D. M. (1994b). *White bears and other unwanted thoughts: Suppression, obsession, and the psychology of mental control.* New York: Guilford Press.

Wegner, D. M. (1997). Why the mind wanders. In J. D. Cohen & J. W. Schooler (Eds.), *Scientific approaches to consciousness* (pp. 295–315). Mahwah, NJ: Erlbaum.

Wegner, D. M. (2002). *The illusion of conscious will.* Cambridge, MA: MIT Press.

Wegner, D. M., Ansfield, M., & Pilloff, D. (1998). The putt and the pendulum: Ironic effects of the mental control of action. *Psychological Science, 9,* 196–199.

Wegner, D. M., Broome, A., & Blumberg, S. J. (1997). Ironic effects of trying to relax under stress. *Behavior Research and Therapy, 35,* 11–21.

Wegner, D. M., Erber, R. E., & Zanakos, S. (1993). Ironic processes in the mental control of mood and mood-related thought. *Journal of Personality and Social Psychology, 65,* 1093–1104.

Wegner, D. M., & Gilbert, D. T. (2000). Social psychology: The science of human experience. In H. Bless & J. Forgas (Eds.), *The message within: Subjective experience in social cognition and behavior* (pp. 1–9). Philadelphia: Psychology Press.

Wegner, D. M., & Gold, D. B. (1995). Fanning old flames: Emotional and cognitive effects of suppressing thoughts of a past relationship. *Journal of Personality and Social Psychology, 68,* 782–792.

Wegner, D. M., Lane, J. D., & Dimitri, S. (1994). The allure of secret relationships. *Journal of Personality and Social Psychology, 66,* 287–300.

Wegner, D. M., & Pennebaker, J. W. (Eds.). (1993). *Handbook of mental control.* Englewood Cliffs, NJ: Prentice Hall.

Wegner, D. M., & Schaefer, D. (1978). The concentration of responsibility: An objective self-awareness analysis of group size effects in helping situations. *Journal of Personality and Social Psychology, 36,* 147–155.

Wegner, D. M., Schneider, D. J., Carter, S. R., & White, T. L. (1987). Paradoxical effects of thought suppression. *Journal of Personality and Social Psychology, 53,* 5–13.

Wegner, D. M., Vallacher, R. R., Macomber, G., Wood, R., & Arps, K. (1984). The emergence of action. *Journal of Personality and Social Psychology, 46,* 269–279.

Wegner, D. M., & Wenzlaff, R. M. (1996). Mental control. In E. T. Higgins & A. Kruglanski (Eds.), *Social psychology: Handbook of basic mechanisms and processes* (pp. 466–492). New York: Guilford Press.

Wegner, D. M., Wenzlaff, R. M., & Kozak, M. (2004). Dream rebound: The return of suppressed thoughts in dreams. *Psychological Science, 15,* 232–236.

Wegner, D. M., & Wheatley, T. (1999). Apparent mental causation: Sources of the experience of will. *American Psychologist, 54,* 480–492.

Weinberg, R. A. (1989). Intelligence and IQ: Landmark issues and great debates. *American Psychologist, 44,* 98–104.

Weinberger, D. A., Schwartz, G. E., & Davidson, R. J. (1979). Low-anxious, high-anxious, and repressive coping styles: Psychometric patterns and behavioral and physiological responses to stress. *Journal of Abnormal Psychology, 88,* 369–380.

Weir, C., Toland, C., King, R. A., & Martin, L. M. (2005). Infant contingency/extinction performance after observing partial reinforcement. *Infancy, 8,* 63–80.

Weisfeld, G. (1999). *Evolutionary principles of human adolescence.* New York: Basic Books.

Weiskrantz, L. (1956). Behavioral changes associated with ablation of the amygdaloid complex in monkeys. *Journal of Comparative and Physiological Psychology, 4,* 381–391.

Weissenborn, R. (2000). State-dependent effects of alcohol on explicit memory: The role of semantic associations. *Psychopharmacology, 149,* 98–106.

Weissman, M. M., Bland, R. C., Canino, G. J., Faravelli, C., Greenwald, S., Hwu, H. G., et al. (1997). The cross-national epidemiology of panic disorder. *Archives of General Psychiatry, 54,* 305–309.

Weissman, M. M., & Markowitz, J. C. (2002). Interpersonal psychotherapy for depression. In I. H. Gotlib & C. L. Hammen (Eds.), *Handbook of depression* (pp. 404–421). New York: Guilford Press.

Weissman, M. M., Markowitz, J. C., & Klerman, G. L. (2000). *Comprehensive guide to interpersonal psychotherapy.* New York: Basic Books.

Wells, G. L., Malpass, R. S., Lindsay, R. C. L., Fisher, R. P., Turtle, J. W., & Fulero, S. M. (2000). From the lab to the police station: A successful application of eyewitness research. *American Psychologist, 55,* 581–598.

Wells, G. L., Small, M., Penrod, S., Malpass, R. S., Fulero, S. M., & Brimacombe, C. A. E. (1998). Eyewitness identification procedures: Recommendations for lineups and photospreads. *Law and Human Behavior, 22,* 603–647.

Wenner, L. A. (2004). On the ethics of product placement in media entertainment. In M. L. Galacian (Ed.), *Handbook of product placement in the mass media* (pp. 101–132). Binghamton, NY: Haworth Press.

Wenzlaff, R. M. (2005). Seeking solace but finding despair: The persistence of intrusive thoughts in depression. In D. A. Clark (Ed.), *Intrusive thoughts in clinical disorders: Theory, research, and treatment* (pp. 54–85). New York: Guilford Press.

Wenzlaff, R. M., & Bates, D. E. (1998). Unmasking a cognitive vulnerability to depression: How lapses in mental control reveal depressive thinking. *Journal of Personality and Social Psychology, 75,* 1559–1571.

Wenzlaff, R. M., & Eisenberg, A. R. (2001). Mental control after dysphoria: Evidence of a suppressed, depressive bias. *Behavior Therapy, 32,* 27–45.

Wenzlaff, R. M., & Grozier, S. A. (1988). Depression and the magnification of failure. *Journal of Abnormal Psychology, 97,* 90–93.

Wenzlaff, R. M., & Wegner, D. M. (2000). Thought suppression. In S. T. Fiske (Ed.), *Annual Review of Psychology* (Vol. 51, pp. 51–91). Palo Alto, CA: Annual Reviews.

Wernicke, K. (1874). *Der Aphasische Symptomenkomplex.* Breslau: Cohn and Weigart.

Wertheimer, M. (1982). *Productive thinking.* Chicago: University of Chicago Press. (Originally published 1945)

Westen, D. (1991). Social cognition and object relations. *Psychological Bulletin, 109,* 429–455.

Whalen, P. J., Rauch, S. L., Etcoff, N. L., McInerney, S. C., Lee, M. B., & Jenike, M. A. (1998). Masked presentations of emotional facial expressions modulate amygdala activity without explicit knowledge. *Journal of Neuroscience, 18,* 411–418.

Whalley, L. J., & Deary, I. J. (2001). Longitudinal cohort study of childhood IQ and survival up to age 76. *British Medical Journal, 322,* 1–5.

Wheatley, T., & Haidt, J. (2005). Hypnotic disgust makes moral judgments more severe. *Psychological Science, 16,* 780–784.

Wheeler, M. A., Petersen, S. E., & Buckner, R. L. (2000). Memory's echo: Vivid recollection activates modality-specific cortex. *Proceedings of the National Academy of Sciences (USA), 97,* 11125–11129.

White, B. L., & Held, R. (1966). Plasticity of motor development in the human infant. In J. F. Rosenblith & W. Allinsmith (Eds.), *The cause of behavior* (pp. 60–70). Boston: Allyn and Bacon.

White, F. J. (1996). Synaptic regulation of mesocorticolimbic dopamine neurons. *Annual Review of Neuroscience, 19,* 405–436.

White, G. M., & Kirkpatrick, J. (Eds.). (1985). *Person, self, and experience: Exploring pacific ethnopsychologies.* Berkeley: University of California Press.

White, N. M., & Milner, P. M. (1992). The psychobiology of reinforcers. *Annual Review of Psychology, 41,* 443–471.

Whorf, B. (1956). *Language, thought, and reality.* Cambridge, MA: MIT Press.

Whybrow, P. C. (1997). *A mood apart.* New York: Basic Books.

Wicker, B., Keysers, C., Plailly, J., Royet, J.-P., Gallese, V., & Rizzolatti, G. (2003). Both of us disgusted in *my* insula: The common neural basis of seeing and feeling disgust. *Neuron, 40,* 655–664.

Wicklund, R. (1975). Objective self-awareness. In L. Berkowitz (Ed.), *Advances in experimental social psychology* (Vol. 8, pp. 233–275). New York: Academic Press.

Widiger, T. A. (2001). The best and the worst of us? *Clinical Psychology: Science and Practice, 8,* 374–377.

Widiger, T. A., & Sankis, L. M. (2000). Adult psychopathology: Issues and controversies. *An Annual Review of Psychology, 51,* 377–404.

Wiederman, M. W. (1997). Pretending orgasm during sexual intercourse: Correlates in a sample of young adult women. *Journal of Sex & Marital Therapy, 23,* 131–139.

Wiener, D. N. (1996). *B. F. Skinner: Benign anarchist.* Boston: Allyn and Beacon.

Wiesenthal, D. L., Austrom, D., & Silverman, I. (1983). Diffusion of responsibility in charitable donations. *Basic and Applied Social Psychology, 4,* 17–27.

Wiggs, C. L., & Martin, A. (1998). Properties and mechanisms of perceptual priming. *Current Opinion in Neurobiology, 8,* 227–233.

Wilcoxon, H. C., Dragoin, W. B., & Kral, P. A. (1971). Illness-induced aversions in rats and quail: Relative salience of visual and gustatory cues. *Science, 171,* 826–828.

Wiley, J. L. (1999). Cannabis: Discrimination of "internal bliss"? *Pharmacology, Biochemistry, & Behavior, 64,* 257–260.

Williams, A. C. (2002). Facial expression of pain: An evolutionary account. *Behavioral and Brain Sciences, 25,* 439–488.

Williams, C. M., & Kirkham, T. C. (1999). Anandamide induces overeating: Mediation by central cannabinoid (CB1) receptors. *Psychopharmacology, 143,* 315–317.

Williams, K. D., Nida, S. A., Baca, L. D., & Latané, B. (1989). Social loafing and swimming: Effects of identifiability on individual and relay performance of intercollegiate swimmers. *Basic and Applied Social Psychology, 10,* 73–81.

Wilson, T. D. (2002). *Strangers to ourselves: Discovering the adaptive unconscious.* Cambridge, MA: Harvard University Press.

Wilson, T. D., Centerbar, D. B., Kermer, D. A., & Gilbert, D. T. (2005). The pleasures of uncertainty: Prolonging positive moods in ways people do not anticipate. *Journal of Personality and Social Psychology, 88,* 5–21.

Wilson, T. D., & Gilbert, D. T. (2003). Affective forecasting. In M. P. Zanna (Ed.), *Advances in experimental social psychology* (Vol. 35, pp. 345–411). New York: Elsevier.

Wilson, T. D., & Lassiter, G. D. (1982). Increasing intrinsic interest with superfluous extrinsic constraints. *Journal of Personality and Social Psychology, 42,* 811–819.

Wilson, T. D., Lindsey, S., & Schooler, T. Y. (2000). A model of dual attitudes. *Psychological Review, 107,* 101–126.

Wilson, T. D., Meyers, J., & Gilbert, D. T. (2003). "How happy was I, anyway?" A retrospective impact bias. *Social Cognition, 21,* 421–446.

Wilson, T. D., & Schooler, J. W. (1991). Thinking too much: Introspection can reduce the quality of preferences and decisions. *Journal of Personality & Social Psychology, 60,* 181–192.

Wilson, T. D., Wheatley, T., Meyers, J., Gilbert, D. T., & Axsom, D. (2000). Focalism: A source of durability bias in affective forecasting. *Journal of Personality and Social Psychology, 78,* 821–836.

Wimmer, H., & Perner, J. (1983). Beliefs about beliefs: Representations and constraining function of wrong beliefs in young children's understanding of deception. *Cognition, 13,* 103–128.

Windeler, J., & Kobberling, J. (1986). Empirische Untersuchung zur Einschatzung diagnostischer Verfahren am Beispiel des Haemoccult-Tests. [An empirical study of the value of diagnostic procedures using the example of the hemoccult test.] *Klinische Wochenscrhrift, 64,* 1106–1112.

Windham, G. C., Eaton, A., & Hopkins, B. (1999). Evidence for an association between environmental tobacco smoke exposure and birthweight: A meta-analysis and new data. *Pediatrics and Perinatal Epidemiology, 13,* 35–57.

Winner, E. (1997). Exceptionally high intelligence and schooling. *American Psychologist, 52,* 1070–1081.

Winter, L., & Uleman, J. S. (1984). When are social judgments made? Evidence for the spontaneousness of trait inferences. *Journal of Personality and Social Psychology, 47,* 237–252.

Winterer, G., & Weinberger, D. R. (2004). Genes, dopamine and cortical signal-to-noise ratio in schizophrenia. *Trends in Neuroscience, 27,* 683–690.

Wise, R. A. (1989). Brain dopamine and reward. *Annual Review of Psychology, 40,* 191–225.

Wise, R. A. (2005). Forebrain substrates of reward and motivation. *Journal of Comparative Neurology, 493,* 115–121.

Wittchen, H., Knauper, B., & Kessler, R. C. (1994). Lifetime risk of depression. *British Journal of Psychiatry, 165,* 16–22.

Wittgenstein, L. (1999). *Philosophical investigations.* Upper Saddle River, NJ: Prentice Hall. (Originally published 1953)

Wixted, J. T., & Ebbensen, E. (1991). On the form of forgetting. *Psychological Science, 2,* 409–415.

Wolf, J. (2003, May 18). Through the looking glass. *The New York Times Magazine,* p. 120.

Wolff, G., Pathare, S., Craig, T., & Leff, J. (1996). Community knowledge of mental illness and reaction to mentally ill people. *British Journal of Psychiatry, 168,* 191–198.

Wollen, K. A., Weber, A., & Lowry, D. (1972). Bizarreness versus interaction of mental images as determinants of learning. *Cognitive Psychology, 3,* 518–523.

Wolpe, J. (1958). *Psychotherapy by reciprocal inhibition.* Stanford, CA: Stanford University Press.

Wong, D. T., Bymaster, F. P., & Engleman, E. A. (1995). Prozac (fluoxetine, Lilly 110140), the first selective serotonin uptake inhibitor and an antidepressant drug: Twenty years since its first publication. *Life Sciences, 57,* 411–441.

Wood, J. M., & Bootzin, R. R. (1990). Prevalence of nightmares and their independence from anxiety. *Journal of Abnormal Psychology, 99,* 64–68.

Wood, J. M., Bootzin, R. R., Rosenhan, D., Nolen-Hoeksema, S., & Jourden, F. (1992). Effects of the 1989 San Francisco earthquake on frequency and content of nightmares. *Journal of Abnormal Psychology, 101,* 219–224.

Wood, J. M., Nezworski, M. T., Lilienfeld, S. O., & Garb, H. N. (2003). *What's wrong with the Rorschach? Science confronts the controversial inkblot test.* New York: Wiley.

Wood, J. M., Nezworski, M. T., & Stejskal, W. J. (1996). The comprehensive system for the Rorschach: A critical examination. *Psychological Science, 7,* 3–10.

Woods, E. R., Lin, Y. G., Middleman, A., Beckford, P., Chase, L., & DuRant, R. H. (1997). The associations of suicide attempts in adolescents. *Pediatrics, 99,* 791–796.

Woods, S. C., Seeley, R. J., Porte, D., Jr., & Schwartz, M. W. (1998). Signals that regulate food intake and energy homeostasis. *Science, 280,* 1378–1383.

Woods, S. M., Natterson, J., & Silverman, J. (1966). Medical students' disease: hypochondriasis in medical education. *Journal of Medical Education, 41,* 785–790.

Woody, S. R., & Sanderson, W. C. (1998). Manuals for empirically supported treatments: 1998 update. *Clinical Psychologist, 51,* 17–21.

Wrangham, R., & Peterson, D. (1997). *Demonic males: Apes and the origin of human violence.* New York: Mariner.

Wren, A. M., Seal, L. J., Cohen, M. A., Brynes, A. E., Frost, G. S., Murphy, K. G., et al. (2001). Ghrelin enhances appetite and increases food intake in humans. *Journal of Clinical Endocrinology and Metabolism, 86,* 5992–5995.

Wrenn, C. C., Turchi, J. N., Schlosser, S., Dreiling, J. L., Stephenson, D. A., Crawley, J. N. (2006). Performance of galanin transgenic mice in the 5-choice serial reaction time attentional task. *Pharmacology Biochemistry and Behavior, 83,* 428–440.

Wright, L. (1994). *Remembering Satan: A case of recovered memory and the shattering of an American family.* New York: Knopf.

Wright, P., Takei, N., Rifkin, L., & Murray, R. M. (1995). Maternal influenza, obstetric complications, and schizophrenia. *American Journal of Psychiatry, 152,* 1714–1720.

Wulf, S. (1994, March 14). Err Jordan. *Sports Illustrated.*

Wundt, W. (1900–20). *Völkerpsychologie. Eine untersuchung der entwicklungsgesetze von sprache, mythos und sitte* [Völkerpsychologie: An examination of the developmental laws of language, myth, and custom]. Leipzig, Germany: Engelmann & Kroner.

Wynn, K. (1992). Addition and subtraction by human infants. *Nature, 358,* 749–750.

Xiaohe, X., & Whyte, K. J. (1990). Love matches and arranged marriages: A Chinese replication. *Journal of Marriage and the Family, 52,* 709–722.

Yamaguchi, S. (1998). Basic properties of umami and its effects in humans. *Physiology and Behavior, 49,* 833–841.

Yamasue, H., Kasai, K., Iwanami, A., Ohtani, T., Yamada, H., Abe, O., et al. (2003). Voxel-based analysis of MRI reveals anterior cingulate gray-matter volume reduction in posttraumatic stress disorder due to terrorism. *Proceedings of the National Academy of Sciences (USA), 100,* 9039–9043.

Yang, S., & Sternberg, R. J. (1997). Conceptions of intelligence in ancient Chinese philosophy. *Journal of Theoretical and Philosophical Psychology, 17,* 101–119.

Yeh, M., Takeuchi, D. T., & Sue, S. (1994). Asian-American children treated in the mental health system: A comparison of parallel and mainstream outpatient service centers. *Journal of Clinical Child Psychology, 23,* 5–12.

Yelsma, P., & Athappilly, K. (1988). Marital satisfaction and communication practices: Comparisons among Indian and American couples. *Journal of Comparative Family Studies, 19,* 37–53.

Yewchuk, C. (1985). Gifted/learning disabled children: An overview. *Gifted Education International, 3,* 122–126.

Yin, R. K. (1970). Face recognition by brain-injured patients: A dissociable ability. *Neuropsychologia, 8,* 395–402.

Young, A. S., Klap, R., Sherbourne, C. D., & Wells, K. B. (2001). The quality of care for depressive and anxiety disorders in the United States. *Archives of General Psychiatry, 58,* 55–61.

Young, P. C. (1948). Antisocial uses of hypnosis. In L. M. LeCron (Ed.), *Experimental hypnosis* (pp. 376–409). New York: Macmillan.

Young, R. M. (1990). *Mind, brain, and adaptation in the nineteenth century: Cerebral localization and its biological context from Gall to Ferrier.* New York: Oxford University Press.

Yucha, C., & Gilbert, C. D. (2004). *Evidence-based practice in biofeedback and neurofeedback.* Colorado Springs, CO: Association for Applied Psychophysiology and Biofeedback.

Yuill, N., & Perner, J. (1988). Intentionality and knowledge in children's judgments of actor's responsibility and recipient's emotional reaction. *Developmental Psychology, 24,* 358–365.

Yuma (Arizona) *Sun.* (2006, May 31). Bribing people to vote will not benefit system. (Retrieved from YumaSun.com on May 31, 2007).

Zahn-Waxler, C., Radke-Yarrow, M., Wagner, E., & Chapman, M. (1992). Development of concern for others. *Developmental Psychology, 28,* 126–136.

Zajonc, R. B. (1968). Attitudinal effects of mere exposure. *Journal of Personality and Social Psychology, 9,* 1–27.

Zajonc, R. B. (1980). Feeling and thinking: Preferences need no inferences. *American Psychologist, 35,* 151–175.

Zajonc, R. B. (1984). On the primacy of affect. In K. R. Scherer & P. Ekman (Eds.), *Approaches to emotion* (pp. 259–270). Hillsdale, NJ: Erlbaum.

Zajonc, R. B. (1989). Feeling the facial efference: Implications of the vascular theory of emotion. *Psychological Review, 96,* 395–416.

Zebrowitz, L. A., Hall, J. A., Murphy, N. A., & Rhodes, G. (2002). Looking smart and looking good: Facial cues to intelligence and their origins. *Personality and Social Psychology Bulletin, 28,* 238–249.

Zebrowitz, L. A., & Montepare, J. M. (1992). Impressions of baby-faced individuals across the life span. *Developmental Psychology, 28,* 1143–1152.

Zeki, S. (1993). *A vision of the brain.* London: Blackwell Scientific Publications.

Zeki, S. (2001). Localization and globalization in conscious vision. *Annual Review of Neuroscience, 24,* 57–86.

Zeman, A. (2002). *Consciousness: A user's guide.* New Haven, CT: Yale University Press.

Zentall, T. R., Sutton, J. E., & Sherburne, L. M. (1996). True imitative learning in pigeons. *Psychological Science, 7,* 343–346.

Zhang, J. (2004, October 2). Prof. Zimbardo faults Rumsfeld for Abu Ghraib. *Stanford Daily.* Retrieved August 2007 from http://daily.stanford.edu/article/2004/10/29/profZimbardoFaultsRumsfeldForAbuGhraib.

Zihl, J., von Cramon, D., & Mai, N. (1983). Selective disturbance of movement vision after bilateral brain damage. *Brain 106,* 313–340.

Zillmann, D., Katcher, A. H., & Milavsky, B. (1972). Excitation transfer from physical exercise to subsequent aggressive behavior. *Journal of Experimental Psychology, 8,* 247–259.

Zimprich, D., & Martin, M. (2002). Can longitudinal changes in processing speed explain longitudinal age changes in fluid intelligence? *Psychology and Aging, 17,* 690–695.

Zola, S. M., & Squire, L. R. (2000). The medial temporal lobe and the hippocampus. In E. Tulving & F. I. M. Craik (Eds.), *The Oxford handbook of memory* (pp. 485–500). New York: Oxford University Press.

Zuckerman, M., DePaulo, B. M., & Rosenthal, R. (1981). Verbal and nonverbal communication of deception. In L. Berkowitz (Ed.), *Advances in experimental social psychology* (Vol. 14, pp. 1–59). New York: Academic Press.

Zuckerman, M., & Driver, R. E. (1985). Telling lies: Verbal and nonverbal correlates of deception. In W. Seigman & S. Feldstein (Eds.), *Multichannel integrations of nonverbal behavior* (pp. 129–147). Hillsdale, NJ: Erlbaum.

Zuckerman, M., Kolin, E. A., Price, L., & Zoob, I. (1964). Development of a sensation-seeking scale. *Journal of Consulting Psychology, 28,* 477–482.

Name Index

A

Aarts, H., 306
Abel, T., 178
Abelson, R. P., 500
Abernathy, A. P., 156
Abramov, I., 138
Abrams, M., 247
Abramson, L. Y., 514
Abromov, I., 137
Acevedo-Garcia, D., 358
Achter, J. A., 363
Ackroff, K., 223
Acocella, J. , 509, 510, 514, 576
Acton, G. S., 344
Adams, C. M., 237
Adams, H. E., 466
Addis, D. R., 103
Adelmann, P. K., 381
Adelson, E. H., 149
Adler, A., 15, 463, 470, 546
Adolph, K. E., 412
Adolphs, R., 97, 382
Adorno, T. W., 455
Aggleton, J., 96
Aharon, I., 237
Ahern, J., 593
Ahlers, M., 368
Ainslie, G., 319
Ainsworth, M. D. S., 423, 424
Albarracin, D., 647
Albee, E., 489
Albert, Prince of England, 328
Alfert, E., 377
Ali, M. (Cassius Marcellus Clay), 86
Alicke, M. D., 484
Allgeier, A. R., 372
Allgeier, E. R., 397
Allen, C. A., 291
Allen, P., 216
Allen, R., 247
Allison, D. B., 393
Alloy, L. B., 514
Allport, G. W., 29, 454, 456, 458, 652
Alt, K. W., 559
Alvarez, L. W., 46
Amabile, T. M., 229, 658
Ambadar, Z., 510
Ambady, N., 357, 380, 383
Ames, A., 148
Ames, M. A., 435
Andersen, H. C., 607
Andersen, S. M., 470, 546
Anderson, C. A., 244, 623, 625, 649

Anderson, C. H., 138
Anderson, E., 178
Anderson, J. R., 190, 203
Anderson, M. C., 465
Anderson, R. C., 181
Anderson, T., 84
Andres, D., 360
Andrewes, D., 108
Andrews, I., 264
Angell, J., 18
Angermeyer, M. C., 500
Angier, N., 39
Angst, J., 512
Ansfield, M., 304, 313
Ansuini, C. G., 434
Antoni, M. H., 611
Antony, M. M., 507, 539, 549, 575
Aral, S. O., 588
Arcari, P. M., 598
Archer, J. E., 624
Archibold, R. C., 401
Argyle, M., 380
Aristotle, 5, 388
Ariyasu, H., 393
Arkes, H. R., 649
Arlitt, A. H., 358
Arlow, J. A., 546
Armstrong, D. M., 300
Arnold, M. B., 374
Arnold, S. E., 524
Arolt, V., 523
Aron, A. P., 372, 633
Aronson, E., 158, 398, 594, 634, 636, 650
Aronson, J., 357, 655
Arps, K., 400
Asch, S. E., 29, 643
Aschoff, J., 309
Aserinsky, E., 311
Ashby, F. G., 272
Ashcraft, M. H., 23
Asher, S. J., 46
Ashmore, R. D., 657
Aslin, R. N., 247
Assanand, S., 614
Astington, J. W., 417, 418
Athappilly, K., 638
Atkinson, G., 328
Atkinson, J. W., 399, 400
Atkinson, L., 425
Atkinson, R. C., 172
Austrom, D., 629
Avolio, A. M., 412
Avolio, B. J., 360

Axel, R., 159
Axelrod, R., 625
Axsom, D., 378
Ayres, C. E., 389
Azam, E., 13
Azuma, H., 350

B

Baars, B. J., 21, 306
Babinsky, R., 382
Backman, C. W., 636
Bachman, J., 433
Back, K., 632
Bäckman, L., 440
Baddeley, A. D., 175, 181
Baer, L., 507, 569
Bagby, R. M., 458
Bahrick, H. P., 176, 188, 189, 201
Bai, D. L., 158
Bailey, J. M., 435
Bailey, R., 363
Baillargeon, R., 414
Baird, J., 418
Baldwin, M. W., 482
Baler, R. D., 84
Baltes, P. B., 360, 362
Balthazard, C., 284
Banaji, M., 660
Bandura, A., 243, 244, 246, 473, 641
Banfield, J. F., 479
Banks, M. S., 410
Banks, C., 658
Banse, R., 379
Barbee, A. P., 635
Barchas, J. D., 85
Bard, P., 370, 371, 372
Bargh, J. A., 307, 308, 381, 399
Bariteau, T. W., Sr., 3
Barker, A. T., 63
Barkow, J., 482
Barlow, D. H., 501, 556, 565, 566
Barnard, P. J., 188
Barndollar, K., 399
Barnier, A. J., 199, 595
Baron, J., 417
Baron-Cohen, S., 418
Barondes, S., 560
Barrett, T. R., 532
Barsalou, L. W., 275
Barston, J. L., 287
Bartlett, F. C., 21, 22, 28, 188
Bartol, C. R., 461
Bartoshuk, L. M., 161, 162
Bashat, D. B., 143

Basquiat, J.-M., 477
Bates, D. E., 514, 515
Bates, J. E., 424, 424
Bateson, G., 30
Batson, C. D., 627
Baudry, M., 178
Bauer, R., 393
Baumeister, R. F., 35, 395, 436, 467, 481, 483, 484, 501, 516, 613, 624, 630, 641, 663
Baxter, L. R., 507
Bayer, T. A., 523
Bayley, P. J., 177
Baylor, D. A., 137
Baylor, G. W., 316
Beall, S. K., 597
Beauchamp, G. K., 161
Beavin, J., 556
Bechara, A., 278
Beck, A. T., 512, 514, 550, 551
Beck, J. G., 506
Becker, J. B., 433, 435
Beckers, G., 63
Becklen, R., 298, 299
Beiser, M., 522
Bekerian, D. A., 188
Békésy, G. von, 153
Belcher, M., 617
Bell, A. P., 435
Bell, J. R., 362
Bellotto, B., 298
Belsky, G., 291
Belsky, J., 423
Beltre, A., 277
Belushi, J., 603
Bem, S. L., 459
Benbow, C. P., 363
Bender, D. S., 528
Bendiksen, M., 510
Benedetti, F., 606
Benes, F. M., 524
Benjamin, L. T., Jr., 13
Bennett, D. J., 71
Benson, D. F., 99, 376
Benson, H., 598
Bereczkei, T., 289
Bergen, J. R., 149
Berger, H., 160, 310
Berger, P. A., 85
Berger, S. A., 201
Berk, J. S., 470, 546
Berkerian, D. A., 197
Berkowitz, L., 623, 624
Berkowitz, O., 646
Berman, D., 326

Bernard, L. L., 389
Bernath, L., 289
Bernieri, F. J., 624
Bernstein, I. L., 222
Berntson, G. G., 630
Berry, D. S., 635
Berry, J. W., 30, 31
Berryman, J., 518
Berscheid, E., 632, 633, 637, 639
Bertelsen, A., 495
Bertelsen, B., 513, 518
Bertenthal, B. I., 158
Bertrand, J., 258
Best, J. B., 23
Bettencourt, B. A., 626
Beunen, G., 432
Beutler, L. E., 573
Bevilacqua, J., 561
Bialystok, E.. 264
Bickerton, D., 257
Bickman, L., 646
Biddle, J. E., 633
Biederman, I., 144
Bierce, A., 660
Bierman, K. L., 437
Billings, F. J., 198
Binet, A., 339, 343, 357, 359, 412
Binik, Y. M., 396
Binkowski, L. A., 467
Binswanger, L., 472
Biswas-Diener, R., 531
Bjork, D. W., 1, 10, 14, 20, 203
Bjork, E. L., 203
Bjork, R. A., 11, 203, 330, 332
Blackmore, S., 335
Blair, I. V., 657
Blair, J., 530
Blakeslee, S., 100, 119
Blanton, H., 71
Blascovich, J., 591, 592
Blasi, A., 428
Blatt, S. J., 514
Blazer, D. G., 502, 503
Bleich, A., 595
Bliss, T. V. P., 178
Bleske, A. L., 27
Block, J., 325
Bloodsworth, K., 196
Bloom, F. E., 85
Bloom, P., 260, 446
Blumberg, S. J., 304, 378
Blume, H. H., 564
Blumenthal, J. A., 591
Bodamer, M., 263
Boden, J. M., 624
Boehm, L. E., 649
Bohan, J. S., 435
Boisvert, C. M., 576
Bolwig, T. G., 507
Boomsma, D., 105
Boon, C., 597
Booth, R. J., 597
Bootzin, R. R., 313, 315
Borden, R., 49
Borkenau, P., 345
Borkevec, T. D., 313
Born, J., 83, 248
Born, R. T., 149
Bornstein, R. F., 632
Boroditsky, L., 267
Bostwick, J. M., 516

Bottone, L., 645
Botwin, M. D., 636
Bouchard, C., 432
Bouchard, T. J., 353, 458, 460
Boucher, J. D., 380
Bourguignon, E., 332
Bower, A. E., 523
Bower, B., 307
Bower, G. H., 172, 173, 200
Bowers, J. M., 197
Bowers, K. S., 284
Bowlby, J., 422, 511
Bowser, R., 313
Bozarth, M. A., 318, 319
Bradbury, T. N., 638, 639
Bradford, D., 562
Bradley, D. C., 149
Bradmetz, J., 417
Braeges, J. L., 429
Brainerd, C. J., 207
Braly, K., 653
Bramlett, M. D., 289, 639
Brammer, M., 122
Branscombe, N. R., 654
Bransford, J. D., 181
Braun, A. R., 316
Breckler, S. J., 200
Brédart, S., 192
Breggin, P. R., 524, 576
Brehm, J. W., 27
Brehm, S. S., 638
Breland, K., 240, 241
Breland, M., 240, 241
Brennan, P. A., 160
Brenneis, C. B., 510
Brennen, T., 192
Brenninkmeijer, V., 594
Breuer, J., 14
Brewer, M. B., 628
Brewer, W. F., 188
Brickman, P., 378
Bridges, P. K., 569
Bridwell, L. G., 391
Broadbent, D. E., 23, 28
Broberg, D. J., 222
Broca, P., 7, 12, 24, 36, 63, 108, 115, 262
Brock, A., 9
Brockner, J., 632
Broderick, C. B., 556
Brody, N., 349
Bromet, E., 592
Brooks, V. E., 340
Brooks-Gunn, J., 301, 433
Broome, A., 304
Brosnan, S. F., 627
Brown, A., 408
Brown, B. B., 437
Brown, F., 204
Brown, J. D., 481, 484, 583
Brown, R., 192, 201, 260, 261
Brown, R. P., 235
Brown, S. A., 322
Brown, S. C., 170
Brown, T. A., 497, 501
Browne, A. J., 540
Brownell, K. D., 394
Brownlee, S., 363
Bruner, J. S., 262
Brunner, D. P., 312
Buchanan, C. M., 433, 435

Buchanan, D. R., 633
Buchanan, J., 367
Buchanan, P. J., 368
Buck, L., 159
Buckley, K. W., 251
Buckman, J., 372
Buckner, R. L., 182, 184, 185, 439
Bucy, P. C., 373, 374
Bull, R., 199
Bullemer, P., 247
Bumpass, L., 638
Bunge, S. A., 376
Bunney, B. S., 237
Bunting, T., 193
Burke, D., 193
Burns, H. J., 197
Burns, L., 615
Burnstein, E., 627
Burris, C. T., 654
Bush, G. W., 50, 199, 306, 308, 618, 659
Bush, J., 116, 659
Bushman, B. J., 484, 623, 625
Busjahn, A., 105
Buss, D. M., 26, 27, 289, 459, 461, 631, 635, 636, 663
Buswell, B. N., 380
Butcher, J. N., 503, 521
Butler, L. D., 199, 508
Butterfield, E. C., 23
Butzlaff, R. L., 526
Buunk, B. P., 594
Buys, C. J., 630
Bymaster, F. P., 86
Byrne, D., 372, 632, 636

C

Caan, W., 113
Cabeza, R., 195, 440
Cabrera, D., 235
Cacioppo, J. T., 630, 647, 648
Cage, N., 155
Cahill, L., 202, 382
Calder, A. J., 374
Calkins, M. W., 32, 36
Call, J., 221
Callaghan, T., 416, 417
Campbell, A., 459
Campbell, B., 637
Campbell, C. M., 157
Campbell, D. T., 628, 647
Campbell, J. D., 481
Campbell, L. A., 497
Campbell, L. C., 156
Campbell, R., 264
Campbell, W. K., 444
Campo, R., 624
Candy, J., 603
Cannon, W. B., 370, 371, 372, 582, 586
Cantanese, K. R., 395
Cantor, N., 476
Caplan, A. L., 70
Capps, L. M., 418
Caramazza, A., 268
Carey, D. P., 140
Carlen, P. L., 323
Carlsmith, J. M., 651
Carlson, C., 598

Carlson, G. E., 380
Carmena, J. M., 92
Carmichael Olson, H., 409
Carolson, E. A., 424
Caron, H. S., 610
Carr, L., 430
Carrell, S. E., 482
Carroll, J. B., 347, 348
Carroll, L. (Charles Lutwidge Dodson), 497
Carson, K. L., 84
Carson, R. C., 503, 521
Carstensen, L. L., 441, 442, 516, 517
Carter, J., 168
Carvallo, M., 483
Carver, C. S., 611
Carville, J., 636
Caspi, A., 424, 435, 437, 458, 460, 636
Cassem, N. H., 607
Cassidy, K. W., 416, 417
Castle, P. H., 543
Castro, F., 86
Castro-Martin, T., 638
Catanese, D., 393
Cates, W., 613
Catrambone, R., 282
Cattell, R. B., 348, 457
Catts, S. V., 362
Caudle, M. L., 511
Ceci, S. J., 169, 343, 360, 361
Celano, M. P., 556
Centerbar, D. B., 378
Chaiken, S., 647
Challis, B. H., 181
Chalmers, D., 295
Chambless, D. L., 574
Chamoun, N., 294
Chan, A. W. Y., 141
Chandrashekar, J., 162
Chang, P. P., 591
Channing, C., 632
Chao, L. L., 268
Chapman, J. G., 629
Charcot, J.-M., 14, 17, 36, 608
Charpentiere, P., 560
Charles, S. T., 441, 442
Charlton, K., 384
Charness, N., 363, 439
Chartrand, T. L., 307, 381, 399
Chase-Landale, P. L., 434
Chavira, D. A., 504
Chebium, R., 196
Cheema, M. A., 568
Cheney, D. L., 254
Cheng, P. W., 626
Cherlin, A. J., 639
Cherry, A., 320
Cherry, C., 299
Chess, S., 424
Chiles, C., 643
Choi, I., 659
Chomsky, N., 24, 28, 36, 246, 256, 259, 260
Chorover, S. L., 338
Christiansen, B. A., 322
Christianson, S.-Å., 201
Chronicle, E. P., 285
Chun, M. M., 115, 141
Churchill, W., 518

Cialdini, R. B., 640, 643, 644, 650, 663
Cicchetti, D., 424
Ciranello, R. D., 85
Cistarelli, L., 502
Clancy, S. A., 576
Clark, K., 32, 33, 34, 36
Clark, L. A., 528
Clark, R. D., 631
Clayton, N. S., 186
Cleckley, H. M., 529
Clinkenbeard, P. R., 363
Clinton, W. J., 187, 188, 634
Cloninger, C. R., 608
Clore, G. L., 387, 636
Clouse, R. E., 511
Coast, J. R., 601
Coates, D., 378
Cobain, K., 516
Coe, C., 602
Coffman, T. L., 653
Cogan, D., 602
Cogan, R., 602
Coghill, R. C., 605
Cohen, A. B., 393
Cohen, D., 524, 625
Cohen, G., 192
Cohen, L., 108
Cohen, L. B., 56
Cohen, N. J., 182, 183
Cohen, P. D. A., 325
Cohen, S., 584, 588, 602, 630
Cohen, S. J., 610
Colder, M., 597
Cole, J. O., 562
Cole, M., 31
Coley, R. L., 434
Colvin, C. R., 345
Commire, A., 251
Condon, J. W., 636
Conger, R. D., 435, 437
Connors, E., 196
Conway, M., 571
Conwell, Y., 517
Cook, D., 46
Cook, E. P., 459
Cook, K. S., 639
Cook, M., 245, 504
Cool, N., 576
Coombs, R. H., 531
Coons, P. M., 509
Cooper, H., 384
Cooper, J., 650
Cooper, J. R., 85
Cooper, M. L., 396
Coppola, A., 155
Coppola, F. F., 155
Corbett, D., 237
Coren, S., 312
Corkin, S., 177
Cornwell, G. T., 434
Correll, J., 656
Corsi, P., 74
Corsini, R. J., 541
Corti, E., 320
Coryell, W., 516, 517
Cosmides, L., 26, 626
Costa, P. T., 457
Costello, N., 461
Cowley, D., 502, 562, 563
Cowling, P., 532

Cox, D., 532
Coyne, J. A., 26
Coyne, J. C., 514
Craighero, L., 78, 245
Craik, F. I. M., 170, 181, 189
Cramer, R. E., 636
Crandall, C., 627
Crane, H., 518
Crano, W. D., 636
Craske, M. G., 505
Crawford, J. R., 359
Crawley, R. A., 204
Creelman, C. D., 127
Crespi, L. P., 237
Crick, N. R., 625
Critelli, J. W., 584
Crnic, K., 423
Crocker, J., 482, 628, 656
Crombag, H. F. M., 197
Cross, P., 484
Crow, T. J., 523
Crowder, R. G., 174
Crowe, R., 492, 506
Cruikshank, G., 511
Csermansky, J. G., 524
Csikszentmihalyi, M., 302, 471
Cumming, S., 569
Cummings, D. E., 391
Cummings, E. M., 423
Cummins, D. D., 291
Cunningham, M. R., 27, 31, 634, 635
Curran, J. P., 633
Curran, T., 184
Curtiss, S., 261
Cuthbert, B. N., 530
Cutler, D. L., 561
Cutler, S., 514
Cytowic, R., 165
Czerny, V., 243

D
da Vinci, L., 409
Dabbs, J. M., 624
D'Agostino, P. R., 659
Dali, S., 477
Dally, P., 489
Dalton, P., 158
Daly, M., 623, 624
Damasio, A. R., 3, 109, 119, 177, 268 375, 387, 458
Damasio, H., 193, 268, 278
Damsma, G., 237
Danesh, J., 529
Daniel, H. J., 636
Daniels, E. A., 520
Dapretto, M., 78
Darley, J. M., 629, 632, 655
Dar-Nimrod, I., 358
Darroch, J. E., 434
Darwin, C., 10, 12, 26, 379, 380, 383, 402
Darwin, C. J., 174
Dasen, P. R., 30
Dauer, W., 97
Davidoff, J., 267
Davidson, P. R., 575
Davidson, R. J., 377, 379, 400, 513, 514, 595
Davies, G., 194
Davies, I. R. L., 267

Davies, N. B., 289
Davies, T., 600
Davis, K., 261
Davis, K. E., 634, 657
Davison, G. C., 507, 519
Dawes, R. M., 128, 274, 291, 453, 573
Dawkins, R. J., 622
Dawood, K., 396
Day, C., 155
De Boeck, P., 399
de Craen, A. J. M., 606
de Geus, E. J. C., 356
de Rosnay, M., 418
De Valois, R. L., 138
de Visser, R., 396
de Waal, F. B. M., 301
De Witte, P., 321
De Wolff, M., 424
Deary, I. J., 343, 344, 346, 359, 360, 364
DeBattista, C., 562
DeCasper, A. J., 410
Deci, E. L., 398, 471, 482, 641
Deese, J., 195
DeFelipe, J., 74
DeLisi, L. E., 523
DeLoache, J. S., 446
Delongis, A., 584
Demb, J. B., 171
Dement, W. C., 112, 311, 312, 313, 314, 315
Dennett, D. C., 294, 298, 510
DePaulo, B. M., 384
Der, G., 344
Dermer, M., 633
DeRosnay, M., 417
Descartes, R., 6, 7, 294, 297
DeSilva, P., 507
DeSimone, M., 169
DesJardin, J. L., 154
Deslauriers, D., 316
Deuenwald, M., 595
Deutsch, M., 625
Devanand, D. P., 510
DeVilliers, P., 418
DeWaal, F. B. M., 627
Di Giulio, G., 573
Diaconis, P., 46
Diallo, A. A., 656
Diamond, M., 119
DiCaprio, L., 111
Dick, P. K., 350
Dickens, W. T., 360
Dickey, C. C., 525
Dickinson, A., 186
Didi-Huberman, G., 608
Diener, E., 531, 629, 630
Dienstbier, R. A., 634
Dijksterhuis, A., 306, 307, 483
Dillbeck, M. C., 332
Dillon, M. E., 320
Dimberg, U., 381, 504
Dimitri, S., 634
Dimsdale, J. E., 87
Dino, M., 633
Dion, K., 633
DiScenna, P., 177
DiTella, R., 444
Dittrich, W. H., 379
Dittus, P. J., 434

Dix, D., 561
Dixon, R. A., 440
DiZio, P., 158
Dobbins, I. G., 184
Dodds, C. M., 141
Dohrenwend, B. S., 584
Dolan, R. J., 173, 288, 430
Dollard, J., 623
Domar, A. D., 598
Domjan, M., 223
D'Onofrio, B., 354
Dorahy, M. J., 510
Dornbusch, S. M., 450
Dorus S., 104
Dostoevsky, F., 303
Douglass, C., 646
Dow, S., 393
Dowling, J. E., 79
Downer, J. D. C., 375
Downhill, J. E., 514
Downie, F., 507
Downing, P. E., 141
Downs, D. L., 641
Draganja, D., 481
Dragoin, W. B., 226
Draguns, J. G., 31
Dreger, A. D., 39
Dreifus, C., 628
Drews, F. A., 129
Drigotas, S. M., 639
Driscoll, R., 634
Driver, R. E., 384
Driver-Linn, E., 378
Druckman, D., 330, 332
Drummond, E., 579
Duchaine, B. C., 73
Duckworth, A. L., 398
Dudycha, G. J., 204
Dudycha, M. M., 204
Duff, K. J., 467
Duffy, V. B., 162
Dunbar, R. I. M., 28
Duncker, K., 281
Dunlap, K., 389
Dunphy, D. C., 437
Durkheim, E., 516
Durrett, C. A., 528
Dutton, D. G., 372, 633
Duval, S., 301
Dworkin, R. H., 156

E
Eacott, M. J., 204
Eagly, A. H., 459, 625, 631, 633
Earls, F., 500
Eaton, W. W., 409, 502, 532
Ebbensen, E., 188
Ebbinghaus, H., 22, 187, 188
Eberhardt, J. L., 661
Eberhardt, N. L., 385
Eccles, J. S., 433, 435
Eddy, D. M., 274
Edgerton, V. R., 91
Edward, R. R., 157
Edwards, C. P., 287
Edwards, M. B., 191
Edwards, W., 274
Ee, J. S., 584
Egeland, B., 425
Eich, J. E., 181, 200
Eichenbaum, H., 182

Eichmann, A., 645
Eilers, R. E., 258
Eimas, P. D., 257
Einstein, A., 492
Einstein, G. O., 191
Eisenberg, A. R., 514
Eisenberg, L. S., 154
Eisenberger, N. I., 630
Ekman, P., 372, 379, 380, 383, 384, 403
Elder, G. H., 435, 437
Eldridge, L. L., 182
Eldridge, M. A., 188
Elfenbein, H. A., 380, 383
El-Hai, J., 579
Ell, S. W., 272
Ellenberger, H. F., 453
Ellicot, A., 518
Ellington, D., 121
Elliot, G. R., 85
Elliott, R., 362
Ellis, A., 550
Ellis, B. J., 432
Ellis, E. M., 596
Ellis, L., 435
Ellison, L., 216
Ellman, S. J., 312
Elman, D., 49
Emerson, R. C., 149
Emmelkamp, P. M. G., 528, 549, 550
Emmons, R. A., 531
Empson, J. A., 313
England, L., 644
Engleman, E. A., 86
Enns, J. T., 165
Epley, N., 306
Erber, R. E., 304, 376
Erffmeyer, E. S., 49
Erickson, E., 470
Ericsson, K. A., 363
Erikson, E., 436
Eron, L. D., 56
Eronen, M., 500
Ervin, C. R., 636
Escher, M. C., 477
Esser, J. K., 630
Etcoff, N., 633
Etheridge, J. B., 532
Evans, F. J., 329
Evans, J. St. B., 287, 288
Evans, P. D., 104
Everson, S. A., 590
Exner, J. E., 453
Eysenck, H. J., 456, 457, 461, 462, 548, 573
Eysenck, S. B. G., 457

F

Fahlman, S., 381
Fahn, S., 608
Falk, R., 46
Fallon, A. E., 382
Fancher, R. E., 6. 8. 9, 13, 18, 37
Fantz, R. L., 414
Farah, M. J., 268, 362
Farley, C., 603
Farrar, M. J., 262
Farries, M. A., 103
Faust, D., 576
Favagehi, M., 588

Fazel, S., 529
Fazio, R. H., 650
Fechner, G. T., 124, 126, 128
Fehr, E., 627
Fein, S., 628, 659
Feinberg, T. E., 458, 477, 487
Feingold, A., 459, 631, 633
Feldman, M. D., 609
Felleman, D. J., 138
Fernald, A., 641
Ferster, C. B., 231
Feske, U., 575
Festinger, L., 632, 650, 651
Fetkewicz, J. M., 199
Fetzer, B. K., 615
Feynman, R., 121
Fibiger, H. C., 237
Fiddler-Woite, J., 434
Fiedler, E. R., 529
Field, G. C., 389
Field, S., 14
Fields, H. L., 606
Fields, J. M., 289
Fiering, C., 363
Fillingim, R. B., 157
Fincham, J. M., 190
Fincher-Kiefer, R., 659
Fink, M., 569
Finkelstein, K. E., 189
Finn, R., 337
Fiorentine, R., 559
Fischer, J., 221
Fischler, C., 214
Fisher, H. E., 638
Fisher, R. P., 181
Fiske, S. T., 655, 659, 660
Fitzgerald, P. B., 568
Fitzpatrick, F., 199
Fleet, R. P., 567
Fleming, R., 585
Fletcher, B., 596
Fletcher, P. C., 173, 520
Flor, H., 100
Florian, V., 612, 636
Flourens, P., 6, 7, 12, 24, 36
Floyd, J., 636
Flynn, J. R., 360
Foa, E. B., 596, 597
Fobes, J. I., 237
Fode, K. L., 50
Fodor, J., 626
Fogassi, L., 245
Fogle, S. M., 597
Foley, D., 502
Folkman, S., 591
Fong, G. T., 616
Fong, G. W., 237
Fontaine, K. R., 393
Ford, G., 344
Fornazzari, L., 323
Forrest, M. S., 575
Fortier, C., 96
Foshay, N. N., 629
Foster, C. A., 444
Foster-Fishman, P. G., 629
Fouts, R. S., 263
Fowler, D., 453
Fox, M. J., 86
Fox, P. T., 115
Frances, R. J., 557
Francis, D., 433

Frank, M. G., 379, 380, 384
Frankl, V., 472
Franklin, J. E., Jr., 557
Franks, J. J., 181
Fraser, S. C., 650
Frease-McMahan, L., 637
Fredrickson, B. L., 441, 531, 583
Freedman, J. L., 637, 650
Freeman, S., 49, 629
Freeman, W., 579
Freeston, I. L., 63
Frensch, P. A., 247
Freud, Amalia, 546
Freud, Anna, 466
Freud, S., 11, 14, 15, 16, 17, 36, 204, 219, 305, 306, 317, 462, 463, 468, 469, 487, 543, 544, 546, 547, 559, 608
Freudenberger, H. J., 594
Freyd, J. J., 198, 199
Frick, R. W., 379
Fried, I., 141, 142
Fried, P. A., 409
Friedberg, F., 575
Friedman, M., 590
Friedman, R. S., 401
Friedman, W. J., 204
Friesen, W. V., 372, 379, 380, 383
Frith, C. D., 430, 520
Frith, U., 78, 418
Frumin, M., 525
Fryer, A. J., 504
Furmark, T., 566
Furumoto, L., 18, 32
Fuster, J. M., 97

G

Gable, S. L., 531
Gabrieli, J. D. E., 376
Gaechter, S., 627
Gage, P., 108, 109, 115, 458
Gais, S., 83, 248
Gal, A., 289
Galanter, E., 125
Galati, D., 380
Galea, S., 592
Galef, B., 225
Galileo, G., 40
Gall, F. J., 6
Gallistel, C. R., 241, 275
Gallup, G. G., 301
Galton, F., 352, 361
Gangestad, S. W., 631, 635
Garb, H. N., 399, 453, 500
Garber, J., 432, 514
Garcia, J., 26, 222
Gardner, B. T., 263
Gardner, H., 350
Gardner, R. A., 263
Gardner, R., 32
Garety, P. A., 532
Garofalo, R., 435
Garry, M., 199
Gary, M. L., 657
Gatz, M., 442
Gauld, A., 327
Gauss, F., 283
Gazzaniga, M. S., 25, 111
Ge, X. J., 435
Geen, R. G., 461, 623
Gegenfurtner, K. R., 137

Geller, D. A., 571
Gelman, R., 275, 280
Genesee, F., 264
Genovese, K., 629
George, C., 423
George, D., 121
George, L. D., 503
George, M. S., 568
Gerard, H. B., 27
Gershoff, E. T., 227
Gerull, F. C., 641
Ghaemi, S. N., 518
Giacino, J. T., 117
Gibb, B. E., 514
Gibbons, F. X., 301
Gibbs, G., 282
Gibbs, N. A., 507
Gick, M. L., 282
Giedd, J. N., 431
Giesler, R. B., 515
Gifford, R. K., 653
Gigerenzer, G., 274, 275, 280, 626
Gigone, D., 629
Gilbert, C. D., 600
Gilbert, D. T., 27, 49, 199, 235, 378, 385, 398, 403, 473, 531, 649, 657, 658, 659, 378
Gilbert, G. M., 653
Gilbertson, M. W., 593
Gill, M. J., 49
Gillham, J. E., 612
Gilligan, C., 428
Gilliland, K., 461
Gilovich, T., 46, 49, 291, 417, 481, 663
Ginzburg, K., 595
Gitelman, D. R., 248
Gitlin, A., 484
Gjernes, M., 405
Gladue, B. A., 435
Glaser, J., 455
Glaser, R., 597
Glass, D. C., 585
Glass, G. V., 573
Gleaves, D. H., 199
Glenwick, D. S., 49
Glick, P., 56
Glisky, E. L., 183
Glynn, S. M., 549
Gneezy, U., 399
Gobert, A., 502
Goddard, H. H., 338
Godden, D. R., 181
Goehler, L. E., 589
Goel, V., 288
Goethe, J. W. von, 516
Goetzman, E. S., 302
Goff, D. M., 562, 563, 568
Goff, L. M., 198
Gold, D., 360
Gold, D. B., 634
Gold, R. B., 434
Golding, J. M., 507
Goldman, M. S., 322
Goldman, R., 648
Gollaher, D., 561
Gollwitzer, P. M., 399
Gomez, C., 300
Good, G. E., 540
Goodale, M. A., 140, 165
Goodman, P., 555

Goodwin, F. K., 518
Gopnik, A., 417, 446
Gopnik, M., 260
Gordon, J., 137
Gordon, P., 421
Gordon, V. V., 434
Gore, A., 199, 308
Gosling, S. D., 460
Gottesman, D., 56
Gottesman, I. I., 104, 354, 522, 523
Gottfredson, L. S., 343, 344, 349, 351
Gottfried, J. A., 160
Gottlieb, A., 446
Gottman, J. M., 638
Gøtzsche, P. C., 606
Gould, M. S., 516
Gouldner, A. W., 642
Goya, F. de, 491
Graber, J. A., 433
Grabham, A., 191
Grabowski, T. J., 268
Grace, A. A., 524
Gracely, R. H., 156
Graf, P., 183, 184
Grafman, J., 657
Grajski, K. A., 101
Grant, B. F., 528, 529
Gray, H. M., 296
Gray, J. A., 461
Gray, K., 296
Graziano, W. G., 625
Greeley, A. M., 332
Green, D. A., 127
Green, L. W., 588
Green, S. K., 633
Greenberg, J., 301, 472, 483, 636
Greenberg, P. E., 540
Greene, D., 229, 398, 549, 641
Greene, J. D., 428, 429
Greenfield, P. M., 437
Greenwald, A. G., 307, 660, 661
Greenwood, M. R. C., 394
Gregg, T. R., 95
Gregory, L. J., 122
Grether, J., 361
Griffiths, P. E., 26
Grisham, J. R., 497
Grockett, L., 435
Groom, R. W., 623
Gropp, E., 391
Gross, J. J., 376, 377
Groth, G., 631
Grotpeter, J. K., 625
Grotzer, T. A., 362
Groves, B., 293
Grozier, S. A., 514
Grudnick, J. L., 344
Gruneberg, M., 11, 37
Guillery, R. W., 95
Gur, R. E., 524
Gurman, A. S., 579
Gurwitz, J. H., 605
Gusnard, D. A., 652
Gustafsson, J.-E., 347
Guthrie, R. V., 33
Guze, S. B., 512

H

Hackett, T. P., 607

Hacking, I., 280
Haider, H., 248
Haidt, J., 380, 382, 428, 429, 531, 638
Hajek, P., 617
Hakuta, K., 264
Halbrooks, D., 198, 199
Haley, A., 354
Hall, G. S., 10, 12, 16, 31, 36, 481
Hall, J. A., 345
Hall, L. K., 201
Hallett, M., 53, 608
Halliday, R., 362
Halpern, B., 161
Halpern, D. F., 357
Halpern, D. V., 301
Hamermesh, D. S., 633
Hamilton, D. L., 653
Hamilton, W. D., 625, 627
Hammen, C. L., 518
Hammersla, J. F., 637
Hammersmith, S. K., 435
Haney, C., 658
Hanlon, C., 260
Hannum, J. W., 599
Hansen, E. S., 507
Hanson, C. J., 601
Hanson, D. R., 104
Happe, F. G. E., 418
Harbluk, J. L., 194
Harding, B., 633
Harding, T., 109
Hare, R. D., 529
Harker, L. A., 380
Harkins, S., 629
Harkness, S., 287
Harlow, H. F., 420
Harlow, J. M., 108, 109
Harlow, M. L., 420
Harris, B., 219
Harris, M. J., 655
Harris, P. L., 418
Harris, V. A., 658
Harsch, N., 201
Hart, B. L., 589
Hart, K., 627
Hartley, M., 251
Hartney, H., 393
Hartshorne, H., 474, 475
Harvald, B., 513, 518
Haselton, M. G., 27
Hasher, L., 275, 280
Hashtroudi, S., 194
Hasselbalch, S., 507
Hasselmo, M. E., 83
Hassmen, P., 600
Hasson, U., 143
Hastie, R., 629
Hatch, R., 651, 652
Hatfield, E., 631, 636, 638
Hathaway, S. R., 452
Hauge, M., 513, 518
Hausser, M., 80
Hawkley, L. C., 630
Haxby, J. V., 141
Hay, P., 569
Hayes, C., 263
Hayes, D. P., 361
Hayes, K., 263
Hayes, S. C., 596
Hayne, H., 31

Heatherton, T. F., 393, 479, 611, 614, 652
Heaton, R., 524
Hebb, D. O., 178
Hebl, M. R., 393
Hecht, S., 134
Hedberg, M., 603
Hedges, M., 543
Heerey, E. A., 418
Hefferkine, R., 555
Heiby, E. M., 567
Heider, F., 56, 657
Heine, S. J., 358
Held, R., 412
Hemingway, E., 518
Hemingway, H., 591
Henderlong, J., 398
Hendler, T., 143
Hendrix, J., 168
Henig, R. M., 577
Henriques, J. B., 514
Henry, W. P., 547
Hepburn, C., 628
Herbener, E. S., 636
Herbert, J. D., 575
Herdt, G., 30, 434
Herek, G. M., 435
Herman, C. P., 614
Herman, J. L., 198
Herman-Giddens, M. E., 432
Hernstadt, R., 247
Herrmann, D. J., 11, 37
Herrnstein, R. J., 20, 364, 389
Hershenson, M., 148
Hertig, J., 193
Hertwig, R., 280
Hess, T. M., 441
Hettema, J. M., 502
Heuer, S. K., 633
Hewstone, M., 628
Heyns, B., 361
Hichwa, R. D., 268
Higgins, E. T., 401, 481
Hilgard, E. R., 328, 329, 330
Hill, G. W., 629
Hiller, J. B., 526
Hilton, J. L., 659
Hilts, P., 177
Hintzman, D. L., 46
Hippocrates, 599
Hirsch, S. R., 523
Hirschberger, G., 636
Hirschfeld, D. R., 504
Hirschfeld, R. M. A., 505
Hirstein, W., 386, 387
Hishakawa, Y., 314
Hitch, G. J., 175
Hitchcock, S. T., 561
Hitler, A., 405
Hoang, H., 277
Hobbes, T., 6
Hobson, J. A., 314, 317, 335
Hodapp, R. M., 154
Hodgkin, A. L., 79, 80
Hodson, G., 628
Hoek, H. W., 392, 408
Hoffman, A., 69
Hoffman, R. E., 568
Hoffman, V., 425
Hoffrage, U., 274, 275, 280
Hofman, Albert, 326

Hogan, D. P., 434
Hollander, E. P., 629
Holloway, G., 314
Holloway, M., 360
Holmbeck, G. N., 437
Holmes, D. S., 601
Holmes, T. H., 582, 612
Holt, J., 301
Holyoak, K. J., 282, 626
Homann, E., 514
Homans, G. C., 639
Hommer, D., 237
Honzik, C. H., 238
Hooley, J. M., 526
Hoon, M. A., 162
Hopkins, B., 409
Horn, J. L., 348
Horney, K., 463, 470, 546, 547
Horta, B. L., 409
Horwitz, J., 531
Horwitz, S., 367
House, J., 601
Houston, M. J., 96
Hovland, C. I., 647, 649
Howard, D. V., 247
Howard, I. P., 144
Howard, J. H., Jr., 247
Howes, M., 204
Howie, P. W., 96
Howland, R. H., 513, 514
Hoyle, R., 598
Hróbjartsson, A., 606
Hsu, L. K. G., 499
Hubbard, E. M., 122
Hubbard, M., 649
Hubel, D. H., 112, 113, 139
Huesmann, L. R., 56
Hug, K., 626
Hughes, D., 503
Hughes, M., 592
Hughes, T., 302
Hughs, S., 433
Hull, C., 390
Humphreys, N., 510
Hunsley, J., 573
Hunt, M., 638
Hunt, R. R., 173
Hunter, J. E., 343
Hunter, R. F., 343
Hunter, S. B., 592
Hurvich, L. M., 137
Huttenlocher, P. R., 431
Huxley, Aldous, 318, 445
Huxley, Andrew F., 79, 80
Hyde, J. S., 428
Hyman, I. E., Jr., 198, 199, 207

I

Iacoboni, M., 78
Iacono, W. G., 522
Ichheiser, G., 658, 659
Inciardi, J. A., 320
Ingersoll, C. D., 122
Ingram, J. A., 510
Ingram, P., 329
Ingram, R. E., 514
Ingvar, M., 362
Inhelder, B., 22
Inoff-Germain, G., 459
Inui, A., 391
Irvine, J. T., 350

Isaacowitz, D. M., 441
Isabelle, R. A., 424
Isacsson, G., 516
Isen, A. M., 387
Israel, L., 195
Ittelson, W. H., 148
Ives, R., 333
Izard, C. E., 380, 381

J

Jablensky, A., 522
Jaccard, J., 434
Jack, T., 471
Jackson, D. D., 556
Jackson, M., 608, 649
Jackson, R. J., 506
Jacobs, B. L., 601
Jacobs, G., 138
Jacobs, S. C., 598
Jacobson, E., 598
Jacobson, N. H., 514
Jacobson, T., 425
Jaffee, S., 428
Jahoda, G., 30
Jakobson, L. S., 140
Jalinous, R., 63
James, T. W., 140
James, W., 1, 2, 3, 4, 5, 9, 10, 12,
    14, 16, 19, 21, 26, 31, 32, 36,
    37, 299, 301, 370, 371, 372,
    389, 458, 478, 481, 530, 625
Jameson, D., 137
Jamison, K. R., 518, 535
Janet, P., 14, 17, 36
Jang, K. L., 504
Janicak, P. G., 568
Janis, I. L., 630
Jankovic, J. J., 608
Janoff-Bulman, R. J., 378
Jarrell, R., 518
Jarvella, R. J., 256
Jason, L. A., 49
Jaynes, J., 301, 305
Jencks, C., 343
Jenike, M. A., 507
Jenkins, H. M., 220
Jenkins, J. M., 373
Jenkins, W. M., 101
Jennings, K., 343
Jennings, P., 616
Jensen, T. S., 100
Jobes, D. A., 517
Joffe, R. T., 458
John Paul II (Pope), 482
John, O. P., 457, 458, 460, 485
Johnson, D. H., 153
Johnson, D. R., 444
Johnson, J. D., 322
Johnson, J. S., 261
Johnson, K., 155
Johnson, L. B., 168
Johnson, M. D., 205
Johnson, M. H., 411
Johnson, M. K., 194
Johnson, N. J., 601
Johnson, R., 418
Johnson, S., 119, 169
Johnson, S. L., 518, 519
Johnson, V. E., 396
Johnston, L., 433.
Johnston, W. A., 129

Johnstone, E. C., 524
Joiner, T. E., Jr., 515, 516
Jolton, J., 56
Jones, A. K., 156
Jones, B. C., 635
Jones, E. E., 654, 657, 658, 659
Jones, E. G., 74
Jones, J. E., 186
Jones, J. T., 483, 636
Jones, K., 561
Jones, L. M., 629
Jones, P., 187
Jonides, J., 440
Jonsson, P., 382
Joplin, J., 168
Jordan, M., 345
Jordan, V., 187, 188
Joseph, S. A., 532
Josephs, R. A., 322, 515
Jost, J. T., 455
Jouvet, M., 316
Joyce, J., 299
Judd, L. L., 512
Jung, C. G., 15, 463, 546
Jurewicz, I., 523

K

Kaal, H. L., 325
Kaas, J. H., 100
Kabnick, K., 614
Kachelski, R. A., 306
Kahlo, F., 477
Kahn, J., 363
Kahn, S., 612
Kahneman, D., 275, 276, 277,
    279, 400, 444
Kalakanis, L., 637
Kalat, J. W., 391
Kalish, D., 238
Kalman, M., 562
Kamil, A. C., 186
Kamin, L. J., 338
Kaminski, J., 221
Kamiya, J., 598
Kandel, E. R., 79, 177, 178, 182
Kanner, A. D., 584
Kant, I., 13, 56
Kanwisher, N., 113, 115, 141
Kaplan, J., 591
Kapur, B. M., 323
Kapur, S., 171
Karg-Palreiro, C., 627
Karlins, M., 653
Karney, B. R., 638, 639
Karno, M., 507
Kashiwagi, K., 350
Kaslow, N. J., 556
Kasparov, G., 295
Kasser, T., 631
Katcher, A. H., 372
Katon, W., 505
Katz, D., 653
Katz, J., 515
Katz, L. C., 159
Katz, R., 513
Kaube, H., 430
Kauffmann, C. D., 568
Kawakami, K., 657
Kay, A., 399
Keefe, F. J., 84, 156
Keisler, D. J., 491

Keith, P. M., 639
Keller, M. B., 495
Kelley, A. E., 237
Kelley, D., 453
Kelley, H. H., 639, 657, 658
Kelley, W. M., 479
Kellman, P. J., 414
Kellogg, A., 1
Kelly, C., 560
Kelly, G., 475, 477
Keltner, D., 373, 379, 380, 418
Kendler, K. S., 502, 504, 506
Kennedy, J., 507
Kennedy, J. F., 160, 201, 659
Kennedy, Q., 441
Kennedy, Robert, 659
Kennedy, Rosemary, 569
Kennedy, S. H., 458
Kennedy, T., 659
Kenrick, D. T., 631
Kenshalo, D. R., 156
Kensinger, E. A., 96, 202
Kephart, W. M., 637
Kepler, J., 40
Kermer, D. A., 378
Kernis, M. H., 482
Kerry, J., 649
Kessinger, T., 193, 194
Kessler, R. C., 490, 496, 500, 502,
    504, 506, 512, 514, 516, 564,
    592
Ketchum, K., 329
Kety, S. S., 516
Keuler, D. J., 200
Kevari, M. K., 184
Keys, C. B., 629
Khalid, R., 399
Kiecolt-Glaser, J. K., 588, 597, 601
Kiehl, K. A., 530
Kihlstrom, J. F., 306, 330, 479,
    510
Kilmister, L., 150
Kim Jong II, 455
Kim, K., 432
King, C. A., 516
King, F., 393
King, M. L., Jr., 657
Kinney, D. A., 437
Kiper, D. C., 137
Kirchner, W. H., 254
Kirk, S. A., 493
Kirker, W. S., 479
Kirkham, T. C., 326
Kirkpatrick, J., 350
Kirsch, I., 571
Kita, S., 262
Kitayama, S., 627
Klein, M., 546, 547
Klein, S. B., 479
Kleinman, A. M., 499
Kleinschmidt, A., 108
Kleitman, N., 311
Klerman, G. L., 547
Klimakhin, V., 399
Klinger, E., 302, 303, 476
Klinger, M. R., 307
Klopfer, B., 453
Kluft, R. P., 509, 510
Kluckhohn, C., 455
Klüver, H., 373, 374
Knauper, B., 512, 516

Knight, J., 633
Knowlton, B. J., 96, 247
Knutson, B., 237, 458
Kobasa, S., 612
Kobberling, J., 274
Koch, C., 141, 142, 297
Kodman, W., 275
Koelling, R. A., 222
Koestner, R., 398, 641
Koffka, K., 13, 142
Kohlberg, L., 427, 428
Kohler, W., 13
Kohut, H., 546, 547
Koivula, N., 600
Kolb, B., 108
Kolotkin, R. L., 393
Komiya, N., 540
Koo, L., 517
Koole, S. L., 483
Koss, M. P., 503
Kosslyn, S. M., 171, 172
Kovalevsky, S., 356
Kowai-Bell, N., 592
Kozak, M., 317
Kraepelin, E., 522
Kraft, T. W., 137
Kral, P. A., 226
Kramer, D. L. F., 184
Kramer, P. D., 564
Kramer, R. M., 630
Krantz, D. S., 589
Kranzler, J. H., 344
Krebs, J. R., 289
Kreider, R. M., 289
Kreiman, G., 141, 142
Kressmann, S., 564
Krimgold, B. K., 358
Krings, T., 2
Kroeze, W. K., 84
Kronig, M. H., 507
Kroonenberg, P. M., 423
Krueger, J. I., 481
Kruetzer, T., 425
Kruger, J., 417
Kruglanski, A. W., 455
Kruk, M. R., 95, 623
Krull, D. S., 649, 659
Kubovy, M., 151
Kuffler, S. W., 134
Kuhl, P., 446
Kuiper, N. A., 479
Kuipers, E., 526
Kulik, J., 201
Kullijian, H., 632
Kumkale, G. T., 647
Kunda, Z., 656
Kunugi, H., 524
Kunz, P. R., 642
Kutchins, H., 493

L

LaBar, K. S., 375
LaBerge, S., 316
Lachman, J. L., 23
Lachman, R., 23
Lackner, J. R., 158
Lagenbucher, J. W., 495
Lai, Y., 316
Lally, M., 344
Lalonde, J. K., 510
Lam, R. W., 512

Lamb, M. E., 423, 425
Lambert, W., 264
Lamberth, J., 636
Lamm, H., 630
Landauer, T. K., 11
Landis, K., 601
Landru, H. D., 529
Lane, J. D., 634
Lang, F. R., 442
Lang, P. J., 530
Lange, C. G., 370, 371, 372
Langer, E. J., 500
Langleben, D. D., 385
Langlois, J. H., 633, 637
Langston, J. W., 85
Larsen, R. J., 27
Larsen, S. F., 201
Larson, C. L., 377
Larson, J. R., 629
Larson, R., 302, 437
Larson-Gutman, M. K., 303
Lashley, K. S., 24
Lassiter, G. D., 384, 398
Last, C. G., 556
Latané, B., 49
Laub, J. H., 433
Laupa, M., 429
Laurence, J., 330
Laureys, S., 117
Lavie, P., 309
Lavoie, K. L., 567
Lavori, P. W., 512
Law, I., 507
Lawton, M. P., 442, 632
Lazarus, R. S., 374, 377, 591
Lea, S., 379
Leary, M. R., 373, 483, 501, 630,
    641
Leary, T., 326
Leaton, R. N., 211
LeBrock, K., 633
Lecky, P., 480
Lecrubier, Y., 565
LeDoux, J. E., 96, 119, 202, 220,
    375, 403, 504
Lee, D. N., 158
Lee, P. A., 432
Lee-Chai, A., 399
Lefcourt, H. M., 476
Lefkowitz, B., 358
Lehman, C. L., 497
Lehman, D. R., 280, 614
Lehman, J. M., 611
Leighton, J. P., 291
Lemmon, H., 359
Lemyre, L., 628
Lenin, V., 647
Lens, W., 399
Lentz, M. J., 312
Leonard, M., 368
Lepage, M., 182
Lepper, M. R., 229, 398, 549, 641,
    649
Lerew, D. R., 506
Leslie, A., 418
Lester, D., 516
Levant, R. F., 567
Levenson, R. W., 372
Levin, K., 595
Levine, J. A., 385
Levine, J. D., 606

Levine, J. M., 629
Levine, M., 561
Levitan, R. D., 458
Levitt, A. J., 458, 512
Levy, J., 110
Lew, A. S., 515
Lewin, K., 22, 28, 29, 31, 474
Lewin, R., 265
Lewinsky, M., 187, 188, 634
Lewis, M., 301
Lewis, R., 524
Lewis-Rivera, L. A., 367
Lewontin, R., 338
Lexenberg, E., 160
Li, H. Z., 540
Li, W., 160
Libet, B., 297
Lickel, B., 592
Liebenluft, E., 517
Lieberman, J., 562
Lieberman, M. D., 27, 461, 630,
    661
Liebler, A., 345
Liebowitz, M. R., 506
Lief, H. I., 199
Lightner, J. M., 604
Lightstone, J., 646
Lilienfeld, S. O., 399, 453, 454,
    575, 579
Lillard, L. A., 443
Lincoln, A., 1, 2, 182, 518, 647
Lindenberger, U., 360
Lindsay, D. S., 194, 198
Lindsay, J. J., 384
Lindsay, S. D., 199
Lindsey, S., 661
Lindsley, O. R., 548
Lindstrom, M., 163
Lindstrom, P., 160
Ling, H., 599
Link, B. G., 500
Link, S. W., 128
Linnaeus, C., 397
Linszen, D. H., 526, 532
Lipetz, M. E., 634
Lipowicz, A., 28
Lippold, S., 633
Lipps, T., 382
Lisanby, S. H., 568
Liszt, F., 121
Little, B. R., 476, 302
Litwin, G. H., 400
Livingstone, M., 113
Locksley, A., 628
Loehlin, J. C., 458
Loftus, E. F., 197, 198, 201, 307,
    329
Logan, A., 506
Logan, G. D., 190
Lohr, B. A., 466
Lohr, J. M., 454, 575, 579
Lømo, W. T., 178
Long, D., 350
Lonner, W. J., 30, 31
Lopez, A. D., 490
Lopez, D. F., 482
Lopiano, L., 606
Lorenz, K., 422
Lorge, I., 647
Losch, M. E., 532
Lowell, R., 518

Lowry, D., 171
Lozano, B. E., 519
Lubinski, D., 343, 363
Luborsky, L., 573
Lucas, J. A., 506
Lucas, R. E., 444, 531
Ludwig, A. M., 309
Luhtanen, R., 628
Lumley, M., 84
Lumsdaine, A. A., 649
Luria, A. R., 203
Lustman, P. J., 511
Luxas, F., 223
Lykken, D. T., 530, 531
Lynch, G. S., 178
Lynch, T., 84
Lynn, M., 633
Lynn, R., 343
Lynn, S. J., 198, 327, 454, 579

M
Ma, Y.-Y., 189
MacCulloch, R. J., 444
MacDonald, S., 31, 205
MacDonald, T. K., 616
MacGregor, J. N., 285
Mack, A. H., 557
Mackin, R., 583
Mackinnon, A., 502
Maclean, P. D., 96
Macmillan, M., 108, 127
Macmillan, N. A., 127
Macomber, G., 400
Macrae, C. N., 479, 652, 656
Maddi, K. L., 612
Maddi, S. R., 612
Madey, S. F., 49, 481
Maes, M., 589
Magder, L., 588
Magee, W. J., 504
Maggi, G., 606
Magnani, F., 176
Magoun, H. W., 93
Maguire, E. A., 101
Mah, K., 396
Maher, A., 595
Mai, N., 149
Maier, S. F., 589
Makin, J. E., 409
Malach, R., 143
Maldonado, J. R., 508
Malina, R. M., 432
Malinoski, P. T., 198
Malle, B. F., 504
Malone, P. S., 649, 658
Malvo, L. B., 367
Manber, R., 313
Mancill, R. B., 497
Mandel, D. R., 280
Mandelbaum, M., 134
Manderscheid, R. W., 522
Mendes, W. B., 592
Mandle, C. L., 598
Mandler, G., 172, 184
Mann, J. J., 516
Mannheim, Z., 387
Manning, C. A., 191
Mannix, L. M., 393
Manson, J. E., 393
Mapplethorpe, R., 410
Maquet, P., 316

Marangell, L. B., 560, 562, 563,
    568
Marcus Aurelius, 377
Marcus, C. C., 557
Marcus, G. B., 200
Marcus, J., 522
Marentette, P. F., 258
Marino, L., 301
Markowitz, J. C., 547
Marks, I. M., 507, 549
Markus, H., 479
Marlatt, G. A., 321, 325
Marmot, M. G., 588, 591
Maroney, Sean, 353
Maroney, Susan, 353
Marr, D., 143
Marsolek, C. J., 272
Martin, A., 99, 184, 268
Martin, B., 367
Martin, G., 517
Martin, J., 367
Martin, L. L., 381
Martin, L. R., 603
Martin, M., 360
Martin, N. G., 460
Marucha, P. T., 588
Maslach, C., 594
Maslow, A. H., 16, 17, 36, 331,
    390, 471, 482, 530
Mason, S. A., 14
Masserman, J. H., 467
Masters, W. H., 396
Matalin, M., 636
Mather, M., 441, 442
Mathis, J. L., 581
Matisse, H., 230
Matschinger, H., 500
Matte, T. D., 408
Matthews, G., 461
Mattick, R. P., 362
Maudsley, H., 520
May, M., 474, 475
May, R., 472
Maynard-Smith, J., 265, 627
McAdams, D., 478
McAndrew, F. T., 380
McArdle, N., 358
McArthur, L. Z., 635
McCann, B., 460
McCann, I. L., 601
McCarley, R. W., 317, 525
McCarthy, R. A., 268
McCartney, K., 359
McCauley, C. R., 382
McCeney, M. K., 589
McClelland, D. C., 399, 454
McClintock, M. K., 160, 434
McCloskey, M., 197
McConkey, K. M., 199
McCrae, R. R., 457
McCreadie, R., 560
McCue, M., 602
McDaniel, M. A., 173, 191,
    361
McDermott, J., 115, 141
McDermott, K. B., 103, 195
McDougall, W., 389, 390
McEvoy, S. P., 129
McFall, R. M., 128
McFarland, B. H., 561
McFarland, C., 200

McFarlane, A. H., 583
McGarrah, A., 337, 338
McGarty, C., 653
McGaugh, J. L., 202
McGee, W. J., 502
McGhee, D. E., 660, 661
McGill, K. L., 583
McGrady, A., 600
McGregor, D., 46
McGue, M., 353, 460
McGuffin, P., 513
McGuire, J. M., 363
McGuire, P. K., 520
McHaffie, J. G., 605
McHugh, P. R., 199
McKetin, R., 73, 362
McKinley, J. C., 452
McKinney, C. H., 598
McLachlan, D. R., 194
McMillan, D., 655
McNally, R. J., 199, 207, 505, 576, 577
McNamara, B., 568
McNeill, D., 192
McNeilly, A. S., 96
McVeigh, T., 193
McWilliams, N., 467
McWilliams, P., 324
Mead, G. H., 479
Mead, M., 30
Meadows, E. A., 597
Mechelli, A., 264
Medin, D. L., 272
Medvec, V. H., 49, 481
Meichenbau, D., 597
Meins, E., 425
Meisel, S. R., 589
Mekel-Bobrov, N., 104
Melon, C., 502
Meltzoff, A. N., 411, 446
Melzack, R., 157
Memon, A., 199
Mendes, W. B., 592
Merikangas, K. R., 512
Mervis, C. B., 258, 269, 271
Merzenich, M. M., 101
Mesmer, F. A., 327
Messer, S. B., 579
Messick, D. M., 639
Mesulam, M. M., 248
Metalsky, G. I., 515
Metcalfe, J., 283
Meter, K., 393
Meyer-Bahlberg, H. F. L., 435
Meyerowitz, R., 562
Meyers, J., 199, 200, 378
Michael, R. T., 434
Michelson, D., 502
Michotte, A., 56
Mignot, E., 313
Miklowitz, D. J., 519
Mikulincer, M., 612, 636
Milavsky, B., 372
Milazzo-Sayre, L. J., 522
Milgram, S., 629, 644, 645, 646
Millan, M. J., 502
Miller, A. J., 71, 645
Miller, D. G., 197
Miller, D. T., 628, 642, 659
Miller, G. A., 23, 175
Miller, I., 518

Miller, I. J., 162
Miller, J., 255
Miller, K. F., 420
Miller, N., 626
Miller, N. E., 392, 600, 647
Miller, T. I., 573
Miller, T. W., 583
Miller, W. R., 559
Millman, L., 382
Mills, J., 634, 650
Mills, P. J., 87
Milne, E., 657
Milner, A. D., 140, 165
Milner, B., 25, 96, 176, 182
Milner, P. M, 95, 237, 374
Milun, R., 624
Mineka, S., 223, 245, 503, 504, 521
Minichiello, W. E., 507
Minsky, M., 297
Mintun, M. A., 113
Miranda, J., 514
Mirenberg, M. C., 483
Mischel, W., 398, 473, 474
Mishkin, M., 139
Mita, T. H., 633
Mitchell, D. R., 530
Mitchell, J. P., 479, 652
Mitchell, K. A., 636
Miura, I. T., 419
Moffitt, T. E., 432, 435
Moghaddam, B., 237
Moise-Titus, J., 56
Mokdad, A. H. P., 612
Monahan, J., 128
Monahan, J. L., 632
Monet, C., 229, 230
Moniz, E., 569
Montepare, J. M., 635
Mook, D. G., 65, 392
Moon, S. M., 29
Moore, A. J., 309
Moore, H., 524
Moore, K. L., 102
Moore, M. K., 411
Moran, J. M., 479
Moray, N., 299
Moreland, R. L., 629
Morgan, D., 379
Morgan, H., 333
Morgenstern, J., 559
Morin, A., 479
Morinan, A., 320
Morison, V., 410
Morris, A. S., 433
Morris, C. D., 181
Morris, E. K., 18
Morris, R. G., 178
Morris, T. L., 504
Morrow, D., 440
Moruzzi, G., 93
Mory, M., 437
Moscovitch, M., 177, 182, 198, 393
Mosher, W. D., 289, 639
Moss, D., 600
Moss, M., 320
Mosteller, F., 46
Motley, M. T., 306
Mounier, D., 316
Mountjoy, C. Q., 513
Moyer, C. A., 599

Mroczek, D. K., 442
Mueller, E. T., 303
Mueller, T. I., 512
Muenter, M. D., 85
Muhammad, J. A., 367
Muhlenbruck, L., 384
Mukherjee, S., 567
Mullen, B., 629
Mullen, M. K., 188, 189
Muller, M. N., 624
Muller, W. E., 564
Multhaup, K. S., 205
Mumford, D. B., 499
Mumme, D. L., 641
Munoz, R. F., 377
Murphy, N. A., 345
Murphy, S. T., 632
Murray, C., 364
Murray, C. J. L., 490
Murray, H. A., 453, 454, 455, 456
Murray, R. M., 520, 523
Musen, G., 96
Musselman, L., 637
Mycielska, K., 4
Myers, D. G., 630
Myers, J., 504

N

Nabokov, V., 121
Nadasdy, A., 254
Nadel, L., 198
Nagasako, E. M., 156
Nagel, T., 295
Nahemow, L., 632
Nakazato, M., 391
Narrow, W. E., 490, 539
Nasar, S., 535
Nash, E., 434
Nash, J., 492, 535
Nash, M., 329
Nasser, M., 499
Nathan, P. E., 495
Natterson, J., 490
Neale, J. M., 507, 519
Neale, M. C., 502
Neilson, T. A., 316
Neimeyer, R. A., 636
Neisser, U., 21, 24, 201, 205, 207, 298, 299, 356, 358, 360
Nelson, C. B. , 592
Nelson, D., 636
Nelson, P., 506
Nemeroff, C. B., 84, 382
Nemeth, C., 643
Nesse, R. M., 507
Nettleback, T., 344
Neu, T. W., 363
Neugebauer, R., 408
Newberg, A., 332
Newell, A., 23
Newman, A. J., 25
Newman, L. S., 467
Newman, M. G., 603
Newport, E. L., 247, 261
Newsom, J. T., 650
Newsome, W. T., 149
Neylan, T. C., 315
Nezworski, M. T., 453
Niaura, R., 591
Nicholson, J., 567
Nicoladis, E., 264

Nicolelis, M. A. L., 92
Nida, S., 629
Nietzsche, F., 587
Nikles, C. D., II, 315
Nikolajsen, L., 100
Nikula, R., 303
Ninan, P. T., 504
Nisbett, R. E., 184, 398, 473, 625, 641, 659
Nishihara, H. K., 143
Nishino, S., 313
Nissen, M. J., 247
Nitschke, J. B., 513
Nixon, R. M., 168
Noel, N. E., 322
Nolen-Hoeksema, S., 514
Norcross, J. C., 541
Norenzayan, A., 659
Norman, W. T., 457
Norton, A. J., 637
Norton, G. R., 506
Nosanchuk, T. A., 646
Nosek, B. A., 661
Novaco, R. W., 597
Nunn, J. A., 122
Nuttin, J. M., 483
Nyberg, L., 182

O

Oakes, L. M., 56
Oaklander, A. L., 156
Oately, K., 373
O'Brien, G. T., 556
Ochsner, K. N., 27, 201, 376, 377
O'Connor, T. G., 422
Odbert, H. S., 456
Oden, M. H., 363
O'Doherty, J., 430
O'Donnell, K., 437
O'Donovan, M. C., 523
Ofshe, R. J., 329, 576
Ohman, A., 223, 245, 504
Ohno, A. A., 94
Okagaki, L., 351
O'Laughlin, M. J., 504
Olausson, P. O., 434
Oldham, J. M., 528
Olds, J., 95, 236, 237, 374
Oleson, K. C., 656
Ollers, D. K., 258
Olson, K., 576
Oltmanns, T. F., 507, 519, 529
Olton, D. S., 186, 240
O'Malley, P., 433
O'Neal, S., 194
O'Neal, T., 46
Orban, G. A., 138
Orme-Johnson, D. W., 332
Ormerod, T. C., 285
Orne, M. T., 329
Ornstein, G. G., 563
Ortiz, V., 628
Orwell, G., 445
Öst, L.-G., 504, 549
Osterloh, M., 401
O'Sullivan, L. F., 397
O'Sullivan, M., 384
Oswald, A. J., 444
Oswald, L., 299
Osypuk, T. L., 358
Owen, A. M., 117

Owen, R. J., 523
Owens, W. A., 360
Ozyurek, A., 262

P
Paige, R. U., 567
Paikoff, R. L., 433
Paivio, A., 11, 172
Palmieri, R. M., 122
Pande, A. C., 563
Pankratz, S., 516
Papez, J. W., 96, 374
Paré, E. B., 149
Parker, D., 284
Parker, K. C. H., 575
Parkinson, B., 376
Parrish, T. B., 160, 248
Parrott, A. C., 320, 323
Parrott, W. G., 376
Parsons, T., 608
Partinen, M., 313
Pasqual-Leone, A., 63, 100
Passini, F. T., 457
Patrick, C. J., 530
Patrick, R., 387
Patterson, C. J., 435
Paul, A. M., 485, 487
Pavlidis, I., 385
Pavlov, I. P., 18, 21, 212, 214,
    215, 216, 218, 219, 220, 223,
    224, 233, 246
Pawlowski, B., 28
Pearce, J. M., 217
Pearlstone, Z., 180
Peaugh, S., 629
Peelen, M. V., 141
Peissig, J. J., 144
Pelham, B. W., 71, 482, 483, 649,
    659
Peltonen, L., 105
Pendergrast, M., 199
Penfield, W., 98, 156
Pennebaker, J. W., 596, 597, 605,
    619, 634
Pentland, J., 198, 199
Perenin, M.-T., 140
Perina, K., 567
Perkins, D. N., 362
Perlis, M. L., 313
Perloff, L. S., 615
Perls, F. S., 555
Perner, J., 416, 427
Perrett, D. I., 113, 635
Perris, C., 515
Perry, C., 330
Perry, Z. W., 655
Persons, J. B., 491
Peschardt, K., 530
Peskin, H., 435
Pete, E., 614
Peters, E. R., 532
Petersen, A. C., 435
Petersen, S. E., 182
Peterson, C., 418, 530
Peterson, D., 624
Peterson, L. R., 174, 175
Peterson, M. J., 174, 175
Peterson, S. E., 25
Petitto, L. A., 258
Petrie, K. P., 597
Petty, R. E., 647, 648

Pfaus, J. G., 237
Phelan, J., 500
Phelps, E. A., 115, 220, 375, 661
Philips, E., 511
Phillips, A. G., 237
Phillips, D. P., 516, 517
Phillips, F., 617
Piaf, E., 449, 450, 463, 465
Piaget, J., 22, 28, 412, 413, 414,
    415, 418, 419, 426, 427, 446
Picasso, P., 229, 230, 492
Pickrell, J. E., 197
Pike, C. L., 635
Pillard, R. C., 435
Pilloff, D., 304
Pinel, E. C., 235, 378
Pinel, J. P. J., 614
Pines, A. M.. 594
Pinker, S., 26, 27, 259, 260, 266,
    291
Pipes, D., 368
Pitman, R. K., 577
Pitt, B., 111
Pittinsky, T. L., 357
Pizlo, F. J., 13
Pizlo, Z., 13
Pizzagalli, D., 513
Plath, S., 518
Plato, 5, 352, 388
Platts, M., 499
Plomin, R., 106, 353, 354, 356,
    358, 460, 502, 513, 518, 611
Plotnik, J. M., 301
Podolski, C.-L., 56
Polivy, J., 614
Pollack, J., 469
Pollard, P., 287
Pons, F., 418
Poole, D. A., 199
Pope, A. W., 437
Porter, E. H., 611
Posey, T. B., 532
Posner, M. I., 113
Post, R. M., 84
Posthuma, D., 356
Postman, L., 189
Power, T., 433
Powers, A. M., 396
Pozos, R., 70
Prasada, S., 259
Pratkanis, A. R., 306, 649
Premack, D., 228
Prentice, D. A., 642
Prescott, C. A., 504
Presley, E. A., 596
Pressman, S. D., 602, 641
Prochaska, J. J., 615
Prodromidis, M., 423
Provine, R. R., 603
Prudic, J., 568
Pruitt, D. G., 625
Przedborski, S., 97
Putnam, F. W., 508, 509
Putnam, K. M., 377, 513
Pyszczynski, T., 301, 472, 483

Q
Quattrone, G. A., 654, 659
Querleu, D., 410
Quiroga, R. Q., 141, 142

R
Rabin, B. M., 222
Rabin, J., 333
Rabin, J. S., 222
Rabinowitz, C., 268
Rachman, S. J., 507
Racine, C. A., 195
Radford, E., 235
Radford, M. A., 235
Rahe, R. H., 582, 612
Raichle, M. E., 113, 190, 652
Rajaram, S., 393
Ralston, A., 157
Ramachandran, V. S., 100, 119,
    122, 386, 387
Ramón y Cajal, S., 74, 75
Ramos, S., 367
Ramus, S. J., 248
Ranvier, L.-A., 81
Rapaport, D., 453
Rapee, R. M., 641
Rapoport, J., 535
Rapport, R., 75
Rapson, R. L., 636
Raskin, N. J., 553
Rasmussen, S., 98, 156
Ratner, R. K., 628
Ray, Man (Emmanuel Radnitzky),
    515
Raybeck, D., 11, 37
Rayner, R., 18, 218, 219
Raz, N., 439
Read, H. L., 152
Read, J., 575
Read, J. D., 198
Read, K. E., 30
Reason, J., 4
Reber, A. S., 246, 247
Reber, P. J., 248. 249
Recanzone, G. H., 101
Rechsthaffen, A., 312
Reddy, L., 141, 142
Reed, G., 194
Reeve, C., 91
Regan, P. C., 636
Regehr, G., 284
Regier, D. A., 490, 500, 507
Reichhardt, T., 65
Reichle, E. D., 301
Reid, S., 636
Reinarman, C., 325
Reinert, G., 362
Reis, S. M., 363
Reiss, D., 301
Reiss, H. T., 632
Reissland, N., 411
Reiter, E. O., 432
Renner, M. J., 583
Repacholi, B. M., 417
Rescorla, R. A., 217, 220, 237
Ressler, K. J., 84
Reyna, V. E., 207
Reynolds, C. A., 442
Rheingold, H., 316
Rhodes, G., 637
Rhue, J. W., 327
Ricci-Bitt, P. E., 380
Rice, C., 306
Rich, C. L., 516
Richards, M. H., 437

Richert, E. S., 363
Richter, J., 507
Richters, J., 396
Rieber, R. W., 7, 9
Riefer, D. M., 184
Rieser-Danner, L. A., 637
Rifkin, L., 523
Riskin, B., 293, 294
Rissel, C., 396
Ritchie, B. F., 238
Rivera, D., 499
Rivet, J. M., 502
Rizzolatti, G., 78, 245
Roberson, D., 267
Roberts, B. W., 458
Roberts, G. A., 520, 600
Robins, E., 512
Robins, L. N., 320, 490, 500, 507,
    512
Robinson, A., 363
Robinson, D. N., 5
Robinson, I. C., 96
Robinson, R. G., 514
Robinson, W. A., 136
Robitzek, E. H., 563
Rockwell, N., 477
Rodgers-Ramachandran, D., 100
Rodieck, R. W., 130
Rodriguez, M. L., 398
Roediger III, H. L., 180, 181, 195,
    198
Roeling, T. A. P., 95
Roethke, T., 518
Rogers, C. R., 16, 17, 36, 471,
    481, 487, 530, 553
Rogers, T. B., 479
Roggman, L. A., 637
Rohsenow, D., 321
Rolls, E. T., 113
Roosevelt, T., 518
Rorschach, H., 453
Rosa, E., 599
Rosa, L., 599
Rosch, E. H., 266, 269, 271
Rose, J. L., 158
Rose, S., 338
Rose, S. P. R., 362
Roseman, I. J., 374
Rosenberg, M., 480
Rosenhan, D., 500
Rosenman, R. H., 590
Rosenstein, M. J., 522
Rosenthal, R., 50, 461, 384, 655
Ross, B. H., 275, 282
Ross, D., 243, 244
Ross, D. F., 196
Ross, L., 473, 649, 658
Ross, M., 200, 571
Ross, S., 243, 244
Roth, B. L., 84
Roth, H. P., 610
Roth, M., 513
Roth, R. H., 85
Rothbart, M. K., 424
Rothbaum, B. O., 538, 575, 596
Rothermundt, M., 523
Rotstein, A. H., 401
Rotter, J. B., 476
Rotton, L., 603
Rounds, J., 599
Rowa, K., 541

Rowland, L. W., 329
Roy-Byrne, P. P., 502, 562, 563
Royzman, E. B., 417
Rozanski, A., 591
Rozin, P., 382, 391, 393, 614
Ruane, M., 367
Rubenstein, A. J., 637
Rubin, B. D., 159
Rubin, E., 143
Rubin, M., 628
Rubin, Z., 638
Rude, S. S., 515
Rudman, L. A., 657
Rugh, D., 320
Rusbult, C. E., 639
Rushton, J. P., 356
Russell, J. A., 370, 382
Rustichini, A., 399
Rutter, M., 104, 422
Ryan, R. M., 398, 471, 482, 641
Ryba, N. J., 162

S

Sachs, J. S., 256
Sackeim, H. A., 510, 567, 568
Sacks, O., 44, 168, 176
Sadalla, E. K., 631
Safer, M. A., 200
Saffran, J. R., 247
Sagi, A., 425
Sahakian, B. J., 362
Sais, E., 264
Sakamoto, J., 230
Salapatek, P., 410
Salge, R. A., 506
Sallis, J. F., 615
Salthouse, T. A., 348, 360, 440
Salvio, M. A., 313
Sammons, M. T., 567
Sampson, R. J., 433
Samuelson, R. J., 186, 240
Sandberg, S., 582
Sanders, D. Y., 641
Sanderson, W. C., 574
Sandin, R. H., 293
Sankis, L. M., 493
Sapirstein, G., 571
Sapolsky, R. M., 588, 619, 625
Saroyan, W., 509
Sarris, V., 13
Sarter, M., 85
Sartre, J.-P., 472
Satcher, D., 434
Saunders, G., 510
Savage, C. R., 171, 173
Savage, P., 410
Savage-Rumbaugh, S., 265
Saver, J. L., 333
Savic, I., 160
Savin-Williams, R. C., 435
Savitsky, K., 306
Sawa, A., 524
Sawyer, T. F., 33
Scarborough, E., 18, 32
Scarr, S., 359
Sczaufca, M., 526
Schabus, M., 117
Schachter, S., 319, 371, 372, 617, 632
Schacter, D. L., 27, 96, 103, 169, 176, 177, 179, 181, 182, 183,

184, 185, 187, 193, 194, 195, 198, 201, 202, 207
Schaefer, D., 629
Schaefer, J. T., 636
Schaeffer, M. A., 585
Schafer, R. B., 639
Schaffer, M. M., 272
Schaie, K. W., 360
Schappell, L., 39, 42
Schappell, R., 39
Schatzberg, A. F., 562, 564
Scheff, T. J., 501
Scheier, M. F., 611
Scherer, K. R., 374, 379, 380
Schiavo, M., 116
Schiavo, T., 116
Schiebel, A. B., 119
Schields, C., 614
Schiff, N. D., 117
Schildkraut, J. J., 513
Schlafly, P., 426
Schmeichel, B. J., 613
Schmidt, F. L., 343
Schmidt, N. B., 506
Schmitt, D. P., 289, 631
Schmitt, W. B., 84
Schnapf, J. L., 137
Schneider, B. H., 425
Schneider, M., 435
Schneider, R., 417
Schneier, F., 504
Schnieder, T., 513
Schnorr, J. A., 172
Schnur, D. B., 567
Schnyer, D. M., 184
Schoeman, R., 481
Scholey, A., 320
Schooler, J. W., 301, 510
Schooler, L. J., 203
Schooler, T. Y., 307, 661
Schouwenburg, H. C., 35
Schrader, S. S., 556
Schreiner, C. E., 152
Schroeder, D. H., 344
Schul, R., 382
Schultz, D. P., 8, 9, 10
Schultz, S. E., 8, 9, 10
Schulze, B., 500
Schwartz, C. E., 424
Schwartz, D., 518
Schwartz, G. E., 595
Schwartz, J. H., 76
Schwartz, J. L. K., 660, 661
Schwartz, S., 316
Schwartzenberg, S., 176
Schwartzman, A. E., 360
Schwarz, N., 387
Sclafani, A., 223
Scoville, W. B., 25, 96, 176
Scribner, S., 287, 349
Secord, P. F., 636
Sedin, D., 353
Sedin, H., 353
Segal, M. W., 632
Segal, Z. V., 514, 551
Segall, M. H., 30, 31
Segerstrom, S. C., 611
Seligman, M. E. P., 398, 504, 514, 530, 573
Selikoff, I. J., 563
Selye, H., 96, 587

Semenza, C., 193
Senghas, A., 262
Serpell, R., 350
Seung-Hui, C., 539
Seyfarth, R. M., 254
Sexton, A., 518
Seymour, B., 430
Shackelford, T. K., 27, 636
Shah, G. M., 520
Shah, J., 401
Shallice, T., 173, 182, 190, 268
Shanker, S. G., 265
Shapiro, C. M., 396
Shapiro, F., 575
Shapiro, L. R., 267
Shapiro, N., 426
Share, L. J., 625
Sharma, Y. S., 631
Sharp, L. K., 597
Shaw, J. C., 23
Shaw, P., 361
Shedler, J., 325
Sheehan, P. W., 199, 328
Sheese, B. E., 625
Sheffield, F. D., 649
Sheingold, K., 205
Shenton, M. E., 525
Shepherd, G. M., 102
Sherburne, L. M., 245
Shereshevskii, S., 203
Sherif, M., 628
Sherman, S. M., 95
Sherrod, D., 585
Sherrod, N. B., 540
Shettleworth, S. J., 186
Shields, B., 513
Shiffman, S., 617
Shih, M., 357
Shimamura, A. P., 194
Shimoda, K., 380
Shiner, R. L., 458
Shiota, M. N., 379
Shiv, B., 388
Shoda, Y., 398, 473, 474
Shomstein, S., 129
Shrager, E. E., 394
Shurgot, B. A., 633
Shweder, R. A., 29, 30
Siegal, J., 316
Siegal, M. 418
Siegel, A., 95
Siegel, B., 70
Siegel, M., 204
Siegel, S., 215
Sigl, J. C., 294
Silberg, J., 104
Silberman, E. K., 544
Silver, R. L., 597
Silverman, I., 629
Silverman, J., 490
Simien, C., 514
Simmel, M., 56
Simon, H. A., 23
Simon, L., 1
Simon, T., 339, 343, 357
Simonides, 171, 172
Simpson, E. L., 428
Simpson, J. A., 631, 637
Singer, B., 573
Singer, J. E., 371, 372, 585, 632
Singer, T., 430

Singh, D., 634, 635
Sipe, K., 368
Skinner, B. F., 11, 19, 20, 21, 24, 36, 37, 225, 226, 228, 231, 232, 233, 234, 235, 236, 242, 243, 251, 259, 260, 390, 473, 548
Skodol, A. E., 528
Slater, A., 410
Slogstad, J., 176
Slone, M., 593
Slotnick, S. D., 195
Smart, L., 624
Smetacek, V., 94
Smetana, J. G., 429
Smith, A., 396
Smith, C. A., 374
Smith, C. M., 420
Smith, E. E., 440
Smith, M. L., 573
Smith, N., 253
Smith, P. K., 306, 432
Smith, P. M., 628
Smith, S. M., 199
Snellen, H., 130
Snyder, M., 655
Snyder, S. H., 524
Sobel, D., 71
Sobell, L. C., 559
Sobell, M. B., 559
Solodky, M., 629
Solomon, H. C., 548
Solomon, J., 423
Solomon, S., 472, 483
Solomon, Z., 595
Somers, M., 410
Sonnby-Borgstrom, M., 382
Sonnega, A., 592
Sorrentino, R. M., 628
Soyinka, W., 351
Spanos, N. P., 509
Spearman, C., 345, 346, 347, 351
Spector, J., 575
Speisman, J. C., 591
Spelke, E. S., 280, 414
Spellman, B. A., 280
Spence, K., 390
Spence, M. J., 410
Spencer, L. G., 491
Spencer, S. J., 302, 628
Sperling, G., 173, 174
Sperry, R. W., 109, 110
Spiegel, D., 199
Spiers, H. J., 101
Spinath, F. M., 354
Spinoza, B., 20
Spiro, A., 442
Spiro, H. M., 609
Spitz, R. A., 420
Spitzer, R. L., 505, 508, 510
Sprecher, S., 200
Spritz, B., 423
Spurling, M., 213
Squire, L. R., 96, 177, 178, 182, 183, 184, 186, 194, 248
Srivastava, S., 457, 458, 485
Sroufe, L. A., 425
Stadler, M. A., 247
Stangor, C., 655
Stark, H., 184
Starkey, P., 280

Starr, J. M., 359
Starr, K., 187
Stasser, G., 629
Staw, B. M., 277
Steadman, H. J., 500
Steele, C. M., 322, 357, 655
Steele, H., 425
Steffen, V. J., 459, 625
Stein, M. B., 504, 593
Stein, Z., 408
Steinbaum, E. A., 392
Steinberg, L., 433
Steinem, G., 426
Steiner, F., 379
Steiner, J. E., 380
Steinman, R. B., 13
Steinmetz, J. L., 658
Stejskal, W. J., 453
Steketee, G. S., 505
Stellar, E., 392, 394
Stellar, J. R., 237, 392
Stelmack, R. M., 461
Stennet, J., 380
Stephens, R. S., 326
Stepper, S., 381
Sterelny, K., 26
Stern, J. A., 330
Stern, L. D., 46
Stern, R., 549
Stern, W., 339, 340
Sternberg, K. J., 423
Sternberg, R. J., 291, 349, 350, 351, 638
Stevens, G., 32
Stevens, J., 172, 393
Stevens, L. A., 79
Stevens, L. C., 601
Stevenson, R. L., 509
Stewart, M., 100
Stewart-Williams, S., 606
Stickgold, R., 312, 315
Stickney-Gibson, M., 201
Stigler, J. W., 30
Stone, A. A., 603
Stone, J., 655
Stone, J. I., 384
Stone, M. B., 122
Stones, M. H., 597
Storms, M. D., 660
Stough, C., 344
Strack, F., 381
Strahan, E. J., 302 308
Strayer, D. L., 129
Streissguth, A. P., 409
Strickland, L. H., 503
Strohmetz, D. B., 642
Strong, R. K., 624
Strosahl, K., 596
Stroup, S., 562
Stuss, D. T., 99, 376
Suchman, A. L., 609
Sue, S., 499
Sullivan, A., 624
Sullivan, H. S., 470, 546, 547
Sullivan, M. A., 29
Sulloway, F. J., 15, 455
Suls, J., 596
Summers, L., 459
Sumner, F. C., 32, 33, 34, 36
Sumner, W., 628
Sun, R., 434

Super, C. M., 287
Susman, S., 437
Susser, E. B., 408
Sussman, L. K., 500
Sutter, M. L., 152
Sutter-Hernandez, J., 322
Sutton, J. E., 256
Suzuki, L. A., 357
Svensson, O., 382
Swann, W. B., 480, 515, 655
Swanson, J. W., 500
Swap, W. C., 632
Swayze II, V. W., 569
Swednsen, J., 519
Swets, J. A., 127, 128
Swinkels, A., 275
Swinson, R. P., 507, 549, 575
Szasz, T., 575
Szathmary, E., 265
Szechtman, H., 330
Szpunar, K. K., 103

T

Tafarodi, R. W., 515, 649
Taft, L., 363
Tajfel, H., 628, 630, 653
Takahashi, K., 423
Takei, N., 523
Takeuchi, D. T., 499
Tam, E. M., 512
Tambor, E. S., 641
Tammet, D., 418
Tamminga, C. A., 84
Tanaka, K., 139, 141
Tang, Y.-P., 179. 362
Tanner, L., 363
Tapert, S. F., 44
Tardif, C., 425
Tarr, M. J., 143, 144
Tart, C. T., 318
Tatum, A., 46
Taubman, O., 612
Tavris, C., 548
Taylor, A. M., 299
Taylor, D., 264
Taylor, E., 14
Taylor, E. H., 523
Taylor, S. E., 204, 484, 602, 609, 619, 659, 660
Taylor, T. J., 265
Teasdale, J. D., 514, 551
Telch, M. J., 506
Tellegen, A., 328, 370, 460, 531
Temerlin, M. K., 500
Tempini, M. L., 193
Tenney, Y. J., 205
Terdal, S. K., 641
Terman, L. M., 340, 342, 351, 356, 357, 363
Terman, M., 568
Tesser, A., 460, 636
Tetirick, J. C., 205
Teyler, T. J., 177
Thaker, G. K., 523
Thaler, R. H., 627
Tharp, R. G., 499
Thase, M. E., 513, 514
Thelen, E., 412
Therriault, N., 376
Thibaut, J. W., 639
Thoma, S. J., 428

Thomas, A., 424
Thomas, G. V., 241
Thompson, C. P., 188
Thompson, D. M., 180
Thompson, P. M., 431, 524, 525
Thomson, D. M., 193, 194
Thorndike, E. L., 224, 225, 233, 243
Thornhill, R., 635
Thurber, J., 400
Thurstone, L. L., 346, 347
Tice, D. M., 35, 516
Tienari, P., 525
Tierney, S., 514
Titchener, E. B., 9, 10, 12, 14, 16, 32, 36, 124
Tittle, P., 445
Titus, W., 629
Toch, H., 629
Todd, J. T., 18
Todes, D. P., 251
Tolin, D. F., 575
Tolman, E. C., 237, 238, 239
Tomaka, J., 591
Tomarken, A. J., 514
Tomkins, S. S., 381
Tonge, J., 333
Tooby, J., 26
Tootell, R. B. H., 149
Torgensen, S., 503, 506
Torrey, E. F., 500, 523
Toth, S. L., 424
Totterdell, P., 376
Towne, W. F., 254
Trachtenberg, S., 393
Tranel, D., 268, 278, 382
Treat, T. A., 128
Trebach, A. S., 324
Treede, R. D., 156
Trevarthen, C., 110
Triesman, M., 299
Triplett, N., 28
Trivers, R. L., 84
Troscianko, T., 379
Trost, M. R., 631, 640, 650
Trötschel, R., 399
Trousdale, W. W., 500
Trull, T. J., 528
Tsien, J., 362
Tsimpli, I-M., 253
Tucker, E., 460
Tuerlinckx, F., 399
Tulving, E., 170, 180, 182, 183, 184, 185, 186
Turiel, E., 428, 429
Turk-Charles, S., 441
Turkheimer, E., 354, 355, 529
Turner, D. C., 362
Turner, J. C., 630, 653
Turvey, M. T., 174
Tversky, A., 275, 276, 277, 279, 400
Twenge, J. M., 444
Tyce, G. M., 85
Tyler, T. R., 644

U

Uesiliana, K., 31
Uleman, J. S., 659
Umberson, D., 601
Underwood, B. J., 189

Ungerleider, L. G., 139
Ursano, R. J., 544
Usher, J. A., 205
Uutela, A., 600

V

Valencia, R. R., 357
Valenstein, E. S., 236
Valentine, T., 192
Valentine, T., 192
Valins, S., 372
Vallacher, R. R., 399, 400, 476, 629
van de Castle, R., 504
van de Castle, S., 504
van den Boon, D. C., 425
Van Dyke, A., 418
Van Essen, D. C., 138
van Gogh, V., 359
Van Halen, E., 121
van Hoeken, D., 392
van IJzendoorn, M. H., 423, 424
van Knippenberg, A., 483
Van Koppen, P. J., 197
Van Lange, P. A. M., 639
van Stegeren, A. H., 375
Van Velzen, C. J. M., 528
Vance, E. B., 396
Vanderplate, C., 588
Vanduffel, W., 138
Vanhanen, T., 343
VanItallie, T. B., 393
Vanyperen, N. W., 594
Vargha-Khadem, F., 185
Verleiger, R., 248
Vesalius, A., 116
Vicary, J., 306, 308
Vighetto, A., 140
Villiers, F., 418
Villiers, G., 418
Virgil, 544
Vitkus, J., 502, 515
Vohs, K. D., 395, 481
Volkow, N. D., 84
von Cramon, D., 149
Von Frisch, K., 254
von Helmholtz, H., 7, 9, 12, 36, 136
von Restorff, H., 173
Vondra, J. I., 425
Vonnegut, K., 535
Vonnegut, M., 535
Vorgos, S., 289
Vortac, O. U., 191
Vuong, Q. C., 143
Vygotsky, L., 419

W

Wade, N. J., 147
Wagenaar, W. A., 197
Wager, T. D., 606
Wagner, A. D., 171, 182
Wagner, A. R., 220
Wagner, N. N., 396
Wagner, U., 248
Wahba, M. A., 391
Wahl, O. F., 523
Waite, L. J., 443
Wakefield, J. C., 27
Wakita, M., 230

Waldfogel, S., 204
Waldman, D. A., 360
Waldmann, M. R., 280
Waldron, M., 354, 355
Walekar, P., 367
Walker, C., 444
Walkenfeld, F. F., 247
Walker, L. J., 428
Walker, M. R., 49
Wall, P. D., 157, 619
Wallace, J., 513
Wallbott, H. G., 379
Wallbom, M., 629
Walster, E., 633. 634, 639
Walster, G. W., 639
Walters, G., 653
Walton, D. N., 286
Waltz, W., 602
Waltzman, S. B., 154
Wander, G., 50
Wang, L. H., 115
Ward, J., 194
Ward, P. B., 362
Warnock, M., 445
Warrington, E. K., 268
Washburn, M. F., 18
Wasserman, S., 414
Watanabe, S., 230
Watkins, L. R., 589
Watkinson, B., 409
Watson, D., 370, 605
Watson, J. B., 18, 19, 21, 24, 36,
   212, 214, 218, 219, 220, 223,
   225, 242, 389, 504
Watson, J. M., 103
Watson, R. I., 124, 126
Watt, H. J., 305
Watters, E., 576
Watzlawick, P., 556
Wearing, D., 207
Weber, A., 171
Weber, E., 126
Weber, R., 656
Wechsler, H., 322
Wechsler, H., 616
Weekes, J. R., 327
Wegener, D. T., 647
Wegner, D. M., 56, 296, 297, 299.
   303, 304, 313, 317, 327, 335,
   376, 399, 400, 473, 476, 507,
   596, 614, 615, 629, 634, 656
Weil, A., 599
Weinberg, M. S., 435
Weinberg, R. A., 359
Weinberger, D. A., 595
Weinberger, D. R., 84
Weinberger, J. L., 611

Weir, C., 233
Weisfeld, G., 437
Weishaar, M., 550
Weiskrantz, L., 374
Weiss, W., 647
Weissenborn, R., 181
Weissman, M. M., 506, 547
Weldon, M. S., 181
Wells, G. L., 196
Wenkstern, D., 237
Wenner, L. A., 163
Wenzlaff, R. M., 317, 507, 514,
   515, 615
Wernicke, C., 108, 115
Wernicke, K., 263
Wertheimer, M., 12, 13, 17, 36,
   149, 283
Werych. J., 162
Wessels, H., 549
Westbrook, G. L., 76
Westen, D., 470
Whalen, P. J., 375
Whalley, L. J., 343, 359
Wheatley, T. P., 56, 378, 429
Wheatstone, C., 146
Wheeler, M. A., 182
Whiffen, V. E., 514
Whishaw, I. Q., 108
White, B. L., 412
White, E., 509
White, F. J., 95
White, G. L., 27
White, G. M., 350
White, N. M., 237
Whitehead, M., 33
Whitehouse, A. M., 499
Whorf, B., 266
Whybrow, P. C., 515, 517, 518
Whyte, K. J., 638
Wicker, B., 430
Wicki, W., 512
Wicklund, R. A., 301, 629
Wickramasekera, I., 600
Widiger, T. A., 453, 493
Wiebe, D., 283
Wiederman, M. W., 396
Wiener, D. N., 19
Wiesel, T. N., 112, 139
Wiesenthal, D. L., 629
Wiggs, C. L., 184
Wightman, L., 541
Wilbur, C., 14
Wilcoxon, H. C., 226
Wiley, J. L., 326
Wilkes, A. L., 653
Wilkinson, D. A., 323
Willerman, B., 636

William, Prince of Wales, 371
Williams, A. C., 608
Williams, C. M., 326
Williams, G. R., 393
Williams, J. M. G., 551
Williams, K. D., 629, 630
Williams, S., 158
Williams, W. M., 343, 361
Willis, H., 628
Wilson, E. O., 26
Wilson, K. G., 596
Wilson, M., 623, 624
Wilson, T. D., 49, 184, 199, 200,
   235, 302, 307, 378, 398, 531,
   661
Wimmer, H., 416
Windeler, J., 274
Windham, G. C., 409
Winner, E., 362
Winslow, L., 372
Winter, L., 659
Winterer, G., 84
Wise, R. A., 236, 318, 319
Wittchen, H. U., 502, 512, 516
Wittgenstein, L., 270
Wixted, J. T., 188
Woite, R. S., 434
Wolf, J., 49
Wolfe, C. T., 482
Wolff, G., 500
Wollen, K. A., 171
Wolpe, J., 548, 549
Wolpert, E., 315
Wonder, S., 121, 380
Wong, A. T., 103
Wong, D. T., 86
Wood, J. M., 315, 399, 453
Wood, R., 400
Wood, W., 459, 631
Woods, E. R., 517
Woods, S. C., 392
Woods, S. M., 490
Woodward, J., 509
Woody, S. R., 574
Woolcott, M., 642
Woolf, L., 489
Woolf, V., 489, 490, 493, 511,
   515, 518
Woollett, K., 101
Worchel, P., 636
Wrangham, R. W., 624
Wren, A. M., 391
Wrenn, C. C., 83
Wright, L., 199
Wright, L. W., Jr., 466
Wright, P., 523
Wright, S., 313

Wu, J., 444
Wulf, S., 345
Wulz, W., 477
Wundt, W., 7, 8, 9, 10, 11, 12, 14,
   16, 21, 30, 32, 36, 121, 124,
   305, 345
Wyatt, J. K., 313
Wynn, K., 421

X

Xiaohe, X., 638
Xu, G., 649

Y

Yamaguchi, S., 161
Yamasue, H., 593
Yang, S., 350
Yantis, S., 129
Yeh, M., 499
Yellon, R., 256
Yelsma, P., 638
Yen, Y., 605
Yewchuk, C., 363
Yin, R. K., 73
Young, A. S., 540
Young, P. C., 329
Young, R. M., 108
Young, T., 136
Yovel, G., 141
Yucha, C., 600
Yuill, N., 427

Z

Zacks, R. T., 275, 280
Zahn-Waxler, C., 429
Zajonc, R. B., 375, 381, 632
Zanakos, S., 304
Zanna, M. P., 302, 616
Zaragoza, M., 197
Zebrowitz, L. A., 345, 635
Zeese, K. B., 324
Zeki, S., 63, 98, 113
Zeman, A., 335
Zentall, T. R., 245
Zettin, M., 193
Zhang, J., 618
Zhu, J., 420
Zihl, J., 149
Zillmann, D., 372
Zimbardo, P. G., 658
Zimprich, D., 360
Zola, S. M., 186
Zola-Morgan, S., 198
Zuckerman, M., 384, 452
Zufall, F., 160
Zuker, C. S., 162
Zuroff, D. C., 514

Subject Index

Note: Page numbers followed by f indicate figures; those followed by t indicate tables.

A1 auditory area, 99, 152, 153f
A1 visual area, 99, 113, 138–139, 138f, 139f
 feature detectors in, 113
Absentmindedness, 4, 189–191, 203
Absolute intelligence, 360
Absolute threshold, 124–125, 125f, 125t
Absolutism, 30
Abstract ideas, understanding of, 416
Abuse, sexual, recovered memories of,
 198–199, 576
Academic careers, 33
Accommodation, 132, 132f
 in cognitive development, 413
Accuracy motive, in social influence, 645–651
Acetylcholine, 83, 83t
Achievement tests. See also Testing
 vs. aptitude tests, 339
Acquired immunodeficiency syndrome, preven-
 tion of, 615–616
Acquisition, in classical conditioning, 214,
 214f
ACTH, 96
 in stress response, 586, 586f
Action potential, 80–81, 80f
 in signaling, 82, 82f
 spontaneous, 127
Activation-synthesis model, 317
Actor-observer effect, 659–660
Adaptation, sensory, 128–129
 dark, 134
 light, 131
Addiction, 318–320. See also Alcohol use/abuse;
 Drug abuse
Additive color mixing, 136–137, 136f
A-delta fibers, 156
Adler, Alfred, 15, 546–547, 546f
Adolescence
 brain development in, 431, 431f
 common goals in, 476
 cultural aspects of, 432, 434, 437
 definition of, 430
 emotions in, 433
 Erikson's developmental tasks of, 436t
 family conflict in, 433, 436–437
 identity formation in, 436–437
 peer relations in, 436–437
 pregnancy in, 434
 protraction of, 432–433
 sexual development in, 430–431, 431f
 storm and stress of, 433

Adrenal androgens
 in sexual desire, 395
 in sexual development, 433–434
 in sexual orientation, 435
Adrenal glands, 96
 in stress response, 586, 586f, 588
Adrenocorticotropic hormone (ACTH), 96
 in stress response, 586, 586f
Adulthood, 438–445. See also Age-related
 changes
 changing orientations in, 441–443
 cognitive performance in, 439–441
 common goals in, 476
 definition of, 438
 emotional experiences in, 442
 Erikson's developmental tasks of, 436t
 marriage in, 443–444, 443f
 memory changes in, 439–441, 441f
 parenthood in, 443–444
 physical decline in, 439–440
 social activity in, 442–443
 temporal orientation in, 441
Advertising
 heuristic persuasion in, 648
 informational influence in, 646
 product placement in, 163
 sensory branding in, 163
 subliminal, 163, 306–308, 308f
Aerobic exercise, in stress management,
 600–601
Affective forecasting, 378
African Americans. See Blacks; Race/ethnicity
Afterimages, color, 137–138, 137f
Age-related changes
 cognitive, 439–440
 in cortical lateralization, 440, 440f
 in happiness, 441, 442–443
 in memory, 193, 439–441, 441f
 physical, 439
Aggression, 623–625. See also Crime; Violence
 alcohol and, 322
 ambient temperature and, 623, 623f
 antisocial personality disorder and, 527t,
 529–530
 causes of, 623–624
 cultural aspects of, 625
 definition of, 623
 frustration and, 623
 gender differences in, 624–625
 group, 628–630
 impulsive, 623–624
 modeling of, 243–244, 244f
 observational learning in, 641

 oral, 468
 premeditated, 623
 status and, 625
 testosterone and, 625
 video games and, 244
Agnosia
 facial, 73, 108, 113
 visual-form, 140
Agonist drugs, 85, 85t
Agoraphobia, 505–506
Agreeableness, 457–458, 457t
AIDS, prevention of, 615–616
Alcohol myopia, 322
Alcohol use/abuse, 321–322, 321t
 abstinence in, 558–559
 in adolescence, 433
 aversion therapy for, 548
 effects of, 321–322
 expectancy theory and, 321–322
 harm reduction approach to, 325
 memory and, 180–181
 in pregnancy, 408–409
 Prohibition and, 324
 risks of, 321t
 self-help groups for, 558–559
 sexual behavior and, 615–616
 suicide and, 517
Alcoholics Anonymous, 558–559
Alertness, intraversion/extraversion and,
 461–462
Algorithms, 275
Allport, Gordon, 29
Alpha waves, 310
 during meditation, 332
Alprazolam, 562
Altered states of consciousness. See also
 Consciousness
 definition of, 309
 drug-induced, 318–327. See also Drug abuse;
 Psychoactive drugs
 in meditation, 331–333, 551, 598
 in peak experiences, 331–333, 471
 religious, 332–333
 sleep as, 309. See also Sleep
Alternative therapies, 564–565
Altruism, 627–628
Alzheimer's disease
 brain activity in, 439f
 daydreaming and, 439f
Ambient temperature, aggression and, 623,
 623f
Ambivalent attachment style, 423
American Journal of Psychology, 10

American Psychological Association, 10, 31–32, 358, 574
  ethical code of, 576–577
American Psychological Society, 32
American Sign Language, 258
  for apes, 263–264
  development of, 262
  language areas and, 25
Ames room, 148, 148f
Amnesia. *See also* Memory
  anterograde, 177
  case examples of, 167–169, 176–177, 182
  childhood, 198, 204–205
  dissociative, 510
  hippocampal damage in, 177
  implicit vs. explicit memory in, 182–186
  posthypnotic, 330
  priming in, 184
  retrograde, 177
  selective drug-induced, 179
Ampakines, 362
Amphetamine, 321t, 323. *See also* Methamphetamine
  agonist effects of, 86
Amplitude, of sound waves, 150, 150f
Amputation, phantom limb syndrome after, 100, 100f
Amygdala, 96–97, 96f, 97f
  in antisocial personality disorder, 530
  in appraisal, 374–375
  in dreaming, 316
  in emotion, 96–97, 374–376, 376f
  in fear, 97, 220, 374–375, 375f, 530
  in fear conditioning, 220
  in memory, 96–97, 202–203, 202f
  structure and function of, 96–97, 96f, 97f
Amyloid plaques, in Alzheimer's disease, 439f
Anal stage, 468–469, 468t
Analgesia. *See also* Anesthesia; Pain
  hypnotic, 330, 330f
Analogical problem solving, 281–282, 282f
Analytic intelligence, 349
Anandamide, 326
Androgens
  in sexual desire, 395
  in sexual development, 433–434
  in sexual orientation, 435
Androgyny, 459
Anesthesia
  hypnosis in, 330, 330f
  level of consciousness during, 293–294
Anger, heart disease and, 590–591
Angst, 472
Animals
  anthropomorphization of, 461
  communication among, 2, 221, 254
  conditioning in. *See* Classical conditioning; Operant conditioning
  emotional expression in, 379, 379f
  experiments on, ethics of, 69
  language in, 221, 263–266
  memory in, 178, 186
  observational learning in, 245
  personality in, 460–461
  self-consciousness in, 301
Anorexia nervosa, 392–393
  cultural aspects of, 499
Anorexigenic signals, in hunger, 391
Antagonist drugs, 85, 85t
Antecedents, behavioral, 548
Anterior capsulotomy, 569

Anterior cingulate cortex
  in hypnosis, 331, 331f
  in pain perception, 605, 606
  in placebo effect, 606, 606f
Anterograde amnesia, 177
Anthropomorphization, 461
Antianxiety medications, 321t, 322–323, 502, 562–563
  with psychotherapy, 565–567
Antidepressants, 513, 563–564
  for bipolar disorder, 564
  definition of, 563
  for depression, 86, 531, 563–564, 565–567
  effectiveness of, 564
  mechanism of action of, 563, 563f
  monoamine oxidase inhibitors, 563
  placebo effect and, 571, 571f
  with psychotherapy, 565–567, 566f
  selective serotonin reuptake inhibitors, 86, 563
  side effects of, 563, 564
  tricyclic, 563
  types of, 563–564
Antipsychotics, 560–562
  atypical, 562
  movement disorders and, 521, 562
  side effects of, 521, 562
Antisocial personality disorder, 527t, 529–531
Anxiety
  pathological. *See* Anxiety disorders
  in psychoanalytic theory, 465
  situational, 501
  stress-related, 592–595
Anxiety disorders, 501–508
  definition of, 501
  generalized, 501–503
  obsessive-compulsive disorder, 506–507
  panic disorder, 505–506
  phobic, 503–505
  posttraumatic stress disorder, 592–595
  societal costs of, 539–540
  treatment of
    antianxiety agents in, 321t, 322–323, 502
    antidepressants in, 564
    combination therapy in, 565–567
    drug therapy in, 562–563, 565–567
    exposure therapy in, 549–550, 549t, 550f
    herbal and natural products in, 565–567
    psychotherapy in, 565–567
Anxiolytics. *See* Antianxiety medications
Anxious/inhibited personality disorders, 527, 527t
Apes
  language learning in, 263–266
  self-consciousness in, 301
Aphasia
  Broca's, 262–263
  definition of, 262
  Wernicke's, 263
Aplysia californica, memory studies in, 178, 178f
Apnea, sleep, 313
Apparent motion, 149
Appearance. *See* Physical attractiveness
Appraisal
  amygdala in, 374–375
  in emotion, 374–376
  reappraisal and, 376–377
Approach motivation, 400–401
Aptitude tests, 339. *See also* Intelligence testing
  gender differences in, 356–357
  group differences in, 356–358
  stereotype threat and, 357–358, 655, 655f

Area A1, 99, 152, 153f
Area V1, 99, 113, 138–139, 138f, 139f
  feature detectors in, 113
Aristotle, 5, 5f, 388, 389
Arousal
  attraction and, 632–633
  emotions and, 370–373, 371f, 373f, 632–633
  intraversion/extraversion and, 461–462
  memory and, 96–97, 201–202
  in panic disorder, 506
  sexual, 396
  sympathetic nervous system in, 88, 88f, 89f
Arranged marriages, 638
Artificial correlation, 59
Artificial grammar, 246–247, 247f
Asch's conformity study, 29, 643, 643f
Assimilation, in cognitive development, 413
Association areas, 99
Association for Psychological Science, 32
Asylums, 561
Ataque de nervios, 499
Atherosclerosis, stress and, 589–591, 591f
Ativan, 562
Attachment, 422–425
  assessment of, 423
  day care and, 426
  definition of, 422
  Harlow's experiment in, 420, 420f
  internal working model of, 424
  life outcomes and, 425
  parental responsiveness and, 424–425
  secure vs. insecure, 423, 423f
  strange situation test for, 423
  temperament and, 424
Attention
  to bodily symptoms, 604–608
  divided, 129, 298–299, 299f
    memory and, 189–190
  joint, 419
  memory and, 189–190
  socioemotional selectivity theory and, 441
Attitudes. *See also* Belief(s)
  conscious vs. unconscious, 660–661
  definition of, 645
  heritability of, 460
  in social influence, 645–651
Attraction, sexual, 632–636. *See also* Physical attractiveness; Sexual attraction
Attributions, 657–660
  actor-observer effect and, 659–660
  correspondence bias and, 658–659
  covariation model of, 657–658, 658f
  definition of, 657
  dispositional, 657
  situational, 657
Atypical antipsychotics, 562
Audition. *See* Hearing
Auditory canal, 151f, 152
Auditory cortex
  in memory, 195
  primary, 99, 152, 153f
  secondary, 153f
Auditory hallucinations
  hypnosis and, 330–331, 331f
  in schizophrenia, 520
Auditory nerve, 151f
Auditory system, structure and function of, 151–152, 151f
Auditory transduction, 152, 152f
Authoritarianism, 455
Autism, 78

cognitive deficits in, 417–418
Autobiographical memory, 478
Autonomic nervous system, 88–89, 88f, 89f
  in emotion, 370–373, 371f, 373f
Availability bias, 275, 275t
Averaging, 46–48
Aversion therapy, 548
Aviophobia, 537, 538, 539
Avoidance motivation, 400–401
Avoidance responses, 596
Avoidant personality disorder, 527t
Axons, 75, 75f
  action potential transmission along, 81, 81f
  giant squid, 79
  myelin sheath of, 81, 81f, 408
  nodes of Ranvier and, 81, 81f
  terminal buttons of, 81

B cells, 588
Babbling, 258
Babies. See Infant(s)
Balance, maintenance of, 158
Balanced placebo design, 322
Barbiturates, 321t, 322–323
Bartlett, Frederic, 21–22
Basal ganglia, 97, 97f
Basilar membrane, 152, 152f, 153
Beauty. See Physical attractiveness
Beck, Aaron T., 550, 550f
Bedlam, 561
Bees, waggle dance of, 254
Behavior
  antecedents of, 548
  attribution of, 657–660
  correlation with personality traits, 474–475
  definition of, 2
  disorganized, in schizophrenia, 521
  group, 628–630
  heritability of, 106–107, 460
  operant, 225–226
  operationalization of, 124
  outcome expectancies and, 476
  overview of, 3
  person-situation controversy and, 474–475
  social, 622–630
  Type A, heart disease and, 590–591
The Behavior of Organisms (Skinner), 19
Behavior therapy, 547–550
  antecedents and consequences in, 548
  aversion therapy in, 548
  cognitive behavioral therapy and, 552–553
  definition of, 548
  effectiveness of, 572–574, 574t
  exposure therapy in, 549–550, 549t, 550f
  response prevention in, 550
  token economies in, 549
  virtual reality in, 537, 538, 539, 550
Behavioral activation system, 461–462
Behavioral inhibition system, 461–462
Behavioral neuroscience, 24–25
Behavioral psychology, 17–21
Behaviorism, 17–21
  conditioning and. See Classical conditioning;
    Operant conditioning
  definition of, 17
  history of, 18–21
  instinct and, 389
  language development and, 259–260
  learning and, 211. See also Learning
  reinforcement in, 19
Belief(s). See also Attitudes

definition of, 645
heritability of, 460
irrational, 551, 551t
  in placebo effect, 606
  political, personality and, 455
  in social influence, 645–651
Belief bias, 287–288
Benzodiazepines, 321t, 322–323, 502, 562
Berm Sex Role Inventory, 459
Beta waves, 310
Beta-blockers, 86–87
Beyond Freedom and Dignity (Skinner), 19
Bias
  availability, 275, 275t
  belief, 287–288
  change, 200
  consistency, 200
  correspondence, 658–659
  definition of, 200
  egocentric, 200–201, 203–204
  hypothesis-confirming, 626
  implicit egotism and, 483
  in intelligence testing, 356–358
  memory and, 199–200, 203–204
  observational, 49–52
  in psychological research, 49–52
  self-enhancing, 200–201, 203–204
  self-serving, 484
  situational, 357–358, 655, 655f
  stereotyping and, 652–657. See also
    Stereotype(s)
  unique invulnerability, 615
Big Five Factor Model, 457–458, 457t
Bilingualism
  cognitive development and, 264
  language learning in, 257, 261
Binocular depth cues, 146–147, 146f, 147f
Binocular disparity, 146, 146f
Biofeedback, 598–600
Biological preparedness, 223
Bipolar cells, 78, 134
Bipolar disorder, 489, 515–519
  definition of, 515
  mania in, 515
  personality traits and, 518–519
  rapid cycling, 516–517
  recurrence in, 516–517
  treatment of, 518, 564
Birth defects, causes of, 408–409
Bitter taste receptors, 161–162
Blacks. See also Cultural factors; Race/ethnicity
  pain perception in, 157
  sexual development in, 432, 432f
Blind observer, 50–51
Blind spot, 134, 134f
Blindness. See also Vision
  facial expressions in, 380, 380f
Blocking, 191–193, 203
Blood pressure, stress and, 589–591
Blushing, 371f, 373
Bobo doll experiment, 243–244, 244f
Body fat, 394, 614
Body mass index, 393, 393t
Body weight. See Weight
Bonding. See Attachment
Borderline personality disorder, 527t
Bottom-up control, in pain perception, 157
Boys. See Gender differences
Brain. See also under Cerebral cortex and specific
    structures
  age-related changes in, 439–440, 439f

cortical lateralization in, 97–98, 109–111,
    110f, 111f
  age-related changes in, 440, 440f
  symmetry of, 440, 440f
development of, 102, 102f. See also Cognitive
    development
  in adolescents, 431, 431f
  evolutionary, 102–104, 408
  intelligence and, 360, 361f
  postnatal, 408
  prenatal, 408
  synaptic pruning in, 431, 431f
evolution of, 102–104, 408
functions of, 91–99
myelination in, 408. See also Myelin sheath
ontogeny of, 102
phylogeny of, 102
plasticity of, 100–101
size of, 408
  intelligence and, 360
structure of, 91–99, 93f–99f
studies of, 107–116
  in brain-injured patients, 63, 108–111
  electroencephalography in, 111–113, 112f,
    310–311, 310f, 311f
  imaging. See Neuroimaging
  in split-brain patients, 109–111, 110f
Brain death, 116–117
Brain injuries
  functional studies in, 63, 108–111, 140
  irreversible, 116–117
  vision impairment and, 140
Brain scanning. See Neuroimaging
Brain surgery, 569
Brave New World (Orwell), 445
Breuer, Joseph, 14
Broadbent, Donald, 23
Broca, Paul, 7, 7f, 24, 63, 262
Broca's aphasia, 262–263
Broca's area, 7, 63, 108, 262–263, 262f
Bulimia nervosa, 392
Burnout, 594–595
Buspirone, 563
Bystander intervention, 629

C fibers, 156
Caffeine, 320
  withdrawal from, 319
Cajal, Santiago Ramón y, 74–75, 76
Calkins, Mary Whiton, 32, 32f
Cancer, lung, in smokers, 616
Cannon-Bard theory, 370–371, 371f, 373
Capgras syndrome, 24, 386–387, 387f
Card selection task, 626–627, 626f
Cardiovascular health, stress effects on,
    589–591, 591f
Career burnout, 594–595
Careers, in psychology, 33–34, 542
Cartesian Theater, 294–295
Case method, 44–45
Catatonia, 521, 521f
Catatonic schizophrenia, 521, 521f, 522t
Catecholamines, in stress reactions, 585–586
Categorization. See Classification; Concepts
    and categories
Category-specific deficits, 268–269
Caudate nucleus, in obsessive-compulsive
    disorder, 507
Causal relationships, 52–67
  causation, 56–64. See also Causation
  correlation, 52–55, 52t, 55f. See also Correlation

Causation, 56–64
  vs. correlation, 56–58. *See also* Correlation
  demonstration of, 58–64. *See also*
    Experiment(s)
  matched pairs technique and, 57–58
  matched samples technique and, 57–58
  statistical significance and, 64
  third-variable problem and, 56–58, 57f
  validity and. *See also* Validity
    external, 65
    internal, 64
Celexa, 563
Cell body, 75, 75f
Cell phones, driving performance and, 129
Cell signaling, 81–87. *See also*
    Neurotransmitters
  synaptic transmission in, 82–83, 82f
Central nervous system, 87–91, 88f. *See also*
    Brain; Spinal cord
  components of, 90–91, 91f
  development of, 102, 102f
  evolution of, 102–104
  hierarchical organization of, 103
Central tendency, descriptions of, 47, 48, 48f
Centration, 415
Cephalocaudal rule, in motor development, 411
Cerebellum, 93, 93f
Cerebral cortex, 95, 95f, 97–99, 97f–99f
  contralateral control in, 97–98, 109–111,
    110f, 111f
  age-related changes in, 440, 440f
  symmetry in, 440, 440f
  development of, intelligence and, 361
Cerebral ventricles, in schizophrenia, 524, 524f
Certainty effect, 279
Change bias, 200
Character Strengths and Virtues (Peterson &
    Seligman), 530
Charcot, Jean-Marie, 14, 608f
Cheating, 474, 475, 626–627, 626f
Chemical signaling, 81–87. *See also*
    Neurotransmitters
  synaptic transmission in, 82–83, 82f
Childhood, definition of, 415
Childhood amnesia, 198, 204–205
Childhood experiences
  false memories of, 197–199, 576
  forgetting of, 198, 204–205
Children. *See also* Adolescence; Infant(s)
  development in, 410–430. *See also*
    Development
    cognitive, 412–419, 413t
    Erikson's stages of, 436t
    moral, 425–430
    motor, 411–412, 411f
    perceptual, 410–411
    social, 420–425
  gifted, 362–363
  language learning in, 221, 257–263
  marital satisfaction and, 444–445, 444f
  memory in, 197–199, 204–205
  taste in, 161, 162
Chimeric face, 110, 111f
Chimpanzees
  language learning in, 263–266
  self-consciousness in, 301, 301f
Chlorpromazine, 560
Chomsky, Noam, 24, 24f, 259, 260
Chromosomes, 104–105, 104f, 407
  definition of, 104
  random distribution of, 105

sex, 105
  in sex determination, 407
Chronic fatigue, 592
Chronic stress, 584
Chronoscope, 42f
Chunking, 175
Cigarette smoking. *See* Smoking
Cilia, 103
Cingulate cortex, in hypnosis, 331, 331f
Cingulotomy, 569
Circadian rhythms, 309
Citalopram, 563
Clark, Kenneth B., 33–34, 34f
Classical conditioning
  acquisition in, 214, 214f
  biological preparedness in, 223
  case study of, 218–219
  cognitive elements of, 220–221
  definition of, 212
  discrimination in, 217–218
  in drug overdose, 215
  evolutionary elements of, 221–223
  expectation in, 220–221, 220f
  extinction in, 214f, 216
  fear, 18, 218–219, 218–220, 218f
  in food aversions, 222
  generalization in, 217, 217f, 218
  neural elements of, 219–220
  vs. operant conditioning, 225
  Pavlov's experiments in, 18, 212–214, 212f,
    213f
  of phobias, 18, 218–219, 218f, 504–505
  Rescorla-Wagner model of, 220–221, 220f,
    237
  response in
    conditioned, 212–214, 213f
    unconditioned, 212–214, 213f
  savings in, 217
  second-order, 215
  social influence and, 641
  spontaneous recovery in, 214f, 216–217
  stimulus in
    conditioned, 212–214, 213f
    unconditioned, 212–213, 213f
Classification
  of concepts, 267–273. *See also* Concepts and
    categories
  deficits in, 268–269
  in organizational encoding, 172–173, 173f
  taxonomic, 397
Claustrophobia, 503
Client-centered therapy, 553–554
Clinical psychologists, 33–34, 542. *See also*
    Psychologists
Clinical trials, 572
Clozapine, 562
Cocaine, 318–319, 321t, 323–324
  agonist effects of, 86
Cochlea, 151f, 152, 152f, 153
Cochlear implants, 154, 154f
Cocktail party phenomenon, 299
Cognition. *See also under* Mental; Thinking;
    Thought
  age-related changes in, 439–441
  in categorization, 267–273
  in classical conditioning, 220–221
  concepts in, 267–273
  in decision making, 273–280
  drug-enhanced, 362
  frontal lobe in, 99
  language and, 266–267

  in operant conditioning, 237–239
  in problem solving, 280–285
  rational choice theory of, 274
  reasoning and, 285–288
  social, 651–660
  socioemotional selectivity theory and, 441
Cognitive behavioral therapy, 552–553
  definition of, 552
  with drug therapy, 565–566, 566f
  effectiveness of, 572–574, 574t
  group, 557–558
Cognitive deficits
  in autism, 417–418
  in dementia, 439f
  implicit learning and, 247–248
Cognitive development, 412–419
  accommodation in, 413
  in adolescents, 431, 431f
  assimilation in, 413
  in autism, 418
  conservation in, 415
  cultural aspects of, 419, 420f
  definition of, 412
  in hearing impaired, 418
  language development and, 266–267, 418
  mental representations in, 416–418
  moral development and, 426–427
  object permanence in, 413–414, 418
  Piaget's theory of, 22, 22f, 412–416
  problem of other minds in, 416–418
  schemas in, 413
  social influences in, 419
  stages of
    concrete operational, 413t, 415–416
    formal operational, 413t, 416
    preoperational, 413t, 415
    sensorimotor, 413–414, 413t
    transitions between, 418
  theory of mind and, 417–418
  zone of proximal development and, 419
Cognitive dissonance, 27, 650–651, 650f, 651f
Cognitive enhancers, 362
Cognitive maps, 238–239, 239f
Cognitive neuroscience, 25
Cognitive psychology, 21–24
  definition of, 21
  history of, 21–24
  technology and, 21, 23
Cognitive Psychology (Neisser), 24
Cognitive restructuring, 551
Cognitive therapy, 550–551
  effectiveness of, 572–574, 574t
Cognitive unconscious, 306–308
Coincidence, 46
Collective unconscious, 546
College students
  current concerns of, 302, 302t
  major life stressors for, 583, 583t
Color blindness, 137
Color deficiency, 137
Color mixing
  additive, 136–137, 136f
  subtractive, 137
Color names, 267
Color-opponent system, 137–138
Color vision, 135–138
  afterimages in, 137–138, 137f
  cones in, 132–134, 133f, 135–138
  impaired, 137
  rods in, 132–134, 133f
  trichromatic color representation in, 136f, 137

Commissures, in flatworms, 103
Committed relationships, 636–639. *See also*
    Marriage; Relationships
Common fate rule, 149
Communication. *See also* Language; Speech
    among animals, 254
    emotional, 377–386
        in schizophrenia, 525–526
    nonverbal. *See* Facial expressions
Comorbidity, 496–497, 497f
    personality disorders in, 528
Companionate love, 638, 638f
Comparison level, 639
Complementary therapies, 564–565
Compliance, therapeutic, 605–606
Composite faces, 637, 637f
Compulsions, 506–507
Computed tomography (CT), 113
Computers, cognitive psychology and, 21, 23
Concepts and categories, 267–273
    brain areas for, 272–273
    critical features of, 271f
    definition of, 267
    exemplar theory of, 272–273, 273f
    family resemblance theory of, 269–270, 270f
    necessary and sufficient conditions for, 269
    perceptual grouping and, 142–143, 142f
    prototype theory of, 271–272, 271f, 273f
    in social cognition, 652
    in stereotyping, 652–657
    variability within, 653–654, 653f
Concordance rates, 502
Concrete operational stage, 413t, 415–416
Conditioned response, 212–214, 213f
Conditioned stimulus, 212–213, 213f
Conditioning. *See* Classical conditioning;
    Operant conditioning
Conduct disorder, 529
Conductive hearing loss, 154. *See also* Hearing
    impairment
Cones, 132–134, 133f, 135–138
Confirmatory factor analysis, 347
Conformity, 643–644, 643f
Congenital abnormalities, causes of, 408–409
Congruence, in person-centered therapy, 554
Conjoined twins, 39
Conjunction fallacy, 276
Conscientiousness, 457–458, 457t
Conscious motivation, 399–400
Conscious will, timing of, 297, 297f
Consciousness, 293–333. *See also under* Mental;
        Mind
    altered states of, 309
    during anesthesia, 293–294
    basic properties of, 298–305
    brain activities and, 297–298
    Cartesian Theater and, 294–295
    content of, 302–305, 302t
    control over, 303–305
    current concerns and, 302–303, 302t
    daydreaming and, 303, 439f
    definition of, 8, 294
    during dreaming, 314–315, 316
    drugs and, 318–327. *See also* Psychoactive
        drugs
    experience and, 294
    filtering of, 299
    full, 300–301
    in functionalism, 10
    during hypnosis, 327–331, 327f–331f
    individual perceptions of, 295–296, 296f

intentionality of, 298
    levels of, 300–301
    during meditation, 331–332
    mind-body problem and, 297–298, 297f
    minimal, 300, 301
    mysteries of, 295–298
    nature of, 298–305
    objects of, 298
    during peak experiences, 331–333
    phenomenology and, 295
    problem of other minds and, 295–296, 296f,
        416–418
    in psychoanalytic theory, 463
    selectivity of, 298–299
    self-consciousness, 301
    during sleep, 309–318. *See also* Sleep
    in structuralism, 8
    study of, difficulty of, 295–298
    thought suppression and, 303–304
    transience of, 299–300
    unconsciousness and, 305–308
    unity of, 298
    zoning out and, 300–301
Consent, informed, 68
Conservation, 415
Conservatism, personality and, 455
Consistency, in social influence, 650–651
Consistency bias, 200
Construct validity, 43, 44f
Contagion, disgust and, 382
Content morphemes, 255
Continuous reinforcement, 232
Contraceptive use
    by adolescents, 434
    factors in, 615–616
Contralateral control, cortical, 97–98, 109–111,
        110f, 111f
Control
    locus of, 476, 476t
    perceived, stress and, 585
Control groups, 60, 60f
Conventional stage, of moral development,
        427–428
Conversion disorder, 543, 607–608
Cooperation, 625–627
    altruism in, 627–628
    in groups, 628–630. *See also* Group(s)
    kin selection and, 627
Coping. *See also* Stress management
    rational, 596–597
    repressive, 595–596
Cornea, 131, 131f
Coronary artery disease, stress and, 589–591,
        591f
Corpus callosum, 98, 98f
    severing of, in split-brain procedure,
        109–111, 110f, 111f
Correlation, 52–55
    artificial, 59
    vs. causation, 56–58. *See also* Causation
    definition of, 53
    direction of, 55, 55f
    illusory, 653, 653f
    imperfect, 55, 55f
    measurement of, 54–55, 55f
    natural, 56
    negative, 54, 55f
    patterns of variation and, 52–54
    perfect, 54–55, 55f
    positive, 54, 55f
    prediction based on, 53–54

significant, 55, 55f
    strength of, 55, 55f
    third-variable, 56–58, 57f, 63–64
Correlation coefficient, 54
Correspondence bias, 658–659
Cortical lateralization, 97–98, 109–111, 110f
    age-related changes in, 440, 440f
    symmetry of, 440, 440f
Cortisol, in stress response, 586, 586f, 588
Cost-benefit ratio, for relationships, 639
Coughing, boredom and, 605
Counseling psychologists, 34. *See also*
        Psychologists
Counselors, 542
Counting ability, cultural aspects of, 419, 420f,
        421
Counting rituals, in obsessive-compulsive dis-
        order, 506–507
Couples therapy, 556–557, 557f
Courage, 530t
Covariation model, 657–658
Cover stories, 50
Creative intelligence, 349
Creativity
    bipolar disorder and, 518, 518t
    in problem solving, 282–285
    in psychological disorders, 489
Crime. *See also* Aggression; Violence
    alcohol and, 322
    antisocial personality disorder and, 527t,
        529–530
    drug abuse and, 324–325, 333
Criminal cases, eyewitness testimony in, 196,
        197–199
Criminal personality, 529–530
Crystallized intelligence, 348–349
Cues, in memory retrieval, 180–181, 191
Cultural factors
    in adolescence, 432, 434
    in aggression, 625
    in attachment, 423
    in cognitive development, 417f, 419, 420f,
        421
    in counting ability, 419, 420f, 421
    in depression, 30–31
    in display rules, 83
    in eating disorders, 499
    in facial expressions, 380, 383
    in intelligence assessment, 350–351,
        356–358
    in mate selection, 289
    in moral reasoning, 428
    in physical attractiveness, 27, 31
    in psychological disorders, 499
    in reasoning, 287
    in sexual development, 432, 432f, 434
Cultural psychology, 29–31
    absolutism in, 30, 31
    definition of, 29
    relativism in, 30–31
Culture-bound syndromes, 499
Curve of forgetting, 187–188, 188f
Cytokines, 589

Daily hassles, stress from, 584
Dark adaptation, 134
Darwin, Charles, 10, 26, 26f, 352, 379
Day care, 426
Daydreaming, 303
    Alzheimer's disease and, 439f
Deafness. *See* Hearing impairment

Death
  brain, 116–117
  fear of, 472–473
    self-esteem and, 483–484
  voodoo, 581, 582
Debriefing, 68–69
Deceptive facial expressions, 383–386
Decision making. *See also* Problem solving
  alcohol effects on, 322
  algorithms in, 275
  availability bias in, 275, 275t
  certainty effect in, 279
  conjunction fallacy and, 276
  expected utility and, 279
  framing effects in, 277
  frequency estimation in, 274, 275, 280
  frequency format hypothesis and, 280
  group, 629–630
  heuristics in, 275
    representativeness, 276–277
  hurried, 307
  impaired, 387–388
  in mate selection, 289
  prefrontal lobe in, 278
  probability estimation in, 274, 275, 276, 280
  prospect theory of, 279–280
  substance abuse and, 278
  sunk-cost fallacy in, 277
  unconscious mind in, 307
Deep structure, of language, 256
Defense mechanisms, 466–467
Definitions, operational, 41, 341
Degree of relatedness, 105
  heritability and, 106–107
Deindividuation, 629
Deinstitutionalization, 561
Déjà vu, 194
Delayed gratification, 398
Delta waves, 310, 310f
Delusions
  incidence of, 532
  in schizophrenia, 520
Demand characteristics, 49–50
Dementia
  brain activity in, 439f
  daydreaming and, 439f
Demyelinating diseases, 76
Dendrites, 75, 75f
Dependence, in drug abuse, 319
Dependent personality disorder, 527t
Dependent variables, 60, 60f
Depressants, 321, 321t
Depression, 511–515
  biological factors in, 513–514
  in bipolar disorder, 489, 515–519, 564. *See also* Bipolar disorder
  brain activity in, 513–514
  cognitive factors in, 514–515
  course of, 512
  cultural aspects of, 30–31
  double, 512
  exercise and, 601
  gender differences in, 512–513
  helplessness theory of, 514
  illness in, 589
  in major depressive disorder, 512
  in personality disorders, 529, 529
  postpartum, 512–513
  psychological factors in, 514–515
  recurrent, 512

in seasonal affective disorder, 512
    phototherapy for, 568, 568f
  social rejection in, 515
  suicide in, 516–517
  symptoms of, 512
  treatment of, 563–569
    drug therapy in, 86, 531, 563–564, 565–567
    electroconvulsive therapy in, 567–568, 568f
    herbal and natural products in, 565–567
    phototherapy in, 568, 568f
    psychotherapy in, 565–567
    transcranial magnetic stimulation in, 568
  unipolar, 512–515
Depth perception, 144–148, 145f, 148f
  binocular cues in, 146–147, 146f, 147f
  monocular cues in, 144–145, 145f, 146f
  motion-based cues in, 147
  pictorial cues in, 145, 146f
Descartes, René, 6, 294, 297
Descriptive statistics, 47–48, 48f
Desensitization, 549–550, 549t, 550f
Development, 405–445
  in adolescence, 430–437. *See also* Adolescence
  in adulthood, 438–445
  cognitive, 412–419
  Erikson's stages of, 436–437, 436t
  in infancy and childhood, 410–430
  language, 257–263
  moral, 425–430
  motor, 411–412, 411f
  perceptual, 410–412
  prenatal, 406–410
  psychosexual, 468–470, 468t
  sexual, 430–436
  social, 420–425, 426
  of vision, 410
Developmental psychology, 405
Developmental tasks, Erikson's, 436–437, 436t
Deviation IQ, 340, 340f
DHEA (dihydroepiandrosterone), in sexual desire, 395
Diagnostic and Statistical Manual of Mental Disorders (DSM-IV-TR), 491–497
  classification in, 494–500, 496t
  comorbidity and, 496–497, 497f
  culture-bound syndromes in, 499
  definitions in, 495
  diagnostic criteria in, 493, 495
    reliability of, 495
  early versions of, 495
  etiology in, 497–498
  Global Assessment of Functioning Scale in, 493, 494t
Diathesis-stress model, 498. *See also* Stress
Diazepam, 562
Dichotic listening, 298–299
Diet, 614, 615. *See also* Eating problems
  hunger and, 391–392
  in pregnancy, 408
Difference thresholds, 126, 135
Diffusion of responsibility, in groups, 629
Digit memory test, 169, 169f
Dihydroepiandrosterone (DHEA), in sexual desire, 395
Discrimination
  in classical conditioning, 217–218
  in groups, 629
  in operant conditioning, 229–230
Discriminative stimulus, 229–230
Discriminatory behavior, definition of, 628

Discriminatory practices. *See also* Bias; Prejudice; Stereotype(s)
  unconscious attitudes and, 660–661
Discursive reasoning, 286–287
Disgust, 382, 429
Disorganized attachment style, 423
Disorganized behavior, in schizophrenia, 521
Disorganized speech, in schizophrenia, 521
Displacement, 467
Display rules, 383
Dispositional attributions, 657
Dissociative disorders, 508–511
  dissociative amnesia, 510
  dissociative fugue, 510
  dissociative identity disorder, 14, 14f, 508–510, 576
Distribution
  frequency, 46–47, 47f, 48
  normal, 47, 47f
Divided attention, 129, 298–299, 299f
  cell phones and driving and, 129
  memory and, 189–190
Divorce, 443–444, 443f. *See also* Marriage
  cost-benefit ratio and, 639
  prevalence of, 636
Dix, Dorothea, 561
Dizygotic twins, 105, 105f, 352. *See also* Twin studies
DNA, structure of, 104, 104f
DNA evidence, vs. eyewitness testimony, 196
Doctor-patient interaction, 609–610
Dogmatism, 40
Door-in-the-face technique, 642
L-Dopa, for Parkinson's disease, 85
Dopamine, 83t, 84
  antipsychotics and, 560, 562
  emotions and, 236–237
  functions of, 83t, 84, 85–86
  in Parkinson's disease, 85, 97
  pleasure/reward and, 236–237
  in schizophrenia, 524, 560
Dopamine hypothesis, 524, 560
Dorsal visual stream, 139–140, 139f
Double depression, 512
Double-blind technique, 572
  in experiments, 572
  in observation, 51
Dramatic/erratic personality disorders, 527, 527t
Dreams/dreaming, 314–318
  activation-synthesis model of, 317
  analysis of, 545
  brain activity during, 316
  consciousness during, 314–315, 316
  content of, 315
    manifest vs. latent, 317
  in Freudian theory, 317
  lucid, 316
  memory and, 314–315
  movement during, 316
  during REM sleep, 311
  theories of, 315–317
  thought suppression and, 317
Drives, 390. *See also* Motivation
Driving, cell phone use and, 129
Drug(s)
  agonist, 85, 85t
  antagonist, 85, 85t
  cognitive enhancer, 362
  consciousness and, 318–327
  memory-enhancing, 179
  prescription of. *See also* Drug therapy

compliance with, 610, 610f
  by psychologists, 567
  psychoactive, 318–327. *See also* Psychoactive drugs
Drug abuse, 318–320
  abused drugs in, 320–327. *See also* Psychoactive drugs
  addiction in, 318–320
  in adolescence, 433
  criminalization of, 324–325, 333
  decision making and, 278
  dependence in, 319
  hallucinations in, 73, 83, 87
  harm reduction approach to, 325
  neurotransmitters and, 85–86, 87
  nonaddictive use in, 320
  operant conditioning in, 236–237
  overdose in, 215
  pleasure center in, 236–237
  risks of, 321t
  societal attitudes toward, 324–325, 333
  suicide and, 517
  tolerance in, 215, 319
  withdrawal symptoms in, 320
Drug therapy, 559–567
  antianxiety agents in, 562–563
  antidepressants in, 563–564
  antipsychotics in, 560–562
  compliance with, 610, 610f
  effectiveness of, 569–574
  evaluation of, 570–572
  herbal and natural products and, 564–565
  mood stabilizers in, 564
  vs. natural improvement, 570
  nonspecific effects of, 570
  placebo effect in, 571, 571f, 606, 606f
  prescribing privileges for, 567
  preventive, 577
  with psychotherapy, 565–567
  reconstructive memory errors and, 571
  side effects of, 575–577
  studies of, 572
DSM-IV-TR. *See Diagnostic and Statistical Manual of Mental Disorders (DSM-IV-TR)*
Dualism, 6
Dynamic unconscious, 305, 463
Dysphasia, genetic, 260–261
Dysthymia, 512

Ear
  in balance, 158
  in hearing, 150–155. *See also* Hearing
  structure and function of, 151–152, 151f
Eardrum, 152f, 153
Eating
  control of, 614–615
  hunger and, 391–392, 392f
  motivation for, 391–394
  reasons for, 393–394
  stress and, 614, 615f
Eating problems, 392–394
  anorexia nervosa, 392–393
  bulimia nervosa, 392
  cultural aspects of, 499
  fussy eaters
    conditioning and, 222
    taste perception and, 162
  obesity, 393–394, 614
Ebbinghaus, Hermann, 22, 187–188, 188f
Echoic memory, 174
Eclectic psychotherapy, 543

Economic status, health and, 588
Ecstasy (MDMA), 321t, 323
Ecstatic religious experiences, 332–333
Edge assignment, 143, 143f
Edge perception, 139, 139f
Education. *See also* Learning
  intelligence and, 360–362
  of psychotherapists, 542
  sex, 434, 616
Effexor, 563–564
Ego, 464
Egocentric bias, 200–201, 203–204
Egocentrism
  in cognitive development, 416–417
  definition of, 416
Elaborative encoding, 170–171, 170f
Elderly. *See also* Adulthood; Age-related changes
  dementia in
    brain activity in, 439f
    daydreaming and, 439f
  Erikson's developmental tasks of, 436t
  memory loss in, 193
Electroconvulsive therapy, 567–568, 568f
Electroencephalography (EEG), 111–113, 112f
  in sleep studies, 310–311, 310f, 311f
Electromagnetic spectrum, 131, 131f
Electromyography (EMG), 42, 42f, 598
Electrooculography (EOG), in sleep studies, 311
Ellis, Albert, 550
Embryonic stage, 407, 407f
Emotion(s), 3, 367–386
  in adolescence, 433
  in adulthood, 442–443
  amygdala in, 96–97, 374–376, 376f
  appraisal in, 374–376
  arousal and, 370–373, 371f, 373f, 632–633
  bodily responses to, 370–373, 371f, 373f
  Cannon-Bard theory of, 370–371, 371f, 373
  definition of, 370
  dimensions of, 369–370
  expression of, 377–386
    in animals, 379, 379f
    cause and effect in, 380–382
    cultural aspects of, 380, 383
    deception in, 383–386
    definition of, 377
    display rules and, 383
    empathy and, 430
    evolution and, 379
    facial, 374–375, 374f, 379–386. *See also* Facial expressions
    means of, 377–379
    negative, 584
    regulation of, 383
    schizophrenia and, 525–526
    in stress management, 597
    universality hypothesis for, 379–380
    vocal, 377–379
  facial feedback hypothesis for, 381–382, 381f
  hedonic principle and, 388
  heuristic, 647–648
  imitation of, 381–382
  James-Lange theory of, 370, 371f, 373
  limbic system in, 374–376, 376f
  mapping of, 369–370, 369f
  memory and, 96, 201–202
  motivation and, 386. *See also* Motivation
  multidimensional scaling of, 369–370, 369f
  in pain perception, 156
  physiology of, 370–373, 371f, 373f
  prediction of, 378

reappraisal of, 376–377
  recognition of, 374–375, 374f
  regulation of, 376–377
  smiling and, 381
  two-factor theory of, 371–373, 371f
  uncertainty and, 378
  valence and, 370
Emotional communication, 377–386
Empathy, 429–430
  in medicine, 609
  in personality disorders, 530
  in person-centered therapy, 554
Empiricism, 5, 40–41
Employment opportunities, in psychology, 33–34, 542
Encoding, 169–173, 169f–173f. *See also* Memory, encoding of
Encoding specificity principle, 180
Endocrine system. *See also* Hormones
  hypothalamic-pituitary-adrenal axis in, 95f, 96, 96f, 586, 586f, 588
  in stress response, 96, 586, 586f, 588, 602
Endorphins (endogenous opiates), 83t, 84, 325
  in placebo effect, 606
Ends-means analysis, 281
Environment
  genes and, 104, 105–106
  shared vs. nonshared, 355
Environmental psychology, 584
Environmental stressors, 582, 584
Epilepsy, ecstatic religious experiences and, 333
Episodic memory, 183f, 185–186. *See also* Memory
Equilibrium, maintenance of, 158
Equity, in relationships, 639
Erikson's developmental tasks, 436–437, 436t
Erotogenic zones, 468, 468t
Erratic personality disorders, 527, 527t
ESP, public opinion on, 46
Estrogen, in sexual desire, 395
Eternal Sunshine of the Spotless Mind, 179
Ethical code, for psychologists, 576–577
Ethical issues, 68–71
  brain death, 116–117
  in experiments, 68–70
  informed consent, 68
Ethnic groups. *See* Race/ethnicity
Etiology, definition of, 497
Evil eye, 499
Evolution
  of brain, 102–104, 408
  classical conditioning and, 221–223
  Darwin's theory of, 10, 26, 352, 379
  emotional expression and, 379
  of language, 254, 262
  mate selection and, 289
  natural selection in, 10, 26
  of nervous system, 102–104, 408
  observational learning and, 245
  operant conditioning and, 239–242
  of personality traits, 461
  reproductive strategies and, 630–640
  sleep and, 312–313
  social behavior and, 622–640
  social role theory and, 459
  survival strategies and, 622–630
Evolutionary psychology, 26–28
  definition of, 26
  history of, 26–28

Excitement phase, of human sexual response, 396–397, 397f
Exemplar theory, 272–273, 273f
Exercise, in stress management, 600–601
Existentialism, 470, 472–473, 480
   Gestalt therapy and, 553, 555
Expectancy theory, alcohol use and, 321–322
Expectation
   bias due to, 49–51
   in classical conditioning, 220–221, 220f
Expected utility, 279
Experience sampling, 302, 302t
Experiment(s), 58–64. *See also* Psychological research
   animal welfare in, 69
   balanced placebo design for, 322
   in clinical trials, 572
   control groups in, 60, 60f
   debriefing after, 68–69
   definition of, 58
   dependent, 60, 60f
   double-blind, 51, 572
   ethical aspects of, 68–70
   experimental groups in, 60, 60f
   hypothesis in, 65–66
   independent, 60, 60f
   informed consent for, 68
   manipulation in, 59–60, 60f
   measurement in, 59, 64. *See also* Measurement
   participant protections in, 68–69
   randomization in, 60–62, 62f
      failure of, 63–64
   results of, statistical significance of, 64
   self-selection in, 61
   in treatment studies, 572–574
   validity of
      external, 65
      internal, 64
   variables in, 53–58, 55f, 57f. *See also* Variable(s)
Experimental group, 60, 60f
Explicit learning, 210
Explicit memory, 183. *See also* Memory
Exposure therapy, 549–550, 549t, 550f, 574t
   virtual reality in, 537, 538, 539, 550
Expressed emotion. *See also* Emotion(s), expression of
   schizophrenia and, 525–526
The Expression of the Emotions in Man and Animals (Darwin), 379
External locus of control, 476, 476t
External validity, 65
Extinction
   in classical conditioning, 214f, 216
   in operant conditioning, 230
Extrasensory perception, public opinion on, 46
Extraversion, 457–458, 457f, 457t
   neurophysiology of, 461–462
   stress and, 518–519
Extrinsic motivation, 397–398
Eye, structure of, 131–132, 131f
Eye gaze, intelligence and, 345
Eye movement, during sleep, 310–311
Eye movement desensitization and reprocessing, 575
Eyewitness testimony
   misattribution and, 196
   suggestibility and, 197–199
Eysenck's personality trait dimensions, 457, 457f

Faces. *See also* Physical attractiveness
   average-looking, 637, 637f
   chimeric, 110, 111f
   composite, 637, 637f
   recognition of
      feature detectors in, 141–144
      impaired, 73, 108, 113
Facial abnormalities, in fetal alcohol syndrome, 409
Facial agnosia, 73, 108, 113
Facial attractiveness. *See* Physical attractiveness
Facial expressions, 374, 374f, 375, 379–386
   action units of, 374, 374f, 375
   in blind persons, 380, 380f
   causes and effects of, 380–382
   cultural aspects of, 380, 383
   deceptive, 383–386
   of disgust, 382, 430
   display rules and, 383
   imitation of, 381–382, 430
      empathy and, 430
      by newborns, 411
   universality of, 379–380
Facial feedback hypothesis, 381–382, 381f
Facial muscles
   reliable, 383
   in smiling, 381, 381f, 383, 383f
Factor analysis, 345–346
   confirmatory, 347
   of personality traits, 456–457
Fallacies
   conjunction, 276
   intervention-causation, 500
   sunk-cost, 277
False belief test, 416, 417f
False memories, 197–199, 576
False recognition, 194–196, 195t
Familiar size, 145
Family, in schizophrenia, 525–526
Family conflict, in adolescence, 433, 436–437
Family resemblance theory, 269–270, 270f
Family therapy, 556–558
Farsightedness, 132, 132f
Fast mapping, 221, 258
   in language development, 258
Fat, body, 394, 614. *See also* Weight
Fathers, satisfaction with parenthood, 444
Fear
   absence of, in temporal lobe syndrome, 373, 374f
   amygdala in, 97, 220, 374–375, 375f, 530
   appraisal in, 374–375
   arousal and, 370–373, 371f, 373f
   conditioned, 18, 218–220, 218f, 504–505
   of death, 472–473
      self-esteem and, 483–484
   of enclosed spaces, 503
   of flying, 537, 538, 539
   insensitivity to, in antisocial personality disorder, 530
   of open spaces, 505–506
   in panic disorder, 505–506
   in phobic disorders, 504–506
   preparedness theory of, 504
   of social situations, 504
Feature detectors, 113, 139
   in edge perception, 139, 139f
   in facial recognition, 141–142
   in object recognition, 141–144
Fechner, Gustav, 124
Feedback

self-concept and, 480
self-esteem and, 482
Females. *See* Gender differences
Fertilization, 406–407, 407f
Fetal alcohol syndrome, 408–409, 409f
Fetal stage, 407f, 408
Fetus
   growth and development of, 102, 102f, 406–410. *See also* Prenatal development
   hearing in, 410
Fight-or-flight response, 586, 586f
Figure-ground illusion, 143, 143f
Filler items, 50
Fixation, 468
Fixed interval schedules of reinforcement, 231–233, 231f
Fixed ratio schedules of reinforcement, 231f, 232–233
Flashbulb memories, 201–202
Flavor, 158, 162–163
Flow, 471, 471f
Fluid intelligence, 348–349
Fluorens, Pierre, 6
Fluoxetine, 563, 564, 571, 571f
Flying, fear of, 537, 538, 539
Flynn effect, 360
fMRI. *See* Functional magnetic resonance imaging
Food aversions, 222
   taste perception and, 162
Foot-in-the-door technique, 650
Forebrain, 95–97, 95f–97f
   development of, 103, 103f
   evolution of, 103–104
Forgetting. *See also* Amnesia; Memory
   absentmindedness and, 189–190
   of childhood memories, 198, 204–205
   transience and, 187–188, 188f, 189f
Formal operational stage, 413t, 416
Fovea, 133, 133f
Framing effects
   in decision making, 277
   in problem solving, 284–285
Fraternal twins, 105, 105f. *See also* Twin studies
   definition of, 352
Free association, 544–545
Free will, Skinnerian view of, 20
Freezing, in rats, 219–220
Frequency, of sound waves, 150, 150f, 151, 152–153
   encoding of, 152–153, 153f
Frequency distributions, 46–47, 47f, 48
Frequency estimation, in decision making, 274, 275, 280
Frequency format hypothesis, 280
Frequency tracking, 280
Freud, Anna, 466
Freud, Sigmund, 14–17, 462–463. *See also* Psychoanalysis; Psychoanalytic theory
Freudian slips, 305–306, 462
Friendships, in adolescence, 437
Frontal lobe, 99
   development of, 431, 431f
   in emotion, 108–111
   in memory
      in encoding, 171, 171f, 173
      in retrieval, 181f, 182, 184, 185f, 194
Frustration-aggression principle, 623
Fugue states, 510
Full consciousness, 300–301
Function morphemes, 255
Functional fixedness, 284–285, 284f

Functional magnetic resonance imaging, 2, 114–115, 115f
  during sleep, 316
Functionalism, 5, 10
Fundamental attribution error, 498
Fusiform gyri, 115
Fussy eaters
  conditioning and, 222
  taste perception and, 162

g (general intelligence), 351
GABA (gamma-aminobutyric acid), 83t, 84
  in anxiety, 502
Gabapentin, 563
Gage, Phineas, 108–109, 109f, 115, 458
Gall, Franz Joseph, 6
Gamma-aminobutyric acid (GABA), 83t, 84
  in anxiety, 502
Ganglia, in flatworms, 103
Ganglion cells, retinal, 134
Gate-control theory, 157
Gay men, 435, 435f
  homophobia and, 466
Gaze, intelligence and, 345
Gender differences
  in aggression, 624–625
  androgyny and, 459
  in depression, 512–513
  in intelligence testing, 356–357
  in mate selection, 289
  in moral reasoning, 428
  in personality, 459
  in reproductive selectivity, 631
  in sexual response, 396–397
  social role theory and, 459
  in stress management, 602
General adaptation syndrome, 587–588, 587f
General intelligence (g), 345–347, 351
Generalization
  in classical conditioning, 217, 217f, 218
  in operant conditioning, 229–230
Generalized anxiety disorder, 501–503
Genes, 104–107, 104f, 407
  chromosomes and, 104–105, 104f
  definition of, 104
  environment and, 104, 105–106
  heritability and, 106–107. See also
    Heritability
  in intelligence, 351–358
  shared, 105
Genetic disorders, polygenic, 518
Genetic dysphasia, 260–261
Genetic engineering, for intelligence, 363
Genital stage, 468t, 470
Geometric elements, in object recognition, 144, 144f
Geons, in object recognition, 144, 144f
Germany, Nazi, research studies in, 70
Germinal stage, 407
Gestalt psychology, 13, 29
  insight problems and, 283
  motion perception and, 149
  object perception and, 142–143, 142f, 147
Gestalt therapy, 555
Ghost sickness, 499
Ghrelin, 391
  in anorexia nervosa, 393
Giant squid axons, 79
Giftedness, 362–363. See also Intelligence
Girls. See Gender differences
Glial cells, 76

Global Assessment of Functioning Scale (DSM-IV-TR), 493, 494t
Glomeruli, olfactory bulb, 159, 159f
Glucocorticoids, in stress response, 588
Glutamate, 83t, 84
  in memory storage, 178–179, 179f
Goals
  outcome expectancies and, 476
  in problem solving, 281
Grammar, 255
  artificial, 246–247, 247f
  innate comprehension of, 260–261
Grateful Dead, 168
Gray matter, in schizophrenia, 525, 525f
Grossly disorganized behavior, in schizophrenia, 521
Group(s), 628–630
  bystander intervention and, 629
  decision making in, 629–630
  definition of, 628
  deindividuation in, 629
  diffusion of responsibility in, 629
  discrimination against, 629
  in-group, 629
  out-group, 629
  prejudice in, 629
  social behavior in, 628–630
  social benefits of, 630
  social loafing in, 629
  stereotyping of, 652–657
Group polarization, 629–630
Group therapy, 557–558
Grouping. See also Concepts and categories
  perceptual, 142–143, 142f
Groupthink, 630
Gustation. See Taste
Gyri, 97
  fusiform, 115

Habituation, 210–211
Hair cells
  in balance, 158
  in hearing, 152, 152f, 153
Hall, G. Stanley, 10, 10f, 16, 16f, 31
Hallucinations
  auditory, hypnosis and, 330–331, 331f
  incidence of, 532
  methamphetamine-induced, 73, 83, 87
  in schizophrenia, 520
Hallucinogens, 326
Haloperidol, 560
Happiness
  age-related changes in, 441, 442–443
  characteristics of, 531
  exercise and, 601
  group belonging and, 630
  health and, 610–617
  hedonic principle and, 388
  heritability of, 531
  investigation of, 530–531
  marriage and, 443–444, 443f, 531
  in motivation, 388
  parenthood and, 443–444
  positive psychology and, 530–531, 612
  prediction of, 378
  promotion of, 530–531
  social connections and, 601–602, 630, 631
Haptic perception, 155–158
Hardiness, 612
Harlow's attachment experiment, 420, 420f
Harm reduction approach, 325

Hashish, 326
Head trauma. See Brain injuries
Health
  exercise and, 601
  hardiness and, 612
  optimism and, 611–612
  personality factors in, 610–612
  psychological factors in, 610–617
  social support and, 601–602
  socioeconomic status and, 588
  stress and, 583, 588–591
Health care providers, patient interaction with, 609–610
Health problems. See Illness
Health promotion, 612–617
  diet in, 614, 615
  safe sex practices in, 615–616
  self-regulation in, 613
  smoking cessation in, 616–617
Health psychology, 582
Hearing, 150–155. See also Sound
  absolute threshold for, 124–125, 125f, 125t
  anatomic aspects of, 151–152, 152f
  auditory transduction in, 152f
  echoic memory and, 174
  false recognition and, 195
  in fetus, 410
  pitch perception in, 152–153
  place code in, 153
  sound localization in, 154
  sound waves in, 150–151, 150f
    amplitude of, 150, 150f
    complexity of, 150f, 151
    frequency of, 150, 150f, 152–153
  temporal code in, 153
  temporal lobe in, 99
Hearing impairment
  causes and prevention of, 154
  cochlear implants for, 154, 154f
  cognitive development and, 418
  conductive, 154
  language areas and, 25
  language development in, 258
  sensorineural, 154
  sign language and, 25, 262
Heart disease, stress and, 589–591, 591f
Hedonic principle, 388, 464, 468, 640–641
Height, in mate selection, 28, 633
Helmholtz, Hermann von, 7, 7f, 136
Helplessness theory, of depression, 514
Hemispheric lateralization, 97–98, 109–111, 110f
  age-related changes in, 440, 440f
  symmetry of, 440, 440f
Herbal products, 564–565
Hereditary Genius (Galton), 352
Heritability, 106–107. See also Genes
  of behavior, 106–107, 389
  of bipolar disorder, 518
  calculation of, 106
  concordance rates and, 502
  of depression, 513
  of happiness, 531
  of instincts, 389
  of intelligence, 106–107, 351–356, 355f
  of obsessive-compulsive disorder, 507
  of panic disorder, 506
  of personality traits, 458–460, 458t
  of phobias, 504
  of psychological disorders, 498
  of schizophrenia, 522–523, 523f
  of sexual orientation, 435

Heritability (continued)
twin studies of. See Twin studies
Heritability coefficient, for intelligence, 353–354
Heroism, 627–628
Heuristic persuasion, 647–648, 648t
Heuristics, 275
definition of, 275
representativeness, 276–277
Hindbrain, 93, 93f
Hipp chronoscope, 42f
Hippocampus, 96, 96f, 97f
in antisocial personality disorder, 530
in fear, 530
long-term potentiation in, 178–179, 179f
in memory, 96, 177, 177f, 178–179, 179f, 181f, 182, 185–186, 195, 195f, 465, 465f
in posttraumatic stress disorder, 593–594, 594f
in repression, 465, 465f
structure and function of, 96, 96f, 97f
Hippocrates, 599, 609
Histrionic personality disorder, 527t
HIV infection, prevention of, 615–616
Hobbes, Thomas, 6
Homeostasis, 390
Homophobia, 466
Homosexuality, 435–436, 435f
Homunculus, 98, 98f, 156
Honeybees, waggle dance of, 254
Hormic psychology, 390
Hormones
of hypothalamic-pituitary-adrenal axis, 96, 586, 586f, 588
pituitary regulation of, 96
in postpartum depression, 512–513
regulation of, 96
sex
in aggression, 624–625
in sexual desire, 395
stress, 96, 586, 586f, 588, 602
Horney, Karen, 546f, 547
Hospitalization, in psychological treatment, 561
Host personality, in dissociative identity disorder, 508
Hostility, heart disease and, 590–591
HPA axis, in stress response, 96, 586, 586f, 588
Huffing, 321t, 322–323
Human immunodeficiency virus infection, prevention of, 615–616
Human sexual response cycle, 396–397, 397f
Humanism, 470–471
Humanistic psychology, 16–17
person-centered therapy and, 553–554
Humanity, 530t
Humor, in stress management, 602–603
Hunger, 391–392, 392f
Hyperopia, 132, 132f
Hypertension, stress and, 589–591
Hypnagogic state, 309
Hypnic jerk, 309
Hypnopompic state, 309
Hypnosis, 327–331, 327f–331f
brain activity during, 330–331, 331f
definition of, 327
effects of, 328–329
Freud's use of, 543
history of, 327
hysteria and, 14
induction of, 327–328

memory and, 329–330
pain perception and, 330, 330f
susceptibility to, 328
Hypnotic analgesia, 330, 330f
Hypochondriasis, 607
Hypothalamic-pituitary-adrenal axis, in stress response, 96, 586, 586f, 588
Hypothalamus, 95, 95f, 96f
in hunger, 392, 392f
in sexual desire, 395
in stress response, 586, 586f, 588
Hypothesis, 65–66
Hypothesis-confirming bias, 626
Hysteria, 14, 543, 608

Iatrogenic illnesses, 576
Iconic memory, 174, 174f
Id, 464
Identical twins, 105, 105f. See also Twin studies
definition of, 352
Identification, 467
Illness
compliance in, 610, 610f
denial of, 605–606
in depression, 589
iatrogenic, 576
misery in, 589
patient experience in, 608–610
patient-practitioner interaction in, 609–610
personality factors in, 611–612
psychology of, 604–610
psychosomatic, 607
secondary gains in, 609
sensitivity to, 604–608
sick role in, 608–609
sickness response in, 589
smoking-related, 616–617
socioeconomic status and, 588
somatoform disorders and, 607–608
stress and, 583, 588–591
symptom recognition in, 604–606
treatment in
avoidance of, 605–606
compliance with, 610, 610f
placebo effect in, 606, 606f
Illusion(s), 12–13, 12f, 13f
Ames room, 148, 148f
of depth and size, 147–148, 148f
figure-ground, 143, 143f
moon, 148, 148f
Mueller-Lyer line, 12, 12f, 147
of unique invulnerability, 615
waterfall, 149
Illusory correlation, 653, 653f
Image-based object recognition, 143
Imagery, visual, encoding of, 171–172, 171f
Imaging studies. See Neuroimaging
Imipramine, with psychotherapy, 565–566, 566f
Imitation, of facial expressions, 381–382, 430
empathy and, 430
in newborn, 411
Immune system, 588
components of, 588, 589
cytokines in, 589
definition of, 588
in sickness response, 589
social support and, 601–602
stress effects on, 588, 589
Implicit egotism, 483
Implicit learning, 210, 246–249

cognitive deficits and, 247–248
definition of, 246
vs. explicit learning, 247–249
neural pathways of, 248–249, 249f
during sleep, 248
Implicit memory, 183–185, 183f. See also Memory
Impossible event test, 414, 414f
Imprinting, 422
Impulse control, 613
Impulsive aggression, 623–624
In vitro fertilization, for intelligence selection, 363
Incest, 429
Independent variables, 60, 60f
Industrial/organizational psychologists, 34
Infant(s)
attachment behavior of, 422–425. See also Attachment
definition of, 410
development in, 410–430. See also Development
cognitive, 413–414, 413t
Erikson's stages of, 436t
language, 247
motor, 411–412, 411f
perceptual, 411–412
facial expressions of, 380
reflexes in, 411
Infantile amnesia, 198, 204–205
Infection. See also Illness
sickness response in, 589
Inferential statistics, 64
Influence. See Social influence
Informational influence, 645–646
Informed consent, 68
In-groups, 629
Inhalant abuse, 321t, 322–323
Inheritance. See Genes; Heritability
Inner ear, 151–152, 151f
in balance, 158
Insecure-avoidant attachment style, 423, 423f
Insecure-resistant attachment style, 423
Insight
in personality disorders, 530
in problem solving, 282–285, 283f
psychoanalytic, 544
Insomnia, 313
Instincts, 389, 390. See also Motivation
Institutional review boards, 68–69
Institutionalization, 561
Instrumental behaviors, 224–225
Insula
in pain perception, 605, 606
in placebo effect, 606, 606f
Intelligence, 337–363
absolute vs. relative, 360
age-related changes in, 360
analytic, 349
brain development and, 361, 361f
components of, 345–351
creative, 349
crystallized, 348–349
cultural aspects of, 350–351, 356–358
definition of, 351
education and, 360–362
environmental effects on, 353–354
eye gaze and, 345
factor analysis for, 345–346
confirmatory, 347
fluid, 348–349

Flynn effect and, 360
general, 345–347, 351
generational changes in, 360
genetic engineering for, 363
genetic factors in, 106–107, 351–358, 353t
giftedness and, 362–363
group differences in, 356–358
heritability coefficient for, 353–354
heritability of, 106–107, 351–356, 355f
hierarchical model of, 347, 347f
improvement of, 360–362
IQ score in, 339–341. *See also* Intelligence testing
judgments of, 345
life outcomes and, 341, 343–344, 343f, 344f, 361–362
middle-level abilities and, 347–351
multiple, 350
practical, 349
primary mental abilities and, 346–347, 347t
relative, 360
in savants, 253, 350, 350f, 363
selection for, 363
social skills and, 362
specific abilities and, 345–347
stability of, 259t, 359–360
twin studies of, 352–353, 353t
two-factor theory of, 346
Intelligence testing, 338–344
age and, 359–360
bias in, 356–358
bottom-up approach to, 347, 348–349, 348f, 359f
consequential behaviors and, 341, 343–344, 344f, 361–362
correlation patterns in, 348, 348f
among relatives, 352–353, 353t
cultural aspects of, 350–351, 356–358
gender differences in, 356–357
group differences in, 356–358
history of, 338–339
hypothetical properties and, 341
logic of, 341–342
predictive value of, 343–344, 343f, 344f
socioeconomic factors in, 357–358
Stanford-Binet test in, 341–342
stereotype threat and, 357–358, 655
top-down approach to, 349–351
Wechsler Adult Intelligence Scale in, 342, 342t
Interactionist theories, of language development, 261
Intermittent reinforcement, 233
Internal locus of control, 476, 476t
Internal validity, 64
Internal working model of attachment, 424
Interneurons, 77, 77f
Interpersonal psychotherapy, 547, 574t
Interposition, in depth perception, 145, 146f
Interval schedules of reinforcement, 231–233, 231f
Intervention-causation fallacy, 500
Intraversion, 457, 457f
neurophysiology of, 461–462
stress and, 519
Intrinsic motivation, 397–398
Introspection, 8, 9, 10
Intrusive memories, 201–203, 204
drug therapy for, 179
Involuntary commitment, 561
Ion channels

action potential and, 80–81, 80f
resting potential and, 79–80, 80f
Ions, 79
Iproniazid, 563
IQ, 339–341. *See also* Intelligence testing
deviation, 340, 340f
group differences in, 356–358
ratio, 339
Iris, 131, 131f
Ironic process of mental control, 304–305
Irrational beliefs, emotional responses to, 551, 551t

James, William, 1, 2, 2f, 4, 5, 7, 9–10, 14, 16, 16f, 31, 32, 478, 530–531, 625
Freud and, 16
James-Lange theory, 370, 371f, 373
Janet, Pierre, 14
Jealousy, 26
Jinjinia bemar, 499
Job opportunities, in psychology, 33–34, 542
Job-related burnout, 594–595
Joint attention, 419
Judgment(s)
alcohol effects on, 322
in decision making, 273–280. *See also* Decision making
rhyme, 170, 171f, 181
semantic, 170, 171f, 181
visual, 170, 171f
Jung, Carl, 15, 546, 546f
Just noticeable difference, 126
Justice, 530t

K complexes, 310, 310f
Kant, Immanuel, 13, 56
Ketamine, 326
Kin selection, 627
Klein, Melanie, 546f, 547
Klüver-Bucy syndrome, 373–374, 374f
Knowledge, 530t
Koffka, Kurt, 13
Kohlberg's moral development theory, 427–428
Kohler, Wolfgang, 13
Kohut, Heinz, 546f, 547
Koro, 499
Kymography, 42f

Labeling, in psychological disorders, 500–501
Language, 253–267. *See also* Speech
in animals, 221, 263–266
brain areas for, 262–263
cognition and, 266–267
definition of, 254
evolution of, 254, 262
functions of, 254
grammar in, 255, 259–261
morphemes in, 255, 255f
morphological rules of, 255
neurology of, 262–263
phonemes in, 254–255, 255f
phonological rules of, 255, 255f
in savant syndrome, 253
sign, 25, 258
for apes, 263–264
evolution of, 262
language areas and, 25
Nicaraguan, 262
structure of, 254–256, 255f
deep vs. surface, 256
symbols in, 380–381

syntactical rules of, 255–256, 256f, 258–259
temporal lobe in, 99
units of, 254–256, 255f
Language acquisition device, 260–261
Language areas
American Sign Language and, 25
in bilingual persons, 264
Broca's, 7, 63, 108, 262–263, 262f
Wernicke's, 108, 262–263, 262f
Language development, 257–263
active vs. passive mastery in, 257
in animals, 221, 263–266
artificial grammar and, 246–247, 247f
in children, 221
cognitive development and, 264, 266–267, 418
critical period for, 261
fast mapping in, 221, 258
grammar learning in, 259
in hearing impairment, 258, 262
implicit learning in, 246–249, 247f
in infants, 247
milestones in, 258–259
neurological specialization in, 262–263
overgeneralization in, 259
in second language learners, 261
cognitive development and, 264
rate of, 257, 264
speech sound discrimination in, 257–258
theories of, 259–262
behavioral, 259–260
interactionist, 261
nativist, 260–261
Lashley, Karl, 24–25, 24f
Latency stage, 468t, 469
Latent content, of dreams, 317
Latent learning, 238, 238f
Lateral geniculate nucleus, 138, 139f
Lateral hypothalamus, in hunger, 392, 392f
Lateral inhibition, 134–135, 135f
Lateralization, cortical, 97–98, 109–111, 110f, 111f
age-related changes in, 440, 440f
symmetry of, 440, 440f
Laughter, in stress management, 602–603
Law of effect, 225
Law of large numbers, 45
L-dopa, for Parkinson's disease, 85
Learning, 209–250
behaviorism and, 211. *See also* Behaviorism
biological preparedness in, 223
in classical conditioning, 212–224. *See also* Classical conditioning
cognitive maps in, 238–239, 239f
context for, 229–230
definition of, 210
explicit, 210
habituation in, 210–211
implicit, 210, 246–249. *See also* Implicit learning
language, 221, 257–263. *See also* Language development
latent, 238, 238f
law of effect and, 225
memory and, 210. *See also* Memory
motivation for, 250
observational, 242–245, 244f, 641
in operant conditioning, 225–229, 237–239. *See also* Operant conditioning
reinforcement in, 19, 250
sleep and, 248, 312

Learning (continued)
  in social cognitive approach, 474
  study skills in, 11
Legal issues
  criminal. See Crime
  eyewitness testimony
    misattribution and, 196
    suggestibility and, 197–199
  informed consent, 68
  prescribing privileges, 567
Length, operational definition of, 41–42
Leptin, 391
Lesbianism, 435, 435f
  homophobia and, 466
Levels of consciousness, 300–301. See also
    Consciousness
Lewin, Kurt, 22, 29
License, parental, 445
Lie detector tests, 385–386, 385f
Life stresses. See Stress; Stressors
Light adaptation, 131, 131f
Light therapy, for seasonal depression, 568,
    568f
Light waves, 130–131, 130t, 131f
Limbic system, 96–97, 96f. See also Amygdala;
    Hippocampus
  in emotion, 374–376, 376f
Linear perspective, in depth perception, 145,
    146f
Lineups, misidentification and, 196
Linguistic relativity hypothesis, 266–267
Listening, dichotic, 298–299
Lithium, 518, 564
Little Albert, 18, 218–219, 218f
Lobotomy, 569
Locus of control, 476, 476t
Logic, 285–286
Loneliness
  brain activity in, 630
  in depression, 515
  in illness, 601–602
  in schizophrenia, 522t
Long-term memory. See also Memory
  storage of, 176–177, 176f, 177f
  types of, 182–186, 183f
Long-term potentiation, 178
Long-term relationships. See Marriage;
    Relationships
Lorazepam, 562
Loudness, 150–151
Love. See also Marriage; Relationships
  companionate vs. passionate, 638, 638f
LSD, 326
Lung cancer, in smokers, 616
Lying, signs of, 383–386
Lymphocytes, 588
Lysergic acid diethylamide, 326

Macrophages, 589
Mad Hatter syndrome, 497
Magnetic resonance imaging (MRI), 113–114,
    114f
  functional, 2, 114–115, 115f
    during sleep, 316
Major depressive disorder, 512–515. See also
    Depression
Mal de ojo, 499
Males. See Gender differences
Malingering, 608–609
Mania, 515–519. See also Bipolar disorder
Manifest content, of dreams, 317

Manipulation, experimental, 59–60, 60f
Maps
  cognitive, 238–239, 239f
  emotional, 369–370, 369f
Marijuana, 326
  decriminalization of, 325
  memory and, 181
Marital therapy, 556–557, 557f
Marriage, 443–444, 443f, 636–639. See also
    Relationships
  arranged, 638
  companionate vs. passionate love in, 638,
    638f
  cultural aspects of, 638
  divorce and, 443–444, 636
  health benefits of, 601
  mate selection and, 289, 631–636. See also
    Mate selection
  satisfaction with, 638–639
Maslow, Abraham, 16–17, 17f, 390
Maslow's hierarchy of needs, 390–391, 391f,
    471
Mass media. See also Movies
  violence in, 244
Massage therapy, 599
Matched pairs technique, 57–58
Matched samples technique, 57–58
Mate selection, 289. See also Marriage;
    Relationships; Reproductive behavior
  height in, 28, 633
  physical factors in, 27, 28, 633–635. See also
    Physical attractiveness
  psychological factors in, 636
  similarity in, 636
  situational factors in, 632–633
Mathematical comprehension, development of,
    419, 420f, 421
MDMA (ecstasy), 321t, 323
Mean, 47, 48, 48f
Means-ends analysis, 281
Means-ends theory, of operant conditioning,
    237–239, 238f, 239f
Measure, definition of, 42
Measurement, 41–44
  detection in, 42, 43
  in experiments, 59, 64
  operational definitions in, 41–43
  power of, 44
  reliability of, 44
  validity of, 43–44, 43f, 44f
Medial forebrain bundle, as reward center,
    236–237, 236f
Medial prefrontal cortex
  in self-concept, 479, 479f
  in social cognition, 652
Median, 47, 48, 48f
Medical conditions. See Health; Illness
Medical model, of psychological disorders, 491
Medications. See Drug therapy
Meditation, 331–332
  mindfulness, 551
  in stress management, 598
Medulla, 93, 93f
Mellaril, 560
Memory, 167–206
  age-related changes in, 193, 439–441, 441f
  amygdala in, 96–97, 202–203, 202f
  in animals, 178, 186
  attention and, 189–190
  autobiographical, 478
  availability bias and, 275

childhood
  loss of, 198, 204–205
  reliability of, 197–199, 204–205, 576
  in children, 198, 204–205
  definition of, 168
  of dreams, 314
  drug enhancement of, 179
  echoic, 174
  emotional arousal and, 96–97, 201–202
  encoding of, 11, 169–173
    attention and, 189–190
    definition of, 169
    elaborative, 170–171, 170f
    judgments and, 170, 171f, 181
    organizational, 172–173, 173f
    prevention of, 577
    during sleep, 312
    specificity principle for, 180
    visual imagery in, 171–172, 171f, 172f
  episodic, 183f, 185–186
  explicit, 183, 183f
  false, 197–199, 576
  flashbulb, 201–202
  formation of, 170
  frontal lobe in, 99
    in encoding, 171, 171f, 173
    in retrieval, 181f, 182, 184, 185f, 194
  hippocampus in, 96, 177, 177f, 178–179,
    179f, 181f, 182, 185–186, 195, 195f, 465,
    465f
  hypnosis and, 329–330
  iconic, 174, 174f
  impaired. See Memory loss
  implicit, 183–185, 183f
  intrusive, 179, 201–203, 204
  learning and, 210. See also Learning
  long-term
    storage of, 176–177, 176f, 177f
    types of, 182–185, 183f
  occipital lobe in, 171, 171f, 172, 182, 184,
    185f, 195
  overview of, 168–169
  personal recollections and, 205
  proactive interference and, 189
  procedural, 183–185, 183f
  prospective, 191
  reconstructive errors in, 571
  recovered, 198–199, 576
  retrieval of, 11, 169, 180–182, 181f
    attempted vs. successful, 181f, 182
    component processes in, 181f, 182
    cues in, 180–181, 191
    definition of, 169
    encoding specificity principle and,
      180–181
    failure of, 191–193
    priming in, 183f, 184–185, 185f
    state-dependent, 181
    transfer-appropriate processing in, 181
  retroactive interference and, 189
  self-relevance and, 479
  semantic, 183f, 185–186
    age-related changes in, 439
  sensory, storage of, 173–174, 174f
  seven sins of, 187–204
    absentmindedness, 189–191, 203
    bias, 199–200, 203–204
    blocking, 191–193, 203
    memory misattribution, 193–196, 203
    persistence, 179, 201–203, 204
    suggestibility, 197–199, 203

transience, 187–188, 188f, 203
usefulness of, 203–204
short-term, 174–175, 175f
sleep and, 248, 312
socioemotional selectivity theory of, 441
source, 194
storage of, 169, 173–180, 174f–177f, 179f
brain areas in, 177, 177f
chunking in, 175
definition of, 173
hippocampus in, 177, 178–179, 179f
long-term, 176–177, 176f, 177f, 183f
long-term potentiation in, 178–179, 179f
neurotransmitters in, 178–179, 179f
rehearsal in, 11, 174–175
sensory, 173–174, 174f
short-term, 174–175, 175f
in studying, 11
temporal lobe in, 171f
tip-of-the-tongue experience and, 191t, 192
types of, 182–22
working, 175
age-related changes in, 439
stream of consciousness and, 300
Memory loss. See also Amnesia
case examples of, 167–169, 176–177, 182
drug-induced, 179
hippocampal damage in, 177
Memory misattribution, 193–196, 203
Memory tests, 169f
in amnesiacs, 184
iconic, 174, 174f
Men. See Gender differences
Menstrual cycle(s)
sexual desire and, 395
synchronization of, 160–161
Mental abilities, primary, 346–347, 347t
Mental control, 303–305. See also
Consciousness
ironic process of, 304–305
Mental health counselors, 542. See also
Psychotherapy
Mental hospitals, 561
Mental representations, in cognitive develop-
ment, 416–418
Mercury poisoning, 497
Mere exposure effect, 632
Mescaline, 326
Mesmerism, 327
Mesolimbic area, in schizophrenia, 560
Metabolism, weight and, 394
Methamphetamine, 321t, 323
hallucinations due to, 73, 83, 87
neurotransmitters and, 83, 87
Method, 40
experimental. See Experiment(s)
Method of loci, 11
Methylphenidate
adverse effects of, 576
cognitive performance and, 362
Microvilli, taste bud, 161
Midbrain, 94–95, 94f
Middle ear, 151–152, 151f
Milgram's obedience experiment, 644–645
Miller, George, 23
Mimicry, of facial expressions, 381–382,
430
empathy and, 430
in newborn, 411
Mind. See also under Consciousness; Mental
definition of, 2

in functionalism, 10
overview of, 2–4
in structuralism, 8
Mind-body problem, 6, 297–298, 297f
Mindbugs, 4
Mindfulness meditation, 551
Minimal consciousness, 300, 301
Minnesota Multiphasic Personality Inventory
(MMPI), 452
Minor tranquilizers, 321t, 322–323
Minorities. See also Cultural factors; Race/
ethnicity
in psychology, 33–34
Mirror neurons, 78
in observational learning, 245
Misattributions, 29–32, 203
memory, 193–196, 203
Misidentification, by eyewitnesses, 196
Modafinil, cognitive performance and, 362
Mode, 47, 48, 48f
Modeling, in observational learning, 243–244,
244f, 641
Monoamine oxidase inhibitors (MAOIs), 563.
See also Antidepressants
Monocular depth cues, 144–145, 145f, 146f
Monosodium glutamate (MSG), 162
Monozygotic twins, 105, 105f. See also Twin
studies
Mood disorders, 511–519
bipolar disorder, 515–519. See also Bipolar
disorder
depression, 511–515. See also Depression
Mood stabilizers, 564
Moon illusion, 148, 148f
Moral development, 425–430
conventional stage of, 427
empathy and, 429–430
gender differences in, 428
moral intuition in, 428–430
moral reasoning in, 426–428
postconventional stage of, 427–428
preconventional stage of, 427
Morphemes, 255, 255f
Morphological rules, 255
Mortality salience, 472–473
self-esteem and, 483–484
Mothers
attachment to, 422–425. See also Attachment
satisfaction with parenthood, 444
voice of, fetal recognition of, 410
working, day care and, 426
Motion. See also Movement
apparent, 149
Motion parallax, 147
Motion pictures. See Movies
Motion sickness, 158
Motivated forgetting, 465
Motivation, 386–401
approach vs. avoidance, 400–401
conscious vs. unconscious, 399–400
definition of, 386
delayed gratification and, 398
drives and, 390
for eating, 391–394
emotions and, 386. See also Emotion(s)
hedonic principle and, 388, 640–641
hedonic principle in, 464, 468
for homeostasis, 390
instinct and, 389, 390
intrinsic vs. extrinsic, 397–399
for learning, 250

need for achievement and, 399
needs and, 390–391, 391f
personality and, 451
priming of, 399
punishment and, 398–399, 398f
for sex, 394–395
social influence and, 640–645
types of, 397–401
for voting, 401
Motor cortex, 98, 99f
Motor development, 411–412, 411f
cephalocaudal, 411
proximodistal, 411
Motor neurons, 77, 77f
Movement. See also Motion
basal ganglia in, 97, 97f
during dreams, 316
frontal lobe in, 99
perception of, 148–149
thought-controlled, 92
visual component of, 140
Movement disorders
drug-related, 521, 562
in schizophrenia, 521
Movies, 12–13, 149
development of, 13, 13f
product placement in, 163
violence in, 244
MPTP intoxication, 86
Mueller-Lyer line, 12, 12f, 147
Multidimensional scaling, 369
Multiple intelligences, 350
Multiple sclerosis, 76
Multitasking, 129
Muscles, facial
reliable, 383
in smiling, 381, 381f, 383, 383f
Myelin sheath, 75f, 76, 408
action potential and, 81, 81f
development of, 408
Myopia, 132, 132f

Names
blocking of, 192–193
color, 267
implicit egotism and, 483
Name-the-letter effect, 483
Narcissism, 484
Narcissistic personality disorder, 527t
Narcolepsy, 314
Narcotics, 321t, 325. See also Drug abuse;
Opiates
Nativism, 5
Nativist theory, of language development,
260–261
Natural correlation, 56
Natural selection, 10, 26
Naturalistic observation, 49
Nature vs. nurture argument, 104, 105–106
Nazi Germany, research studies in, 70
Nearsightedness, 132, 132f
Necker cube, 300, 300f
Need for achievement, 399
Needs. See also Motivation
Maslow's hierarchy of, 390–391, 391f, 471
self-actualization and, 471
Negative correlation, 54, 55f
perfect, 54–55, 55f
Negative emotions, expression of, 584
Negative reinforcement, 226–227, 227t. See also
Punishment; Reinforcement

Negative symptoms, in schizophrenia, 521, 522t, 560
Negative thinking, in depression, 514–515
Neisser, Ulric, 21, 24
Nerves, myelination of, 75f, 76, 408
  action potential and, 81, 81f
  development of, 408
Nervous system
  autonomic, 88–89, 88f, 89f
    in emotion, 370–373, 371f, 373f
  central, 87–91, 88f. See also Brain; Central nervous system; Spinal cord
  definition of, 87
  development of
    evolutionary, 102–104
    postnatal, 408
    prenatal, 102, 102f, 408
  divisions of, 87–89, 88f, 89f
  evolution of, 102–104
  invertebrate, 103, 103f
  organization of, 87–101
  parasympathetic, 88–89, 88f, 89f
  peripheral, 87–88, 88f
  somatic, 87–88, 88f
  sympathetic, 88, 88f, 89f, 96
    activation of, 96
Neural development, 102, 102f
Neural tube, 102
Neuroimaging, 2–3
  computed tomography in, 113
  magnetic resonance imaging in, 113–114
    functional, 2, 25
  positron emission tomography in, 25, 25f, 114–115, 115f
  transcranial magnetic stimulation in, 63
Neuroimmunology, 588
Neurons, 74–83
  action potential of, 80–81, 80f
  auditory receptor, 152
  bipolar, 78
  components of, 75–76, 75f
  definition of, 74
  early studies of, 74–75, 75f
  electrochemical action of, 79–81
  interneurons, 77, 77f
  in memory storage, 178–179, 179f
  mirror, 78, 245
  motion-sensitive, 149
  motor, 77, 77f
  number of, 74
  olfactory receptor, 158–159, 159f
  plasticity of, 100–101
  postsynaptic, 82, 82f
  presynaptic, 82, 82f
  resting potential of, 79–80
  sensory, 77, 77f
  synapses between, 76, 76f
Neuroscience
  behavioral, 24–25
  cognitive, 25
Neurosis
  definition of, 494
  in DSM-II, 495
Neuroticism, 457–458, 457t
Neurotransmitters, 81–87
  in anxiety, 502
  in bipolar disorder, 518
  definition of, 81
  in depression, 513
  diversity of, 83
  drug effects on, 85–87

enzyme deactivation of, 82–83, 82f
functions of, 83t
imbalances of, 94
in phobic disorders, 504
receptors for, 81, 82, 82f, 83
release of, 82, 82f
reuptake of, 82, 82f
in schizophrenia, 524, 560
synaptic strengthening and, 178–179, 179f
in synaptic transmission, 82–83
types of, 83–84, 83t
Newborns. See also Infant(s)
  development of, 410–411
Nicaraguan sign language, 262
Nicotine. See Smoking
Night terrors, 314
Night vision, rods in, 132–134, 133f
Nightmares, 315, 316
Nine-dot problem, 285, 285f
NMDA receptors, in memory storage, 178–179, 179f
Nodes of Ranvier, 81, 81f
Noise, 126
  stress due to, 584, 585
Noncompliance, with treatment, 610
Nondirective psychotherapy, 554
Nonhuman primates
  language learning in, 263–266
  self-consciousness in, 301
Non-REM sleep, 311
Nonshared environment, 355
Nontasters, 162
Norepinephrine, 83t, 84
  in bipolar disorder, 518
  in depression, 513
  functions of, 83t, 84, 86
Norm(s), 642
  conformity and, 643–644
  definition of, 642
  obedience and, 644–645
  of reciprocity, 642
Normal distribution, 47, 47f
Normative influence, 642
Nose, anatomy of, 158, 159f
NREM sleep, 311
Nucleus, 75, 75f
Nucleus accumbens, pleasure/reward and, 236, 236f, 237
Nutrition, 614, 615. See also Eating problems
  fetal development and, 408
  hunger and, 391–392
Nutritional supplements, 564–565

Obedience, social influence in, 644–645
Obesity, 393–394, 614
Object permanence, 413–414, 418
Object recognition, 141–144, 141f–144f
  distributed representation in, 141
  edge assignment in, 143, 143f
  figure-ground relationship in, 143, 143f
  geons in, 144, 144f
  image-based, 143
  modular view of, 141
  parts-based, 143–144
  perceptual constancy and, 142
  perceptual grouping rules and, 142, 142f
  template in, 143
  theories of, 143–144
Observation, 41–52
  bias in, 49–52
  blind observer and, 50–51

demand characteristics and, 49–50
expectations in, 49–51
measurement in, 41–44
naturalistic, 49
participants in, 50
sampling in, 44–48
Observational learning, 242–245, 244f, 641
Obsessive-compulsive disorder, 506–507
  psychosurgery for, 569
Obsessive-compulsive personality disorder, 527t
Occipital lobe, 98, 98f
  area V1 of, 138–139, 138f. See also Primary visual cortex
  association areas of, 99
  development of, 431, 431f
  in memory, 171, 171f, 172, 182, 184, 185f, 195
  in object recognition, 141–142
  in vision, 98
Occupational burnout, 594–595
Odd/eccentric personality disorders, 527, 527t
Odorant molecules, 158
Oedipus conflict, 469
Off-center cells, 134–135, 135f
Olanzepine, 562
Olfaction. See Smell
Olfactory bulb, 159–160, 159f
Olfactory receptor neurons, 158–159, 159f
On-center cells, 134–135, 135f
One Flew Over the Cuckoo's Nest (Kesey), 567
Ontogeny, of brain, 102
Openness to experience, 457–458, 457t
Operant behavior, 225
Operant chamber, 226, 226f
Operant conditioning, 224–242, 548
  antecedents and consequences in, 548
  in aversion therapy, 548
  in behavior therapy, 548–550
  vs. classical conditioning, 225
  cognitive elements of, 237–238
  cognitive maps and, 238–239
  context in, 229–230
  definition of, 224
  discrimination in, 229–230
  in drug abuse, 236–237
  early studies of, 224–225
  evolutionary aspects of, 239–242
  extinction in, 230
  generalization in, 229–230
  latent learning and, 238, 238f
  law of effect and, 225
  neural elements of, 236–237, 236f
  overjustification effect and, 229, 250
  Premack principle and, 228
  reinforcement in, 19, 225–229, 227t. See also Reinforcement
  reinforcement schedules in, 231–233, 231f
  shaping in, 233–235, 234f
  superstitious behavior and, 235
  Tolman's means-ends theory of, 237–239, 238f, 239f
Operational definitions, 41, 341
Operationalization, 124
Opiates
  abuse of, 321t, 325
  endogenous, 83t, 84, 325
    in placebo effect, 606
Optic ataxia, 140
Optic flow, 147
Optic nerve, 133f, 134, 138, 139f
Optical illusions. See Illusion(s)

Optimism, 530–531. *See also* Happiness
  health and, 612
    positive psychology and, 530–531, 612
Oral aggression, 468
Oral stage, 468, 468t
Orexigenic signals, in hunger, 391
Organizational encoding, 172–173, 173f
Orgasm, 396–397, 397f
The Origin of Species (Darwin), 10
Ossicles, 151f, 152
Outcome expectancies, 476
Outcome studies, 572
Outer ear, 151–152, 151f
Out-groups, 629
Overdose, in drug abuse, 215
Overjustification effect, 229, 250
Overweight, 393, 393t
Ovulation, sexual desire and, 395
Oxytocin, 96
  in stress response, 602

Pain
  avoidance of, 388
  brain activity in, 605, 605f
  congenital insensitivity to, 156
  endorphins and, 83t, 84, 325, 606
  gate-control theory of, 157
  in hypnosis, 330, 330f
  perception of, 156–157
  phantom limb, 100, 110f
  placebo effect and, 606
  racial differences in, 157
  referred, 156
  sensitivity to, 605, 605f
Pain withdrawal reflex, 90, 90f, 156
Panic disorder, 505–506
Papillae, taste buds in, 161, 161f
Paralysis
  in spinal cord injuries, 90–91
  thought-controlled movement in, 92
Paranoid personality disorder, 527t
Parasympathetic nervous system, 88–89, 88f, 89f
Parent, attachment to, 422–425. *See also* Attachment
Parenthood
  licensing for, 445
  satisfaction with, 443–444
Parietal lobe, 98, 99f
  development of, 431, 431f
  in meditation, 332
  in reasoning, 288, 288f
Parkinson's disease
  dopamine in, 85, 97
  substantia nigra in, 97
  treatment of, 85
Parkinson's-like symptoms, in MPTP abusers, 85–86
Paroxetine, 563
Parts-based object recognition, 143–144
Passionate love, vs. companionate love, 638, 638f
Patient experience, 608–610
Patient-physician interaction, 609–610
Pavlov, Ivan, 18, 212
Pavlovian conditioning, 18, 212–224, 212f, 213f. *See also* Classical conditioning
Paxil, 563
PCP, 326
Peak experiences, 471
  consciousness during, 331–333

Peer nomination, 528–529
Peer relations, in adolescence, 437
Perception, 123. *See also* Sensation
  absolute thresholds in, 124–125, 125f, 125t
  auditory, 150–155. *See also* Hearing
  definition of, 123
  difference thresholds in, 126, 135
  haptic, 155–158
  illusions and. *See* Illusion(s)
  of light, 130–135
  noise and, 126
  olfactory, 158–161. *See also* Smell
  pain, 156–157
  psychophysics of, 124–128
  receptive fields in, 134–135
  subliminal, 163, 306–308, 308f
  tactile, 98, 124–125, 155–156
  taste, 124–125, 125t, 161–163
  visual, 130–149. *See also* Vision
Perceptual confirmation, of stereotypes, 655
Perceptual constancy, 142
Perceptual grouping, 142–143, 142f
Perceptual sensitivity, measurement of, 128
Perfect correlation, 54–55, 55f
Periaqueductal gray, 157
Peripheral nervous system, 87–88, 88f
Peripheral vision, 133
Perls, Fritz, 555
Perseverance effect, 649
Persistent memories, 201–203, 204
  drug therapy for, 179
Persistent vegetative state, 116–117
Personal constructs, 475
Personal names
  blocking of, 192–193
  implicit egotism and, 483
Personal recollections, 205. *See also* Memory
Personality. *See also* Personality traits
  in animals, 460–461
  authoritarian, 455
  behavioral activation/inhibition system and, 461–462
  criminal, 529–530
  definition of, 450
  development of, 450
    psychoanalytic view of, 468–470, 468t
    psychosexual development and, 468–470, 468t
  environmental factors in, 460
  evolutionary aspects of, 461
  existential approach to, 470, 472–473
  gender differences in, 459
  genetic aspects of, 458–460
  goals and, 476
  hardiness and, 612
  health and, 610–612
  humanist approach to, 470–472
  influences on, 451
  locus of control and, 476, 476t
  measurement of, 451–454
  motivations and, 451
  multiple, 508–510
  neurophysiology of, 461–462
  outcome expectancies and, 476
  overview of, 450–451
  personal constructs and, 475
  person-situation controversy and, 474–475
  psychodynamic view of, 462–470
  self-actualization and, 471
  self-concept and, 477–480
  self-esteem and, 478, 480–485

situational consistency of, 474–475
  social role theory of, 459
  social-cognitive approach to, 473–477
  stability of, 458
    self-reflection and, 480
  stress effects and, 518–519
  unconditional positive regard and, 471
Personality assessment
  applications of, 485
  in employment, 485
  inventories in, 451–452
  Minnesota Multiphasic Personality Test in, 452
  projective tests in, 452–454, 453t
  response style in, 452
  Rorschach Inkblot Test in, 453–454, 453f, 463
  self-reports in, 452, 452t
  test validity in, 485
  Thematic Apperception Test in, 453–454, 453f
Personality changes, 449–485
  in brain-injured patients, 109
Personality disorders, 526–531
  antisocial, 527t, 529–531
  anxious/inhibited, 527, 527t
  avoidant, 527t
  borderline, 527t
  classification of, 527–528, 527t
  common feature of, 529
  comorbid, 528
  definition of, 526
  dependent, 527t
  diagnosis of, 528–529
  dramatic/erratic, 527, 527t
  histrionic, 527t
  narcissistic, 527t
  obsessive-compulsive, 527t
  odd/eccentric, 527, 527t
  paranoid, 527t
  peer nominations for, 528–529
  schizoid, 527t
  schizotypal, 527t
Personality inventories, 451–452
Personality traits, 454–462
  authoritarianism, 455
  behavioral correlates of, 474–475
  Big Five, 457–458, 457t
  conservatism, 455
  core, 456–458
  Eysenck's classification of, 457, 457f
  factor analysis of, 456–457
  heritability of, 458–460, 458t
  hierarchy of, 456–457, 456f
  in personality disorders, 528
  in self-schemas, 479
  stress response and, 590–591, 603
Person-centered therapy, 553–554
Person-situation controversy, 474–475
Persuasion, 647–648. *See also* Social influence
  heuristic, 647–648, 648t
  perseverance effect in, 649
  sleeper effect in, 649
  subliminal, 163, 306–308, 308f
  systematic, 647, 648, 648t
  unbelieving effect in, 649
Pessimism
  health and, 611–612
  reduction of, 611–612
PET scans, 25, 25f, 114–115, 115f
Peyote, 326

Phallic stage, 468t, 469
Phantom limb syndrome, 100, 100f
Phencyclidine (PCP), 326
Phenomenology, 295
Pheromones, 160
Phi phenomenon, 149
Philosophical empiricism, 5
Philosophy, 5–7
Phobias, 503–505
  agoraphobia, 505–506
  air travel, 537, 538, 539
  biological preparedness and, 223
  conditioned, 18, 218–219, 218f, 223,
    504–505
  exposure therapy for, 549–550, 549t, 550f
  preparedness theory of, 504
  social, 504
  specific, 503–504
Phonemes, 254–255, 255f
Phonological rules, 255
Photopigments, 132, 136
Photoreceptors, 132–134, 133f
Phototherapy, for seasonal depression, 568,
  568f
Phototransduction, 132–134
Phrases, 255, 255f
Phrenology, 6, 6f
Phylogeny, of brain, 102
Physical attractiveness, 633–635
  arousal and, 632–633
  averageness in, 637
  cultural aspects of, 27, 31, 634–635
  evolutionary aspects of, 634–635
  sexual attraction and, 23, 633–635
  social aspects of, 633–634
Physical dependence, in drug abuse, 319
Physician-patient interaction, 609–610
Physiological psychology, 24–25
Physiology, 7–9
Piaget, Jean, 22, 22f, 412–416, 412f
Piaget's cognitive development stages, 412–416
  moral reasoning and, 426–427
Pictorial depth cues, 145, 146f
Pinna, 151f, 152
Pitch, 150
  perception of, 152–153
Pituitary gland, in stress response, 95f, 96, 96f,
  586, 586f
Place code, 153
Placebo effect, 571, 571f, 606
Placenta, 408
Plaques, amyloid, in Alzheimer's disease, 439f
Plasticity, brain, 100–101
Plateau phase, of human sexual response,
  396–397, 397f
Plato, 5, 5f, 352, 388
Pleasure centers, 236–237, 236f
Pleasure principle, 388, 464, 468, 640–641
Poisoning
  food aversions and, 162, 222
  mercury, 497
Polarization, group, 629–630
Political conservatism, personality and, 455
Polygenic disorders, 518
Polygraphs, 385–386, 385f
Pons, 93f, 94
Population, sampling, 45
Positional perception, 157–158
Positive correlation, 54, 55f
  perfect, 54–55, 55f
Positive psychology, 530–531, 612

Positive punishment, 226–227, 227t
Positive reinforcement, 226–227, 227t
Positron emission tomography, 25, 25f,
  114–115, 115f
Postconventional stage, of moral development,
  427–428
Posthypnotic amnesia, 330
Postpartum depression, 512–513
Postsynaptic neurons, 82, 82f
Posttraumatic stress disorder, 592–595
  eye movement desensitization and reprocess-
    ing for, 575
  prevention of, 577, 595–597. See also Stress
    management
Potassium ion channels
  action potential and, 79, 80–81, 80f
  resting potential and, 79, 80f
Poverty, health and, 588
Power, in measurement, 44
Practical intelligence, 349
Practical reasoning, 286–287
Pragnanz, law of, 142
Preconsciousness, 463
Preconventional stage, of moral development,
  427–428
Predictive validity, 43, 44f
Prefrontal cortex
  age-related changes in, 439
  in decision making, 278
  in depression, 513–514
  development of
    in adolescence, 431, 431f
    intelligence and, 361, 361f
  in self-concept, 479, 479f
  in substance abuse, 278
Pregnancy. See also Reproductive behavior
  adolescent, 434
  alcohol use in, 408–409
  diet in, 408
  fetal development in, 406–410. See also
    Prenatal development
  infections in, schizophrenia and, 523
  prevention of, 434, 615–616
  smoking in, 409
  teratogens in, 408–409
Pre-implantation genetic diagnosis, for intelligence selection, 363
Prejudice. See also Bias; Stereotype(s)
  definition of, 628
  in groups, 629
  unconscious, 660–661
Premack principle, 228
Premeditated aggression, 623
Prenatal development, 406–410
  embryonic stage in, 407, 407f
  environmental influences on, 408–410
  fetal stage in, 407f, 408
  germinal stage in, 407
  intrauterine environment in, 408–410
  of nervous system, 102, 102f, 408
  nutrition in, 408
Preoperational stage, 413t, 415
Preparedness theory
  of obsessive-compulsive disorder, 507
  of phobias, 504
Prescribing privileges, for psychologists, 567
Presynaptic neurons, 82, 82f
Primary auditory cortex, 99, 152, 153f
Primary caregiver, attachment to, 422–425. See
  also Attachment
Primary mental abilities, 346–347, 347t

Primary reinforcement, 227
Primary sex characteristics, 431
Primary visual cortex, 99, 113, 138–139, 138f,
  139f
  feature detectors in, 113
Priming, 183f, 184–185, 185f
  of motivation, 399
Principles of Physiological Psychology (Wundt), 8
The Principles of Psychology (James), 1, 4, 10
Prisoner's dilemma, 625–626, 626f
Proactive interference, 189
Probability estimation, in decision making,
  274, 275, 276, 280
Problem of other minds, 295–296, 296f
  in cognitive development, 416–418
Problem solving, 280–285. See also Decision
  making
  analogical, 281–282
  creativity and insight in, 282–285
  framing in, 284–285
  functional fixedness in, 284–285, 284f
  for ill-defined vs. well-defined problems,
    280–281
  means-ends analysis in, 281
Procedural memory, 183–185, 183f. See also
  Memory
Process studies, 572
Procrastination, 35
Prodigies, 350, 362–363. See also Savants
Product placement, 163
Professors, of psychology, 33
Prognosis, of psychological disorders, 497
Projection, 466–467
Projective tests
  in personality assessment, 452–454, 453f
  in psychodynamic approach, 463
Propranolol, 86–87
  memory encoding and, 577
Prosopagnosia, 73, 108, 113
Prospect theory, 279–280
Prospective memory, 191. See also Memory
Prototype theory, 271–272, 271f, 273f
Proximity, attraction and, 632–633
Proximodistal rule, for motor development,
  411
Prozac, 86, 563, 564, 571, 571f
Psilocybin, 326
Psychiatric labeling, 500–501
Psychiatric social workers, 542
Psychiatrists, 542
  prescription privileges of, 567
Psychoactive drugs, 318–327
  alcohol, 321–322, 321t. See also Alcohol
    use/abuse
  barbiturates, 321t, 322–323
  benzodiazepines, 321t, 322–323
  caffeine, 319, 320
  dangers of, 321t
  definition of, 318
  depressants, 321, 321t
  hallucinogens, 326
  marijuana, 326
  narcotics, 321t, 324–325
  toxic inhalants, 321t, 322–323
  types of, 320–327
  use vs. abuse of, 318–320. See also Drug abuse
Psychoanalysis, 15, 543, 543f
  vs. cognitive behavioral therapy, 552
  definition of, 543
  dream analysis in, 545
  duration of, 544

effectiveness of, 574
free association in, 544–545
insight in, 544
interpretation in, 545
of psychoanalysts, 545
resistance in, 544–545
transference in, 546
Psychoanalytic theory, 14–17. *See also*
Psychoanalysis; Psychodynamic approach
anxiety in, 465
defense mechanisms in, 466–467
definition of, 15
dreams in, 317
ego in, 464
id in, 464
influence of, 26–27
inner conflict in, 465–467
personality in, 461–470
pleasure principle in, 464
vs. psychodynamic approach, 463
psychosexual stages in, 468–470, 468t
reality principle in, 464
superego in, 464
unconscious in, 305–306, 463
Psychodynamic approach, 463–470
definition of, 463
projective tests in, 463
vs. psychoanalytic theory, 463. *See also*
Psychoanalytic theory
Psychodynamic therapy, 543–547, 543f. *See
also* Psychoanalysis
vs. cognitive behavioral therapy, 552
definition of, 543
effectiveness of, 572–574, 574t
Psychological dependence, in drug abuse, 319
Psychological disorders, 489–533
anxiety disorders, 501–508
bipolar disorder, 515–519
causes of, 497–500
classification of, 494–501. *See also Diagnostic
and Statistical Manual of Mental Disorders
(DSM-IV-TR)*
comorbidity in, 496–497, 497f, 528
continuum of, 493
creativity in, 489
cultural aspects of, 499
definition of, 490
depression, 511–515
diagnosis of, 491–492, 493, 495
diathesis-stress model of, 498. *See also* Stress
dissociative, 508–511
exercise and, 601
genetic factors in, 498
incidence of, 490
integrative approach to, 397, 497–498
labeling and, 500–501
medical model of, 491
mood disorders, 511–519
natural improvement in, 570, 572
vs. normality, 492–493, 532
outcome in, 497
overview of, 490
polygenic, 518
prognosis of, 497
schizophrenia, 519–522, 522t
societal attitudes toward, 490–491
societal costs of, 539–540
stigma of, 500, 540–541
treatment of, 537–577
barriers to, 540–541
dangers of, 575–577

effectiveness of, 569–574
electroconvulsive therapy in, 567–568, 568f
evaluation of, 570–572
eye movement desensitization and reprocessing in, 575
history of, 561
illusions of, 570–571, 572
institutionalization in, 561
intervention-causation fallacy and, 500
medical and biological, 559. *See also* Drug
therapy
vs. natural improvement, 570, 572
need for, 539–540
nonspecific effects of, 570
phototherapy in, 568, 568f
placebo effect in, 571, 571f, 606, 606f
providers of, 542
psychosurgery in, 569
psychotherapy in, 541–559. *See also*
Psychotherapy
reconstructive memory errors and, 571
selection of, 540–541
studies of, 572
transcranial electrical stimulation in, 568
Psychological research
animal welfare in, 69
bias in, 49–52
careers in, 33
case method in, 44–45
causal relationships in, 52–67. *See also* Causal
relationships
descriptive statistics in, 47–48, 48f
double-blind technique in, 51, 572
ethical aspects of, 68–70
experimentation in, 58–64. *See also*
Experiment(s)
informed consent for, 68
measurement in, 41–44. *See also* Measurement
methods of, 40–70
observation in, 41–52. *See also* Observation
operational definitions in, 41
outcome studies in, 572
participant protections in, 68–69
process studies in, 572
sampling in, 44–48
third-variable problem in, 57–58, 57f
treatment studies in, 572–574
Psychological therapy. *See* Psychological disorders, treatment of
Psychologists, 542
clinical, 33–34, 542
counseling, 34
education and training of, 542
ethical code for, 576–577
industrial/organizational, 34
misconduct of, 576–577
prescribing privileges for, 567
research, 33
school, 34
selection of, 542
types of, 542
Psychology
behavioral, 17–21
careers in, 33–34, 542
clinical, 33–34, 542
cognitive, 21–24
cultural, 29–31. *See also* Cultural factors
definition of, 2
developmental, 405
education and training in, 33
environmental, 584

evolutionary, 26–28
Gestalt, 13, 29. *See also* Gestalt psychology
health, 582
history of, 1–12
hormic, 390
humanistic, 16–17
methods of, 40–70. *See also* Psychological
research
minorities in, 32–33
overview of, 1–4
philosophy and, 5–7
physiological, 24–25
physiology and, 7–9
profession of, 31–34
professional organizations for, 31–32
social, 28–29, 621–661
stimulus-response, 19
subfields of, 27, 33–34, 34f
cooperative endeavors of, 27
women in, 32
The Psychology of Everyday Life (Freud), 306
Psychoneuroimmunology, 588
Psychopaths, 529
Psychopharmacology, 560. *See also* Drug
therapy
Psychophysics, 124–128
signal detection theory and, 126–128, 127f
Psychosexual development, stages of, 468–470,
468t
Psychosis. *See also* Schizophrenia
definition of, 495
treatment of, 560–562
Psychosomatic illness, 607
Psychosurgery, 569
Psychotherapy, 541–559
access to, 540–541
barriers to, 540–541
behavioral, 547–550
cognitive, 550–551
couples, 556–557, 557f
dangers of, 575–577
definition of, 541
with drug therapy, 565–567
eclectic, 543
education and training for, 542–543
effectiveness of, 569–574
evaluation of, 570–572
existential, 553, 555
family, 556–558
Gestalt, 555
group, 557–558
humanistic, 553–554
interpersonal, 547
intervention-causation fallacy and, 500
vs. natural improvement, 570
need for, 539–540
nondirective, 554
nonspecific effects of, 570
person-centered, 553–554
placebo effect in, 571, 571f, 606, 606f
providers of, 542
psychoanalytic, 463, 543–546, 543f. *See also*
Psychoanalysis
psychodynamic, 463, 543–547, 543f
rational emotive, 550–551
reconstructive memory errors and, 571
studies of, 572–574
types of, 542–543, 543f
selection of, 540–541
Puberty, 430–431, 431f
timing of, 432, 432f, 435

Punishment. *See also* Reinforcement
  definition of, 226
  motivation and, 398–399, 398f
  negative, 226–227, 227t
  neutrality of, 228
  in operant conditioning, 226–228, 227t
    secondary, 227–228
  positive, 226–227, 227t
  in social influence, 641
Pupil, 131, 131f
Pure tone, 150
Purkinje cells, 77–78, 77f, 93
Puzzle box, 224–225, 224f, 225f
Pyramidal cells, 77f, 78

Race/ethnicity
  diversity among psychologists and, 33–34
  intelligence and, 351
  intelligence testing and, 356–358, 655
  pain perception and, 157
  sexual development and, 432, 432f
  situational bias and, 357–358
  stereotype threat and, 357–358, 655, 655f
  stereotypes and, 652–657. *See also* Stereotype(s)
Radiological studies. *See* Neuroimaging
Random sampling, 66–68
Randomization, 60–62, 62f
  failure of, 63–64
Range, 47, 48f
Rape, alcohol and, 322
Rape victims
  avoidance responses in, 596
  rational coping by, 596
Rapid cycling bipolar disorder, 516–517
Ratio IQ, 339
Rational choice theory, 274
Rational coping, 596–597
Rational emotive behavior therapy, 550–551
Rationalization, 466
Raven's Progressive Matrices Test, 349, 349f, 357
Rayner, Rosalie, 18, 218–219, 218f
Reaction formation, 466
Reaction time, 7, 9
  implicit learning and, 247
  measurement of, 42f
Reality principle, 464
Reappraisal, 376–377
Reasoning, 285–288. *See also* Problem solving
  belief bias and, 287–288
  brain activity in, 288, 288f
  cultural aspects of, 287
  definition of, 285
  discursive, 286–287
  logical, 285–286
  practical, 286–287
  syllogistic, 287–288
  theoretical, 286–287
Rebound effect, in thought suppression, 303–304, 304f
Receptive fields, 134
  of retinal ganglion cells, 134–135, 134f, 135f
Receptors
  neurotransmitter, 81, 82, 82f, 83
  NMDA, in memory storage, 178–179, 179f
  olfactory, 158
  pain, 155f
  photoreceptors, 132–134, 133f
  taste, 161–162
  thermal, 155
  touch, 155–156, 155f
Reciprocal altruism, 627

Reciprocity norm, 642
Recovered memories, 198–199, 576. *See also* Memory
Referred pain, 156
Reflexes
  in infants, 411
  pain withdrawal, 90, 90f, 156
  spinal, 90, 90f
Refractive errors, 132, 132f
Refractory period, 81
Reframing, 597
  in problem solving, 284–285
Regression, 467
Regression to the mean, 576
Rehearsal, 11, 174–175
  spaced, 11
Reinforcement, 19, 225–229, 227t
  continuous, 232
  definition of, 226
  extrinsic vs. intrinsic, 228–229
  intermittent, 233
  limits on, 228–229
  negative, 226–227, 227t. *See also* Punishment
  neutrality of, 228
  overjustification effect and, 229, 250
  positive, 226–227, 227t
  Premack principle and, 228
  primary, 227
  secondary, 227–228
  in shaping, 233–235, 234f
  in skills training, 549
  in social influence, 641
  token economy in, 549
Reinforcement schedules, 231–233, 231f
Reinforcers, 226
Rejection. *See also* Social isolation
  brain activity in, 630
Relatedness, degree of, 105
  heritability and, 106–107
Relationships
  committed, 636–639
    companionate vs. passionate love in, 638, 638f
    comparison level in, 639
    cost-benefit calculation for, 639
    equity in, 639
  peer, in adolescence, 437
  secret, appeal of, 634
  social exchange in, 639
Relative intelligence, 360
Relativism, 30
Relaxation response, 598
Relaxation techniques
  in stress management, 598, 599
  in systematic desensitization, 549
Reliability, 44
Reliable muscles, 383
Religious experiences, ecstatic, 332–333
REM sleep, 310–311, 310f, 311f
Representative samples, 66–67
Representative variables, 64–66
Representativeness heuristics, 276–277
Repression, 305, 465
Repressive coping, 595–596
Reproductive behavior, 631–640
  attraction and, 632–636
    physical factors in, 27, 28, 633–635. *See also* Physical attractiveness
    psychological factors in, 636
    situational factors in, 632–633
  gender differences in, 631
  pheromones in, 160–161, 160f

relationships and, 637–639
  secret relationships and, 634
  selectivity in, 631
Reproductive costs, mate selection and, 289
Reproductive cycle, sexual desire and, 395
Reproductive technology, for intelligence selection, 363
Rescorla-Wagner model, 220–221, 220f, 237
Research. *See* Experiment(s); Psychological research
Resistance, in psychoanalysis, 544–545
Resolution phase, of human sexual response, 396–397, 397f
Resonance, 151
Response, 18
Response prevention, 550
Resting potential, 79–80
Reticular formation, 93, 93f
  in intraversion/extraversion, 461–462
Retina, 131f, 132
  blind spot in, 134, 134f
  phototransduction in, 132–134
  visual processing in, 138
Retinal ganglion cells, 134
  on-/off-center, 134–135, 135f
  receptive fields of, 134–135, 134f, 135f
Retrieval cues, 180–181, 191. *See also* Memory, retrieval of
Retroactive interference, 189
Retrograde amnesia, 177
Reversibility, 415
Reversible figure-ground relationship, 143, 143f
Reward centers, 236–237, 236f
Rewards, 226–227, 227t. *See also* Classical conditioning; Operant conditioning; Reinforcement
  in social influence, 641
Rhyme judgments, 170, 171f, 181
Risk-benefit analysis, 68
Risperidone, 562
Ritalin
  adverse effects of, 576
  cognitive performance and, 362
Rituals, in obsessive-compulsive disorder, 506–507
Rods, 132–134, 133f
Rogers, Carl, 16–17, 17f, 553–554
Rok-Jooi, 499
Roles
  changing, in adulthood, 443–445
  gender. *See* Gender differences
Romantic relationships, 636–639. *See also* Marriage; Relationships; Reproductive behavior
  secret, appeal of, 634
Rorschach Inkblot Test, 453, 453f, 463
Rosenberg Self-esteem Scale, 480, 480t
Rotter's Locus of Control Scale, 476, 476t
Rubin image, 143
Rule of contagion, 382
Rule of similarity, 382

s (specific abilities), 351
Safe sex practices, 615–616
St. John's wort, 564, 565
St. Mary's of Bethlehem Hospital, 561
Salt taste receptors, 161
Saltatory conduction, 81
Sample, definition of, 45
Sampling, 44–48
  averaging in, 46–48

experience, 302, 302t
  frequency distributions in, 46–47, 47f, 48
  law of large numbers in, 45
  population in, 45
  random, 66–67. *See also* Randomization
  representative samples in, 66–67
Satiety, 391, 392, 392f
Savants, 363
  artistic, 350, 350f
  autistic, 418
  definition of, 350
  language, 253
Savings, in classical conditioning, 217
Scans. *See* Neuroimaging
Schedules of reinforcement, 231–233, 231f
Schemas, 413
  self, 479
Schizoid personality disorder, 527t
Schizophrenia, 519–522
  age at onset of, 522
  biochemical factors in, 523–524
  biological factors in, 522–525
  brain activity in, 524, 560
  catatonic, 521, 521f, 522t
  causes of, 522–526
  definition of, 519–520
  disorganized, 522t
  dopamine hypothesis for, 524, 560
  expressed emotion and, 525–526
  family factors in, 525–526
  genetic factors in, 522–523, 523f
  neuroanatomy in, 524–525, 524f, 525f
  neurotransmitters in, 524, 560
  paranoid, 522t
  prenatal/perinatal factors in, 523
  psychological factors in, 525–526
  residual, 522t
  symptoms of, 520–521, 522t
    negative, 521, 522t, 560
  treatment of, 560–562
  types of, 521, 522t
  undifferentiated, 522t
Schizotypal personality disorder, 527t
School psychologists, 34
Seasonal affective disorder, 512. *See also*
    Depression
  phototherapy for, 568, 568f
Second language learning
  cognitive development and, 264
  timing of, 257, 261
Secondary punishment, 227–228
Secondary reinforcement, 227–228
Secondary sex characteristics, 431, 432f
Second-order conditioning, 215
Secret relationships, appeal of, 634
Secure attachment style, 423, 423f
Sedatives, for insomnia, 313
Seizures, ecstatic religious experiences and, 333
Selective serotonin reuptake inhibitors (SSRIs),
    86, 563. *See also* Antidepressants
Self-actualization, 471
Self-concept, 477–480
  behavior and, 480
  causes and effects of, 479–480
  consensus-based, 479–480
  definition of, 478
  feedback and, 480
  organization of, 478–479
  stability of, 479–480
Self-consciousness, 301
Self-enhancing bias, 200–201, 203–204

Self-esteem, 480–485
  assessment of, 480, 480t
  definition of, 480
  in depression, 515
  desire for, 482–485
  fear of death and, 483–484
  feedback and, 482
  implicit egotism and, 483
  importance of, 480
  influences on, 481–482
  life outcomes and, 480
  vs. narcissism, 484
  security and, 483
  sources of, 480–482
Self-fulfilling prophecy, in stereotyping,
    655–656, 655f
Self-help groups, 558–559
Self-information processing, 479
Self-interest, cooperation and, 625–628
Self-narrative, 478
Self-regulation, 613
Self-relevance, 479
Self-reports, in personality assessment, 452,
    452t
Self-schemas, 479
Self-selection, 61
Self-serving bias, 484
Self-verification, 480
Selye's general adaptation syndrome, 587–588,
    587f
Semantic judgments, 170, 171f, 181
Semantic memory, 183f, 185–186. *See also*
    Memory
  age-related changes in, 439
Semicircular canals, 151f, 158
Sensation, 121–163. *See also specific senses*
  absolute thresholds for, 124–125, 125f, 125t
  definition of, 123
  perception and, 123
  perceptual constancy and, 142
  perceptual grouping and, 142–143, 142f
  psychophysics of, 124–128
  receptive fields in, 134–135
  signal detection in, 126–128
  transduction in, 123
Sensation-seeking scale, 452, 452t
Sensorimotor stage, 413–414, 413t
Sensorineural hearing loss, 154. *See also*
    Hearing impairment
Sensory adaptation, 128–129
Sensory branding, 163
Sensory development, 410–411. *See also*
    Development
Sensory disturbances, in schizophrenia, 520
Sensory memory store, 173–174, 174f
Sensory neurons, 77, 77f
Sensory processing, thalamus in, 95, 95f
Serial killers, 367–368
Serial reaction time task, 247
Serotonin, 83t, 84
  antipsychotics and, 562
  in bipolar disorder, 518
  in depression, 513
  in obsessive-compulsive disorder, 507
Seven sins of memory, 187–204. *See also*
    Memory, seven sins of
Sex, motivation for, 394–395
Sex chromosomes, 105, 407
Sex determination, 407
Sex differences. *See* Gender differences
Sex education, 434, 616

Sex hormones
  in sexual desire, 395
  in sexual development, 433–434
  in sexual orientation, 435
Sex roles. *See* Gender differences
Sexual abuse, recovered memories of, 198–199,
    576
Sexual activity, 396–397
  of adolescents, 434, 434f
  contraception and, 434, 615–616
  gender differences in, 396–397
  risk reduction for, 615–616
  unwanted pregnancy and, 434, 615–616
Sexual assault, alcohol and, 322
Sexual assault victims
  avoidance responses in, 596
  rational coping by, 596
Sexual attraction, 632–635. *See also*
    Relationships
  physical factors in, 27, 28, 633–635. *See also*
    Physical attractiveness
  psychological factors in, 636
  similarity in, 636
  situational factors in, 632–636
Sexual behavior
  alcohol effects on, 322
  pheromones in, 160–161, 160f
Sexual development, 430–436
  cultural aspects of, 432, 432f, 434
  puberty in, 430–431, 431f, 432, 432f
  sexual awakening in, 433–434, 434f
  sexual debut and, 434, 434f
  sexual orientation and, 435–436, 435f
Sexual interest, 394–395
  age at onset of, 433–434
Sexual orientation, 435–436, 435f
  homophobia and, 466
Sexual response
  autonomic nervous system in, 89
  hypothalamus in, 95
Sexual response cycle, 396–397, 397f
Sexually transmitted diseases, 612–613,
    613t
  prevention of, 615–616
Shape perception, 139, 139f
Shaping, 233–235, 234f
Shared environment, 355
Shock therapy, 567–568, 568f
Shook yong, 499
Short-term memory store, 174–175, 175f. *See
    also* Memory
Sick role, 608–609
Sickness response, 589. *See also* Illness
Sight. *See* Vision
Sign language, 25, 258
  for apes, 263–264
  evolution of, 262
  language areas and, 25
  Nicaraguan, 262
Signal detection theory, 126–128, 129
Signaling, 81–87. *See also* Neurotransmitters
  synaptic transmission in, 82–83, 82f
Significance, experimental, 64
Signs, vs. symbols, 380–381
Situational attributions, 657
Situational bias, in testing, 357–358, 655,
    655f
Size
  familiar, 145
  perception of, 144–148
Skills training, 549

Skinner, B. F., 19–21, 19f, 24, 225–227, 236, 390, 473, 548
Skinner box, 19, 19f, 226, 226f
Sleep, 309–318
  dreaming in, 311, 314–317. *See also* Dreams/dreaming
  electroencephalography in, 310–311, 310f, 311f
  electrooculography in, 311
  evolution and, 312–313
  lack of, 312–313
  learning and, 248, 312
  memory consolidation during, 312
  need for, 312–313
  non-REM, 311
  purpose of, 312–313
  REM, 310–311, 310f, 311f
  stages of, 309–311, 310f, 311f
Sleep apnea, 313
Sleep cycle, 309–311
Sleep deprivation, 312–313
Sleep disorders, 313–314
Sleep paralysis, 314
Sleep spindles, 310, 310f
Sleeper effect, 649
Sleepwalking, 313–314
Slips of speech, 305–306, 462
Smell, 158–161. *See also under* Olfactory
  absolute threshold for, 124–125, 125t
  anatomical aspects of, 158–159, 159f
  in flavor, 158, 162–163
  olfactory receptor neurons in, 158–159, 159f
  pheromones and, 160–161, 160f
Smiling. *See also* Facial expressions
  emotional effects of, 381
  fake, 383, 383f
Smoking
  cessation of, 319–320, 617
  health risks of, 616–617
  in pregnancy, 409
Snellen chart, 130, 130f
Social acceptance, motivational effects of, 641–645
Social behavior, 622–630
  aggressive, 623–625. *See also* Aggression
  altruistic, 627–628
  cooperative, 625–627
  definition of, 623
  evolutionary perspective on, 622–640
  in groups, 628–630
  relationships in, 636–639
Social cognition, 651–660
  attributions and, 657–660
  categorization in, 652. *See also* Concepts and categories
  definition of, 652
  medial prefrontal cortex in, 652
  stereotyping and, 652–657
Social cognitive approach, 473–477
  locus of control and, 476, 476t
  outcome expectancies and, 476
  personal constructs in, 475
  person-situation controversy and, 474–475
  trait-behavior correlation and, 474–475
Social development, 420–425
  in adolescence, 432–433, 436–437
  in adulthood, 442–443
  attachment in, 422–425. *See also* Attachment
  cognitive development and, 419

day care and, 426
  imprinting in, 422
  temperament and, 424
Social exchange, 639
Social feedback
  self-concept and, 480
  self-esteem and, 482
Social influence, 622, 640–651
  accuracy motive in, 645–651
  attitudes and beliefs and, 645–651
  cognitive dissonance and, 650–651, 651f
  conformity and, 643–644
  consistency in, 650–651
  definition of, 640
  door-in-the-face technique and, 650
  foot-in-the-door technique and, 650
  hedonic motive in, 640–641
  informational, 645–646
  normative, 642–643
  obedience and, 644–645
  observational learning and, 641
  perseverance effect in, 649
  persuasion in, 647–648
  rewards and punishment in, 640–641
  sleeper effect in, 649
  social acceptance and, 641–645
  susceptibility to, 640
  unbelieving effect in, 649
Social isolation
  brain activity in, 630
  in depression, 515
  in illness, 601–602
  in schizophrenia, 522t
Social loafing, 629
Social norms. *See* Norm(s)
Social phobia, 504
  exposure therapy for, 549
Social psychology, 28–29, 621–661
  definition of, 28, 621–661
  history of, 28–29
  social behavior and, 622–640
  social cognition and, 651–660
  social influence and, 640–651
Social referencing, 419
Social role theory, 459
Social support. *See also* Relationships
  definition of, 601
  in stress management, 601–602
Social workers, 542
Sociobiology (Wilson), 26
Socioeconomic status, health and, 588
Socioemotional selectivity theory, 441
Sociopaths, 529
Sodium ion channels, action potential and, 80–81, 80f
Sodium lactate, in panic disorder, 506
Somatic nervous system, 87–88, 88f
Somatization disorder, 607
Somatoform disorders, 607–608
Somatosensory cortex, 98, 99f
  in pain perception, 156
Somnambulism, 313–314
Soul, location of, 297, 297f
Sound
  localization of, 154
  loudness (intensity) of, 150
  perception of. *See* Hearing
  pitch of, 150
  quality of, 151
  resonance of, 151
  timbre of, 150

Sound waves, 150–153, 150f
  amplitude of, 150–151, 150f
  complexity of, 150f, 151
  frequency of, 150, 150f, 152–153
    encoding, 152–153, 153f
Sour taste receptors, 161
Source memory, 194
Spaced rehearsal, 11
Spatial dimension, of time, 267
Specific phobia, 504–505
  exposure therapy for, 549
Speech. *See also* Language
  babbling and, 258
  development of, 258
  disorganized, in schizophrenia, 521
  emotional content of, 377–379
  slips of, 305–306, 462
  telegraphic, 258–259
Speech deficits
  in Broca's aphasia, 262
  in Wernicke's aphasia, 262
Speech sounds, discrimination of, 257–258
Sperm, 406–407, 407f
Spinal cord, 87, 88f
  development of
    evolutionary, 102–104
    prenatal, 102, 408
  injuries of, 90–91
    thought-controlled movement and, 92
  myelination of, 408. *See also* Myelin sheath
  structure and function of, 90–91, 90f, 91f
Spinal reflexes, 90, 90f
Spiritual experiences, ecstatic, 332–333
Split-brain procedures, 109–111, 110f, 111f
Spontaneous action potential, 127
Spontaneous recovery, in classical conditioning, 214f, 216–217
Spouse selection. *See* Mate selection
S-R psychology, 19
Standard deviation, 47
Standardized testing. *See also* Intelligence testing
  aptitude vs. achievement, 339
  gender differences in, 356–357
  group differences in, 356–358
  stereotype threat and, 357–358, 655, 655f
Stanford-Binet test, 341–342
Stanford prison experiment, 658
State-dependent retrieval, 181
Statistical significance, 64
Statistics
  descriptive, 47–48, 48f
  inferential, 64
Status, aggression and, 625
Stereoscope, 146
Stereotype(s), 652–657
  automatic/unconscious nature of, 656–657
  definition of, 652
  illusory correlation and, 653, 653f
  inaccuracy of, 653
  inferences and, 653
  overuse of, 653–654
  perceptual confirmation of, 655
  as self-fulfilling prophecy, 655–656, 655f
  self-perpetuation of, 655–656
  subtyping and, 656
  test performance and, 357–358, 655, 655f
Stereotype threat, 357–358, 655, 655f
Stigmatization, of psychological disorders, 500, 540

Cherrise Lewis

Professor Saunders

Psychology

October 21st, 2008

The Seven Sins of Memory

Memory is described as our ability to store and retrieve information over time, but there are always instances in which our memory can fail us. These instances are known as the seven sins of memory. The seven sins of memory are: transience, absentmindness, blocking, memory misattribution, suggestibility, bias, and persistence. The sins that I fear and seem to me to be the most dreadful out of the seven are transience, blocking, and persistence.

Transience is the inability to remember events with the passage of time. I fear this one because although we can't escape the process of aging and, as we age our memory beings to fade with us; there have been a few occasions where the time has only been five minutes and I have already forgotten what as learned and what was said. When I was in my first year of high school, my English class was reading the Greek tragedy Antigone, and we had numerous homework assignments that involved reading on our own. When it came time to do my homework, I found myself forgetting what I read five minutes ago and had to go back and reread on a numerous amount of occasions. I also fear this the most because when it comes to cases where relationships are involved I find myself lying

Stimulants, 321t, 323–324
Stimulus
  definition of, 7
  discriminative, 229–230
  habituation to, 210–211
Stimulus control, 229–230
Stimulus generalization, 217, 217f
Stimulus-response (S-R) psychology, 19
Storage, of memories. *See* Memory, storage of
Strange situation test, 423
Stream of consciousness, 299–300
Stress
  anxiety disorders and, 503
  in bipolar disorder, 518–519
  brain activity in, 585, 586f
  burnout from, 594–595
  chronic, 584
  chronic fatigue and, 592
  in college students, 583, 583t
  coping with, 595–604. *See also* Stress
    management
  definition of, 582
  in depression, 514–515
  in diathesis-stress model, 498
  eating and, 614, 615f
  endorphins and, 325
  health effects of, 581–582
  job-related, 594–595
  memory and, 202–203
  perceived control over, 585
  personality factors in, 518–519
  physical reactions to, 585–591
    cardiovascular, 589–591, 591f
    catecholamines in, 585–586
    fight-or-flight response in, 586, 586f
    general adaptation syndrome in, 587–588,
      587f
    hippocampus in, 593–594, 594f
    hormonal, 96, 586, 586f, 588, 602
    immunologic, 588, 589
    sickness response in, 589
  posttraumatic stress disorder and,
    592–595
  primary appraisal of, 591–595
  in psychological disorders, 498
  psychological reactions to, 591–595
    gender differences in, 602
    tend-and-befriend, 602
  resistance to, 612
  secondary appraisal of, 591
  self-regulation and, 614–617
  sources of, 582–585. *See also* Stressors
  warnings and, 618
Stress hormones, 96, 586, 586f, 588, 602
Stress inoculation training, 597
Stress management, 595–604
  aerobic exercise in, 600–601
  avoidance responses in, 596
  biofeedback in, 598–600
  body management in, 598–601
  gender differences in, 602
  hardiness and, 612
  humor in, 602–603
  massage therapy in, 599
  mind management in, 595–597
  personality factors in, 518–519
  reframing in, 597
  relaxation therapy in, 598, 599
  repressive coping in, 595–596
  situation management in, 601–604
  social support in, 601–602

stress inoculation training in, 597
  therapeutic touch in, 599
Stress response, 585
  physical, 585–591. *See also* Stress, physical
    reactions to
  psychological, 591–595. *See also* Stress, psy-
    chological reactions to
Stressors, 582–585
  chronic, 584
  definition of, 582
  environmental, 584
  major life, 582–583, 583t
Striatum, 97
Stroke
  memory impairment in, 193
  prosopagnosia after, 73, 108
Structuralism, 5, 8–9
  vs. functionalism, 10
Study skills, 11
Studying, procrastination and, 35
Subcortical structures, 95–96, 95f, 96f
Sublimation, 467
Subliminal perception, 163, 306–308, 308f
Substance abuse. *See* Alcohol use/abuse; Drug
    abuse
Substantia nigra, 95
Subtractive color mixing, 136–137, 136f
Subtyping, 656
Successive approximation, in shaping,
    233–235
Suggestibility, 197–199, 203
Suicide, 489, 516–517
Sulci, 97
Sullivan, Harry Stack, 546f, 547
Sumner, Francis Cecil, 32f, 33
Sunk-cost fallacy, 277
Suo yang, 499
Superego, 464
Superstitious behavior, 235
Supertasters, 162
Support groups, 558–559
Surface structure, of language, 256
Surgical anesthesia, level of consciousness dur-
    ing, 293–294
Surveys, filler items in, 50
Survival advantages. *See also* Evolution
  of aggression, 623–625
  of altruism, 627–628
  of cooperation, 625–627
  of group membership, 628–630
Survivor, 622–623
Sweet taste receptors, 161, 162
Sybil (Schreiber), 14
Syllogistic reasoning, 287–288
Symbols, vs. signs, 380–381
Sympathetic nervous system, 88, 88f, 89f
  activation of, 96
Synapses, 76, 76f
  strengthening of, long-term potentiation and,
    178–179, 179f
Synaptic pruning, 431, 431f
Synaptic transmission, 82–83, 82f
Synesthesia, 121–122, 122f
Syntactical rules, 255–256, 256f, 258–259
Systematic desensitization, 549–550, 549t,
    550f
  virtual reality in, 537, 538, 539, 550
Systematic persuasion, 647, 648, 648t

T cells, 588
T mazes, 240f

Tabula rasa, 5
Tactile perception. *See* Touch
Tardive dyskinesia, 562
Taste, 161–163, 161f
  absolute threshold for, 124–125, 125t
Taste buds, 161, 161f
Tasters, 162
Taxonomy, 397
Tay-Sachs disease, 358
Teaching machines, 20
Tectum, 94, 94f
Teenagers. *See* Adolescence
Tegmentum, 94–95, 94f
Telegraphic speech, 258–259
Television, violence on, 244
Temperament, 424
Temperance, 530t
Temperature, aggression and, 623, 623f
Template, in object recognition, 143
Temporal code, 153
Temporal lobe, 99
  in classification, 268, 268f
  development of, 431, 431f
  in emotion, 373–374
  in fear, 373–374
  in memory encoding, 171f
  in object recognition, 141–142
  in reasoning, 288, 288f
Temporal lobe syndrome, 373–374, 374f
Teratogens, 408–409
Terminal buttons, 81
Terrorism warnings, 618
Testing
  aptitude vs. achievement, 339
  gender differences in, 356–357
  group differences in, 356–358
  intelligence, 338–344. *See also* Intelligence
    testing
  stereotype threat and, 357–358, 655, 655f
Testosterone
  aggression and, 625
  in sexual desire, 395
  in sexual development, 433–434
  in sexual orientation, 435
Texture gradient, in depth perception, 145,
    146f
Thalamus, 95, 95f, 96f
  in fear, 375
  in pain perception, 157, 605, 606, 606f
  in placebo effect, 606, 606f
  in visual processing, 138
Thematic Apperception Test, 399, 453–453,
    453f
Theoretical reasoning, 286–287
Theories, 65
Theory of mind, 417–418
Therapeutic touch, 599
Therapy. *See* Treatment
Theta waves, 310, 310f
Thinking. *See also under* Cognition; Cognitive;
    Thought
  irrational, 551, 551t
  negative, in depression, 514–515
Thioridazine, 560
Third-variable problem, 56–58, 57f,
    63–64
Thorazine, 560
Thorndike, Edward, 224–225
Thought control, 92
Thought suppression, 303–304, 304f
  in depression, 514–515